TREASURY of the WORLD'S GREAT SERMONS

OTHER SERMON RESOURCES BY WARREN W. WIERSBE

TREASURY of the WORLD'S GREAT SERMONS

Biographical Introductions and Compilation by

WARREN W. WIERSBE

kregel
PUBLICATIONS

Grand Rapids, MI 49501

Cover Design: Alan G. Hartman

Library of Congress Cataloging Card Number 77-72366

ISBN 0-8254-4002-5 (paperback)

6 7 8 9 Printing / Year 97 96

Printed in the United States of America

CONTENTS

FOREWORD

Samuel Johnson once said that "a library must be very imperfect if it has not a numerous collection of sermons." That was in 1781, when the publishing of sermons was a popular thing, and when people actually took time to read and discuss them. Today, alas, the situation is different! I fear that many pastors' libraries lack good sermon collections, and, of course, they are the poorer because of it; and so are their congregations. It is to help remedy this deficiency that this present volume has been published.

The basis for this book is *The World's Great Sermons,* a ten-volume set edited by Grenville Kleiser and published by Funk & Wagnall's in 1909. I have long considered this set to be one of the finest collections of sermons available in the English language. For one thing, it includes sermons from every major period of church history, and from men of different ecclesiastical and doctrinal persuasions. There are theologians like John Calvin and Jonathan Edwards, as well as evangelists like Christmas Evans and pulpiteers like C. H. Spurgeon, Campbell Morgan, and Alexander Maclaren. Many of the classic sermons are included, such as John Bunyan's "The Heavenly Footman," F. W. Robertson's "The Loneliness of Christ," and Charles Spurgeon's "Songs In The Night." But there are also numerous messages that will be new even to the connoisseur of sermonic literature. For variety and solid content, *Treasury of The World's Great Sermons* is a superior collection.

But we have also added material from another ten-volume set, *Modern Sermons By World Scholars,* edited by Robert Scott and William C. Stiles, and also published in 1909 by Funk & Wagnall's. While many of the preachers who contributed to this publication are today unknown or forgotten, there are several that must never be forgotten, and we have included them. For example, Walter F. Adeney is here. He edited *The Century Bible,* wrote nine volumes of *The Pulpit Commentary,* and contributed two volumes to *The Expositor's Bible.* We have included Hugh Black, who assisted the great Alexander Whyte in Edinburgh; W. G. Moorehead, who helped edit *The Scofield Reference Bible;* A. T. Pierson, missionary leader and Bible teacher; James Orr, whose *The Virgin Birth* is still a classic; and many others. We have met these men as scholars and theologians, but now we may meet them as preachers.

I wish I had owned a collection like this when I was beginning my ministry. Why? Well, for one thing, I would have been exposed much sooner to the most important preachers in church history. As it was, I had to discover many of these men on my own, and I really needed to meet them sooner. Also, a volume like this is a treasury for devotional reading and homiletical study. For many years, I have tried to read a sermon a day for my own spiritual welfare. I have also taken time to study other men's sermons to learn from them how better to proclaim the Word of God. In other words, a book like this is both a *treasury* and a *tool,* and wise is the pastor who makes good use of it!

Three basic principles governed the selections: (1) the preachers, (2) the historical value of the sermons, and (3) the homiletics and contents of the sermons. We have tried to include as many of the "great preachers" as possible as well as some who were great in their day and need to be rediscovered. Some of these sermons are classics and should be read by every intelligent Christian. "The Expulsive Power Of A New Affection" is one of them, and so is "The Loneliness Of Christ." I need not explain that the inclusion of a sermon does not mean we endorse the preacher's theology, because, quite frankly, some of them we disagree with! But no sermon is here by accident; each one has a permanent value for the church today.

The best thing any serious Christian could do (and this means laymen as well as pastors) would be to keep this volume handy and read in it regularly. The younger preacher in particular ought to live in it until the preachers and their preaching become alive and meaningful to him. He ought to seek out their books and add them to his library. Before long, he will have a collection of the best sermonic literature of the ages to enrich his own life and ministry.

I commend my friend Robert Kregel for making the best of these two valuable sets available to a new generation of students and others who love good preaching. My prayer is that all of us will find in *Treasury of the World's Great Sermons* the kind of spiritual enjoyment and enlargement that will help us to enrich others.

The Moody Church   *Warren W. Wiersbe*
Chicago, Illinois

WALTER F. ADENEY

1849-1920

TRUTH IN JESUS

BIOGRAPHICAL NOTE

PRINCIPAL of Lancashire Independent College 1903 -1909; born Ealing, Middlesex, England; educated New College, London; seventeen years Congregational minister at Acton; fourteen years professor of New Testament exegesis and Church history at Hackney College, London; lecturer in history of doctrine at the University of Manchester; editor of the "Century Bible"; D.D. from St. Andrew's, Scotland; author of "The Hebrew Utopia," "From Christ to Constantine," "From Constantine to Charles the Great," "Theology of the New Testament" (which has been translated into Japanese), "Ezra, Nehemiah and Esther," "Canticles and Lamentations" (Expositor's Bible), "Women of the New Testament," "How to Read the Bible," "A Century's Progress," "St. Luke and Galatians and Thessalonians" (Century Bible), etc.

"As truth is in Jesus."—Eph. 4 : 21.

WE hear this phrase very frequently quoted, but too often in ways that miss the pith and point of it. Sometimes it is used quite indefinitely, for the whole realm of Christian doctrine; and sometimes it is applied in a peculiar manner to a singularly constricted scheme of ideas to which its admirers confine that great word "gospel." Both of these usages show a failure to catch the original tone of the phrase.

This should be suggested to us by the simplicity of the name of our Lord. It is just "Jesus"—the bare personal name, shorn of all titles and honors, of all reference to His kingship and divine nature. That is quite unusual in the epistles—most unusual with Paul. In the epistles—especially in Paul's Epistles—we nearly always have some such expression as "Jesus Christ," "Christ Jesus," "Christ" alone, "the Lord," "the Lord Jesus Christ." But when we go back to the gospels we come upon the simple name "Jesus." In a word, that is the name our Lord bears in the gospels, while "Christ" is specifically His name in the epistles.

Now this is not merely a question of words. "Jesus" was our Lord's personal name, the name by which He was known in His boyhood and obscurity at Nazareth, before any dreamed who He was, and what He was to become; it was the name by which He was known to the end by those people who rejected His high claims.

Why, then, does Paul here strip the name of the titles of honor and reverence which the disciples had learned to attach to it? If we examine a few of their passages in the epistles where this is done, we shall see that they all point in one and the same direction. They all call our attention to the earthly life of our Lord, to that life which we have in the gospel story.

Truth in Jesus, then, is truth in the life of Jesus on earth; to us it is truth contained and revealed in the gospel story.

But, you will ask, why, then, was this not stated more clearly? Why do we not read "the truth which Jesus taught?" Because, there is a closer relation between Jesus and truth than there is between the mere teacher and his lesson. As a matter of fact, I suppose nobody can teach well any truth except that which is in him. A man must have assimilated an idea and made it part of himself before he can impart it effectively to others. Phillips Brooks tells us—and none knew it better than he—that a sermon should be truth passing through the experience of the preacher, and Henry Ward Beecher once said, ''Preaching is the preacher laying his heart on the people.''

But it is even more than that with our Lord's teaching of truth; because His vital and personal relation to it is peculiarly intimate. John the Baptist was ''a voice crying in the wilderness''—a voice, the message everything, the speaker a negligible quantity. But Jesus is more than a voice—He is truth incarnate. So He can say, ''I am the light of the world,'' ''I am the truth.''

We often hear of the return to Christ which our age has witnessed, and if we ask, what are the most modern ideas in religion? the answer is, ''The ideas of the Sermon on the Mount.'' Apparently some people are just discovering these ideas for the first time—to them; and the discovery is a perfect revelation for them. But we have not all the truth Jesus is prepared to give us when we have His words. The words of Him who spake as never man spake are of incomparable worth. When a scrap of a papyrus containing six or eight very doubtful sentences ascribed to our Lord is discovered, its contents are devoured with the keenest interest. There is an admirable little book entitled, ''The Master's Guide,'' in which the sayings of Jesus collected from the New Testament are arranged under the headings of various topics. You can not read such a book without feeling that what it contains is altogether unique. Here we have the regalia of the kingdom of heaven, every sentence a gem. And yet we should be heavy losers if we gave up the four gospels in exchange for such a book as this. It is not enough to know what Jesus said. We want to know Jesus Himself, Jesus as He is revealed in deed and life as well as in word and teaching. Here we have the truth He brings to us in its fulness and vitality and power—''as truth is in Jesus.''

Now we are often reminded that this is an age when Pilate's weary question—perhaps I should say his cynical question: ''What is truth?'' is being asked with a new intensity of interest. It is an age of many questions. Unfortunately, it is also an age of many answers, an age of many voices all clamorous for a hearing, each offering its own solution of the riddles of existence. If any of us are driven to seek peace in the intellectual Nirvana of agnosticism, it is not for want of a gospel, it is rather from the bewilderment of the claims of too many gospels. But how otherwise are we to escape from this confusion of cries, this babel of utterances, and all the perplexity it engenders and the despair of ever reaching truth to which it points?

I answer, we must turn a deaf ear to the whole of them, and seek truth in Jesus. We must leave the library and enter our chamber;

take with us our New Testament; turn to the gospels; make a study of them—a study with this specific end in view—to discover truth.

Immediately we begin thus to study Jesus, so to say, at first hand in these gospel portraits, one characteristic most strikes us. As a leader He is quite sure of what He has to say. There is a ring of certainty in all His words. Never was there a teacher more positive, if you like to put it so, more dogmatic. We have our views, we cherish our opinions, we balance arguments and measure probabilities. You never find Jesus doing anything of the kind. You never hear Him talking of His views or His opinions; you never hear Him speaking in our hazy style: ''On the whole, considering all the facts of the case, I am inclined to venture the assertion that this or that may turn out to be the explanation of it.'' If you discovered a new *logion* in language such as that, you would declare it a forgery beyond doubt. For the style of Jesus, even when dealing with the most profound mysteries of existence, is thus: ''Verily, verily, I say unto you.'' I do not say that He claimed omniscience on earth. He even repudiated it. But what He did assert He asserted with unhesitating decision.

But is it enough to be positive? We all of us know very positive people—popes who claim infallibility, altho no Vatican council has voted it them—and we are not inclined to surrender our judgment to them on demand. Do we not often find people to be positive exactly in proportion to the limited range of their knowledge? The less a person knows the more sure he is of everything; while the wider his horizon becomes, the slower and more hesitating he will be in making a distinct assertion.

It is not enough, then, to say that anyone is very positive. We must first face the question as to who it is that speaks to us with this singular decisiveness. I doubt not there are many among us who are perfectly satisfied on that point, who are well assured that Jesus is the very Son of God dwelling ever in the bosom of the Father, who can almost see the angels ascending and descending on the Son of Man.

But if it be the case that we have not all reached this position of calm assurance, if the uncertainty and questioning of the age have driven some of us into wondering thoughts about the very being and nature of Christ, how is it possible to take His direct assurance as the settlement of all doubt? We must begin at a more preliminary stage.

Consider the case of the expert, who condescends to leave his advanced studies for a little while, and instruct us in some of the more elementary principles of his science. What a firm grip he has of the subject! With what ease he moves from point to point! His only difficulty is not to go too far, and lead his audience out of their depth. Plainly, he is master of the situation. And when he sits down nothing pleases him better than to be questioned on anything in the lecture. At once he is ready to explain it more fully, and his *ex tempore* explanation is as learned and as masterly as the set lecture. You can not take him at a disadvantage. You can sit at the feet of such a man with the utmost confidence. Clearly he has a right to speak with authority.

Now is it not clear, when you study the gospel story, that Jesus is an expert in religion, by the side of whom the greatest theologian appears but as an amateur dabbling in a subject too large for him? It may seem almost irreverent to use such a title as "expert" for Jesus Christ; He is so much more. But then He is at least that. Here, surely, we may be all agreed. What is to us, alas! too much a strange subject, one that we neglect for a multitude of minor interests, was to Him a region in which He was perfectly at home. He lived in it and spoke out from it as from the depths of His daily experience.

It is as when a party of travelers climbing some wild and dangerous mountain find themselves enveloped in cloud. All trace of direction is lost. A yawning gulf may be at their feet. But one is well on in advance of the rest. He has reached the ridge and passed the cloud; and he calls back to the others, "It is all clear here; I can see the way right on to the summit; follow me and you will be safe." His position of advance gives him authority to speak. As we listen to the voice of Jesus coming to us through the clinging mists that blot out the landscapes for us and chill our hearts, we discover that this is a voice from the heights. Is it nothing that Jesus can say, "Follow me! He that followeth me shall not walk in darkness?" He, too, is on the mountain above us—how far exalted, perhaps we may not yet see; but, at all events, well in advance—yes, and well in advance of all the world's great thinkers and teachers of religion. Is it nothing that from this high ground He speaks with the voice of sure knowledge and decisive utterance? And then, as I have said, it is not only by His words that He guides us. His person, His life, His character are luminous and illuminating.

Let us see how this conception of truth, as truth is in Jesus, may apply to various regions of thought and life, and consider what answer to the questions that most perplex us may be found in the Jesus of the gospels, in the actual contents of these records. The inquiry is not mystical; it is literary and historical. As such it may not be finally satisfactory to all minds, still it is the path of light.

First, let us look at the region of the practical. The deepest, darkest doubt—a doubt vastly more unsettling than any amount of speculative uncertainty, worse even than what is called religious skepticism, because it cuts at the root of all religion and all goodness—is moral doubt. So long as a man can keep "conscience as the noontide clear," with unhesitating faith in goodness and unwavering determination to pursue it at all hazards, he can never be utterly at sea. All may seem lost, sky and ocean mixed in the fury of tempest; and yet, while the anchor of conscience holds, the vessel will ride the storm. But if this anchor is dragged, if the very fundamental ideas of right and wrong are tossing in confusion, the peril is great indeed. There is absolutely nothing to prevent drifting on to the rocks. It is no longer the eclipse of faith. It is the shipwreck of faith. Beware of that horror of horrors—moral skepticism.

But how is it to be escaped? When we turn from theory to fact, the world, as we see it, does not seem to show that sharp distinction, that impassable gulf, that vast distance as from pole to pole, between good and evil. The two are strangely intermingled. If even a good man looks down into the lower regions of his nature, he may be startled to discover there the lurking possibilities of the crimes of a Borgia. When some one who has been respected universally as a pillar of virtue suddenly falls, or is suddenly found out in some base action, the sight of such unexpected wickedness sends a shock through society, and tempts the world to say that all men are alike; or with the only difference that some sin openly while others hide their misdeeds; that some are honest knaves and the rest but hypocrites.

This miserable cynicism must shrink for very shame in the presence of Jesus Christ. Will anybody venture to read the story of His life and still maintain that there is no reality in goodness? For see what it comes to! If virtue is a myth, if the moral law is an illusion, if there is no essential distinction between good and evil, then there is no essential distinction between Jesus Christ and Judas Iscariot. And by all the appalling distance from the awful purity of the Savior to the sordid vileness of the traitor, the essential distinction between good and evil is proved to us. If not in St. Francis, if not in John, if in no saint, or martyr, or apostle, still, as the last resort, in Jesus, assuredly, we can see the moral law vindicated. He magnifies this law and makes it honorable. He established the eternal reality of goodness. That truth we may see in Jesus.

The frequency of failure provokes the further question whether life is not altogether a mistake. As some lives are spent, it is difficult to resist that dismal conclusion. There are stained and misshapen lives that appear like spots and blotches in creation, their very existence a blight upon society. Are there not, too, multitudes of lives which, if not thus stamped with offensiveness, yet are no comfort to the livers of them and no blessing to others—poor, withered, doleful lives spent in a round of weary drudgery, with no prospect of relief but by the merciful hand of death? I am afraid it must be admitted there are ways of living that do not seem to make life worth the trouble of lungs in drawing breath, and heart in driving blood to keep them going. It is possible for any of us to live in such a mode—servile in poverty or self-indulgent in luxury. It might be well for all of us occasionally to put the question to ourselves point blank, Are we living in a way that is worth all the cost to ourselves and others?

But can anybody ask that question concerning Jesus Christ? To His contemporaries He was a failure, meeting the doom of the enthusiast who braves the conventions of the world, cut off in young manhood, tortured and killed by the death of the vilest criminal. And yet, we know that He did not fail. If ever any life was a success, the life of Jesus was. It was the life which reversed the whole course of history, and laid the foundation of the upward movement of mankind. Life a failure? Apparently so in some instances, as far as we can see in this world; but not the life of the Crucified. And, therefore, we may conclude that just in proportion as we follow Christ our lives, too, will not fail. I do not know what to say of many lives, but looking at it in the light of truth, I am perfectly certain that the Christian life, the life of self-denial and service, cross-bearing and Christ-likeness, is not and can not be a failure. This is as the truth of life is in Jesus.

The same rule applies when we turn to more mysterious regions of speculative inquiry. Questions are raised concerning the nature of Christ, such questions as rent the Church in fierce internal conflicts in the ages of the great Christian fathers. Out of these conflicts came the creeds that were to settle the dogmas of the believer for all subsequent ages. But to many of us these creeds are not final utterances. They affirm, they do not prove, neither do they explain. To some people they only appear to "darken counsel with words without knowledge." It is not thus that we determine any truth of science. Why should we expect to settle theological truth in so preposterous a method of finality? Why should the twentieth century bow down to the fourth century, dumb and submissive, in this the most difficult of questions, and in this alone? Surely, we have learned a more excellent way. The naturalist is not satisfied to study in old libraries; he examines the

objects of nature. It is this inductive method of Bacon that opened the door to science. Is it unreasonable to apply the same method in religion? If we do, the right way to know Christ is not to analyze creeds, it is to make a study of the Jesus of the gospels. What a picture we have there—babe of Bethlehem, boy at Nazareth, carpenter in the workshop, preacher by the lakeside, brother in the home, healer of the sick, victim on the cross, firstborn from the dead! Watch Him as He moves along His brief, strange course. Humblest of men, yet making the highest claims; most modest, yet never confessing to a fault.

A person of dull conscience may defend himself against all fault-finding. As a rule, this unruffled sense of rectitude is exactly proportionate to the torpor of conscience. The awakened conscience is self-accusing. And so it comes about that the holiest man is the most eager to repudiate the title to holiness, that the saint is the first to confess himself a sinner.

But Jesus makes no such confession. He is keenly alive to the evil of sin, and He is unfaltering in the denunciation of hypocrisy. We can not say He is callous and indifferent to evil. Yet He never confesses sin of His own; claiming to forgive sin in others, He always speaks as tho there were none in Himself. And His life bears out this personal conviction. Neither is He conscious of sin, nor can anybody detect it in Him. This is the first wonder of His life—the sinlessness of Jesus. In this He is quite alone and apart. How shall we explain it? He gives us His own explanation: "I and my Father are one." Apostles, evangelists, those who watched Him most closely, who knew Him best, give the same explanation when they describe Him as the Son of God. I can see no other adequate explanation of the gospel record than this assertion of the divinity of Christ. This is not merely a dogma of the creeds—it is a truth in Jesus, a truth in the gospels, a truth that shines out of the ancient pages; to my mind and to many minds the only way of accounting for what is recorded there.

Again, it may be that we are opprest with the larger mystery of existence. What is the meaning of this vast, perplexing system of things, in the midst of which we live, which we call universe? Is it but an interminable nexus of forces, or is there mind behind force? Is there God? If so, what is God? The existence of the world points to a cause; the order of the universe suggests a mind; the beauty of nature a soul; the bountifulness of life a heart. And yet, when we have reached these conclusions, Mill's terrible indictment of nature confronts us. Apparently all is not wise and good. Earthquakes, famine, flood, plague—what are these?

But here is the dilemma—if there is no God, in the end we must go back to chance, and chaos is the parent of all things. Evolution introduces an orderly process, but it is only a process, a method, not a cause. Evolution inspired by God is a sublime theory of creation. Evolution without God is but a product of chance. Then even with this theory we are forced back on something like the daring epicurean notion so brilliantly set forth by the Roman poet Lucretius—a fortuitous concourse of atoms, falling, as he had it, through space, and jostling one another incessantly in the vast cascade of them till they ultimately chance to fall into a condition of order. If that be true, then Jesus Christ is the result of such a chance, a product of blind and purposeless evolution—His life but as one speck of foam flung up from the dark ocean of existence.

And further, if there is no mind in the universe, if the brain secretes thought as the liver secretes bile, then we must come to this wild and desperate conclusion that the Sermon on the Mount and the parable of the prodigal son are by-products of certain chance combinations of phosphates and nitrates in the brain of an organism to which we misleadingly attach the greatest of names. It is abhorrent to state such a conclusion; yet we must be honest; we must be consistent. There is no alternative. This is the conclusion to which we must be driven on the materialistic hypothesis.

Philosophers have described animals as automatons, and there are men whose sheer animalism of existence encourages the hypothesis. These are the excuses for materialism. But it breaks down utterly in the presence of Jesus. The credulity of the Christian is as nothing to the credulity of the materialist who can believe that all we read in the gospel story is but a fine and vaporous emanation of chemical elements. The being of God and the existence of mind, of soul, of spirit, are vindicated by the very being of Jesus. These truths are to be seen in Him.

There is one more question to which I wish to apply this solvent of the truth that is found in the gospels, the truth as it is in Jesus—the question of a future life. We must all feel that much of what is said on this subject will not bear a very close scrutiny. There are times when we can not be satisfied with conventional notions. When we stand by the open grave of a very dear friend, or when the doctor has warned us that we should do well to put our affairs in order, as the summons may come to us at any moment; when it has become clear that close at hand

"the shadow sits and waits for us," then, in these moments of intense reality, we can not be satisfied with the flowers of hymnology and pulpit eloquence, and we ask in grim earnest Job's straight question: "If a man die shall he live again?"

What is Christ's answer to that pregnant question. It is a very remarkable answer—quite one by itself—reticent, yet clear and positive. Jesus paints no fancy pictures of elysian fields where happy souls walk in meads of asphodel; He draws no plan of a heavenly city with gates of pearl and streets of gold. To the curiosity that hungers for information about the forms and manners of the life beyond He is perfectly silent. But to the deeper hunger for life after death He is most reassuring. He is as positive on this subject as on any other. His words are few, but they are quite clear and absolutely unwavering. While we halt and hesitate, and falter and tremble, before the mystery of death, He, above our mists, standing there in the light, is certain. Surely, this means much!

What can be more decisive than such words as these: "He that believeth in me, tho he were dead, yet shall he live"; "in my Father's house are many places of rest. If it were not so I would have told you." I do not know any statement of the case more exact and true than that in Richard Baxter's most honest hymn:

> My knowledge of that life is small,
> The eye of faith is dim;
> But 'tis enough that Christ knows all,
> And I shall be with Him.

And here we have a further confirmation beyond the words and direct teaching of Jesus—His own resurrection. Jesus was raised up from the dead; He came back from beyond the shadows—the first-born among many brethren. That is in the record of the gospels. The very existence of the Church—itself a resurrection after the despair of Calvary—is witness to the resurrection of Jesus, and that in turn is witness to the life eternal.

To any, then, who may be distrest by the wild, free questions of our day; to any who may be bewildered by the hosts of conflicting voices each offering its own reply, this is one way of life and guidance. Study the gospels. Come to a first-hand knowledge of Jesus. Learn of Him. Consider what a Master of His subject He is, how clear His vision, how serene His assurance, how positive His utterance, how real His life! All else may waver; mists may gather round the cherished convictions of childhood. Jesus abides, the light of the world and the light of the ages. In Him shall we see light.

SAINT AUGUSTINE

354-430

THE RECOVERY OF SIGHT BY THE BLIND

BIOGRAPHICAL NOTE

SAINT AUGUSTINE (Aurelius Augustinus), one of the greatest theological fathers of the Church, was born at Tagaste, 354 A.D., and became devoted to the study of Cicero. As a Manichean he occasioned great anxiety to his mother Monica. Eventually embracing Christianity, he was baptized by Ambrose of Milan (387), on which occasion, tradition says, the Te Deum was composed by himself and his baptizer. Appointed to the See of Hippo in 395, he threw himself into the conflict against heresy and schism, his principal opponents being the Donatists and Pelagians. His sermons, powerful as they are, disappoint the modern reader by their fantastic and allegorical interpretation of Scripture, but his "Confessions," in which he details the history of his early life and conversion, present a wonderful picture of personal experience. He is styled by Harnack "the first modern man." He died at Hippo in 430.

Have mercy on us, O Lord, thou Son of David.— Matt. xx., 30.

I. YE know, holy brethren, full well as we do, that our Lord and Savior Jesus Christ is the physician of our eternal health; and that to this end we task the weakness of our natures, that our weakness might not last forever. For He assumed a mortal body, wherein to kill death. And, "though He was crucified through weakness," as the apostle saith, yet He "liveth by the power of God." They are the words, too, of the same apostle: "He dieth no more, death hath no more dominion over Him." These things, I say, are well known to your faith. And there is also this which follows from them, that we should know that all the miracles which He did on the body avail to our instruction, that we may from them perceive that which is not to pass away, nor to have any end. He restored to the blind those eyes which death was sure some time to close; He raised Lazarus to life who was to die again. And whatever He did for the health of bodies, He did it not to this end that they should be forever; whereas, at the last, He will give eternal health even to the body itself. But because those things which were not seen were not believed; by means of those temporal things which were seen, He built up faith in those things which were not seen.

II. Let no one then, brethren, say that our Lord Jesus Christ doeth not those things now, and on this account prefer the former to the present ages of the Church. In a certain place, indeed, the same Lord prefers those who do not see and yet believe to them who see and therefore believe. For even at that time so irresolute was the infirmity of His disciples that they thought that He whom they saw to have risen again must be handled, in order that they might believe. It was not enough for their eyes that they had seen Him, unless their hands also were applied to His limbs, and the scars of His recent wounds were touched: that this disciple, who was in doubt, might cry suddenly when he had touched and recognized the scars, "My Lord and my God." The scars manifested Him who had healed all wounds in others. Could not the Lord have risen again without scars? Yes, but He knew the wounds which were in the hearts of His disciples, and to heal them He had preserved the scars on His own body. And what said the Lord to him

6

who now confest and said, "My lord, and my God?" "Because thou hast seen," He said, "thou hast believed; blessed are they who have not seen, and yet have believed." Of whom spake He, brethren, but of us? Not that He spoke only of us, but of those also who shall come after us. For a little while when He had departed from the sight of men, that faith might be established in their hearts, whosoever believed, believed tho they saw Him not, and great has been the merit of their faith; for the procuring of which faith they brought only the movement of a pious heart, and not the touching of their hands.

III. These things, then, the Lord did to invite us to the faith. This faith reigneth now in the Church, which is spread throughout the whole world. And now, He worketh greater cures, on account of which He disdained not then to exhibit those lesser ones. For as the soul is better than the body, so is the saving health of the soul better than the health of the body. The blind body doth not now open its eyes by a miracle of the Lord, but the blinded heart openeth its eyes to the word of the Lord. The mortal corpse doth not now rise again, but the soul doth rise again which lay dead in a living body. The deaf ears of the body are not now opened; but how many have the ears of their heart closed, which yet fly open at the penetrating word of God, so that they believe who did not believe, and they live well who did live evilly, and they obey who did not obey; and we say, "such a man is become a believer," and we wonder when we hear of them whom once we had known as hardened. Why, then, dost thou marvel at one who now believes, who is living innocently, and serving God, but because thou dost behold him seeing, whom thou hadst known to be blind; dost behold him living whom thou hast known to be dead; dost behold him hearing whom thou hadst known to be deaf? For consider that there are those who are dead in another than the ordinary sense, of whom the Lord spoke to a certain man who delayed to follow the Lord, because he wished to bury his father; "Let the dead," said He, "bury their dead." Surely these dead buriers are not dead in body; for if this were so, they could not bury dead bodies. Yet doth He call them dead; where but in the soul within? For as we may often see in a household, itself sound and well, the master of the same house lying dead; so in a sound body do many carry a dead soul within; and these the apostle arouses thus, "Awake, thou that sleepest, and arise from the dead, and Christ shall give thee light." It is the same who giveth sight to the blind that awakeneth the dead. For it is with His voice that the cry is made by the apostle to the dead. "Awake thou that sleepest." And

the blind will be enlightened with light, when he shall have risen again. And how many deaf men did the Lord see before His eyes, when He said, "He that hath ears to hear let him hear." For who was standing before Him without his bodily ears? What other ears, then, did He seek for, but those of the inner man?

IV. Again, what eyes did He look for when He spake to those who saw indeed, but who saw only with the eyes of the flesh? For when Philip said to Him, "Lord, show us the Father and it sufficeth us": he understood, indeed, that if the Father were shown him, it might well suffice him; when He that was equal to the Father had sufficed not? And why did He not suffice? Because He was not seen. And why was He not seen? Because the eye whereby He might be seen was not yet whole. For this, namely, that the Lord was seen in the flesh with the outward eyes, not only the disciples who honored Him saw, but also the Jews who crucified Him. He, then, who wished to be seen in another way, sought for other eyes. And, therefore, it was that to him who said, "Show us the Father, and it sufficeth us," He answered, "Have I been so long time with you, and yet hast thou not known Me, Philip? He who hath seen Me hath seen the Father also." And that He might in the meanwhile heal the eyes of faith, He has first of all given him instructions regarding faith, that so he might attain to sight. And lest Philip should think that he was to conceive of God under the same form in which he then saw the Lord Jesus Christ in the body, he immediately subjoined, "Believest thou not that I am in the Father, and the Father in me?" He had already said, "He who hath seen me hath seen the Father also." But Philip's eye was not yet sound enough to see the Father, nor, consequently, to see the Son, who is Himself coequal with the Father. And so Jesus Christ took in hand to cure, and with the medicine and salve of faith to strengthen the eyes of his mind, which as yet were weak and unable to behold so great a light, and He said, "Believest thou not that I am in the Father, and the Father in Me?" Let not him, then, who can not yet see what the Lord will one day show him, seek first to see what he is to believe; but let him first believe that the eye by which he is to see may be healed. For it was only the form of the servant which was exhibited to the eyes of servants; because if "He who thought it not robbery to be equal with God" could have been now seen as equal with God by those whom He wished to be healed, He would not have needed to empty Himself and to take the form of a servant. But because there was no way whereby God could be seen, but whereby man could be seen there was;

therefore, He who was God was made man, that that which was seen might heal that whereby He was not seen. For He saith Himself in another place, "Blessed are the pure in heart, for they shall see God." Philip might, of course, have answered and said, Lord, do I see Thee? Is the Father such as I see Thee to be? Forasmuch as Thou hast said, "He who hath seen Me hath seen the Father also?" But before Philip answered thus, or perhaps before he so much as thought it, when the Lord had said, "He who hath seen Me hath seen the Father also," He immediately added, "Believest thou not that I am in the Father, and the Father in me?" For with that eye he could not yet see either the Father, or the Son who is equal with the Father; but that his eye might be healed for seeing, he was anointed unto believing. So, then, before thou seest what thou canst not now see, believe what as yet thou seest not. "Walk by faith," that thou mayest attain to sight. Sight will not gladden him in his home whom faith consoleth not by the way. For, so says the apostle, "As long as we are in the body we are absent from the Lord." And he subjoins immediately why we are still "absent or in pilgrimage," tho we have now believed; "For we walk by faith," he says; "not by sight."

V. Our whole business, then, brethren, in this life is to heal this eye of the heart whereby God may be seen. To this end are celebrated the Holy Mysteries; to this end is preached the Word of God; to this end are the moral exhortations of the Church, those, that is, that relate to the corrections of manners, to the amendment of carnal lusts, to the renouncing the world, not in word only, but in a change of life: to this end is directed the whole aim of the Divine and Holy Scriptures, that that inner man may be purged of that which hinders us from the sight of God. For as the eye which is formed to see this temporal light, a light tho heavenly yet corporeal, and manifest, not to men only, but even to the meanest animals (for this the eye is formed to this light); if anything be thrown or falls into it, whereby it is disordered, is shut out from this light; and tho it encompasses the eye with its presence, yet the eye turns itself away from, and is absent from it; and tho its disordered condition is not only rendered absent from the light which is present, but the light to see which it was formed is even painful to it, so the eye of the heart too, when it is disordered and wounded, turns away from the light of righteousness, and dares not and can not contemplate it.

VI. And what is it that disorders the eye of the heart? Evil desire, covetousness, injustice, worldly concupiscence; these disorder, close, blind the eye of the heart. And yet, when the eye of the body is out of order, how is the physician sought out, what an absence of all delay to open and cleanse it, that they may be healed whereby this outward light is seen! There is running to and fro, no one is still, no one loiters, if even the smallest straw fall into the eye. And God, it must be allowed, made the sun which we desire to see with sound eyes. Much brighter, assuredly, is He who made it; nor is the light with which the eye of the mind is concerned of this kind at all. That light is eternal wisdom. God made thee, O man, after His own image. Would He give thee wherewithal to see the sun which He made, and not give thee wherewithal to see Him who made thee, when He made thee after His own image? He hath given thee this also; both hath He given thee. But much thou dost love these outward eyes, and despisest much that interior eye; it thou dost carry about bruised and wounded. Yea, it would be a punishment to, if thy Maker should wish to manifest Himself unto thee, it would be a punishment to thine eye, before that it is cured and healed. For so Adam in Paradise sinned, and hid himself from the face of God. As long, then, as he had the sound heart of a pure conscience, he rejoiced at the presence of God; when that eye was wounded by sin, he began to dread the divine light, he fled back into the darkness, and the thick covert of trees, flying from the truth, and anxious for the shade.

VII. Therefore, my brethren, since we too are born of him, and as the apostle says, "In Adam all die"; for we were all at first two persons; if we were loath to obey the physician, that we might not be sick; let us obey Him now, that we may be delivered from sickness. The Physician gave us precepts, when we were whole; He gave us precepts that we might not need a physician. "They that are whole," He saith, "need not a physician, but they that are sick." When whole, we despised these precepts, and by experience have felt how to our own destruction we despised His precepts. Now we are sick, we are in distress, we are on the bed of weakness; yet let us not despair. For because we could not come to the Physician, He hath vouchsafed to come Himself to us. Tho despised by man when he was whole, He did not despise him when he was stricken. He did not leave off to give other precepts to the weak, who would not keep the first precepts, that he might not be weak; as tho He would say, "Assuredly thou hast by experience felt that I spoke the truth when I said, Touch not this. Be healed then now, at length, and recover the life thou hast lost. Lo, I am bearing thine infirmity; drink then the bitter cup. For thou hast of thine own self made those my so sweet precepts, which were given to thee when whole, so toilsome. They were despised, and so thy distress began; cured thou canst not be, except thou drink the bitter cup, the cup of temptations, wherein this life abounds, the cup of tribulation, anguish, and suffering. Drink then," He says, "drink, that thou mayest live." And that the sick man may not make answer, "I can not, I can not bear it, I will not drink"; the Physician, all whole tho He be, drinketh first, that the sick man may not hesitate to drink. For what bitterness is there in this cup which He hath not drunk? If it be contumely, He heard it first when He drove out the devils. "He hath a devil, and by Beelzebub He casteth out devils." Whereupon, in order to comfort the sick, He saith, "If they have called the Master of the house Beelzebub, how much more shall they call them of His household?" If pains are this bitter cup, He was bound, and scourged, and crucified. If death be this bitter cup, He died also. If infirmity shrink with horror from any particular kind of death, none was at that time more ignominious than the death of the cross. For it was not in vain that the apostle, when setting forth His obedience, added, "He became obedient unto death, even the death of the cross."

VIII. But because He designed to honor His faithful ones at the end of the world, He hath first honored the cross in this world; in such wise that the princes of the earth who believe in Him have prohibited any criminal from being crucified; and that cross which the Jewish persecutors with great mockery prepared for the Lord, even kings, His servants, at this day, bear with great confidence on their foreheads. Only the shameful nature of the death which our Lord vouchsafed to undergo for us is not now so apparent, Who, as the apostle says, "Was made a curse for us." And when, as He hung, the blindness of the Jews mocked Him, surely He could have come down from the cross, who, if He had not so willed, had not been on the cross; but it was a greater thing to rise from the grave than to come down from the cross. Our Lord, then, in doing these divine and in suffering these human things, instructs us by His bodily miracles and bodily patience, that we may believe and be made whole to behold those things invisible which the eye of the body hath no knowledge of. With this intent, then, He cured those blind men of whom the account has just now been read in the Gospel. And consider what instruction He has by this cure conveyed to the man who is sick within.

IX. Consider the issue of the thing, and the order of the circumstances. Those two blind men sitting by the wayside cried out, as the Lord passed by, that He would have mercy upon them. But they were restrained from crying out by the multitude which was with the Lord. Now do not suppose that this circumstance is left without a mysterious meaning. But they overcame the crowd who kept them back by the great perseverance of their cry, that their voice might reach the Lord's ears; as tho he had not already anticipated their thoughts. So then the two blind men cried out that they might be heard by the Lord, and could not be restrained by the multitude. The Lord "was passing by," and they cried out. The Lord "stood still," and they were healed. "For the Lord Jesus stood still, and called them, and said, What wilt ye that I shall do unto you? They say unto Him, That our eyes may be opened." The Lord did according to their faith, He recovered their eyes. If we have now understood by the sick, the deaf, the dead, the sick, and deaf, and dead within; let us look out in this place also for the blind within. The eyes of the heart are closed; Jesus passeth by that we may cry out. What is meant by "Jesus passeth by?" Jesus is doing things which last but for a time. What is meant by "Jesus passeth by?" Jesus doth things which pass by. Mark and see how many things of His have passed by. He was born of the Virgin Mary; is He being born always? As an infant He was suckled; is He suckled always? He ran through the successive ages of life until man's full estate; doth He grow in body always? Boyhood succeeded to infancy, to boyhood youth, to youth man's full stature in several passing successions. Even the very miracles which He did are passed by; they are read and believed. For because these miracles are written that so they might be read, they passed by when they were being done. In a word, not to dwell long on this, He was crucified; is He hanging on the cross always? He was buried, He rose again, He ascended into heaven, now He dieth no more, death hath no more dominion over Him. And His divinity abideth ever, yea, the immortality of His body now shall never fail. But nevertheless all those things which were wrought by Him in time have passed by; and they are written to be read, and they are preached to be believed. In all these things, then, Jesus passeth by.

X. And what are the two blind men by the wayside but the two people to cure whom Jesus came? Let us show these two people in the Holy Scriptures. It is written in the Gospel, "Other sheep I have which are not of this fold; them also must I bring, that there may be one fold and one Shepherd." Who then are the two people? One the people of the Jews, and the other of the Gentiles. "I am not sent," He saith, "but unto the lost sheep of the house of Israel." To whom did He say this? To the disciples; when that woman of Canaan, who confest herself to be a dog, cried out that she might be found worthy of the crumbs from the Master's table. And because she was found worthy, now were the two people to whom He had come made manifest, the Jewish people, to wit, of whom He said, "I am not sent but unto the lost sheep of the house of Israel"; and the people of the Gentiles, whose type this woman exhibited, whom He had first rejected, saying, "It is not meet to cast the children's bread to the dogs"; and to whom, when she said, "Truth, Lord, yet the dogs eat of the crumbs which fall from their master's table," He answered, "O woman, great is thy faith; be it unto thee even as thou wilt." For of this people also was that centurion of whom the same Lord saith, "Verily I say unto you, I have not found so great faith, no, not in Israel," because he had said, "I am not worthy that Thou shouldst come under my roof, but speak the word only, and my servant shall be healed." So then the Lord even before His passion and glorification pointed out two people, the one to whom He had come because of the promises to the Fathers, and the other whom for His mercy's sake He did not reject; that it might be fulfilled which had been promised to Abraham, "In thy seed shall all the nations be blessed."

XI. Attend, now, dearly beloved. The Lord was passing by, and the blind men cried out. What is this "passing by?" As we have already said, He was doing works which passed by. Now upon these passing works is our faith built up. For we believe on the Son of God, not only in that He is the Word of God, by whom all things were made; for if He had always continued in the form of God, equal with God, and had not emptied Himself in taking the form of a servant, the blind men would not even have perceived Him, that they might be able to cry out. But when he wrought passing works, that is, when He humbled Himself, having become obedient unto death, even the death of the cross, the two blind men cried out, Have mercy on us, thou Son of David. For this very thing that He, David's Lord and Creator, willed also to be David's son, He wrought in time, He wrought passing by.

XII. Now what is it, brethren, to cry out unto Christ, but to correspond to the grace of Christ by good works? This I say, brethren, lest haply we cry aloud with our voices, and in our lives be dumb. Who is he that crieth out to Christ, that his inward blindness may be driven away by Christ as He is passing by, that is, as He is dispensing to us those temporal sacraments, whereby we are instructed to receive the things which are eternal? Who is he that crieth out unto Christ? Whoso despiseth the world, crieth out unto Christ. Whoso despiseth the pleasures of the world, crieth out unto Christ. Whoso saith, not with his tongue but with his life, the world is crucified unto me, and I unto the world, crieth out unto Christ. Whoso disperseth abroad and giveth to the poor, that his righteousness may endure forever, crieth out unto Christ. For let him that hears, and is not deaf to the sound, sell that ye have, and give to the poor; provide yourselves bags which wax not old, a treasure in the heavens that faileth not; let him as he hears the sound as it were of Christ's footsteps passing by cry out in response to this in his blindness; that is, let him do these things. Let his voice be in his actions. Let him begin to despise the world, to distribute to the poor his goods, to esteem as nothing worth what other men love, let him disregard injuries, not seek to be avenged, let him give his cheek to the smiter, let him pray for his enemies; if any one who have taken away his goods, let him not ask for them again; if he have taken anything from any man, let him restore fourfold.

XIII. When he shall begin to do all this, all his kinsmen, relations, and friends will be in commotion. They who love the world will oppose him. What madness this! You are too extreme! What! Are not other men Christians? This is folly, this is madness. And other such like things do the multitude cry out to prevent the blind from crying out. The multitude rebuked them as they cried out; but did not overcome their cries. Let them who wish to be healed understand what they have to do. Jesus is now also passing by; let them who are by the wayside cry out. These are they, who know God with their lips, but their heart is far from Him. These are by the wayside, to whom, as blinded in heart, Jesus gave His precepts. For when those passing things which Jesus did are recounted, Jesus is always represented to us as passing by. For even unto the end of the world there will not be wanting blind men sitting by the wayside. Need then there is that they who sit by the wayside should cry out. The multitude that was with the Lord would repress the crying of those who were seeking for recovery. Brethren, do you see my meaning? For I know not how to speak, but still less do I know how to be silent. I will speak then, and speak plainly. For I fear Jesus passing by and Jesus standing still; and therefore I can not keep silence. Evil and unknown Christians who are truly earnest and wish to do the commandments of God, which are written in the Gospel. This multitude which is with the Lord hinders those who are crying out, hinders those, that is, who are doing well, that they may not by perseverance be healed. But let them cry out, and not faint; let them not be led away as if by the authority of numbers; let them not imitate those who become Christians before them, who live evil lives themselves, and are jealous of the good deeds of others. Let them not say, "Let us live as these so many live." Why not rather as the Gospel ordains? Why dost thou wish to live according to the remonstrances of the multitude who would hinder them, and not after the steps of the Lord who passeth by? They will mock, and abuse, and call thee back; do thou cry out till thou reach the ears of Jesus. For they who shall persevere in doing such things as Christ hath enjoined, and regard not the multitude that hinder them, nor think much of their appearing to follow Christ, that is of their being called Christians; but who love the light which Christ is about to restore to them more than they fear the uproar of those who are hindering them; they shall on no account be separated from Him, and Jesus will stand still, and make them whole.

XIV. For how are our eyes made whole? That as by faith we perceive Christ passing by in the temporal economy, so we may attain to the knowledge of Him as standing still in His unchangeable eternity. For there is the eye made whole when the knowledge of Christ's divinity is attained. Let your love apprehend this; attend ye to the great mystery which I am to speak of. All the things which were done by our Lord Jesus Christ, in time, graft faith in us. We believe on the Son of God, not on the word only, by whom all things were made; but on this very word, "made flesh that He might dwell among us"; who was born of the Virgin Mary; and the rest which the Faith contains, and which are represented to us that Christ might pass by, and that the blind, hearing His footsteps as He passeth by, might by their works cry out, by their life exemplifying the profession of their faith. But now in order that they who cry out may be made whole, Jesus standeth still. For he saw Jesus now standing still, who says, "Though we have known Christ after the flesh, yet now henceforth know we Him no more." For he saw Christ's divinity as far as in this life is possible. There is then in Christ the divinity, and the humanity. The divinity standeth still, the humanity passeth by. What means "the divinity standeth still?" It changeth not, is not shaken, doth not depart away. For He did not so come to us as to depart from the Father; nor did He so ascend as to change His place. When He assumed flesh, it changed place; but God assuming flesh, seeing He is not in place, doth not change His place. Let us then be touched by Christ standing still, and so our eyes be made whole. But whose eyes? The eyes of those who cry out when He is passing by; that is, who do good works through that faith which hath been dispersed in time, to instruct in our infancy.

XV. Now what thing more precious can we have than the eye made whole? They rejoice who see this created light which shines from heaven, or even that which is given out from a lamp. And how wretched do they seem who can not see this light? But wherefore do I speak, and talk of all these things, but to exhort you all to cry out, when Jesus passeth by. I hold up this light which perhaps ye do not see as an object of love to you, holy brethren. Believe, while as yet ye see it not; and cry out that ye may see. How great is thought to be the unhappiness of men who do not see this bodily light? Does any one become blind; immediately it is said: "God is angry with him, he has committed some wicked deed." So said Tobias's wife to her husband. He cried out because of the kid, lest it had come of theft; he did not like to hear the sound of any stolen thing in his house; and she, maintaining what she had done, reproached her husband; and when he said, "Restore it if it be stolen"; she answered insultingly, "Where are thy righteous deeds?" How great was her blindness who maintaineth the theft; and how clear a light he saw, who commanded the stolen thing to be restored! She rejoiced outwardly in the light of the sun; he inwardly in the light of righteousness. Which of them was in the better light?

XVI. It is to the love of this light that I would exhort you, beloved; that ye would cry out by your works, when the Lord passeth by; let the voice of faith sound out, that Jesus was standing still, that is, the unchangeable, abiding wisdom of God, and the majesty of the Word of God, by which all things were made, may open your eyes. The same Tobias, in giving advice to his son, instructed him to this, to cry out; that is, he instructed him to good works. He told him to give to the poor, charged him to give alms to the needy, and taught him, saying, "My son, alms suffereth not to come into darkness." The blind gave counsel for receiving and gaining sight. "Alms," saith he, "suffereth not to come into darkness." Had his son in astonishment answered him, "What then, father, hast thou not given alms, that thou speakest to me in blindness; art not thou in darkness, and yet thou dost say to me, Alms suffereth not to come into darkness?" But no, he knew well what the light was concerning which he gave his son instruction, he knew well what he saw in the inner man. The son held out his hand to his father, to enable him to dwell in heaven.

XVII. To be brief; that I may conclude this sermon, brethren, with a matter which touches me very nearly, and gives me much pain, see what crowds there are which rebuke the blind as they cry out. But let them not deter you. whosoever among this crowd desire to be healed; for there are many Christians in name, and in works ungodly; let them not deter you from good works. Cry out amid the crowds that are restraining you, and calling you back, and insulting you, whose lives are evil. For not only by their voices, but by evil works, do wicked Christians repress the good. A good Christian has no wish to attend the public shows. In this very thing, that he bridles his desire of going to the theater, he cries out after Christ, cries out to be healed. Others run together thither, but perhaps they are heathens or Jews? Ah! indeed, if Christians went not to the theaters, there would be so few people there that they would go away for very shame. So then Christians run thither also, bearing the Holy Name only to their condemnation. Cry out then by abstaining from going, by repressing in thy heart this worldly concupiscence; hold on with a strong and persevering cry unto the ears of the Savior, that Jesus may stand still and heal thee. Cry out amid the very crowds, despair not of reaching the ears of the Lord. For the blind man in the Gospel did not cry out in that quarter where no crowd was, that so they might be heard in that direction, where there was no impediment from persons hindering them. Amid the very crowds they cried out; and yet the Lord heard them. And so also do ye even amid sinners, and sensual men, amid the lovers of the vanities of the world, there cry out that the Lord may heal you. Go not to another quarter to cry out unto the Lord, go not to heretics and cry out unto Him there. Consider, brethren, how in that crowd which was hindering them from crying out, even there they who cried out were made whole.

THE GREAT
BISHOP BASIL

329-379

THE CREATION
OF THE WORLD

BIOGRAPHICAL NOTE

BASIL, bishop of Cæsarea in Cappadocia, and styled "The Great," was the founder of Eastern monasticism, defender of the Nicene doctrines and doctor of the Church. He was born at Cæsarea in 329, and was thoroughly educated in all that a teacher like Libanius could impart at Rome, and Himerius at Constantinople. Returning home, he plunged into the pleasures of social life, but was induced by his sister to visit the hermits of Syria, Palestine and Egypt. Attracted during his travels to the religious life, he secluded himself in a lonely spot in inclement Pontus.

During his monastic life of seven years (357-364) he formulated the monastic rule still observed by Eastern monks. Ordained presbyter in 364, he labored in founding religious institutions of various kinds. He attracted notice by his growing Nicene predilections, and was elected bishop of his native town (370) and virtual primate of Asia Minor. His conduct in dealing with the Arians was uncompromising yet conciliating. As a theologian he stands next to his brother Gregory and to Athanasius, but he excels them both in the literary charm and variety of his Greek style. He died in 379.

The earth was without form and void.—Gen. i., 2.

IN the few words which have occupied us this morning we have found such a depth of thought that we despair of penetrating farther. If such is the forecourt of the sanctuary, if the portico of the temple is so grand and magnificent, if the splendor of its beauty thus dazzles the eyes of the soul, what will be the holy of holies? Who will dare to try to gain access to the innermost shrine? Who will look into its secrets? To gaze into it is indeed forbidden us, and language is powerless to express what the mind conceives.

However, since there are rewards, and most desirable ones, reserved by the just Judge for the intention alone of doing good, do not let us hesitate to continue our researches. Altho we may not attain to the truth, if, with the help of the Spirit, we do not fall away from the meaning of Holy Scripture, we shall not deserve to be rejected, and with the help of grace, we shall contribute to the edification of the Church of God.

"The earth," says Holy Scripture, "was without form and void"—*i.e.*, invisible and unfinished. The heavens and the earth were created together. How, then, is it that the heavens are perfect whilst the earth is still unformed and incomplete? In one word, what was the unfinished condition of the earth and for what reason was it invisible? The fertility of the earth is its perfect finishing; growth of all kinds of plants, the up-springing of tall trees, both productive and unfruitful, flowers' sweet scents and fair colors, and all that which, a little later, at the voice of God came forth from the earth to beautify her, their universal mother.

As nothing of all this yet existed, Scripture is right in calling the earth "without form." We could also say of the heavens that they were still imperfect and had not received their natural adornment, since at that time they did not shine with the glory of the sun and of the moon, and were not crowned by the choirs of the stars. These bodies were not yet created. Thus you will not diverge from the truth in saying that the heavens also were "without form." The earth was invisible for two reasons: it may be because man, the spectator, did not yet exist, or because, being submerged under the waters which overflowed the surface, it could not be seen, since the waters had not yet been gathered together into their own places, where God afterward collected them and gave them the name of sea.

What is invisible? First of all, that which

our fleshly eye can not perceive—our mind, for example; then that which, visible in its nature, is hidden by some body which conceals it, like iron in the depths of the earth. It is in this sense that the earth, in that it was hidden under the waters, was still invisible. However, as light did not yet exist, and as the earth lay in darkness because of the obscurity of the air above it, it should not astonish us that for this reason Scripture calls it "invisible."

But the corrupters of the truth, who, incapable of submitting their reason to Holy Scripture, distort at will the meaning of the Holy Scriptures, pretend that these words mean matter. For it is matter, they say, which from its nature is without form and invisible—being by the conditions of its existence without quality and without form and figure. The Artificer submitting it to the working of His wisdom clothed it with a form, organized it, and thus gave being to the visible world.

If the matter is uncreated, it has a claim to the same honors as God, since it must be of equal rank with Him. Is this not the summit of wickedness that utter chaos, without quality, without form or shape, ugliness without configuration, to use their own expression, should enjoy the same prerogatives as He who is wisdom, power, and beauty itself, the Creator and the Demiurge of the universe enjoys? This is not all. If the matter is so great as to be capable of being acted on by the whole wisdom of God, it would in a way raise its hypostasis to an equality with the inaccessible power of God, since it would be able to measure by itself all the extent of the divine intelligence.

If it is insufficient for the operations of God, then we fall into a more absurd blasphemy, since we condemn God for not being able, on account of the want of matter, to finish His own works. The ·resourcelessness of human nature has deceived these reasoners. Each of our crafts is exercised upon some special matter—the art of the smith upon iron, that of the carpenter on wood. In all there is the subject, the form and the work which results from the form. Matter is taken from without—art gives the form—and the work is composed at the same time of form and of matter.

Such is the idea that they make for themselves of the divine work. The form of the world is due to the wisdom of the supreme Artificer; matter came to the Creator from without; and thus the world results from a double origin. It has received from outside its matter and its essence, and from God its form and figure. They thus come to deny that the mighty God has presided at the formation of the universe, and pretend that he has only brought a crowning contribution

to a common work; that he has only contributed some small portion to the genesis of beings; they are incapable, from the debasement of their reasonings, of raising their glances to the height of truth. Here, below, arts are subsequent to matter—introduced into life by the indispensable need of them. Wool existed before weaving made it supply one of nature's imperfections. Wood existed before carpentering took possession of it, and transformed it each day to supply new wants and made us see all the advantages derived from it, giving the oar to the sailor, the winnowing-fan to the laborer, the lance to the soldier.

But God, before all those things which now attract our notice existed, after casting about in His mind and determining to bring into being that which had no being, imagined the world such as it ought to be, and created matter in harmony with the form which He wished to give it. He assigned to the heavens the nature adapted for the heavens, and gave to the earth an essence in accordance with its form. He formed, as he wished, fire, air, and water, and gave to each the essence which the object of its existence required.

Finally he welded all the diverse parts of the universe by links of indissoluble attachment and established between them so perfect a fellowship and harmony that the most distant, in spite of their distance, appeared united in one universal sympathy. Let those men, therefore, renounce their fabulous imaginations, who in spite of the weakness of their argument, pretend to measure a power as incomprehensible to man's reason as it is unutterable by man's voice.

God created the heavens and the earth, but not only one-half of each; He created all the heavens and all the earth, creating the essence with the form. For He is not an inventor of figures, but the Creator even of the essence of beings. Further, let them tell us how the efficient power of God could deal with the passive nature of matter, the latter furnishing the matter without form, the former possessing the science of the form without matter, both being in need of each other; the Creator in order to display his art, matter in order to cease to be without form and to receive a form. But let us stop here and return to our subject.

"The earth was invisible and unfinished." In saying "In the beginning God created the heavens and the earth" the sacred writer passed over many things in silence—water, air, fire, and the results from them, which, all forming in reality the true complement of the world, were, without doubt made at the same time as the universe. By this silence history wishes to train the activity of our intelligence, giving it a weak point for starting, to impel it to the discovery of the truth.

Thus, we are told of the creation of water; but, as we are told that the earth was invisible, ask yourself what could have covered it and prevented it from being seen? Fire could not conceal it. Fire brightens all about it, and spreads light rather than darkness around. No more was it air that enveloped the earth. Air by nature is of little density and transparent. It receives all kinds of visible objects and transmits them to the spectators. Only one supposition remains: that which floated on the surface of the earth was water, the fluid essence which had not yet been confined to its own place.

Thus the earth was not only invisible; it was still incomplete. Even to-day excessive damp is a hindrance to the productiveness of the earth. The same cause at the same time prevents it from being seen and from being complete, for the proper and natural adornment of the earth is its completion: corn waving in the valleys, meadows green with grass and rich with many-colored flowers, fertile glades and hilltops shaded by forests. Of all this nothing was yet produced; the earth was in travail with it in virtue of the power that she had received from the Creator. But she was waiting for the appointed time and the divine order to bring forth.

"Darkness was upon the face of the deep." A new source for fables and most impious imaginations may be found by distorting the sense of these words at the will of one's fancies. By "darkness" these wicked men do not understand what is meant in reality—air not illumined, the shadow produced by the interposition of a body, or finally a place for some reason deprived of light. For them "darkness" is an evil power, or rather the personification of evil, having his origin in himself in opposition to, and in perpetual struggle with, the goodness of God. If God is light, they say, without any doubt the power which struggles against Him must be darkness, "darkness" not owing its existence to a foreign origin, but an evil existing by itself. "Darkness" is the enemy of souls, the primary cause of death, the adversary of virtue. The words of the prophet, they say in their error, show that it exists and that it does not proceed from God. From this what perverse and impious dogmas have been imagined! What grievous wolves, tearing the flock of the Lord, have sprung from these words to cast themselves upon souls! Is it not from hence that have come forth Marcions and Valentinuses and the detestable heresy of the Manicheans which you may, without going far wrong, call the putrid humor of the churches?

O man, why wander thus from the truth and imagine for thyself that which will cause thy perdition? The word is simple and within the comprehension of all. "The earth was invisible." Why? Because the "deep" was spread over its surface. What is "the deep?" A mass of water of extreme depth. But we know that we can see many bodies through clear and transparent water. How, then, was it that no part of the earth appeared through the water? Because the air which surrounded it was still without light and in darkness. The rays of the sun, penetrating the water, often allow us to see the pebbles which form the bed of the river, but in a dark night it is impossible for our glance to penetrate under the water. Thus, these words, "the earth was invisible," are explained by those that follow; "the deep" covered it and itself was in darkness. Thus the deep is not a multitude of hostile powers, as has been imagined; nor "darkness" an evil sovereign force in enmity with good. In reality two rival principles of equal power, if engaged without ceasing in a war of mutual attacks, will end in self-destruction.

But if one should gain the mastery it would completely annihilate the conquered. Thus, to maintain the balance in the struggle between good and evil is to represent them as engaged in a war without end and in perpetual destruction, where the opponents are at the same time conquerors and conquered. If good is the stronger, what is there to prevent evil from being completely annihilated? But if that be the case, the very utterance of which is impious, I ask myself how it is that they themselves are not filled with horror to think that they have imagined such abominable blasphemies.

It is equally impious to say that evil has its origin from God; because the contrary can not proceed from its contrary. Life does not engender death; darkness is not the origin of light; sickness is not the maker of health. In the changes of conditions there are transitions from one condition to the contrary; but in genesis each being proceeds from its like and from its contrary. If, then, evil is neither uncreated nor created by God, from whence comes its nature? Certainly, that evil exists no one living in the world will deny. What shall we say, then? Evil is not a living animated essence: it is the condition of the soul opposed to virtue, developed in the careless on account of their falling away from good.

Do not, then, go beyond yourself to seek for evil, and imagine that there is an original nature of wickedness. Each of us—let us acknowledge it—is the first author of his own vice.

Among the ordinary events of life, some come naturally, like old age and sickness; others by chance, like unforeseen occurrences, of which the origin is beyond ourselves, often sad, sometimes fortunate—as, for instance, the discovery of a treasure when digging a well, or the meeting of a mad dog when going to the market-place.

Others depend upon ourselves; such as ruling one's passions, or not putting a bridle on one's pleasures; the mastery of anger, or resistance against him who irritates us; truth-telling or lying, the maintenance of a sweet and well-regulated disposition, or of a mood fierce and swollen and exalted with pride. Here you are the master of your actions. Do not look for the guiding cause beyond yourself, but recognize that evil, rightly so called, has no other origin than our voluntary falls. If it were involuntary, and did not depend upon ourselves, the laws would not have so much terror for the guilty, and the tribunals would not be so pitiless when they condemn wretches according to the measure of their crimes.

But enough concerning evil rightly so called. Sickness, poverty, obscurity, death, finally all human afflictions, ought not to be ranked as evils, since we do not count among the greatest boons things which are their opposites. Among these afflictions some are the effect of nature, others have obviously been for many a source of advantage. Let us be silent for the moment about these metaphors and allegories, and, simply following without vain curiosity the words of Holy Scripture, let us take from darkness the idea which it gives us.

But reason asks, Was darkness created with the world? Is it older than light? Why, in spite of its inferiority, has it preceded it? Darkness, we reply, did not exist in essence; it is a condition produced in the air by the withdrawal of light. What, then, is that light which disappeared suddenly from the world so that darkness should cover the face of the deep? If anything had existed before the formation of this sensible and perishable world, no doubt we conclude it would have been in the light. The orders of angels, the heavenly hosts, all intellectual natures named or unnamed, all the ministering spirits, did not live in darkness, but enjoyed a condition fitted for them in light and spiritual joy.

No one will contradict this, least of all he who looks for celestial light as one of the rewards promised to virtue—the light which, as Solomon says, is always a light to the righteous, the light which made the apostle say, "Giving thanks unto the Father, which hath made us meet to be partakers of the inheritance of the saints in light." Finally, if the condemned are sent into outer darkness, evidently those who are made worthy of God's approval are at rest in heavenly light. When, then, according to the order of God, the heaven appeared, enveloping all that its circumference included, a vast and unbroken body separating outer things from those which it enclosed, it necessarily kept the space inside in darkness for want of communication with the outer light.

Three things are, indeed, needed to form a shadow: light, a body, a dark place. The shadow of heaven forms the darkness of the world. Understand, I pray you, what I mean, by a simple example—by raising for yourself at midday a tent of some compact and impenetrable material, you shut yourself up in sudden darkness. Suppose that original darkness was like this, not subsisting directly by itself, but resulting from some external causes. If it is said that it rested upon the deep, it is because the extremity of air naturally touches the surface of bodies; and as at that time the water covered everything, we are obliged to say that darkness was upon the face of the deep.

"And the Spirit of God moved upon the face of the waters?" Does this Spirit mean the diffusion of air? The sacred writer wishes to enumerate to you the elements of the world, to tell you that God created the heavens, the earth, water and air, and that the last was now diffused and in motion; or rather, that which is truer and confirmed by the authority of the ancients, by the Spirit of God he means the Holy Spirit. It is, as has been remarked, the special name, the name above all others that Scripture delights to give to the Holy Spirit, and by the Spirit of God the Holy Spirit is meant, the Spirit, namely, which completes the divine and blessed Trinity. You will always find it better, therefore, to take it in this sense. How, then, did the Spirit of God move upon the waters? The explanation that I am about to give you is not an original one, but that of a Syrian who was as ignorant in the wisdom of this world as he was versed in the knowledge of the truth.

He said, then, that the Syriac word was more expressive, and that, being more analogous to the Hebrew term, it was a nearer approach to the Scriptural sense. This is the meaning of the word: by "moved" the Syrians, he says, understand brooded over. The Spirit cherished the nature of the waters as one sees a bird cover the eggs with her body and impart to them vital force from her own warmth. Such is, as nearly as possible, the meaning of these words—the Spirit moved: that is, prepared the nature of water to produce living beings: a sufficient proof for those who ask if the Holy Spirit took an active part in the creation of the world.

"And God said, Let there be light." The first word uttered by God created the nature of light; it made darkness vanish, dispelled gloom, illuminated the world, and gave to all being at the same time a sweet and gracious aspect. The heavens, until then enveloped in darkness, appeared with that beauty which they still present to our eyes.

The air was lighted up, or rather made the light circulate mixed with its substance, and, distributing its splendor rapidly in every direction, so dispersed itself to its extreme limits. Up it sprang to the very ether and heaven. In an instant it lighted up the whole extent of the world, the north and the south, the east and the west. For the ether also is such a subtle substance and so transparent that it needs not the space of a moment for light to pass through it. Just as it carries our sight instantaneously to the object of vision, so without the least interval, with a rapidity that thought can not conceive, it receives these rays of light in its uttermost limits. With light the ether becomes more pleasing and the waters more limpid. These last, not content with receiving its splendor, return it by the reflection of light and in all directions send forth quivering flashes. The divine word gives every object a more cheerful and a more attractive appearance, just as when men pour in oil into the deep sea they make the place about them smooth. So, with a single word and in one instant the Creator of all things gave the boon of light to the world.

"Let there be light." The order was itself an operation, and a state of things was brought into being than which man's mind can not even imagine a pleasanter one for our enjoyment. It must be well understood that when we speak of the voice, of the word, of the command of God, this divine language does not mean to us a sound which escapes from the organs of speech, a collision of air struck by the tongue; it is a simple sign of the will of God, and, if we give it the form of an order, it is only the better to impress the souls whom we instruct.

"And God saw the light, that it was good." How can we worthily praise light after the testimony given by the Creator to its goodness? The word, even among us, refers the judgment to the eyes, incapable of raising itself to the idea that the senses have already received. But if beauty in bodies results from symmetry of parts and the harmonious appearance of colors how, in a simple and homogeneous essence like light, can this idea of beauty be preserved? Would not the symmetry in light be less shown in its parts than in the pleasure and delight at the sight of it? Such is also the beauty of gold, which it owes, not to the happy mingling of its parts, but only to its beautiful color, which has a charm attractive to the eyes.

Thus, again, the evening star is the most beautiful of the stars: not that the parts of which it is composed form a harmonious whole, but thanks to the unalloyed and beautiful brightness which meets our eyes. And further, when God proclaimed the goodness of light, it was not in regard to the charm of the eye, but as a provision for future advantage, because at that time there were as yet no eyes to judge of its beauty.

"And God divided the light from the darkness." That is to say, God gave them natures incapable of mixing, perpetually in opposition to each other, and put between them the widest space and distance.

"And God called the light day, and the darkness he called night." Since the birth of the sun, the light that it diffuses in the air when shining on our hemisphere is day, and the shadow produced by its disappearance is night. But at that time it was not after the movement of the sun, but following this primitive light spread abroad in the air or withdrawn in a measure determined by God, that day came and was followed by night.

"And the evening and the morning were the first day." Evening is then the boundary common to day and night; and in the same way morning constitutes the approach of night to day. It was to give day the privileges of seniority that Scripture put the end of the first day before that of the first night, because night follows day: for, before the creation of light, the world was not in night, but in darkness. It is the opposite of day which was called night, and it did not receive its name until after day. Thus were created the evening and the morning. Scripture means the space of a day and a night, and afterward no more says day and night, but calls them both under the name of the more important: a custom which you will find throughout Scripture. Everywhere the measure of time is counted by days without mention of nights. "The days of our years," says the Psalmist; "few and evil have the days of the years of my life been," said Jacob; and elsewhere "all the days of my life."

"And the evening and the morning were the first day," or, rather, one day.—(Revised Vers). Why does Scripture say "one day," not "the first day?" Before speaking to us of the second, the third, and the fourth days, would it not have been more natural to call that one the first which began the series? If it, therefore, says "one day," it is from a wish to determine the measure of day and night and to combine the time that they contain. Now, twenty-four hours fill up the space of one day—we mean of a day and of a night; and if, at the time of the solstices, they have not both an equal length, the time marked by Scripture does not the less circumscribe their duration. It is as tho it said: Twenty-four hours measure the space of a day, or a day is in reality the time that the heavens, starting from one point, take to return thither. Thus, every time that, in the revolution of the sun, evening and morning occupy the world, their periodical succession never exceeds the space of one day.

But we must believe that there is a mysterious reason for this? God, who made the nature of time, measured it out and determined it by intervals of days; and, wishing to give it a week as a measure, he ordered the week to resolve from period to period upon itself, to count the movement of time, forming the week of one day revolving seven times upon itself: a proper circle begins and ends with itself. Such is also the character of eternity, to revolve upon itself and to end nowhere. If, then, the beginning of time is called "one day" rather than "the first day," it is because Scripture wishes to establish its relationship with eternity. It was, in reality, fit and natural to call "one" the day whose character is to be one wholly separated and isolated from all others. If Scripture speaks to us of many ages, saying everywhere "age of age, and ages of ages," we do not see it enumerate them as first, second, and third. It follows that we are hereby shown, not so much limits, ends, and succession of ages as distinctions between various states and modes of action. "The day of the Lord," Scripture says, "is great and very terrible," and elsewhere, "Woe unto you that desire the day of the Lord: to what end is it for you? The day of the Lord is darkness and not light."

A day of darkness for those who are worthy of darkness. No; this day without evening, without succession, and without end is not unknown to Scripture, and it is the day that the Psalmist calls the eighth day, because it is outside this time of weeks. Thus, whether you call it day or whether you call it eternity, you express the same idea. Give this state the name of day; there are not several, but only one. If you call it eternity still it is unique and not manifold. Thus it is in order that you may carry your thoughts forward toward a future life that Scripture marks by the word "one" the day which is the type of eternity, the first-fruits of days, the contemporary of light, the holy Lord's day.

But while I am conversing with you about the first evening of the world, evening takes me by surprise and puts an end to my discourse. May the Father of the true light, who has adorned day with celestial light, who has made to shine the fires which illuminate us during the night, who reserves for us in the peace of a future age a spiritual and everlasting light, enlighten your hearts in the knowledge of truth, keep you from stumbling, and grant that "you may walk honestly as in the day." Thus shall you shine as the sun in the midst of the glory of the saints, and I shall glory in you in the day of Christ, to whom belong all glory and power for ever and ever. Amen.

RICHARD BAXTER

1615-1691

MAKING LIGHT OF CHRIST AND SALVATION

BIOGRAPHICAL NOTE

RICHARD BAXTER, was born in 1615, at Rowton, near Shrewsbury, in England. After surmounting great difficulties in securing an education for the ministry he was ordained in 1638, in the Church of England, his first important charge being that of Kidderminster, where he established his reputation as a powerful evangelical and controversial preacher. Altho opposed to Cromwell's extreme acts, he became a chaplain in the army of the Rebellion. His influence was all on the side of peace, however, and at the Restoration he was appointed chaplain to Charles II.

Baxter left the Church of England on the promulgation of the Act of Uniformity, and in 1662 retired to Acton in Middlesex, where he wrote most of his works. The Acts of Indulgence enabled him to return to London, where he remained until Judge Jeffreys imprisoned and fined him on a charge of sedition. He was the most prolific writer and controversialist of his day among nonconformists. Baxter left only two works which seem likely to be of ever fresh interest, "The Saint's Rest" and "Calls to the Unconverted." He died in London in 1691.

But they made light of it.—Matt. xxii., 5.

BELOVED hearers; the office that God hath called us to is, by declaring the glory of His grace, to help under Christ to the saving of men's souls. I hope you think not that I come hither to-day on another errand. The Lord knows I had not set a foot out-of-doors but in hope to succeed in this work for your souls. I have considered, and often considered, what is the matter that so many thousands should perish when God hath done so much for their salvation; and I find this that is mentioned in my text is the cause. It is one of the wonders of the world, that when God hath so loved the world as to send His Son, and Christ hath made a satisfaction by His death sufficient for them all, and offereth the benefits of it so freely to them, even without money or price, that yet the most of the world should perish; yea, the most of those that are thus called by His Word! Why, here is the reason—when Christ hath done all this, men make light of it. God hath showed that He is not unwilling; and Christ hath showed that He is not unwilling that men should be restored to God's favor and be saved; but men are actually unwilling themselves. God takes not pleasure in the death of sinners, but rather that they return and live. But men take such pleasure in sin that they will die before they will return. The Lord Jesus was content to be their physician, and hath provided them a sufficient plaster of His own blood: but if men make light of it, and will not apply it, what wonder if they perish after all? This Scripture giveth us the reason of their perdition. This, sad experience tells us, the most of the world is guilty of. It is a most lamentable thing to see how most men do spend their care, their time, their pains, for known vanities, while God and glory are cast aside; that He who is all should seem to them as nothing, and that which is nothing should seem to them as good as all; that God should set mankind in such a race where heaven or hell is their certain end, and that they should sit down, and loiter, or run after the childish toys of the world, and so much forget the prize that they should run for. Were it but possible for one of us to see the whole of this business as the all-seeing God doth; to see at one view both heaven and hell, which men are so near; and see what most men in the world are minding, and what they are doing every day, it would be the saddest sight that could be imagined. Oh, how should we marvel at their madness, and lament their self-delusion! O poor distracted world! what is it you run after? and what is it that you neglect? If God had never told them what they were sent into the world to do, or whither they were going, or what was before them in another world, then they had been excusable; but He hath told them over and over, till they were weary of it. Had He left it doubtful, there had been some excuse; but it is His sealed word, and they profess to believe it, and would take it ill of us if we should question whether they do believe it or not.

Beloved, I come not to accuse any of you particularly of this crime; but seeing it is the commonest cause of men's destruction, I suppose you will judge it the fittest matter for our inquiry, and deserving our greatest care for the cure. To which end I shall, (1) endeavor the conviction of the guilty; (2) shall give them such considerations as may tend to humble and reform them; (3) I shall conclude with such direction as may help them that are willing to escape the destroying power of this sin.

And for the first, consider: It is the case of most sinners to think themselves freest from those sins that they are most enslaved to; and one reason why we can not reform them is because we can not convince them of their guilt. It is the nature of sin so far to blind and befool the sinner, that he knoweth not what he doth, but thinketh he is free from it when it reigneth in him, or when he is committing it: it bringeth men to be so much unacquainted with themselves that they know not what they think, or what they mean and intend, nor what they love or hate, much less what they are habituated and disposed to. They are alive to sin, and dead to all the reason, consideration, and resolution that should recover them, as if it were only by their sinning that we must know that they are alive. May I hope that you that hear me to-day are but willing to know the truth of your case, and then I shall be encouraged to proceed to an inquiry. God will judge impartially; why should not we do so? Let me, therefore, by these following questions, try whether none of you are slighters of Christ and your own salvation. And follow me, I beseech you, by putting them close to your own hearts, and faithfully answering them.

Things that men highly value will be remembered; they will be matter of their freest and sweetest thoughts. This is a known case.

Do not those then make light of Christ and salvation that think of them so seldom and coldly in comparison of other things? Follow thy own heart, man, and observe what it daily runneth after; and then judge whether it make not light of Christ.

We can not persuade men to one hour's sober consideration what they should do for an interest in Christ, or in thankfulness for His love, and yet they will not believe that they make light of Him.

Things that we highly value will be matter of our discourse; the judgment and heart will command the tongue. Freely and delightfully will our speech run after them. This also is a known case.

Do not those men make light of Christ and salvation that shun the mention of His name, unless it be in a vain or sinful use? Those that love not the company where Christ and salvation is much talked of, but think it troublesome, precise discourse: that had rather hear some merry jests, or idle tales, or talk of their riches or business in the world; when you may follow them from morning to night, and scarce have a savory word of Christ; but perhaps some slight and weary mention of Him sometimes; judge whether these make not light of Christ and salvation. How seriously do they talk of the world and speak of vanity! but how heartlessly do they make mention of Christ and salvation!

The things that we highly value we would secure the possession of, and therefore would take any convenient course to have all doubts and fears about them well resolved. Do not those men then make light of Christ and salvation that have lived twenty or thirty years in uncertainty whether they have any part in these or not, and yet never seek out for the right resolution of their doubts? Are all that hear me this day certain they shall be saved? Oh, that they were! Oh, had you not made light of salvation, you could not so easily bear such doubting of it; you could not rest till you had made it sure, or done your best to make it sure. Have you nobody to inquire of, that might help you in such a work? Why, you have ministers that are purposely appointed to that office. Have you gone to them, and told them the doubtfulness of your case, and asked their help in the judging of your condition? Alas! ministers may sit in their studies from one year to another, before ten persons among a thousand will come to them on such an errand! Do not these make light of Christ and salvation? When the gospel pierceth the heart indeed, they cry out, "Men and brethren, what shall we do to be saved?" Trembling and astonished, Paul cries out, "Lord, what wilt Thou have me to do?" And so did the convinced Jews to Peter. But when hear we such questions?

The things that we value do deeply affect us, and some motions will be in the heart according to our estimation of them. O sirs, if men made not light of these things, what working would there be in the hearts of all our hearers! What strange affections would it raise in them to hear of the matters of the world to come! How would their hearts melt before the power of the gospel! What sorrow would be wrought in the discovery of their sins! What astonishment at the consideration of their misery! What unspeakable joy at the glad tidings of salvation by the blood of Christ! What resolution would be raised in them upon the discovery of their duty! Oh, what hearers should we have, if it were not for this sin! Whereas now we are liker to weary them, or preach them asleep with matters of this unspeakable moment. We talk to them of Christ and salvation till we make their heads ache: little would one think by their careless carriage that they heard and regarded what we said, or tho we spoke at all to them.

Our estimation of things will be seen in the diligence of our endeavors. That which we highliest value, we shall think no pains too great to obtain. Do not those men then make light of Christ and salvation that think all too much that they do for them; that murmur at His service, and think it too grievous for them to endure? that ask His service as Judas of the ointment. What need this waste? Can not men be saved without so much ado? This is more ado than needs. For the world they will labor all the day, and all their lives; but for Christ and salvation they are afraid of doing too much. Let us preach to them as long as we will, we can not bring them to relish or resolve upon a life of holiness. Follow them to their houses, and you shall not hear them read a chapter, nor call upon God with their families once a day; nor will they allow Him that one day in seven which He hath separated to His service. But pleasure, or worldly business, or idleness, must have a part. And many of them are so far hardened as to reproach them that will not be as mad as themselves. And is not Christ worth the seeking? Is not everlasting salvation worth more than all this? Doth not that soul make light of all these that thinks his ease more worth than they? Let but common sense judge.

That which we most highly value, we think we can not buy too dear. Christ and salvation are freely given, and yet the most of men go without them because they can not enjoy the world and them together. They are called but to part with that which would hinder them Christ, and they will not do it. They are called but to give God His own, and to resign all to His will, and let go the profits and pleasures of this world, when they must let go either Christ or them, and they will not. They think this too dear a bargain, and say they can not spare these things: they must hold their credit with men; they must look to their estates: how shall they live else? They must have their pleasure, whatsoever becomes

of Christ and salvation: as if they could live without Christ better than without these; as if they were afraid of being losers by Christ, or could make a saving match by losing their souls to gain the world. Christ hath told us over and over that if we will not forsake all for Him we can not be His disciples. Far are these men from forsaking all, and yet will needs think that they are His disciples indeed.

That which men highly esteem, they would help their friends to as well as themselves. Do not those men make light of Christ and salvation that can take so much care to leave their children portions in the world, and do so little to help them to heaven? that provide outward necessaries so carefully for their families, but do so little to the saving of their souls? Their neglected children and friends will witness that either Christ, or their children's souls, or both, were made light of.

That which men highly esteem, they will so diligently seek after that you may see it in the success, if it be a matter within their reach. You may see how many make light of Christ, by the little knowledge they have of Him, and the little communion with Him, and the communication from Him; and the little, yea, none, of His special grace in them. Alas! how many ministers can speak it to the sorrow of their hearts, that many of their people know almost nothing of Christ, tho they hear of Him daily! Nor know they what they must do to be saved: if we ask them an account of these things, they answer as if they understood not what we say to them, and tell us they are no scholars, and therefore think they are excusable for their ignorance. Oh, if these men had not made light of Christ and their salvation, but had bestowed but half as much pains to know and enjoy Him as they have done to understand the matters of their trades and callings in the world, they would not have been so ignorant as they are: they make light of these things, and therefore will not be at the pains to study or learn them. When men that can learn the hardest trade in a few years have not learned a catechism, nor how to understand their creed, under twenty or thirty years' preaching, nor can abide to be questioned about such things, doth not this show that they have slighted them in their hearts? How will these despisers of Christ and salvation be able one day to look Him in the face, and to give an account of these neglects?

Thus much I have spoken in order to your conviction. Do not some of your consciences by this time smite you, and say, I am the man that have made light of my salvation? If they do not, it is because you make light of it still, for all that is said to you. But because, if it be the will of the Lord, I would fain have this damning distemper cured, and am loath to leave you in such a desperate condition, if I knew how to remedy it, I will give you some considerations, which may move you, if you be men of reason and understanding, to look better about you; and I beseech you to weigh them, and make use of them as we go, and lay open your hearts to the work of grace, and sadly bethink you what a case you are in, if you prove such as make light of Christ.

Consider, 1. Thou makest light of Him that made not light of thee who deserve it. Thou wast worthy of nothing but contempt. As a man, what art thou but a worm to God? As a sinner, thou art far viler than a toad: yet Christ was so far from making light of thee and thy happiness, that He came down into the flesh, and lived a life of suffering, and offered Himself a sacrifice to the justice which thou hadst provoked, that thy miserable soul might have a remedy. It is no less than miracles of love and mercy that He hath showed to us; and yet shall we slight them after all?

Angels admire them, whom they less concern, and shall redeemed sinners make light of them? What barbarous, yea, devilish—yea, worse than devilish—ingratitude is this! The devils never had a savior offered to them; but thou hast, and dost thou yet make light of Him?

2. Consider, the work of man's salvation by Jesus Christ is the masterpiece of all the works of God, wherein He would have His love and mercy to be magnified. As the creation declareth His goodness and power, so doth redemption His goodness and mercy; He hath contrived the very frame of His worship so that it shall much consist in the magnifying of this work; and, after all this, will you make light of it? "His name is wonderful." "He did the work that none could do." "Greater love could none show than His." How great was the evil and misery that He delivered us from! the good procured from us! All are wonders, from His birth to His ascension; from our new birth to our glorification, all are wonders of matchless mercy—and yet do you make light of them?

3. You make light of matters of greatest excellency and moment in the world: you know not what it is that you slight: had you well known, you would not have done it. As Christ said to the woman of Samaria, "Hadst thou known who it is that speaketh to thee, thou wouldst have asked of Him the waters of life"; had they known they would not have crucified the Lord of Glory. So, had you known what Christ is, you would not have made light of Him; had you been one day in heaven, and but seen what they possess, and seen also what miserable souls must endure that are shut out, you would never sure have made so light of Christ.

O sirs, it is no trifles or jesting matters that the gospel speaks of. I must needs profess to you that when I have the most serious thoughts of these things myself, I am ready to marvel that such amazing matters do not overwhelm the souls of men; that the greatness of the subject doth not so overmatch our understandings and affections as even to drive men besides themselves, but that God hath always somewhat allayed it by the distance; much more that men should be so blockish as to make light of them. O Lord, that men did but know what everlasting glory and everlasting torments are: would they then hear us as they do? would they read and think of these things as they do? I profess I have been ready to wonder, when I have heard such weighty things delivered, how people can forbear crying out in the congregation; much more how they can rest till they have gone to their ministers, and learned what they should do to be saved, that this great business might be put out of doubt. Oh, that heaven and hell should work no more on men! Oh, that everlastingness work no more! Oh, how can you forbear when you are alone to think with yourselves what it is to be everlastingly in joy or in torment! I wonder that such thoughts do not break your sleep, and that they come not in your mind when you are about your labor! I wonder how you can almost do anything else! how you can have any quietness in your minds! How you can eat, or drink, or rest, till you have got some ground of everlasting consolations! Is that a man or a corpse that is not affected with matters of this moment? that can be readier to sleep than to tremble when he heareth how he must stand at the bar of God? Is that a man or a clod of clay that can rise or lie down without being deeply affected with his everlasting estate? that can follow his worldly business and make nothing of the great business of salvation or damnation; and that when they know it is hard at hand? Truly, sirs, when I think of the weight of the matter, I wonder at the very best of God's saints upon the earth that they are no better, and do no more in so weighty a case. I wonder at those whom the world accounteth more holy than needs, and scorns for making too much ado, that they can put off Christ and their souls with so little; that they pour not out their souls in every supplication; that they are not more taken up with God; that their thoughts be more serious in preparation for their account. I wonder that they be not a hundred times more strict in their lives, and more laborious and unwearied in striving for the crown, than they are. And for myself, as I am ashamed of my dull and careless heart, and of my slow and unprofitable course of life, so the Lord knows I am ashamed of every sermon that I preach: when

I think what I have been speaking of, and who sent me, and that men's salvation or damnation is so much concerned in it, I am ready to tremble lest God should judge me as a slighter of His truth and the souls of men, and lest in the best sermon I should be guilty of their blood. Methinks we should not speak a word to men in matters of such consequence without tears, or the greatest earnestness that possibly we can: were not we too much guilty of the sin which we reprove, it would be so. Whether we are alone, or in company, methinks our end, and such an end, should still be in our mind, and before our eyes; and we should sooner forget anything, and set light by anything, or by all things, than by this.

Consider, 4. Who is it that sends this weighty message to you? Is it not God Himself? Shall the God of heaven speak and men make light of it? You would not slight the voice of an angel or a prince.

5. Whose salvation is it that you make light of? Is it not your own? Are you no more near or dear to yourselves than to make light of your own happiness or misery? Why, sirs, do you not care whether you be saved or damned? Is self-love lost? are you turned your own enemies? As he that slighteth his meat doth slight his life, so if you slight Christ, whatsoever you may think, you will find it was your own salvation that you slighted. Hear what He saith, "All they that hate me love death."

6. Your sin is greater, in that you profess to believe the gospel which you make so light of. For a profest infidel to do it that believes not that ever Christ died, or rose again, or doth not believe that there is a heaven or hell, this were no such marvel—but for you, that make it your creed, and your very religion, and call yourselves Christians, and have been baptized into this faith, and seemed to stand to it, this is the wonder, and hath no excuse. What! believe that you shall live in endless joy or torment, and yet make no more of it to escape torment, and obtain that joy! What! believe that God will shortly judge you, and yet make no preparation for it! Either say plainly, I am no Christian, I do not believe these wonderful things, I will believe nothing but what I see, or else let your hearts be affected with your belief, and live as you say you do believe. What do you think when you repeat the creed, and mention Christ's judgment and everlasting life?

7. What are these things you set so much by as to prefer them before Christ and the saving of your soul? Have you found a better friend, a greater and a surer happiness than this? Good Lord! what dung is it that men make so much of, while they set so light by everlasting glory? What toys are they that are daily taken up with, while matters of life and death are neglected? Why, sirs, if you had every one a kingdom in your hopes, what were it in comparison of the everlasting kingdom? I can not but look upon all the glory and dignity of this world, lands and lordships, crowns and kingdoms, even as on some brain-sick, beggarly fellow, that borroweth fine clothes, and plays the part of a king or a lord for an hour on a stage, and then comes down, and the sport is ended, and they are beggars again. Were it not for God's interest in the authority of magistrates, or for the service they might do Him, I should judge no better of them. For, as to their own glory, it is but a smoke: what matter is it whether you live poor or rich, unless it were a greater matter to die rich than it is? You know well enough that death levels all. What matter is it at judgment, whether you be to answer for the life of a rich man or a poor man? Is Dives, then, any better than Lazarus? Oh, that men knew what poor, deceiving shadow they grasp at while they let go the everlasting substance! The strongest, and richest, and most voluptuous sinners do but lay in fuel for their sorrows, while they think they are gathering together a treasure. Alas! they are asleep, and dream that they are happy; but when they awake, what a change will they find! Their crown is made of thorns; their pleasure hath such a sting as will stick in the heart through all eternity, except unfeigned repentance do prevent it. Oh, how sadly will these wretches be convinced ere long, what a foolish bargain they made in selling Christ and their salvation for these trifles! Let your farms and merchandise, then, save you, if they can, and do that for you that Christ would have done. Cry then to Baal, to save thee! Oh, what thoughts have drunkards and adulterers, etc., of Christ, that will not part with the basest lust for Him? "For a piece of bread," saith Solomon, "such men do transgress."

8. To set so light by Christ and salvation is a certain mark that thou hast no part in them, and if thou so continue, that Christ will set as light by thee: "Those that honor him he will honor, and those that despise him shall be lightly esteemed." Thou wilt feel one day that thou canst not live without Him; thou wilt confess then thy need of Him; and then thou mayest go look for a savior where thou wilt; for He will be no Savior for thee hereafter, that wouldst not value Him, and submit to Him here. Then who will prove the loser by thy contempt? Oh, what a thing will it be for a poor miserable soul to cry to Christ for help in the day of extremity, and to hear so sad an answer as this! Thou didst set lightly by Me and My law in the day of thy prosperity, and I will now set as light by thee in the day of thy adversity. Read Prov. i., 24, to the end. Thou

that, as Esau, didst sell thy birthright for a mess of pottage, shalt then find no place for repentance, tho thou seek it with tears. Do you think that Christ shed His blood to save them that continue to make light of it? and to save them that value a cup of drink or a lust before His salvation? I tell you, sirs, tho you set so light by Christ and salvation, God doth not so: He will not give them on such terms as these: He valueth the blood of His Son, and the everlasting glory, and He will make you value them if ever you have them. Nay, this will be thy condemnation, and leaveth no remedy. All the world can not save him that sets lightly by Christ. None of them shall taste of His supper. Nor can you blame Him to deny you what you made light of yourselves. Can you find fault if you miss of the salvation which you slighted?

9. The time is near when Christ and salvation will not be made light of as now they are. When God hath shaken those careless souls out of their bodies, and you must answer for all your sins in your own name, oh, then, what would you not give for a Savior! When a thousand bills shall be brought in against you, and none to relieve you, then you will consider, Oh! Christ would now have stood between me and the wrath of God; had I not despised Him, He would have answered all. When you see the world hath left you, and your companions in sin have deceived themselves and you, and all your merry days are gone, then what would you not give for that Christ and salvation that now you account not worth your labor! Do you think that when you see the judgment seat, and you are doomed to everlasting perdition for your wickedness, that you should then make as light of Christ as now? Why will you not judge now as you know you shall judge then? Will He then be worth ten thousand worlds? And is He not now worth your highest estimation and dearest affection?

10. God will not only deny thee that salvation thou madest light of, but He will take from thee all that which thou didst value before it: he that most highly esteems Christ shall have Him, and the creatures, so far as they are good here, and Him without the creature hereafter, because the creature is not useful; and he that sets more by the creature than by Christ, shall have some of the creature without Christ here, and neither Christ nor it hereafter.

So much of these considerations, which may show the true face of this heinous sin.

What think you now, friends, of this business? Do you not see by this time what a case that soul is in that maketh light of Christ and salvation? What need then is there that you should take heed lest this should prove your own case! The Lord knows it is too common a case. Whoever is found guilty at the last of this sin, it were better for that man he had never been born. It were better for him he had been a Turk or Indian, that never had heard the name of a Savior, and that never had salvation offered to him: for such men "have no cloak for their sin." Besides all the rest of their sins, they have this killing sin to answer for, which will undo them. And this will aggravate their misery, that Christ whom they set light by must be their Judge, and for this sin will He judge them. Oh, that such would now consider how they will answer that question that Christ put to their predecessors: "How will ye escape the damnation of hell?" or, "How shall we escape if we neglect so great salvation?" Can you escape without a Christ? or will a despised Christ save you then? If he be accurst that sets light by father or mother, what then is he that sets light by Christ? It was the heinous sin of the Jews, that among them were found such as set light by father and mother. But among us, men slight the Father of Spirits! In the name of God, brethren, I beseech you to consider how you will then bear this anger which you now make light of! You that can not make light of a little sickness or want, or of natural death, no, not of a toothache, but groan as if you were undone; how will you then make light of the fury of the Lord, which will burn against the contemners of His grace! Doth it not behoove you beforehand to think of these things?

Dearly beloved in the Lord, I have now done that work which I came upon; what effect it hath, or will have, upon your hearts, I know not, nor is it any further in my power to accomplish that which my soul desireth for you. Were it the Lord's will that I might have my wish herein, the words that you have this day heard should so stick by you that the secure should be awakened by them, and none of you should perish by the slighting of your salvation. I can not follow you to your several habitations to apply this word to your particular necessities; but oh, that I could make every man's conscience a preacher to himself that it might do it, which is ever with you! That the next time you go prayerless to bed, or about your business, conscience might cry out, Dost thou set no more by Christ and thy salvation? That the next time you are tempted to think hardly of a holy and diligent life (I will not say to deride it as more ado than needs), conscience might cry out to thee, Dost thou set so light by Christ and thy salvation? That the next time you are ready to rush upon unknown sin, and to please your fleshly desires against the command of God, conscience might cry out, Is Christ and salvation no more worth than to cast them away, or venture them for thy lust? That when you are following the world with your most eager desires, forgetting the world to come, and the change that is a little before you, conscience might cry out to you, Is Christ and salvation no more worth than so? That when you are next spending the Lord's day in idleness or vain sports, conscience might tell you what you are doing. In a word, that in all your neglects of duty, your sticking at the supposed labor or cost of a godly life, yea, in all your cold and lazy prayers and performances, conscience might tell you how unsuitable such endeavors are to the reward; and that Christ and salvation should not be so slighted. I will say no more but this at this time, it is a thousand pities that when God hath provided a Savior for the world, and when Christ hath suffered so much for their sins, and made so full a satisfaction to justice, and purchased so glorious a kingdom for His saints, and all this is offered so freely to sinners, to lost, unworthy sinners, even for nothing, that yet so many millions should everlastingly perish because they make light of their Savior and salvation, and prefer the vain world and their lusts before them. I have delivered my message, the Lord open your hearts to receive it. I have persuaded you with the word of truth and soberness; the Lord persuade you more effectually, or else all this is lost. Amen.

HENRY WARD BEECHER

1813-1887

IMMORTALITY

BIOGRAPHICAL NOTE

HENRY WARD BEECHER, preacher, orator, lecturer, writer, editor, and reformer, was born at Litchfield, Connecticut, in 1813. He was by nature and training a great pulpit orator. Mr. Beecher kept himself in perfect physical condition for his work. He has described a course of vocal exercises which he pursued in the open air for a period of three years. "The drill I underwent," he says, "produced, not a rhetorical manner, but a flexible instrument, that accommodated itself readily to every kind of thought and every shape of feeling."

He had deep sympathy for all men, and this with his intense dramatic power often carried him into the wildest and most exalted flights of oratory. Phillips Brooks styled him the greatest preacher in America, and he is generally regarded as the most highly gifted of modern preachers. He was fearless, patriotic, clear-headed, witty, and self-sacrificing. Dr. Wilkinson calls him "the greatest pulpit orator the world ever saw." He died in 1887.

If in this life only we have hope in Christ, we are of all men most miserable.—I Cor. xv., 19.

THIS is not the declaration of a universal principle: it is biographical and personal. And yet, there is in it a principle of prime importance. It is true that Paul and his compeers had sacrificed everything that was dear to man for the sake of Christ. Paul had given up the place that he held among his countrymen, and the things which surely awaited him. He had consented to be an exile. Loving Palestine and the memory of his fathers, as only a Jew could love, he found himself an outcast, and despised everywhere by his own people. And the catalog that he gives of the sufferings which he felt keenly; which perhaps would not have been felt by a man less susceptible than he, but which were no less keen in his case—that catalog shows how much he had given up for Christ. And if it should turn out that after all he had followed a mere fable, a myth; that Christ was but a man; that, dying, He had come to an end; that He stayed dead, and that there was no resurrection, no future, but only that past through which he waded, and that present in which he was suffering, then, surely, it would be true that of all men he was most miserable.

This is the biographical view; but it may be said of all men, in this respect, that no persons can so ill afford to lose faith of immortality as those who have had all their affections burnished, deepened and rendered sensitive by the power of Christianity. When Christianity has had the education of generation after generation, and has shaped the style of its manhood, and ordained the institutions by which its affections have been enlarged and purified; when, in short, generations of men have been intimately the children of Christianity, to take away from them the faith of immortality would be a cruelty which could have no parallel in the amount of suffering which it would entail.

It is not necessarily true that men without a hope of Christianity would have no incitement to virtue—certainly not in the ordinary way in which it is put to us. Abstractly, it is said that virtue is its own reward—and it is. If there was enough of it to amount to anything, it would be a great, an exceeding great, reward; but where it is a spark; a germ; where it is struggling for its own existence; where it bears but a few ripe fruits, the reward is hardly worth the culture. If all that we get is what we have in this life, it is but little.

Many men are favorably organized and favorably situated; they have an unyearning content; things seem good enough for them; and they do not understand why it is that persons should desire immortality and glory —that is, at first. In general, I think there are few persons that live long in life who do not, sooner or later, come to a point in which they wake up to the consciousness of a need of this kind. It is not always true in the case of persons of refined moral and intellectual culture that they are conscious of needing a belief in immortality; but a belief in immortality is the unavoidable result and the indispensable requirement of all true manhood. When you look at growth, not in each particular case, but largely, as it develops itself in communities; when you consider it, not only in a single individual, but in whole communities, as they develop from childhood to manhood, or from barbarism through semi-civilization to civilization and refinement, the law of development is always away from animal life and its sustaining appetites and passions toward the moral and the intellectual. That is the direction in which unfolding takes place.

The naturalist watches the insect, and studies all the stages through which it goes, till it becomes a perfect insect. We look at a seed, and see how it develops stem and leaf and blossom all the way through, till we find out what the plant is in its final and perfect condition. And in studying men to know what is the perfect condition of manhood, looking at them from the beginning to the end, which way does manhood lie, in the direction of the bodily appetites and senses, or in the other direction?

Men come into life perfect animals. There is very little that culture does in that direction, giving them a little more or a little less use of themselves, as the case may be. That which we mean when we speak of developing manhood in a child, is something more than the development of symmetry of form and power of physical organization. When we speak of the civilization and refinement of the race at large, development does not mean bodily power or bodily skill: it means reason; moral sense; imagination; profounder affection; subtler, purer, sweeter domestic relations. Manhood grows away from bodily conditions, without ever leaving them. The body becomes a socket, and the soul is a lamp in it. And if you look narrowly at what we mean by growth in mankind, whether it be applied to the individual or to the race, you will find that we mean an unfolding which takes a man

away from the material toward that which is subtler, more spiritual, existing outside of the ordinary senses, tho acting from them, as something better than bone and muscle, nerve and tissue.

All development, then, is from the animal toward the spiritual and the invisible. This is the public sentiment of mankind even in the lower forms of society. What are considered heroic traits, the things which bring admiration to men, if narrowly examined will be found to be not the things which belong to men as brutes—tho these things may be employed by them as instruments. Even in the cases of such men as Samson and Hercules, who were rude, brute men, it was not their strength that drew admiration to them: it was their heroism; it was their patriotism; it was that which they did by their strength for their kind, and not for themselves. And in lower societies it is courage, it is self-devotion, it is the want of fear, it is the higher form of animal life, that attracts admiration. But as we develop out of barbarous into civilized conditions, we admire men, not because they can lift so much, or throw such heavy weights, or endure such hardships of body. Admiration on these accounts has its place; but higher than these is the power of thought, the power of planning, the power of executing, the power of living at one point so as to comprehend in the effects produced all circuits of time in the future. Thought-power; emotion; moral sense; justice; equity in all its forms; higher manhood, and its branches, which stretch up into the atmosphere and reach nearest to the sun—these are something other than those qualities which develop earliest, and are lowest—nearest to the ground.

True manhood, then, has its ripeness in the higher faculties. Without disdaining the companionship of the body the manhood of man grows away from it—in another direction. There is not simply the ripening of the physical that is in man; but there is, by means of the physical, the ripening of the intellectual, the emotional, the moral, the esthetic life, as well as the whole spiritual nature.

When reason and moral sense are developed, there will inevitably spring up within a man an element the value of which consists in perpetuating things—in their continuance. It is spontaneous and universal for one to seek to perpetuate, to extend life. I do not mean by this that one wants to live a great while; but men are perpetually under the unconscious influence of this in their nature: the attempt to give form and permanence to that which is best in their manhood. We build, to be sure, primarily, to cover ourselves from the elements; but we very soon cease to build for that only: we not merely build for protection from cold and from wet, but we build for gratification. We build to gratify the sense of beauty, the sense of convenience, and the sense of love. And we go on beyond that: we build in order that we may send down to those who are to come after us a memorial of our embodied, incarnated thoughts. In other words, when men build, they seek, by incarnation, to render things permanent which have existed only as thoughts or transient emotions. There is a tendency to incarnate the fugitive elements in men, and give them permanence. And the element of continuing is one of the elements which belong to the higher manhood.

This throws light upon the material growths of society. Men strive to perpetuate thoughts and feelings which are evanescent unless they are born into matter. Men build things for duration. There is this unconscious following out of things to make them last; to give them long periods. And it opens up to men the sense of their augmented being. Largeness of being is indissolubly connected with extended time of being.

We admire the pyramids, not because they have been associated with so many histories, but because they have stood so many ages. We admire old trees, not because so many tribes have sat under them, nor because so many events have taken place beneath them, but simply because they have age with them. For there are mute, inexplicable feelings connected with the mere extension of time which belong to the higher development of manhood in us. Frangible things are of less value than things that are infrangible. Things that last are of more value, on the same plane, than their congeners are that do not last.

Who can equal the pictures which are painted on the panes of glass in our winter rooms? Where can you find a Lambineau, or any painter who can give a mountain scenery such as we have for nothing, every morning, when we wake up, and such as the sun outside, or the stove inside, destroys before ten o'clock? These pictures are not valued as are those which are painted on canvas, and which are not half so good; but the element of enduring is with the latter, while the element of evanescence is with the former. Tho the pictures on the pane are finer than those on the canvas, they lack the element of time, on which value so largely depends. The soul craves, hungers for, this quality of continuance as an element for measuring the value of things. This element of time is somewhat felt in the earlier conditions of humanity; but it grows with the development of men, and attaches itself to every part of human life.

I never saw a diamond that was so beautiful as are the dew-drops which I see on my lawn in summer. What is the difference between a dew-drop and a diamond? One goes in a moment; it flashes and dies; but the other endures; and its value consists in its endurance. There are hundreds of things which are as beautiful as a diamond in their moment; but the endurance of the diamond is measured by ages, and not by moments, and so carries on the value.

I do not draw these reasonings very close as yet—I do not desire to put too much emphasis upon them; but I think you will see that there is a drift in them, and that they will bear, at last, an important relation to this question of immortality. The element of manhood carries with it a very powerful sense of the value of existence. The desire to live is a blind instinct. A happy experience brings to this instinct many auxiliaries—the expectation of pleasure; the wish to complete unfinished things; the clinging affection to those that have excited love; and habits of enterprise.

Besides all these, is a development of the sense of value in simply being. We have said that in external matters the continuity of being is an element of value in the judgment which mankind at large have put upon things. We say that the same is true in respect to the inward existence—to manhood itself. The savage cares very little for life. He lives for to-day; and in every to-day he lives for the hour. Time is of the least importance to him. The barbarian differs from the savage in this: that he lives to-day for to-morrow, perhaps, but not for next year. The semi-civilized man lives for next year; but only for the year, or for years. The civilized man begins to live in the present for the future. And the Christian civilized man begins to live with a sense of the forever.

The extension of the sense of time goes on with the development of manhood in men. The sweet, the tender, the loving, the thoughtful, the intellectual, live not simply with a sense of life as a pleasure-bringer: there grows up in them, with their development toward manhood, an intrinsic sense of the value of being itself. The soul knows the cargo that it carries. It knows that that cargo is destined to immortality. As men are conscious of seeing more, of thinking more, and of feeling more; as thought becomes more precious; as emotion becomes deeper and more valuable; so men more and more feel that they cannot afford to have such things go to waste.

A man who takes in his hands a lump of mud and molds it to some pleasing form, cares but little when, dropping it, he sees it flatten on the ground. The man that grinds a crystal, and sees it broken, thinks of it for a moment, perhaps, with regret, but soon forgets it. No one, however, can see an organized thing, having its uses, and indicating exquisite skill and long experience, dashed to pieces without pain. But what is anything that is organized in life worth in comparison with the soul of a man? And if that soul be pure, and sweet, and deep, and noble, and active, and fruitful, who can, without a pang, look at it, and think that it must in an instant go to nothing, dissolving again as an icicle from a roof in the spring?

The feeling is not the fruit of mere reflection. It is instinctive. It is universal. Men do not cultivate it on purpose. They cannot help having it. No man of moral culture can regard human life as without immortality except with profound melancholy. No man that is susceptible to reflectiveness can bear to think of man's existence here without the bright background of another life.

The sense of the continuity of existence is grounded in men, and grows with their refinement and development and strength, and gives color to their life, and change to their opinions, it may be.

To men who have developed moral sense and intellectual culture, every element of value in life is made precious by some conscious or some unconscious element of time and continuance. It is the nature of our better faculties, in their better states, to place a man in such relations to everything that is most precious to him, that it gives him pleasure in the proportion in which it seems to be continuous and permanent, and gives him pain in the proportion in which it seems to be evanescent and perishing.

We are building a crystal character with much pain and self-denial; and it is to be built as bubbles are blown? What is finer in line than the bubble? What is more airy? Where are pictures more exquisite, where are colors more tender and rich and beautiful—and where is there anything that is born so near to its end as a bubble? Is the character which we are building with so much pain and suffering and patience, with so much burden of conscience, and with so much aspiration; is the character which we are forming in the invisible realm of the soul—is that but a bubble? Is that only a thin film which reflects the transient experiences of a life of joy or sadness, and goes out? Then, what is life worth? If I had no function but that of a pismire; if I were a beetle that rolled in the dirt, and yet were clothed with a power of reflection, and knew what the depths of feeling were, what intense emotions were, and what struggling and yearning were; if, being a mere insect, I had all the works in the intellect of man, and all the aspiration that goes with spiritual elements; if I were but a leaf-cutter, a bug in the soil, or about the same thing on a little larger pattern, and were to be blotted out at death, what would be the use of my trying to grow? If by refining and whetting our faculties they become more susceptible to pleasure, they become equally susceptible to pain. And in this great, grinding, groaning world, pain is altogether out of proportion to pleasure, in an exquisite temperament. The finer men are the better they are, if they are forever; but the finer men are the worse they are if they are only for a day; for they have a disproportion of sensibility to suffering over and above present remuneration and conscious enjoyment.

Men feel an intrinsic sense of personality and personal worth. They have self-esteem, which is the only central, spinal, manly faculty which gives them a sense of personal identity and personal value, and which is an auxiliary counselor of conscience itself. This sense of "I" demands something more than a short round of physical life, to be followed by extinction. I am too valuble to perish so; and every step in life has been training me in the direction of greater value. As men grow broader, and stronger, and finer, and deeper, and sweeter, they become more and more conscious of the intrinsic value of their being, and demand for themselves a harbor in order that they may not be wrecked or foundered.

Nor do I think that there can be found, to any considerable extent, or developed, friendships which shall not, with all their strength and with all their depth, resist the conception of dissolution or of fading. For friendships are not casual likings. Friendships are not merely the interchange of good nature, and the ordinary friendly offices of good neighborhood. These things are friendly, but they do not comprise friendship. Two trees may grow contiguous, and throw their shade one over upon the other; but they never touch nor help each other; and their roots quarrel for the food that is in the ground. But two vines, growing over a porch, meet each other, and twine together, and twist fiber into fiber and stem into stem, and take shape from each other, and are substantially one. And such are friendships. Now, one cannot have his life divided as two trees are. He cannot enter into partnership with others, and be conscious that that partnership shall be but for an hour or for a moment. The sanctity, the honor, the exaltation, the exhilaration of a true and manly friendship lies in the thought of its continuance. There can be no deep friendship which does not sign for endlessness.

Still more is this true of love: not that rudimentary form which seeks lower fruitions, and which is often but little more than passion done up in friendship; but that higher love which manifests itself chiefly in the spiritual realm; that love which is not forever asking, but forever giving; that love which is not centripetal, but centrifugal; that love which, like a mother's, gives for the pleasure of giving; that love which reveres; that love which looks up; that love which seeks to exalt its object by doing what is pleasant and noble; that love which demands continuance, elevation, yea, grandeur, it may be, in the thing beloved. How little will such a love tolerate the idea of evanescence, the dread of discontinuing! Can such a love do other than yearn for immortality?

So then, if you take the thought, it is this: that if men develop, they come under the dominion of higher faculties; and that it is then their nature to stamp on all their occupations, on their self-consciousness, on the whole development of their affections, the need of continuance, of immortality. There are, therefore, in the growth of the mind itself, as a department of nature, these elements of conviction. The mind cannot do other than develop in itself a faith in immortality.

It may be said, and it sometimes is said, that the origin of the belief of existence out of the body, of spiritual existence, may be traced directly back to the dreams of the barbarous ages, to a period when men were so low that they did not recognize the difference between a dream and a waking reality—to a time when persons dreamed that their friends came back to them, and waked up and believed that they had been back. Thus, it is said, began the thought of continuity of life after death. For my part, I do not care how it began. The question is not how it started; the question is, What becomes of it now that it has begun? No matter how it was born, what purpose is it to serve? What is it adapted to do? How is it calculated to influence our manhood? In what way shall it be employed to lead man God-ward? How shall it be used to work most effectually in the direction of civilization and refinement? It so fits every human soul, that men will not let it go. They cling to it with their inward and best nature.

All experiences of human life fall in with this tendency of the mind. When men look out upon the incoherent and unmannerly course of things in time, I can understand how, believing in the future, they may live with patience; but in every age of the world where the clear light of immortality has not shone, men have mostly been discouraged, have been generally indifferent to public superiority, and have taken no interest in things done for the sake of humanity. Such is the worthlessness of time, to the thought of those that have no faith in the future, that they have cared for little except present physical enjoyment. And on the whole, when such men crowd together, and tribes take the place of individuals, or kingdoms take the place of tribes, with all their complications in the working out of their clashing results, they look upon human life, and feel that the world is not worth living for. Things are so uncertain, products are in such disproportion to their causes, or to the expectations of men, that if there is to be nothing but this life,

then, "Eat, drink and be merry, for tomorrow we die," is not only the philosophy of the epicurean, but the temptation of the most wise and frugal and self-restraining. The nature of life to a man who is highly educated requires that he should believe in the continuity and existence of the myriads that he sees in such a state of quarreling infelicity and wretchedness in this mortal condition. The utter futility of the best part of man's life here, the total bankruptcy of his best endeavors, the worthlessness of his career from the material standpoint, makes it imperative on him to believe that he shall have another chance in another sphere of being.

Is it enough to have been born, to have lived till one is of age, and then to be launched out to founder in mid-ocean? Is it enough that one should devote the best part of his life to the building of a character, only to see the fabric which he has constructed tumbling about his ears? Is this enough in the day of distress and bankruptcy? Is it enough, in the time when a man's ambitions are crossed, and the sky is dark, and he can do nothing but stand amid the ruins of his hopes and expectations? Is not the thought revolting to every instinct of manhood?

But if there is another life; if all our labor has this value in it, that while a man is building up his outward estate, if it is certain that the man himself will live, no matter what becomes of his property and his reputation, then all his endeavors have endless scope, and his life becomes redeemable and radiant.

Nowhere else so much as in the realm of grief, I think, is the question of immortality interpreted. It is true that the first shock of overwhelming grief sometimes drives faith out of the mind; that it sometimes staggers the reason; that it sometimes dispossesses the moral sense of its accustomed health, and leaves the mind in weakness. As in a fever, the natural eye can see nothing aright, and things then seem to dance in the air, and take on grotesque forms, so persons who are bewildered with first sorrow oftentimes see things amiss. And there is no skepticism which is so deep and pulseless as that which often takes possession of people in the first great overmastering surprize and shock of grief. But after one had recovered a little, and the nerve has come to its wonted sensibility, the faith of immortality returns. There is that in every soul which knows what is the strength of life and noble deeds and aspirations; and therefore there is that in every soul which calls out for immortality.

I cannot believe, I will not believe, when I walk upon the clod, that it is my mother that I tread under foot. She that bore me, she that every year more than gave birth to me out of her own soul's aspiration—I will not believe that she is dust. Everything within me revolts at the idea.

Do two persons walk together in an inseparable union, mingling their brightest and noblest thoughts, striving for the highest ideal, like flowers that grow by the side of each other, breathing fragrance each on the other, and shining in beauty each for the other; are two persons thus twined together and bound together for life, until in some dark hour one is called and the other is left; and does the bleeding heart go down to the grave and say, "I return dust to dust?" Was that dust, then? That trustworthiness; that fidelity; that frankness of truth; that transparent honesty; that heroism of love; that disinterestedness; that fitness and exquisiteness of taste; that fervor of love; that aspiration; that power of conviction; that piety; that great hope in God—were all these elements in the soul of the companion that had disappeared but just so many phenomena of matter? And have they already collapsed and gone, like last year's flowers struck with frost, back again to the mold? In the grief of such an hour one will not let go the hope of resurrection.

Can a parent go back from the grave where he has laid his children and say, "I shall never see them more?" Even as far back as the dim twilight in which David lived, he said, "Thou shalt not come to me, but I shall go to thee"; and is it possible for the parental heart to stand in our day by the side of the grave, where the children have been put out of sight, and say, "They neither shall come to me, nor shall I go to them; they are blossoms that have fallen; they never shall bring forth fruit"? It is unnatural. It is hideous. Everything that is in man, every instinct that is best in human nature repels it.

Is not the human soul, then, itself a witness of the truth of immortality?

Men say, "You cannot prove it. There is no argument that can establish it. No man has seen it, and it cannot be substantiated. It is not a ponderable thing." Men demand that we should prove things by straight lines; by the alembic; by scales; by analysis; but I say that there is much in nature which is so high that scales and rules and alembics cannot touch it. And is not man's soul a part of nature—the highest part?

I hold that even the materialist may believe in immortality. For, altho there is a gross kind of materialism, there may be a materialism which is consistent with a belief in immortality. Because, on the supposition that the mind is matter, it must be admitted that it is incomparably superior to any other matter that we are familiar with. Is there any matter outside of mind that produces thought and feeling such as we see evolved among men? If it be the theory that mind is matter, and if the matter of which the mind is composed be

so far above all other kinds of matter in its fruit and product, is it not on so high a plane as presumably not to be subject to the lower and coarser forms of examination and test? I know no reason why cerebral matter may not be eternal. I do not belong to those who take that material view of the mind; but I do not know that immortality is inconsistent even with materialism; and how much more easily may it be reconciled to the view of those who believe in the ineffable character, the imponderable, spiritual condition, of the soul!

In addition to these arguments, when we come to the Word of God, we hear the voices of those who sang and chanted in the past. We hear the disciple crying out, "Christ is risen!" and we hear the apostle preaching this new truth to mankind. So that now the heavens have been broken open. The secrets of the other life have been revealed. And is there not a presumption, following the line of a man's best manhood, that immortality is true? Does one need to go into a rigorous logical examination of this subject? Should one stand jealously at the side of the sepulcher of Christ, and examine this matter as a policeman examines the certificate of a suspected man, or as one takes money from the hand of a cheating usurer and goes out to see if it is gold? Shall one stand at the door from which issue all the hopes that belong to the best part of man; shall one look upon that which is demanded by the very nature of his better manhood, and question it coldly, and tread it under foot?

What do we gain by obliterating this fair vision? Why should not heaven continue to shine on? Why should we not look into it, and believe that it is, and that it waits for us? Have we not the foretokens of it? Is not the analogy of the faculties one that leads us to believe that there is some such thing? Does not the nature of every man that is high and noble revolt at flesh and matter? Are they not rising toward the ineffable? Are not all the intuitions and affections of men such that, the better they are, the more they have of things that are manly, the more indispensable it is that they should have endurance, etherealization, perpetuation?

The heart and flesh cry out for God. They cry out for immortality. Not only does the Spirit from the heavenly land say to every toiling, yearning, anxious soul, "Come up hither," but every soul that is striving upward has in it, if not a vocalized aspiration, yet a mute yearning—a voice of the soul— that cries out for heaven,

"As the hart panteth after the waterbrooks, so panteth my soul after thee, O God!"

On such a day as this, then, in a community of moral feeling, how blest is the truth which comes to us, that we are not as the beasts that die; that we are as the gods that live! That for which we were made is immortality; and our journey is rough, straight, sharp, burdensome, with many tears. Our journey is not to the grave. I am not growing into old age to be blind, and to be deaf, and to be rheumatic, and to shrink a miserable cripple into the corner, shaking and tottering and forgetting all that I ever knew. The best part of me is untouched. The soul; the reason; the moral sense; the power to think; the power to will; the power to love; the power to admire purity, and to reach out after it—that is not touched by time, tho its instrument and means of outer demonstration be corroded and failing. No physical weakness touches the soul. Only the body is touched by sickness. And shake that down! Shake it down! Let it go! For, as the chrysalis bursts open, and the covering which confines the perfected insect is dropt, that he may come out into brightness of form and largeness of life, so this body is but a chrysalis; and when we break through it, we rise on wings by the attraction of God, and by the propulsion of our own inevitable desire and need, and are forever with the Lord.

LYMAN BEECHER

1775-1863

THE GOVERNMENT OF GOD DESIRABLE

BIOGRAPHICAL NOTE

LYMAN BEECHER was born in New Haven, Conn., in 1775. He graduated from Yale in 1797, and in 1798 took charge of the Presbyterian Church at Easthampton, Long Island. He first attracted attention by his sermon on the death of Alexander Hamilton, and in 1810 became pastor of the Congregational Church at Litchfield, Conn. In the course of a pastorate of 16 years, he preached a remarkable series of sermons on temperance and became recognized as one of the foremost pulpit orators of the country. In 1826 he went to Boston as pastor of the Hanover Street Congregational Church. Six years later he became president of the Lane Theological Seminary in Ohio, an office he retained for twenty years. In 1852 he returned to Boston and subsequently retired to the house of his son, Henry Ward Beecher, where he died in 1863. His public utterances, whether platform or pulpit, were carefully elaborated. They were delivered extemporaneously and sparkled with wit, were convincing by their logic, and conciliating by their shrewd common sense.

Thy will be done in earth as it is in heaven.—Matthew vi., 10.

IN this passage we are instructed to pray that the world may be governed, and not abandoned to the miseries of unrestrained sin; that God Himself would govern, and not another; and that God would administer the government of the world, in all respects, according to His own pleasure. The passage is a formal surrender to God of power and dominion over the earth, as entire as His dominion is in His heaven. The petition, therefore, "Thy will be done," contains the doctrine:

That it is greatly to be desired that God should govern the world, and dispose of men, in all respects, entirely according to His own pleasure.

The truth of this doctrine is so manifest, that it would seem to rank itself in the number of self-evident propositions, incapable of proof clearer than its own light, had not experience taught that, of all truths, it is the most universally and bitterly controverted. Plain as it is, it has occasioned more argument than any other doctrine, and, by argument merely, has gained fewer proselytes; for it is one of those controversies in which the heart decides wholly, and argument, strong or feeble, is alike ineffectual.

This consideration would present, on the threshold, a hopeless impediment to further progress, did we not know, also, that arguments a thousand times repeated, and as often resisted, may at length become mighty through God, to the casting down of imaginations, and every high thing that exalteth itself against the knowledge of God. I shall, therefore, suggest several considerations, to confirm this most obvious truth, that it is desirable that God should govern the world entirely according to His own good pleasure.

1. It is desirable that God should govern the world, and dispose of all events, according to His pleasure, because He knows perfectly in what manner it is best that the world should be governed.

The best way of disposing of men and their concerns is that which will effectually illustrate the glory of God. The glory of God is His benevolence, and His natural attributes for the manifestation of it, and sun of the moral universe, the light and life of His kingdom. All the blessedness of the intelligent creation arises, and ever will arise, from the manifestation and apprehension of the glory of God.

It was to manifest this glory that the worlds were created. It was that there might be creatures to behold and enjoy God, that His dominions were peopled with intelligent beings. And it is that His holy subjects may see and enjoy Him, that He upholds and governs the universe. The entire importance of our world, therefore, and of men and their concerns, is relative, and is great or small only as we are made to illustrate the glory of God. How this important end shall be most effectually accomplished none but Himself is able to determine. He, only, knows how so to order things as that the existence of every being, and every event, shall answer the purpose of its creation, and from the rolling of a world to the fall of a sparrow shall conspire to increase the exhibitions of the divine character, and expand the joy of the holy universe.

An inferior intelligence at the helm of government might conceive very desirable purposes of benevolence, and still be at a loss as to the means most fit and effectual to accomplish them. But, with God, there is no such deficiency. In Him, the knowledge which discovered the end discovers also, with unerring wisdom, the most appropriate means to bring it to pass. He is wise in heart; He hath established the world by His wisdom and stretched out the heavens by His discretion. And is He not wise enough to be intrusted with the government of the world? Who, then, shall be His counsellor? Who shall supply the deficiencies of His skill? Oh, the presumption of vain man! and, oh! the depths both of the wisdom and knowledge of God!

2. It is desirable that God should govern the world according to His own pleasure, because He is entirely able to execute His purposes.

A wise politician perceives, often, both the end and the means; and is still unable to bring to pass his counsels, because the means, though wise, are beyond his control. But God is as able to execute as He is to plan. Having chosen the end, and selected the means, his counsels stand. He is the Lord God omnipotent. The whole universe is a storehouse of means; and when He speaks every intelligence and every atom flies to execute His pleasure. The omnipotence of God, in giving efficacy to His government, inspires and perpetuates the ecstasy of heaven. "And a voice came out from the throne, saying, Praise our God. And I heard as it were the voice of a great multitude, and as the voice of many waters, and as the voice of many thunderings, saying Alleluia, the Lord God omnipotent reigneth." What will that man do in heaven, who is afraid and reluctant to commit to God the government of the earth? And what will become of those who, unable to frustrate His counsels, murmur and rebel against His providence?

3. It is desirable that God should govern the world according to His pleasure, because the pleasure of God is always good.

The angels who kept not their first estate, and many wicked men, have great knowledge, and skill, and power: and yet, on these accounts, are only the more terrible; because they employ these mighty faculties to do evil. And the government of God, were He a being of malevolence, armed as He is with skill and power, would justly fill the universe with dismay. But, as it is, brethren, "let not your hearts be troubled." With God there is no perversion of attributes. He is as good as He is wise and powerful. God is love! Love is that glory of God which He has undertaken to express to His intelligent creation in His works. The sole object of the government of God, from beginning to end, is, to express His benevolence. His eternal decrees, of which so many are afraid, are nothing but the plan which God has devised to express His benevolence, and to make His kingdom as vast and as blest as His own infinite goodness desires. It was to show His glory—to express, in action, His benevolence—that He created all the worlds that roll, and rejoice, and speak His name, through the regions of space. It is to accomplish the same blest design, that He upholds, and places under law, every intelligent being, and directs every event, causing every movement, in every world, to fall in, in its appointed time and place, and to unite in promoting the grand result—the glory of God, and the highest good of His kingdom. And is there a mortal, who, from this great system of blest government, would wish this earth to be an exception? What sort of beings must those be who are afraid of a government administered by infinite benevolence, to express, so far as it can be expressed, the infinite goodness of God? I repeat the question,—What kind of characters must those be who feel as if they had good reason to fear a government the sole object of which is to express the immeasurable goodness of God?

4. It is greatly to be desired that God should govern the world according to His pleasure, because it is His pleasure to rule as a moral governor.

A moral government is a government exercised over free agents, accountable beings; a government of laws, administered by motives.

The importance of such a government below is manifest from the consideration, that it is in His moral government, chiefly, that the glory of God is displayed.

The superintendence of an empty world, or a world of mere animals, would not exhibit, at all, the moral character of God. The glory of God, shining in His law, could never be made manifest, and the brighter glory of God, as displayed in the gospel, must remain forever hid; and all that happiness of which we are capable, as moral beings, the joys of religion below, and the boundless joys of heaven above, would be extinguished, in a moment, by the suspension of the divine moral government.

Will any pretend that the Almighty cannot maintain a moral government on earth, if He governs according to His own pleasure? Can He wield the elements, and control, at His pleasure, every work of His hands, but just the mind of man? Is the most noble work of God—that which is the most worthy of attention, and in reference to which all beside is upheld and governed—itself wholly unmanageable? Has Omnipotence formed minds, which, the moment they are made, escape from His hands, and defy the control of their Maker? Has the Almighty erected a moral kingdom which He cannot govern without destroying its moral nature? Can He only watch, and mend, and rectify, the lawless wanderings of mind? Has He filled the earth with untamed and untamable spirits, whose wickedness and rebellion He can merely mitigate, but cannot control? Does He superintend a world of madmen, full of darkness and disorder, cheered and blest by no internal pervading government of His own? Are we bound to submit to all events, as parts of the holy providence of God; and yet, is there actually no hand of God controlling the movements of the moral world? But if the Almighty can, and if he does, govern the earth as a part of His moral kingdom, is there any method of government more safe and wise than that which pleases God? Can there be a better government? We may safely pray, then, "Thy will be done in earth as it is in heaven," without fearing at all the loss of moral agency; for all the glory of God, in His Law and Gospel, and all the eternal manifestations of glory to principalities and powers in heavenly places, depend wholly upon the fact, that men, though living under the government of God, and controlled according to His pleasure, are still entirely free, and accountable for all the deeds done in the body. There could be no justice in punishment and no condescension, no wisdom, no mercy, in the glorious gospel, did not the government of God, though administered according to His pleasure, include and insure the accountable agency of man.

Seeing, therefore, that all the glory of God, which He ever proposes to manifest to the intelligent creation, is to be made known by the Church, and is to shine in the face of Jesus Christ, and is to depend upon the perfect consistency of the moral government of God with human freedom, we have boundless assurance that, among His absolute, immutable, eternal purposes, one, and a leading one, is, so to govern the world according to His counsels, that, if men sin, there shall be complete desert of

punishment, and boundless mercy in their redemption.

5. It is greatly to be desired that God should rule in the earth according to His pleasure, because it is His pleasure to govern the world in mercy, by Jesus Christ.

The government is in the hand of a Mediator, by whom God is reconciling the world to Himself, not imputing their trespasses to them that believe. Mercy is the bestowment of pardon upon the sinful and undeserving. Now, mankind are so eminently sinful, that no government but one administered in infinite mercy, could afford the least consolation. Had any being but the God of mercy sat upon the throne, or any will but His will prevailed, there would have been no plan of redemption, and no purposes of election, to perplex and alarm the wicked. There would have been but one decree, and that would have been, destruction to the whole race of man. Are any reluctant to be entirely in the hands of God? Are they afraid to trust Him to dispose of soul and body, for time and eternity? Let them surrender their mercies, then, and go out naked from that government which feeds, protects and comforts them. Let them give up their Bibles, and relinquish the means of grace, and the hopes of glory, and descend and make their bed in hell, where they have long since deserved to be, and where they long since would have been, if God had not governed the world according to His own good pleasure. If they would escape the evils which they fear from the hand of God, let them abandon the blessings they receive from it, and they will soon discover whether the absolute dominion of God, and their dependence upon Him, be, in reality, a ground of murmuring and alarm. Our only hope of heaven arises from being entirely in the hands of God. Our destruction could not be made more certain than it would be were we to be given up to our own disposal, or to the disposal of any being but God. Would sinful mortals change their own hearts? Could the combined universe, without God, change the depraved affections of men? Surely, then, we have cause for unceasing joy, that we are in the hands of God; seeing He is a God of mercy, and has decreed to rule in mercy, and actually is administering the government of the world in mercy, by Jesus Christ.

We have nothing to fear, from the entire dominion of God, which we should not have cause equally to fear, as outcasts from the divine government; but we have everything to hope, while He rules the earth according to His most merciful pleasure. The Lord reigneth; let the earth rejoice, let the multitude of the isles be glad. It is of the Lord's mercies that we are not consumed, because His compassions fail not.

6. It is greatly to be desired that God

should dispose of mankind according to His pleasure, because, if He does so, it is certain that there will be no injustice done to anyone.

He will do no injustice to His holy kingdom by any whom He saves. He will bring none to heaven who are not holy, and prepared for heaven. He will bring none there in any way not consistent with His perfections, and the best good of His kingdom; none in any way but that prescribed in the gospel, the way of faith in Jesus Christ, of repentance for sin, and of good works as the constituted fruit and evidence of faith.

Earthly monarchs have their favorites, whom, if guilty of a violation of the laws, they will often interpose to save, although the welfare of the kingdom requires their punishment. But God has no such favorites—He is no respecter of persons: He spared not the angels: and upon the earth distinctions of intellect, or wealth, or honor, will have no effect; he only that believeth shall be saved. The great and the learned shall not be obtruded upon heaven without holiness because they are great or learned; and the humble and contrite shall not be excluded because they are poor, or ignorant, or obscure. God has provided a way for all men to return to Him. He has opened the door of their prison, and set open before them a door of admission into the kingdom of His dear Son; and commanded and entreated them to abandon their dreary abode, and come into the glorious liberty of the sons of God. But all, with one consent, refuse to comply. Each prefers his own loathsome dwelling to the building of God, and chooses, stedfastly, the darkness of his own dungeon, to the light of God's kingdom. But, as God has determined that the redemption of His Son shall not be unavailing through human obstinacy, so He hath chosen, in Christ, multitudes which no man can number, that they should be holy and without blame before Him in love. And in bringing these sons and daughters to glory, through sanctification of the Spirit, and belief of the truth, He will introduce not one whom all the inhabitants of heaven will not hail joyfully, as the companion of their glory. And if God does in the earth just as He pleases, He will make willing, and obedient, and bring to heaven, just those persons who it was most desirable should come. And He will bring just as many obstinate rebels to abandon their prison, and enter cheerfully His kingdom, as infinite wisdom, goodness, and mercy, see fit and desire. He will not mar His glory, or the happiness of His kingdom, by bringing in too many, nor by omitting to bring in enough. His redeemed kingdom, as to the number and the persons who compose it, and the happiness included in it, will be such as shall be wholly satisfactory to God, and to every subject of His kingdom.

And if God governs according to His pleasure, He will do no injustice to His impenitent enemies. He will send to misery no harmless animals without souls—no mere machines—none who have done, or even attempted to do, as well as they could. He will leave to walk in their own way none who do not deserve to be left; and punish none for walking in it who did not walk therein knowingly, deliberately and with wilful obstinacy. He will give up to death none who did not choose death, and choose it with as entire freedom as Himself chooses holiness; and who did not deserve eternal punishment as truly as Himself deserves eternal praise. He will send to hell none who are not opposed to Him, and to holiness, and to heaven; none who are not, by voluntary sin and rebellion, unfitted for heaven, and fitted for destruction, as eminently as saints are prepared for glory. He will consign to perdition no poor, feeble, inoffensive beings, sacrificing one innocent creature to increase the happiness of another. He will cause the punishment of the wicked to illustrate His glory, and thus indirectly to promote the happiness of heaven. But God will not illumine heaven with His glory, and fill it with praise, by sacrificing helpless, unoffending creatures to eternal torment; nor will He doom to hell one whom He will not convince also, that he deserves to go thither. The justice of God, in the condemnation of the impenitent, will be as unquestionable, as His infinite mercy will be in the salvation of the redeemed.

If the will of God is done on earth, among men, there will be no more injustice done to the inhabitants of the earth than there is done to the blessed in heaven. Was it ever known —did any ever complain—was it ever conceived—that God was a tyrant, in heaven? Why, then, should we question the justice of His government on earth? Is He not the same God below as above? Are not all His attributes equally employed? Does He not govern for the same end, and will not His government below conspire to promote the same joyful end as His government above?

7. It is greatly to be desired that God should govern the world according to His pleasure, because His own infinite blessedness, as well as the happiness of His kingdom, depends upon His working all things according to the counsel of His own will.

Could the Almighty be prevented from expressing the benevolence of His nature, according to His purposes, His present boundless blessedness would become the pain of ungratified desire. God is love, and His happiness consists in the exercise and expression of it, according to His own eternal purpose, which He purposed in Christ Jesus before the world began. It is therefore declared, ''The Lord hath made all things for himself;'' that is, to express and gratify His infinite benevolence. The moral excellence of God does not consist in quiescent love, but in love active, bursting forth, and abounding. Nor does the divine happiness arise from the contemplation of idle perfections, but from perfections which comprehend boundless capacity, and activity in doing good.

From what has been said, we may be led to contemplate with satisfaction the infinite blessedness of God.

God is love! This is a disposition which, beyond all others, is happy in its own nature. He is perfect in love; there is, therefore, in His happiness no alloy. His love is infinite; and, of course, His blessedness is unbounded. If the little holiness existing in good men, though balanced by remaining sin, occasions, at times, unutterable joy, how blessed must God be, who is perfectly and infinitely holy! It is to be remembered, also, that the benevolence of God is at all times perfectly gratified. The universe which God has created and upholds, including what He has done, and what He will yet do, will be brought into a condition which will satisfy His infinite benevolence. The great plan of government which God has chosen, and which His power and wisdom will execute, will embrace as much good as in the nature of things is possible. He is not, like erring man, straitened and perplexed, through lack of knowledge or power. There is in His plan no defect, and in His execution no failure. God, therefore, is infinitely happy in His holiness, and in the expression of it which it pleases Him to make.

The revolt of angels, the fall of man, and the miseries of sin, do not, for a moment, interrupt the blessedness of God. They were not, to Him, unexpected events, starting up suddenly while the watchman of Israel slumbered. They were foreseen by God as clearly as any other events of His government, and have occasioned neither perplexity nor dismay. With infinite complacency He beholds still His unshaken counsels, and with almighty hand rolls on His undisturbed decrees. Surrounded by unnumbered millions, created by His hand, and upheld by His power, He shines forth, God over all, blest for ever. What an object of joyful contemplation, then, is the blessedness of God! It is infinite; His boundless capacity is full. It is eternal; He is God blest forever. The happiness of the created universe is but a drop—a drop to the mighty ocean of divine enjoyment. How delightful the thought, that in God there is such an immensity of joy, beyond the reach of vicissitude! When we look around below, a melancholy sensation pervades the mind. What miserable creatures! What a wretched world! But when, from this scene of darkness and misery, we look up to the throne of God, and behold Him, high above the darkness and

miseries of sin, dwelling in light inaccessible and full of glory, the prospect brightens. If a few rebels, who refuse to love and participate in His munificence, are groping in darkness on His footstool, God is light, and in Him there is no darkness at all.

Those who are opposed to the decrees of God, and to His sovereignty, as displayed in the salvation of sinners, are enemies of God.

They are unwilling that His will should be done in earth as it is in heaven; for the decrees of God are nothing but His choice as to the manner in which He will govern His own kingdom. He did not enter upon His government to learn wisdom by experience. Before they were yet formed, His vast dominion lay open to His view; and before He took the reins of created empire, He saw in what manner it became Him to govern. His ways are everlasting. Known unto God are all His works from the beginning. To be opposed to the decrees of God, therefore, is to be unwilling that God should have any choice concerning the government of the world. And can those be willing that God should govern the world entirely according to His pleasure who object to His having any pleasure upon the subject? To object to the choice of God, with respect to the management of the world, because it is eternal, is to object to the existence of God. A God of eternal knowledge. without an eternal will or choice, would be a God without moral character.

To suppose that God did not know what events would exist in His kingdom, is to divest Him of omniscience. To suppose that He did know, and did not care,—had no choice, no purpose,—is to blot out His benevolence, to nullify His wisdom and convert His power into infinite indolence. To suppose that He did know, and choose, and decree, and that events do not accord with His purposes, is to suppose that God has made a world which He can not govern; has undertaken a work too vast; has begun to build, but is not able to finish. But to suppose that God did, from the beginning, behold all things open and naked before Him, and that He did choose, with unerring wisdom and infinite goodness, how to govern His empire,—and yet at the same time, to employ heart, and head, and tongue, in continual opposition to this great and blessed truth,—is, most clearly, to cherish enmity to God and His government.

To object to the choice of God because it is immutable, is to cavil against that which constitutes its consummating excellence. Caprice is a most alarming feature in a bad government; but in a government absolutely perfect, none, surely, can object to its immutability, but those, who, if able, would alter it for the worse.

To say that, if God always knew how to govern so as to display His glory, and bless His kingdom, and always chooses thus to govern, there can be, therefore, no accountable agency in the conduct of His creatures, is to deny the possibility of a moral government, to contradict the express testimony of God; and this, too, at the expense of common sense, and the actual experience of every subject of His moral government on earth.

From the character of God, and the nature of His government, as explained in this discourse, may be inferred, the nature and necessity of unconditional submission to God.

Unconditional submission is an entire surrender of the soul to God, to be disposed of according to His pleasure,—occasioned by confidence in His character as God.

There are many who would trust the Almighty to regulate the rolling of worlds, and to rule in the armies of heaven, just as He pleases; and devils they would consign to His disposal, without the least hesitation; and their own nation, if they were sure that God would dispose of it according to their pleasure; even their own temporal concerns they would risk in the hands of God, could they know that all things would work together for their good; their souls, also, they would cheerfully trust to His disposal, for the world to come, if God would stipulate, at all events, to make them happy.

And to what does all this amount? Truly, that they care much about their own happiness, and their own will, but nothing at all about the will of God, and the welfare of His kingdom. He may decree, and execute His decrees, in heaven, and may turn its inhabitants into machines, or uphold their freedom, as He pleases; and apostate spirits are relinquished to their doom, whether just or unjust. It is only when the government of God descends to particulars, and draws near and enters their own selfish enclosures, and claims a right to dispose of them, and extends its influence to the unseen world, that selfishness and fear take the alarm. Has God determined how to dispose of my soul? Ah! that alters the case. If He can, consistently with freedom, govern angels, and devils, and nations, how can He govern individuals? How can He dispose of me according to His eternal purpose and I be free? Here reason, all-penetrating, and all-comprehensive, becomes weak; the clouds begin to collect, and the understanding, veiled by the darkness of the heart, can "find no end, in wandering mazes lost."

But if God has purposes of mercy in reserve for the sinner, he is convinced, at length, of his sin, and finds himself in an evil case. He reforms, prays, weeps, resolves, and re-resolves, regardless of the righteousness of Christ, and intent only to establish a righteousness of his own. But, through all his windings, sin cleaves to him, and the law, with its fearful curse, pursues him. Whither shall he flee? What shall he do? A rebel heart, that will not bow, fills him with despair. An angry God, who will not clear the guilty, fills him with terror. His strength is gone, his resources fail, his mouth is stopped. With restless anxiety, or wild amazement, he surveys the gloomy prospect. At length, amidst the wanderings of despair, the character of God meets his eye. It is new, it is amiable, and full of glory. Forgetful of danger, he turns aside to behold this great sight; and while he gazes, new affections awake in his soul, inspiring new confidence in God, and in His holy government. Now God appears qualified to govern, and now he is willing that He should govern, and willing himself to be in the hands of God, to be disposed of according to His pleasure. What is the occasion of this change? Has the divine character changed? There is no variableness with God. Did he, then, misapprehend the divine character? Was all this glory visible before? Or has a revelation of new truth been granted? There has been no new revelation. The character now admitted is the same which just before appeared so gloomy and terrible. What, then, has produced this alteration? Has a vision of angels appeared, to announce that God is reconciled? Has some sudden light burst upon him, in token of forgiveness? Has Christ been seen upon the cross, beckoning the sinner to come to Him? Has heaven been thrown open to his admiring eyes? Have enrapturing sounds of music stolen upon the ear, to entrance the soul? Has some text of Scripture been sent to whisper that his sins are forgiven, tho no repentance, nor faith, nor love, has dawned in his soul? And does he now submit, because God has given him assurance of personal safety? None of these. Considerations of personal safety are, at the time, out of the question.

The change produced, then, is the effect of benevolence, raising the affections of the soul from the world, and resting them upon God. Holiness is now most ardently loved. This is seen to dwell in God and His kingdom, and to be upheld and perfected by His moral government. It is the treasure of the soul, and all the attributes of God stand pledged to protect it. The solicitude, therefore, is not merely, What will become of me? but, What, O Lord, will become of Thy glory, and the glory of Thy kingdom? And in the character of God, these inquiries are satisfactorily answered. If God be glorified, and His kingdom upheld and made happy, the soul is satisfied. There is nothing else to be anxious about; for individual happiness is included in the general good, as the drop is included in the ocean.

HUGH BLACK

1869-1953

THE ATTRACTION OF THE PRESENT

BIOGRAPHICAL NOTE

PROFESSOR of practical theology Union Theological Seminary, New York, 1906-1929; born at Rothesay, Scotland, March 26, 1869; educated at Rothesay Academy; Glasgow University, 1883-87; Free Church College, Glasgow, 1887-91; ordained 1891; minister of Sherwood Church, Paisley, Scotland, 1891-96; St. George's United Free Church, Edinburgh, 1896-1906; came to the United States, 1906; author of "The Dream of Youth," "Friendship," "Culture and Restraint," "Practise of Self-Culture," "Listening to God," "Christ's Service of Love," "The Gift of Influence," etc.

"And Esau said, Behold, I am at the point to die; and what profit shall this birthright do to me?"—Genesis 25 : 32.

WE can not suppress a natural sympathy with Esau in this scene between the two brothers. He seems as much sinned against as sinning, and in comparison with the cunning, crafty character of Jacob he appears the better of the two. His very faults lean to virtue's side, we think, as we look at his bold, manly, impulsive figure. There is nothing of the cold calculating selfishness, the astute trickery, the determination to get his pound of flesh, which make his brother appear mean beside him. With our swift and random and surface judgments we are inclined to think it unjust that Esau should be set aside in the great history of grace for one who could be guilty of both malice and fraud in advancing his own interests. We are not at present dealing with the character of Jacob or we would see that this hasty judgment, true so far as it goes, is something less even than half the truth, and that tho he here and elsewhere sinned and was punished through all his life for his subtlety and selfishness, yet he was not the monster of unbrotherly malice merely which this scene might suggest, and that he had qualities of heart and spirit which made it inevitable that he, and not Esau, should be chosen for the line of God's purpose. Our subject is Esau and his weakness and fall in the presence of his overmastering temptation.

Esau's good qualities are very evident, being of the kind easily recognized and easily popular among men, the typical sportsman who is only a sportsman, bold and frank and free and generous, with no intricacies of character, impulsive and capable of magnanimity, the very opposite of the prudent, dexterous, nimble man of affairs, rather reckless indeed and hot-blooded and passionate. His virtues are already, we see, dangerously near to being vices. Being largely a creature of impulse, he was in a crisis the mere plaything of animal passion, ready to satisfy his desire without thought of consequences. Without self-control, without spiritual insight, without capacity even to know what spiritual issues were, judging things by immediate profit and material advantage, there was not in him depth of nature out of which a really noble character could be cut. This damning lack of self-control comes out in the passage of our text, the transaction of the birthright. Coming from the hunt hungry and faint, he finds Jacob cooking porridge of lentils and asks for it. The sting of ungovernable appetite makes him feel as if he would die if he did not get it. Jacob takes advantage of his brother's appetite and offers to barter his dish of pottage for Esau's birthright.

There would be some superstition in the minds of both of them as to the value of the birthright. Both of them valued it as a vague advantage, carrying with it a religious worth, but it meant nothing tangible; and here was Esau's temptation, terribly strong to a man of his fiber. He was hungry, and before his fierce desire for the food actually before him such a thing as a prospective right of birth seemed an ethereal thing of no real value. If he thought of any spiritual privilege the birthright might be supposed to confer, it was only to dismiss the thought as not worth considering. Spiritual values had not a high place in his standard of things. He could not be unaware of the material advantages the possession of the birthright would one day mean. He must have known that it was something to be recognized as the eldest son, with special rights of inheritance and precedence and authority after his father's death. These things were real enough to him, even tho he might have no notion of a deeper meaning in being the heir of the promise. But in the grip of his appetite even these temporal advantages were too distant to weigh much. In the presence of immediate satisfaction the distant appeared shadowy and unreal and not worth sacrificing present enjoyment for. 'He feels he is going to die, as a man of his type is always sure he will die if he does not get what he wants when the passion is on him; and supposing he does die, it will be poor consolation that he did not barter this intangible and shadowy blessing of his birthright. "Behold I am at the point to die; and what profit shall this birthright do to me?"

The Bible writers speak of Esau always with a certain contempt, and with all our appreciation of his good natural qualities, his courage and frankness and good humor, we can not help sharing in the contempt. The man who has no self-control, who is swept away by every passion of the moment, whose life is bounded by sense, who has no appreciation of the higher and larger things which call for self-control, that man is, after all, only a superior sort of animal, and not always so very superior at that. The author of the Epistle to the Hebrews calls Esau "a profane person who for one morsel of meat sold his birthright." "Profane" means not blasphemous but simply secular, a man who is not touched to finer issues, judging things by coarse earthly standards, without spiritual aspiration or insight, feeling every sting of flesh keenly, but with no sting of soul toward God. Bold and manly and generous and with many splendid constitutional virtues he may be, but the man himself lacks susceptibility to the highest motives of life. He is easily bent by every wind of impulse, and is open without defense to animal appetite. He is capable of despising the intangible blessing of such a thing as a birthright, even tho he feel it to be a holy thing, because he can not withstand present need. A profane, a secular person as Esau, is the judgment of the New Testament.

The scene where he surrendered his birthright did not settle the destiny of the two brothers—a compact like this could not stand good forever, and in some magical way substitute Jacob for Esau in the line of God's great religious purpose. But this scene, tho it did not settle their destiny in that sense, revealed their character, the one essential thing which was necessary for the spiritual succession to Abraham; and Esau failed here in this test as he would fail anywhere. His question to reassure himself, "What profit shall this birthright do to me?" reveals the bent of his life and explains his failure. True self-control means willingness to resign the small for the sake of the great, the present for the sake of the future, the material for the sake of the spiritual, and that is what faith makes possible. Of course, Esau did not think he was losing the great by grasping at the small. At the moment the birthright, just because it was distant, appeared insignificant. He had no patience to wait, no faith to believe in the real value of anything that was not material, no self-restraint to keep him from instant surrender to the demand for present gratification.

This is the power of all appeal to passion, that it is present, with us now, to be had at once. It is clamant, imperious, insistent, demanding to be satiated with what is actually present. It has no use for a far-off good. It wants immediate profit. This is temptation, alluring to the eye, whispering in the ear, plucking by the elbow, offering satisfaction now. Here and now—not hereafter; this thing, that red pottage there—not an ethereal unsubstantial thing like a birthright! What is the good of it if we die? And we are like to die if we do not get this gratification the senses demand. In the infatuation of appetite all else seems small in comparison; the birthright is a poor thing compared to the red pottage.

It is the distortion of vision which passion produces, the exaggeration of the present which temptation creates, making the small look like the great, and discrediting the value of the thing lost. The vivid lurid description in the Proverbs of the young man void of understanding snared in the street by the strange woman gives both these elements of the effect of passion, the weak surrender to impulse, and the distortion of vision which blinds to the real value of what is given up for the gratification. "He goeth straightway as an ox goeth to the slaughter, till a dart strike through his liver; as a bird hasteth to the snare, and knoweth not that it is for his life."

But it is not merely lack of self-control which Esau displays by the question of our text. It is also lack of appreciation of spiritual values. In a vague way he knew that the birthright meant a religious blessing, and in the grip of his temptation that looked to him as purely a sentiment, not to be seriously considered as on a par with a material advantage. The profane man, the secular man, may not be just a creature of impulse, he may have his impulses in good control, but he has no place for what is unseen. He asks naturally, What shall it profit? Men who judge by the eye, by material returns only, who are frankly secular, think themselves great judges of profit, and they too would not make much of a birthright if it meant only something sentimental, as they would call it. The real and not the ideal, the actual and not the visionary, the thing seen and not the thing unseen—they would not hesitate more than Esau over the choice between the pottage and the birthright. They judge by substance, and do not understand about the faith which is the substance of things hoped for, the evidence of things not seen.

How easy it is for all of us to drift into the class of the profane, the secular persons as Esau; to have our spiritual sensibility blunted; to lose our appreciation of things unseen; to be so taken up with the means of living that we forget life itself and the things that alone give it security and dignity! How

easy, when soul wars with sense, to depreciate everything that is beyond sense, and let the whole moral tone be relaxed! There is much cause for the apostle to warn us to "Look diligently lest there be among us any profane person as Esau who for one morsel of meat sold his birthright."

We, too, can despise our birthright by living far below our privileges, and far below our spiritual opportunities. We have our birthright as sons of God, born to an inheritance as joint-heirs with Christ. We belong by essential nature not to the animal kingdom, but to the kingdom of Heaven; and when we forget it and live only with reference to the things of sense and time, we are disinheriting ourselves as Esau did. The secular temptation strikes a weak spot in all of us, suggesting that the spiritual life, God's love and holiness, the kingdom of Heaven and His righteousness, the life of faith and prayer and communion, are dim and shadowy things, as in the land that is very far off. "What profit shall this birthright do to me?"

What shall it profit? seems a sane and sensible question, to be considered in a businesslike fashion. It is the right question to ask, but it has a wider scope and another application. What profit the mess of pottage if I lose my birthright? What profit the momentary gratification of even imperious passion if we are resigning our true life, and losing the clear vision and the pure heart? What profit to make only provision for the flesh, if of the flesh we reap but corruption? What profit the easy self-indulgence, if we are bartering peace and love and holiness and joy? "What shall it profit a man if he shall gain the whole world (and not merely a contemptible mess of pottage) and lose his own soul?" What profit if in the insistence of appetite men go like an ox to the slaughter, knowing not that it is for their life? "Thus Esau despised his birthright."

HUGH BLAIR

1718-1800

THE HOUR AND THE EVENT OF ALL TIME

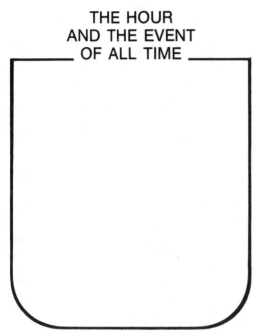

BIOGRAPHICAL NOTE

HUGH BLAIR, the preacher and divine, was born in Edinburgh, 1718. He entered the university of his native town and graduated in 1739. Two years later he was licensed to preach; he was ordained minister of Colossie, Fife, in 1742, but returned to Edinburgh and in 1762 was made regius professor of rhetoric and belles-lettres to the university. He became a member of the great literary club, the Poker, where he associated with Hume, A. Carlyle, Adam Ferguson, Adam Smith and others, and enjoyed a high reputation as a preacher and critic. The lectures he published on style are elegantly written, but weak in thought, and his sermons share the same fault. They are composed with great care, and sometimes a single discourse cost him a week's labor, but they are formal and destitute of feeling and sometimes even affected in style. Blair was notable for fastidiousness in dress and manners, and took very seriously the reputation he was given for refinement and common-sense as one of the moderate divines. He died in 1800.

Jesus lifted up His eyes to heaven, and said, Father! the hour is come.—John xvii., 1.

THESE were the words of our blest Lord on a memorable occasion. The feast of the Passover drew nigh, at which He knew that He was to suffer. The night was arrived wherein He was to be delivered into the hands of His enemies. He had spent the evening in conference with His disciples, like a dying father in the midst of his family, mingling consolations with His last instructions. When He had ended His discourse to them, "he lifted up his eyes to heaven," and with the words which I have now read, began that solemn prayer of intercession for the Church, which closed His ministry. Immediately after, He went forth with His disciples into the garden of Gethsemane and surrendered Himself to those who came to apprehend Him.

Such was the situation of our Lord at the time of His pronouncing these words. He saw His mission on the point of being accomplished. He had the prospect full before Him of all that He was about to suffer—"Father! the hour is come." What hour? An hour the most critical, the most pregnant with great events, since hours had begun to be numbered, since time had begun to run. It was the hour at which the Son of God was to terminate the labors of His important life by a death still more important and illustrious; the hour of atoning, by His sufferings, for the guilt of mankind; the hour of accomplishing prophecies, types, and symbols, which had been carried on through a series of ages; the hour of concluding the old and of introducing into the world the new dispensation of religion; the hour of His triumphing over the world, and death, and hell; the hour of His creating that spiritual kingdom which is to last forever. Such is the hour. Such are the events which you are to commemorate in the sacrament of our Lord's Supper.

I. This was the hour in which Christ was glorified by His sufferings. The whole of His life had discovered much real greatness under a mean appearance. Through the cloud of His humiliation, His native luster often broke forth; but never did it shine so bright as in this last, this trying hour. It was indeed the hour of distress and of blood. He knew it to be such; and when He uttered the words of the text, He had before His eyes the executioner and the cross, the scourge, the nails, and the spear. But by prospects of this nature His soul was not to be overcome. It is distress which ennobles every great character; and distress was to glorify the Son of God. He was now to teach all mankind by His example, how to suffer and to die. He was to stand forth before His enemies as the faithful witness of the truth, justifying by His behavior the character which He assumed, and sealing by His blood the doctrines which He taught.

What magnanimity in all His words and actions on this great occasion! The court of Herod, the judgment-hall of Pilate, the hill of Calvary, were so many theaters prepared for His displaying all the virtues of a constant and patient mind. When led forth to suffer, the first voice which we hear from Him is a generous lamentation over the fate of His unfortunate tho guilty country; and to the last moment of His life we behold Him in possession of the same gentle and benevolent spirit. No upbraiding, no complaining expression escaped from His lips during the long and painful approaches of a cruel death. He betrayed no symptom of a weak or a vulgar, of a discomposed or impatient mind. With the utmost attention of filial tenderness He committed His aged mother to the care of His beloved disciple. With all the dignity of a sovereign He conferred pardon on a fellow-sufferer. With a greatness of mind beyond example, He spent His last moments in apologies and prayers for those who were shedding His blood.

By wonders in heaven and wonders on earth was this hour distinguished. All nature seemed to feel it; and the dead and the living bore witness of its importance. The veil of the temple was rent in twain. The earth shook. There was darkness over all the land. The graves were opened, and "many who slept arose, and went into the holy city." Nor were these the only prodigies of this awful hour. The most hardened hearts were subdued and changed. The judge who, in order to gratify the multitude, passed sentence against Him, publicly attested His innocence. The Roman centurion who presided at the execution, "glorified God," and acknowledged the Sufferer to be more than man. "After he saw the things which had passed, he said, Certainly this was a righteous person: truly this was the Son of God." The Jewish malefactor who was crucified with Him addrest Him as a king, and implored His favor. Even the crowd of insensible spectators, who had come forth as to a common spectacle, and who began with clamors and insults, "returned home smiting their breasts." Look back on the heroes, the philosophers, the legislators of old. View them in their last moments. Recall

every circumstance which distinguished their departure from the world. Where can you find such an assemblage of high virtues, and of great events, as concurred at the death of Christ? Where so many testimonials given to the dignity of the dying person by earth and by heaven?

II. This was the hour in which Christ atoned for the sins of mankind, and accomplished our eternal redemption. It was the hour when that great sacrifice was offered up, the efficacy of which reaches back to the first transgression of man, and extends forward to the end of time; the hour when, from the cross, as from a high altar, the blood was flowing which washed away the guilt of the nations.

This awful dispensation of the Almighty contains mysteries which are beyond the discovery of man. It is one of those things into which "the angels desire to look." What has been revealed to us is, that the death of Christ was the interposition of heaven for preventing the ruin of human kind. We know that under the government of God misery is the natural consequence of guilt. After rational creatures had, by their criminal conduct, introduced disorder into the divine kingdom, there was no ground to believe that by their penitence and prayers alone they could prevent the destruction which threatened them. The prevalence of propitiatory sacrifices throughout the earth proclaims it to be the general sense of mankind that mere repentance was not of sufficient avail to expiate sin or to stop its penal effects. By the constant allusions which are carried on in the New Testament to the sacrifices under the law, as pre-signifying a great atonement made by Christ, and by the strong expressions which are used in describing the effects of His death, the sacred writers show, as plainly as language allows, that there was an efficacy in His sufferings far beyond that of mere example and instruction. The nature and extent of that efficacy we are unable as yet fully to trace. Part we are capable of beholding; and the wisdom of what we behold we have reason to adore. We discern, in this plan of redemption, the evil of sin strongly exhibited and the justice of the divine government awfully exemplified, in Christ suffering for sinners. But let us not imagine that our present discoveries unfold the whole influence of the death of Christ. It is connected with causes into which we can not penetrate. It produces consequences too extensive for us to explore. "God's thoughts are not as our thoughts." In all things we "see only in part"; and here, if anywhere, we see also "as through a glass, darkly."

This, however, is fully manifest, that redemption is one of the most glorious works of the Almighty. If the hour of the creation of the world was great and illustrious, that hour when, from the dark and formless mass, this fair system of nature arose at the divine command, when "the morning-stars sang together, and all the sons of God shouted for joy," no less illustrious is the hour of the restoration of the world; the hour when, from condemnation and misery, it emerged into happiness and peace. With less external majesty it was attended; but it is, on that account, the more wonderful that, under an appearance so simple, such great events were covered.

III. In this hour the long series of prophecies, visions, types, and figures were accomplished. This was the center in which they all met: this the point toward which they had tended and verged, throughout the course of so many generations. You behold the law and the prophets standing, if we may speak so, at the foot of the cross, and doing homage. You behold Moses and Aaron bearing the Ark of the Covenant; David and Elijah presenting the oracle of testimony. You behold all the priests and sacrifices, all the rites and ordinances, all the types and symbols assembled together to receive their consummation. Without the death of Christ, the worship and ceremonies of the law would have remained a pompous, but unmeaning, institution. In the hour when He was crucified, "the book with the seven seals" was opened. Every rite assumed its significancy; every prediction met its event; every symbol displayed its correspondence.

The dark and seemingly ambiguous method of conveying important discoveries under figures and emblems was not peculiar to the sacred books. The spirit of God in presignifying the death of Christ, adopted that plan, according to which the whole knowledge of those early ages was propagated through the world. Under the veil of mysterious allusion, all wisdom was then concealed. From the sensible world images were everywhere borrowed to describe things unseen. More was understood to be meant than was openly exprest. By enigmatical rites the priests communicated his doctrines; by parables and allegories the philosopher instructed his disciples; even the legislator, by figurative sayings, commanded the reverence of the people. Agreeably to this prevailing mode of instruction, the whole dispensation of the Old Testament was so conducted as to be the shadow and figure of a spiritual system. Every remarkable event, every distinguished personage, under the law, is interpreted in the New Testament, as bearing reference to the hour of which we treat. If Isaac was laid upon the altar as an innocent victim; if David was driven from his throne by the wicked, and restored by the hand of God; if the brazen serpent was lifted up to heal the people; if the rock was smitten by Moses, to furnish drink in the wilderness; all were types of Christ and alluded to His death.

In predicting the same event the language of ancient prophecy was magnificent, but seemingly contradictory: for it foretold a Messiah, who was to be at once a sufferer and a conquerer. The Star was to come out of Jacob, and the Branch to spring from the stem of Jesse. The Angel of the Covenant, the desire of all nations, was to come suddenly to His temple; and to Him was to be "the gathering of the people." Yet, at the same time, He was to be "despised and rejected of men"; He was to be "taken from prison and from judgment," and to be "led as a lamb to the slaughter." Tho He was "a man of sorrows, and acquainted with grief," yet "the Gentiles were to come to his light, and kings to the brightness of his rising." In the hour when Christ died, those prophetical riddles were solved: those seeming contradictions were reconciled. The obscurity of oracles, and the ambiguity of types vanished. The "sun of righteousness" rose; and, together with the dawn of religion those shadows passed away.

IV. This was the hour of the abolition of the law, and the introduction of the gospel; the hour of terminating the old and of beginning the new dispensation of religious knowledge and worship throughout the earth. Viewed in this light, it forms the most august era which is to be found in the history of mankind. When Christ was suffering on the cross, we are informed by one of the evangelists that He said, "I thirst"; and that they filled a sponge with vinegar, and put it to His mouth. "After he had tasted the vinegar, knowing that all things were now accomplished, and the Scriptures fulfilled, he said, It is finished"; that is, this offered draft of vinegar was the last circumstance predicted by an ancient prophet that remained to be fulfilled. The vision and the prophecy are now sealed: the Mosaic dispensation is closed. "And he bowed his head and gave up the ghost."

"It is finished." When He uttered these words He changed the state of the universe. At that moment the law ceased, and the gospel commenced. This was the ever memorable point of time which separated the old and the new worlds from each other. On one side of the point of separation you behold the law, with its priests, its sacrifices, and its rites, retiring from sight. On the other side you behold the gospel, with its simple and venerable institutions, coming forward into view. Significantly was the veil of the temple rent in this hour; for the glory then departed from between the cherubim. The legal high priest delivered up his urim and thummim, his breast-plate, his robes, and his incense: and Christ stood forth as the great high priest of all succeeding generations. By that one sacrifice which He now offered, He abolished sacrifices forever. Altars on which the fire had blazed for ages, were now to smoke no more. Victims were no more to bleed. "Not with the blood of bulls and goats, but with his own blood he now entered into the holy place, there to appear in the presence of God for us."

This was the hour of association and union to all the worshipers of God. When Christ said, "It is finished," He threw down the wall of partition which had so long divided the Gentile from the Jew. He gathered into one all the faithful out of every kindred and people. He proclaimed the hour to be come when the knowledge of the true God should be no longer confined to one nation, nor His worship to one temple; but over all the earth, the worshipers of the Father should serve Him "in spirit and in truth." From that hour they who dwelt in the "uttermost ends of the earth, strangers to the covenant of promise," began to be "brought nigh." In that hour the light of the gospel dawned from afar on the British Islands.

During a long course of ages, Providence seemed to be occupied in preparing the world for this revolution. The whole Jewish economy was intended to usher it in. The knowledge of God was preserved unextinguished in one corner of the world, that thence, in due time, might issue forth the light which was to overspread the earth. Successive revelations gradually enlarged the views of men beyond the narrow bounds of Judea, to a more extensive kingdom of God. Signs and miracles awakened their expectation and directed their eyes toward this great event. Whether God descended on the flaming mountain, or spoke by the prophet's voice; whether He scattered His chosen people into captivity, or reassembled them in their own land, He was still carrying on a progressive plan, which was accomplished at the death of Christ.

Not only in the territories of Israel, but over all the earth, the great dispensations of Providence respected the approach of this important hour. If empires rose or fell; if war divided, or peace united, the nations; if learning civilized their manners, or philosophy enlarged their views; all was, by the secret decree of Heaven, made to ripen the world for that "fulness of time," when Christ was to publish the whole counsel of God. The Persian, the Macedonian, the Roman conqueror, entered upon the stage each at his predicted period. The revolutions of power, and the succession of monarchies, were so arranged by Providence, as to facilitate the progress of the gospel through the habitable world, after the day had arrived, "when the stone which was cut out of the mountain without hands, should become a great moun-

tain and fill the earth." This was the day which Abraham saw afar off, and was glad. This was the day which "many prophets, and kings, and righteous men desired to see, but could not"; the day for which "the earnest expectation of the creature," long opprest with ignorance, and bewildered in superstition, might be justly said to wait.

V. This was the hour of Christ's triumph over all the powers of darkness; the hour in which He overthrew dominions and thrones, "led captivity captive, and gave gifts unto men." The contest which the kingdom of darkness had long maintained against the kingdom of light was now brought to its crisis. The period was come when "the seed of the woman shall bruise the head of the serpent." For many ages the most gross superstition had filled the earth. "The glory of the incorruptible God" was everywhere, except in the land of Judea, "changed into images made like to corruptible man, and to birds, and beasts, and creeping things." The world, which the Almighty created for Himself, seemed to have become a temple of idols. Even to vices and passions altars were raised; and what was entitled religion, was in effect a discipline of impurity. In the midst of this universal darkness, Satan had erected his throne, and the learned and the polished, as well as the savage nations, bowed down before him. But at the hour when Christ appeared on the cross, the signal of His defeat was given. His kingdom suddenly departed from Him; the reign of idolatry passed away: He was beheld to fall "like lightning from heaven." In that hour the foundation of every pagan temple shook. The statue of every false god tottered on its base. The priest fled from his falling shrine; and the heathen oracles became dumb forever.

As on the cross Christ triumphed over Satan, so He overcame His auxiliary, the world. Long had it assailed Him with its temptations and discouragements; in this hour of severe trial He surmounted them all. Formerly He had despised the pleasures of the world. He now baffled its terrors. Hence He is justly said to have "crucified the world." By His sufferings He ennobled distress; and He darkened the luster of the pomp and vanities of life. He discovered to His followers the path which leads, through affliction, to glory and to victory; and He imparted to them the same spirit which enabled Him to overcome. "My kingdom is not of this world. In this world ye shall have tribulation, but be of good cheer, I have overcome the world."

Death also, the last foe of man, was the victim of this hour. The formidable appearance of the specter remained; but his dart was taken away. For, in the hour when Christ expiated guilt, He disarmed death, by securing the resurrection of the just. When

He said to His penitent fellow sufferer, "To-day thou shalt be with me in paradise," He announced to all His followers the certainty of heavenly bliss. He declared the cherubim to be dismissed and the flaming sword to be sheathed, which had been appointed at the fall, to keep from man "the way of the tree of life." Faint, before this period, had been the hope, indistinct the prospect, which even good men enjoyed of the heavenly kingdom. Life and immortality were now brought to light. From the hill of Calvary the first clear and certain view was given to the world of the everlasting mansions. Since that hour they have been the perpetual consolation of believers in Christ. Under trouble, they soothe their minds; amid temptation, they support their virtue; and in their dying moments enable them to say, "O death! where is thy sting? O grave! where is thy victory"?

VI. This was the hour when our Lord erected that spiritual kingdom which is never to end. How vain are the counsels and designs of men! How shallow is the policy of the wicked! How short their triumphing! The enemies of Christ imagined that in this hour they had successfully accomplished their plan for His destruction. They believed that they had entirely scattered the small party of His followers, and had extinguished His name and His honor forever. In derision they addrest Him as a king. They clothed Him with purple robes; they crowned Him with a crown of thorns; they put a reed into His hand; and, with insulting mockery, bowed the knee before Him. Blind and impious men! How little did they know that the Almighty was at that moment setting Him as a king on the hill of Zion; giving Him "the heathen for his inheritance, and the uttermost parts of the earth for his possession"! How little did they know that their badges of mock royalty were at that moment converted into the signals of absolute dominion, and the instruments of irresistible power! The reed which they put into His hands became "a rod of iron," with which He was to "break in pieces his enemies," a scepter with which He was to rule the universe in righteousness. The cross which they thought was to stigmatize Him with infamy, became the ensign of His renown. Instead of being the reproach of His followers, it was to be their boast and their glory. The cross was to shine on palaces and churches throughout the earth. It was to be assumed as the distinction of the most powerful monarchs, and to wave in the banner of victorious armies when the memory of Herod and Pilate should be accurst, when Jerusalem should be reduced to ashes, and the Jews be vagabonds over all the world.

These were the triumphs which commenced at this hour. Our Lord saw them already in their birth; He saw of the travail of His soul, and was satisfied. He beheld the Word of God going forth, conquering, and to conquer; subduing, to the obedience of His laws, the subduers of the world; carrying light into the regions of darkness, and mildness into the habitations of cruelty. He beheld the Gentiles waiting below the cross, to receive the gospel. He beheld Ethiopia and the Isles stretching out their hands to God; the desert beginning to rejoice and to blossom as the rose; and the knowledge of the Lord filling the earth, as the waters cover the sea. Well pleased, He said, "It is finished." As a conqueror He retired from the field, reviewing His triumphs: "He bowed his head and gave up the ghost." From that hour, Christ was no longer a mortal man, but "Head over all things to the Church," the glorious King of men and angels, of whose dominion there shall be no end. His triumphs shall perpetually increase. "His name shall endure forever; it shall last as long as the sun; men shall be blest in him, and all nations shall call him blest."

Such were the transactions, such the effects, of this ever-memorable hour. With all those great events was the mind of our Lord filled, when He lifted His eyes to heaven, and said, "Father! the hour is come."

From this view which we have taken of this subject, permit me to suggest what ground it affords to confide in the mercy of God for the pardon of sin; to trust to His faithfulness for the accomplishment of all His promises; and to approach to Him, with gratitude and devotion, in acts of worship.

In the first place, the death of Christ affords us ground to confide in the divine mercy for the pardon of sin. All the steps of that high dispensation of Providence, which we have considered, lead directly to this conclusion, "He that spared not his own Son, but delivered him up for us all, how shall he not with him also freely give us all things?" This is the final result of the discoveries of the gospel. On this rests the great system of consolation which it hath reared up for men. We are not left to dubious and intricate reasonings concerning the conduct which God may be expected to hold toward His offending creatures: but we are led to the view of important and illustrious facts which strike the mind with evidence irresistible. For it is possible to believe that such great operations, as I have endeavored to describe, were carried on by the Almighty in vain? Did He excite in the hearts of His creatures such encouraging hopes, without any intention to fulfil them? After so long a preparation of goodness, could He mean to deny forgiveness to the penitent and the humble? When overcome by the sense of guilt, man looks up with an astonished eye to the justice of his Creator, let him recollect that hour of which the text speaks, and be comforted. The signals of divine mercy, erected in his view, are too conspicuous to be either distrusted or mistaken.

In the next place, the discoveries of this hour afford the highest reason to trust in the divine faithfulness for the accomplishment of every promise which remains yet unfulfilled. For this was the hour of the completion of God's ancient covenant.

It was the "performance of the mercy promised to the fathers." We behold the consummation of a great plan, which, throughout a course of ages, had been uniformly pursued; and which, against every human appearance, was, at the appointed moment, exactly fulfilled." No length of time alters His purpose. No obstacles can retard it. Toward the ends accomplished in this hour, the most repugnant instruments were made to operate. We discern God bending to His purpose the jarring passions, the opposite interests, and even the vices of men; uniting seeming contrarieties in His scheme; making "the wrath of man to praise him"; obliging the ambition of princes, the prejudices of Jews, the malice of Satan, all to concur, either in bringing forward this hour, or in completing its destined effects. With what entire confidence ought we to wait for the fulfilment of all His other promises in their due time, even when events are most embroiled and the prospect is most discouraging: "Altho thou sayst thou canst not see him, yet judgment is before him; therefore trust thou in him." Be attentive only to perform thy duty; leave the event to God, and be assured that, under the direction of His Providence, "all things shall work together" for a happy issue.

Lastly, the consideration of this whole subject tends to excite gratitude and devotion, when we approach to God in acts of worship. The hour of which I have discust, presents Him to us in the amiable light of the deliverer of mankind, the restorer of our forfeited hopes. We behold the greatness of the Almighty, softened by the mild radiance of condescension and mercy. We behold Him diminishing the awful distance at which we stand from His presence, by appointing for us a mediator and intercessor, through whom the humble may, without dismay, approach to Him who made them. By such views of the divine nature, Christian faith lays the foundation for a worship which shall be at once rational and affectionate; a worship in which the light of the understanding shall concur with the devotion of the heart, and the most profound reverence be united with the most cordial love. Christian faith is not a system of speculative truths. It is not a lesson of moral instruction only. By a train of high discoveries which it reveals, by a succession of interesting objects which it places in our view, it is calculated to elevate the mind, to purify the affections, and by the assistance of devotion, to confirm and encourage virtue. Such, in particular, is the scope of that divine institution, the sacrament of our Lord's Supper. To this happy purpose let it conduce, by concentering in one striking point of light all that the gospel has displayed of what is most important to man. Touched with such contrition for past offenses, and filled with a grateful sense of divine goodness, let us come to the altar of God, and, with a humble faith in His infinite mercies, devote ourselves to His service forever.

WILLIAM ERNEST BLOMFIELD

1862-1934

THE IMPERATIVE CLAIMS OF CHRIST UPON HIS FOLLOWERS

BIOGRAPHICAL NOTE

PRESIDENT of the Baptist College, Rawdon, Leeds, 1904-1934; born Rayleigh, Essex, England, October 23, 1862; educated at the nonconformist grammar school, Regents Park College, London; graduated London University (B.A.), 1883; assistant minister of Elm Road Baptist church, Beckenham; sole minister, 1885,6; minister of Turret Green church, Ipswich, 1886-95; graduated (B.D.) at St. Andrew's University, 1892; minister of Queen's Road church, Coventry, 1895-1904; received diploma, fellow of Senatus Academicus, 1898, for proficiency in knowledge of Hebrew and Greek Testaments.

"And it came to pass, that, as they went in the way, a certain man said unto him, Lord, I will follow thee whithersoever thou goest. And Jesus said unto him, Foxes have holes, and birds of the air have nests; but the Son of man hath not where to lay his head. And he said unto another, Follow me. But he said, Lord, suffer me first to go and bury my father. Jesus said unto him, Let the dead bury their dead: but go thou and preach the kingdom of God. And another also said, Lord, I will follow thee; but let me first go bid them farewell which are at home at my house. And Jesus said unto him, No man, having put his hand to the plough, and looking back, is fit for the kingdom of God."—Luke 9: 57-62.

WE have a parallel to this narrative in Matthew's Gospel. There are, however, two points of divergence from Luke's version. There is no mention of the third would-be disciple, and what is still more worthy of observation, the historic setting of the narrative is absolutely different. In Matthew the incidents take place early in the Galilean ministry, in Luke they are found when that ministry had definitely closed. It is quite impossible to reconcile the two evangelists, and I think we may regard Luke's setting of the story as likely to be the more accurate. To Matthew the question of chronological sequence was one of subordinate importance. His mind and heart were arrested by the sayings of Jesus, and they are everything to him. Accordingly, in the Sermon on the Mount, he groups together logia which may have been spoken on divers occasions, and in the thirteenth chapter he gives us a string of seven parables which few intelligent readers can think were spoken at one and the same time. Luke was more of the historian, and tells us in the preface to his gospel that it was his purpose "to write in order." We accept, then, the sequence of events as narrated in this chapter. And if we grasp the situation here revealed we shall understand more clearly the sternness and severity with which Jesus addrest these men about whom I want to speak.

Our Lord had ended His Galilean ministry. A definite crisis is marked by verse 51. He set His face stedfastly to go to Jerusalem. Mark, according to his wont, gives us a still more striking picture. Jesus strode in front of His disciples, and as they followed they were amazed and afraid. A great fear and awe fell upon them as they looked upon the resolute Savior hastening to meet His cross. It was amid the feelings awakened by such a crisis that these three men met Christ. Will they become His disciples? Have they some good thing in their hearts toward Him? Then

48

let them at once translate thought into decisive action. It was no time for temporizing and delay. Jesus needed men who understood the hour and its solemn call. Half-hearted disciples, followers who had a mere sentimental liking for Him but who gave the "first" place to any other interest, were of no use to His kingdom. He must have men who, for weal or wo, without reserve or hesitation, yet with knowledge and intelligence, would follow in His train. Decision firm and irrevocable must now be made. Never more would Christ pass this way. Thus bearing in mind the gravity of the crisis, we shall find some clue to the hard sayings in our text. Here are three men. The first brings Christ an unconditional offer of allegiance, and is repelled. The second is called by Christ to a great work and the reluctance shown by the man is rebuked. The third is a volunteer, but a double-minded man who has to be sharply reminded that thoroughness is an essential requisite for service in the kingdom. And we may see here three permanent types of human character—the impulsive, the diffident, the irresolute.

"Lord, I will follow thee whithersoever thou goest." It was a fine offer. There was no reserve or limit to it. Jesus had not many such, and we might suppose that He would have promptly accepted the allegiance of this generous heart. One feature of the heavenly life is that the Lamb's servants follow "whithersoever he leadeth." Here is a man who is ready to begin the heavenly life of perfect surrender on earth. Yet the volunteer is met with the chilling rejoinder, "Foxes have holes, the birds of heaven have nests, but the Son of man has not where to lay his head."

There is not a trace of insincerity in the man. Nor is there any sign that he was filled with self-complacency at the splendor of his own deed. All seems genuine and modest enough. But Christ's answer reveals a man who was easily swayed by the feeling of the moment, who would be the victim of any sudden impulse, easily moved by superficial excitement to the utterance of tremendous words whose implications he had never realized. He was simply thoughtless, the kind of man who would begin to build without first considering if he had wherewith to complete the costly enterprise. And so Jesus flings him back upon himself and bids him reflect. The man had been attracted by our Lord as many amiable people are attracted to-day. He had sat perhaps among the mountain lilies and listened to those wonderful beatitudes, or he had stood by the lake with the summer sun gleaming upon its waters as Jesus taught the multitudes from the boat, or he had heard of the wondrous works of Him who rebuked the storm and the angrier

passions which rage in human breasts. The rapt face of the young Prophet of Nazareth and His words of wisdom and grace had been an irresistible spell upon this open, ingenuous nature. He would fain follow Him and listen to the flow of golden speech every day, and so he cries, "Lord, I will follow thee whithersoever thou goest." But Christ knew the shallowness of this man's religion. In effect He says, "Understandest thou what thou sayest? Wilt thou indeed follow me whithersoever I lead? My way is not always amongst flower-clad hills nor by the quiet lakeside; it leads sometimes into the wilderness and amidst stony paths where the feet ache and bleed. Even now the Master thou wouldst serve goes to meet a cruel doom at the hands of men. Wilt thou follow Him there and share His cup of pain? It is no light thing for a scribe accustomed to a life of cultured ease to become the follower of One who is a homeless fugitive upon the face of the earth." This was not the only time Jesus checked emotional excitability. Once when He was preaching, a woman, carried away by His personal charm, exclaimed, "Blesséd is the womb that bare thee, and the paps which thou hast sucked," And He met this gush of sentiment with the quiet answer, "Yea, rather blesséd are they that hear the word of God and keep it." On another occasion He saw the multitudes following Him, and He turned and said, "If any man cometh to me and hateth not his father, mother, wife, brethren, sisters, yea, and his own life also, he can not be my disciple."

Herein I see the kindness of Christ. He would save a man from the pain and humiliation which ever come to him who begins a high enterprise whose difficulties and disappointments he has neither gaged nor suspected. Is there any picture more pitiable in Bunyan's allegory than that of Pliable, who had thoughtlessly set out on pilgrimage, and who at last is found sneaking among his former companions, his own self-respect gone, and himself the object of their mockery and contempt? It had been better for him not to have known the way of life than, having known it, to depart from the way of righteousness.

Not less clear is the wisdom of Christ's candor. Much as He suffered when men went back and walked no more with Him, it were better so than that they should follow Him under illusions. Fair-weather disciples are out of place in a kingdom where patient endurance is an inexorable necessity. The failure of this type of character is graphically depicted in the parable of the sower. These are they who hear the word and—alas for the fatal word!—immediately with joy receive it. Yet have they no root in themselves, but are only temporary, and when tribulation or persecution arise because of the word, immediately—the declension is as swift as the profession—they are made to stumble. The reminder is not an untimely one for these days of revival. "A man who is touched only on the surface of his soul by a religious movement and has yielded to the current without understanding what it means, whither it tends, and what it involves, is doomed to apostasy in the season of trial. When the tide of enthusiasm subsides and he is left to himself to carry on single-handed the struggle with temptation, he has no heart for the work, and his religion withers like the corn growing on rocky places under the scorching heat of the summer sun" (Bruce). Therefore, count the cost before thou takest upon thy lips so great a pledge as this: "Lord, I will follow thee whithersoever thou goest."

The diffident man is another type of character. He does not proffer his allegiance. He is timid and shy in the presence of great demands and heroic tasks. Jesus has looked into the soul of this man and seen the stuff of which apostles, missionaries, confessors and martyrs are made. And He summons him to the sublime work of preaching the gospel of the kingdom. The retiring man pleads home duties. Elsewhere we read of one who had married a wife, and therefore could not come. Here we have a man who pleads the claims of filial piety. "Suffer me first to go and bury my father." The ordinary interpretation of these words is that this man's father was dead, and that he simply sought permission to wait till the funeral was over. It may be so, or it may be that this was a proverbial way of sacrificing Christ to the claims of family affection. He shrinks from the high calling and excuses himself by saying that there are ordinary every-day duties to be done. It is an Eastern way of declaring that other claims take precedence of some great demand made upon him, and he says that he will obey when he has buried his father. Take it in either sense, the word of Christ is clear, and the principle on which it is based is indisputable. There are crises in life when the duty of burying one's father must be subordinated to a more imperious call. When in the hour of an empire's peril, the summons comes to a soldier to fight his country's battle, his oath to his king must be preferred before piety to parents, however right and beautiful that may be under ordinary circumstances. Christ always claims to stand first. Whoever loves father or mother more than Him is not worthy of Him. Not that He was indifferent to the sacred ties of home life. In His own mortal agony He commended Mary to the beloved disciple. In the chapter immediately before that from which my text is taken, He claimed the right to send a man home to be a missionary there when the man would fain have

remained at His side. Christ claims the rights of absolute ownership over every one of us. And surely this fact leads to faith in His higher nature. No one man of a particular race and age can be the one absolute authority for all men of all ages and all races unless he is something more than man, however great and good. What think ye of Christ? Who is He that He may command us all as He wills and look for our unhesitating and unreserved obedience?

Consider, too, the principle of Christ's answer to this man. "Let the dead bury their own dead." Let those who have no spiritual life in them attend to the tasks which need no spiritual life for their discharge, but let the man who is fitted for high work which only a rare soul can accomplish devote himself to it as to his heaven-appointed mission. This has been called Christ's law of economy in the service of the kingdom. Every man is bound to serve where he can be and do the most for his king. He must trade with his pound and make it yield all that is possible. If one has in him the capacity of a great statesman—ah, what would we not give for such an one at the present hour!—he has no right to be following the plow. If a young man is gifted with the spiritual vision and power of expression which made the prophet of the Lord, he is guilty of unholy waste if he stands behind a counter measuring off calico. It is related of the late Dr. Parker that he said: "I came early to the conclusion that the Almighty did not intend me to carry bricks and mortar up a ladder." He was right. Not that these tasks are common or unclean.

> Who sweeps a room as for thy laws,
> Makes that and the action fine.

But myriads can attend to these duties, while the statesman, the missionary, the preacher, are few and far to seek. Do I speak to any man who has heard Christ's call to preach the gospel of the kingdom? It is not for us to run unless we are bidden. No man taketh this honor to himself but he that is called of God. If, however, thou hast heard the voice of Jesus, I would pray that thou mayest have no rest till thou hast yielded Him obedience. Listen to His own word: "Let the dead bury their own dead, but go thou and publish abroad the kingdom of God."

The irresolute man is he who said, "Lord, I will follow thee, but let me first bid them farewell who are at my house." The natural request was met with what seems an unreasonable answer. A similar petition was made by Elisha to Elijah when he was called to the prophetic office. And Elijah granted it. Is Elijah more considerate and human than Jesus? We must look beneath the surface. Martin Luther says, in commenting upon this verse, "The New Testament was written for men with heads upon their shoulders." Elijah granted the request because it was safe to grant it. Jesus saw here a man easily led away, to whom the farewell visit would be fatal. Once in the family circle all kinds of obstacles would be put in his way; tender reproaches and tearful pleadings would be leveled against his resolve; heart-moving pictures would be put before him of the perils which must attend the man who was wild enough to throw in his lot with Jesus of Nazareth. And under the warmth of home affection his little courage would melt away. To go home would be to say farewell to the kingdom forever. Therefore, in a graphic way, our Lord reminds this volunteer that half-hearted men are useless in the service of God. He who puts his hand to the plow must give eye and mind to his work or he will be the derision of the field when the furrow is complete. Even with our heavy instruments drawn by two horses (sometimes more intelligent than the man behind) attention to the business in hand is essential to success. But with the Hebrew plow of much lighter construction, with only one stilt to guide it, leaving the other hand free to use the goad to the often untractable ox, undivided interest was indispensable.

Let us lay to heart the truth. The half-hearted are not fit for the kingdom of God. Are they fit for any kingdom worth the having? No man can make a scholar who is not prepared to scorn delights and live laborious days. No young man will be successful in business if his chief thought all day is of the hour when he may escape from the office to his football or golf. Ay, no man can be a king in the sphere of athletics unless he is prepared to pay the price of self-control and severe training. How, then, should we be fit for the highest kingdom if, while we profess to be Christ's, our hearts are not wholly His but with the world? Yes, it is hard to be a Christian. And the Lord in very kindness and truth tells us that nothing less than personal devotion to Himself will carry us through. There are hours in life when we have to learn with pain the lesson of forgetting the past. Bright and beautiful and not unholy as it was, we may not nurse and fondle it, for God has called us to a new work which demands all our strength, and there may not be a look behind. The Master here spoke out of the depth of His own experience. His face was now set to Jerusalem. Behind Him lay the happy home of Nazareth, and warm hearts and kindly friends were in the northern province. It was not easy to turn to the unloving city, and Peter sought to dissuade Him from the sorrow and suffering which lay in His God-appointed path. But the well-meant entreaty was rejected as a temptation from hell. It was a temptation to look back. He could not afford to palter with it, to give it lodgment for one moment. How much less may we? Has the world been gaining too much influence over us? Has its spell weakened our hold of the plow? Then let us look to Him who can reenforce our will and give us a single heart. The sorrow of looking back is this, that it never ends there. In the long run it means going back from the plow altogether. "Demas hath forsaken me, having loved this present world." It can not be otherwise. That love of the world is the backward look, which, persisted in, issues in apostasy. Consider Him who endured to the end lest ye be weary and faint in your mind. Pray to Him who giveth power to the faint. Then grip the plow more earnestly, and press on. Be not of them who draw back unto perdition and in whom God has no pleasure, rather aspire to be of that elect company who believe unto the saving of the soul.

EDWARD INCREASE BOSWORTH

1861-1926

THE MEANING OF LIFE

BIOGRAPHICAL NOTE

PROFESSOR of New Testament language and literature, Oberlin Theological Seminary, Ohio, 1892-1926; dean 1903-1924; born Dundee, Ill., January 10, 1861; graduated from Elgin Academy, Ill., 1877; student Oberlin College, 1879-81; graduated from Yale, 1883; Oberlin Theological Seminary, 1886; student at the University of Leipsic, 1890,1; Congregational clergyman; pastor, Mt. Vernon, Ohio, 1886,7; professor of English Bible, 1887-90; author of "Studies in the Acts and Epistles," "Studies in the Teaching of Jesus and His Apostles," "Studies in the Life of Jesus Christ," etc.

"If a son, then an heir."—Gal. 4 : 7.

THERE is one story that never fails to interest men. It is the story of the real experiences of a human life. If an old man should rise in any audience and describe with absolute frankness the most vitally important experiences of his life, he would hold the attention of his audience to the end. He would describe his earliest recollections of home, parents, brothers and sisters. He would tell of his first boy friend. He would describe the way in which he earned his first dollar. He would tell how he first met, learned to love and asked in marriage her who afterward became his wife. He would speak of the holy sensation of fatherhood that welled up in his heart as he held his first-born in his arms. He would speak of the dumb outcry of his heart as he held the same child in his arms and watched its breathing slowly cease. He would tell the story of the great loves and hates of his life. He would speak of the timid wonder or eager anticipation with which now, in his old age, he looks out upon a near eternity.

God is the supreme inventive genius of the universe. Men are possest of wonderful inventive genius that has exprest itself in all the countless devices of modern civilization. We may say of them in homely phrase that in this particular they simply "take after" their Father, who is Himself the supreme inventive genius. So far as we know, the supreme product of His infinite inventive genius is the situation which we call plain, commonplace daily life. Nothing else is more wonderful than the daily relation of a man to his personal and physical environment, that we call plain daily life.

What is the meaning of this experience, the story of which never fails to interest men? What is the purpose of this situation devised by the infinite ingenuity of God? What is life for? The answer is to be sought from the standpoint of the text—the Fatherhood of God: "If a son, then an heir." God appears as a Father of sons whom He wishes to be His heirs. Human life is a situation devised by the infinite ingenuity of God, in which to train sons for an inheritance of power by teaching them to use power in a friendly spirit.

There are certain things implied in this statement of the purpose of life. It is implied that God is a Father who has vast power to bequeath. The evidences of it are on every side. It is said that if one of the fiery whirlstorms on the sun should occur on the surface of the earth, it would be in the Gulf of Mexico thirty seconds after it had left the St. Lawrence, and everything in its track would be a hot vapor. The words that God left ringing in the ears of men, when He launched the race upon its career, were calculated to arouse expectation of power: "Subdue the earth," "Have dominion." The words which Jesus spoke to His fellow men at the close of His life of marvelous manifestation of power were also calculated to make them expect to exercise power. "He that believeth on me, the works that I do shall he do also, and greater works than these shall he do."

It is implied that God is an ambitious Father, ambitious to see His sons make the most of themselves. We sometimes think of God as a Sovereign whose plans are good for the world as a whole, but involve so much of hardship and limitation for the individual that a man may well wish to have the least possible personal connection with them. Such is not Paul's thought. To him God is indeed a Sovereign, but a sovereign Father, ambitious to see His sons become His heirs.

It is implied also that God is a conscientious Father, too conscientious to allow His sons to become His heirs unless they are fit to possess that which He would bequeath. Heirship was once synonymous with license. The heir to the throne was allowed certain exemptions from ordinary obligations. He might gratify his appetites with a disregard of consequences unpardonable in the case of other men. But with advancing ideas of the responsibilities inseparable from the possession of power this idea is largely passing away. He who would inherit must be trained into fitness for the inheritance. It is said that one of the present European sovereigns gave little promise as a child of ever being fit for the inheritance that would naturally come to him. His father, however, was a conscientious man, and systematically set about the process of making his son fit for heirship. He provided for his physical development, gave him military training, educated him in the branches of learning most essential to statesmanship, and in every way so devoted himself to the preparation of his son for the responsibilities of heirship that, finally, when the prince inherited the kingdom, few rulers were better fitted than he for the responsibilities of power.

That human life is a situation devised by the infinite ingenuity of God, in which to teach His sons to use power in a friendly spirit is evident from several considerations:

The nature of life as revealed in its two most characteristic features shows that it is intended to serve this purpose. It may seem difficult to determine what features of life ought to be selected as characteristic. We naturally look for something very generally present in life and of fundamental significance. Perhaps, nothing more exactly meets this requirement than the phenomenon of human suffering, and the family.

Suffering is a universal and vitally significant feature of human life. Who escapes it? It begins with the physical pains of infancy. How many thousands lie to-day suffering in hospitals! How many millions suffer pain outside the merciful ministrations of the hospital! But who is there who lives long without knowing something of the suffering that is keener than bodily pain, the suffering of the soul, in all the violent passion or steady, relentless oppression of sorrow in its manifold forms? We may be unable to form a complete philosophy of suffering, but this much is at once evident: It makes a powerful appeal for the friendly use of power. Especially is this seen to be the case in our day when easy combination and swift transmission of power make it possible for a large number of men, each of whom has a little power, quickly to apply that power in a friendly way to any remote point of need. It is possible for thousands of persons, each with a small amount of personal power represented in his single dollar, to accumulate a sum of money within a few hours in the hands of a reliable central agency that will cable it to the other side of the world and release it there in some form of personal activity that shall be the friendly relief of suffering.

By the side of the phenomenon of suffering stands the family as a great characteristic feature of human life. A large part of the significance of the family consists in the training it affords its members in the friendly use of power. A little child is born into the world, "an appetite and a cry." Very soon an appeal is made to the little soul for love. It is the appeal of the mother's eyes. The appeal of the father is soon made and felt to be different from that of the mother. In time a third appeal is made by the baby brother, and a fourth, different from the other three, by the baby sister. The child becomes a man and loves a woman. The appeal of the wife for love; that is, for the friendly use of power, differs from any that have preceded it. When a baby boy lies in the father's arms a new appeal is made, and the appeal of the baby girl touches a new chord in the father's heart. The seven-fold appeal of father, mother, brother, sister, wife, son, daughter, which is experienced in the fully developed family relationship, constitutes an appeal for the friendly use of power that can be matched by no creation of the imagination. When one looks, therefore, into the nature of human life as exprest in its two characteristic features, human suffering and the family, he is constrained to regard it as a situation devised by the infinite ingenuity of God in which to teach His children to use power in a friendly spirit, and presumably with reference to giving them larger bequests of power.

The truth of this proposition also becomes evident when we recognize that this conception underlay Jesus' theory of life. When the rich young senator came to Him as to an expert professional prophet, asking Him to specify something the doing of which would guarantee him the advantages of "eternal life," Jesus simply directed him to begin at once to use the power he already possest in a friendly spirit. He pointed out to him the suffering on every side and told him to begin to use his possessions in relieving it.

Jesus' general teaching regarding the proper use of money is based on this theory of life. "Make to yourselves friends," he said, "by means of the mammon of unrighteousness, so that when it shall fail they may receive you into eternal tabernacles" (Luke, 16 : 9). That is, a man's money power is to be used in a friendly spirit that will lay the foundations for eternal friendships. When two men meet for the first time in the age to come, it will be discovered that one is there because of the friendly spirit in which the other once used his money to meet the great needs of those whom he did not then know personally, and who perhaps lived in other lands. Jesus regarded money as a comparatively low form of power put into a man's hands for a little time in order that he might learn to use it in a friendly way and so prepare himself to be trusted with higher forms of power. "If, therefore, ye have not been faithful in the use of unrighteous mammon, who will commit to your trust the true riches?" How can the Church expect God to trust it with any such large degree of prayer power as is described in the great promises of achievement through prayer, until it has first learned to use the lower money power in a friendly spirit? Jesus regarded money as something that really belongs to another. It often comes to us by inheritance from another, and is certain at death to pass from us to another. It remains in our hands a little while in order that by using it in a friendly way we may be prepared to inherit some higher form of power that we can carry out into the eternal future as our permanent possession. "And if ye have not been faithful in that which is another's, who will give you that which is your own?"

Jesus not only held this view of life as a theory, but He actually used human life as a situation in which to prepare men for an inheritance of power by teaching them to use power in a friendly way. The salvation which He brings to men is one which saves them to this kind of life. There is no more striking evidence of the seriousness of sin than the fact that the powerful appeal made by life itself is not sufficient to induce men to use power in a friendly way. There is still need that a great Savior should enter the situation and bring the persuasive power of His own friendly personality to bear upon men. But human life, as we have conceived it, is a situation big enough for, and suitable to, the operations of a great Savior. It affords Him the opportunity He needs to link men's lives in with His own ever-present life, and to train them through personal association with Himself in the friendly use of power. He not only pointed out the suffering poor to the rich young man who came inquiring about eternal life, and directed him to use his money in their relief, but He said also, "Come, follow me." He proposed to attach the man permanently to Himself and to the friendly enterprise into which He was leading His disciples. The disciples of Jesus were a company of men being personally trained by Him in the friendly use of power. They were to be specialists in friendship: "By this shall all men know that ye are my disciples, if ye have love one to another." The Church of Jesus Christ is not a club which men and women join for what they can get out of it, but it is a company of men and women banded together to be trained by the living Lord in the friendly use of power. They keep the search-light of their investigation playing all round the world's horizon, and when it falls upon some point of special need, to that point some members of this Christly company hasten with power for its relief.

It is further evident that human life is a situation devised by the infinite ingenuity of God in which to prepare sons for an inheritance of power by teaching them to use power in a friendly spirit, because human life has actually been serving this purpose. When we look back over the long history of human life in the world, it is evident that God has fairly been crowding more power into the hands of men, as fast as they have learned to use what they already had with even an imperfect degree of friendliness. This is seen, for instance, in the case of explosives. Men in the brutal first century of our era could not be trusted to use the power of modern explosives. We see evidences enough of brutality still, but if some new explosive should be discovered that would destroy the lives of a million men in an instant, there is now a friendly sentiment in the hearts of men that would instantly demand the elimination of this explosive from modern warfare.

In the industrial development of our day, increasing power is being put into the hands of employers and employed, as men are able to use it with increasing, tho imperfect, friendliness. Once neither employers nor employed could have been safely trusted with the power that organization has given to both parties, but now the growing sense of responsibility for the general welfare makes it safe to give larger power to both. It seems probable that vast industrial enterprises conducive to human welfare lie just ahead of us, which can be undertaken only when men have been trained to use power with a friendliness that will make it safe to trust them with the great increase of power that these enterprises will demand.

Human life, then, by its very nature, by Jesus' theory and use of it, by what it has already accomplished through the centuries, is seen to be a situation devised by the infinite ingenuity of God, in which to train sons for an inheritance of power by teaching them to use power in a friendly spirit.

It is in the light of this conception of the meaning of life that the peril of living appears. The danger is that men will refuse to learn the friendly use of power, and therefore be unable to inherit the bequests of power that would naturally await them. Such failure means unspeakable loss. He who throws himself athwart the deep trend of the long evolution of life inevitably suffers indescribable disaster. It is of him that the most ominous words of Jesus are spoken. The power that he has will be taken from him and be given to him that has shown himself fit to be trusted with large and growing grants of power—"Take away the talent from him and give it to him that hath ten talents." From the farmer who refuses to sow his seed the seed shall be taken and given to him who has it in abundance and is willing to sow it, for seed must be sown that God's children may have bread. "He will be cast out into the outer darkness," eliminated from Jesus' civilization of friendly workmen. Over against these busy friendly workmen, to whom, as they work together, God gives growing grants of power, the persistently selfish man putters away ever more feebly and painfully in his little lonely self-made hell. The peril is that men will not see the significance of plain daily life, with its commonplace and constantly recurring opportunity to learn to use power in a friendly spirit. The men that stood for judgment before the Son of Man cried out in surprised chagrin, "When saw we thee hungry and thirsty?" They had not noticed the significance of daily life. It is those with the least power, one-talent people, who are in greatest danger. They are too proud to do the little they can do because it will appear to others to be so little — "Others can do it so much better than I." Or the little power they possess is not sufficiently impressive to overcome the wicked lethargy of their anemic good will—"It is too much trouble." So they merit the descriptive words of Jesus, "wicked and slothful," proud and lazy, and pass out into the sphere of self-wrecked personalities.

But, on the other hand, this view of the meaning of life gives birth to a great hope. The man who has only a little power, and who faithfully uses it in the friendly spirit of a son of God, is certain to inherit vastly increased power. He lives in a generous economy in which he who is "faithful over a few things" will surely be "set over many things." It is this conception of the future life as one of achievement that appeals to the strong men of our age. We do not like to think of the future life as one of endless rest. We do not care to sing:

> There shall I bathe my weary soul
> In seas of endless rest,
> And not a wave of trouble roll
> Across my peaceful breast.

Tennyson rather has struck the chord to which our age responds, when he says of his departed friend:

> And doubtless unto thee is given
> A life that bears immortal fruit
> In those great offices that suit
> The full-grown energies of heaven.

The thought of "the full-grown energies of heaven" and the opportunity for their exercise that "heaven" must afford, makes immortality seem worth while. The sons of God are to inherit a career. Men may walk the shores of the "silent sea" not shivering and cowering with fear of death, but feeling rather as Columbus did when he finally got his three ships, and sailed away expecting to find opportunity for great achievements beyond. They may walk the shore like spiritual vikings, ready to start out on a beneficent career of high adventure. They may feel an enthusiasm for eternity which will

> Greet the unseen with a cheer!

But all this future outlook is for him who has present insight into the meaning of daily life and who puts himself under the daily discipline of Jesus. The homespun language of Sam Foss expresses his deep desire.

> Let me live in a house by the side of the road,
>   Where the race of men go by—
> The men who are good and the men who are bad,
>   As good and as bad as I.
> I would not sit in a scorner's seat,
>   Or hurl the cynic's ban;
> Let me live in a house by the side of the road
>   And be a friend to man.

Human life is a situation devised by the infinite ingenuity of God, in which to prepare sons for an inheritance of power by teaching them to use power in a friendly spirit. "If a son, then an heir."

LOUIS BOURDALOUE

1632-1704

THE PASSION OF CHRIST

BIOGRAPHICAL NOTE

LOUIS BOURDALOUE was born at Bourges, in 1632. At the age of sixteen he entered the order of the Jesuits and was thoroughly educated in the scholarship, philosophy and theology of the day. He devoted himself entirely to the work of preaching, and was ten times called upon to address Louis XIV and his court from the pulpit as Bossuet's successor. This was an unprecedented record and yet Bourdaloue could adapt his style to any audience, and "mechanics left their shops, merchants their business, and lawyers their court house" to hear him. His high personal character, his simplicity of life, his clear, direct, and logical utterance as an accomplished orator united to make him not only "the preacher of kings but the king of preachers." Retiring from the pulpit late in life he ministered to the sick and to prisoners. He died in Paris, 1704.

And there followed him a great company of people, and of women, which also bewailed and lamented him. But Jesus turning unto them, said, ''Daughters of Jerusalem, weep not for me, but weep for yourselves, and for your children.''—Luke xxiii., 27, 28.

THE passion of Jesus Christ, however sorrowful and ignominious it may appear to us, must nevertheless have been to Jesus Christ Himself an object of delight, since this God-man, by a wonderful secret of His wisdom and love, has willed that the mystery of it shall be continued and solemnly renewed in His Church until the final consummation of the world. For what is the Eucharist but a perpetual repetition of the Savior's passion, and what has the Savior supposed in instituting it, but that whatever passed at Calvary is not only represented but consummated on our altars? That is to say, that He is still performing the functions of the victim anew, and is every moment virtually sacrificed, as tho it were not sufficient that He should have suffered once; at least that His love, as powerful as it is free, has given to His adorable sufferings that character of perpetuity which they have in the Sacrament, and which renders them so salutary to us. Behold, Christians, what the love of God has devised; but behold, also, what has happened through the malice of men! At the same time that Jesus Christ, in the sacrament of His body, repeats His holy passion in a manner altogether mysterious, men, the false imitators, or rather base corrupters of the works of God, have found means to renew this same passion, not only in a profane, but in a criminal, sacrilegious, and horrible manner!

Do not imagine that I speak figuratively. Would to God, Christians, that what I am going to say to you were only a figure, and that you were justified in vindicating yourselves to-day against the horrible expressions which I am obliged to employ! I speak in the literal sense, and you ought to be more affected with this discourse, if what I advance appears to you to be overcharged; for it is by your excesses that it is so, and not by my words. Yes, my dear hearers, the sinners of the age, by the disorders of their lives, renew the bloody and tragic passion of the Son of God in the world; I will venture to say that the sinners of the age cause to the Son of God, even in the state of glory, as many new passions as they have committed outrages against Him by their actions! Apply yourselves to form an idea of them; and in this picture, which will surprise you, recognize what you are, that you may weep bitterly over yourselves! What do we see in the passion of Jesus Christ? A divine Savior betrayed and abandoned by cowardly disciples, persecuted by pontiffs and hypocritical priests, ridiculed and mocked in the palace of Herod by impious courtiers, placed upon a level with Barabbas, and to whom Barabbas is preferred by a blind and inconstant people, exposed to the insults of libertinism, and treated as a mock king by a troop of soldiers equally barbarous and insolent; in fine, crucified by merciless executioners! Behold, in a few words, what is most humiliating and most cruel in the death of the Savior of the world! Then tell me if this is not precisely what we now see, of what we are every day called to be witnesses. Let us resume; and follow me.

Betrayed and abandoned by cowardly disciples; such, O divine Savior, has been Thy destiny. But it was not enough that the apostles, the first men whom Thou didst choose for Thine own, in violation of the most holy engagement, should have forsaken Thee in the last scene of Thy life; that one of them should have sold Thee, another renounced Thee, and all disgraced themselves by a flight which was, perhaps, the most sensible of all the wounds that Thou didst feel in dying. This wound must be again opened by a thousand acts of infidelity yet more scandalous. Even in the Christian ages we must see men bearing the character of Thy disciples, and not having the resolution to sustain it; Christians, prevaricators, and deserters from their faith; Christians ashamed of declaring themselves for Thee, not daring to appear what they are, renouncing at least in the exterior what they have profest, flying when they ought to fight; in a word, Christians in form, ready to follow Thee even to the Supper when in prosperity, and while it required no sacrifice, but resolved to abandon Thee in the moment of temptation. It is on your account, and my own, my dear hearers, that I speak, and behold what ought to be the subject of our sorrow.

A Savior mortally persecuted by pontiffs and hypocritical priests! Let us not enter, Christians, into the discussion of this article, at which your piety would, perhaps, be offended, and which would weaken or prejudice the respect which you owe to the ministers of the Lord. It belongs to us, my brethren, to meditate to-day on this fact in the spirit of holy compunction; to us consecrated to the ministry of the altars, to us priests of Jesus Christ, whom God has chosen in His Church to be the dispensers of His sacraments. It does not become me to remonstrate in this place. God forbid that I should undertake to judge those who sustain the sacred office! This is not the duty of humility to which my condition calls me. Above all, speaking as I do, before many ministers, the irreprehensible

life of whom contributes so much to the edification of the people, I am not yet so infatuated as to make myself the judge, much less the censor of their conduct.

But tho it should induce you only to acknowledge the favors with which God prevents you, as a contrast, from the frightful blindness into which He permits others to fall, remember that the priests and the princes of the priests, are those whom the evangelist describes as the authors of the conspiracy formed against the Savior of the world, and of the wickedness committed against Him. Remember that this scandal is notoriously public, and renewed still every day in Christianity. Remember, but with fear and horror, that the greatest persecutors of Jesus Christ are not lay libertines, but wicked priests; and that among the wicked priests, those whose corruption and iniquity are covered with the veil of hypocrisy are His most dangerous and most cruel enemies. A hatred, disguised under the name of zeal, and covered with the specious pretext of observance of the law, was the first movement of the persecution which the Pharisees and the priests raised against the Son of God. Let us fear lest the same passion should blind us! Wretched passion, exclaims St. Bernard, which spreads the venom of its malignity even over the most lovely of the children of men, and which could not see a God upon earth without hating Him! A hatred not only of the prosperity and happiness, but what is yet more strange, of the merit and perfection of others! A cowardly and shameful passion, which, not content with having caused the death of Jesus Christ, continues to persecute Him by rending His mystical body, which is the Church; dividing His members, which are believers; and stifling in their hearts that charity which is the spirit of Christianity! Behold, my brethren, the subtle temptation against which we have to defend ourselves, and under which it is but too common for us to fall!

A Redeemer reviled and mocked in the palace of Herod by the impious creatures of his court! This was, without doubt, one of the most sensible insults which Jesus Christ received. But do not suppose, Christians, that this act of impiety ended there. It has passed from the court of Herod, from that prince destitute of religion, into those even of Christian princes. And is not the Savior still a subject of ridicule to the libertine spirits which compose them? They worship Him externally, but internally how do they regard His maxims? What idea have they of His humility, of His poverty, of His sufferings? Is not virtue either unknown or despised? It is not a rash zeal which induces me to speak in this manner; it is what you too often witness, Christians; it is what you perhaps feel in yourselves; and a little reflection upon the manners of the court will convince you that there is nothing that I say, which is not confirmed by a thousand examples, and that you yourselves are sometimes unhappy accomplices in these crimes.

Herod had often earnestly wished to see Jesus Christ. The reputation which so many miracles had given Him, excited the curiosity of this prince, and he did not doubt but that a man who commanded all nature might strike some wonderful blow to escape from the persecution of His enemies. But the Son of God, who had not been sparing of His prodigies for the salvation of others, spared them for Himself, and would not say a single word about His own safety. He considered Herod and his people as profane persons, with whom he thought it improper to hold any intercourse, and he preferred rather to pass for a fool than to ratisfy the false wisdom of the world. As His kingdom was not of this world, as He said to Pilate, it was not at the court that He designed to establish Himself. He knew too well that His doctrine could not be relished in a place where the rules of worldly wisdom only were followed, and where all the miracles which He had performed had not been sufficient to gain men full of love for themselves and intoxicated with their greatness. In this corrupted region they breathe only the air of vanity; they esteem only that which is splendid; they speak only of preferment: and on whatever side we cast our eyes, we see nothing but what either flatters or inflames the ambitious desires of the heart of man.

What probability then was there that Jesus Christ, the most humble of all men, should obtain a hearing where only pageantry and pride prevail? If He had been surrounded with honors and riches, He would have found partisans near Herod and in every other place. But as He preached a renunciation of the world both to His disciples and to Himself, let us not be astonished that they treated Him with so much disdain. Such is the prediction of the holy man Job, and which after Him must be accomplished in the person of all the righteous; "the upright man is laughed to scorn." In fact, my dear hearers, you know that, whatever virtue and merit we may possess, they are not enough to procure us esteem at court. Enter it, and appear only like Jesus Christ, clothed with the robe of innocence; only walk with Jesus Christ in the way of simplicity; only speak as Jesus Christ to render testimony to the truth, and you will find that you meet with no better treatment there than Jesus Christ. To be well received there, you must have pomp and splendor. To keep your station there, you must have artifice and intrigue. To be favorably heard there, you must have complaisance and flattery. Then all this is opposed to Jesus Christ; and the court being what it is—that is to say,

the kingdom of the prince of this world—it is not surprizing that the kingdom of Jesus Christ can not be established there. But wo to you, princes of the earth! Wo to you, men of the world, who despise this incarnate wisdom, for you shall be despised in your turn, and the contempt which shall fall upon you shall be much more terrible than the contempt which you manifest can be prejudicial.

A Savior placed upon a level with Barabbas, and to whom Barabbas is preferred by a blind and fickle rabble! How often have we been guilty of the same outrage against Jesus Christ as the blind and fickle Jews! How often, after having received Him in triumph in the sacrament of the communion, seduced by cupidity, have we not preferred either a pleasure or interest after which we sought, in violation of His law, to this God of glory! How often divided between conscience which governed us, and passion which corrupted us, have we not renewed this abominable judgment, this unworthy preference of the creature even above our God! Christians, observe this application; it is that of St. Chrysostom, and if you properly understand it, you must be affected by it. Conscience, which, in spite of ourselves, presides in us as judge, said inwardly to us, "What art thou going to do? Behold thy pleasure on the one hand, and thy God on the other: for which of the two dost thou declare thyself? for thou canst not save both; thou must either lose thy pleasure or thy God; and it is for thee to decide." And the passion, which by a monstrous infidelity had acquired the influence over our hearts, made us conclude—I will keep my pleasure. "But what then will become of thy God," replied conscience secretly, "and what must I do, I, who can not prevent myself from maintaining His interests against thee?" I care not what will become of my God, answered passion insolently; I will satisfy myself, and the resolution is taken. "But dost thou know," proceeded conscience by its remorse, "that in indulging thyself in this pleasure it will at last submit thy Savior to death and crucifixion for thee?" It is of no consequence if He be crucified, provided I can have my enjoyments. "But what evil has He done, and what reason hast thou to abandon Him in this manner?" My pleasure is my reason; and since Christ is the enemy of my pleasure, and my pleasure crucifies Him, I say it again, let Him be crucified.

Behold, my dear hearers, what passes every day in the consciences of men, and what passes in you and in me, every time that we fall into sin, which causes death to Jesus Christ, as well as to our souls! Behold what makes the enormity and wickedness of this sin! I know that we do not always speak, that we do not always explain ourselves in such express terms and in so perceptible a manner;

but after all, without explaining ourselves so distinctly and so sensibly, there is a language of the heart which says all this. For, from the moment that I know that this pleasure is criminal and forbidden of God, I know that it is impossible for me to desire it, impossible to seek it, without losing God; and consequently I prefer this pleasure to God in the desire that I form of it, and in the pursuit that I make after it. This, then, is sufficient to justify the thought of St. Chrysostom and the doctrine of the theologians upon the nature of deadly sin. . . .

That there are men, and Christian men, to whom, by a secret judgment of God, the passion of Jesus Christ, salutary as it is, may become useless, is a truth too essential in our religion to be unknown, and too sorrowful not to be the subject of our grief. When the Savior from the height of His cross, ready to give up His spirit, raised this cry toward heaven, "My God, my God, why hast thou forsaken me?" there was no one who did not suppose but that the violence of His torments forced from Him this complaint, and perhaps we ourselves yet believe it. But the great Bishop Arnauld de Chartres, penetrating deeper into the thoughts and affections of this dying Savior, says, with much more reason, that the complaint of Christ Jesus to His Father proceeded from the sentiment with which He was affected, in representing to Himself the little fruit which His death would produce; in considering the small number of the elect who would profit by it; in foreseeing with horror the infinite number of the reprobate, for whom it would be useless: as if He had wished to proclaim that His merits were not fully enough nor worthily enough remunerated; and that after having done so much work He had a right to promise to Himself a different success in behalf of men. The words of this author are admirable: Jesus Christ complains, says this learned prelate, but of what does He complain? That the wickedness of sinners makes Him lose what ought to be the reward of the conflicts which He has maintained; that millions of the human race for whom He suffers will, nevertheless, be excluded from the benefit of redemption. And because He regards Himself in them as their head, and themselves, in spite of their worthlessness, as the members of His mystical body; seeing them abandoned by God, He complains of being abandoned Himself: "My God, my God, why hast thou forsaken me?" He complains of what made St. Paul groan when, transported with an apostolic zeal, he said to the Galatians: "What, my brethren, is Jesus Christ then dead in vain? Is the mystery of the cross then nothing to you? Will not this blood which He has so abundantly shed have the virtue to sanctify you?"

But here, Christians, I feel myself affected with a thought which, contrary as it appears to that of the apostle, only serves to strengthen and confirm it. For it appears that St. Paul is grieved because Jesus Christ has suffered in vain; but I, I should almost console myself if He had only suffered in vain, and if His passion was only rendered useless to us. That which fills me with consternation is, that at the same time that we render it useless to ourselves, by an inevitable necessity it must become pernicious; for this passion, says St. Gregory of Nazianzen, "partakes of the nature of those remedies which kill if they do not heal, and of which the effect is either to give life or to convert itself into poison; lose nothing of this, I beseech you." Remember, then, Christians, what happened during the judgment and at the moment of the condemnation of the Son of God.

When Pilate washed his hands before the Jews and declared to them that there was nothing worthy of death in this righteous man, but that the crime from which he freed himself rested upon them, and that they would have to answer for it, they all cried with one voice that they consented to it, and that they readily agreed that the blood of this just man should fall upon them and upon their children. You know what this cry has cost them. You know the curses which one such imprecation has drawn upon them, the anger of heaven which began from that time to burst upon this nation, the ruin of Jerusalem which followed soon after —the carnage of their citizens, the profanation of their temple, the destruction of their republic, the visible character of their reprobation which their unhappy posterity bear to this day, that universal banishment, that exile of sixteen hundred years, that slavery through all the earth—and all in consequence of the authentic prediction which Jesus Christ made to them of it when going to Calvary, and with circumstances which incontestably prove that a punishment as exemplary as this can not be imputed but to decide which they had committed in the person of the Savior; since it is evident, says St. Augustine, that the Jews were never further from idolatry nor more religious observers of their law than they were then, and that, excepting the crime of the death of Jesus Christ, God, very far from punishing them, would, it seems, rather have loaded them with His blessings. You know all this, I say; and all this is a convincing proof that the blood of this God-man is virtually fallen upon these sacrilegious men, and that God, in condemning them by their own mouth, altho in spite of Himself, employs that to destroy them which was designed for their salvation.

But, Christians, to speak with the Holy Spirit, this has happened to the Jews only as a figure; it is only the shadow of the fearful curses of which the abuse of the merits and passion of the Son of God must be to us the source and the measure. I will explain myself. What do we, my dear hearers, when borne away by the immoderate desires of our hearts to a sin against which our consciences protest? And what do we, when, possest of the spirit of the world, we resist a grace which solicits us, which presses us to obey God? Without thinking upon it, and without wishing it, we secretly pronounce the same sentence of death which the Jews pronounced against themselves before Pilate, when they said to him, "His blood be upon us." For this grace which we despise is the price of the blood of Jesus Christ, and the sin that we commit is an actual profanation of this very blood. It is, then, as if we were to say to God: "Lord, I clearly see what engagement I make, and I know what risk I run, but rather than not satisfy my own desires, I consent that the blood of Thy Son shall fall upon me. This will be to bear the chastisement of it, but I will indulge my passion; Thou hast a right to draw forth from it a just indignation, but nevertheless I will complete my undertaking."

Thus we condemn ourselves. And here, Christians, is one of the essential foundations of this terrible mystery of the eternity of the punishment with which faith threatens us, and against which our reason revolts. We suppose that we can not have any knowledge of it in this life, and we are not aware, says St. Chrysostom, that we find it completely in the blood of the Savior, or rather in our profanation of it every day. For this blood, my brethren, adds this holy doctor, is enough to make eternity not less frightful, but less incredible. And behold the reason: This blood is of an infinite dignity; it can therefore be avenged only by an infinite punishment. This blood, if we destroy ourselves, will cry eternally against us at the tribunal of God. It will eternally excite the wrath of God against us. This blood, falling upon lost souls, will fix a stain upon them, which shall never be effaced. Their torments must consequently never end.

A reprobate in hell will always appear in the eyes of God stained with that blood which he has so basely treated. God will then always abhor him; and, as the aversion of God from His creature is that which makes hell, it must be inferred that hell will be eternal. And in this, O my God, Thou art sovereignly just, sovereignly holy, and worthy of our praise and adoration. It is in this way that the beloved disciple declared it even to God Himself in the Apocalypse. Men, said he, have shed the blood of Thy servants and of Thy prophets; therefore they deserve to drink it, and to drink it from the cup of Thine indig-

nation. "For they have shed the blood of saints and prophets, and thou hast given them blood to drink." An expression which the Scripture employs to describe the extreme infliction of divine vengeance. Ah! if the blood of the prophets has drawn down the scourge of God upon men, what may we not expect from the blood of Jesus Christ? If the blood of martyrs is heard crying out in heaven against the persecutors of the faith, how much more will the blood of the Redeemer be heard!

Then once more, Christians, behold the deplorable necessity to which we are reduced. This blood which flows from Calvary either demands grace for us, or justice against us. When we apply ourselves to it by a lively faith and a sincere repentance, it demands grace; but when by our disorders and impieties we check its salutary virtue, it demands justice, and it infallibly obtains it. It is in this blood, says St. Bernard, that all righteous souls are purified; but by a prodigy exactly opposite, it is also in this same blood that all the sinners of the land defile themseles, and render themselves, if I may use the expression, more hideous in the sight of God.

Ah! my God, shall I eternally appear in thine eyes polluted with that blood which washes away the crimes of others? If I had simply to bear my own sins, I might promise myself a punishment less rigorous, considering my sins as my misfortune, my weakness, my ignorance. Then, perhaps, Thou wouldst be less offended on account of them. But when these sins with which I shall be covered shall present themselves before me as so many sacrileges with respect to the blood of Thy Son; when the abuse of this blood shall be mixed and confounded with all the disorders of my life; when there shall not be one of them against which this blood shall not cry louder than the blood of Abel against Cain; then, O God of my soul! what will become of me in thy presence? No, Lord, cries the same St. Bernard affectionately, suffer not the blood of my Savior to fall upon me in this manner. Let it fall upon me to sanctify, but let it not fall upon me to destroy. Let it fall upon me in a right use of the favors which are the divine overflowings of it, and not through the blindness of mind and hardness of heart which are the most terrible punishments of it. Let it fall upon me by the participation of the sacred Eucharist, which is the precious source of it, and not by the maledictions attached to the despisers of Thy sacraments. In fine, let it fall upon me by influencing my conduct and inducing the practise of good works, and let it not fall upon me for my wanderings, my infidelities, my obstinacy, and my impenitence. This, my brethren, is what we ought to ask to-day from Jesus Christ crucified. It is with these views that we ought to go to the foot of the cross and catch the blood as it flows. He was the Savior of the Jews as well as ours, but this Savior, St. Augustine says, the Jews have converted into their judge. Avert from us such an evil. May He Who died to save us be our Savior. May He be our Savior during all the days of our lives. And may His merits, shed upon us abundantly, lose none of their efficacy in our hands, but be preserved entire by the fruits we produce from them. May He be our Savior in death. And at the last moment may the cross be our support, and thus may He consummate the work of our salvation which He has begun. May He be our Savior in a blest eternity, where we shall be as much the sharer in His glory as we have been in His sufferings.

JOHN C. BOWMAN

1849-1920

PRAYER IN THE NAME OF JESUS

BIOGRAPHICAL NOTE

PRESIDENT of the Theological Seminary of the Reformed Church, Lancaster, Pa., and professor of practical theology; born at Chambersburg, Pa.; after completing his course in Franklin and Marshall College and the theological seminary at Lancaster, Pa., entered the ministry as pastor of the Reformed church, Shepherdstown, W. Va.; later became pastor of the Reformed church, Hanover, Pa.; for sixteen years was professor of New Testament exegesis in the theological seminary at Lancaster, Pa.

"And whatsoever ye shall ask in my name that will I do, that the Father may be glorified in the Son. If ye shall ask anything in my name, I will do it."— John 14 : 13, 14.

IF one may discriminate as to the relative value and importance of the several religious disciplines, I should assign the first place to prayer. It relates itself to all other religious observances and activities as cause to effect. It serves, as no other agency can serve, to bring and keep the soul of man in touch with God, as the source and support of his spiritual life, and as a strong rock and tower of defense in the midst of life's perils.

The text is found in what is known as the discourse of Jesus in the upper room at Jerusalem. It was spoken on one of the days of the last week of Jesus, shortly before He proceeded to Olivet, accompanied by His disciples. Its significance, therefore, is enhanced by the solemnity which attaches to a final message. The words clearly indicate a confidential and spiritual relationship between Jesus and His disciples, such as had not previously existed; and they invest the prayer-problem with a meaning which carries with it corresponding difficulties. Frequently, on former occasions, Jesus had spoken to His disciples of the necessity and efficacy of prayer, and He confirmed His instruction by His example. The several instances of the praying of Jesus, recorded in the gospels, indicate the rule, the habit of His life. At the tomb of Lazarus, while addressing the Father, (John 11:42), He says, "I knew that thou hearest me always." The word "always" evidently implies the regular habit of prayer. But the words of the text have very special significance in that they contain the promise that the time is drawing near when the disciples shall pray "in the name of Jesus"; and whatsoever they shall ask in His name, shall be given them.

The philosophy of prayer, which satisfies both the faith and the reason of a Christian, rests on certain assumptions, namely, that God is; that He is infinitely wise and good; that, as a father, He has a loving care for His children; that He is ever willing to help them in accordance with their need; and, further, that His help is conditioned by their desire and their cooperation. Prayer is the expression of confidence in the Father's wisdom and love; also, of the dependence, need, and desire of the supplicating child. Prayer, therefore, is the bond of union between God and His children, the indispensable condition of the bestowal and the reception of divine

62

blessing. But what of the reign of law? The reign of law, wrongly viewed, is an objection and an obstacle to prayer. The reign of law, rightly viewed, is an incentive to prayer. The universality of law does not mean that law works as an unconscious and unintelligent force, but that God works everywhere and in all things conformably to His will and to the designed purposes of creation. Christian prayer does not contradict the divine method; it does not attempt to constrain the will of God to an accommodative compliance with the desires or whims of fallible children. It is, rather, the means by which we lift ourselves up into correspondence with the purposes and the methods of God. It is the harmonizing of our will with the will of God.

In the bestowal of natural blessings God's laws do not dispense with human cooperation. They demand it. It is part of the reign of law that man must work in harmony with nature in order to obtain what nature has in store. It is God's method to open to those who knock; to give to those who ask. In the spiritual kingdom there must ever be a recognition and application of a similar principle. It is not the province of prayer to attempt to withstand the invariable laws established by divine wisdom. That were folly. Prayer seeks correspondence with God's method; and it is in harmony with the divine method, as well as with the law of human personality, that the bestowal of spiritual blessings should be conditioned by conscious human need and earnest desire. The idea of obtaining spiritual blessings without asking, without the free human will cooperating with the divine will, is irrational. It is indeed unthinkable in the light of our knowledge of spiritual life and a human personality.

Prayer is dependence upon divine guidance; it is the craving of divine help; it is the desire to live conformably to the will of Him who is infinitely wise and good; and thus, by glorifying Him, glorify our own nature.

What I have said by way of positive statement concerning the nature and the purpose of prayer is, by implication, an answer to the question as to the efficacy of prayer. It is the height of folly to attempt to prove the efficacy of prayer to those who do not pray, or who doubt the efficacy of prayer. In the very nature of things the efficacy of prayer can be known only to those who observe the habit of prayer. It should count for something that the best and wisest of all ages have prayed, and were helped by prayer as by no other means. It should count for much that Jesus prayed. Shall He be convicted of folly? But the argument most convincing is the argument from experience. Has any one observed the habit of uplifting his mind daily to the throne of God, his thought communing with the Highest? Has any one

habitually and fervently prayed in the name of Jesus? If so, for him there is no question as to the efficacy of prayer.

This brings us now to the consideration of the warrant for the high claim made by Jesus. In our text the prayer-problem is conjoined with that of the person of Christ. Prayer is the communion of man with God. How do we know God? How shall we come to Him? Not otherwise than through the revelations which He has made of himself. God in nature, through its varied forms, has revealed, and ever continues to reveal, His wisdom, His power, and His goodness. And through these lower forms, as Bryant in his "Thanatopsis" teaches, nature, or God in nature, "speaks a various language." And by means of these visible manifestations of the divine, the spirit of worship may be evoked. We lose nothing and may gain much by accepting the truth of natural religion. But this can not satisfy the aspirations and longings of the human heart, craving for communion with God through the highest and fullest revelation which He has made of Himself. Where do we find this? In Jesus Christ; in the moral perfections disclosed through His character and ministry.

In the discourses which lead up to the great pronouncement of the text, and in those which follow it, Jesus claims for Himself unique, ethical sonship with God; an incomparable closeness of fellowship with the Father. "The Father is in me and I in the Father." "I and my Father are one." "I speak that which I have seen with my Father." "If I do not the works of my Father, believe me not." "I do always the things which are pleasing to God." "My meat is to do the will of him who sent me."

These are but a few of the many passages taken from the teaching of Jesus, as set forth in the Fourth Gospel, which enforce the claim of Jesus to a perfect moral union with God. This claim is not weakened by the supposititious theory that the representation of the teaching of Jesus in the Fourth Gospel is colored by the thought of a theological interpreter. Admitting such inference, yet we may maintain that the coloring does not obscure or weaken, but that it enriches the truth of the teaching of Jesus. The primary question is: Has the claim of Jesus, made through His direct teaching, or through that which has been credited to Him, been made good? Has it been fully vindicated? If so, on what basis? I answer: on the basis of what Jesus was, in His character and in His life, as revealed unto men during his earthly ministry; as authenticated unto men throughout the entire period of Christian history; and as authenticated unto men to-day. In Jesus Christ, as revealed unto men, there is given the highest and fullest revelation of God. In the moral perfections of His manhood, in the superior excellences of His character, in His flawless virtues, in His unsurpassed and unsurpassable ideals, there is given all-sufficient proof that he is the Son of God; so that, both to Christian faith and enlightened reason, the claim of the divinity of Jesus Christ is fully justified.

And as Jesus is the highest revelation which God has made of Himself, so by virtue of that fact, in Jesus do we find the true mediator between God and man. No one can come to the Father but by him. He is the way, the truth, the life. "There is none other name under heaven given among men, whereby we must be saved." If, therefore, we would go to God in prayer, to commune with Him, to seek His help, we would go to Him preferably in the form in which He has most fully manifested Himself; that is, in Jesus Christ our Lord. And, further, if we would satisfy the aspirations of the heart to worship God, while we may praise Him in all his works, in His manifestations in nature, in His providential dealings with men and nations; and while we would heed His voice "spoken unto the fathers in the prophets, by divers portions and in divers manners," yet, would we speak to Him and have Him speak to us, we come to Him as He has revealed Himself in His Son; and we worship God in Christ.

The claim of Jesus to perfect unity and fellowship with the Father being warranted by His character and His life, we can the more clearly apprehend the meaning of the phrase "in my name," as this appears in the double promise: "Whatsoever ye shall ask in my name, that will I do." "If ye shall ask anything in my name, I will do it." "In my name"—this is the first occurrence of the phrase in the teaching of Jesus, and implies an advance in thought as it does in revelation. It is something of which the Old Testament saints, and even the New Testament disciples, previous to this time, had not known. But let us not be misled by the very frequent, and perhaps too common, if not irreverent, use of the name of Jesus in prayer. The use of the name of Jesus in prayer, in itself, is no warrant of efficacy. It possesses no spell by means of which a Simon Magus can work wonders. It will not serve as an incantation to be used by the seven sons of Sceva against an evil spirit. Nor is an answer promised to the Christian's prayer because it is summarily concluded by the solemn appeal "in Jesus' name," or, "for Jesus' sake," however sincere may be one's dependence on the vicarious work of Jesus.

The name of Jesus, just as the name of God, expresses the sum of the qualities which mark the nature or character of the person. It is the embodiment and presentation of what Jesus is, demanding our recognition of

the same. To believe in the name of Jesus is to accept as truth the revelation contained in the title. It is to acknowledge and appropriate Jesus in all that He is, and in all that He does for men.

To pray in the name of Jesus designates, on the part of the Christian, a holy and exalted state and action of the spirit corresponding to that of Jesus while praying to the Father. The phrase, "In the name of Jesus," expresses a spiritual realm of life with which the mind of the Christian is enveloped, and implies that, moving in this realm of thought and life, the Christian is *en rapport* with the mind of Jesus. It means the identification of the disciple with his Lord. "In the name of Jesus," designates a relationship to Jesus analogous to that which Jesus sustained to the Father. "I am in the Father, and the Father in me." "I in them and they in me that they may be perfected in one." "He that abideth in me and I in him, the same bringeth forth much fruit." "If ye abide in me and my word abide in you, ye shall ask what ye will, and it shall be done unto you." In all these sayings there is set forth the thought of a profound spiritual kinship and fellowship, implying an essential unity and community of life. Similarly, in the teaching of Paul do we find frequent use of the phrases "in Christ," "in Christ Jesus," "in the Lord." The significance of the preposition "in," according to such New Testament usage, far transcends its ordinary meaning. Indeed, there is no single word in our language which can serve as its full equivalent. "In the name of Jesus" designates a vital, spiritual union with Christ, which is the basis, the explanation, and inspiration of the Christian's whole manner of life. It denotes the aim and quality of every virtue and of every act. At the same time it carries with it the promise and pledge of heavenly power and blessedness. We have to do, then, not with a figure of speech, in our interpretation of the words of the text: "Whatsoever ye shall ask in my name that will I do," but with a fact no less real than that of our spiritual union with Jesus, corresponding to the union which holds between Him and the Father. "In the name of Jesus" impresses the fact of a constant, spiritual environment, in which the personality is implanted, and upon which it ever depends as its source of sustenance and as the incentive to all action.

If the name of Jesus, as embracing the revelation of the Father in the Son, be the element in which the prayerful activity moves, then is the answer fully assured; as much so as tho Jesus Himself offered the prayer. Manifestly, no thought or desire which is alien to the spirit of Jesus, and inconsistent with His ideals, can shield itself under the shelter of His name. That only can be in His name which expresses the spirit exhibited by Jesus in His life, and which promotes the ends for which Jesus lived. That only can be prayed in His name which brings to clear expression the principles by which His life was regulated, and the faith by which His conduct was inspired.

And whatsoever is prayed in His name shall be granted. "Whatsoever" designates the boundless scope of prayer as the expression of human need and of all lawful human desires. "Whatsoever ye shall ask"—this is the pledge that every need of the religious nature, indeed, of the entire proper nature of man, shall find enduring satisfaction in what Jesus has to give. "Whatsoever ye shall ask in my name" breathes all the solicitude and tenderness of the Father-heart, and of the Savior's love in the care of supplicating children as regards their individual or personal needs.

Further, the name of Jesus betokens the comprehensiveness of the Savior's love. It uplifts the thought and the desire of the individual into the realm of a world-wide loving care. It is the inspiration of all home and foreign missionary activity. Approaching the Father in the name of the Son, we place ourselves in intelligent correspondence with the divine kingdom and the divine purpose; and from the largess of God's love we may draw the stores of good things which God wills to give for the well-being not simply of the individual or of the family, but of the Church, of the nation, of mankind. All these boundless stores of blessings are open to those who pray in the name of Jesus.

"In the name of Jesus," while it is the sure pledge of answer to prayer, it is at the same time a severe test of the purity and sincerity of prayer. It is the sure standard by which we distinguish true prayer from prayer expressive of selfish desire, unholy cravings, impure thoughts, emotions, aspirations, born of the will of the flesh and not of the will of God. Prayer in the name of Jesus accepts Jesus as the guide to prayer and as our example in thought, purpose, and life. If we seek to commune with Jesus, as He communed with the Father; if we seek to do His will as He sought to do the Father's will; if we, in our lives, seek to glorify Him as He glorified the Father; then will be realized the blessedness, the joy, and the peace which accompany the constant habit of prayer. And in our life's experience we shall find all-sufficient testimony to the uplifting power and saving efficacy of prayer.

LEWIS ORSMOND BRASTOW

1834-1912

THE REALITY OF THE UNSEEN

BIOGRAPHICAL NOTE

PROFESSOR emeritus in Yale University; born in Brewer, Me., March 23, 1834; graduated from Bowdoin College in 1857, and from Bangor Theological Seminary in 1860; received the degree of D.D. from Bowdoin College, and A.M. from Yale University; pastor of the South Congregational church at St. Johnsbury, Vt., from 1861 to 1873; and of the First Congregational church of Burlington, Vt., 1873-84; professor of practical theology in Yale Divinity School, 1885-1907; chaplain of the Twelfth Regiment of Vermont Volunteer Infantry in 1862 and 1863, and a member of the Vermont Constitutional Convention in 1870; author of "Representative Modern Preachers," "The Modern Pulpit," etc.

"While we look not at the things which are seen, but at the things which are not seen."—2 Cor. 4 : 18.

IT should not be difficult to believe in an unseen world and an unseen life. Such belief is normal, for it is a product of the unperverted constitution of the human soul. And yet confessedly the whole matter is becoming invested with a large measure of uncertainty. The notion gets currency that men know only what they see, and that they only guess at what they can not see. They are forced to deal practically with the seen, and they indulge the fancy that they only consent to deal speculatively with the unseen. They have senses, and they are surrounded by objects that impress themselves upon those senses. They have material wants and what they see supplies those wants. Here are the wants and over there in the world of sense are the instruments, the agencies and the objects of supply. These are the facts with which the average man concerns himself, and he is sure that no one can deny them.

Men have business occupations. They force them to deal with what they see, what they can know about and accomplish through the agency of the things that are seen seems to them to determine the practical worth of their lives. In all this they think themselves to be on solid ground. The world that is seen is very real to them. There is no possibility of delusion here. Besides, it is a pleasant thing to live.

Of course, there are hardships, but, on the whole, to most men material existence is a pleasant thing; and so it comes about, for these and other obvious reasons, that a superficial, sensuous habit of mind is fixt. The unseen life loses its hold of men because they lose their hold of it. Much that is said about it fails to reach them, and they come to regard it as wholly beyond their range. They tell us that there is a vast deal of romancing about it, which may be considerably more than half true. But why should they leap to the conclusion that therefore an invisible world is a fundamental delusion? Why should they assume that, because things that are seen are to them the only real things, they are the only things they can know, and that they are responsible only with respect to the things they thus know?

And now, as against all this, whether said or thought—and it is perhaps more often thought than said—and as against the false attitude of mind behind it, in as friendly and non-polemical a temper as is possible, I want to make a plea for the things that are unseen.

At the outset, let us note that they are, in fact, the first things. There must be some first things—things to start with. There is bottom somewhere. Things haven't always been just as they are now. There is somewhere a point of departure. Now these first things, things to start with, things that stand at least at the beginning of the material universe, if they do not antedate it, are either identical with and are a constituent qualitative part of the realm of the seen, or they belong to a realm that is relatively independent of it and antedates it, the realm of the unseen. The crucial question is, which? Human intelligence, with inconsiderable exceptions, has always referred them to the realm of the unseen. They exist before the things that are seen. If there were not already realities one can not see, there never would be things one can see. The unseen is always back of the seen. It is the vice of men's thinking, as well as living, that they reverse the order. It is a modern fashion to undertake to get on without the presupposition of an invisible order that antedates the visible order. What we see is the first thing and the only thing. Everything unseen falls somewhere within its limits, and has no existence independently of it.

We have no knowledge of anything unseen that is not identical with and inseparable from the realm of the seen. The whole universe of real existence is crowded within its bounds. There is no personal soul, because it can not be seen. The only soul a man has is a product of material energy. There is no thought, feeling, hope, aspiration, prayer, that is not the product of material force. There is no heaven, no ideal world, because the world of visible actuality discloses no trace of one. There is no God, because this material world does not bring Him before their eyes, or present Him to their intelligence out of what the senses recognize. God and heaven and the soul must be found within the limits of recognized phenomena or there is none. All this is an irrational reversal of order. The unseen is first. Nothing can be adequately explained without it. Behind the commonest thing that exists there is something one can not see.

Thus the idea, the purpose, the plan of a thing is before the thing itself. This idea, purpose, plan, no one sees. One sees only the thing itself. But it is precisely what lies behind it that makes it what it is, and not something else or whatever might happen. The ideas—the patterns of things, are always in the mind to begin with, and always out of sight. If a man sees a thing that he understands—understands because it has a definite meaning and object which he can interpret, he, as by a kind of instinct, assumes that some meaning, some purpose, went into it.

The plan of one's house is in the mind before the eyes behold it; and it is the plan that makes it what it is—a structure put together for a specific, intelligible object—and not something else, or whatever might happen. A man's business plan for the day is before the business itself; and it is the plan that constitutes it an orderly sequence of transactions, and not a medley of blind and meaningless motions. It is the plan that one does not see. One sees only its products. There is a standard of right action. It is something that no one sees. One sees only the act. But the act would have no significance whatever apart from its reference to the standard that tests it. That is, what one sees finds all its moral character in its connection with what one can not see. It is matter of commonest experience, then, that in practical life the unseen is always before the seen. And it is worth while to pause just here for a moment to add that the thought or the plan of a thing in the mind is a different thing in kind, belongs to a different realm of substances, from the thing itself as recognized by the senses. There is no similarity in kind, no substantive likeness between a man's business acts and their practical results and the place of his business in the mind; or between the materials of his houses and the conception of the house, as he has thought it out. And until it can be shown that the idea of a thing may be defined in precisely the same terms that define the thing itself, men are bound to acknowledge that the unseen part of a thing is of a different order and substance from the visible product itself. A man's thought must be defined in different terms from the visible products of them.

Now, let it be remembered that the visible universe must have had some sort of beginning. No matter by what process the things we see began to be, whether the process of their becoming was sudden or slow and gradual—enough that they began to be. That beginning presupposes something that started it, and that something belongs to a realm behind, above and superior to it, and it is an invisible realm. What we see is matter—if, indeed, we do see much of it anyhow—which is an open question. But at any rate, we see nothing else. What lies behind the universe we can not see. And what is it? Is it some blind, brute, invisible energy, of which one can know nothing? Is it unintelligible and unknowable? If the material universe were itself utterly unintelligible, then one might call the energy behind it unintelligible with some show of reason. But if we can understand anything about the things we see, if we can trace any order, any plan, any adaptation of means to ends, if the universe has any meaning whatever to us, then we certainly find the traces of thought in it. The thought that enters our minds concerning it answers to the thought that went into it. Things that have intelligent plan are thought out. And things that are intelligently thought out have an intelligent origin. What has thought in it has mind back of it; and a planning mind is a self-conscious mind; and a self-conscious mind is a personal mind—and that yields the primal conception of God.

An invisible God is before a visible universe. The seen is a product of the unseen. In the fullest and best sense, I can believe in what I see only as I believe in what I can not see. If I am constrained to believe in this reality—of the material universe—I am constrained to believe in the existence and priority of God.

And that brings me to note that things unseen are, in fact, the real things. If they are the first things, of course they are the real things. If God is before the world and if He made it, He is far more real than His handiwork. The reality of things made is conditioned by the reality of the maker. If an ideal world exists in the order of thought and of time before the actual world of sense, it is, in the truest sense, the more real world. If mind exists before matter, mind is the reality and matter is real only as conditioned by it. What men call reality is often, in fact, only a show. It is easy to confound seeming with reality. It is important to know what is real and what is only phenomenal. What seems belongs only to the outside of things. What is real belongs to the inside. One fancies that what he sees is the only real thing because he sees it. But what, in fact, does one see? He sees only the surface of it. If he gets hold of anything more, it is the mind—not the eyes—that gets into contact with it. And that more lies utterly beyond the reach of the eyes; it is entirely invisible. Here is a book one opens and reads. Now what takes place? Certain impressions are made upon the retina of the eye. These sensations travel inward a certain distance and then, as sensations, stop. As physical sensations, they get no farther. By a process which no man knows and perhaps no man ever will know, they utterly change their character and are transmuted from sensations into thoughts. Well, now, if there be nothing more than what one has seen in the book, it has no meaning. It is a mass of paper, printer's ink and unintelligible marks that are not even signs. If there be nothing in the reader behind his physical sensations, what he sees will remain only a mass of physical sensations that will leave no result in his intelligence. The book is a mass of unintelligible color and form. It is only a show. It has no reality, because it has no meaning. It is not the impression made on the senses that is the real thing; it is not the outside but the inside that is the real thing. It is not letters or words or sounds, but thought, that is the reality of language. Without ideas, which no man sees, what we call language were only a jargon—a nothingness of sounds. Mind is the reality of language. What the book contains makes it a book, and not a mass of paper, printer's ink, and type. The reality of anything is found in its significance. If it have no meaning, it has no reality. It is a fantom show. The Buddhist regards the material universe as only a fantom of the unreality. It is all unreal to him—a passing show.

> We are no other than a moving row
> Of magic shadow shapes that come and go,
> Round with this sun-illumined lantern held
> In midnight by the Master of the show.
>
> Impotent pieces in the game he plays
> Upon his checker-board of nights and days,
> Hither and thither moves and checks and slays,
> And one by one back into the closet lays.
>
> And that inverted bowl we call the sky,
> Whereunder crawling, cooped, we live and die,
> Lift not your hands to it for help—for it
> As impotently rolls as you or I.

And what wonder? He has lost the key. It can mean nothing to him. He has lost God. The Master of the show that holds the magic shadow-shapes is as unreal as the shapes themselves. He has no wisdom, no benevolence, no intelligence. What can be the meaning and the end of a world that has no creator? What wonder that the Buddhist fancies life a sort of wandering sea—restless and aimless! What wonder that for him the problem of existence is to get out of conscious insignificance into unconscious nothingness! What wonder that he knows no higher bliss than to be extinguished!

This universe is God's book. If it be not this, will you tell me what it is? What you read in it, not what you see at the surface of it, secures for it reality. To any man who looks only at the outside of the world and lives only in its shows it will be unreal. It will be a hollow world, whatever his theory about it. The man whom we call a worldling is the man who lives on the outside of things—in its shows and not in its realities. Such a man can not know much about this world. He may fancy that he does, but he is mistaken. He may seem to be a worldly-wise man, but he does not get at the inner reality of the world in which he lives. He is an unreal character. The unreality of his life makes him such.

You can not see God, nor heaven, nor eternity, nor the soul; but they are far more real than anything you can see. You can not define them in terms that define matter, but they give it whatever best significance it has; and apart from them, it were not better, even at its best, than the mud of the streets or the dust of the desert.

I see an old friend who is mourning for the beloved taken from his side. He says to me: "The world is insignificant, it amounts to nothing." And I make answer: "Yes, save as it is held in connection with an invisible and a higher world and so interpreted and understood and evaluated." And he replies with that tone of weariness and disheartenment with which we are becoming so familiar in our day: "We know little or nothing about that other world." And again I answer: "Little, indeed, about its details, but something surely about its simple outline reality. That other world is as real as this world. In a sort, it is even more so; for it is the ideal world that exalts the real world, and it is this ideal world that is, therefore, the truly real one." If God and that higher world and life were more real to men, this world and life would be more real. They could not be insignificant and contemptible. If a man loses his hold of the unseen, he will lose what is best in his own earthly life. The world is hollow without God. Earthly life is indeed insignificant without a heavenly life beyond. Worldliness is unreality. Only the things that are unseen are the primal and regulative realities.

And so we come to note that the things that are unseen are the controlling things. They command us, and they ought to control us. They have the authority, and they ought to have the power. All legitimate ultimate authority belongs to the unseen realm. If the seen masters a man, it usurps authority. No man can rightly be mastered by his senses. Every civilized man knows that he should not allow his senses to tyrannize over him. You never saw a man that had a particle of self-respect left who was willing to proclaim outright: "I propose to give full rein to my sensuous propensities. I mean to let the material world dominate me." Such a man proclaims his own degradation and ruin. He is a lost man, and it will take a mighty power to save him. If there is a relic of manhood left in any man, he will revolt from degradation to a merely animal and material life.

The problem of life is, after all, simple. It is this: "Which shall control you—the seen or the unseen?" The struggle of life is here. If the people about us are mastered by their senses, mastered by a shallow and gross materialism, as they are, they know better. No man becomes a sensualist, or materialist, or world-monger and keeps a good conscience. It is sin to be mastered by the seen. The first sinner in that old Biblical story, so full of profound significance, was mastered by the seen rather than the unseen. Sense and conscience contended for the mastery, and sense won. But the man was dishonored. The fall of man is his descent into subordination to a sensuous life. The redemption of man is his recovery to the realm of the spirit, the realm of the invisible. Religion is identified with the realm of the unseen, and the claims of religion are the claims of the unseen; and so long as it truly represents the unseen, it is only religion that can save the world. When it panders to the visible and material, it becomes idolatry, and its power is broken. The purity of religion is in its faithful devotion to an invisible ideal, and its power is realized through faith and not through sight. The claims of religion are rational. They are simply this: What is first and most real and authoritative should control you. God keeps the realities of religion before us in order that the unseen order may control us. It is religion—it is a practical recognition of the supreme invisible ideal that rescues the world from the abyss of materialism. In every variety of ways, God is trying to keep the realities of an invisible world and life open to us. The end of all our worship, of all our sacraments, the end of all grace and all severity, the end of all our suffering and our dying, is to keep this unseen world and life and all unseen powers before the soul. And the noblest characters of human history have been controlled by the unseen. The noblest lives have been shaped by it. A Being whom our eyes have never seen on earth and shall never see, has ruled the best part of the world for almost two thousand years. Jesus Christ is more commanding and controlling in influence, that the world has not seen Him and can not see Him. If we should see Him, we should probably degrade Him. It was expedient for this world that He should go. The world knows Him best unseen. And it may be that those of our friends whom we love best and whom we have "lost a while" are far more influential with us for good that they have gone from us into the unseen world. Elisha, in that strange Old Testament story, wanted a double portion of Elijah's spirit, and Elijah named what seems at first a singular, but when we come to think of it, after all, a natural condition. Let him behold the prophet—his spiritual father—depart and it should come. The unique sphere of the prophet is the realm of the invisible. Elijah translated is a greater power than Elijah in the flesh. And so God often lets us behold our beloved pass into the unseen world that, rapt from our sight, a mightier influence may come upon us.

The best race of history worshiped an unseen God. It was the realm of the unseen that made Hebrewism what it was. Only when the visible supplanted the invisible in the grand old worship was it corrupted and shorn of its power. The prophet-souls have always been men of the invisible. Faith in the unseen has mastered them. God has been more real, in a sort, than the world, the unseen future and the unseen "city that hath foundations whose builder and maker is God" have been, in a sort, more real than the visible present, and faith has been more real and more potent than sight.

The unseen has doubtless been too often a dark and tyrannical power. The sinful and ignorant soul has stocked it with all mischiefs. Superstition has often displaced religion. But the fact still remains that it has been a great and ennobling power in the lives of men, and that even in the lower and more degraded forms of religion, it has not been without its uplift from the beginning until now.

It is the unseen realm that abides. "The things that are unseen are eternal." Nothing else abides. The fact is set and kept before us continually. Every change, every loss and disappointment, proclaims it. Strange that what goes so speedily, so easily, so suddenly, should be so important, so real, so controlling! It marks a singular perversion in our nature that it is so. Men are saying: "What I see is to me the only reality"; and yet its very transitoriness should remind them that there must be somewhere some reality behind it or beyond it or it is the veriest mockery of unreality. How can a man call the property, to the acquisition of which he devotes all his energies and which may slip from him at any moment, in the highest sense a real thing? How can he call the visible form of his friend the only or chief reality as related to his friendship, when he knows that this friend may, at any hour, pass from his gaze? Surely the properties and the friends we see and may lose at any moment must stand for unseen realities of far greater importance and value. These unseen realities that abide ought to be the priceless realities just because they abide. That they do abide is involved in what they are. If God and heaven and eternity and the soul with all its higher powers are realities at all, they abide just because they are what they are; and we need familiarity with these unseen realities in order to realize the transitoriness of the seen. The man who lives wholly in his senses, will live as if this world were to last forever. It is the one who lives above them that will live otherwise. You can not fatally disappoint the man who knows that the things that are seen are temporal. He is the man that knows this world. But the one who never gets used to the changes and losses

of life because he does not like them and will not accept them, is doomed to perpetual disappointment.

Those who live wholly in the seen are always cheating themselves. They want what they see to last. But it is a very unaccommodating world. It does not last and was not made to last. Yet men persist in living as tho it were to endure, and so at last they feel themselves deluded and mocked and even wronged. A man may say, "Let us eat and drink, for to-morrow we die," but the fact is, that he does not expect to die to-morrow, nor the next day, nor for an indefinite time to come. He clings to life, and death is his last and bitterest disappointment. We need to be familiar with the unseen if we would get wonted to the solemn realities of a transitory life. Let a man live that life which is in its nature eternal, the life that is unseen, the "life that is hid with Christ in God," and he will not know the disappointments of this transitory sphere. He will not live as if time were eternity. He will know this world for what it is and what it is worth.

But we need also to be reminded, and often startlingly, of the transitoriness of the seen in order to make us more familiar with the unseen, and more completely committed to it. And God is not slow to furnish such reminders. The language of all change, all loss, all disappointment, the language of sickness and pain and death, is a double language. It says: "The things that are seen are, indeed, temporal; but the things that are unseen are eternal." God says: "I take what you see that I may give you what you can not see. I substitute the invisible for the visible. I take your beloved from before your eyes that I may give him back to your soul, more beloved, more precious, yea, more real than ever before. I take your property that I may substitute for it character more precious than gold, yea, than much fine gold." To interpret all this, to know the true meaning of this world, to know the inner meaning of our life, to know it in all its wondrous greatness and glory, with all its loss and pain and sorrow and darkness, its bewildering confusion and its final death, we need religion; we need immediate contact with God; we need the vision of the unseen; need culture of the "faith talent," of the religious instinct and impulses; need to live more in meditation of and fellowship with super-worldly realities, that so God may meet us and teach us and strengthen us and lift us up.

JOHN A. BROADUS

1827-1895

LET US HAVE PEACE WITH GOD

BIOGRAPHICAL NOTE

JOHN A. BROADUS was born in Virginia in 1827. His preeminence as a preacher was attained while he was chiefly occupied as professor of New Testament Interpretation and Homiletics in the Baptist Theological Seminary at Louisville, Kentucky. (Originally established at Greenville, South Carolina.) For many years Dr. Broadus was regarded as the foremost preacher of the South, and was in demand on many important public occasions for sermons and addresses. It has been said that "the thought and the language of his sermons lingered in the mind like strains of melodious and inspiring music." The sermon here given is characteristic of the earnest simplicity of his style, and of the theological and philosophical bent of his homiletic methods. He died in 1895.

Therefore being justified by faith, let us have peace with God, through our Lord Jesus Christ.—Romans v., 1. (R. V.)

IT is nearly four centuries ago now, that a young professor from the north of Germany went to Rome. He was a man of considerable learning and of versatile mind. Yet he did not go to Rome to survey the remains of antiquity or the treasures of modern art. He went to Rome because he was in trouble about his sins and could find no peace. Having been educated to regard Rome as the center of the Christian world, he thought he would go to the heart of things and see what he could there find. He had reflected somewhat at home, and had talked with other men more advanced than himself, on the thought that the just shall live by faith; but still that thought had never taken hold of him. We read—some of you remember the story quite well—how one day, according to the strange ideas that prevailed and still prevail at Rome, he went climbing up a stairway on his knees, pausing to pray on every step, to see if that would not help him about his sins. Then, as he climbed slowly up, he seemed to hear a voice echoing down the stairway, "The just shall live by faith; the just shall live by faith." And so he left alone his dead works, he arose from his knees and went down the stairway to his home to think about that great saying, "The just shall live by faith."

It is no wonder that with such an experience, and such a nature, Martin Luther should have lived to shake the Christian world with the thought that justification by faith is the great doctrine of Christianity, "the article of a standing or a falling church." It is no wonder that John Wesley, rising up with living earnestness when England was covered with a pall of spiritual death, should have revived the same thought—justification by faith.

Yet it is not true that the doctrine of justification by faith is all of the gospel. It is true that the doctrine of justification by faith is simply one of the several ways by which the gospel takes hold of men. You do not hear anything of that doctrine in the Epistles of John. He has another way of presenting the gospel salvation, namely, that we must love Christ, and be like Him, and obey Him.

I think sometimes that Martin Luther made the world somewhat one-sided by his doctrine of justification by faith; that the great mass of the Protestant world are inclined to suppose there is no other way of looking on the gospel. There are very likely some here to-day who would be more imprest by John's way of presenting the matter; but probably, the majority would be more imprest by Paul's way, and it is our business to present now this and now that, to present first one side and then the other. So we have here before us to-day Paul's great doctrine of justification by faith, in perhaps one of his most striking statements. "Therefore, being justified by faith, let us have peace with God through our Lord Jesus Christ."

My friends, we talk and hear about these gospel truths, and repeat these Scripture words, and never stop to ask ourselves whether we have a clear idea of what is meant. What does Paul mean when he talks about being justified? There has been a great deal of misapprehension as to his meaning. Martin Luther was all wrong in his early life, because he had been reared up in the idea that a justified man means simply a just man, a good man, and that he could not account himself justified or hope for salvation until he was a thoroughly good man. Now, the Latin word from which we borrow our word "justified" does not mean to make just, and as the Romanists use the Latin, their error is natural. But Paul's Greek word means not to make just, but to regard as just, to treat as just. That is a very important difference—not to make just, but to regard and treat as just. How would God treat you, if you were a righteous man; if you had, through all your life, faithfully performed all your duties, conforming to all your relations to your fellow beings—how would He regard and treat you? He would look upon you with complacency. He would smile on you as one that was in His sight pleasing. He would bless you as long as you lived in this world, and, when you were done with this world, He would delight to take you home to His bosom, in another world, because you would deserve it.

And now as God would treat a man who was just because he deserved it, so the gospel proposes to treat men who are not just and who do not deserve it, if they believe in the Lord Jesus Christ. He will treat them as just, tho they are not just, if they believe in Christ; that is to say, he will look upon them with His favor; He will smile upon them in His love; He will bless them with every good as long as they live, and when they die He will delight to take them home to His own bosom, tho they never deserved it, through His Son, Jesus Christ. That is what Paul means by justification. And when Martin Luther found

that out he found peace. This Epistle to the Romans had always stopt his progress when reading the New Testament. He would read, in the Latin version, "For therein is revealed the justice of God," and he felt in his heart that God's justice must condemn him. But now he came to see what was really meant by the righteousness of God, the righteousness which God provides and bestows on the believer in Jesus. A sinful man, an undeserving man, may get God Almighty's forgiveness and favor and love, may be regarded with complacency and delight, tho he does not deserve it, if he believes in the Lord Jesus Christ. That is justification by faith.

It is one thing to take hold of this matter in the way of doctrinal conception and expression, and of course, God be thanked! it is another thing to receive it in the heart. There are many people who get hold of it all in the heart with trust and peace that never have a correct conception of it as a doctrine. Yet I suppose it is worth while that we should endeavor to see these things clearly. Other things being equal, they will be the holiest and most useful Christians who have the clearest perception of the great facts and truths of the gospel. So I recommend to you that whenever any one tries to explain to you one of these great doctrinal truths, you shall listen with fixt attention and see if you can not get a clearer view of the gospel teachings on that subject, for it will do you good.

Now let us come to the second thought here, viz., being justified by faith. A man might say, if God proposes to deal with those who are not just, as if they were, why does He condition it upon believing in the gospel of Jesus Christ? Why can not God proclaim a universal amnesty at once, and be done with it, to all His sinful, weak children, and treat them all as if they were just, without their believing? I don't think this is hard to see. God does not merely propose to deal with us for the time being as if we were just, but He proposes in the end to make us actually just. It would be an unsatisfactory salvation to a right-minded man if God proposed merely to exempt us from the consequences of our sins and not to deliver us from our sins. You do not want merely to escape punishment for sin without ever becoming good; you want to be righteous and holy; you want to be delivered from sin itself as well as from the consequences of sin. And this gospel, which begins by its proclamation that God is willing to treat men as just, altho they are not just, does not stop there. It proposes to be the means by which God will take hold of men's characters and make them just, make them holy. You may, for the moment, conceive of such a thing as that God should make a proclamation of universal amnesty, and treat all men as if they were just; but that would not make them any better. The gospel is not merely to deliver us from the consequence of sin, but to deliver us from the power of sin. You can conceive of an amnesty as to the consequence of sin, which should extend to persons that will not even believe there is such an amnesty; but you can not see how the gospel is to have any power in delivering us from the dominion of sin, unless we believe the gospel. It can do so only through belief. Therefore it is not possible that a man should be justified without belief. I think it is useful that we should thus try to see that this is not a matter of mere arbitrary appointment on the part of the sovereign Power of the universe, but that the condition is necessary —that it can not be otherwise. "Being justified by faith," it reads; and we can not be justified without faith, because the same gospel is also to take hold of us and make us just.

And now, some one who feels a little freshened interest in this subject, some man who has never got hold of the gospel faith, says to himself: "I wonder if the preacher is going to explain to me what believing is, what faith is. I never heard any one succeed in explaining faith." Well, if you will pardon me, the best explanation of faith I ever heard was given by a negro preacher in Virginia. As the story was told me, one Sunday afternoon, a few years ago, some negroes were lying on the ground together, and one of them spoke and said, "Uncle Reuben, can you explain this: Faith in de Lord, and faith in de debbil?" "To be sure I can. There is two things: in de fust place, faith in de Lord, and then faith in de debbil. Now, in the fust place, fustly, there is faith. What is faith? Why, faith is jes faith. Faith ain't nothing less than faith. Faith ain't nothing more than faith. Faith is jest faith —now I done splain it." Really, that man was right, there is nothing to explain. Faith is as simple a conception as the human mind can have. How, then, can you explain faith? You are neither able to analyze it into parts, nor can you find anything simpler with which to compare it. So also as to some other things, that are perfectly easy and natural in practical exercise, and can not be explained.

What is love? Well, I won't go into an elaborate metaphysical definition of love, but if I wanted a child to love me, I should try to exhibit myself in such a character to him and act in such ways that the little child would see in me something to love, and would feel like loving. There would then be no need of an explanation of what love is. Did you ever hear a satisfactory definition of laughter? If you wanted to make a man laugh, would you attempt to define laughter to him? You might possibly succeed in making a laughable

definition; but otherwise definitions won't make a man laugh. You would simply say or do something ludicrous, and he would laugh readily enough if he was so disposed; and if the man be not in a mood for laughing, all your explanations are utterly useless. And so what is faith? There is nothing to explain. Everybody knows what faith is. If you want to induce a man to believe in the Lord Jesus Christ, you must hold up the Lord to him in His true character, and then, if he is in a mood to believe, he will believe, and if he is disinclined to belief, all your explanations will be fruitless. The practical result may even be obstructed by attempts to explain. What is faith? You know what faith is. Every one knows.

Well, then, a man might say, "If you mean by faith in the Lord the simple idea of believing what the Scripture says concerning Him, the idea of believing its teachings about the Lord Jesus Christ to be true, if that is what faith means, then all of us are believers, all have faith." I am afraid not. I am afraid there are some here who have not faith. Has a man faith in the Lord Jesus Christ who simply does not disbelieve in him? I may not deny that what the gospel says is true, but is that believing? Yonder sits a gentleman; suppose some one should come hastily up the aisle, calling his name, and say, "Your house is afire." The gentleman sits perfectly quiet and looks unconcerned, as people so often do when listening to preaching. The man repeats it: "I say your house is afire." But still he sits in his place. Some one near him says, "You hear what that man says. Do you believe it?" "Yes, I believe it," he carelessly replies, and does not stir. You would all say, "The man is insane, or certainly he does not believe it; for if he did, he would not sit perfectly still and remain perfectly unconcerned." Even so when the preacher speaks of sin and guilt and ruin, of God's wrath and the fire that is not quenched; or when he stands with joyful face and proclaims to his hearers that for their sin and ruin there is a Savior; and they say they believe, and yet look as if it were of no concern to them at all; then I say they do not believe it—the thing is not possible. They may not disbelieve it; they may not care to make an attempt to overturn it; they may be in a sort of negative mood; but they do not believe it.

With that statement I suppose there are a great many of us who concur and who will at once say, "Often I fear that I do not really believe it. If I did believe it, the gospel would have more power over my heart and more power over my life than it does have. And what, oh, what shall I do?" The preacher has to remind you of that father to whom the Savior came when the disciples

had tried in vain to heal his suffering child.
Jesus said to him: "All things are possible to
him that believeth;" and he replied: "I believe; help thou my unbelief." That should
be your cry: "I believe; help thou my unbelief." The man would not deny that he believed, and yet felt bound to add that he knew
he did not believe as he ought to. Now the
comfort is, that He who sees all hearts accepted that man's confessedly imperfect faith,
and granted his request. That has often been
the preacher's comfort as he uttered the same
cry, "I believe; help thou my unbelief"; and
God give it as a comfort to you! But do not
content yourself with such a state of things,
with any such feeble, half-way believing.
Nay, let us cherish all that tends to strengthen
our faith in the gospel; let us read the Word
of God, praying that we may be able to believe; let us say from day to day, as the disciples said: "Lord, increase our faith."

The text proceeds: "Therefore, being justified by faith, let us have peace with God."
Instead of the declaration, "We have peace
with God," the best authorities for the text
make it an exhortation, "Let us have peace
with God"; and so the revised version reads.
Some critics admit that the documents require
us so to read, but say that they can see no
propriety in an exhortation at this point—
that it seems much more appropriate to understand the apostle as asserting a fact. Yet
I think we can see meaning and fitness in the
text as corrected: "Being justified by faith,
let us have peace with God."

Let us have peace with God, notwithstanding our unworthiness. My friends, we can not
have peace with God so long as we cling to
the notion that we are going to deserve it.
Just there is the difficulty with many of those
who are trying to be at peace with God. They
have been clinging to the thought that they
must first become worthy, and then become
reconciled to God; and they will have to see
more clearly that they must come to Christ in
order that, being reconciled, they may be
made good, may become worthy. We may
say there are two conceivable ways to have
peace with God. It is conceivable to have
peace with God through our worthiness, and
it is conceivable and also practicable to have
peace with God through our Lord Jesus
Christ, tho we be unworthy. Then let us have
peace with Him, altho so unworthy, through
our Lord Jesus Christ.

Again, let us have peace with God, tho we
are still sinful and unholy, tho we know we
come far short in character and in life of
what God's children ought to be. We must
be, ought to be, intensely dissatisfied with ourselves; but let us be satisfied with our Savior,
and have peace with God through Him; not
content with the idea of remaining such as we
are, but, seeing that the same gospel which

offers us forgiveness and acceptance offers us
also a genuine renewal through our Lord
Jesus Christ, and promises that finally we
shall be made holy, as God is holy, shall indeed
be perfect, as our Father in heaven is perfect.
Let us rejoice in the gracious promise of
that perfect life, and, while seeking to be
what we ought to be, let us have peace with
God. Our sanctification is still sadly imperfect—the best of us well know that, and probably the best of us feel it most deeply; but if
we believe in the Lord Jesus Christ, our justification is perfect. We can never be more
justified than we are now justified, tho we
shall be more and more made holy as long as
we live, and at last made perfectly holy as we
pass into the perfect world. My brethren,
do think more and talk more of that. It is
an intensely practical matter, not only for
your comfort but for the strength of your
life. If we believe in the Lord Jesus Christ,
altho we are painfully conscious that we are
far from being in character and life what we
ought to be, yet, through the perfect justification which we have at once, we shall in the
end by His grace be made perfectly holy.

Let us have peace with God, tho we have
perpetual conflict with sin. What a singular
idea! Peace with God, and yet conflict, yes,
perpetual conflict, with a thousand forms of
temptation to sin, temptations springing from
spiritual tempters—perpetual conflict, and yet
peace with God. Is not that conceivable? Is
not that possible? In this conflict we are on
the Lord's side; in this conflict the Lord is
on our side; and so, tho the battle must be
waged against every form of sin, we may have
peace with God.

And finally, let us have peace with God tho
He leaves us to suffer a thousand forms of
distress and trial. "Let us have peace with
God through our Lord Jesus Christ, by whom
also we have had access by faith into this
grace wherein we stand; and let us rejoice in
hope of the glory of God. And not only so,
but let us also rejoice in our tribulations;
knowing that tribulation worketh patience;
and patience, proving; and proving, hope;
and hope maketh not ashamed, because the
love of God hath been shed abroad in our
hearts through the Holy Ghost which was
given unto us." Surely man may have peace
with God, tho he be left to suffer. For none
of these things can separate us from God's
love. Who shall separate us from Christ's
love? "For I am persuaded that neither
death nor life, neither angels nor principalities
nor powers, neither things present nor things
to come, neither height nor depth, nor any
other creature, shall be able to separate us
from the love of God which is in Christ Jesus
our Lord." When we are in trouble, let us take
fast hold upon that great thought, that trouble
does not divide us from the love of God. Yea,

God's peace can conquer trouble, and guard us, as in a fortress, against its assaults. "In nothing be anxious; but in everything, by prayer and supplication, with thanksgiving, let your requests be made known unto God. And the peace of God, which passeth all understanding, shall guard your hearts and your thoughts in Christ Jesus."

PHILLIPS BROOKS

1835-1893

THE PRIDE OF LIFE

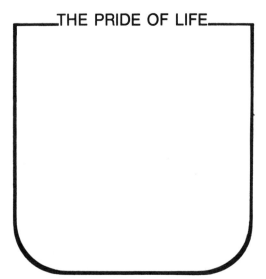

BIOGRAPHICAL NOTE

PHILLIPS BROOKS was born at Boston, Mass., in 1835, graduated at Harvard in 1855 and studied theology at the P. E. Seminary, Alexandria, Va. He was elected rector of the Church of the Advent, Philadelphia, in 1859, and three years later to that of Holy Trinity in the same city. In 1869 he became rector of Trinity Church, Boston, and was consecrated Bishop of Massachusetts in 1891. He died in 1893. He was in every sense a large man, large in simplicity and sympathy, large in spiritual culture. In his lectures to the students at Yale he spoke of the preparation for the ministry as being nothing less than the making of a man. Said he:

"It cannot be the mere training to certain tricks. It cannot be even the furnishing with abundant knowledge. It must be nothing less than the kneading and tempering of a man's whole nature till it becomes of such a consistency and quality as to be capable of transmission. This is the largeness of the preacher's culture." Doctor Brastow describes him thus: "The physical equipment was symbol of his soul; and the rush of his speech was typical of those mental, moral, and spiritual energies that were fused into unity and came forth in a stream of fiery intensity."

The pride of life.—1 John ii., 16.

JOHN is giving his disciples the old warning not to love the world, that world which then and always is pressing on men's eyes and ears and hearts with all its loveliness and claiming to be loved. "Love not the world, neither the things that are in the world. . . . For all that is in the world, the lust of the flesh, and the lust of the eyes, and the pride of life, is not of the Father, but is of the world."

What is the pride of life? Pride is one of those words which hover in the middle region between virtue and vice. The materials which under one set of circumstances and in one kind of character make up an honorable self-respect, seem so often to be precisely the same as those which under another set of circumstances and in another kind of character make up arrogance and self-conceit. This last is the tone evidently in which John speaks. So it is with most moral minglings. All character is personal, determined by some force that blends the qualities into a special personality. The same apparent qualities unite into the most various results. It is like the delicate manufacture of mosaics. The skilful workers of Rome or Venice put in the same ingredients in nature and amount, and the composition comes out at one time dull and muddy and at another time perfectly clear and lustrous. Some subtle difference in the mixture of the constituents or in the condition of the atmosphere or in the heat of the furnace alters the whole result. So out of life we may say in its various minglings there come various products in character, either humility or thankfulness or contentment or self-respect, from some failure of the qualities to meet in perfect union, from some fault in the shape or misregulation of the temperature of the human furnace in which they are fused, this degenerate and confused result of pride which yet is often so near to, that we can see how it was only some slightest cause, some stray and unguarded draft across the surface that hindered it from being, one of the clear and lustrous combinations of the same material. But that fact makes it no better. The muddy glass is no more useful because it is made of the same components as the clear glass. There is nothing still to be done with it but to throw it away.

What then is the pride of life which is bad,

which "is not of the Father, but is of the world"? Life itself we know is of the Father. In whatever sense we take that much-meaning word, life is God's gift. The mere physical being, if that be life, is the creation of His mighty word. The continuance, the prolongation of the vital function, if that be life, that too is the result of His never-sleeping care. The surrounding circumstances, the scenery of our experience, if that be life, is also of His arranging. The spiritual vitality, all the higher powers as we call them, of thought and feeling and conscience, if they be life, no hand but His strung and tuned their manifold and subtle cords. Everywhere there is no life but what He gives. It is not of the world. In no sense does any creative power of being issue either from the material earth, or from the social system, or from the mass of conventional laws and standards, each of which is sometimes, in different uses of the word, characterized as "the world." They may all influence and change and give character to life, but none of them can create it.

And perhaps this brings us to what we want. The world may give a certain character or shape to life, even altho it cannot create it. Now pride is a certain character or shape of life. It is a term of description not of the material of life but of a particular result of that material fused into a particular furnace. In general the shape of life which pride describes may be otherwise characterized as arrogant self-reliance or self-sufficiency. We may reach more minute definitions of it before we are done, but this seems to make the meaning plain when it is said that the pride of life is not of the Father, but of the world. Life comes from God. It is the world's influence that shapes that life, which has no moral character in itself, into arrogance and self-sufficiency, makes it up into pride instead of into humility, and so leaves as the result the pride of life. The pride of life, then, is God's gift which means dependence changed and distorted into independence, revolt and disobedience.

Most necessary is it that in all we say we should keep clear in mind that the first gift is God's. The substance of life is His. All evil is misuse, otherwise repentance must be cursed with misanthropy and hopelessness instead of being as it always ought to be, the very birthplace of hope, the spring of a new life from the worn-out failure of an old, back into the possibility of life that is older still, as old as man's first creation.

Let us see where the pride of life shows itself. First of all doubtless in the mere exuberance of animal strength. To be well and strong, full of spirit and physical vitality, this is beyond all doubt one of the most precious gifts of God. We never can forget the large strong physical strain with which our

Bible opens, the torrent of health and full life that seems to pour down to us out of those early days when the world was young, when the giants made the earth shake under their mighty tread and the patriarchs outlived the forests with their green old years. The fulness of physical vitality is of God, to be accepted as His benefaction, to be cultivated and cared for with the reverence that His gifts demand. And round the mere physical life group a whole circle of tastes and enjoyments and exercises which belong with the sensuous more than with the intellectual or moral part of us, and whose full life seems to be dependent upon the fulness of physical being, the mere perception of beauty, the love of comfort, the delight in enterprise and adventure and prowess. The sum of all these is what we call full physical life. It is what gives youth its most generous charm and makes it always poetic with its suggested powers and unaccomplished possibilities.

But yet this mere fulness of life as we all know has its dangers. Mere health is overbearing by its very nature. There is a lack of sympathy in it. Not knowing suffering itself, it is not respectful of suffering in others. It is not careful of inflicting suffering. The full blood sings of nothing but itself. It is careless of others. It is careless of God, not malignantly cruel, nor deliberately atheistic, but selfish with a sort of self-absorption which is often very gracious in its forms and infidel with a mere forgetfulness of God. Who of us does not know, and who of us, wavering between his standards and his feelings, has not very often found it hard to tell just how he ought to value the enthusiastic and arrogant self-sufficiency of healthy youth?

It is this, I take it, that is described here as "the pride of life." Wherever there is eager and full-blooded youth there it appears. It breaks out in the wild and purposeless mob of lower city life, in the impatience and insubordination of the country boy who longs to be free from his father's farm, in the crude skepticism of college students' first discussions of religion. It is jealous of slight, of insult, of the least suspicion of restraint or leading. It belongs to strong young nations as well as to strong young men. By it they flaunt defiance in the face of the world and are afraid of the imputation of prudence. It is what you can see in the faces of any group of eager young men as you pass them on the street. Sometimes it makes them attractive and sometimes it makes them detestable. It turns the noble youth into a hero and the mean youth into a bully. A fine nature it leads into the most exquisite tastes and encircles it with art and music. A coarse nature it plunges into the vilest debauchery and vice. In good fortune it makes the temper carelessly benignant. In bad fortune it makes the temper recklessly defiant. It works these very different effects but is always the one same spirit still,—the pride of life. The gift of life which came from God, taken possession of by the world and tamed into self-sufficiency, a thing not of the Father, but of the world, who does not know in himself, or see in somebody he watches, something of this pure pride in life? Just to live is so attractive that the higher ends and responsibilities of living drift away out of sight. This instinctive almost physical selfishness is the philosophy of more than we think both of the good and of the bad that is in young people.

I have seen too much of it to undervalue the sweet and sober piety of old age. There is a beauty in it that is all its own. A softness and tenderness and patience and repose in the western sky that the bolder glories of the east where the morning breaks never can attain. Many and many of the best men we have known have been old men, but no one looks at men's progress without feeling that a great deal of what passes for growth in goodness as men grow old is in reality only the deadening of the pride of life from the dying-down of the life itself. Many and many a man who passes for a sober, conscientious, religious sort of man at fifty, if you put back into his cooled blood the hot life he had at twenty-five would be the same reckless, profligate, arrogant sinner that he was then. It is the life, not the pride, that he has lost. Many and many a man thinks that he has saved his house from conflagration because he sees no flame, when really the flame is hidden only because the house is burnt down and the fire is still lurking among the ashes, hunting out any little prey that is left and hungrily waiting for more fuel to light up the darkness again. One thing at least is true, that the goodness of old age in what we may call its passive forms, humility, submission, patience, faith, is necessarily far more hard to recognize and be sure of than the same goodness in a younger man. What you call piety may be only deadness.

And young men are often pointed just to this old age as the golden time when they will be religious as they cannot be now. They look to it themselves. "You are full of the pride of life," men say to them; "Ah, wait! By and by the life will flag. The senses will grow dull, the tastes will stupefy, the enterprise will flicker out, and the days come in which your soul will say 'I have no pleasure in them.' Just wait for that! Then your pride will go too, and then you will need and seek your God." It is a poor taunt and a poorer warning. If you have nothing better to say to make men use their powers rightly than to tell them that they will lose their powers some day, the answer will always be, "Well, I will wait until that losing day comes before I worry." If you tell a young man that his life is short, the old bacchanalian answer is the first one, "Live while we live." You must somehow get hold of that, you must persuade him that the true life now is the holy life, that life, this same life that he prizes, ought to breed humility and faith, not arrogance and pride, or else you must expect to talk to the winds. It surely is important that the conversion of the pride of life must come not by the putting-out of life but by making it a source of humility instead of pride. The humbleness of life. How can it come? By clearer and deeper truthfulness to let us see what the real facts of the case are, that is all; but that is very hard, so hard that it can be brought about by no other than the Almighty Holy Ghost. Let me see that this physical life of mine, having no true character of its own, is made to be a great machinery for simply conducting the knowledge and the love of God into my life; let all my study of the exquisite adaptations of the physical organs for their work be sanctified with this idea, this ever-pervading consciousness that eye and ear and hand are doors for the knowledge and the love of Him to enter by, and that all their marvelous mechanism is only the perfecting of hinges and bolt that He may enter more impressively and lovingly and entirely; let me learn that every bright taste or fine instinct or noble appetite is a ray of sunlight, not the sun, is the projection into my life of some force above, outside of me, which I can find only by climbing back along the ray that is projected, up to it; let me see all animal life a study and preparation for this final life of man, sensations and perceptions, growing clearer and clearer as we rise in the scale until in man they are fit to convey this knowledge which man alone can have, the knowledge of God; let me see this, and I must be ashamed to make that life a thing of pride which might be the seat of such an exalted and exalting dependence and humility. I am unwilling that those well-built cisterns which ought to be so full of God should hold nothing but myself, as if one crept into his aqueduct and closed it up where the water came into it from the fountain and lived in it for a house and found it very dry.

We see clearly enough what the change is that is needed. It is to substitute for self-consciousness as the result of life the ever-abiding consciousness of God. Do you ask how it shall be done? Ah, my dear friends, that is the very miracle of the gospel. I can tell you only this about it, which the Lord has told us all before: "Except a man be born again, he cannot see the kingdom of God." The kingdom of God, that region of life in which God is the life's King. And again: "If any man love me he will keep my words and my Father will love him and we will come unto him and make our abode with him." "We will come to him!" That is what we want, for that is the source of all humility, the coming of God into us, and the condition is love and obedience, the spiritual and the active forms of faith. That is all we can say. And that is enough, for in that this at least is clear, that such a conversion is a work that God has undertaken to do for us, that He asks of us nothing but submission to His willing helpfulness, and that being a transformation of life, it may, nay it must, be done while life is in possession, it can be done best when life is in its fullest. We have not to wait till movement is slow and color is dull. We are not tempted to make a vacancy and call it piety; but when man's life is so full that it tempts him daily to self-consciousness and pride, then let him open it wide to the consciousness of God and ennoble it with the full dignity of that humility whose first condition is the presence of God in the soul that He built for His own inhabiting.

There is a condition possible where the life shall flow with God as fully and freely as it ordinarily flows with self, where the greater volume it acquires, it only bears the more of Him; where every joy delights in Him, and every power depends on Him, and the whole man lives in Him and knows it. It is not a constant effort. It is the spontaneous direction of the whole nature. It is the new condition of the Christian who has been exalted from the human pride into the divine humility of life, out of self to God.

But I suggested at the outset that the word life was used in various meanings, and in connection with one or two of them I should like to develop a little what is meant by this phrase the "pride of life." Life sometimes familiarly signifies what we otherwise call circumstances. A man is said to "get on in life," not with reference to his growing older or growing healthier, but as he grows more rich, more prosperous. The pride of life in this sense would be the pride of success, which we see wherever men are struggling in this world of competition. Look at the young merchant who is making a living. Things go well with him. He rises from stratum to stratum of that commercial system whose geology is the ever-eluding study of the toilers of the street. He grows rich. His store begins to spread with the pressure of new enterprises. His house begins to blossom into the rich bloom of luxury. He is greeted with a new respect. He is courted with an eagerness he never knew before. Friends gather about him. His word has weight. His name means money. He is successful. What is the result? Those facts in themselves signify nothing, let us remember, but material capable of being made into one thing or another wholly its opposite. These are the gift of the Father, every one

of them, all that profusion of life. But there is a possible effect of them all in character, a pride, which is not of the Father, but of the world. With a morbid sympathy the man assimilates all that is poor and mean and worldly out of his prosperity, and rejects, because he has no affinity for it, all that is good and sweet and heavenly. He is chilled and narrowed and embittered. All the old sweetness and humility fade out of his nature. Need I tell you of it? Our streets are full of the pride of life. Its types only, its outer types flash in the splendid carriages and blaze in the fronts of gaudy houses and sweep the floors of drawing-rooms and the aisles of churches. Those types, the mere outward trappings of success, are not wherein the badness lies. The reality is in the hard hearts and selfish tempers and undocile minds which, in the splendor or the squalidness of wealth, show the sad ruin of self-sufficient success, the pride of life.

The pride of life kills out the life itself. Is there a sadder picture than you have in the life of a man, old or young, to whom God has sent prosperity, who by his own act then turns that prosperity into a failure by being proud of it? Christ Himself has told us how it is. The life is more than meat. He has no tolerance for this little meaning of a word that He made so large. The life is more than meat. Yes, life is meat and man, and to lose the best manhood to get the meat, to lose the soul to save the body, to fail of heaven above you and before you that you may own the ground under your feet, that is not success but failure. "In all time of our prosperity, Good Lord deliver us!" May God help you who are prosperous.

I would speak again of what is called intellectual life, the life of thought. It is "of the Father," indeed. We picture to ourselves the pure joy of God in thought. Free from so many of our cumbrous processes, free from the limitations of slow-moving time, free from all imperfection, with an instantaneous thought as is His being, the intellect that is the center of all reason revolves in its unfathomed majesty. And man thinks too. God makes him think. God gives him powers to think with, and then, as when you pour for your child a stream of water out of your cisterns upon the wheels of the machinery that you have first built for him, God gives man thoughts to exercise his power of thinking upon. Can anything be more humble? The power was from God, the thoughts by which the power moves were God's thoughts first. "Oh, God, I think Thy thoughts after Thee," cried John Kepler, when he caught sight of the great law of planetary motion. But mere thought, self-satisfied, seeking no unity in God, owning no dependence, boasting of itself, counting it hardship that it cannot know all where it knows so much, this is the pride of thought, and this is not of the Father, but is of the world. How arrogant it is! How it is jealous of dictation, how it chafes under a hand that presses it down and a voice that says to it, "Wait! what thou knowest not now thou shalt know hereafter." How carefully it limits its kind of evidence, shutting out everything that sounds like personal communication, revelation, in its impatient independence; how studiously it orphans itself. And then how, in some moods, orphaned by its arrogance, it suddenly becomes intensely cognizant of its orphanage, and the child's hunger for a Father takes possession of its heart and it is dreary and miserable!

I always know, when I speak thus of types of men, that you will think that I am talking of those types in their extreme specimens. I am not speaking to-day of the miracles of physical vitality, nor of the over-successful men with their colossal fortunes, nor of the mighty thinkers only. We all have our certain share in these various kinds of life, and each of us may make his little share a seed of pride. We are strangely ingenious here. We have an easy faculty of persuading ourselves that ours is best of everything and growing arrogant, unfilial and worldly over it. I speak to the men confident in their youth and health, to the merchants strong in their business credit, to the thoughtful brains at work over their problems of settling the universe for themselves. I warn them all against the pride of life. I would try to show them all that the same material which is capable of being made into pride is capable also of being made into humility. I would tell them therefore that they have not to be made old or sick or poor or stupid before they can be made humble, that the best humility, as well as the hardest, is that which can come to them here, right in the midst of their strength and wealth and study!

Do you ask how that can be? It is time that I tried to tell you, tried to tell how one may be full of life and yet be free from the pride of life. That question must somehow be answered, or else the world will be condemned to choose forever between an arrogant prosperity and a salvation by misery, distress and disaster, by death. What do we need for the salvation of a prosperous life? The answer in one word is consecration. Consecration, that is what we need. There have been men in whom life seemed complete who have yet walked very humbly. They had no pride of life. And why? Because always before them and above them there stood some great principle, some idea, some duty to which their life belonged, not to themselves. All work is modest, all idle self-contemplation is vain. And what the young man needs with his vague aspirations and conceits is to make him-

self the servant of some worthy purpose. And what the merchant needs with his growing business is to count himself the steward of some worthy Master. And what the student needs with his active mind is to trace the footsteps of the God of wisdom in the path he walks and to count the reaching nearer to Him the true prize and object of all thinking. Consecration! We are proud of life because we do so little with it. It is as if the bearer of dispatches sat down calmly and boasted of the well-made box in which they had been given to him, and never bore them to their destination. Life is force, to be transmitted and delivered to a purpose and an end. It loses its true nature and sweetness, it corrupts into pride, when it is robbed of its true purpose and cherished only for itself.

We can find our example of the consecrated man wherever we see true lives lived in history or about us now, in the Bible or in common life. Moses, David, Paul! But why look at the poor, imperfect copies when in our Lord Himself we have the consummate human life clothed in the wondrous humility of His appointed work. The life of lives! and yet was ever any life so utterly free from the tawdry pride that makes our poor achievements so wretched and unsatisfying. You say He cut Himself off from all that men are proud of. Not so. He gave up house and home, but he carried about with Him always the devotion of the people, the mystery of unknown power and the consciousness of great work and influence, the very things that have always seduced the best men most and in their highest labors made them proud. You say He was divine and so could not be humble. Yes, but He was profoundly human also, and humility is not subserviency or meanness. It is a grace not unworthy of, nay, necessary to, even the perfect humanity. But one thing stands out always: His was the consecrated life. It was all given to its purpose. "He was called Jesus because he should save his people from their sins." "Wist ye not that I must be about my Father's business?" "Behold we go up to Jerusalem and the Son of Man shall be betrayed." "To this end was I born and for this cause came I into the world, that I should bear witness unto the truth." Everywhere the consecration, a life appointed to an end, the face set to Jerusalem, the hands and feet waiting for the cross! Meanwhile it was the fullest life, but lived so high that the "pride of life" lay all below under His feet and out of sight.

And our life must be consecrated even as His was. What shall the consecration be? Far be it from me to undervalue the exaltation into humility that comes to a man when he consecrates himself to any great and noble cause. I believe that it helps to save any man from pride when he gives himself to his family or his country or his fellow men, to truth, to liberty, to purity, to anything outside of and above himself, but there is a consecration higher and fuller and more saving than any such can be. We go back to the Cross. Jesus is dying there for us. He dies and we are saved. What then? When a soul "knows its full salvation" and sees it all bought by, all wrapt up in, that Redeemer, then in the outburst of a grateful love, he gives himself to the Redeemer Christ. There is no hesitation, no keeping back of anything. He is all offered up to Christ; and then to serve that Christ, to follow Him, to do His will, to enter into Him, that is the one great object of the whole consecrated life, and in that consecration, the straining of the life toward that One Object, the "pride of life" is swept down and drowned. Not merely the life then, but the use of the life, comes from the Father. It is not of the world. The soul is saved!

The salvation of the Cross! Its center is the forgiveness of sins which the cross alone made possible; but is not its issue here, in the lifting of the soul above the pride of life and consecrating it in the profoundest gratitude to "Him who redeemed us and washed us from sins in His own blood"? What humility! What self-forgetfulness! What unworldliness! What utter childhood to the Father!

My friends, my people, would you be saved, saved from your sins, saved from yourselves, saved from the pride of life? You must be His that you may not be your own! He died for you that you might not henceforth live to yourself but unto Him. You must be consecrated to your Savior. If there is one soul in my church to-day who is weary and dissatisfied with his self-slavery, I offer him Jesus for Savior, for Master! If any man thirst let him come unto Him and drink. Turn unto Him and be ye saved! You can, you must! His service is life, life in its fullest because life in humility. Outside of His gospel and His service there is the pride of life, and the pride of life is death.

JOHN BUNYAN

1628-1688

THE HEAVENLY FOOTMAN

BIOGRAPHICAL NOTE

JOHN BUNYAN was born in the village of Elstow, near Bedford, England, in 1628. Because of his fearless preaching he was imprisoned in Bedford jail from 1660 to 1672, and again for six months in 1675, during which latter time it is said his wonderful "Pilgrim's Progress" was written. While his sermons in their tedious prolixity share the fault of his time, they are characterized by vividness, epigrammatic wit, and dramatic fervor. The purity and simplicity of his style have been highly praised, and his unflinching faith has been the inspiration of many a hesitating soul. Among his best known works are "The Holy War," "Grace Abounding in the Chief of Sinners," and "Sighs from Hell." He died in London in 1688.

So run that ye may obtain.—I Cor. ix., 24.

HEAVEN and happiness is that which every one desireth, insomuch that wicked Balaam could say, "Let me die the death of the righteous, and let my last end be like his." Yet, for all this, there are but very few that do obtain that ever-to-be-desired glory, insomuch that many eminent professors drop short of a welcome from God into this pleasant place. The apostle, therefore, because he did desire the salvation of the souls of the Corinthians, to whom he writes this epistle, layeth them down in these words such counsel, which if taken, would be for their help and advantage.

First, Not to be wicked, and sit still, and wish for heaven; but to run for it.

Secondly, Not to content themselves with every kind of running, but, saith he, "So run that ye may obtain." As if he should say, some, because they would not lose their souls, begin to run betimes, they run apace, they run with patience, they run the right way. Do you so run. Some run from both father and mother, friends and companions, and thus, they may have the crown. Do you so run. Some run through temptations, afflictions, good report, evil report, that they may win the pearl. Do you so run. "So run that ye may obtain."

These words were taken from men's running for a wager; a very apt similitude to set before the eyes of the saints of the Lord. "Know you that they which run in a race run all, but one obtaineth the prize? So run that ye may obtain." That is, do not only run, but be sure you win as well as run. "So run that ye may obtain."

I shall not need to make any great ado in opening the words at this time, but shall rather lay down one doctrine that I do find in them; and in prosecuting that, I shall show you, in some measure, the scope of the words.

The doctrine is this: They that will have heaven, must run for it; I say, they that will have heaven, they must run for it. I beseech you to heed it well. "Know ye not, that they which run in a race run all, but one obtaineth the prize? So run ye." The prize is heaven, and if you will have it, you must run for it. You have another scripture for this in the xii. of the Hebrews, the 1st, 2d, and 3d verses: "Wherefore seeing also," saith the apostle, "that we are compassed about with so great a cloud of witnesses, let us lay aside every weight, and the sin which doth so easily beset us, and let us run with patience the race that is set before us.'' And let us run, saith he. Again, saith Paul, ''I so run, not as uncertainly: so fight I,'' etc.

But before I go any farther:

1. Fleeing. Observe, that this running is not an ordinary, or any sort of running, but it is to be understood of the swiftest sort of running; and therefore, in the vi. of the Hebrews, it is called a fleeing: ''That we might have strong consolation, who have fled for refuge, to lay hold on the hope set before us.'' Mark, who have fled. It is taken from that xx. of Joshua, concerning the man that was to flee to the city of refuge, when the avenger of blood was hard at his heels, to take vengeance on him for the offense he had committed; therefore it is a running or fleeing for one's life: a running with all might and main, as we use to say. So run.

2. Pressing. Secondly, this running in another place is called a pressing. ''I press toward the mark''; which signifieth, that they that will have heaven, they must not stick at any difficulties they meet with; but press, crowd, and thrust through all that may stand between heaven and their souls. So run.

3. Continuing. Thirdly, this running is called in another place, a continuing in the way of life. ''If you continue in the faith grounded, and settled, and be not moved away from the hope of the gospel of Christ.'' Not to run a little now and then, by fits and starts, or half-way, or almost thither, but to run for my life, to run through all difficulties, and to continue therein to the end of the race, which must be to the end of my life. ''So run that ye may obtain.'' And the reasons are:

(1.) Because all or every one that runneth doth not obtain the prize; there may be many that do run, yea, and run far too, who yet miss of the crown that standeth at the end of the race. You know all that run in a race do not obtain the victory; they all run, but one wins. And so it is here; it is not every one that runneth, nor every one that seeketh, nor every one that striveth for the mastery that hath it. ''Tho a man do strive for the mastery,'' saith Paul, ''yet he is not crowned, unless he strive lawfully''; that is, unless he so run, and so strive, as to have God's approbation. What, do you think that every heavy-heeled professor will have heaven? What, every lazy one? every wanton and foolish professor, that will be stopt by anything, kept back by anything, that scarce runneth so fast heavenward as a snail creepeth on the ground? Nay, there are some professors that do not go on so fast in the way of God as a snail doth go on the wall; and yet these think that heaven and happiness is for them. But stay, there are many more that run than there be that obtain; therefore he that will have heaven must run for it.

(2.) Because you know, that tho a man do run, yet if he do not overcome, or win, as well as run, what will they be the better for their running? They will get nothing. You know the man that runneth, he doth do it to win the prize; but if he doth not obtain it, he doth lose his labor, spend his pains and time, and that to no purpose; I say, he getteth nothing. And ah! how many such runners will there be found in the day of judgment? Even multitudes, multitudes that have run, yea, run so far as to come to heaven-gates, and not able to get any farther, but there stand knocking when it is too late, crying, Lord! Lord! when they have nothing but rebukes for their pains. Depart from Me, you come not here, you come too late, you run too lazily; the door is shut. ''When once the master of the house is risen up,'' saith Christ, ''and hath shut to the door, and ye begin to stand without, and to knock, saying, Lord, Lord, open to us, I will say, I know you not, depart,'' etc. Oh, sad will the state of those be that run and miss; therefore, if you will have heaven, you must run for it; and ''so run that ye may obtain.''

(3.) Because the way is long (I speak metaphorically), and there is many a dirty step, many a high hill, much work to do, a wicked heart, world, and devil to overcome; I say, there are many steps to be taken by those that intend to be saved, by running or walking in the steps of that faith of our father Abraham. Out of Egypt thou must go through the Red Sea; thou must run a long and tedious journey, through the vast howling wilderness, before thou come to the land of promise.

(4.) They that will go to heaven they must run for it; because, as the way is long, so the time in which they are to get to the end of it is very uncertain; the time present is the only time; thou hast no more time allotted thee than thou now enjoyest: ''Boast not thyself of to-morrow, for thou knowest not what a day may bring forth.'' Do not say, I have time enough to get to heaven seven years hence; for I tell thee, the bell may toll for thee before seven days more be ended; and when death comes, away thou must go, whether thou art provided or not; and therefore look to it; make no delays; it is not good dallying with things of so great concernment as the salvation or damnation of thy soul. You know he that hath a great way to go in a little time, and less by half than he thinks of, he had need to run for it.

(5.) They that will have heaven, they must run for it; because the devil, the law, sin, death, and hell follow them. There is never a poor soul that is going to heaven, but the devil, the law, sin, death, and hell, make after the soul. ''The devil, your adversary, as a roaring lion, goeth about, seeking whom he may devour.'' And I will assure you, the devil is nimble, he can run apace, he is light of foot, he hath overtaken many, he hath turned up their heels, and hath given them an everlasting fall. Also the law, that can shoot a great way, have a care thou keep out of the reach of those great guns, the Ten Commandments. Hell also hath a wide mouth; it can stretch itself farther that you are aware of. And as the angel said to Lot, "Take heed, look not behind thee, neither tarry thou in all the plain" (that is, anywhere between this and heaven), "lest thou be consumed"; so I say to thee, Take heed, tarry not, lest either the devil, hell or the fearful curses of the law of God do overtake thee, and throw thee down in the midst of thy sins, so as never to rise and recover again. If this were all considered, then thou, as well as I, wouldst say, They that will have heaven must run for it.

(6.) They that go to heaven must run for it; because perchance the gates of heaven may be shut shortly. Sometimes sinners have not heaven-gates open to them so long as they suppose; and if they be once shut against a man, they are so heavy that all the men in the world, nor all the angels in heaven, are not able to open them. "I shut, and no man can open," saith Christ. And how if thou shouldst come but one quarter of an hour too late? I tell thee, it will cost thee an eternity to bewail thy misery in. Francis Spira can tell thee what it is to stay till the gate of mercy be quite shut; or to run so lazily that they be shut before you get within them. What, to be shut out! what, out of heaven! Sinner, rather than lose it, run for it; yea, "and so run that thou mayst obtain."

(7.) Lastly, because if thou lose, thou losest all, thou losest soul, God, Christ, heaven, ease, peace, etc. Besides, thou layest thyself open to all the shame, contempt, and reproach, that either God, Christ, saints, the world, sin, the devil, and all can lay upon thee. As Christ saith of the foolish builder, so I will say of thee, if thou be such a one who runs and misses; I say, even all that go by will begin to mock at thee, saying, This man began to run well, but was not able to finish. But more of this anon.

Quest. But how should a poor soul do to run? For this very thing is that which afflicteth me sore (as you say), to think that I may run, and yet fall short. Methinks to fall short at last, oh, it fears me greatly. Pray tell me, therefore, how I should run.

Ans. That thou mayst indeed be satisfied in this particular, consider these following things.

The first direction: If thou wouldst so run as to obtain the kingdom of heaven, then be sure that thou get into the way that leadeth thither: For it is a vain thing to think that ever thou shalt have the prize, tho thou runnest never so fast, unless thou art in the way that leads to it. Set the case, that there should be a man in London that was to run to York for a wager; now, tho he run never so swiftly, yet if he run full south, he might run himself quickly out of breath, and be never nearer the prize, but rather the farther off. Just so is it here; it is not simply the runner, nor yet the hasty runner, that winneth the crown, unless he be in the way that leadeth thereto. I have observed, that little time which I have been a professor, that there is a great running to and fro, some this way, and some that way, yet it is to be feared most of them are out of the way, and then, tho they run as swift as the eagle can fly, they are benefited nothing at all.

Here is one runs a-quaking, another a-ranting; one again runs after the baptism, and another after the Independency: here is one for Freewill, and another for Presbytery; and yet possibly most of all these sects run quite the wrong way, and yet every one is for his life, his soul, either for heaven or hell.

If thou now say, Which is the way? I tell thee it is Christ, the Son of Mary, the Son of God. Jesus saith, "I am the way, the truth, and the life; no man cometh to the Father but by me." So then thy business is (if thou wouldst have salvation), to see if Christ be thine, with all His benefits; whether He hath covered thee with His righteousness, whether He hath showed thee that thy sins are washed away with His heart-blood, whether thou art planted into Him, and whether you have faith in Him, so as to make a life out of Him, and to conform thee to Him; that is, such faith as to conclude that thou art righteous, because Christ is thy righteousness, and so constrained to walk with Him as the joy of thy heart, because he saveth thy soul. And for the Lord's sake take heed, and do not deceive thyself, and think thou art in the way upon too slight grounds; for if thou miss of the way, thou wilt miss of the prize, and if thou miss of that I am sure thou wilt lose thy soul, even that soul which is worth more than the whole world.

Mistrust thy own strength, and throw it away; down on thy knees in prayer to the Lord for the spirit of truth; search His word for direction; flee seducers' company; keep company with the soundest Christians, that have most experience of Christ; and be sure thou have a care of Quakers, Ranters, Freewillers: also do not have too much company with some Anabaptists, tho I go under that name myself. I will tell thee this is such a serious matter, and I fear thou wilt so little regard it, that the thought of the worth of the thing, and of thy too light regarding of it, doth even make my heart ache whilst I am writing to thee. The Lord teach thee the way by His Spirit, and then I am sure thou wilt know it. So run.

The second direction: As thou shouldst get into the way, so thou shouldst also be much in studying and musing on the way. You know men that would be expert in anything, they are usually much in studying of that thing, and so likewise is it with those that quickly grow expert in any way. This therefore thou shouldst do; let thy study be much exercised about Christ, which is the way, what He is, what He hath done, and why He is what He is, and why He hath done what is done; as why "He took upon Him the form of a servant" (Phil. ii.); why He was "made in the likeness of man"; why He cried; why He died; why He "bare the sin of the world"; why He was made sin, and why He was made righteousness; why He is in heaven in the nature of man, and what He doth there. Be much in musing and considering of these things; be thinking also enough of those places which thou must not come near, but leave some on this hand, and some on that hand; as it is with those that travel into other countries; they must leave such a gate on this hand, and such a bush on that hand, and go by such a place, where standeth such a thing. Thus therefore you must do: "Avoid such things, which are expressly forbidden in the Word of God." Withdraw thy foot far from her, "and come not nigh the door of her house, for her steps take hold of hell, going down to the chambers of death." And so of everything that is not in the way, have a care of it, that thou go not by it; come not near it, have nothing to do with it. So run.

The third direction: Not only thus, but in the next place, thou must strip thyself of those things that may hang upon thee, to the hindering of thee in the way to the kingdom of heaven, as covetousness, pride, lust, or whatever else thy heart may be inclining unto, which may hinder thee in this heavenly race. Men that run for a wager, if they intend to win as well as run, they do not use to encumber themselves, or carry those things about them that may be a hindrance to them in their running. "Every man that striveth for the mastery is temperate in all things"; that is, he layeth aside everything that would be anywise a disadvantage to him; as saith the apostle, "Let us lay aside every weight, and the sin that doth so easily beset us, and let us run with patience the race that is set before us." It is but a vain thing to talk of going to heaven, if thou let thy heart be encumbered with those things that would hinder. Would you not say that such a man would be in danger of losing, tho he run, if he fill his pockets with stones, hang heavy garments on his shoulders, and get lumpish shoes on his feet? So it is here; thou talkest of going to heaven, and yet fillest thy pockets with stones —i.e., fillest thy heart with this world, lettest that hang on thy shoulders, with its profits

and pleasures. Alas! alas! thou art widely mistaken: if thou intendest to win, thou must strip, thou must lay aside every weight, thou must be temperate in all things. Thou must so run.

The fourth direction: Beware of by-paths; take heed thou dost not turn into those lanes which lead out of the way. There are crooked paths, paths in which men go astray, paths that lead to death and damnation, but take heed of all those. Some of them are dangerous because of practise, some because of opinion, but mind them not; mind the path before thee, look right before thee, turn neither to the right hand nor to the left, but let thine eyes look right on, even right before thee; "Ponder the path of thy feet, and let all thy ways be established." Turn not to the right hand nor to the left. "Remove thy foot far from evil." This counsel being not so seriously taken as given, is the reason of that starting from opinion to opinion, reeling this way and that way, out of this lane into that lane, and so missing the way to the kingdom. Tho the way to heaven be but one, yet there are many crooked lanes and by-paths that shoot down upon it, as I may say. And again, notwithstanding the kingdom of heaven be the biggest city, yet usually those by-paths are most beaten, most travelers go those ways; and therefore the way to heaven is hard to be found, and as hard to be kept in, by reason of these. Yet, nevertheless, it is in this case as it was with the harlot of Jericho; she had one scarlet thread tied in her window, by which her house was known: so it is here, the scarlet streams of Christ's blood run throughout the way to the kingdom of heaven; therefore mind that, see if thou do not find the besprinkling of the blood of Christ in the way, and if thou do, be of good cheer, thou art in the right way; but have a care thou beguile not thyself with a fancy; for then thou mayst light into any lane or way; but that thou mayst not be mistaken, consider, tho it seem never so pleasant, yet if thou do not find that in the very middle of the road there is written with the heart-blood of Christ, that he came into the world to save sinners, and that we are justified, tho we are ungodly, shun that way; for this it is which the apostle meaneth when he saith, "We have boldness to enter into the holiest by the blood of Jesus, by a new and living way which He hath consecrated for us, through the vail—that is to say, His flesh." How easy a matter it is in this our day, for the devil to be too cunning for poor souls, by calling his by-paths the way to the kingdom. If such an opinion or fancy be but cried up by one or more, this inscription being set upon it by the devil, "This is the way of God," how speedily, greedily, and by heaps, do poor simple souls throw away themselves upon it; especially if it be daubed over with a few

external acts of morality, if so good. But it
is because men do not know painted by-paths
from the plain way to the kingdom of heaven.
They have not yet learned the true Christ,
and what His righteousness is, neither have
they a sense of their own insufficiency; but
are bold, proud, presumptuous, self-conceited.
And therefore,

The fifth direction: Do not thou be too much
in looking too high in thy journey heavenward. You know men that run a race do not
use to stare and gaze this way and that,
neither do they use to cast up their eyes too
high, lest haply, through their too much gazing with their eyes after other things, they in
the mean time stumble and catch a fall. The
very same case is this: if thou gaze and stare
after every opinion and way that comes into
the world, also if thou be prying overmuch
into God's secret decrees, or let thy heart too
much entertain questions about some nice
foolish curiosities, thou mayst stumble and
fall, as many hundreds in England have done,
both in ranting and quakery, to their own
eternal overthrow, without the marvelous
operation of God's grace be suddenly
stretched forth to bring them back again.
Take heed, therefore; follow not that proud,
lofty spirit, that, devil-like, can not be content
with his own station. David was of an excellent spirit, where he saith, "Lord, my heart
is not haughty, nor mine eyes lofty, neither
do I exercise myself in great matters, or
things too high for me. Surely I have behaved and quieted myself as a child that is
weaned of his mother: My soul is even as a
weaned child." Do thou so run.

The sixth direction: Take heed that you
have not an ear open to every one that calleth
after you as you are in your journey. Men
that run, you know, if any do call after them,
saying, I would speak with you, or go not too
fast and you shall have my company with
you, if they run for some great matter, they
use to say, Alas! I can not stay, I am in haste,
pray talk not to me now; neither can I stay
for you, I am running for a wager: if I win
I am made; if I lose I am undone, and therefore hinder me not. Thus wise are men when
they run for corruptible things, and thus
shouldst thou do, and thou hast more cause
to do so than they, forasmuch as they run for
things that last not, but thou for an incorruptible glory. I give thee notice of this betimes, knowing that thou shalt have enough
call after thee, even the devil, sin, this world,
vain company, pleasures, profits, esteem among
men, ease, pomp, pride, together with an innumerable company of such companions; one
crying, Stay for me; the other saying, Do not
leave me behind; a third saying, And take
me along with you. What, will you go, saith
the devil, without your sins, pleasures, and
profits? Are you so hasty? Can you not
stay and take these along with you? Will you
leave your friends and companions behind
you? Can you not do as your neighbors do,
carry the world, sin, lust, pleasure, profit, esteem among men, along with you? Have a
care thou do not let thine ear open to the
tempting, enticing, alluring, and soul-entan-
gling flatteries of such sink-souls as these are.
"My son," saith Solomon, "if sinners entice
thee, consent thou not."

You know what it cost the young man whom
Solomon speaks of in the vii. of the Proverbs,
that was enticed by a harlot: "With much
fair speech she won him, and caused him to
yield, with the flattering of her lips she forced
him, till he went after her as an ox to the
slaughter, or as a fool to the correction of the
stocks"; even so far, "till the dart struck
through his liver," and he knew not "that it
was for his life." "Hearken unto me now
therefore," saith he, "O ye children, and attend to the words of my mouth, let not thine
heart incline to her ways, go not astray in her
paths, for she hast cast down many wounded,
yea, many strong men have been slain (that
is, kept out of heaven); by her house is the
way to hell, going down to the chambers of
death." Soul, take this counsel, and say,
Satan, sin, lust, pleasure, profit, pride, friends,
companions, and everything else, let me alone,
stand off, come not nigh me, for I am running for heaven, for my soul, for God, for
Christ, from hell and everlasting damnation;
if I win, I win all; and if I lose, I lose all;
let me alone, for I will not hear. So run.

The seventh direction: In the next place,
be not daunted tho thou meetest with never
so many discouragements in thy journey
thither. That man that is resolved for heaven,
if Satan can not win him by flatteries, he will
endeavor to weaken him by discouragements;
saying, Thou art a sinner, thou hath broken
God's law, thou art not elected, thou comest
too late, the day of grace is passed, God doth
not care for thee, thy heart is naught, thou
art lazy, with a hundred other discouraging
suggestions. And thus it was with David,
where he saith, "I had fainted, unless I had
believed to see the loving-kindness of the
Lord in the land of the living." As if he
should say, the devil did so rage, and my heart
was so base, that had I judged according to
my own sense and feeling, I had been absolutely distracted; but I trusted to Christ in the
promise, and looked that God would be as
good as his promise, in having mercy upon
me, an unworthy sinner; and this is that
which encouraged me, and kept me from
fainting. And thus must thou do when Satan,
or the law, or thy own conscience, do go about
to dishearten thee, either by the greatness of
thy sins, the wickedness of thy heart, the
tediousness of the way, the loss of outward
enjoyments, the hatred that thou wilt pro-

cure from the world or the like; then thou must encourage thyself with the freeness of the promises, the tender-heartedness of Christ, the merits of His blood, the freeness of His invitations to come in, the greatness of the sin of others that have been pardoned, and that the same God, through the same Christ, holdeth forth the same grace as free as ever. If these be not thy meditations, thou wilt draw very heavily in the way of heaven, if thou do not give up all for lost, and so knock off from following any farther; therefore, I say, take heart in thy journey, and say to them that seek thy destruction, "Rejoice not against me, O my enemy, for when I fall I shall arise, when I sit in darkness the Lord shall be a light unto me." So run.

The eighth direction: Take heed of being offended at the cross that thou 'must go by before thou come to heaven. You must understand (as I have already touched) that there is no man that goeth to heaven but he must go by the cross. The cross is the standing way-mark by which all they that go to glory must pass.

"We must through much tribulation enter into the kingdom of heaven." "Yea, and all that will live godly in Christ Jesus shall suffer persecution." If thou art in thy way to the kingdom, my life for thine thou wilt come at the cross shortly (the Lord grant thou dost not shrink at it, so as to turn thee back again). "If any man will come after me," saith Christ, "let him deny himself, and take up his cross daily, and follow me." The cross it stands, and hath stood, from the beginning, as a way-mark to the kingdom of heaven. You know, if one ask you the way to such and such a place, you, for the better direction, do not only say, This is the way, but then also say, You must go by such a gate, by such a stile, such a bush, tree, bridge, or such like. Why, so it is here; art thou inquiring the way to heaven? Why, I tell thee, Christ is the way; into Him thou must get, into His right-eousness, to be justified; and if thou art in Him, thou wilt presently see the cross, thou must go close by it, thou must touch it, nay, thou must take it up, or else thou wilt quickly go out of the way that leads to heaven, and turn up some of those crooked lanes that lead down to the chambers of death.

It is the cross which keepeth those that are kept from heaven. I am persuaded, were it not for the cross, where we have one professor we should have twenty; but this cross, that is it which spoileth all.

The ninth direction: Beg of God that He would do these two things for thee: First, enlighten thine understanding: And, secondly, inflame thy will. If these two be but effectually done, there is no fear but thou wilt go safe to heaven.

One of the great reasons why men and women do so little regard the other world is because they see so little of it: And the reason why they see so little of it is because they have their understanding darkened: And therefore, saith Paul, "Do not you believers walk as do other Gentiles, even in the vanity of their minds, having their understanding darkened, being alienated from the life of God through the ignorance (or foolishness) that is in them, because of the blindness of their heart." Walk not as those, run not with them: alas! poor souls, they have their under-standings darkened, their hearts blinded, and that is the reason they have such undervalu-ing thoughts of the Lord Jesus Christ, and the salvation of their souls. For when men do come to see the things of another world, what a God, what a Christ, what a heaven, and what an eternal glory there is to be en-joyed; also when they see that it is possible for them to have a share in it, I tell you it will make them run through thick and thin to enjoy it. Moses, having a sight of this, because his understanding was enlightened, "He feared not the wrath of the king, but chose rather to suffer afflictions with the peo-ple of God than to enjoy the pleasures of sin for a season. He refused to be called the son of the king's daughter"; accounting it wonderful riches to be accounted worthy of so much as to suffer for Christ with the poor despised saints; and that was because he saw Him who was invisible, and had respect unto the recompense of reward. And this is that which the apostle usually prayeth for in his epistles for the saints, namely, "That they might know what is the hope of God's calling, and the riches of the glory of his inheritance in the saints; and that they might be able to comprehend with all saints, what is the breadth, and length, and depth, and height, and know the love of Christ, which passeth knowledge." . . .

The tenth direction: Cry to God that He would inflame thy will also with the things of the other world. For when a man's will is fully set to do such or such a thing, then it must be a very hard matter that shall hinder that man from bringing about his end. When Paul's will was set resolvedly to go up to Je-rusalem (tho it was signified to him before what he should there suffer), he was not daunted at all; nay, saith he, "I am ready (or willing) not only to be bound, but also to die at Jerusalem for the name of the Lord Jesus." His will was inflamed with love to Christ; and therefore all the persuasions that could be used wrought nothing at all.

Your self-willed people, nobody knows what to do with them: we use to say, he will have his own will, do all what you can. Indeed, to have such a will for heaven, is an admirable advantage to a man that undertaketh a race thither; a man that is resolved, and hath his will fixt, saith he, I will do my best to advantage myself; I will do my worst to hinder my enemies; I will not give out as long as I can stand; I will have it or I will lose my life; "tho he slay me, yet will I trust in him. I will not let thee go except thou bless me." I will, I will, I will, oh this blest inflamed will for heaven! What is it like? If a man be willing, then any argument shall be a matter of encouragement; but if unwilling, then any argument shall give discouragement; this is seen both in saints and sinners; in them that are the children of God, and also those that are the children of the devil. As,

1. The saints of old, they being willing and resolved for heaven, what could stop them? Could fire and fagot, sword or halter, stinking dungeons, whips, bears, bulls, lions, cruel rackings, stoning, starving, nakedness, etc., "and in all these things they were more than conquerors, through him that loved them"; who had also made them "willing in the day of his power."

2. See again, on the other side, the children of the devil, because they are not willing, how many shifts and starting-holes they will have. I have a married wife, I have a farm, I shall offend my landlord, I shall offend my master, I shall lose my trading, I shall lose my pride, my pleasures, I shall be mocked and scoffed, therefore I dare not come. I, saith another, will stay till I am older, till my children are out, till I am got a little aforehand in the world, till I have done this and that and the other business; but, alas! the thing is, they are not willing; for, were they but soundly willing, these, and a thousand such as these, would hold them no faster than the cords held Samson, when he broke them like burnt flax. I tell you the will is all: that is one of the chief things which turns the wheel either backward or forward; and God knoweth that full well, and so likewise doth the devil; and therefore they both endeavor very much to strengthen the will of their servants; God, He is for making of His a willing people to serve Him; and the devil, he doth what he can to possess the will and affection of those that are his with love to sin; and therefore when Christ comes closer to the matter, indeed, saith He, "You will not come to me. How often would I have gathered you as a hen doth her chickens, but you would not." The devil had possest their wills, and so long he was sure enough of them. Oh, therefore cry hard to God to inflame thy will for heaven and Christ: thy will, I say, if that be rightly set for heaven, thou wilt not be beat off with discouragements; and this was the reason that when Jacob wrestled with the angel, tho he lost a limb, as it were, and the hollow of his thigh was put out of joint as he wrestled with him, yet saith he, "I will not," mark, "I will not let thee go except thou bless me."

Get thy will tipped with the heavenly grace, and resolution against all discouragements, and then thou goest full speed for heaven; but if thou falter in thy will, and be not found there, thou wilt run hobbling and halting all the way thou runnest, and also to be sure thou wilt fall short at last. The Lord give thee a will and courage.

Thus I have done with directing thee how to run to the kingdom; be sure thou keep in memory what I have said unto thee, lest thou lose thy way. But because I would have thee think of them, take all in short in this little bit of paper.

1. Get into the way. 2. Then study on it. 3. Then strip, and lay aside everything that would hinder. 4. Beware of by-paths. 5. Do not gaze and stare too much about thee, but be sure to ponder the path of thy feet. 6. Do not stop for any that call after thee, whether it be the world, the flesh, or the devil: for all these will hinder thy journey, if possible. 7. Be not daunted with any discouragements thou meetest with as thou goest. 8. Take heed of stumbling at the cross. 9. Cry hard to God for an enlightened heart, and a willing mind, and God give thee a prosperous journey.

Provocation: Now that you may be provoked to run with the foremost, take notice of this. When Lot and his wife were running from curst Sodom to the mountains, to save their lives, it is said, that his wife looked back from behind him, and she became a pillar of salt; and yet you see that neither her example, nor the judgment of God that fell upon her for the same, would cause Lot to look behind him. I have sometimes wondered at Lot in this particular; his wife looked behind her, and died immediately, but let what would become of her, Lot would not so much as once look behind him to see her. We do not read that he did so much as once look where she was, or what was become of her; his heart was indeed upon his journey, and well it might: there was the mountain before him, and the fire and brimstone behind him; his life lay at stake, and he had lost it if he had looked behind. Do thou so run and in thy race remember Lot's wife, and remember her doom; and remember for what that doom did overtake her; and remember that God made her an example for all lazy runners, to the end of the world; and take heed thou fall not after the same example. But,

If this will not provoke thee, consider thus, 1. Thy soul is thine own soul, that is either to be saved or lost; thou shalt not lose my soul by thy laziness. It is thine own soul, thine own ease, thine own peace, thine own advantage or disadvantage. If it were my own that thou art desired to be good unto, methinks reason should move thee somewhat to pity it. But, alas! it is thine own, thine own soul. "What shall it profit a man if he shall gain the whole world, and lose his own soul?'' God's people wish well to the souls of others, and wilt not thou wish well to thine own? And if this will not provoke thee, then think.

Again, 2. If thou lose thy soul, it is thou also that must bear the blame. It made Cain stark mad to consider that he had not looked to his brother Abel's soul. How much more will it perplex thee to think that thou hadst not a care of thine own? And if this will not provoke thee to bestir thyself, think again.

3. That, if thou wilt not run, the people of God are resolved to deal with thee even as Lot dealt with his wife—that is, leave thee behind them. It may be thou hast a father, mother, brother, etc., going post-haste to heaven, wouldst thou be willing to be left behind them? Surely no.

Again, 4. Will it not be a dishonor to thee to see the very boys and girls in the country to have more with them than thyself? It may be the servants of some men, as the housekeeper, plowman, scullion, etc., are more looking after heaven than their masters. I am apt to think, sometimes, that more servants than masters, that more tenants than landlords, will inherit the kingdom of heaven. But is not this a shame for them that are such? I am persuaded you scorn that your servants should say that they are wiser than you in the things of this world; and yet I am bold to say that many of them are wiser than you in the things of the world to come, which are of greater concernment.

Expostulation. Well, then, sinner, what sayest thou? Where is thy heart? Wilt thou run? Art thou resolved to strip? Or art thou not? Think quickly, man; have no dallying in this matter. Confer not with flesh and blood; look up to heaven, and see how thou likest it; also to hell, and accordingly devote thyself. If thou dost not know the way, inquire at the Word of God; if thou wantest company, cry for God's Spirit; if thou wantest encouragement, entertain the promises. But be sure thou begin betimes; get into the way, run apace, and hold out to the end; and the Lord give thee a prosperous journey. Farewell.

DAVID J. BURRELL

1849-1926

HOW TO BECOME A CHRISTIAN

BIOGRAPHICAL NOTE

DAVID JAMES BURRELL was born at Mount Pleasant, Pennsylvania, in 1849. He graduated from Yale College in 1867. From 1891 to 1909 he was pastor of the Marble Collegiate Church, New York, which was founded in 1628. Dr. Burrell was unusually popular as a pulpit preacher, and attracted many young people to his evening services. His delivery was clear-cut and vigorous, and often he rose to dramatic heights of eloquence. His gesture was marked by grace and appropriateness, and his illustrations were always chosen with felicity. His sermons were stenographically reported and printed each week in pamphlets for wide distribution.

And there arose no small stir about that way.
—Acts xix., 23.

THE name by which the early Christians were familiarly known was "The people of that way." In the year 36 the Sanhedrin issued a commission to Saul of Tarsus authorizing him to arrest any whom he might find "of the way, whether they were men or women, and to bring them bound unto Jerusalem." (Acts ix., 2.) In the year 58, twenty-two years later, the same Saul, now an apostle of Christ, made a defense from the steps of the Castle of Antonia, in which he said, "I persecuted this way unto the death, binding and delivering into prison both men and women" (Acts xxii., 4).

The name thus given to the followers of Christ is significant for many reasons. The question has been raised in some quarters as to whether religion is dogma or life. In fact, our religion in the last reduction is neither dogma nor life; it is a way from sin into the Kingdom of God. Its bed-rock is truth, its pavement is character, its destination is eternal life.

It is a plain way; as indicated in the prophecy, "A highway shall be there and a way, and it shall be called the way of holiness; the wayfaring man tho a fool shall not err therein." Nevertheless, to the unsaved no question is more bewildering than this: "What shall I do that I may inherit eternal life?" In the Pocono Mountains, last summer, I found it very difficult to keep in the old Indian trail; tho it was easy enough for my comrade, who had been born and bred in the vicinity. A letter lies before me, written by a man of affairs, in which he says, "All my life I have been an attendant at church; I would like to be a Christian, but I confess that I have never yet learned how to set about it."

It is my present purpose to make this matter as clear as I can. Let it be said at the outset that one thing only is needful in order to become a follower of Christ—to wit, that one shall believe in Him, but, before we come to that, we must touch upon a matter of preliminary importance.

A man must repent before he believes in Christ (Mark i., 15). Now repentance is not a saving grace, having value only as it leads to something further on. The pain of a physical malady has no curative virtue; but it is this pain that inclines the patient to ring the doctor's bell. So John the Baptist goes before Christ with his cry, "Repent ye!" Since without repentance there is no adequate sense of need, nor disposition to accept Christ.

Let us get a clear understanding of repentance. It suggests at the outset, an apprehension of sin as a fact; not a figment of the imagination, not "a belief of mortal mind"; not an infection due to environment, and therefore involving no personal accountability; but a distinct, flagrant violation of holy law, by which the sinner is brought into rebellion against God.

And sin must be apprehended, furthermore, as a calamitous fact, that is, involving an adequate penalty: "The soul that sinneth, it shall die." A true penitent recognizes the justice of the punishment which is imposed upon him; as did the repentant thief, when he said to his comrade, "We indeed are condemned justly." One who spends his time in trying to explain away hell and "the unquenchable fire" and "the worm that dieth not," is not a penitent man.

And sin must be furthermore recognized as a concrete or personal fact. It is not enough to acknowledge the incontrovertible presence of sin in the world around us. The important thing is, that this sin inheres in me. So David prayed, "Have mercy upon me, O God, according unto thy loving kindness; for I have sinned and done this evil in thy sight." He had always known, in general terms, that adultery was a fearful thing; but when it pointed its gaunt finger at him in the watches of the night and hissed, "Bathsheba!" it brought him to his knees.

And this conviction of sin must be followed by a resolution to forsake it. The true penitent fears his sin, hates it, loathes it, abhors it, and determines to quit it.

But observe, all this is merely preliminary to the one thing needful. There is no virtue in repentance *per se*. The penitent is not saved; he has only discovered his need of salvation. He knows his malady; now how shall he be cured of it? To pause here is death. One in a sinking boat must not be satisfied with stopping the leak; the boat must be baled out. A man head over ears in debt can not recover his credit by resolving to pay cash in the future; he must somehow cancel his past obligations. If a penitent were never to commit another sin, the "handwriting of ordinances" would still be against him. The record of the past remains; and it will confront him in the judgment unless it be disposed of. The past. The mislived past! What shall be done about it?

This brings us to the matter in hand: What shall I do to be saved? or How shall I become a Christian?

Our Lord at the beginning of His ministry said to Nicodemus, "God so loved the world, that he gave his only begotten Son, that whosoever believeth on him, should not perish, but have everlasting life." And to make the matter perfectly clear to this learned rabbi, He resorted to the kindergarten method, using an object-lesson: "As Moses lifted up the serpent in the wilderness, even so must the Son of man be lifted up (that is, crucified), that whosoever believeth in him should not perish, but have eternal life." So the one thing needful is to believe in Christ.

The same truth was repeated over and over in the teachings of Jesus and of His disciples as well. To the jailer of Philippi who, in sudden conviction, was moved to cry, "What shall I do?" the answer of Paul was, "Believe on the Lord Jesus Christ and thou shalt be saved."

But what is it to "believe in Christ?" It is easy to say, "Come to Christ" and "Accept Christ" and "Believe in Him"; but just here occurs the bewilderment. These are oftentimes mere shop-worn phrases to the unsaved, however simple they may appear to those who have entered on the Christian life.

To believe in Christ is, first, to credit the historic record of His life. Once on a time He lived among men, preached, wrought miracles, suffered and died on the accurst tree. So far all will agree; but there is clearly no saving virtue in an intellectual acceptance of an undisputed fact.

It means, second, to believe that Jesus was what He claimed to be. And His claim is perfectly clear. To the woman of Samaria who sighed for the coming of Messiah He said, "I that speak unto thee am he." No reader of the Scripture could misunderstand His meaning, since the prophecy of the Messiah runs like a golden thread through all its pages from the protevangel, "The seed of the woman shall bruise the serpent's head," to the prediction of Malachi, "The Sun of righteousness shall arise with healing in his beams."

But, more than this, Jesus claimed that as Messiah He was the only begotten and co-equal Son of God. He came forth from God and, after finishing His work, was to return to God and reassume "the glory which he had with the Father before the world was." It was this oft repeated assertion which so mortally offended the Jews as to occasion His arrest on the charge of blasphemy. He persisted in His claim, and was put to death for "making himself equal to God." It must be seen, therefore, that no man can be said to believe in Christ who is not prepared to affirm, without demur or qualification, that He was what He claimed to be.

It means, third, to believe that Jesus did what He said He came into the world to do. And here again there can be no doubt or peradventure. He said, "The Son of man came not to be ministered unto, but to minister and to give his life a ransom for many." His death was to be the purchase price of redemption. In the wilderness He was tempted to turn aside from His great purpose. The adversary led Him to a high place, and with a wave of his hand, directed His thought to the kingdoms of this world, saying, "All these are mine. I know thy purpose: thou art come to win this world by dying for it. Why pay so great a price? I know thy fear and trembling—for thou art flesh—in view of the nails, the fever, and dreadful exposure, the long agony. Why pay so great a price? I am the prince of this world. One act of homage, and I will abdicate. Fall down and worship me!" Never before or since has there been such a temptation, so specious, so alluring. But Jesus had covenanted to die for sinners. He knew there was no other way of accomplishing salvation for them. He could not be turned aside from the work which He had volunteered to do. Therefore He put away the suggestion with the words, "Get thee behind me, Satan! I can not be moved! I know the necessity that is laid upon me. I know that my way to the kingdom is only by the cross. I am therefore resolved to suffer and die for the deliverance of men."

On a later occasion, on His way to Jerusalem—that memorable journey of which it is written. "He set his face stedfastly" to go toward the cross—He spoke to His disciples of His death. He had been with them now three years, but had not been able fully to reveal His mission, because they were "not strong enough to bear it." A man with friends, yet friendless, lonely in the possession of His great secret, He had longed to give them His full confidence, but dared not. Now, as they journeyed southward through Cæsarea Philippi, He asked them, "Who do men say that I am?" And they answered, "Some say John the Baptist; others, Elias; others, Jeremias, or one of the prophets." And he saith, "But who say ye that I am?" Then Peter—brave, impulsive, glorious Peter—witness his good confession: "Thou art the Christ, the Son of the living God!" The hour had come. His disciples were beginning to know Him. He would give them His full confidence. So as they journeyed on toward Jerusalem He told them all how He had come to redeem the world by bearing its penalty of death; "He began to show them how he must suffer many things of the elders and chief priests and scribes, and be killed." At that point Peter could hold his peace no longer, but began to rebuke him, saying, "Be it far from thee, Lord! To suffer? To die? Nay, to reign in Messianic splendor!" And Jesus turning, said unto him, "Get thee behind me, Satan!"—the very words with which He had repelled the same suggestion in the wilderness. As He looked on His disciple, He saw not Peter, but Satan—

perceived how the adversary had for the moment taken possession, as it were, of this man's brain and conscience and lips. "Get thee behind me, Satan! I know thee! I recognize thy crafty suggestion; but I am not to be turned aside from my purpose. Get thee behind me! Thou art an offense unto me. Thy words are not of divine wisdom, but of human policy. Thou savorest not the things that be of God, but those that be of men!"

From this we conclude that the vicarious death of Jesus is the vital center of His gospel, and that any word which contravenes it is in the nature of a Satanic suggestion. It follows that no man can truly believe in Christ without assenting to the fact that the saving power is in His death; as it is written, "The blood of Jesus Christ cleanseth from all sin," and, "Without the shedding of blood there is no remission." He came into the world to die for sinners, that they by His death might enter into life; He came to take our place before the bar of the offended law, to be "wounded for our transgressions and bruised for our iniquities, that by his stripes we might be healed"; He came to "bear our sins in his own body on the tree"; and to believe in Christ is to believe that He did what He came to do.

It means, fourth—and now we come to the very heart of the matter—to believe that Christ means precisely what He says. He says to the sinner, "The Son of man hath power on earth to forgive sins." He says, "Him that cometh unto me, I will in no wise cast out." He says, "He that believeth in me hath everlasting life." At this point belief means personal appropriation; acceptance, immediate, here, now. It is to make an end of doubt and perplexity and all questionings, by closing in with the overtures of divine mercy. It is to lay down one's arms and make an unconditional surrender. It is to take the proffered hand of the Savior in an everlasting covenant of peace. It is to say, "My Lord, my life, my sacrifice, my Savior and my all!"

But just here is where many hesitate and fail. They do not "screw their courage to the sticking point." They come up to the line, but do not take the step that crosses it. They put away the outstretched hand, and so fall short of salvation.

The will must act. The prodigal in the far country will stay there forever unless his resolution cries, "I will arise and go!" The resolution is an appropriating act. It makes Christ mine; it links my soul with His, as the coupler binds the locomotive to the loaded train. It grasps His outstretched hand; it seals the compact and inspires the song:

'Tis done, the great transaction's done,
  I am my Lord's and He is mine!
He drew me, and I followed on,
  Charmed to confess the voice divine.

High heaven that hears the solemn vow,
That vow renewed shall daily hear;
Till in life's latest hour I bow
And bless in death a bond so dear!

Now this is all. The man who really believes on Christ is saved by that alone. He can never be lost. As Wesley sang, "Christ and I are so joined, He can't go to heaven and leave me behind." But salvation from the penalty of sin is not the whole of salvation; only the beginning of it.

The sequel to "becoming a Christian" is following Christ. "Salvation" is a large word, including growth in character and usefulness and all the high attainments which are included in a genuine Christian life. This is what Paul means when he says, "Work out your own salvation with fear and trembling, for it is God that worketh in you." Work it out! Work your salvation out to its uttermost possibilities! Be a maximum Christian; not content with being saved "so as by fire," but craving "an abundant entrance" into the kingdom. All this is accomplished in the close and faithful following of Christ.

This "following" is the sure test and touchstone by which a man determines whether he has really come to Christ and believes in Him. Our "good works" are not meritorious as having any part in our deliverance from condemnation; but they are the acid test of our faith; and they also determine the quality of the heaven that awaits us. And, in this sense, "they shall in no wise lose their reward." To use a rude figure; a man going to an entertainment gets a ticket of admission, but for his reserved seat he pays something more. "The just shall live by faith;" but the abundance of their life is determined by the product of their faith. Wherefore, he loses much who, while believing in Christ, follows Him afar off.

To follow Christ at the best, means to regard Him as our Priest, our only Priest, whose sacrifice is full and sufficient for us. We forsake all other plans of salvation and trust simply and solely to the merit of His atoning blood.

To follow Christ means to regard Him as our only Prophet or Teacher. All preachers, ecclesiastical councils, historic creeds and symbols are remanded to a subordinate place. His word is ultimate for us.

To follow Christ means to regard Him as our King. He reigns in us and over us. His love constrains us. His wish is our law. His authority is final. "Whatsoever he saith unto you, do it."

And to follow Christ means to do all this in the open. It may be that some who refuse to confess Christ are ultimately saved by Him; but the presumption is immensely against the man who lives that way. "Stand forth into the midst!" "Quit thyself like a man!"

In closing, we return to iterate and reiterate the proposition that our salvation from sin and spiritual death is by faith in Christ and by that only. Let no side issues enter here to confuse and bewilder us. "He that believeth shall be saved."

That is final and conclusive. Our deliverance is wholly of grace: we do not earn it. "The wages of sin is death: but the gift of God is eternal life."

Long as I live, I'll still be crying
Mercy's free!

And therefore all the glory is unto God: "Of whom are we in Christ Jesus, who is made unto us wisdom and righteousness and sanctification and redemption; that, according as it is written, if any man glory, let him glory in the Lord."

Nevertheless, the benefit of the gift is conditioned on our acceptance of it. The manna lies about our feet "white and plenteous as hoar frost," but it will not save us from famishing unless we gather it up and eat it. The water gushes from the rock, but we shall die of thirst unless we dip it up and drink it. Christ on the cross saves no man; it is only when Christ is appropriated that He saves us. We must make Him ours. We must grasp His extended hand. Luther said, "The important thing is the possessive pronoun, first person singular." One of the fathers said, "It is the grip on the Blood that saves us." Christ stands waiting—he offers life for the taking. Who will have it? The worst of sinners can make it his very own by saying with all his heart, "I will! I do!"

HORACE BUSHNELL

1802-1876

UNCONSCIOUS INFLUENCE

BIOGRAPHICAL NOTE

HORACE BUSHNELL was born at Litchfield, Connecticut, in 1802. Graduated at Yale 1827. In 1833 he became pastor of the North Congregational Church, Hartford, Conn., resigned in 1859 and died in 1876. He wrote many theological works. Among them "Christian Nurture" (1847), a book now looked upon as of classical authority. Considerable discussion among Calvinists was aroused by his "Nature and the Supernatural," and his "The Vicarious Sacrifice" (1865) as being out of accord with the accepted creeds of the Congregational churches. He lacked the sympathy and dramatic instinct necessary to great oratorical achievement, but his sermons prove by their profound suggestiveness that he was a man of keen spiritual insight, and preached with force and impressiveness. His influence upon the ministers of America in modifying theology and remolding the general type of preaching is fairly comparable with that of Robertson.

Then went in also that other disciple.—John xx., 8.

IN this slight touch or turn of history, is opened to us, if we scan closely, one of the most serious and fruitful chapters of Christian doctrine. Thus it is that men are ever touching unconsciously the springs of motion in each other; thus it is that one man, without thought or intention, or even a consciousness of the fact, is ever leading some other after him. Little does Peter think, as he comes up where his doubting brother is looking into the sepulcher, and goes straight in, after his peculiar manner, that he is drawing in his brother apostle after him. As little does John think, when he loses his misgivings, and goes into the sepulcher after Peter, that he is following his brother. And just so, unaware to himself, is every man, the whole race through, laying hold of his fellow-man, to lead him where otherwise he would not go. We overrun the boundaries of our personality— we flow together. A Peter leads a John, a John goes after Peter, both of them unconscious of any influence exerted or received. And thus our life and conduct are ever propagating themselves, by a law of social contagion, throughout the circles and times in which we live.

There are, then, you will perceive, two sorts of influence belonging to man; that which is active or voluntary, and that which is unconscious—that which we exert purposely or in the endeavor to sway another, as by teaching, by argument, by persuasion, by threatenings, by offers and promises, and that which flows out from us, unaware to ourselves, the same which Peter had over John when he led him into the sepulcher. The importance of our efforts to do good, that is of our voluntary influence, and the sacred obligation we are under to exert ourselves in this way, are often and seriously insisted on. It is thus that Christianity has become, in the present age, a principle of so much greater activity than it has been for many centuries before; and we fervently hope that it will yet become far more active than it now is, nor cease to multiply its industry, till it is seen by all mankind to embody the beneficence and the living energy of Christ Himself.

But there needs to be reproduced, at the same time, and partly for this object, a more thorough appreciation of the relative importance of that kind of influence or beneficence which is insensibly exerted. The tremendous weight and efficacy of this, compared with the other, and the sacred responsibility laid upon us in regard to this, are felt in no such degree or proportion as they should be; and the consequent loss we suffer in character, as well as that which the Church suffers in beauty and strength, is incalculable. The more stress, too, needs to be laid on this subject of insensible influence, because it is insensible; because it is out of mind, and, when we seek to trace it, beyond a full discovery.

If the doubt occur to any of you, in the announcement of this subject, whether we are properly responsible for an influence which we exert insensibly; we are not, I reply, except so far as this influence flows directly from our character and conduct. And this it does, even much more uniformly than our active influence. In the latter we may fail of our end by a want of wisdom or skill, in which case we are still as meritorious, in God's sight, as if we succeeded. So, again, we may really succeed, and do great good by our active endeavors, from motives altogether base and hypocritical, in which case we are as evil, in God's sight, as if we had failed. But the influences we exert unconsciously will almost never disagree with our real character. They are honest influences, following our character, as the shadow follows the sun. And, therefore, we are much more certainly responsible for them, and their effects on the world. They go streaming from us in all directions, tho in channels that we do not see, poisoning or healing around the roots of society, and among the hidden wells of character. If good ourselves, they are good; if bad, they are bad. And, since they reflect so exactly our character, it is impossible to doubt our responsibility for their effects on the world. We must answer not only for what we do with a purpose, but for the influence we exert insensibly. To give you any just impressions of the breadth and seriousness of such a reckoning I know to be impossible. No mind can trace it. But it will be something gained if I am able to awaken only a suspicion of the vast extent and power of those influences, which are ever flowing out unbidden upon society, from your life and character.

In the prosecution of my design, let me ask of you, first of all, to expel the common prejudice that there can be nothing of consequence in unconscious influences, because they make no report, and fall on the world unobserved. Histories and biographies make little account of the power men exert insensibly over each other. They tell how men have led armies, established empires, enacted laws, gained causes, sung, reasoned, and taught—always occupied in setting forth what they do with a purpose. But what they do without purpose, the streams of influence that flow out from their persons unbidden on the world, they can not trace or compute, and seldom even men-

tion. So also the public laws make men responsible only for what they do with a positive purpose, and take no account of the mischiefs or benefits that are communicated by their noxious or healthful example. The same is true in the discipline of families, churches, and schools; they make no account of the things we do, except we will them. What we do insensibly passes for nothing, because no human government can trace such influences with sufficient certainty to make their authors responsible.

But you must not conclude that influences of this kind are insignificant, because they are unnoticed and noiseless. How is it in the natural world? Behind the mere show, the outward noise and stir of the world, nature always conceals her hand of control, and the laws by which she rules. Who ever saw with the eye, for example, or heard with the ear, the exertions of that tremendous astronomic force, which every moment holds the compact of the physical universe together? The lightning is, in fact, but a mere firefly spark in comparison; but, because it glares on the clouds, and thunders so terribly in the ear, and rives the tree or the rock where it falls, many will be ready to think that it is a vastly more potent agent than gravity.

The Bible calls the good man's life a light, and it is the nature of light to flow out spontaneously in all directions, and fill the world unconsciously with its beams. So the Christian shines, it would say, not so much because he will, as because he is a luminous object. Not that the active influence of Christians is made of no account in the figure, but only that this symbol of light has its propriety in the fact that their unconscious influence is the chief influence, and has the precedence in its power over the world. And yet, there are many who will be ready to think that light is a very tame and feeble instrument, because it is noiseless. An earthquake, for example, is to them a much more vigorous and effective agency. Hear how it comes thundering through solid foundations of nature. It rocks a whole continent. The noblest works of man —cities, monuments, and temples—are in a moment leveled to the ground, or swallowed down the opening gulfs of fire. Little do they think that the light of every morning, the soft, and genial, and silent light, is an agent many times more powerful. But let the light of the morning cease and return no more, let the hour of morning come, and bring with it no dawn; the outcries of a horror-stricken world fill the air, and make, as it were, the darkness audible. The beasts go wild and frantic at the loss of the sun. The vegetable growths turn pale and die. A chill creeps on, and frosty winds begin to howl across the freezing earth. Colder, and yet colder, is the night. The vital blood, at length, of all creatures, stops congealed. Down goes the frost toward the earth's center. The heart of the sea is frozen; nay, the earthquakes are themselves frozen in, under their fiery caverns. The very globe itself, too, and all the fellow planets that have lost their sun, are become mere balls of ice, swinging silent in the darkness. Such is the light, which revisits us in the silence of the morning. It makes no shock or scar. It would not wake an infant in his cradle. And yet it perpetually new creates the world, rescuing it each morning, as a prey, from night and chaos. So the Christian is a light, even ''the light of the world,'' and we must not think that, because he shines insensibly or silently, as a mere luminous object, he is therefore powerless. The greatest powers are ever those which lie back of the little stirs and commotion of nature; and I verily believe that the insensible influences of good men are much more potent than what I have called their voluntary, or active, as the great silent powers of nature are of greater consequence than her little disturbances and tumults. The law of human influences is deeper than many suspect, and they lose sight of it altogether. The outward endeavors made by good men or bad to sway others, they call their influence; whereas, it is, in fact, but a fraction, and, in most cases, but a very small fraction, of the good or evil that flows out of their lives. Nay, I will even go further. How many persons do you meet, the insensible influence of whose manners and character is so decided as often to thwart their voluntary influence; so that, whatever they attempt to do, in the way of controlling others, they are sure to carry the exact opposite of what they intend! And it will generally be found that, where men undertake by argument or persuasion to exert a power, in the face of qualities that make them odious or detestable, or only not entitled to respect, their insensible influence will be too strong for them. The total effect of the life is then of a kind directly opposite to the voluntary endeavor, which, of course, does not add so much as a fraction to it.

I call your attention, next, to the twofold powers of effect and expression by which man connects with his fellow man. If we distinguish man as a creature of language, and thus qualified to communicate himself to others, there are in him two sets or kinds of language, one which is voluntary in the use, and one that is involuntary; that of speech in the literal sense, and that expression of the eye, the face, the look, the gait, the motion, the tone of cadence, which is sometimes called the natural language of the sentiments. This natural language, too, is greatly enlarged by the conduct of life, that which, in business and society, reveals the principles and spirit of men. Speech, or voluntary language, is a door to the soul, that we may open or shut at will; the other is a door that stands open evermore, and reveals to others constantly, and often very clearly, the tempers, tastes, and motives of their hearts. Within, as we may represent, is character, charging the common reservoir of influence, and through these twofold gates of the soul pouring itself out on the world. Out of one it flows at choice, and whensoever we purpose to do good or evil to men. Out of the other it flows each moment, as light from the sun, and propagates itself in all beholders.

Then if we go to others, that is, to the subjects of influence, we find every man endowed with two inlets of impression; the ear and the understanding for the reception of speech, and the sympathetic powers, the sensibilities or affections, for tinder to those sparks of emotion revealed by looks, tones, manners and general conduct. And these sympathetic powers, tho not immediately rational, are yet inlets, open on all sides, to the understanding and character. They have a certain wonderful capacity to receive impressions, and catch the meaning of signs, and propagate in us whatsoever falls into their passive molds from others. The impressions they receive do not come through verbal propositions, and are never received into verbal propositions, it may be, in the mind, and therefore many think nothing of them. But precisely on this account are they the more powerful, because it is as if one heart were thus going directly into another, and carrying in its feelings with it. Beholding, as in a glass, the feelings of our neighbor, we are changed into the same image, by the assimilating power of sensibility and fellow-feeling. Many have gone so far, and not without show, at least, of reason, as to maintain that the look or expression, and even the very features of children, are often changed by exclusive intercourse with nurses and attendants. Furthermore, if we carefully consider, we shall find it scarcely possible to doubt, that simply to look on bad and malignant faces, or those whose expressions have become infected by vice, to be with them and become familiarized to them, is enough permanently to affect the character of persons of mature age. I do not say that it must of necessity subvert their character, for the evil looked upon may never be loved or welcomed in practise; but it is something to have these bad images in the soul, giving out their expressions there, and diffusing their odor among the thoughts, as long as we live. How dangerous a thing is it, for example, for a man to become accustomed to sights of cruelty? What man, valuing the honor of his soul, would not shrink from yielding himself to such an influence? No more is it a thing of indifference to become accustomed to look on the manners, and receive the bad expression of any kind of sin.

The door of involuntary communication, I have said, is always open. Of course we are communicating ourselves in this way to others at every moment of our intercourse or presence with them. But how very seldom, in comparison, do we undertake by means of speech to influence others! Even the best Christian, one who most improves his opportunities to do good, attempts but seldom to sway another by voluntary influence, whereas he is all the while shining as a luminous object unawares, and communicating of his heart to the world.

But there is yet another view of this double line of communication which man has with his fellow-men, which is more general, and displays the import of the truth yet more convincingly. It is by one of these modes of communication that we are constituted members of voluntary society, and by the other, parts of a general mass, or members of involuntary society. You are all, in a certain view, individuals, and separate as persons from each other; you are also, in a certain other view, parts of a common body, as truly as the parts of a stone. Thus if you ask how it is that you and all men came without your consent to exist in society, to be within its power, to be under its laws, the answer is, that while you are a man, you are also a fractional element of a larger and more comprehensive being, called society—be it the family, the church, the state. In a certain department of your nature, it is open; its sympathies and feelings are open. On this open side you will adhere together, as parts of a larger nature, in which there is a common circulation of want, impulse, and law. Being thus made common to each other voluntarily, you become one mass, one consolidated social body, animated by one life. And observe how far this involuntary communication and sympathy between the members of a state or a family is sovereign over their character. It always results in what we call the national or family spirit; for there is a spirit peculiar to every state and family in the world. Sometimes, too, this national or family spirit takes a religious or an irreligious character, and appears almost to absorb the religious self-government of individuals. What was the national spirit of France, for example, at a certain time, but a spirit of infidelity? What is the religious spirit of Spain at this moment, but a spirit of bigotry, quite as wide of Christianity and destructive of character as the spirit of falsehood? What is the family spirit in many a house, but the spirit of gain, or pleasure, or appetite, in which everything that is warm, dignified, genial, and good in religion, is visibly absent? Sometimes you will almost fancy that you see the shapes of money in the eyes of children. So it is that we are led on by nations, as it were, to good

or bad immortality. Far down in the secret foundations of life and society there lie concealed great laws and channels of influence, which make the race common to each other in all the main departments or divisions of the social mass, laws which often escape our notice altogether, but which are to society as gravity to the general system of God's works.

But these are general considerations, and more fit, perhaps, to give you a rational conception of the modes of influence and their relative power, than to verify that conception, or establish its truth. I now proceed to add, therefore, some miscellaneous proofs of a more particular nature.

And I mention, first of all, the instinct of imitation in children. We begin our mortal experience, not with acts grounded in judgment or reason, or with ideas received through language, but by simple imitation, and, under the guidance of this, we lay our foundations. The child looks and listens, and whatsoever tone of feeling or manner of conduct is displayed around him, sinks into his plastic, passive soul, and becomes a mold of his being ever after. The very handling of the nursery is significant, and the petulance, the passion, the gentleness, the tranquillity indicated by it, are all reproduced in the child. His soul is a purely receptive nature, and that for a considerable period, without choice or selection. A little further on he begins voluntarily to copy everything he sees. Voice, manner, gait, everything which the eye sees, the mimic instinct delights to act over. And thus we have a whole generation of future men, receiving from us their beginnings, and the deepest impulses of their life and immortality. They watch us every moment, in the family, before the hearth, and at the table; and when we are meaning them no good or evil, when we are conscious of exerting no influence over them, they are drawing from us impressions and molds of habit, which, if wrong, no heavenly discipline can wholly remove; or, if right, no bad associations utterly dissipate. Now it may be doubted, I think, whether, in all the active influence of our lives, we do as much to shape the destiny of our fellow-men as we do in this single article of unconscious influence over children.

Still further on, respect for others takes the place of imitation. We naturally desire the approbation or good opinion of others. You see the strength of this feeling in the article of fashion. How few persons have the nerve to resist a fashion! We have fashions, too, in literature, and in worship, and in moral and religious doctrine, almost equally powerful. How many will violate the best rules of society, because it is the practise of the circle! How many reject Christ because of friends or acquaintance, who have no suspicion of the influence they exert, and will not have, till the last days show them what they have done! Every good man has thus a power in his person, more mighty than his words and arguments, and which others feel when he little suspects it. Every bad man, too, has a fund of poison in his character, which is tainting those around him, when it is not in his thoughts to do them injury. He is read and understood. His sensual tastes and habits, his unbelieving spirit, his suppressed leer at religions, have all a power, and take hold of the heart of others, whether he will have it so or not.

Again, how well understood is it that the most active feelings and impulses of mankind are contagious. How quick enthusiasm of any sort is to kindle, and how rapidly it catches from one to another, till a nation blazes in the flame! In the case of the Crusades you have an example where the personal enthusiasm of one man put all the states of Europe in motion. Fanaticism is almost equally contagious. Fear and superstition always infect the mind of the circle in which they are manifested. The spirit of war generally becomes an epidemic of madness, when once it has got possession of a few minds. The spirit of party is propagated in a similar manner. How any slight operation in the market may spread, like a fire, if successful, till trade runs wild in a general infatuation, is well known. Now, in all these examples, the effect is produced, not by active endeavor to carry influence, but mostly by that insensible propagation which follows, when a flame of any kind is once more kindled.

It is also true, you may ask, that the religious spirit propagates itself or tends to propagate itself in the same way? I see no reason to question that it does. Nor does anything in the doctrine of spiritual influences, when rightly understood, forbid the supposition. For spiritual influences are never separated from the laws of thought in the individual, and the laws of feeling and influence in society. If, too, every disciple is to be an "epistle known and read of all men," what shall we expect, but that all men will be somehow affected by the reading? Or if he is to be a light in the world, what shall we look for, but that others, seeing his good works, shall glorify God on his account? How often is it seen, too, as a fact of observation, that one or a few good men kindle at length a holy fire in the community in which they live, and become the leaven of general reformation! Such men give a more vivid proof in their persons of the reality of religious faith than any words or arguments could yield. They are active; they endeavor, of course, to exert a good voluntary influence; but still their chief power lies in their holiness and the sense they produce in others of their close relation to God.

It now remains to exhibit the very important fact, that where the direct or active influence of men is supposed to be great, even this is due, in a principal degree, to that insensible influence by which their arguments, reproofs, and persuasions are secretly invigorating. It is not mere words which turn men; it is the heart mounting, uncalled, into the expression of the features; it is the eye illuminated by reason, the look beaming with goodness; it is the tone of the voice, that instrument of the soul, which changes quality with such amazing facility, and gives out in the soft, the tender, the tremulous, the firm, every shade of emotion and character. And so much is there in this, that the moral stature and character of the man that speaks are likely to be well represented in his manner. If he is a stranger, his way will inspire confidence and attract good will. His virtues will be seen, as it were, gathering round him to minister words and forms of thought, and their voices will be heard in the fall of his cadences. And the same is true of bad men, or men who have nothing in their character corresponding to what they attempt to do. If without heart or interest you attempt to move another, the involuntary man tells what you are doing in a hundred ways at once. A hypocrite, endeavoring to exert a good influence, only tries to convey by words what the lying look, and the faithless affectation, or dry exaggeration of his manner perpetually resists. We have it for a fashion to attribute great or even prodigious results to the voluntary efforts and labors of men. Whatever they effect is commonly referred to nothing but the immediate power of what they do. Let us take an example, like that of Paul, and analyze it. Paul was a man of great fervor and enthusiasm. He combined, withal, more of what is lofty and morally commanding in his character, than most of the very distinguished men of the world. Having this for his natural character, and his natural character exalted and made luminous by Christian faith, and the manifest indwelling of God, he had of course an almost superhuman sway over others. Doubtless he was intelligent, strong in argument, eloquent, active, to the utmost of his powers, but still he moved the world more by what he was than by what he did. The grandeur and spiritual splendor of his character were ever adding to his active efforts an element of silent power, which was the real and chief cause of their efficacy. He convinced, subdued, inspired, and led, because of the half-divine authority which appeared in his conduct, and his glowing spirit. He fought the good fight, because he kept the faith, and filled his powerful nature with influences drawn from higher worlds.

And here I must conduct you to a yet higher example, even that of the Son of God, the light of the world. Men dislike to be swayed by direct, voluntary influence. They are jealous of such control, and are therefore best approached by conduct and feeling, and the authority of simple worth, which seem to make no purposed onset. If goodness appears, they welcome its celestial smile; if heaven descends to encircle them, they yield to its sweetness; if truth appears in the life, they honor it with a secret homage; if personal majesty and glory appear, they bow with reverence, and acknowledge with shame their own vileness. Now it is on this side of human nature that Christ visits us, preparing just that kind of influence which the spirit of truth may wield with the most persuasive and subduing effect. It is the grandeur of His character which constitutes the chief power of His ministry, not His miracles or teachings apart from His character. Miracles were useful, at the time, to arrest attention, and His doctrine is useful at all times as the highest revelation of truth possible in speech; but the greatest truth of the gospel, notwithstanding, is Christ Himself —a human body becomes the organ of the divine nature, and reveals, under the conditions of an earthly life, the glory of God! The Scripture writers have much to say, in this connection, of the image of God; and an image, you know, is that which simply represents, not that which acts, or reasons, or persuades. Now it is this image of God which makes the center, the sun itself, of the gospel. The journeyings, teachings, miracles, and sufferings of Christ, all had their use in bringing out this image, or what is the same, in making conspicuous the character and feelings of God, both toward sinners and toward sin. And here is the power of Christ—it is that God's beauty, love, truth, and justice shines through Him. It is the influence which flows unconsciously and spontaneously out of Christ, as the friend of man, the light of the world, the glory of the Father, made visible. And some have gone so far as to conjecture that God made the human person, originally, with a view to its becoming the organ or vehicle by which He might reveal His communicable attributes to other worlds. Christ, they believe, came to inhabit this organ, that He might execute a purpose so sublime. The human person is constituted, they say, to be a mirror of God; and God, being imaged in that mirror, as in Christ, is held up to the view of this and other worlds. It certainly is to the view of this; and if the Divine nature can use the organ so effectively to express itself unto us, if it can bring itself, through the looks, tones, motions, and conduct of a human person, more close to our sympathies than by any other means, how can we think that an organ so communicative, inhabited by us, is not always breathing our spirit and transferring our image insensibly to others?

I have protracted the argument on this subject beyond what I could have wished, but I can not dismiss it without suggesting a few thoughts necessary to its complete practical effect.

One very obvious and serious inference from it, and the first which I will name, is, that it is impossible to live in this world and escape responsibility. It is not that they alone, as you have seen, who are trying purposely to convert or corrupt others, who exert an influence; you can not live without exerting influence. The doors of your soul are open on others, and theirs on you. You inhabit a house which is well-nigh transparent; and what you are within, you are ever showing yourself to be without, by signs that have no ambiguous expression. If you had the seeds of a pestilence in your body, you would not have a more active contagion than you have in your tempers, tastes, and principles. Simply to be in this world, whatever you are, is to exert an influence—an influence, too, compared with which mere language and persuasion are feeble. You say that you mean well; at least, you think you mean to injure no one. Do you injure no one? Is your example harmless? Is it ever on the side of God and duty? You can not reasonably doubt that others are continually receiving impressions from your character. As little you can doubt that you must answer for these impressions. If the influence you exert is unconsciously exerted, then it is only the most sincere, the truest expression of your character. And for what can you be held responsible, if not for this? Do not deceive yourselves in the thought that you are at least doing no injury, and are, therefore, living without responsibility; first, make it sure that you are not every hour infusing moral death insensibly into your children, wives, husbands, friends, and acquaintances. By a mere look or glance, not unlikely, you are conveying the influence that shall turn the scale of some one's immortality. Dismiss, therefore, the thought that you are living without responsibility; that is impossible. Better is it frankly to admit the truth; and if you will risk the influence of a character unsanctified by duty and religion, prepare to meet your reckoning manfully, and receive the just recompense of reward.

The true philosophy or method of doing good is also here explained. It is, first of all and principally, to be good—to have a character that will of itself communicate good. There must and will be active effort where there is goodness of principle; but the latter we should hold to be the principal thing, the root and life of all. Whether it is a mistake more sad or more ridiculous, to make mere stir synonymous with doing good, we need not inquire; enough, to be sure that one who has taken up such a notion of doing good, is for that reason a nuisance to the Church. The Christian is called a light, not lightning. In order to act with effect on others, he must walk in the Spirit, and thus become the image of goodness; he must be so akin to God, and so filled with His dispositions, that he shall seem to surround himself with a hallowed atmosphere. It is folly to endeavor to make ourselves shine before we are luminous. If the sun without his beams should talk to the planets, and argue with them till the final day, it would not make them shine; there must be light in the sun itself; and then they will shine, of course. And this, my brethren, is what God intends for you all. It is the great idea of His gospel, and the work of His spirit, to make you lights in the world. His greatest joy is to give you character, to beautify your example, to exalt your principles, and make you each the depository of His own almighty grace. But in order to do this, something is necessary on your part—a full surrender of your mind to duty and to God, and a perpetual desire of this spiritual intimacy; having this, having a participation thus of the goodness of God, you will as naturally communicate good as the sun communicates his beams.

Our doctrine of unconscious and undesigning influence shows how it is, also, that the preaching of Christ is often unfruitful, and especially in times of spiritual coldness. It is not because truth ceases to be truth, nor, of necessity, because it is preached in a less vivid manner, but because there are so many influences preaching against the preacher. He is one, the people are many; his attempt to convince and persuade is a voluntary influence; their lives, on the other hand, and especially the lives of those who profess what is better, are so many unconscious influences ever streaming forth upon the people, and back and forth between each other. He preaches the truth, and they, with one consent, are preaching the truth down; and how can he prevail against so many, and by a kind of influence so unequal? When the people of God are glowing with spiritual devotion to Him, and love to men, the case is different; then they are all preaching with the preacher, and making an atmosphere of warmth for his words to fall in; great is the company of them that publish the truth, and proportionally great its power. Shall I say more? Have you not already felt, my brethren, the application to which I would bring you? We do not exonerate ourselves; we do not claim to be nearer to God or holier than you; but, ah! you know how easy it is to make a winter about us, or how cold it feels! Our endeavor is to preach the truth of Christ and His cross as clearly and as forcefully as we can. Sometimes it has a visible effect, and we are filled with joy; sometimes it has no effect, and then we struggle on, as we must, but under great oppression. Have we none among you that preach against us in your lives? If we show you the light of God's truth, does it never fall on banks of ice; which if the light shows through, the crystal masses are yet as cold as before? We do not accuse you; that we leave to God, and to those who may rise up in the last day to testify against you. If they shall come out of your own families; if they are the children that wear your names, the husband or wife of your affections; if they declare that you, by your example, kept them away from Christ's truth and mercy, we may have accusations to meet of our own, and we leave you to acquit yourselves as best you may. I only warn you, here, of the guilt which our Lord Jesus Christ will impute to them that hinder His gospel.

JOHN CALVIN

1509-1564

ENDURING PERSECUTION FOR CHRIST

BIOGRAPHICAL NOTE

JOHN CALVIN was born in 1509, at Noyon, France. He has been called the greatest of Protestant commentators and theologians, and the inspirer of the Puritan exodus. He often preached every day for weeks in succession. He possest two of the greatest elements in successful pulpit oratory, self-reliance and authority. It was said of him, as it was afterward said of Webster, that "every word weighed a pound." His style was simple, direct, and convincing. He made men think. His splendid contributions to religious thought, and his influence upon individual liberty, give him a distinguished place among great reformers and preachers. His idea of preaching is thus exprest in his own words: "True preaching must not be dead, but living and effective. No parade of rhetoric, but the Spirit of God must resound in the voice in order to operate with power." He died at Geneva in 1564.

Let us go forth therefore unto Him without the camp bearing His reproach.—Hebrews xiii., 13.

ALL the exhortations which can be given us to suffer patiently for the name of Jesus Christ, and in defense of the gospel, will have no effect if we do not feel assured of the cause for which we fight. For when we are called to part with life, it is absolutely necessary to know on what grounds. The firmness necessary we can not possess, unless it be founded on certainty of faith.

It is true that persons may be found who will foolishly expose themselves to death in maintaining some absurd opinions and dreams conceived by their own brain, but such impetuosity is more to be regarded as frenzy than as Christian zeal; and, in fact, there is neither firmness nor sound sense in those who thus, at a kind of haphazard, cast themselves away. But, however this may be, it is in a good cause only that God can acknowledge us as His martyrs. Death is common to all, and the children of God are condemned to ignominy and tortures as criminals are; but God makes the distinction between them, inasmuch as He can not deny His truth. On our part, then, it is requisite that we have sure and infallible evidence of the doctrine which we maintain; and hence, as I have said, we can not be rationally imprest by any exhortations which we receive to suffer persecution for the gospel, if no true certainty of faith has been imprinted in our hearts. For to hazard our life upon a peradventure is not natural, and tho we were to do it, it would only be rashness, not Christian courage. In a word, nothing that we do will be approved of God if we are not thoroughly persuaded that it is for Him and His cause we suffer persecution, and the world is our enemy.

Now, when I speak of such persuasion, I mean not merely that we must know how to distinguish between true religion and the abuses or follies of men, but also that we must be thoroughly persuaded of the heavenly life, and the crown which is promised us above, after we shall have fought here below. Let us understand, then, that both of these requisites are necessary, and can not be separated from each other. The points, accordingly, with which we must commence are these: We must know well what our Christianity is, what the faith which we have to hold and follow, what the rule which God has given us; and we must be so well furnished with such instructions as to be able boldly to condemn all the falsehoods, errors, and superstitions which Satan has introduced to corrupt the pure simplicity of the doctrine of God. Hence, we ought not to be surprized that, in the present day, we see so few persons disposed to suffer for the gospel, and that the greater part of those who call themselves Christians know not what it is. For all are, as it were, lukewarm; and instead of making it their business to hear or read, count it enough to have had some slight taste.of Christian faith. This is the reason why there is so little decision, and why those who are assailed immediately fall away. This fact should stimulate us to inquire more diligently into divine truth, in order to be well assured with regard to it.

Still, however, to be well informed and grounded is not the whole that is necessary. For we see some who seem to be thoroughly imbued with sound doctrine, and who, notwithstanding, have no more zeal or affection than if they had never known any more of God than some fleeting fancy. Why is this? Just because they have never comprehended the majesty of the Holy Scriptures. And, in fact, did we, such as we are, consider well that it is God who speaks to us, it is certain that we would listen more attentively, and with greater reverence. If we would think that in reading Scripture we are in the school of angels, we would be far more careful and desirous to profit by the doctrine which is propounded to us.

We now see the true method of preparing to suffer for the gospel. First, We must have profited so far in the school of God as to be decided in regard to true religion and the doctrine which we are to hold; and we must despise all the wiles and impostures of Satan, and all human inventions, as things not only frivolous but also carnal, inasmuch as they corrupt Christian purity; therein differing, like true martyrs of Christ, from the fantastic persons who suffer for mere absurdities. Second, Feeling assured of the good cause, we must be inflamed, accordingly, to follow God whithersoever He may call us: His Word must have such authority with us as it deserves, and having withdrawn from this world, we must feel as it were enraptured in seeking the heavenly life.

But it is more than strange that,tho the light of God is shining more brightly than it ever did before, there is a lamentable want of zeal! If the thought does not fill us with shame, so much the worse. For we must shortly come before the great Judge, where the iniquity which we endeavor to hide will be brought forward with such upbraidings that we shall be utterly confounded. For, if we are obliged to bear testimony to God,

according to the measure of the knowledge which He has given us, to what is it owing, I would ask, that we are so cold and timorous in entering into battle, seeing that God has so fully manifested Himself at this time that He may be said to have opened to us and displayed before us the great treasures of His secrets? May it not be said that we do not think we have to do with God? For had we any regard to His Majesty we would not dare to turn the doctrine which proceeds from Him into some kind of philosophic speculation. In short, it is impossible to deny that it is our great shame, not to say fearful condemnation, that we have so well known the truth of God, and have so little courage to maintain it!

Above all, when we look to the martyrs of past times, well may we detest our own cowardice! The greater part of those were not persons much versed in Holy Scripture, so as to be able to dispute on all subjects. They knew that there was one God, whom they behooved to worship and serve—that they had been redeemed by the blood of Jesus Christ, in order that they might place their confidence of salvation in Him and in His grace—and that, all the inventions of men being mere dross and rubbish, they ought to condemn all idolatries and superstitions. In one word, their theology was in substance this—There is one God who created all the world, and declared His will to us by Moses and the prophets, and finally by Jesus Christ and His apostles; and we have one sole Redeemer, who purchased us by His blood, and by whose grace we hope to be saved: All the idols of the world are curst, and deserve execration.

With a system embracing no other points than these, they went boldly to the flames, or to any other kind of death. They did not go in twos or threes, but in such bands that the number of those who fell by the hands of tyrants is almost infinite! We, on our part, are such learned clerks that none can be more so (so at least we think), and, in fact, so far as regards the knowledge of Scripture, God has so spread it out before us that no former age was ever so highly favored. Still, after all, there is scarcely a particle of zeal. When men manifest such indifference, it looks as if they were bent on provoking the vengeance of God.

What then should be done in order to inspire our breasts with true courage? We have, in the first place, to consider how precious the confession of our faith is in the sight of God. We little know how much God prizes it, if our life, which is nothing, is valued by us more highly. When it is so, we manifest a marvelous degree of stupidity. We can not save our life at the expense of our confession without acknowledging that we hold it in higher estimation than the honor of God and the salvation of our souls.

A heathen could say that "It was a miserable thing to save life by giving up the only things which made life desirable!" And yet he and others like him never knew for what end men are placed in the world, and why they live in it. It is true they knew enough to say that men ought to follow virtue, to conduct themselves honestly and without reproach; but all their virtues were mere paint and smoke. We know far better what the chief aim of life should be, namely, to glorify God, in order that He may be our glory. When this is not done, wo to us! And we can not continue to live for a single moment upon the earth without heaping additional curses on our heads. Still we are not ashamed to purchase some few days to languish here below, renouncing eternal kingdom by separating ourselves from Him by whose energy we are sustained in life.

Were we to ask the most ignorant, not to say the most brutish, persons in the world why they live, they would not venture to answer simply that it is to eat, and drink, and sleep; for all know that they have been created for a higher and holier end. And what end can we find if it be not to honor God, and allow ourselves to be governed by Him, like children by good parents; so that after we have finished the journey of this corruptible life, we may be received into His eternal inheritance? Such is the principal, indeed the sole end. When we do not take it into account, and are intent on a brutish life, which is worse than a thousand deaths, what can we allege for our excuse? To live and not know why is unnatural. To reject the causes for which we live, under the influence of a foolish longing for a respite of some few days, during which we are to live in the world, while separated from God—I know not how to name such infatuation and madness!

But as persecution is always harsh and bitter, let us consider how and by what means Christians may be able to fortify themselves with patience, so as unflinchingly to expose their life for the truth of God. The text which we have read out, when it is properly understood, is sufficient to induce us to do so. The apostle says, Let us go forth from the city after the Lord Jesus, bearing His reproach. In the first place, he reminds us, altho the swords should not be drawn against us nor the fires kindled to burn us, that we can not be truly united to the Son of God while we are rooted in this world. Wherefore a Christian, even in repose, must always have one foot lifted to march to battle, and not only so, but he must have his affections withdrawn from the world, altho his body is dwelling in it. Grant that this at first sight seems to us hard, still we must be satisfied

with the words of St. Paul (I Thess. iii.), that we are called and appointed to suffer. As if He had said, Such is our condition as Christians; this is the road by which we must go if we would follow Christ.

Meanwhile, to solace our infirmity and mitigate the vexation and sorrow which persecution might cause us, a good reward is held forth: In suffering for the cause of God, we are walking step by step after the Son of God, and have Him for our guide. Were it simply said that to be Christians we must pass through all the insults of the world boldly, to meet death at all times and in whatever way God may be pleased to appoint, we might apparently have some pretext for replying that it is a strange road to go at peradventure. But when we are commanded to follow the Lord Jesus, His guidance is too good and honorable to be refused. Now, in order that we may be more deeply moved, not only is it said that Jesus Christ walks before us as our Captain, but that we are made conformable to His image; so St. Paul says in the eighth chapter to the Romans that God hath ordained all those whom He hath adopted for His children, to be made conformable to Him who is the pattern and head of all.

Are we so delicate as to be unwilling to endure anything? Then we must renounce the grace of God by which He has called us to the hope of salvation. For there are two things which can not be separated—to be members of Christ, and to be tried by many afflictions. We certainly ought to prize such a conformity to the Son of God much more than we do. It is true, that in the world's judgment there is disgrace in suffering for the gospel. But since we know that believers are blind, ought we not to have better eyes than they? It is ignominy to suffer from those who occupy the seat of justice, but St. Paul shows us by his example that we have to glory in scourings for Jesus Christ, as marks by which God recognizes us and avows us for His own. And we know what St. Luke narrates of Peter and John (Acts v., 41); namely, that they rejoiced to have been counted worthy to suffer infamy and reproach for the name of the Lord Jesus.

Ignominy and dignity are two opposites: so says the world, which, being infatuated, judges against all reason, and in this way converts the glory of God into dishonor. But, on our part, let us not refuse to be vilified as concerns the world, in order to be honored before God and His angels. We see what pains the ambitious take to receive the commands of a king, and what a boast they make of it. The Son of God presents His commands to us, and every one stands back. Tell me, pray, whether in so doing are we worthy of having anything in common with Him? there is nothing here to attract our sensual nature, but such notwithstanding are the true escutcheons of nobility in the heavens. Imprisonment, exile, evil report, imply in men's imagination whatever is to be vituperated; but what hinders us from viewing things as God judges and declares them, save our unbelief? Wherefore, let the name of the Son of God have all the weight with us which it deserves, that we may learn to count it honor when He stamps His marks upon us. If we act otherwise our ingratitude is insupportable.

Were God to deal with us according to our desserts, would He not have just cause to chastise us daily in a thousand ways? Nay more, a hundred thousand deaths would not suffice for a small portion of our misdeeds! Now, if in His infinite goodness He puts all our faults under His foot and abolishes them, and instead of punishing us according to our demerit, devises an admirable means to convert our afflictions into honor and a special privilege, inasmuch as through them we are taken into partnership with His Son, must it not be said, when we disdain such a happy state, that we have indeed made little progress in Christian doctrine?

Accordingly, St. Peter, after exhorting us (I Peter iv., 15) to walk so purely in the fear of God, as not to suffer as thieves, adulterers, and murderers, immediately adds, that if we must suffer as Christians, let us glorify God for the blessing which He thus bestows upon us. It is not without cause he speaks thus. For who are we, I pray, to be witnesses of the truth of God, and advocates to maintain His cause? Here we are poor worms of the earth, creatures full of vanity, full of lies, and yet God employs us to defend His truth—an honor which pertains not even to the angels of heaven! May not this consideration alone well inflame us to offer ourselves to God to be employed in any way in such honorable service?

Many persons, however, can not refrain from pleading against God, or, at least, from complaining against Him for not better supporting their weakness. It is marvelously strange, they say, how God, after having chosen us for His children, allows us to be trampled upon and tormented by the ungodly. I answer: Even were it not apparent why He does so, He might well exercise His authority over us, and fix our lot at His pleasure. But when we see that Jesus Christ is our pattern, ought we not, without inquiring further, to esteem it great happiness that we are made like Him? God, however, makes it very apparent what the reasons are for which He is pleased that we should be persecuted. Had we nothing more than the consideration suggested by St. Peter (I Peter i., 7), we were disdainful indeed not to acquiesce in it. He says that since gold and silver, which are only corruptible metals, are purified and tested by fire, it is but reasonable that our faith, which surpasses all the riches of the world, should be so tried.

It were easy indeed for God to crown us at once without requiring us to sustain any combats; but as it is His pleasure that until the end of the world Christ shall reign in the midst of His enemies, so it is also His pleasure that we, being placed in the midst of them, shall suffer their oppression and violence till He deliver us. I know, indeed, that the flesh rebels when it is to be brought to this point, but still the will of God must have the mastery. If we feel some repugnance in ourselves, it need not surprize us; for it is only too natural for us to shun the cross. Still let us not fail to surmount it, knowing that God accepts our obedience, provided we bring all our feelings and wishes into captivity, and make them subject to Him.

When prophets and apostles went to death, it was not without feeling some inclination to recoil. "They shall carry thee whither thou wouldst not," said our Lord Jesus Christ to Peter. (John xxi., 18. When such fears of death arise within us, let us gain the mastery over them, or rather let God gain it; and meanwhile, let us feel assured that we offer Him a pleasing sacrifice when we resist and do violence to our inclinations for the purpose of placing ourselves entirely under His command: This is the principle war in which God would have His people to be engaged. He would have them strive to suppress every rebellious thought and feeling which would turn them aside from the path to which He points. And the consolations are so ample that it may well be said, we are more than cowards if we give away!

In ancient times vast numbers of people, to obtain a simple crown of leaves, refused no toil, no pain, no trouble; nay, it even cost them nothing to die, and yet every one of them fought for a peradventure, not knowing whether he was to gain or to lose the prize. God holds forth to us the immortal crown by which we may become partakers of His glory: He does not mean us to fight at haphazard, but all of us have a promise of the prize for which we strive. Have we any cause then to decline the struggle? Do we think it has been said in vain that if we die with Jesus Christ we shall also live with Him? Our triumph is prepared, and yet we do all we can to shun the combat.

But it is said that all we teach on this subject is repugnant to human judgment. I confess it. And hence when our Savior declares, "Blest are they which are persecuted for righteousness' sake" (Matt. v., 10), He gives utterance to a sentiment which is not easily received in the world. On the contrary, He wishes to account that as happiness which in the judgment of sense is misery. We seem to ourselves miserable when God leaves us to be trampled upon by the tyranny and cruelty of our enemies; but the error is that we look not to the promises of God, which assure us that all will turn to our good. We are cast down when we see the wicked stronger than we, and planting their foot on our throat; but such confusion should rather, as St. Paul says, cause us to lift up our heads. Seeing we are too much disposed to amuse ourselves with present objects, God in permitting the good to be maltreated, and the wicked to have sway, shows by evident tokens that a day is coming on which all that is now in confusion will be reduced to order. If the period seems distant, let us run to the remedy, and not flatter ourselves in our sin; for it is certain that we have no faith if we can not carry our views forward to the coming of Jesus Christ.

To leave no means which may be fitted to stimulate us unemployed, God sets before us promises on the one hand and threatenings on the other. Do we feel that the promises have not sufficient influence, let us strengthen them by adding the threatenings. It is true we must be perverse in the extreme not to put more faith in the promises of God, when the Lord Jesus says that He will own us as His before His Father, provided we confess Him before men. (Matt. x., 32; Luke xii., 8.) What should prevent us from making the confession which He requires? Let men do their utmost, they can not do worse than murder us! and will not the heavenly life compensate for this? I do not here collect all the passages in Scripture which bear on this subject: they are so often reiterated that we ought to be thoroughly satisfied with them. When the struggle comes, if three or four passages do not suffice, a hundred surely ought to make us proof against all contrary temptations.

But if God can not will us to Himself by gentle means, must we not be mere blocks if His threatenings also fail? Jesus Christ summons all those who from fear of temporal death shall have denied the truth, to appear at the bar of God his Father, and says, that then both body and soul will be consigned to perdition. (Matt. x., 28; Luke xii., 5.) And in another passage He says that He will disclaim all those who shall have denied Him before men. (Matt. x., 33; Luke xii., 10.) These words, if we are not altogether impervious to feeling, might well make our hair stand on end. Be this as it may, this much is certain; if these things do not move us as they ought, nothing remains for us but a fearful judgment. (Heb. x., 27.) All the words of Christ having proved unavailing, we stand convinced of gross infidelity.

It is in vain for us to allege that pity should be shown us, inasmuch as our nature is so frail; for it is said, on the contrary, that Moses, having looked to God by faith, was fortified so as not to yield under any temptation. Wherefore, when we are thus soft and easy to bend, it is a manifest sign, I do not say that we have no zeal, no firmness, but that we know nothing either of God or His kingdom. When we are reminded that we ought to be united to our Head, it seems to us a fine pretext for exemption to say that we are men. But what were those who have trodden the path before us? Indeed, had we nothing more than pure doctrine, all the excuses we could make would be frivolous; but having so many examples which ought to supply us with the strongest proof, the more deserving are we of condemnation.

There are two points to be considered. The first is, that the whole body of the Church in general has always been, and to the end will be, liable to be afflicted by the wicked, as is said in the Psalms (Psalms cxxix., 1), "From my youth up they have tormented me, and dragged the plow over me from one end to the other." The Holy Spirit there brings in the ancient Church, in order that we, after being much acquainted with her afflictions, may not regard it as either new or vexatious when the like is done to ourselves in the present day. St. Paul, also, in quoting from another Psalm (Rom. vii., 36; Psalm xliv., 22), a passage which says, "We have been led like sheep to the slaughter"; shows that that has not been for one age only, but is the ordinary condition of the Church, and shall be.

Therefore, on seeing how the Church of God is trampled upon in the present day by proud worldlings, how one barks and another bites, how they tortue, how they plot against her, how she is assailed incessantly by mad dogs and savage beasts, let it remind us that the same thing was done in all the olden time. It is true God sometimes gives her a truce and time of refreshment, and hence in the Psalm above quoted it is said, "He cutteth the cords of the wicked"; and in another passage (Psalm cxxv., 3), "He breaks their staff, lest the good should fall away, by being too hardly pressed." But still it has pleased Him that His Church should always have to battle so long as she is in this world, her repose being treasured up on high in the heavens. (Heb. iii., 9.)

Meanwhile, the issue of her afflictions has always been fortunate. At all events, God has caused that tho she has been prest by many calamities, she has never been completely crusht; as it is said (Psalm vii., 15), "The wicked with all their efforts have not succeeded in that at which they aimed." St. Paul glories in the fact, and shows that this is the course which God in mercy always takes. He says (I Cor. iv., 12) that we endure tribulations, but we are not in agony; we are impoverished, but not left destitute; we are persecuted, but not forsaken; cast down, but we perish not; bearing everywhere in our body the mortification of the Lord Jesus, in order that His life may be manifested in our mortal bodies. Such being, as we see, the issue which God has at all times given to the persecutions of His Church, we ought to take courage, knowing that our forefathers, who were frail men like ourselves, always had the victory over their enemies by remaining firm in endurance.

I only touch upon this article briefly to come to the second, which is more to our purpose, viz., that we ought to take advantage of the particular examples of the martyrs who have gone before us. These are not confined to two or three, but are, as the apostle says (Heb. xii., 1), "So great a cloud of witnesses." By this expression he intimates that the number is so great that it ought, as it were, completely to engross our sight. Not to be tedious, I will only mention the Jews, who were persecuted for the true religion, as well under the tyranny of King Antiochus as a little after his death. We can not allege that the number of sufferers was small, for it formed, as it were, a large army of martyrs. We can not say that it consisted of prophets whom God had set apart from common people, for women and young children formed part of the band. We can not say that they got off at a cheap rate, for they were tortured as cruelly as it was possible to be. Accordingly, we hear what the apostle says (Heb. xi., 35), that some were stretched out like drums, not caring to be delivered, that they might obtain a better resurrection; others were proved by mockery and blows, or bonds and prisons; others were stoned or sawn asunder; others traveled up and down, wandering among mountains and caves.

Let us now compare their case with ours. If they so endured for the truth which was at that time so obscure, what ought we to do in the clear light which is now shining? God speaks to us with open mouth; the great gate of the kingdom of heaven has been opened, and Jesus Christ calls us to Himself, after having come down to us that we might have him, as it were, present to our eyes. What a reproach would it be to us to have less zeal in suffering for the gospel than those who had only hailed the promises afar off—who had only a little wicket opened whereby to come to the kingdom of God, and who had only some memorial and type of Jesus Christ? These things can not be exprest in a word, as they deserve, and therefore I leave each to ponder them for himself.

The doctrine now laid down, as it is general, ought to be carried into practise by all Christians, each applying it to his own use according as may be necessary. This I say, in order that those who do not see themselves in apparent danger may not think it superfluous as regards them. They are not at this hour in the hands of tyrants, but how do they know what God means to do with them hereafter? We ought therefore to be so forearmed that if some persecution which we did not expect arrives, we may not be taken unawares. But I much fear that there are many deaf ears in regard to this subject. So far are those who are sheltered and at their ease from preparing to suffer death when need shall be that they do not even trouble themselves about serving God in their lives. It nevertheless continues true that this preparation for persecution ought to be our ordinary study, and especially in the times in which we live.

Those, again, whom God calls to suffer for the testimony of His name ought to show by deeds that they have been thoroughly trained to patient endurance. Then ought they to recall to mind all the exhortations which were given them in times past, and bestir themselves just as the soldier rushes to arms when the tempest sounds. But how different is the result. The only question is how to find out subterfuges for escaping. I say this in regard to the greater part; for persecution is a true touchstone by which God ascertains who are His. And few are so faithful as to be prepared to meet death boldly.

It is a kind of monstrous thing, that persons who make a boast of having a little of the gospel, can venture to open their lips to give utterance to such quibbling. Some will say, What do we gain by confessing our faith to obstinate people who have deliberately resolved to fight against God? Is not this to cast pearls before swine? As if Jesus Christ had not distinctly declared (Matt. viii., 38) that He wishes to be confest among the perverse and malignant. If they are not instructed thereby, they will at all events remain confounded; and hence confession is an odor of a sweet smell before God, even tho it be deadly to the reprobate. There are some who say, What will our death profit? Will it not rather prove an offense? As if God hath left them the choice of dying when they should see it good and find the occasion opportune. On the contrary, we approve our obedience by leaving in His hand the profit which is to accrue from our death.

In the first place, then, the Christian man, wherever he may be, must resolve, notwithstanding dangers or threatings, to walk in simplicity as God has commanded. Let him guard as much as he can against the ravening of the wolves, but let it not be with carnal craftiness. Above all, let him place his life in the hands of God. Has he done so?

Then if he happens to fall into the hands of the enemy, let him think that God, having so arranged, is pleased to have him for one of the witnesses of His Son, and therefore that he has no means of drawing back without breaking faith with Him to whom we have promised all duty in life and in death—Him whose we are and to whom we belong, even though we should have made no promise.

In saying this I do not lay all under the necessity of making a full and entire confession of everything which they believe, even should they be required to do so. I am aware also of the measure observed by St. Paul, altho no man was ever more determined boldly to maintain the cause of the gospel as he ought. And hence it is not without cause our Lord promises to give us, on such an occasion, "a mouth and wisdom" (Luke xxi., 15); as if he had said, that the office of the Holy Spirit is not only to strengthen us to be bold and valiant, but also to give us prudence and discretion, to guide us in the course which it will be expedient to take.

The substance of the whole is, that those who are in such distress are to ask and obtain such prudence from above, not following their own carnal wisdom, in searching out for a kind of loop-hole by which to escape. There are some who tell us that our Lord Himself gave no answer to those who interrogated Him. But I rejoin, First, That this does not abolish the rule which He has given us to make confession of our faith when so required. (I Peter iii., 15.) Secondly, That He never used any disguise to save His life: and, Thirdly, That He never gave an answer so ambiguous as not to embody a sufficient testimony to all that He had to say; and that, moreover, He had already satisfied those who came to interrogate Him anew, with the view not obtaining information, but merely of laying traps to ensnare Him.

Let it be held, then, as a fixed point among all Christians, that they ought not to hold their life more precious than the testimony to the truth, inasmuch as God wishes to be glorified thereby. Is it in vain that He gives the name of witnesses (for this is the meaning of the word martyr) to all who have to answer before the enemies of the faith? Is it not because He wished to employ them for such a purpose? Here every one is not to look for his fellow, for God does not honor all alike with the call. And as we are inclined so to look, we must be the more on our guard against it. Peter having heard from the lips of our Lord Jesus (John xxi., 18) that he should be led in his old age where he would not, asked, What was to become of his companion John? There is not one among us who would not readily have put the same question; for the thought which instantly rises in our mind is, Why do I suffer rather than others? On the contrary, Jesus Christ exhorts all of us in common, and each of us in particular, to hold ourselves "ready," in order that according as He shall call this one or that one, we may march forth in our turn.

I explained above how little prepared we shall be to suffer martyrdom, if we be not armed with the divine promises. It now remains to show somewhat more fully what the purport and aim of these promises are—not to specify them all in detail, but to show the principal things which God wishes us to hope from Him, to console us in our afflictions. Now these things, taken summarily, are three. The first is, that inasmuch as our life and death are in His hand, He will preserve us by His might that not a hair will be plucked out of our heads without His leave. Believers, therefore, ought to feel assured into whatever hands they may fall, that God is not divested of the guardianship which He exercises over their persons. Were such a persuasion well imprinted on our hearts, we should be delivered from the greater part of the doubts and perplexities which torment us and obstruct us in our duty.

We see tyrants let loose: thereupon it seems to us that God no longer possesses any means of saving us, and we are tempted to provide for our own affairs as if nothing more were to be expected from Him. On the contrary, His providence, as He unfolds it, ought to be regarded by us as an impregnable fortress. Let us labor, then, to learn the full import of the expression, that our bodies are in the hands of Him who created them. For this reason He has sometimes delivered His people in a miraculous manner, and beyond all human expectation, as Shadrach, Meshach, and Abednego, from the fiery furnace, Daniel from the den of lions; Peter from Herod's prison, where he was locked, chained, and guarded so closely. By these examples He meant to testify that He holds our enemies in check, altho it may not seem so, and has power to withdraw us from the midst of death when He pleases. Not that He always does it; but in reserving authority to Himself to dispose of us for life and for death, He would have us to feel fully assured that He has us under His charge; so that whatever tyrants attempt, and with whatever fury they may rush against us, it belongs to Him alone to order our life.

If He permits tyrants to slay us, it is not because our life is not dear to Him, and held in a hundred times greater honor than it deserves. Such being the case, having declared by the mouth of David (Psalm cxvi., 13), that the death of the saints is precious in His sight, He says also by the mouth of Isaiah (xxvi., 21), that the earth will discover the blood which seems to be concealed. Let the enemies of the gospel, then, be as prodigal as they will of the blood of martyrs, they shall have to render a fearful account of it even to its last drop. In the present day, they indulge in proud derision while consigning believers to the flames; and after having bathed in their blood, they are intoxicated by it to such a degree as to count all the murders which they commit mere festive sport. But if we have patience to wait, God will show in the end that it is not in vain He has taxed our life at so high a value. Meanwhile, let it not offend us that it seems to confirm the gospel, which in worth surpasses heaven and earth.

To be better assured that God does not leave us as it were forsaken in the hands of tyrants, let us remember the declarations of Jesus Christ, when He says (Acts ix., 4) that He Himself is persecuted in His members. God had indeed said before, (Zech. ii., 8), "He who touches you touches the apple of mine eye." But here it is said much more expressly, that if we suffer for the gospel, it is as much as if the Son of God were suffering in person. Let us know, therefore, that Jesus Christ must forget Himself before He can cease to think of us when we are in prison, or in danger of death for His cause; and let us know that God will take to heart all the outrages which tyrants commit upon us, just as if they were committed on His own Son.

Let us now come to the second point which God declares to us in His promise for our consolation. It is, that He will so sustain us by the energy of His Spirit that our enemies, do what they may, even with Satan at their head, will gain no advantage over us. And we see how He displays His gifts in such an emergency; for the invincible constancy which appears in the martyrs abundantly and beautifully demonstrates that God works in them mightily. In persecution there are two things grievous to the flesh, the vituperation and insult of men, and the tortures which the body suffers. Now, God promises to hold out His hand to us so effectually, that we shall overcome both by patience. What He thus tells us He confirms by fact. Let us take this buckler, then, to ward off all fears by which we are assailed, and let us not confine the working of the Holy Spirit within such narrow limits as to suppose that He will not easily defeat all the cruelties of men.

Of this we have had, among other examples, one which is particularly memorable. A young man who once lived with us here, having been apprehended in the town of Tournay, was condemned to have his head cut off if he recanted, and to be burned alive if he continued steadfast to his purpose. When asked what he meant to do, he replied simply, "He who will give me grace to die patiently for His name, will surely give me grace to bear the fire." We ought to take this expression not as that of a mortal man, but as that of the Holy Spirit, to assure us that God is not less powerful to strengthen us, and render us victorious over tortures, than to make us submit willingly to a milder death. Moreover, we oftentimes see what firmness he gives to unhappy malefactors who suffer for their crimes. I speak not of the hardened, but of those who derive consolation from the grace of Jesus Christ, and by His means, with a peaceful heart, undergo the most grievous punishment which can be inflicted. One beautiful instance is seen in the thief who was converted at the death of our Lord. Will God, who thus powerfully assists poor criminals when enduring the punishment of their misdeeds, be so wanting to His own people, while fighting for His cause, as not to give them invincible courage?

The third point for consideration in the promises which God gives His martyrs is, the fruit which they ought to hope for from their sufferings, and in the end, if need be, from their death. Now, this fruit is, that after having glorified His Name—after having edified the Church by their constancy—they will be gathered together with the Lord Jesus into His immortal glory. But as we have above spoken of this at some length, it is enough here to recall it to remembrance. Let believers, then, learn to lift up their heads towards the crown of glory and immortality to which God invites them, thus they may not feel reluctant to quit the present life for such a recompense; and, to feel well assured of this inestimable blessing, let them have always before their eyes the conformity which they thus have to our Lord Jesus Christ; beholding death in the midst of life, just as He, by the reproach of the cross, attained to the glorious resurrection, wherein consists all our felicity, joy, and triumph.

ALEXANDER CAMPBELL

1788-1866

THE MISSIONARY CAUSE

BIOGRAPHICAL NOTE

ALEXANDER CAMPBELL, founder of the "Campbellites" or Disciples of Christ, was born in Ireland in 1788, and received his education in Glasgow University. In 1809 he emigrated to the United States and took charge of a Presbyterian congregation in Bethany, Va. He did not long remain in this pastorate, but proceeded to institute a sect based upon the abolition of all confessions and formularies and the acknowledgment of the text of the Holy Scriptures as the sole creed of the Church. In 1841 he founded Bethany College (Bethany, Va.), and remained its president until his death in 1866. In 1823 he founded the *Christian Baptist,* changed its name in 1829 to the *Millennial Harbinger,* but abandoned it three years before his death. He was a prolific controversial writer and published over fifty volumes, among which were hymn books and a translation of the New Testament.

He that winneth souls is wise.—Prov. xi., 30.

THE missionary cause is older than the material universe. It was celebrated by Job—the oldest poet on the pages of time.

Jehovah challenges Job to answer Him a few questions on the institutions of the universe. "Gird up now thy loins," said He; "and I will demand of thee a few responses. Where wast thou when I laid the foundations of the earth? Declare, if thou hast understanding. Who has fixt the measure thereof? Or who has stretched the line upon it? What are the foundations thereof? Who has laid the corner-stone thereof when the morning stars sang together, and all the sons of God shouted for joy? Who shut up the sea with doors when it burst forth issuing from the womb of eternity—when I made a cloud its garment, and thick darkness its swaddling band? I appointed its limits, saying, Thus far shalt thou come, but no farther; and here shall the pride of thy waves be stayed.

"Has the rain a father? Who has begotten the drops of the dew? Who was the mother of the ice? And the hoar-frost of heaven, who has begotten it? Can mortal man bind the bands of the Seven Stars, or loose the cords of Orion? Can he bring forth and commission the twelve signs of the Zodiac, or bind Arcturus with his seven sons?

"Knowest thou, oh man, the missionaries of the starry heavens? Canst thou lift up thy voice to the clouds, that abundance of waters may cover thee? Canst thou command the lightnings, so that they may say to thee, Here we are? Who can number the clouds in wisdom? Or who can pour out the bottles of heaven upon the thirsty fields?"

If such be a single page in the volume of God's physical missionaries, what must be its contents could we, by the telescope of an angel, survey one single province of the universe, of universes, which occupy topless, bottomless, boundless space!

We have data in the Bible, and, in the phenomena of the material universe, sufficient to authorize the assumption that the missionary idea circumscribes and permeates the entire area of creations.

Need we inquire into the meaning of a celestial title given to the tenantries of the heaven of heavens? But you all, my Christian brethren, know it. You anticipate me. The sweet poet of Israel told you long since, in his sixty-eighth ode, that the chariots of God are about twenty thousand of angels.[1]

And what is an angel but a messenger, a missionary? Hence the seven angels of the seven-churches in Asia were seven missionaries, or messengers, sent to John in his exile; and by these John wrote letters to the seven congregations in Asia.

Figuratively, God makes the winds and lightnings his angels, his messengers of wrath or of mercy, as the case may be.

But we are a missionary society—a society assembled from all points of the compass, assembled, too, we hope, in the true missionary spirit, which is the spirit of Christianity in its primordial conception. God Himself instituted it. Moses is the oldest missionary whose name is inscribed on the rolls of time.

He was the first divine missionary, and, if we except John the Baptist, he was the second in rank and character to the Lord Messiah Himself.

Angels and missionaries are rudimentally but two names for the same officers. But of the incarnate Word, God's only begotten Son, He says, "Thou art my son, the beloved, in whom I delight." And He commands the world of humanity to hearken to Him. He was, indeed, God's own special ambassador, invested with all power in heaven and on earth —a true, a real, an everlasting plenipotentiary, having vested in Him all the rights of God and all the rights of man. And were not all the angels of heaven placed under Him as His missionaries, sent forth to minister to the heirs of salvation?

His commission, given to the twelve apostles, is a splendid and glorious commission. Its preamble is wholly unprecedented—"All authority in heaven and on earth is given to me." In pursuance thereof, he gave commission to His apostles, saying, "Go, convert all the nations, immersing them into the name of the Father, and of the Son, and of the Holy Spirit; teaching them to observe all things whatever I have commanded you; and, lo, I am with you always, even to the end of the world." Angels, apostles and evangelists were placed under this command, and by Him commissioned as His ambassadors to the world.

The missionary institution, we repeat, is older than Adam—older than our earth. It is coeval with the origin of angels.

Satan had been expelled from heaven before Adam was created. His assault upon our mother Eve, by an incarnation in the most

subtle animal in Paradise, is positive proof of the intensity of his malignity to God and to man. He, too, has his missionaries in the whole area of humanity. Michael and his angels, or missionaries, are, and long have been, in conflict against the devil and his missionaries. The battle, in this our planet, is yet in progress, and therefore missionaries are in perpetual demand. Hence the necessity incumbent on us to carry on this warfare as loyal subjects of the Hero of our redemption.

The Christian armory is well supplied with all the weapons essential to the conflict. We need them all. "We wrestle not against flesh and blood, but against principalities, against powers, against the rulers of the darkness of this world, against wicked spirits in the regions of the air." Hence the need of having our "loins girded with the truth"; having on the breastplate of righteousness, our feet shod with the preparation to publish the gospel of peace, taking the shield of faith, the helmet of salvation and the sword of the Spirit, the Word of God, always praying and making supplication for our fellow-missionaries and for all saints.

The missionary fields are numerous and various. They are both domestic and foreign. The harvest is great in both. The laborers are still few, comparatively very few, in either of them.

The supply is not a tithe of the demand. The Macedonians cry, "Come over and help us;" "Send us an evangelist;" "Send us missionaries;" "The fields are large, the people are desirous, anxious, to hear the original gospel. What can you do for us?" Nothing! Nothing! My brethren, ought this so to be?

Schools for the prophets are wanting. But there is a too general apathy or indifference on the subject. We pray to the Lord of the harvest to send our reapers to gather it into His garner. But what do we besides praying for it? Do we work for it? Suppose a farmer should pray to the Lord for an abundant harvest next year, and should never, in seed-time, turn over one furrow or scatter one handful of seed: what would we think of him? Would not his neighbors regard him as a monomaniac or a simpleton? And wherein does he excel such a one in wisdom or in prudence who prays to the Lord to send out reapers—missionaries, or evangelists—to gather a harvest of souls, when he himself never gives a dollar to a missionary, or the value of it, to enable him to go into the field? Can such a person be in earnest, or have one sincere desire in his heart to effect such an object or purpose? We must confess that we could have no faith either in his head or in his heart.

The heavenly missionaries require neither gold nor silver, neither food nor raiment. Not so the earthly missionaries. They themselves,

---

[1] This is an exact literal version of *Rebotayim alphey shenan.* The Targum says, "The chariots of God are two myriads—and two thousand angels draw them." A myriad is 10,000—two myriads 20,000. "To know this," Adam Clarke says, "we must die."

their wives and children, demand both food and clothing, to say nothing of houses and furniture. Their present home is not

"The gorgeous city, garnish'd like a bride,
  Where Christ for spouse expected is to pass,
The walls of, jasper compass'd on each side,
  And streets all paved with gold, more bright than glass."

If such were the missionary's home on earth, he might, indeed, labor gratuitously all the days of his life. In an humble cottage—rather an unsightly cabin—we sometimes see the wife of his youth, in garments quite as unsightly as those of her children, impatiently waiting "their sire's return, to climb to his knees the envied kiss to share." But, when the supper table is spread, what a beggarly account of almost empty plates and dishes! Whose soul would not sicken at such a sight? I have twice, if not thrice, in days gone by, when travelling on my early missionary tours —over not the poorest lands nor the poorest settlements, either—witnessed some such cases, and heard of more.

I was then my own missionary, with the consent, however, of one church. I desired to mingle with all classes of religious society, that I might personally and truthfully know, not the theories, but the facts and the actualities, of the Christian ministry and the so-called Christian public. I spent a considerable portion of my time during the years 1812, '13, '14, '15, '16, traveling throughout western Virginia, Pennsylvania, and Ohio.

I then spent seven years in reviewing my past studies, and in teaching the languages and the sciences—after which I extended my evangelical labors into other States and communities, that I might still more satisfactorily apprehend and appreciate the *status,* or the actual condition, of the nominally and profest religious or Christian world.

Having shortly after my baptism connected myself with the Baptist people, and attending their associations as often as I could, I became more and more penetrated with the conviction that theory had usurped the place of faith, and that consequently, human institutions had been, more or less, substituted for the apostolic and the divine.

During this period of investigation I had the pleasure of forming an intimate acquaintance with sundry Baptist ministers, East and West, as well as with the ministry of other denominations. Flattering prospects of usefulness on all sides began to expand before me and to inspire me with the hope of achieving a long-cherished object—doing some good in the advocacy of the primitive and apostolic gospel—having in the year 1820 a discussion on the subject of the first positive institution enacted by the Lord Messiah, and in A. D. 1823 another on the same subject—

the former more especially on the subject and action of Christian baptism, the latter more emphatically on the design of that institution tho including the former two.

These discussions, more or less, embraced the rudimental elements of the Christian institution, and gave to the public a bold relief outline of the whole genius, spirit, letter and doctrine of the gospel.

Its missionary spirit, tho not formally propounded, was yet indicated, in these discussions; because this institution was the terminus of the missionary work. It was a component element of the gospel, as clearly seen in the commission of the enthroned Messiah. Its preamble is the superlative fact of the whole Bible. We regret, indeed, that this most sublime preamble has been so much lost sight of even by the present living generation. If we ask when the Church of Jesus Christ began or when the reign of the Heavens commenced, the answer, in what is usually called Christendom, will make it either to be contemporaneous with the ministry of John the Harbinger, or with the birth of the Lord Jesus Christ. We will find one of these two opinions almost universally entertained. The Baptists are generally much attached to John the Baptist; the Pedobaptists, to the commencement of Christ's public ministry. John the Baptist was the first Christian missionary with a very considerable class of living Baptists; the birth of Christ is the most popular and orthodox theory at the respective meridians of Lutheranism, Calvinism, and Arminianism.

But, by the more intelligent, the resurrection, or the ascension of the Lord Jesus Christ, is generally regarded as the definite commencement of the Christian age or institution.

Give us Paul's or Peter's testimony, against that of all theologians, living or dead. Let us look at the facts.

Did not the Savior teach His personal pupils, or disciples, to pray, "Thy kingdom" —more truthfully, "Thy reign—come"? Does any king's reign or kingdom commence with his birth? Still less with his death? Did not our Savior Himself, in person, decline the honors of a worldly or temporal prince? Did He not declare that His kingdom "is not of this world"? Did He not say that He was going hence, or leaving this world, to receive or obtain a kingdom? And were not the keys of the kingdom first given to Peter to open, to announce it? And did he not, when in Jerusalem, on the first Pentecost, after the ascension of the Lord Jesus, make a public proclamation, saying, "Let all the house of Israel know assuredly that God has made (or constituted) the identical Jesus of Nazareth, the son of Mary, both the Lord and the Christ, or the anointed Lord"?

Do kings reign before they are crowned?

Before they are anointed? There was not a Christian Church on earth, or any man called a Christian, until after the consecration and coronation of Jesus of Nazareth as the Christ of God.

The era of a son's birth was never, since the world began, the era of his reign or of the commencement of it. It is a strange fact, to me a wonderful fact, and, considering the age in which we live, an overwhelming fact, that we, as a community, are the only people on the checkered map of all Christendom, Greek, Roman, Anglican or American, that preach and teach that the commonly called Christian era is not the era or the commencement of the Christian Church or kingdom of the Lord Jesus the Christ.

The kingdom of the Christ could not antedate His coronation. Hence Peter, in announcing His coronation, after His ascension, proclaimed, saying, "Let all the house of Israel know assuredly that God has made—*touton ton Ieesoun*—the same, the identical Jesus whom you have crucified, both Lord and Christ"; or, in other words, has crowned Him the legitimate Lord of all. Then indeed His reign began. Then was verified the oracle uttered by the royal bard of Israel, "Jehovah said to my Jehovah"—or, "the Lord said to my Lord,"—"Sit thou on my right hand till I make thy foes thy footstool."

Hence He could say, and did say, to His apostles, "All authority in the heavens and on the earth is given to me." In pursuance thereof, "Go you into all the world, proclaim the gospel to the whole creation; assuring them that everyone who believes this proclamation and is immersed into the name of the Father, and of the Son, and of the Holy Spirit, shall be saved."

Here, then, the missionary field is declared to be the whole world—the broad earth. They were, as we are afterwards informed, to begin at the first capital in the land of Judea, then to proceed to Samaria, the capital of the ten tribes, and thence to the last domicile of man on earth.

There was, and there is still, in all this arrangement, a gracious and a glorious propriety.

The Jews had murdered the Messiah under the false charge of an impostor. Was it not, then, divinely grand and supremely glorious to make this awfully bloodstained capital the beginning, the fountain, of the gospel age and mission? Hence it was decreed that all the earth should be the parish, and all the nations and languages of earth the objects, and millions of them the subjects, of the redeeming grace and tender mercies of our Savior and our God.

What an extended and still extending area is the missionary field! There are the four mighty realms of Pagandom, of Papaldom, of Mohammedandom and of ecclesiastic Sectariandom. These are, one and all, essentially and constitutionally, more or less, not of the apostolic Christendom.

The divinely inspired constitution of the Church contains only seven articles. These are the seven hills, not of Rome, but of the true Zion of Israel's God. Paul's summary of them is found in the following words: "One body, one spirit, one hope, one Lord, one faith, one baptism, and one God and Father of all."

The clear perception, the grateful reception, the cordial entertainment of these seven divinely constructed and instituted pillars, are the alone sufficient, and the all-sufficient, foundation — the indestructible basis — of Christ's kingdom on this earth, and of man's spiritual and eternal salvation in the full enjoyment of himself, his Creator, his Redeemer, and the whole universe of spiritual intelligence through all the circles and the cycles of an infinite, an everlasting future of being and of blessedness.

The missionary spirit is, indeed, an emanation of the whole Godhead. God the Father sent His Son, His only begotten Son, into our world. The Son sent the Holy Spirit to bear witness through His twelve missionaries, the consecrated and Heaven-inspired apostles. They proclaimed the glad tidings of great joy to all people—to the Jews, to the Samaritans, to the Gentiles, of all nations, kindreds and tongues. They gave in solemn charge to others to sound out and proclaim the glad tidings of great joy to all people. And need we ask, is not the Christian Church itself, in its own institution and constitution, virtually and essentiallly a missionary institution? Does not Paul formally state to the Thessalonians in his first epistle that from them sounded out the Word of the Lord not only in Macedonia and in Achaia, but in every place?

No man can really or truthfully enjoy the spiritual, the soul-stirring, the heart-reviving honors and felicities of the Christian institution and kingdom, who does not intelligently, cordially and efficiently espouse the missionary cause.

In other words, he must feel, he must have compassion for his fellow man; and, still further, he must practically sympathize with him in communicating to his spiritual necessities as well as to his physical wants and infirmities. The true ideal of all perfection—our blest and blissful Redeemer—went about continually doing good—to both the souls and the bodies of his fellow men; healing all that were, in body, soul or spirit, opprest by Satan, the enemy of God and of man.

To follow his example is the grand climax of humanity. It is not necessary to this end that he should occupy the pulpit. There are, as we conceive, myriads of Christian men in the private walks of life, who never aspired to the "sacred desk," that will far outshine, in eternal glory and blessedness, hosts of the reverend, the boasted and the boastful right reverend occupants of the sacred desks of this our day and generation.

But Solomon has furnished our motto:— "He that winneth " or taketh "souls is wise" (Prov. xi. 30). Was he not the wisest of men, the most potent and the richest of kings, that ever lived? He had, therefore, all the means and facilities of acquiring what we call knowledge—the knowledge of men and things; and, consequently, the value of men and things was legitimately within the area of his understanding; or, in this case, we might prefer to say, with all propriety, within the area of his comprehension.

Need I say that comprehension incomparably transcends apprehension? Simpletons may apprehend, but only wise men can comprehend anything. Solomon's rare gift was, that both his apprehension and his comprehension transcended those of all other men, and gave him a perspicacity and promptitude of decision never before or since possest by any man. His oracles, indeed, were the oracles of God. But God especially gave to him a power and opportunity of making one grand experiment and development for the benefit of his living contemporaries, and of all posterity, to whom God presents his biography, his Proverbs and his Ecclesiastes.

"The winning of souls" is, therefore, the richest and best business, trade or calling, according to Solomn, ever undertaken or prosecuted by mortal man. Paul was fully aware of this, and therefore had always in his eye a "triple crown"—"a crown of righteousness," a "crown of life," a "crown of glory." And even in this life he had "a crown of rejoicing," in prospect of an exceeding and eternal weight of glory, imperishable in the heavens.

There is, too, a present reward, a present pleasure, a present joy and peace which the wisdom, and the riches, and the dignity, and the glory, and the honors of this world never did, never can, and consequently never will, confer on its most devoted and persevering votaries.

There is, indeed, a lawful and an honorable covetousness, which any and every Christian, man and woman, may cultivate and cherish.

Paul himself justifies the poetic license, when he says, "Covet earnestly the best gifts."

The best gifts in his horizon, however, were those which, when duly cultivated and employed, confer the greatest amount of profit and felicity upon others. We should, indeed, desire, even covet, the means and the opportunities of beatifying and aggrandizing one another with the true riches, the honors and

the dignities that appertain to the spiritual, the heavenly and the eternal inheritance.

But we need not propound to your consideration or inquiry the claims—the paramount, the transcendent claims—which our enjoyment of the gospel and its soul-cheering, soul-animating, soul-enrapturing influences present to us as arguments and motives to extend and to animate its proclamation by every instrumentality and means which we can legitimately employ, to present it in all its attractions and claims upon the understanding, the conscience and the affections of our contemporaries, in our own country and in all others, as far as our most gracious and bountiful Benefactor affords the means and the opportunities of co-operating with Him, in the rescue and recovery of our fellow men, who, without such means and efforts, must forever perish, as aliens and enemies, in heart and in life, to God and to His divinely-commissioned ambassador, the glorious Messiah.

We plead for the original apostolic gospel and its positive institutions. If the great apostles Peter and Paul—the former to the Jews and the latter to the Gentiles—announced the true gospel of the grace of God, shall we hesitate a moment on the propriety and the necessity, divinely imposed upon us, of preaching the same gospel which they preached, and in advocating the same institutions which they established, under the plenary inspiration and direction of the Holy Spirit? Can we improve upon their institutions and enactments? What means that singular imperative enunciated by the evangelical prophet Isaiah (Isa. viii.), "Bind up the testimony, seal the law among my disciples?" What were its antecedents? Hearken! The prophet had just foretold. He, the subject of this oracle, viz: "The desire of all nations," was coming to be a sanctuary; but not a sanctuary alone, but for a stone of stumbling and a rock of offense (as at this day) to both the houses of Israel—for a gin and for a snare to the inhabitants of Jerusalem.

The Church, therefore, of right is, and ought to be, a great missionary society. Her parish is the whole earth, from sea to sea, and from the Euphrates to the last domicile of man.

But the crowning and consummating argument of the missionary cause has not been fully presented. There is but one word, in the languages of earth, that fully indicates it. And that word indicates neither less nor more than what is represented—literally, exactly, perspicuously represented—by the word philanthropy. But this being a Greek word needs, perhaps in some cases, an exact definition. And to make it memorable we will preface it with the statement of the fact that this word is found but twice in the Greek original New Testament (Acts xxviii., 2, and

Titus iii., 4.). In the first passage this word is, in the common version, translated "kindness," and in the second, "love toward man." Literally and exactly, it signifies the love of man, objectively; but, more fully exprest, the love of one to another.

The love of God to man is one form of philanthropy; the love of angels to one man is another form of philanthropy; and the love of man to man, as such, is the true philanthropy of the law. It is not the love of one man to another man, because of favors received from him; this is only gratitude. It is not the love of one man to another man, because of a common country: this is mere patriotism. It is not the love of man to man, because of a common ancestry: this is mere natural affection. But it is the love of man to man, merely because he is a man. This is pure philanthropy. Such was the love of God to man as exhibited in the gift of His dearly beloved Son as a sin-offering for him. This is the name which the inspired writers of the New Testament give it. So Paul uses it, Titus iii. and iv. It should have been translated, "After that the kindness and philanthropy of God our Savior appeared." Again, Acts xxviii., 2, "The barbarous people of the Island of Melita showed us no little philanthropy. They kindled a fire for us on their island, because of the impending rain and the cold."

There are, indeed, many forms and demonstrations of philanthropy. For one good man another good man might presume to die. But the philanthropy of God to man incomparably transcends all other forms of philanthropy known on earth or reported from heaven.

While we were sinners, in positive and actual rebellion against our Father and our God, He freely gave up His only begotten and dearly beloved Son, as a sin-offering for us, and laid upon Him, or placed in His account, the sin, the aggregate sin, of the world. He became in the hand of His Father and our Father a sin-offering for us. He took upon Himself, and His Father "laid upon him, the iniquity of us all." Was ever love like this? Angels of all ranks, spirits of all capacities, still contemplate it with increasing wonder and delight.

This gospel message is to be announced to all the world, to men of every nation under heaven. And this, too, with the promise of the forgiveness of sins and of a life everlasting in the heavens, to everyone who will cordially accept and obey it.

WILLIAM B. CARPENTER

1841-1918

THE AGE OF PROGRESS

BIOGRAPHICAL NOTE

WILLIAM BOYD CARPENTER, English divine, was born in 1841 in Liverpool, educated at the Royal Institution and Cambridge University, where he was appointed Hulsean lecturer in 1878. After holding several curacies he was appointed vicar of Christ Church, Lancaster Gate, in 1879. He held also a canonry of Windsor until 1884, when he was consecrated bishop of Ripon. In 1887 he delivered the Bampton lectures. He has published a large number of works, among which may be reckoned "Commentary on Revelation" (1879); "Lectures on Preaching" (1895); and a "Popular History of the Church of England" (1900).

And the sons of the prophets said unto Elisha, Behold now, the place where we dwell with thee is too strait for us. Let us go, we pray thee, unto Jordan, and take thence every man a beam, and let us make a place there where we may dwell. And he answered, Go ye.—II Kings vi., 1, 2.

THERE are two conditions of real personal power in the world. One is that we should be able to look above this earth and see some heavenly light surrounding everything we meet. We call this, in ordinary language, asserting the power of insight, and it is that which redeems life from being regarded as commonplace. Everything is tinged with heavenliness for those who see heaven's light above all; and the possession of this power gives that dignity of conception to life which is one of the secrets of power. But there is another condition also, and that is that there shall be the strength of personal assertiveness. A man may be possest of never so much insight, and yet he may lack that robustness of personal character which can make itself felt among his fellows; he may, in fact, be deficient in the powers of personal action.

Now these two gifts Elisha possest. He possest the loftiness of insight. He had seen when his master was taken up the glimpse of the fiery chariot which took him into the heavens, and from that time forward his life was tinged with the consciousness of heaven. Nothing could be mean or low to a man who had beheld that first vision of God. This was, as it were, an enduring and abiding background of all his after-conceptions. So in the hour when it seemed as tho beleagured by armies and enemies, that there was no power of release, his eyes, as it were, were still open to behold the heavenly brightness about him. He possest also that power of personal assertiveness. Standing in front of the Jordan, he smote aside every difficulty which hindered him commencing his career.

But there is a third qualification still which is needed, in order that these two powers may be brought, as it were, into practical contact with life. Great men, it has been said by one of our own great teachers, are men who live very largely in their own age; that is to say, they are persons the drift and set of whose mind does not belong to the generation before themselves exactly, altho they may be possest of powers of insight, nor to the generation after their own age, but have much power of sympathy and comprehensiveness toward the interests and exigencies of their own time. They are men to use the phrase, who are in touch with their own age. And therefore it is, tho a man may be possest of so much insight that heavenly light breathes upon all things, tho he may have a certain robust assertiveness and energy of character, yet if he have no power of adjusting his capacities, so to speak, in language understood of the men among whom he moves, all that power will, for the practical purpose of life, be thrown away.

Elisha possest the two. Does he possess the third? Is he a man, in fact, who can make his influence felt among the men of his day? Is he in touch with his time? Can he be a man capable, not only of acting for himself, but capable, by that subtle and magical influence, of arousing the activity of others? For a man may, indeed, hold a position of isolated splendor, which may produce the admiration of the men of his day; but to be a real prophet, I take it, is to be able to merge largely our own individuality into the individualities of others, and to be not so much the cause of admiration as the cause of activity.

Now I think that the scene will explain to us that Elisha was largely possest of that gift. If you watch it you will see that here is a scene which has since then often been exhibited in the story of all great movements. One of the great conditions of life is the capacity to expand. Dead things may indeed crystallize into a sort of cold uniformity, but that which has life in it is always possest of expansive energy. Here are these sons of the prophets becoming conscious that the place where they dwell is too strait for them. It is a movement which, as it were, arises outside the prophet's suggestion; he is not the one who tells them that the place is too strait. They gather themselves together and say, "The place is too strait for us; let us go and build a larger and ampler habitation for ourselves." And immediately you watch him in the midst of these men whose minds are alive to the spirit of progress. He identifies himself with their aspirations; he is one with them in the movement; he does not coldly frown upon their glorious aspirations, which are from the extension of their own institutions, but rather makes himself one with them. Not only so. See how he allies himself to their individual life. He does not even dictate to them the whole method of the movement; each man shall be free, he says, to choose his beam. When they say, Let us go and select our own beam for our own habitation, be it so. He is not to frown down their individual efforts, but, at the same time, by going with them he preserves the coherence, as it were, of their work. He allows the freest scope of individual activity, but yet preserves them in the great unification of their work. And when the episode happens which often does happen in the story of great movements—when the hour comes when one man's heart is smitten through with despondency, when the work is still before him, but the power of carrying on the work has dropt from his hand, slipping into the stream which is ever ready to drown our best ambitions and endeavors—Elisha stands beside a man in despondency, cheers his spirit, which is overwhelmed by hopelessness, and restores to him hope, capacity, and power. I say this is a man who is, in a great sense, a true prophet of his day, not simply posing for personal admiration, not merely asserting himself and destroying the capabilities of those about him, but with that sweet flexibility and that wondrous firmness combined, which is capable of giving movement to the young life about him and at the same time drawing them into the one great purpose of existence.

And thus it seems to me that the scene spreads beyond its own age. It is a type of all great movements, and it gives us a fitting attitude of those who would direct and control such movements. Here is the prophet in relation to the idea of the age of progress. The place is too strait for us. It is not the cry of the Jewish Church only; it is the cry of all ages. "The place is too strait." You and I might say that is a vision of the growth of Christendom; the place is too strait. The little upper chamber at Jerusalem did not suffice for the three thousand converts. "The place is too strait," they are forced to exclaim. The limits of Judea are too small for the ever-extending energy of Christianity. Every land and every nationality must be brought within its sway, and the workers shall be as the workers in this scene, manifold. Here shall be men like St. Paul, who shall go, with a strong forensic sense of what the gospel is, to speak it to the hearts of men who need it, and lift them high above commonplace things. Here shall be one like St. John, reposing upon the bosom of his Lord, and able to unfold to them heavenly visions and the anticipations of the outgrowth and development of the world. Here is one who, like Origen shall collate, like Jerome shall translate, like Augustine shall expound, like the men of later ages shall preach the spirit of reformation. The place is too strait, but given to each man his individual freedom, the power and the expansion of the Church goes on.

But is it not true that while, on the one side, we might say that this is a glorious picture, untouched and untinged by any dark lines, the moment that we begin to look at it in its practical form we begin to see the difficulties of its development? Let us go unto Jordan, and let us take each man our own beam. As long as the expansion of the Church is in the direction of the increase of its numbers or accession of new territories, so long indeed the men who have had the spirit of zeal have been willing to sanction such extension. But there comes a time when the consciousness of its expansion does not move according to the line of numbers merely, but it moves according to the line of new institutions and of new thoughts. How, then, will it be received by those into whose hand is placed the responsibility of its guidance? "The place is too strait for us;" so they cried in the early Church when they found that Judaic institutions were too narrow for the spirit of Christianity. The new wine could not be left in old bottles. "The place is too strait for us;" so they cried when they found within the bosom of the medieval Church that there was not the opportunity for the expansion of their spiritual life and the development of their missionary energy. But has it always been true that the spirit of this religious zeal which longs for new developments and new departures has been received with the spirit of wisdom? You and I know full well that the history of the Church of Christ is the history of a thousand regrets. Did the medieval Church never regret the act by which it drove forth the Waldenses into schism? Has our Church never regretted the day when it looked askance at the work of John Wesley? You know full well, whatever might have been the feeling of earlier times, there is growing up among us a larger and wider spirit, catching—shall I say?—the true directing spirit which shone thus in the life of Elisha; and believing that it is possible after all that each man may have his function in life, and each man, choosing his beam, may in bearing that beam be building up the temple of God. But, alas! it is hard for men to believe it. Still, even now, the spirit of prejudice surrounds every aspect with which we regard life and Church movement. It is difficult for a man bred in one communion, for example, to believe in the types of saintship which have become the favorites of another; harder, perhaps, for men bred in the very heart of Rome to believe in the spirit of saintship which dwelt in the breast of Molinos; hard for those dwelling in the heart of Protestantism to understand Bonaventura or Xavier; hard for one who has been taught in Presbyterian lines to believe in that sanctity which descends to us as an heritage from Cosin and Ken; and difficult, perhaps, for Episcopalians to recognize the sanctity which dwelt in Richard Baxter and John Bunyan. . . .

You may believe that there is the danger of the Church—shall I say?—growing stereotyped in its forms, by checking the freedom of individual life. There is the danger, on the other side, of the Church, as it were, spreading itself in the aggregation of splendid individualities; and because men believe intensely in their own mission, because they can not but see that the beam which they are hewing down is one of paramount importance to take some place in supporting the temple of God, they are inclined to prefer the attitude of isolation. Is this wise, and is it well? Pardon me if I ask you to say that this spirit, if allowed to grow, is a spirit which, from its various aspects, is one which, by all means in our power, we ought to set our faces against. Our own beam is not the temple of God. Each move and form of religious thought is not comprehensive of the whole; but it is here where men, choosing their own beam, begin to believe in their own, and their own alone, and seek to impose that little thing of their own as tho it were an absolute necessity of every portion of God's Church, that you get the spirit of actual division. "The whole is greater than its part." If we could only bring the aphorisms of ordinary life into the bearings of the Church of God we should be happier. But, let me assure you, when a man has his beam, and tells me that that beam will be built into the temple of God, will support its roof, and perhaps be the very thing which will add new dignity to the splendid arch which will spring from it, I am content to accept it. Let him believe anything that will beautify and extend. But when he tells me that it is catholicity to believe in his beam being all, he simply, as it were, sins against the very thing he is seeking to maintain. It is a sign of intellectual mediocrity; it is the spirit of sectarianism; it is the spirit ultimately of skepticism. When a man believes that pious views, which have been found profitable to his own soul, are to be made the rule for the whole catholic Church; when he tells me that special hours for special services are essential for the well-being of all Christian souls; when he tells me that special attitudes in the house of God are essential to catholicity, it is intellectual mediocrity, as the brilliant French poet has written which can not comprehend anything beyond itself. It is a spirit of sectarianism; for what, I pray, do you mean by sectarianism, if it is not this spirit, that you exaggerate your own particular doctrine into such proportions as to make men feel that there is none other than that? You are of your own little Church, and you are doubtful of the rest of the world. That is the spirit of sectarianism, and that, if you understand it rightly, is the only fault of skepticism for to believe that God is to be narrowed down to the conception of such a thing as that, to believe that God's temple is to be brought down to the measure of your own little beam, is to believe with such a stunted growth, such a stunted conception of God, that it is practically denying Him altogether.

Sometimes I venture to think that we have lost faith in Christ altogether. We believe in a Church which can be manipulated by human wisdom, we believe in a Church which can be galvanized by organization, but we can not believe in a Church whose development is being overruled by the guiding spirit and eternal presence of Christ Himself. If you take a large view of Christianity the danger becomes yours. Some, indeed, hew down beams for the temple of God not themselves knowing of that temple into which they are placed; for I do believe that in the development of God's great world the efforts of earnest and honest men who know not indeed in what direction their efforts are tending will be found to have been real efforts for the promotion of something, for the bringing out of some truth, for the establishment of some truth by which the Church may live, on which the Church may build, of whom the whole building, fitly framed together and compacted by that which every joint supplies, shall thus grow into the holy temple of the Lord.

But the scene is not the scene merely of these activities uncrossed by a single reverse. Here is the accident, here is the time in which men begin to feel that their power has left them. One, in hewing down his beam, animated by a spirit of a little overeagerness, perhaps gifted with that egotism of his work which made him develop it more rapidly than that of his fellows, strikes too hard a blow, and the loose ax-head slips off the haft and falls into the stream. Immediately he is face to face with, and conscious of, that most painful consciousness which can ever visit the heart of man—the contradiction between the grandness of the work and the ideal of the work which he has to achieve and his own impotence. There is the beam, and all about me are the workers, and the house is to be built for the sons of the prophets. But here, in my hand I hold this simple haft, bereft of the power of doing my share in that great work. It is a picture which has been repeated often and often. Does there not come a time when we feel that the power, as it were, of things has forsaken us? There was a time when our creeds afforded us great delight. We believed in God; we believed in redemption; we believed in the Spirit which could guide human affairs; we moved to our work full of the exuberance of confidence in that faith. But behold, there has come a time when we, perhaps almost unconsciously, lose the very thing which has given us hope.

Now whenever a new doctrine or new truth has come up in the history of the Church, it has been held, in the first instance, by men who lived by it and tied their own lives to it. No power of that ax-head slipt off into life's stream. They knew what they were doing. When men brought out the doctrine of the inspiration of the Bible, they knew what they were doing; they hewed down the trees about them, and they really believed it. Their lives were created by this truth. So when they believed in the real presence of Christ, they believed that Christ was really present. It was no fiction. When they believed in the doctrine of justification by faith, they believed that God had taken them into His own hands, that God had grasped their lives, and God Himself was behind their lives. Truth was to them truth, and it was a consecrated thing; but remember that truth, which is a flower, has its roots there, and it is only as you grasp it by its roots it becomes true to you. Truth is not a thing of the intellect only; it descends into our moral nature, it grafts upon our affections and conscience; the moment I cut it away from it it ceases to be truth; it becomes dogma—for the sake of distinction. That is to say, the men of our age who do not live by that truth wish, as it were, to attach that truth to them; they wish to make it actually the cry of party. They stole the wand of the enchanter, but they had not the power of the enchanter. They knew that they had the flower, but the flower cut away from its moral root had no force and no vitality, and therefore it crystallizes it. Hence, the natural history of a doctrine is this: when men are taking it rightly, using it as for God, rightly handling it, it is a power in their hands. Taken up for their own purposes, for the purpose of satisfying an indolent understanding, for the purpose of evading the claims of God which other truths may be making upon their minds, it then becomes evacuated of its power; it is impotent, it is buried underneath the stream of constantly changing time.

And, then, how shall it be restored? By again, I say, being taken up out of the stream by the true handle. If you wish to restore the power of truth, you must see that it is the truth which has a claim upon your moral being. For just as we are told that the sun may pour down its beams eternally upon the face of the moon, burning and blistering with its rays its surface, and that there everything remains cold and frozen underneath those beams, because no sweet atmosphere can hold the sunbeams in its fold, so it is true that when you take truth and use it from its false side, it shall pour its brightest rays into your intellect, not the dry light which Bacon meant, but the false light which some substitute for it. You receive a true light upon your understanding, and there is no moral atmosphere upon your nature to embrace those sunbeams, to keep them and make them your own, and make them your life blood by their presence. If thus we take truth it becomes false to us, a buried and useless thing. But if you take truth from its moral side, and approach it from its moral and spiritual side, it shall again become a power in your nature.

When men believed in the inspiration of God and the Bible it was a power to them; but when this dropt down into a belief that every jot and tittle was part and parcel of God's inspiration, then they merely crystallized into a dogma what was a great and living truth. When men ask us, Are the doctrines of Christianity dead; are they played out? my answer is, They are dead to those who use them wrongly, as all truth is dead to those who have no moral love of truth—dead to those who will use them as charms and incantations, sewing them, as the Pharisees sewed some texts, into the border of their robes; dead, indeed, they are to those who are not making them part of their own life, but not dead to those who, tho they may not be able to formulate their view into any way that will satisfy a partizan section of Christianity, yet feel that to them the old inspiration is life. God's living voice will speak to them godlike in every line, to them because they believe in a Christ behind all these truths, and that these are but the endeavors of men to express the power of the living thought and voice of God. Then to them ordinances will live; a real presence will be about their path. Sacraments and ordinances will live because something lives behind them. They are not using them falsely but reverently, and truly God has spoken to their souls; He has put back the truths into their hearts by the handle of some new-found life.

It is the same with our own lives; often and often it happens that you feel life has lost its power and charm; its vigor was once great. I came up, for instance, into the midst of my fellows here, with all the enthusiasms of university life, and I rejoiced in them; but now, somehow or other, the novelty has gone away, and the interest has palled, and I do not care. Life has lost its meaning to me, and I do not feel that life is worth living at all. Yes, it is a contradiction in your own mind between the conception of life as in your nobler moments you form it and your own impotence. Has the ax-head gone? Has it slipt into the water? How can it be restored? The first thing a man discovers in his own impotence, is that the power which was in his hands was not his own.

It is only when you and I see this that we can take it up again. Take life, and make it the reason for indulgence; take amusements, and make them the instruments for mere enjoyment; take study, and make it the reason for mere pride; and you will find the ax-head will slip off. All the knowledge you possess will be like blinded knowledge, capable of being applied to nothing. But believe it to be your own, given you of God—these hands, this brain, this heart, God's, not your own; these ordinances of religion God's, not your own; these teachings of the Church in all ages God's varied voice, which, if heard aright, shall blend into one mold in your ears. Take it up as His, and not your own; lift up your life right reverently; bend as you receive it from His hand, who can alone give you the restored fulness of His powers. You are surrounded by workers; your mind is often disturbed among the many cries and many sounds; but believe it, each of you has your own beam, and God can put into your hand the weapon which you are to use in hewing it down. Go forward, and be not afraid.

THOMAS CHALMERS

1780-1847

THE EXPULSIVE POWER OF A NEW AFFECTION

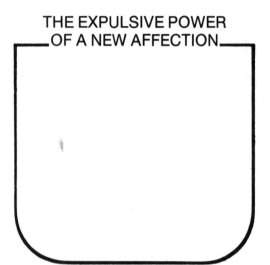

BIOGRAPHICAL NOTE

THOMAS CHALMERS, theologian, preacher and philanthropist, was born at Anstruther, near St. Andrews, Scotland, in 1780. In his thirty-fifth year he experienced a profound religious change and became a pronounced, tho independent, evangelical preacher. On being appointed to the Tron Church in Glasgow, he set about to face what he called "the home heathenism." During the week days he delivered his series of "Astronomical Discourses," in which he endeavored to bring science into harmony with Christianity. His "Commercial Discourses" were designed to Christianize the principles of trade. But he reduced pauperism chiefly by fighting against intemperance in Glasgow. On being transferred to St. John's Parish, the largest, but poorest in the city, he made Edward Irving his assistant. In 1828 he was called to the chair of theology in Edinburgh University.

But it was as a preacher that he exerted most influence by bringing the evangelical message into relations with the science, the culture, the thinking of his age. In doing this he carried his hearers away by the blazing force of his eloquence. Many times in his preaching he was "in an agony of earnestness," and one of his hearers speaks of "that voice, that face, those great, simple, living thoughts, those floods of resistless eloquence, that piercing, shattering voice!" He died in 1847.

Love not the world, neither the things that are in the world. If any man love the world, the love of the Father is not in him.—1 John ii., 15.

THERE are two ways in which a practical moralist may attempt to displace from the human heart its love of the world; either by a demonstration of the world's vanity, so as that the heart shall be prevailed upon simply to withdraw its regards from an object that is not worthy of it; or, by setting forth another object, even God, as more worthy of its attachment; so as that the heart shall be prevailed upon, not to resign an old affection which shall have nothing to succeed it, but to exchange an old affection for a new one. My purpose is to show, that from the constitution of our nature, the former method is altogether incompetent and ineffectual—and that the latter method will alone suffice for the rescue and recovery of the heart from the wrong affection that domineers over it. After having accomplished this purpose, I shall attempt a few practical observations.

Love may be regarded in two different conditions. The first is when its object is at a distance, and when it becomes love in a state of desire. The second is when its object is in possession, and then it becomes love in a state of indulgence. Under the impulse of desire, man feels himself urged onward in some path or pursuit of activity for its gratification. The faculties of his mind are put into busy exercise. In the steady direction of one great and engrossing interest, his attention is recalled from the many reveries into which it might otherwise have wandered; and the powers of his body are forced away from an indolence in which it else might have languished; and that time is crowded with occupation, which but for some object of keen and devoted ambition, might have driveled along in successive hours of weariness and distaste—and tho hope does not always enliven, and success does not always crown the career of exertion, yet in the midst of this very variety, and with the alternations of occasional disappointment, is the machinery of the whole man kept in a sort of congenial play, and upholden in that tone and temper which are most agreeable to it; insomuch that, if through the extirpation of that desire which forms the originating principle of all this movement, the machinery were to stop, and to receive no impulse from another desire substituted in its place, the man would be left with all his propensities to action in a state of most painful and unnatural abandonment. A sensitive being suffers, and is in violence, if, after having thoroughly rested from his fatigue, or been relieved from his pain, he continue in possession of powers without any excitement to these powers; if he possess a capacity of desire without having an object of desire; or if he have a spare energy upon his person, without a counterpart, and without a stimulus to call it into operation. The misery of such a condition is often realized by him who is retired from business, or who is retired from law, or who is even retired from the occupations of the chase, and of the gaming-table. Such is the demand of our nature for an object in pursuit, that no accumulation of previous success can extinguish it—and thus it is, that the most prosperous merchant, and the most victorious general, and the most fortunate gamester, when the labor of their respective vocations has come to a close, are often found to languish in the midst of all their acquisitions, as if out of their kindred and rejoicing element. It is quite in vain, with such a constitutional appetite for employment in man, to attempt cutting away from him the spring or the principle of one employment, without providing him with another. The whole heart and habit will rise in resistance against such an undertaking. The else unoccupied female, who spends the hours of every evening at some play of hazard, knows as well as you, that the pecuniary gain, or the honorable triumph of a successful contest, are altogether paltry. It is not such a demonstration of vanity as this that will force her away from her dear and delightful occupation. The habit can not so be displaced as to leave nothing but a negative and cheerless vacancy behind it—tho it may be so supplanted as to be followed up by another habit of employment, to which the power of some new affection has constrained her. It is willingly suspended, for example, on any single evening, should the time that is wont to be allotted to gaming be required to be spent on the preparations of an approaching assembly.

The ascendant power of a second affection will do what no exposition, however forcible, of the folly and worthlessness of the first, ever could effectuate. And it is the same in the great world. You never will be able to arrest any of its leading pursuits by a naked demonstration of their vanity. It is quite in vain to think of stopping one of these pursuits in any way else but by stimulating to another. In attempting to bring a worthy man, intent and busied with the prosecution of his objects, to a dead stand, you have not merely to encounter the charm which he annexes to these objects, but you have to encounter the pleasure which he feels in the very prosecution of them. It is not enough, then, that you dissipate the charm by your moral and eloquent and affecting exposure of its illusiveness. You must address to the eye of his mind another object, with a charm powerful enough to dispossess the first of its influence, and to engage him in some other prosecution as full of interest and hope and congenial activity as the former. It is this which stamps an impotency on all moral and pathetic declamation about the insignificance of the world. A man will no more consent to the misery of being without an object, because that object is a trifle, or of being without a pursuit, because that pursuit terminates in some frivolous or fugitive acquirement, than he will voluntarily submit himself to the torture, because that torture is to be of short duration. If to be without desire and without exertion altogether is a state of violence and discomfort, then the present desire, with its correspondent train of exertion, is not to be got rid of simply by destroying it. It must be by substituting another desire, and another line or habit of exertion in its place, and the most effectual way of withdrawing the mind from one object is not by turning it away upon desolate and unpeopled vacancy, but by presenting to its regards another object still more alluring.

These remarks apply not merely to love considered in its state of desire for an object not yet obtained. They apply also to love considered in its state of indulgence, or placid gratification, with an object already in possession. It is seldom that any of our tastes are made to disappear by a mere process of natural extinction. At least, it is very seldom that this is done through the instrumentality of reasoning. It may be done by excessive pampering, but it is almost never done by the mere force of mental determination. But what can not be thus destroyed, may be dispossest—and one taste may be made to give way to another, and to lose its power entirely as the reigning affection of the mind. It is thus that the boy ceases, at length, to be the slave of his appetite; but it is because a manlier taste has now brought it into subordination, and that the youth ceases to idolize pleasure; but it is because the idol of wealth has become the stronger and gotten the ascendency, and that even the love of money ceases to have the mastery over the heart of many a thriving citizen; but it is because, drawn into the whirl of city politics, another affection has been wrought into his moral system, and he is now lorded over by the love of power. There is not one of these transformations in which the heart is left without an object. Its desire for one particular object may be conquered; but as to its desire for having some one object or other, this is unconquerable. Its adhesion to that on which it has fastened the preference of its regards, can not willingly be overcome by the rending away of a simple separation. It can be done only by the application of something else, to which it may feel the adhesion of a still stronger and more powerful preference. Such is the grasping tendency of the human heart, that it must have a something to lay hold of—and which, if wrested away without the substitution of another something in its place, would leave a void and a vacancy as painful to the mind as hunger is to the natural system. It may be dispossest of one object, or of any, but it can not be desolated of all. Let there be a breathing and a sensitive heart, but without a liking and without affinity to any of the things that are around it, and in a state of cheerless abandonment, it would be alive to nothing but the burden of its own consciousness, and feel it to be intolerable. It would make no difference to its owner, whether he dwelt in the midst of a gay and a goodly world, or, placed afar beyond the outskirts of creation, he dwelt a solitary unit in dark and unpeopled nothingness. The heart must have something to cling to—and never, by its own voluntary consent, will it so denude itself of all its attachments that there shall not be one remaining object that can draw or solicit it.

The misery of a heart thus bereft of all relish for that which is wont to minister enjoyment, is strikingly exemplified in those who, satiated with indulgence, have been so belabored, as it were, with the variety and the poignancy of the pleasurable sensations that they have experienced, that they are at length fatigued out of all capacity for sensation whatever. The disease of ennui is more frequent in the French metropolis, where amusement is more exclusively the occupation of higher classes, than it is in the British metropolis, where the longings of the heart are more diversified by the resources of business and politics. There are the votaries of fashion, who, in this way, have at length become the victims of fashionable excess; in whom the very multitude of their enjoyments has at last extinguished their power of enjoyment; who, with the gratifications of art and nature at command, now look upon all that is around them with an eye of tastelessness; who, plied with the delights of sense and of splendor even to weariness, and incapable of higher delights, have come to the end of all their perfection, and, like Solomon of old, found it to be vanity and vexation. The man whose heart has thus been turned into a desert can vouch for the insupportable languor which must ensue, when one affection is thus plucked away from the bosom, without another to replace it. It is not necessary that a man receive pain from anything, in order to become miserable. It is barely enough that he looks with distaste to everything, and in that asylum which is the repository of minds out of joint, and where the organ of feeling as well as the organ of

intellect has been impaired, it is not in the cell of loud and frantic outcries where you will meet with the acme of mental suffering; but that is the individual who outpeers in wretchedness all his fellows, who throughout the whole expanse of nature and society meets not an object that has at all the power to detain or to interest him; who neither in earth beneath, nor in heaven above, knows of a single charm to which his heart can send forth one desirous or responding movement; to whom the world, in his eye a vast and empty desolation, has left him nothing but his own consciousness to feed upon, dead to all that is without him, and alive to nothing but to the load of his own torpid and useless existence.

We know not a more sweeping interdict upon the affections of nature, than that which is delivered by the apostle in the verse before us. To bid a man into whom there is not yet entered the great and ascendant influence of the principle of regeneration, to bid him withdraw his love from all the things that are in the world, is to bid him give up all the affections that are in his heart. The world is the all of a natural man. He has not a taste, nor a desire, that points not to a something placed within the confines of its visible horizon. He loves nothing above it, and he cares for nothing beyond it; and to bid him love not the world is to pass a sentence of expulsion on all the inmates of his bosom. To estimate the magnitude and the difficulty of such a surrender, let us only think that it were just as arduous to prevail on him not to love wealth, which is but one of the things in the world, as to prevail on him to set wilful fire to his own property. This he might do with sore and painful reluctance, if he saw that the salvation of his life hung upon it. But this he would do willingly if he saw that a new property of tenfold value was instantly to emerge from the wreck of the old one. In this case there is something more than the mere displacement of an affection. There is the overbearing of one affection by another. But to desolate his heart of all love for the things of the world without the substitution of any love in its place, were to him a process of as unnatural violence as to destroy all the things he has in the world, and give him nothing in their room. So if to love not the world be indispensable to one's Christianity, then the crucifixion of the old man is not too strong a term to mark that transition in his history, when all old things are done away, and all things are become new.

The love of the world can not be expunged by a mere demonstration of the world's worthlessness. But may it not be supplanted by the love of that which is more worthy than itself? The heart can not be prevailed upon to part with the world, by a simple act of resignation. But may not the heart be prevailed upon to admit into its preference another, who shall subordinate the world, and bring it down from its wonted ascendency? If the throne which is placed there must have an occupier, and the tyrant that now reigns has occupied it wrongfully, he may not leave a bosom which would rather detain him than be left in desolation. But may he not give way to the lawful Sovereign, appearing with every charm that can secure His willing admittance, and taking unto Himself His great power to subdue the moral nature of man, and to reign over it? In a word, if the way to disengage the heart from the positive love of one great and ascendant object is to fasten it in positive love to another, then it is not by exposing the worthlessness of the former, but by addressing to the mental eye the worth and excellence of the latter, that all old things are to be done away, and all things are to become new.

This, we trust, will explain the operation of that charm which accompanies the effectual preaching of the gospel. The love of God, and the love of the world, are two affections, not merely in a state of rivalship, but in a state of enmity, and that so irreconcilable that they can not dwell together in the same bosom. We have already affirmed how impossible it were for the heart, by any innate elasticity of its own, to cast the world away from it, and thus reduce itself to a wilderness. The heart is not so constituted, and the only way to dispossess it of an old affection is by the expulsive power of a new one. Nothing can exceed the magnitude of the required change in a man's character—when bidden, as he is in the New Testament, to love not the world; no, nor any of the things that are in the world—for this so comprehends all that is dear to him in existence as to be equivalent to a command of self-annihilation. But the same revelation which dictates so mighty an obedience places within our reach as mighty an instrument of obedience. It brings for admittance, to the very door of our heart, an affection which, once seated upon its throne, will either subordinate every previous inmate, or bid it away. Beside the world it places before the eye of the mind Him who made the world, and with this peculiarity, which is all its own—that in the gospel do we so behold God as that we may love God. It is there, and there only, where God stands revealed as an object of confidence to sinners—and where our desire after Him is not chilled into apathy by that barrier of human guilt which intercepts every approach that is not made to Him through the appointed Mediator. It is the bringing in of this better hope, whereby we draw nigh unto God —and to live without hope is to live without God, and if the heart be without God the world will then have all the ascendency. It is God apprehended by the believer as God in Christ who alone can dispost it from this as-

cendency. It is when He stands dismantled of the terrors which belong to Him as an offended lawgiver, and when we are enabled by faith, which is His own gift, to see His glory in the face of Jesus Christ, and to hear His beseeching voice, as it protests good-will to men, and entreats the return of all who will to a full pardon, and a gracious acceptance— it is then that a love paramount to the love of the world, and at length expulsive of it, first arises in the regenerating bosom. It is when released from the spirit of bondage, with which love can not dwell, and when admitted into the number of God's children, through the faith that is in Christ Jesus, the spirit of adoption is poured upon us—it is then that the heart, brought under the mastery of one great and predominant affection, is delivered from the tyranny of its former desires, and in the only way in which deliverance is possible. And that faith which is revealed to us from heaven, as indispensable to a sinner's justification in the sight of God, is also the instrument of the greatest of all moral and spiritual achievements on a nature dead to the influence, and beyond the reach of every other application.

Let us not cease then to ply the only instrument of powerful and positive operation, to do away from you the love of the world. Let us try every legitimate method of finding access to your hearts for the love of Him who is greater than the world. For this purpose let us, if possible, clear away that shroud of unbelief which so hides and darkens the face of Deity. Let us insist on His claims to your affection; and whether in the shape of gratitude, or in the shape of esteem, let us never cease to affirm that in the whole of that wondrous economy, the purpose of which is to reclaim a sinful world unto Himself, He, the God of love, so sets Himself forth in characters of endearment that naught but faith, and naught but understanding are wanting, on your part, to call forth the love of your hearts back again.

And here let me advert to the incredulity of a worldly man when he brings his own sound and secular experience to bear upon the high doctrines of Christianity, when he looks on regeneration as a thing impossible, when, feeling, as he does, the obstinacies of his own heart on the side of things present, and casting an intelligent eye, much exercised perhaps in the observation of human life, on the equal obstinacies of all who are around him, he pronounces this whole matter about the crucifixion of the old man, and the resurrection of a new man in his place, to be in downright opposition to all that is known and witnessed of the real nature of humanity. We think that we have seen such men, who, firmly trenched in their own vigorous and home-bred sagacity, and shrewdly regardful of all that passes before them through the week, and upon the scenes of ordinary business, look on that transition of the heart by which it gradually dies unto time, and awakens in all the life of a new-felt and ever-growing desire toward God, as a mere Sabbath speculation; and who thus, with all their attention engrossed upon the concerns of earthliness, continue unmoved, to the end of their days, among the feelings, and the appetites, and the pursuits of earthliness. If the thought of death, and another state of being after it, comes across them at all, it is not with a change so radical as that of being born again that they ever connect the idea of preparation. They have some vague conception of its being quite enough that they acquit themselves in some decent and tolerable way of their relative obligations; and that, upon the strength of some such social and domestic moralities as are often realized by him in whose heart the love of God has never entered, they will be transplanted in safety from this world, where God is the Being with whom, it may almost be said that, they have had nothing to do, to that world where God is the Being with whom they will have mainly and immediately to do throughout all eternity. They will admit all that is said of the utter vanity of time, when taken up with as a resting-place. But they resist every application made upon the heart of man, with the view of so shifting its tendencies that it shall not henceforth find in the interests of time all its rest and all its refreshment. They, in fact, regard such an attempt as an enterprise that is altogether aerial—and with a tone of secular wisdom, caught from the familiarities of every day of experience, do they see a visionary character in all that is said of setting our affections on the things that are above; and of walking by faith; and of keeping our hearts in such a love of God as shall shut out from them the love of the world; and of having no confidence in the flesh; and of so renouncing earthly things as to have our conversation in heaven.

Now, it is altogether worthy of being remarked of those men who thus disrelish spiritual Christianity, and, in fact, deem it an impracticable acquirement, how much of a piece their incredulity about the demands of Christianity, and their incredulity about the doctrines of Christianity, are with one another. No wonder that they feel the work of the New Testament to be beyond their strength, so long as they hold the words of the New Testament to be beneath their attention. Neither they nor anyone else can dispossess the heart of an old affection, but by the impulsive power of a new one—and, if that new affection be the love of God, neither they nor anyone else can be made to entertain it, but on such a representation of the Deity as shall draw the heart of the sinner toward Him. Now it is just

their belief which screens from the discernment of their minds this representation. They do not see the love of God in sending His Son into the world. They do not see the expression of His tenderness to men, in sparing Him not, but giving Him up unto the death for us all. They do not see the sufficiency of the atonement, or of the sufferings that were endured by Him who bore the burden that sinners should have borne. They do not see the blended holiness and compassion of the Godhead, in that He passed by the transgressions of His creatures, yet could not pass them by without an expiation. It is a mystery to them how a man should pass to the state of godliness from a state of nature—but had they only a believing view of God manifest in the flesh, this would resolve for them the whole mystery of godliness. As it is, they can not get quit of their old affections, because they are out of sight from all those truths which have influence to raise a new one. They are like the children of Israel in the land of Egypt, when required to make bricks without straw they cannot love God, while they want the only food which can aliment this affection in a sinner's bosom—and however great their errors may be, both in resisting the demands of the gospel as impracticable, and in rejecting the doctrines of the gospel as inadmissible, yet there is not a spiritual man (and it is the prerogative of him who is spiritual to judge all men) who will not perceive that there is a consistency in these errors.

But if there be a consistency in the errors, in like manner, is there a consistency in the truths which are opposite to them? The man who believes in the peculiar doctrines will readily bow to the peculiar demands of Christianity. When he is told to love God supremely, this may startle another, but it will not startle him to whom God has been revealed in peace, and in pardon, and in all the freeness of an offered reconciliation. When told to shut out the world from his heart, this may be impossible with him who has nothing to replace it—but not impossible with him who has found in God a sure and satisfying portion. When told to withdraw his affections from the things that are beneath, this were laying an order of self-extinction upon the man, who knows not another quarter in the whole sphere of his contemplation to which he could transfer them, but it were not grievous to him whose view had been opened to the loveliness and glory of the things that are above, and can there find, for every feeling of his soul, a most ample and delighted occupation. When told to look not to the things that are seen and temporal, this were blotting out the light of all that is visible from the prospect of him in whose eye there is a wall of partition between guilty nature and the joys of eternity—but he who believes that

Christ has broken down this wall finds a gathering radiance upon his soul, as he looks onward in faith to the things that are unseen and eternal. Tell a man to be holy—and how can he compass such a performance, when his fellowship with holiness is a fellowship of despair? It is the atonement of the cross reconciling the holiness of the lawgiver with the safety of the offender, that hath opened the way for a sanctifying influence into the sinner's heart, and he can take a kindred impression from the character of God now brought nigh, and now at peace with him. Separate the demand from the doctrine, and you have either a system of righteousness that is impracticable, or a barren orthodoxy. Bring the demand and the doctrine together, and the true disciple of Christ is able to do the one, through the other strengthening him. The motive is adequate to the movement; and the bidden obedience to the gospel is not beyond the measure of his strength, just because the doctrine of the gospel is not beyond the measure of his acceptance. The shield of faith, and the hope of salvation, and the Word of God, and the girdle of truth, these are the armor that he has put on; and with these the battle is won, and the eminence is reached, and the man stands on the vantage ground of a new field and a new prospect. The effect is great, but the cause is equal to it, and stupendous as this moral resurrection to the precepts of Christianity undoubtedly is, there is an element of strength enough to give it being and continuance in the principles of Christianity.

The object of the gospel is both to pacify the sinner's conscience and to purify his heart; and it is of importance to observe, that what mars the one of these objects mars the other also. The best way of casting out an impure affection is to admit a pure one; and by the love of what is good to expel the love of what is evil. Thus it is, that the freer gospel, the more sanctifying is the gospel; and the more it is received as a doctrine of grace, the more will it be felt as a doctrine according to godliness. This is one of the secrets of the Christian life, that the more a man holds of God as a pensioner, the greater is the payment of service that He renders back again. On the venture of "Do this and live," a spirit of fearfulness is sure to enter; and the jealousies of a legal bargain chase away all confidence from the intercourse between God and man; and the creature striving to be square and even with his creator is, in fact, pursuing all the while his own selfishness instead of God's glory; and with all the conformities which he labors to accomplish, the soul of obedience is not there, the mind is not subject to the law of God, nor indeed under such an economy ever can be. It is only when, as in the gospel, acceptance is bestowed as a

present, without money and without price, that the security which man feels in God is placed beyond the reach of disturbance, or that he can repose in Him as one friend reposes in another; or that any liberal and generous understanding can be established betwixt them, the one party rejoicing over the other to do him good, the other finding that the truest gladness of his heart lies in the impulse of a gratitude by which it is awakened to the charms of a new moral existence. Salvation by grace—salvation by free grace—salvation not of works, but according to the mercy of God, salvation on such a footing is not more indispensable to the deliverance of our persons from the hand of justice than it is to the deliverance of our hearts from the chill and the weight of ungodliness. Retain a single shred or fragment of legality with the gospel, and you raise a topic of distrust between man and God. You take away from the power of the gospel to melt and to conciliate. For this purpose the freer it is the better it is. That very peculiarity which so many dread as the germ of Antinomianism, is, in fact, the germ of a new spirit and a new inclination against it. Along with the lights of a free gospel does there enter the love of the gospel, which, in proportion as you impair the freeness, you are sure to chase away. And never does the sinner find within himself so mighty a moral transformation as when, under the belief that he is saved by grace, he feels constrained thereby to offer his heart a devoted thing, and to deny ungodliness.

To do any work in the best manner, you would make use of the fittest tools for it. And we trust that what has been said may serve in some degree for the practical guidance of those who would like to reach the great moral achievement of our text, but feel that the tendencies and desires of nature are too strong for them. We know of no other way by which to keep the love of the world out of our heart than to keep in our hearts the love of God— and no other way by which to keep our hearts in the love of God, than by building ourselves on our most holy faith. That denial of the world which is not possible to him that dissents from the gospel testimony, is possible, even as all things are possible, to him that believeth. To try this without faith is to work without the right tool or the right instrument. But faith worketh by love; and the way of expelling from the heart the love that transgresseth the law is to admit into its receptacles the love which fulfilleth the law.

Conceive a man to be standing on the margin of this green world, and that, when he looked toward it, he saw abundance smiling upon every field, and all the blessings which earth can afford scattered in profusion throughout every family, and the light of the sun sweetly resting upon all the pleasant habitations, and the joys of human companionship brightening many a happy circle of society; conceive this to be the general character of the scene upon one side of his contemplation, and that on the other, beyond the verge of the goodly planet on which he was situated, he could descry nothing but a dark and fathomless unknown. Think you that he would bid a voluntary adieu to all the brightness and all the beauty that were before him upon earth, and commit himself to the frightful solitude away from it? Would he leave its peopled dwelling places, and become a solitary wanderer through the fields of nonentity? If space offered him nothing but a wilderness, would he for it abandon the home-bred scenes of life and cheerfulness that lay so near, and exerted such a power of urgency to detain him? Would not he cling to the regions of sense, and of life, and of society? Shrinking away from the desolation that was beyond it, would not he be glad to keep his firm footing on the territory of this world, and to take shelter under the silver canopy that was stretched over it?

But if, during the time of his contemplation, some happy island of the blest had floated by, and there had burst upon his senses the light of surpassing glories, and its sounds of sweeter melody, and he clearly saw there a purer beauty rested upon every field, and a more heartfelt joy spread itself among all the families, and he could discern there a peace, and a piety, and a benevolence which put a moral gladness into every bosom, and united the whole society in one rejoicing sympathy with each other, and with the beneficent Father of them all. Could he further see that pain and mortality were there unknown, and above all, that signals of welcome were hung out, and an avenue of communication was made before him—perceive you not that what was before the wilderness, would become the land of invitation, and that now the world would be the wilderness? What unpeopled space could not do, can be done by space teeming with beatific scenes, and beatific society. And let the existing tendencies of the heart be what they may to the scene that is near and visible around us, still if another stood revealed to the prospect of man, either through the channel of faith or through the channel of his senses—then, without violence done to the constitution of his moral nature, may he die unto the present world, and live to the lovelier world that stands in the distance away from it.

THOMAS KELLY CHEYNE

1841-1915

─ FAITH AND PROGRESS ─

BIOGRAPHICAL NOTE

ORIEL professor of interpretation of Scripture in Oxford with the duties and emoluments annexed to a canon of Rochester; in 1908 almost retired from direct teaching; born in London, September 18, 1841; was educated at Merchant Taylors' School; Worcester College, Oxford; Göttingen; in 1866, he gained the chancellor's English essay prize, and in the same year took orders in the Anglican Church; from 1868 to 1882 he was fellow, and for part of that time lecturer of Baliol College; in 1889 became Bampton lecturer; visited America in 1897, and lectured in various library and academic centers on "Jewish Religious Life After the Exile"; a contributor to the "Polychrome Bible" (Edited by Professor Haupt), coeditor with Dr. J. S. Black of the "Encyclopedia Biblica," 1899-1903; author of "Bible Problems," "Traditions and Beliefs," "The Decline and Fall of the Kingdom of Judah," etc.

"And the Lord said unto Moses, 'Wherefore criest thou unto me? Speak unto the children of Israel tnat they go forward.'"—Exod. 14 : 15.

FAITH and progress go together; without faith there can be no sound progress. The soul of the Christian is, in fact, oftentimes the arena of a controversy between these two powers. Little Faith says: "Oh, that it were as in the ancient days, when God raised up great personalities to lead and to teach His people; or, better still, when He, whom the Christian tradition calls indifferently Son of man and Son of God, set up in human hearts a kingdom of love which is now hard prest by its foes." Little Faith, who is not to be confounded with No Faith, and has her own theory of the future of the Church, looks forward to a time when the Lord of Hosts will bring forth from His quiver another "polished shaft," another uniquely gifted leader, and so excuses herself for the want of a more cheerful courage, a more strenuous endeavor. Great Faith replies that that very prophecy to which allusion is made is spoken, not of any individual, but of the ideal Israel—the ideal Church, and that that very Moses, who is the type of extraordinary religious leaders and prophets, conceived the idea of a stage of developments when all true Israelites would be prophets, because in that day the Lord would have put His own Spirit upon each of them.

Too much converse with men of low ideals tends to give the advantage to the first of these vices; Israel by the Red Sea is the type of Little Faith; it needs a Moses to speak to the people that they go forward. But the type of Great Faith is Abraham, who, when he had been inwardly called, "went out," as the New Testament puts it, "not knowing whither he went."

Far be it from me to assert that any one of us can dictate the exact course which the movement of mankind shall take. If we believe that the host in which we are marching is not left to itself, but is being led to a goal which will realize our highest aspirations, we must neither rejoice overmuch at our temporary successes, nor be unduly disappointed at our temporary failures. We can not, for instance, by any personal efforts simply recall the past. Reactions which may appear to issue in a mere revival of past forms may really contain the germs of something to a large extent new both in form and in substance. To those who are unduly sad at the disappearance of much that was beautiful in the past, I may quote those words of

Richard Froude, the friend of Newman and brother of the well-known historian: "Mournest thou, poor soul? and thou wouldst yet call back the things which shall not, can not be? Heaven must be won, not dream'd; thy task is set; peace was not made for earth, nor rest for thee."

It is true, a heaven upon earth may seem a contradiction in terms. But it certainly is the dream or vision of heaven which encourages the worker to contend earnestly in the cause of progress, and it will at any rate mark our arrival at the end of a fresh stage in our march, when, in the words of Joel, "Your old men shall dream dreams, and your young men shall see visions." For must we not admit that when old men and young shall dream heavenly dreams, that is, and whatever be their earthly disguise, shall lead hidden lives in that ideal world whose center is God, the kingdom of heaven will be at hand?

"Your young men shall see visions." The visions of one age may not be quite those of another; the outlines of Utopia change. I will not be so rash as to attempt to describe all these visions. But there is, at any rate, one dream to which I should like to give a brief and loving mention—it is the dream to which that great seer among the poets, John Milton, gave the name of a "New Reformation." The shape which, according to him, the newly reformed religion should take does not concern us; it is the spirit of his words which has a permanent value. And when we try to provide a form for this spirit, it is surely the point of view of our own century that we must adopt. What then, more definitely, should be our point of view? It is that of men who have had a longer experience than the men of Milton's age. We—whether young or old, it matters not—represent not only the catholic movement but the evangelical, not merely the conservative side but the progressive. We do not contemptuously reject the traditions of the Church; we have studied them more deeply than Milton's generation could do, and we are aware of the spiritual treasures which they often contain. But we also do justice to the new facts of history, science, and Biblical criticism which the more fully awakened thought of the last two centuries has brought to light, to the new facts of a more advanced moral experience which we owe to Protestant or evangelical piety.

And what is our aim in this movement for a second Reformation? Some of us will say, To remove any hindrances which may exist to perfect sincerity of speech. It is this no doubt, but a broader and more general statement can be ventured upon; it is to strengthen the hold of religion upon modern men and women by presenting it to them in a simplified form. The fact is undeniable that many Christian people to-day stumble at the multitudinous forms with which, in the course of centuries, the historic Church has become laden. These forms were anciently, to educated people, the symbols of deep ideas, and it is these ideas, in so far as they are still felt to be truths, which need to be restated, and if the old meaning should not be simple or deep enough, then a new or partly new meaning must be substituted. A religion complicated with conceptions which are no longer intelligible can not suffice to the Church of Christ in this century. Indeed, we may seriously doubt whether a religion of a highly intellectual character ever did suffice to the whole Church of Christ. There were, in the olden times at least, two types of the Christian religion—the type which appealed to the poor and the suffering, and the type which supplied the wants of the intellectual minority. The question which now meets us is this: Whether, even for the intellectual of our day, a simpler form of religion would not be the most beneficial. And in favor of this view let us remember that the religion of Jesus Christ was preeminently a simple religion. In all things He appears to have been a lover of simplicity, but especially in religion. Those words of His, addrest to the busy and anxious-minded Martha, "Few things are needful," may be applied without violence to the religion which He taught and by which he lived.

I do not, of course, deny that deep, even if simple, ideas will always require intellectual gifts, denied to the multitude, for their complete appreciation. But I think that sometimes, at least, the experience of the Christian life has an effect on the intellect; that is, it clears up the mental vision, and suggests presentiments of deep truths. There must be some bridge of transition between the religion of the wise and that of the multitude. It is not for the intellectual impoverishment of the Christian religion that I plead, but for its simplification. It may take a long time to bring this about, but when all our old men dream this dream, and all our young men see this vision, it will only remain for some gifted church-leader to make it a reality. And meantime what is there to prevent the ordinary Christian from exercising the right and performing the duty of private judgment by simplifying his religion for himself, a task for which in these days the help of sincere thinkers and writers is so abundantly available? Is it not in your power to preach, not a superficial but a simple gospel, a gospel which makes a man strong to think, strong to do, and strong to bear?

There is a place for theology, not only in the circle of the sciences, but in the Christian Church. Those who pursue theology as a branch of knowledge can also, if they will, be ministers of the household of faith. It is essential that the great religious problems arising out of natural science and the criticism of the Bible should be treated by those who have equally at heart the truth of science and the truth of religion. Neither in our own nor in any following age will the former problems be finally solved, but partial and temporary solutions must, at any rate, be found, and we may live in hope that, by learning to understand each other, men of science and theologians will be enabled to cooperate in such partial solutions.

As for the difficulties arising from the other source—namely, the analytic criticism of the Bible—the remedy lies close at hand. The criticism of the Bible is now becoming more constructive, more synthetic than of old. There are a sufficient number of reasonably well-assured details to justify our taking in hand the preliminary history of the Christian religion. It is only as yet in an early stage, some branches of this great study being more advanced than others. Still it exists, and neither popes nor bishops can thrust it out of the Church. And what is it that makes synthetic criticism a religous remedy for the difficulties arising from the older analytic criticism? It is the fact that this study centers in what many students do not hesitate to call the rediscovery (to however limited an extent) of the personality of Jesus. That personality, according to them, was indeed partly influenced by the ideas and imaginations of the time, but it contained an element of strange originality, an originality derived not from the intellect but from personal religious experience. Even if you go no further, the new study (as I may in some sense call it) of the personality of the Lord Jesus ought to act as a purifier and preserver of Christian faith.

I have said that the object of the "New Reformation" is to strengthen the hold of religion upon modern men and women, by presenting it to them in a simplified form. Old forms of truth have to be restated, first of all, so as to be intelligible; next, so as to be in fuller harmony with the religion of Jesus; and lastly, so as not to conflict with views of nature and of the historical origin of the Bible, which we could not, even if we would, repudiate. The "New Reformation," then, makes an appeal to the intellect of the ordinary modern Christian. It is bound to do so, for the difficulties of such a person are largely intellectual. But it can not stop short here. It is bound also to appeal to the Christian conscience. Among those words of Jesus which stand at the head of our sacred forms are some which seem to cut at the root of

much in the existing social system. The Christian conscience acknowledges that these words are right, and that we ought to find some way of giving them effect. So that the "New Religious Reformation" is the ally of social reformation, tho it can not commit itself as a movement to more than great principles of action. But still more, the movement appeals to the Christian conscience, inasmuch as it demands a reformation or a new creation of the inner man. Christian people have to be stirred up—indeed, they want to be stirred up—to purer and nobler living, and those especially who wish, on intellectual grounds, to help this movement must first of all seek to be reformed, remade themselves.

But how, we may ask, can we succeed in realizing this high ambition—of simplifying and vitalizing religion? Not by mere endeavors on the part of individuals can religion be remade. There is a well-known, eloquent passage in which Milton has described his vision of the "New Reformation." He represents England as a Samson awaking out of his sleep, and shaking his invincible locks. Alas! our prophet was too forgetful of human weakness. England was destined to be taken captive by worse foes than the Philistines, and her blind poet learned to sympathize all too fully with the defeated champion. Not to Samson, proud of his natural strength, would I desire to compare the England of my vision, but to David, who overthrew the Philistine giant in the power of an invincible faith. And since the new England can only arise through the earnest efforts of a continually renewed band of reformers, I would compare these reformers (as I see them in vision) to the multitude of the first Christian disciples who were of one heart and one soul. The *odium theologicum* has become proverbial. Let it not slip in among those who contend together against the formalism and conventionalism of religion. "Let nothing be done through strife or vain glory." Let the privilege of working together be a sufficient reward, and let differences of mere opinion be no bar to perfect communion of soul. There is room in the movement which I contemplate for great variety of opinion; indeed, variety is indispensable for success. Let us respect one another's individualities, and not seek to recast the workers in one mold. Our methods and opinions may differ in some points; but our aim is one, and our spirit is one. We are modern men, and desire to speak in modern speech to men of our own age. The difficulties of our undertaking may be great, but those who have dreamed our dream, and seen our vision, are conscious of an inner voice which says, "Speak unto the children of Israel that they go forward."

JOHN CHRYSOSTOM

347-407

EXCESSIVE GRIEF AT THE DEATH OF FRIENDS

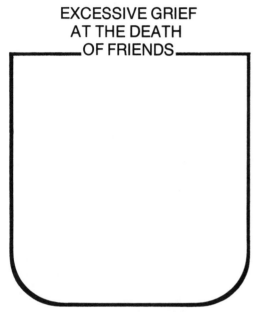

BIOGRAPHICAL NOTE

CHRYSOSTOM (that is, "Of the Golden Mouth") was a title given to John, Archbishop of Constantinople. He was born of a patrician family at Antioch about 347, and owed much to the early Christian training of his Christian mother, Anthusa. He studied under Libanius, and for a time practised law, but was converted and baptized in 368. He made a profound study of the Scriptures, the whole of which, it is said, he learned to repeat by heart.

Like Basil and Gregory he began his religious life as a hermit in the desert. After six years he returned to Antioch, where he gained reputation as the greatest preacher in the Eastern Church. Raised to the metropolitan See of Constantinople in 397, his fulminations against the corruptions of the court caused him to be banished, after a stormy ministry of six years. He was recalled in response to popular clamor, but removed again, and shortly after died, in 407. He was a great exegete, and showed a spirit of intellectual liberty which anticipated modern criticism. Sermons to the number of one thousand have been attributed to him.

But I would not have you to be ignorant, brethren, concerning them which are asleep, that ye sorrow not.
—I Thess. iv., 13.

WE have occupied four days in explaining to you the parable of Lazarus, bringing out the treasure that we found in a body covered with sores; a treasure, not of gold and silver and precious stones, but of wisdom and fortitude, of patience and endurance. For as in regard to visible treasures, while the surface of the ground shows only thorns and briers, and rough earth, yet, let a person dig deep into it, abundant wealth discovers itself; so it has proved in respect to Lazarus. Outwardly, wounds; but underneath these, unspeakable wealth; a body pining away, but a spirit noble and wakeful. We have also seen an illustration of that remark of the apostle's —in proportion as the outward man perishes, the inward man is renewed.

It would, indeed, be proper to address you to-day, also, on this same parable, and to enter the lists with those heretics who censure the Old Testament, bringing accusations against the patriarchs, and whetting their tongues against God, the Creator of the universe. But to avoid wearying you and reserving this controversy for another time, let us direct the discourse to another subject; for a table with only one sort of food produces satiety, while variety provokes the appetite. That it may be so in regard to our preaching, let us now, after a long period, turn to the blest Paul; for very opportunely has a passage from the apostle been read to-day, and the things which are to be spoken concerning it are in harmony with those that have lately been presented. Hear, then, Paul this day proclaiming—"I would not have you to be ignorant concerning them which are asleep, that ye sorrow not even as others which have no hope." The parable of Lazarus is the evangelical chord; this passage is the apostolic note. And there is concord between them; for we have, on that parable, said much concerning the resurrection and the future judgment, and our discourse now recurs to that theme; so that, tho it is on apostolic ground we are now toiling, we shall here find the same treasure. For in treating the parable, our aim was to teach the hearers this lesson, that they should regard all the splendors of the present life as nothing, but should look forward in their hopes, and daily reflect on the decisions which will be here-after pronounced, and on that fearful judgment, and that Judge who can not be deceived. On these things Paul has counseled us to-day in the passages which have been read to us. Attend, however, to his own words—"I would not have you to be ignorant, brethren, concerning them which are asleep, that ye sorrow not, even as others which have no hope. For if we believe that Jesus died and rose again, even so them also which sleep in Jesus will God bring with him."—I Thess. iv., 13, 14.

We ought here, at the outset, to inquire why, when he is speaking concerning Christ, he employs the word death; but when he is speaking of our decease he calls it sleep, and not death. For he did not say, Concerning them that are dead: but what did he say? "Concerning them that are asleep." And again—"Even so them also which sleep in Jesus will God bring with Him." He did not say, Them that have died. Still again—"We who are alive and remain unto the coming of the Lord shall not prevent them that sleep." Here, too, he did not say—Them that are dead; but a third time, bringing the subject to their remembrance, for the third time called death a sleep. Concerning Christ, however, he did not speak thus; but how? "For if we believe that Jesus died." He did not say, Jesus slept, but He died. Why now did he use the term death in reference to Christ, but in reference to us the term sleep? For it was not casually, or negligently, that he employed this expression, but he had a wise and great purpose in so doing. In speaking of Christ, he said death, so as to confirm the fact that Christ had actually suffered death; in speaking of us, he said sleep, in order to impart consolation. For where resurrection had already taken place, he mentions death with plainness; but where the resurrection is still a matter of hope, he says sleep, consoling us by this very expression, and cherishing our valuable hopes. For he who is only asleep will surely awake; and death is no more than a long sleep.

Say not a dead man hears not, nor speaks, nor sees, nor is conscious. It is just so with a sleeping person. If I may speak somewhat paradoxically, even the soul of a sleeping person is in some sort asleep; but not so the soul of a dead man; that is awake.

But, you say, a dead man experiences corruption, and becomes dust and ashes. And what then, beloved hearers? For this very reason we ought to rejoice. For when a man is about to rebuild an old and tottering house, he first sends out its occupants, then tears it down, and rebuilds anew a more splendid one. This occasions no grief to the occupants, but rather joy; for they do not think of the demolition which they see, but of the house which is to come, tho not yet seen. When God is about to do a similar work, he destroys our body, and removes the soul which was dwelling in it as from some house, that he may build it anew and more splendidly, and again bring the soul into it with greater glory. Let us not, therefore, regard the tearing down, but the splendor which is to succeed.

If, again, a man has a statue decayed by rust and age, and mutilated in many of its parts, he breaks it up and casts it into a furnace, and after the melting he receives it again in a more beautiful form. As then the dissolving in the furnace was not a destruction but a renewing of the statue, so the death of our bodies is not a destruction but a renovation. When, therefore, you see as in a furnace our flesh flowing away to corruption, dwell not on that sight, but wait for the recasting. And be not satisfied with the extent of this illustration, but advance in your thoughts to a still higher point; for the statuary, casting into the furnace a brazen image, does not furnish you in its place a golden and undecaying statue, but again makes a brazen one. God does not thus; but casting in a mortal body formed of clay, he returns to you a golden and immortal statue; for the earth, receiving a corruptible and decaying body gives back the same, incorruptible and undecaying. Look not, therefore, on the corpse, lying with closed eyes and speechless lips, but on the man that is risen, that has received glory unspeakable and amazing, and direct your thoughts from the present sight to the future hope.

But do you miss his society, and therefore lament and mourn? Now is it not unreasonable, that, if you should have given your daughter in marriage, and her husband should take her to a distant country and should there enjoy prosperity, you would not think the circumstance a calamity, but the intelligence of their prosperity would console the sorrow occasioned by her absence; and yet here, while it is not a man, nor a fellow servant, but the Lord Himself who has taken your relative, that you should grieve and lament?

And how is it possible, you ask, not to grieve, since I am only a man? Nor do I say that you should not grieve: I do not condemn dejection, but the intensity of it. To be dejected is natural; but to be overcome by dejection is madness, and folly, and unmanly weakness. You may grieve and weep; but give not way to despondency, nor indulge in complaints. Give thanks to God, who has taken your friend, that you have the opportunity of honoring the departed one, and of dismissing him with becoming obsequies. If you sink under depression, you withhold honor from the departed, you displease God who has taken him, and you injure yourself;

but if you are grateful, you pay respect to him, you glorify God, and you benefit yourself. Weep, as wept your Master over Lazarus, observing the just limits of sorrow, which it is not proper to pass. Thus also said Paul —"I would not have you to be ignorant concerning them which are asleep, that ye sorrow not as others who have no hope. Grieve," says he; "but not as the Greek, who has no hope of a resurrection, who despairs of a future life."

Believe me, I am ashamed and blush to see unbecoming groups of women pass along the mart, tearing their hair, cutting their arms and cheeks—and all this under the eyes of the Greeks. For what will they not say? What will they not declare concerning us? Are these the men who reason about a resurrection? Indeed! How poorly their actions agree with their opinions! In words, they reason about a resurrection: but they act just like those who do not acknowledge a resurrection. If they fully believed in a resurrection, they would not act thus; if they had really persuaded themselves that a deceased friend had departed to a better state, they would not thus mourn. These things, and more than these, the unbelievers say when they hear those lamentations. Let us then be ashamed, and be more moderate, and not occasion so much harm to ourselves and to those who are looking on us.

For on what account, tell me, do you thus weep for one departed? Because he was a bad man? You ought on that very account to be thankful, since the occasions of wickedness are now cut off. Because he was good and kind? If so, you ought to rejoice; since he has been soon removed, before wickedness had corrupted him, and he has gone away to a world where he stands even secure, and there is no reason even to mistrust a change. Because he was a youth? For that, too, praise Him that has taken him, because he has speedily called him to a better lot. Because he was an aged man? On this account, also, give thanks and glorify Him that has taken him. Be ashamed of your behavior at a burial. The singing of psalms, the prayers, the assembling of the (spiritual) fathers and brethren—all this is not that you may weep, and lament, and afflict yourselves, but that you may render thanks to Him who has taken the departed. For as when men are called to some high office, multitudes with praises on their lips assemble to escort them at their departure to their stations, so do all with abundant praise join to send forward, as to greater honor, those of the pious who have departed. Death is rest, a deliverance from the exhausting labors and cares of this world. When, then, thou seest a relative departing, yield not to despondency; give thyself to reflection; examine thy conscience;

cherish the thought that after a little while this end awaits thee also. Be more considerate; let another's death excite thee to salutary fear; shake off all indolence; examine your past deeds; quit your sins, and commence a happy change.

We differ from unbelievers in our estimate of things. The unbeliever surveys the heavens and worships them, because he thinks them a divinity; he looks to the earth and makes himself a servant to it, and longs for the things of sense. But not so with us. We survey the heavens and admire Him that made them; for we do not believe them to be a god, but a work of God. I look on the whole creation, and am led by it to the Creator. He looks on wealth, and longs for it with earnest desire; I look on wealth, and contemn it. He sees poverty, and laments; I see poverty, and rejoice. I see things in one light; he in another. Just so in regard to death. He sees a corpse, and thinks of it as a corpse; I see a corpse, and behold sleep rather than death. And as in regard to books, both learned persons and unlearned see them with the same eyes, but not with the same understanding—for to the unlearned the mere shapes of letters appear, while the learned discover the sense that lies within those letters—so in respect to affairs in general, we all see what takes place with the same eyes, but not with the same understanding and judgment. Since, therefore, in all other things we differ from them, shall we agree with them in our sentiments respecting death?

Consider to whom the departed has gone, and take comfort. He has gone where Paul is, and Peter, and the whole company of the saints. Consider how he shall arise, with what glory and splendor. Consider that by mourning and lamenting thou canst not alter the event which has occurred, and thou wilt in the end injure thyself. Consider whom you imitate by so doing, and shun this companionship in sin. For whom do you imitate and emulate? The unbelieving, those who have no hope; as Paul has said—"That ye sorrow not, even as others who have no hope." And observe how carefully he expresses himself; for he does not say, Those who have not the hope of a resurrection, but simply, Those who have no hope. He that has no hope of a future retribution has no hope at all, nor does he know that there is a God, nor that God exercises a providential care over present occurrences, nor that divine justice looks on all things. But he that is thus ignorant and inconsiderate is more unwise than a beast, and separates his soul from all good; for he that does not expect to render an account of his deeds cuts himself loose from all virtue, and attaches himself to all vice. Considering these things, therefore, and reflecting on the folly and stupidity of the heathen, whose associates we become by our lamentations for the dead, let us avoid this conformity to them. For the apostle mentions them for this very purpose, that by considering the dishonor into which thou fallest, thou mightest recover thyself from this conformity, and return to thy proper dignity.

And not only here, but everywhere and frequently, the blest Paul does the same. For when he would dissuade from sin, he shows with whom we become associated by our sins, that, being touched by the character of the persons, thou shouldest avoid such companionship. To the Thessalonians, accordingly, he says, Let every one "possess his vessel in sanctification and honor, not in the lust of concupiscence, even as the Gentiles which know not God." And again—"Walk not as the other Gentiles in the vanity of their mind." Thus also here—"I would not have you to be ignorant, brethren, concerning them which are asleep, that ye sorrow not even as others who have no hope." For it is not the nature of things, but our own disposition, which makes us grieve; not the death of the departed, but the weakness of those who mourn.

We ought, therefore, to thank God not only for the resurrection, but also for the hope of it; which can comfort the afflicted soul, and bid us be of good cheer concerning the departed, for they will again rise and be with us. If we must have anguish, we should mourn and lament over those who are living in sin, not over those who have died righteously. Thus did Paul; for he says to the Corinthians—"Lest when I come to you God shall humble me among you and that I shall bewail many." He was not speaking of those who had died, but of those who had sinned and had not repented of the lasciviousness and uncleanness which they had committed; over these it was proper to mourn. So likewise another writer admonishes, saying—"Weep over the dead, for the light has failed; and weep over the fool, for understanding has failed" (Eccles. xxii., 10). Weep a little for the dead; for he has gone to his rest; but the fool's life is a greater calamity than death. And surely if one devoid of understanding is always a proper object of lamentation, much more he that is devoid of righteousness and that has fallen from hope toward God. These, then, let us bewail; for such bewailing may be useful. For often while lamenting these, we amend our own faults; but to bewail the departed is senseless and hurtful. Let us not, then, reverse the order, but bewail only sin; and all other things, whether poverty, or sickness, or untimely death, or calumny, or false accusation, or whatever human evil befalls us, let us resolutely bear them all. For these calamities, if we are

watchful, will be the occasions of adding to our crowns.

But how is it possible, you ask, that a bereaved person, being a man, should not grieve? On the contrary, I ask, how is it that being a man he should grieve, since he is honored with reason and with hopes of future good? Who is there, you ask again, that has not been subdued by this weakness? Many, I reply, and in many places, both among us and among those who have died before us. Job, for instance; the whole circle of his children being taken away, hear what he says —"The Lord gave; the Lord hath taken away; blessed be the name of the Lord." A wonderful saying, even when merely heard; but if you examine it closely, your wonder will greatly increase.

For consider; Satan did not take merely half and leave half, or take the larger number and leave the rest; but he gathered all the fruit, and yet did not prevail in uprooting the tree; he covered the whole sea with waves, and yet did not overwhelm the bark; he despoiled the tower of its strength, and yet could not batter it down. Job stood firm, tho assailed from every quarter; showers of arrows fell, but they did not wound him. Consider how great a thing it was, to see so many children perish. Was it not enough to pierce him to the quick that they should all be snatched away?—altogether and in one day; in the flower of life; having shown so much virtue; expiring as by a stroke of vengeance; that after so many sorrows this last should be inflicted; that the father was fond of them, and that the deceased were worthy of his affection. When a man loses vicious children, he does indeed suffer grief, but not intense grief; for the wickedness of the departed does not allow the sorrow to be poignant. But when children are virtuous, an abiding wound is inflicted, the remembrance is indelible, the calamity is inconsolable; there is a double sting, from nature, and from the virtuous character of the departed.

That Job's children were virtuous, appears from the fact that their father was particularly solicitous in regard to them, and rising up offered sacrifices in their behalf, fearing lest they might have committed secret sins; and no consideration was more important in his esteem than this. Not only the virtue of the children is thus shown, but also the affectionate spirit of the father. Since, therefore, the father was so affectionate, showing not only a love for them which proceeded from nature, but that also which came from their piety, and since the departed were thus virtuous, the anguish had a threefold intensity. Still further; when children are torn away separately, the suffering has some consolation; for those that are left alleviate the sorrow over the departed; but when the whole circle is gone, to what one of all his numerous children can the childless man now look?

Besides these causes of sorrow, there was a fifth stroke. What was that? That they were all snatched away at once. For if in the case of those who die after three or five days of sickness, the women and all the relatives bewail this most of all, that the deceased was taken away from their sight speedily and suddenly, much more might he have been distrest, when thus deprived of all, not in three days, or two, or one, but in one hour! For a calamity long contemplated, even if it be hard to bear, may fall more lightly through this anticipation; but that which happens contrary to expectation and suddenly is intolerable.

Would you hear of a sixth stroke? He lost them all in the very flower of their age. You know how very overwhelming are untimely bereavements, and productive of grief on many scores. The instance we are contemplating was not only untimely, but also violent; so that here was a seventh stroke. For their father did not see them expire on a bed, but they are all overwhelmed by the falling habitation. Consider then; a man was digging in that pile of ruins, and now he drew up a stone, and now a limb of a deceased one; he saw a hand still holding a cup, and another right hand placed on the table, and the mutilated form of a body, the nose torn away, the head crusht, the eyes put out, the brain scattered, the whole frame marred, and the variety of wounds not permitting the father to recognize the beloved countenances. You suffer emotions and shed tears at merely hearing of these things: what must he have endured at the sight of them? For if we, so long after the event, can not bear to hear of this tragedy, tho it was another man's calamity, what an adamant was he to look on these things, and contemplate them, not as another's, but his own afflictions! He did not give way to dejection, nor ask, "What does this mean? Is this the recompense for my kindness? Was it for this that I opened my house, that I might see it made the grave of my children? Did I for this exhibit every parental virtue, that they should endure such a death?" No such things did he speak, or even think; but steadily bore all, tho bereaved of them after bestowing on them so much care. For as an accomplished statuary framing golden images adorns them with great care, so he sought properly to mold and adorn their souls. And as a husbandman assiduously waters his palm-trees, or olives, inclosing them and cultivating them in every suitable way; so he perpetually sought to enrich each one's soul, as a fruitful olive, with increasing virtue. But he saw the trees overthrown by the assault of the evil spirit, and exposed on the earth, and enduring that miserable kind of death; yet he uttered no reviling word, but rather blest God, thus giving a deadly blow to the devil.

Should you say that Job had many sons, but that others have frequently lost their only sons, and that his cause of sorrow was not equal to theirs, you say well; but I reply, that Job's cause of sorrow was not only equal, but far greater. For of what advantage was it to him that he had many children? It was a severer calamity and a more bitter grief to receive the wound in many bodies.

Still, if you wish to see another holy man having an only son, and showing the same and even greater fortitude, call to mind the patriarch Abraham, who did not indeed see Isaac die, but, what was much more painful, was himself commanded to slay him, and did not question the command, nor repine at it, nor say, "Is it for this thou hast made me a father, that thou shouldest make me the slayer of my son? Better it would have been not to give him at all, than having given him thus to take him away. And if thou choosest to take him, why dost thou command me to slay him and to pollute my right hand? Didst thou not promise me that from this son thou wouldst fill the earth with my descendants? How wilt thou give the fruits, then, if thou pluck up the root? How dost thou promise me a posterity, and yet order me to slay my son? Who ever saw such things, or heard of the like? I am deceived; I have been deluded." No such thing did he say, or even think; he said nothing against the command, he did not ask the reasons; but hearing the Word—"Take thy son, thine only son whom thou lovest, and carry him up to one of the mountains which I shall show thee," he complied so readily as even to do more than was commanded. For he concealed the matter from his wife, and he left the servants at the foot of the Mount in ignorance of what was to be done, and ascended, taking only the victim. Thus not unwillingly, but with promptness, he obeyed the command. Think now what it was, to be conversing alone with his son, apart from all others, when the affections are the more fervently excited, and attachment becomes stronger; and this not for one, or two, but for several days. To obey the command speedily would have been wonderful; but not so wonderful as, while his heart was burdened and agitated for many days, to avoid indulging in human tenderness toward his son. On this account God appointed for him a more extended arena, and a longer racecourse, that thou mightest the more carefully observe his combatant. A combatant he was indeed, contending not against a man, but against the force of nature. What language can describe his fortitude? He brought forward his son, bound him, placed him on the wood, seized the sacrificial knife, was just on the point of dealing the stroke. In what manner to express myself properly, I know not; he only would know, who did these things. For no language can describe how it happened that his hand did not become torpid, that the strength of his nerves did not relax, that the affecting sight of his son did not overpower him.

It is proper here, too, to admire Isaac. For as the one obeyed God, so did the other obey his father; and as the one, at God's bidding him to sacrifice, did not demand an account of the matter, so the other, when his father was binding him and leading him to the altar, did not say, "Why art thou doing this?"—but surrendered himself to his father's hand. And then was to be seen a man uniting in his own person the father and the sacrificing priest; and a sacrifice offered without blood, a whole burnt offering without fire, an altar representing a type of death and the resurrection. For he both sacrificed his son and he did not sacrifice him. He did not sacrifice him with his hand, but in his purpose. For God gave the command, not through desire to see the flowing of the blood, but to give you a specimen of steady purpose, to make known throughout the world this worthy man, and to instruct all in coming time that it is necessary to prefer the command of God before children and nature, before all things, and even life itself. And so Abraham descended from the Mount, bringing alive the martyr Isaac. How can we be pardoned then, tell me, or what apology can we have, if we see that noble man obeying God with so much promptness and submitting to Him in all things, and yet we murmur at His dispensations? Tell me not of grief, nor of the intolerable nature of your calamity; rather consider how in the midst of bitter sorrow you may yet rise superior to it. That which was commanded to Abraham was enough to stagger his reason, to throw him into perplexity, and to undermine his faith in the past. For who would not have then thought that the promise which had been made him of a numerous posterity was all a deception? But not so Abraham. And not less ought we

to admire Job's wisdom in calamity; and particularly, that after so much virtue, after his alms and various acts of kindness to men, and tho aware of no wrong either in himself or his children, yet experiencing so much affliction, affliction so singular, such as had never happened even to the most desperately wicked, still he was not affected by it as most men would have been, nor did he regard his virtue as profitless, nor form any ill-advised opinion concerning the past.

By these two examples, then, we ought not only to admire virtue, but to emulate and imitate it. And let no one say these were wonderful men. True, they were wonderful and great men. But we are now required to have more wisdom than they, and than all who lived under the Old Testament. For "except your righteousness exceed that of the Scribes and Pharisees, ye shall not enter into the kingdom of heaven." Gathering wisdom, then, from all quarters, and considering what we are told concerning a resurrection and concerning these holy men, let us frequently recite it to our souls, not only when we are actually in sorrow, but also while we are free from distress. For I have now addrest you on this subject, tho no one is in particular affliction, that when we shall fall into any such calamity, we may, from the remembrance of what has been said, obtain requisite consolation. As soldiers, even in peace, perform warlike exercises, so that when actually called to battle and the occasion makes a demand for skill, they may avail themselves of the art which they have cultivated in peace; so let us, in time of peace, furnish ourselves with weapons and remedies, that whenever there shall burst on us a war of unreasonable passions, or grief, or pain, or any such thing, we may, well armed and secure on all sides, repel the assaults of the evil one with all skill, and wall ourselves round with right contemplations, with the declarations of God, with the examples of good men, and with every possible defense. For so shall we be able to pass the present life with happiness, and to attain to the kingdom of heaven, through Jesus Christ, to whom be glory and dominion, together with the Father and the Holy Spirit, forever and ever. Amen.

WILLIAM NEWTON CLARKE

1841-1912

THE CHRISTIAN DOCTRINE OF SALVATION

BIOGRAPHICAL NOTE

Ex-Professor of Christian theology, Colgate University; born at Cazenovia, N. Y., December 2, 1841; graduated Colgate (then Madison) University, 1861; Hamilton Theological Seminary, 1863; received the degree of D.D. from Colgate in 1878; Yale, 1900; University of Chicago, 1901; pastor of Baptist churches in Keene, N. H., 1863-69; Newton Centre, Mass., 1869-80; Montreal, Quebec, 1880-83; Hamilton, N. Y., 1887-90; professor of Toronto Baptist College, 1883-87; author of "Commentary on the Gospel of Mark," "Outline of Christian Theology," "What Shall We Think of Christianity?" "Can I Believe in God the Father?" "A Study of Christian Missions," "The Use of the Scriptures in Theology," "The Christian Doctrine of God."

"For by grace are ye saved through faith, and that not of yourselves, it is the gift of God."—Ephes. 2 : 8.

I CAN scarcely claim this as a text, for I shall not unfold it. But I shall be quite content if I can declare as the Christian doctrine the truth which it utters, that salvation is the gift of God. The more gladly do I use it, also, because it sounds, to my ear at least, more like a strain from a psalm of praise than like a calm prose sentence; and surely, the Christian doctrine of salvation ought to ring like a strain from a psalm of praise.

The Christian doctrine of salvation must be identical at heart with the Christian message of salvation. Through all ages the Church of Christ has been a herald, a preacher of salvation to the world, and her work of heralding has continued till now. She has made her proclamation with joy, for she bears a glorious message; the sermon has been a psalm, and the preaching praise. In another department of thought she has her doctrine of salvation. She distinguishes it from her message, but yet the two are one. There can be no real message that differs from the doctrine, and there can be no real doctrine that differs from the message.

As for the proclamation, the Church of Christ is preaching salvation until now, and is preaching what she has always preached. The message of salvation has been always the same. One conception of salvation has been held always, everywhere and by all. In all parts and periods of Christendom the message has been unchanging, and the doctrine one. One salvation has been preached by Paul and Apollos, by Irenæus, Origen, Tertullian and Chrysostom, by Augustine and Pelagius, by Anselm and Abelard, Aquinas and Scotus, by Francis, Dominic and Bernard, by Luther and Loyola, by Calvin and Arminius, by Pascal and George Fox, by the Westminster Divines and John Wesley, by Edwards, Chalmers and Schleiermacher, by Maurice, Newman and Spurgeon, by Leo XIII, Martineau, Phillips Brooks and Joseph Parker. And the patriarchs of the Greek Church, and the popes, bishops and parish priests of the Roman Church, and the pastors and teachers of the Protestants in all lands, have heralded the same: and the common salvation that these many men have preached is the one that is to be described and held forth to-day, in the Christian doctrine of salvation.

It must be confest that this claim of unity and identity is not obviously true, and that there are many reasons why some may hear it without believing it. But that is because many influences have conspired to hide the one reality under numerous disguises. Sometimes it almost seems as if infinite labor and pains must have been expended in pursuit of this most undesirable end. One doctrine has been variously clad: or, one reality has been identified with so many special interpretations, and associated with so many forms of definition and defense, as to deceive even those who were most anxious to discover the unity. Swift tho it must be, the mention of some of these diversifying causes will best prepare us for considering the doctrine which remained the same beneath them all.

In the early Christian circle, the message and doctrine of salvation were often exprest in forms of Jewish symbolism; and ever since there have been those who took the Jewish symbolism for the very substance of the doctrine. Later, again and again, the message and the doctrine were wrought out in forms of philosophy—forms that must needs change with the changing human thought; and there have always been those who could not carry the thought of the salvation without some forms of philosophy. Many different elements in Christian faith and doctrine have been held as indispensable to the doctrine of salvation, and held so piously and firmly as to divide their advocates sometimes into bands that almost forgot that they all believed in one salvation. Some have been sure that the Christian doctrine of salvation could not exist apart from certain views of the Trinity, or some special interpretation concerning the two natures in the person of Christ. Some have tied the doctrine in with a definite teaching on original sin. Some have thought that salvation required a scheme of universal predestination, with particular redemption and atonement limited to the elect; others that it required a strong doctrine of free will in man and universal grace in God. Some could not conceive of the doctrine of salvation except as a doctrine of substitutionary atonement, with penal justice satisfied in the death of Christ; others, repudiating this, have insisted upon a doctrine of due vindication to God's government as righteous, while sin was forgiven; while others still have thought it enough if Christ by life and death revealed the saving love of God and brought His appeal to a sinful world. Some have bound to the doctrine a strict limitation of gracious opportunity to this present life; while others have felt that a real doctrine of divine salvation naturally carried with it a larger hope. The majority of all who have proclaimed salvation have held that it was mediated through the ministrations of the Church, the kindly mother who provides for her children's needs; and these have insisted upon the helpfulness,

or the indispensableness, of the sacraments as channels of saving grace. But others have insisted that personal faith is the direct and only indispensable approach to God, even ruling sacraments out as intruders. Many have declared that the doctrine of salvation could not stand without the inspiration of the Scriptures, and have built the theoretical possibility of salvation upon assent to all that the Bible teaches, if not to all that it contains; while some have seemed to represent that the message and doctrine of salvation must carry alone the whole substance of systematic theology. Most especially has it been held that every conception of salvation that a Biblical writer recorded must be regarded as permanently authoritative, and any true doctrine of salvation must be able to accommodate within itself every expression of Scripture on the subject, in its original meaning. So there have been many variant heralds of salvation, and they have been so intense and conscientious and loyal in their devotion to what they deemed sacred because divine as almost to lose sight of what they held in common. When nearer approach to unity was really made, still the one doctrine has been emphasized on so many sides, and exhibited in so many lights, as scarcely to be recognizable as one. In very loyalty to salvation itself, the message of salvation has been burdened with many a heavy weight, and the doctrine of salvation has been deprived of much of its singleness and simplicity.

Yet no one of the matters that have now been mentioned is indispensable to the message of salvation, or belongs necessarily to the doctrine. We may all deny this statement in our controversial moods, and consider it dangerously latitudinarian; but in our more reflective and religious moods, when we are remembering how men have been saved, our denial fades into silence, for we thankfully own that men have found salvation in connection with every one of the many forms of proclamation and of doctrine. The interpretations are various, and conflicting, too, but the one gospel of Christ is the power of God unto salvation, under them all. One of them may be truer than another, and more harmonious with the central spirit and life, and in selecting the truest we may differ still; but the indispensable doctrine of salvation must be something that lies back of all the modes and theories and is operative through them all. There must be one central truth about salvation, from which the vitality of all the various preachings of salvation proceeds.

This one doctrine of salvation is not difficult of discovery. Certainly, it should not be, for it is the common stock of all the preachings, the doctrines and the experiences. What all the preachers have preached and all the teachers have taught ought not to be so very hard to find. It is written in the New Testament, and has been sung in the hymns of the singing Church in all ages. Our Lord Jesus Himself declared it, and the apostles, and the fathers, and the popes, and the reformers, and the ministers who offered salvation this morning. This common doctrine I must now endeavor to present. Would that I could do this more worthily, but the defect will be in me, not in the doctrine. It will be a defect in spirit and power, not in abundance of divine material lying ready to my hand.

To begin with, the doctrine of salvation presupposes a world of sin. Not, indeed, that everything in the world is sin, for it is not. Mankind has solid virtues, and has always possest enough of good to hold together in its life, and move on from lower to higher things. Nevertheless, it is a world of sin. We find a race in which evil has become established and entrenched, and a common life in which evil battles with good, too often getting the advantage. The race is made up of individuals who do not live up to themselves, but fall below their best, and violate their acknowledged law. When they look fairly at themselves they are self-condemned. Sin brings its blame, and its shame; it makes men guilty, before their own consciences and before God. It brings innumerable woes, it paralyzes good endeavor, it corrupts religion, it makes man a tormentor or a corrupter of his fellow, it banishes the consolations of life, it darkens the future. No indictment of its evils that we could make would be complete. However, it came so, here, as a matter of plain fact, is a race involved in sin. Degrees of involvement vary, but the fact is everywhere.

This is one of the great realities of existence for us. It is a reality that we were born to and always live with. This is a sinful world, and we are sinful beings. Sometimes we do not feel it, but whether we feel it or not, it is true. Along with our sin, we bear the burden of our feebleness, our immaturity, our imperfectness; and our sinfulness is the chief hindrance to our rising out of this into our normal life.

Over against this fact stands another— God. He is a living God. The Christian doctrine knows nothing of any lifeless, mindless order. It does not admit that men, such as they are, are the highest moral beings that exist. God lives. As for God, He is good. In the Christian doctrine, God is such a being as Jesus Christ declared; He is such a God as we know when we have truly learned of Jesus. Seen by the light of the Christian revelation, God is utterly without fault, and full of all goodness. He is more full of the glory of holiness than the sun is of light, and from Him streams forth love unlimited, as from the sun streams warmth. He is an absolutely good and perfect God. We can attribute to Him traits that imply the littleness and faultiness of our humanity, but if we do so we are wrong—they are not His. He is all good, and good in the supreme degree.

It would be no help or comfort to set these two great realities over against each other, if they were separate. A sinful world would be no better for a good God if He were apart and had no care for it. But the Christian doctrine of salvation consists in the announcement of what God is to the world and the world to Him. God loves the world. It is His, for He caused it to be, and He bears it upon His heart. God is love, and toward this sinful world His love flows out. Love is desire to bless, and to possess; and all language whereby we describe human love is colorless and powerless in comparison with the great reality of the love of God, who desires to bless and to possess this humanity which He has brought into being. Sin has not extinguished or dimmed this love; it has only given it the form of desire to save. He who loves a sinful world must desire to deliver it from sin. This desire the Christian doctrine of salvation declares to be characteristic of the living God.

With these realities in mind, who can doubt what will come next? A divine movement, an act, a work. The heart of love leaps forth to meet the need. By the divine love the holy God and the sinful world are brought together. There is a mission of love to the world. The source of it is in God, who, out of His own free and unbought compassion, does this deed. "God so loved the world that he gave his only begotten Son, that whosoever believeth in him might not perish, but have eternal life."

How can I set forth the meaning and power of this mission of love from God to men? The Christian preaching of salvation is preaching of Jesus Christ. God sent Him, God gave Him, and in His coming God came to save—this has always been the burden of the glad announcement. But all that we have in Him, no preaching has ever told. In Him has been seen the revelation of God, and the God revealed. He that hath seen Him hath seen the Father. In Him besides seeing God we see man also, for He is the type of all human excellence. Thus God and man at once we behold in Him, and from Him we learn how to conceive of both. But He has come to save us. Jesus Christ is the expression of that love of God whereby He seeks to save. In Him God's redeeming love and strength are brought to the weakness and need of sinful men. Christ is the living evidence—nay, Christ is the very act—of that redeeming love which bursts all barriers and finds the needy. Love is sacrifice—and if God is love, then God is sacrifice; sacrifice for the objects of His love is of His nature. So the mission of Christ means sacrifice—sacrifice not in the pictorial manner that innumerable altars have exhibited, but sacrifice in the real sense that befits the heart of God. His saving love is love unto the uttermost, love inexhaustible. Unto death it goes, even the death of the cross, for the sins of the world. Whenever any Christian has preached salvation, in any church or sect or school of thought, he has pointed to the cross for perfect and constraining evidence of the unfathomable love wherewith God hath loved us in Christ, and the certainty of salvation for all who receive and appropriate His grace.

A sinful world, a holy Savior-God, a mission of saving love in Christ—these are the elements of the Christian message of salvation and of the doctrine also. But these are not the whole of it. What comes of it? This is not salvation; there must be a result in us men. If Christ dies for our salvation, we must receive the benefit in our experience. Accordingly there goes out a power from the living God for fulfilment of his saving purpose. There comes the living Holy Spirit, God in us, to accomplish what was intended. Men are to be saved.

And what is it to be saved? We have not defined our chief word as yet, but we can define it. When a man is saved, according to the Christian doctrine, at least three things occur in his case. First, he is brought out of that wrong and distorted relation to God in which sin has placed him; he receives the unspeakably precious gift of divine forgiveness, and comes to his true place as a child of his heavenly Father. He is brought home, henceforth to live at home with his God. Next, under the influence of divine love and truth, by the touch of the divine Spirit, the man is brought out of the character that sin has fastened upon him. He is new-made, and made such as he ought to be. Not at a stroke, but stroke by stroke, step by step, the change comes about. The graces of right character and the powers that transform conduct take hold upon him, and he becomes what a man ought to be, in godliness and manliness, in purity and truth and helpfulness, in brotherly kindness and righteousness among men. And, third, all this is done in the field not of his mortality, but of his immortality, so that he is brought out of the destiny that sin would make for him. Now there is born to him a living hope of endless salvation, growing ever nearer to perfection in the endless life unseen. Thus the man is saved. In all these, his relation to God, his character and his destiny, the man is normalized—if we wish a modern name for it; he is made what he ought to be, and set about the life that normally belongs to a human being. And this,

according to the Christian doctrine of salvation, is the work of God upon a man. It is not mere growth, or evolution; it is the gift and operation of the living God, wherein He claims for His own the creature who is His by right. Therefore, since God is in it all, salvation makes a religious man; and at the same time it makes a right ethical man. The ethical and the religious go hand in hand, and in both God is the inspiration.

One thing must be added, implied already, but not always set in its true place in the doctrine of salvation. No man liveth unto himself. The saved man is the Lord's, Christ's, and therefore lives for what Christ lived for; namely, for the good of others. Modern study has wrought out the doctrine that man is not merely an individual, but a social being, whose very personality implies relations with other human beings. Yet this doctrine is not modern. There has been a long period of excessive and hurtful individualism; it may be that now the doctrine of Jesus Christ is coming to its own. If he receives the full Christian salvation, the new man finds his place in the kingdom of God, and lives his life in the great world, filling his place among men as a child of God. His entire life is the field upon which his salvation is to be lived out. Salvation is salvation to service, out of selfishness into the life of love. And thus it is plain how salvation may be more than an individual experience. There is a salvation for society, as well as for the individual. The world, the race, can in this high sense be normalized by the grace of God, as well as the single person; and nothing less than this is the purpose of the God of the world in becoming Savior.

And this one word must still be added to the description: there is no one form of experience in which alone this salvation can be realized. In the many types of mankind and the many modes of life, "God fulfils himself in many ways." He must, if He is to work His will. His salvation demands nothing but its own reality. Modes and forms may vary, as they must; and tho the modes and forms be so various that we men can scarcely recognize the unity, still the one salvation may proceed in power. God is too great to insist upon unessential things, and great enough to work His one work in a thousand ways. Therefore it is that His salvation has free course. He was saving men before Christ came, on the same principle as now; and He alone knows how wide is the range of His gracious work among the sinful sons of men. Only, His salvation does demand its own reality.

This is the Christian doctrine of salvation: a world of sin, a God who loves it, a mission of Christ in which divine redeeming love is exprest unto the uttermost, a restoration and normalizing of sinful men, who now become new creatures, growing like to God revealed in Christ. Or, again, Sin—God of the Savior heart; Christ, the messenger-Savior, who works out God's salvation; forgiveness and transformation for men, until they are Christ-like lovers and doers of the good. This is what we preach, and our fathers preached it, and so did the apostles, and the Lord. This is what we have proclaimed, and that means that this is the substance of our doctrine.

Is it not plain that the message and the doctrine are one? I claim for this outline which I have sketched, that it contains what preachers in all Christian ages have uttered with one accord, and that it contains nothing that they have not uttered with one accord. This is the common substance of the Christian tidings about salvation. Inconsistently enough, I know, has this common substance been held, and preached. It has often been combined with ideas that did not match its quality, and has thus sometimes been unwittingly contradicted by men who were proclaiming it with all their hearts. Nevertheless, this doctrine has been the heart of the preaching, and the source of its power. Special forms of the doctrine have had their special kinds of power, and of usefulness; but the steady power of the Christian teaching about salvation has dwelt in the broad, unspecialized good news of free saving love from God in Christ, forgiving and transforming men. This power shines forth in all the special forms, and about it all subsidiary powers have gathered. The doctrine has often changed its appearance, as we have seen, one form following another, to be superseded in its turn. But for the central truth which I have now set forth, there can be no substitute in Christianity. This is Christianity.

As for the various and often conflicting forms of the doctrine, they came naturally, and inevitably. There are various causes for them. For one thing, if a truth is greater than a man, how can one-sidedness in his apprehension of it be prevented? He can not see all round it; one must see it from one side, and another from another, and then they will differ. Generations will differ, as well as individuals. Moreover, Jesus Christ's conception of God is an infinitely high and exacting truth, to which no generation, and no soul, has ever yet done full justice. In order to think of salvation as Jesus thought of it, we must think of God as Jesus thought of Him, and must read moral meanings as He read them. This has never been fully done, and so the Christian doctrine of salvation has never been fully Christian. Forgive me for saying so, but in the outline that I have now given, I have endeavored, humbly and afar off, to introduce no element that was not present in Jesus' own revelation of the Father, and to give the central place to the

qualities in God that He made central. Whether or not I have been successful, this is the right way to approach the subject; but the inability of the Christian people in all ages to do full justice to Jesus' conception of God has prevented the doctrine of salvation from coming to its full simplicity and glory.

Moreover, it is to be remembered that not all our ideas have come from Jesus. All Christian minds contain some things that they possess because they have learned of Jesus, and some that they possess altho they have learned of Jesus; and good discrimination between the two classes is rare. The first disciples, we know, received the Master's teachings into minds that were full of Jewish notions, and therefore misunderstood Him. We wrong them if we blame them for this, or reckon them exceptional. All men do the same. A new mental or spiritual possession falls into blending with what was present in mind and heart before it came, and blends again with what enters afterward. The genuine Christian teaching has never been kept distinct from other matters, for it could not be. The great and ancient human world has its vast stock of pagan-born ideas of God, the influence of which has never yet been wholly banished from any country or church. Christ negatives all conceptions of God that are born of groveling before power, or of guilty fear that can not see truly, or of moral ignorance; but his negative has not done its perfect work, and unworthy elements enter into all human thought of God and what he does toward us. Thus there is abundant reason for variation and imperfection in the Christian doctrine. And sometimes the variations serve their age, and bring real salvation home according to the heart and life, and convey the central doctrine to its triumph.

One class of variations comes in with the rising of questions about the guilt of sin. Conscience lives and does its work, and by and by it is said, "Sin is a dreadful thing; how can God forgive it?" Then come in the suggestions—and they have been many—that something must be offered to God by way of propitiation. I once heard a useful pastor in the region of New York give thanks for "the precious blood, whereby the burning throne is sprinkled over and God is rendered placable." Oftener, however, the thought has been that something must be offered to God for the removal of His difficulties, that he may be able to forgive. Sometimes the difficulty is that all sin absolutely must be punished; sometimes that His government must be guarded from dishonor when He forgives; and the doctrine of salvation declares that Christ has been punished for our sins, or else that He has suffered sufficiently for the vindication of God's moral government, and now

God can forgive. By the aid of these proposals for dealing with the guilt of sin, innumerable conscience-burdened souls have found relief and peace. Yet there sometimes comes a clear flash of the glory of God as Jesus Christ revealed Him, and we wonder what He needs that any offer Him, in order that He may forgive. Yonder, in the Pharisee's house, bows the repenting harlot over the feet of Jesus, shaken with an agony of remorse, yet weeping tears of love and joy in response to the holy love that has sought and found her in her sin; and the word goes forth, "Thy sins are forgiven thee, thy faith hath saved thee, go in peace," and we feel that it is right. God's difficulties, rendering this scene incomplete—we are not so sure of them when we hear the voice of Jesus, and perceive what manner of God we have by His revealing.

Another class of variations comes in with the realization of human weakness. Experience speaks, saying, "Salvation is a great and holy thing; it means much; it calls for strenuousness of heart and life; and how shall weak human nature hold itself to the strain of spirit which it requires?" Multitudes on multitudes must needs have it, but are not the most of them as sheep wandering in the wilderness, feeble, incompetent, unable? Then come in the suggestions of efficient help. Shall not the Church bear her children on her heart? Shall she not feed them with the bread of life? Can she not make salvation sure to them? May not the merits of her saints be handed over for the help of these her feeble little ones? It is theirs to take from her what the Lord and Savior has put into her keeping for their benefit. Through the sacraments which she administers, they may receive the gift; and then the way is short to the insisting that through her sacraments they must receive the gift, which is not otherwise to be had. Is not this the best hope of the multitude? And by this means many do receive the genuine blessing. Through sacraments which they deem indispensable, they do receive the grace of God unto salvation. The heart of a little child can take the salvation of God through sacraments; but by and by it dawns upon the soul, and upon the world, that the heart of a little child can take the grace of God without sacraments, going straight to the heart of God by simple faith, and finding there all fulness. Did not the Lord promise the child-like heart exactly this? Is not the soul's faith the directest answer to God's grace? and may not even the weak rise thus directly to the source of strength? The shortest way to God is the best. "If ye then, being evil," said Jesus, "know how to give good gifts to your children, how much more shall your heavenly Father give good things to them that

ask him?" That is the manner of God that He is. Straight from God comes the gift: "He that spared not his own Son but delivered him up for us all, how shall he not with him also freely give us all things?" Straight to God goes the soul: "Let the wicked forsake his way, and the unrighteous man his thoughts, and let him return unto the Lord and he will have mercy upon him, and unto our God for he will abundantly pardon."

But amid all the varieties, there stands firm and forever the one common doctrine—sin, God, love, Christ, forgiveness, renovation. These are facts, spiritual realities. "When," cried Thomas Erskine, "when shall we begin to realize that Christianity is not a religion got up either by God or man, but that it is the practical acknowledgment of man's actual condition as a spiritual being, of God's mind toward him, and of the relation in which he stands to God and to his fellow creatures?" When a man takes himself for what he is, and God for what He is, then he is in the way of salvation; for then he arises and goes to his Father, and God is to him all that it is in God's heart to be, forgiving his sins and letting His own helpful holy love renew and sustain him ever after; and in this coming together of God as He is and man as he is, Christ, the messenger, mediator, revealer of God, Christ, the brother, finder, bringer of man, is the efficient Savior. His cross is the meeting-point. There God shows us how He hates our sins and loves our souls; and there we bow, and give ourselves away to Him who hath loved us and given Himself for us.

The twentieth century needs the doctrine and message of salvation as much as ever did the first. The world of to-day needs to believe in salvation, in order that it may experience salvation, throughout the length and breadth of its life. The world needs to be normalized—that is, to be delivered from its evil, and brought to itself and its God. It is not that the world is suffering for this or that particular form of the idea of salvation, as the thought of the past has developed it; it needs the doctrine itself, in its great central meaning. Our world needs to believe in sin as a dreadful fact, to believe in the perfect God, to believe in the mission of love in Christ for salvation, and to believe in the power that can transform men, and man, and bring in the normal character and life. We should not think that the time offers no encouragement to the proclamation of this divine reality. I think we do our generation some injustice when we say that it has no sense of sin. Rather is it true that the sense of sin which our generation does possess in part is the key for the understanding of our present hopes. Self-searching is far less abundant now than it used to be, and the consciousness of personal guilt is not as easily aroused as once it was. Individual experience has retired from the front, and the old scrutiny has been turned off from it. This seems a loss. But the change has not been made without some gain. There is slowly rising in our time a social sense of sin. We are called to feel our unity with mankind, and to pass moral judgment upon events and characters in the light of their relation to the common life of man. There appear faint and crude foreshadowings of a time when sin will be understood to consist more in standing for one's self in selfish isolation, and righteousness and help will be accounted the primary virtues. Awful commentaries on the meaning of selfishness are being written in our day, and are beginning to be read with understanding. Slowly the absolute necessity of the mind of Christ in the common life is coming to be discerned. All this, our inmost hearts unhesitatingly declare, is good and right, and part of that forward movement for which we pray. It is the mission of the gospel of Christ to overcome our selfishness, and that can be done only by fastening our very hearts to the cause of righteousness and help toward men.

Toward this transfer of vital interest from the personal to the universal, from self to the common cause, Christ is leading on. But it is plain what we need. We need more than human interest; we need salvation—we, the men and women of this day. We need to have Christ's estimate of sin for our own, as distinctly as we have our habitual estimates of worldly values. We need to discern the God and Father of Christ who loves our selfish world and longs to save it from itself, as we perceive the sun in the heavens. We need to learn the lesson of the cross, or of salvation by love and self-sacrifice, as well as we learn the principles and methods of our common business. And we need to believe in the reality of the power that can conquer evil, as we believe in electricity, tho invisible, and what it can perform. There are forces all around us that would trample down our faith in the divine realities. Therefore let us consecrate ourselves daily in a strong and simple devotion to God and the soul, to Christ and salvation, to fellowship and the common task of the heavenly kingdom.

JOHN CLIFFORD

1836-1923

THE FORGIVENESS OF SINS

BIOGRAPHICAL NOTE

JOHN CLIFFORD, Baptist divine, was born at Lawley, Derbyshire, in 1836. He was educated at the Baptist College, Nottingham, and University College, London. He has had much editorial as well as ministerial experience and has published a number of works upon religious, educational and social questions. The Rev. William Durban, the editor, writing from London of John Clifford in the *Homiletic Review*, styles him "the renowned Baptist preacher, undoubtedly the most conspicuous figure in his own denomination." He speaks of "the profundity of thought," "simplicity and beauty of diction," the "compactness of argument" and "instructive expository character" of this preacher's discourses.

I believe in the forgiveness of sins.—Apostles' Creed.

THIS is the first note of personal experience in the Apostles' Creed. We here come into the society of men like John Bunyan and go with them through the wicketgate of repentance, through the Slough of Despond, getting out on the right side of it, reaching at length the cross, to find the burden fall from our backs as we look upon Him who died for us; and then we travel on our way until we come to the River of Death and cross it, discovering that it is not so deep after all, and that on the other side is the fulness of the life everlasting.

It is a new note, and it is a little surprizing —is it not?—to most students of this creed that we should have to travel through so many clauses before we reach it. It scarcely seems to be in keeping with the spirit and temper of the early Christian Church that we should have all this analysis of thought, this statement of the facts of Christian revelation, this testimony as to the power of the Holy Spirit, before we get any utterance as to that individual faith by which the Christian Church has been created, and owing to which there has been the helpful and inspiring fellowship of the saints.

I say it is a new note, but it is fundamental. When the Creed does touch the inward life, it goes straight to that which is central—to that which is preeminently evangelical. Without the doctrine of the forgiveness of sins you could have no good news for a sinful world; but with the assertion of this faith as the actual faith of the man, you have possibilities of service, the upspringing of altruism, the conquest of self, the enthronement of Christ, the advancement of humanity after the likeness of Jesus Christ.

A note it is which is not only fundamental but most musical, harmonious and gladdening. In the ancient Psalms we hear it oft—"Bless the Lord, O my soul, and all that is within me bless his holy name, who forgiveth all thine iniquities, who healeth all thy diseases." It recurs in the prophets: "I, the Lord, am he that blotteth out thy sins; yea, tho they be as a thick cloud, I will blot them out." It is the highest note reached by the singers of the Old Testament; but it comes to us with greater resonance and sweetness from the lips of the men who have stood in the presence of Jesus Christ, and who are able to say, as they look into the faces of their fellows: "Be it known unto you that through this man is

143

preached unto you the forgiveness of sins from which you could not have been freed by the law of Moses.'' With emphasis, with strength, with fulness of conviction, with gladdening rapture, these men proclaimed their faith in the forgiveness of sins, and tho the Creed of the churches travels slowly after the faith of the early Church, its last note sounds out a note of triumph: ''I believe in the forgiveness of sins, the resurrection of the body, and life everlasting.''

It is the crown of the whole Creed. It is the flowering of the truths that are contained in the Creed. Let a man understand God, and let him have such a vision of the Eternal as Job had, and he is constrained to say, ''I abhor myself and repent in dust and ashes.'' He desires first and chiefly to know that the true relation between the human spirit and God which has been broken by sin has at length been rearranged, and that sin is no longer an obstacle to the soul's converse with a holy God, but that the ideal relation of the human spirit with the divine spirit is reestablished by the proclamation of forgiveness. For, as you know, pardon is not the extinguishing of a man's past; that cannot be done. What has been done by us of good or evil abides, it endures; not God Himself can extinguish the deeds of the past. What forgiveness does is this: it rearranges the relations between the spirit of man and our Father, so that the sins of the past are no longer an obstacle to us in our speech with Him, our trust in Him —our using the energies of God for the accomplishment of His purposes. It is the restoration of the human spirit to right relations with God. Forgiveness of sins comes, therefore, at the very start of a right life. It is the beginning. All else in the spiritual life succeeds upon this.

I know there is a theory among us, and I am prepared to endorse it, that, if we are trained by godly parents in godly homes, we may grow into the spiritual life, pass into it, as it were, by stages which it is impossible for us to register. We are largely unconscious of these spiritual ascents; they are being made by the gracious use of influences that are in our environment, that reach us through sanctified folk, and we travel on from strength to strength, and, then, perchance, in our young manhood or womanhood, there comes a crisis of revelation, and we discover that we are in such relations with God our Father, Redeemer, and Renewer as fill us with peace, create hope and conscious strength. But I assure you that in addition to this experience there will come, it may be early, it may be late, some moment in the life when there is discovered to the individual spirit making that ascent a sense of the awful heinousness of sin; and tho we may not have such a unique experience of evil as the Apostle Paul had, and

become so conscious of it as to feel, as it were, that it is a dead body that we have to carry about with us as we go through life, interfering with the very motions of our spirit; yet we do approximate to it, and it is through these approximations to the Apostle Paul that we are lifted to the heights of spiritual achievement, and are qualified for sympathy with a sin-stricken world, and inspired by and nourished in a passionate enthusiasm to serve that world by bringing it into right relations with God.

When, therefore, a man says, ''I believe in God the Father Almighty, maker of heaven and earth,'' he is asserting that which, being turned to its full and true use, carries him to this goal, ''I believe in the forgiveness of sins.'' For a full and true doctrine of God can only be heartily welcomed when it is associated with the message of the forgiveness of sins. Otherwise the visions of the eternal Power may start in us the cry of Peter: ''Depart from me, for I am a sinful man, O Lord.'' When a man asserts his faith in Jesus Christ, God's only Son, our Lord, who was crucified, who suffered under Pontius Pilate, who died on the cross; he is himself asserting his faith in the great purpose for which God sent His Son; even to take away the sin of the world, to make an end of iniquity, to bring in an everlasting righteousness; and so out of that faith he prepared for the response which the soul makes to the workings of the Spirit, the Holy Ghost within him, and he is able to say from his own knowledge of what God has been to him, ''I believe in the forgiveness of sins.''

Friends, you have said this again and again, some of you hundreds of times. You have asserted it week by week. What did you mean by it? What exactly was the thought in your heart as the words passed over your lips, ''I believe in the forgiveness of sins''? Was it simply the recognition of a universal amnesty for a world of rebels? Was it merely the assertion of your confidence in the goodness of God irrespective of His holiness? Or when you uttered that faith of yours, did it mean that you were able to say, ''My sins, which were many, are all forgiven. My sins are forgiven, not may be—that pardon is a glorious possibility only—but are forgiven, not will be forgiven at some future time. I am now at peace with God through faith in our Lord Jesus Christ''? Could you say that? Was that what it meant; or was it simply the repetition of a phrase which has been handed down to you by your predecessors, and which you took up as part of an ordered service, without putting the slightest fiber of your soul into it?

Depend upon it, the mere recitation of a creed will not bring you God's peace, it will not open your heart to the access of His infinite calm. It will not secure you that emancipation from evil which will mean immediate dedication of yourself to work for the emancipation of the world. You must know of yourself, of your own heart and consciousness, that God has forgiven you. And if you do get that consciousness, that moment of your life will be marked indelibly upon the tablet of your memory. The dint will go so deeply into your nature that it will be impossible for you to forget it. Speaking for myself, I can at this moment see the whole surroundings of the place and time when to me there came the glad tidings, "God has forgiven you." "God was in Christ, reconciling the world unto himself, not reckoning unto men their trespasses."

Do you believe in the forgiveness of sins? Then preach it. Tell it to other people. Let your neighbors know about it. I do not mean by preaching at the street corners, but by getting into such close affectionate touch with your friends as that you shall be able to persuade them to disinter the thoughts of their own hearts, and show the sorrows that are there—sorrows produced by sin. For, believe me, behind all the bright seeming of human countenances there is a subtle bitterness gnawing constantly at the heart, consequent upon the consciousness of failure—the sense of having broken the law of God. I know that hundreds of people go into the church and tell God that they are miserable sinners. They do that in a crowd; it is saying nothing. They no more think of saying it in such a way as to place themselves apart from their fellows than they would of saying: "I am a thief!"

Do you believe in the forgiveness of sins? What, then, are you going to do with your faith?

Prove your faith by your works. Every time you ask God for forgiveness you should feel yourself pledged to a most strenuous and resolute fight with the sin you ask God to forgive. The acceptance of pardon pledges you to the pursuit of holiness, and yet we have to keep on with this doctrine, because it is not only the very beginning of the Christian life, but also the continuous need of that life.

We have to say night by night, "Forgive the ill that I this day have done." And if we say it as we ought, as really believing that God forgives us, so that we may not lose heart, may never encourage despair of final victory, we shall get up next morning resolved to make a fiercer fight than ever with the evil that sent us on our knees last night. Do you believe in the forgiveness of sins? Let the joy of it come to you, and as your own heart overflows with the fulness of that joy, declare unto others God's salvation, and teach transgressors His way. Do you believe in the forgiveness of sins? Then find in that faith an impact to obedience to the law of Jesus: "Be ye perfect even as your Father in heaven is perfect"; and do not forget that He who begins the good work in you with His pardon will carry it on to the day of Jesus Christ; so that you may add the last words of the Creed: "I believe in the resurrection from the dead and in the life everlasting."

It is not altogether a good sign that we have pushed eternity out of our modern thought. Confronted as man is every moment by a sense of the fragility and the brevity of human life, it is not surprizing that we should welcome everybody who comes with a message concerning eternity.

Is there not, in truth, beauty in the old Anglo-Saxon story of the bird that shot in at one open window of the large assembly hall and out at another, where were gathered together a great company of thanes and vassals; and when the missionary was asked to speak to them concerning God and His salvation, the thane who was presiding rose and said, recalling the bird's speedy flight from side to side of the hall, "Such is our life, and if this man can tell us anything concerning the place to which we are going, let him stand up and be heard." Brothers, a few days may carry us into eternity. "Boast not thyself of to-morrow, thou knowest not what a day may bring forth." Strong, hopeful, rich in promise of service is to-day; to-morrow friends may be weeping, kith and kin full of sorrow for our departure. This life does not end all; we are going to an eternity of blessedness, to progress without limit, to an assimilation with God that shall know no sudden break or failure, but shall be perfect, even as He is perfect.

CAMDEN M. COBERN

1855-1920

A PLACE BETTER THAN PARADISE

BIOGRAPHICAL NOTE

PROFESSOR of English Bible, and philosophy of religion, Allegheny College, Meadville, Pa., 1906-1915; born in Uniontown, Pa., April 19, 1855; received A.B., A.M. and D.D. from Allegheny College; S.T.B. and Ph.D. from Boston University; and Litt.D. from Lawrence University; was the pastor of important churches such as Ann Arbor, Mich., Trinity church, Denver, and St. James, Chicago; gave courses of Bible lectures in different cities; known on both continents as the man who discovered the "bricks without straw" which the Israelites made in Egyptian bondage; was with the world's most famous excavator, Dr. W. M. Flinders Petrie, visiting him while he was digging up the archeological remains of several cities in Egypt and Palestine; author of a large work on Egypt, a critical commentary on Daniel, etc.

"The place whereon thou standest is holy ground."— Exod. 3 : 5.

A POOR man, an old man, a lonely man is tending his sheep on Mount Horeb. He is a failure. He had a chance once. Once he lived in the city and was thought well of at court; but because of certain ideals of his he threw up all this—and has missed a career. He was a big man in a big place once; but that was long ago. He is a nobody now. He has been a nobody for forty years. He has grown slow of tongue. He has lost his courtly bearing, and in appearance as in speech has become a rustic. If he had only been a little less impulsive, a little less patriotic or conscientious, he might have made quite a success in life. Poor old man—a little man in a little place! But God still remembers him. Others forget him, but what a blest thing it is that God even remembers the little man in the little place.

But are we absolutely sure, after all, that Moses is a smaller man than he was forty years ago? No. He has been hidden and forgotten, but he is still the big man—so big that he can take the biggest task ever given by the Almighty to a mortal man for two thousand years. He is a greater man than he was forty years ago. He was not great enough then for this great task of nation-building. The desert has been his teacher. The God of the sky and of the heart has been teaching him self-poise and self-mastery. He has had time and chance to get away from the little things of the city and the court and think of the big things of life; to think and grow. Do not pity Moses because he lost half a lifetime in the country. That made him. That was part of God's plan for him and the world. God's man need not be in a hurry to get into a big place. If he is God's man, God will lead him and give him a task big enough for his fullest powers.

What did Moses learn in the desert? He learned its resources, its hidden springs, its oases. He learned the ways of the desert folk and made blood-brotherhood with them. It was God's plan to thus prepare allies for the mightiest deliverance of a slave people known to history.

One day the new call came to the new stupendous task for which the old little task had prepared him. A bush began to burn as he passed by, and continued to burn, and was not consumed. "And Moses said, I will turn aside now and see this great sight why the bush is not burnt. And when Jehovah saw that he turned aside to see, God called unto him." That was the test. It is so to-day.

We talk of the dead-line. That is the test as to whether a man has reached it. When a man has lost inquisitiveness for new truth, when he has lost interest in the new things of the new present, when he has become too old to "turn aside to see," then he has reached the dead-line. Then even God Almighty can not use him as a leader. But when he finds God in the novelties of daily life, then the place where he stands may become holy ground.

What makes a particular spot "holy ground"? Is it holy because God is there? No. God is everywhere. Why is this particular spot holy? Because God and man are here together, and the man recognizes God's presence and finds his world task.

It is a holy moment and a holy place when God and I are linked together eternally and I make the soul-thrilling discovery that He needs me to help Him save the world. That is a place better than heaven, where a man hears the voice of the Eternal saying, "I need you," and joins partnership with the omnipotent God—omnipotent and yet not able, as the human heart is now constructed, to "make a best man without man's best to help Him." To be called to such work is better than to be called to go to Paradise in a chariot of fire. There is a good deal of sham in much of our talk about wanting to go to heaven. I believe in heaven; but I don't want to go yet. Earth is better for me now. If there were twenty air-ships anchored in front of this church at this very minute, each bound for the New Jerusalem, all of them manned by angels in white robes and carrying a written guarantee from the King of Heaven that they would make the journey safely, I would not apply for passage. I can not conceive of anything in heaven equal to the task given me here and now of helping the Christ to conquer this earth. Why did God, when Cornelius prayed, send to Joppa for Peter, calling upon him to make that long trip to Cæsarea and tell that heathen how to be saved? Why did not God send His angel? Because no angel could tell that story. Only the man who has fought the beast in himself and got the victory through Christ's help can tell the power of Jesus' blood. No archangel could do that. Why did not God Himself whisper to Cornelius the way of life? Was it that He was unwilling to take away that possible star out of Peter's crown, or is the human agency in salvation a necessity which even the great God acknowledges? In any case, how glad Peter must have been that he did not get to heaven too soon! He wanted to go once on the Mount of Transfiguration— or at least to turn that mountain into Paradise and stay there—but how glad he ought to have been that he was still on the earth and able to help this One, greater than Moses,

in the one and only task greater than the deliverance of an enslaved nation—the deliverance of an enslaved world.

It is better than heaven to feel that God is using me as He could not use an angel and as He could not use me in heaven.

That there is a mystery about the Omnipotent using and needing human help to save and uplift the world we must admit. But we must also admit the fact. The battle-hymn of the old church army was "The sword of the Lord and of Gideon." That was big honor for Gideon. It is doubtful if that battle would have been won without Gideon. So in the New Testament: would Jesus have worked the miracle of feeding the five thousand if there had been no boy there willing to do his part? Did not the boy help Jesus work the miracle? So we help Him work His miracles of healing now. Does He not say distinctly that we have a part which if we fail to do will affect His power to save? He could do no mighty works in one place because of their unbelief in the olden time. He is crippled in His saving work now in the same way. Yes, and by our inactivity. "We are members of his body," wrote the apostle and some eighteen hundred years ago or more an ancient reader added, and wisely, "Of his flesh and of his bones" (Eph. 5:30). That is, we are as necessary to Him in this one particular work as hands and feet are necessary to us in doing our work. "Ye are the body of Christ and severally members thereof." The body is not one member, but many; and each member is needed. "God hath set the members each one of them in the body even as it pleased him" (1 Cor. 12). Too often when the Christ would do some mighty works today the body is paralyzed through which He seeks to act. Ye are His very flesh and bones! This is His second incarnation in human flesh. What honor is this that I may be His hand to help Him lift up the fallen. Can any better task come to us in any other world? Perhaps a greater task may come, but not this task— and to neglect this is to fail to do a work which is more important now than any joy which heaven could give us.

But not only the spots devoted to what we call religious work are sacred. The whole man is sacred, and the whole work of God's man is sacred work. It is not one day in seven and one place in Palestine and one man in a nation, but all God's men are priests, and the temple is in the man's own heart and the sacred work is all the work of the daily human Christian toil. As in the making of the tabernacle, God inspired men to spin and work in wood and brass; so now the work on the farm or in the store or in the home may be as sacred toil, and as truly religious as the words spoken in the pulpit or the testimony given in the prayer-meeting. The steps of a good man

are ordered of the Lord; not simply his steps
when he travels to the house of God, but
when he goes to his business office and about
his every-day duties. Man's religious life
extends through seven days of the week and
twenty-four hours of each day. He does not
lose his religion, even when he is asleep. To
sleep when it is time to sleep, and to laugh
when it is time to laugh, and to work when it
is time to work, is just as religious as to say
one's prayers. It is just as Christian a duty
to saw wood or deliver mail or build a house,
or put in the plumbing so it will stay, or keep
the accounts so that no recording angel can
find fault with them, as it is to go to the communion table. God wants religious men as
world-workers. Not to provide for the things
of one's own household is to be worse than an
infidel. To fail to provide the necessary
things for the wife and children of one's
household in order to get to the prayer-meeting is a sin. To be diligent in business is as
much a duty as to trust in God. To take care
of the house and the children is a higher duty
than to go to the missionary rally. If one or
the other must be given up, it should be the
latter. The religious value of good cooking
has never yet been sufficiently discust. Our
distinctions between secular and religious activities are artificial and unbiblical. It is
religious to do one's daily task as "unto the
Lord." As Hiram Golf said, There is such
a thing as being a shoemaker "by the grace
of God." Good shoes are just as necessary as
good sermons. The cobbler who fails to mend
the shoe religiously, and so allows William
Runkles' youngest to catch cold and die, will
find at the judgment day what it means to
be false to one's daily religious task. A defective cap used in a drill-hole yesterday exploded prematurely and blew twenty-eight
men into eternity. What shall be said of the
man who made that defective cap? Careless-
ness in stitching a saddle-girth, it has been
said, caused a general to fall from his horse
at a critical moment and a great battle to be
lost. The man who made that saddle-girth,
stopping to take a glass of beer and thus carelessly losing a stitch, or the army contractor
who furnished poor thread instead of the best,
did not do their daily tasks religiously—and
in the judgment day, if the universe is governed justly, they must suffer penalty. It
is a great thing when a man realizes that "the
place where thou standest is holy ground."
God is here! The task I do is under His eye
and according to His will, and this seemingly
small task is to take its place in the large
scheme for bringing in the heavenly kingdom
upon the earth.

There are no "little" unimportant things
in an immortal life, which is a part of a
divine plan for the coming future. All human
life is sacred when the man who lives the
life is God's man. It is better than heaven to
help God make the "new heaven and the new
earth" which is to come.

It is better to be on the wicked earth helping to make it better with God looking on ap-
provingly, than to be singing hallelujahs with
holy angels. If God wanted us in heaven He
could easily provide transportation. Where
He wants us to be is better for us than paradise. If we are where God wants us to be,
then the place where we stand is holy ground.

THEODORE L. CUYLER

1822-1909

THE
VALUE OF LIFE

BIOGRAPHICAL NOTE

THEODORE LEDYARD CUYLER, Presbyterian divine, was born at Aurora, New York, in 1822. He took his degree at · Princeton in 1841, and studied theology in Princeton Seminary. He was ordained to the ministry in 1848, but after discharging the duties of three pastoral positions, took up the prosecution of more general activities, including temperance and philanthropic work. He has been a voluminous writer, having contributed some four thousand articles to leading religious organs.

The spirit of God hath made me, and the breath of the Almighty hath given me life.—Job xxxiii., 4.

THERE are two conflicting theories, now-adays, as to the origin of man. One theory brings him upward from the brute, the other, downward from God; one gives him an ascent from the ape, the other a descent from the Almighty. I shall waste no time in refuting the first theory. The most profound physicist of Europe, Professor Virchow, of Berlin, has lately asserted that this theory of man's evolution from the brute has no solid scientific foundation. Why need you and I seek to disprove what no man has ever yet proved or will prove? The other theory of man's origin comes down to us in the oldest book in existence, the Book of Job, and tallies exactly with the narrative in the next oldest books, those compiled by Moses: "The spirit of God hath made me, and the breath of the Almighty hath given me life." That is the Bible account of your ancestry and mine.

We make a great deal of ancestry. The son of a duke may become a duke; the child of a king has royal blood in his veins; and a vast deal of honor is supposed to descend with an honorable descent. Grant this true, it proves a great deal; it proves more than some of us imagine. It proves that there is something grander than for man to have for his sire a king or an emperor, a statesman or a conqueror, a poet or a philosopher. It looks to the grandest genealogy in the universe, the ancestry of a whole race; not a few favored individuals, but all humanity. My brethren, fellow sharers of immortality, open this family record. Trace your ancestry back to the most august parentage in the universe: One is our Father, God; One our elder brother, Jesus. We all draw lineage from the King of kings and the Lord of lords. Herein consists the value and dignity of human life. I go back to the origin of the globe. I find that for five days the creative hand of the Almighty is busy in fitting up an abode of palatial splendor. He adorns it; He hollows the seas for man's highway, rears the mountains for his observatories, stores the mines for his magazines, pours the streams to give him drink, and fertilizes the fields to give him daily bread. The mansion is carpeted with verdure, illuminated with the greater light by day, lesser lights by night. Then God comes up to the grandest work of all. When the earth is to be fashioned and the ocean to be poured into its bed, God simply says, "Let them be," and they are. When man is to be created, the Godhead seems to make a solemn pause, retires into the recesses of His own tranquillity, looks for a model, and finds it in Himself. "And God said, let us make man in our image, after our likeness. . . . So God created man in his own image, in the image of God created he him; male and female created he them. . . . So God breathed into man's nostrils the breath of life and he became a living soul." No longer a beautiful model, no longer a speechless statue, but vivified. Life, that subtle, mysterious thing that no physicist can define, whose lurking place in the body no medical eye hath yet found out—life came into the clay structure. He began to breathe, to walk, to think, to feel in the body the "nephesh": the word in the Hebrew means, in the first place, the breath of life, then, finally, by that immortal essence called the soul.

Now, it is not my intention to enter into any analysis of this expression, "the spirit," but talk to you on life, its reach and its revenue, its preciousness and its power, its rewards and its retributions, life for this world and the far-reaching world beyond. Life is God's gift; your trust and mine. We are the trustees of the Giver, unto whom at last we shall render account for every thought, word and deed in the body.

I. In the first place, life, in its origin, is infinitely important. The birth of a babe is a mighty event. From the frequency of births, as well as the frequency of deaths, we are prone to set a very low estimate on the ushering into existence of an animate child, unless the child be born in a palace or a presidential mansion, or some other lofty station. Unless there be something extraordinary in the circumstances, we do not attach the importance we ought to the event itself. It is only noble birth, distinguished birth, that is chronicled in the journals or announced with salvos of artillery. I admit that the relations of a prince, of a president and statesman, are more important to their fellow men and touch them at more points than those of an obscure pauper; but when the events are weighed in the scales of eternity, the difference is scarcely perceptible. In the darkest hovel in Brooklyn, in the dingiest attic or cellar, or in any place in which a human being sees the first glimpse of light, the eye of the Omniscient beholds an occurrence of prodigious moment. A life is begun, a life that shall never end. A heart begins to throb that shall beat to the keenest delight or the acutest anguish. More than this—a soul commences a career that shall outlast the earth on which it moves. The soul enters upon an existence that shall be untouched by time, when the sun is extinguished like a taper in the sky, the moon blotted out, and the heavens have been rolled together as a vesture and changed forever.

The Scandinavians have a very impressive allegory of human life. They represent it as a tree, the "Igdrasil" or the tree of existence, whose roots grow deep down in the soil of mystery; the trunk reaches above the clouds; its branches spread out over the globe. At the foot of it sit the Past, the Present, and the Future, watering the roots. Its boughs, with their unleafing, spread out through all lands and all time; every leaf of the tree is a biography, every fiber a word, a thought or a deed; its boughs are the histories of nations; the rustle of it is the noise of human existence onward from of old; it grows amid the howling of the hurricane, it is the great tree of humanity. Now in that conception of the half savage Norsemen, we learn how they estimated the grandeur of human life. It is a transcendent, momentous thing, this living, bare living, thinking, feeling, deciding. It comes from God; He is its Author; it should rise toward God, its Giver, who is alone worthy of being served; that with God it may live forever.

II. In the next place, human life is transcendently precious from the services it may render to God in the advancement of His glory. Man was not created as a piece of guesswork, flung into existence as a waif. There is a purpose in the creation of every human being. God did not breathe the breath of life into you, my friend, that you might be a sensuous or a splendid animal. That soul was given you for a purpose worthy of yourself, still more of the Creator.

What is the purpose of life? Is it advancement? Is it promotion? Is it merely the pursuit of happiness? Man was created to be happy, but to be more—to be holy. The wisdom of those Westminster fathers that gathered in the Jerusalem chamber, wrought it into the well-known phrase, "Man's chief end is to glorify God and enjoy him forever." That is the double aim of life: duty first, then happiness as the consequence; to bring in revenues of honor to God, to build up His kingdom, spread His truth; to bring this whole world of His and lay it subject at the feet of the Son of God. That is the highest end and aim of existence, and every one here that has risen up to that purpose of life lives. He does not merely vegetate, he does not exist as a higher type of animal: he lives a man's life on earth, and when he dies he takes a man's life up to mingle with the loftier life of paradise. The highest style of manhood and womanhood is to be attained by consecration to the Son of God. That is the only right way, my friends, to employ these powers which you have brought back to your homes from your sanctuary. That is the only idea of life which you are to take to-morrow into the toils and temptations of the week. That is the only idea of life that you are to carry unto God in your confessions and thanksgivings in the closet. That is the only idea of life on which you are to let the transcendent light of eternity fall. These powers, these gifts, the wealth earned, the influence imparted, all are to be laid at the feet of Him who gave His life for you. Life is real, momentous, clothed with an awful and an overwhelming responsibility to its possessor. Nay, I believe that life is the richest of boons, or the most intolerable of curses.

Setting before you the power of a well-spent life, I might of course point first to the radiant pathway that extended from Bethlehem's manger to the cross of Calvary. All along that path I read the single purpose of love, all embracing and undying: "My meat is to do the will of him that sent me. . . . I have glorified thee on earth, I have finished the work thou gavest me to do." Next to that life we place the life begun on the road to Damascus. In him Christ lived again, with wondrous power, present in the utterances and footsteps of the servant. "For me to live is Christ:" that is the master passion of Paul. Whether he ate or drank, gained or lost, wrought or suffered, Christ filled the eye and animated every step. The chief end of Paul was to glorify his Savior; and of the winding-up of that many-sided term of existence he could exclaim, not boastfully, but gladly: "I have fought the good fight; I have finished my course; I have kept the faith: Henceforth there is laid up for me a crown of righteousness."

I found myself lately studying with intense interest the biography of Baxter. For half a century that man gave himself to the service of Jesus with a perseverance and industry that shames such loiterers as you and I. Just think of a man that twice on every Lord's day proclaimed the gospel of his Master with most elaborate care and unflinching diligence; on the first two days of the week spent seven hours each day in instructing children of the parish, not omitting a single one on account of poverty or obscurity; think of him as devoting one whole day of each week to care for their bodily welfare, devoting three days to study, during which he prepared one hundred and sixty instructive volumes saturated with the spirit of the word, among them that immortal "Saints' Everlasting Rest," that has guided so many a believer up to glory. The influence of one such life as that changed the whole aspect of the town of Kidderminster. When he came to it, it swarmed with ignorance, profligacy, Sabbath-breaking, vice; when he left it the whole community had become sober and industrious, and a large portion converted and godly. He says: "On the Lord's Day evening you may hear hundreds of families in their doors singing psalms or reading the Bible, as you pass along the streets." Sixteen hundred sat down at one time to his communion-table. Nearly every house became a house of prayer. Such was one life, the life of a man much of the time an invalid, crying out often unto God for deliverance from the most excruciating bodily pains. Such was one life on which was a stamped "Holiness to Jesus," and out of which flowed the continual efflux of Christian power and beneficence. Such a man never dies. Good men live forever. Old Augustine lives to-day in the rich discourses inspired by his teachings. Lord Bacon lives in the ever-widening circles of engines, telegraph and telephones which he taught men how to invent. Elizabeth Fry lives in the prison reformers following her radiant and beneficial footsteps. Bunyan lies in Bunhill Fields, but his bright spirit walks on the earth in the "Pilgrim's Progress." Calvin sleeps at Geneva, and no man knoweth his sepulcher to this day, but his magnificent "Vindication of God's Sovereignty" will live forever. We hail him as in one sense an ancestor of our republic. Wesley slumbers beside the City Road Chapel; his dead hand rings ten thousand Methodist church bells round the globe. Isaac Watts is dead, but in the chariot of his hymns tens of thousands of spirits ascend to-day in majestic devotion. Howard still keeps prisons clean. Franklin protects our dwellings from lightnings. Dr. Duncan guards the earnings of the poor in the savings-bank. For a hundred years Robert Raikes has gathered his Sunday-schools all over Christendom; and Abraham Lincoln's breath still breathes through the life of the nation to which, under God, he gave a new birth of freedom. The heart of a good man or a good woman never dies. Why, it is infamy to die and not be missed. Live, immortal friend, live as the brother of Jesus, live as a fellow workman with Christ in God's work. Phillips Brooks once said to his people: "I exhort you to pray for fulness of life—full red blood in the body, full and honest truth in the mind, fulness of consecrated love to the dying Savior in the heart."

III. In the next place, life is infinitely valuable, not only from the dignity of its origin and the results and revenues it may reach, but from the eternal consequences flowing from it. Ah, this world, with its curtaining of light, its embroideries of the heavens, and its carpeting of verdure, is a solemn vestibule to eternity. My hearer, this world on which you exhibit your nature this morning is the porch of heaven or the gateway of hell. Here you may be laying up treasures through Christ and for Christ, to make you a millionaire to all eternity. Here, by simply refusing to hearken, by rejecting the cross, by grieving the Spirit, you may kindle a flame that shall consume and give birth to a worm of remorse that shall prey on your soul forever and ever. In this brief twenty years, thirty, or forty, you must, without mistake, settle a question, the decision of which shall lift you to the indescribable heights of rapture or plunge you to the depths of darkness and despair. I am a baby at the thought of the word "eternity"; I have racked this brain of mine, in its poverty and its weakness, and have not the faintest conception of it, any more than I have of the omnipresence of Jehovah; yet one is as real as the other, and you and I will go on in the continuation of an existence that outnumbers the years as the Atlantic drops outnumber the drops of a brook; an existence whose ages are more than the stars that twinkled last night in the firmament—an existence interminable, yet all swinging on the pivot of that life in that pew. It is overpowering.

How momentous, then, is life! How grand its possession! what responsibility in its very breath! what a crime to waste it! what a glory to consecrate it! what a magnificent outcome when it shall shuffle off the coil, and break itself free from its entanglements, and burst into the presence of its Giver, and rise into all the transcendent glories of its life everlasting!

In view of that, what a solemn thing it is to preach God's word, and to stand between the living and the dead! And in view of life, its preciousness and power, its far-reaching rewards and punishments, let me say here, in closing, that there are three or four practical considerations that should be prest home upon us and carried out by us:

1. The first practical thought is, how careful you and I ought to be to husband it. The neglect of life is a sin; it is an insult to God; it is tampering with the most precious trust He bestows. The care of life is a religious duty. A great deal of your happiness depends on it, and I can tell you, my Christian brother, a great deal of your spiritual growth and capacity for usefulness depends on the manner in which you treat this marvelous mechanism of the body. Your religious life is affected by the condition of the body in which the spirit tabernacles. It is not only lying lips, it is "the wilful dyspeptic, that is an abomination to the Lord." Any one that recklessly impairs, imperils and weakens bodily powers by bad hours, unwholesome diet, poisonous stimulants or sensualities, is a suicide; and there are some men, I am afraid, in this congregation that yield themselves such unpitied bond-slaves to the claims of business, that they are shortening life by years and impairing its powers every day. Thousands of suicides are committed every year in Brooklyn by a defiance of the simplest laws of self-preservation and health. What shall we say of him who opens a haunt of temptation, sets out his snares and deliberately deals out death by the dram? So many pieces of silver for so many ounces of blood, and an immortal soul tossed into the balance! If I could let one ray of eternity shine into every dramshop, methinks I could frighten the poison seller back from making his living at the mouth of the pit.

2. Again, in this view of the value of life, what a stupendous crime wanton war becomes —offensive war, such war as multitudes have dashed into from the lust of conquest or the greed of gold. When war is to be welcomed, rather than a nation should commit suicide and the hopes of men perish, then with prayers and self-consecration may the patriot go out to the battle and the sacrifice; but offensive war is a monster of hell. With all our admiration for Napoleon's brilliant and unsurpassed genius, there are passages in his life that make my blood sometimes tingle to the finger ends, and start the involuntary hiss at the very thought of such a gigantic butcher of his fellow creatures. If that man knew that a battery could be carried only at the cost of a legion of men, he never hesitated to order their sacrifice as lightly as he would the life of a gnat. I read that, after what is called his splendid victory of Austerlitz was over and the triumph was won and the iron crown of empire was fixt on his brow, as he stood on the high ground he saw a portion of the defeated Russians making a slow, painful retreat over a frozen lake. They were in his power; he rode up to a battery, and said, "Men you are losing time! fire on those masses; they must be swallowed up! fire on that ice!" The order was executed. Shells were thrown, and went crashing through the brittle bridge of ice, and amid awful shrieks hundreds upon hundreds of poor wretches were buried in the frozen waters of that lake. I believe the dying shrieks of his fellow creatures will haunt the eternity of a man who prostituted the most magnificent powers the Creator fashioned in this our century of time to the awful work of shortening life, tormenting his fellow creatures and sending a million unbidden before God.

3. Once more I emphasize upon you, my beloved people, life, its preciousness and power, its rewards and its retributions. And yet, what a vapor, what a flight of an arrow, what a tale that is told! Short, yet infinite in its reach and its retribution! When life is represented as an arrow flight and a vapor, it is not that it may be underrated in its infinite importance, but only that we may be pushed up to the right sense of its brevity. Everything in God's world ennobles humanity and exhibits life as earnest, solemn, decisive,

momentous. The highest ends are proposed to it while it exists, the most magnificent rewards are held out at the termination of its consecrated vitalities. At the end of it is the great white throne, and the decisions of the judgment. Some of you, turning from this discourse this morning, may say it was nothing but sacred poetry because your life is only the steady, monotonous round of a mill-horse—to-morrow across the ferry, home at night—through its routine in the shop, in the counting-room, in the family, on the Sabbath in church—and say, "I see nothing in my life that thus sparkles or shines or has this sublime characteristic!" Ah, my friend, grant that your life may be the mill-round of the mill-horse; you turn a shaft that reaches through the wall into eternity, and the humblest life in this house sets in motion revolving wheels that shall at last grind out for God's garner the precious grain, or else the worthless chaff of a wasted existence. So again I say, life is the porch of eternity, the only one we shall ever have; and you are to decide now whether it shall be the uplift from strength to strength, from glory to glory, or the plunge downward and still downward and deeper downward to darkness and eternal death.

My friend, what sort of a life are you living? A really earnest, humble consecration to God? Go on. Live, as I mean to do, as long as God shall spare power and intellectual faculty to serve Him. Live as long as you can, as largely as you can; and then carry all life's accumulation and lay it down at the feet of Him whose heart broke for you and me on the cross of Calvary, and say: "Master, here I am, and the life Thou hast given me."

ROBERT W. DALE

1829-1890

THE ARGUMENT FROM EXPERIENCE

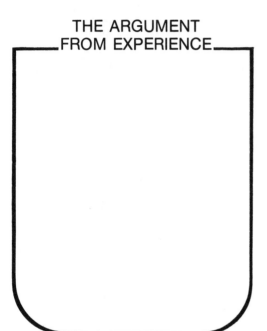

BIOGRAPHICAL NOTE

ROBERT WILLIAM DALE was born in London, England, in 1829 and died in 1895. His long and fruitful ministry was confined to Birmingham, where he preached with great power. He believed, as he once said, that if a minister had anything from God to say to his fellow men, they would gladly come to hear him. He favored extemporaneous preaching, was a devoted student of English style, and advocated in his Yale lectures a more thorough attention to this important subject. He said:

"There is no reason why, when you have at your service the noblest language for an orator that was ever spoken by the human race, you should be satisfied with the threadbare phrases, the tawdry, tarnished finery, the patched and ragged garments, with the smell like that of the stock of a second-hand clothes shop, with which half-educated and ambitious declaimers are content to cover the nakedness of their thought. You can do something better than this, and you should resolve to do it."

THERE are large numbers of people who suppose that modern science and modern criticism have destroyed the foundations of faith, and who can not understand how it is possible, in these days, for intelligent, open-minded, educated men to believe in the Lord Jesus Christ.

There are many persons who are convinced that the ascertained conclusions of modern science and of modern criticism are destructive of the authority which has been attributed both to the Jewish and the Christian Scriptures, that the traditional opinions concerning the authorship and the dates of many of the books of the Old Testament are false; and that most of the writings contained in the New Testament are spurious. Or, if some of the extreme conclusions of the destructive criticism are not regarded as finally established, it is known that great names can be quoted for, as well as against, them. And as it is assumed that the Jewish and the Christian Scriptures are the foundations of Christian faith, that we must believe in the genuineness and historical trustworthiness of these ancient books, and even in their inspiration, before we can believe in Christ, they argue that, until these discussions are finally closed in favor of the traditional opinions, faith in Christ is impossible. The controversies have not, in any large number of cases, destroyed faith where faith already existed; but where faith does not exist, they appear to very many persons to create an insuperable obstacle to faith.

To such persons, if they are serious and well informed, there is something perplexing in the persistency of the faith of the great majority of Christian believers. Among those who remain Christian there are men whose intellectual vigor, patience, and keenness are equal to their own; men who are their equals in general intellectual culture, and who know as much as they know about the currents of modern thought; candid men; men who are incorruptible in their loyalty to truth; men who have a due sense of the immense importance, in relation to the higher life of the human race, of the questions at issue:

How is it that the faith in Christ of such men is unshaken?

The substance of the answer that I make here to the question, why it is that those who believe in Christ continue to believe, may be given in a single sentence: Whatever may have been the original grounds of their faith, their faith has been verified in their own personal experience.

They have trusted in Christ for certain great and wonderful things, and they have received great and wonderful things. They have not perhaps received precisely what they expected when their Christian life began, for the kingdom of heaven cannot be really known until a man has entered into it; but what they have received assures them that Christ is alive, that He is within reach, and that He is the Savior and Lord of men.

That they have received these blessings in answer to their faith in Christ is a matter of personal consciousness. They know it, as they know that fire burns.

Their experience varies. Some of them would say they can recall acts of Christ in which His personal volition and His supernatural power were as definitely manifested as in any of the miracles recorded in the four Gospels. They were struggling unsuccessfully with some evil temper—with envy, jealousy, personal ambition—and could not subdue it. They hated it; they hated themselves for being under its tyranny; but expel it they could not. If it seemed supprest for a time, it returned; and returned with its malignant power increased rather than diminished. They scourged themselves with scorpions for yielding to it; still they yielded. In their despair they appealed to Christ; and in a moment the evil fires were quenched, and they were never rekindled. These instantaneous deliverances are perhaps exceptional; but to those who can recall them they carry an irresistible conviction that the living Christ has heard their cry and answered them.

The more ordinary experiences of the Christian life, tho less striking, are not less conclusive. The proof that Christ has heard prayer is not always concentrated into a moment, but is more commonly spread over large tracts of time. Prayer is offered for an increase of moral strength in resisting temptation, or for the disappearance of reluctance in the discharge of duties which are distasteful, or for a more gracious and kindly temper, or for patience and courage in bearing trouble, or for self-control, or for relief from exhausting and fruitless anxiety; and the answer comes. It comes gradually, but still it comes. We had lost hope. It seemed as if all our moral vigor was dying down, and as if nothing could restore it. The tide was slowly ebbing, and we were powerless to recall the retreating waters; but after we prayed it ceased to ebb; for a time it seemed stationary; then it began to flow; and tho with many of us it has never reached the flood, the wholesome waters have renewed the energy and the joy of life.

Or we prayed to Christ to liberate us from some evil habit. The chains did not fall away at His touch, like the chains of Peter at the touch of the angel; but in some mysterious way they were loosened, and at the same time we received accessions of strength. The old habit continued to trouble us; it still impeded our movements: but we could move; we recovered some measure of freedom, and were conscious that we were slaves no longer. There still remained a mechanical and automatic tendency to the evil ways of thinking, speaking, or acting; but we had become vigilant and alert, and were prompt to resist the tendency as soon as it began to work; and we were strong enough to master it. In the course of time the tendency became weaker and weaker, and at last, in some cases, it almost disappeared.

Some men have appealed to Christ when they have been seized with a great horror through the discovery of their guilt. It was not the awful penalty which menaces the impenitent that haunted and terrified them. Nor was their distress occasioned chiefly by the consciousness of moral evil. They feared the penalty, and they were humiliated and shamed by the contrast between ideal goodness and their own moral and spiritual life; but what stung and tortured them, sunk them into despair, filled heaven and earth with a darkness that could be felt, and made life intolerable, was their guilt—guilt which they had incurred by their past sins, and which they continued to incur by their present sinfulness.

When once this sense of guilt fastens itself on a man, he cannot shake it off at will. The keen agony may gradually pass into a dull, dead pain; and after a time, the sensibility of the soul may seem to be wholly lost; but a man can never be sure that the horror will not return.

The real nature of this experience is best seen when it has been occasioned by the grosser and more violent forms of crime. Men who have committed murder, for example, have been driven almost insane by the memory of their evil deed. Their agony may have had nothing in it of the nature of repentance; they were not distrest because their crime had revealed to them the malignity and the fierce strength of their passions; they had no desire to become gentle and kindly. They were filled with horror and remorse by their awful guilt. They felt that the crime was theirs, and would always continue to be theirs; that it would be theirs if it remained concealed as truly as if it were known; indeed, it seemed to be in some terrible way more truly theirs so long as the secret was kept. It was not the fear of punishment that convulsed them; they have sometimes brought on themselves public indignation and abhorrence, and have condemned themselves to the gallows by confessing their crime in order to obtain relief from their agony.

Suppose that a man possest by this great horror discovered that, in some wonderful way, the dark and damning stain on his conscience had disappeared; that, altho he had done the deed, the iron chain which bound him to the criminality of it had been broken; that before God and man and his own conscience he was free from the guilt of it;—the supposition, in its completeness, is an impossible one; but if it were possible, the discovery would lift the man out of the darkness of hell into the light of heaven.

But to large numbers of Christian men a discovery which in substance is identical with this has actually come in response to their trust in Christ. Nothing is more intensely real than the sense of guilt; it is as real as the eternal distinction between right and wrong in which it is rooted. And nothing is more intensely real than the sense of release from guilt which comes from the discovery and assurance of the remission of sins. The evil things which a man has done cannot be undone; but when they have been forgiven through Christ, the iron chain which so bound him to them as to make the guilt of them eternally his has been broken; before God and his own conscience he is no longer guilty of them. This is the Christian mystery of justification, which, according to Paul—and his words have been confirmed in the experience of millions of Christian men—is "the power of God unto salvation to every one that believeth." It changes darkness into light; despair into victorious hope; prostration into buoyancy and vigor. It is one of the supreme motives to Christian living, and it makes Christian living possible. The man who has received this great deliverance is no longer a convict, painfully observing all prison rules with the hope of shortening his sentence, but a child in the home of God.

There are experiences of another kind by which the faith of Christian men is verified. Of these one of the most decisive and most wonderful is the consciousness that through Christ he has passed into the eternal and divine order. He belongs to two worlds. He is just as certain that he is environed by things unseen and eternal as that he is environed by things seen and temporal. In the power of the life given to him in the new birth he has entered into the kingdom of God. He is conscious that that diviner region is now the native land of his soul. It is there that he finds perfect rest and perfect freedom. It is a relief to escape to its eternal peace and glory from the agitations and vicissitudes, the sorrows and successes, of this transitory world. It is not always that he is vividly conscious of belonging to that eternal order; this supreme blessedness is reserved for the great

hours of life; but he knows that it lies about him always, and that at any moment the great Apocalypse may come. And even when it is hidden, its "powers" continue to act upon him, as the light and heat of the sun pass through the clouds by which the burning splendor is softened and concealed.

Further, "in Christ" Christian men know God; they know Him for themselves. The mere conception of God is as different from the immediate knowledge of Him as the mere conception of the Matterhorn from the actual vision of it as an external objective grandeur; and it is not the conception of God, but God Himself, that fills them with awe and wonder, and with a blessedness which trembles into devout fear. Sometimes the "exceeding weight of glory" is too great to bear, and human infirmity is relieved when the vision passes. At other times God is more than a transcendent glory to be contemplated and adored. His infinite love, to use Paul's words, is shed abroad in their hearts, like the sun's heat under tropical heavens; it is immediately revealed. How, they can not tell, any more than they can tell how the material world is revealed to sense; they only know that, apart from any self-originated effort, apart from any movement of their own towards Him, the eternal Spirit draws near to their spirit and reveals God's love to them. It is as if the warm streams of the love which have their fountains in the depths of His infinite life were flowing round them and into them. They are conscious of that love for them of which God is conscious.

And this blessedness is not the prerogative of elect saints, or of those who may be said to have a natural genius for spiritual thought. It is the common inheritance of all that are "in Christ," altho there is reason to fear that many Christian people rarely reach the height of its joy. But among those who reach it are men of every degree of intellectual rank and every variety of moral and spiritual temperament. It is reached by ignorant men, whose thoughts are narrow and whose minds are inert, as well as by men with large knowledge and great powers of speculation; by men destitute of imagination, as well as by men whose imagination kindles as soon as it is touched by the splendors of nature or by the verses of poets. Men whose life moves slowly and sluggishly reach it, as well as men who are impulsive, ardent, and adventurous. And where this experience is known, it becomes an effective force in the moral life. Peter, writing to slaves, says, "For this is acceptable, if through consciousness of God a man endureth griefs, suffering wrongfully."

I have said that "in Christ" men know God—not merely through Christ. It is true that during His earthly ministry He revealed God; so that, in answer to the prayer of one of His disciples, "Show us the Father, and it sufficeth us," He said, "Have I been so long time with you, and dost thou not know me, Philip? he that hath seen me hath seen the Father." That revelation has eternal power and value; but there are other words spoken by Christ that same night which suggest that it is not merely by the revelation of God during His earthly ministry that Christ has made it possible for men to know the Father. He said: "I am the true vine, and ye are the branches. . . . Abide in me, and I in you. As the branch cannot bear fruit of itself, except it abide in the vine; so neither can ye, except ye abide in me. He that abideth in me, and I in him, the same beareth much fruit: for apart from me ye can do nothing." It is not certain that when Paul wrote his Epistle to the Galatian Christians he had heard of these words; but what they meant he had learnt for himself. He said, "I live: and yet no longer I, but Christ liveth in me." In various measures the experience of Paul has been the experience of Christian men ever since. Their relationship to Christ—their conscious relationship to Christ—has been most mysterious, but most intimate and most certain. They have meditated on the infinite love which moved Him to descend from the heights of God and to become man, upon His graciousness and gentleness, His purity, His spontaneous goodness, His pity for suffering, His merciful words to the sinful, His patience and His long-suffering, and His fiery indignation against hypocrisy; they have meditated on His teaching, on all the words of His that have been preserved concerning the love and grace of God, concerning the remission of sins, the gift of eternal life, the judgment to come, the eternal blessedness of the righteous, and the doom of the lost; they have felt the spell and the charm of that ideal perfection to which He calls them in His precepts, and which He illustrated and transcended in His own character: but they have been conscious that it was not merely by the power of the great and pathetic story of His earthly history, or by the power of His spiritual and ethical teaching, that He gives to men the life of God, and constantly renews, sustains, and augments it. They shared the very life of their Lord. He lived in them. They lived in Him. And it was in the power of this common life that they knew God.

Nor is it only the immediate knowledge of God that is rendered possible by this union with Christ. Christian men are conscious that they do not receive strength from Christ for common duty, as they might receive strength from One who, while He conferred the grace, stood apart from them, but that in some wonderful way they are strong in the strength of Christ Himself. They are too often drawn down into the region of baser forces, and then

they fall; but their very failure verifies the truth of their happier experiences, for it brings home to them afresh what they are apart from Christ; and when they recover their union with Him—which indeed had not been lost, tho for a time it was not realized—they recover their power.

The man who has had, and who still has, such experiences as these will listen with great tranquillity to criticisms which are intended to shake the historical credit of the four Gospels, altho the story they contain may have been the original ground of his faith in Christ. The criticism may be vigorous; he may be wholly unable to answer it: but what then? Is he to cease to believe in Christ? Why should he?

Let me answer these questions by an illustration. Towards the close of our Lord's ministry, when He was in the neighborhood of Jericho—just leaving the city or just entering it—Bartimeus, a blind man, who was begging at the side of the road, heard that Jesus of Nazareth was passing by, and He appealed to the great Prophet to have mercy upon him. Jesus answered his appeal, and gave him sight. Now it is possible that Bartimeus may have been told by some passing traveler, of whom he knew nothing, the story of a similar miracle which Jesus had worked a few weeks before in Jerusalem, and this may have been the ground, and the only ground, of his confidence in our Lord's supernatural power. If, after he had received his sight, some sagacious friend of his had asked him how it was that he came to believe that the Nazarene Teacher could give sight to the blind, nothing would have been easier than for his friend to show that, whether the story of the Jerusalem miracle was true or not, Bartimeus had no trustworthy evidence of its truth. A tale told by an unknown stranger! This was no sufficient reason for believing that Jesus had given sight to a man born blind. Did the stranger who told the tale know the beggar who was said to have been cured? Was it certain that the man was blind? Had the stranger examined his eyes the very morning of the day on which he received sight? Was it certain that the vision was not gradually returning? Was the stranger present when Jesus made the clay, and put it on the blind man's eyes; close enough to see that no delicate operation was performed during the process? The sending of the blind man to wash at the Pool of Siloam was suspicious: what could that washing have to do with a miracle? Did the stranger go with the man to the pool, and keep his eye upon him while he was there? Was it quite certain that the blind beggar who was sent to Siloam was the man who came back to the city and declared that Jesus had healed him? Might not one man have been sent to the pool, and another man have come back to Jerusalem? It looked very much as if there were some previous understanding between the blind man and the Nazarene Prophet. The Prophet had rich friends; they could have made it worth the man's while to come into the plot. Had Bartimeus considered all these difficulties? Was it not more probable that the stranger's story should be false than that the miracle should be true? Would it not be well for Bartimeus to suspend his faith in Jesus until he had made further inquiries about the miracle?

We can imagine the answer of Bartimeus. I think that he would have said: "At first I believed in the power of Jesus of Nazareth, because I was told that He had given sight to another blind man; now I am sure of His power, because He has given sight to me. It is possible, as you say, that the story about the blind man in Jerusalem is not true. You have asked me many questions which I can not answer. I can not explain why he should have been sent to the Pool of Siloam. I acknowledge that the evidence which I have for the miracle is not decisive. As Jesus has restored my sight, I think that the story is probably true; but whether the story is true or not can not disturb my faith in Him, for if He did not heal the other man, He has healed me."

And so the faith in the living Christ of those who have had the great experiences of His power and grace which I have described is not shaken by any assaults on the historical trustworthiness of the story of His earthly ministry. Much less can it be shaken by discussions concerning the nature and origin of the ancient Scriptures of the Jewish people. Their confidence in the books, both of the Old Testament and the New, may perhaps have to be suspended until the controversies of scholars are closed, or until, on historical and critical grounds, they can see their own way to firm and definite conclusions about the main questions at issue; but not their confidence in Christ. They may be uncertain about the books; they are sure about Him. Both Christian scholars and the commonalty of Christian people approach the controversies on these ancient records with a settled faith in the power and grace and glory of Christ. Their faith in Him rests on foundations which lie far beyond the reach of scientific and historical criticism. They know for themselves that Christ is the Savior of men: for they have received through Him the remission of their own sins; He has translated them into the divine kingdom; He has given them strength for righteousness, and through Him they have found God.

WILLIAM THEOPHILUS DAVISON

1846-1935

THE TREASURE-HOUSE OF THE KINGDOM

BIOGRAPHICAL NOTE

PRINCIPAL of Richmond College, England, 1909; born at Bath, England, 1846; educated at Kingswood School; graduated (M.A.) at the London University in 1871; has held various pastorates in the Wesleyan Methodist Church from 1868-81; was for ten years professor of Biblical literature in Richmond College and for thirteen years professor of theology in Handsworth; in 1905, he returned as theological professor to Richmond College; was a member of faculty of theology of London University, and in 1901 was president of the Wesleyan Methodist Conference; author of "The Christian Conscience," "The Praises of Israel," "Wisdom Literature of the Old Testament," "The Lord's Supper," "Strength for the Way," "Psalms" in "Century Bible."

"And he said unto them, Therefore every scribe who hath been made a disciple to the kingdom of heaven is like a man that is a householder, which bringeth forth out of his treasure things new and old."—Matt. 13 : 52.

WE can not be sure of the exact scope of the figure employed in our text. Is this householder providing food for the multitude, various provision for various needs, "all manner of precious fruits, new and old" (Song 7 : 13), new confections and old wine—that is far better than the crude must of yesterday? Or is he, as is common in the East, unfolding the resources of a rich wardrobe, so many changes of raiment, brand-new fabrics of latest style, old laces and gold-embroidered garments possessing dignity and historic interest? Or rather, jewels and furniture of diverse history and value, heirlooms from a distant past, bright new ornaments, carved chests from the stores of ancient kings? It matters not. We spoil the illustration by narrowing it down to detail; let it stand in its original breadth and generality—he bringeth forth out of his treasure things new and old. The application to our own time, a period in which so much is said of the old faith and the new knowledge, may well prove to be fruitful and instructive.

Every teacher must be first a learner, every real learner ought to become in his own measure a teacher. This is true in all departments of life; we can not teach what we do not know, we can not know without learning by the methods proper to the subject. The learned man is called a scholar because he is content to acknowledge ignorance, to open his mind and sit at the feet of those who are wiser than he. In science we must observe, collect instances, experiment, verify. In metaphysics we analyze, discriminate, reason, confirm. In art students open their eyes and heart to receive lessons of beauty, patiently toil over technical processes, submitting to laws which it is painful to obey in order to communicate delight which it is a joy to impart. The successful manufacturer and the skilled artizan, the craftsman and the laborer of all types, are not exempt from laws which apply to all human acquisitions and achievements.

Not least is this the case in the sphere of religion. Those who carried God's message of old time were men who had been taught of God. The prophet who would speak a word in season to him who is weary must be one who has learned divine lessons, who has been awakened morning by morning to be taught the highest love. The ready tongue can only be inspired by the willing and waiting heart. The priest who was to help in the work of revealing God to man and bringing man near to God needed long and careful training. The "wise man," who taught in proverbs might be supposed to be educated in society, the possessor of a shrewd eye and a ready wit, but he, more, perhaps, than other teachers, had learned the lesson that the fear of the Lord is the beginning of wisdom and that the secret of the Lord is with them that fear Him.

In later times another type of teacher had come to the front, and in the time of Christ he was known as the "scribe." He spent his time in mastering the details of an ecclesiastical code, becoming familiar with traditional precedents and decisions, that he might hand them on and add to their numbers—a doctor, a lawyer, a rabbi, a teacher of the schools. He is not lovely in our eyes. But it must be remembered that he had conscientiously taken much trouble to master what was esteemed the highest knowledge attainable: he had studied, arranged, codified and made the subject his own; he built a hedge round the law and a hedge round that hedge, his whole object being to keep God's commandments inviolate and the name of Him who had given them sacred, as in a very holy of holies.

Then had come One who taught "not as the scribes." His words carried their own weight, were stamped with their own credentials, proclaimed their own authority. None could hear them unmoved and their main teaching was concerning God. The Father was made known by the Son as never before; the truth revealed concerning Him lived, palpitated and glowed in the very utterance; it was brought home with immediate directness to men's business and bosoms; the kingdom of which others had had much to say took on new meaning and character, it was not to come with "observation"—the craning of the neck into the distance to watch for an unimaginable portent — it was in their very midst.

Christ proclaimed a new spiritual order, to attain which there was no need to climb the heaven or cross the sea; men had but to look within and search around them. No new God was declared, yet the new light shed on the nature of Him whom the fathers had known and worshiped gave an altogether new idea of His mind and will, and altogether new conceptions of what was meant by His tabernacling among men and the establishment of His dominion upon earth. The message came, Repent, change both mind and habit from the old hard, selfish, conventional ways; be born again, become as little children with simple, wondering, trustful and obedient hearts; be baptized, not only with water to cleanse from the evil of the past, but with the Holy Spirit and with fire to purify from within and inform with new celestial energy. Above all, love; love God with heart and mind and soul and strength, love man as man, whether friendly or hostile, generous or ungrateful; so shall new relations between God and men usher in a new heaven and a new earth, a new social organism of renovated spirits, a kingdom whose full coming shall mean that the will of God is done on earth as it is in heaven.

Hence arose a new world, of which Christ Himself is the center. "My disciple" is a more frequent phrase with Him than "disciple of the kingdom," but the two mean the same thing. A new sort of scribism, this. You shall learn, He says, not necessarily from books and manuscripts. Not that there is any need to despise a good book, "the precious life-blood of a master-spirit embalmed and treasured up to a life beyond life." You shall learn, not necessarily dogmas of the schools. Not that men should decry healthy doctrine, the best thoughts on the most sacred subjects framed in the best words attainable. You shall learn, not necessarily from carefully compiled ethical codes. Not that any wise man will slight or disregard these precepts of highest sanction and most sacred obligation, the behests of a duty which may be the "stern daughter of the voice of God," but which also means "the Godhead's most benignant grace."

Doctrines, traditions, laws, principles are inculcated—but alive, not dead; no fossils, but instinct with vital energy. The school of this kingdom is one of spiritual experience; its training is not one of poring over musty tomes, or repeating parrot-like phrases which are only half-understood and wholly uncared for. A man can not enter the kingdom, can not even see it, without a new nature; wise men may miss it, while babes enjoy it. Learn of me, says the Teacher, in simplicity and meekness, throwing aside prejudice, selfishness and hardness of heart, opening wide the doors of affection and trustfulness, gaining fuller insight into the will of God by unfailing obedience to His voice when heard—"if any man willeth to do his will, he shall know of the doctrine." For all is embodied in Him who is the way, the truth and the life. Whoever seeks to embody living truths in abstract propositions—and no true teacher ever does—Jesus Christ does not make disciples thus. He came to be the truth, not simply to declare it. Only the Son can reveal the Father, the nature of the kingdom can only be seen in its King. His are words which are spirit and life, indeed, and in Him is a fountain of redeeming energy enabling men to realize their meaning in action. Learn of me, says the lowliest of all masters; drink not from the pool, not from the cistern, not from the reservoir, but from the fountain of life indeed.

So the first disciples found it and generations of Christ's followers since. Those who have learned of Him have had placed in their hands a talisman, with its secret watchword, opening up mountain-caves close by their side, rich in treasure, a key to the knowledge of nature, man and God. Jesus said nothing about nature in the modern sense of the word, but the whole world was His; as all our science can not make it ours. He knew man perfectly, the best as well as the worst of human nature; none exposed more sternly than He the evil of hardness and hypocrisy, none more tenderly pitied man's weakness and waywardness, yearning after the lost and giving Himself to the uttermost in order to reclaim them. Christ understood man and nature because He knew God. Others guess and wonder and dream, He knows. Where other religious teachers scatter a few clouds from the lower firmament of the spiritual sky He shoots up a straight shaft of access into the farthest azure, and a vision of glory appears, indeed, such as can never be forgotten or lost. When a "scribe" is made a disciple of this kingdom and knows God and man and nature as Christ makes him, he has found a new world such as eye sees not, ear hears not, and which can not otherwise enter into the heart of man.

Read the seven parables of this chapter or other chapters. Read the Beatitudes, learn the Lord's Prayer, sit at Jesus' feet to hear His words. Draw still nearer, that you may understand Himself and that kingdom which, because it is His, it must be our first aim to seek and to make our own in His way. Look to Him as Savior, as well as Revealer. Trust Him as He offers on the cross one sacrifice for sins forever, and as He is declared to be the Son of God with power by the resurrection from the dead. Receive His Holy Spirit into the heart and let Him do His work of cleansing, renewing and purifying to the uttermost. Jesus says still to His disciples, Abide in me and I in you; and then, Ask what ye will and it shall be done unto you. If ye abide in my word, then are ye truly my disciples; and you shall know the truth and the truth shall make you free.

"Have ye understood all these things?" It is a searching question. Religiously educated, professing and calling ourselves Christians, taught the catechism as children, having known the Bible all our lives, accepting an orthodox creed and perhaps attending the holy communion—it may still be that in the inner springs of our nature we have not yet been made disciples to the kingdom of heaven. The promise of the parable is only to such.

But all may become disciples if they will; the way is open and the grace is free. The blind from birth may have eyesight given him; the half-cured who see men as trees walking, by an added touch may be enabled clearly to scan the horizon far and near. Those whose eyes have thus been opened will easily follow on to explore.

The abundance of the householder's store is exprest by a notable phrase, "things, new and old." Why is it used? Why does not Jesus say things great and small, things useful and beautiful, things suitable for rich and poor, old and young, wise and simple? The form may be proverbial, or it may be considered generally suitable in describing a storehouse. But it probably contains a deeper significance. Jesus as a teacher had often to face this question of old and new in the realm of truth and to declare what was his attitude to both in a time of transition. The Jews were particularly tenacious of tradition, and in all ages religious people have been naturally conservative. They are usually disturbed, if not alarmed, by the cry, "Thou bringest certain strange things to our ears." It is, therefore, the relation between past and future that is in the mind of the Master when He uses this phrase; the relative claims of venerable, mature experience, on the one hand, and the fresh, vigorous, earnest thought of the moment; on the other the relation of successive generations to one another, the perennial contest between the *laudator temporis acti*, the tenacious upholder of the customary ideas of the past and the eager young life full of hope and clamorous for the satisfaction of the pressing needs of to-day. Hence our Lord describes the resources of a true disciple of the kingdom as sufficient for all emergencies. The supply in His treasure-house is adequate and abundant, both of things new and old.

How does the doctrine of the kingdom preserve the unity of these two? The arguments of those who plead the claims of either old or new taken separately are well known. Apart from that shallowest and laziest of pleas which obstructs all progress because "what was good enough for our fathers is good enough for us," the better part of human nature is rightly enlisted in defense of truth already assimilated and positions already attained. In religion especially the value of existing grounds of trust causes men rightly to cling to revelations already made and to contend earnestly for the forms in which they have been delivered. Further protection for the sacred truth is afforded by ethical precepts or religious ceremonies; these in turn become sacrosanct, and further doctrine is formulated to secure them in their place. Thus the process of overlaying the original deposit of truth is continued till the very significance of the original is lost and the Jewish scribes, who most honor the law, make it void through their tradition.

On the other hand, the intellectually restless and eager are represented by the vivacious and versatile Athenians, who "spent their time in nothing else but either to tell or to hear some new thing." Novelty may become in itself an excellence, and accepted truth be discarded merely because it is familiar. The paradoxical is considered in itself admirable because it stimulates the intellectually jaded palate. The world of ideas changes for some thinkers like the book of fashions in dress; last season's garb is considered ugly simply because it is no longer worn. For them the stigma of dulness attaches to all that is based on precedent and authority; prejudice is raised against the old, since by its very definition it has had its day, and is fit only to make way for something else.

In true religion each of these tendencies is wrong if it be taken alone. There must be a reasoned relation between the abiding and the transient; no religion can meet the needs of man which does not on the one hand preserve unchanged the eternal principles of right and wrong, both human and divine, and on the other take full account of new conditions, new knowledge, and new requirements, as the generations succeed one another in unending procession. In Christianity the unity between these conflicting elements may always be preserved by men who are made disciples to the kingdom that can not be moved. There may be a removing of those things that are shaken, as of things that have been made; but the things which can not be shaken will remain. These householders bring forth from their treasure things new and old, both equally valuable and easily and harmoniously blended.

Christ Himself furnishes the supreme example of this. We know how, early in His ministry, the objection was raised: "What is this—a new teaching?" How, in the Sermon on the Mount, He said that He came not to destroy but to fulfil; that no jot or tittle of the law should fail till it had been fulfilled. In the brief parable of Luke 5: 39, Christ laid stress on the value of the old, as such, and more than once He upheld the judgments of those who spoke from Moses' seat because of the place from which the words were spoken. Yet He protested against pouring new wine into old wine-skins. He superseded that which had been said "to them of old time" by His authoritative word, "I say unto you," for a greater than Jonah, a greater than Solomon, a greater than Moses, is here. Without breaking with the past, He vindicated the rights and the duties of the present; without proclaiming a revolution, He accomplished

one; while upholding the law and the prophets, He showed how the gospel realized and surpassed both. If ever there was a teacher who brought forth for His treasure things new and old, it was He who spoke this parable.

The servant was to be even as his lord. Christ declares here that those who followed Him would be like Him in their blending of old faith and new knowledge. The best-known example is that of the apostle Paul. Who, more completely than he, realized this combination? Brought up as a Pharisee, he never lost his zeal for righteousness. When he preached Christ crucified, it was only that that end should be attained for which the law had striven but had not been strong enough to secure. He pleads continually, "It is written," yet is so convinced of the paramount importance of the message entrusted to him that if an angel from heaven should preach any other gospel than this, he must be anathema. So with the other apostles; from Pentecost onward, they followed their Lord faithfully and closely, but not slavishly. They did not put forth a replica of the Sermon on the Mount, tho echoes of it are found in the epistles of Peter and James. But they were enlightened by the promised Spirit to understand the supreme importance of the person and the work of Christ on earth and its consummation in heaven; and they rightly put this in the forefront of their message. There were various types of apostolic teaching. The writers of the New Testament do not mechanically copy or imitate one another. The early sermons in the Acts are, in some respects, unlike the teaching that went before and that which followed afterward. Peter, James, John, Stephen, Paul, the writer of Hebrews and of the Apocalypse—how various are these, yet how true, every one of them, to the great central principles of Christ and His kingdom! We need not go beyond the New Testament to find striking illustration of how possible it is for the Christian householder to bring out of the same rich gospel treasure-house things new and old.

The history of Christendom is a running commentary on the same text. What a manifold and complex development has been that of the Christian religion; how difficult it is at this moment to define its essential character, so as to include its almost infinitely various forms and manifestations! There have been periods in its history when a clinging to old and stereotyped forms has endangered the very life of its spirit, as well as periods during which a readiness to change the form of faith has well-nigh caused the substance to disappear. But, on the whole, it has preserved its continuity while spreading into all regions of the world and translating its message into alien climes and other tongues.

The curve described by the development of Christianity may be determined by two foci: belief in Jesus Christ, Son of God and Son of man, and the historical revelation given in Him; the gift of the Holy Spirit whose work it is to glorify Christ, to take of the things that are His, bring them to remembrance, and so to teach them to the Church that it may assimilate, adapt and apply to new needs the truth, "as truth is in Jesus." The process has not been without its dangers. Serious mistakes have been made, as all must acknowledge except those who consider the Church, as such, to be infallible. But, taking a broad view of Christianity through the centuries, it is remarkable how the two extremes have been avoided. On the one hand, the danger of restricting its development as Islam is fossilized by the dead hand of the Koran; on the other, the snapping of those sacred links of continuity which bind together all who call themselves Christians in loyal allegiance to Him whose name they bear.

Doctrines have changed their form while preserving their substance. It took three centuries to frame the creed of Nicæa, and some important articles of faith, on sin and grace, atonement and justification, were still more gradually wrought out. Some of these, perhaps, need reminting if they are to be made current coin for the circulation of to-day. The ethical principles laid down in the New Testament are continually receiving new illustration and new applications which may sometimes seem to make the old obsolete. But as Jesus drew from the old law the two great commandments on which He sought to base the conduct of His followers, so the great moral principles of the New Testament, tenaciously held by the Church as beyond change and repeal, are brought freshly to bear upon a perpetually changing civilization. New problems affecting the family, slavery, the position of woman, or international wars, are continually arising, and fresh appeal is continually being made to the disciples of the kingdom for their solution. These do not profess to be able to answer all questions, to remove all difficulties; but it is part of their work in the world to show how those who have learned in Christ's school, can bring the old truth which they assuredly believe, to bear upon hitherto unanticipated problems and practically revolutionized conditions of society.

It is in this way that the kingdom itself is to come among men. For the kingdom is coming, not come; the Church is making, not made. Christendom is, in a sense, a word of the past; its history may be traced out and written down. In a sense, it is a word of the present, representing a mighty living force to-day. Still more is it a word of the future, for as yet we have not been able to see what "Christianity" fully means. He was right who, in answer to the question, Is the Christian religion "played out"? replied, It has not yet been tried. The disciples of the kingdom are, as yet, far from having exhausted the resources of the treasure-house entrusted to their care.

Ours is an age of transition. Every age forms a bridge between that which precedes and that which follows it, but to our own seems to be entrusted a specially difficult task of assimilating new knowledge, meeting new conditions, abandoning old forms and revivifying old truths. Those on whom such work is specially incumbent need not be discouraged; those who see the process going on around them need not despair. The Christ of the New Testament is for us the Way, the Truth and the Life; not the Christ of the Sermon on the Mount, still less the shadowy personage who is all that remains when certain critics of the Gospels have eliminated from the text whatever does not please them. The Christ of the New Testament, as the Redeemer of men, is the treasure-house, and the Holy Spirit whom He promised enables us to make its contents our own. He is the way-guide into all the truth, new and old, that we need for the journey of life. Forms of dogma which have commended themselves to the Church in past centuries may change, but Jesus Christ is the same yesterday, to-day and forever. The gospel of salvation in Him is sufficient for the individual, the nation and the race; it need not be changed, and it can not be given up without darkening the hope of the world. But the task of bringing it to bear with new power upon new generations and new intellectual and social conditions is continually laid upon Christ's Church; it is one of which she must not complain and must not grow weary. In accomplishing it, Christ's disciples fulfil the design of their Master and work out at the same time their own salvation and that of the world whom He came to save.

Spirit, who makest all things new,
Thou leadest onward: we pursue
    The heavenly march sublime.
'Neath thy renewing fire we glow,
And still from strength to strength we go,
    From height to height we climb.

To thee we rise, in thee we rest;
We stay at home, we go in quest,
    Still thou art our abode.
The rapture swells, the wonder grows,
As full on us new life still flows
    From our unchanging God.

JAMES DENNEY

1856-1917

THE PRIMARY MARKS OF CHRISTIANITY

BIOGRAPHICAL NOTE

PROFESSOR of New Testament language, literature and theology, United Free Church College, Glasgow, Scotland; born Paisley, February 5, 1856; educated Highlanders' Academy, Greenock; Glasgow University and Free Church College; D.D. Glasgow, Chicago Theological Seminary, Princeton University and Aberdeen; minister of Free Church, Broughty Ferry, 1886-97; author of "The Epistle to the Thessalonians," "Second Epistle to the Corinthians" ("Expositor's Bible"), "Studies in Theology," "The Epistle to the Romans" ("Expositor's Greek Testament"), "Gospel Questions and Answers," "The Death of Christ," "The Atonement and the Modern Mind," "Jesus and the Gospel," etc.

"Where is boasting, then? It is excluded. By what law? of works? Nay: but by the law of faith. Therefore we conclude that a man is justified by faith without the deeds of the law. Is he the God of the Jews only? is he not also of the Gentiles? Yes, of the Gentiles also: Seeing it is one God, which shall justify the circumcision by faith, and uncircumcision through faith. Do we then make void the law through faith? God forbid: yea, we establish the law."—Romans 3 : 27-31.

A T first sight this is a difficult and intractable passage. Our minds are hurried abruptly from one question to another, and we fail to see how the questions are connected, or what is their significance when we take them altogether. Readers who are more familiar with the verses which precede than with almost anything in the New Testament, relax their attention unintentionally when they come to the words, "that he might be just, and the justifier of him which believeth in Jesus." They feel that there they have got to the heart of the matter—the revelation of God in a manner which is at once the vindication of His own character and the hope of sinful men. Their minds rest, and can not but rest there, and they go over and over the wonderful verses in which Paul interprets for all time the mystery of the cross: Christ Jesus, whom God set forth in propitiatory power, through faith in His blood, with a view to demonstrating His righteousness, that he might be just himself, and justify all who believe in Jesus. But Paul does not himself stop at that point. The sight of Christ on His cross thus interpreted, of Christ a propitiation in his blood, of the Lamb of God bearing the sin of the world, searched and quickened his whole being. We read in one of the gospels, of the men who put Jesus to death, that sitting down they watched him there. So we must conceive Paul's attitude as he writes this passage. He writes with his eye on the Son of God crucified for our sins. His heart is being searched and sounded by the revelation of the cross, and as these swift far-reaching questions rise in quick succession to his lips, we see how he is being moved within. Each of them is prompted by the cross. It is the power of Christ's passion, descending into the apostle's heart and making itself intelligible there, which comes out in them. Each of them is itself a revelation. Each of them implicitly asserts a truth which belongs to the very essence of the Christian faith. All of them together may be said to exhibit the notes of true Christianity as understood by Paul. They may be various, but they are not incoherent; they are connected by their common relation to the cross; they find their unity and their impulse there.

As Paul contemplates Christ a propitiation in his blood, the first question prompted by the sight is, Where is boasting then? And he answers in a word, Excluded. Standing by Mount Calvary, and realizing that there is no way to God but that way, we become conscious of an infinite obligation to Christ. The deepest, strongest, most omnipresent of all Christian feelings is the feeling of debt. The one thing a man can not do, who has taken home to his heart the significance of the cross, is to make claims as of right against God. He feels that he is debtor to Christ for what he can never repay. Christ has done for him what he could not do for himself, and what no effort could ever enable him to do; He has made atonement for his sins; and as this truth, on which all his hope depends, sinks into his mind and masters it, his soul is flooded with a sense of obligation to Christ in which all other feelings are swallowed up. Boasting is excluded; it is peremptorily and finally excluded; the Christian's whole life is a life of debt to God.

It may seem to some that a truth so obvious is hardly worth stating, either by an apostle or by a modern preacher. But to Paul it was a great revelation, and a stage comes in every serious religious life in which it has to be learned anew. There is, as Dr. Chalmers said, a "natural legality" in the heart of man which urges him to seek righteousness "as it were of works," instead of submitting to the righteousness of God. Even a Christian lapses half unconsciously into this unchristian attitude; he tries to be good, so to speak, without God; he tries to achieve some character or virtue out of his own resources, and clothes himself in that character or virtue to challenge God's approbation. True, he can only do this when the cross has sunk below his horizon; but it does sometimes sink; and it needs the painful experience of failure to bring him back to it, and to teach him that he must owe the power of the new life to the atonement. What Paul felt with startling force as he looked at Christ crucified, has found expression in every variety of Christian creed. All churches confess with one heart, tho in different forms of speech, that in our spiritual life we begin by being, and must forever continue to be, God's debtors. We can have no relation to him but that of owing him all we are and all we hope to become. Salvation is of the Lord; and the moment we are influenced by any other thought, it ceases to be operative in us. This is what the Lutheran Church means when following in the train of Paul, it teaches that we are justified by faith alone, without works of law. What does that mean, as a religious truth, but this: that before we have done anything, before we can do anything, nay, in order that we may be able to do anything, the mercy of God is there for us sinners in Jesus Christ; there, before our faces, independent of any action of ours, an inconceivable unmerited mercy, which we can only welcome, and to which we must be indebted forever? This, too, is the Calvinistic doctrine of election. For what does that mean (as a doctrine based on experience) but this: that the initiative of salvation lies with God? that the Master can always say to the disciple, Ye have not chosen me, but I have chosen you? and that the disciple must always say to the Master, Not unto us Lord, not unto us, but unto thy name be the glory? The religious import of Calvinism is precisely that of the Lutheran doctrine of justification by faith; it is justification by faith exprest in the form of a doctrine of the divine sovereignty. And the same may be said even of what seem to be intellectually poor and unworthy, even degrading and superstitious modes of expressing the truth. The sacramentarianism of the Roman Catholic or of the Anglican Church, which ascribes a peculiar sanctity to sacramental elements, and makes them in themselves vehicles of grace, would never command the influence it does unless it represented, as it were, to the very senses, the truth (for surely it is the truth) that the grace of God is independent of our deserts, antecedent to our exertions, and that our sole relation to God must be that of being His debtors for it. Lutherans, Calvinists, or Catholics, to call them so—Paul anticipated every particle of the truth enshrined in their characteristic and fundamental doctrines when he exprest the first conviction generated in his heart by the cross in the swift question and answer, Where is boasting then? It is excluded. Humility, as Calvin puts it, is the first, second, and third thing in the Christian religion.

There can be no doubt that this necessity of coming under an infinite obligation to Christ is the great difficulty in the way of the acceptance of Christianity. It is still what it was when Paul preached—the offense or stumbling-block of the cross. It was not the cross itself which was or which is an offense: it was the cross interpreted as Paul interpreted it, the cross a propitiation for sin, the cross requiring men from the very beginning to humble themselves in a way they had never dreamed of, and to owe their very being as children of God, having access to the Father, to what had been done for them by another. Yet this is the test of Christianity. It is not the man who admires Christ, or who essays to imitate Him, or who exalts Him as the measure and standard of perfection, who is the Christian according to the New Testament; it is the man who is debtor to Christ for the forgiveness of his sins, and for every hope of holiness and impulse to it. Try yourself by that.

Humility is sometimes discredited in the Church because it is misunderstood. It is regarded as an artificial depreciation of one's self in comparison with others. But that has no connection with humility as it is represented here. Humility is simply the recognition of the real relation between ourselves and God. To be humble is to be in one's spirit and temper what we are in point of fact—God's debtors; debtors forever, debtors all the time, to God's redeeming love in Christ. This habit of mind has nothing to do, as is sometimes supposed, with low spirits. It is not characterized by want of hope or inspiration. On the contrary, the most unmistakable indication that the Church lives in the sense of its infinite obligations to Christ is the intensity and fervor of its praise. Boasting is excluded, says Paul; yet did any man ever boast as he? Why, he uses this very word boasting, or words of the same root, over fifty times in his epistles. There is no word he could less afford to dispense with. What he does exclude, or rather what the cross excludes, is that self-confidence in which a man would be independent of God; but when that goes, then room is made for boasting in the Lord. Put the atonement out of the Church's faith, and adoration dies on her lips. You may have complacent or sentimental hymns; you may have insincere or flattering hymns; you will have no doxologies like those of the New Testament. It is when the sense of what we owe to Christ strikes into our hearts as it struck into the hearts of the apostles that we can say with them, "Unto him that loved us, and washed us from our sins in his own blood, . . . to him be glory and dominion for ever and ever." That is the beginning of Christianity, and the end of it. It is the exaltation of Christ in the inspiration of what we owe to him.

But as Paul contemplates the cross, another question rises swiftly in his mind. The cross is a revelation of God; it is the final and supreme revelation; for whom is it meant? The question may seem to us almost unreal, but it was a question of fateful importance then. God had had a people peculiarly His own; He had been a God of Jews in a sense in which He had not been the God of other nations. Whatever difficulties we may have in adjusting it to our general conceptions of human history, the fact remains that God had been present in the history of Israel in a manner and to issues to which He had not been present in the history of other races. He had been the God of Abraham, of Isaac and of Jacob, the God of Moses and the prophets, the God of the pious souls who wrote the Psalms, as He had not been the God of the Gentile

world. This had been in point of fact the method of His dealing with the human race, and whatever problems it may present to our apologetics, it is useless to quarrel with the way God has made and ruled His world. Salvation is of the Jews, let comparative religion say what it will. But God's revelation of Himself to the Jews culminated in the cross, and as Paul looked at it, the truth rose upon his mind that the limitations of the earlier stages of the true religion had passed away. The deliverance from Egypt, the restoration from Babylon, the interpretation of history by Amos and Isaiah and Jeremiah—these might have significance only for the Hebrew race; but Christ on His cross is propitiation for sin. Christ bearing sin, Christ dying in love and dying for righteousness' sake: to whom is that intelligible? to whom does it appeal? To what, rather, let us ask, did it appeal in Paul himself? Was it to the Jew or to the Pharisee? No, it was to the man in Paul that Christ appealed from His cross. It was to the conscience stricken with sin, and doomed to impotence and despair. And as Paul realized this he realized at the same time the great truth which is peculiarly associated with his name—that the gospel is not for a nation, but for all mankind. Is God, the God who reveals Himself at the cross, a God of Jews only? No! there is nothing in the world so universally intelligible as the cross. Make it visible, and there is not a man on earth who may not know what it means and respond to its power. "I, if I be lifted· up from the earth, will draw all men unto myself." The second characteristic, then, of the true religion, which will live in the heart of every man who knows what it is, is its universality. The cross appeals to me not in virtue of anything which distinguishes me from others, but in virtue of that in which I am one with every member of the human race. It was the sense of this which made Paul a missionary. I am debtor, he said, not to Christ only, but to Jew and Greek, to wise and unwise. The gospel is not ours; we have no interest in it, and no hope in it, that is not common to the whole family of man. To exclude any section of humanity from it, on any ground whatever, is to disinherit ourselves.

One is tempted to remark in passing that this throws an interesting light on the distinction that is popular in some circles, not to say fashionable, between Paulinism and Christianity. Paul is represented as a person of such abnormal individuality that his interpretation of Christianity must be heavily discounted, or, indeed, completely ignored. It is hardly worth while trying to understand him, let alone feeling under any obligation as far as possible to agree with him. Perhaps it is pleasant to have the consciousness of superiority to the protest of evangelists and of theologians, but it is surely a case in which to rejoice with trembling. May we not rather say that Paul became the first of missionaries, and established, as he does in this passage, the missionary character of the Christian religion just because he had eliminated from his gospel all that belonged to the Jew or the Pharisee, all that could be characterized as personality or idiosyncrasy, and saw confronting each other and calling to each other, as deep calls unto deep, the infinite love of God in the cross of Jesus, and the hopeless sin and misery of man. Those who contrast Christianity and Paulinism provoke one to say that they understand neither Christ nor Paul. Paulinism will go out of fashion only when sin and grace have ceased to need and to seek each other, and if it does, Christianity will perish with it.

Commonplace as it ought to be—an immediate inference from the fact that the cross appeals directly and exclusively to what is human in man—the truth which is involved in the question, Is He a God of Jews only? is one that is far from commanding practical acceptance in Christendom. It is traversed still, as it was in ancient times, by national pride. It is traversed by that national Pharisaism which disbelieves in the character or in the Christianity of other peoples, and regards them as all, somehow, in the sight of heaven, less favored races. It is traversed even in the Church itself by the ecclesiastical exclusiveness which would confine the redeeming force of the cross of Christ to the boundaries of some particular organization. It is traversed by all who, on whatever ground, are opposed to the work of Christian missions. Such opponents are not to be found only outside of the Church; they are numerous and sometimes they are audible within. Now no one would assert that all missions have answered the hopes with which they were set on foot, and least of all, would any missionary assert that no mistakes have been made, that no wrong methods have been tried, or that nothing remains to be learned from experience. But that does not touch on the great question, whether God is the God of all, and whether the revelation of God made in Christ the propitiation for sin, is one which is meant for all, which all need, and which all are capable of receiving. When that question is raised, it can only be by those who have the whole significance of the cross yet to discover. The man who has seen what Paul saw, who has felt what Paul felt, dares not limit the range of that divine appeal. He dare not say, This speaks to me, and exerts its power over me; it has meaning and virtue for those who have been brought so far in the life of the soul without its help; but there are races to whom it does not speak, and to

whom it will not speak for generations to come; they must be raised by some other discipline to the level at which in the long run they may see and comprehend and be subdued by the cross. Such a line of argument is not only confuted by all the experiences with which our missionary reports are crowded; it is confuted *ab initio* by the inspired insight of Paul. The discipline of law and of labor is no doubt indispensable in human life, as indispensable within the bounds of Christendom as beyond them. But it is not the discipline of law and of labor which qualifies us to appreciate the gospel; it is the discipline of sin, of failure, of despair. And the gospel comes not to put the finishing touches to a work which has been carried so far in independence of it; it comes to initiate the divine life in the soul. Law and labor can cooperate with it: they can do nothing of consequence without it, and they can not take its place. As long as the cross is visible, God speaks from it to the world in a language that all the world can understand; He proclaims a message from it that all the world needs to hear. Is He a God of Britons only? or of white men only? Who that has bowed down, as Paul did in his soul's great need, and received the atonement, but must answer with him, No! not of Britons only, or of white men only, but of all; the God of Kaffirs and Hindus and Chinamen, exactly as He is our God; and there is that in every race, underneath the dark skin and the alien traditions, which leaps up as it does in us to the reconciling love of God. That is why we are debtors to all, and have no liberty and no inclination to listen to those who decry mission work. If there is any meaning in the cross, it means that there are no step-children in the family of God. The most superior person must sink or swim with all his kind.

There is another side to this which must not be overlooked. If there are those for whom the gospel as Paul preached it is supposed to be as yet too good, there are those, on the other hand, who are supposed to be too good for the gospel in this particular shape. They do not deny that in some large indefinite sense the world has been indebted to Christ and is indebted to Him still; the leaven has leavened the lump, and in the process they, too, have in a measure been changed; but it is unnecessary, many think, to go further. There is no need, certainly, to disparage this collective impersonal Christianity; we ought to thank God that there is so much of it as there is. But to any one standing where Paul stood, feeling in his own spirit what Paul felt, how inconsiderable a thing it is. Christianity means nothing whatever unless it means the sense of obligation to Christ; but what does this sense of obligation itself mean, when we keep it out of relation to the personal Savior, and to the divine supernatural deeds on which the hope of the world depends? When we think of the Son of God bearing the sin of the world, can we believe that it will ever be less than the first interest of every man that breathes to know Him, to come under the infinite obligation to Him which constitutes Christianity, to call Him for what He has done Redeemer and Lord? No inheritance of science or philosophy, no advance of art or civilization can ever make the atonement less than essential. There is something in the cross of Christ which strikes deeper into the heart of man than all these elevating and refining powers, and which works miracles in it that none of them can work; and therefore we are debtors to the wise and to the Greek, to that modern intelligence which is often said to be alienated from the gospel, as much as to the barbarians and the uncultured. I believe it is from the cross, as a center, interpreted as Paul interpreted it—from the place at which a supernatural person achieved a supernatural work—that the modern mind, so far as it has been estranged from the New Testament mode of thinking, will be won for that mode of thinking again. The Christian view of all things will be recovered when the soul comes into the Christian relation to Christ bearing the sin of the world. A missionary society naturally thinks of those who have never heard Christ's name; but it is not they only who need the reconciliation; it is not they only to whom God appeals in His Son; it is not they only for whom Christ died; and if we would do justice to the revelation of the cross, we must make it our calling to carry it not only to what are visibly the dark places of the earth, but to those also that boast of their enlightenment. Is God the God of barbarous races only? Is He not also the God of the races which have produced art and science and philosophy? Yes, He is their God, too; and as their need of reconciliation is the same, it appeals to them on the same terms.

We can not think of this common appeal of the reconciling love of God to all men without distinction without being disappointed with the smallness of the results achieved. The cross has not yet done much, we are tempted to say, to unite the human race. Even Christian nations are at war with each other. If they are not at war, they live in a chronic state of mutual envy, hatred and suspicion, which is morally if not materially as disastrous as war itself. Within a Christian nation there is strife and estrangement of classes; in spite of the all-reconciling symbol which is over them, men are arrayed in opposing camps, which represent hostile interests, and neither love nor trust each other. Nay, the Church itself is rent in pieces by questions of order and organization, and men unchurch each other over matters like these. The only explanation of such things is that the cross meanwhile has sunk beneath the horizon. If it were visible, if men saw what it meant, this would be impossible. The common relation to the cross would subdue to itself every other relation in human life.

This brings us to Paul's third and last question, Do we make void the law through faith? The question may seem unprovoked, but it was a very real one then, and it resumes its reality as soon as the gospel exerts its power on a great scale. The gospel is a proclamation of the free forgiveness of sins, and the forgiveness of sins is capable both of being misinterpreted and abused. It was misinterpreted and abused in the apostolic age. It was regarded by some people as giving a license to sin with impunity. The enemies of Paul, who affected zeal for righteousness, slanderously insinuated that such was his teaching. He made void the law through faith, they said. In modern language, he abolished morality with his religion. The forgiveness of sins, freely bestowed upon faith, acted as a solvent on morality; the atonement was an opiate to the conscience; the man who accepted it did not take life seriously any more. This problem of the relation of faith and law, religion and morality, pardon and the good life, often comes up anew; there are always people full of moral interest, and especially of interest in their own morality—their very own—to deprecate the Pauline emphasis on the cross. When the objection was actually made to Paul's gospel that it was unfavorable to morality, that it meant, in plain English, let us do evil that good may come, the more sin the more grace, he denounced it indignantly as a slander. The people who say anything of the kind incur the just judgment of God. There are still people who ought to be answered so. Even here, where it is rather the inevitable consequences of the cross with which he is dealing, Paul repels rather than refutes the idea that faith makes void the law, or that the cross of Christ as he has interpreted it is hostile to morality. The very contrary, he maintains, is the case. "We establish the law." It gets its due for the first time in the lives of Christian men reconciled to God by the blood of the cross. The righteousness of the law is fulfilled in them, walking as they do, not after the flesh, but after the spirit.

There are many ways in which this can be brought out. It can be proved by looking at what the cross of Christ was, even historically. The cross establishes the law, indicates morality, because it triumphs over the one thing which more persistently and insinuatingly than anything else tends to undermine it. The one undying enemy of Christ, it has been said, is the great God Pan: in other words, it is the feeling which creeps upon us insensibly that all things are one, and one with a unity in which all differences disappear. Truth and falsehood, right and wrong, nature and spirit, necessity and freedom, the personal and the impersonal, that which we inherit and that which we earn for ourselves—all these are perpetually in process of interpenetration and of transformation into each other. The differences between them are evanescent and unreal, even the difference between right and wrong. And suddenly, in this world of moral haze and uncertainty, where all things are in flux and nothing sure, we come upon the cross, and One hanging on it who died for the difference, and made it as real as His agony and passion, as eternal as the being of God which He revealed. Of all who are interested in morality, the Christian is pledged by the cross to an interest the most passionate and profound. There is a challenge in the very aspect of it. It calls aloud, Who is on the Lord's side? for the Lord has a side. It binds every man who owes allegiance to it to resist, even unto blood, striving against sin.

The falsehood of the suggestion that the Christian religion abolishes morality—or that forgiveness favors sin—is seen more clearly still if we think how forgiveness has just been connected by Paul with Christ as a propitiation for sin. If God's forgiveness meant indulgence if it had no content but this, that God simply took no notice of sin, no doubt the charge would often be true. But the only forgiveness of which the New Testament speaks is that which is bestowed at the cross; and is there anything there which speaks of indulgence? At the cross of Christ sin is judged as well as pardoned; and the sinner who takes into his heart the Christian forgiveness, the forgiveness preached at the cross, takes into his heart along with it God's annihilating sentence on his sin. Christ bore our sins; that is how they are pardoned; and the virtue of His submission to their doom enters into the Christian along with pardon, so that he is dead to sin. It is because Christ's death has this character, because it is a death in which He is bearing sin that sinners have a point of attachment in Christ, and can become one with Him. If Christ were the holy one of God and we could say no more of Him than that, who could approach Him? Who could dare, to use the language which is so common, to identify himself' with Him? But He is the Holy One of God bearing our sin; that is what He is at the cross, and that is our point of contact with Him; it is as He dies in our place, bearing our burden, that He draws us to Himself and unites our life to His own; and the new life that we live in Him is not a life to which law is indifferent; it is a life into which the awful sanctity of the law has en-

tered once for all through the death of Jesus. This is the experience and the gospel of the apostle; and we can understand the indignation with which he repels a charge which virtually meant that Christ had died in vain.

And once more, we can give an experimental proof that religion does not abolish morality; only the forgiven man, it may be boldly maintained, exhibits goodness in its true proportions. The law is only established; that is, it only gets justice done to it when it is written on the heart. But it can not be written on the heart till the heart is made tender, and the heart is not made really tender by anything but that humility which is born in it as it stoops to be forgiven for Christ's sake. It is this which makes it sensitive to all its obligations both to God and man, and not till then does morality get justice in a man's life. The man who is proud of his integrity, and who needs no repentance nor forgiveness, thinks he is fulfilling the law; it does not occur to him that the only fulfilling of the law is love, and that love in Christian proportions and Christian intensity is the response of the soul to what God has done for us in Christ at the cross. We love, with the only love which does justice to the law, with the only love which works righteousness and holiness of truth—we love because He first loved us. And according to the plainest teaching of the New Testament, we do not know what God's love is until we learn it at the cross, "Herein is love, not that we loved God, but that He loved us, and sent His son to be the propitiation for our sins." The saint never lived who did not rest his sanctity from beginning to end on the forgiveness of sins. The blood of Christ is no opiate to the conscience; it is a slander so to say, a blind and fatal guiltiness so to think; it is the quickening of the conscience, it is death to sin and life to God.

Such are the thoughts that rise in Paul's mind as he contemplates Christ set forth in his blood, a propitiation for sin. Whatever else they are, they are great thoughts; they are thoughts of that order, the truth of which is seen not in the light we can cast upon them, but in the light which they cast upon everything else. The Christian Church is passing through a hard and perplexing time; not a time of persecution, but one of indifference and even of contempt, in which injustice is easy. There are many who tell us that it is permanently discredited, and that the difficulty felt in almost all the Christian communities of obtaining ministers and missionaries is an unmistakable indication of this. We have heard such things before; they have been often heard in the course of Christian history. The way to meet them and defeat them is not to minimize the gospel, not to reduce it to its lowest terms or to what we consider such, but to maintain it in the integrity of the apostolic testimony. It is by its greatness it must prevail, by the sense in it of a breadth and length and depth and height passing knowledge. Intelligence may be alienated by the trivial; but great ideas, great truths, great problems, great tasks, always fascinate and subdue it again. We are debtors both to Greeks and barbarians, both to the wise and to the foolish; let us preach to them all Christ crucified, the power of God and the wisdom of God; and if we do it with this apostolic comprehension, in the sense of what we owe to God, in the sense of the appeal which His love makes to all without distinction, in the sense, too, of a new obligation to a holy life, we can leave it to God to make it salvation to every one who believes.

SAMUEL ROLLES DRIVER

1846-1914

THE HEBREW PROPHETS

BIOGRAPHICAL NOTE

REGIUS professor of Hebrew and canon of Christ church, Oxford, England, 1883-1914; born Southampton, October 2, 1846; educated at Winchester College; New College, Oxford; fellow of New College, 1870-83; tutor of New College, 1875-83; member of Old Testament Revision Committee, 1876-84; D.Litt., Dublin, 1892; D.D., Glasgow, 1901; Aberdeen, 1906; D.Litt., Cambridge, 1905; fellow of the British Academy, 1902; author of "A Treatise on the Use of the Tenses in Hebrew," "Isaiah, His Life and Times," "Notes on the Hebrew Text of the Books of Samuel," "An Introduction to the Literature of the Old Testament," "Sermons on Subjects Connected with the Old Testament," commentaries on the books of the Bible, etc.

"Attend unto me, O my people; and give ear unto me, O my nation; for a law shall go forth from me, and I will make my judgment to rest for a light of the peoples."—Isaiah 51 : 4.

THE prophets are at once the most brilliant product of the genius of Israel, and a unique phenomenon in history. The "prophet" is one who speaks on behalf of or for another; this is the sense which the word had among the Greeks, who used it specially of one who interpreted the obscure utterances of a deity; and it is the sense which the word bears in the Old Testament in the Book of Exodus (7 : 1, 2), for example, Aaron, speaking to the people in Moses' name, is called his "prophet." The prophet is one who speaks for God, comes forward in His name and declares His will or His purpose to His people. The prophets are at one in declaring their firm and unwavering belief that they are the organs and instruments of the Most High, and that their utterances about Him come at His prompting, and are invested with His authority. The phrases which they habitually use are, "Thus saith Jehovah," "Hear ye Jehovah's word." While we can not doubt the inspiration of the prophets, we must be careful not to think of their inspiration too mechanically. Especially, we must not think of God as dictating to the prophets the very words which they are to use. In all inspiration there are two factors, a human as well as a divine factor. The divine thought, implanted (as we may suppose) by an extraordinary quickening and exaltation of his natural faculties in the prophet's soul, takes there the shape which the prophet's own individuality impresses upon it; he speaks "for" God, but he throws the thought which he expresses into his own words and literary form; the phraseology, the rhetoric, the poetry, the imagery, and also the feelings and the emotions (which are sometimes very palpable) are his own; it is these personal characteristics which impart to the writings of each individual prophet their own distinctive character. And in estimating the writings of the prophets, and comparing them with one another, account must always be taken of this varying human element, which, in a greater or less degree, is invariably present in them.

I may now pass on to illustrate some of the principal ways in which the activity of the prophets displayed itself. And, firstly, notice briefly the part which the prophets played as statesmen. Jehovah was the national God of Israel; Church and State were closely allied; and the truest interests of the one were also the interests of the other. The prophets

possest an insight and independence which
fitted them, in an exceptional degree, to be
the political advisers of their nation. They
saw more clearly than their contemporaries
the bearing upon Israel of the movements and
tendencies operative about them; they interpreted beforehand the signs of the times, and
warned their countrymen how to face the future. In earlier times they are influential in
setting up or dethroning dynasties; at a later
time they stand beside the king to admonish
or advise. Saul, the first king of Israel, was
appointed through the instrumentality of a
prophet; Samuel saw that the time had come
when Israel needed the unifying and consoli-
dating influences which in those days could
be wielded only by a monarch; he anointed
Saul and instructed him how to act. Jeroboam was encouraged to assume the leadership of the Ten Tribes by the prophet Ahijah.
Jehu, again, who overthrew the dynasty of
Omri, was anointed at the instance of Elijah
and Elisha. But we can study the political
action of the prophets more distinctly in the
case of those whose writings remain to witness to it. These prophets attack the popular
statesmanship of the day; they unmask the
fallacies underlying it, and expose its short-
sightedness. They also denounce the national
sins and shortcomings, showing how they must
inevitably end in national disaster. Thus
Amos sees society in the northern kingdom, in
spite of the brilliancy and long prosperity of
Jeroboam's reign, morally vitiated and corrupt; the nobles of Samaria, so far from
evincing anxiety for the public weal, "put
far the evil day," and are abandoned to self-
indulgence and luxury; he sees only too truly
what will happen when the Assyrian draws
near; ruin and exile will be his nation's doom.
The event proved signally the accuracy of his
forecasts. Within sixteen years the inhabitants of the northeastern districts were transported by Tiglath-pileser to Assyria; within
thirty years the northern kingdom had ceased
to exist.

Isaiah, a little later, displays conspicuously
the qualities of a clear-sighted and consistent
statesman. The age was one in which the
danger that threatened Judah was entangle-
ment with foreign powers; and Isaiah lays
down the principles by which her actions
should be guided. In the panic caused by the
Syro-Ephraitish invasion (Is. 7 : 2) Isaiah
alone retained his calmness, and estimated the
danger at its just proportions. At that time
he discountenanced the application to Assyria
for help, for he foresaw the complications
that would in all probability result from it;
when, however, Ahaz had taken this step and
the Assyrian protectorate had been actually
accepted by Judah, he acquiesces, and all his
efforts are directed toward averting a rup-
ture. From the first he saw the hollowness

of Egyptian promises; again and again he
keenly satirizes the folly of trusting to them;
and it was doubtless owing chiefly to his influence that the alliance with Egypt was deferred for so many years. In the end, however, in 700 B.C., the party opposed to him
prevailed; and Judah, relying upon Egypt
and other neighbors, revolted from Assyria.
The sequel showed the soundness of Isaiah's
judgment. As before, whenever it came to a
contest of strength, the help of Egypt was of
no avail, and Jerusalem was only saved from
destruction by an occurrence which could not
have been calculated upon, and which was the
termination of a crisis, that, so far as we can
judge, would not have arisen at all had
Isaiah's counsels been listened to in the first
instance.

To pass now to a second aspect of the prophet's work: The prophets were the teachers
of a pure and spiritual religion, and of an
elevated morality. Their teaching on these
subjects has now become so completely part
of the common stock of Christian theology
and ethics, that we do not always remember
how much of it is due, in the first instance, to
the initiative. We may be better able to appreciate this if we view them historically.
Amos and Hosea, the two earliest prophets
whose writings have been preserved to us,
lived in the early and middle part of the
eighth century B.C.; and when these prophets
wrote, the greater part of the Old Testament
was still unwritten; if we bear this fact in
mind we shall perhaps be in a better position
to realize the originality and creative power
of the great prophets. The foundations of
Israel's religion had indeed been laid in the
distant past. The earlier parts of the historical books, which are the work of men of
prophetical spirit, had shown generally that
Jehovah was a God of righteousness Himself,
who loved righteousness in men; and history
had produced many examples of men who had
striven to rule their lives accordingly; but
the great prophets who followed developed
both theology and ethics in many directions,
and gave them new and important practical
applications. Nathan, we remember, rebuked
David fearlessly for his great sin. Elijah was
the champion alike of religion and morality;
he fought, and fought successfully, the great
battle of Jehovah against Baal; and he pronounced sentence upon Ahab and Jezebel for
the mock trial and murder of Naboth.

When we come to the prophets whose writings have been preserved to us, we find that,
while, of course, there are many fundamental
truths, which are proclaimed by all alike,
there is mostly some particular principle upon
which each lays stress. Amos, for instance,
the first of these prophets, shows remarkable
originality and breadth of view. He opens
his book with a survey of the nations around

Israel; and fastening upon some offense against common humanity of which each has been guilty, declares the judgment impending upon it. But he does not end there; Israel and Judah are included in his count, "because they sold the righteous for silver, and the poor for the sake of a pair of shoes." He thus transcends the limits of Jewish particularism; he teaches the impartiality with which Jehovah views all nations, and shows, in opposition to what was the current belief at the time, that He demands of Israel, His chosen and privileged people, precisely the same standard of equity and right which He exacts of other nations. Hosea, the prophet of religious emotion, lays stress upon the love with which Jehovah regards Israel; and while reproaching Israel for the imperfect manner in which His love was requited by it, deduces the lesson that the individual Israelite who seeks to participate in God's love must show love, on his own part, to his brother man. Isaiah is filled with the sense of the majesty of Israel's God; alike in nature and in history he sees Jehovah reveal Himself in grandeur; the whole earth is full of His glory; and his description of Jehovah seated upon His heavenly throne, or of the "day" on which He will manifest Himself against all that is "proud and lofty," or the imposing imagery under which he represents Him as striking down the hosts of Assyria (Is. 30 : 27-32), are sufficient evidence how fitted his genius was to conceive and express this aspect of the divine nature. The author of the discourses of Deuteronomy, who was a prophet intermediate in time between Isaiah and Jeremiah, and who in some respects developed the teaching of Hosea, insists with that warmth and persuasive eloquence which is peculiarly his own upon the sole divinity of Jehovah, as opposed to the inroads which heathenism was at the time making into Judah; He insists that Jehovah is the only God, a pure and spiritual being, who has loved Israel and is worthy to receive Israel's undivided love in return; Israel is to be a holy nation; its members are never to forget that they are the servants of a holy and loving God, and love is to be the guiding principle of their conduct, whether toward God or man. Jeremiah deplores the abandonment of Jehovah by His people for "other gods," and seeks to recall Judah to a sense of the claims which Jehovah has upon its reverence and love. The great prophet of the Exile, the author of chapters 40-66 of Isaiah, when his contemporaries doubted Jehovah's power to bring home His people from Babylon, preaches in language more exalted and impressive than is to be found in any other part of the Bible the transcendence, the omnipotence, the infinitude of Israel's God, the first and the last, the creator and sustainer of the universe, the incomparable One, who stands nevertheless in intimate relation with the earth, whose throne is indeed the heavens, but who dwells also with the humble and contrite heart; who has, moreover, His purposes of salvation, which, tho they are directed with special affection toward Israel, comprehend within their ultimate scope all the kindreds of the earth. Isaiah can depict, in unrivaled imagery, the majesty of Jehovah; but the great prophet of the Exile stands alone in the splendid comprehensiveness with which he proclaims the immensity of the divine nature and the boundlessness of its operation. And so we see how each prophet dwells upon and develops some particular aspect of truth, partly such as his own character and genius were adapted to apprehend, partly such as was fitted to meet the needs of the age in which he wrote.

Ethically, the prophets play largely the rôle of what we should call social reformers. They attack the abuses always conspicuous in an Eastern aristocracy; they assert with an earnestness and eloquence, which can never lose their spell, the claims of honesty, justice, philanthropy, and mercy. Certainly, the most ancient Hebrew legislation known to us, the Decalog and the Book of the Covenant (Ex. 20 : 23) fully recognize such claims. But the prophets develop and apply to new situations the principles implied in the old legislation, and reaffirm them with fresh energy. Listen thus to Amos: "Forasmuch, therefore, as ye trample upon the poor, and take exactions from him of wheat: ye have built houses of hewn stone, but ye shall not dwell in them; ye have planted pleasant vineyards, but ye shall not drink the wine thereof" (Amos 5 : 11). "Seek good and not evil, that ye may live; and so Jehovah, the God of hosts, shall be with you, as ye say. Hate the evil and love the good, and establish judgment in the gate"—the place where justice was administered—"it may be that Jehovah, the God of hosts, will be gracious to the remnant of Joseph" (Amos 5 : 14, 15). Micah and other prophets speak similarly: Isaiah, for instance (ch. 5), inveighs at length against the sins of a selfish and debased aristocracy, and shows how they were working their natural effects by disintegrating and weakening the national character. Nor must I omit to notice here the wonderful spiritualization of (chiefly) the old legislation of the "Book of the Covenant" in Deuteronomy, in which civil and ceremonial statutes are made the expression of a great and moral and spiritual ideal, which is designed to comprehend and govern the entire life of the community.

The prophets are again the warm and earnest advocates of a spiritual service of God. The Jews were too often apt to become formalists in their religious observances: they thought that if they were sufficiently frequent in their attendance at the temple, and in offering sacrifices, it was of little moment what their conduct in other respects might be; they were secure of Jehovah's favor. The prophets, on the contrary, teach that God requires the service of the heart. Of their memorable declarations on this subject, I can now only remind you of two. Amos, addressing the Israelites who thronged the great sanctuary at Bethel, and maintained there a splendid ceremonial, cries out, in Jehovah's name: "I hate, I despise your feasts, and I will take no delight in your solemn assemblies. Yea, tho ye offer me your burnt offerings and meal offerings, I will not accept them; neither will I regard the peace offerings of your fat beasts. Take thou away from me the noise of thy songs; for I will not hear the melody of thy lyres. But let judgment roll down as waters, and righteousness as a mighty stream" (Amos 5 : 21-24). And so, again, in the dark days of Manasseh, when heathen rites made their way into Judah, and it was asked by many what offerings might be of sufficient value to propitiate the Deity:

Wherewith shall I come before Jehovah,
And bow myself before the high God?
Shall I come before Him with burnt offerings,
With calves of a year old?
Will Jehovah be pleased with thousands of rams,
Or with ten thousands of rivers of oil?
Shall I give my first-born for my transgression,
The fruit of my body for the sin of my soul?

Micah answers by setting forth an ideal of religion which has never been surpassed:

He hath shewed thee, O man, what is good:
And what doth Jehovah require of thee,
But to do justly, and to love mercy,
And to walk humbly with thy God?
                              (Micah 6 : 6-8).

As their writings sufficiently show, the prophets were primarily the teachers of their own generation. It is the political mistakes, the social abuses, the religious and moral shortcomings of their own age which they set themselves to correct. It was their own contemporaries whom they sought in the first instance to recall to a high ideal of faith and practise. To be sure, they assert principles of universal validity, and capable, therefore, of application in new and altered circumstances; but the special forms which these principles assume in their hands show that the aim which they had in view is to meet the needs of their own time. Prophecy subserved moral purposes; and its primary motive was the practical guidance, in life and thought, of those among whom the prophet lived. This fact affords us a criterion for estimating the temporal predictions of the prophets. The prophets unquestionably possess the gift of uttering temporal predictions, which were truly fulfilled, in accordance with their expectations; but these predictions relate to the immediate or proximate future; and they are given for the warning or encouragement of the people, as the case may be, in the particular circumstances in which they are situated at the time; they stand consequently in a direct relation to the age in which the prophets themselves lived.

I have already noticed how Amos' predictions of the end of the northern kingdom were fulfilled. I can now only notice besides the brilliant series of predictions in which Isaiah foretold alike the siege of Jerusalem and the fate of the besiegers. All, so far as we can see, was calm on the political horizon, when, in the summer of B.C. 702, Isaiah amazed the people of Jerusalem by this startling announcement: "Ah! Ariel, Ariel, the city where David encamped, add ye a year to the [current] year; let the feasts run their round; then will I distress Ariel, and there shall be mourning and lamentation. And I will camp against thee round about, and will lay siege against thee with a fort, and I will raise siege works against thee. . . . But the multitude of thy foes shall be like small dust, and the multitude of the terrible ones as the chaff that passeth away; yea, it shall be at an instant suddenly" (Isaiah 29 : 1-5). The people only stared at the prophet in blank incredulity (ver. 9, R. V. margin). But the event showed that he had seen truly. Next year, Judah and many of its neighbors revolted from the Assyrians; Sennacherib started to quell the rebellion; and as he drew nearer and nearer to Jerusalem, Isaiah accompanied his movements with a whole series of prophecies, all describing, under varying imagery, a sudden and mysterious disaster which would disperse his forces and release Judah from her peril. Thus, in chapter 10, he imagines Sennacherib drawing nearer and nearer to Jerusalem from the north, until at last at Nob, a height about a mile north of the city, he swings his hand audaciously at the temple hill; the prize seems already within his grasp; when his army, figured as a huge forest, is mown down suddenly by an unseen hand: "Behold! the Lord, Jehovah of hosts, will lop the boughs with terror: and the high ones of stature will be hewn down, and the lofty will be brought low, and he will strike down the thickets of the forest with iron, and Lebanon will fall by a mighty one" (Is. 10 : 33, 34). And a little later, perhaps when the troops of Sennacherib were massing close at hand in the Philistine territory, he paints the splendid scene: "The nations make an uproar like the roaring of many waters, but he will rebuke them, and they shall flee far off; and they shall be chased as the chaff of the mountains before the wind, and like the whirling dust before the storm. At eventide behold confusion; before the morning, he is not" (Is. 17 : 13, 14).

And still later, when to human eyes it must have seemed that the toils had finally closed about the city: "At the noise of the tumult the peoples are fled; at the lifting up of thyself the nations are scattered" (Is. 33 : 3). And, as we know from the historical books, the army of Sennacherib was, in fact, when the doom of the city was to all appearance sealed, cut off unexpectedly by what must in reality have been a pestilence, while pressing on into Egypt. It would not be difficult to adduce other examples of the remarkable prevision possest by the prophets; but I must pass on.

Already, however, even in the few quotations which I have given, we may observe a fact which is worthy of our attention. The prophets are nearly always poets; hence, tho they no doubt utter sometimes matter-of-fact predictions, they very frequently clothe the thought which they have to express in an imaginative dress, or develop it with poetic imagery; and this imaginative element in their predictions has often nothing corresponding to it in the fulfilment. Thus Isaiah pictures Sennacherib approaching Jerusalem from the north, and having his army suddenly cut off at Nob; but in point of fact, neither of these things happened; he sent Rabshakeh against Jerusalem from Lachish in the southwest, and his army perished in or near Egypt. The essence of Isaiah's prophecy is fulfilled; but not the particular form in which its essential idea is exprest. Similarly in chapter 30: the great storm by which he pictures the Assyrian army as dispersed, and the huge funeral pyre which he imagines prepared to receive the Assyrian king and his army, are but poetical figures under which he depicts the completeness of the Assyrians' ruin; nothing corresponded to them in the fulfilment. We have thus a warning against interpreting the imagery of the prophets too literally.

The last characteristic of the prophets to which I shall be able to refer—their anticipation of an ideal future, of a time when the kingdom of God, unmarred by the presence of sin or trouble, will be established upon earth (or in the broader sense of the expression) of the Messianic age. The representations of this ideal future are poetically conceived, and hence vary often in details; but there are few prophets in whose writings, in one form or another, they do not form a characteristic feature. Thus Hosea closes his prophecy with a beautiful picture of Israel penitent, flourishing and spreading like a fruitful vine under the protecting favor of its God. Isaiah, after his impressive description of the "day" of Jehovah, sweeping away from Judah every object of pride and delight, and leaving the city desolate and empty, goes on abruptly to hold out before his hearers a vision of the new glory which is to follow (Chap. 4): "In that day shall the growth of Jehovah be for beauty and for glory, and the fruit of the land for majesty and adornment, unto the escaped of Israel. And it shall come to pass that he that is left in Zion and that remaineth in Jerusalem shall be called holy, even every one that is written down for life in Jerusalem" (Is. 4 : 2, 3). The picture is that of a remnant that will survive the judgment, and under changed and brighter auspices form the nucleus of an ideal community in the future. A new glory and ornament will appear, and take the place of that which has been swept away. The very growth of the land, for those that escape, fostered by Jehovah's care, will be clad with preternatural splendor. The inhabitants of Zion will realize the ideal character of the nation; every one of the survivors, "written down for life in Jerusalem"—i.e., inscribed in the register of its living citizens—shall be called "holy" (Ex. 19 : 6). By "life" Isaiah means not life hereafter, but life on earth under new conditions; a glorified life freed from sin and trouble. The community is, moreover, not merely purified morally, provision is also made for its continued safety. It is defended by the protecting presence of Jehovah, described, in imagery suggested by the story of the Exodus, as "a cloud and smoke by day, and the shining of a flaming fire by night";

a pavilion, or canopy, spread out over the whole site of Zion, will shelter it both from the sultry heat and from the violent storms to which an Eastern climate is always exposed. This is a single picture; but it is typical of many which appear in Isaiah, as also in other prophets. What the prophets love to depict, after the troubles of the present are over, is the advent of an age in which the unworthy members of a community having been removed, the survivors, purified and regenerate, realize the ideal holiness of the nation, and inspired by feelings of gratitude and devotion, live a life of ideal felicity in their own land.

A frequent but not a constant figure in these ideal pictures of the future is the ideal king, commonly known as the Messiah (i.e., the "anointed one"—a term based on the expression "Jehovah's anointed," often used in the Old Testament of the Israelitish king). David and Solomon had both left brilliant memories behind them; for centuries the monarchy had been the center and pivot of the State; and so the prophets, especially Isaiah, conceived the portrait of an ideal king, who, in contrast to the imperfect rulers of their own day, would realize the highest possibilities of earthly monarchy, sitting on the throne of David, governing Israel with perfect justice and perfect wisdom, and securing for his subjects perfect peace. As Isaiah had drawn the picture of the ideal king, so the author of Isaiah 40 : 66 draws a picture of the personified genius of the nation—Jehovah's "servant," as he is termed. Israel was the prophetic nation; it had received in the past the call to be the witness to God upon earth, and the organ and channel of revelation, but it had only imperfectly fulfilled its destiny; and so, upon the basis of the actual but imperfect Israel, the prophet rises to the conception of the ideal Israel, the Israel true to its destiny; and so vivid is the personification that the figure assumes, in his hands, the features and form of an individual who exhibits in their perfection the typical excellences of the nation, and may, therefore, be not unsuitably described as the personified genius of Israel. In virtue of his prophetic office Jehovah's "servant" has a mission, not to Israel only, but to the world (Is. 49 : 6); in pursuing his course, he meets contumely, persecution, and even death; but being innocent himself, his sufferings are efficacious for the good of others; finally, as the reward for his obedience, amazing greatness, such as even kings will marvel at (Is. 52 : 14) is in store for him afterward. The character is a wonderful one: it is instinct with singular sweetness, sympathy and tenderness; it is drawn by the prophet with great completeness; and it is introduced by him into his discourse with surprizing dramatic force.

There is one more feature in the prophets' outlook into the future to which I must refer, and that is their catholicity. They look forward to the time when the Gentiles will be admitted to the religious privileges of the chosen people. In the striking prophecy with which his second chapter opens, Isaiah poetically imagines the temple hill elevated so that it may be conspicuous afar, and then he pictures the nations streaming to it as to their spiritual metropolis, eager to listen to the divine instruction proceeding from it; and afterward he views in succession Ethiopia, Egypt, Tyre, and even Assyria, doing homage in the future to Israel's God. Jehovah's servant, of whom I have just spoken, is also commissioned to proclaim the truth possest by Israel to the world: he is equipped as a prophet, with God's spirit resting upon him; and his work is to "bring forth judgment [i.e., religion] to the nations"; to adopt the fine figure of another passage, he is to be a "light of the Gentiles" (Is. 42 : 1, 6). It is the same prophet who declares that the temple is to be a "house of prayer for all nations" (Is. 56 : 7).

These ideals form a striking and most characteristic feature in the writings of the prophets, and the question arises, How are they to be interpreted? What is to be said about their fulfilment? A careful comparison of the prophecies between themselves and with history shows that in interpreting them there are certain principles which must be remembered, if we are to avoid error. There is, of course, no question that the two great ideals I have spoken of, the ideal king and the personified genius of the nation, were fulfilled in the person of our Lord Jesus Christ. The two ideals which in the Old Testament are always distinct, were in the end fulfilled in union in Him. On the one hand, He is the king, the prince of peace, whose rule over the hearts of men is prefigured by Isaiah in his wonderful picture of the just and perfect administration of the shoot out of the stock of Jesse. On the other hand, as teacher, prophet, example, and sacrifice, He exhibited in their completeness the character which had before been imperfectly realized, whether by individual Israelites, or by the nation collectively: He thus corresponded precisely to the figure which I have called the personified genius of the nation, portrayed by the second Isaiah. But even here, if we look carefully, we shall see exemplified some of those principles of interpretation of prophecy to which I have alluded. In the first place, as I have said before, the prophets were preeminently poets; as poets, and especially as Oriental poets, they are endowed with imagination; they project bold ideals; they paint the future in brilliant colors; but we must beware of looking at details too narrowly, or expecting the fulfilment to be too literal. Secondly, they were seldom able to emancipate themselves entirely from the local and temporal limitations of the age in which they lived; and thirdly, they generally believed that the immediate future would see their ideals realized. Now, it is doubtful if any of their ideals have been realized in the precise form in which they themselves pictured them. Christ did not, and does not, sit upon a literal throne of David, or reign in the actual city of Jerusalem; still less did He, as Micah expressly says that the ideal ruler of Israel would do (Mic. 5 : 6), ward off the Assyrian when he invaded their territory; when Christ was born the Assyrian empire had long ceased to be. But, in fact, the kingdom of the prophets is in the fulfilment transformed: the glorified earthly kingdom, with a visible center at Zion, has given place to a spiritual "kingdom of heaven," with no local center; and spiritual blessings take the place of the material benefits to be conferred by the rule of Isaiah's or Micah's ideal king.

So, again, it is clear that the prophets greatly foreshorten the future. Under the strain and anxiety of a great national crisis, they idealize the age which is to begin when it is past; they picture it as marked by the reign of goodness and felicity. We have seen one of Isaiah's visions of this golden future. The great prophet of the Exile pictures in even more dazzling colors the splendor of the restored Jerusalem, the perfections of its inhabitants; the profound impression that it would make upon the world, the deference and respect which would be paid to it by all nations. But neither of thèse visions was realized as the prophet saw it. Jerusalem was, indeed, delivered from the Assyrian, and the exiles did return to Palestine; thus far both prophets foretold truly, but no great national reformation, no great national exaltation, followed either one event or the other. The prophets did not realize the complexity of human nature, or the force of evil habit upon it; they did not perceive how gradual all moral change must be; they did not understand what centuries must elapse, and what new and varied influences must be brought to bear upon human character, before the conditions of a perfect social state could be even approximately satisfied.

Their visions are great ones; no more ennobling and inspiring ideals of the possibilities of human life, or of the destinies of human society, are to be found in all literature. But they must be read and interpreted as ideals. The imaginative garb in which the prophets set forth the future must be recognized; it must be recognized that they are largely not predictions of fact, and that in the form in which they are set forth they contain many details which have not been realized in the past, and can not be realized in the future. I say can not be realized in the future, because the circumstances under which alone their realization was possible have passed away and can not be reproduced. Whatever the future course of history may be, it is contrary to the fundamental teaching of the New Testament to suppose, for instance, that Israel should ever become the priestly caste, with the Gentiles standing toward it in the subordinate position of laity, or that Jerusalem should become the actual and visible religious center of the world, to be visited, week by week, and month by month, by pilgrims from all nations, to observe the Jewish feasts of the Sabbath and the new moon (Is. 59 : 6; 66 : 23; cf. Zech. 14 : 16, 17). But the most catholic of the prophets are unable entirely to rise above the national and religious limitations of their age, or to avoid conceiving the future under the time-honored forms of their own dispensation.

When, however, due allowance has been made for the imaginative language employed often by the prophets, and for the national and temporal limitations which thus cling to them, their visions of the future are seen to be vivid and true expressions of the real purposes of God toward man. When, to the great majority of those who were to witness it, the return of a few thousand Jews to Palestine must have seemed an event of absolute indifference, the prophet of the Exile affirmed that it was fraught with the world-wide consequences for the spiritual future of mankind. Again, the event showed that he saw truly. The return to Palestine prevented the Jews from being lost among the nations, as their brethren of the ten tribes had been lost. Israel returned, and resumed its national life and organization; and so, when the fulness of time had come, the transformation of the old Jewish religion into a form adapted for other nations was found to be possible, and the faith of Christ was diffused among the Gentiles by the agency of the apostles. The consummation to which the prophets had often pointed was thus inaugurated; and the words of the passage which I have chosen for my text, as marking one of the culminating points of Old Testament prophecy, were fulfilled: Jehovah's "teaching" had gone forth, and He had made His "judgment"—i.e. His religion—"to rest for a light of the peoples."

HENRY DRUMMOND

1851-1897

THE GREATEST THING IN THE WORLD

BIOGRAPHICAL NOTE

HENRY DRUMMOND, author and evangelist, was born at Stirling, Scotland, in 1851. His book, "Natural Law in the Spiritual World," caused much discussion and is still widely read. His "Ascent of Man" is regarded by many as his greatest work. The address reprinted here has appeared in hundreds of editions, and has been an inspiration to thousands of peoples all over the world. There is an interesting biography of Drummond by Professor George Adam Smith, his close friend and colaborer. He died in 1897.

Tho I speak with the tongues of men and of angels, and have not love, &c.—I Cor. xiii.

EVERY one has asked himself the great question of antiquity as of the modern world: What is the *summum bonum*—the supreme good? You have life before you. Once only you can live it. What is the noblest object of desire, the supreme gift to covet?

We have been accustomed to be told that the greatest thing in the religious world is faith. That great word has been the key-note for centuries of the popular religion; and we have easily learned to look upon it as the greatest thing in the world. Well, we are wrong. If we have been told that, we may miss the mark. I have taken you, in the chapter which I have just read, to Christianity at its source; and there we have seen, "The greatest of these is love." It is not an oversight. Paul was speaking of faith just a moment before. He says, "If I have all faith, so that I can remove mountains, and have not love, I am nothing." So far from forgetting, he deliberately contrasts them, "Now abideth faith, hope, love," and without a moment's hesitation the decision falls, "The greatest of these is love."

And it is not prejudice. A man is apt to recommend to others his own strong point. Love was not Paul's strong point. The observing student can detect a beautiful tenderness growing and ripening all through his character as Paul gets old; but the hand that wrote, "The greatest of these is love," when we meet it first, is stained with blood.

Nor is this letter to the Corinthians peculiar in singling out love as the *summum bonum*. The masterpieces of Christianity are agreed about it. Peter says, "Above all things have fervent love among yourselves." Above all things. And John goes further, "God is love." And you remember the profound remark which Paul makes elsewhere, "Love is the fulfilling of the law." Did you ever think what he meant by that? In those days men were working their passage to heaven by keeping the ten commandments, and the hundred and ten other commandments which they had manufactured out of them. Christ said, I will show you a more simple way. If you do one thing, you will do these hundred and ten things, without ever thinking about them. If you love, you will unconsciously fulfil the whole law. And you can readily see for yourselves how that must be so. Take any of the commandments. "Thou shalt have no other gods before me." If a man love God, you will not require to tell him that. Love is the fulfilling of that law. "Take not his name in vain." Would he ever dream of taking His name in vain if he loved Him? "Remember the Sabbath day to keep it holy." Would he not be too glad to have one day in seven to dedicate more exclusively to the object of his affection? Love would fulfil all these laws regarding God. And so, if he loved man, you would never think of telling him to honor his father and mother. He could not do anything else. It would be preposterous to tell him not to kill. You could only insult him if you suggested that he should not steal —how could he steal from those he loved? It would be superfluous to beg him not to bear false witness against his neighbor. If he loved him it would be the last thing he would do. And you would never dream of urging him not to covet what his neighbors had. He would rather that they possest it than himself. In this way "Love is the fulfilling of the law." It is the rule for fulfilling all rules, the new commandment for keeping all the old commandments, Christ's one secret of the Christian life.

Now, Paul had .earned that; and in this noble eulogy he has given us the most wonderful and original account extant of the *summum bonum*. We may divide it into three parts. In the beginning of the short chapter, we have love contrasted; in the heart of it, we have love analyzed; toward the end, we have love defended as the supreme gift.

Paul begins contrasting love with other things that men in those days thought much of. I shall not attempt to go over those things in detail. Their inferiority is already obvious.

He contrasts it with eloquence. And what a noble gift it is, the power of playing upon the souls and wills of men, and rousing them to lofty purposes and holy deeds. Paul says, "If I speak with the tongues of men and of angels, and have not love, I am become as sounding brass, or a tinkling cymbal." And we all know why. We have all felt the brazenness of words without emotion, the hollowness, the unaccountable unpersuasiveness, of eloquence behind which lies no love.

He contrasts it with prophecy. He contrasts it with mysteries. He contrasts it with faith. He contrasts it with charity. Why is love greater than faith? Because the end is greater than the means. And why is it greater than charity? Because the whole is greater than the part. Love is greater than faith, because the end is greater than the means. What is the use of having faith? It is to connect the soul with God. And what is the object of connecting man with God? That he may become like God. But God is love. Hence faith, the means, is in order to love, the

end. Love, therefore, obviously is greater than faith. It is greater than charity, again, because the whole is greater than a part. Charity is only a little bit of love, one of the innumerable avenues of love, and there may even be, and there is, a great deal of charity without love. It is a very easy thing to toss a copper to a beggar on the street; it is generally an easier thing than not to do it. Yet love is just as often in the withholding. We purchase relief from the sympathetic feelings roused by the spectacle of misery, at the copper's cost. It is too cheap—too cheap for us, and often too dear for the beggar. If we really loved him we would either do more for him, or less.

Then Paul contrasts it with sacrifice and martyrdom. And I beg the little band of would-be missionaries—and I have the honor to call some of you by this name for the first time—to remember that tho you give your bodies to be burned, and have not love, it profits nothing—nothing! You can take nothing greater to the heathen world than the impress and reflection of the love of God upon your own character. That is the universal language. It will take you years to speak in Chinese, or in the dialects of India. From the day you land, that language of love, understood by all, will be pouring forth its unconscious eloquence. It is the man who is the missionary, it is not his words. His character is his message. In the heart of Africa, among the great lakes, I have come across black men and women who remembered the only white man they ever saw before—David Livingstone; and as you cross his footsteps in that dark continent, men's faces light up as they speak of the kind doctor who passed there years ago. They could not understand him; but they felt the love that beat in his heart. Take into your new sphere of labor, where you also mean to lay down your life, that simple charm, and your life-work must succeed. You can take nothing greater, you need take nothing less. It is not worth while going if you take anything less. You may take every accomplishment; you may be braced for every sacrifice; but if you give your body to be burned, and have not love, it will profit you and the cause of Christ nothing.

After contrasting love with these things, Paul, in three verses, very short, gives us an amazing analysis of what this supreme thing is. I ask you to look at it. It is a compound thing, he tells us. It is like light. As you have seen a man of science take a beam of light and pass it through a crystal prism, as you have seen it come out on the other side of the prism broken up into its component colors—red, and blue, and yellow, and violet, and orange, and all the colors of the rainbow —so Paul passes this thing, love, through the magnificent prism of his inspired intellect, and it comes out on the other side broken up into its elements. And in these few words we have what one might call the spectrum of love, the analysis of love. Will you observe what its elements are? Will you notice that they have common names; that they are virtues which we hear about every day, that they are things which can be practised by every man in every place in life; and how, by a multitude of small things and ordinary virtues, the supreme thing, the *summum bonum*, is made up?

The spectrum of love has nine ingredients:

Patience—"Love suffereth long."
Kindness—"And is kind."
Generosity—"Love envieth not."
Humility—"Love vaunteth not itself, is not puffed up."
Courtesy—"Doth not behave itself unseemly."
Unselfishness—"Seeketh not her own."
Good temper—"Is not easily provoked."
Guilelessness—"Thinketh no evil."
Sincerity—"Rejoiceth not in iniquity, but rejoiceth in the truth."

Patience, kindness, generosity, humility, courtesy, unselfishness, good temper, guilelessness, sincerity—these make up the supreme gift, the stature of the perfect man. You will observe that all are in relation to men, in relation to life, in relation to the known to-day and the near to-morrow, and not to the unknown eternity. We hear much of love to God; Christ spoke much of love to man. We make a great deal of peace with heaven; Christ made much of peace on earth. Religion is not a strange or added thing, but the inspiration of the secular life, the breathing of an eternal spirit through this temporal world. The supreme thing, in short, is not a thing at all, but the giving of a further finish to the multitudinous words and acts which make up the sum of every common day.

There is no time to do more than to make a passing note upon each of these ingredients. Love is patience. This is the normal attitude of love; love passive, love waiting to begin; not in a hurry; calm; ready to do its work when the summons comes, but meantime wearing the ornament of a meek and quiet spirit. Love suffers long; beareth all things; believeth all things; hopeth all things. For love understands, and therefore waits.

Kindness. Love active. Have you ever noticed how much of Christ's life was spent in doing kind things—in merely doing kind things? Run over it with that in view, and you will find that He spent a great proportion of His time simply in making people happy, in doing good turns to people. There is only one thing greater than happiness in the world, and that is holiness; and it is not in our keeping; but what God has put in our power is the happiness of those about us, and that is largely to be secured by our being kind to them.

"The greatest thing," says some one, "a man can do for his Heavenly Father is to be kind to some of his other children." I wonder why it is that we are not all kinder than we are? How much the world needs it. How easily it is done. How instantaneously it acts. How infallibly it is remembered. How superabundantly it pays itself back—for there is no debtor in the world so honorable, so superbly honorable, as love. "Love never faileth." Love is success, love is happiness, love is life. "Love," I say, with Browning, "is energy of life."

For life, with all it yields of joy or wo
And hope and fear,
Is just our chance o' the prize of learning love—
How love might be, hath been indeed, and is.

Where love is, God is. He that dwelleth in love dwelleth in God. God is love. Therefore love. Without distinction, without calculation, without procrastination, love. Lavish it upon the poor, where it is very easy; especially upon the rich, who often need it most; most of all upon our equals, where it is very difficult, and for whom perhaps we each do least of all. There is a difference between trying to please and giving pleasure. Give pleasure. Lose no chance of giving pleasure. For that is the ceaseless and anonymous triumph of a truly loving spirit. "I shall pass through this world but once. Any good thing therefore that I can do, or any kindness that I can show to any human being, let me do it now. Let me not defer it or neglect it, for I shall not pass this way again."

Generosity. "Love envieth not." This is love in competition with others. Whenever you attempt a good work you will find other men doing the same kind of work, and probably doing it better. Envy them not. Envy is a feeling of ill-will to those who are in the same line as ourselves, a spirit of covetousness and detraction. How little Christian work even is a protection against unchristian feeling! That most despicable of all the unworthy moods which cloud a Christian's soul assuredly waits for us on the threshold of every work, unless we are fortified with this grace of magnanimity. Only one thing truly needs the Christian envy, the large, rich, generous soul which "envieth not."

And then, after having learned all that, you have to learn this further thing, humility—to put a seal upon your lips and forget what you have done. After you have been kind, after love has stolen forth into the world and done its beautiful work, go back into the shade again and say nothing about it. Love hides even from itself. Love waives even self-satisfaction. "Love vaunteth not itself, is not puffed up."

The fifth ingredient is a somewhat strange one to find in this *summum bonum*: Courtesy.

This is love in society, love in relation to etiquette. "Love doth not behave itself unseemly." Politeness has been defined as love in trifles. Courtesy is said to be love in little things. And the one secret of politeness is to love. Love can not behave itself unseemly. You can put the most untutored persons into the highest society, and if they have a reservoir of love in their hearts, they will not behave themselves unseemly. They simply can not do it. Carlyle said of Robert Burns that there was no truer gentleman in Europe than the plowman-poet. It was because he loved everything—the mouse, the daisy, and all the things, great and small, that God had made. So with this simple passport he could mingle with any society, and enter courts and palaces from his little cottage on the banks of the Ayr. You know the meaning of the word "gentleman." It means a gentle man —a man who does things gently with love. And that is the whole art and mystery of it. The gentle man can not in the nature of things do an ungentle and ungentlemanly thing. The ungentle soul, the inconsiderate, unsympathetic nature can not do anything else. "Love doth not behave itself unseemly."

Unselfishness. "Love seeketh not her own." Observe: Seeketh not even that which is her own. In Britain the Englishman is devoted, and rightly, to his rights. But there come times when a man may exercise even the higher right of giving up his rights. Yet Paul does not summon us to give up our rights. Love strikes much deeper. It would have us not seek them at all, ignore them, eliminate the personal element altogether from our calculations. It is not hard to give up our rights. They are often external. The difficult thing is to give up ourselves. The more difficult thing still is not to seek things for ourselves at all. After we have sought them, bought them, won them, deserved them, we have taken the cream off them for ourselves already. Little cross then perhaps to give them up. But not to seek them, to look every man not on his own things, but on the things of others —id opus est. "Seekest thou great things for thyself?" said the prophet; "seek them not." Why? Because there is no greatness in things. Things can not be great. The only greatness is unselfish love. Even self-denial in itself is nothing, is almost a mistake. Only a great purpose or a mightier love can justify the waste. It is more difficult, I have said, not to seek our own at all, than, having sought it, to give it up. I must take that back. It is only true of a partly selfish heart. Nothing is a hardship to love, and nothing is hard. I believe that Christ's yoke is easy. Christ's "yoke" is just His way of taking life. And I believe it is an easier way than any other. I believe it is a happier way than any other. The most obvious lesson in Christ's teaching is that there is no happiness in having and getting anything, but only in giving. I repeat, there is no happiness in having or in getting, but only in giving. And half the world is on the wrong scent in the pursuit of happiness. They think it consists in having and getting, and in being served by others. It consists in giving and serving others. He that would be great among you, said Christ, let him serve. He that would be happy, let him remember that there is but one way—it is more blest, it is more happy, to give than to receive.

The next ingredient is a very remarkable one: good temper. "Love is not easily provoked." Nothing could be more striking than to find this here. We are inclined to look upon bad temper as a very harmless weakness. We speak of it as a mere infirmity of nature, a family failing, a matter of temperament, not a thing to take into very serious account in estimating a man's character. And yet here, right in the heart of this analysis of love, it finds a place; and the Bible again and again returns to condemn it as one of the most destructive elements in human nature.

The peculiarity of ill temper is that it is the vice of the virtuous. It is often the one blot on an otherwise noble character. You know men who are all but perfect, and women who would be entirely perfect, but for an easily ruffled, quick-tempered, or "touchy" disposition. This compatibility of ill temper with high moral character is one of the strangest and saddest problems of ethics. The truth is, there are two great classes of sins— sins of the body, and sins of the disposition. The Prodigal Son may be taken as a type of the first, the Elder Brother of the second. Now society has no doubt whatever as to which of these is the worse. Its brands fall without a challenge, upon the Prodigal. But are we right? We have no balance to weigh one another's sins, and coarser and finer are but human words; but faults in the higher nature may be less venial than those in the lower, and to the eye of Him who is love, a sin against love may seem a hundred times more base. No form of vice, not worldliness, not greed of gold, not drunkenness itself, does more to unchristianize society than evil temper. For embittering life, for breaking up communities, for destroying the most sacred relationships, for devastating homes, for withering up men and women, for taking the bloom off childhood, in short, for sheer gratuitous misery-producing power, this influence stands alone. Look at the Elder Brother, moral, hard-working, patient, dutiful—let him get all credit for his virtues—look at this man, this baby, sulking outside his own father's door. "He was angry," we read, "and would not go in." Look at the effect upon the father, upon the servants, upon the happiness of the guests. Judge of the effect upon the Prodigal—and how many prodigals are kept out of the kingdom of God by the unlovely character of those who profess to be inside? Analyze, as a study in temper, the thunder-cloud itself as it gathers upon the Elder Brother's brow. What is it made of? Jealousy, anger, pride, uncharity, cruelty. self-righteousness, touchiness, doggedness, sullenness—these are the ingredients of this dark and loveless soul. In varying proportions, also, these are the ingredients of all ill temper. Judge if such sins of the disposition are not worse to live in, and for others to live with, than sins of the body. Did Christ indeed not answer the question Himself when He said, "I say unto you, that the publicans and the harlots go into the kingdom of heaven before you." There is really no place in heaven for a disposition like this. A man with such a mood could only make heaven miserable for all the people in it. Except, therefore, such a man be born again, he can not, he simply can not, enter the kingdom of heaven. For it is perfectly certain—and you will not misunderstand me—that to enter heaven a man must take it with him.

You will see then why temper is significant. It is not in what it is alone, but in what it reveals. This is why I take the liberty now of speaking of it with such unusual plainness. It is a test for love, a symptom, a revelation of an unloving nature at bottom. It is the intermittent fever which bespeaks unintermittent disease within; the occasional bubble escaping to the surface which betrays some rottenness underneath; a sample of the most hidden products of the soul dropt involuntarily when off one's guard; in a word, the lightning form of a hundred hideous and unchristian sins. For a want of patience, a want of kindness, a want of generosity, a want of courtesy, a want of unselfishness, are all instantaneously symbolized in one flash of temper.

Hence it is not enough to deal with the temper. We must go to the source, and change the inmost nature, and the angry humors will die away of themselves. Souls are made sweet not by taking the acid fluids out, but by putting something in—a great love, a new spirit, the spirit of Christ. Christ, the spirit of Christ, interpenetrating ours, sweetens, purifies, transforms all. This only can eradicate what is wrong, work a chemical change, renovate and regenerate, and rehabilitate the inner man. Will-power does not change men. Time does not change men. Christ does. Therefore, "Let that mind be in you which was also in Christ Jesus." Some of us have not much time to lose. Remember, once more, that this is a matter of life or death. I can not help speaking urgently, for myself, for yourselves. "Whoso shall offend one of these little ones, which believe in me, it were better for him that a millstone were hanged about his neck, and that he were drowned in the depth of the sea." That is to say, it is the deliberate verdict of the Lord Jesus that it is better not to live than not to love. *It is better not to live than not to love.*

Guilelessness and sincerity may be dismissed almost without a word. Guilelessness is the grace for suspicious people. And the possession of it is the great secret of personal influence. You will find, if you think for a moment, that the people who influence you are people who believe in you. In an atmosphere of suspicion men shrivel up; but in that other atmosphere they expand, and find encouragement and educative fellowship. It is a wonderful thing that here and there in this hard, uncharitable world there should still be left a few rare souls who think no evil. This is the great unworldliness. Love "thinketh no evil," imputes no bad motive, sees the bright side, puts the best construction on every action. What a delightful state of mind to live in! What stimulus and benediction even to meet with it for a day! To be trusted is to be saved. And if we try to influence or elevate others, we shall soon see that success is in proportion to their belief of our belief in them. For the respect of another is the first restoration of the self-respect a man has lost; our ideal of what he is becomes to him the hope and pattern of what he may become.

"Love rejoiceth not in iniquity, but rejoiceth in the truth." I have called this sincerity from the words rendered in the Authorized Version by "rejoiceth in the truth." And, certainly, were this the real translation, nothing could be more just. For he who loves will love truth not less than men. He will rejoice in the truth—rejoice not in what he has been taught to believe; not in this Church's doctrine or in that; not in this ism or in that ism; but "in the truth." He will accept only what is real; he will strive to get at facts; he will search for truth with an humble and unbiased mind, and cherish whatever he finds at any sacrifice. But the more literal translation of the Revised Version calls for just such a sacrifice for truth's sake here. For what Paul really meant is, as we there read, "Rejoiceth not in unrighteousness, but rejoiceth with the truth," a quality which probably no one English word—and certainly not sincerity—adequately defines. It includes, perhaps more strictly, the self-restraint which refuses to make capital out of others' faults; the charity which delights not in exposing the weakness of others, but "covereth all things"; the sincerity of purpose which endeavors to see things as they are, and rejoices to find them better than suspicion feared or calumny denounced.

So much for the analysis of love. Now the business of our lives is to have these things in our characters. That is the supreme work to which we need to address ourselves in this world to learn love. Is life not full of opportunities for learning love? Every man and woman every day has a thousand of them. The world is not a playground; it is a school-room. Life is not a holiday, but an education. And the one eternal lesson for us all is how better we can love. What makes a man a good cricketer? Practise. What makes a man a good artist, a good sculptor, a good musician? Practise. What makes a man a good linguist, a good stenographer? Practise. What makes a man a good man. Practise. Nothing else. There is nothing capricious about religion. We do not get the soul in different ways, under different laws, from those in which we get the body and the mind. If a man does not exercise his arm he develops no biceps muscle; and if he does not exercise his soul, he acquires no muscle in his soul, no strength of character, no vigor of moral fiber nor beauty of spiritual growth. Love is not a thing of enthusiastic emotion. It is a rich, strong, manly, vigorous expression of the whole round Christian character—the Christlike nature in its fullest development. And the constituents of this great character are only to be built up by ceaseless practise.

What was Christ doing in the carpenter's shop? Practising. Tho perfect, we read that He learned obedience, and grew in wisdom and in favor with God. Do not quarrel, therefore, with your lot in life. Do not complain of its never-ceasing cares, its petty environment, the vexations you have to stand, the small and sordid souls you have to live and work with. Above all, do not resent temptation; do not be perplexed because it seems to thicken round you more and more, and ceases neither for effort nor for agony nor prayer. That is your practise. That is the practise which God appoints you; and it is having its work in making you patient, and humble, and generous, and unselfish, and kind, and courteous. Do not grudge the hand that is molding the still too shapeless image within you. It is growing more beautiful, tho you see it not, and every touch of temptation may add to its perfection. Therefore keep in the midst of life. Do not isolate yourself. Be among men, and among things, and among troubles, and difficulties, and obstacles. You remember Goethe's words: *Es bildet ein Talent sich in der Stille, Doch ein Character in dem Strom der Welt.* "Talent develops itself in solitude; character in the stream of life." Talent develops itself in solitude—the talent of prayer, of faith, of meditation, of seeing the unseen; character grows in the stream of the world's life. That chiefly is where men are to learn love.

How? Now how? To make it easier, I have named a few of the elements of love. But these are only elements. Love itself can never be defined. Light is a something more than the sum of its ingredients—a glowing, dazzling, tremulous ether. And love is something more than all its elements—a palpitating, quivering, sensitive, living thing. By synthesis of all the colors, men can make whiteness, they can not make light. By synthesis of all the virtues, men can make virtue, they can not make love. How then are we to have this transcendent living whole conveyed into our souls? We brace our wills to secure it. We try to copy those who have it. We lay down rules about it. We watch. We pray. But these things alone will not bring love into our nature. Love is an effect. And only as we fulfil the right condition can we have the effect produced. Shall I tell you what the cause is?

If you turn to the Revised Version of the First Epistle of John you will find these words: "We love because he first loved us." "We love," not "We love him." That is the way the old version has it, and it is quite wrong. "We love—because he first loved us." Look at that word "because." It is the cause of which I have spoken. "Because he first loved us," the effect follows that we love, we love Him, we love all men. We can not help it. Because He loved us, we love, we love everybody. Our heart is slowly changed. Contemplate the love of Christ, and you will love. Stand before that mirror, reflect Christ's character, and you will be changed into the same image from tenderness to tenderness. There is no other way. You can not love to order. You can only look at the lovely object, and fall in love with it, and grow into likeness to it. And so look at this perfect character, this perfect life. Look at the great sacrifice as He laid down Himself, all through life, and upon the cross of Calvary; and you must love Him. And loving Him, you must become like Him. Love begets love. It is a process of induction. Put a piece of iron in the presence of an electrified body, and that piece of iron for a time becomes electrified. It is changed into a temporary magnet in the mere presence of a permanent magnet, and as long as you leave the two side by side they are both magnets alike. Remain side by side with Him who loved us, and gave Himself for us, and you too will become a permanent magnet, a permanently attractive force; and like Him you will draw all men unto you; like Him you will be drawn unto all men. That is the inevitable effect of love. Any man who fulfils that cause must have that effect produced in him. Try to give up the idea that religion comes to us by chance, or by mystery, or by caprice. It comes to us by natural law, or by spiritual law, for all law is divine. Edward Irving went to see a dying boy once, and when he entered the room he just put his hand on the sufferer's head, and said, "My boy, God loves you," and went away. And the boy started from his bed, and called out to the people in the house, "God loves me! God loves me!" It changed that boy. The sense that God loved him overpowered him, melted him down, and began the creating of a new heart in him. And that is how the love of God melts down the unlovely heart in man, and begets in him the new creature, who is patient and humble and gentle and unselfish. And there is no other way to get it. There is no mystery about it. We love others, we love everybody, we love our enemies, because He first loved us.

Now, I have a closing sentence or two to add about Paul's reason for singling out love as the supreme possession. It is a very remarkable reason. In a single word it is this: it lasts. "Love," urges Paul, "never faileth." Then he begins one of his marvelous lists of the great things of the day, and exposes them one by one. He runs over the things that men thought were going to last, and shows that they are all fleeting, temporary, passing away.

"Whether there be prophecies, they shall fail." It was the mother's ambition for her boy in those days that he should become a prophet. For hundreds of years God had never spoken by means of any prophet, and at that time the prophet was greater than the king. Men waited wistfully for another messenger to come, and hung upon his lips when he appeared as upon the very voice of God. Paul says, "Whether there be prophecies, they shall fail." This book is full of prophecies. One by one they have "failed"; that is, having been fulfilled their work is finished; they have nothing more to do now in the world except to feed a devout man's faith.

Then Paul talks about tongues. That was another thing that was greatly coveted. "Whether there be tongues, they shall cease." As we all know, many, many centuries have passed since tongues have been known in this world. They have ceased. Take it in any sense you like. Take it, for illustration merely, as languages in general—a sense which was not in Paul's mind at all, and which tho it can not give us the specific lesson will point the general truth. Consider the words in which these chapters were written— Greek. It has gone. Take the Latin—the other great tongue of those days. It ceased long ago. Look at the Indian language. It is ceasing. The language of Wales, of Ireland, of the Scottish Highlands is dying before our eyes. The most popular book in the English tongue at the present time, except the Bible, is one of Dickens' works, his "Pickwick Papers." It is largely written in the language of London street-life, and experts assure us that in fifty years it will be unintelligible to the average English reader.

Then Paul goes further, and with even greater boldness adds, "Whether there be knowledge, it shall vanish away." The wisdom of the ancients, where is it? It is wholly gone. A schoolboy to-day knows more than Sir Isaac Newton knew. His knowledge has vanished away. You put yesterday's newspaper in the fire. Its knowledge has vanished away. You buy the old editions of the great encyclopedias for a few cents. Their knowledge has vanished away. Look how the coach has been superseded by the use of steam. Look how electricity has superseded that, and swept a hundred almost new inventions into oblivion. One of the greatest living authorities, Sir William Thompson, said the other day, "The steam-engine is passing away." "Whether there be knowledge, it shall vanish away." At every workshop you will see, in the back yard; a heap of old iron, a few wheels, a few levers, a few cranks, broken and eaten with rust. Twenty years ago that was the pride of the city. Men flocked in from the country to see the great invention; now it is superseded, its day is done. And all the boasted science and philosophy of this day will soon be old. But yesterday, in the University of Edinburgh, the greatest figure in the faculty was Sir James Simpson, the discoverer of chloroform. The other day his successor and nephew, Professor Simpson, was asked by the librarian of the university to go to the library and pick out the books on his subject that were no longer needed. And his reply to the librarian was this: "Take every text-book that is more than ten years old, and put it down in the cellar." Sir James Simpson was a great authority only a few years ago; men came from all parts of the earth to consult him; and almost the whole teaching of that time is consigned by the science of to-day to oblivion. And in every branch of science it is the same. "Now we know in part. We see through a glass darkly."

Can you tell me anything that is going to last? Many things Paul did not condescend to name. He did not mention money, fortune, fame; but he picked out the great things of his time, the things the best men thought had something in them, and brushed them peremptorily aside. Paul had no charge against these things in themselves. All he said about them was that they would not last. They were great things, but not supreme things. There were things beyond them. What we are stretches past what we do, beyond what we possess. Many things that men denounce as sins are not sins; but they are temporary. And that is a favorite argument of the New Testament. John says of the world, not that it is wrong, but simply that it "passeth away." There is a great deal in the world that is delightful and beautiful; there is a great deal in it that is great and engrossing; but it will not last. All that is in the world, the lust of the eye, the lust of the flesh, and the pride of life, are but for a little while. Love not the world therefore. Nothing that it contains is worth the life and consecration of an immortal soul. The immortal soul must give itself to something that is immortal. And the immortal things are: "Now abideth faith, hope, love, but the greatest of these is love."

Some think the time may come when two of these three things will also pass away—faith into sight, hope into fruition. Paul does not say so. We know but little now about the conditions of the life that is to come. But what is certain is that love must last. God, the eternal God, is love. Covet therefore that everlasting gift, that one thing which it is certain is going to stand, that one coinage which will be current in the universe when all the other coinages of all the nations of the world shall be useless and unhonored. You will give yourselves to many things, give yourselves first to love. Hold things in their proportion. *Hold things in their proportion.* Let at least the first great object of our lives be to achieve the character defended in these words, the character—and it is the character of Christ—which is built round love.

I have said this thing is eternal. Did you ever notice how continually John associates love and faith with eternal life? I was not told when I was a boy that "God so loved the world that he gave his only begotten son, that whosoever believeth in him should have everlasting life." What I was told, I remember, was, that God so loved the world that, if I trusted in Him, I was to have a thing called peace, or I was to have rest, or I was to have joy, or I was to have safety. But I had to find out for myself that whosoever trusteth in Him—that is, whosoever loveth Him, for trust is only the avenue to love—hath everlasting life. The gospel offers a man life. Never offer men a thimbleful of gospel. Do not offer them merely joy, or merely peace, or merely rest, or merely safety; tell them how Christ came to give men a more abundant life than they have, a life abundant in love, and therefore abundant in salvation for themselves, and large in enterprise for the alleviation and redemption of the world. Then only can the gospel take hold of the whole of a man, body, soul, and spirit, and give to each part of his nature its exercise and reward. Many of the current gospels are addrest only to a part of man's nature. They offer peace, not life; faith, not love; justification, not regeneration. And men slip back again from such religion because it has never really held them. Their nature was not all in it. It

offered no deeper and gladder life-current than the life that was lived before. Surely it stands to reason that only a fuller love can compete with the love of the world.

To love abundantly is to live abundantly, and to love forever is to live forever. Hence, eternal life is inextricably bound up with love. We want to live forever for the same reason that we want to live to-morrow. Why do we want to live to-morrow? It is because there is some one who loves you, and whom you want to see to-morrow, and be with, and love back. There is no other reason why we should live on than that we love and are beloved. It is when a man has no one to love him that he commits suicide. So long as he has friends, those who love him and whom he loves, he will live; because to live is to love. Be it but the love of a dog, it will keep him in life; but let that go and he has no contact with life, no reason to live. He dies by his own hand. Eternal life is to know God, and God is love. This is Christ's own definition. Ponder it. "This is life eternal, that they might know thee the only true God, and Jesus Christ whom thou hast sent." Love must be eternal. It is what God is. On the last analysis, then, love is life. Love never faileth, and life never faileth, so long as there is love. That is the philosophy of what Paul is showing us; the reason why in the nature of things love should be the supreme thing—because it is going to last; because in the nature of things it is an eternal life. It is a thing that we are living now, not that we get when we die; that we shall have a poor chance of getting when we die unless we are living now. No worse fate can befall a man in this world than to live and grow old all alone, unloving and unloved. To be lost is to live in an unregenerate condition, loveless and unloved; and to be saved is to love; and he that dwelleth in love dwelleth already in God; for God is love.

Now I have all but finished. How many of you will join me in reading this chapter once a week for the next three months? A man did that once and it changed his whole life. You might begin by reading it every day, especially the verses which describe the perfect character. "Love suffereth long, and is kind; love envieth not; love vaunteth not itself." Get these ingredients into your life. Then everything that you do is eternal. It is worth doing. It is worth giving time to. No man can become a saint in his sleep; and to fulfil the condition required demands a certain amount of prayer and meditation and time, just as improvement in any direction, bodily or mental, requires preparation and care. Address yourselves to that one thing; at any cost have this transcendent character exchanged for yours. You will find as you look back upon your life that the moments that stand out, the moments when you have really lived, are the moments when you have done things in a spirit of love. As memory scans the past, above and beyond all the transitory pleasures of life, there leap forward those supreme hours when you have been enabled to do unnoticed kindnesses to those around about you, things too trifling to speak about, but which you feel have entered into your eternal life. I have seen almost all the beautiful things God has made; I have enjoyed almost every pleasure that He has planned for man; and yet as I look back I see standing out above all the life that has gone four or five short experiences when the love of God reflected itself in some poor imitation, some small act of love of mine, and these seem to be the things which alone of all one's life abide. Everything else in all our lives is transitory. Every other good is visionary. But the acts of love which no man knows about, or can ever know about, they never fail.

In the Book of Matthew, where the judgment day is depicted for us in the imagery of One seated upon a throne and dividing the sheep from the goats, the test of a man then is not, "How have I believed?" but "How have I loved?" The test of religion, the final test of religion, is not religiousness, but love. I say the final test of religion at that great day is not religiousness, but love; not what I have done, not what I have believed; not what I have achieved, but how I have discharged the common charities of life. Sins of commission in that awful indictment are not even referred to. By what we have not done, by sins of omission, we are judged. It could not be otherwise. For the withholding of love is the negation of the spirit of Christ, the proof that we never knew Him, that for us He lived in vain. It means that He suggested nothing in all our thoughts, that He inspired nothing in all our lives, that we were not once near enough to Him to be seized with the spell of His compassion for the world. It means that

> I lived for myself, I thought for myself,
>   For myself, and none beside—
> Just as if Jesus had never lived,
>   As if He had never died.

It is the Son of Man before whom the nations of the world shall be gathered. It is in the presence of humanity that we shall be charged. And the spectacle itself, the mere sight of it, will silently judge each one. Those will be there whom we have met and helped; or there, the unpitied multitude whom we neglected or despised. No other witness need be summoned. No other charge than lovelessness shall be preferred. Be not deceived. The words which all of us shall one day hear sound not of theology but of life, not of churches and saints but of the hungry and the poor, not of creeds and doctrines but of shelter and clothing, not of Bibles and prayer-books but of cups of cold water in the name of Christ. Thank God the Christianity of to-day is coming nearer the world's need. Live to help that on. Thank God men know better, by a hairbreadth, what religion is, what God is, who Christ is, where Christ is. Who is Christ? He who fed the hungry, clothed the naked, visited the sick. And where is Christ? Where?—Whoso shall receive a little child in My name receiveth Me. And who are Christ's? Every one that loveth is born of God.

TIMOTHY DWIGHT

1752-1817

THE SOVEREIGNTY OF GOD

BIOGRAPHICAL NOTE

TIMOTHY DWIGHT was born at Northampton, Massachusetts, in 1752. He graduated from Yale in 1769, served as chaplain in the army during the Revolutionary War and was chosen president of his university in 1795. He died, after holding that office for twelve years, in 1817. Lyman Beecher, who attributed his conversion to him, says: "He was of noble form, with a noble head and body, and had one of the sweetest smiles that ever you saw. When I heard him preach on 'the harvest is passed, the summer is ended, and we are not saved,' a whole avalanche rolled down on my mind. I went home weeping every step."

O Lord, I know that the way of man is not in himself: it is not in man that walketh to direct his steps.
—Jeremiah x., 23.

FEW of this audience will probably deny the truth of a direct Scriptural declaration. With as little reason can it be denied that most of them apparently live in the very manner in which they would live if the doctrine were false: or that they rely, chiefly at least, on their own sagacity, contrivance and efforts for success in this life and that which is to come. As little can it be questioned that such self-confidence is a guide eminently dangerous and deceitful. Safe as we may feel under its direction, our safety is imaginary. The folly of others in trusting to themselves we discern irresistibly. The same folly they perceive, with equal evidence, in us. Our true wisdom lies in willingly feeling, and cheerfully acknowledging, our dependence on God; and in committing ourselves with humble reliance to His care and direction.

With these observations I will now proceed to illustrate the truth of the doctrine. The mode which I shall pursue will, probably, be thought singular. I hope it will be useful. Metaphysical arguments, which are customarily employed for the purpose of establishing this and several other doctrines of theology, are, if I mistake not, less satisfactory to the minds of men at large than the authors of them appear to believe. Facts, wherever they can be fairly adduced for this end, are attended with a superior power of conviction; and commonly leave little doubt behind them. On these, therefore, I shall at the present time rely for the accomplishment of my design. In the first place, the doctrine of the text is evident from the great fact that the birth and education of all men depend not on themselves.

The succeeding events of life are derived, in a great measure at least, from our birth. By this event, it is in a prime degree determined whether men shall be princes or peasants, opulent or poor, learned or ignorant, honorable or despised; whether they shall be civilized or savage, freemen or slaves, Christians or heathens, Mohammedans or Jews.

A child is born of Indian parents in the western wilderness. By his birth he is, of course, a savage. His friends, his mode of life, his habits, his knowledge, his opinions, his conduct, all grow out of this single event. His first thoughts, his first instructions, and all the first objects with which he is conversant, the persons whom he loves, the life to which he assumes are all savage. He is an Indian from the cradle; he is an Indian to the grave. To say that he could not be otherwise, we are not warranted; but that he is not is certain.

Another child is born of a Bedouin Arab. From this moment he begins to be an Arabian. His hand is against every man; and every man's hand is against him. Before he can walk, or speak, he is carried through pathless wastes in search of food; and roams in the arms of his mother, and on the back of a camel, from spring to spring, and from pasture to pasture. Even then he begins his conflict with hunger and thirst; is scorched by a vertical sun; shriveled by the burning sand beneath; and poisoned by the breath of the simoom. Hardened thus through his infancy and childhood, both in body and mind, he becomes, under the exhortations and example of his father, a robber from his youth; attacks every stranger whom he is able to overcome; and plunders every valuable thing on which he can lay his hand.

A third receives his birth in the palace of a British nobleman; and is welcomed to the world as the heir apparent of an ancient, honorable and splendid family. As soon as he opens his eyes on the light, he is surrounded by all the enjoyments which opulence can furnish, ingenuity contrive, or fondness bestow. He is dandled on the knee of indulgence; encircled by attendants, who watch and prevent alike his necessities and wishes; cradled on down; and charmed to sleep by the voice of tenderness and care. From the dangers and evils of life he is guarded with anxious solicitude. To its pleasures he is conducted by the ever-ready hand of maternal affection. His person is shaped and improved by a succession of masters; his mind is opened, invigorated and refined by the assiduous superintendence of learning and wisdom. While a child he is served by a host of menials and flattered by successive trains of visitors. When a youth he is regarded by a band of tenants with reverence and awe. His equals in age bow to his rank; and multitudes, of superior years acknowledge his distinction by continual testimonies of marked respect. When a man, he engages the regard of his sovereign; commands the esteem of the senate; and earns the love and applause of his country.

A fourth child, in the same kingdom, is begotten by a beggar, and born under a hedge. From his birth he is trained to suffering and hardihood. He is nursed, if he can be said to be nursed at all, on a coarse, scanty and precarious pittance; holds life only as a tenant at will; combats from the first dawnings of intellect with insolence, cold and nakedness; is originally taught to beg and to steal; is driven from the doors of men by the porter or the house dog; and is regarded as an alien from the family of Adam. Like his kindred worms, he creeps through life in the dust; dies under the hedge, where he is born; and is then, perhaps, cast into a ditch, and covered with earth by some stranger, who remembers that, altho a beggar, he still was a man.

A child enters the world in China; and unites, as a thing of course, with his sottish countrymen in the stupid worship of the idol Fo. Another prostrates himself before the Lama, in consequence of having received his being in Tibet, and of seeing the Lama worshiped by all around him.

A third, who begins his existence in Turkey, is carried early to the mosque; taught to lisp with profound reverence the name of Mohammed; habituated to repeat the prayers and sentences of the Koran as the means of eternal life; and induced, in a manner irresistible, to complete his title to Paradise by a pilgrimage to Mecca.

The Hindu infant grows into a religious veneration for the cow; and perhaps never doubts that, if he adds to this solemn devotion to Juggernaut, the Gooroos, and the Dewtahs, and performs carefully his ablutions in the Ganges, he shall wash away all his sins, and obtain, by the favor of Brahma, a seat among the blest.

In our own favored country, one child is born of parents devoted solely to this world. From his earliest moments of understanding, he hears and sees nothing commended but hunting, horse-racing, visiting, dancing, dressing, riding, parties, gaming, acquiring money with eagerness and skill, and spending it in gaiety, pleasure and luxury. These things, he is taught by conversation and example, constitute all the good of man. His taste is formed, his habits are riveted, and the whole character of his soul is turned to them before he is fairly sensible that there is any other good. The question whether virtue and piety are either duties or blessings he probably never asks. In the dawn of life he sees them neglected and despised by those whom he most reverences; and learns only to neglect and despise them also. Of Jehovah he thinks as little, and for the same reason as a Chinese or a Hindu. They pay their devotions to Fo and to Juggernaut: he his to money and pleasure. Thus he lives, and dies, a mere animal; a stranger to intelligence and morality, to his duty and his God.

Another child comes into existence in the mansion of knowledge and virtue. From his infancy, his mind is fashioned to wisdom and piety. In his infancy he is taught and allured to remember his Creator; and to unite, first in form and then in affection, in the household devotions of the morning and evening.

God he knows almost as soon as he can know anything. The presence of that glorious being he is taught to realize almost from the cradle; and from the dawn of intelligence to understand the perfections and government of his Creator. His own accountableness, as soon as he can comprehend it, he begins to feel habitually, and always. The way of life through the Redeemer is early, and regularly explained to him by the voice of parental love; and enforced and endeared in the house of God. As soon as possible, he is enabled to read, and persuaded to "search the Scriptures." Of the approach, the danger and the mischiefs of temptations, he is tenderly warned. At the commencement of sin, he is kindly checked in his dangerous career. To God he was solemnly given in baptism. To God he was daily commended in fervent prayer. Under this happy cultivation he grows up "like an olive-tree in the courts of the Lord"; and, green, beautiful and flourishing, he blossoms; bears fruit; and is prepared to be transplanted by the divine hand to a kinder soil in the regions above.

How many, and how great, are the differences in these several children! How plainly do they all, in ordinary circumstances, arise out of their birth! From their birth is derived, of course, the education which I have ascribed to them; and from this education spring in a great measure both character and their destiny. The place, the persons, the circumstances, are here evidently the great things which, in the ordinary course of Providence, appear chiefly to determine what the respective men shall be; and what shall be those allotments which regularly follow their respective characters. As, then, they are not at all concerned in contriving or accomplishing either their birth or their education; it is certain that, in these most important particulars, the way of man is not in himself. God only can determine what child shall spring from parents, wise or foolish, virtuous or sinful, rich or poor, honorable or infamous, civilized or savage, Christian or heathen.

I wish it to be distinctly understood, and carefully remembered, that "in the moral conduct of all these individuals no physical necessity operates." Every one of them is absolutely a free agent; as free as any created agent can be. Whatever he does is the result of choice, absolutely unconstrained.

Let me add, that not one of them is placed in a situation in which, if he learns and performs his duty to the utmost of his power, he will fail of being finally accepted.

Secondly. The doctrine is strikingly evident from this great fact, also, that the course of life, which men usually pursue, is very different from that which they have intended.

Human life is ordinarily little else than a collection of disappointments. Rarely is the life of man such as he designs it shall be. Often do we fail of pursuing, at all, the business originally in our view. The intentional farmer becomes a mechanic, a seaman, a merchant, a lawyer, a physician, or a divine. The very place of settlement, and of residence through life, is often different, and distant, from that which was originally contemplated. Still more different is the success which follows our efforts.

All men intend to be rich and honorable; to enjoy ease; and to pursue pleasure. But how small is the number of those who compass these objects! In this country, the great body of mankind are, indeed, possest of competence; a safer and happier lot than that to which they aspire; yet few, very few are rich. Here, also, the great body of mankind possess a character, generally reputable; but very limited is the number of those who arrive at the honor which they so ardently desire, and of which they feel assured. Almost all stop at the moderate level, where human efforts appear to have their boundary established in the determination of God. Nay, far below this level creep multitudes of such as began life with full confidence in the attainment of distinction and splendor.

The lawyer, emulating the eloquence, business, and fame of Murray or Dunning, and secretly resolved not to slacken his efforts until all his rivals in the race for glory are outstript is often astonished, as well as broken-hearted, to find business and fame pass by his door, and stop at the more favored mansion of some competitor, in his view less able, and less discerning, than himself.

The physician, devoted to medical science, and possest of distinguished powers of discerning and removing diseases, is obliged to walk; while a more fortunate empiric, ignorant and worthless, rolls through the streets in his coach.

The legislator beholds with anguish and amazement the suffrages of his countrymen given eagerly to a rival candidate devoid of knowledge and integrity; but skilled in flattering the base passions of men, and deterred by no hesitations of conscience, and no fears of infamy, from saying and doing anything which may secure his election.

The merchant often beholds with a despairing eye his own ships sunk in the ocean; his debtors fail; his goods unsold, his business cramped; and himself, his' family and his hopes ruined; while a less skilful but more successful neighbor sees wealth blown to him by every wind, and floated on every wave.

The crops of the farmer are stinted; his cattle die; his markets are bad; and the purchaser of his commodities proves to be a cheat, who deceives his confidence and runs away with his property.

Thus the darling schemes and fondest hopes

of man are daily frustrated by time. While sagacity contrives, patience matures, and labor industriously executes, disappointment laughs at the curious fabric, formed by so many efforts and gay with so many brilliant colors, and while the artists imagine the work arrived at the moment of completion, brushes away the beautiful web, and leaves nothing behind.

The designs of men, however, are in many respects not infrequently successful. The lawyer and physician acquire business and fame; the statesman, votes; and the farmer, wealth. But their real success, even in this case, is often substantially the same with that already recited. In all plans, and all labors, the supreme object is to become happy. Yet, when men have actually acquired riches and honor, or secured to themselves popular favor, they still find the happiness, which they expected, eluding their grasp. Neither wealth, fame, office, nor sensual pleasure can yield such good as we need. As these coveted objects are accumulated, the wishes of man always grow faster than his gratifications. Hence, whatever he acquires, he is usually as little satisfied as before, and often less.

A principal design of the mind in laboring for these things is to become superior to others. But almost all rich men are obliged to see, and usually with no small anguish, others richer than themselves; honorable men, others more honorable; voluptuous men, others who enjoy more pleasure. The great end of the strife is therefore unobtained; and the happiness expected never found. Even the successful competitor in the race utterly misses his aim. The real enjoyment existed, altho it was unperceived by him, in the mere strife for superiority. When he has outstript all his rivals the contest is at an end: and his spirits, which were invigorated only by contending, languish for want of a competitor.

Besides, the happiness in view was only the indulgence of pride, or mere animal pleasure. Neither of these can satisfy or endure. A rational mind may be, and often is, so narrow and groveling as not to aim at any higher good, to understand its nature or to believe its existence. Still, in its original constitution, it was formed with a capacity for intellectual and moral good, and was destined to find in this good its only satisfaction. Hence, no inferior good will fill its capacity or its desires. Nor can this bent of its nature ever be altered. Whatever other enjoyment, therefore, it may attain, it will, without this, still crave and still be unhappy.

No view of the ever-varying character and success of mankind in their expectations of happiness, and their efforts to obtain it, can illustrate this doctrine more satisfactorily than that of the progress and end of a class of students in this seminary. At their first appearance here they are all exactly on the same level. Their character, their hopes and their destination are the same. They are enrolled on one list; and enter upon a collegiate life with the same promise of success. At this moment they are plants, appearing just above the ground; all equally fair and flourishing. Within r short time, however, some begin to rise above others; indicating by a more rapid growth a structure of superior vigor, and promising both more early and more abundant fruit. . . .

Were I to ask the youths who are before me what are their designs and expectations concerning their future life, and write down their several answers, what a vast difference would ultimately be found between those answers and the events which would actually befall them! To how great a part of that difference would facts, over which they could have no control, give birth! How many of them will in all probability be less prosperous, rich, and honorable than they now intend: how many devoted to employments of which at present they do not even dream; in circumstances, of which they never entertained even a thought, behind those whom they expected to outrun, poor, sick, in sorrow or in the grave.

First. You see here, my young friends, the most solid reasons for gratitude to your Creator.

God, only, directed that you should be born in this land, and in the midst of peace, plenty, civilization, freedom, learning and religion; and that your existence should not commence in a Tartarian forest or an African waste. God, alone, ordered that you should be born of parents who knew and worshiped Him, the glorious and eternal Jehovah; and not of parents who bowed before the Lama or the ox, an image of brass or the stock of a tree. In the book of His counsels, your names, so far as we are able to judge, were written in the fair lines of mercy. It is of His overflowing goodness that you are now here; surrounded with privileges, and beset with blessings, educated to knowledge, usefulness and piety, and prepared to begin an endless course of happiness and glory. All these delightful things have been poured into your lap, and have come, unbidden, to solicit your acceptance. If these blessings awaken not gratitude, it can not be awakened by the blessings in the present world. If they are not thankfully felt by you, it is because you know not how to be thankful. Think what you are, and where you are; and what and where you just as easily might have been. Remember that, instead of cherishing tender affections, imbibing refined sentiments, exploring the field of science, and assuming the name and character of the sons of God, you might as easily have been dozing in the smoke of a wigwam, brandishing a tomahawk, or dancing round an emboweled captive; or that you might yourself have been emboweled by the hand of superstition, and burnt on the altars of Moloch. If you remember these things, you can not but call to mind, also, who made you to differ from the miserable beings who have thus lived and died.

Secondly. This doctrine forcibly demands of you to moderate desires and expectations.

There are two modes in which men seek happiness in the enjoyments of the present world. "Most persons freely indulge their wishes, and intend to find objects sufficient in number and value to satisfy them." A few "aim at satisfaction by proportioning their desires to the number and measure of their probable gratifications." By the doctrine of the text, the latter method is stamped with the name of wisdom, and on the former is inscribed the name of folly. Desires indulged grow faster and farther than gratifications extend. Ungratified desire is misery. Expectations eagerly indulged and terminated by disappointment are often exquisite misery. But how frequently are expectations raised only to be disappointed, and desires let loose only to terminate in distress! The child pines for a toy: the moment he possesses it, he throws it by and cries for another. When they are piled up in heaps around him, he looks at them without pleasure, and leaves them without regret. He knew not that all the good which they could yield lay in expectation; nor that his wishes for more would increase faster than toys could be multiplied, and is unhappy at last for the same reason as at first: his wishes are ungratified. Still indulging them, and still believing that the gratification of them will furnish the enjoyment for which he pines, he goes on, only to be unhappy.

Men are merely taller children. Honor, wealth and splendor are the toys for which grown children pine; but which, however accumulated, leave them still disappointed and unhappy. God never designed that intelligent beings should be satisfied with these enjoyments. By his wisdom and goodness they were formed to derive their happiness and virtue.

Moderated desires constitute a character fitted to acquire all the good which this world can yield. He who is prepared, in whatever situation he is, therewith to be content, has learned effectually the science of being happy, and possesses the alchemic stone which will change every metal into gold. Such a man will smile upon a stool, while Alexander at his side sits weeping on the throne of the world.

The doctrine of the text teaches you irresistibly that, since you can not command gratifications, you should command your de-sires; and that, as the events of life do not accord with your wishes, your wishes should accord with them. Multiplied enjoyments fall to but few men, and are no more rationally expected than the highest prize in a lottery. But a well-regulated mind, a dignified independence of the world, and a wise preparation to possess one's soul in patience, whatever circumstances may exist, is in the power of every man, and is greater wealth than that of both Indies, and greater honor than Cæsar ever acquired.

Thirdly. As your course and your success through life are not under your control, you are strongly urged to commit yourselves to God, who can control both.

That you can not direct your course through the world, that your best concerted plans will often fail, that your sanguine expectations will be disappointed, and that your fondest worldly wishes will terminate in mortification can not admit of a momentary doubt. That God can direct you, that He actually controls all your concerns, and that, if you commit yourselves to His care, He will direct you kindly and safely, can be doubted only of choice. Why, then, do you hesitate to yield yourselves and your interests to the guidance of your Maker? There are two reasons which appear especially to govern mankind in this important concern; they do not and will not realize the agency of God in their affairs; and they do not choose to have them directed as they imagine He will direct them. The former is the result of stupidity; the latter, of impiety. Both are foolish in the extreme, and not less sinful than foolish.

The infinitely wise, great and glorious benefactor of the universe has offered to take men by the hand, lead them through the journey of life, and conduct them to His own house in the heavens. The proof of His sincerity in making this offer has been already produced. He has given His own Son to live, and die, and rise, and reign, and intercede for our race. "Herein is love," if there ever was love; "not that we have loved him, but that he has loved us." That He, who has done this, should not be sincere is impossible. St. Paul, therefore, triumphantly asks what none can answer: "He, that spared not his own Son, but delivered him up for us all, how shall he not with him also freely give us all things?" Trust, then, His word with undoubting confidence; take His hand with humble gratitude, and with all thy heart obey His voice, which you will everywhere hear, saying, "this is the way, walk ye therein." In sickness and in health, by night and by day, at home and in crowds, He will watch over you with tenderness inexpressible. He will make you lie down in green pastures, lead you beside the still waters and guide you in paths of righteousness, for His name's sake. He will prepare a table before you in the presence of your enemies, and cause your cup to run over with blessings. When you pass through the waters of affliction He will be with you, and through the rivers they shall not overflow you. When you walk through the fire, you shall not be burned; neither shall the flame kindle on you. From their native heavens He will commission those charming twin sisters, goodness and mercy, to descend and "follow you all your days."

But if you wish God to be your guide and your friend, you must conform to His pleasure. Certainly you can not wonder that the infinitely Wise should prefer His own wisdom to yours, and that He should choose for His children their allotments, rather than leave them to choose for themselves. That part of His pleasure, which you are to obey, is all summed up in the single word duty, and it is perfectly disclosed in the Scriptures. The whole scheme is so formed as to be plain, easy, profitable, and delightful; profitable in hand, delightful in the possession. Every part and precept of the whole is calculated for this end, and will make you only wise, good, and happy.

Life has been often styled an ocean, and our progress through it a voyage. The ocean is tempestuous and billowy, overspread by a cloudy sky, and fraught beneath with shelves and quicksands. The voyage is eventful beyond comprehension, and at the same time full of uncertainty, and replete with danger. Every adventurer needs to be well prepared for whatever may befall him, and well secured against the manifold hazards of losing his course, sinking in the abyss, or of being wrecked against the shore.

These evils have all existed at all times. The present, and that part of the past which is known to you by experience, has seen them multiplied beyond example. It has seen the ancient and acknowledged standards of thinking violently thrown down. Religion, morals, government, and the estimate formed by man of crimes and virtues, and of all the means of usefulness and enjoyment, have been questioned, attacked, and in various places, and with respect to millions of the human race, finally overthrown. A licentiousness of opinion and conduct, daring, outrageous, and rending asunder every bond formed by God or man, has taken place of former good sense and sound morals, and has long threatened the destruction of human good. Industry, cunning, and fraud have toiled with unrivaled exertions to convert man into a savage and the world into a desert. A wretched and hypocritical philanthropy, also, not less mischievous, has stalked forth as the companion of these ravages: a philanthropy born in a dream, bred in a hovel, and living only in professions. This guardian genius of human interests, this friend of human rights, this redresser of human wrongs, is yet without a heart to feel, and without a hand to bless. But she is well furnished with lungs, with eyes, and a tongue. She can talk, and sigh, and weep at pleasure, but can neither pity nor give. The objects of her attachment are either knaves and villains at home, or unknown sufferers beyond her reach abroad. To the former, she ministers the sword and the dagger, that they may fight their way into place, and power, and profit. At the latter she only looks through a telescope of fancy, as an astronomer searches for stars invisible to the eye. To every real object of charity within her reach she complacently says, "Be thou warmed, and be thou filled; depart in peace."

By the daring spirit, the vigorous efforts, and the ingenious cunning so industriously exerted on the one hand, and the smooth and gentle benevolence so softly profest on the other, multitudes have been, and you easily may be, destroyed. The mischief has indeed been met, resisted, and overcome; but it has the heads and the lives of the hydra, and its wounds, which at times have seemed deadly, are much more readily healed than any good man could wish, than any sober man could expect. Hope not to escape the assaults of this enemy: To feel that you are in danger will ever be a preparation for your safety. But it will be only such a preparation; your deliverance must ultimately and only flow from your Maker. Resolve, then, to commit yourselves to Him with a cordial reliance on His wisdom, power, and protection. Consider how much you have at stake, that you are bound to eternity, that your existence will be immortal, and that you will either rise to endless glory or be lost in absolute perdition. Heaven is your proper home. The path, which I have recommended to you, will conduct you safely and certainly to that happy world. Fill up life, therefore, with obedience to God, with faith in the Lord Jesus Christ, and repentance unto life, the obedience to the two great commands of the gospel, with supreme love to God and universal good-will to men, the obedience to the two great commands of the law. On all your sincere endeavors to honor Him, and befriend your fellow men, He will smile; every virtuous attempt He will bless; every act of obedience He will reward. Life in this manner will be pleasant amid all its sorrows; and beams of hope will continually shine through the gloom, by which it is so often overcast. Virtue, the seed that can not die, planted from heaven, and cultivated by the divine hand, will grow up in your hearts with increasing vigor, and blossom in your lives with supernal beauty. Your path will be that of the just, and will gloriously resemble the dawning light, "which shines brighter and brighter, to the perfect day.'' Peace will take you by the hand, and offer herself as the constant and delightful companion of your progress. Hope will walk before you, and with an unerring finger point out your course; and joy, at the end of the journey, will open her arms to receive you. You will wait on the Lord, and renew your strength; will mount up with wings as eagles; will run, and not be weary; will walk, and not faint.

J. OSWALD DYKES

1835-1912

THE CHAMPION WHO SLAYS THE DRAGON

BIOGRAPHICAL NOTE

EX-PRINCIPAL and Barbour professor of divinity in Theological College of Presbyterian Church of England, 1888-1907; born Port Glasgow, Scotland, August 14, 1835; educated at Dumfries Academy, Edinburgh University and New College, Heidelberg and Erlangen; ordained at East Kilbride, 1859; colleague to Dr. Candlish in Free St. George's church, Edinburgh, 1861; resigned through ill-health, 1864; spent three years without charge in Melbourne, Australia; minister of Regent Square church, London, 1869-88; author of "The Beatitudes of the Kingdom," "Laws of the Kingdom," "Relations of the Kingdom," "From Jerusalem to Antioch," "Abraham the Friend of God," "Daily Prayers for the Household," "Sermons," etc.

"It shall bruise thy head and thou shalt bruise his heel."--Gen. 3 : 15.

MOST nations which have achieved independence and renown, have either possest or fabled in the dawn of their origin some famous national hero—the champion and the deliverer of his people. Indeed, the earliest names that have struggled down to us, encrusted with legend, from dim ages, are probably the names of strong and valiant men who in their day wrought a kind of deliverance on the earth. In the most primitive times of all the contest was necessarily with hostile powers of nature; the monster of the forest or the pestilential swamp. How many a dragon legend is to be found in traditional story; how many a giant to be slain; how many a tale of romantic exploit by adventurous pioneers, who pierced the savage wildernesses of the world to clear its forests, slay its wolves, drain and till its fens, till the land grew safe and healthy for human habitation. Within historic periods, the task of a national champion has more often been to contend with hostile tribes, to fire his countrymen with the love of freedom or to lead their resistance against some more powerful neighbor. But whether it be in the legend of a Hercules or Perseus, or of Romulus or Arthur, or in the more sober pages which record the name of Leonidas or Tell, Wallace or Washington, all such champions represent a battle which has never ceased since the world was—the ancient endless battle of spirit against brute strength or craft, of order against lawless self-will, of liberty against tyranny, of light against darkness. It is with good right that such tales, dear to the heart of boyhood, linger on in the memory of grown men. For they all preserve some obscure episode or another in the struggle between the seed of the woman and the seed of the serpent. Strangely distorted as they may be or drest in allegory and in fable, they do serve for unconscious types of His mighty task who from the beginning has been the expected champion of human deliverance.

In men of this heroic type no nation's story was ever richer than the sacred annals of the Jews, with one notable distinction. Such names as Moses, Joshua, Samson, Gideon, David, represent deliverances wrought for their fellow countrymen indeed; yet deliverances in which, not man, but God Himself was the evident and acknowledged Deliverer, even more than in the case of their fellow Semites, tho the trait is a Semitic one. In

194

the nation's perils, whether from the Egyptian, or the Bedouin, or the Canaanite, warrior after warrior was raised up, champion after champion, stout of heart and strong of arm; yet always he bore Jehovah's direct commission; always he acted in Jehovah's name; always it was not his bow or sword the people were taught to extol, but the outstretched arm of Israel's God and King. While most other nations, therefore, semi-deified their ancient heroes, this was the language of the Hebrew poet:

Thou art my king, O God! command deliverances
    for Jacob!
Through thee will we push down our enemies:
Through thy name will we tread them under that
    rise up against us.

One example will show how this continued to be the sentiment of the best men in the nation till the close of its career. The last of Israel's great "deliverances" was that from the bondage in Babylon. In speaking of this, the most eloquent of its prophets depicts Jehovah as contemplating "with dismay" the waste and wrongful ruin inflicted upon His repentant people by heathen hands. "Wondering" that no man arose to redress such oppression, He Himself, Jehovah, arms Himself for the combat. With justice for a breastplate, salvation for a head-piece, and the zeal of an avenger for a warrior's crimson cloak, the Almighty descends into the arena against Israel's adversaries:

His own arm—it brought him salvation;
And his righteousness—it sustained him!

Thus by worthier and still worthier instances do we approach that supreme Hero and Deliverer of mankind, divine yet human, who, predicted in the infancy of our race, was manifested in its old age. Fulfiller of all Gentile and Hebrew hope, greater than all Gentile or Hebrew precedent, Jesus is the champion of all men's cause, who in single combat has overthrown the giant dragon, fountain of unnumbered woes, and won for every nation rest and liberty and prosperous life.

Keeping in view this aspect of our Lord's work, foreshadowed in the first prophecy, let me single out in a few sentences some of His characteristics as the ideal champion—dragon-slayer, and rescuer of men from evil.

In the first place our Lord stands alone in this, that He aims at the deliverance of all men from all evil. In other words, it is rescue universal He seeks to compass, and rescue complete. Not the men of a tribe or of a land only, but man as man, human nature and the human family in its integrity. As much as this is implied in the title given Him in this ancient oracle—"the seed of the woman." And the same idea is continued in the title (with a similar meaning) which He adopted for Himself: "the Son of man." It is as One qualified to represent every other human being, the Head therefore and the champion of us all, that He enters the lists. And the deliverance is to be as thorough as its benefits will be wide. For He fights not against this or that form of evil, for this or that single blessing; but against the head seat and fontal source of all human ill, that He may restore us to the whole of our forfeited inheritance. His adversary is the ancient serpent, to whose craft human innocence fell a prey. In him is summed up, as in a single head, the whole of that alien and hostile force with which, under its innumerable hydra shapes, men have been contending from the beginning. In these combatants are incarnated, as it were, two realms of good and evil. "He shall bruise thy head."

From this we gather, in the second place, the region and character of the struggle. Human nature and human life are devastated by a malignant power, not native to us, but intruding from without. Where is its chief seat or citadel? When our Lord Himself described His task under this figure of a combat with the ruler of the darkness, He spoke of "the strong man armed," as one whose goods must lie in peace so long as he held possession of his "house," his central fortress and habitation of strength, where like a robber chieftain he sits secure, lording it over the whole territory of this world. Now, what is this "house" of Satan, where first he must be mastered and bound, if ever the goods he has ravished from us are to be restored? It is the moral nature and moral choice of man himself. It is by perverting to sin the tastes and preferences of each of us, as of the first human pair, that evil gains admittance to the true citadel of life. The central seat of the mischiefs that afflict mankind lies there: in a heart turned aside from God, subdued to lawless desire and preferring evil to good. All evils flow from choosing the bad; and choosing the bad from distrust of God. Within the wide circumference of physical lies moral evil; and at the core of moral you lay your finger on religious evil—the sin of an ungodly nature. Here sits the grisly king that holds us captive; and here must the true Deliverer grapple with the power that has ruined man. It follows that the theater of this tremendous conflict is to be sought inside of man's own spiritual being. Have we not here the key to the mysterious experience of temptation which, like a dark thread, traversed and colored the earthly life of Jesus? From His first great trial in the wilderness to His last in the olive-garden, Jesus' life was a struggle against evil choice, conducted within the recesses of His own personal life; a fight for purity and goodness and pious trust against every form of seductive or appalling evil, fought out in His own human soul. The weapons of His warfare were not carnal, but spiritual. He fought first to safeguard the citadel of His personal integrity and holiness. Like the ideal knight of romance, He became invincible only by being pure. To borrow His own words: The prince of this world came, but found nothing of his own in Him.

It is quite in harmony with this inward and moral character of Christ's own conflict that His victory should always work from within men outward. The evils of life which are the first to arrest attention and claim deliverance of some sort, are such as affect the body and its outward well-being; physical evils, first of all, in the wild beasts and savage and destructive elements which have to be overcome if human life is to grow orderly, settled and civilized. There, also, are the oppression of man's rights by his stronger fellow man; individual slavery, serfdom, subjection of woman, military oppression of one tribe by another, feudal lordship over vassals, despotic forms of government. Even now the evils we most keenly realize and of which we most loudly complain are such as arise out of social or political causes. Ignorance, pauperism, class legislation, expensive justice, preventible disease, contests of labor with capital—such are the modern ills to which brave men toil to apply a remedy. True successors they of their forefathers who fought the savage beast or curbed the rage of kings. The form of the contest has changed, but we have still, under other forms, to compel the elements of nature to minister to human welfare; still to check, if we can not prevent, the wasteful action of social injustice and selfish passion. But while all other champions of human deliverance are thus operating on the outside, more or less, Jesus to this hour continues to act by preference from within. He did not ride abroad redressing wrongs; nor does He yet. He did not make war in His own day upon unequal laws or domestic slavery or military despotism. No more is it here that we are now to look for His peculiar sphere. But knowing that if once the individual will be renewed, all other reforms will follow of themselves, Christ goes to the root of the disorder. He acts on units first in order to act the better on the mass. He aims at religious, that He may achieve moral, social, and political regeneration. He addresses to each of us His gracious word and desires leave to put forth within us His regenerating power. Within your soul He wants to be master in the name of God—to break down the fortress of pride, to sweeten the sour temper, to bridle the hot lips of passion, to reconcile you to the dominion of your

Heavenly Father, to restore to the little inner realm of your heart order and law and peace and purity and sweet graciousness. For if that be but done, and the serpent of selfishness within you wounded to death, and the strong evil power of ungodly preference and rebellious will chained, then full well does He know that in the train of that victory will flow all victories, and that spiritual deliverance will be the harbinger of all deliverances.

Here, then, is a champion fit for such of us—(pity they should be so few!)—as desire above all things to subdue sin within themselves. If this be the enterprise on which you are bent—to slay the dragons of pride, temper, lust and ungodliness within you—be sure One is at your side who fighteth for you! This is His elected field of combat, and these spiritual enemies who oppress your better will, and threaten forever to quench the life of faith—these are the foes He has faced in personal encounter and subdued. Cling to His aid and faint not! Grasp His weapons and strike hard! Lean your feebleness against Christ's mighty arm and hide you beneath the shield of His protection: for this is He by whom "the principalities" have been worsted, "the rulers of the darkness of this world," the "spiritual wickedness" that sits in "heavenly" places! This is He who bruised the serpent's head.

In the third place, the character of Jesus Christ is our ideal of the hero. I said His weapons were spiritual, not carnal. They were so because the struggle is a moral one within the heart. Unlike in this all His types in romance or in heroic tale, nevertheless He required for His enterprise the same high qualities of soul which men praise in them. What are the hard tasks given to the sons of men? To face physical peril with material weapons; to beard the lion like David or rend him like Samson; to brave toil and exposure and fatigue, whether in battle or in exile, or in pioneering the steps of the colonist and the trader in arctic frost or tropic swamp; to lead a philanthropic movement or advocate a just reform in its early unpopular days when public ridicule assails it—these all are enterprises of very dissimilar character and all of them unlike our Lord's contest with sin. Yet the qualities which these call forth and exercise in brave men were still more demanded for His work. What is the type of nobleness men style heroic? What ideal floats before the enthusiastic imagination when in youth we picture to ourselves the chivalrous champion of right against powerful wrong? On the one side, the manful virtues: strength, skill, endurance of hardship, tenacity of purpose, fearless valor, indifference to blows or pain, and the power to smite evil with unsparing hand. Yet on the other side—no less tenderness to the weak, pity for the opprest, magnanimity, generosity, scorn of all meanness, hatred of all cruelty and lies. My friends, I am describing Jesus Christ. If it be not actually from Himself we have drawn our ideal of the blameless hero, at least in Him is that ideal realized. True, He wore no sword of steel. With no earthly arms He fought, but with saintly meekness, with continual prayer, with words of heavenly truth, with deeds of gentle kindness. All the resistance which He offered to evil was the resistance of His will to sin; to armed hostility, to brute force He offered none. He gave His wrist to the fetter and His back to the scourge. He let the serpent bite Him in the heel, the lowest and only vulnerable part, which was His material life and fleshly mortal body. That heel of His He suffered to be stung unresisting; yet with the very heel that was stung did He crush the serpent's head. For in such a contest of spiritual and moral forces, material defeat is often the substance of victory. In physical weakness Jesus discovered His true strength— strength to endure for love's and justice's sake. Thus He overcame, not by material, but moral forces: in meekness, not in pride; suffering a seeming defeat, not with the insolence of a triumph. He crowned bleeding brows with a coronet of thorn and wielded a reed.for a rod of power. But from His example heroism learned a new nobleness. What tenacity was His to a generous enterprise! What firmness of moral fiber, true as steel to duty! What silent courage to sustain disaster hopefully and take buffets without complaint! What prodigality of Himself! What unselfish sacrifice for others! What fearlessness of foes in earth or hell! What amazing strength of soul veiled under lamblike submission! As the contest was without parallel, so was this a hero without compeer!

Of one heroic attribute, at the least, has He need to this hour. A victory which is spiritual is a hidden victory. A deliverance which begins within man's soul and works thence outward is slow to become apparent. The spiritual intelligences in heaven and earth, who look beneath the surface, know that the fatal dominion of Satan over man has long been a broken and a doomed dominion. The first sinful soul whom the cross of Jesus turned into a penitent and His grace lifted to Paradise was token enough that the head of the evil one was bruised, sin, in principle at least, destroyed, death (as Paul says) abolished, and victory won for mankind over its ancient foe. Yet because the rescue and the victory lie within the spiritual sphere, in

the change of each man's relations to God and the renewal of each man's will, therefore they are realized but slowly, man by man, and they do not at first betray themselves by any material consequences. The bruising of Jesus' heel we see; for that was physical suffering. The crushing of Satan's head we do not see; for that was a moral conquest. Hence is this champion robbed of His meed of laurel. Men will not praise what they can not see; nor applaud a success that leaves the physical condition of humanity where it was. Very slowly indeed, and in a very partial measure, Christ has shown Himself able to better the social, political, and even material condition of the nations. That has come about very fitfully, very gradually, and very imperfectly. Yet to this extent and no further is Christ owned by the world at large as a benefactor. His real claim, His great achievement, the world overlooks. Let us try to be wiser than the world! Ask for eyes to see things spiritual. Pray to be no longer blind to the true meaning of Christ's work or the true glory of His conquest. Enter by faith into the victory He achieved for you over sin and Satan, over death and hell; and by faith and prayer and spiritual effort make that victory your own. He bruised Satan for you; in you He will bruise him likewise. He will enable you to bruise him. He will make you sharers in His own inward and moral supremacy over temptation, fear, unbelief, fleshly desire, and spiritual pride—helping you also to plant your foot upon the head of every sin that lifts itself within your soul. It may be you, too, will suffer in the process. It may be your heel must be stung. It may be you have to pay with material loss or bodily pain for each moral victory you win. It may be, therefore, that no splendid or pleasant fruits of conquest are yours to boast of in this life. Meantime your victory over the dragon may be as far from apparent as your Lord's. Yet wait. I said He had still need of one attribute of heroes. Here it is: Patience to wait for the fruits of victory. This also belongs to the conquest of faith over sense, of spirit over matter. To believe that the dragon's head is bruised; that the lord of the castle is bound and his power passed into better hands; that all things therefore will be righted one day, and the real conqueror crowned, and His true followers made glad, and all old things pass and all things grow new; to believe this now, when little or nothing of it is to be seen; to believe in it, I say, and to wait for it and in patience work for it: here is the faith and patience of the saints!

JONATHAN EDWARDS

1703-1758

SINNERS
IN THE HANDS OF
AN ANGRY GOD

BIOGRAPHICAL NOTE

JONATHAN EDWARDS, the new New England divine and metaphysician, was born at East Windsor, Connecticut, in 1703. He graduated early from Yale College, where he had given much attention to philosophy, became tutor of his college, and at 19 began to preach. His voice and manner did not lend themselves readily to pulpit oratory, but his clear, logical and intense presentation of the truth produced a profound and permanent effect upon his hearers. He wrote what is considered the most important philosophical treatise of his time. His place among the thinkers of the world is high. He had gifts of intellect and imagination. He was one of the greatest preachers of his age. His most widely quoted sermon, "Sinners in the Hands of an Angry God," is the most famous discourse of its time and perhaps the most terrifying sermon ever preached. It is marked with utter sincerity and a profound conviction that drives the preacher to declare the "whole truth of God"; so that he, with those he would arouse, may escape the awful judgment. Not pleasant reading, but it is perhaps profitable in such a time as this. He died in 1758.

Their foot shall slide in due time. — Deut. 32:35

In this verse is threatened the vengeance of God on the wicked, unbelieving Israelites, who were God's visible people, and lived under means of grace; and who, notwithstanding all God's wonderful works that He had wrought toward that people, yet remained, as is expressed in the twenty-eighth verse, void of counsel, having no understanding in them; and that, under all the cultivations of heaven, brought forth bitter and poisonous fruit; as in the two verses next preceding the text.

The expression that I have chosen for my text, "Their foot shall slide in due time," seems to imply the following things, relating to the punishment and destruction that these wicked Israelites were exposed to:

1. That they were always exposed to destruction; as one that stands or walks in slippery places is always exposed to fall. This is implied in the manner of their destruction's coming upon them, being represented by their foot's sliding. The same is expressed in the seventy-third Psalm: "Surely Thou didst set them in slippery places; Thou castedst them down into destruction."

2. It implies that they were always exposed to sudden, unexpected destruction. As he that walks in slippery places is every moment liable to fall, he can not foresee one moment whether he shall stand or fall the next; and when he does fall, he falls at once, without wavering, which is also expressed in the seventy-third Psalm: "Surely Thou didst set them in slippery places: Thou castedst them down into destruction: how are they brought into desolation as in a moment!"

3. Another thing implied is, that they are liable to fall of themselves, without being thrown down by the hand of another; as he that stands or walks on slippery ground needs nothing but his own weight to throw him down.

4. That the reason why they are not fallen already, and do not fall now, is only that God's appointed time is not come. For it is said that when that due time or appointed time comes, "their feet shall slide." Then they shall be left to fall, as they are inclined by their own weight. God will not hold them up in these slippery places any longer, but will let them go; and then, at that very instant, they shall fall into destruction; as he that stands on such slippery, declining ground, on the edge of a pit, that he cannot stand alone, when he is let go he immediately falls and is lost.

The observation from the words that I would now insist upon is this:

There is nothing that keeps wicked men at any one moment out of hell, but the mere pleasure of God.

By the mere pleasure of God, I mean his sovereign pleasure, his arbitrary will, restrained by no obligation, hindered by no manner of difficulty any more than if nothing else but God's mere will had, in the last degree, or in any respect whatsoever, any hand in the preservation of wicked men one moment.

The truth of this observation may appear by the following considerations:

1. There is no want of power in God to cast wicked men into hell at any moment. Men's hands cannot be strong, when God rises up. The strongest have no power to resist him, nor can any deliver out of his hands.

He is not only able to cast wicked men into hell, but he can most easily do it. Sometimes an earthly prince meets with a great deal of difficulty in subduing a rebel, who has found means to fortify himself, and has made himself strong by the number of his followers. But it is not so with God. There is no fortress that is any defense from the power of God. Though hand join in hand, and a vast multitude of God's enemies combine and associate themselves, they are easily broken in pieces. They are as great heaps of light chaff before the whirlwind; or large quantities of dry stubble before devouring flames. We find it easy to tread on and crush a worm that we see crawling on the earth; so it is easy for us to cut or singe a slender thread that anything hangs by: thus easy is it for God when he pleases, to cast his enemies down to hell. What are we, that we should think to stand before Him, at whose rebuke the earth trembles, and before whom the rocks are thrown down?

2. They deserve to be cast into hell; so that divine justice never stands in the way; it makes no objection against God's using his power at any moment to destroy them. Yea, on the contrary, justice calls aloud for an infinite punishment of their sins. Divine justice says of the tree that brings forth such grapes of Sodom, "Cut it down, why cumbereth it the ground?" — Luke 13:7. The sword of divine justice is every moment brandished over their heads and it is nothing but the hand of arbitrary mercy, and God's mere will that holds it back.

3. They are already under a sentence of condemnation to hell. They do not only justly deserve to be cast down thither, but the sentence of the law of God, that eternal and immutable rule of righteousness that God has fixed between him and mankind, is gone out against them, and stands against them; so that they are bound over already to hell. John 3:18 — "He that believeth not is condemned already." So that every unconverted man properly belongs to hell; that is his place;

from thence he is. John 8:23 — "Ye are from beneath"; and thither he is bound; it is the place that justice, and God's Word, and sentence of his unchangeable law, assign to him.

4. They are now the objects of that very same anger and wrath of God, that is expressed in the torments of hell; and the reason why they do not go down to hell at each moment, is not because God, in whose power they are, is not at present very angry with them; as he is with many miserable creatures now tormented in hell, who there feel and bear the fierceness of his wrath. Yea, God is a great deal more angry with great numbers that are now on earth, yea doubtless with some who may read this book, who, it may be are at ease, than he is with many of those that are now in the flames of hell.

So it is not because God is unmindful of their wickedness, and does not resent it, that he does not let loose his hand, and cut them off. God is not altogether such a one as themselves, though they may imagine him to be so. The wrath of God burns against them, their damnation does not slumber; the pit is prepared, the fire is made ready, the furnace is now hot, ready to receive them; the flames do now rage and glow. The glittering sword is whetted, and held over them, and the pit hath opened its mouth under them.

5. The devil stands ready to fall upon them, and seize them as his own, at what moment God shall permit him. They belong to him; he has their souls in his possession, and under his dominion. The Scripture represents them as his goals — Luke 11:21. The devils watch them; they are ever by them, at their right hand; they stand waiting for them, like greedy hungry lions, that see their prey, and expect to have it, but are for the present kept back. If God should withdraw his hand, by which they are restrained, they would in one moment fly upon their poor souls. The old serpent is gaping for them; hell opens its mouth wide to receive them; and if God should permit it, they would be hastily swallowed up and lost.

6. There are in the souls of wicked men those hellish principles reigning, that would presently kindle and flame out into hell fire, if it were not for God's restraints. There is laid in the very nature of carnal men, a foundation for the torments of hell. There are those corrupt principles, in reigning power in them, and in full possession of them, that are seeds of hell fire. The principles are active and powerful, exceedingly violent in their nature; and if it were not for the restraining hand of God upon them, they would soon breakout; they would flame out after the same manner as the same corruption, the same enmity, does in the hearts of damned souls, and would beget the same torments as they do in them. The souls of the wicked are

in Scriptures compared to the troubled sea —
Isaiah 57:20. For the present, God restrains
their wickedness by his mighty power, as he
does the raging waves of the troubled sea,
saying "Hitherto shalt thou come, and no
further," but if God should withdraw that
restraining power, it would soon carry all
before it. Sin is the ruin and misery of the
soul; it is destructive in its nature; and if God
should leave it without restraint, there would
need nothing else to make the soul perfectly
miserable. The corruption of the heart of the
man is immoderate and boundless in its fury;
and while wicked men live here, it is like fire
pent up by the course of nature; and as the
heart is now a sink of sin, so, if sin was not
restrained, it would immediately turn the
soul into a fiery oven, or furnace of fire and
brimstone.

7. It is no security to wicked men for one
moment, that there are no visible means of
death at hand! It is no security to a natural
man, that he is now in health, and that he
does not see which way he should now immediately go out of the world by any accident, and that there is no visible danger, in
any respect, in his circumstances. The
manifold and continual experience of the
world, in all ages, shows this is no evidence
that a man is not on the very brink of eternity
and that the next step will not be into
another world. The unseen, unthought-of-
ways and means of persons going suddenly
out of the world are innumerable and inconceivable. Unconverted men walk over the
pit of hell on a rotten covering, and there are
innumerable places in this covering so weak
that they will not bear their weight, and these
places are not seen. The arrows of death fly
unseen at noon-day; the sharpest sight cannot discern them. God has so many different
unsearchable ways of taking wicked men out
of the world and sending them to hell, that
there is nothing to make it appear that God
had need to be at the expense of a miracle, or
to go out of the ordinary course of His
providence to destroy any wicked man, at
any moment. All the means that there are of
sinners going out of the world, are so in God's
hands, and so universally and absolutely subject to His power and determination, that it
does not depend at all the less on the mere
will of God, whether sinners shall at any moment go to hell, than if means were never
made use of, or at all concerned in the case.

8. Natural men's prudence and care to
preserve their own lives, or the care of others
to preserve them, do not secure them a moment. To this, divine providence and universal experience do bear testimony. There is
this clear evidence that men's own wisdom is
no security to them from death; that, if it
were otherwise, we should see some difference
between the wise and politic men of the world
and others, with regard to their liableness to
early and unexpected death; but how is it in
fact? "How dieth the wise man? as the fool"
— Ecclesiastes 2:16.

9. All wicked men's pains and contrivances
which they use to escape hell, while they continue to reject Christ, and so remain wicked
men, do not secure them from hell one moment. Almost every natural man that hears
of hell, flatters himself that he shall escape it;
he depends upon himself for his own security;
he flatters himself in what he has done, in
what he is now doing, or what he intends to
do; every one lays out matters in his own
mind, how he shall avoid damnation, and
flatters himself that he contrives well for
himself, and that his schemes will not fail.
They hear indeed that there are but few saved, and that the greater part of men that have
died heretofore, are gone to hell; but each one
imagines that he forms plans to effect his escape better than others have done. He does
not intend to go to that place of torment; he
says within himself, that he intends to take
effectual care, and to order matters so for
himself as not to fail.

But the foolish children of men miserably
delude themselves in their own schemes, and
in confidence in their own strength and
wisdom; they trust to nothing but a shadow.
The greater part of those who heretofore have
lived under the same means of grace, and are
now dead, are undoubtedly gone to hell; and
it was not because they were not as wise as
those who are now alive, it was not becuase
they did not lay out matters as well for
themselves to secure their own escape. If we
could come to speak with them, and inquire
of them, one by one, whether they expected,
when alive, and when they used to hear about
hell, ever to be subjects of that misery, we,
doubtless, should hear one and another
reply, "No, I never intended to come here: I
had arranged matters otherwise in my mind;
I thought I should contrive well for myself; I
thought my scheme good. I intended to take
effectual care; but it came upon me unexpectedly; I did not look for it at that time,
and in that manner; it came as a thief. Death
outwitted me: God's wrath was too quick for
me. O my cursed foolishness! I was flattering
myself, and pleasing myself with vain dreams
of what I would do hereafter; and when I was
saying peace and safety, then sudden
destruction came upon me."

10. God has laid himself under no obligation, by any promise, to keep any natural
man out of hell one moment. God certainly
has made no promises either of eternal life, or
of any deliverance or preservation from eternal death, but what are contained in the
covenant of grace, the promises that are given
in Christ, in whom all the promises are yea
and amen. But surely they have no interest in
the promise of the covenant of grace who are
not the children of the covenant, who do not

believe in any of the promises, and have no interest in the Mediator of the covenant.

So that, whatever some have imagined and pretended about promises made to natural men's earnest seeking and knocking, it is plain and manifest, that whatever pains a natural man takes in religion, whatever prayers he makes, till he believes in Christ, God is under no manner of obligation to keep him a moment from eternal destruction.

So that thus it is that natural men are held in the hand of God over the pit of hell; they have deserved the fiery pit, and are already sentenced to it; and God is dreadfully provoked: his anger is as great towards them as those that are actually suffering the execution of the fierceness of His wrath in hell; and they have done nothing in the least to appease or abate that anger, neither is God in the least bound by any promise to hold them up for one moment. The devil is waiting for them, hell is gaping for them, the flames gather and flash about them, and would fain lay hold on them, and swallow them up; the fire pent up in their own hearts is struggling to break out; and they have no interest in any Mediator; there are no means within reach that can be any security to them. In short they have no refuge, nothing to take hold of; all that preserves them every moment is the mere arbitrary will, and uncovenanted, unobliged forbearance of an incensed God.

Application

The use of this awful subject may be for awakening unconverted persons to a conviction of their danger. This that you have heard is the case of every one out of Christ. That world of misery, that lake of burning brimstone, is extended abroad under you. There is the dreadful pit of the glowing flames of the wrath of God; there is hell's wide gaping mouth open; and you have nothing to stand upon, nor anything to take hold of, there is nothing between you and hell but the air; it is only the power and mere pleasure of God that holds you up.

You are probably not sensible of this; you find you are kept out of hell, but do not see the hand of God in it, but look at other things, as the good state of your bodily constitution, your care of your own life, and the means you use for your own preservation. But indeed these things are nothing; if God should withdraw His hand, they would avail no more to keep you from falling, than the thin air to hold up a person who is suspended in it.

Your wickedness makes you, as it were, heavy as lead, and to rend downwards with great weight and pressure towards hell, and if God should let you go, you would immediately sink, and swiftly descend and plunge into the bottomless gulf; and your healthy constitution, and your own care and prudence,

and best contrivance, and all your righteousness, would have no more influence to uphold you, and keep you out of hell, than a spider's web would have to stop a falling rock. Were it not for the sovereign pleasure of God, the earth would not bear you one moment, for you are a burden to it; the creation groans with you; the creature is made subject to the bondage of your corruption, not willingly; the sun does not willingly shine upon you, to give you light to serve sin and Satan; the earth does not willingly yield her increase, to satisfy your lusts; nor is it willingly a stage for your wickedness to be acted upon; the air does not willingly serve you for breath to maintain the flame of life in your vitals, while you spend your life in the service of God's enemies. God's creatures are good, and were made for men to serve God with; and do not willingly subserve any other purpose, and groan when they are abused to purposes so directly contrary to their nature and end. And the world would spew you out, were it not for the sovereign hand of Him who hath subjected it in hope. There are the black clouds of God's wrath now hanging directly over your heads, full of the dreadful storm, and big with thunder; and were it not for the restraining hand of God they would immediately burst forth upon you. The sovereign pleasure of God, for the present, stays His rough wind, otherwise it would come with fury; and your destruction would come like a whirlwind, and would be like the chaff of the summer threshing-floor.

The wrath of God is like great waters that are restrained for the present; but they increase more and more, and rise higher and higher, till an outlet is given; and the longer the stream is stopped the more rapid and mighty is its course when once it is let loose. It is true, that judgment against your evil works has not been executed hitherto; the floods of God's vengeance have been withheld; but your guilt in the meantime is constantly increasing, and you are every day treasuring up more wrath; the waters are constantly rising and waxing more and more mighty; and there is nothing but the mere pleasure of God that holds the waters back, that are unwilling to be stopped, and press hard to go forward. If God should only withdraw His hand from the floodgate, it would immediately fly open, and the fiery floods of the fierceness and wrath of God, would rush forth with inconceivable fury, and would come upon you with omnipotent power; and if your strength were ten thousand times greater than it is, yea, ten thousand times greater than the strength of the stoutest, sturdiest devil in hell, it would be nothing to withstand or endure it.

The bow of God's wrath is bent, and the arrow made ready on the string; and justice directs the bow to your heart, and strains at the bow: and it is nothing but the mere pleasure of God, and that of an angry God, without any promise or obligation at all, that keeps the arrow one moment from being made drunk with your blood.

Thus all you that never passed under a great change of heart, by the mighty power of the Spirit of God upon your souls; all you that were never born again, and made new creatures, and raised from being dead in sin, to a state of new, and before altogether unexperienced light and life, are in the hands of an angry God. However you may have reformed your life in many things and many have had religious affections, and may keep up a form of religion in your families and closets, and in the house of God, it is nothing but his mere pleasure that keeps you from being this moment swallowed up in everlasting destruction.

However unconvinced you may now be of the truth of what you hear, by and by you will be fully convinced of it. Those that are gone from being in the like circumstances with you, see that it was so with them; for destruction came suddenly upon most of them; when they expected nothing of it, and while they were saying, Peace and safety. Now they see, that those things on which they depended for peace and safety, were nothing but thin air and empty shadows.

The God that holds you over the pit of hell, much in the same way as one holds a spider, or some loathesome insect, over the fire, abhors you, and is dreadfully provoked; His wrath towards you burns like fire; he looks upon you as worthy of nothing else but to be cast into the fire; He is of purer eyes than to bear to have you in His sight; you are ten thousand times more abominable in His eyes than the most hateful venomous serpent is in ours. You have offended Him infinitely more than ever a stubborn rebel did his prince; and yet, it is nothing but His hand that holds you from falling into the fire every moment. It is to be ascribed to nothing else, that you did not go to hell the last night; that you were suffered to awake again in this world, after you closed your eyes to sleep; and there is no other reason to be given, why you have not dropped into hell since you arose in the morning, but that God's hand has held you up. There is no other reason to be given, while you have been reading this address, but His mercy; yea, no other reason can be given why you do not this very moment drop down into hell.

O sinner, consider the fearful danger you are in! It is a great furnace of wrath, a wide and bottomless pit, full of the fire of wrath that you are held over in the hand of that God whose wrath is provoked and incensed as much against you as against many of the damned in hell. You hang by a slender thread, with the flames of divine wrath flashing about it and ready every moment to singe it, and burn it asunder; and you have no interest in any Mediator, and nothing to lay hold of to save yourself, nothing to keep off the flames of wrath, nothing of your own, nothing that you have done, nothing that you can do, to induce God to spare you one moment.

And consider here more particularly.

1. Whose wrath it is. It is the wrath of the infinite God. If it were only the wrath of man, though it were of the most potent prince, it would be comparatively little to be regarded. The wrath of kings is very much dreaded, especially of absolute monarchs, who have the possessions and lives of their subjects wholly in their power, to be disposed of at their mere will. Proverbs 20:2 — "The fear of a king is as the roaring of a lion; whoso provoketh him to anger, sinneth against his own soul." The subject who very much enrages an arbitrary prince, is liable to suffer the most extreme torments that human art can invent, or human power can inflict. But the greatest earthly potentates, in their greatest majesty and strength, and when clothed in their greatest terrors are but feeble, despicable worms of the dust, in comparison with the great and almighty Creator and King of heaven and earth. It is but little that they can do, when most enraged, and when they have exerted the utmost of their fury. All the kings of the earth, before God, are as grasshoppers; they are nothing, and less than nothing: both their love and their hatred are to be despised. The wrath of the great King of kings, is as much more terrible than theirs, as his majesty is greater. "And I say unto you, my friends, Be not afraid of them that kill the body, and after that, have no more that they can do. But I will forewarn you whom ye shall fear; Fear him, which after he hath killed, hath power to cast into hell; yea, I say unto you. Fear him" — Luke 12:4, 5.

2. It is the fierceness of his wrath that you are exposed to. We often read of the fury of God; as in Isaiah 59:18 "According to their deeds, accordingly he will repay, fury to his adversaries." So Isaiah 66:15 — "For, behold, the Lord will come with fire, and with his chariots like a whirlwind to render his anger with fury, and his rebuke with flames of fire." And so also in many other places. Thus we read of "the winepress of the fierceness and wrath of Almighty God" — Revelation 19:15. The words are exceedingly terrible. If it had only been said, "the wrath of God," the words would have implied that which is unspeakably dreadful; but it is said, "the fierceness and wrath of God"; the fury of God! the fierceness of Jehovah! Oh how dreadful must that be! Who can utter or conceive what such expressions carry in them? But it is also, "the fierceness and wrath of

Almighty God." As though there would be a very great manifestation of His almighty power in what the fierceness of His wrath should inflict; as though Omnipotence should be, as it were, enraged, and exerted, as men are wont to exert their strength in the fierceness of their wrath. O! then, what will be the consequence? what will become of the poor worm that shall suffer it? whose hands can be strong; and whose heart can endure? To what a dreadful inexpressible, inconceivable depth of misery must the poor creature be sunk, who shall be the subject of this!

Consider this, you that yet remain in an unregenerate state. That God will execute the fierceness of His anger, implies, that he will inflict wrath without any pity. When God beholds the ineffable extremity of your case, and sees your torment to be so vastly disproportioned to your strength, and sees how your poor soul is crushed, and sinks down, as it were, into an infinite gloom; he will have no compassion upon you, he will not forbear the execution of his wrath, or in the least lighten his hand: there shall be no moderation or mercy, nor will God then at all stay his rough wind: he will have no regard to your welfare, nor be at all careful lest you should suffer too much in any other sense, than only that you shall not suffer beyond what strict justice requires: nothing shall be withheld, because it is so hard for you to bear. "Therefore will I also deal in fury; mine eye shall not spare, neither will I have pity; and though they cry in mine ears with a loud voice, yet will I not hear them" — Ezekiel 8:18. Now, God stands ready to pity you; this is the day of mercy; you may cry now with some encouragement of obtaining mercy. But when once the day of mercy is passed, your most lamentable and dolorous cries and shrieks will be in vain; you will be wholly lost and thrown away of God, as to any regard to your welfare. God will have no other use to put you to, but to suffer misery; you may be continued in being to no other end! for you will be a vessel of wrath fitted to destruction; and there will be no other use of this vessel, but only to be filled full of wrath. God will be so far from pitying you when you cry to him, that it is said he will only "laugh and mock." "Because I have called, and ye refused; I have stretched out my hand, and no man regarded; but ye have set at nought all my counsel, and would none of my reproof; I also will laugh at your calamity; I will mock when your fear cometh; when your fear cometh as desolation, and your destruction cometh as a whirlwind; when distress and anguish cometh upon you. Then shall they call upon me, but I will not answer; they shall seek me early, but they shall not find me; for that they hated knowledge, and did not choose the fear of the Lord: they would none of my counsel; they despised all my reproof. Therefore shall they eat of the fruit of their own way, and be filled with their own devices. For the turning away of the simple shall slay them, and the prosperity of fools shall destroy them" — Proverbs 1:24-32.

How awful are those words of the great God. "I will tread them in mine anger, and will trample them in my fury; and their blood shall be sprinkled upon my garments, and I will stain all my raiment" — Isaiah 63:3. It is, perhaps, impossible to conceive of words that carry in them greater manifestations of these three things namely, contempt, hatred, and fierceness of indignation. If you cry to God to pity you, he will be so far from pitying you in your doleful case, or showing you the least reward or favor, that instead of that, he will only tread you under foot: and though he will know that you cannot bear the weight of Omnipotence treading upon you, yet he will not regard that, but he will crush you under his feet without mercy; he will crush out your blood, and make it fly, and it shall be sprinkled on his garments, so as to stain all his raiment. He will not only hate you, but he will have you in the utmost contempt; no place shall be thought fit for you, but under his feet, to be trodden down as the mire of the streets.

3. The misery you are exposed to is that which God will inflict, to the end that he might show what the wrath of Jehovah is. God hath had it on his heart to show to angels and men, both how excellent his love is, and also how terrible his wrath is. Sometimes earthly kings have a mind to show how terrible their wrath is, by the extreme punishments they would execute on those that provoked them. Nebuchadnezzar, that mighty and haughty monarch of the Chaldean empire, was willing to show his wrath, when enraged with Shadrach, Meshach, and Abednego; and accordingly gave order that the burning, fiery furnace should be heated seven times hotter than it was before; doubtless, it was raised to the utmost degree of fierceness that human art could raise it. But the great God is also willing to show his wrath, and magnify his awful majesty and mighty power in the extreme sufferings of his enemies. "What if God, willing to show his wrath, and to make his power known, endured with much long-suffering the vessels of wrath fitted to destruction?" — Romans 9:22. And seeing this is his design, and what he has determined, even to show how terrible the unmixed, unrestrained wrath, the fury and fierceness of Jehovah is, he will do it to effect. There will be something accomplished and brought to pass that will be dreadful with a witness. When the great and angry God hath risen up and executed his awful vengeance on the poor sinner, and the wretch is actually suffering the infinite weight and

power of his indignation, then will God call upon the whole universe to behold the awful majesty and mighty power that is to be seen in it. "And the people shall be as the burnings of lime, as thorns cut up shall they be burned in the fire. Hear, ye that are afar off, what I have done; and ye that are near, acknowledge my might. The sinners in Zion are afraid; fearfulness hath surprised the hypocrites. Who among us shall dwell with the devouring fire? Who among us shall dwell with everlasting burnings?" — Isaiah 33: 12-14.

Thus it will be with you that are in an unconverted state, if you continue in it; the infinite might, and majesty, and terribleness, of the omnipotent God, shall be magnified upon you in the ineffable strength of your torments. You shall be tormented in the presence of the holy angels, and in the presence of the Lamb; and when you shall be in this state of suffering, the glorious inhabitants of heaven shall go forth and look on the awful spectacle, that they may see what the wrath and fierceness of the Almighty is; and when they have seen it, they will fall down and adore that great power and majesty. "And it shall come to pass that from one new moon to another, and from one Sabbath to another, shall all flesh come to worship before me, saith the Lord. And they shall go forth and look upon the carcasses of the men that have transgressed against me; for their worm shall not die, neither shall their fire be quenched; and they shall be an abhorring unto all flesh" — Is. 66:23,24.

4. It is everlasting wrath. It would be dreadful to suffer this fierceness and wrath of Almighty God one moment; but you must suffer it to all eternity. There will be no end to this exquisite horrible misery. When you look forward, you shall see a long forever, a boundless duration, before you, which will swallow up your thoughts, and amaze your souls; and you will absolutely despair of ever having any deliverances, any end, any mitigation, any rest at all; you will know certainly that you must wear out long ages millions of millions of ages, in wrestling and conflicting with this almighty merciless vengeance; and then when you have so done, when many ages have actually been spent by you in this manner, you will know that all is but a point to what remains. So that your punishment will indeed be infinite. O, who can express what the state of a soul in such circumstances is! All that we can possibly say about it, gives but a very feeble, faint representation of it; it is inexpressible and inconceivable: for, "Who knoweth the power of God's anger?"

How dreadful is the state of those who are daily and hourly in danger of this great wrath and infinite misery! But this is the dismal case of every soul in this congregation that has not been born again, however moral and strict, sober and religious, they may otherwise be. Oh that you would consider it, whether you be young or old! There is reason to fear that there are many in this congregation who have heard the gospel, who will actually be the subjects of this very misery to all eternity. We know not who they are, or what thoughts they now have. It may be they are now at ease, and hear all these things without much disturbance, and are now flattering themselves that they are not the persons, promising themselves that they shall escape. If we knew that there was one person, and but one, of those that we know, that was to be the subject of this misery, what an awful thing would it be to think of! If we knew who it was, what an awful sight would it be to see such a person! How might every Christian lift up a lamentable and bitter cry over him! But alas! instead of one, how many is it likely will remember this discourse in hell! And some may be in hell in a very short time, before this year is out. And it would be no wonder if some who sit in this meeting and are now in health, and quiet and secure, may be there before tomorrow morning. Those of you who finally continue in a natural condition who may keep out of hell longest, will be there in a little time! Your damnation does not slumber; it will come swiftly, and, in all probability, very suddenly, upon many of you. You have reason to wonder that you are not already in hell. It is doubtless the case of some whom you have seen and known, that never deserved hell more than you, and that heretofore appeared as likely to have been now alive as you. Their case is past all hope. They are crying in extreme misery and perfect despair; but here you are in the land of the living, blessed with Bibles and sabbaths, and ministers, and have an opportunity to obtain salvation. What would not those poor damned, hopeless souls give for one day's opportunity such as you now enjoy?

And now you have an extraordinary opportunity, a day wherein Christ has thrown the door of mercy wide open, and stands calling, and crying with a loud voice to poor sinners, a day wherein many are flocking to him, and pressing into the kingdom of God; many are daily coming from the east, west, north, and south; many that were very lately in the same miserable condition that you are in are now in a happy state with their hearts filled with love to Him who has loved them, and washed them from their sins in his own blood, and rejoicing in hope of the glory of God. How awful is it to be left behind at such a day to see so many others feasting, while you are pining and perishing! To see so many rejoicing and singing for joy of heart, while you have cause to mourn for sorrow of heart, and to howl for vexation of spirit! How can you rest one moment in such a condition? Are not your souls as precious as the souls of those who are flocking from day to day to Christ?

Are there not many who have lived long in the world, who are not to this day born again, and so are aliens from the commonwealth of Israel, and have done nothing ever since they have lived, but treasure up wrath against the day of wrath? O sirs! your case, in an especial manner, is extremely dangerous. Your guilt and hardness of heart are extremely great. Do not you see how generally persons of your years are passed over and left, in the dispensations of God's mercy? You had need to consider yourselves, and wake thoroughly out of sleep: you cannot bear the fierceness and wrath of the infinite God.

And you, young man, and young woman, will you neglect this precious season which you now enjoy, when so many others of your age are renouncing all youthful vanities, and flocking to Christ? You especially have now an opportunity, but if you neglect it, it will soon be with you as it is with those persons who spent all the precious days of youth in sin, and are now come to such a dreadful pass in blindness and hardness.

And you children, who are unconverted, do not you know that you are going down to hell, to bear the dreadful wrath of that God, who is now angry with you every day and every night? Will you be content to be the children of the devil, when so many of the children of the land are converted, and are becoming the holy and happy children of the King of kings?

And let every one that is yet out of Christ, and hanging over the pit of hell, whether they be old men and women, or middle aged, or young people, or little children, now hearken to the loud calls of God's word and providence. This acceptable year of the Lord, a day of great mercy to some will doubtless be a day of as remarkable vengeance to others. Men's hearts harden, and their guilt increases apace at such a day as this, if they neglect their souls. Never was there a period when so many means were employed for the salvation of souls, and if you entirely neglect them, you will eternally curse the day of your birth. Now, undoubtedly it is, as it was in the days of John the Baptist, the axe is laid at the root of the trees, and every tree which brings not forth good fruit, may be hewn down, and cast into the fire.

Therefore, let every one that is out of Christ, now awake and flee from the wrath to come. The wrath of Almighty God is now undoubtedly hanging over every unregenerate sinner. Let every one flee out of Sodom: "Escape for your lives, look not behind you, escape to the mountain, lest you be consumed."

CHRISTMAS EVANS

1766-1838

THE FALL
AND
RECOVERY OF MAN

BIOGRAPHICAL NOTE

CHRISTMAS EVANS, a Welsh Baptist preacher, was born at Isgaerwen, Cardiganshire, South Wales, in 1766. Brought up as a Presbyterian, he turned Baptist in 1788, and was ordained the following year and ministered among the Baptists in Carmaerthenshire. In 1792 he became a sort of bishop to those of his denomination in Anglesey, where he took up his residence. After a somewhat stormy experience with those he undertook to rule, he removed to Carmaerthen in 1832. He distinguished himself by his debt-raising tours, in which his eloquence brought him much success. It is said that once when he was preaching on the subject of the prodigal son, he pointed to a distant mountain as he described the father seeing him while yet a great way off, whereupon thousands in his congregation turned their heads in evident expectation of seeing the son actually coming down the hills. He died in 1838.

For if, through the offense of one, many be dead, much more the grace of God, and the gift by grace, which is by one man, Jesus Christ, hath abounded unto many.—Romans v., 15.

MAN was created in the image of God. Knowledge and perfect holiness were imprest upon the very nature and faculties of his soul. He had constant access to his Maker, and enjoyed free communion with Him, on the ground of his spotless moral rectitude. But, alas! the glorious diadem is broken; the crown of righteousness is fallen. Man's purity is gone, and his happiness is forfeited. "There is none righteous; no, not one." "All have sinned, and come short of the glory of God." But the ruin is not hopeless. What was lost in Adam is restored in Christ. His blood redeems us from the bondage, and His gospel gives us back the forfeited inheritance. "For if, through the offense of one, many be dead; much more the grace of God, and the gift by grace, which is by one man, Jesus Christ, hath abounded unto many." Let us consider, first, the corruption and condemnation of man; and secondly, his gracious restoration to the favor of his offended God.

I. To find the cause of man's corruption and condemnation, we must go back to Eden. The eating of the "forbidden tree" was "the offense of one," in consequence of which "many are dead." This was the "sin," the act of "disobedience," which "brought death into the world, and all our wo." It was the greatest ingratitude to the divine bounty, and the boldest rebellion against the divine sovereignty. The royalty of God was contemned; the riches of His goodness slighted; and His most desperate enemy preferred before Him, as if he were a wiser counsellor than infinite wisdom. Thus man joined in league with hell against heaven; with demons of the bottomless pit against the almighty maker and benefactor; robbing God of the obedience due to His command and the glory due to His name; worshiping the creature instead of the creator; and opening the door to pride, unbelief, enmity, and all the wicked and abominable passions. How is the "noble vine," which was planted "wholly a right seed," "turned into the degenerate plant of a strange vine"!

Who can look for pure water from such a fountain? "That which is born of the flesh is flesh." All the faculties of the soul are corrupted by sin; the understanding dark; the will perverse; the affections carnal; the conscience full of shame, remorse, confusion, and mortal fear. Man is a hard-hearted and stiff-necked sinner; loving darkness rather than light, because his deeds are evil; eating sin like bread, and drinking iniquity like water; holding fast deceit, and refusing to let it go. His heart is desperately wicked; full of pride, vanity, hypocrisy, covetousness, hatred of truth, and hostility to all that is good.

This depravity is universal. Among the natural children of Adam, there is no exemption from the original taint. "The whole world lieth in wickedness." "We are all as an unclean thing, and all our righteousness is as filthy rags." The corruption may vary in the degrees of development, in different persons; but the elements are in all, and their nature is everywhere the same; the same in the blooming youth, and the withered sire; in the haughty prince, and the humble peasant; in the strongest giant, and the feeblest invalid. The enemy has "come in like a flood." The deluge of sin has swept the world. From the highest to the lowest, there is no health or moral soundness. From the crown of the head to the soles of the feet, there is nothing but wounds, and bruises, and putrefying sores. The laws, and their violation, and the punishments everywhere invented for the suppression of vice, prove the universality of the evil. The bloody sacrifices, and various purifications, of the pagans, show the hand-writing of remorse upon their consciences; proclaim their sense of guilt, and their dread of punishment. None of them are free from the fear which hath torment, whatever their efforts to overcome it, and however great their boldness in the service of sin and Satan. "Mene! Tekel!" is written on every human heart. "Wanting! wanting!" is inscribed on heathen fanes and altars; on the laws, customs, and institutions of every nation; and on the universal consciousness of mankind.

This inward corruption manifests itself in outward actions. "The tree is known by its fruit." As the smoke and sparks of the chimney show that there is fire within; so all the "filthy conversation" of men, and all "the unfruitful works of darkness" in which they delight, evidently indicate the pollution of the source whence they proceed. "Out of the abundance of the heart the mouth speaketh." The sinner's speech betrayeth him. "Evil speaking" proceeds from malice and envy. "Foolish talking and jesting" are evidence of impure and trifling thoughts. The mouth full of cursing and bitterness, the throat an open sepulcher, the poison of asps under the tongue, the feet swift to shed blood, destruction and misery in their paths, and the way of peace unknown to them, are the clearest and amplest demonstration that men "have gone out of the way," "have together become unprofitable." We see the bitter fruit of the same corruption in robbery, adultery, gluttony, drunkenness, extortion, intolerance, persecution, apostasy, and every evil work—in all false religions; the Jew, obstinately adhering to the carnal ceremonies of an abrogated law; the Mohammedan, honoring an impostor, and receiving a lie for a revelation from God; the papist, worshiping images and relics, praying to departed saints, seeking absolution from sinful men, and trusting in the most absurd mummeries for salvation; the pagan, attributing divinity to the works of his own hands, adoring idols of wood and stone, sacrificing to malignant demons, casting his children into the fire or the flood as an offering to imaginary deities, and changing the glory of the incorruptible God into the likeness of the beast and the worm.

"For these things' sake the wrath of God cometh upon the children of disobedience." They are under the sentence of the broken law; the malediction of eternal justice. "By the offense of one, judgment came upon all men unto condemnation." "He that believeth not is condemned already." "The wrath of God abideth on him." "Curst is every one that continueth not in all things written in the book of the law, to do them." "Wo unto the wicked; it shall be ill with him, for the reward of his hands shall be given him." "They that plow iniquity, and sow wickedness, shall reap the same." "Upon the wicked the Lord shall rain fire, and snares, and a horrible tempest; this shall be the portion of their cup." "God is angry with the wicked every day; if he turn not he will whet his sword; he hath bent his bow, and made it ready."

Who shall describe the misery of fallen man! His days, tho few, are full of evil. Trouble and sorrow press him forward to the tomb. All the world, except Noah and his family, are drowning in the deluge. A storm of fire and brimstone is fallen from heaven upon Sodom and Gomorrah. The earth is opening her mouth to swallow up alive Korah, Dathan, and Abiram. Wrath is coming upon "the beloved city," even "wrath unto the uttermost." The tender and delicate mother is devouring her darling infant. The sword of men is executing the vengeance of God. The earth is emptying its inhabitants into the bottomless pit. On every hand are "confused noises, and garments rolled in blood." Fire and sword fill the land with consternation and dismay. Amid the universal devastation wild shrieks and despairing groans fill the air. God of mercy! is Thy ear heavy, that Thou canst not hear? or Thy arm shortened, that Thou canst not save? The heavens above are brass, and the earth beneath is iron; for Jehovah is pouring His indignation upon His adversaries, and He will not pity or spare.

Verily, "the misery of man is great upon him"! Behold the wretched fallen creature!

The pestilence pursues him. The leprosy cleaves to him. Consumption is wasting him. Inflammation is devouring his vitals. Burning fever has seized upon the very springs of life. The destroying angel has overtaken the sinner in his sins. The hand of God is upon him. The fires of wrath are kindling about him, drying up every well of comfort, and scorching all his hopes to ashes. Conscience is chastizing him with scorpions. See how he writhes! Hear how he shrieks for help! Mark what agony and terror are in his soul, and on his brow! Death stares him in the face, and shakes at him his iron spear. He trembles, he turns pale, as a culprit at the bar, as a convict on the scaffold. He is condemned already. Conscience has pronounced the sentence. Anguish has taken hold upon him. Terrors gather in battle array about him. He looks back, and the storms of Sinai pursue him; forward, and hell is moved to meet him; above, and the heavens are on fire; beneath, and the world is burning. He listens, and the judgment trump is calling; again, and the brazen chariots of vengeance are thundering from afar; yet again, the sentence penetrates his soul with anguish unspeakable—"Depart! ye accurst! into everlasting fire, prepared for the devil and his angels!"

Thus, "by one man, sin entered into the world, and death by sin; and so death passed upon all men, for that all have sinned." They are "dead in trespasses and sins," spiritually dead, and legally dead; dead by the mortal power of sin, and dead by the condemnatory sentence of the law; and helpless as sheep to the slaughter, they are driven fiercely on by the ministers of wrath to the all-devouring grave and the lake of fire!

But is there no mercy? Is there no means of salvation? Hark! amid all this prelude of wrath and ruin, comes a still small voice, saying: "Much more the grace of God, and the gift by grace, which is by one man, Jesus Christ, hath abounded unto many."

II. This brings us to our second topic, man's gracious recovery to the favor of his offended God.

I know not how to present to you this glorious work, better than by the following figure. Suppose a vast graveyard, surrounded by a lofty wall, with only one entrance, which is by a massive iron gate, and that is fast bolted. Within are thousands and millions of human beings, of all ages and classes, by one epidemic disease bending to the grave. The graves yawn to swallow them, and they must all perish. There is no balm to relieve, no physician there. Such is the condition of man as a sinner. All have sinned; and it is written, "The soul that sinneth shall die." But while the unhappy race lay in that dismal prison, Mercy came and stood at the gate, and wept over the melancholy scene, exclaiming—"Oh, that I might enter! I would bind up their wounds; I would relieve their sorrows; I would save their souls!" An embassy of angels, commissioned from the court of heaven to some other world, paused at the sight, and heaven forgave that pause. Seeing Mercy standing there, they cried:—"Mercy! canst thou not enter? Canst thou look upon that scene and not pity? Canst thou pity, and not relieve?" Mercy replied: "I can see!" and in her tears she added, "I can pity, but I can not relieve!" "Why canst thou not enter?" inquired the heavenly host. "Oh!" said Mercy, "Justice has barred the gate against me, and I must not—can not unbar it!" At this moment, Justice appeared, as if to watch the gate. The angels asked, "Why wilt thou not suffer Mercy to enter?" He sternly replied: "The law is broken, and it must be honored! Die they, or Justice must!" Then appeared a form among the angelic band like unto the Son of God. Addressing Himself to Justice, He said: "What are thy demands?" Justice replied: "My demands are rigid; I must have ignominy for their honor, sickness for their health, death for their life. Without the shedding of blood there is no remission!" "Justice," said the Son of God, "I accept thy terms! On me be this wrong! Let Mercy enter, and stay the carnival of death!" "What pledge dost thou give for the performance of these conditions?" "My word; my oath!" "When wilt thou perform them?" "Four thousand years hence, on the hill of Calvary, without the walls of Jerusalem." The bond was prepared, and signed and sealed in the presence of attendant angels. Justice was satisfied, the gate was opened, and Mercy entered, preaching salvation in the name of Jesus. The bond was committed to patriarchs and prophets. A long series of rites and ceremonies, sacrifices and obligations, was instituted to perpetuate the memory of that solemn deed. At the close of the four thousandth year, when Daniel's "seventy weeks" were accomplished, Justice and Mercy appeared on the hill of Calvary. "Where," and Justice, "is the Son of God?" "Behold him, answered Mercy, "at the foot of the hill!" And there He came, bearing His own cross, and followed by His weeping church. Mercy retired, and stood aloof from the scene. Jesus ascended the hill like a lamb for the sacrifice. Justice presented the dreadful bond, saying, "This is the day on which this article must be canceled." The Redeemer took it. What did He do with it? Tear it to pieces, and scatter it to the winds? No! He nailed it to His cross, crying, "It is finished!" The victim ascended the altar. Justice called on Holy Fire to come down and consume the sacrifice. Holy Fire replied: "I come! I will consume the sacrifice, and then I will burn up the world!" It fell upon the Son of God, and rapidly consumed His humanity; but when it touched His deity, it expired. Then was there darkness over the whole land, and an earthquake shook the mountain; but the heavenly host broke forth in rapturous song—"Glory to God in the highest! on earth peace! good will to man!"

Thus grace has abounded, and the free gift has come upon all, and the gospel has gone forth proclaiming redemption to every creature. "By grace ye are saved, through faith; and that not of yourselves; it is the gift of God; not of works, lest any man should boast." By grace ye are loved, redeemed, and justified. By grace ye are called, converted, reconciled and sanctified. Salvation is wholly of grace. The plan, the process, the consummation are all of grace. "Where sin abounded, grace hath much more abounded." "Through the offense of one, many were dead." And as men multiplied, the offense abounded. The waters deluged the world, but could not wash away the dreadful stain. The fire fell from heaven, but could not burn out the accurst plague. The earth opened her mouth, but could not swallow up the monster sin. The law thundered forth its threat from the thick darkness on Sinai, but could not restrain, by all its terrors, the children of disobedience. Still the offense abounded, and multiplied as the sands on the seashore. It waxed bold, and pitched its tents on Calvary, and nailed the Lawgiver to a tree. But in that conflict sin received its mortal wound. The victim was the victor. He fell, but in His fall He crusht the foe. He died unto sin, but sin and death were crucified upon His cross. Where sin abounded to condemn, grace hath much more abounded to justify. Where sin abounded to corrupt, grace hath much more abounded to purify. Where sin abounded to harden, grace hath much more abounded to soften and subdue. Where sin abounded to imprison men, grace hath much more abounded to proclaim liberty to the captives. Where sin abounded to break the law and dishonor the Lawgiver, grace hath much more abounded to repair the breach and efface the stain. Where sin abounded to consume the soul as with unquenchable fire and a gnawing worm, grace hath much more abounded to extinguish the flame and heal the wound. Grace hath abounded! It hath established its throne on the merit of the Redeemer's sufferings. It hath put on the crown, and laid hold of the golden scepter, and spoiled the dominion of the prince of darkness, and the gates of the great cemetery are thrown open, and there is the beating of a new life-pulse throughout its wretched population and immortality is walking among the tombs!

This abounding grace is manifested in the gift of Jesus Christ, by whose mediation our reconciliation and salvation are effected. With Him, believers are dead unto sin, and alive unto God. Our sins were slain at His cross, and buried in His tomb. His resurrection hath opened our graves, and given us an assurance of immortality. "God commendeth his love toward us, in that while we were yet sinners, Christ died for us; much more, then, being now justified by his blood, we shall be saved from the wrath through him; for if, when we were enemies, we were reconciled to God by the death of his Son, much more, being reconciled, we shall be saved by his life."

"The carnal mind is enmity against God; it is not subject to the law of God, neither indeed can be." Glory to God, for the death of His Son, by which this enmity is slain, and reconciliation is effected between the rebel and the law! This was the unspeakable gift that saved us from ruin; that wrestled with the storm, and turned it away from the devoted head of the sinner. Had all the angels of God attempted to stand between these two conflicting seas, they would have been swept to the gulf of destruction. "The blood of bulls and goats, on Jewish altars slain," could not take away sin, could not pacify the conscience. But Christ, the gift of divine grace, "Paschal Lamb by God appointed," a "sacrifice of nobler name and richer blood than they," bore our sins and carried our sorrows, and obtained for us the boon of eternal redemption. He met the fury of the tempest, and the floods went over His head; but His offering was an offering of peace, calming the storms and the waves, magnifying the law, glorifying its Author, and rescuing its violator from the wrath and ruin. Justice hath laid down his sword at the foot of the cross, and amity is restored between heaven and earth.

Hither, O ye guilty! come and cast away your weapons of rebellion! Come with your bad principles and wicked actions; your unbelief, and enmity, and pride; and throw them off at the Redeemer's feet! God is here waiting to be gracious. He will receive you; He will cast all your sins behind His back, into the depths of the sea; and they shall be remembered against you no more forever. By Heaven's "unspeakable gift," by Christ's invaluable atonement, by the free, infinite grace of the Father and Son, we persuade you, we beseech you, we entreat you, "be ye reconciled to God"!

It is by the work of the Holy Spirit with us that we obtain a personal interest in the work wrought on Calvary for us. If our sins are canceled, they are also crucified. If we are reconciled in Christ, we fight against our God no more. This is the fruit of faith. "With the heart man believeth unto righteousness.'' May the Lord inspire in every one of us that saving principle!

But those who have been restored to the divine favor may sometimes be cast down and dejected. They have passed through the sea, and sung praises on the shore of deliverance; but there is yet between them and Canaan "a waste howling wilderness," a long and weary pilgrimage, hostile nations, fiery serpents, scarcity of food, and the river of Jordan. Fears within and fightings without, they may grow discouraged, and yield to temptation and murmur against God, and desire to return to Egypt. But fear not, thou worm Jacob! Reconciled by the death of Christ; much more, being reconciled, thou shalt be saved by His life. His death was the price of our redemption; His life insures liberty to the believer. If by His death He brought you through the Red Sea in the night, by His life He can lead you through the river Jordan in the day. If by His death He delivered you from the iron furnace in Egypt, by His life He can save you from all perils of the wilderness. If by His death He conquered Pharaoh, the chief foe, by His life He can subdue Sihon, king of the Amorites, and Og, the king of Bashan. "We shall be saved by his life." Because He liveth, we shall live also. "Be of good cheer!" The work is finished; the ransom is effected; the kingdom of heaven is open to all believers. "Lift up your heads and rejoice," "ye prisoners of hope!" There is no debt unpaid, no devil unconquered, no enemy within your hearts that has not received a mortal wound! "Thanks be unto God, who giveth us the victory, through our Lord Jesus Christ!"

ANDREW MARTIN FAIRBAIRN

1838-1912

CHRIST IN GALILEE

BIOGRAPHICAL NOTE

Ex-principal of Mansfield College, Oxford, England; born November 4, 1838, near Edinburgh, Scotland; educated universities of Edinburgh, Berlin, and at Evangelical Union Theological Academy, Glasgow; D.D., Edinburgh and Yale; LL.D., Aberdeen, and D.Litt., Oxford; minister Evangelical Union Congregational church, Bathgate, West Lothian, 1860-72; E. U. Congregational church, St. Paul's Street, Aberdeen, 1872-77; principal of Airedale College, 1877-86; Mansfield College, Oxford, from its foundation, 1886; Muir lecturer, University of Edinburgh, 1878-82; Gifford lecturer, University of Aberdeen, 1882-84; Lyman Beecher lecturer, University of Yale, 1891,2; Haskell lecturer, 1898,9; author of "Studies in the Philosophy of Religion and History," "Studies in the Life of Christ," "The City of God," "Religion in History and in Modern Life," "Christ in Modern Theology," "Christ in the Centuries," "Catholicism, Roman and Anglican," "The Philosophy of the Christian Religion," etc.

"Now after that John was put in prison, Jesus came into Galilee, preaching the gospel of the kingdom of God."—Mark 1 : 14.
"And he said unto them, Go ye into all the world, and preach the gospel to every creature."—Mark 16 : 15.

OF these texts, the one describes Christ's acts in founding His kingdom, and the other states the commission He gave to the men who had as their duty and mission to extend and perpetuate the kingdom He had founded. There are two points from which these two acts may be viewed—the contemporary and the historical. If we try to see this act of founding as contemporaries, what visions will these simple words of Mark call up, "Jesus came into Galilee, preaching the gospel of the kingdom of God?" He will appear before us as a Jew, lowly born, humbly bred, without the manners of the court or the capital, without the learning of the school, or the culture of the college; a mere peasant, as it were, just like the unlettered workmen of Nazareth, or the toil-stained rustics of Galilee. He becomes a preacher, just as Amos the herdsman of Tekoah and multitudes more of His people had done, but He is flouted by the Pharisees, contradicted by the scribes, hated and persecuted by the priests. In a word, He is despised and rejected of the official guardians of religion, and heard gladly by the common people alone. The men He gathers round Him are, like Himself, without the delicate thought or the fastidious speech—not always accurate or pure—of the man of conscious culture, or the thorough knowledge of all that is superficial in man, which marks the person high in place and familiar with affairs. Now, what would men accustomed to a perspective given by those who are accounted pillars in Church and State think of this preacher and His rustic band? Pascal puts the matter far too mildly when he says Jesus Christ lived in such obscurity that the great historians of the world who are concerned with the affairs of State have hardly noticed Him. He who from the heavens watcheth the ways of men might well laugh in infinite irony as He heard the poet praise Cæsar as divine, or the historian bid all eyes to behold the acts of Pilate, and blind as death to the deeds of Christ. If the historian had tried to notice and to describe Him, what would he have said? Something like this: "In those days one Jesus of Nazareth, a carpenter, began to preach, and gathered around Him certain ignorant fisher-folk after the manner of His kind, but all the people of repute held aloof, and the chief

211

priest, with adroit and most excellent diplomacy, when this Jesus became troublesome, induced the procurator to crucify Him." Had we depended on the historian of great deeds there would have been the limit of his vision, and it would mark the immensity of his ignorance and our own. Happily, eyes truer and keener of sight watched His coming, and by their help we can see the entrance into the world of the greatest person and the most creative truth, and the process by which they slowly penetrated the spirit of man, and worked his saving. It was Godlike that He should enter and begin in silent lowliness. All God's great works are silent. They are not done amid rattle of drums and flare of trumpets. Light as it travels makes no noise, utters no sound to the ear. Creation is a silent process; nature rose under the Almighty hand without clang or clamor, or noises that distract and disturb. So, when Jesus came, being of God, His coming was lowly. The most common of all things known of men is birth; the most strange and wonderful of all the things that come to man is the child that is born; but the most marvelous of all births is the birth of Him that Herod stayed not to watch, and Rome did not know, but which all the after ages have turned back to regard as the supreme coming of God into man. And as the child came, so came the King, founding His kingdom by humble word, by lowly deed, by life among men; amid His own people, at the side of His own sea, in His own province of Galilee, He preached the gospel of the kingdom. When the moment came that His work was done, and He had to pass to the Father, His going was as silent as His coming, noted only by the men who loved Him; and that departure was no evening shading into darkest night; it is a day that can never set, but only be absorbed into the splendor of His own coming, the everlasting glory of His eternal home. The two texts put together will give us two distinct truths or messages, which yet are one. One is the personal ministry of Christ, the other is the apostolic ministry of His people as the continuation and realization of His own.

Starting with His personal ministry, there are three things growing out of this text that are notable: There is, first, the place where it is exercised—Galilee; there is, secondly, the men among whom it is exercised—the disciples, called from sea and boat; and there is, thirdly, the substance of His preaching—the gospel of the kingdom of God.

Note the place, Galilee, the circle of the Gentiles. Where would you have thought Jesus would go to found His kingdom, to begin His ministry? Why, of course, if He had been an astute man of the world, up there, at Jerusalem. There was the great temple of His people, there the ornate and ancient priesthood, there the extended and venerated worship, there the historical associations of His race and of its king. Was ever city so loved by men as was Jerusalem? Poets praised it; beautiful for situation, the joy of the whole earth was Mount Zion. The people had loved it; there Solomon had planted his temple; and there, amid poverty, pain and war, a few returned exiles had built another and still more gracious; there the people of God had known the siege of the heathen; there they had known the deliverance of the Most High. The great prophet of the exile had broken into immortal poetry in praise of that city where God dwelt, and toward which all nations should come. Athens may be the eye of Greece, illustrious in wisdom; Rome may be the synonym of imperial and ecclesiastical power; Mecca may speak of a prophet that conquered by the sword, and Benares of one that rules as with a rod of iron millions of our race; but Jerusalem is preeminent as the city of faith, the birthplace of a religion whose very stones were dear to those that loved her. There, then, it might have seemed, Jesus would begin to exercise His ministry. There were rabbis to listen to Him, there were priests to support Him, there were scribes to report Him; all around it seemed the firm soil for His work; but nay, tho He knew that a prophet must perish in Jerusalem, the ministry that was to be fruitful for all time must be exercised elsewhere. He would not throw His soul into the midst of conflict, while conflict would have soiled the serenity of His soul. He would not seek the men bound to fashion and form and place, He would seek those that would gather around Him, ready to be made by His work. He did not need to nurse human sin; left to itself it would breed passion, create jealousy, make the awful hour of His agony and the awful majesty of His cross. But He had to seek love, nurse it and cultivate it, and gather it to His bosom, and bear it there. He wanted the silence that was nurture, He wanted the obscurity that was growth, He wanted the cloistered security of nature, as it were, where His own loved people would learn to know and would learn to love Him, and be made fit to be preachers to all ages and models for all time. Tho of humble birth, scorned by the proud of blood and culture, He had the supernal wisdom, and saw in the quiet of His own province the ministry that could be a well of truth and grace.

Then there is the second point, the men among whom His ministry is exercised. Here, again, you would have imagined that wisdom would have gone in search of the priests and the scribes, and the great men of culture and of training. Nature, once it is formed, is very hard to reform, and the danger of getting hold of a man of great ancestral rights is that he will adhere to the rights till they become great human wrongs. These men with their fashions of robe and garment, these men with their positions and postures, with their incense and altars—what had they in common with Him who wanted not things, but men?

But, on the other hand, see how easily and completely the unformed can be formed by Him who knows how to make them. These disciples had the simplicity of children; they were malleable, they were soft in His plastic hand; He could take them and He could make them, and when they were made they would be the men He desired. And note one wondrous thing! The people, the common people, as proud men say, are apt to fanaticism; they love the intense passion after small things that we call by that unkindly name. But no men ever became less fanatics, more perfectly human enthusiasts than the simple men Jesus formed. Fanaticism is zeal for trifles, enthusiasm is zeal for humanity. Fanaticism is external, is the devotion of a spirit thrown over upon, as it were, a ceremony or a rite; enthusiasm is the concentration, complete and absolute, of a spirit, of all that is ethical and spiritual and good for men. Fanaticism guards the altar, or the alb, or the outer decoration; enthusiasm seeks to recreate the inner and the ideal man of men. Fanaticism marked the priests of Jerusalem; enthusiasm marked the apostles in Galilee. Fanaticism guards a city and keeps it sacred; enthusiasm takes a religion and makes it universal. The one guards what it will not part with, for it is its strength; the other spreads what it lives by, for it is its glory. So Christ created enthusiasts, and left the fanatics to build and possess the city and die by the hands of Rome.

But along with this wondrous power to make out of the common the great enthusiasm of humanity lies another. Did you ever think or feel what a wondrous pathos there is in the speechlessness of the common people? Think how, through long generations, they have remained at home with thoughts in them they can not speak, with ideals before them they can not explain, with the whole inarticulate world passionate for birth. There is a wondrous pathos in the inarticulate multitude. But yet, when the inarticulate finds speech what speech it is! All the world is dumb till one bright day a William Shakespeare is born, and thereafter she is immortal and silent nevermore. The Vale of Annan is a name until one day Thomas Carlyle lives and his great Galloway voice goes wandering through the ages. Tinkers are but people to be shunned; their speech is not the speech of the parlor or of the lecture-room. One day a John Bunyan lives and brings into being a ''Pilgrim's Progress'' and a ''City of Mansoul'' that remain things of beauty and joys forever. Give to the inarticulate the moment

of speech, and there bursts into being all that nature made, that art may follow after but can never overtake or create.

So Jesus, out of the bosom of the inarticulate, forth from the midst of the pathetically dumb, calls these men, fashions them, forms them, preaches to them, makes within them the kingdom of God to live; and lo! it lives, and their eloquence, their speech, immortal as His own, changes and saves the world.

As to the substance of His preaching—He came preaching the gospel of the kingdom of God. The time He came was the time fulfilled; then the long waiting was at an end. Now was the great moment of deliverance and of speech; and this gospel of the kingdom spoke of God whose kingdom it was, and such a God! No harsh, severe fate, no blind, almighty will, no narrow, exclusive sovereign; but that gracious, infinite King, who, reigning in the heavens, reigned over all men, and sought to make in all men His reign supreme. As is the Gods, so is the realm. It is inner, ''for the kingdom of heaven is within you.'' It is outer, for the kingdom of God is around you. It is present, for it is here. It is coming ever more progressively as the ages go on. In this realm there rules a Lord, and the Lord that rules is love; in it there are relations, and the relation Godward is at once that of subject and son, and the relation manward is at once that of Savior and brother. Within this kingdom man knows blessedness, and into it he can enter on two great conditions—he must repent, and he must believe. Let him try to come in with his sin, and for him there is no entrance; let him try to enter out of love of profit and power, without faith, and for him it has no being. It is large enough to embrace the world, yet so small, so exclusive, that the men it embraces are men who love righteousness and have faith. This kingdom he preaches, so that men everywhere may hear, and tho they stand in outer relations where they did, they are new men, and all their world is new.

Compare this kingdom and the gospel concerning it with other kindred messages. Compare the society and the kingdom of Jesus with, say, a great pagan ideal, the ideal that lives partly in the ''Republic'' and partly in the laws of Plato. No more splendid discipline for the fashioning of intellect has ever been made by man than these books of ancient Plato; never a more impracticable dream— incapable of realization, and, were it capable, disastrous in its very being—was ever dreamt by man. Christ's is an ideal and a reality. It is not for the closet, but for the city and the mart. Men everywhere must be within it, and if they are within it, are new. Then there stands a realized religious ideal in what is known and named as Buddhism. With all its wealth of ethical ideal, the Buddhistic nation is marked by two things—a complete separation of the initiated disciple from the world and the duties that most ameliorate its hard and painful lot; and secondly, by an estimate of life that is the child of despair, hatred of being, rather than a love of men. There is an infinite difference between pity for human suffering and love for human souls. Never has the pity for human suffering been more nobly exprest than in Buddha; nowhere, save in Christ, have you the consuming, passionate, saving love of souls. The difference is infinite. You may so pity suffering that you hate life, for in living, men endure pain; but if you love souls, then you hate sin, you hate sorrow, you hate whatever adds to the element of life the ingredient of pain. In Christ you have, therefore, these two things—direct, immediate, face to face, interpenetrated being, saved society, a world to be saved, and you have a saved society penetrated and possest by the passion to save—the love that can redeem.

I pass on from the Master and His personal mission to the apostolic mission as the continuation of the Master's. Here I want especially to observe that the method He followed His disciples were to follow, what He did and was they were to do and be. He was a preacher, they were to be preachers; His message was the gospel of God, their message was to be the same gospel. Now, if men are to accomplish the work they are sent to do by Christ, it must be in the method and the spirit, by the gospel and the mission Jesus gave and Jesus is.

If we take our stand on history as it has been fulfilled up to this present moment, what strikes us? Why, this; the marvelous success of Christ's plan. If He had gone to Jerusalem, think you Christianity would have ever been anything else than redrest Judaism? Think you, had He called men who regarded Him from above downward, as a lesson to be used rather than obeyed, that He would have been anything else than a lost name in history? See, 'y following the plan He took what has been accomplished! Here are we, sections and representatives of the people who use the English tongue. In this kingdom, away with our kin beyond the sea, in America, in our colonies, well-nigh 120,000,000 of men use our tongue and hold our faith. Over on the Continent, of Europe 200,000,000 of men have the same faith, disguised in varied forms. Where lies the movement and the mind of the world? With these people, made by these people. They everywhere constitute the very heart and the very spirit of man. Take, as a type, out of the great multitude this very city [London], the immensest, most populous, richest, poorest, the most ubiquitous city, in

a sense, in all the experience of man; her energies run to the uttermost parts of the earth; her eyes are everywhere; where wealth is to be found, there some of her myriad hands are groping; where money is wanting, there some one or several of her myriad money-lenders are prepared to offer for sale; wherever there is man there is the feeling of this great city, and she seeks ever to draw toward herself from all parts of the world, to enlarge, to enrich, and to impoverish. What now stands in this great city for all that is ameliorating, progressive, orderly, potent in good? Let any stranger come up her ancient river, and high, overtopping all her towers and palaces, rises the lofty dome of St. Paul's. Is it under the dome where your men coin their money? Is it from that lordly peak they look for markets throughout the world? Nay! There, amid all their warehouses, reigning over all their daily interests, stands a symbol of their faith. Higher up the river lie the ashes of our most illustrious dead, shadowed and consecrated by the name of the Crucified. Why are they there, but to express this: the faith of our people is the most sacred thing our people have? They love to enshrine the names they love in a symbol of their faith. Pass through the streets, and mark, in places where they are needed huge hospitals rise. There, in the crowded ward where lie the suffering and the sick, moving with a soft foot, and speaking with a gentle voice, so excellent a thing in women, are those who are set to heal and to help the suffering. There the knife of the surgeon has ceased from its cruel power of slaying, and turned into a beneficent minister of health and life; there the physician seeks to battle with grim disease and make the sound body for the sound mind to dwell in. Pass on, and you will see in every street a building consecrated to sacred use. There lives a man given up to the service of men, with the message meant for their healing, with a word meant for their saving, to be a man who is a man of God amid men and of men. Here there are books to be read, and social societies to publish and to disperse them; there are societies to shelter the innocent, prosecute the guilty; to reach out to the poor, to ameliorate the lot of the sad; societies designed to heal every ill flesh is heir to, to breathe health into sickness, to create purity in guilt, to surround helpless infancy with the strong hands of gracious protection. And if you ask what is the mainspring of all these, giving them purpose, giving them power, what man dare to say other than this, "They are the creation of the Christ that preached the gospel in Galilee, and the creation of men who preach His gospel in the England of to-day."

FREDERICK W. FARRAR

1831-1903

WORK
IN THE
GROANING CREATION

BIOGRAPHICAL NOTE

FREDERICK WILLIAM FARRAR was born in Bombay, India, in 1831. He was educated at King's College, London, and at Trinity College, Cambridge. He became dean of Canterbury in 1895, and died in 1903. His Life of Christ, the most widely read of his many religious works, has been translated into many languages— even into Japanese. The following illustrates his power of emphasis.

"There, amid those voluptuous splendors, Pilate, already interested, already feeling in this prisoner before him some nobleness which touched his Roman nature, asking Him in pitying wonder, 'Art thou the King of the Jews?'—Thou poor, worn, tear-stained outcast, in this hour of Thy bitter need—O pale, lonely, friendless, wasted man, in Thy poor peasant garments, with Thy tied hands and the foul traces of the insults of Thine enemies on Thy face and on Thy robes—Thou, so unlike the fierce, magnificent Herod, whom this multitude which thirsts for Thy blood acknowledged as their sovereign—art Thou the King of the Jews?'"

And God saw everything that he had made, and behold it was very good.—Gen. i., 31.

For we know that the whole creation groaneth and travaileth in pain together until now.—Rom. viii., 22.

And there shall be no more curse.—Rev. xxii., 3.

IN those three texts you have the past, the present, the future of our earth; what was, what is, what shall be; the perfectness which man has marred, the punishment which he is enduring, the hope to which he looks. What share we may have in the marring or the mending of this our transitory dwelling, that is our main subject to-day.

We see some glimpses at least of the truth that actively by sympathy, by thoughtfulness, by charity, by unselfishness, by loving one another;—that even passively by abstaining from the fashionable and universal vice of biting and devouring one another;—we see that by honesty, by self-reverence, by reverence for others, by obeying the golden rule of "doing unto others as we would they should do unto us," we may do very much to limit the realm of sorrow, and to substitute a golden for an iron scepter in its sway over human hearts. We see, too, that our own inevitable trials and humiliations,—all the neglect, all the insult, all the weariness, all the disappointment, all the ingratitude, which may befall us,—can be better borne if we be cheerful and active in doing good. Labor for God is the best cure for sorrow, and the best occupation of life.

Can we to-day push the inquiry yet further, and learn whether it is in our power in any way to mend the flaw which runs for us through the material world; or in any way to diminish for ourselves and for mankind the pressure of that vast weight of laws which exercises over us, undoubtedly, a sway of awful potency? The whole creation groaneth and travaileth in pain together until now; can we—not by any strength of ours, but because God permits and desires it, can we do anything to hasten that blest hour for which we wait—the hour of the new creation; of the adoption, to wit, the redemption of our body; of the restitution of all things; of the *palingenesia* of the world?

I think we can. I know that the supposed helplessness of man is a favorite topic of modern materialism, which makes of man the irresponsible tool of forces which he can not resist, the sport and prey of dumb powers which are alike inexorable and passionless. This philosophy—if we may call it a philosophy—laughs to scorn the notion of a miracle, and makes virtue and vice not the conscious choice of free beings, but the inevitable result of material causes and hereditary impulses, of which in all but semblance, we are the mere automata and slaves. My brethren, into all these speculations of a baseless atheism, I need not enter. To us, nature means nothing but the sum total of phenomena which God has created; and since in the idea of nature is included the idea of God, a miracle becomes as natural and as easily conceivable as the most ordinary occurrence. And we know that we are free, that God does not mock us, that we can abhor that which is evil, and cleave to that which is good. The laws of nature are nothing, then, for us but observed sequences, and we do not admit that there is anything fearful in their uniformity. It is true that nature drives her plowshare straight onwards, and heeds not what may be lying in the furrow; it is true that therefore she shows an apparent indifference to human agony; it is true that if the fairest and sweetest child which earth ever saw be left at play in the face of the advancing tide, the tide will still advance and drown the little life; it is true that the fire in its ruthless vividness will roll over the loveliest maiden whose rich dress should catch its flame. It is a law that resistance must be equal to force, and that if there be a certain amount of pressure of vibration, whatever comes of it, a structure will give way, even though, alas, it hurl nearly a hundred human beings, with one flash of horror, into the gulf of death. But is this any reason for a fierce arraignment of nature, as tho she were execrably ruthless, and execrably indifferent? Not so, my brethren. Death whenever it comes is but death. None of us has any promise of this or that amount of life. It needs no railway accident, no sinking ship, or breaking ice, or burning town, or flame from heaven, or arrow in the darkness, or smiting of the sun by day, or the moon by night, to cut short our days. An invisible sporule in the air may do it, or a lesion no bigger than a pin's point.

"He ate, drank, laughed, loved, lived, and liked life
    well;
Then came—who knows?—some gust of jungle wind,
A stumble on the path; a taint i' the tank;
A snake's nip; half a span of angry steel;
A chill; a fishbone; or a falling tile,—
And life is over, and the man is dead."

But is this any reason why we should look on ourselves as victims of dead irresponsible forces? Why so? Death is but death, and if we live faithfully, death is our richest birthright. "Were you ready to die that you jumped into the stormy sea to save that child's life?" said a gentleman to an English sailor. "Should I have been better prepared, sir," the sailor answered, "if I had shirked my duty?" A sudden death is often, and in many respects, the most merciful form of death; and the apparently terrible death of a few may save the lives of many hundreds. The uniformity of nature may sometimes wear the aspect of passionless cruelty; but as we learn more and more to observe and to obey her laws, we find more and more that they work for countless ends of beneficence and beauty, that out of seeming evil she works real good, out of transient evil enduring good. The fires which rend the earthquake and burst from the volcano, are the quickening forces of the world; her storms lash the lazy atmosphere which otherwise would stagnate into pestilence, and it is for man's blessing, not for his destruction, that her waters roll and her great winds blow.

But are we, after all, so very helpless before the aggregate of these mighty forces, as materialism loves to represent? Not so! "Thou madest him to have dominion over the works of thy hands," said the Psalmist, "Thou hast put all things under his feet." "Replenish the earth, and subdue, and have dominion," said the first utterance of God to man. And what is this but an equivalent of the latest utterances of science, that "the order of nature is ascertainable by our faculties to an extent which is practically unlimited, and that our volition counts for something in the course of events"? Man has done much to make the world in all senses a worse place for himself, but he has also, thank God, done much to make it better, and he may, to an almost unspeakable extent, remedy for himself and for his race the throes and agonies of the groaning universe. God meant His earth to be a more blest place for us than it is, and in every instance men have made it more blest when they have read the open secrets, by virtue of which, for our excitement, if not for our reward, "herbs have their healing, stones their preciousness, and stars their times." Ancient nations have shuddered at the awfulness of the sea. It drowns ship and sailor; but "trim your sail, and the same wave which drowns the bark is cleft by it, and bears it along like its own foam, a plume and a power." The lightning shatters tower and temple; but once learn that it is nothing but the luminous all-pervading fluid which you may evolve by rubbing a piece of amber, and brush out of a child's fair hair, and then with no more potent instrument than a boy's kite you may dash harmless to the earth the all-shattering brand which was the terror of antiquity; nay, you may seize it by its wing of fire, and bid it carry your messages around the girdled globe. Zymotic diseases smite down the aged and young, but, when you have learnt that they are caused by myriads of invisible germs which float in the water or the air, you have but to observe the commonest rules of sanitary science, to filter and boil the dangerous water, to insure free currents of air, to breathe as nature meant you to breathe, through the nostrils, and not through the throat, and you rob them of half their deadliness. Why has smallpox been stayed in its loathly ravages, and deprived of its hideous power? Why does the Black Death rage no longer, as it raged among the monks of this Abbey four centuries ago? Why do we not have pestilence, like that great plague of London, which destroyed 7,165 persons in a single week? Why has jail fever disappeared? Why are the cities of Europe horrified no longer by the hideousness of medieval leprosy? Because men live amid cleaner and purer surroundings. Because rushes are no longer strewn over floors which had been suffered to be saturated with the organic refuse of years. Because the simplest laws of nature are better understood. Because, in these respects, men have remedied by God's aid, some of those miseries for which the Savior sighed.

And this amelioration of man's miseries is a great, and noble, and Christlike work. Would that there were no other side to the picture! Man, alas! also has done, and may do, infinite mischief to the world he lives in. He may cut down the forests on the hills, and so diminish the necessary rain. He may pluck up the grasses on the shore, and so lay waste whole acres to the devastating sands. He may poison the sweet, pure rivers of his native soil, till their crystal freshness is corrupted into deathful and putrescent slime. He may herd together, as we suffer our poor to do, in filthy tenements which shall breed every species of disease and vice. He may indulge or acquiesce in senseless fashions and pernicious vanities which shall mean not only wasteful ugliness and grotesque extravagance, but leave shattered health and ruined lives, to the mothers of his race. He may in greed of competition extirpate the game of the forest, the fishes of the sea. He may destroy the exquisite balance of nature, by shooting down or entrapping the sweet birds of the air, till his vines and his harvests are devastated by the insects on which they feed. He may suffer the chimneys of his manufactories to poison the atmosphere with black smoke and sulphurous acid, till his proudest cities are stifled at noonday, as we all have seen in London for these many weeks, with the unclean mirk of midnight fogs. He may suffer noxious gases to be vomited upon the breeze, till the most glorious buildings in his cities corrode and crumble—as the stones of this Abbey are doing—under their influence,—till the green woods blacken into leafless wastes, and life is lived at miserable levels of vitality under the filthy reek. There is hardly any limit to the evil, no less than to the good, which man may do to this his earthly environment. Nor is it less deplorable that he may go out of his way to do endless mischief to himself by his misuse or abuse of the properties of things. From the dried capsules of the white poppy he extracts opium, and he grows acres of poppies that with thousands of chests of that opium he may degrade into decrepitude and wretchedness the most populous nations upon earth. Nature gives him the purple grape and the golden grain, and he mashes them and lets them rot and seethe, and assists, and superintends, and retards their decomposition, till he has educed from them a fermented intoxicating liquor; and not content with this luxury, he pours it into Circean cups of degrading excess; not content with even fermentation, he further, by distillation, extracts a transparent, mobile, colorless fluid, which is the distinctive element in ardent spirits, and these, whatever may be their legitimate use in manufacture or in medicine, he has so horribly abused that they have become to mankind, the *spiritus ardentes* indeed, but not of heaven—fiery spirits of the abyss, which have decimated nations, ruined continents, shortened millions of lives, and turned for millions of God's children, and millions of Christ's little ones, life into an anguish, and earth into a hell. Do not say we can do nothing to soften for man the deadly agencies which are working in the world,—for all this mischief, and incalculably more than this, is man's own doing.

But let me ask you to glance for a moment at one of the beneficent secrets which nature has yielded up to man. Have you ever realized, with heartfelt gratitude to God, the priceless boon which He has granted to this generation in the diminution of pain? One of our best surgeons has just told us the strange yet simple story of this discovery, from the first dim intimation of the possibility in 1789, till in 1846 it might almost be said that in Europe we could name the month, before which all operative surgery was agonizing, and after which it was painless. But what an immense, what an enormous boon is this application of anodynes! "Past all counting is the sum of happiness enjoyed by the millions who have, in the last thirty-three years, escaped the pain that was inevitable in surgical operations; pain made more terrible by apprehension; more keen by close attention; sometimes awful in a swift agony; sometimes prolonged beyond even the most patient endurance, and then renewed in memory, and terrible in dreams. This will never be felt again." And besides this abolition of pain, it would take long to tell how chloroform and ether "have enlarged the field of useful surgery, making many things easy which were difficult, many safe which were perilous, many practical which were nearly impossible." But another lesson this eminent man of science draws, which bears directly on our subject, is that while we are profanely decrying nature, discoveries the most blest, boons the most priceless, may lie close to us and yet God leave us to discover them; and that we may endure many needless miseries, falsely accusing nature and even God, only because we have neither hope enough to excite intense desire, nor desire enough to encourage hope. We wonder that for forty years the discovery of anesthetics was not pursued, tho, after the pregnant hint of Sir H. Davy, it lay but half hidden under so thin a veil. Our successors will wonder at us, as we at those before us, that we were as blind to who can tell how many great truths, which, they will say, were all around us, within reach of any clear and earnest mind. They will wonder at the quietude with which we stupidly acquiesce in, or immorally defend, the causes which perpetuate and intensify our habitual miseries. Our fathers needlessly put up with these miseries "as we now put up with typhoid fever and sea-sickness; with local floods and droughts; with waste of health and wealth in pollutions of rivers; with hideous noises, and foul smells"; with the curse of alcoholic poisoning, and many other miseries. Our successors, when they have remedied or prevented these, will look back on them with horror, and on us with wonder and contempt, for what they will call our idleness or blindness, or indifference to suffering. Alas! in the physical as in the moral world, we murmur at the evils which surround us, and we do not remove them. We multiply those evils, and make life wretched, and then curse nature because it is wretched, and neglect or fling away the precious gifts and easy remedies which would make it blest. And is it not so in the spiritual world? Nine-tenths of our miseries are due to our sins. Yet the remedy of our sins is close at hand. We have a Savior; we have been commemorating His birth, but we live and act as tho He were dead; in our own lives and those of others we suffer those miseries to run riot which He came to cure; we talk and live as tho those remedies were undiscoverable, while from day to day His Word is very nigh us, even in our mouths and in our hearts!

For one sermon you hear about work for the secular amelioration of the suffering world for which Christ sighed, you may (I suppose) hear fifty on passing ecclesiastical controversies and five thousand about individual efforts for personal salvation. And yet one pure, self-sacrificing deed, one word of generosity to an opponent, one kindly act to aid another, may have been better for you in God's sight and far harder for you to do, than to attend in the year the 730 daily services which this Abbey provides. Yes, I am glad that I have preached to you to-day the duty of what some would call secular work—as tho secular work were not often the most profoundly religious work!—for the amelioration of the world. And I say, it were better for you to have made but two blades of grass grow where one grew before, than if, with the hollow, hateful, slanderous heart of some false prophets of modern religionism, you were every morning to do whatever modern thing may be analogous to binding your fringes with blue, and broadening your phylacteries,—to making the hilltops blaze with your sacrificial fires, building here seven altars, and offering a bullock and a ram on every altar. And so, my brethren, let us leave this Abbey to-day with conceptions of duty larger and more hopeful; with more yearning both after the sympathy of Christ and after His activity; with more faith to see that the world would not be so utter a ruin but for our perversity; with more hope to be convinced that even we can help to redeem its disorders, and restore its pristine perfectness. Let us obey the command, "Ephphatha, Be opened!" Let us lift up our eyes to see that, tho the air around us is colorless, the far-off heaven is blue. Let us see and be thankful for the beauty of the world, the sweet air, the sunshine, the sea, the splendid ornaments of heaven, the ever-recurring circles of the divine beneficence. Let us learn the secrets of the mighty laws which only crush us when we disobey them, and which teach us, with divine inflexibility, that as we sow we reap. Let us not hinder the students of science in their patient toil and marvelous discovery by the crude infallibilities of our ignorant dogmatism. Let us believe—for we were saved in hope—that "Utopia itself is but another word for time"; and that, if our own work seems but infinitesimal, yet "there are mites in science, as well as in charity, and the ultimate results of each are alike important and beneficial." And so the more we share in the sigh and in the toil of the Savior, the more shall we share in His redeeming gladness.

FRANCOIS FENELON

1651-1715

THE SAINTS CONVERSE WITH GOD

BIOGRAPHICAL NOTE

FRANÇOIS DE SALIGNAC DE LA MOTHE-FÉNELON, Archbishop of Cambray, and private tutor to the heir-apparent of France, was born of a noble family in Périgord, 1651. In 1675 he received holy orders, and soon afterward made the acquaintance of Bossuet, whom he henceforth looked up to as his master. It was the publication of his "De l'Éducation des Filles" that brought him his first fame, and had some influence in securing his appointment in 1689 to be preceptor of the Duke of Burgundy. In performing this office he thought it necessary to compose his own text-books, such as would teach the vanity of worldly greatness and the loftiness of virtue. He was promoted to the archbishopric of Cambray in 1695, and subsequently became entangled in the religious aberrations of Madame Guyon. Fénelon came into controversy with Bossuet, whose severity against his friend was rebuked by the Pope, who, nevertheless, condemned some of the Archbishop of Cambray's views. Fénelon submitted, and withdrew to his diocesan see, where he died in 1715. His deep spirituality and eloquence are exemplified in the following sermon.

Pray without ceasing.—I Thess. v., 17

OF all the duties enjoined by Christianity none is more essential, and yet more neglected, than prayer. Most people consider this exercise a wearisome ceremony, which they are justified in abridging as much as possible. Even those whose profession or fears lead them to pray, do it with such languor and wanderings of mind that their prayers, far from drawing down blessings, only increase their condemnation. I wish to demonstrate, in this discourse, first, the general necessity of prayer; secondly, its peculiar duty; thirdly, the manner in which we ought to pray.

First. God alone can instruct us in our duty. The teachings of men, however wise and well disposed they may be, are still ineffectual, if God do not shed on the soul that light which opens the mind to truth. The imperfections of our fellow creatures cast a shade over the truths that we learn from them. Such is our weakness that we do not receive, with sufficient docility, the instructions of those who are as imperfect as ourselves. A thousand suspicions, jealousies, fears, and prejudices prevent us from profiting, as we might, by what we hear from men; and tho they announce the most serious truths, yet what they do weakens the effect of what they say. In a word, it is God alone who can perfectly teach us.

St. Bernard said, in writing to a pious friend—If you are seeking less to satisfy a vain curiosity than to get true wisdom, you will sooner find it in deserts than in books. The silence of the rocks and the pathless forests will teach you better than the eloquence of the most gifted men. "All," says St. Augustine, "that we possess of truth and wisdom is a borrowed good flowing from that fountain for which we ought to thirst in the fearful desert of this world, that, being refreshed and invigorated by these dews from heaven, we may not faint upon the road that conducts us to a better country. Every attempt to satisfy the cravings of our hearts at other sources only increases the void. You will be always poor if you do not possess the only true riches." All light that does not proceed from God is false; it only dazzles us; it sheds no illumination upon the difficult paths in which we must walk, along the precipices that are about us.

Our experience and our reflections can not, on all occasions, give us just and certain rules of conduct. The advice of our wisest and most sincere friends is not always sufficient; many things escape their observation, and many that do not are too painful to be spoken. They suppress much from delicacy, or sometimes from a fear of transgressing the bounds that our friendship and confidence in them will allow. The animadversions of our enemies, however severe or vigilant they may be, fail to enlighten us with regard to ourselves. Their malignity furnishes our self-love with a pretext for the indulgence of the greatest faults. The blindness of our self-love is so great that we find reasons for being satisfied with ourselves, while all the world condemn us. What must we learn from all this darkness? That it is God alone who can dissipate it; that it is He alone whom we can never doubt; that He alone is true, and knoweth all things; that if we go to Him in sincerity, He will teach us what men dare not tell us, what books can not—all that is essential for us to know.

Be assured that the greatest obstacle to true wisdom is the self-confidence inspired by that which is false. The first step toward this precious knowledge is earnestly to desire it, to feel the want of it, and to be convinced that they who seek it must address themselves to the Father of lights, who freely gives to him who asks in faith. But if it be true that God alone can enlighten us, it is not the less true that He will do this simply in answer to our prayers. Are we not happy, indeed, in being able to obtain so great a blessing by only asking for it? No part of the effort that we make to acquire the transient enjoyments of this life is necessary to obtain these heavenly blessings. What will we not do, what are we not willing to suffer, to possess dangerous and contemptible things, and often without any success? It is not thus with heavenly things. God is always ready to grant them to those who make the request in sincerity and truth. The Christian life is a long and continual tendency of our hearts toward that eternal goodness which we desire on earth. All our happiness consists in thirsting for it. Now this thirst is prayer. Ever desire to approach your Creator and you will never cease to pray.

Do not think that it is necessary to pronounce many words. To pray is to say, Let Thy will be done. It is to form a good purpose; to raise your heart to God; to lament your weakness; to sigh at the recollection of your frequent disobedience. This prayer demands neither method, nor science, nor reasoning; it is not essential to quit one's employment; it is a simple movement of the heart toward its Creator, and a desire that whatever you are doing you may do it to His glory. The best of all prayers is to act with a pure intention, and with a continual reference to the will of God. It depends much upon ourselves whether our prayers be efficacious. It is not by a miracle, but by a movement of the heart that we are benefited; by a submissive spirit. Let us believe, let us trust, let us hope, and God never will reject our prayer. Yet how many Christians do we see strangers to the privilege, aliens from God, who seldom think of Him, who never open their hearts to Him; who seek elsewhere the counsels of a false wisdom, and vain and dangerous consolations, who can not resolve to seek, in humble, fervent prayer to God, a remedy for their griefs and a true knowledge of their defects, the necessary power to conquer their vicious and perverse inclinations, and the consolations and assistance they require, that they may not be discouraged in a virtuous life.

But some will say, "I have no interest in prayer; it wearies me; my imagination is excited by sensible and more agreeable objects, and wanders in spite of me."

If neither your reverence for the great truths of religion, nor the majesty of the ever-present Deity, nor the interest of your eternal salvation, have power to arrest your mind and engage it in prayer, at least mourn with me for your infidelity; be ashamed of your weakness, and wish that your thoughts were more under your control; and desire to become less frivolous and inconstant. Make an effort to subject your mind to this discipline. You will gradually acquire habit and facility. What is now tedious will become delightful; and you will then feel, with a peace that the world can not give nor take away, that God is good. Make a courageous effort to overcome yourself. There can be no occasion that more demands it.

Secondly. The peculiar obligation of prayer. Were I to give all the proofs that the subject affords, I should describe every condition of life, that I might point out its dangers, and the necessity of recourse to God in prayer. But I will simply state that under all circumstances we have need of prayer. There is no situation in which it is possible to be placed where we have not many virtues to acquire and many faults to correct. We find in our temperament, or in our habits, or in the peculiar character of our minds, qualities that do not suit our occupations, and that oppose our duties. One person is connected by marriage to another whose temper is so unequal that life becomes a perpetual warfare. Some, who are exposed to the contagious atmosphere of the world, find themselves so susceptible to the vanity which they inhale that all their pure desires vanish. Others have solemnly promised to renounce their resentments, to conquer their aversions, to suffer with patience certain crosses, and to repress their eagerness for wealth; but nature prevails, and they are vindictive, violent, impatient, and avaricious.

Whence comes it that these resolutions are so frail? That all these people wish to improve, desire to perform their duty toward God and man better, and yet fail? It is because our own strength and wisdom, alone, are not enough. We undertake to do everything without God; therefore we do not succeed. It is at the foot of the altar that we must seek for counsel which will aid us. It is with God that we must lay our plans of virtue and usefulness; it is He alone that can render them successful. Without Him, all our designs, however good they may appear, are only temerity and delusion. Let us then pray that we may learn what we are and what we ought to be. By this means we shall not only learn the number and the evil effects of our peculiar faults, but we shall also learn to what virtues we are called, and the way to practise them. The rays of that pure and heavenly light that visit the humble soul will beam on us and we shall feel and understand that everything is possible to those who put their whole trust in God. Thus, not only to those who live in retirement, but to those who are exposed to the agitations of the world and the excitements of business, it is peculiarly necessary, by contemplation and fervent prayer, to restore their souls to that serenity which the dissipations of life and commerce with men have disturbed. To those who are engaged in business, contemplation and prayer are much more difficult than to those who live in retirement; but it is far more necessary for them to have frequent recourse to God in fervent prayer. In the most holy occupation a certain degree of precaution is necessary.

Do not devote all your time to action, but reserve a certain portion of it for meditation upon eternity. We see Jesus Christ inviting His disciples to go apart, in a desert place, and rest awhile, after their return from the cities, where they had been to announce His religion. How much more necessary is it for us to approach the source of all virtue, that we may revive our declining faith and charity, when we return from the busy scenes of life, where men speak and act as if they had never known that there is a God! We should look upon prayer as the remedy for our weakness, the rectifier of our own faults. He who was without sin prayed constantly; how much more ought we, who are sinners, to be faithful in prayer!

Even the exercise of charity is often a snare to us. It calls us to certain occupations that dissipate the mind, and that may degenerate into mere amusement. It is for this reason that St. Chrysostom says that nothing is so important as to keep an exact proportion between the interior source of virtue and the external practise of it; else, like the foolish virgins, we shall find that the oil in our lamp is exhausted when the bridegroom comes.

The necessity we feel that God should bless our labors is another powerful motive to prayer. It often happens that all human help is vain. It is God alone that can aid us, and it does not require much faith to believe that it is less our exertions, our foresight, and our industry than the blessing of the Almighty that can give success to our wishes.

Thirdly. Of the manner in which we ought to pray. 1. We must pray with attention. God listens to the voice of the heart, not to that of the lips. Our whole heart must be engaged in prayer. It must fasten upon what it prays for; and every human object must disappear from our minds. To whom should we speak with attention if not to God? Can He demand less of us than that we should think of what we say to Him? Dare we hope that He will listen to us, and think of us, when we forget ourselves in the midst of our prayers? This attention to prayer, which it is so just to exact from Christians, may be practised with less difficulty than we imagine. It is true that the most faithful souls suffer from occasional involuntary distractions. They can not always control their imaginations, and, in the silence of their spirits, enter into the presence of God. But these unbidden wanderings of the mind ought not to trouble us; and they may conduce to our perfection even more than the most sublime and affecting prayers if we earnestly strive to overcome them, and submit with humility to this experience of our infirmity. But to dwell willingly on frivolous and worldly things during prayer, to make no effort to check the vain thoughts that intrude upon this sacred employment and come between us and the Father of our spirits—is not this choosing to live the sport of our senses, and separated from God?

2. We must also ask with faith; a faith so firm that it never falters. He who prays without confidence can not hope that his prayer will be granted. Will not God love the heart that trusts in Him? Will He reject those who bring all their treasures to Him, and repose everything upon His goodness? When we pray to God, says St. Cyprian, with entire assurance, it is Himself who has given us the spirit of our prayer. Then it is the Father listening to the words of His child; it is He who dwells in our hearts, teaching us to pray. But must we confess that this filial confidence is wanting in all our prayers? Is not prayer our resource only when all others have failed us? If we look into hearts, shall we not find that we ask of God as if we had never before received benefits from Him? Shall we not discover there a secret infidelity that renders us unworthy of His goodness?

Let us tremble, lest, when Jesus Christ shall judge us, He pronounce the same reproach that He did to Peter, "O thou of little faith, wherefore didst thou doubt?"

3. We must join humility with trust. Great God, said Daniel, when we prostrate ourselves at Thy feet, we do not place our hopes for the success of our prayers upon our righteousness, but upon Thy mercy. Without this disposition in our hearts, all others, however pious they may be, can not please God. St. Augustine observes that the failure of Peter should not be attributed to insincerity in his zeal for Jesus Christ. He loved his Master in good faith; in good faith he would rather have died than have forsaken Him; but his fault lay in trusting to his own strength, to do what his own heart dictated.

It is not enough to possess a right spirit, an exact knowledge of duty, a sincere desire to perform it. We must continually renew this desire, and enkindle this flame within us, at the fountain of pure and eternal light.

It is the humble and contrite heart that God will not despise. Remark the difference which the evangelist has pointed out between the prayer of the proud and presumptuous Pharisee and the humble and penitent publican. The one relates his virtues, the other deplores his sins. The good works of the one shall be set aside, while the penitence of the other shall be accepted. It will be thus with many Christians. Sinners, vile in their own eyes, will be objects of the mercy of God; while some, who have made professions of piety, will be condemned on account of the pride and arrogance that have contaminated their good works. It will be so because these have said in their hearts, "Lord, I thank thee that I am not as other men are." They imagine themselves privileged; they pretend that they alone have penetrated the mysteries of the kingdom of God; they have a language and science of their own; they believe that their zeal can accomplish everything. Their regular lives favor their vanity; but in truth they are incapable of self-sacrifice, and they go to their devotions with their hearts full of pride and presumption. Unhappy are those who pray in this manner! Unhappy are those whose prayers do not render them more humble, more submissive, more watchful over their faults, and more willing to live in obscurity!

4. We must pray with love. It is love says St. Augustine, that asks, that seeks, that knocks, that finds, and that is faithful to what it finds. We cease to pray to God as soon as we cease to love Him, as soon as we cease to thirst for His perfections. The coldness of our love is the silence of our hearts toward God. Without this we may pronounce prayers, but we do not pray; for what shall lead us to meditate upon the laws of God if it be not the love of Him who has made these laws? Let our hearts be full of love, then, and they will pray. Happy are they who think seriously of the truths of religion; but far more happy are they who feel and love them! We must ardently desire that God will grant us spiritual blessings; and the ardor of our wishes must render us fit to receive the blessings. For if we pray only from custom, from fear, in the time of tribulation—if we honor God only with our lips, while our hearts are far from Him—if we do not feel a strong desire for the success of our prayers—if we feel a chilling indifference in approaching Him who is a consuming fire—if we have no zeal for His glory—if we do not feel hatred for sin, and a thirst for perfection, we can not hope for a blessing upon such heartless prayers.

5. We must pray with perseverance. The perfect heart is never weary of seeking God. Ought we to complain if God sometimes leaves us to obscurity, and doubt, and temptation? Trials purify humble souls, and they serve to expiate the faults of the unfaithful. They confound those who, even in their prayers, have flattered their cowardice and pride. If an innocent soul, devoted to God, suffer from any secret disturbance, it should be humble, adore the designs of God, and redouble its prayers and its fervor. How often do we hear those who every day have to reproach themselves with unfaithfulness toward God complain that He refuses to answer their prayers! Ought they not to acknowledge that it is their sins which have formed a thick cloud between Heaven and them, and that God has justly hidden Himself from them? How often has He recalled us from our wanderings! How often, ungrateful as we are, have we been deaf to His voice and insensible to His goodness! He would make us feel that we are blind and miserable when we forsake Him. He would teach us, by privation, the value of the blessings that we have slighted. And shall we not bear our punishment with patience? Who can boast of having done all that he ought to have done; of having repaired all his past errors; of having purified his heart, so that he may claim as a right that God should listen to his prayer? Most truly, all our pride, great as it is, would not be sufficient to inspire such presumption! If then, the Almighty do not grant our petitions, let us adore His justice, let us be silent, let us humble ourselves, and let us pray without ceasing. This humble perseverance will obtain from Him what we should never obtain by our own merit. It will make us pass happily from darkness to light; for know, says St. Augustine that God is near to us even when He appears far from us.

6. We should pray with a pure intention. We should not mingle in our prayers what is false with what is real; what is perishable

with what is eternal; low and temporal interests with that which concerns our salvation.
Do not seek to render God the protector of
your self-love and ambition, but the promoter
of your good desires. You ask for the gratification of your passions, or to be delivered
from the cross, of which He knows you have
need. Carry not to the foot of the altar irregular desires and indiscreet prayers. Sigh
not for vain and fleeting pleasures. Open
your heart to your Father in heaven, that
His Spirit may enable you to ask for the true
riches. How can He grant you, says St.
Augustine, what you do not yourself desire to
receive? You pray every day that His will
may be done, and that His kingdom may come.

How can you utter this prayer with sincerity
when you prefer your own will to His, and
make His law yield to the vain pretexts with
which your self-love seeks to elude it? Can
you make this prayer—you who disturb His
reign in your heart by so many impure and
vain desires? You, in fine, who fear the coming of His reign, and do not desire that God
should grant what you seem to pray for? No!
If He, at this moment, were to offer to give
you a new heart, and render you humble,
and willing to bear the cross, your pride would
revolt, and you would not accept the offer; or
you would make a reservation in favor of
your ruling passion, and try to accommodate
your piety to your humor and fancies!

WILLIAM GOODELL FROST

1854-1938

LEADERSHIP

BIOGRAPHICAL NOTE

PRESIDENT of Berea College 1893-1920; born LeRoy, N. Y., July 2, 1854; entered Beloit College, 1872; graduated from Oberlin, 1876; studied at Wooster and Harvard universities, also at Göttingen University, Germany; graduated in theology Oberlin, 1879; received the degree of Ph.D. from Wooster, 1891; D.D. from Oberlin, 1893, and Harvard, 1907; author of "Inductive Studies in Oratory," "Greek Primer," etc.

"And there arose not a prophet since in Israel, like unto Moses, whom the Lord knew face to face."— Deut. 34 : 10.

MOSES was the ideal national hero of the Hebrew race. His story was learned by heart by every Hebrew child. His precepts and examples were the law in every Israelitish home. So far as the Jews surpassed the Philistines, and the Egyptians, and the nations round about, in character and spiritual ideals, it was largely through the influence of this ideal character of Moses.

And in the larger Israel of which we are a part, this same man Moses is an inspirer still, not as a national hero merely, but as one of the great spiritual leaders of the human race. Even those who may doubt the historical accuracy of some portions of the ancient record, can not fail to find in the ideal Moses an object-lesson of abiding power.

Moses was a lawgiver like Lycurgus; a scientist, learned in all the learning of the Egyptians, like Pythagoras; a statesman like Solon; a warrior like Pericles. But all these distinctions are passed over by the inspired historian, who names the one great character of the man in our text: "There arose not a *prophet* since in Israel, like unto Moses, whom the Lord knew face to face."

The word prophet means a spokesman— one who speaks not for himself but for God. The prophet is not merely one who foretells future events—he is one who tells us the great principles of the universe, the laws of well-being and destruction, of right and wrong; one who gives us the mind of God.

There should be a prophetic element in every Christian man or woman. In enumerating spiritual gifts, Paul refers to the gift of prophesy as the most choice. The gift of healing is wonderful. The gift of tongues is wonderful. "I would," says the apostle, "that ye all spake with tongues, but rather that ye should prophesy." Every spirit-born soul should have some insight into the things of God which would enable him to speak with authority. And it is this speaking for God that is needed in every age, every nation, every community. We are all called to be prophets, and if we study Moses we shall be studying one who stands near the head of our profession, one who exemplifies in large outlines and on a sublime scale that prophetic mission which belongs to all who are truly born of God. What Moses was to his age and people, that in our measure you and I should be in our own homes, and among our own neighbors.

We can summarize the career of this great prophet in a few words: he was born in adversity, educated in solitude, and called into public service against his will. He worked against all human probabilities; he was rejected by those he benefited; and he brought others to a land of plenty which he himself was forbidden to enter. All these are types of things in the experience of every true Christian.

He was born in adversity. How many millions of children have had their little hearts thrilled by the story of the childhood of Moses! There was the mother, the slave-mother, in her humble home. She was wondering whether her new-born babe should be a girl to share her slavery, or a boy to be put to death by the cruelty of Pharaoh. It was a boy, and she hid him through three anxious months. Then with loving hands she made the little ark, the floating cradle, and laid it in the reeds of the river, and set her daughter to watch it. And now when she has done her utmost and her best, divine Providence comes in. The daughter of Pharaoh comes down to the river. She sees the ark and sends her maid to fetch it. The princess and her maids are gathered around the strange cradle and the weeping child when his sister timidly approaches. Then said his sister unto Pharaoh's daughter, "Shall I go and call to thee a nurse of the Hebrew women, that she may nurse the child for thee?" And Pharaoh's daughter said to her, "Go." And the maid went and called the child's mother!

However wise and great Moses may become, he can never forget the story of his childhood. And the world can never forget it. The poorest and the rudest of all the people who hear about Moses will not be altogether awed by his greatness, or chilled by the distance between him and themselves. Yes, this greatest of prophets was the child of a slave-mother—he was once a foundling on the banks of the Nile.

And he was educated in solitude. Solitude is a university where all of us may take courses if we will. Solitude means reflection. It means studying over the experiences of life. It means quiet listening to the voices of one's own spirit, and to the voice of God. Moses had his preparatory course at the court of Pharaoh. He learned all of man's wisdom as it was at that time developed by the foremost nation of the world. But after that preparatory course, he was banished to the wilderness. For forty years he was a shepherd in the mountains. He learned lessons from the wild-flowers and the brooks. He watched the shy gazelles and the soaring eagles. He traced out the constellations of the stars. He thought over all he had learned in Egypt, and new ideas which were not of Egypt were born in his soul. When a man is listening, and when human teachers are silent, then God teaches. And so it came to pass that Moses, all unconsciously, was educated for his high career, and led at last to the burning bush where God gave him his great commission.

He was called against his will. Moses had no desire to be a ruler. Place and power had no attractions for him. He had seen the vanity of all that years before when he was living at the court, and called the son of Pharaoh's daughter.

There are many high places in this world which have to be filled. And there is always a crowd of applicants and aspirants and candidates, men who have little idea of the work and service for which the public offices exist, but whose heads are turned by the glamour and distinction of publicity.

A public office is a public service, and as a rule the higher the office the more severe the service. One who truly realizes the severity of public service, and has a high ideal of that service, can never be an eager candidate.

Moses was fully aware of his own deficiencies, and had very high notions of the kind of man who ought to be God's representative in bringing the children of Israel out of Egypt. And the Lord said, "Come now, and I will send thee unto Pharaoh, that thou mayest bring forth my people the children of Israel out of Egypt." And Moses said unto God, "Who am I, that I should go unto Pharaoh, and that I should bring forth the children of Israel out of Egypt?" And God said, "Certainly I will be with thee." And Moses answered and said, "But, behold, they will not believe me; for they will say, 'The Lord hath not appeared unto thee.'" Then the Lord gave him the power of working miracles with his rod and with his hand. But Moses said unto the Lord, "O my Lord, I am not eloquent, but am of a slow tongue." And the Lord said, "I will be with thy mouth; and teach thee what thou shalt say." Then this modesty of Moses became a fault. He could mention no other objections, but he said, "O my Lord, send I pray thee by the hand of him whom thou wilt send." That meant, send some one else, not me. And the anger of the Lord was kindled against Moses. And he said, "I will send Aaron with thee." So Moses was persuaded with reluctance to enter upon his great mission. He went from a sense of duty. He acted to please God, and to save his nation. And so he moved forward with that irresistible power which belongs to one who is not fighting for himself but for others.

Moses worked against human probabilities. He undertook something which was not likely to succeed. The chances were against him.

Humanly speaking, there was no prospect that Pharaoh would let the people go, or that the people would prove worthy of the efforts put forth in their behalf.

This is the very essence of heroism. The hero risks defeat. He sees something which ought to be done. It never has been done. A thousand selfish obstacles stand in the way of its being done. A thousand wise men say it never can be done. But the hero sees it ought to be done. He fixes his attention upon that one point—it ought to be done, it ought to be done. Gradually there rises within him the faith that what ought to be done can be done. He does not know that it can be done, but he believes that it can be done. Really his faith is in a God who stands for all that ought to be done, and who has the power to do things which are from a human standpoint impossible. The hero changes the old motto as Lincoln did, and says, Right makes might.

So Moses became a hero before he ever left his mountain home. He became ready at God's command to attempt the impossible. And so he started out with his brother who was a weakling, and his simple shepherd's rod, to cope with the wisdom and the power of Egypt, and the folly and weakness of his own people.

We too often think of a great leader as he appears on the day of triumph, and forget the toils which brought that triumph to pass. Let us think of Moses waiting through anxious hours and days in the court of Pharaoh's palace. Let us remember how he had to plan the march, the camp, the order, the security, the sustenance of the great moving nation. The early dawn brought suitors to his tent. There were quarrels to settle, disputes to arbitrate, mistakes to be corrected. Each hour of the day brought its new and unexpected perplexities. Moses must know how the advance-guard is moving, and he must know how the rear-guard is following. He must see to it that none stray off and are lost in the desert. And when night falls and other men have sunk into repose, the wearied leader must make the last rounds of the encampment, he must see that the fires are covered, and the guards posted, and the flocks and herds secure. And then he must snatch the uninterrupted hours of night to plan for the morrow. A million thoughtless, thankless people are happy and secure because of the night watches of that faithful leader.

He was rejected by those he sought to benefit. It began in Egypt. The first result of his appeal to Pharaoh was to make the bondage of the Hebrews more bitter, and like thoughtless children they turned against their friend. And they said unto Moses, "You have brought evil upon us, and put a sword into the hand of our enemies to slay us."

And again at the Red Sea, when the children of Israel lifted up their eyes, and "behold the Egyptians marched after them," they were sore afraid, and they said unto Moses, "Because there were no graves in Egypt, hast thou taken us away to die in the wilderness? For it had been better for us to serve the Egyptians, than that we should die here." But the patient leader said, "Fear ye not, stand still, and see the salvation of the Lord."

And again a little further on the people forgot this great deliverance, and complained for lack of food, saying, "Would to God we had died by the hand of the Lord in the land of Egypt, when we sat by the flesh-pots, and when we did eat bread to the full; for ye have brought us forth into this wilderness, to kill this whole assembly with hunger." But the prophet answered, "The Lord heareth your murmurings; for what are we, that ye murmur against us?" And the quails and the manna were sent them for food.

And again at Rephidim, the children of Israel did chide with Moses, and said, "Wherefore is it that thou hast brought us up out of Egypt, to kill us and our children and our cattle with thirst?" And Moses cried unto the Lord saying, "What shall I do unto this people? They be almost ready to stone me." And the Lord said unto Moses, "Take thy rod, wherewith thou smotest the river, . . . and smite the rock, and there shall come water out of it, that the people may drink." And Moses did so, in the sight of the elders of Israel. And he called the name of the place . . . Meribah, because of the chiding of the children of Israel, and because they tempted the Lord, saying, "Is the Lord among us or not?"

And a little later in the history we see the difference between the true leader and the false one. Aaron was the brother of Moses, but he was by no means of the same temper. Moses desired to lead the people for their good. Aaron desired to lead them merely to be a leader, not caring which way they went. The time came when Moses was withdrawn. For many days he was with God, in the mount, out of their sight. "And when the people saw that Moses delayed to come down, . . . the people gathered themselves together unto Aaron, and said unto him, Up, make us gods which shall go before us; as for this Moses, the man that brought us up out of the land Egypt, we wot not what has become of him." There was Aaron's opportunity. Had he been a true leader he would have turned the people in the right direction. But he was weak and afraid. He was not man enough to lead them, and so he let them lead him. He said, yes, if you desire to do this wicked, foolish thing, I will show you how. If you will put me at the head of the procession I will go anywhere you say. And so Aaron takes their golden ornaments, and makes the golden calf, and plans for them a feast of idolatry and sin. There is the base leader, the man who loves a conspicuous position, but who does not use that position for the people's good. He does not watch by night for the people's welfare. He brings no message from Jehovah. He has no influence, no authority for good. He is ready to march at the head of the procession in any foolish, wicked enterprise the people may wish to take up.

Moses returns, and who shall describe his heart. "The Lord said unto Moses, I have seen this people, and behold it is a stiff-necked people; now, therefore, let me alone that my wrath may wax hot against them, that I may consume them, and I will make of thee a great nation. And Moses besought the Lord his God and said, 'Why doth thy wrath wax hot against thy people?'" There is the great leader and prophet as an intercessor. He pleads for those who have wronged him and his God. He thinks not of their perversity, but of their danger, and their need. He has the same temper as a shepherd for his foolish flock, as a mother for her silly child. He loves them in their weakness and even in their sins, and such generous and loving intercession prevails—the Lord repented of the evil which He thought to do unto His people.

We can take but one more of these instances in which the prophet was rejected by those he sought to benefit. In these cases it was their lack of faith—they could not believe that God could deliver them, and give them food and drink—and their quick forgetfulness when Moses was out of their sight. There is still another way in which a true prophet or leader is sure to be rejected. The time came when they grew jealous of his power, and other people desired to take his place.

Korah, Dathan and Abiram, with two hundred and fifty men of renown in the congregation, "gathered themselves together against Moses and against Aaron, and said unto them, 'Ye take too much upon you; wherefore lift ye up yourselves above the congregation of the Lord?'" Moses was the meekest man that ever lived, but that did not prevent him from being accused of pride and ambition. None of these two hundred and fifty men of renown had received any revelation from the Lord, none of them had any plan for the benefit of their country. But they desired to occupy Moses' position. The prophet gave a wise answer. He put forth no claim for himself. He simply said, "The Lord shall show whom he hath chosen." And the Lord did show. The two hundred and fifty men of renown were swallowed up, and Moses was permitted to lead on the procession toward the promised land.

And so at last we see this man Moses bringing the others into the land of promise which he was not himself permitted to enter. Pharaoh and his Egyptians are sunk in the Red Sea. Sihon, king of the Amorites, and Og, king of Bashan, have been overcome. Midian has been punished and conquered. The long wilderness road has been traversed at last. "The promised land" is before us! That is the land to which Abraham came. It is the land whereon Isaac and Jacob and the patriarchs pitched their tents and fed their flocks. For four hundred years every Hebrew mother has sung to her children of this wonderful promised land—the land of vines and pomegranates, the land of wine, and milk, and honey. And now it is no longer a song and a tradition only, but a reality. Yesterday we saw a distant mountain top which they told us was in that promised land. To-day it is in plain sight, just across the river, and that is it—the promised land! We are each of us to have a home there, a part of the great pasture where Abraham and Isaac and Jacob used to encamp, where Isaac met Rebecca, where Jacob saw the wonderful ladder, and wrestled with the angel. We are all to have an inheritance there—in a few days we shall go over and take possession.

But we shall go over without our great leader. Moses is forbidden to enter this promised land. It must always be told as a part of his story that he sinned. And sin must be punished, even the sin of a good man. Back there at the rock of Meribah, even when he was working the great miracle that brought the water for the thirsty thousands, Moses sinned. He spake unadvisedly with his lips; he failed that one time in not giving God the glory. He was impatient and wilful.

"And Moses went up from the plains of Moab into the mountain of Nebo, to the top of Pisgah, that is over against Jericho. And the Lord showed him all the land of Gilead unto Dan, and all Naphtali, and the land of Ephraim and Manassah, and all the land of Judah, unto the utmost sea, and the south, and the plain of the valley of Jericho, the city of palm-trees, unto Zoar. And the Lord said unto him, 'This is the land which I sware unto Abraham, unto Isaac, and unto Jacob, saying, I will give it unto thy seed. I have caused thee to see it with thine eyes, but thou shalt not go over thither.' So Moses, the servant of the Lord, died there in the land of Moab, according to the word of the Lord. And he buried him in a valley in the land of Moab, over against Bethpeor; but no man knoweth of his sepulcher unto this day. And Moses was a hundred and twenty years old when he died; his eye was not dim, nor his natural force abated. And the children of Israel wept for Moses in the plains of Moab forty days." "And there arose not a prophet since in Israel like unto Moses, whom the Lord knew face to face."

And now, beloved, what has Moses to do with us? We wonder at his courage, we admire his wisdom and patience, we weep at his death. He is a sublime spectacle, as we gaze upon him. Can we come nearer to him, and find enough in his experience which is like that which is in our experience, so that he can be to us an example?

We can certainly learn from the example of Moses that a humble birth is no bar to greatness. Being born in adversity does not insure a man's greatness, but neither does it hinder it. None of us can say, "I would be better if I had been born in a palace, if I had been cradled in luxury." Do not believe it. There are too many great men whose origin was lowly. Beginning with Moses in his ark of bulrushes in the river, we may find a long line of the children of poverty and adversity who have been raised up to greatness of spirit and of service. Let every child of the cottage, every son of toil, every daughter of obscurity, take courage. God calls such as you to be his prophets—his spokesmen.

And we may learn something from the education of Moses in the mountain solitudes. Doubtless one mind may be much more capable than another, but all minds are alike in this; they are strengthened and enlightened by reflection. When the mind is still and quiet, and yet awake, it gathers strength, and balance, it receives impressions that come from some mysterious source outside its own consciousness. The man or woman who is never alone, who lives in an unceasing round of activity, amusement, company, excitement, never grows wise or great. Our very studies fail to profit us unless we take time to reflect upon them. Here is the great opportunity for all whose lot is cast in solitary places. They need not sleep, they need not stagnate, they need not pass the days without improvement. Here is the great use and value of the Sabbath—its voice summons a crazy world to reflection. Let us all find time to spend as Moses on the mountain tops, with thought, reflection, and worship.

And we may learn something from Moses about public life, and public duties. He was slow to accept a public office, because he realized the burden of it, and was not dazzled by the outside show. It is a great responsibility to guide my own steps aright; how much greater if another is to follow me. The fool says, "Make me an officer, a captain, a governor; I want to wear the badge and the title, and to ride at the head of the procession." The wise man says, "How do I know that I am the best man to lead the army or to rule the state?" It would have been better for Braddock and for the world, if he had never been general. It would have been better for many a man if he had never won

the office in which he afterward disgraced himself. When we undertake any responsibility let us be sure that the Lord calls us, and that He is ready to go with us, and guide and sustain and instruct us.

But on the other hand when God does call us, we can go forward in confidence and courage. "I will be with thy mouth," saith the Lord. He will qualify you for every task He sets before you.

And there is another great thought here. Moses was not a king, or president, but a prophet, and that is a more important office. The great world is being slowly pushed toward righteousness not so much by its conspicuous office-holders as by its prophets in obscure places—the teachers, mothers, preachers, who speak for God in remote homes and churches. When all these are bold and faithful, we have a public sentiment which will control our governors and legislatures whether they be good or bad.

You or I may not be called to speak as Moses did, to an entire nation, but we are called to speak for God each in his own circle. This speaking for God is not a self-assertion, and it is not done with the desire to override others but to do them good. To this prophetic life every one of us is certainly called. God wishes in solitude to teach us His will and way, and then to have us boldly and lovingly proclaim that will and way of God to our neighbors. So each one of us will lead some fellow mortal into the promised land.

Moses was rejected by those he sought to benefit. So it will be with us. Let no one set out to be a prophet expecting to receive his main reward in this present life, at the hands of those he benefits. It is very important to understand this principle at the outset. If the people were all prophets they would not need a Moses. He comes to them precisely because they are blind and need a guide. The very business of a prophet is to contend against unbelief and ingratitude. He should not be angry at the unbelief and ingratitude he is sent to cure any more than a doctor should be angry at finding his patients maimed or diseased. It is his business to deal with those who are defective. A prophet must study the symptoms and conditions of the unbelieving multitude, and learn how to cure that unbelief. He must expect to find people unbelieving and unappreciative, but if he can not change them he must simply conclude that he is an unskilful prophet!

And finally Moses brought others to a land of plenty which he was not permitted himself to enter. This, too, is the common experience of those who are leaders of men. It takes a lifetime to transform a community, and when the community is transformed the man or woman who has done it passes to a higher reward than any this earth can give. It is not always so, but this is the rule. William of Orange secured the freedom of his country, but he was struck down by an assassin before he himself knew that his work had been a success. Abraham Lincoln restored the Union, but he was not permitted to live out his days in the country he had saved. And so many a teacher and many a parent dies without being permitted to see the pupil or the son whom they have started in the path of honor—they are not permitted to live to see him win his highest attainments.

These things are said in order that none of us may set our hearts upon that which may disappoint us. Do not be a prophet for the sake of being adored by the people you benefit, and do not be a prophet for the sake of the enjoyment of bringing people into the promised land. It will be enough, and more than enough, if you can see that promised land, even by faith, afar off. Be a prophet because God calls you, and because in that high calling you are brought near to Him.

The glory and the greatness of Moses lay in the fact that he was one who spoke for God, and one whom the Lord knew face to face. This high commission of spokesman for the Almighty, and this intimacy of being known by the Lord, is not confined to the few and the great. The mother of Moses, whose very name has been forgotten, also spoke for God when she ordered the hiding of the child, and the Lord knew her in her humility and her affliction. The rulers of hundreds, and the rulers of fifties, and the rulers of tens, who were appointed to share the burdens of Moses, all these became spokesmen for God in their several places, and the Lord knew them also.

WASHINGTON GLADDEN

1836-1918

THE PRINCE OF LIFE

BIOGRAPHICAL NOTE

WASHINGTON GLADDEN, Congregational divine, was born at Pottsgrove, Pa., in 1836. After graduating at Williams College he was ordained pastor, and occupied pulpits in Brooklyn, Morrisania, N. Y., and Springfield, Mass., until 1882, when he assumed charge of the First Congregational Church of Columbus, Ohio. He has also occupied editorial positions, and has published many books on social and civil reform and the practical application of Christian truth to popular and common life. His style, whether he was writing or speaking, combined vigor with grace.

And killed the prince of life, whom God hath raised from the dead.—Acts iii., 15.

THIS is the phrase with which Peter, in his great speech in the temple porch, describes the Master whose disciple he had been for three years, whose death he had witnessed on Calvary, and to whose resurrection from the dead he is now bearing witness. "The prince of life!" It is one of the many great titles conferred upon the Lord by those who loved Him. Reverence and devotion fell from their lips in lyrical cadences whenever they spoke of Him, and they wreathed for Him garlands of words with which they loved to deck His memory. He was "the Prophet of the Highest"; He was "the Great High Priest"; He was "the Shepherd of the Sheep"; He was "the Captain of Salvation"; He was "the First Born of Many Brethren"; He was "Redeemer," "Reconciler," "Savior." Gratitude and affection shaped many a tender phrase in which to describe Him, but there is none, perhaps, more luminous or more comprehensive than this with which the impulsive Peter, facing the men who had put Him to death, gave utterance to his loyalty. Its pertinence is confirmed by the word of Jesus Himself, in one of the sayings in which He described His mission: "I am come that ye might have life, and that ye might have it abundantly." Author and Giver of life He was, and what He gave He gave with princely munificence—freely, unstintedly.

The phrase seems to be one on which we may fitly dwell to-day, since the day of the year which commemorates His birth occurs on the day of the week which celebrates His resurrection. Both events proclaim Him the Prince of Life. In the one He is the Bringer of new life, in the other He is the Victor over death; and thus He becomes, in the impassioned confessions of the apostle, the Alpha and the Omega, the Author and the Finisher of Faith, the First and the Last and the Living One.

Those who are familiar with the New Testament narration do not need to have their attention called to the constant ministry of this Son of Man to the vital needs of men. The impartation of life seems to have been His main business. Somehow it came to be believed by the multitude, at the very beginning of His public ministry, that He possest some power of communicating life. The wonderful works ascribed to Him are nearly all of this character. The healing of the sick, the cleansing of the lepers, all resulted from the reenforcement of the vital energies of the sufferers. When He laid His hand upon men, new life seemed to speed through their veins. We have known some who seemed to have, in some imperfect way, this quickening touch. It is a physiological fact that warm blood from the veins of a thoroughly healthy person, transfused through the veins of one who is emaciated or exhausted, quickens the wavering pulse and brings life to the dying. It may be that through the nerve tissues, as well as through the veins, the same vitalizing force may be communicated, and that those who are in perfect health, both of body and of mind, may have the power of imparting life to those who are in need of it. The miracles of healing ascribed to Jesus must have been miracles in the literal sense; they were wonders, marvels—for that is what the word miracle means; that they were interruptions or violations of natural law is never intimated in the New Testament; they may have been purely natural occurrences, taking place under the operation of natural laws with which we are not familiar. We are far from knowing all the secrets of this wonderful universe; the time may come when these words of Jesus will have larger meaning than we have ever given them: "If ye abide in me, the works that I do shall ye do also, and greater works than these shall ye do, because I go unto my Father."

The fact to be noted is, however, that the people with whom Jesus was brought into contact were made aware in many ways of the impartation of His Life to them. "Of His fulness," said John, "we all received, and grace for grace." There seemed to be in Him a plenitude of vitality, from which health and vigor flowed into the lives of those who came near to Him. Nor does this seem to have been any mere physical magnetism; there is no intimation that His physical endowments were exceptional; the restoring and invigorating influence oftener flowed from a deeper source. The physical renewal came as the result of a spiritual quickening. He reached the body through the soul. The order was, first, "Thy sins be forgiven thee"; then, "Arise and walk." If the spirit is thoroughly alive, the body more quickly recovers its lost vigor. And it was mainly in giving peace to troubled consciences and rest to weary souls that He conferred upon those who received Him the great boon of life.

Thus Jesus proved Himself "the Prince of Life." In the early ages of the Church the Holy Spirit, the Comforter, came to be described as "the Lord and Giver of Life"; but that was because He was believed to be the Continuator of the work of Jesus—the spiritual Christ.

There seems to be in this conception a great and beautiful revelation of the essential nature of Christianity. There are many ways of conceiving of this, but I am not sure that any one of them is more significant than that which we are now considering. Those words of Jesus to which I have before referred are wonderful words when we come to think upon them. They occur in that discourse in which He describes Himself first as the Good Shepherd, and contrasts Himself with the thieves and robbers who have been ravaging the flock. "The thief cometh not," He says, "but that he may steal and kill and destroy; I came that they may have life, and may have it abundantly." Have we not here the great fundamental distinction between men—the line that separates the evil from the good, the just from the unjust, the sheep from the goats—that distinction which Jesus marks so clearly in His parable of judgment, and which must never, in our interpretations or philosophizings, be blotted or blurred? Some are life-givers; some are life-destroyers. "The thief cometh not but that he may steal and kill and destroy; I came that they may have life, and may have it abundantly."

I do not suppose that Jesus meant in this to declare that there is a large class of persons whose entire purpose it is to steal and kill and destroy; probably there are none so malevolent that they do not cherish some kindly impulses and perform some generous deeds. It is a distinction between acts, or perhaps between tendencies of character, that He is making. He speaks in the concrete, as He always does; but He expects us to make the proper application of His words. The fact to which He guides our thought is this—that there are ways of living, forms of conduct, which are predatory and destructive of life, and other ways that tend to make life increase and abound. When Jesus contrasts His own conduct, as one who gives life and gives it abundantly, with the thieves and robbers who kill and destroy, we must interpret the conduct of those whom He describes as destructive of life—as tending to the diminution of life. Indeed, it is a very deep and awful truth that all our social action tends in one or other of these directions. Life, in its proper relation, is the one supreme and central good; the life of the body is the supreme good of the body; the life of the spirit is the supreme good of the spirit. And you can rightly estimate any act or habit or tendency of human conduct only by determining whether it increases and invigorates the life of men, body and spirit, or whether it reduces or diminishes their life. Good men are adding to the life of those with whom they have to do; evil men are debilitating and depleting the life of those with whom they have to do.

Even in our economic relations the final

effect of all our conduct upon those with whom we deal is to replenish or diminish their life. The wage question is at bottom a question of more or less life for the wage-worker. Starvation wages are wages by which the hold upon life of the wage-earner and his wife and children is weakened. Systems of industry are good in proportion as they enlarge and invigorate the life of the whole population; evil in proportion as they lessen and weaken its life. So all industrial and national policies are to be judged by the amount of life which they produce and maintain—life of the body and of the spirit. Those strong words of John Ruskin are the everlasting truth:

"There is no wealth but life—life including all its powers of love, of joy and of admiration. That country is the richest which nourishes the greatest number of noble and happy human beings; that man is richest who, having perfected the functions of his own life to the utmost, has also the widest helpful influence, both personal and by means of his possessions, over the lives of others."

We have here, as you see, the Christian conception—the very word of the Prince of Life, of Him who came that we might have life, and that we might have it abundantly. And when His kingdom has come, this will be the end for which wealth is sought and used in every nation.

It is possible to use wealth so that it shall be productive of life; so that the entire administration of it shall tend to the enlargement and enrichment of the life of men; so that the labor which it employs shall obtain an increasing share of the goods which it produces; so that all the conditions under which that labor is performed shall be favorable to health and life and happiness; so that the spiritual life, also, of all who are employed shall be nourished by inspiring them with good-will and kindness, with the confidence in man which helps us to have faith in God. Such an administration of wealth is perhaps the very best testimony to the reality of the truth of the Christian religion which it is possible to bear in this day and generation. One who handles capital with this clear purpose can do more to establish in the earth the kingdom of heaven than any minister or missionary can do.

But it is possible to use wealth in the opposite way, so that it shall be destructive rather than productive of life. A man may manage his industry in such a way that the last possible penny shall be taken from wages and added to profit; in such a way that the health of his employees shall be impaired and their happiness blighted and their hope taken away. He may do this while maintaining an outwardly religious behavior and giving large sums to philanthropy. But such a handling of wealth does more to make infidels than any heretical teacher or lecturer ever did or can do.

The fact needs to be noted that all the predatory schemes by which capital is successfully inflated and nefariously manipulated, and the community is thus burdened, are deadly attacks upon the life of the people. They filch away the earnings of the laboring classes. They increase the cost of rent and transportation and all the necessaries of life. They extort from the people contributions for which no equivalent has been given, of commodity or service. Thus the burden of toil is increased and the reward of industry is lessened for all who work; the surplus out of which life would be replenished is consumed, and the amount of life in the nation at large is lessened. Every one of those schemes of frenzied finance about which we are reading in these days is a gigantic bloodsucker, with ten million minute tentacles which it stealthily fastens upon the people who do the world's work, and each one of the victims must give up a little of his life for the aggrandizement of our financial Titans. When such schemes flourish, by which men's gains are suddenly swollen to enormous proportions, somebody must be paying for it, and life is always the final payment. It all comes out of the life of the people who are producing the world's wealth. The plethora of the few is the depletion of the millions. In every great aggregation of workers, the faces of the underfed are a little paler and the pulses of the children beat a little less joyously, and the feet are hastened on that journey to the tomb—all because of those who come to steal and to kill and to destroy.

Such is the contrast between beneficent business and maleficent business. The good business employs men, feeds them, clothes them, shelters them, generously distributes among them the goods that nourish life; the bad business contrives to levy tribute on the resources out of which they are fed and clad and nourished, and thus enriches itself by impoverishing the life of the multitude.

And I suppose that we should all find, whether we are engaged in what is called business or not, that the work which we are doing, the way in which we are spending our time and gaining our income, is tending either to the enlargement and increase of the life of those with whom we have to do or to the impoverishment and destruction of their life; and that this is the final test by which we must be judged—are we producers of life or destroyers of life? Is there more of life in the world—more of physical and spiritual life—because of what we are and what we do, or is the physical and spiritual vitality of men lessened by what we are and what we do? Are we helping men to be stronger and sounder in body and mind and soul for the work of life, or are we making them feebler in muscle and will and moral stamina?

When Jesus Christ came into the world the civilization prevailing—if such it could be called—was under the dominion of those who came to steal and to kill and to destroy. Rome was the world, and the civilization of Rome, with all its splendor, was at bottom a predatory civilization. It overran all its neighbors that it might subjugate and despoil them; its whole social system was based on a slavery in which the enslaved were merely chattels; the life of its ruling class was fed by the literal devouring of the lives of subject classes. Of course, this civilization was decadent. That terrible decline and fall which Gibbon has pictured was in full progress. It was in the midst of this awful scene that Jesus was born in Bethlehem of Judea. Can anyone doubt that His heart was full of divine compassion for those who were trampled on and preyed upon by the cruel and the strong, for those whose lives were consumed by the avarice and greed of their fellows? What did He mean when, at the beginning of His ministry in the synagog where He had always worshiped, He took in his hand the roll of the prophet Isaiah and read therefrom: "The Spirit of the Lord is upon me, because he hath anointed me to preach good tidings to the poor; he hath sent me to proclaim release to the captives and recovery of sight to the blind, to set at liberty them that are bruised, to proclaim the acceptable year of the Lord"—adding as He sat down, under the gaze of the congregation, "To-day hath this scripture been fulfilled in your ears"? What could He have meant but this, that it was His mission to change the entire current and tendency of human life; to put an end to the plunderers and devourers; to chain the wolfish passion in human hearts which prompts men to steal and to kill and to destroy; to inspire them with His own divine compassion; to give life and to give it abundantly? And is it not true that so far as men do receive of His fulness, so far as they are brought under the control of His spirit, they do cease to be destroyers and devourers of the bodies and souls of their fellows, and become helpers, saviors, life-bringers? And is not this included in His meaning when He says: "I am come that they may have life, and that they may have it abundantly"?

To-day, then, we hail Him as Prince of Life, the glorious Giver to men of the one supreme and crowning good. And the manner of the giving is not hard to understand. He gives life by kindling in our hearts the flame of sacred love. Love is life. Love to God and man brings the soul into unity with itself; it is obeying its own organic law, and obedience to its law brings to any organism life and health and peace. If the spirit of Christ has become the ruling principle of our conduct, then we have entered into life, and it is a life that knows no term; it is the immortal life. If the spirit of Christ has entered into our lives, then in all our relations with others life is increased; we are by nature givers of good; out of our lives are forever flowing healing, restoring, saving, vitalizing influences; and when all the members of the society in which we move have received this spirit and manifest it, there are none to bite and devour, to hurt and destroy; the predatory creatures have ceased their ravages, and the world rejoices in the plenitude of life which He came to bring.

We hail Him, then, to-day, as the Lord and Giver of life. We desire to share with Him the unspeakable gift, and to share it, as best we may, with all our fellow men. What we freely receive from Him, we would freely give. What the whole world needs to-day is life, more life, fuller life, larger life. We spend all our energies in heaping up the means of life, and never really begin to live; our strength is wasted, our health is broken, our intellects are impoverished, our affections are withered, our peace is destroyed in our mad devotion to that which is only an adjunct or appendage of life. Oh, if we could only understand how good a thing it is to live, just to live, truly and freely and largely and nobly, to live the life that is life indeed!

Shall we not draw to this Prince of Life and take from Him the gift that He came to bring? Is not this the one thing needful? We are reading and hearing much in these days of the simple life. What is it but the life into which they are led who take the yoke of this Master upon them and learn of Him? It is a most cheering omen that this little book of Pastor Wagner's is falling into so many hands and uttering its ingenuous and persuasive plea before so many minds and in so many homes. If we heed it, it must bring us back to the simplicity of Christ. Pastor Wagner is only preaching over again the Sermon on the Mount; it is nothing but the teaching of Jesus brought down to this day and applied to the conditions of our complex civilization. It is the true teaching; none of us can doubt it. And I wish that we could all begin the new year with the earnest purpose to put ourselves under the leadership of the Prince of Life. I know that we should find His yoke easy and His burden light, and that there would be rest for our souls in the paths into which He would lead us. We should know, if we shared His life, that we were really living; and we should know also that we were helping others to live; that we were doing what we could to put an end to the ravages of the destroyers and the devourers, and to fill the earth with the abundance of peace.

Is not this, fellow men, the right way to

live! Does not all that is deepest and divinest in you consent to this way of life into which Jesus Christ is calling us, as the right way, the royal way, the blessed way? Choose it, then, with all the energy of your volition, and walk in it with a glad heart and a hope that maketh not ashamed.

CHARLES GORE

1853-1932

THE EFFICACY OF PRAYER

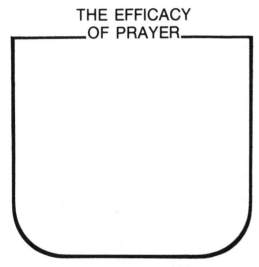

BIOGRAPHICAL NOTE

CHARLES GORE, Bishop of Birmingham since 1905, was born in 1853. He was educated at Harrow and Balliol College, Oxford (Scholar), and became Chaplain in Ordinary to the King in 1901, being appointed Bishop of Worcester in 1902. A leading social reformer, his sermons are largely devoted to a consideration of sociological problems ; he was a worker on behalf of the poor, whose misery had drawn his active sympathies, and a strong opponent of sweating in every form. His belief was that " the law should be so amended as to empower the Church with the right of progress, though, at the same time, a community must be secured against passing waves of feeling." Bishop Gore was a typical representative of that most modern of Anglican schools of thought, the wing of the clergy at once High and Broad. His preaching was eloquent yet simple, and he delighted in treating at one time some sociological problem, illuminating it with Christian doctrine ; and at another some profound and controversial topic, handling this with acute acumen. His sermons were often dogmatic, but were always popularly intelligible, and he is recognised as being eminently a " people's prelate."

M Y subject is the Efficacy of Prayer. Prayer is asking. It is the creature asking the Creator. And by the efficacy of prayer we mean that something comes of our asking, for God hears and answers as we ask. And my desire is, if I can, to reinforce in you the will to pray by removing some of those obstacles which, in the minds of good people, very often impede them in taking pains about prayer. . . . Therefore, I ask your attention to four plain points in regard to prayer, if, it may be, I may remove some of those obstacles, conscious or half-unconscious, which impede you and me from taking the pains and giving the systematic energy we might to this life of prayer, and finding what is always the consequence, our delight and our fruit therein.

Let your imagination grasp the vast place which prayer holds in the whole history of our humanity. Man, as you look at him broadly, does set his faculties to move in three directions. He moves out toward Nature to draw out its resources for his advantage ; and that is civilization. Its history begins where the savage hunts his prey, or scratches the soil and throws in his grains for the beginning of agriculture. It passes through all that 'varied history of industry which reaches up to that vast complexity of the modern system of civilization, by which the resources of the furthest corners of the earth are brought together to the centers where men live, for their convenience and for their luxury. Man moves out toward nature to appropriate its resources ; but he moves out also toward his fellow-men, and that is the history of society. It has its rude beginnings in the tribe and in the family ; it advances through all human history ; it reaches to that point of infinite complexity in which the life of nations in themselves, and the life of nations one with another, is presented to our minds. Man moves out toward nature ; it is the history of civilization. He moves out toward his fellow men ; it is the history of society. But he moves out also toward God. Look at the savage ; look at man in every stage of civilization ; it bridges over his rudest beginning up to the point of his greatest advance. Everywhere in the works which men work, in the structures which they build, in the language which they speak, you observe a good third part of their energy preoccupied with prayer. The religion of which prayer is the characteristic act sets its stamp everywhere on human history. It has, like civilization, like society, a checkered but a definite progress.

It passes through that progress most conspicuously in the Old Testament; for at the beginning of the Old Testament you see a worship which has conspicuous affinity with the worship of a merely savage tribe ; while at the top it reaches up to that supreme worship which is the worship of the Son of Man. It reaches there its climax. It is the heritage of that society which was founded by Jesus of Nazareth. It has its center in the Lord's Prayer ; at the altar it radiates out to consecrate and to bring down blessing upon the whole of life. But contemplate the greatness of the place which prayer occupies in human activity, and ask yourselves, as you are reasonable men, whether you can possibly believe that an activity so regular, so constant, so progressive, so universal, can be based on any mere figment or dream of the imagination. It is one of the most solid results of scientific inquiry that no human faculty can develop or subsist unless it is what scientific men call in correspondence with its environment. That phrase means that no faculty can come into existence or maintain itself unless it is really useful, unless it really corresponds with some fact external to man, is in real relation with nature as it is. The eye could not have developed or subsisted unless there had been the reality called light to evoke it and to make it useful. And all this activity of prayer, seen in its various strange forms till it reaches up to rational consistency in the prayers of the Son of Man—all this activity of prayer could not have been evoked, could not have developed, could not have subsisted unless man by praying had been really in relation to the God Who hears ; unless all this activity of prayer had been in real correspondence with the fact, and the most fundamental fact on which the universe is built.

There is no doubt that a great many people recognize in a vague sort of way that somehow prayer is a real activity of human life. They can not so far separate themselves from the inner man as to deny that. But to kneel down and pray for this or that seems to postulate a knowledge of God about me, and attention of God to me in particular which, when I consider the vastness of the universe, appears altogether preposterous to suppose.

Brethren, there are a great many cases in which we need to distinguish between our imagination and our reason. This is one. True it is that the imagination of man falls absolutely baffled before the task of imagining how the conscience of God and the activity of God which are over all things absolutely can still comprise an individual knowledge, and an individual attention directed to every particular atom and part of that great universe. Our imagination, I say, is absolutely baffled. But you know quite well that if you take the elementary facts with which physical science deals, like the existence of ether, on which all modern theories of light and heat are based,

or the vastness of the solar system, in the same degree your imagination is absolutely baffled. You may not be able to draw a mental picture of things which still your reason may postulate, may force you to believe. Now let your reason go to work, and you will find that it comes very near to postulating about God just this very thing which you find it so hard to imagine. For think a moment ; in ourselves, as our knowledge or our activity grows to perfection, it passes out of being merely vague into being definite, detailed, particular. If I go into a schoolroom where there are boys, I know nothing about them except what vague and general knowledge I have of boys as a whole. But the schoolmaster knows them better ; that means he knows them more particularly as individuals, with individual histories, with characteristics, and powers, and faults. Or ask in what the preeminent physician is distinguished from the ordinary doctor. It is, I suppose, in this—that he has, while possessing a broader experience, at the same time a more individual insight into particular cases. All human knowledge and action as it advances to perfection both widens in range, while at the same time it becomes more detailed in application. Carry up that thought until you can perceive the perfect consciousness of God, and you will find that it postulates that God's knowledge and action shall be at once over all His creatures whatsoever ; but that the universal range and scope of the divine attributes shall diminish not one whit from their particular and personal application, so that God created us, and loves us, and knows us, and deals with us one by one as individually, as particularly, as if there were no one other created, or none so loved. Prayer is possible as the real request addressed by an individual soul out of its individual needs to the Almighty and Universal Father because that Fatherhood of God is not wider in its range than it is absolutely particular and individual in its protecting, in its creating, in its predestinating love.

But God knows so much better than I do what I want. That prayer, the asking God out of my short-sighted folly to give me this or that, is surely a very ignorant procedure. Had I not better put a general trust in God and go on my way submitting to His providence ? That is one of the cases in which a thought can take very devout expression while at the same time it may cut at the root of practical religion. For, brethren, we all know that this appeal—we need not pray because God knows already what we want—allows even too easily of our going on our way and practically leaving God out of our lives. Our Lord knew well enough that the object of prayer was not to inform God ; your Father knoweth what things ye have need of before ye ask it. The object of prayer is not to inform God ; but it is to train us in habits of personal intercourse with God, of personal sonship toward Him.

We are made for sonship,—sonship is personal correspondence, personal, intelligent cooperation with God. It is a gradually increasing power of familiarity with God : of intercourse with Him, of approach toward Him as person to person.

Well, then, prayer is made necessary for us simply in order that by this necessity for praying, for asking, we may be, as it were, constrained again and again to come before God and, by asking, familiarize ourselves with Him ; and as we ask, and as we receive, grow into correspondence, intelligent personal correspondence with God our Father. Who that has prayed diligently, and experienced an answer, does not know that that one experience has done more for the life of religion in his or her soul than a great deal of reading or thinking. That consciousness of our relation to God is a thing which will develop through all eternity ; but it has its beginning here, and the reason why God makes things depend upon our asking for them is that we may be thus educated into such personal intercourse with Him that that truth of sonship may never be merged and lost as it is merged and lost in all that direction of life which, unconsecrated by prayer, moved away from God.

But then, lastly, we get to what in a great many people's minds is the heart of the difficulty. I grant all you say about the meaning of prayer ; I grant all you say, this or that man will urge. I grant all you say about its place in human history ; I would fain pray, I should feel its reasonableness, I should indeed experience the spiritual exaltation which it would give my life ; but surely prayer is one of those things which was possible in old days, but is not really possible now when once we have grasped that the world is governed by fixed, unalterable laws. If all this world is the seat of the operation of fixed laws, then surely it is, indeed, purposeless to think to bend down to the level of our wishes and our short-sighted ideas that fixed and unchangeable system. Surely fixed laws, once grasped by the imagination and the mind, render impossible the real action of prayer. To pray is, after all, to anyone who conceives the world as modern knowledge forces us to conceive it,—to pray is, after all, only like a bird beating its wings against the bars of an iron cage.

Brethren, this is one of those difficulties which find their strength in people's minds so largely because they do not have the courage or take the pains to think them out to the bottom. The answer to it lies, I think, in two directions. It is indeed a complete destruction of the idea of prayer that the world should be governed by fixed laws, if prayer is in any sense conceived of as an attempt to bend down the wisdom of God to the level of our folly. But by law what do you mean ? You mean the method by which things work. Law is not a power ; it is only a method. The uni-

versality of law means that God works everywhere and in all things by constant and unchangeable method. This is observed not only in the wide things, in the vast movements of solar systems, but in the tiniest details of nature, so that all the intricacies of the wing of a butterfly are as much the result in each detail of the universal law or method by which God works in all things as the vastest cosmic movements. Everywhere God works by law, by order, by method. But if our Lord taught us anything He taught us this, that prayer is not the attempt to drag down the divine operations to the level of our folly ; prayer is a method by which we lift up ourselves into correspondence with the methods of God. It is not the bringing of the methods of God down to our level ; it is the lifting up of our will in correspondence with the method of God.

We shall have occasion to notice this at greater length when we come to think about the special lessons which our Lord taught us about prayer. But grasp now that if this be granted, that prayer is not an attempt on our part to make God work otherwise than by the method of law, but is simply one way in which we men correspond with the method of God in the universe ; and you will see, I think, that all that difficulty about prayer and law is, if not destroyed and abolished, at least reduced to a position where it can have no reasonable effect upon our lives. For this we must grant, God works everywhere by law. But that does not mean that He dispenses with our cooperation. God works everywhere by law. It is by law that gold comes into existence ; it is by law that gold is drawn out of the earth ; it is by law it is purified ; it is by law it is put into circulation as a medium of currency ; all that is by law, but it does not happen without human cooperation. The universe is a universe of law ; but it postulates our cooperation if we are to receive its benefit. The world is a universe of law ; but I shall get nothing of the good things I might get out of the world unless I show an active initiative ; unless I take trouble and pains ; unless by diligence and fruitful correspondence with the law of the world I obtain those things which are within my grasp. Now, here is a mystery. How is it that if the world is governed by law there is room for my free will, for my cooperation ? How is it that if the world is governed by law I cannot simply sit still and say, Whatever comes to me will come to me; and whatever will not come to me will not come to me ; I can do nothing. I am in a world of fixed law.

There is a mystery. At present I will not say a word in attempting to solve it. I say, let our freedom be, if you will, denied in theory, you must admit it in fact ; you must day by day, moment by moment, act as if everything depended on your cooperation with the system of nature, and it is only in proportion to your initiative, your vigorous will, your constant energy, that you get what nature can afford to you. But I am sure that I am not exaggerating when I say this—there is in regard to prayer absolutely no more difficulty in connection with the reign of law than there is in regard to any other form of activity. There is the same mystery everywhere about human free will. We leave it altogether aside; but we know this, that there are multitudes of things in nature which are laid there in store for me, but which will not come to be mine unless I energetically work for them, unless I energetically correspond with the method of nature. Exactly as truly there are stores of blessings which God intends for you, but which He will not give to you unless you energetically correspond with His law, with His method, by prayer. Prayer is as fruitful a correspondence with the method of God as work—as fruitful and as necessary. Some things you can obtain by work without prayer; some things you can obtain by prayer without other work; some things by the combination of working and praying : but no things at all without your cooperation; and cooperation by prayer has no kind of rational difficulty attendant upon it which does not attend equally upon cooperation by the method of work. You have no kind of right to put the reign of law as an obstacle to prayer unless you are prepared to make the reign of law an obstacle to your doing anything to get your own living. . . . .

It is true that the man of prayer who approaches the Father in the name of the Son, in intelligent correspondence with the divine kingdom and divine purpose, draws out of the largeness of the love of God infinite stores of good things which God wills to give to him, and thru him to his family, his Church, his nation, humanity—stores of good things which are there in the providence of God waiting to comfort him, but will not be given him except he prays.

DAVID GREGG

1846-1919

THE SACRAMENTAL WAGONS

BIOGRAPHICAL NOTE

EX-PRESIDENT of Western Theological Seminary, Allegheny, Pa.; born Pittsburg Pa., March 25, 1846; at the age of twenty-three entered on an eighteen-year pastorate in the Scotch Covenanter Church, New York; pastor Park Street Congregational church, Boston, for four years; when Dr. Theodore L. Cuyler resigned the pastorate of the Lafayette Avenue Presbyterian church, Brooklyn, he was called to be his successor, where he remained fourteen years; president of the Western Theological Seminary four years, resigning from ill health, whereupon the trustees of the seminary made him president emeritus and lecturer extraordinary; author of "Between the Testaments" (which has been translated into Greek and published in Athens), "The Value of Literature in the Construction of the Sermon"

*"And when he [Jacob] saw the wagons which Joseph had sent to carry him, the spirit of Jacob, their father, revived. And Israel said, It is enough."—*Genesis 45 : 27.

OUR text is part of the story of the patriarch Jacob. As a mere piece of history, this story of the father of the twelve tribes of Israel is a veritable gem in literature. It is full of information and thrill and fascination. But the story is more than a mere piece of history. It is a type of spiritual things. It is a prefiguration of the destiny of the good. It is one form of God's covenant with His own. It is a symbol of greater and higher realities. It is a parable illustrative of the operation of divine principles in the life of God's elect. And it is an assurance of God's overrule in the affairs of mankind. Such is the use which the New Testament teaches us to make of Old Testament biography. It teaches us to convert it into the sacramental; and to work it over into a gospel of spirit and of power.

In its inclusiveness, this story of Jacob reminds one of the famous jewel in the crown-room at Dresden. The jewel is a perfect silver egg. When the secret spring of the silver egg is prest, a golden yolk opens into view. When the spring of the yolk is prest, a beautiful bird appears. When the spring in the wings of the bird is prest, a matchless crown of precious gems falls into the hand. Each treasure includes a greater treasure. Such a multifold treasure is the story of this Old Testament saint, which opens before us on the sacred page. It is a piece of fascinating history. It is a spiritual type. It is a glorious prefiguration. It is one of faith's symbols. It is a sacramental parable full of sacramental facts and inspirations and assurances.

The point where we strike the story is the point where the wagons of the long-lost Joseph come to take the aged patriarch to a renewed fellowship and to a grander life, and to the beginning of a more glorious future. As we see the patriarch, he is sitting at the tent-door looking Egyptward. These sad words are still in his heart: "Joseph is not, and Simeon is not; and ye will take Benjamin away. All these things are against me." All the boys of the family are down in Egypt, for they have taken Benjamin away. The patriarch is alone. He sits at the tent-door awaiting the return of his sons. He is praying for their safety, and especially for the safety of Benjamin, Rachel's boy.

Suddenly, in the dim distance, he catches sight of a cloud of dust which rises in the air. This brings him at once to his feet, that he may peer into the distance. His heart says, "There are my sons, and God be praised." But it immediately asks, "Are they all there?" As he talks with himself, the company comes within full sight so that he can discern full outlines. Then he begins to count: "One, two, three, four, five, six, seven, eight, nine. Nine! Are there only nine? Ah, then my dark foreboding has become a reality. Mischief has befallen Benjamin by the way. I should never have allowed him to go." These words no sooner fall from his lips than he sees the form of a tenth person; and his soul cries "Benjamin is safe, God be doubly praised!" Then comes the eleventh form into sight, and he cries, "They are all there! Simeon has been set free!" Blest be God, who hath not turned my prayer from Him, nor His mercy from me!" What a heart relief for Jacob! It is the sun flashing in crimson and gold through the black cloud which he saw above his head, and from which he expected only the deadly storm.

But wait! Jacob sees beyond his sons another cloud of dust. Another company comes into sight. What can that be? To his consternation, it is a company of Egyptians. Is it a pursuit? Does it mean that the might of Egypt is hurled against his little home? Is the return of his sons to end in a worse sorrow? Who can tell the anxious questions that filled the heart of the patriarch, from the time he discerned the Egyptian wagons, until his sons reached him and explained all?

The first thing that gave Jacob relief was the happy faces of his returning sons. They were different men from what they were when they returned from Egypt the first time. Scarcely had he gotten relief from the sight of their happy faces, than he was subjected to a shock of joy, as his sons told him the whole story of their glad faces in this one sentence: "Joseph is yet alive, and is governor over all the land of Egypt."

Do you want a picture of sudden surprize? You have it here. Do you want to see a human heart leap from fear and grief into happy assurance and faith? You see it here. Do you want to see how the soul can paint for itself a dark present and a black future, while the real facts warrant a picture as bright as the sun? You can see that here. The absence of Joseph and Simeon and Benjamin, which was so lamented by Jacob, was working out a magnificent destiny for the household of Jacob. We can credit the narrative when it tells us that the sudden declaration of the sons of Jacob caused their father's heart to faint, for he believed them not. "Joseph is yet alive!" The very joy wrapt up in the assertion was so great that it hindered faith. "Governor over all the land of Egypt!" Methinks I hear Jacob talking with himself, and saying: "If he were

alive, by what means could my shepherd lad rise to the highest seat of government in that great land? Ah, these, my sons, are too cruel in their treatment of me. If Joseph were alive, he would be here himself."

It was natural for Jacob to be incredulous at first, and to hold on to his incredulity until he received some evidence from Joseph himself. Remember what he had to argue down before he could believe. He felt that he had irresistible presumptive evidence that Joseph had been torn to pieces by wild beasts. He had to argue that down. He had in his possession the blood-stained coat; and he brought it out and held it up before his sons. He had to contradict the coat, and charge it with black falsehood. He had to turn back the whole tide and current of his feelings, from that dismal day when he accepted the account of Joseph's death as a fact. He had to give up the rest of acquiescence for the restlessness of a revived hope. He had to unsettle everything.

The incredulity of Jacob did not strike his sons as strange. They accepted it as a matter of course; hence they began to persuade him. They told him all that they had seen and all that Joseph had said. They gave him every confirming detail. They pointed to the costly changes of raiment from the palace, which Joseph had sent, and to the full provisions from Goshen, the land of plenty; and to the many rich gifts of Joseph's love. They made these material things talk and bear testimony. And then, to climax everything, they took Jacob, their father, out to look at the wagons, with their Egyptian drivers. They explained to him the purpose of the wagons and read him the invitation from Joseph, which they embodied. This was a masterstroke. For when Jacob saw the wagons his heart revived, his doubts vanished, and his faith leapt into full growth. The wagons were symbols to his faith and spake to him as nothing else could speak. When he heard the story which the wagons told, he believed all that his sons declared. He said, "It is enough."

But why should these sons be believed on account of the wagons? Jacob once believed them when they made Joseph's coat speak. What assurance has he that they have put the voice of truth into the wagons? There is a vast difference between the coat and the wagons. These sons could control the coat; but they could not control the wagons. The wagons belonged to royalty; and only some one in the royal palace, some one connected with the throne of Egypt, could send them. Now, who in all the world could have enough interest in this lame old shepherd to send for him, and to bestow such royal gifts upon him, except one, and that one Joseph? Joseph was in the wagons; Joseph's love, Joseph's desire; and because of this they spake to the father's heart. Their message brought a glow of joy into his faded cheek, and infused a new elasticity into his limbs, and breathed vigor and vitality into all his powers. Old and weary as he was, he at once determined to go and see his son. His new faith gave him a new life. Making use of the wagons, he went to Egypt and to his son. He saw Joseph wearing the crown of an unsullied manhood as well as the royal ring of favor; and his gray hairs, which he said would be brought with sorrow to the grave, fell in joy upon the neck of the one for whom he had mourned until grief had whitened them.

As we look at the effect which the glad message, "Joseph is yet alive," had upon Jacob, we see the wisdom of Joseph in the way he dealt with his father. One would naturally say, "Now that Joseph knows everything, why not go himself and see his father and bring him to Egypt?" If the simple words "Joseph is yet alive" caused such a shock, and set the tide of life rolling backward upon his heart until he swooned, what think ye would have been the shock had Joseph himself stept unexpectedly into his father's presence? Do you not know that joy, as well as grief, has the power to kill? The daily press tells this story: A young man left his fatherland and sailed from Germany to America. He left behind him the betrothed of his heart, with the promise that he would send for her as soon as his gains warranted. Manfully he wrought his way up the hill of fortune, and faithfully he kept his promise. His affianced landed safely in New York and sent a telegram to Chicago, announcing the time her train was due. The engine came thundering into the Union station, and the two met and spake each other's name. It was a lover's greeting, full of romance from real life. It was a moment of grateful joy. The greeting given, the affianced husband gently sought to disengage himself from the clasped hands, which were around his broad and manly shoulders. But, as he did so, he found his betrothed in his arms, dead. She died from very joy. The method which Joseph adopted was such as would prevent the shock of joy being too great. The glad tidings were given gradually, and the meeting of great joy was gradually brought about.

As we read how the wagons of Joseph wrought conviction in Jacob and gave him strong and active and vigorous faith, we see the value of those things which we call outward evidences. The wagons were outward evidences. They were a separate and distinct testimony to the reality of what his sons declared. They confirmed the words of his sons. They were outward arguments, proving the things which the sons asked the father to believe. They so settled things, that there was

no way open for Jacob to introduce or to entertain a single doubt. Faith only was the order of the day.

Has God outside arguments and external evidences to prove the reality of the religion which He has asked us to espouse? Has Christianity such testimony to offer on behalf of itself and its doctrines? Are there not sacramental wagons, laden with such irresistible proof, that in espousing the Christian religion we build our soul and rest our faith upon veritable facts?

For example, we are asked to believe in the doctrine of God's fatherly care over us. We believe that doctrine because of what God is in Himself. We reason thus: "Since God is the author of fatherhood, He must have the father-heart. We can trust the father-heart." But is there not an external argument proving His fatherly care? There is. There is a sacramental wagon, and He sends that wagon to us laden with fatherly gifts. The sun rolling in its orbit is God's wagon; and out from this wagon there is tossed upon the earth golden grain for bread, and brilliant flowers for beauty, and all manner of luscious fruit for luxury, and flashing beams which give tonic and light and life.

For example, we are asked to believe in the Christian religion, and in the historicity of its founder, Jesus Christ. We accept the Christian religion because of what it is in itself. It is full of purity and love and heavenliness and grand and inspiring ideals. It is its own argument. Because of its very essence, it is irresistible. While this is so, still we instinctively ask: "Are there not external and historical evidences in favor of Christ and Christianity?" The human soul demands a religion that is really and truly historic. We want to know in very deed that the prophetic Christ has become the historic Christ. We want fixedness and certainty in our religion; for only when our religion is a fixt certainty can it dominate and rule us, and fill us with the rest and peace of God. God knows this; hence, He gives us external as well as internal evidences. He gives us material facts—facts that are visible and tangible and usable. He gives us effects which call for adequate causes. He gives us collateral securities. He gives us Christic verities. He gives us monumental ordinances, and holy days, and continuing institutions. He gives us historical certainties, which are acting forces and factors in the world's life. He gives us facts which are contemporaneous with the essential things which we are asked to believe; and which are forever married to these things. Now all of these things—holy days, institutions, ordinances, collateral securities, contemporaneous facts, effects which call for adequate causes, visible certainties—all these external evidences deal with the very roots of our religion. They talk, they suggest, they argue, they prove, they give testimony, they confirm and establish the essentialities of our faith. They leave us no logical resting-place, save a willing and loving and final surrender to Jesus Christ. These things are the glory of the world. They are historical certainties, which come directly from the historic Christ and which lead directly to the historic Christ. They are sacramental wagons from our New Testament Joseph; and they speak incontrovertibly relative to Him, and His life, and His rule, and His saving purposes.

Let me name these! They are the great outstanding and active forces of our Christianity. They are, the Lord's Day, the Christian Church, the New Testament and the Lord's Supper. These are all sacramental wagons laden with spiritual gifts. They are living voices talking for Christ. They are all of them facts before our eyes, and they challenge an explanation. Where did they originate? What do they mean? What continues them? To what do they testify? My fellow men, answer these questions truthfully and you will have a complete vindication of Christ and Christianity. They bear the same relation to Christianity that Independence Day bears to the American republic; and they are just as worthy of credence. They all proclaim Christ, and they all proclaim the gospel of Christ. They are the external evidences of our religion. Certainly each of these externals gives us a fearless challenge.

You hear the challenge of the Lord's Day! It says: "O man, harken unto me. I, the first day of the week, am now the Sabbath of the Lord. I own your conscience. I call you to rest and to worship. I have not always been the Sabbath. For thousands of years the seventh day of the week was the Sabbath of the Lord. Tell me what great revolution dethroned that day, and enthroned me? It must have been a splendid fact that did this! Cause and effect, and effect and cause, must match. Now what was that fact? It was the splendid fact for which I stand, and which I herald to mankind, viz., on the first day of the week Jesus Christ rose from the dead. "Joseph is yet alive!" I, the great Christ-day of Christendom, am a contemporaneous fact with the fact of the Master's resurrection. If this be not my origin, disprove it. For twenty centuries I have done my duty and borne my testimony relative to the empty tomb. Fifty-two times a year I have uttered the cry, 'The Lord is risen!' Five thousand two hundred times each century I have repeated it. In the twenty centuries of the Christian Era, I have set forth the risen Savior no less than one hundred and four thousand times. Now, you have my challenge on your hands, and I leave it with you." My fellow men, if each Lord's Day be a sacramental wagon, we have

had during the Christian dispensation no less than one hundred and four thousand sacramental wagons from our New Testament Joseph, freighted with the hope of life and immortality.

You hear the challenge of the Christian Church! It says: "I owe myself and my all to Jesus Christ, my head. I came from Him. There was a time when He only existed. Then came John the Baptist; and from that day I began to take on my growth. This is my story in epitome: First there were one; then two; then five; then twelve; then seventy; then one hundred and twenty; then five hundred; then three thousand; then fellowships of believers sprang up everywhere in the Holy Land; then the gospel boldly marched into all nations, until now, I count as my own four hundred million souls. I have come down the centuries through the apostolic succession, i.e., the succession of the Godly. I have come down through the creeds of Christendom; I have come down through the catacombs of Rome, and by means of the blood of martyrs, and the zeal of the missionary of the cross. I have come down the ages through architecture and painting and sculpture and music. I am a triumphant fact calling for faith. Explain me, O man, if you can, apart from the historic Christ!"

You know the challenge of the New Testament! It is the greatest small book in the libraries of earth. It is an easy thing to take into one's hand the New Testament and turn its pages; but do you estimate the New Testament aright? It is colossally sublime. It has no parallel in human language. It is the power of God among men. It is the critic of our thoughts. And it is all this because it enshrines the Christ. It exists to perpetuate the Master. The pens that wrote it were pens in the hands of men who either associated with Christ or with His disciples. Have you not often remarked this fact that contemporary literature takes no notice of the Master? The great writers of Greece and Rome who have the ear of the world ignore His existence. But He suffered not from this. His own wrote Him up with inspired pens and gave Him a literature that threw all other literatures into eclipse. My fellow men, Jesus Christ can for all time safely commit Himself to the New Testament. This is the challenge of the New Testament: "O man, match the divine Christ who walks my pages as the inspirational personage of all time." We do not wish to take up the challenge, and we do not wish to take it up because we are completely and absolutely satisfied with the New Testament Christ. He carries in Him the most glorious destiny possible to man.

You know the challenge of the Lord's Supper! Its challenge is perhaps the boldest and most satisfactory of all the challenges. It is perhaps the most heavily laden with good things of all the sacramental wagons which come to us from the palace of the king. We know that it carries in it the cross, and the communion of the saints. It is a glorious fellowship. It brings us the faith of scores of generations of believers, and the hosannahs of tens and tens of thousands of the saints. The Master says of it: "It is the New Testament in my blood." It is very bold in its self-assertion. In its challenge it names dates and places; a most dangerous thing to do, unless one is absolutely certain of his facts. It says: "I was instituted in Jerusalem, and in the upper room, and on the night in which the Master was betrayed." If it were not instituted then and there, it would be self-confuting. In view of this its challenge is the climax of boldness and honesty. It is all that any incredulous Jacob can ask. "It is enough."

Satisfied that the Lord's Supper is all that it claims to be, let us ascertain briefly just what it means to us; and what its sacred symbols utter to us on behalf of our New Testament Joseph, who is on the throne of heaven! And here we may be helped by the wagons which Joseph sent to Jacob.

The wagons declare to Jacob that there is somebody in Egypt who knows him and is thinking of him. The sacramental symbols declare to us that there is somebody in heaven who knows us and is thinking of us.

The wagons were expressly for Jacob. Joseph could not have spoken more distinctly or recognizably to Jacob, if he had spoken to him through the telephone of the twentieth century. The wagons annihilated distance. In them Joseph thought aloud and audibly; and his father heard his thoughts. As he listened to the story of the wagons, his heart said to him, "I am known in Egypt; and there is one exalted mind there who is thinking of me. He individualizes me." Are not these the very thoughts which communicants have as they receive the sacramental elements? "This is my body broken for you." What are these words but a personal address individualizing each disciple upon the part of the Master? Child of God, whoever you are, you are known in heaven, and in the sacrament of the Church. God sends you a personal assurance of your salvation through the cross of Christ.

The wagons declare to Jacob that there is somebody in Egypt who is planning for his comfort and making rich provision for him. The sacramental symbols declare to us that there is somebody in heaven planning for our comfort and making a rich provision for us.

Joseph's wagons and gifts were earnests of the future, and as such they gave Jacob confidence and satisfaction. The wagons were prophecies and promises. Because of them Jacob knew that Goshen, the choice valley of Egypt, was sure. Is not the Lord's Supper an earnest to us? Is it not the Master saying "Blésséd are they who are bidden to the marriage supper of the Lamb?" It is a foretaste of the fellowship of heaven. Men and women of God, overlook not the provision which God has made for His own. He has wagons for every spiritual Jacob. No Jacob need go footsore and weary through life. Every Jacob who walks and plods does so because he persistently refuses to ride. The wagons of God are running along every highway over which God calls us to travel. They are the golden-wheeled chariots of the promises; and they run hither and thither all through human life. Does God call you to run along the pathway of orphanage? There is a golden-wheeled chariot running that way: "I will be a father to the fatherless." Does God call you to run along the way of widowhood? There is a golden-wheeled chariot running that way: "I will be the husband of the widow." Does God call you to travel the *via dolorosa?* There is a golden-wheeled chariot running that way: "I will be with thee in six troubles, and in seven troubles I will deliver thee."

The wagons declare to Jacob that there is somebody in Egypt who loves him and can not be satisfied without his presence. The sacramental symbols declare to us there is somebody in heaven who loves us, and who can not be satisfied without our presence.

Joseph lived in the palace, and had the run of the kingdom; but there was a place in his life which his father only could fill, and that is why he sent the wagons. What do the sacramental symbols tell us but this: Tho heaven be full of glories, it will never satisfy God if His people be absent. It is a great thought, and it is full of comfort, viz., heaven will not be perfect to God until every wagon is in, and every saved soul has been brought home.

E. GRIFFITH-JONES

1860-1942

THE RELEASE OF SPIRITUAL POWER

BIOGRAPHICAL NOTE

PRINCIPAL and professor of theology and homiletics at the Yorkshire United Independent College, Bradford, England, since 1907; born at Merthyr-Tydfil, South Wales, in 1860; educated at the Presbyterian College, Carmarthen, 1875-78; New College and University College, London, 1880-85; graduated from the London University, 1882; served in the Congregational ministry at St. John's Wood, London, 1885-87; Llanelly, South Wales, 1887-90; Mount View, Strand Green, London, 1890-98; Balhan, 1898-1907; author of "The Ascent Through Christ," "Types of Christian Life," "The Master and His Method," "The Economics of Jesus," "Faith and Verification," etc.

"And behold, I send forth the promise of my Father upon you: but tarry ye in the city, until ye be clothed with power from on high."—Luke 24 : 49.

PERHAPS there is no feature of the last hundred years which will be considered in future ages so remarkable as the release of the natural forces pent up in all forms of matter, and their utilization in the service of humanity which has been achieved during this time. Mr. Alfred Russel Wallace, in his book on "The Wonderful Century," draws an instructive contrast between the beginning and the end of the period in this particular. In 1800 the human race, in respect to its control over the wild untutored forces of nature, was in much the same position as in the days of Hannibal; indeed, more advance has been made in the sovereignty over nature during this century than in the six or seven thousand years since the building of the pyramids. It is not merely that knowledge has advanced by leaps and bounds, that new sciences have been born and old ones perfected, that the lines of research have been pushed "many a furlong further into chaos," that a flood of light has been shed on the method of creation, on the origins of life, and on the development of the universe from its primal simplicity to the ordered complexities of its present state. It is all this, but it is more. It is that that kind of knowledge has vastly increased which means the unlocking of doors, the opening of secret places, the taming, as it were, of gigantic forces for the benefit of the race in all directions. The universe has been rediscovered from the human standpoint. We have found out that nature is not dead, but sleeping; that she hides behind her gentle, placid face a perfect whirlwind of pent-up force; that every particle of matter is a center of energy; that what we call solid substances are, really, but a system of interlocked but fiercely gyrating force-centers. The tremendous power of the new explosives is probably only a suggestion of the energies that slumber in every brick in our walls, in every flagstone beneath our feet, in every particle of food which we digest; and we have only to discover the secret of disturbing this equilibrium of matter to be able to blow the very globe into space. The puny body of man has always been the least important part of him; it is now of less account to him than ever, for the earth is being transformed into a kind of organism of which he is the nerve center; he is multiplying his limbs like a centipede, and forcing inanimate

244

nature to supply him with organs of motion which enable him to put distance and time to defiance. Already he can burrow in the earth like a mole, skim the ocean like a gull, and soon he will be able to fly over the continents like an eagle. By means of his far-reaching electric antennæ, he can speak and hear at a distance, see what takes place miles away, and draw pictures with the intangible pencil of light. In these days, when we can take a photograph through a brick wall, and carry on a conversation through miles of mountain or across vast stretches of ocean, there seems little else to expect by way of fresh wonders. And yet, we know that we have scarcely tapped the vast storage battery of natural force; and who shall tell what shall be in the end thereof?

All this is by way of preamble to a still more wonderful vision. Christianity was born of two great events. The first was the coming of Jesus in the flesh, which was the dawn of a new science—the revelation of God, which had been hidden in a mystery from the foundation of the world, a revelation which was also a redemption; the second was the descent of the Spirit at Pentecost, which brought into the world a new power. Jesus brought us the gospel, the "good news" of God, of His willingness to forgive, and save, and renew the spiritual forces of life; and at Pentecost the Holy Spirit of promise came as a spiritual force, which transformed the "knowledge of God" into the "power of God." Luke gives us the story of the revelation, a revelation in deed and in suffering, as well as in word, in his gospel; and he gives the story of how this was transformed into the spirit of power in the Acts.

At the time when this text was spoken, the disciples stood midway between these two critical events. The gospel of redemption had received its finishing touch in the resurrection of our Lord from the dead; the fair fabric of the perfect life was complete from base to pinnacle. But as yet the forces concentrated in that holy and beautiful gospel of truth and life and love were inoperative; the secret of turning the new knowledge of God into the power of God was not yet theirs. And Jesus, in His parting message, told them to wait. They must not hurry the process; they were not to be impatient; presently something would happen to them, if only they would prepare themselves quietly for it, which would bring the full fruits of His gospel within their reach. Meanwhile they were to "tarry in the city until" the hour when "the Spirit of power" would break forth from the unseen, and the Word would no longer be "with" them as an incarnate Presence, but "in" them as an immanent life. "And, behold, I send forth the promise of the Father upon you; but tarry ye in the city, until ye be clothed with power from on high."

Of what kind of situation does this remind us? How shall I phrase the parallel I wish to draw more vividly?

I think of a tidal channel, and of a vessel ready for a long and adventurous voyage. The cargo is all on board, the steam is in the boilers, the fires are burning brightly in the furnaces. All the arrangements for the voyage have been completed; there is nothing wanted so far as preparedness is concerned. But there is no movement seaward. The captain and the crew are waiting for something; something that can neither be hurried nor controlled. That something is the rising of the tide. The vessel is made for the sea, not the land, and whatever her equipment, she will not move till that tide lifts her, and provides the channel deep enough for her displacement. But directly that tide does come, the engines will begin to throb, the vast bulk will begin to move, the helm will begin to direct her course, and so the voyage will be started.

Or, I think of something else, still nearer the heart of my subject. I think of the trees in winter, standing leafless and rugged against a pale sky, or fighting with rude and stormy winds; and of the brown fields, and of the gardens where no flowers grow. The world seems dead; life seems as tho it had fled away to some younger planet. But we know better than that, for we have seen this before. Life is really busy, not, indeed, with the twigs and leaves and blossoms, but with the roots of life. Far below the surface they are storing up the moisture, and transforming the soil by that hidden process of vital chemistry which goes on all the winter, into "something new and strange." Yet nothing seems to happen at all for a long time. Week follows week, and month crawls after month, with no sign of life anywhere. The roots, indeed, can do no more; they are full of sap; but they are powerless to lift it through trunk and branch to the buds at their extremities. But wait a little longer, till the poor old earth that has lost the fires of her youth, and now depends on the kindly sun for her annual quickening, has turned herself toward the cherishing heat that pours down upon her; and one day you realize suddenly that the leaves are out, and that spring has come, clothing the world in garments of beauty and light.

Now, there are periods of recurring spiritual barrenness and inability that come upon the souls of men, alternating with periods of freshness and vitality. It is difficult to account for the law of periodicity which somehow rules the forces of religious progress, but that there is such a law is unquestionable. There are times of creative power in the career of nations, as well as individuals; when great thinkers, great poets, great preachers rise, and mighty movements are set going, and mighty things are done; and there are other periods when it would seem as tho heaven had retired to some distant part of the sky, and all things great and good were impossible. Am I wrong in thinking that just now we are rather in the trough than on the crest of the wave? Not only in matters of religion, but in matters of social and political progress, we are not having an easy or happy time. Immense efforts are being made to better the world. It is an age of reformers. Every one is a reformer nowadays; utopias are thick as blackberries in September; the State is split up into parties who are fiercely contending as to who shall be the first to put the world right. New theologies battle with old theologies, till the air is thick with dust, and the combatants can scarcely see or hear one another for the noise and clamor. And yet somehow nothing seems to be happening. The vessel of progress labors heavily as tho in a place where two (or many) seas meet, and men turn hither and thither, uncertain as to whom to listen to, and in what direction to trace their steps. There is much effort, but little progress; much turmoil, but little life; many voices, but no all-commanding message that carries conviction. Our churches are marking time, and many of them are living on their past; there is a sense of disillusionment and fear in the dumb, unthinking multitude that has largely lost faith in its religious leaders. We seem to be between two worlds, "one dead, the other powerless to be born." In theology, especially, we are in a distracted and troublous state; and when theology is distracted, religion is paralyzed, for if our ideas of God and the soul are in utter confusion, how shall we act confidently and live happily, or do anything noble and good? I do not wish to put the case too strongly, or to give forth a Cassandra message; and yet, who can deny that these things are so? And if these things are so, what are we to do or think? Let me ask you to come back to the text, and the situation it embodied. These men, who were about to part from their Master for the last time in visible form, were in just this situation that I have described. They were in a strait between two great epochs in their life, and in their relation with Him. The period of their earthly communion with Him was over. They were not quite ripe for the period of His spiritual presence within their hearts. They had received the gospel in all its fulness; they had seen and come to know the Father through the Son; but they had not come to that experience which would turn the knowledge they had into power. What was lacking in their experience before the power would come?

Two things were lacking: First, they lacked that insight into the meaning of the wonderful Life that had been lived in their presence, which enabled them to understand the gospel which it embodied. Tho Jesus had been with them for several years in daily communion; tho they had heard His message, and witnessed the great deeds He had wrought, and felt the perpetual play of His love around them; tho they had seen Him die, and rise again from the dead, they were not possest of the key to the mystery of their Master's person and purpose. In a sense, they were too near the events to realize their tremendous importance; too much under the spell of the physical presence of Christ to know Him for what and who He was. A period of quiet meditation over all that they had seen and felt and handled of the Word of Life was needed, during which the strange, harrowing, soul-stirring events through which they had passed, might have time and opportunity to range themselves in order and fall into their natural perspective. Great events do not unfold their significance to us at the moment; they need a certain distance in order to be seen in their majesty of meaning; they can be duly interpreted only when thrown up into relief against the background of time and circumstance. And so they were told to tarry a while in the city and spend their time in thought and prayer for light on the mystery and perplexity that filled their minds. And that light which they needed could only come from above. They were to wait in faith and hope, sure that their Master would not fail them in their need. The promise was given to them, "And behold! I send forth the promise of my Father upon you." The spirit of truth was to lead them into all the truth concerning Himself. Enlightenment must precede realization; the power could only come through illumination.

But even this was not enough. It would be a great mistake to imagine that the disciples entered at Pentecost into the fulness of either the light or the power of the Christian faith. In the first blaze of that sunrise, they were filled with enough light to give them great power—a power that swept multitudes into the fold of believers, and created the first church. But it is clear that it was long ere they realized the manifold meanings of the gospel which they preached with such acceptance; and the means by which they came into the fulness of light and power was self-forgetful service, the outpouring of their hearts in love and solicitude over the souls of their fellow men. The gospel light and the gospel power were only slowly and gradually revealed as they "lived the life," and tested the truth in the stress and storm of their experience of its value. The New Testament literature is the record of successive stages in the expansion of the light of the knowledge of the love of God shining in the face of Jesus Christ, and in the deepening and spreading of the power that slumbered in it. By preaching and teaching in many lands; by meeting persecutions and distresses, and sorrows manifold, in the name and for the sake of their Master, with unflinching courage, and unwearied love, and unbroken patience, and undying hope; by working for the gospel, and by suffering for it, they lived their way into its innermost secret and power; and so Christianity became a "light to the Gentiles" and a power that "turned the world upside down."

We have been passing recently through a kind of *résumé* of the experience of the first Christians in our relation to the story and person of Jesus Christ. The cry of the last fifty years in theology has been "back to Christ," the idea being that it was our duty to come into fresh and living acquaintance with the human life of Jesus in its historical environment, and as He lived and moved among men. To this end all the resources of scholarship, critical and historical, have been directed. Every foot of ground has been traversed, every line of literature has been ransacked that could enrich our materials for seeing Jesus; who and what manner of man He was. The result is now practically complete. We are not likely to know more about the man, Christ Jesus, than has been already ascertained. And we may as well be thankful for the wonderful freshening of the world's interest in the human Christ. It has brought home, as never before, the sense of His oneness with ourselves. It has opened out as never before the naturalness, as well as the unspeakable beauty and loftiness of the perfect life He lived. And this it has done to most of us without removing from the personality of Jesus that element of a divine mystery which in all ages has been the crowning attribute of His nature, as well as the deepest source of His fascination and ascendency over the human soul. Let us devoutly thank God for all that criticism—historical, textual, rational, spiritual, and whatnot—has done for the better realization of Jesus Christ as a man among men—and the man of all men.

And yet, can we really say that this closer knowledge has done very much so far for a clearer understanding of His divine message for our own day and generation? Is the meaning of Christ as clear to us as to our forefathers, who had so distorted and unreal an idea of the earthly conditions of the incarnation of the Son of God? Is it not true that with less knowledge they had more light than we seem to have? Did not they live nearer than we do to Him who once appeared in the flesh, but who is evermore with His

people by His Spirit? Have we not been burrowing too much in the far-off centuries for Him who was once dead, but who is alive for evermore? The Jesus who lived in the first century will be nothing better than a picturesque and beautiful figure in history unless we can realize that He has been at work through all the centuries between, and that we can never understand Him nor receive the promise of the Father from Him till we say with Paul: "Yea, even tho we have known him after the flesh, yet know we him so no more." There is nothing the Church needs just now more than a fresh grasp of the meaning of the gospel of the divine Person for our own day and generation. We need the light that we may realize the power.

This light can only come as it came to the first disciples: first, by waiting upon God in humble dependence on His holy spirit which can only come from Himself; and then by a courageous application of the light we have to the needs and problems, individual and social, of the day. The secret of Christ can only be learned by those who are prepared to receive His influence into their heart of hearts, and then to obey His word with a willing mind and a single eye. It is because there is so little of this among us that our religion has fallen into temporary disrepute among those who need it most, the toiling masses for whom the great heart of Jesus agonized and yearned so deeply, and for whom He died, and for whom He now lives and works in the unseen world, which we think of as so far, but which is so terribly beautifully near to us all. "The word is still nigh thee, even at the doors." And when that power once more comes—as come it will—what then?

Ah, then once more we shall see signs and wonders. Right through the ages we can see that power at work, now silently gathering force in secret channels, anon swelling into a flood, inundating multitudes, filling the Church with energy, and overflowing into the wide world with its healing, uplifting, enabling influence. I believe that through these lean and barren years this power has been gathering force for a fresh advance, and that we are on the eve of a great outpouring of spiritual blessing throughout the world. It may not come along the old paths—indeed, it has never come as men expected it to come; it always cuts its own channels and shapes its own instruments of expression; there is always a great unexpectedness about a spiritual revival, both in its methods and in its results. Our wisdom will be to be open-minded as well as open-hearted, and to welcome the light as it breaks into power, however unfamiliar the way in which it will come. "The wind [spirit] bloweth where it listeth; thou hearest the sound thereof, but canst not tell whence it cometh nor whither it goeth."

But if we do not know in what manner God will express His will and send forth His spirit into our midst, we do know what its outcome will be. Now as ever, it will issue in a renewed sense of the forgiving love of God in Christ; now, as ever, it will cleanse guilty consciences from their sorrow and their despair through faith in the eternal cross; now, as ever, it will move the hopeless and helpless to turn to the Lord with the immemorial cry, "What must I do to be saved?" with a sense of victory over the sin that doth so easily beset them. Old things will pass away; behold, all things shall become new.

And the evangel to the individual will not be the only note of the coming revival. The times are ripe for a great social evangel; and it will come, if we only wait and work in faith. Not by hard mechanical schemes and artificial man-made utopias will this good thing for which we are all waiting and praying come; but by filling all parties in Church and State with a new enthusiasm for humanity; by breaking down the suspicions and the antagonisms of class against class; by filling men with a passion for righteousness and a love for what is just and fair between those who think and those who work, those who lead and those who can only follow. Grant this new temper—and a new temper always follows a new revival of spiritual life, whether in the individual or the community—and all our insoluble enigmas will become easy to deal with; the impossibilities of to-day will become the commonplaces of to-morrow. I venture to call you away from the poor polemics of the hour to the larger duty that presses at our door and demands our undivided attention. We may well forget the clashings of new theologies and old, with all their unworthy suspicions and recriminations and personalities, and to set ourselves to the real task of

the hour, which is to wait on God, and join hands in doing His work. The world is athirst for the living God, and the living God is athirst for the world. Shall we, then, divide into parties, and schools, and coteries of thought? Shall we say again, "I am of Paul," and "I am of Apollos," and "I am of Christ?" "Is Christ, then, divided?" Rather let us lift up our eyes, and see the fields, how they are already ripe unto harvest, and verily the laborers are few. Let us pray that the Lord of harvest may send His servants into the harvest; let us pray that He may make us ready to toil and to suffer and to bleed in the sacred holy task of winning the world to Him who is its Lord and their Savior. The more I study the conditions and temper of our age, the more is the impression borne in on my mind that great social and religious forces are moving in uneasy slumber, and that they will break forth presently into activity. The question is, Who shall stand at the side of the reawakened Demos and say: "Loose him, and let him go?" Shall it be the spirit of Christ or the spirit of secularism? Is religion to be degraded into a department of economics, or is it to hold its place at the source and head of things—the great moving, inspiring force for social progress and for personal salvation? The result will depend on the attitude taken by the Church of Christ in this hour of crisis and trial. Our opportunity, I believe, is almost unparalleled in the history of our faith, to carry the gospel of the blesséd God to a weary and hungry world; and in doing this we shall be as one heart and one mind, as were the disciples when the spirit fell on their wondering hearts, kindling tongues of flame and setting loose torrents of renewing power.

FRANK W. GUNSAULUS

1856-1921

THE BIBLE VS. INFIDELITY

BIOGRAPHICAL NOTE

FRANK WAKELY GUNSAULUS was born at Chesterville, Ohio, in 1856. He graduated from Ohio Wesleyan University in 1875. For some years he was pastor of Plymouth Church, Chicago, and then became pastor of Central Church, Chicago. He was president of the Armour Institute of Technology. He was a fascinating speaker, having a clear, resonant voice, and a dignified presence. His mind was a storehouse of the best literature, and his English style was noted for its purity and richness. He is the author of several books and was in popular demand as a lecturer.

There are, it may be, so many kinds of voices in the world, and none of them is without signification.— I Cor. xiv., 10.

OURS is a voiceful era. Perhaps, as the ages come and go and man's life grows richer, its questions more restless for answer, its moral supports called upon to bear heavier interests of faith, its enterprises more often and searchingly compelled to defend themselves, the voices of time will be increasingly potent and worthy of his attention. A singularly suggestive collection of messages fills the air to-day, and all of these voices speak of one theme—the Bible.

Anarchy, which is always atheistic, holds its converse in the places of evil which this book's message would close forever; the foes of that civilization builded on its laws and stimulated by its hopes asks us to condemn it as worthy only of caricature, vituperation, and hate. Let us find a path of duty to-day, not refusing to listen to any of these voices, but asking that other voices also may help us to the truth.

The preacher's message is a book called the Bible. That is only the literary form of his message—telling its history. Even that form, which is much less divine as paper and ink are less lofty in the scale than humanity, has worked wonders. To-day, the Bible offers the nineteenth-century infidel as testimony of the influence it has. It has force enough to make infidelity preach tearfully and well about man, woman, and child. Skepticism did not do so well until the Bible came. The Bible has furnished the eloquence of infidelity with such a man as Shakespeare to talk about; no student of literature could imagine Shakespeare without the Bible and the Bible's influence upon him as he created his dreams. It furnished an Abraham Lincoln for an orator to compare favorably with incomplete ideas of Almighty God; but it seems to have been unable to show the critic that Christian ideas of Almighty God made Lincoln so love the Lord's Prayer that he wanted a church builded with this as its creed. It would seem that any general denunciation or humorous caricature of a book which has worked such an amazing effect in literature as has the Bible would be tempered by some recognition of the fact that these other minds—poets, orators, sages, and scientists—have found illumination and help in its pages. Liberal Christianity will be intellectually broad. Certainly the greatest of modern pagans, Goethe, will not be accused of favoritism toward the Bible, yet he said: "I esteem the gospels to be thoroughly genuine, for there shines forth from them the reflected splendor of a sublimity, proceeding from the person of Jesus Christ, of so divine a kind as only the divine could ever have manifested upon earth." The Earl of Rochester saw that the only liberalism which objects to the Bible, in its true uses, is the liberalism of licentiousness; and he left this saying: "A bad heart is the great argument against this holy book." And Faraday, weeping, said: "Why will people go astray when they have this blest book to guide them?"

If we turn to literature we encounter many such liberal thinkers as Theodore Parker, who calmly informs us: "This collection of books has taken such a hold upon the world as has no other. The literature of Greece, which goes up like incense from that land of temples and heroic deeds, has not half the influence of this book. It goes equally to the cottage of the plain man and the palace of the king. It is woven into the literature of the scholar and colors the talk of the street." That is the voice of the liberalism which includes rather than excludes.

These were men not of the band of evangelical Christian preachers, who are roughly classed as a set of persons unable to tell the truth about the Bible, for fear they may lose their means of subsistence; these are men who know the true mission of the Bible. It is not to furnish a picture of life in the time of Moses such as life ought to be, a portrait of a David for the imitation of men, a statue of a warrior in a time of barbarism who shall command my obedience to his commands now, an idea of God wrought out in ignorance and darkness, which has no self-development within it. The mission of the Bible is to furnish a humanly written account of a people, just as human as we, in whom, by divine inspiration, the soul of truth so lived and worked as to develop, in gradual course, by laws, by hopes, by loves, by life, a living, and, at last, perfectly authoritative ideal of righteousness, but more than all a gradual growth of such moral power as would be commanding in the redeeming self-sacrifice and love of Jesus Christ. Every page of the Old Testament was only preparatory, as the thorny bush is preparatory for the rose. Christ is the end of the long, weary human history that leads to Him. If the laws of Sinai had been enough, there never would have been a Calvary. No one for a moment dreams that the God of nature could have brought forth such a fruit as the life and ideas of Jesus without a tree of such a history a tree rooted in the ground, storm-twisted, gnarled, and valuable only for its fruit. We are not asked to eat the roots and bark and branches; only the

fruit has an appeal to us. Its appeal is to our hunger, its authority lies in the fact that it satisfies our hunger.

It has satisfied the hunger of men whose liberalism came from their being made liberally. Large and capacious souls of mighty yearnings are they. They stand in contrast with the puny critics who assert that the Bible fails to feed them, because they have never tasted its nourishment.

Liberal Christianity, separating itself from the dogmatism which would make Christianity a book religion, worshiping a literary idol rather than loving a human revelation of the divine, knows it is not an ignorant lot of men and women who have received most from the Bible and spoken most gratefully of its message. When we think of sending the Bible to barbarism, with the hope of creating in its stead civilization, we can look into the face of John Selden, one of the most illustrious of English lawyers, when he says: "I have surveyed most of the learning that is among the sons of men, yet at this moment I can recall nothing in them on which to rest my soul, save one from the sacred Scriptures, which rises much on my mind. It is this: 'The grace of God, which bringeth salvation, hath appeared unto all men, teaching us that denying ungodliness and worldly lusts, we should live soberly, righteously, and godly in this present world, looking for that blest hope and the glorious appearing of the great God and our Savior Jesus Christ, who gave himself for us that he might redeem us unto himself, a peculiar people zealous of good works.'" Liberal religion must include Selden. We will not be deterred from giving the Bible to heathenism of any kind when we remember that Sir William Jones has left these words: "The Scriptures contain more true sublimity, more exquisite beauty, and finer strains of poetry and eloquence than could be collected from all other books that were ever composed in any age or in any idiom." Liberal religion must be as broad as Sir William Jones.

This is a very needy world, and many are the institutions of evil that need to be changed for institutions of goodness. If we are to believe the eloquence of hopeless unbelief, we ourselves will only be the slaves of a fatalism which says that man is but a result of forces; that what we call crime is but a part of the necessary course of things, and that there is no such thing as moral responsibility. This makes all reform or efforts at staying the tide of evil useless. Oftentimes the heart of the man who has ceased to read his Bible gets the victory over this dreadful philosophy, and it is not remarkable that the skeptic becomes the exponent of freedom, charging like a host of war upon all institutions of slavery. Liberal theology puts its one hand on the dogmatist who tells him to accept literal infallibility, and its other on the sincere lover of men who has lost his Bible entirely. And liberalism says: It is in just such moments that we trust our Bible the most, and we remember that William Wilberforce, who lifted the chains from the bondmen, has said: "I never knew happiness until I found Christ as a Savior. Read the Bible! Read the Bible! Through all my perplexities and distresses I never read any other book, I never knew the want of any other." We are certainly not despising the science which is worthy of a name, nor are we forgetting any proposition which has found a place in the world's thought, if we look into the face of Sir John Herschel, who tells us that "all human discoveries seem to be made only for the purpose of confirming more and more strongly the truths contained in the holy Scriptures." It is truly no part of wisdom for us to conclude that for scientific reasons we ought to forsake our Bible when Professor Dana avers: "The grand old book of God still stands; and this old earth, the more its leaves are turned and pondered, the more will it sustain and illustrate the sacred Word."

Surely it is not the hour dogmatically to withdraw this book, which has proved the basis of civilization. Professor Lyell, the great English geologist, tells us: "In the year 1806 the French Institute enumerated no less than eighty geological theories which were hostile to the Scriptures, but not one of these theories is held to-day." Bacon's remark is still true: "There never was found in any age of the world either religion or law that did so highly exalt the public good as the Bible." And John Marshall and Prince Bismarck agree with Daniel Webster when he says: "If we abide by the principles taught in the Bible our country will go on prospering and to prosper; but if we and our posterity neglect its instructions and authority no man can tell how sudden a catastrophe may overwhelm us and bury all our glory in profound obscurity." There is not an anarchist in America who does not clap his hands when he hears a Bible with the Ten Commandments and the Sermon on the Mount denounced. Indeed, the civilization in which we stand, as compared with the barbarism out of which we have been led by the Bible, would make William Henry Seward's assertion only a mild statement of the truth when he says: "The whole hope of human progress is suspended on the ever-growing influence of the Bible." I prefer lawyers like these to lead American public opinion. Part of the service of these men has been that they have shown theology that the Bible is not a set of texts on a dead level of authority and equal value, but the revealing, slow and sure, of an inspiration obeyed by a certain people in the realm of morals like that inspiration obeyed by another people in the realm of art, and its test is: Does the Bible's ultimate message, its crowning commandment of Christ's life and love, produce goodness in morals? just as the test of the long revelation of beauty in his ancestors and the Greek is, does its ultimate commandment produce goodness in art.

Christianity does not ask: "What think ye of the Bible?" It asks: "What think ye of Christ?" There the throne is set, and so majestic is His glory that the moment we come into His presence we are judged. The Judge of the earth has taken His place in thought, history and hope. He is not on trial, and He asks no question as to what man thinks of the book which has enthroned Him in literature. The test is placed in my conduct and yours; each may say with Michael Bruce, who left these words on the fly-leaf of his Bible:

'Tis very vain of me to boast
How small a price this Bible cost;
The day of judgment will make clear
'Twas very cheap or very dear.

Shall we go forward with our Bible or backward without it? Infidelity has always forgotten that, so far as it has an eye for liberty and humanity, the Christianity not of sects but of the Bible has furnished it and trained it. The liberalism which puts its Bible aside will acknowledge that a Christless humanity culminated in Rome. Skepticism is often eloquent when it tries to show how much "fragments of Roman art" had to do with the making of modern civilization. Now, as Rome marks the height to which humanity without a Bible ascended, it would seem that this would be just the point where free and untrammeled thought and the fullest intellectual liberty would be found. Right there, where a Christless race was supreme, ought to be the place where the liberty abounded which the religion of Christ is said to destroy.

Whose program for the production of intellectual and spiritual liberty can liberals accept? Hoarse is the cry: The Bible is to be cast out. We look and behold men who have these opinions sitting on the throne of the Cæsars. Now, one would suppose the intellect of that whole realm would have fair play. There was no Bible there to fetter or to annoy. This ought to be the halcyon age for "the liberty of man, woman and child." These rulers have the same dignified abhorrence for all kinds of religion. The skeptic Lucretius says: "The fear of the lower world must be sent headlong forth. It poisons life to its lowest depths; it spreads over all things the blackness of death; it leaves no pleasure unalloyed." I match the Roman with the phrase of a recent orator of this school who spoke of the soldiers dead, as now "sleeping beneath the shadows of the clouds, careless alike of sunshine or of storm, each in the windowless palace of rest." There was no window in the grave when more illustrious and original skeptics talked about it. Modern infidelity has many expressions on the future after death which sound like the old Roman distich, "I was not, and became; I was, and am no more."

Its orator, bending over the body of his dear brother, said nothing more touching than did Tacitus over the grave of Agricola, as he wrote: "If there is a place for the spirits of the pious; if, as the wise suppose, great souls do not become extinct with their bodies; if"—oh, that age of "if" ought to have been an age when every brain was free and no thought or sentiment were a chain. The Bible of Christianity was not powerful enough to throttle anybody. Its pages were not all written; its authors were hunted and outcast. Morals, too, ought to have been all right, for we are told that they are independent of God and Christ.

But what is the fact? Strangely enough, in that age, when nearly every monarch, or poet, or philosopher was a humorous skeptic and they had no Christian religion to "bind their hands," in an age when nothing but this sort of infidelity was supreme, Seneca, to whom connoisseurs in ethics blandly turn when they grow weary of the strenuous Paul or the pensive John, Seneca, while he wrote a book on poverty, has a fortune of $15,000,000, with a house full of citrus tables made of veined wood brought from Mount Atlas. While he framed moral precepts which we are besought to substitute for the Sermon on the Mount, he was openly accused of constant and shameless iniquity, and was leading his distinguished and tender pupil, Nero, into those practises and preparing him for those atrocities which Seneca himself had upon his own soul while he wrote his book on clemency. At that hour the Bible Christianity offered to the world's heart and aspiration, not a book, not a theorist of morals, but a man for the leadership of humanity, and, of that Man the literary and calm French skeptic says: "Jesus will never be surpassed." In the age of Rome, when people were not burdened by churches or Bibles, Lucian says: "If any one loves wealth and is dazed by gold; if any one measures happiness by purple and power; if any one brought up among flatterers and slaves has never had a conception of liberty, frankness and truth; if any one has wholly surrendered himself to pleasure, full tables, carousals, lewdness, sorcery, and deceit, let him go to Rome."

There was no Bible either to preach against it or to interfere with it. These things were the product then, as they are now, of infidelity. Whenever the world wishes a civilization so barbarous as that, the reviler of the Bible must create it, for they have the applause of evil and the good-will of crime. In

the age of Rome, when this skepticism was the creed of the State, Nero got tired of the goddess Astarte, and murdered his own brother, his wife, and his mother, and the senate was so affected with the same opinion that they heard his justification and proceeded to heap new honors upon him. He threw the preacher Paul into jail, but there Paul wrought out the impulse of Europe. In the age when the great Livy said that "neglect of gods" had come, Caligula let loose his imperial frenzy, and every stream of blood that could be sent toward the sea carried its red tide. In that age when, like later eloquent critics, Ennius said that he did not believe that the gods thought of human beings, "for if the gods concerned themselves about the human race the good would prosper and the bad suffer," the courtesan was kept for pleasure and the wife for domestic slavery. In that happy age of unbelief, when Menander sung "the gods do not care for men," "the homes were," according to Juvenal, "broken up before the nuptial garland faded"; and according to Tertullian, "they married only to be divorced." Friends exchanged wives; infanticide and other hellish crimes were common. This is what that spirit, in its purity, did for the home, when there was no Bible to read at its hearthstone and no New Testament to put into the hands of young lovers departing to make a new rooftree.

Labor will some day be too liberal to give up its Bible. In that age, when "God was dead"; in that age, when "the gods had abdicated"; they said, "the mechanic's occupation is degrading. A workshop is incompatible with anything noble." The curse of slavery had blotted the name of labor, and they agreed that "a purchased laborer is better than a hired one," and thousands of prison-like dwellings rose to conceal the myriads of slaves. In that age Nero, who had the same opinion about God which the vaunting spirit which calls itself liberal has to-day, had a "golden house" as large as a city, with colonnades a mile long, and within it a statue of Nero 120 feet high. That is what the theory of infidelity did for labor and the working man when it was on the throne. Do you wonder that from that day to this the "carpenter's son" of the Bible has been scoffed at by this infidelity?

In that age, when the theories of infidelity ruled, the gladiators made wet with their blood the great enclosure of the arena. The women and timid girls of Rome gave lightly the sign of death. The crowd shook the building with applause as the palpitating body was dragged by a hook into the deathchamber, and slaves turned up the bloody soil and covered the blood-dabbled earth with sand that the awful amusement might go on. All this was allowed by infidelity in its purity, before it had been influenced by the Christian's Bible into believing that such things are atrocious.

Oh, when I hear infidelity prate of the horrors of slavery and defend a Godless theory of the State, I remember that those who had it in its purity did not regard the slave as a man. When I read the story of slavery and hear an exponent of free thought say, "The doctrine that woman is a slave or serf of man —whether it comes from hell or heaven, from God or demon, from the golden streets of the New Jerusalem, or the very Sodom of perdition—is savagery pure and simple," I say, "That is so, but just that was the ruling idea when infidelity was on the throne of Rome." And only where the Bible has gone and triumphed has woman the privileges which are thus praised.

When I hear it said: "Slavery includes all other crimes. It is the joint product of the kidnaper, pirate, thief, murderer, and hypocrite. It degrades labor and corrupts leisure. To lacerate the naked back, to sell wives, to steal babes, to debauch your soul—this is slavery," I answer: "That is so," and I add that all these and a thousand other damnable features of slavery were seen in Rome when the whole Roman people felt and spoke about the message of the Bible just as your type of liberalism does to-day.

To all this wretched state of man what offers came from Seneca, whom skepticism quotes as a moralist? Why, he said: "Admire only thyself"; and when he saw that a man must get out of himself, he said: "Give thyself to philosophy." Not philosophy, but the power of the Bible's Christ has lifted man upward to his highest life.

If ever anti-Christianity had a chance to show its beauty, it was when it was at its supreme strength, and when Christianity was a babe in the manger; and these are only suggestions of the hell it dug for man at Rome. You say that it was not what skepticism is at the present day, and I acknowledge that it is so. Why? Because nineteen centuries have rolled like waves of light between, and Christ has improved it in spite of itself. Never had the world so good a chance to see what almost absolute skepticism and unbelief could and would do for the liberty of the human soul as then. But when the thrones of Rome were occupied with men who held the same opinion of the Bible as he does to-day, what was the freedom of the race?

The scene all comes back. Here is a little, obscure set of poor people who follow the words and life of the son of a carpenter. They are powerful in nothing that Rome calls power. But Rome says that they shall not think that way. Celsus, from whom our less scholarly skepticism is ready to borrow arguments, was not enough for the new thought

in the arena of debate, and they cried for another arena. Let us remember that unbelief, in its purity at that date, was so offended at nothing as at the fact that the Church said: "Christian justice makes all equal who bear the name of man," and that Paul said: "There is neither bond nor free, but ye are all one in Christ Jesus." Nothing so offended the representative of free thought in that period as the fact that a rich Roman, in the time of Trajan, having become a Christian, presented freedom to his 1,250 slaves on an Easter day. And, in all that time, when poor Christians with the funds of the Church were privately buying the freedom of slaves, I do not find that a base liberalism believed in liberty. Neither did it believe in freedom of thought. It is the blossom of egotism; it has nothing to which it bows; it beholds no majesty to which it can look up. It is sublime self-conceit, and it has no hesitancy in telling the whole human race that at its grandest moments it has been wrong. This egotism dared to become active in Rome, and it asked the Christians, in the person of the Emperor, to worship him, and to strew incense about him. "I will honor the Emperor," said Theophilus, "not by worshiping him, but by praying for him." Such men as that infidelity kindly put to death. Around their quivering limbs the infidelity of that day made the fagots to flame, and it taught the red tongues of cruel death to creep about their smoking bodies.

Men who believed that the Bible's influence was what infidelity says it is, made the funeral pyre for Polycarp, the populace bringing fuel for the fire, and while the flames made a glory of their lambent glare, he cried out: "Six and eighty years have I served him and he has done me nothing but good, and how could I curse him, my Lord and Savior. If you would know what I am, I tell you frankly, I am a Christian." He did his own thinking, and was brave enough to avow his opinion, for which hate of Christianity duly burned him. This was the way infidelity treated free speech. In that way it unchained the soul of Polycarp. Infidelity's idea of Christianity sent the martyrs of Numidia and Paulus out of the world while they were praying for their murderers. Who believed in freedom then? Infidelity's idea of the message of the Bible followed the Christian like a wild beast, and in the catacomb of Calixtus drew from the pursued soul the pathetic exclamation: "Oh, sorrowful times, when we can not even in caves escape our foes!" And all this was true, because they said, "Recompense to no man evil for evil"; "Pray for them that despitefully use you and persecute you."

This spirit of hate has had at least one holiday at the expense of Christian faith. On the night of the 18th of July, 64, Rome was swept with fire. Six days and nights it raged. Ruined was the world's metropolis and excited were the wo-stricken people. Nero, whose opinions of Christianity, by the way, were wonderfully like the orator's, was king, and the people suspected that this royal monster did it. Men told of how he exulted over the sea of flame as he watched it from the tower of Mæcenas; and whatever the truth of this may be, it is certain that for the rage of the people Nero must have a victim, and Tacitus tells us that he charged the Christians with the crime. Then opened in Rome the awful carnival of bloodshed that the orator never mentions, in which horrible modes of torture and excruciating methods of producing pain vied with each other in satisfying the demands of death. Women bound to raging bulls and dragged to death were not without the companionship of others who, in the evening, in Nero's garden, were coated with pitch, covered with tar, bound to stakes of pine, lighted with fire, and sent to run aflame with the hatred of Christianity. Through the crowd of sufferers a gentleman, who was ultra-liberal as the orator, drove about, fantastically attired as a charioteer, and the people were wild with delight. Domitian had the same ideas, and severe were his persecutions of the new heresy. This was the day on which infidelity was so full of the love of freedom that it cried: "The Christians to the lions!"

And so I might recount to you how for hundreds of years the Church found out how early and unchristianized infidelity loved freedom of thought. To a type of liberals, it has for years seemed a joy to go to the places in the old world and note how intolerant the Church has been. Now I suggest to any one that he go and visit some of the places where men who thought of Christianity as negativism thinks showed their faith and its fruits. Let him go to the Colosseum and ask the winds that moan over its ruins what they know of the history of infidelity. The winds will hush in that wreck of stupendous magnificence, and with an eloquence gathered from seventeen centuries they will tell him a story that will cause a flow of tears, for much of infidelity is of noble heart. They will tell him how the marble seats were crowded with thousands; again will sweep upward the shout of the excited throng; before him there will lie a half-dead Christian martyr, and near that pool of blood will stand a lion who has satiated his horrid thirst.

They will tell him how infidelity made that splendid place a temple of the furies, how it laughed and yelled and applauded, as it amused itself with that spectacle of horror. They will tell him how the underground passages served to keep and cage wild beasts, and how those who then hated Christianity starved the fierce lion until his eyes rolled in hot

hunger and his teeth were sharpened with its agony. They will tell him how the infidelity of that day put balls of fire on the backs of the lions, and how the madness of their passion was increased by scattering hated colors about, tearing the beasts with iron hooks and beating them with cruel whips. They will tell how the Christian was made to fight these infuriated beasts without weapons, while infidelity was frantic with applause. It said "no" to the torn body yonder, that was mangled and supplicating in blood for life. I would have him stand there until, in after years, in a nobler strain than that of Byron, he could say:

And thou didst shine, thou rolling moon, upon
All this, and cast a wide and tender light,
Which softened down the hoar austerity
Of rugged desolation.

.   .   .   .

Till the place
Became religion, and the heart ran o'er
With silent worship of the great of old!
The dead but sceptered sovereigns who still rule
Our spirits from their urns.

So long as I know what this book has been and done, so long as man's history will not allow me to risk the interests of society with the infidelity which has so often demoralized it, so long will I yearn to get the Bible and its message to all men. It has been our world's best book. With this book as inspiration and resource, William Tyndale and Miles Coverdale were so to continue and complete the task of The Venerable Bede and John Wyclif as to make an epoch in the history of that language to be used by Shakespeare and Burke—an era as distinct as that which Luther's Bible so soon should mark in the history of a language to be such a potent instrument in the hands of Goethe and Hegel. For this very act of heresy, Tyndale was to be called "a full-grown Wyclif," and Luther "the redeemer of his mother-tongue." With the Bible, Calvin was to conceive republics at Geneva, and Holbein to paint, in spite of the iconoclasm of the Reformation, the faces of Holy Mother and Saint, and in spite of the cruelty of the Church, scripturally conceived satires illustrating the sale of indulgences. With that book Gustavus Vasa was to protect and nurture the freedom of the land of flowing splendors, while Angelo was transcribing sacred scenes upon the Sistine vault or fixing them in stone. Reading this book, More was to die with a smile; Latimer, Cranmer, and Ridley to perish while illuminating with living torches, and the Anabaptist to arouse the sympathies of Christendom by his agonies. With this book in hand, Shakespeare was to write his plays; Raleigh was to die, knight, discoverer, thinker, statesman, martyr; Bacon to lay the foundation of modern scientific research—three stars in the majestic constellation about Henry's daughter. With this Bible open before them the English nation would behold the Spanish Armada dashed to pieces upon the rocks, while Edmund Spenser mingled his delicious notes with the tumult of that awful wreck.

This book was to produce the edict of Nantes, while John of Barneveld would give new life to the command of William the Silent —"Level the dikes; give Holland back to the ocean, if need be," thus making preparation for the visit of the Mayflower pilgrims to Leyden or Delfthaven. Their eyes resting upon its pages, Selden and Pym were to go to prison, while Grotius dreamed of the rights of man in peace and war, and Guido and Rubens were painting the joys of the manger or the sorrows of Calvary. His hand resting upon this book, Oliver Cromwell would consolidate the hopes and convictions of Puritanism into a sword which should conquer at Nasby, Marston Moor and Dunbar, leave to the throne of Charles I. a headless corpse, and create, if only for an hour's prophecy, a commonwealth of unbending righteousness. With that volume in their homes, the Swede and the Huguenot, the Scotch-Irishman and the Quaker, the Dutchman and the freedom-loving cavalier, were to plan pilgrimages to the West, and establish new homes in America. With that book in the cabin of the *Mayflower*, venerated and obeyed by sea-tossed exiles, was to be born a compact from which should spring a constitution and a government for the life of which all these nationalities should willingly bleed and struggle, under a conqueror who should rise from the soil of the cavaliers, and unsheath his sword in the colony of the Puritans.

Out of that Bible were to come the "Petition of Right," the national anthem of 1628, the "Grand Remonstrance," and "Paradise Lost." With it, Blake and Pascal should voyage heroically in diverse seas. In its influence Jeremy Taylor should write his "Liberty of Prophesying," Sir Matthew Hale his fearless replies, while Rembrandt was placing on canvas little Dutch children, with wooden shoes, crowding to the feet of a Jewish Messiah.

Its lines, breathing life, order, and freedom, would inspire John Bunyan's dream, Algernon Sidney's fatal republicanism, and Puffendorf's judicature. With them, William Penn would meet the Indian of the forest, and Fénelon, the philosopher, in his meditative solitude. Locke and Newton and Leibnitz would carry it with them in pathless fields of speculation, while Peter the Great was smiting an arrogant priest in Russia, and William was ascending the English throne. From its poetry Cowper, Wordsworth, Tennyson, and Browning would catch the divine afflatus; from its statesmanship Burke, Romilly, and Bright would learn how to create and redeem institutions; from its melodies Handel, Bach, Mendelssohn, and Beethoven would write oratorios, masses, and symphonies; from its declaration of divine sympathy Wilberforce, Howard, and Florence Nightingale were to emancipate slaves, reform prisons, and mitigate the cruelties of war; from its prophecies Dante's hope of a united Italy was to be realized by Cavour, Garibaldi, and Victor Emmanuel. Looking upon the family Bible as he was dying, Andrew Jackson said: "That book, sir, is the rock on which the Republic rests"; and with her hand upon that book, Victoria, England's queen, was to sum up her history as a power amid the nations of the earth, when, replying to the question of an ambassador: "What is the secret of England's superiority among the nations?" she would say: "Go tell your prince that this is the secret of England's political greatness."

Beloved friends, when spurious liberalism, with all her literature, produces such a roll-call as this; when out of her pages I may see coming a nobler set of forces for the making of manhood, then, and only then, will I give up my Bible; then, and only then, will I cease to pray and labor that it may be given to all the world.

THOMAS GUTHRIE

1803-1873

THE NEW HEART

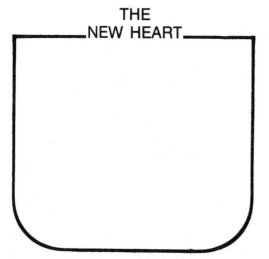

BIOGRAPHICAL NOTE

THOMAS GUTHRIE, preacher, philanthropist, and social reformer, was born at Brechin, Forfarshire, Scotland, in 1803. He spent ten years at the University of Edinburgh and was licensed to preach by the Presbytery of Brechin in 1825. In 1830 he was ordained minister of Arbirlot. After a valuable experience in evangelical preaching among the farmers, weavers and peasants of his congregation, he became one of the ministers of Old Greyfriars Church, Edinburgh, in 1827. Lord Cockburn described his sermons in that city as appealing equally "to the poor woman on the steps of the pulpit" as to the "stranger attracted solely by his eloquence." He was a great temperance advocate, becoming a total abstainer in 1844, and has been styled "the apostle of the ragged school movement." Retiring from the active work of the ministry in 1864, he still remained in public life until he died in 1873. Through long practise, Dr. Guthrie delivered his memorized discourses as tho they fell spontaneously from his lips. His voice has been described as powerful and musical. He was fond of vivid illustration, and even on his death bed, as he lay dying in the arms of his sons, he exclaimed: "I am just as helpless in your arms now as you once were in mine."

A new heart also will I give you, and a new spirit will I put within you; and I will take away the stony heart out of your flesh, and I will give you an heart of flesh.—Ezekiel xxxvi., 26.

As in a machine where the parts all fit each other, and, bathed in oil, move without din or discord, the most perfect harmony reigns throughout the kingdom of grace. Jesus Christ is the "wisdom," as well as the "power" of God; nor in this kingdom is anything found corresponding to the anomalies and incongruities of the world lying without. There we sometimes see a high station disgraced by a man of low habits; while others are doomed to an inferior condition, who would shine like gilded ornaments on the very pinnacles of society. That beautiful congruity in Christ's kingdom is secured by those who are the objects of saving mercy being so renewed and sanctified that their nature is in harmony with their position, and the man within corresponds to all without.

Observe how this property of "new" runs through the whole economy of grace. When mercy first rose upon this world, an attribute of Divinity appeared which was new to the eyes of men and angels. Again, the Savior was born of a virgin; and He who came forth from a womb where no child had been previously conceived, was sepulchered in a tomb where no man had been previously interred. The infant had a new birthplace, the crucified had a new burial-place. Again, Jesus is the mediator of a new covenant, the author of a new testament, the founder of a new faith. Again, the redeemed receive a new name; they sing a new song; their home is not to be in the old, but in the new, Jerusalem, where they shall dwell on a new earth, and walk in glory beneath a new heaven. Now it were surely strange, when all things else are new, if they themselves were not to partake of this general renovation. Nor strange only, for such a change is indispensable. A new name without a new nature were an imposture. It were not more an untruth to call a lion a lamb, or the rapacious vulture by the name of the gentle dove, than to give the title of sons of God to the venomous seed of the serpent.

Then, again, unless man received a new nature, how could he sing the new song? The raven, perched on the rock, where she whets her bloody beak, and impatiently watches the dying struggles of some unhappy lamb can not tune her croaking voice to the rich, mellow music of a thrush; and, since it is out of the abundance of the heart that the mouth speaketh, how could a sinner take up the strain and sing the song of saints? Besides, unless a man were a new creature, he were out of place in the new creation. In circumstances neither adapted to his nature, nor fitted to minister to his happiness, a sinner in heaven would find himself as much out of his element as a finny inhabitant of the deep, or a sightless burrower in the soil, beside an eagle, soaring in the sky, or surveying her wide domain from the mountain crag.

In the works of God we see nothing more beautiful than the divine skill with which He suits His creatures to their condition. He gives wings to birds, fins to fishes, sails to the thistleseed, a lamp to light the glowworm, great roots to moor the cedar, and to the aspiring ivy her thousand hands to climb the wall. Nor is the wisdom so conspicuous in nature, less remarkable and adorable in the kingdom of grace. He forms a holy people for a holy heaven—fits heaven for them, and them for heaven. And calling up His Son to prepare the mansions for their tenants, and sending down His Spirit to prepare the tenants for their mansions, He thus establishes a perfect harmony between the new creature and the new creation.

You can not have two hearts beating in the same bosom, else you would be, not a man, but a monster. Therefore, the very first thing to be done, in order to make things new, is just to take that which is old out of the way. And the taking away of the old heart is, after all, but a preparatory process. It is a means, but not the end. For, strange as it may at first sound, he is not religious who is without sin. A dead man is without sin; and he is sinless, who lies buried in dreamless slumber, so long as his eyes are sealed. Now, God requires more than a negative religion. Piety, like fire, light, electricity, magnetism, is an active, not a passive element; it has a positive, not merely a negative existence. For how is pure and undefiled religion defined? "Pure religion and undefiled is to visit the fatherless and widows in their affliction." And on whom does Jesus pronounce His beatitude? "If ye know these things, happy are ye if ye do them." And what is the sum of practical piety—the most portable form in which you can put an answer to Saul's question, "Lord, what wouldst thou have me to do?" What but this, "Depart from evil, and do good." Therefore, while God promises to take the stony heart out of our flesh, He promises more. In taking away one heart, He engages to supply us with another; and to this further change and onward stage in the process of redemption, I now proceed to turn your attention.

By way of general observation, I remark that our affections are engaged in religion.

An oak—not as it stands choked up in the crowded wood, with room neither to spread nor breathe, but as it stands in the open field, swelling out below where it anchors its roots in the ground, and swelling out above where it stretches its arms into the air,—presents us with the most perfect form of firmness, self-support, stout and sturdy independence. So perfectly formed, indeed, is the monarch of the forest to stand alone, and fight its own battles with the elements, that the architect of the Bell Rock lighthouse is said to have borrowed his idea of its form from God in nature, and that, copying the work of a divine Architect, he took the trunk of the oak as the model of a building which was to stand the blast of the storm, and the swell of the winter seas.

Observe, that although the state of the natural affections does not furnish any certain evidence of conversion, it is the glory of piety that these are strengthened, elevated, sanctified by the change. The lover of God will be the kindest, best, wisest lover of his fellow-creatures. The heart that has room in it for God, grows so large, that it finds room for all God's train, for all that He loves, and for all that He has made; so that the Church, with all its denominations of true Christians, the world, with all its perishing sinners, nay, all the worlds which He has created, find orbit-room to move, as in an expansive universe, within the capacious enlargement of a believer's heart. For while the love of sin acts as an astringent—contracting the dimensions of the natural heart, shutting and shriveling it up—the love of God expands and enlarges its capacity. Piety quickens the pulse of love, warms and strengthens our heart, and sends forth fuller streams of natural affection toward all that have a claim on us, just as a strong and healthy heart sends tides of blood along the elastic arteries to every extremity of the body.

This new heart, however, mainly consists in a change of the affections as they regard spiritual objects. Without again traveling over ground which we have already surveyed, just look at the heart and feelings of an unconverted man. His mind being carnal, is enmity or hatred against God. This may be latent, not at first sight apparent, nor suspected, but how soon does it appear when put to the proof? Fairly tried, it comes out like those unseen elements which chemical tests reveal. Let God, for instance, by His providences or laws, thwart the wishes or cross the propensities of our unrenewed nature—let there be a collision between His will and ours—and the latent enmity flashes out like latent fire when the cold black flint is struck with steel.

In conversion God gives a new spirit. Conversion does not bestow new faculties. It does not turn a weak man into a philosopher. Yet, along with our affections, the temper, the will, the judgment partake of this great and holy change. Thus, while the heart ceases to be dead, the head, illuminated by a light within, ceases to be dark; the understanding is enlightened; the will is renewed; and our whole temper is sweetened and sanctified by the Spirit of God. To consider these in their order, I remark—

By this change the understanding and judgment are enlightened. Sin is the greatest folly, and the sinner the greatest fool in the world. There is no such madness in the most fitful lunacy. Think of a man risking eternity and his everlasting happiness on the uncertain chance of surviving another year. Think of a man purchasing a momentary pleasure at the cost of endless pain. Think of a dying man living as if he were never to die. Is there a convert to God who looks back upon his unconverted state, and does not say with David, "Lord, I was as a beast before Thee."

Now conversion not only restores God to the heart, but reason also to her throne. Time and eternity are now seen in their just proportions—in their right relative dimensions; the one in its littleness, and the other in its greatness. When the light of heaven rises on the soul, what grand discoveries does she make —of the exceeding evil of sin, of the holiness of the divine law, of the infinite purity of divine justice, of the grace and greatness of divine love. On Sinai's summit and on Calvary's cross, what new, sublime, affecting scenes open on her astonished eyes! She now, as by one convulsive bound, leaps to the conclusion that salvation is the one thing needful, and that if a man will give all he hath for the life that now is, much more should he part with all for the life to come. The Savior and Satan, the soul and body, holiness and sin, have competing claims. Between these reason now holds the balance even, and man finds, in the visit of converting grace, what the demoniac found in Jesus' advent. The man whose dwelling was among the tombs, whom no chains could bind, is seated at the feet of Jesus, "clothed, and in his right mind."

By this change the will is renewed. Bad men are worse, and good men are better than they appear. In conversion the will is so changed and sanctified, that altho a pious man is in some respects less, in other respects he is more holy than the world gives him credit for. The attainments of a believer are always beneath his aims; his desires are nobler than his deeds; his wishes are holier than his works. Give other men their will, full swing to their passions, and they would be worse than they are; give that to him, and he would be better than he is. And if you have experienced the gracious change, it will be your daily grief that you are not what you not only know you

should be, but what you wish to be. To be complaining with Paul, "When I would do good, evil is present with me; that which I would I do not, and what I would not, that I do," is one of the best evidences of a gracious, saving change.

Children of God! let not your souls be cast down. This struggle between the new will and the old man—painful and prolonged altho it be—proves beyond all doubt the advent of the Holy Spirit. Until the Savior appeared there was no sword drawn, nor blood shed in Bethlehem, nor murderous decree issued against its innocents—they slept safely in their mothers' bosoms, Herod enjoyed his security and pleasure, and Rachel rose not from her grave to weep for her children because they were not. Christ's coming rouses all the devil in the soul. The fruits of holy peace are reaped with swords on the fields of war; and this struggle within your breast proves that grace, even in its infancy a cradled Savior, is engaged in strangling the old Serpent. When the shadow of calamity falls on many homes, and the tidings of victory come with sad news to many a family, and the brave are lying thick in the deadly breach, men comfort us by saying, that there are things worse than war. That is emphatically true of this holy war. Rejoice that the peace of death is gone.

By conversion the temper and disposition are changed and sanctified. Christians are occasionally to be found with a tone of mind and a temper as little calculated to recommend their faith as to promote their happiness. I believe that there are cases in which this is due to a deranged condition of the nervous system, or the presence of disease in some other vital organ. These unhappy persons are more deserving of our pity than our censure. This is not only the judgment of Christian charity, but of sound philosophy, and is a conclusion to which we are conducted in studying the union between mind and body, and the manner in which they act and re-act upon each other. So long as grace dwells in a "vile body," which is the seat of frequent disorder and many diseases—these infirmities of temper admit no more, perhaps, of being entirely removed, than a defect of speech, or any physical deformity. The good temper for which some take credit may be the result of good health and a well-developed frame—a physical more than a moral virtue; and an ill temper, springing from bad health, or an imperfect organization, may be a physical rather than a moral defect—giving its victim a claim on our charity and forbearance. But, admitting this apology for the unhappy tone and temper of some pious men, the true Christian will bitterly bewail his defect, and, regretting his infirmity more than others do a deformity, he will carefully guard and earnestly pray against it. Considering it as a thorn in his flesh, a messenger of Satan sent to buffet him, it will often send him to his knees in prayer to God, that the grace which conquers nature may be made "sufficient for him."

I pray you to cultivate the temper that was in Jesus Christ. Is he like a follower of the Lamb who is raging like a roaring lion? Is he like a pardoned criminal who sits moping with a cloud upon his brow? Is he like an heir of heaven, like a man destined to a crown, who is vexed and fretted with some petty loss? Is he like one in whose bosom the dove of heaven is nestling, who is full of all manner of bile and bitterness? Oh, let the same mind be in you that was in Jesus. A kind, catholic, gentle, loving temper is one of the most winning features of religion; and by its silent and softening influence you will do more real service to Christianity than by the loudest professions, or the exhibition of a cold and skeleton orthodoxy. Let it appear in you, that it is with the believer under the influence of the Spirit as with fruit ripened beneath the genial influences of heaven's dews and sunbeams. At first hard, it grows soft; at first sour, it becomes sweet; at first green, it assumes in time a rich and mellow color; at first adhering tenaciously to the tree, when it becomes ripe, it is ready to drop at the slightest touch. So with the man who is ripening for heaven. His affections and temper grow sweet, soft, mellow, loose from earth and earthly things. He comes away readily to the hand of death, and leaves the world without a wrench.

In conversion God gives a heart of flesh. "I will give you a heart of flesh."

Near by a stone, a mass of rock that had fallen from the overhanging crag, which had some wild flowers growing in its fissures, and on its top the foxglove, with its spike of beautiful but deadly flowers, we once came upon an adder as it lay in ribbon coil, basking on the sunny ground. At our approach the reptile stirred, uncoiled itself, and raising its venomous head, with eyes like burning coals, it shook its cloven tongue, and, hissing, gave signs of battle. Attacked, it retreated; and, making for that gray stone, wormed itself into a hole in its side. Its nest and home were there. And in looking on that shattered rock —fallen from its primeval elevation—with its flowery but fatal charms, the home and nest of the adder, where nothing grew but poisoned beauty, and nothing dwelt but a poisoned brood, it seemed to us an emblem of that heart which the text describes as a stone, which experience proves is a habitation of devils, and which the prophet pronounces to be desperately wicked. I have already explained why the heart is described as a stone. It is cold as a stone; hard as a stone; dead and insensible as a stone. Now, as by the term

"flesh" we understand qualities the very opposite of these, I therefore remark that—

In conversion a man gets a warm heart.

Let us restrict ourselves to a single example. When faith receives the Savior, how does the heart warm to Jesus Christ! There is music in His name. "His name is an ointment poured forth." All the old indifference to His cause, His people, and the interests of His kingdom, has passed away; and now these have the warmest place in a believer's bosom, and are the object of its strongest and tenderest affections. The only place, alas! that religion has in the hearts of many is a burial-place; but the believer can say with Paul, "Christ liveth in me." Nor is his heart like the cottage of Bethany, favored only with occasional visits. Jesus abides there in the double character of guest and master, its most loving and best loved inmate; and there is a difference as great between that heart as it is, and that heart as it was, as between the warm bosom where the Infant slept or smiled in Mary's arms and the dark, cold sepulcher where weeping followers laid and left the Crucified.

Is there such a heart in you? Do you appreciate Christ's matchless excellences? Having cast away every sin to embrace him, do you set him above your chiefest joy? Would you leave father, mother, wife, children, to follow Him, with bleeding feet, over life's roughest path? Rather than part with Him, would you part with a thousand worlds? Were He now on earth, would you leave a throne to stoop and tie His latchet? If I might so speak, would you be proud to carry His shoes? Then, indeed, you have got the new, warm heart of flesh. The new love of Christ, and the old love of the world, may still meet in opposing currents; but in the war and strife of these antagonistic principles, the celestial shall overpower the terrestrial, as, at the river's mouth, I have seen the ocean tide, when it came rolling in with a thousand billows at its back, fill all the channel, carry all before its conquering swell, dam up the fresh water of the land, and drive it back with resistless power.

In conversion a man gets a soft heart.

As "flesh," it is soft and sensitive. It is flesh, and can be wounded or healed. It is flesh, and feels alike the kiss of kindness and the rod of correction. It is flesh; and no longer a stone, hard, obdurate, impenetrable to the genial influences of heaven. A hard block of ice, it has yielded to the beams of the sun, and been melted into flowing water. How are you moved now, stirred now, quickened now, sanctified now, by truths once felt no more than dews falling out of starry heavens, in soft silence upon rugged rock. The heart of grace is endowed with a delicate sensibility, and vibrates to the slightest touch of a Savior's fingers. How does the truth of God affect it now! A stone no longer, it melts under the heavenly fire—a stone no longer, it bends beneath the hammer of the word; no longer like the rugged rock, on which rains and sunbeams were wasted, it receives the impression of God's power, and retains the footprints of His presence. Like the flowers that close their eyes at night, but waken at the voice of morning, like the earth that gapes in summer drought, the new heart opens to receive the bounties of grace and the gifts of heaven. Have you experienced such a change? In proof and evidence of its reality, is David's language yours—"I have stretched out my hands unto thee. My soul thirsteth after thee as a thirsty land"?

In conversion a man gets a living heart.

The perfection of this life is death—it is dead to be sin, but alive to righteousness, alive to Christ, alive to everything which touches His honor, and crown, and kingdom. With Christ living in his heart, the believer feels that now he is not himself, not his own; and, as another's, the grand object of his life is to live to Christ. He reckons him an object worth living for, had he a thousand lives to live; worth dying for, had he a thousand deaths to die. He says with Paul, "I am crucified with Christ, nevertheless I live." In the highest sense alive, he is dead, dead to things he was once alive to; and he wishes that he were more dead to them, thoroughly dead. He wishes that he could look on the seductions of the world, and sin's voluptuous charms, with the cold, unmoved stare of death, and that these had no more power to kindle a desire in him than in the icy bosom of a corpse. "Understandest thou what thou readest?"

It is a mark of grace that the believer, in his progress heavenward, grows more and more alive to the claims of Jesus. If you "know the love of Christ," His is the latest name you will desire to utter; His is the latest thought you will desire to form; upon Him you will fix your last look on earth; upon Him your first in heaven. When memory is oblivious of all other objects—when all that attracted the natural eye is wrapt in the mists of death, when the tongue is cleaving to the roof of our mouth, and speech is gone, and sight is gone, and hearing gone, and the right hand, lying powerless by our side, has lost its cunning, Jesus! then may we remember Thee! If the shadows of death are to be thrown in deepest darkness on the valley, when we are passing along it to glory, may it be ours to die like that saint, beside whose bed wife and children once stood, weeping over the wreck of faded faculties, and a blank, departed memory. One had asked him, "Father, do you remember me?" and received no answer; and another, and another, but still no

answer. And then, all making way for the venerable companion of a long and loving pilgrimage—the tender partner of many a past joy and sorrow, his wife draws near. She bends over him, and as her tears fall thick upon his face, she cries, "Do you not remember me?" A stare, but it is vacant. There is no soul in that filmy eye; and the seal of death lies upon these lips. The sun is down, and life's brief twilight is darkening fast into a starless night. At this moment, one calm enough to remember how the love of Christ's spouse is "strong as death," a love that "many waters can not quench," stooped to his ear, and said, "Do you remember Jesus Christ?" The word was no sooner uttered than it seemed to recall the spirit, hovering for a moment, ere it took wing to heaven. Touched as by an electric influence, the heart beat once more to the name of Jesus; the features, fixt in death, relax; the countenance, dark in death, flushes up like the last gleam of day; and, with a smile in which the soul passed away to glory, he replied, "Remember Jesus Christ! dear Jesus Christ! He is all my salvation, and all my desire."

By conversion man is ennobled.

While infidelity regards man as a mere animal, to be dissolved at death into ashes and air, and vice changes man into a brute or devil, Mammon enslaves him. She makes him a serf, and condemns him to be a gold-digger for life in the mines. She puts her collar on his neck, and locks it; and bending his head to the soil, and bathing his brow in sweat, she says, Toil, toil, toil; as if this creature, originally made in the image of God, this dethroned and exiled monarch, to save whom the Son of God descended from the skies, and bled on Calvary, were a living machine, constructed of sinew, bone, and muscle, and made for no higher end than to work to live, and live to work.

Contrast with these the benign aspect in which the gospel looks on man. Religion descends from heaven to break our chains. She alone raises me from degradation, and bids me lift my drooping head, and look up to heaven. Yes; it is that very gospel which by some is supposed to present such dark, degrading, gloomy views of man and his destiny, which lifts me from the dust to set me among princes—on a level with angels—in a sense above them. To say nothing of the divine nobility grace imparts to a soul which is stamped anew with the likeness and image of God, how sacred and venerable does even this body appear in the eye of piety! No longer a form of animated dust; no longer the subject of passions shared in common with the brutes; no longer the drudge and slave of Mammon, the once "vile body" rises into a temple of the Holy Ghost. Vile in one sense it may be; yet what, although it be covered with sores?

What, although it be clothed in rags? What, although, in unseemly decrepitude, it want its fair proportions? That poor, sickly, shattered form is the casket of a precious jewel. This mean and crumbling tabernacle lodges a guest nobler than palaces may boast of; angels hover around its walls; the Spirit of God dwells within it. What an incentive to holiness, to purity of life and conduct, lies in the fact that the body of a saint is the temple of God, a truer, nobler temple than that which Solomon dedicated by his prayers, and Jesus consecrated His presence! In popish cathedrals, where the light streamed through painted window, and the organ pealed along lofty aisles, and candles gleamed on golden cups and silver crosses, and incense floated in fragrant clouds, we have seen the blinded worshiper uncover his head, drop reverently on his knees, and raise his awestruck eye on the imposing spectacle; we have seen him kiss the marble floor, and knew that sooner would he be smitten dead upon that floor than be guilty of defiling it. How does this devotee rebuke us! We wonder at his supersitition; how may he wonder at our profanity! Can we look on the lowly veneration he expresses for an edifice which has been erected by some dead man's genius, which holds but some image of a deified virgin, or bones of a canonized saint, and which, proudly as it raises its cathedral towers, time shall one day cast to the ground, and bury in the dust; can we, I say, look on that, and, if sensible to rebuke, not feel reproved by the spectacle? In how much more respect, in how much holier veneration should we hold this body? The shrine of immortality, and a temple dedicated to the Son of God, it is consecrated by the presence of the Spirit—a living temple, over whose porch the eye of piety reads what the finger of inspiration has written: "If any man defile the temple of God, him shall God destroy; for the temple of God is holy, which temple ye are."

JOHN NEWMAN HALL

1816-1902

CHRISTIAN VICTORY

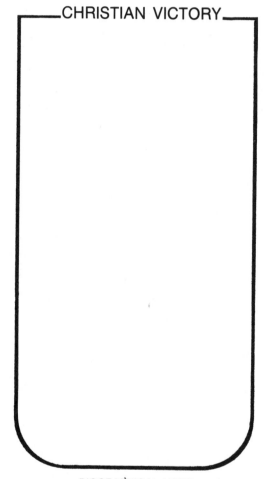

BIOGRAPHICAL NOTE

JOHN CHRISTOPHER NEWMAN HALL, Congregational divine, was born at Maidstone, Kent, in 1816. He was widely known as a writer, lecturer, and preacher of great eloquence. During the American Civil War he was enthusiastic in advocating the cause of the North, and subsequently two extended tours in the United States brought him international fame. His tract, "Come to Jesus," published in 1846, has been translated into over twenty languages. He died in 1902.

To him that overcometh will I give to eat of the hidden manna, and will give him a white stone, and in the stone a new name written, which no man knoweth saving he that receiveth it.—Rev. ii., 17.

THE Christian life is often compared in Scripture to a warfare. Followers of Jesus are "soldiers." They are exhorted to put on "the whole armor of God." They "fight the good fight of faith." Some of you have been engaged in the conflict: others have more recently entered upon it. But, whether young or old in the Christian career, all find it necessary to be constantly stirred up to watchfulness against the never-ceasing assaults of the foe. It is not enough to put on the armor and to commence the battle. He that overcometh, and he alone, will receive the salutation, "Well done, good and faithful servant,"—he alone shall "lay hold upon eternal life."

But we are not left to fight without encouragement. As generals before a battle go in front of their troops to stimulate them to valor, so Christ, the Captain of our Salvation, leads on the consecrated hosts of His elect; and having himself set us a glorious example of valor and victory, animates us to follow in His footsteps by the "exceeding great and precious promises" of His word. Christian warrior! let your eye be lifted up to Him. Behold Him beckoning you onward. Listen to Him, as from His throne of glory He exhorts you to persevering valor against the foe; and pray earnestly that His promise may be fulfilled in your case: "To him that overcometh will I give to eat of the hidden manna, and will give him a white stone, and in the stone a new name written, which no man knoweth saving he that receiveth it."

Let us consider first, the promise; then, the condition attached to it.

I. The promise. This is twofold,—the hidden manna and the white stone.

1. The hidden manna.—God fed the Israelites in the wilderness with manna. A portion of this was laid by in the ark, and thus was hidden from public view. It is here referred to as a figurative representation of the spiritual blessings bestowed upon the victor in the heavenly fight. Christ, speaking of the manna as a type of Himself, said, "I am the bread which came down from heaven." The manna in the wilderness sustained the life of the Israelites.

But there is another life more important than that of the body. By sin the soul is dead, dead toward God. By the Holy Spirit, the "dead in trespasses and sins" are "quickened," or made alive. As the life of the new-born infant cannot be preserved without food, so the new spiritual life which God imparts needs continual support. Both the life, and the nourishing of it, come from Christ, and Christ alone. By His sacrifice that life becomes possible; and by His spirit working within our hearts that life becomes actual. He sustains as well as imparts spiritual vitality. He is the food of our faith: "believe in the Lord Jesus Christ, and thou shalt be saved." He is the food of our love: "we love him because he first loved us." He is the food of our obedience: "the love of Christ constraineth us." He is the food of our peace: for when "justified by faith, we have peace with God through Jesus Christ our Lord." He is the food of our joy: for if "we joy in God" it is "through Jesus Christ our Lord."

The manna which sustained the Israelites was evidently the gift of God. And so this "hidden manna" is from heaven. It is no contrivance of man—no philosophy of human invention. It is a divine plan for the salvation of our ruined race. "God so loved the world that he gave his only begotten Son, that whosoever believeth in him should not perish but should have everlasting life." That manna in the wilderness was sweet to the taste; yet they who fed on it grew weary of it. But the more we eat of the bread of life, the more we relish it—the greater is our appetite for it. That manna in the wilderness was needed daily. And so with this heavenly bread. Yesterday's supply will not suffice for to-day. The prayer is as needful for the soul as for the body: "Give us this day our daily bread." But if that manna was needed daily, so it was supplied; none went in vain at the appointed season—and no soul that "hungers and thirsts after righteousness" is sent empty away. The manna was supplied to the Israelites till they came to the promised land—so God has promised that His grace shall not fail His people through their wanderings.

It is spoken of as the "hidden manna." Such is the Christian's life. "Our life is hid with Christ in God." The outward effects of it may be seen, but the inner life is invisible. So is the nourishing of the life. You may see the Christian on his knees, you may hear the words which he utters, but you cannot see the streams of divine influence which are poured into his spirit; nor hear the sweet whispers of divine love which fill him with joy; nor comprehend the peace passing all understanding which he is permitted to experience. Unbelievers are often amazed at what they see in the Christian. He is troubled on every side, yet not in despair. Waves of sorrow beat upon his frail vessel, yet it does not sink. Men now threaten, now allure, but he holds on his way. What to others is an irresistible charm, is no attraction to him. What is a terror to others, deters not him. Why does he not faint beneath the burden? why does he not sink in the storm? Because he eats of the "hidden manna." "The secret of the Lord is with them that fear him." "He hath taken him into his banqueting-room, and the banner over him is love."

Were this promise merely the reward of final victory, that victory itself would never be gained. We need to eat this manna during our pilgrimage. We cannot live without it. Every act of overcoming will be followed by a verification of the promise, "I will give him to eat of the hidden manna." Yet we must look beyond the present life for its full accomplishment. "To him that overcometh" at the last "shall be given the hidden manna," in a sense of which at present we have but a very faint conception.

As the manna was hidden in the ark, and that ark was hidden behind the curtain of the Holy of Holies, so the Christian's hope, "as an anchor of the soul, sure and stedfast, enters into that which is within the veil." Those joys we cannot yet conjecture; their splendor is too intense; we should be blinded by excessive light; we should be overpowered by the excellent glory.

One look of heaven would unfit us for earth. It is wisely appointed that at present this manna should in one sense be hidden, even from ourselves. We are as yet but babes—such strong meat would not suit us now; we must be content with simpler fare. But oh! if the manna, tho at present so partially and imperfectly appreciated, can produce such peace and joy, what must be the bliss of entering into the holiest of all, and there, in the presence of God Himself, feasting on it eternally! Unceasing, unlimited reception of divine influences into the soul!

Uninterrupted fellowship with Him who is the only fountain of life, and purity, and happiness! Perfect love! But at present such full fruition is "hidden." "Now we see through a glass darkly"; "now we know but in part"; "it doth not yet appear what we shall be." But how unspeakably blest are they to whom, partially in this world and perfectly in the next, the promise shall be verified: "To him that overcometh will I give to eat of the hidden manna"!

2. The white stone.—Reference is made to the *tessera hospitalis*, the tally or token of hospitality employed by the ancients. At a time when houses of public entertainment were less common, private hospitality was the more necessary. When one person was received kindly by another, or a contract of

friendship was entered into, the *tessera* was given. It was so named from its shape, being four-sided; it was sometimes of wood; sometimes of stone; it was divided into two by the contracting parties; each wrote his own name on half of the *tessera;* then they exchanged pieces, and therefore the name or device on the piece of *tessera* which each received, was the name the other person had written upon it, and which no one else knew but him who received it. It was carefully prized, and entitled the bearer to protection and hospitality.

Plautus, in one of his playes, refers to this custom. Hanno inquires of a stranger where he may find Agorastocles, and discovers to his surprize that he is addressing the object of his search.

"If so," he says, "compare, if you please, this hospitable *tessera;* here it is; I have it with me."

Agorastocles replies, "It is the exact counterpart; I have the other part at home."

Hanno responds, "O my friend! I rejoice to meet thee; thy father was my friend, my guest; I divided with him this hospitable *tessera.*" "Therefore," said Agorastocles, "thou shalt have a home with me, for I reverence hospitality."

Beautiful illustration of gospel truth! The Savior visits the sinner's heart, and being received as a guest, bestows the white stone, the token of His unchanging love. It is not we who in the first instance desire this compact. Far from it.

But Jesus, anxious to bless us, kindly forces Himself on our regard. By His spirit, he persuades us to give Him admission to our hearts. "Behold, I stand at the door and knock; if any man hear my voice and open the door, I will come in to him, and will sup with him, and he with me." We often disregarded His appeal. Yet, with what condescending kindness did he persevere! And when at length we opened the door, we saw Him laden with blessings which He had been long waiting to bestow. The feast which was then spread was all of His providing. He who went to be "the guest of one that was a sinner," inverts the usual course. He invites Himself and brings the feast. What have we fit to set before so august and holy a visitant? But He who chooses the sinner's heart as His banqueting-chamber, spreads there His choicest gifts, His exceeding great and precious promises, His finished sacrifice, His human sympathy, His perfect example, His pure precepts, His all-prevailing intercession, the various developments of His infinite love.

He "sups with us," and makes us "sup with Him." He enrolls our name among His friends. "He makes an everlasting covenant with us, ordered in all things and sure." He promises never to leave nor forsake us. He

tells us we "shall never perish." He gives us the *tessera*, the white stone!

Is not this "the witness of the Spirit," the "earnest of the promised possession"? Does not "the Spirit witness with our spirit that we are born of God"? Does not our experience of the friendship of Jesus correspond with what we are taught of it in the Scriptures? "I know in whom I have believed, and am persuaded that he is able to keep that which I have committed unto him, against that day." The "love of God is shed abroad" in the heart of the believer. He says, with humble confidence, "My Lord, and my God!"

On this white stone is inscribed a "new name." The part of the *tessera* which each of the contracting parties received contained the name of the other. And, therefore, "the new name" on the "white stone," which he that overcometh receives, is that of Him who gives. By the unbeliever, God is known as Power, as Majesty, as Justice. He is dreaded. "The carnal mind is enmity against God." The Christian alone knows Him as "Love!" Jehovah has now "a new name." He was once a ruler—now He is Friend; He was once judge—now He is Father.

Do you know God by His "new name"? Do you so know Him as to wish no longer to hide from Him, but to hide in Him, as the only home the universe can furnish in which you can be safe and happy? Have you learned to say, "Our Father which art in heaven"? If we have, indeed, received this "white stone," let us continually be reading the "new name" engraven on it. Here I am assured that the Holy Ghost is my teacher, my guide, my comforter; that the eternal Word, the only begotten Son, is my Savior, my Friend, my Brother; that the infinite Jehovah is my Father, and that "like as a father pitieth his children, so the Lord pitieth them that fear him."

We are told that no man knoweth this new name, "saving he that receiveth it." He knows it for himself, but no one else can read it for him. Thus it resembles the "hidden manna." The frivolous may deride, fools may mock, the unbeliever may deny, the sceptic may bring forth his objections in all the pride of a false philosophy; but the Christian, even if unable to reply to the caviller, or to make intelligible to any other mind his own strong assurance, has an evidence within him which nothing can shake, for God has written on his heart "His new best name of Love."

Fellow pilgrims to the heavenly Canaan, how precious is this token! We are travelers through the desert; for tho the enjoyments of earth are many, yet this life, compared with what is to come, is a wilderness. We are away from home; we are exposed to privations, tempests, foes; we constantly need a refuge. But we are never far from the house of a friend. Everywhere, in every city and in every village, on the desert and on the ocean, in the solitude of secrecy, and in the solitude of a crowd, in the bustle of business, and in the sick chamber, a Friend is at hand, who will always recognize the white stone He gave us, a token of His love. We have only to present it to claim the fulfilment of His promise.

How wide will the door be thrown open for our reception! What divine entertainment we shall receive! what safety from peril! what succor in difficulty! what comfort in trouble! what white raiment! what heavenly food! O that we valued the *tessera* more, that we sought more frequent interviews with our heavenly Friend, that we more habitually resorted as invited guests to Jesus, and dwelt in Him as the home of our souls! We shall never find the door closed against us; we shall never be received reluctantly; He will never allow us to think that we are intruders. Jesus is never ashamed of His poor relations, nor treats them coldly because they need His help. The greater our distress, the more shall we prove His liberality and tender sympathy.

And as regards this stone, as well as the hidden manna, we can look beyond the present life. A day is coming when we shall be compelled to leave the homes of earth, however endeared. We must embrace for the last time the friends united to us as our own souls. Tho we have traveled along the road many a year together, we must now separate, and go alone. They may accompany us to the river side, but we must cross it by ourselves. What cheering voice will greet us then? What kind roof will receive us then? What loving friend will welcome us then?

But we shall not have left our best treasure behind us! No! we shall carry the white stone with us; and with this we shall look for no inferior abode, but with unhesitating step shall advance at once right up to the palace of the Great King. We present the *tessera;* the "new name" is legible upon it; the angelic guards recognize the symbol; the everlasting gates lift up their heads; and the voice of Jesus Himself invites us to enter, saying, "Come, ye blessed of my Father, inherit the kingdom!"

Such is the welcome that every soul shall experience to whom the promise is fulfilled: "I will give him a white stone, and in the stone a new name written, which no man knoweth, saving he that receiveth it."

II. The condition annexed to the promise, "To him that overcometh!"

A great war is going on between the Church and the powers of darkness. It is not an affair of strategy between two vast armies, wherein skilful maneuvers determine the issue, many on either side never coming into actual combat; but every Christian has to fight hand to hand with the enemy. We cannot be lost in the crowd. We may not stand in the middle of the hollow square, without sharing the perils of the outer rank. Every Christian must not only occupy his post in the grand army, but must personally grapple with the foe.

Before conversion there was no fighting. The devil's suggestions and the heart's inclination were allied. Then we did the enemy's bidding, or were lulled to sleep by his intoxicating cup. But when light shone into the soul, and we strove to escape, the struggle began. God, as our Creator and Redeemer, justly demands our obedience and love. Whatever interferes with these claims, is an enemy summoning us to battle. The world of frivolity is our foe. How numerous and insinuating are its temptations—the more perilous because of the difficulty of defining them!

Moreover, lawful pleasures and necessary cares become dangerous when they cease to be subordinate to the love of God. The enjoyments He bestows and the labors He appoints are calculated to minister to godliness,—and yet they may be perverted to idolatry by our forgetting Him on whom our highest thoughts should be fixt. What danger is there that things in themselves holy and beautiful may thus become pernicious and destructive!

The flesh, too, furnished its contingent to the army of our foes. Not that any of our natural appetites, being divinely bestowed, can have in them the nature of sin. No! the flesh, as God made it, is pure and holy. But those instincts, which, regulated by the revealed will of their Author, are "holiness to the Lord," may, by unhallowed gratification, become those "fleshly lusts which war against the soul." As we carry about with us these animal propensities, there is necessity for constant vigilance lest our own nature, being abused, should become our destroyer.

Inbred depravity lurks in the heart of even the true believer. Tho dethroned, it is not completely expelled. With what selfishness, covetousness, vanity, hastiness of temper, uncharitableness, have we not to contend! Who has not some sin which most easily besets him? How varied are the forms of unbelief! Spiritual pride, too, corrupts our very graces, piety itself furnishing an occasion of evil, so that when we have conquered some temptation or performed some duty, our victory is often tarnished, our holy things corrupted, by our falling into the snare of self-complacency.

Above all, there is that great adversary who "goeth about as a roaring lion, seeking whom he may devour." He avails himself of the world, and the flesh, and the infirmities of the spirit, to tempt the soul of sin. This is no fable, altho one of Satan's most skilful stratagems is to make men disbelieve in his existence. Overlooked or despised, a foe is already half victorious. But the Captain of our Salvation, in His word, often warns us both of the craft and of the violence of our adversary. We sometimes read of "the wiles of the devil"; and sometimes of "the fiery darts of the wicked one." They who fail to watch and pray, are sure to be vanquished by such a foe.

These are our enemies! And if we would possess the promise we must "overcome." A mere profession of religion is of no avail. It is not enough for our name to appear on the muster-roll of the camp. Many wear the soldier's dress who know nothing of the soldier's heart. Many are glad to glitter on the grand parade who fall off from the hard-fought, blood-stained battle-field. It is not enough to buckle on our armor; many do this, and lay it aside again. We must devote ourselves to this great daily battle of life.

There is no exemption of persons. Women must fight, as well as men; the tender and timid must be as Amazons in the conflict. Children must carry the shield, and wield the sword. The aged and infirm must keep the ranks. The sick and wounded must not be carried to the rear. No substitute can be provided, and there is no discharge in this war.

There is no exemption on account of circumstances. The rich and poor, the learned and the unlearned, the cheerful and the sad, all must fight. No accumulation of trouble, no unexpected death of friends, can be an excuse for laying down our arms. We must go to the marriage feast, and we must attend the funeral procession, as warriors, wearing our armor and grasping our weapons. We must be like those spoken of by Nehemiah, "every man with one hand wrought in the work, and with the other hand held a weapon."

There is no exemption of place. Foes lie in wait for the Christian wherever he goes—in the mart of commerce, in the busy workshop, when he returns to his home, when he rests on his bed, in the bustle of the day, in the silence of the night, in the circle of his friends, in the bosom of his family, in society, alone, in the city, in the fields, in his walks of benevolence, in his private meditations, in the church, in his secret retirement, when he worships with the great congregation, and when he enters his closet and shuts the door. He can never elude the enemy; he carries the foe in his own breast; the conflict ceases not!

There is no exemption of time, no season of rest. No truce is sounded. Satan never beats a retreat, except to lead us into an ambuscade. No white flag comes out that can be trusted. If we parley it is at our peril; if we pause, we are wounded or taken captive. Wars on earth may often terminate by mutual agreement. It is a war of extermination; no quarter is given; either we must trample Satan under foot, or Satan will drag us down to hell!

It is a warfare until death. While we are in the body it will be always true—"We wrestle." The oldest Christian cannot lay aside his weapons. "Having done all, stand." A great word that! "Having done all!" "What!" you may say, "after a long life of conflict, surely I may put aside my armor, and sheathe my sword, and recline on some sunny bank, and enjoy myself after my victory!"

No; you must not expect it; "having done all" it is enough if you stand at bay on the battle-ground; all you can hope for in this world is to maintain your post, still defying the foe, who will be still meditating fresh attacks. You will never be able to say with St. Paul, "I have finished my course."

It is not the appearance of fighting. It is not a few faint, irresolute strokes. "So fight I," said the Apostle, "not as one that beateth the air." We must be resolute, determined, in earnest, giving our enemy no advantage. We must "not give place to the devil." We must watch against the smallest beginnings of sin. By "keeping the heart with all diligence," by putting on "the whole armor of God," by having faith as our shield, righteousness as our breastplate, the hope of salvation as our helmet, by keeping "the sword of the Spirit" bright with exercise, "praying with all prayer," standing near our Captain, looking to Him, relying upon Him, knowing that "without Him we can do nothing,"—so must we fight! All this is necessary, if we would overcome.

It is not so easy to fight this fight as some suppose. It is not a true faith merely, an evangelical creed, a scriptural church, a comfortable sermon once or twice a week, a little Sabbath-keeping, an agreeable pause in your pleasures, giving to them a new relish—it is not this which constitutes Christianity. You that think religion so very easy a thing, have a care at least, lest when too late, you find that you know not what true religion meant.

Easy? A depraved being to trample upon his lusts—a proud being to lie prostrate with humility and self-reproach—they that are "slow of heart to believe," to receive the gospel as little children?

Easy? To "crucify the flesh," "to deny ungodliness," "to cut off a right hand, and to pluck out a right eye"?

Easy? To be in the world, and yet not of the world—to come out from it, not by the seclusion of the cloister, but by holiness of life—to be diligent in its duties, yet not absorbed by them; appreciating its innocent delights, and yet not ensnared by them; beholding its attractions and yet rising superior to them?

Easy? To live surrounded by objects which appeal to the sight, and yet to endure as seeing what is invisible?

Easy? To pray and see no answer to prayer, and still pray on—to fight this battle, and find fresh foes ever rising up, yet still to fight on—to be harassed with doubts and fears, and yet walk on in darkness, tho we see no light, staying ourselves upon God?

Easy? To be preparing for a world we have never visited, in opposition to so much that is captivating in a world where we have always dwelt, whose beauties we have seen, whose music we have heard, whose pleasures we have experienced?

Easy? To resist that subtle foe who has cast down so many of the wise and the mighty?

Easy? When Jesus says it is a "strait gate," and that if we would enter we must "strive," bidding us "take up our cross daily, deny ourselves and follow him"? Ah! it is no soft flowery meadow, along which we may languidly stroll, but a rough, craggy cliff that we must climb. "To him that overcometh!" It is no smooth, placid stream, along which we may dreamily float, but a tempestuous ocean we must stem. "To him that overcometh!" It is no easy lolling in a cushioned chariot, that bears us on without fatigue and peril. The trumpet has sounded to arms; it is not peace, but war, war for liberty, war for life, on the issue of which our everlasting destiny depends! If we are to be saved. we must "overcome."

But tho the conflict is arduous, the encouragments are great. We have armor of proof. We have a mighty Champion. Victory is ensured to the brave. Others who stood on the same battle-field and fought with the same enemies, are now enjoying an eternal triumph. Not one faithful warrior ever perished. Their foes were not fewer than ours, their strength was not greater. They overcame by the same "blood of the Lamb" on which we rely.

"Once they were mourning here below,
    And wet their couch with tears;
They wrestled hard, as we do now,
    With sins, and doubts, and fears."

But they are wearing their crowns, they are enjoying their rest; and the feeblest and most unworthy of our own day, trusting in the same Savior, shall inherit the same promise. Then let us overcome. Sheathe not the sword, and it shall never be wrested from you; lay not down the shield, and no fiery dart shall ever penetrate it; face the foe, and he shall never trample you down, never drive you back.

Listen to your Captain; how He animates you onward! Look to the crown he is ready to bestow upon you; eat of the hidden manna which He gives; read the name in the "white stone,"—the name of God,—His name of love, recorded for your encouragement; and thus be animated to walk worthy of this holy alliance, and not to allow the foe to wrench from you such an assurance of divine favor, such a passport to heavenly bliss.

A little more conflict, and that "white stone" shall introduce you to the inheritance above, where, in the everlasting repose of the inner sanctuary, you shall without intermission eat of the hidden manna.

"Then let my soul march boldly on,
    Press forward to the heavenly gate;
There peace and joy eternal reign,
    And glittering robes for conquerors wait."

Some of you may consider this subject visionary and unreal. You say, "I know nothing of this warfare. I know what the conflict of business is, the race of fashion, the bustle of toil or pleasure; but to anxiety about spiritual things I am a stranger."

You are enjoying peace—but—what peace? There is a captive in a dungeon—his limbs are fast chained to the walls—yet he is singing songs. How is it? Satan has given him to drink of his drugged cup, and he does not know where he is. Look at that other. He says, "it is peace." There is truly no fighting, but he is groveling in the dust, and the heel of his foe is upon his neck. Such is the peace of every one going on in his wickedness, unpardoned and unsaved. "Taken captive by the devil at his will."

Chained in Satan's boat, you are swiftly gliding down the stream to ruin, and because it is smooth, you dream that it is safe! What is the difference between the saint and the sinner? Not that in the saint there is no sin. Not that in the sinner there is never a thought about God. The difference is this—that the saint is overcoming his sin; but the sin is overcoming the sinner. Oh, what a terrible thing if sin have the upper hand! No "hidden manna" is yours. The symbols of religion you may look at, but real religion must be a stranger to you. You know not its enjoyment. You do not taste it. It is a hidden thing. Heaven too will be hidden. You hear of its gates of pearl—but they will never open to you. You may catch the distant accents of its songs—but in those songs you will never join. And that "white stone" cannot be yours. You have no joyful anticipation of heaven—but a fearful looking-for of fiery indignation —or else the insensate resolve not to think at all. And the "new name"—no! you cannot read it! You know God by no such name as makes you seek His company. The thought of Him renders you unhappy, and therefore you banish it from your mind. You are not now alarmed, but soon the spell may be broken, and you may find the chains riveted upon your soul forever.

I fancy I hear you say, "I wish that before it is too late, I could escape! But mine is a hopeless case. My heart is hardened against the gospel, and evil habit has so got the mastery over me, that I have no power to begin this conflict!"

No, you have no power; but One has visited this world, and taken our nature, who can help you. The mighty Son of God became the suffering Son of Man that He might be the liberator of our enslaved race. He burst open the prison doors, that captive souls might escape. He stands near you, ready to break off your fetters and strengthen you to fight the enemy who has so long opprest you. Tell Him your simple but sad tale; how helpless, how miserable, how ruined you are! Tell Him you want to be saved, but know not how to begin the work, and ask Him both to begin and complete it for you! Let your prayer be this: "Be merciful to me, a sinner"; and He who "came to destroy the works of the devil," He "whose nature and property is ever to have mercy and to forgive," will receive your "humble petitions; and tho you be tied and bound with the chain of your sins, He, in the pitifulness of His great mercy, will loose you."

He will pardon your past shameful concessions to the foe, and, arraying you in "the whole armor of God," and animating you with His Holy Spirit, He will enable you so to fight against the world, the flesh, and the devil, that you also shall share in the prize of them that overcome; you also shall eat of the "hidden manna," and receive the "white stone."

ROBERT HALL

1764-1831

MARKS OF LOVE TO GOD

BIOGRAPHICAL NOTE

ROBERT HALL, Baptist divine, was born at Arnesby, near Leicester, England, in 1764. Destined for the ministry, he was educated at the Baptist Academy at Bristol, and preached for the first time in 1779. In 1783 he began his ministry in Bristol and drew crowded congregations of all classes. The tradition of Hall's pupit oratory has secured his lasting fame. Many minds of a high order were fascinated by his eloquence, and his conversation was brilliant. His treatment of religious topics had the rare merit of commending evangelical doctrine to people of taste. Dugald Stewart declares that his writings and public utterances exhibited the English language in its perfection. He died in 1831.

But I know you, that ye have not the love of God in you.—John v., 42.

THE persons whom our Lord addrest in these words made a high profession of religion, valued themselves upon their peculiar opportunities of knowing the true God and His will, and proclaimed themselves as the Israel and the temple of the Lord, while they despised the surrounding pagans as those who were strangers to the divine law. Yet the self-complacent Pharisees of our Savior's age were as far from the love of God, he assures them in the text, as any of those who had never heard of His name. In this respect, many of "the first were last, and the last first." The rejection of the gospel evinces a hardness of heart which is decisive against the character; and, in the case of the Pharisees, it gave ample evidence that they possest no love of God. Had they really known God, as our Lord argues, they would have known Himself to be sent by God: whereas, in proving the bitter enemies of Christ, they proved that they were in a state of enmity against God. By parity of reason, we, my brethren, who know God and His Word in the way of Christian profession, ought not to take it for granted that we possess the love of God, and are in the way of eternal life; the same self-delusion may overtake us also; and similar admonitions may be no less necessary to many present, than to the Pharisees of old. Suffer then, my brethren, the word of exhortation, while I invite each individual seriously to consider this subject, with a view to the discovery of his real character.

In proceeding to lay down certain marks of grace, let it be premised, that either these marks partake of the nature of true religion, or they do not. If they do, they must be identified with it, and here the mark is the thing: if they do not partake of its nature, some of them may exist as indications where genuine religion is not. It is necessary, then, that we combine a variety of particular signs of grace: any one taken by itself, may, or may not, exist, without true religion; but where many are combined, no just doubt can remain.

Whether you have the love of God in your soul presents a most critical subject of inquiry; since the love of God will be acknowledged by all to be the great, the essential, principle of true religion. The simple question, then, to which I would call your attention, is this: "Am I, or am I not, a sincere lover of the Author of my being?"

In endeavoring to assist you in the decision of this momentous question, as it respects yourselves, I shall entreat your attention while I suggest a variety of marks which indicate love to God; and supposing the conviction produced by the statement to be, that you have not the love of God, I shall point out the proper improvement of such a conviction.

In suggesting various marks by which you may ascertain whether you love God or not, I would mention the general bent and turn of your thoughts, when not under the immediate control of circumstances; for these, you are aware, give a new and peculiar bias to our thoughts, and stamp them with an impress of their own. There is an infinite variety of thoughts continually passing through the mind of every individual: of these, some are thrown up by occasions; but others, and often the greater part, follow the habitual train of our associations. It is not to thoughts of the former kind that I refer; it is to those of the latter class—those involuntary thoughts which spring up of themselves in the mind of every person: it is these, not the former, that afford clear indication of the general temper and disposition. The question I would propose to you is, What is the bent of your thoughts when, disengaged from the influence of any particular occurrence, you are left to yourselves, in the intervals of retirement and tranquillity, in the silence of the midnight watches, and, in short, whenever your mind is left free to its own spontaneous musings? Are the thoughts most familiar to your mind, at such times, thoughts of God and the things of God—or are they thoughts that turn upon the present world and its transient concerns? Are they confined, for the most part, within the narrow circle of time and sense; or do they make frequent and large excursions into the spiritual and eternal world? The answer to this question will go far to decide whether you have, or have not, the love of God. It is impossible that such an object as the divine Being should be absent long from your thoughts; impossible that His remembrance should long remain merged in the stream of other imaginations; unless you are supposed chargeable with a decided indifference to divine things! Unless you are destitute of love to God you can never be so utterly uncongenial in sentiment and feeling with the psalmist, when he says, "My mouth shall praise thee with joyful lips, while I meditate upon thee in the night watches." "How precious are thy thoughts unto me, O God!" When that man of God gazed upon the starry heavens, his mind was not merely wrought into astonishment at the physical energy there displayed; he was still more deeply lost in grateful admiration of the mercy of Providence as manifested to man—a sinful child of dust, and yet visited by God in the midst of so magnificent a universe! But when day passes after day, and night after night, without any serious thoughts of God, it is plain that He is not the home of your mind, not your portion, center, and resting-place: and if this is the case, it is equally plain that you are not in a state of acceptance with Him; since nothing can be more certain than that, as our thoughts are, such must be our character. I do not ask what are your thoughts at particular times, or under the influence of some particular event: there may be little difference, on some occasions, between those who remember, and those who neglect, God habitually. The charge against the ungodly is, that "God is not in all their thoughts." If there are any here who feel this charge as bearing against themselves, let them take that solemn warning given by God himself at the close of the fiftieth psalm, "Oh, consider this, ye that forget God, lest I tear you in pieces, and there be none to deliver you!"

Let me request you to consider seriously how you stand disposed to the exercises of religion. If God is the object of your love, you will gladly avail yourselves of the most favorable opportunities of cultivating a closer friendship with the Father of your spirits: on the contrary, he who feels no regard for these opportunities, proves that he has no love to God, and will never be able to establish the conviction that God is his friend. Wherever there exists a sincere friendship, opportunities of cultivating it are gladly embraced, and the opposite privations are regretted. Where a habitual neglect of sacred exercises prevails it must be interpreted as if it said, like those whom the prophet describes, "Cause the Holy One of Israel to cease from amongst us. Depart from us, for we desire not the knowledge of thy way!" If your closets seldom witness your private devotions, if your moments in retirement are languid and uninteresting—your religion can have no hold on your heart; and the reason why your religion has no hold on your heart is because you have no love of God. There are some whose religion sits easy and delightful upon them; its acts and functions are free and lively: there are others who seem to bear their religion as a burden, to drag their duties as a chain—as no vital part of themselves, but rather a cumbrous appendage: this is a decisive and melancholy symptom of a heart alienated from God. There is no genuine religion, no real contact of the heart with the best of beings, unless it makes us continually resort to Him as our chief joy. The psalmist is always expressing his fervent desires after God: after the light of the divine countenance, and the sense of the divine favor: but do you suppose such desires peculiar to the state of believers under the Old Testament? No, my brethren; there exist more abundant reasons than ever, since the gospel of Christ has been displayed in all the glorious fulness of its blessings, why our souls should be inflamed with such feelings as those which inspired the psalmist, when he exclaimed, "As the hart panteth for the water-brooks, so longeth my soul after thee, O God!"

If you would ascertain whether you love God, consider how you stand affected toward the Word of God. We can entertain no just thoughts of God, but such as we derive from His own Word: we can acquire no true knowledge of God, nor cherish any suitable affections toward Him, unless they are such as His own revelation authorizes. Otherwise we must suppose that revelation insufficient for its specific purposes, and set the means against the end. All, therefore, who sincerely love God, are students of His Word; they here, also accord in soul with the psalmist, and like him, can say, "O how I love thy word! in it is my meditation all the day:" they eat it as food for their souls, and find it sweeter than honey. They go to it as to an inexhaustible fountain, and drink from it streams of sacred light and joy. A neglected Bible is too unambiguous a sign of an unsanctified heart; since that blest book can not fail to attract every one that loves its divine Author. How is it possible to delight in God, and yet neglect that Word which alone reveals Him in His true and glorious character—alone discovers the way by which He comes into unison with us, and condescends to pardon us, to love us, and to guide us through all this mysterious state of being? It is observable that the only persons who are inattentive to their own sacred books are to be found among Christians. Mohammedans commit large portions of the Koran to memory; the Jews regard the Old Testament with reverence; the Hindu Brahmans are enthusiastically attached to their Shastra; while Christians alone neglect their Bible. And the reason is, that the Scriptures are so much more spiritual than the religious books received by others; they afford so little scope for mere amusement or self-complacency; they place the reader alone with God; they withdraw him from the things that are seen and temporal, and fix him among the things that are unseen and eternal; they disclose to his view at once the secret evils of his own condition, and the awful purity of that Being with whom he has to do. No wonder the ungodly man hates their light, neither comes to their light, but retires from it farther and farther into the shades of guilty ignorance. How melancholy the infatuation of such a character!

Estimate your character in respect to your love of God, by reflecting, with what sentiments you regard the people of God. God has a people peculiarly His own: they are not of that world to which they outwardly belong —not conformed to it in the spirit of their mind; they stand apart, many of them at least, in conspicuous conformity to Jesus Christ, and in earnest expectation of the glory which He had promised. How, then, do you regard these decided followers of God? Do you shun their society with aversion and secret shame; or do you enjoy their communion as one of the most delightful among your Christian privileges? Are you content merely to be the companion of those who "have a name to live, but are dead": or can you say with the psalmist, "My delight is in the excellent of the earth"? or, with the beloved disciple, "We know that we have passed from death unto life, because we love the brethren"? for, as he adds, "He that loveth him that begot, loveth him that is begotten"; if you do not love the image which you have seen, how can you love the unseen original? If the features of holiness and grace in the creature are not attractive to your view, how can your affections rise to the perfect essence? How can you ascend to the very sun itself, when you can not enjoy even the faint reflection of its glory? He who knew the heart, could alone say to those around Him, "I know you, that ye have not the love of God in you": but tho none can address you now in the same tone of divine authority, yet we may hear it uttered by a voice—the voice of your own conscience: you may know, without any perturbations of hope or fear, by the spiritual insensibility and inaction of your soul—by this you may know, with equal certainty as by a voice from heaven, that you have not the love of God in you.

Consider the disposition you entertain toward the person and office of the Son of God. "If ye had loved the Father, ye would have loved me also," was the constant argument of Jesus Christ to those Pharisees whom He addresses in the text. For Jesus Christ is the express image of God: the effulgence of the divine character is attempered in Him, to suit the views of sinful humanity. In the life of Jesus Christ we see how the divine Being conducts Himself in human form and in our own circumstances: we behold how He bears all the sorrows, and passes through all the temptations, of flesh and blood. Such, indeed, is the identity, so perfect the oneness of character, between the man Christ Jesus and the divine Being—that our Savior expressly assures us, "He that hath seen me, hath seen the Father; I and my Father are one." The purpose for which God was manifested in the flesh was not to reveal high speculations concerning the nature of the Deity: it was to bear our sorrows, and to die for our sins. But can you contemplate Him, thus stooping to your condition, thus mingling with every interest of your own, and not be moved by such a spectacle?—not be attracted, fixt, filled with grateful astonishment and devotion—crucified, as it were, on the cross of Christ, to the flesh, and to the world? What mark, then, of our possessing no love of God can equal this, that we are without love to Jesus Christ?—that neither the visibility of His divine excellence, nor His participation of all our human sufferings, can reach our hearts and command our affections?

In examining whether you love God, examine how you are affected by His benefits. These are so numerous and so distinguished that they ought to excite our most ardent gratitude: night and day they are experienced by us; they pervade every moment of our being. We know that favors from an enemy derive a taint from the hands through which they are received, and excite alienation rather than attachment: but the kindness of a friend, by constantly reminding us of himself, endears that friend more and more to our hearts; and thus, he that has no love to God receives all His favors without the least attraction toward their Author, whom he regards rather as an enemy than as a friend. But the Christian feels his love of God excited by every fresh goodness. The mercies of God have accompanied you through every stage of your journey; and they are exhibited to you in His word as stretching through a vast eternity. Are these the only benefits you can receive without gratitude, and suffer to pass unregarded How, then, can any love of God dwell in your bosom?

Consider, in the next place, in what manner you are imprest by the sense of your sins. The question is not whether you have any sins,—none can admit a doubt on this point; the only inquiry is, how you are affected by those sins? Are they remembered by you with a sentiment of tender regret, of deep confusion and humiliation, that you should ever have so requited such infinite goodness? And is this sentiment combined with a sacred resolution to go and sin no more,—to devote yourself to the service of your divine Benefactor? If you can live without an habitual sense of penitential tenderness and reverential fear, be assured you can not love God; you have no experience of those Scripture declarations: "They shall fear the Lord and his goodness in the latter days;" "There is forgiveness with thee, that thou mayst be feared;" you know not that "the goodness of God leadeth to repentence." If the mind is softened by the love of God, all His favors serve to inflame its gratitude, and confirm its devotion to His will: but he who has no love of God in his soul, thinks of nothing but how he may escape from God's hand, and selfishly devours all His favors, without an emotion of gratitude to the Giver.

Finally, let me remind you to consider how you are affected to the present world. If you could only be exempt from its afflictions, would you wish it to be your lasting home? If you could surround yourself with all its advantages and enjoyments, would you be content to dwell in it forever? Yet you know that it is a place of separation and exile from the divine majesty; that it is a scene of darkness, in comparison with heaven, very faintly illuminated with the beams of His distant glory; that its inhabitant is constrained to say, "I have heard of thee by the hearing of the ear, but mine eye hath not yet seen thee";—while heaven is the proper dwelling-place of God and His people! Could you then consent to remain here always, without ever seeing as you are seen—seeing light in His light—without ever beholding His glory; without ever drinking at the fountain, and basking in that presence which is fulness of joy, and life forevermore? always to remain immersed in the shadows of time—entombed in its corruptible possessions? never to ascend up on high to God and Christ and the glories of the eternal world? If such is the state of your spirit, you want the essential principle of a Christian—you want the love of God. The genuine Christian, the lover of God, is certain to feel himself a "stranger on the earth." No splendor, no emolument of this world,—not all the fascinations of sensual pleasure,—can detain his heart below the skies, or keep him from sympathizing with the sentiment of the psalmist: "As for me, I shall behold thy face in righteousness; I shall be satisfied when I wake in thy likeness." I do not ask whether you have, at present, "a desire to depart": perhaps you may not be as yet sufficiently prepared and established to entertain so exalted a desire; but still, if you have received a new heart, you will deprecate nothing so much as having your portion in this life,—as having your eternal abode on earth. It is the character of faith to dwell much in eternity: the apostle says, in the name of all real believers, "We look not at the things that are seen, but the things that are not seen; for the things that are seen are temporal, but the things that are not seen are eternal."

And now, my brethren, supposing the preceding remarks to have produced in any of you the conviction that you have not the love of God in you, permit me very briefly to point out the proper improvement of such a conviction.

First, it should be accompanied with deep humiliation. If you labored under the privation of some bodily organ, requisite to the discharge of an animal function, you would feel it as in some degree a humiliating circumstance; but what would be any defect of this kind, however serious, in comparison with that great want under which you labor—

the want of piety, the calamity of a soul estranged from the love of God! What are the other subjects of humiliation compared with this—a moral fall, a spiritual death in sin: and this, unless it be removed, the sure precursor of the second death—eternal ruin! "This is a lamentation indeed, and it shall be for a lamentation."

Suppose the children of a family, reared and provided for by the most affectionate of parents, to rise up in rebellion against their father, and cast off all the feelings of filial tenderness and respect; would any qualities those children might possess, any appearance of virtue they might exhibit in other respects, compensate for such an unnatural, such an awful deformity of character? Transfer this representation to your conduct in relation to God: "If I," says He, "am a father, where is my fear? if I am a master, where is my honor?" "Hear, O heavens, and give ear, O earth! I have nourished and brought up children, and they have rebelled against me: the ox knoweth his owner, and the ass his master's crib: but Israel doth not know, my people doth not consider."

And let your humiliation be accompanied with concern and alarm. To be alienated from the great Origin of being; to be severed, or to sever yourself from the essential Author and element of all felicity, must be a calamity which none can understand, an infinite wo which none can measure or conceive. If the stream is cut off from the fountain, it soon ceases to flow, and its waters are dissipated in the air: and if the soul is cut off from God, it dies! Its vital contact with God,—its spiritual union with the Father of spirits through the blest Mediator, is the only life and beauty of the immortal soul. All, without this, are dead—"dead in trespasses and sins"! A living death—a state of restless wanderings, and unsatisfied desires! What a condition theirs! And, oh! what a prospect for such, when they look beyond this world! who will give them a welcome when they enter an eternal state?

What reception will they meet with, and where? What consolation amid their losses and their sufferings, but that of the fellow-sufferers plunged in the same abyss of ruin? Impenitent sinners are allied to evil spirits, they have an affinity with the kingdom of darkness; and when they die, they are emphatically said to "go to their own place"!

This is an awful state for any to be in at present; but, blest be God, it is not yet a hopeless situation. Let no person say, "I find by what I have heard, that I do not love God, and therefore I can entertain no hope." There is a way of return and recovery open to all. Jesus Christ, my dear brethren, proclaims to you all, "I am the way. No man can come to the Father but by me":—but every one that will may come by this new and living way; and, if you lose life eternal, you lose it because—according to his words just before the text—because "you will not come to Christ that you may have life." If you feel the misery, deformity, and danger of your state, then listen to His invitation, and embrace His promise. See the whole weight of your guilt transferred to His cross! See how God can be at once the just and the justifier! Take of the blood of sprinkling, and be at peace! His blood cleanseth from all sin: He will send that Spirit into your heart which will manifest Him to you; and where that Spirit is, there is liberty and holy love. He is the mystical ladder, let down from heaven to earth, on which angels are continually ascending and descending, in token of an alliance established between God and man. United by faith to Jesus Christ, you shall become a habitation of God through the Spirit; the Father will make you a partaker of His love, the Son of His grace, angels of their friendship; and you shall be preserved, and progressively sanctified, until, by the last change, all remains of the great epidemic source of evils shall be forever removed from your soul; and the love of God shall constitute your eternal felicity.

THOMAS CUMING HALL

1858-1936

THE CHANGING
AND THE CHANGELESS
IN RELIGIOUS LIFE

BIOGRAPHICAL NOTE

PROFESSOR of theology, Union Theological Seminary, New York, 1898-1929; born in Armagh, Ireland, September 25, 1858; graduated from Princeton, 1879; received degree of D.D. from Hamilton and Union Theological Seminary; was pastor in Omaha in 1883-86; in charge of the Forty-first Street Presbyterian, and later of the Fourth Presbyterian church, Chicago; author of "The Power of an Endless Life," "The Social Significance of the Evangelical Revival in England," "The Synoptic Gospels," etc.

"For we through the Spirit wait for the hope of righteousness."—Gal. 5 : 5.

THIS letter marks Paul's struggle with the older conservative forces from Jerusalem. These teachers from Jerusalem represented, it is quite true, an older stratum of thought than that of Paul. In the beginning all Christians had been Jews. The doorway into the Christian Church had, in the beginning, been solely through Judaism. Jesus had been a faithful Jew, going to the synagog, submitting to the ordinances of Judaism, taking his part in the regular services. He never broke with Judaism, only Judaism cast him out. These teachers from Jerusalem, therefore, felt that Paul was an innovator, and they had history on their side. But this was not their only difficulty; they also saw in Paul a great danger to the moral life of the community. This danger comes out strongly in the passage we have chosen. Paul was preaching as the central doctrine of Christianity faith energizing through love.

Now there is something to be said for these teachers from Jerusalem. Not only had they history on their side, but they had a very definite and concrete principle; and over against this principle Paul's teaching seemed obscure and hazy. Paul spoke of faith energizing through love. He preached of liberty in Christ Jesus, of freedom in the Spirit. But who was to decide the limits of freedom, who could really separate between liberty and license? They felt that Paul himself was nebulous and hazy; he kept the Sabbath, but he taught his Galatian church they were not to keep the Sabbath. The council at Jerusalem had strictly prohibited eating meat offered to idols, but Paul said that when they went to the house of the heathen they could eat it, asking no questions. Paul kept vows and went up with shaven head to Jerusalem, but to the heathen church he taught freedom from vows and reliance solely upon an inner life. Over against this ambiguous teaching of Paul they could put definite, concrete law. They had the Old Testament, which Paul pretended also to honor; they had the council at Jerusalem, which Paul had also promised to obey; they knew exactly the limits of liberty and freedom, for it lay only within the definite closed system of the written law. Moses and the prophets and Jesus Christ, these were the ultimate authority, and all liberty that strayed beyond these was license and sin.

Moreover, these teachers of Jerusalem could actually point to the ill effects of Paul's teaching. They had only to go to the church at Corinth and see in its confusions the evil effects of Paul's principle of liberty. What was the good of singing a magnificent hymn to love to a people that could not even keep sober at the communion table? What was the good of painting in the most glowing colors the fruits of the spirit to a people practising a form of incest abhorrent even to the heathen world? These teachers of Jerusalem felt that a great moral issue was involved; that Paul was breaking down the barriers that divided between the righteousness of the past and the licentiousness of the pagan community.

And in truth the law had functioned with extraordinary efficiency as a barrier between the Jewish world and the pagan corruptions. As one may see in East-Side streets in New York to-day, so in the Jewish community in the old Roman world, the legal arrangements isolated the Jewish community and gave to religious orthodoxy its one chance to stamp itself upon the youthful mind. They did not always succeed; they do not now always succeed; a large percentage broke away from law and were lost in the pagan tide, but a small minority always remained faithful and bore aloft the banner of righteousness according to Moses and the worship of Jehovah according to the ancient prophets. Why should not Christianity enter into this splendid Jewish heritage, preserve intact this wonderful isolation, and thus screen the Christian Church from the pagan world with equal effectiveness?

It is the old tragic struggle between law and authority, between the principle of life and progress and the timidity and natural fear that would seek to anchor itself in the past, to remain the same even if the whole world changed. And Paul saw more deeply into the real spirit of the struggle than did these teachers from Jerusalem. The letter to the Galatians and the letter to the Romans may be almost summed up in the words of our text: "We, through the Spirit, wait for the hope of righteousness."

It is a tragic struggle because so much may be said on both sides. The past has had its triumphs, authority has yet its function; we are the children of the past; we have all been under authority. So largely has authority functioned in life that it must loom large on the horizon of us all; as children we obeyed our parents, as students we were under the authority of teachers; as citizens we feel that large sections of our life are under the authority of the community. We need the pressures of authority; who of us does not turn eagerly to the authority of the expert, feeling his own incompetence and glad in the last resort to trust to one more fully fitted? And authority is so definite—brings with it a sense of peace; relieves us from the strain and

struggle of our own decision, so that it is indeed a tragic moment when the boy or girl discovers that father and mother are not infallible, that the religious teacher makes mistakes even in morals, that the professor has already become antiquated, who once seemed so far in the van. Paul's principle of liberty seems desperately dangerous in the presence of immaturity and the raw inexperience of the average human life. And yet, the question can never be actually put down—was Paul not right? Is his principle not the fundamental religious one?

True it is, that the teachers of Jerusalem, in a large way, won their battle. Paul's principle was obscured, and unstable men wrested it to their own destruction. Much of the outward form of Judaism disappeared; but the Church became another synagog, the New Testament writings a simple addition to the law and the prophets, the fathers of the Church a new school of scribes, the creedal utterances a new *mischna* and a new interpretation of law. The irony of the situation is most plainly seen when we realize that poor Paul's own writings became an addition to the law he dreaded.

His principle was never wholly lost sight of, in spite of the substantially authoritative character of Augustine's system. Augustine at his best was profoundly Pauline, and there were voices of heretics all through the ages who raised again the cry of freedom. Yes, even within the Church men like Jovianus and Claudius stood strongly for the same freedom wherewith Christ had made us free. And at each religious revival men like Luther stood up to assert once more that we dare not identify our faith with even the fairest triumphs of the past; that if we were to be found faithful we, too, through the Spirit, must wait for the hope of righteousness, and that this faith, energizing by love, was more than law and larger and more effective than any tradition.

What is, then, the inwardness of this struggle? The essence of it is that which Paul clearly saw to be a contradiction between attitudes toward life where compromise is impossible; that this Galatian church had to choose between the teachers of Jerusalem and the teachings of Jesus Christ—and Paul was right. He had better understood Jesus than these teachers from Jerusalem, for Jesus had stood against all authority and defied it in the name and in the power of an inward assurance. "Ye have heard, Jesus said, how they of old time said unto you, but I say unto you." This Jesus taught as one having authority within; this Jesus broke the Sabbath day in the name of God and said the Sabbath was made for man and not man for the Sabbath; this Jesus broke the Levitical law in the name of humanity and healed the sick, and let the hungry feed themselves on the Sabbath day in the assurance that he was Lord of the Sabbath. It was this defiance of the outward law, it was this break with external authority, that cost the great innovator his life, and Paul felt, and felt rightly, that the cross of Christ was made vain and that the death of Jesus was bereft of significance if the faith of Jesus was buried again under the burdens of external enactment.

And history has been with Paul. All that he foresaw in writing to the Galatians took place, and all too speedily. Formalism, legalism, priestcraft and imperial ambition swallowed up the beautiful gospel of the Nazarene and left the church of the Middle Ages the merest caricature of Paul's community of propaganda.

And when, after Luther, authority in the Puritan State again asserted itself to a lesser degree, all the evils against which the Reformation contended reasserted themselves—formalism, hypocrisy, sectarianism, dogged the steps of the Reformation Church. Protestantism took no part in the evangelization of the world into which Jesuitism threw itself. Protestantism failed to organize her forces on any principle larger than the broken fragments of scholastic creeds. Protestantism had to wait for the great evangelical revival before she again began to realize that her strength is the life of faith. and that we who are really Protestants through the Spirit must wait for the hope of righteousness; and that our principle is not law and external authority, but faith, and faith only, working by love.

It is this venture of faith that marks the movement of the modern religious world. The triumphs of the past are but the stepping-stones to the victories of the future. We must realize that the function of the past was principally as a training-ground for the freedom to make new and more glorious pasts. A really modern Protestantism stands firmly upon the same inward assurance that gave Paul his power of prophecy and which spoke the life-giving word in Jesus Christ.

But it may be said we are not Pauls, and least of all are we to put ourselves on a level with Jesus Christ. This is fundamentally wrong. The faith of Paul is to be our faith; and tho we are not on a level with Jesus Christ, if we follow His leadership it is that we may, as He promised, become sons of God. Authority and law have only temporary place in the household of God, and Paul is right in interpreting Jesus as calling to us to become the sons of God and to enter into the freedom of sonship. It is a tremendous venture of faith; it involves, indeed, immense moral, intellectual, and spiritual risks, but it is the risk of the religious life; it is the inevitable outcome of the life of faith; it is because we believe in God that we, through the Spirit, wait for the hope of righteousness. Our faces are to the future. The past has its messages for us, but they are not final. The past had its triumphs, but they are only the foretaste of still larger victory. The past had its life, but to seek to go back to it is but to find it death. We wait for a hope of righteousness, the larger vision of new heavens and new earth, organized in the beauty of God's holiness on the basis of loving faith, energizing effectively along all lines of life and in the tragic conflict between external authority and living faith, the great heroes of the past—Paul, Augustine, Origen—yes, even some of those who, like Gregory the Great and Leo the First, and the great Hildebrand, summon us to take part with the best in Luther and Calvin and Wesley in building into the new world the triumphant faith that God is a living God and that we, through the Spirit, work and wait with Him for the coming, completer vision of righteousness, holiness and peace.

NEWELL DWIGHT HILLIS

1858-1929

GOD THE UNWEARIED GUIDE

BIOGRAPHICAL NOTE

NEWELL DWIGHT HILLIS was born at Magnolia, Iowa, in 1858. He first became known as a preacher of the first rank during his pastorate over the large Presbyterian church in Evanston, Illinois. This reputation led to his being called to the Central Church, Chicago, in which he succeeded Dr. David Swing, and where from the first he attracted audiences completely filling one of the largest auditoriums in Chicago. In 1899 he was called to Plymouth Church, Brooklyn, to succeed Dr. Lyman Abbott in the pulpit made famous by the ministry of Henry Ward Beecher. By his strong personality and mental gifts he drew to his church a large and eager following. His best known books are "A Man's Value to Society," and "The Investment of Influence."

Comfort ye, comfort ye, my people, saith your God, &c.—Isaiah xl., 1-31. *He shall not fail, nor be discouraged.*—xliv., 4.

THIS is an epic of the unwearied God, and the fainting strength of man. For splendor of imagery, for majesty and elevation, it is one of the supreme things in literature. Perhaps no other Scripture has exerted so profound an influence upon the world's leaders. Luther read it in the fortress of Salzburg, John Brown read it in the prison at Harper's Ferry. Webster made it the model of his eloquence, Wordsworth, Carlyle and a score of others refer to its influence upon their literary style, their thought and life. Like all the supreme things in eloquence, this chapter is a spark struck out of the fires of war and persecution. Its author was not simply an exile—he was a slave who had known the dungeon and the fetter. Bondage is hard, even for savages, naked, ignorant, and newly drawn from the jungle, but slavery is doubly hard for scholars and prophets, for Hebrew merchants and rulers.

This outburst of eloquence took its rise in a war of invasion. When the northern host swept southward, and overwhelmed Jerusalem, the onrushing wave was fretted with fire; later, when the wave of war retreated, it carried back the detritus of a ruined civilization. The story of the siege of Jerusalem, the assault upon its gates, the fall of the walls, all the horrors of famine and of pestilence, are given in the earlier chapters of this wonderful book. The homeward march of the Persian army was a kind of triumphal procession in which the Hebrew princes and leaders walked as captives. The king marched in the guise of a slave, with his eyes put out, followed by sullen princes, with bound hands, and unsubdued hearts. As slaves the Hebrews crossed the Euphrates at the very point where Xenophon crossed with his immortal ten thousand. In the land of bondage the exiles were planted, not in military prisons, but in gangs, working now in the fields, now in the streets of the city, and always under the scourge of soldiers. When thirty years had passed the forty thousand captives were scattered among the people, one brother in the palace, and another a slave in the fields. Soon their religion became only a memory, their language was all but forgotten, their old customs and manner of life were utterly gone.

But God raised up two gifted souls for just such an emergency as this. One youth, through sheer force of genius, climbed to the position of prime minister, while a young girl through her loveliness came to the king's palace. One day an emancipation proclamation went forth, from a king who had come to believe in the unseen God who loved justice, and would overwhelm oppression and wrong. The good news went forth on wings of the wind. Making ready for their return to their homeland, all the captives gathered on the outskirts of the desert. It was a piteous spectacle. The people were broken in health, their beauty marred, their weapon a staff, their garments the leather coat, their provisions pieces of moldy bread, and their path fifteen hundred miles of sands, across the desert. To such an end had come a disobedient and sinful generation!

In that hour, beholding these exiles and captives, a flood of emotions rushed over the poet; he saw those bound who should conquer; he saw that men were slaves who should be kings. Then, with a rush, an immeasurable longing shivers through him like a trumpet call. Oh, to save them! To perish for their saving! To die for their life, to be offered for them all! In an abandon of grief and sympathy, he began to speak to them in words of comfort and hope. At first these exiles, dumb with pain and grief, listened, but listened with no light quivering in the eye, and no hope flitting like sunshine across the face. Their yesterdays held bondage, blows and degradation; their to-morrow held only the desert and the return to a ruined land. Then the word of the Lord came upon the poet. What if the night winds did go mourning through the deserted streets of their capital! What if their language had decayed and their institutions had perished? What if the farmer's field was only a waste of thorns and thickets, and the towns become heaps and ruins! What if the king of Babylon and his army has trampled them under foot, as slaves trample the shellfish, crushing out the purple dye that lends rich color to a royal robe? "Comfort ye, comfort ye, my people." Is the way long and through a desert? "Every valley shall be exalted, every mountain and hill shall be made low." Has slavery worn man's strength to nothingness until he is as weak as the broken reed and the withered grass? The spirit of the Lord will revive the grass, trampled down by the hoofs of war horses. Soon the bruised root shall redden into the rose and the fluted stem climb into the tree. And think you if God's winds can transform a spray and twig into a trunk fit for foundation of house or mast of ship, that eternal arms can not equip with strength the hand of patriot?

Is the Shepherd and Leader of His little flock unequal to their guidance across the desert? "Behold the Lord will come with a strong arm; he shall feed his flock like a shepherd and he shall gather the lambs in his arms and carry them in his bosom." What! Man's hand unequal to the task of rebuilding Jerusalem? Hath not God pledged His strength to the worker, that God whose arm strikes out worlds as the smith strikes out sparks upon the anvil? Is not man's helper that God who dippeth up the seas in the hollow of His hand? Who weighs the mountains with scales and the hills in the balance? What! Thine enemies too strong for thee? Why, God looketh upon all the nations and enemies of the earth as but a drop in the bucket. He sendeth forth His breath, and the tribes disappear as dust is blown from the balance. Then the trumpet call shivered through these exiles. "Hast thou not known? Have the sons of the fathers never heard of the everlasting God, the Lord, Creator of the ends of the earth? Fainteth not, neither is weary!" Heavy is the task, but the Eternal giveth power and strength. Even tho young patriots and heroes faint and fall, they that wait upon the Lord shall renew their strength. While fulfilling their task of rebuilding they shall mount up with wings as eagles, they shall run and not be weary, they shall walk and not faint. Oh, what a word is this! What page in literature is comparable to it for comfort! Wonderful the strength of the warrior! Mighty the influence of the statesman! All powerful seems the inventor, but greater still the poet who dwells above the clang and dust of time, with the world's secret trembling on his lips.

He needs no converse nor companionship,
In cold starlight, whence thou can not come,
The undelivered tidings in his breast,
Will not let him rest.
He who looks down upon the immemorable throng,
And binds the ages with a song.
And through the accents of our time,
There throbs the message of eternity.

And so the unwearied God comforted the fainting strength of man.

Primarily, this glorious outburst was addrest to the exiles as heads of families. The father's strength was broken and his children had been crusht and ground to earth. The ancient patrimony was gone; he had gathered his little ones in from the huts where slaves dwelt. He was leading his little band of pilgrims into a desert. But the prophet spoke to the exiles as to men who believed that the family was the great national institution. With us, the family is important, but with these Hebrew exiles the family was everything. For them the home was the spring from whence the mighty river rolled forth. The family was the headwaters of national, industrial, social and religious life. Every father was revered as the architect of the family fortune. The first ambition of every young Hebrew was to found a family. Just as abroad, a patrician gentleman builds a baronial mansion, fills it with art treasures, hangs the shields and portraits of his ancestors upon the walls, hoping to hand the mansion forward to generations yet unborn, so every worthy Hebrew longed to found a noble family. How keen the anguish, therefore, of this exile in the desert! What a scene is that of the exiles upon the edge of the desert. Darkness is upon the land and the fire burns low into coals. Worn and exhausted, children are sleeping beside the mother. Here is an old man, lying apart, broken and bitter in spirit—one son stands forth a dim figure—looking down upon his aged parents, upon the wife of his bosom and upon his little children. Standing under the stars, he meditates his plans. How shall he care for these, when he returns to his ruined estate? In the event of death, what arm shall lift a shield above these little ones? What if sickness or death pounce upon a home as an eagle upon a dove, as wolves upon lambs, or as brigands descend from the mountains upon sleeping herdsmen!

Every founder of a family knows the agony of such an hour! We are in a world where men are never more than a few weeks from possible poverty and want; little wonder then that all men seek to provide for the future of the home and the children. But to the exile standing in the darkness, with love that broods above his babes, there comes this word of comfort: God's solicitude for you and yours will not let Him slumber or sleep! God will lift up a highway for the feet of the little band of pilgrims. The eternal God shall be thy guide in the march through the desert. His pillar of cloud by day and of fire by night shall stand in the sky; He shall lead the flock like a shepherd; He shall gather the little ones in His arms, and carry the children in His bosom. And if the father fall on the march, the wings of the Eternal shall brood the babes that are left. His right arm shall be a sword and His left arm a shield. The eternal God fainteth not, neither is weary. Having time to care for the stars, and to lead them forth by name, He hath time and thought also for His children. What a word is this for the home! What comfort for all whose hearts turn toward their children! What a pledge to fathers for generations yet unborn! This truth arms every parent for any emergency. For God is round about every home as the mountains are round about Jerusalem, for bounty and protection.

But the sage was also thinking of men whose hopes were broken, and whose lives were baffled and beaten. These exiles, crossing the desert, might have claimed for themselves the poet's phrase, "Lo, henceforth I am a prisoner of hope." Like Dante, they might have cried, "For years my pillow by night has been wet with tears, and all day long have I held heartbreak at bay." For these whose glorious youth had been exhausted by bondage, life had run to its very dregs. Gone the days of glorious strength! Gone all the opportunities that belong to the era when the heart is young, the limitations of life had become severe! Environment often is a cage against whose iron bars the soul beats bloody wings in vain!

How many men are held back by one weak nerve, or organ! How many are shut in, and limited, and just fall short of supreme success because of an hereditary weakness, handed on by the fathers! How many made one mistake in youth in choosing the occupation and discovered the error when it was too late! How many erred in judgment in their youth, through one critical blunder, that has been irretrievable, and whose burden is henceforth lasht to the back! In such an hour of depression, Isaiah assembles the exiles, and exclaims, "Comfort ye, comfort ye, my people. Tho your young men faint and be weary, tho the strong utterly fail, yet God is the unwearied one; with his help thou shalt take thy burden, and mount up with wings as eagles; with his unwearied strength thou shalt run with thy load and not be weary, and walk and not faint." For this is the experience of persecution and the reward of sorrow, bravely borne that the fainting strength of man is supplemented by the sure help of the unwearied God.

Therefore, in retrospect, exiles, prisoners, martyrs, who have believed in God seem fortunate. The endungeoned heroes often seem the children of careful good fortune and happiness. The saints, walking through the fire, stand forth as those who are dear unto God. How the point of view changes events. Kitto was deaf, and in his youth his deafness broke his heart, but because his ears were closed to the din of life, he became the great scholar of his time, and swept the treasures of the world into a single volume, an armory of intellectual weapons. Fawcett was blind, but through that blindness became a great analytic student, a master of organization, and served all England in her commerce. John Bright was broken-hearted, standing above the bier, but Richard Cobden called him from his sorrow to become a voice for the poor, to plead the cause of the opprest, and bring about the Corn Laws for the hungry workers in the factories and shops. Comfort ye, comfort ye, my people.

Let the exile say unto himself: "Your warfare is accomplished; your iniquity is pardoned; the Lord's hand will give unto thee double for all thy sins that are forgiven.'' The great faiths and convictions of the prophets and law-givers, your language and your laws and your liberties, have not been destroyed by captivity; rather slavery has saved them. At last you know their value; in contrast with the idolatry of the Euphrates, the jargon of tongues, the inequality of rights, the organization of justice and oppression, how wonderful the equity of the laws of Moses! How beautiful the faith of the fathers! How surely founded the laws of God. Henceforth idolatry, injustice and sin became as monstrous in their ugliness as they were wicked in their essence. Everything else might go, but not the faith of the fathers. Persecution was like fire on the vase; it burned the colors in. Little wonder that the tradition tells us that for the next hundred years, at stated periods, all the people in the land came together, while a reader repeated this chapter on the unwearied God and the fainting strength of man that had recovered unto hope, men whose hopes had been baffled and beaten.

The thought of an unwearied God is also the true antidote to despondency. The ground of optimism is in God. When that great thinker described certain people as without God and without hope, there was sure logic in his phrase, for the Godless man is always the hopeless man. Between no God anywhere and the one God who is everywhere, there is no middle ground. Either we are children, buffeted about by fate and circumstances, with events tossing souls about in an eternal game of battledore and shuttlecock, or else the world is our Father's house, and God standeth within the shadow, keeping watch above His own. For the man who believes in God, who allies himself to nature, who makes the universe his partner, there is no defeat, and no death, and no interruption of his prosperity. Concede that there is a God, and it follows as a logical necessity that He will not permit any enemy to ruin your life and His plans. For a man who holds this faith it follows that there can be no defeat, or failure. Indeed, the essential difference between men is the difference in their relation toward God. Here are the biographies of two great men. Both are men of genius, both are marvelously equipped, but their end was, oh, how different. One is Martin Luther, who stood forth alone, affirming his religious freedom, in the face of enemies and devils thick as the tiles on the roofs of the houses. The few friends Luther had shut him up in a fortress to save his life, but Luther mightily believed in God. With the full consent of his marvelous gifts, he surrendered his life to the will of God. Knowing that his days were as brief as the withering grass, he allied himself with the Eternal. In his discouragement he read these words, ''The Everlasting God fainteth not, neither is weary.'' In that hour Martin Luther shouted for joy. The beetling walls of the fortress were as tho they were not. Victorious he went forth, in thought, ranging throughout all Germany. And going out, he went up and down the land telling the people that God would protect him, and soon Germany was free.

Goethe tells us that Luther was the architect of modern German language and literature, and stamped himself into the whole national life. The Germany of the Kaiser is simply Martin Luther written large in fifty millions of men. But what made Luther? There was some hidden energy and spirit within him! What was this spirit in him? The spirit of beauty turned a lump of mud into that Grecian face about which Keats wrote his poem. The spirit of truth changes a little ink into a beautiful song. The spirit of strength and beauty in an architect changes a pile of bricks into a house or cathedral or gallery. And the thought of our unwearied God changed the collier's son into the great German emancipator. But over against this man, who never knew despondency, after his vision hour, stands another German. He, too, was a philosopher, clothed with ample power, and blest with oportunity. But he did evil in his life, and then the heart lost its faith, and hope utterly perished. The more he loved pleasure and pursued self, the more cynical and bitter he became. Pessimism set a cold, hard stamp upon his face, and marred his beauty. Cynicism lies like a black mark across his pages. At last, in his bitterness, the philosopher tells us the whole universe is a mirage, and that yonder summer-making sun is a bubble that repeats its iridescent tints in the colors of the rainbow. Despair ate out his heart. He became the most miserable of men, and knew no freedom from sorrow and pain. And lo, now the man's philosophy has perished like a bubble, his influence has utterly disappeared, for his books are unread, while only an occasional scholar chances upon his name, tho the great summer-making sun still shines on and Luther's eternal God fainteth not, neither is weary.

Are you weak, oh, patriot? Remember God is strong. Do your days of service seem short, until your life is scarcely longer than the flower that blooms to-day and is gone to-morrow? God is eternal, and He will take care of your work. Are you sick with hope long deferred? Hope thou in God; He shall yet send succor. Have troubles driven happiness from thee, as the hawk drives the young lark or nightingale from its nest? Return unto thy rest, troubled heart, for the Lord will deal bountifully with thee. Are you anxious for your children? God will bring the child back from the far country. For the child hath wandered far, the golden thread spun in a mother's heart is an unbroken thread that will draw him home! For things that distress you to-day, you shall thank God to-morrow. Nothing shall break the golden chain that binds you to God's throne. Are you hopeless and despondent because of your fainting strength? Remember that the antidote for despondency is the thought of the unwearied God, who is doing the best He can for you, and whose ceaseless care neither slumbers nor sleeps.

Little wonder therefore that God became all and in all to this feeble band of captives, journeying across the desert back to their ruined life and land. God had taken away earthly things from them, that He might be their all and in all. When the earth is made poor for us, sometimes the heavens become rich. God closed the eyes of Milton to the beauty in land and sea and sky, that he might see the companies of angels marching and countermarching on the hills of God. He closed the ears of Beethoven, that he might hear the music of St. Cecilia falling over heaven's battlements. He gave Isaiah a slave's hut, that he might ponder the house not made with hands, eternal in the heavens. How is it that this prophet and poet has become companion of the great ones of the earth? At the time Isaiah rebelled against his bondage, but when it was all over, and the fitful fever had passed, and the fleshly fetters had fallen, he smiled at the things that once alarmed him, as he recalled his fainting strength and the unwearied God.

Gone—that ancient capital. Babylon is a heap. Jerusalem a ruin! But this epic of the unwearied Guide still lives! Isaiah, can never die! Can a chapter die that has cheered the exile in his loneliness, that has comforted the soldier upon his bivouac, that has braced the martyr for his execution, that has given songs at midnight to the prisoners in the dungeon? Out of suffering and captivity came this song of rest and hope. At last the poet praised the eternal God for his bonds and his imprisonment. Oh, it is darkness that makes the morning light so welcome to the weary watcher. It is hunger that makes bread sweet. It is pain and sickness that gives value to the physician and his medicine. It is business trouble that makes you honor your lawyer and counselor, and it is the sense of need that makes God near.

Are there any merchants here who are despondent? Remember the eternal God and make your appeal to the future. Are there any parents whose children have wandered far? When they are old, the children will return to the path of faith and obedience. Are there any in whom the immortal hope burns low? The smoking flax He will not quench, but will fan the flame into victory. Look up to-day; be comforted once more. Work henceforth in hope. Live like a prince. Scatter sunshine. Let your atmosphere be happiness. If troubles come, let them be the dark background that shall throw your hope and faith into bolder relief. God hath set His heart upon you to deliver you. Tho your hand faint, and the tool fall, the eternal God fainteth not, neither is weary. He will bring thy judgment unto victory, immortalize thy good deeds, and crown thy career with everlasting renown.

HENRY SCOTT HOLLAND
1847-1918

THE STORY
OF A DISCIPLE'S FAITH

BIOGRAPHICAL NOTE

HENRY SCOTT HOLLAND, English clergyman and author, was born at Wimbledon in 1847. He was educated at Eton and Oxford, at which university he was distinguished for learning and character. In 1884 he was appointed Canon of St. Paul's Cathedral, London. He has published "Logic and Life"; "Creed and Character," and other volumes.

Then went in also that other disciple which came first to the sepulchre, and he saw and believed.—John xx., 8.

JOHN, the beloved disciple, has given his witness, has made his confession. What he once touched, and tasted, and handled, that he has declared unto us. It was the shining, the epiphany of God the Father which he and the twelve had discovered, tabernacled close at their side in the body of Christ. "We saw his glory, the glory as of God himself." So he pronounces. Yet still his listeners sit on about his feet. They hear great words, but these words are the end of a long and anxious meditation. The apostle is giving us, is giving them his completed conclusions—yes, and they have accepted the conclusions; they hold them fast. But it is not enough to know what they ought to believe, tho that is much—they must also know the process by which the conclusion is to be reached. They must reproduce in themselves the living story of its formation. They must be conscious of its stages, its degrees, and its growth. They can not surely be as reapers entering into the labors of others who went forth weeping with good seed. They must feel their own faith grow, first the blade, then the ear, and so at last, in ample richness, the full corn in the ear; and therefore they went on wondering. "Let us hear it all," they say; "tell us of that day when first it came to you that something wonderful was there. Tell us how you slowly learned the great mystery; and then tell us when and how it was that the full truth broke from your heart and from your lips. Tell us this, that so we, too, may say with you and with ten thousand times ten thousand: 'Worthy is the Lamb that was slain.'"

This is the question that St. John sets himself to answer; and you can see that it is so by this, that he begins his gospel, not with our Lord's own beginning, the baptism by John, but with the day on which the disciples began to believe on Him; and he ends it, not with our Lord's own ending, His ascension, but with the first completed confession of Jesus by an apostle—the confession of Thomas. This achieved, his gospel is done; he has nothing to add but one scene that to him was full of tender personal interest.

The Fourth Gospel tells us how the apostolic faith was built and established. Let us carefully turn to it, for it is a revelation of the apostle's own heart. The old man himself is bidding us draw near and taste of his own experiences. He unlocks his soul to us that he may help us to mount up into his assured peace, so calm, so sure, so strong. He sits there murmuring always his: "Come, Lord Jesus, even come"; and round about him, enthroned in the majesty of age, is that mysterious silence in which the voices of the Spirit and the Bride say: "Come." And yet he can turn from that upward vision and bend his eyes back on us—on us, so perplexed, and troubled, and hesitating, and fearful, and bewildered. He can yearn to make us fellowship in his joy. "Little children, it is the last hour. Even now are there many antichrists. And now, my little children, abide in him. My little children, let no man lead you astray, for this is the true God and eternal life; and therefore, O my children, keep yourselves from idols." So tender, so beseeching, the fatherly love! And in the name of that love he sets himself to tell the story of his own conversion, how he had begun. He can recall every tiny detail of that first critical hour. It began on the day when John the Baptist cast off the hopes that were so eagerly bent upon him; for he it was, the Baptist, and not the Lord Jesus, who first woke in their hearts that spiritual movement which became Christianity. He roused first the cry of the new faith, and passionately they had given him their souls—they and all who, seeing John, mused in their hearts what would be the Christ. Even the Pharisees of Jerusalem felt the excitement and shared the hope; and it was to their deputation that the Baptist made his great repudiation: "No; I am not it, not the Christ; no, nor Elias, nor a prophet. I am nought but a flying cry in the wilderness, a cry that floats by on the wind and perishes. Not I, but another—another who comes after me; yea, who is now standing among you, even tho you know it not." So he confest. He denied not, but confest; so brave a heart he had! All those hearts were at his service, a world of devotion all lying there at his feet; but he would not be tempted. He knew his own limits; he would have none of it. He confest, and denied not: "I am not the Christ."

And then came the great moment. It was the very next day after the great confession —so exact is the apostle's memory. The very day after, John saw Jesus coming toward him, and a wonderful word broke from him: "Behold the Lamb of God, which taketh away the sins of the world." Taketh away the sin! Oh, the peace of such a promise to those who had been washed in Jordan, and had repented, and had confest, and yet found their burden of sin as miserable, as intolerable as ever! The words haunted them; and when, the day following, John uttered them again,

two of them at least could not rest. Their hearts burned to know more. Who is this strange visitant—so quiet, so silent, so unobserved? He makes no sign. He says no word. He invites no attention. He does not even stop to look. He just passes by; and, lo! He is already passed—in another moment He will have gone. They must act for themselves then. They will force Him to stop and tell them the secret. So two of them that heard John speak followed Him—two of them, and John the beloved, who now tells us the story, was one of the two. And now that they followed, He, the Stranger, must turn and speak. For the first time, then, He looked upon them with that look which again and again had power to draw a soul, by one glance, out of the night of sin into the life of eternal light. He turned and saw them following, and it was then they heard His voice first speak— that voice which by its cry could raise the dead. "Whom seek ye?" That was all. And they—they hardly knew what to say—only they must see Him, must go with Him; and they stammered out: "Rabbi, where dwellest thou?" And He said: "Come and see."

Come and see! It was all as quiet and natural and easy as any ordinary interview. No one could have seen anything unusual. Just a few words of salutation—just three short sentences that could be said in half a minute. And yet that sealed their lot for eternity. That was the moment of decision. "Come and see." They went and saw. So intense is the apostle's memory of that blest hour that he can never forget the very hour of the day. It was just ten o'clock when he got to the house. They stopt there with Him that night; and in the morning they were sure of what they had found—so sure that neither of them could rest until he had hurried off with the good news to find and bring his brother. Andrew found his brother before John could find James; or else it was that both went at once to seek for Peter, and Andrew found him first. Anyhow, when Peter was found, both were prepared to assert, "We have found the Christ." And so they brought the great chief to his Master; and in a moment the Master knew what He had won in that loyal, loving soul, and He turned those deep eyes upon him, and named him by his new name. "Thou art Simon, the son of Jonas; thou shalt be called Cephas."

So it all began. The very next day after that the Master Himself added one other to the number—Philip a friend of Peter's and Andrew's—and Philip brought Nathaniel; and these were the little band whom the Master took with Him from Jordan to Cana— the seed of that great Church which now reigns from Babylon to Rome.

"And what next"—so the listeners ask— "what was the next step made?" Three days later, at Cana, for the first time, came that strange secret of which the apostle had spoken. The glory shone out with a sudden flash from the deeps within Him; a word of power leapt out—very quietly. Very few saw or knew it. But as the few saw there the white water redden into wine, they knew, and felt the wonder of that change which had passed over their own being. That word of power was at its work within them, transforming them from out of sickly impotence into splendid energy. They saw now what it was that had happened when the Lord spoke, that it would have the same power whether He spoke to matter or spirit, to body or soul; whether He said: "Thy sins be forgiven thee," or "Rise up and walk." As water into wine, so the old into the new.

So the light flashed; so the secret made its first disclosure. It had vanished again, for His hour had not yet come; but they had seen it, and this is John's enduring record, remembered by us this day, that there first at Cana Jesus manifested His glory, and there His disciples first believed in Him.

And what next did they learn? It was at Jerusalem, the Passover feast. The Master made His first entry and startled them, for He who was so quiet and reserved burned with a sudden fury as He looked upon the temple of Jehovah. Very, very rarely did He show Himself excited or disturbed; but then He was terrible. He bound together a scourge of small cords. He drove the cattle in front of Him; He dashed over the money-changers' tables. And John can recall still the look of the coins as they poured down upon the pavement. And they, the disciples, wondered at the violence of the emotion, until a word from an old Psalm came into their minds, and they remembered how it was written that the zeal of the Lord's house should be in a prophet's heart like a devouring fire.

At that time, too, the Lord Himself gave a sign and spoke a word, which at the time the disciples could make nothing of, and forgot. It was about the temple being destroyed and raised again in three days. They forgot it; but long after, when He had risen from the dead, the old words came back to them: "After three days I shall raise it again"; and they remembered then how He had spoken them two years before His death, and as they remembered, they believed. . . .

And how can we stop to follow the apostle through all the wonderful story? Yet just one thing we can not pass over—the awful hours of crisis in Galilee. It came just when all looked brightest, when the people were rushing round Him, and would have made Him a king. They would have gone with Him to the death. But He—He threw it all away to the winds. He hurried off the twelve in a body across the lake, for they had caught the crowd's enthusiasm, and could not be calmed. He scattered the crowd; He fled back Himself alone into the dark hills, and on the morrow at Capernaum, He broke it all down by a word which staggered the rising belief. It was a saying about His body and His blood—a very hard saying. Not only were the Pharisees furious, but His own followers were dumfounded. They could not bear it, could not believe. They fell away, and walked no more with Jesus.

"And you, O disciple dearly loved, what of you and your brethren?" "Most terrible, most bitter that hour, my children," the old man answers. "We walked trembling, quaking, behind him. We were cowed and disheartened, until he the Master felt himself the chill of our dismay, and He turned to us and challenged our failing faith. 'Will ye also go away?' Oh, the shame of being open to a charge of such meanness! The very tenderness of the question and of the reproach recalled and recovered us. We knew nothing. We could explain nothing. Every clue was lost. The darkness was thickening over our heads, our hearts were failing for fear, our souls were sinking in the great water-floods, earth was falling from us; struggle, and anguish, and doubt shook us with wild alarm; and yet, even so as he turned his eyes upon us, the old unconquerable faith woke, and stirred, and quickened; and with a rush, as of a mighty wind, it lifted us; and out from Peter's lips broke the words which saved us— the words which sealed us to Him forever: 'Will we go away? Nay, Lord, to whom shall we go? Thou hast the words of eternal life!' So we spoke with burning hearts, and yet through and through us still those strange eyes of His pierced. Deep below all our emotion He penetrated. Quite calmly He weighed its worth; and in one of us even then He detected a flaw which would widen and worsen. One of us, He knew, hung back from echoing St. Peter's confession. One spirit there was there that could not throw off its dismay, one dark spirit in whom the hard saying was the seed of bitter and poisonous fruit. 'Have I not chosen you twelve, and yet one of you is a devil?' He spoke of Judas Iscariot, who should betray him."

So they followed and clung, the trembling band; clung through all the harrowing days in which the Jewish enmity hardened itself into the hate of hates; clung even tho their souls fell away from the rapture of St. Peter to the desperate wail of Thomas: "Let us go with him that at least we may die with him"; clung even through the terrors of that last evening, when they sat shaking with the very shudder of death, and the soul of the Master Himself was trouble-tossed, and there was the scent of treachery in the air, and the end was very near, and He spake dim, dark words that they could not follow—only they knew one thing, that He was to be taken from them, and they sat shrouded in a mighty sorrow such as no assurances even of His could lessen or lift. One moment there was indeed even then in which they seemed suddenly to lay hold of His meaning. "Now we believe," they cried. "Now we are sure that thou camest forth from God." So they cried, and yet He met their professions with a sorrowful hesitation. "Do ye now believe? Yea; the hour is all but come when ye will all flee and leave me alone." How sad and cowed they felt at the rebuff! Were they then never to rise into the joy of clear and entire belief? Yes; it came at last. Blest assurance! Let John tell how it was reached by him.

Two points he singles out for himself as marking epochs of his own conviction, and in them both we are let inside the workings of his innermost mind. And how curious, yet how natural is the working! For in every hour of agony the mind becomes strangely and fearfully alert to very little things. It is sensitive to sudden and ineffaceable impressions. It is touched into the swiftest and subtlest activity by the tiniest touches of detail. Often in the supreme moment of a dark tragedy, the fibers of the imagination seem to close round some minute incident, like the ticking of a clock in the hush of a death-chamber; and never throughout the long years that follow can it detach that tiny incident from its memory of the black hour. And so with St. John. He stood below the bitter cross, and he saw the nails beaten through the hands and feet, and he heard the last loud cry, and yet still his despair hung heavy as death upon his soul, until, just at the touch of the soldier's spear, there broke from the dead side a little jet of blood and water. What was it that he saw and felt? What was it that so startled him? Why could that little jet of blood and water never pass out of his sight? Why should it haunt him sixty years after, as still his heart wonders over the mysterious witness of the water and the blood? We can not tell. Perhaps he could never tell. Only his spirit woke with a start. Only a strange tremor shook him, and somehow just then, just at that little pivot moment, he must break off all his story, to declare with abrupt and quivering emphasis: "This is the disciple that wrote these things. He it is who saw the water and the blood, and he knows that his record is true."

And once again, in the haste of the resurrection morning, what was the moment and what was the scene which turned his despair into belief? It was the moment at which he stooped down and saw within the empty tomb the folded napkin and the linen clothes. What did he notice? Why, that the napkin that had been round the Master's head was not lying with the linen clothes, but was rolled up in a place by itself. A tiny, tiny thing! Yet somehow it was that which he saw and never forgot. It was that which he could never omit from his story of the resurrection—the rolled-up napkin lying apart from the linen clothes. Was it the sudden sense that struck him of order and seemliness as of a thing premeditated, intended? Was it the reaction of detecting the quiet tokens of deliberate purpose there, where all had seemed to him a very chaos of confusion? Who can say? Only just then a key was somewhat turned and a bolt shot back somewhere within his breast, and a secret flashed in upon him, and a thrill of insight rushed over him, and his blindness fell off as it had been scales, and a quiver of hope shot up like a flame, and a new light broke over him, and he passed at one bound out of death into life. "Then entered in, therefore, that other disciple which came first to the tomb, and he saw and believed."

My brethren, where do you stand? How far have you come in this pathway of faith? Are you yet at the beginning, looking wistfully, with hungry eyes, after a hundred gallant human heroes who point you this way and that? Are you musing in your heart which of them may be your guide and master, which is the Christ? Good, and fair, and high they may be; but they must all confess it, they can not deny it—they are not the Christ. And all of them who are honest will earnestly assure you, "It is not I, but another." Oh, and that that other even now standeth among you, tho you know Him not yet; and there is a voice gone out upon Him which has gone out upon none other ever born of woman, with this witness, "Behold the Lamb of God, which taketh away the sin of the world!"

Consider it. What an assurance! Who is there that has ever been brave enough to accept such a salutation without a whisper of protest, without a shadow of a scruple? Who is this that dares to stand up before the entire mass of His fellows and say, "Come, all who are weary and heavy-laden—come, all who are burdened sorely with sin—come all to me—I will give you rest?" Who is He? Look at Him. He is passing even now before you. Follow Him. He is very quiet, and still, and silent; but follow Him. He will turn at last and speak, and invite you—invite you a little further. "Master, where dwellest thou?" "Come and see."

O Jesus, Lord and lover of souls, there are many of us laden with sickness and sin, so many that are sad with doubt and fear, that are asking: "Master, where dwellest thou?" Oh, let them even come home with Thee and see. Go and see. Abide with Him, talk with Him. Wait upon Him. Learn His words. Take up His gospels. Read them with care, with silence to yourself, with thought and prayer. Abide with Him one night at least, that you may in the morning be able to tell your fellows: "I have found the Christ." And then suddenly, now and again, a light flashes, and a glory is made manifest to you. Some touch of Divine benediction will break out of the secret silence, some sudden joy, some gift of power. It is as at Cana with you when the water ran into wine.

Yet this when it comes, remember, is not the end. It is but a pledge. You may not cling to the blessings and the gifts of faith. They flash and disappear, and you will not be surprized to find that you have yet a long road to travel—a road of disappointment, of increasing failure, of gathering pain, of enlarging doubt—doubt! why not? Doubt of the ways and the methods of God. Doubt of the path as the darkness encompasses, doubt of Christ's meaning, of His wisdom, of His readiness, of His care, of His guidance. The obscurity may even deepen as you advance along the road of faith. The storm may grow blacker and fiercer, for the higher your faith in God, the darker will be your despair at His failure to make His name good. And you will find Him fail. He will seem to come so little way in the world; He will seem to miss opportunities. It is very hard to believe in One in whom others believe less and less every day. And then it is, when all are falling away and the hard sayings of theology begin to harass and repel, then it is that you must call with all your might upon the St. Peter within you that you may have the heart of fire that will feel but one thing, will feel that if the world fell into ruins, and if the power of God Himself be hidden, yet there stands the Christ still facing you with the question: "Will you go away? Will you fail as others failed me?" Will you feel then but this, just that you must send out your faith in the one passionate cry: "Lord, thou art there, and that is all. Thou hast the words of eternal life. To whom can I go? Tho all men forsake thee yet will not I; and in spite of all, I believe, and am sure that thou art the Christ, the holy one of God?" That is the faith which is felt indeed as a rock under the feet, and to such faith the love of God will make itself more and more

manifest. You will so trust Him in the black night, you who can walk on knowing nothing but that Christ goes before you, you who mutually cling with the violence of an ineradicable love to Him Who has enthralled you, you will find yourselves carried on day after day, you know not how, until at last you find yourselves enclosed in some upper chamber with the Master. Yes, and there the secrets of His love are disclosed, and the mysteries of His counsels, and the hidden wonder of His victory, and the strange glory of His consolation. You will not know or understand all; you will feel yourselves held in the grasp of a wisdom that reaches far and away beyond your little day. You will inquire with stammering lips as Philip and Judas, not Iscariot, and Thomas stammered in the upper chamber before you, and the answer that He gives will be but dim; and yet you will know enough to make you absolutely sure that the truth as you hold it in Jesus is the truth that holds the world in one in God, and you will be able to cry in glimpses of peculiar manifestation: "Lord, now speakest thou plainly, and speakest no parable. Now I believe, and have known, and am sure that thou camest forth from God." And yet even that faith, the faith of roused feelings, may lapse again; even that moment of blessing may lose its power over you. Yes, for only when you become convinced not only of your possession of a Teacher who once came on earth from God, but more, of a Lord living on the far side of death, living in the might of a resurrection life, able to stand by you in that lifegiving might as you keep there with the faithful in the upper chamber—able to feed you with His life now from that home of His beyond the grave—only then, when you so receive Him, and take of Him, and taste Him, and know yourselves quickened in Him—only so will your last doubt pass away from you, only so will the close of the crown of your faith be obtained, and you will end—as the story of St. John ends—with the cry of doubting Thomas, with his last doubt scattered—the cry in which the perfected apostolic faith at last saluted its rising Master—"Jesus Christ, my Lord and my God."

THOMAS HOOKER

1586-1647

THE ACTIVITY OF FAITH
OR
ABRAHAM'S IMITATORS

BIOGRAPHICAL NOTE

THOMAS HOOKER, graduate and fellow of Cambridge, England, and practically founder of Connecticut, was born in 1586. He was dedicated to the ministry, and began his activities in 1620 by taking a small parish in Surrey. He did not, however, attract much notice for his powerful advocacy of reformed doctrine, until 1629, when he was cited to appear before Laud, the Bishop of London, whose threats induced him to leave England for Holland, whence he sailed with John Cotton, in 1633, for New England, and settled in Newtown, now Cambridge, Mass.

Chiefly in consequence of disagreements between his own and Cotton's congregation he, with a large following, migrated in 1636 to the Connecticut Valley, where the little band made their center at Hartford. Hooker was the inspirer if not the author of the Fundamental Laws and was of wide political as well as religious influence in organizing "The United Colonies of New England" in 1643—the first effort after federal government made on this continent. He was an active preacher and prolific writer up to his death in 1647.

And the father of circumcision to them who are not of circumcision only, but who also walk in the steps of that faith of our father Abraham, which he had, being yet uncircumcized.—Romans iv., 12.

I PROCEED now to show who those are, that may, and do indeed, receive benefit as Abraham did. The text saith, "They that walk in the steps of that faith of Abraham:" that man that not only enjoyeth the privileges of the Church, but yieldeth the obedience of faith, according to the Word of God revealed, and walketh in obedience, *that* man alone shall be blest with faithful Abraham.

Two points may be here raised, but I shall hardly handle them both; therefore I will pass over the first only with a touch, and that lieth closely couched in the text.

That faith causeth fruitfulness in the hearts and lives of those in whom it is.

Mark what I say: a faithful man is a fruitful man; faith enableth a man to be doing. Ask the question, by what power was it whereby Abraham was enabled to yield obedience to the Lord? The text answereth you, "They that walk in the footsteps" not of Abraham, but "in the footsteps of the faith of Abraham." A man would have thought the text should have run thus: They that walk in the footsteps of Abraham. That is true, too, but the apostle had another end; therefore he saith, "They that walk in the footsteps of the faith of Abraham," implying that it was the grace of faith that God bestowed on Abraham, that quickened and enabled him to perform every duty that God required of him, and called him to the performance of. So that I say, the question being, whence came it that Abraham was so fruitful a Christian, what enabled him to do and to suffer what he did? surely it was faith that was the cause that produced such effects, that helped him to perform such actions. The point then you see is evident, faith it is that causeth fruit.

Hence it is, that of almost all the actions that a Christian hath to do, faith is still said to be the worker. If a man pray as he should, it is "the prayer of faith." If a man obey as he should, it is the obedience of faith. If a man war in the Church militant, it is "the fight of faith." If a man live as a Christian and holy man, he "liveth by faith." Nay, shall I say yet more, if he died as he ought, "he dieth by faith." "These all died in faith." What is that? The power of faith that directed and ordered them in the cause of their death, furnished them with grounds and

287

principles of assurance of the love of God, made them carry themselves patiently in death. I can say no more, but with the apostle, "Examine yourselves, whether ye be in the faith." Why doth not the apostle say, Examine whether faith be in you, but "whether ye be in the faith"? His meaning is, that as a man is said to be in drink, or to be in love, or to be in passion, that is, under the command of drink, or love, or passion; so the whole man must be under the command of faith (as you shall see more afterward). If he prays, faith must indite his prayer; if he obey, faith must work; if he live, it is faith that must quicken him; and if he die, it is faith that must order him in death. And wheresoever faith is, it will do wonders in the soul of that man where it is; it can not be idle; it will have footsteps, it sets the whole man on work; it moveth feet, and hands, and eyes, and all parts of the body. Mark how the apostle disputeth: "We having the same spirit of faith, according as it is written, I believed, and therefore have I spoken, we also believe, and therefore speak." The faith of the apostle, which he had in his heart, set his tongue agoing. If a man have faith within, it will break forth at his mouth. This shall suffice for the proof of the point; I thought to have prest it further, but if I should, I see the time would prevent me.

The use, therefore, in a word, is this: if this be so, then it falleth foul, and is a heavy bill of indictment against many that live in the bosom of the Church. Go thy ways home, and read but this text, and consider seriously but this one thing in it: That whosoever is the son of Abraham, hath faith, and whosoever hath faith is a walker, is a marker; by the footsteps of faith you may see where faith hath been. Will not this, then, I say, fall marvelous heavy upon many souls that live in the bosom of the Church, who are confident, and put it out of all question, that they are true believers, and make no doubt but what they have faith? But look to it, wheresoever faith is, it is fruitful. If thou art fruitless, say what thou wilt, thou hast no faith at all. Alas, these idle drones, these idle Christians, the Church is too full of them; Men are continually hearing, and yet remain fruitless and unprofitable; whereas if there were more faith in the world, we should have more work done in the world; faith would set feet, and hands, and eyes, and all on work. Men go under the name of professors, but alas! they are but pictures; they stir not a whit; mark, where you found them in the beginning of the year, there you shall find them in the end of the year, as profane, as worldly, as loose in their conversations, as formal in duty as ever. And is this faith? Oh! faith would work other matters, and provoke a soul to other passages than these.

But you will say, may not a man have faith, and not that fruit you speak of? May not a man have a good heart to Godward, altho he can not find that ability in matter of fruitfulness?

My brethren, be not deceived; such an opinion is a mere delusion of Satan; wherever faith is it bringeth Christ into the soul; mark that, "Whosoever believeth, Christ dwelleth in his heart by faith. And if Christ be in you," saith the apostle, "the body is dead, because of sin, but the spirit is life, because of righteousness." If Christ be in you, that is, whosoever believeth in the Lord Jesus, Christ dwells in such a man by faith; now if Christ be in the soul, the body can not be dead; but a man is alive, and quick, and active to holy duties, ready, and willing, and cheerful in the performance of whatsoever God requireth. Christ is not a dear Savior, nor the Spirit a dead Spirit: the second Adam is made a quickening spirit. And wherever the Spirit is, it works effects suitable to itself. The Spirit is a spirit of purity, a spirit of zeal, and where it is it maketh pure and zealous. When a man will say he hath faith, and in the mean time can be content to be idle and unfruitful in the work of the Lord, can be content to be a dead Christian, let him know that his case is marvelously fearful: for if faith were in him indeed it would appear; ye can not keep your good hearts to yourselves; wherever fire is it will burn, and wherever faith is it can not be kept secret. The heart will be enlarged, the soul quickened, and there will be a change in the whole life and conversation, if ever faith takes place in a man. I will say no more of this, but proceed to the second point arising out of the affirmative part.

You will say, what fruit is it then? Or how shall a man know what is the true fruit of faith, indeed, whereby he may discern his own estate? I answer, the text will tell you: "He that walketh in the footsteps of that faith of Abraham." By footsteps are meant the works the actions, the holy endeavors of Abraham; and where those footsteps are there is the faith of Abraham. So that the point of instruction hence is thus much (which indeed is the main drift of the apostle).

That, Every faithful man may, yea doth, imitate the actions of faithful Abraham.

Mark what I say; I say again, this is to be the son of Abraham, not because we are begotten of him by natural generation, for so the Jews are the sons of Abraham; but Abraham is our father because he is the pattern for the proceeding of our faith. "Thy father was an Amorite," saith the Scripture: that is, thou followest the steps of the Amorites in thy conversation. So is Abraham called the "father of the faithful," because he is the copy of their course, whom they must follow in those services that God calleth for. So the point is clear, every faithful man may, yea doth, and must imitate the actions of faithful Abraham. It is Christ's own plea, and He presseth it as an undeniable truth upon the hearts of the Scribes and Pharisees, that bragged very highly of their privileges and prerogatives, and said, "Abraham is our father." "No (saith Christ), if ye were Abraham's children ye would do the works of Abraham." To be like Abraham in constitution, to be one of his blood, is not that which makes a man a son of Abraham, but to be like him in holiness of affection, to have a heart framed and a life disposed answerably to his. The apostle in like manner presseth this point when he would provoke the Hebrews, to whom he wrote, to follow the examples of the saints: "Whose faith (says he) follow, considering the end of their conversation." So the apostle Peter presseth the example of Sarah upon all good women: "Whose daughter ye are (saith he) as long as ye do well."

For the opening of the point, and that ye may more clearly understand it, a question here would be resolved, what were "the footsteps of the faith of Abraham"? which way went he? This is a question, I say, worthy the scanning, and therefore (leaving the further confirmation of the point, as already evident enough) I will come to it that you may know what to settle your hearts upon.

I answer, therefore, there are six footsteps of the faith of Abraham, which are the main things wherein every faithful man must do as Abraham did, in the work of faith—I mean in his ordinary course; for if there be any thing extraordinary no man is bound to imitate him therein; but in the works of faith, I say, which belongeth to all men, every man must imitate Abraham in these six steps, and then he is in the next door to happiness, the very next neighbor, as I say, to heaven.

The first advance which Abraham made in the ways of grace and happiness, you shall observe to be a yielding to the call of God. Mark what God said to Abraham: "Get thee out of thy country, and from thy kindred, and from thy father's house, unto a land that I will show thee; and Abraham departed," saith the text, "as the Lord had spoken unto him." Even when he was an idolater, he is content to lay aside all and let the command of God bear the sway; neither friends, nor kindred, nor gods can keep him back, but he presently stoopeth to the call of God. So it is, my brethren, with every faithful man. This is his first step: he is content to be under the rule and power of God's command. Let the Lord call for him, require any service of him, his soul presently yieldeth, and is content to be framed and fashioned to God's call, and returneth an obedient answer thereto; he is content to come out of his sins,

and out of himself, and to receive the impressions of the Spirit. This is that which God requireth, not only of Abraham, but of all believers: "Whosoever will be my disciple," saith Christ, "must forsake father, and mother, and children, and houses, and lands; yea, and he must "deny himself, and take up his cross and follow me." This is the first step in Christianity, to lay down our own honors, to trample upon our own respects, to submit our necks to the block, as it were, and whatever God commands, to be content that His good pleasure should take place with us.

Then Abraham, as doth every faithful soul, set forward, in this wise: He showed that whenever faith cometh powerfully into the heart, the soul is not content barely to yield to the command of God, but it breatheth after His mercy, longeth for His grace, prizeth Christ and salvation above all things in the world, is satisfied and contented with nothing but with the Lord Christ, and altho it partake of many things below, and enjoy abundance of outward comforts, yet it is not quieted till it rest and pitch itself upon the Lord, and find and feel that evidence and assurance of His love, which He hath promised unto and will bestow on those who love Him. As for all things here below, he hath but a slight, and mean, and base esteem of them. This you shall see apparent in Abraham. "Fear not, Abraham (saith God), I am thy shield, and thy exceeding great reward." What could a man desire more? One would think that the Lord makes a promise here large enough to Abraham, "I will be thy buckler, and exceeding great reward." Is not Abraham contented with this? No; mark how he pleadeth with God: "Lord God (saith he), what wilt thou give me, seeing I go childless?" His eye is upon the promise that God had made to him of a son, of whom the Savior of the world should come. "O Lord, what wilt thou give me?" as if he had said, What wilt Thou do for me? alas! nothing will do my soul good unless I have a son, and in him a Savior. What will become of me so long as I go childless, and so Saviorless, as I may so speak? You see how Abraham's mouth was out of taste with all other things, how he could relish nothing, enjoy nothing in comparison of the promise, tho he had otherwise what he would, or could desire. Thus must it be with every faithful man. That soul never had, nor never shall have Christ, that doth not prize Him above all things in the world.

The next step of Abraham's faith was this, he casteth himself and flingeth his soul, as I may say, upon the all-sufficient power and mercy of God for the attainment of what he desireth; he rolleth and tumbleth himself, as it were, upon the all-sufficiency of God. This you shall find in Rom. iv. 18, where the apostle, speaks of Abraham, who "against hope, believed in hope"; that is, when there was no hope in the world, yet he believed in God, even above hope, and so made it possible. It was an object of his hope, that it might be in regard of God, howsoever there was no possibility in regard of man. So the text saith, "he considered not his own body now dead, when he was about a hundred years old, neither yet the deadness of Sarah's womb, but was strong in faith." He cast himself wholly upon the precious promise and mercy of God.

But he took another step in true justifying faith. He proved to us the believer is informed touching the excellency of the Lord Jesus, and that fulness that is to be had in Him, tho he can not find the sweetness of His mercy, tho he can not or dare not apprehend and apply it to himself, tho he find nothing in himself, yet he is still resolved to rest upon the Lord, and to stay himself on the God of his salvation, and to wait for His mercy till he find Him gracious to his poor soul. Excellent and famous is the example of the woman of Canaan. When Christ, as it were, beat her off, and took up arms against her, was not pleased to reveal Himself graciously to her for the present, "I am not sent (saith He) but to the lost sheep of the house of Israel; and it is not meet to take the children's bread, and to cast it to the dogs"; mark how she replied, "Truth, Lord, I confess all that; yet notwithstanding, the dogs eat of the crumbs that fall from their master's table." Oh, the excellency, and strength, and work of her faith! She comes to Christ for mercy, He repelleth her, reproacheth her, tells her she is a dog; she confesseth her baseness, is not discouraged for all that, but still resteth upon the goodness and mercy of Christ, and is mightily resolved to have mercy whatsoever befalleth her. Truth, Lord, I confess I am as bad as Thou canst term me, yet I confess, too, that there is no comfort but from Thee, and tho I am a dog, yet I would have crumbs. Still she laboreth to catch after mercy, and to lean and to bear herself upon the favor of Christ for the bestowing thereof upon her. So it must be with every faithful Christian in this particular; he must roll himself upon the power, and faithfulness, and truth of God, and wait for His mercy (I will join them both together for brevity's sake, tho the latter be a fourth step and degree of faith); I say he must not only depend upon God, but he must wait upon the Holy One of Israel.

But a further step of Abraham's faith appeared in this: he counted nothing too dear for the Lord; he was content to break through all impediments, to pass through all difficulties, whatsoever God would have, He had of him. This is the next step that Abraham went; and this you shall find when God put him upon trial. The text saith there "that God did tempt Abraham," did try what He would do for Him, and He bade him, "Go, take thy son, thine only son, Isaac, whom thou lovest, and slay him"; and straight Abraham went and laid his son upon an altar, and took a knife, to cut the throat of his son—so that Abraham did not spare his son Isaac, he did not spare for any cost, he did not dodge with God in this case; if God would have anything, He should have it, whatsoever it were, tho it were his own life, for no question Isaac was dearer to him than his own life. And this was not his case alone, but the faithful people of God have ever walked the same course. The apostle Paul was of the same spirit; "I know not (saith he) the things that shall befall me, save that the Holy Ghost witnesseth in every city, saying that bonds and afflictions abide me: but none of these things move me, neither count I my life dear unto myself, so that I might finish my course with joy, and the ministry which I have received of the Lord Jesus, to testify the Gospel of the grace of God." O blest spirit! here is the work of faith. Alas! when we come to part with anything for the cause of God, how hardly comes it from us! "But I (saith he) pass not, no, nor is my life dear unto me." Here, I say, is the work of faith, indeed, when a man is content to do anything for God, and to say if imprisonment, loss of estate, liberty, life, come, I pass not, it moveth me nothing, so I may finish my course with comfort. Hence it was that the saints of God in those primitive times "took joyfully the spoiling of their goods." Methinks I see the saints there reaching after Christ with the arms of faith, and how, when anything lay in their way, they were content to lose all, to part with all, to have Christ. Therefore saith Saint Paul, "I am ready not to be bound only, but also to die at Jerusalem for the name of the Lord Jesus." Mark, rather than he would leave his Savior, he would leave his life, and the men would have hindered him, yet was resolved to have Christ, howsoever, tho he lost his life for Him. Oh, let me have my Savior, and take my life!

The last step of all is this: when the soul is thus resolved not to dodge with God, but to part with anything for Him, then in the last place there followeth a readiness of heart to address man's self to the performance of whatsoever duty God requireth at his hands; I say this is the last step, when, without consulting with flesh and blood, without hammering upon it, as it were, without awkwardness of heart, there followeth a readiness to obey God; the soul is at hand. When Abraham was called, "Behold (saith he) here I am." And so Samuel, "Speak, Lord, for thy servant heareth," and so Ananias, "Behold, I am here, Lord." The faithful soul is not to seek, as an evil servant that is gone a roving after his companions, that is out of the way when his master would use him, but is like a trusty servant that waiteth upon his master, and is ever at hand to do His pleasure. So you shall see it was with Abraham, when the Lord commanded him to go out of his country, "he obeyed, and went out, not knowing whither he went"; he went cheerfully and readily, tho he knew not whither; as who would say, if the Lord calls, I will not question, if He command I will perform, whatever it be. So it must be with every faithful soul—we must blind the eye of carnal reason, resolve to obey, tho heaven and earth seem to meet together in a contradiction, care not what man or what devil saith in this case, but what God will have done, do it; this is the courage and obedience of faith. See how Saint Paul, in the place before named, flung his ancient friends from him, when they came to cross him in the work of his ministry. They all came about him, and because they thought they should see his face no more, they besought him not to go up to Jerusalem. Then Paul answered, "What, mean ye to weep, and to break my heart?" as who should say, It is a grief and a vexation to my soul, that ye would burden me, that I can not go with readiness to perform the service that God requireth at my hands. The like Christian courage was in Luther when his friends dissuaded him to go to Worms: "If all the tiles in Worms were so many devils (said he) yet would I go thither in the name of my Lord Jesus." This is the last step.

Now gather up a little what I have delivered. He that is resolved to stoop to the call of God; to prize the promises, and breathe after them; to rest upon the Lord, and to wait His time for bestowing mercy upon him; to break through all impediments and difficulties, and to count nothing too dear for God; to be content to perform ready and cheerful obedience; he that walketh thus, and treadeth in these steps, peace be upon him; heaven is hard by; he is as sure of salvation as the angels are; it is as certain as the Lord liveth that he shall be saved with faithful Abraham, for he walketh in the steps of Abraham, and therefore he is sure to be where he is. The case, you see, is clear, and the point evident, that every faithful man may, and must, imitate faithful Abraham.

It may be here imagined, that we draw men up to too high a pitch; and certainly, if this be the sense of the words, and the meaning of the Holy Ghost in this place, what will become of many that live in the bosom of the Church? Will you therefore see the point confirmed by reason? The ground of this doctrine stands thus: every faithful man hath the same faith, for nature and for work, that Abraham had; therefore, look what nature

his faith was of, and what power it had; of the same nature and power every true believer's faith is. Briefly thus: the promises of God are the ground upon which all true faith resteth; the Spirit of God it is that worketh this faith in all believers; the power of the Spirit is that that putteth forth itself in the hearts and lives of all the faithful; gather these together: if all true believers have the same promises for the ground of their faith; have one and the same spirit to work it; have one and the same power to draw out the abilities of faith, then certainly they can not but have the very self-same actions, having the very self-same ground of their actions.

Every particular believer (as the apostle Peter saith) "hath obtained the like precious faith." Mark, that there is a great deal of copper faith in the world—much counterfeit believing; but the saints do all partake of "the like precious faith." As when a man hath but a sixpence in silver, or a crown in gold, those small pieces, for the nature, are as good as the greatest of the same metal; so it is with the faith of God's elect. And look as it is in grafting; if there be many scions of the same kind grafted into one stock, they all partake alike of the virtue of the stock; just so it is here. The Lord Jesus Christ is the stock, as it were, into which all the faithful are grafted by the spirit of God and faith; therefore, whatsoever fruit one beareth, another beareth also: howsoever, there may be degrees of works, yet they are of the same nature. As a little apple is the same in taste with a great one of the same tree, even so every faithful man hath the same holiness of heart and life, because he hath the same principle of holiness. The fruit indeed that one Christian bringeth may be but poor and small in comparison with others, yet it is the same in kind; the course of his life is not with so much power and fulness of grace, it may be, as another's, yet there is the same true grace, and the same practise, in the kind of it, for truth, however in degree it differ.

Let us now come to see what benefit we may make to ourselves of this point, thus proved and confirmed; and, certainly, the use of this doctrine is of great consequence. In the first place, it is a just ground of examination. For if it be true (as can not be denied, the reasons being so strong, and arguments so plain) that every son of Abraham followeth the steps of Abraham, then here you may clearly perceive who it is that hath saving faith indeed, who they be that are true saints and the sons of Abraham. By the light of this truth, by the rule of this doctrine, if you would square your courses, and look into your conversations, you can not but discern whether you have faith or no. That man whose faith showeth itself and putteth itself forth in its several conditions, agreeably to the faith of Abraham, that man that followeth the footsteps of the faith of Abraham, let him be esteemed a faithful man, let him be reckoned for a true believer.

You that are gentlemen and tradesmen, I appeal to your souls whether the Lord and His cause is not the loser this way? Doth not prayer pay for it? Doth not the Word pay for it? Are not the ordinances always losers when anything of your own cometh in competition? Is it not evident, then, that you are not under the command of the Word? How do you tremble at the wrath and threatenings of a mortal man? and yet, when you hear the Lord thunder judgments out of His Word, who is humbled? When He calls for fasting, and weeping, and mourning, who regards it? Abraham, my brethren, did not thus: these were none of his steps; no, no: he went a hundred miles off this course. The Lord no sooner said to him, "Forsake thy country and thy kindred, and thy father's house," but he forsook all, neither friend nor father prevailed to detain him from obedience, but he stooped willingly to God's command.

There are a sort that come short of being the sons of Abraham, and they are the close-hearted hypocrites. These are a generation that are of a more refined kind than the last, but howsoever they carry the matter very covertly, yea, and are exceeding cunning; yet the truth will make them known. Many a hypocrite may come thus far, to be content to part with anything, and outwardly to suffer for the cause of God, to part with divers pleasures and lusts, and to perform many holy services. But here is the difference between Abraham and these men: Abraham forsook his goods and all, but your close-hearted hypocrites have always some god or other that they do homage to—their ease, or their wealth, or some secret lust, something or other they have set up as an idol within them—and so long as they may have and enjoy that, they will part with anything else. But thou must know that, if thou be one of Abraham's children, thou must come away from thy gods—the god of pride, of self-love, of vainglory—and leave worshiping of these, and be content to be alone by God and His truth. This shall suffice for the first use; I can not proceed further in the pressing thereof, because I would shut up all with the time.

The second use is a word of instruction, and it shall be but a word or two; that if all the saints of God must walk in the same way of life and salvation that Abraham did, then there is no byway to bring a man to happiness. Look, what way Abraham went, you must go; there are no more ways: the same course that he took must be a copy for you to follow, a rule, as it were, for you to square

your whole conversation by. There is no way but one to come to life and happiness. I speak it the rather to dash that idle device of many carnal men, that think the Lord hath a new invention to bring them to life, and that they need not go the ordinary way, but God hath made a shorter cut for them. Great men and gentlemen think God will spare them. What, must they be humbled, and fast, and pray? That is for poor men, and mean men. Their places and estates will not suffer it; therefore surely God hath given a dispensation to them. And the poor men, they think it is for gentlemen that have more leisure and time: alas! they live by their labor, and they must take pains for what they have, and therefore they can not do what is required. But be not deceived; if there be any way beside that which Abraham went, then will I deny myself. But the case is clear, the Lord saith it, the Word saith it; the same way, the same footsteps that Abraham took, we must take, if ever we will come where Abraham is.

You must not balk in this kind, whoever you are; God respecteth no man's person. If you would arrive at the same haven, you must sail through the same sea. You must walk the same way of grace, if you would come to the same kingdom of glory. It is a conceit that harboreth in the hearts of many men, nay, of most men in general, especially your great wise men and your great rich men, that have better places and estates in the world than ordinary. What, think they, may not a man be saved without all this ado? What needs all this? Is there not another way besides this? Surely, my brethren, you must teach our Savior Christ and the apostle Paul another way. I am sure they never knew another; and he that dreameth of another way must be content to go beside. There is no such matter as the devil would persuade you; it is but his delusion to keep you under infidelity, and so shut you up to destruction under false and vain conceits. The truth is, here is the way, and the only way, and you must walk here if ever you come to life and happiness. Therefore, be not deceived, suffer not your eyes to be blinded; but know, what Abraham did, you must do the same, if not in action, yet in affection. If God say, forsake all, thou must do it, at least in affection. Thou must still wait upon His power and providence; yield obedience to Him in all things; be content to submit thyself to His will. This is the way you must walk in, if you ever come to heaven.

The last use shall be a use of comfort to all the saints and people of God, whose consciences can witness that they have labored to walk in the uprightness of their heart as Abraham did. I have two or three words to speak to these.

Be persuaded out of the Word of God, that your course is good, and go on with comfort, and the God of heaven be with you; and be sure of it, that you that walk with Abraham shall be at rest with Abraham; and it shall never repent you of all the pains that you have taken. Haply it may seem painful and tedious to you; yet, what Abigail said to David, let me say to you: "Oh," saith she, "let not my lord do this: when the Lord shall have done to my lord according to all the good that he hath spoken concerning thee, and shall have appointed thee ruler over Israel, this shall be no grief unto thee, nor offense of heart, that thou hast shed blood causeless, or that my lord hath avenged himself." My brethren, let me say to you, you will find trouble and inconveniences and hard measure at the hands of the wicked in this world. Many Nabals and Cains will set themselves against you; but go on, and bear it patiently. Know it is a troublesome way, but a true way; it is grievous but yet good; and the end will be happy. It will never repent you, when the Lord hath performed all the good that He hath spoken concerning you.

Oh! to see a man drawing his breath low and short, after he hath spent many hours and days in prayer to the Lord, grappling with his corruptions, and striving to pull down his base lusts, after he hath waited upon the Lord in a constant course of obedience. Take but such a man, and ask him, now his conscience is opened, whether the ways of holiness and sincerity be not irksome to him, whether he be not grieved with himself for undergoing so much needless trouble (as the world thinks it); and his soul will then clear this matter. It is true he hath a tedious course of it, but now his death will be blest. He hath striven for a crown, and now beholds a crown. Now he is beyond the waves. All the contempts, and imprisonments, and outrages of wicked men are now too short to reach him. He is so far from repenting, that he rejoiceth and triumpheth in reflecting back upon all the pains, and care, and labor of love, whereby he hath loved the Lord Jesus, in submitting his heart unto Him.

Take me another man, that hath lived here in pomp and jollity, hath had many livings, great preferments, much honor, abundance of pleasure, yet hath been ever careless of God and of His Word, profane in his course, loose in his conversation, and ask him upon his death-bed, how it standeth with him. Oh! wo the time, that ever he spent it as he hath done. Now the soul begins to hate the man, and the very sight of him that hath been the instrument with it in the committing of sin. Now nothing but gall and wormwood remaineth. Now the sweetness of the adulterer's lust is gone, and nothing but the sting of conscience remaineth. Now the covetous man must part with his goods, and the gall of asps must stick behind. Now the soul sinks within, and the heart is overwhelmed with sorrow. Take but these two men, I say, and judge by their ends, whether it will ever repent you that you have done well, that you have walked in the steps of the faith of Abraham.

My brethren, howsoever you have had many miseries, yet the Lord hath many mercies for you. God dealeth with His servants, as a father doth with his son, after he hath sent him on a journey to do some business; and the weather falleth foul, and the way proveth dangerous, and many a storm, and great difficulties are to be gone through. Oh, how the heart of that father pitieth his son! How doth he resolve to requite him, if he ever live to come home again! What preparation doth he make to entertain, and welcome him; and how doth he study to do good unto him! My brethren, so it is here; I beseech you, think of it, you that are the saints and people of God. You must find in your way many troubles and griefs (and we ought to find them), but be not discouraged. The more misery, the greater mercy. God the Father seeth His servants: and if they suffer and endure for a good conscience, as His eye seeth them, so His soul pitieth them. His heart bleeds within Him for them; that is, He hath a tender compassion of them, and He saith within Himself, Well, I will requite them if ever they come into My kingdom; all their patience, and care, and conscience in walking My ways, I will requite; and they shall receive a double reward from Me, even a crown of eternal glory. Think of these things that are not seen; they are eternal. The things that are seen are temporal, and they will deceive us. Let our hearts be carried after the other, and rest in them forever!

JOHN HOWE

1630-1705

THE REDEEMER'S TEARS OVER LOST SOULS

And when He was come near, He beheld the city, and wept over it, saying, If thou hadst known, even thou, at least in this thy day, the things which belong to thy peace! But now they are hid from thine eyes.
—Luke xix., 41, 42.

SUCH as live under the gospel have a day, or a present opportunity, for the obtaining the knowledge of those things immediately belonging to their peace, and of whatsoever is besides necessary thereunto. I say nothing what opportunities they have who never lived under the gospel, who yet no doubt might generally know more than they do, and know better what they do know. It suffices who enjoy the gospel to understand our own advantages thereby. Nor, as to those who do enjoy it, is every one's day of equal clearness. How few, in comparison, have ever seen such a day as Jerusalem at this time did! made by the immediate beams of the Sun of Righteousness! our Lord Himself vouchsafing to be their Instructor, so speaking as never man did, and with such authority as far outdid their other teachers, and astonished the hearers. In what transports did He use to leave those that heard Him, wheresoever He came, wondering at the gracious words that came out of His mouth! And with what mighty and beneficial works was He wont to recommend His doctrine, shining in the glorious power and savoring of the abundant mercy of Heaven, so that every apprehensive mind might see the Deity was incarnate. God was come down to entreat with men, and allure them into the knowledge and love of Himself. The Word was made flesh. What unprejudiced mind might not perceive it to be so? He was there manifested and vailed at once; both expressions are made concerning the same matter. The divine beams were somewhat obscured, but did yet ray through that vail; so that His glory was beheld of the only-begotten Son of His Father, full of grace and truth.

This Sun shone with a mild and benign, but with a powerful, vivifying light. In Him was life, and that life was the light of men. Such a light created unto the Jews this their day. Happy Jews, if they had understood their own happiness! And the days that followed to them (for a while) and the Gentile world were not inferior, in some respects brighter and more glorious (the more copious gift of the Holy Ghost being reserved unto the crowning and enthroning of the victorious

Redeemer), when the everlasting gospel flew like lightning to the uttermost ends of the earth, and the word which began to be spoken by the Lord Himself was confirmed by them that heard Him, God also Himself bearing them witness with signs, and wonders, and gifts of the Holy Ghost. No such day hath been seen this many an age. Yet whithersoever this same gospel, for substance, comes, it also makes a day of the same kind, and affords always true tho diminished light, whereby, however, the things of our peace might be understood and known. The written gospel varies not, and if it be but simply and plainly proposed (tho to some it be proposed with more advantage, to some with less, still we have the same things immediately relating to our peace extant before our eyes. . . .

This day hath its bounds and limits, so that when it is over and lost with such, the things of their peace are forever hid from their eyes. And that this day is not infinite and endless, we see in the present instance. Jerusalem had her day; but that day had its period, we see it comes to this at last, that now the things of her peace are hid from her eyes. We generally see the same thing, in that sinners are so earnestly prest to make use of the present time. To-day if you will hear His voice, harden not your hearts. They are admonished to seek the Lord while He may be found, to call upon Him when He is nigh. It seems some time He will not be found, and will be far off. They are told this is the accepted time, this is the day of salvation. . . . As it is certain death ends the day of grace with every unconverted person, so.it is very possible that it may end with divers before they die; by their total loss of all external means, or by the departure of the blest Spirit of God from them; so as to return and visit them no more.

How the day of grace may end with a person, is to be understood by considering what it is that makes up and constitutes such a day. There must become measure and proportion of time to make up this (or any) day, which is as the substratum and ground forelaid. Then there must be light superadded, otherwise it differs not from night, which may have the same measure of mere time. The gospel revelation some way or other, must be had, as being the light of such a day. And again there must be some degree of liveliness, and vital influence, the more usual concomitant of light; the night doth more dispose men to drowsiness. The same sun that enlightens the world disseminates also an invigorating influence. If the Spirit of the living God do no way animate the gospel revelation, and breathe in it, we have no day of grace. It is not only a day of light, but a day of power, wherein souls can be wrought upon, and a people made willing to become the Lord's. As

the Redeemer revealed in the gospel, is the light of the world, so He is life to it too, tho neither are planted or do take root everywhere. In Him was life and that life was the light of men. That light that rays from Him is vital light in itself, and in its tendency and design, tho it be disliked and not entertained by the most. Whereas therefore these things must concur to make up such a day; if either a man's time, his life on earth, expire, or if light quite fail him, or if all gracious influence be withheld, so as to be communicated no more, his day is done, the season of grace is over with him. Now it is plain that many a one may lose the gospel before his life end; and possible that all gracious influence may be restrained, while as yet the external dispensation of the gospel remains. A sinner may have hardened his heart to that degree that God will attempt him no more, in any kind, with any design of kindness to him, not in that more inward, immediate way at all—*i.e.*, by the motions of His Spirit, which peculiarly can impart nothing but friendly inclination, as whereby men are personally applied unto, so that can not be meant; nor by the voice of the gospel, which may either be continued for the sake of others, or they contained under it, but for their heavier doom at length. Which, tho it may seem severe, is not to be thought strange, much less unrighteous.

It is not to be thought strange to them that read the Bible, which so often speaks this sense; as when it warns and threatens men with so much terror. For if we sin wilfully after that we have received the knowledge of the truth, there remaineth no more sacrifice for sins, but a fearful looking for judgment, and fiery indignation, which shall devour the adversaries. He that despised Moses's law died without mercy, under two or three witnesses; of how much sorer punishment, suppose ye, shall he be thought worthy who hath trodden under foot the Son of God, and hath counted the blood of the covenant, wherewith He was sanctified, an unholy thing, and hath done despite unto the Spirit of grace? And when it tells us, after many overtures made to men in vain, of His having given them up. "But my people would not hearken to my voice; and Israel would none of me; so I gave them up unto their own hearts' lust: and they walked in their own counsels;" and pronounces, "Let him that is unjust be unjust still, and let him which is filthy be filthy still," and says, "In thy filthiness is lewdness, because I have purged thee, and thou wast not purged; thou shalt not be purged from thy filthiness any more, till I have caused my fury to rest upon thee." Which passages seem to imply a total desertion of them, and retraction of all gracious influence. And when it speaks of letting them be under the gospel, and the ordinary means of salvation, for the most direful purpose: as that, "This child (Jesus) was set for the fall, as well as for the rising, of many in Israel"; as that, "Behold, I lay in Zion a stumbling, and a rock of offense"; and, "The stone which the builders refused, is made a stone of stumbling, and a rock of offense, even to them which stumble at the word, being disobedient, whereunto also they were appointed"; with that of our Savior Himself, "For judgment I am come into this world, that they which see not might see; and that they which see, might be made blind." And most agreeable to those former places is that of the prophet, "But the word of the Lord was unto them precept upon precept, line upon line, here a little and there a little; that they might go, and fall backward, and be broken, and snared, and taken." And we may add, that our God hath put us out of doubt that there is such a sin as that which is eminently called the sin against the Holy Ghost; that a man in such circumstances, and to such a degree, sin against that Spirit, that He will never move or breathe upon him more, but leave him to a hopeless ruin; tho I shall not in this discourse determine or discuss the nature of it. But I doubt not it is somewhat else than final impenitency and infidelity; and that every one that dies, not having sincerely repented and believed, is not guilty of it, tho every one that is guilty of it dies impenitent and unbelieving, but was guilty of it before; so it is not the mere want of time that makes him guilty. Whereupon, therefore, that such may outlive their day of grace, is out of the question. . . .

Wherefore, no man can certainly know, or ought to conclude, concerning himself or others, as long as they live, that the season of grace is quite over with them. As we can conceive no rule God hath set to Himself to proceed by, in ordinary cases of this nature; so nor is there any He hath set unto us to judge by, in this case. It were to no purpose, and could be of no use to men to know so much; therefore it were unreasonable to expect God should have settled and declared any rule, by which they might come to the knowledge of it. As the case is then, viz.: there being no such rule, no such thing can be concluded; for who can tell what an arbitrary, sovereign, free agent will do, if he declare not his own purpose himself? How should it be known, when the Spirit of God hath been often working upon the soul of man, that this or that shall be the last act, and that he will never put forth another? And why should God make it known? To the person himself whose case it is, 'tis manifest it could be of no benefit. Nor is it to be thought the Holy God will ever so alter the course of His own proceedings but that

it shall be finally seen to all the world that every man's destruction was entirely, and to the last, of himself. If God had made it evident to a man that he were finally rejected, he were obliged to believe it. But shall it ever be said, God hath made anything a man's duty which were inconsistent with his felicity. The having sinned himself into such a condition wherein he is forsaken of God is indeed inconsistent with it. And so the case is to stand—i.e., that his perdition be in immediate connection with his sin, not with his duty; as it would be in immediate, necessary connection with his duty, if he were bound to believe himself finally forsaken and a lost creature. For that belief makes him hopeless, and a very devil, justifies his unbelief in the gospel, toward himself, by removing and shutting up, toward himself, the object of such a faith, and consequently brings the matter to this state that he perishes, not because he doth not believe God reconcilable to man, but because, with particular application to himself, he ought not so to believe. And it were most unfit, and of very pernicious consequence, that such a thing should be generally known concerning others. . . .

But tho none ought to conclude that their day or season of grace is quite expired, yet they ought to deeply apprehend the danger, lest it should expire before their necessary work be done and their peace made. For tho it can be of no use for them to know the former, and therefore they have no means appointed them by which to know it, 'tis of great use to apprehend the latter; and they have sufficient ground for the apprehension. All the cautions and warnings wherewith the Holy Spirit abounds, of the kind with those already mentioned, have that manifest design. And nothing can be more important, or opposite to this purpose, than that solemn charge of the great apostle: "Work out your own salvation with fear and trembling"; considered together with the subjoined ground of it; "For it is God that worketh in you to will and to do of his own good pleasure." How correspondent is the one with the other; work for He works: there were no working at all to any purpose, or with any hope, if He did not work. And work with fear and trembling, for He works of His own good pleasure, q. d., " 'Twere the greatest folly imaginable to trifle with One that works at so perfect liberty, under no obligation, that may desist when He will; to impose upon so absolutely sovereign and arbitrary an Agent, that owes you nothing; and from whose former gracious operations not complied with you can draw no argument, unto any following ones, that because He doth, therefore He will. As there is no certain connection between present time and future, but all time is made up of undepending, not strictly coherent, moments, so as no man can be sure, because one now exists, another shall; there is also no more certain connection between the arbitrary acts of a free agent within such time; so that I can not be sure, because He now darts in light upon me, is now convincing me, now awakening me, therefore He will still do so, again and again." Upon this ground then, what exhortation could be more proper than this? "Work out your salvation with fear and trembling." What could be more awfully monitory and enforcing of it than that He works only of mere good will and pleasure? How should I tremble to think, if I should be negligent, or undutiful, He may give out the next moment, may let the work fall, and me perish? And there is more especial cause for such an apprehension upon the concurrence of such things as these:

1. If the workings of God's Spirit upon the soul of a man have been more than ordinarily strong and urgent, and do not now cease: if there have been more powerful convictions, deeper humiliations, more awakened fears, more formed purposes of a new life, more fervent desires that are now vanished, and the sinner returns to his dead and dull temper.

2. If there be no disposition to reflect and consider the difference, no sense of his loss, but he apprehends such workings of spirit in him unnecessary troubles to him, and thinks it well he is delivered and eased of them.

3. If in the time when he was under such workings of the Spirit he had made known his case to his minister, or any godly friend, whose company he now shuns, as not willing to be put in mind, or hear any more of such matters.

4. If, hereupon he hath more indulged sensual inclination, taken more liberty, gone against the check of his own conscience, broken former good resolutions, involved himself in the guilt of any grosser sins.

5. If conscience, so baffled, be now silent, lets him alone, grows more sluggish and weaker, which it must as his lusts grow stronger.

6. If the same lively, powerful ministry which before affected him much, now moves him not.

7. If especially he is grown into a dislike of such preaching—if serious godliness, and what tends to it, are become distasteful to him—if discourses of God, and of Christ, of death and judgment, and of a holy life, are reckoned superflous and needless, are unsavory and disrelished—if he have learned to put disgraceful names upon things of this import, and the persons that most value them live accordingly—if he hath taken the seat of the scorner, and makes it his business to deride what he had once a reverence for, or took some complacency in.

8. If, upon all this, God withdraw such a ministry, so that he is now warned, admonished, exhorted and striven with, as formerly, no more. Oh, the fearful danger of that man's case! Hath he no cause to fear lest the things of his peace should be forever hid from his eyes? Surely he hath much cause of fear, but not of despair. Fear in this case would be his great duty, and might yet prove the means of saving him—despair would be his very heinous and destroying sin. If yet he would be stirred up to consider his case, whence he is fallen, and whither he is falling, and set himself to serious seekings of God, cast down himself before Him, abase himself, cry for mercy as for his life, there is yet hope in his case. God may make here an instance what He can obtain of Himself to do for a perishing wretch. But if with any that have lived under the gospel, their day is quite expired, and the things of their peace now forever hid from their eyes, this is in itself a most deplorable case, and much lamented by our Lord Jesus Himself. That the case is in itself most deplorable, who sees not? A soul lost! a creature capable of God! upon its way to Him! near to the kingdom of God! shipwrecked in the port! Oh, sinner, from how high a hope art thou fallen! into what depths of misery and wo! And that it was lamented by our Lord is in the text. He beheld the city (very generally, we have reason to apprehend, inhabited by such wretched creatures) and wept over it. This was a very affectionate lamentation. We lament often, very heartily, many a sad case for which we do not shed tears. But tears, such tears, falling from such eyes! the issues of the purest and best-governed passion that ever was, showed the true greatness of the cause. Here could be no exorbitancy or unjust excess, nothing more than was proportional to the occasion. There needs no other proof that this is a sad case than that our Lord lamented it with tears, which that He did we are plainly told, so that, touching that, there is no place for doubt. All that is liable to question is, whether we are to conceive in Him any like resentments of such cases, in His present glorified state? Indeed, we can not think heaven a place or state of sadness or lamentation, and must take heed of conceiving anything there, especially on the throne of glory, unsuitable to the most perfect nature, and the most glorious state. We are not to imagine tears there, which, in that happy region are wiped away from inferior eyes— no grief, sorrow, or sighing, which are all fled away, and shall be no more, as there can be no other turbid passion of any kind. But when expressions that import anger or grief are used, even concerning God Himself, we must sever in our conception everything of imperfection, and ascribe everything of real perfection. We are

not to think such expressions signify nothing that they have no meaning, or that nothing at all is to be attributed to Him under them. Nor are we again to think they signify the same thing with what we find in ourselves, and are wont to express by those names. In the divine nature there may be real, and yet most serene, complacency and displacency—viz., that, unaccompanied by the least commotion, that impart nothing of imperfection, but perfection rather, as it is a perfection to apprehend things suitably to what in themselves they are. The holy Scriptures frequently speak of God as angry, and grieved for the sins of men, and their miseries which ensue therefrom. And a real aversion and dislike is signified thereby, and by many other expressions, which in us would signify vehement agitations of affection, that we are sure can have no place in Him. We ought, therefore, in our own thoughts to ascribe to Him that calm aversion of will, in reference to the sins and miseries of men in general; and in our own apprehensions to remove to the utmost distance from Him all such agitations of passion or affection, even tho some expressions that occur carry a great appearance thereof, should they be understood according to human measures, as they are human forms of speech. As, to instance in what is said by the glorious God Himself, and very near in sense to what we have in the text, what can be more pathetic than that lamenting wish, "Oh, that my people had hearkened unto me, and Israel had walked in my ways!" But we must take heed lest, under the pretense that we can not ascribe everything to God that such expressions seem to import, we therefore ascribe nothing. We ascribe nothing, if we do not ascribe a real unwillingness that men should sin on, and perish, and consequently a real willingness that they should turn to Him, and live, which so many plain texts assert. And therefore it is unavoidably imposed upon us to believe that God is truly unwilling of some things which He doth not think fit to interpose His omnipotency to hinder, and is truly willing of some things which He doth not put forth His omnipotency to effect.

We can not, therefore, doubt but that,

1. He distinctly comprehends the truth of any such case. He beholds, from the throne of His glory above, all the treaties which are held and managed with sinners in His name, and what their deportments are therein. His eyes are as a flame of fire, wherewith He searcheth hearts and trieth reins. He hath seen therefore, sinner, all along every time an offer of grace hath been made to thee, and been rejected; when thou hast slighted counsels and warnings that have been given thee, exhortations and treaties that have been prest upon thee for many years together,

and how thou hast hardened thy heart against reproofs and threatenings, against promises and allurements, and beholds the tendency of all this, what is like to come to it, and that, if thou persist, it will be bitterness in the end.

2. That He hath a real dislike of the sinfulness of thy course. It is not indifferent to Him whether thou obeyest or disobeyest the gospel, whether thou turn and repent or no; that He is truly displeased at thy trifling, sloth, negligence, impenitency, hardness of heart, stubborn obstinacy, and contempt of His grace, and takes real offense at them.

3. He hath real kind propensions toward thee, and is ready to receive thy returning soul, and effectually to mediate with the offended majesty of Heaven for thee, as long as there is any hope in thy case.

4. When He sees there is no hope, He pities thee, while thou seest it not, and dost not pity thyself. Pity and mercy above are not names only; 'tis a great reality that is signified by them, and that hath place here in far higher excellency and perfection than it can with us poor mortals here below. Ours is but borrowed and participated from that first fountain and original above. Thou dost not perish unlamented even with the purest heavenly pity, tho thou hast made thy case incapable of remedy; as the well tempered judge bewails the sad end of the malefactor, whom justice obliges him not to spare or save.

And that thou mayst not throw away thy soul and so great a hope, through mere sloth and loathness to be at some pains for thy life, let the text, which hath been thy directory about the things that belong to thy peace, be also thy motive, as it gives thee to behold the Son of God weeping over such as would not know those things. Shall not the Redeemer's tears move thee? O hard heart! Consider what these tears import to this purpose.

1. They signify the real depth and greatness of the misery into which thou are falling. They drop from an intellectual and most comprehensive eye, that sees far and pierces deep into things, hath a wide and large prospect; takes the comfort of that forlorn state into which unreconcilable sinners are hastening, in all the horror of it. The Son of God did not weep vain and causeless tears, or for a light matter; nor did He for Himself either spend His own or desire the profusion of others' tears. "Weep not for me, O daughters of Jerusalem," etc. He knows the value of souls, the weight of guilt, and how low it will press and sink them; the severity of God's justice and the power of His anger, and what the fearful effects of them will be when they finally fall. If thou understandest not these things thyself, believe Him that did; at least believe His tears.

2. They signify the sincerity of His love and pity, the truth and tenderness of His com-

passion. Canst thou think His deceitful tears? His, who never knew guile? Was this like the rest of His course? And remember that He who shed tears did, from the same fountain of love and mercy, shed blood too! Was that also done to deceive? Thou makest thyself a very considerable thing indeed, if thou thinkest the Son of God counted it worth His while to weep, and bleed, and die, to deceive thee into a false esteem of Him and His love. But if it be the greatest madness imaginable to entertain any such thought but that His tears were sincere and unartificial, the natural, genuine expression of undissembled benignity and pity, thou art then to consider what love and compassion thou art now sinning against; what bowels thou spurnest; and that if thou perishest, 'tis under such guilt as the devils themselves are not liable to, who never had a Redeemer bleeding for them, nor, that we ever find, weeping over them.

3. They show the remedilessness of thy case if thou persist in impenitency and unbelief till the things of thy peace be quite hid from thine eyes. These tears will then be the last issues of (even defeated) love, of love that is frustrated of its kind design. Thou mayst perceive in these tears the steady, unalterable laws of heaven, the inflexibleness of the divine justice, that holds thee in adamantine bonds, and hath sealed thee up, if thou prove incurably obstinate and impenitent, unto perdition; so that even the Redeemer Himself, He that is mighty to save, can not at length save thee, but only weep over thee, drop tears into thy flame, which assuage it not; but (tho they have another design, even to express true compassion) do yet unavoidably heighten and increase the fervor of it, and will do so to all eternity. He even tells thee, sinner, "Thou hast despised My blood; thou shalt yet have My tears." That would have saved thee, these do only lament thee lost. But the tears wept over others, as lost and past hope, why should they not yet melt thee, while as yet there is hope in thy case? If thou be effectually melted in thy very soul, and looking to Him whom thou hast pierced, dost truly mourn over Him, thou mayst assure thyself the prospect His weeping eye had of lost souls did not include thee. His weeping over thee would argue thy case forlorn and hopeless; thy mourning over Him will make it safe and happy. That it may be so, consider, further, that,

4. They signify how very intent He is to save souls, and how gladly He would save thine, if yet thou wilt accept of mercy while it may be had. For if He weep over them that will not be saved, from the same love that is the spring of these tears, would saving mercies proceed to those that are become willing to receive them. And that love that wept over them that were lost, how will it glory in them that are saved! There His love is disappointed and vexed, crossed in its gracious intendment; but here, having compassed it, how will He joy over thee with singing, and rest in His love! And thou also, instead of being revolved in a like ruin with the unreconciled sinners of old Jerusalem, shalt be enrolled among the glorious citizens of the new, and triumph together with them in glory.

WILLIAM DEWITT HYDE

1858-1917

THE SINS THAT CRUCIFIED JESUS

BIOGRAPHICAL NOTE

PRESIDENT of Bowdoin College 1885-1917; born Winchendon, Mass., September 23, 1858; graduated Harvard University, 1879; received the degree of D.D. from Harvard, and LL.D. from Syracuse; author of "Practical Ethics," "Social Theology," "Practical Idealism," "The Evolution of a College Student," "God's Education of Man," "The Art of Optimism," etc.

"For envy the chief priests had delivered him up."—Mark 15 : 10.

"Then one of the twelve, called Judas Iscariot, went unto the chief priests and said unto them, 'What will ye give me and I will deliver him unto you?' And they covenanted with him for thirty pieces of silver. And from that time he sought opportunity to betray him."—Matt. 26 : 14-16.

"And the whole multitude of them arose and led him unto Pilate, and they began to accuse him, saying, 'We found this fellow perverting the nation and forbidding to give tribute to Cæsar, saying that he himself is Christ, a king.' "—Luke 23 : 1, 2.

"And so Pilate, willing to content the people, released Barabbas unto them and delivered Jesus, when he had scourged him, to be crucified."—Mark 15 : 15.

THESE four texts give consecutively the sins that were immediately responsible for the crucifixion of our Lord.

These self-same sins, envy, avarice, slander, and servility, are most common in our midst to-day. Who is there among us that can plead "not guilty" to each of these four charges which the record brings against the crucifiers of our Lord? Yet the prevalence of these sins detracts nothing from their heinous and deadly character. The fact that these so common sins are the sins of Christ's murderers ought to deepen our abhorrence of them. The fact that, whenever we are envious, or avaricious; whenever we give currency to scandal, or yield to the pressure of evil influence, we are joining the company of these abhorred chief priests and elders; of the odious Judas and the detested Pilate, ought to make us more on our guard against them.

The first and chief of the sins that led to Christ's death was envy. "For envy the chief priests delivered him up."

The chief priests were the prime movers. The rest were but tools in their hands. Power and privilege and influence of all kinds, and especially ecclesiastical power and privilege and influence, have always been found dangerous gifts to trust in frail human hands. Insolence and arrogance, perversion and abuse, have almost invariably sprung from long-continued ecclesiastical authority, whether among Jews or Christians, Catholics or Protestants, Episcopalians or Congregationalists. The chief priests formed a pontifical clique, an ecclesiastical ring. The control of the temple was in their hands. They bestowed the patronage. Out of the expenses connected with the observance of a system of religious rites which they had made more and more elaborate and costly, they took their commissions. They had been looked up to with unquestioning reverence all their lives by the unlettered multitude. They had always had the satisfaction of running things their own way; and without knowing when or how they had come, as men generally do in such cases, to identify their own way with God's way.

Their reasoning was simple, if not sound. "This," they said, "is a divinely ordered system of worship; we are the divinely established administrators of it. Therefore, our views and notions about religious matters are God's purposes and plans. Therefore, it is God's will that whoever opposes us should be put out of the way." If this reasoning is not satisfactory to a dispassionate observer, it no doubt was all-conclusive to these chief priests, who had centuries of tradition behind them and an abundance of conceit within them. In every age since then, and in cases before our eyes to-day, men, without a tenth part of the excuse for it, have found, and are still finding, just such reasoning amply satisfactory. The line between self-deception and hypocrisy is a very shadowy one; and we should never bring a charge of the latter unless we have given due allowance to every indication of the possible presence of the former. Had nothing happened to disturb them, no doubt these chief priests and scribes would have gone down to history with quite as much of a halo about their memories as has attached to the average priest and bishop and prelate and secretary of religious boards and moderator of church assemblies the world over.

In their day, however, something did come to pass. From despised Nazareth, out of provincial Galilee, there came a teacher, a preacher, a healer of disease, a forgiver of sins, a king of men, the Son of God. In the name of His Heavenly Father, he cleared the temple of dove-sellers and money-changers. He substituted prayer for merchandise as a condition of acceptance with the Temple's God. He taught plain, honest-hearted men, and poor, humble women, that God was their Father, and that He listened more willingly to their own heartfelt stammerings of penitence and devotion than to the pompous rites and elaborate ceremonies which the chief priests celebrated in the temple. He told repentant publicans and sinners that forgiveness was not to be purchased from a reluctant tyrant, of whom the heartless and mercenary priests were the vice-regents, but was to be gratefully received in humble trust as the free gift of a loving Father, of whom He Himself was the anointed messenger and faithful witness and true Son.

The chief priests saw that He was superseding them. The common people were hearing Him gladly; and in proportion as they followed Him the spell of obsequious reverence with which they had regarded the long-robed priests and broad-phylacteried Pharisees was broken. For this cause they envied Him, and "for envy delivered Him up." In this the chief priests were not sinners above

men in similar position always and everywhere. Can you tell me of a single church reform, either in doctrine or policy, that did not have to meet opposition from this very source? A healthy conservatism is indispensable to safe and sure advance. Conservatives are as conscientious in their obstruction of new movements as progressive spirits are in pushing forward new views and measures. Yet when we have made all allowance for the conscientious distrust of innovation which is constitutional to many minds; while we rejoice that every new movement has to run the gantlet of honest opposition; still we are compelled to recognize the fact that the dread, on the part of somebody or other, of being superseded, the reluctance to give up the relative importance and prominence and leadership which they have previously held, invariably comes in and gives to every controversy about religious matters that personal bitterness which renders such controversies so deplorable. Even in the local church, when there ought to be the closest love and fellowship, it is often found to be almost impossible to advocate seriously a new measure of any sort without meeting an outcropping of this same malicious envy which crucified our Lord.

How, then, shall we guard against this most deadly of sins, in ourselves? We must make sure whenever we support a side that we are seeking, with a single eye, the highest good of the universal or the local church, or of the community interested in the question. We must make sure that we are willing to have our views, and even ourselves with them, displaced by better measures and more efficient men if such there shall prove to be. Thus only can there be the fullest and fairest discussion of every proposed change of doctrine. Thus each side of the question can be fully, fairly, candidly, forcibly set forth. Thus will truth ultimately triumph, and no injury be done. Let us remember that to have part or lot in any controversy on one side or the other in the spirit of envy, because somebody else, with some other doctrine, is gaining more favor than we with ours, is to take our place in the verdict of history and before the judgment-seat of God by the side of the men who for envy put to death our Lord.

The second of the sins that crucified Jesus was money-loving. "Then one of the twelve called Judas Iscariot went unto the chief-priests and said unto them, 'What will ye give me and I will deliver him unto you.' And they covenanted with him for thirty pieces of silver. And from that time he sought opportunity to betray him."

Now we all recognize that money, as it is the symbol of the universal product of human toil, is, in itself, a good. And if money is good, then money-getting and money-making are most worthy objects of human ambition and endeavor. Money-loving, however, is a very different thing from money-making and money-getting. Every honest laborer is a money-getter; every upright merchant is a money-maker. But only knaves and misers are money-lovers. Love is personal. Persons alone are worthy of being the objects of our love. When a man cares more for money than for men; when he will sacrifice the human welfare of others or himself for the sake of money, then he becomes a money-lover, and joins the company of Judas. And the money-lovers of our day are just as guilty, just as murderous, just as odious as was ever Judas Iscariot. As John Ruskin has well said: "We do great injustice to Iscariot in thinking him wicked above all common wickedness. He was only a common money-lover, and like all money-lovers the world over, didn't understand Christ; couldn't make out the worth of Him, or the meaning of Him. Now this is the money-lover's idea the world over. He does not hate Christ, but can not understand Him, does not care for Him, sees no good in that benevolent business; makes his own little job out of it come what will."

Do you ask who are the money-loving Judases of our day? They are, as has been said, the men who in any way whatsoever are sacrificing human welfare to their own love of gain. Honest work and honest trade, besides contributing to the gain of the workman or tradesman, also contributes an equivalent to the welfare of other men and women. Any form of work or trade which fails to benefit others as well as yourself has the Judas brand upon it. The kinds of work and trade that bear this brand are various. For instance, take the plumber, who, to gain an extra profit for himself, does defective work; and months afterward, a child of the unsuspecting family that comes to occupy the house, pays the penalty with its innocent young life. Is that money-loving plumber less a murderer than the money-loving Judas? A workman in a foundry finds a gap as large as a man's hand in a casting destined for an important place in an ocean steamer. I could name the shop where this was done. The workman takes a piece of cold iron, heats it and hammers it into the gap, smooths over the surface and thereby saves the thousand dollars it would cost to reject the piece and cast a new one. This very hour some ocean steamer, I know not whether passenger or freight, is carrying human lives on such security as that wedge of iron can give to that faulty casting. If ever disaster shall bring the passengers and crew of that vessel to a watery grave, will the money-loving foreman, who ordered that thing done to save expense, be less a murderer than the money-loving

Judas? A merchant adulterates his groceries or his drugs and sells them as genuine. And some poor invalid, on the margin of life, fails to get the nutriment or remedial effect expected. Is that merchant less guilty than Judas? An employer of labor screws down the wages of his workmen to the lowest notch, in order that his company's dividends may be ten or twelve per cent.; and from lack of healthful tenements, from inability to provide sufficiently nourishing food, and competent care and nursing, the families of his workmen show an abnormal death-rate. What is the difference between the policy of that employer and the policy of Judas? "Inasmuch as ye have done it unto one of the least of these my brethren, ye have done it unto me." There are factories and stores in our large cities where no girl can gain promotion, or gain a decent livelihood save at the cost of what is more precious to her than life. Think you the stockholders and agents and overseers of such concerns are anywise better than the betrayer of our Lord?

To take but a single instance more. In nearly every large town of these United States there are men engaged in a traffic which involves as its direct consequence, as some compute, sixty thousand deaths a year, to say nothing of the untold shame and degradation and misery and wo which follows in the train of that murderous traffic. The principle at the bottom of this business— that which makes men cling to it so fondly, is not that liquor-sellers love to bring wo and poverty and disease and death upon their fellows—not that—but simply the fact that liquor-selling happens to be the way in which a certain class of men find that, with least expenditure of hard labor, they can get the greatest money returns. It is not the love of liquor, strong as that is; it is the infinitely stronger, infinitely more murderous and heartless love of money that makes the liquor traffic so hard to exterminate.

Instances might be multiplied indefinitely. The betrayals and murders and robberies that go on in this land every year due to this Judas motive of money-loving are countless in number. Only the recording angel can trace the subtle workings of this murderous principle, and assign to you and me whatever share of responsibility our dishonesty, our selfishness, our avarice, our money-loving lays upon us.

Let us, then, realize the worth of money; let us be as diligent as may be in all honest efforts to earn and save it. But may we be careful that no piece of silver goes into our pockets which directly or indirectly represents unnecessary privation or want or injury or disability to any fellow man. As we would shun the remorse and condemnation that befell Judas, may we be free ourselves from all complicity with business schemes in which the gain to ourselves is based on a corresponding loss or injury to others.

The third sin which contributed to our Lord's crucifixion was slander. ''And the whole multitude of them arose and led him unto Pilate, and they began to accuse him, saying, We found this fellow perverting the nation and forbidding to give tribute to Cæsar, and saying that he himself is Christ a king.''

The sin of slander, you observe, is the one of which the multitude were guilty. Slander is the weapon of the ignoble rabble who have not influence or power enough to stand up by themselves and strike an open blow on their own responsibility. Just so to-day, the meanest feature about malicious gossip and scandal is that it is sure to be the work of some one who is sheltered behind his or her insignificance. The scandal-monger does the devil's retail business. Scandal consists of putting a grain of truth with a bushel of surmises, inferences, misinterpretations and innuendoes and peddling the product as unquestioned fact. In the case before us, the grain of truth was that Jesus had announced a spiritual kingdom. That He meant a temporal kingdom was at best an inexcusable misunderstanding; that He was a rival of Cæsar was nonsense; that He forbade to give tribute to Cæsar was the exact opposite of the truth, and that He perverted the nation was a downright lie. We detest and abominate that lying, yelling rabble that thronged the Judgment Hall of Pilate with cries of ''Crucify him, Crucify him.'' But have we never repeated an uninvestigated charge? Have we never put a bad interpretation on conduct which yet was susceptible of honorable interprétation? Have we never, as a man was being condemned unheard, added our voices to the clamor? Have we never whispered behind a person's back what we would not have had the courage to say to his face? Have we never allowed our prejudices to color our interpretations of another's conduct? It is to be hoped that we are not. But if we have, then let us remember that those acts of ours are precisely on a level with the slanderous accusations of this mob that clamored for the crucifixion of our Lord. And let us in the future beware how we lend our lips to slanderous accusations which reduce us to a level with these most detestable of our Lord's murderers.

In the fourth place, to crown the whole, we have Pilate's servility. ''And so Pilate, willing to content the people, released Barabbas unto them, and delivered Jesus, when he had scourged him, to be crucified.''

Pilate did not want to do it; he had resorted to every device; he had left no stone unturned by which he might avoid this unjust act. But he was willing to content the people, and so he yielded. And so, notwithstanding his real love of justice, and his abhorrence and shrinking from the injustice of this deed, he did it; and his name has gone down to all ages as one who sanctioned and authorized the central crime of history.

And he likewise is the type of the sinners of our own day. Nineteen-twentieths of all the sins committed to-day are done in just the way that Pilate committed this. A young man does not wilfully and deliberately ruin his health and reputation and fortune and character in drink and dissipation. He first gets entangled with a company, or, as he says, ''gets into a crowd,'' ''goes with a set of fellows,'' and, willing to please them, he takes step after step, reluctantly and in secret unwillingness, on the downward road that leads to death. A man does not willingly become a defaulter and a thief: but he gets drawn into extravagant ways of living, and willing to keep up his standing with a fashionable circle, willing to gratify the pride and vanity of his own family, reluctantly and unwillingly he takes the secret steps that ultimately lead to exposure, ruin and disgrace.

A man does not willingly and deliberately pass all his days without an open, full whole-souled committal of his ways unto the Lord, and find himself at last face to face with a neglected, injured, unknown and untrusted God. No man sits down and with full and deliberate intent does that. How then comes it about that in so many cases the thing is done? The reason is that you are associated at home, in business and in society, with men and women who know you pretty thoroughly. They know your weak points, just as well as this multitude knew the vulnerable points in Pilate's record. To come out squarely and openly on the Lord's side, would surprize them; would make talk; perhaps provoke criticism and in general stir up the comfortable relation in which you now stand to them. They might think you were setting yourself up as an example for them. Your act might be a silent condemnation of their indifference. It might set them to serious thinking. For the time being, at least, the relations between yourself and them would not be so easy-going and comfortable and sympathetic as they now are. And willing to content them and leave these things undisturbed, you go on risking your own soul, and placing yourself side by side with Pilate, who for no deeper reason and with no more malicious intention became partner in the crucifixion of the Lord.

It is precisely the same willingness to content somebody else which made Pilate deliver up Jesus to be scourged and crucified, that causes vast multitudes of men and women here in our midst and everywhere to-day, to deliver over the Church of Christ to languish and suffer, and perhaps to die, for the lack of that hearty, thorough, whole-souled support which, in their secret hearts, they feel and know they ought to give it.

I suspect there is scarcely a man or woman among us who has not at some time or other been guilty of one or all of these very sins which contributed to the crucifixion of our Lord. This I do know; that if there is a soul to-day who is above these very sins, it is because the grace of God has lifted you and is still holding you above them. Between the ranks of the crucifiers and the followers of Jesus there is no middle ground. "He that is not with me is against me," says Jesus. I know enough of human nature to say that if there is a soul to-day that has not repented of his sinfulness, made confession and received the grace of Christ, he is not only capable of each and all these sins, but is yielding to them day after day. If there is one of the profest followers of Christ, whose hold on Christ has weakened, whose communion with Him has become less deep and full and constant, I know that he is finding these sins creeping back into his life to mar and defile it. From these very sins that crucified our Lord, nothing short of the constant presence and power of the Spirit of Christ Himself can keep us.

If this study of the sins that crucified our Lord brings home to you and me an unsuspected depth of sinfulness within our hearts; if it classes us with men whose names we have been wont to speak with bated breath, nevertheless let us not despair. For you and me, who have done these very things unto our Lord in doing them to our fellow men; for us, as for those whose envy and avarice and slander and servility were directed against His person, He prays: "Father, forgive them, for they know not what they do." Not only will Christ pardon these deep-seated, daily sins of ours, but he will give us power to rise above them. As has been said, there is no other way given among men whereby our human hearts can rise above these easily besetting sins except that of letting the love of Christ lift us up out of them.

Christ is able to save to the uttermost. From even these deeply ingrained traits of character and lines of habitual conduct, He can rescue us. Do you doubt it? Do you ask how? Let us take these very sins one by one:

First, envy. Do you find it difficult, at times impossible, to look on your neighbor who is richer than yourself, who has an easier time, who is more popular, more beautiful, who is a better housekeeper, who excels you in your particular line of business, your profession, your art, your music; who has op-portunities thrown in his way which you have struggled all your life to secure in vain—do you, I say, find it difficult to repress the feeling of envy that arises spontaneously at the thought of this more favored one? The love of Christ will lift you clear above all that. He will teach you that a man can have nothing really and lastingly good unless God gives it to Him. He will fill your mind and heart and hands with thoughts and deeds of loving service to Him, which, with the talents, the opportunities, the means, and the accomplishments you already have, you can perform, and in which and for which you can, day by day, receive His approval and enjoy His fellowship and love. Entering heartily and self-forgetfully into this service for Christ and with Christ, you will consider yourself the most highly favored of mankind. You will be only thankful if others can perform this same Christian service in a more effective manner and in a wider sphere. And for all who have not learned this blesséd secret of doing whatever their hands find to do contentedly, humbly and cheerfully for Christ's sake—for all such, whether they be above you or below you in outward advantages and accomplishments you can have nothing but pity and sorrow to think that with all their opportunities they are missing the one thing which can give to life, under any conditions, a real joy and satisfaction. As John the Baptist said of Jesus, you will gladly say of every one who can do more and better work in any line than yourself, "He must increase and I must decrease." And your joy will be just as great in the total good accomplished as tho your part in producing it was greater, and your honor connected with it more generally recognized.

Secondly, money-loving; avarice. Do you find yourself tempted to put the question, "What will it pay?" "How much can I make out of it?" above the question, "How will this bargain affect my fellow man?" Do you find yourself making trades where you would not willingly yourself take the consequences which these trades bring on the men you trade with? Do you find a tendency to treat your debtor, your workman, your servant, as you would not willingly be treated yourself, if you were in debt, if you were earning wages by the daily labor of your hands? Has this habit of getting as much out of everybody and giving as little back as possible so become a habit with you that you never think of the privation, the suffering, the disappointment your dealing brings to others? The love of the Christ, who gave, not His money alone, but His very life for men; the love of the Christ to whom all, even the lowliest, the least deserving, the most wayward, are still brethren and sisters, to be blest, and helped, and loved, and saved;

this love of Christ, really coming into your heart and taking possession of your life, will take out of you all that is accurst in the thirst for gold; and at the same time it will leave you thrifty, industrious and economical; and protect you from future poverty and want quite as effectively as these close-fisted, avaricious ways which you have come to regard as your only safeguard. In the face of all temptations to do wrong for the money it will bring, you will be able to say with Peter, "Thy silver perish with thee."

Thirdly. Is it the habit of running from house to house with the wretched tale of some fellow creature's misdoings, real or fancied, that likens you to these murderers of Jesus? Is that little member about the use of which James gives us so many warnings, the one which leads you most frequently into unchristlike conduct? If so, then your fault is one of the most difficult of all to cure. Yet even from malicious gossip and scandal, the grace of Christ can keep you. Let the pity and compassion of Him who said to the convicted woman, "Neither do I condemn thee; go and sin no more"—let the broad, human sympathy of Him who found even publicans and harlots more congenial to His spirit than their censorious and self-righteous accusers, once gain complete admission to your breast, and you will find it as impossible to speak harshly of a brother's sin or a sister's fall, to find satisfaction in discussing iniquity, as it is now seemingly impossible to avoid it. You will still see with sorrow the evil and sin there is in human hearts and lives. When called upon to act with reference to a man who has done wrong, you will not ignore his misdeeds; when it is necessary to reprove directly, or to warn those interested indirectly, of a bad man's character, you will not hesitate to do it. But from out a heart in which Christ is present at the time, no unnecessary word of fault-finding or ill-willed gossip can ever pass.

Fourthly, compliance and servility. Are you accustomed to think what this, that, and the other one will say about you; how they will feel toward you; what possibly they may do to you before you make up your mind what to do in any given case? In other words, are you the slave of your associates? Let the life of Him, who, when advised to alter his course for fear that Herod might kill Him, replied: "Go and say to that fox, behold I cast out devils and perform cures to-day and to-morrow, and the third day I am perfected. Howbeit I must go on my way to-day and to-morrow and the day following"; let the spirit of Him who drove out the sellers of doves and overthrew the tables of the money-changers in the temple, not deigning to give answer to the chief priests who asked by what authority He acted; let the majestic calmness of Him who would not in the slightest respect explain away his lofty claims before the Roman procurator who was to decide between release and crucifixion; let this manly independence that Christ displayed once get hold of you, and this excessive regard for what folks will say and think about you will instantly vanish.

To all who are disposed to criticize you after you have decided to take a given course, because God calls you that way, you will be able to say with Paul: "With me it is a very small thing that I should be judged of you or of man's judgment. He that judgeth me is God."

Thus for each and all of these sins, the grace of Christ can pardon us, and from them His spirit can preserve us.

In view of the presence of these same sinful tendencies within us; in view of the prevalence of these very evils in our midst to-day; in view of our Lord's words: "Inasmuch as ye have done it unto one of the least of these, my brethren, ye have done it unto me," shall we not, with deeper contrition and more heartfelt confession of our sins, betake ourselves to Christ for His forgiveness and His saving power; that both now and in the great day when the men of every age and every nation shall be assembled before the judgment-seat of God, we may be found, not in the company of the traitor Judas, the envious Caiaphas, the malignant Annas, the slanderous rabble and the servile Pilate; but may ours be the blessed fellowship in Christ with the impetuous but repentant Peter, the faithful Marys, and the loving John.

CHARLES E. JEFFERSON

1860-1937

THE RECONCILIATION

BIOGRAPHICAL NOTE

CHARLES EDWARD JEFFERSON was born at Cambridge, Ohio, in 1860. He came to public attention by the effectiveness of his preaching during a most successful pastorate in Chelsea, Mass., from which he was called to the Broadway Tabernacle, New York, in 1897. During his New York pastorate the Tabernacle at 34th Street has been sold and a unique structure, including an apartment tower ten stories high, has been built farther up-town. Dr. Jefferson has published several successful books. He had a mellow, sympathetic voice, of considerable range and flexibility, and he spoke in an easy, conversational style.

Christ died for our sins.—1 Cor. xv., 3.

I WANT to think with you this morning about the doctrine of the Atonement. Having used that word atonement once, I now wish to drop it. It is not a New Testament word, and is apt to lead one into confusion. You will not find it in your New Testament at all, providing you use the Revised Version. It is found in the King James Version only once, and that is in the fifth chapter of Paul's letter to the Romans; but a few years ago, when the revisers went to work, they rubbed out the word and would allow it no place whatever in the entire New Testament. They substituted for it a better word—reconciliation—and that is the word that will probably be used in the future theology of the Church. It is my purpose, then, this morning, to think with you about the doctrine of the reconciliation, or, to put it in a way that will be intelligible to all the boys and girls, I want to think with you about the "making up" between God and man.

Christianity is distinctly a religion of redemption. Its fundamental purpose is to recover men from the guilt and power of sin. All of its history and its teachings must be studied in the light of that dominating purpose. We are told sometimes that Jesus was a great teacher, and so He was, but the apostles never gloried in that fact. We are constantly reminded that He was a great reformer, and so He was, but Peter and John and Paul seemed to be altogether unconscious of that fact. It is asserted that He was a great philanthropist, a man intensely interested in the bodies and the homes of men, and so of course He was, but the New Testament does not seem to care for that. It has often been declared that He was a great martyr, a man who laid down His life in devotion to the truth, and so He was and so He did, but the Bible never looks at Him from that standpoint or regards Him in that light. It refuses to enroll Him among the teachers or reformers or philanthropists or the martyrs of our race. According to the apostolic writers, Jesus is the world's Redeemer, He was manifested to take away sin. He is the Lamb of God that taketh away the sin of the world. The vast and awful fact that broke the apostles' hearts and sent them out into the world to baptize the nations into His name, was the fact which Paul was all the time asserting, "He died for our sins."

No one can read the New Testament without seeing that its central and most conspicuous fact is the death of Jesus. Take, for instance, the gospels, and you will find that over one-quarter of their pages are devoted to the story of His death. Very strange is this indeed, if Jesus was nothing but an illustrious teacher. A thousand interesting events of His career are passed over, a thousand discourses are never mentioned, in order that there may be abundant room for the telling of His death. Or take the letters which make up the last half of the New Testament; in these letters there is scarcely a quotation from the lips of Jesus. Strange indeed is this if Jesus is only the world's greatest teacher. The letters seem to ignore that He was a teacher or reformer, but every letter is soaked in the pathos of His death. There must be a deep and providential reason for all this. The character of the gospels and the letters must have been due to something that Jesus said or that the Holy Spirit inbreathed. A study of the New Testament will convince us that Jesus had trained His disciples to see in His sufferings and death the climax of God's crowning revelation to the world. The key-note of the whole gospel story is struck by John the Baptist in his bold declaration, "Behold the Lamb of God, which taketh away the sin of the world." In that declaration there was a reference to His death, for the "lamb" in Palestine lived only to be slain. As soon as Jesus began His public career He began to refer in enigmatic phrases to His death. He did not declare His death openly, but the thought of it was wrapt up inside of all He said. Nicodemus comes to Him at night to have a talk with Him about His work, and among other things, Jesus says, "As Moses lifted up the serpent in the wilderness so shall the Son of man be lifted up." Nicodemus did not know what He meant—we know. He goes into the temple and drives out the men who have made it a den of thieves, and when an angry mob surrounds Him He calmly says, "Destroy this temple, and in three days I will raise it up." They did not know what He meant—we know. He goes into the city of Capernaum, and is surrounded by a great crowd who seem to be eager to know the way of life. He begins to talk to them about the bread that comes down from heaven, and among other things He says, "The bread which I will give is my flesh, which I will give for the life of the world." They did not understand what He said—we understand it now. One day in the city of Jerusalem He utters a great discourse upon the good shepherd. "I am the good shepherd," He says; "the good shepherd giveth his life for the sheep." They did not understand Him—we do. In the last week of His earthly life

it was reported that a company of Greeks had come to see Him. He falls at once into a thoughtful mood, and when at last He speaks it is to say that "I, if I be lifted up, will draw all men unto me." The men standing by did not understand what He said—we understand. All along His journey, from the Jordan to the cross, He dropt such expressions as this: "I have a baptism to be baptized with; and how am I straitened till it be accomplished." Men did not know what He was saying—it is all clear now.

But while He did not talk openly to the world about His death, He did not hesitate to speak about it to His nearest friends. As soon as He found a man willing to confess that He was indeed the world's Messiah, the Son of the living God, He began to initiate His disciples into the deeper mysteries of His mission. "From that time," Matthew says, "he began to show, to unfold, to set forth the fact that he must suffer many things and be killed." Peter tried to check Him in this disclosure, but Jesus could not be checked. It is surprising how many times it is stated in the gospels that Jesus told His disciples He must be killed. Matthew says that while they were traveling in Galilee, on a certain day when the disciples were much elated over the marvelous things which He was doing, He took them aside and said "Let these words sink into your ears: I am going to Jerusalem to be killed." Later on, when they were going through Perea, Jesus took them aside and said, "The Son of man must suffer many things, and at last be put to death." On nearing Jerusalem His disciples became impatient for a disclosure of His power and glory. He began to tell them about the grace of humility. "The Son of man," He said, "is come, not to be ministered unto, but to minister, and to give his life a ransom for many." On the last Tuesday of His earthly life He sat with His disciples on the slope of the Mount of Olives, and in the midst of His high and solemn teaching He said, "It is only two days now until I shall be crucified." And on the last Thursday of His life, on the evening of His betrayal, He took His disciples into an upper room, and taking the bread and blessing it, He gave it to these men, saying, "This is my body which is given for you." Likewise after supper He took the cup, and when He had blest it gave it to them, saying, "This is my blood of the covenant which is shed for you and for many for the remission of sins. Do this in remembrance of me." It would seem from this that the one thing which Jesus was desirous that all His followers should remember was the fact that He had laid down His life for them. One can not read the gospels without feeling that he is being borne steadily and irresistibly toward the cross.

When we get out of the gospels into the

epistles we find ourselves face to face with the same tragic and glorious fact. Peter's first letter is not a theological treatise. He is not writing a dissertation on the person of Christ, or attempting to give any interpretation of the death of Jesus; he is dealing with very practical matters. He exhorts the Christians who are discouraged and downhearted to hold up their heads and to be brave. It is interesting to see how again and again he puts the cross behind them in order to keep them from slipping back. "Endure," he says, "because Christ suffered for us. Who his own self bore our sins in his own body on the tree." The Christians of that day had been overtaken by furious persecution. They were suffering all sorts of hardships and disappointments. But "suffer," he says, "because Christ has once suffered for sins, the just for the unjust, that he might bring us to God." Certainly the gospel, according to St. Peter, was: Christ died for our sins.

Read the first letter of St. John, and everywhere it breathes the same spirit which we have found in the gospels and in St. Peter. John punctuates almost every paragraph with some reference to the cross. In the first chapter he is talking about sin. "The blood of Jesus Christ," he says, "cleanses us from all sins." In the second chapter he is talking about forgiveness, and this leads him to think at once of Jesus Christ, the righteous, "who is the propitiation for our sins, and not for ours only but for the sins of the whole world." In the third chapter he is talking about brotherly love. He is urging the members of the Church to lay down their lives, one for another, "Hereby perceive we the love of God, because he laid down his life for us." In the fourth chapter he tells of the great mystery of Christ's love: "Herein is love, not that we loved God, but that he loved us, and sent his Son to be the propitiation for our sins." To the beloved disciple evidently the great fact of the Christian revelation is that Christ died for our sins.

But it is in the letters of Paul that we find the fullest and most emphatic assertion of this transcendent fact. It will not be possible for me to quote to you even a half of what he said on the subject. If you should cut out of his letters all the references to the cross, you would leave his letters in tatters. Listen to him as he talks to his converts in Corinth: "First of all I delivered unto you that which I also received, how that Christ died for our sins." That was the foremost fact, to be stated in every letter and to be unfolded in every sermon. To Saul of Tarsus, Jesus is not an illustrious Rabbi whose sentences are to be treasured up and repeated to listening congregations; He is everywhere and always the world's Redeemer. And throughout all of Paul's epistles one hears the same jubilant, triumphant declaration, "I live by the faith of the Son of God, who loved me and gave himself for me."

Let us now turn to the last book of the New Testament, the Book of the Revelation. What does this prophet on the Isle of Patmos see and hear, as he looks out into future ages and coming worlds? The book begins with a doxology: "Unto him that loved us, and washed us from our sins in his own blood, to him be glory and dominion forever and ever." John looks, and beholds a great company of the redeemed. He asks who these are, and the reply comes back, "These are they who have washed their robes and made them white in the blood of the Lamb." He listens, and the song that goes up from the throats of the redeemed is, "Worthy art thou to take the book, and to open the seals thereof; for thou wast slain and didst purchase us for God with thy blood." At the center of the great vision which bursts upon the soul of the exiled apostle, there is a Lamb that was slain. Whatever we may think of Jesus of Nazareth, there is no question concerning what the men who wrote the New Testament thought. To the men who wrote the book, Jesus was not a Socrates or a Seneca, a Martin Luther or an Abraham Lincoln. His life was not an incident in the process of evolution, His death was not an episode in the dark and dreadful tragedy of human history. His life is God's greatest gift to men, His death is the climax and the crowning revelation of the heart of the eternal. You can not open the New Testament anywhere without the idea flying into your face, "Christ died for our sins."

How different all this is from the atmosphere of the modern Church. When you go into the average church to-day, what great idea meets you? Do you find yourselves face to face with the fact that Christ died for our sins? I do not think you will often hear that great truth preached. In all probability you will hear a sermon dealing with the domestic graces, or with business obligations, or with political duties and complications. You may hear a sermon on city missions, or on foreign missions; you may hear a man dealing with some great evil, or pointing out some alarming danger, or discussing some interesting social problem, or urging upon men's consciences the performance of some duty. It is not often in these modern days that you will hear a sermon dealing with the thought that set the apostles blazing and turned the world upside down. And right there, I think, lies one of the causes of the weaknesses of the modern Church. We have been so busy attending to the things that ought to be done, we have had no time to feed the springs that keep alive these mighty hopes which make us Christian men. What is the secret of the strength of the Roman Catholic Church? How is it that she pursues her conquering way, in spite of stupidities and blunders that would have killed any other institution? I know the explanations that are usually offered, but it seems to me they are far from adequate. Somebody says, But the Roman Catholic Church does not hold any but the ignorant. That is not true. It may be true of certain localities in America, but it is not true of the nations across the sea. In Europe she holds entire nations in the hollow of her hand; not only the ignorant, but the learned; not only the low, but the high; not only the rude, but the cultured, the noble, and the mighty. It will not do to say that the Roman Catholic Church holds nòbody but the ignorant. But even if it were true, it would still be interesting to ascertain how she exercises such an influence over the minds and hearts of ignorant people—for ignorant people are the hardest of all to hold. When you say that the Church can hold ignorant men, you are giving her the very highest compliment, for you are acknowledging that she is in the possession of a power which demands an explanation. The very fact that she is able to bring out such hosts of wage-earning men and women in the early hours of Sunday morning, men and women who have worked hard through the week, and many of them far into the night, but who are willing on the Lord's Day to wend their way to the house of God and engage in religious worship, is a phenomenon which is worth thinking about. How does the Roman Catholic Church do it? Somebody says she does it all by appealing to men's fears, she scares men into penitence and devotion. Do you think that that is a fair explanation? I do not think so. I can conceive how she might frighten people for one generation, or for two, but I can not conceive how she could frighten a dozen generations. One would suppose that the spell would wear off by and by. There is a deeper explanation than that. The explanation is to be found in the spiritual nature of man. The Roman Catholic leaders, notwithstanding their blunders and their awful sins, have always seen that the central fact of the Christian revelation is the death of Jesus, and around that fact they have organized all their worship. Roman Catholics go to mass; what is the mass? It is the celebration of the Lord's Supper. What is the Lord's Supper? It is the ceremony that proclaims our Lord's death until He comes. The hosts of worshipers that fill our streets in the early Sunday morning hours are not going to church to hear some man discuss an interesting problem, nor are they going to listen to a few singers sing; they are going to celebrate once more the death of the Savior of the world. In all her cathedrals Catholicism places the stations of the cross, that they may tell to the eye the

story of the stages of His dying. On all her altars she keeps the crucifix. Before the eyes of every faithful Catholic that crucifix is held until his eyes close in death. A Catholic goes out of the world thinking of Jesus crucified. So long as a Church holds on to that great fact, she will have a grip on human minds and hearts that can not be broken. The cross, as St. Paul said, a stumbling-block to the Jews and foolishness to the Greeks, is the power of God unto salvation to every one that believes. The Catholic Church has picked up the fact of Jesus' death and held it aloft like a burning torch. Around the torch she has thrown all sorts of dark philosophies, but through the philosophies the light has streamed into the hearts and homes of millions of God's children.

Protestantism has prospered just in proportion as she has kept the cross at the forefront of all her preaching. The missionaries bring back the same report from every field, that it is the story of Jesus' death that opens the hearts of the pagan world. Every now and then a denomination has started, determined to get rid of the cross of Jesus, or at least to pay scant attention to it, and in every case these denominations have been at the end of the third or fourth generation either decaying or dead. There is no interpretation of the Christian religion that has in it redeeming power which ignores or belittles the death of Christ.

If Protestantism to-day is not doing what it ought to do, and is manifesting symptoms which are alarming to Christian leaders, it is because she has in these recent years been engaged so largely in practical duties as to forget to drink inspiration from the great doctrines which must forever furnish life and strength and hope. If you will allow me to prophesy this morning, I predict that the preaching of the next fifty years will be far more doctrinal than the preaching of the last fifty years has been. I imagine some of you will shudder at that. You say you do not like doctrinal preaching, you want preaching that is practical. Well, pray, what is practical preaching? Practical preaching is preaching that accomplishes the object for which preaching is done, and the primary object of all Christian preaching is to reconcile men to God. The experience of 1900 years proves that it is only doctrinal preaching that reconciles the heart to God. If, then, you really want practical preaching, the only preaching that is deserving the name is preaching that deals with the great Christian doctrines. But somebody says, I do not like doctrinal preaching. A great many people have said that within recent years. I do not believe they mean what they say. They are not expressing with accuracy what is in their mind. They do like doctrinal preaching if they are intelligent, faithful Christians, for doctrinal preaching is bread to hearts that have been born again. When people say they do not like doctrinal preaching, they often mean that they do not like preaching which belongs to the eighteenth or seventeenth or sixteenth centuries. They are not to be blamed for this. There is nothing that gets stale so soon as preaching. We can not live upon the preaching of a bygone age. If preachers bring out the interpretations and phraseology which were current a hundred years ago, people must of necessity say, "Oh, please do not give us that, we do not like such doctrinal preaching." But doctrinal preaching need not be antiquated or belated, it may be fresh, it may be couched in the language in which men were born, it may use for its illustrations the images and figures and analogies which are uppermost in men's imagination. And whenever it does this there is no preaching which is so thrilling and uplifting and mighty as the preaching which deals with the great fundamental doctrines.

In one sense, the Christian religion never changes, in another sense it is changing all the time. The facts of Christianity never change, the interpretations of those facts alter from age to age. It is with religion as it is with the stars, the stars never change. They move in their orbits in our night sky as they moved in the night sky of Abraham when he left his old Chaldean home. The constellations were the same at the opening of our century as they were when David watched his flocks on the old Judean hills. But the interpretations of the stars have always changed, must always change. Pick up the old charts which the astrologers made and compare them with the charts of astronomers of our day. How vast the difference! Listen to our astronomers talk about the magnitudes and distances and composition of the stars, and compare with their story that which was written in the astronomy of a few centuries ago. The stellar universe has not changed, but men's conceptions have changed amazingly. The facts of the human body do not change. Our heart beats as the heart of Homer beat, our blood flows as the blood of Julius Cæsar flowed, our muscles and nerves live and die as the nerves and muscles have lived and died in the bodies of men in all the generations—and yet, how the theories of medicine have been altered from time to time. A doctor does not want to hear a medical lecturer speak who persists in using the phraseology and conceptions which were accepted by the medical science of fifty years ago. Conceptions become too narrow to fit the growing mind of the world, and when once outgrown they must be thrown aside. As it is in science, so it is in religion. The facts of Christianity never change, they are fixt stars in the firmament of moral truth. Forever and forever it will be true that Christ died for our sins, but the interpretations of this fact must be determined by the intelligence of the age. Men will never be content with simple facts, they must go behind them to find out an explanation of them. Man is a rational being, he must think, he will not sit down calmly in front of a fact and be content with looking it in the face, he will go behind it and ask how came it to be and what are its relations to other facts. That is what man has always been doing with the facts of the Christian revelation, he has been going behind them and bringing out interpretations which will account for them. The interpretations are good for a little while, and then they are outgrown and cast aside.

A good illustration of the progressive nature of theology is found in the doctrine of the atonement. All of the apostles taught distinctly that Christ died for our sins. The early Christians did not attempt to go behind that fact, but by and by men began to attempt explanations. In the second century a man by the name of Irenæus seized upon the word "ransom" in the sentence, "The Son of man is come to give his life a ransom for many," and found in that word "ransom" the key-word of the whole problem. The explanation of Irenæus was taken up in the third century by a distinguished preacher, Origen. And in the fourth century the teaching of Origen was elaborated by Gregory of Nyssa. According to the interpretation of these men, Jesus was the price paid for the redemption of men. Paul frequently used the word redemption, and the word had definite meanings to people who lived in the first four centuries of the Christian era. If Christ was indeed a ransom, the question naturally arose, who paid the price? The answer was, God. A ransom must be paid to somebody—to whom was this ransom paid? The answer was, the devil. According to Origen and to Gregory, God paid the devil the life of Jesus in order that the devil might let humanity go free. The devil, by deceit, had tricked man, and man had become his slave—God now plays a trick upon the devil, and by offering him the life of Jesus, secures the release of man. That was the interpretation held by many theologians for almost a thousand years, but in the eleventh century there arose a man who was not satisfied with the old interpretation. The world had outgrown it. To many it seemed ridiculous, to some it seemed blasphemous. There was an Italian by the name of Anselm who was an earnest student of the Scriptures, and he seized upon the word "debt" as the key-word of the problem. He wrote a book, one of the epoch-making books of Christendom, which he called "Cur Deus Homo." In this book Anselm elaborated his interpretation of the reconciliation. "Sin," he said, "is debt, and sin against an infinite being is an infinite debt. A finite being can not pay an infinite debt, hence an infinite being must become man in order that the debt may be paid. The Son of God, therefore, assumes the form of man, and by his sufferings on the cross pays the debt which allows humanity to go free.'' The interpretation was an advance upon that of Origen and Gregory, but it was not final. It was repudiated by men of the twelfth and thirteenth centuries, and finally, in the day of the Reformation, it was either modified or cast away altogether.

Martin Luther, Calvin, and the other reformers seized upon the word ''propitiation,'' and made that the starting-point of their interpretation. According to these men, God is a great governor and man has broken the divine law—transgressors must be punished—if the man who breaks the law is not punished, somebody else must be punished in his stead. The Son of God, therefore, comes to earth to suffer in His person the punishment that rightly belongs to sinners. He is not guilty, but the sins of humanity are imputed to Him, and God wreaks upon Him the penalty which rightfully, should have fallen on the heads of sinners. That is known as ''the penal substitution theory.''

It was not altogether satisfactory, many men revolted from it, and in the seventeenth century a Dutchman, Hugo Grotius, a lawyer, brought forth another interpretation, which is known in theology as ''the governmental theory.'' He would not admit that Christ was punished. His sufferings were not penal, but illustrative. ''God is the moral governor,'' said Grotius, ''his government must be maintained, law can not be broken with impunity. Unless sin is punished the dignity of God's government would be destroyed. Therefore, that man may see how hot is God's displeasure against sin, Christ comes into the world and suffers the consequences of the transgressions of the race. The cross is an exhibition of what God thinks of sin.'' That governmental theory was carried into England and became the established doctrine of the English Church for almost three hundred years. It was carried across the ocean and became the dominant theory in the New Haven school of theologians, as represented by Jonathan Edwards, Dwight, and Taylor. The Princeton school of theology still clung to the penal substitution theory, and it was the clashing of the New Haven school and the Princeton school which caused such a commotion in the Presbyterian Church of sixty years ago. They are antiquated. They are too little. They seem mechanical, artificial, trivial. We can say of the governmental theory what Dr. Hodge said, ''It degrades the work of Christ to the level of a governmental contrivance.'' If I should attempt to preach

to you the governmental theory as it was preached by theologians fifty years ago, you would not be interested in it. There is nothing in you that would respond to it. You would simply say, ''I do not like doctrinal preaching.'' Or if I should go back and take up the penal substitution theory in all its nakedness and hideousness, and attempt to give it to you as the correct interpretation of the gospel, you would rise up in open rebellion and say, ''We will not listen to such preaching.'' If I should go back and take up the Anselmic theory and attempt to show how an infinite debt must be paid by infinite suffering, you would say: ''Stop, you are converting God into a Shylock, who is demanding His pound of flesh. We prefer to think of Him as our heavenly Father.'' If I should go further back and take up the old ransom theory of Origen and Gregory, I suspect that some of you would want to laugh. You could not accept an interpretation which represents God as playing a trick upon Satan in order to get humanity out of his grasp. No, those theories have all been outgrown. We have come out into larger and grander times. We have higher conceptions of the Almighty than the ancients ever had. We see far deeper into the Christian revelation than Martin Luther or John Calvin ever saw. These old interpretations are simply husks, and men and women will not listen to the preaching of them. If, now and then, a belated preacher attempts to preach them, the people say, ''If that is doctrinal preaching, please give us something practical.''

And so the Church is to-day slowly working out a new interpretation of the great fact that Christ died for our sins. The interpretation has not yet been completed, and will not be for many years. I should like this morning simply to outline in a general way some of the more prominent features of the new interpretation. The Holy Ghost is at work. He is taking the things of Christ and showing them unto us. The interpretation of the reconciliation of the future will be superior in every point to any of the interpretations of the past.

The new interpretation is going to be simple, straightforward, and natural. The death of Christ is not going to be made something artificial, mechanical, or theatrical. It is going to be the natural conception of the outflowing life of God.

The new interpretation is going to start from the Fatherhood of God. The old theories were all born in the counting-room, or the court-house. Jesus went into the house to find His illustrations for the conduct of the heavenly Father. He never went into the court-house, nor can we go there for analogies with which to image forth His dealings with our race. It was His custom to say, ''If you, being evil, know how to give good gifts unto your children, how much more shall your Father which is in heaven give good things to them that ask him.''

The new interpretation is going to be comprehensive. It is going to be built, not on a single metaphor, but on everything that Jesus and the apostles said. Right there is where the old interpretations went astray. They seized upon one figure of speech and made that the determining factor in the entire interpretation. Jesus said many things, and so did His apostles, and all of them must contribute to the final interpretation.

Two things are to be hereafter made very clear: The first is that God reveals Himself in Jesus Christ. The old views were always losing sight of that great fact. There was always a dualism between God and Christ. I remember what my conception was when I was a boy. I thought that God was a strict and solemn and awful king, who was very angry because men had broken His law. He was just, and His justice had no mercy in it. Christ, His Son, was much better-natured and more compassionate, and He came forth into our world to suffer upon the cross that God's justice might relax a little, and His heart be opened to forgive our race. I supposed that that was the teaching of the New Testament, it certainly was the teaching of the hymns in the hymn-book, if not of the preachers. And when I became a young man, I supposed that that was the teaching of the Christian religion. My heart rebelled against it. I would not accept it. I became an infidel. A man can not accept an interpretation of God that does not appeal to the best that is in him. No man can accept a doctrine that darkens his moral sense, or that confuses the distinction between right and wrong. I would not accept the old interpretation because my soul rose in revolt against it. I shall never forget how, one evening in his study, a minister, who had outgrown the old traditions, explained to me the meaning of the reconciliation. He assured me that God is love, invisible, eternal. Christ, His Son, is also love. In becoming at one with the Son we become at one with the Father. This is the at-one-ment. And when that truth broke upon me my heart began to sing:

> Just as I am—Thy love unknown
> Hath broken every barrier down;
> Now, to be Thine, yea, Thine alone,
> O Lamb of God, I come!

I wonder in telling this if I have not spoken the experience of many of you this morning. It is impossible to love God if we feel that He is stern and despotic, and must be appeased by the sufferings of an innocent man. The New Testament nowhere lends any support to that idea. Everywhere the New Testament assures us that God is the lover of men, that He initiates the movement for man's redemption. "God so loved the world that he gave his only begotten Son. . . ." "Herein is love: not that we loved God, but that he loved us." "God commendeth his love toward us, in that, while we were yet sinners, Christ died for us." "The Father spared not his own Son, but delivered him up for us all." "He that hath seen me hath seen the Father." "I and my Father are one." These are only a few of the passages in which we are told that God is our Savior. When an old Scotchman once heard the text announced, "God so loved the world that he gave his only begotten Son," he exclaimed, "Oh, that was love indeed! I could have given myself, but I never could have given my boy." This, then, is the very highest love of which it is possible for the human mind to think: the love of a father that surrenders his son to sufferings and death.

And this brings us to the second great truth which is outgrowing increasingly clear in the consciousness of the Church. The death of Jesus is the revelation of an experience in the heart of God. God is the sin-bearer of the world. He bears our sins on His mind and heart. There are three conceptions of God: the savage, the pagan, and the Christian. God, according to the savage conception, is vengeful, and capricious, and vindictive. He is a great savage hidden in the sky. We have all outgrown that. According to the pagan idea, He is indifferent to the wants and woes of men. He does not care for men. He is not interested in them. He does not sympathize with them. He does not suffer over their griefs. He does not feel pain or sorrow. I am afraid that many of us have never gotten beyond the pagan conception of the Almighty. But according to the Christian conception, God suffers. He feels, and because He feels, He sympathizes, and because He sympathizes, He suffers. He feels both pain and grief. He carries a wound in His heart. We men and women sometimes feel burdened because of the sin we see around us; shall not the heavenly Father be as sensitive and responsive as we men? But somebody says that God can not be happy then. Of course he can not be happy. Happiness is not an adjective to apply to God. Happy is a word that belongs to children. Children are happy, grown people never are. One can be happy when the birds are singing and the dew is on the grass, and there is no cloud in all the sky, and the crape has not yet hung at the door. But after we have passed over the days of childhood, there is happiness no longer. Some of us have lived too long and borne too much ever to be happy any more. But it is possible for us to be blest. We may pass into the very blessedness of God. The highest form of blessedness is suffering for those we love, and shall not the Father of all men have in His own eternal heart that experience which we confess to be the highest form of blessedness? This is the truth which is dawning like a new revelation on the Church: the humanity of God. It is revealed in the New Testament, but as yet we have only begun to take it in. God is like us men. We are like Him. We are made in His image. We are His children, and He is our Father. If we are His children, then we are His heirs, and joint heirs with Christ. Not only our joys, but our sorrows also, are intimations and suggestions of experiences in the infinite heart of the Eternal.

HERRICK JOHNSON

1832-1913

THE CHANGELESS CHRIST

BIOGRAPHICAL NOTE

EX-PROFESSOR of homiletics, McCormick Theological Seminary, Chicago; born Kaughnewaga, N. Y., September 22, 1832; graduated from Hamilton College, 1857; Auburn Theological Seminary, 1860; received D.D. from Western Reserve College, LL.D. from Wooster University, D.C.L. from Omaha University; ordained to Presbyterian ministry, 1860; pastor in Troy, N. Y., 1860-62; of the Third church, Pittsburg, 1862-67; of the First church, Philadelphia, 1868-74; professor of homiletics and pastoral theology, Auburn Theological Seminary, 1874-80; pastor of Fourth Presbyterian church, Chicago, 1880-83; author of "Christianity's Challenge," "Revivals: Their Place and Power," "Plain Talks about the Theatre," "Presbyterian Book of Forms," "From Love to Praise," etc.

"Jesus Christ is the same yesterday and to-day; yea, and forever."—Heb. 13 : 8.

CHANGE is stamped upon everything earthly. Nature takes on ever-varying moods. Society is in a constant state of transformation. When we visit old scenes and renew old associations, we find they are not what they were before. Even the old homestead, hallowed by tender memories, and tho kept through generations, must needs have its beloved face marred by patches of repair. Time makes furrows in the cheeks that were once full, and dims the eyes that once flashed like jewels. The soul behind the eyes is also changed with the changing years; so that neither the form nor the spirit of friends remains the same to us.

And there is a sense, of course, in which we would not have this otherwise. What would nature be without her infinite variety? A particular sunset, however gorgeous and brilliant its hues, would grow absolutely unbearable with exact, monotonous, daily repetition.

Think of life, fixt in grooves, and stamped with changelessness. It would be living death. Precious and matchless as infancy is, what mother would have her babe remain a babe? Her chief joy is that her new-born child grows. An old infant! What an anomaly! Think of a mother carrying about in her arms and hugging to her bosom a twenty- or thirty-year-old baby! The very suggestion is both ludicrous and repugnant.

No, we love change. A world of ravishing delight comes to us through the law of development. Things that grow, having life in them, how they outrival the lifeless things manufactured in shops! The top of creation is man, and he is fullest of changing moods and wills.

If, therefore, it should be written of things and men, of nature and society, "the same yesterday, to-day and forever," this world would be a desert.

Yet this is exactly what has been written of Jesus Christ, and written of Him, too, as if it were His unique, peculiar crown and glory! There must be a sense, therefore, in which for Him to be the same to-day and to-morrow and evermore would be occasion of unspeakable comfort.

And we do not need to think long or far to find this sense. It is at the door of our daily life. It enters into our most cherished relationships. It furnishes the basis for trust. The uniformity of nature is what gives us faith in nature. It is belief in the changeless order that makes vast enterprises possible. It is confidence in man's continuing as he is that leads to far-reaching ventures and compacts. Just as we count on the constancy of a friend, do we trust that friend.

Unchangeableness is therefore a peerless quality when we conceive of it as unity, but not uniformity; constancy, but not mechanical rigidity; the play of an infinite variety, with the fixedness of eternal principle.

What is it we want most in a bosom friend, when we and that friend come together again after long separation? That he be the same dear old trusted companion to whom we breathed our confidences, and with whom we walked in most loving and joy-giving fellowship in other years. How eagerly we look into his eyes, wondering if he is still the very same! Well, when we part with the best friend, we can not be quite sure he will be the same when we come back. But who of us has not at times wished he could be sure!

Blesséd be God! there is one being who changes not. And it is of Jesus Christ our Lord, "the chief among ten thousand" and "the one altogether lovely," that this matchless word is spoken.

So, if we wish to know what Jesus is, we only need to find out what He was, when He walked among men. What He was in the yesterday of His earthly life, He is in the to-day of His heavenly life, and shall be forever.

What was He in His earthly life? For one thing, He was always approachable. This is one of the most remarkable qualities with which Christ is stamped in the gospel record. And is it not one of the rarest in the personal history of men? From the very necessities of public and official life, as men grow famous and come in touch with wider and wider interests, they get hedged about with more or less of circumstance and condition that hinder familiar and unimpeded approach to them. It was the setting aside of many of these stately forms and regulations by the beloved Abraham Lincoln, and the living in constant sympathetic relation with the people, the door of his great nature being ever open to their need, that so endeared this martyred hero to the popular heart.

And friendship has one of its sweetest phases in this—the approachableness it invites and furnishes. Just as we find ourselves barred from access by the conventionalities or the engagements of life, do the shadows fall on our hearts. Watch a little child. Where does it fly when trouble comes? To the one place always open to it, the one covert where shelter has never been refused—the mother's bosom. One of the glories of true motherhood is approachableness. One of the curses of a home is to have this quality farmed out to a hired nurse.

A Savior, to meet the need of simple, struggling, suffering, and often impotent and sometimes despairing men, must be always approachable. If there is even an hour when He can not be reached, in that hour a sinner may perish. There must be no exigencies of government, no demands of multitudinous host, no public honor, no private feasts, to keep Him from the approach of one who needs His help.

And Jesus met this condition to the full. He was always approachable. On the public road, in the midst of the joyful acclaims of the multitude hailing Him as King, a blind beggar could come to Him and receive sight. In the crowded house a paralytic of years could be brought to him and get the power to take up his bed and walk. At a private feast a woman that had sinned, a harlot of the street, could come to Him, and, bathing His feet with her penitent tears, receive from His lips the gracious words, "Go in peace: thy sins be forgiven thee." Thank God, He was never shut away from the people He came to save. He had no private quarters. No inner office stamped "No admittance" and too sacred for the intrusion of honest inquiry. There was no place where He could not be sought and found. He had no business, and allowed none, that kept Him from the business of healing and helping men—of seeking and saving the lost. He was occupied with nothing that shut His ear against the cry of want. When alone in the solitude of the night, a ruler of the Jews came to Him, and got instruction as to the kingdom of God. When weary, sitting at the well, travel-worn and seeking rest, a Samaritan woman came to Him, and got from Him a cup of living water for her thirsty soul. When asleep in the ship, timid disciples came to Him, and, waking Him, could find a calm, both for their affrighted spirits and the tossing sea. When on a march of triumph, when in a desert place, when tempted, when dying—from first to last there was never an hour He could not be got at.

He had no preengagements, not one. Anybody could come to Him—absolutely anybody. The loving, of course, could come. Love makes a way in where nothing else can. We all welcome this angel guest. And Jesus did. The visits of love seemed a solace to this sad, great heart. Mary with her cruse of precious ointment; the other Mary with her heart swept clean of devilish possessions; the soiled woman with nothing but her grateful tears; Peter with his bruised and penitent spirit; Paul with his flaming ardor of devotion, loving possibly deepest and most fervently— these all found Jesus always approachable.

But the doubting also could come to Him. Fearing, challenging, wondering, questioning —no matter! What honest doubter ever failed of being met by Him as Thomas was; not to be rebuked for his doubt, but to be trusted out of it, if he only came. Jesus had no thunders for this honest soul that trembled and questioned and would put his Lord to the proof. He welcomed the doubter, tenderly met his need, and furnished the evidence. And He is the same yesterday and to-day and forever.

The heavy-hearted came, too, and were never turned away without the burden being lifted off. The poor, the sick, the lame, the halt, the blind, the palsied, the bruised ones, the tired and lonely, with strength clean gone, the hungry wanting bread, and the heart-hungry starving on the husks of formalism— how they flocked to Him; and always to find Him!

And even the outcasts came; the publicans and the harlots. And by these He was approachable, as by all the rest. He never broke a bruised reed, not one. "Send her away, she crieth after us," said His disciples. But Christ sent nobody away, until the need was met. There were brought unto Him little children that He should put His hands on them and pray. And the disciples rebuked them. What rudeness these mothers were guilty of, thus interrupting Christ in the midst of His wondrous speech! And of what use could He be to babes? Ah! those well-meaning but blinded disciples; they did not know Him. He said, "Suffer the little children to come unto me, and forbid them not." Does this not seem almost best of all, that He was always approachable by the children?

Mothers! He is the changeless Christ. Do you take in all the meaning there is to you in this wondrous word? Picture that scene! Think of that listening crowd, the weighty divine speech that was dropping from those sacred lips, the strange interruption, the mothers bringing their babes, the rebuking disciples, and Jesus saying, "Suffer the little children to come"—and remember, He is the same to-day and forever, thinking just as much of babes now as then; and just as sure to lay His hands upon your little ones and speak His blessing on them, and interest Himself in their behalf now as when He took the children in His arms at Capernaum.

But again: Jesus on earth was always ready to hear prayer. What we want in a helper is to hear us when we cry to him. Does God hear prayer? Will He hear prayer in any conceivable circumstances? Jesus did. Blind Bartimæus sat by the wayside begging. He heard the tramp and roar of a great multitude. He inquired what it meant. They told him "Jesus of Nazareth passeth by." And the blind man cried out, saying, "Jesus, have mercy on me." And Jesus caught the cry of the wayside beggar, stood still, stopt the journey to Jerusalem, hushed the hosannas, commanded the blind man to be brought to Him, and gave him his sight.

Again, when Christ was dying, when the agony of death was on Him, when the burden of a sinful world was on His heart, when a jeering mob beneath the cross on which He was crucified railed at Him with awful imprecations and blasphemy—amid all that babel of hell, He caught the cry of the penitent thief and answered it, commanding for him an entrance into paradise.

Prayer was never offered to Him in this earthly life that He did not listen to. No sounding hallelujahs of a triumph march, no raging passions of men bent upon His life, no occupation of absorbing interest, whether in deed or speech, could stop His ear from listening to the cry of a human heart. Amid any confusion of tongues and any babel of angry noises of conflicting interests and claims, He always heard prayer.

Just as there are ears strung with such exquisite delicacy of adaptation that they will detect in any flood of tumultuous harmony the chords for which they have an affinity— so Jesus seemed strung to catch the notes of prayer; and He caught them whenever they were struck, no matter with what roar of other voices the air was filled.

You who pray; you who sometimes cry and get no answer; you who have hesitated to pray, thinking that it could not be that the ascended Lord would hear—do you think He has lost that exquisitely tender and sympathetic relation to human need, since He went to heaven? No! In this respect, as in the others I have named He is the same for evermore—the changeless Christ. And therefore there can be no vast concerns of His mediatorial kingdom, no bursts of rapture by angelic hosts, no trumpet-notes of redemption's victory, and no shoutings of the multitudes of the saved, that can make Him deaf to the cry of a penitent or believing heart on earth.

Reader, looking upon this page and reading it, are you a sinner blinded by sin and wanting sight? Are you a Christian father or mother having a child that needs the touch of the divine healer? Are you a doubter, wondering if the gospel story can be true? Pray! O I beseech you, speak to this changeless Christ, who caught every cry that was ever made to Him when He was here. He is the same to-day and forever.

This blessèd Lord Jesus when on earth forgave sin.

Take the instances in His life that set this forth with a luminous fulness and a blessèd emphasis. Recall Zacchæus, the despised publican, the sinner, desiring to see that blessèd face, "whose very looks, he was told, shed peace upon restless spirits and fevered hearts"; and trembling with desire and expectation, he found Jesus desiring to see him. Seeking Jesus, he himself was sought. He found there were two seeking. And as the good old Scotch woman said, "Where there are twa seekin', there'll always be a findin'."

Zacchæus was met with sympathy and forgiveness. But what did the sneering Pharisees say? They said, "Jesus has gone to be guest with him that is a sinner." As if Jesus had not left heaven on that very business! Zacchæus a sinner! Yes; but it is a saying worthy of all acceptation that Jesus Christ came into the world to save sinners. Zacchæus lost! Yes; but the Son of Man is come to seek and save that which is lost.

Take the case of the publican, who, with the Pharisee, went up to the temple to pray. "God, I thank thee that I am not as other men are," prayed the Pharisee. "God be merciful to me a sinner," prayed the publican. Who did Jesus say went down to his house justified? "Justified?" asked an old soldier to whom this parable was read as he lay dying. He was scarred by sin as well as by battle. His face was seamed and ridged with the hoofs of appetite. He had been an awful sinner. But he had been touched in camp by the Christlike courage and tenderness and fidelity of a young comrade soldier. And this soldier of Christ had read to him the parable of the Pharisee and the publican, and had taught him to pray, "God be merciful to me a sinner"—"Justified," asked the dying veteran, "Did Jesus say that?" "Yes," was the reply, "Jesus said the publican went down to his house justified." "God be merciful to me a sinner," broke from the trembling lips. And that day he was with Jesus in paradise. And this Savior of sinners to-day is just the same.

Mark another trait of this Jesus of Nazareth. He was always ready to sympathize and help.

Have you ever noticed how often the Gospels speak of Jesus as moved with compassion? Seeing the man bound by Satan, lo! many years, Christ was moved with compassion. Seeing the multitude scattered abroad as sheep without a shepherd, He was moved with compassion. The beggars at the Jericho gate moved him with compassion. A leper moved Him with compassion. Most touching instance of all, they were carrying out of the city of Nain "one that was dead, the only son of his mother, and she was a widow." And when the Lord saw her, He had compassion.

Right up into heaven He carried this sympathetic nature; and the writer of the Epistle to the Hebrews refers to Him there, making intercession for us, a high priest, sympathetic still; able to be touched with the feeling of our infirmities (συμπαθησαι). No wonder the sacred writer adds, "Let us therefore draw near with boldness unto the throne of grace, that we may receive mercy and find grace to help us in time of need."

Blesséd be God for the changeless Christ. What an argument this puts into the mouth of prayer. Thou hast been my help, cries the psalmist; therefore, leave me not; neither forsake me, O God of my salvation! We can plead God's past goodness as a reason for continued goodness. We can ask Him for more because He has given us so much.

And what a sense of Christ's nearness this theme gives us. Our Lord has not gone on a journey. He is not asleep. He is not hedged about with infinite dignities. He is never behind locked doors. He has no preengagements. On earth He was always approachable. He is just so now. On earth He was always ready to forgive sin and to sympathize with the bruised and broken-hearted, and He is just so now. On earth He was always ready to hear prayer. And He is just so now—the same yesterday, to-day and forever.

JOHN H. JOWETT

1864-1923

COURAGE AND HOPE

BIOGRAPHICAL NOTE

JOHN HENRY JOWETT, Congregational divine, was born at Barnard Castle, Durham, in 1864, and educated at Edinburgh and Oxford universities. In 1889 he was ordained to St. James's Congregational Church, Newcastle-on-Tyne, and in 1895 was called and began his pastorate of Carr's Lane Congregational Church, Birmingham, where he took first rank among the leading preachers of Great Britain. He is the author of several important books.

Rejoicing in hope.—Romans xii., 12.

THAT is a characteristic expression of the fine, genial optimism of the Apostle Paul. His eyes are always illumined. The cheery tone is never absent from his speech. The buoyant and springy movement of his life is never changed. The light never dies out of his sky. Even the gray firmament reveals more hopeful tints, and becomes significant of evolving glory. The apostle is an optimist, "rejoicing in hope," a child of light wearing the "armor of light," "walking in the light" even as Christ is in the light.

This apostolic optimism was not a thin and fleeting sentiment begotten of a cloudless summer day. It was not the creation of a season; it was the permanent pose of the spirit. Even when beset with circumstances which to the world would spell defeat, the apostle moved with the mien of a conqueror. He never lost the kingly posture. He was disturbed by no timidity about ultimate issues. He fought and labored in the spirit of certain triumph. "We are always confident." "We are more than conquerors through Him that loved us." "Thanks be unto God who giveth us the victory through our Lord Jesus Christ."

This apostolic optimism was not born of sluggish thinking, or of idle and shallow observation. I am very grateful that the counsel of my text lifts its chaste and cheery flame in the twelfth chapter of an epistle of which the first chapter contains as dark and searching an indictment of our nature as the mind of man has ever drawn. Let me rehearse the appalling catalog that the radiance of the apostle's optimism may appear the more abounding: "Senseless hearts," "fools," "uncleanness," "vile passions," "reprobate minds," "unrighteousness, wickedness, covetousness, maliciousness; full of envy, murder, strife, deceit, malignity, whisperers, backbiters, hateful to God, insolent, haughty, boastful, inventors of evil things, without understanding, covenant breakers, without natural affection, unmerciful." With fearless severity the apostle leads us through the black realms of midnight and eclipse. And yet in the subsequent reaches of the great argument, of which these dark regions form the preface, there emerges the clear, calm, steady light of my optimistic text. I say it is not the buoyancy of ignorance. It is not the flippant, lighthearted expectancy of a man who knows nothing about the secret places of the night. The counselor is a man who has steadily gazed at light at its worst, who has digged through the outer walls of convention and respectability, who has pushed his way into the secret chambers and closets of life, who has dragged out the slimy sins which were lurking in their holes, and named them after their kind—it is this man who when he has surveyed the dimensions of evil and misery and contempt, merges his dark indictment in a cheery and expansive dawn, in an optimistic evangel, in which he counsels his fellow-disciples to maintain the confident attitude of a rejoicing hope.

Now, what are the secrets of this courageous and energetic optimism? Perhaps, if we explore the life of this great apostle, and seek to discover its springs, we may find the clue to his abounding hope. Roaming then through the entire records of his life and teachings, do we discover any significant emphasis? Preeminent above all other suggestions, I am imprest with his vivid sense of the reality of the redemptive work of Christ. Turn where I will, the redemptive work of the Christ evidences itself as the base and groundwork of his life. It is not only that here and there are solid statements of doctrine, wherein some massive argument is constructed for the partial unveiling of redemptive glory. Even in those parts of his epistles where formal argument has ceased, and where solid doctrine is absent, the doctrine flows as a fluid element into the practical convictions of life, and determines the shape and quality of the judgments. Nay, one might legitimately use the figure of a finer medium still, and say that in all the spacious reaches of the apostle's life the redemptive work of his Master is present as an atmosphere in which all his thoughts and purposes and labors find their sustaining and enriching breath. Take this epistle to the Romans in which my text is found. The earlier stages of the great epistle are devoted to a massive and stately presentation of the doctrines of redemption. But when I turn over the pages where the majestic argument is concluded, I find the doctrine persisting in a diffused and rarefied form, and appearing as the determining factor in the solution of practical problems. If he is dealing with the question of the "eating of meats," the great doctrine reappears and interposes its solemn and yet elevating principle: "destroy not him with thy meat for whom Christ died." If he is called upon to administer rebuke to the passionate and unclean, the shadow of the cross rests upon his judgment. "Ye are not your own; ye are bought with a price." If he is portraying the ideal relationship of husband and wife, he sets it in the light of redemptive glory: "Husbands, love your wives, even as Christ also loved the church, and gave himself up for it." If he is seeking to cultivate the grace of liberality, he brings the heavenly air around about the spirit. "Ye know the grace of our Lord Jesus Christ, that tho he was rich, yet for your sakes he became poor." It interweaves itself with all his salutations. It exhales in all his benedictions like a hallowing fragrance. You can not get away from it. In the light of the glory of redemption all relationships are assorted and arranged. Redemption was not degraded into a fine abstract argument, to which the apostle had appended his own approval, and then, with sober satisfaction, had laid it aside, as a practical irrelevancy, in the stout chests of orthodoxy. It became the very spirit of his life. It was, if I may be allowed the violent figure, the warm blood in all his judgment. It filled the veins of all his thinking. It beat like a pulse in all his purposes. It determined and vitalized his decisions in the crisis, as well as in the lesser trifles of the common day. His conception of redemption was regulative of all his thought.

But it is not only the immediacy of redemption in the apostle's thought by which I am imprest. I stand in awed amazement before its vast, far-stretching reaches into the eternities. Said an old villager to me concerning the air of his elevated hamlet, "Ay, sir, it's a fine air is this westerly breeze; I like to think of it as having traveled from the distant fields of the Atlantic!" And here is the Apostle Paul, with the quickening wind of redemption blowing about him in loosening, vitalizing, strengthening influence, and to him, in all his thinking, it had its birth in the distant fields of eternity! To the apostle redemption was not a small device, an afterthought, a patched-up expedient to meet an unforseen emergency. The redemptive purpose lay back in the abyss of the eternities, and in a spirit of reverent questioning the apostle sent his trembling thoughts into those lone and silent fields. He emerged with whispered secrets such as these: "fore-knew," "fore-ordained," "chosen in him before the foundation of the world," "eternal life promised before times eternal," "the eternal purpose which he purposed in Christ Jesus our Lord."

Brethren, does our common thought of redemptive glory reach back into this august and awful presence? Does the thought of the modern disciple journey in this distant pilgrimage? Or do we now regard it as unpractical and irrelevant? There is no more insidious peril in modern religious life than the debasement of our conception of the practical. If we divorce the practical from the sublime, the practical will become the superficial, and will degenerate into a very lean and forceless thing. When Paul went on this lonely pilgrimage his spirit acquired the pos-

ture of a finely sensitive reverence. People
who live and move beneath great domes acquire a certain calm and stately dignity. It
is in companionship with the sublimities that
awkwardness and coarseness are destroyed.
We lose our reverence when we desert the
august. But has reverence no relationship
to the practical? Shall we discard it as an
irrelevant factor in the purposes of common life? Why, reverence is the very clue
to fruitful, practical living. Reverence is
creative of hope; nay, a more definite emphasis can be given to the assertion; reverence is
a constituent of hope. Annihilate reverence,
and life loses its fine sensitiveness, and when
sensitiveness goes out of a life the hope that
remains is only a flippant rashness, a thoughtless impetuosity, the careless onrush of the
kine, and not a firm, assured perception of a
triumph that is only delayed. A reverent
homage before the sublimities of yesterday
is the condition of a fine perception of the
hidden triumphs of the morrow. And, therefore, I do not regard it as an accidental conjunction that the psalmist puts them together
and proclaims the evangel that "the Lord
taketh pleasure in them that fear him, in them
that hope in his mercy." To feel the days
before me I must revere the purpose which
throbs behind me. I must bow in reverence if
I would anticipate in hope.

Here, then, is the Apostle Paul, with the
redemptive purpose interweaving itself with
all the entanglements of his common life, a
purpose reaching back into the awful depths
of the eternities, and issuing from those
depths in amazing fulness of grace and glory.
No one can be five minutes in the companionship of the Apostle Paul without discovering
how wealthy is his sense of the wealthy, redeeming ministry of God. What a wonderful consciousness he has of the sweep and
fulness of the divine grace! You know the
variations of the glorious air: "the unsearchable riches of Christ"; "riches in glory in
Christ Jesus"; "all spiritual blessings in the
heavenly places in Christ"; "the riches of
his goodness and forbearance and long-suffering." The redemptive purpose of God bears
upon the life of the apostle and upon the
race whose privileges he shares, not in an uncertain and reluctant shower, but in a great
and marvelous flood. And what to him is
the resultant enfranchisement? What are
the spacious issues of the glorious work? Do
you recall those wonderful sentences, scattered here and there about the apostle's writings, and beginning with the words "but
now"? Each sentence proclaims the end of
the dominion of night, and unveils some
glimpse of the new created day. "But now!"
It is a phrase that heralds a great deliverance!
"But now, apart from the law the righteousness of God hath been manifested." "But

now, being made free from sin and become
servants to God." "But now in Christ Jesus
ye that once were far off are made nigh in
the blood of Christ." "But now are ye light
in the Lord." "Now, no condemnation to
them that are in Christ Jesus." These represent no thin abstractions. To Paul the realities of which they speak were more real than
the firm and solid earth. And is it any wonder
that a man with such a magnificent sense of
the reality of the redemptive works of Christ,
who felt the eternal purpose throbbing in the
dark background and abyss of time, who conceived it operating upon our race in floods
of grace and glory, and who realized in his
own immediate consciousness the varied
wealth of the resultant emancipation—is it
any wonder that for this man a new day had
dawned, and the birds had begun to sing and
the flowers to bloom, and a sunny optimism
had taken possession of his heart, which found
expression in an assured and rejoicing hope?

I look abroad again over the record of
this man's life and teachings, if perchance I
may discover the secrets of his abiding optimism, and I am profoundly imprest by his
living sense of the reality and greatness of his
present resources. "By Christ redeemed!"
That is not a grand finale; it is only a glorious
inauguration. "By Christ redeemed; in
Christ restored"; it is with these dynamics of
restoration that his epistles are so wondrously
abounding. In almost every other sentence
he suggests a dynamic which he can count
upon as his friend. Paul's mental and spiritual outlook comprehended a great army of
positive forces laboring in the interests of
the kingdom of God. His conception of life
was amazingly rich in friendly dynamics! I
do not wonder that such a wealthy consciousness was creative of a triumphant optimism.
Just glance at some of the apostle's auxiliaries: "Christ liveth in me!" "Christ liveth
in me! He breathes through all my aspirations. He thinks through all my thinking.
He wills through all my willing. He loves
through all my loving. He travails in all
my labors. He works within me 'to will and
to do of his good pleasure.'" That is the
primary faith of the hopeful life. But see
what follows in swift and immediate succession. "If Christ is in you, the spirit is life."
"The spirit is life!" And therefore you find
that in the apostle's thought dispositions are
powers. They are not passive entities. They
are positive forces vitalizing and energizing
the common life of men. My brethren, I am
persuaded there is a perilous leakage in this
department of our thought. We are not bold
enough in our thinking concerning spiritual
realities. We do not associate with every mode
of the consecrated spirit the mighty energy of
God. We too often oust from our practical
calculations some of the strongest and most

aggressive allies of the saintly life. Meekness is more than the absence of self-assertion; it is the manifestation of the mighty power of God. To the Apostle Paul love exprest more than a relationship. It was an energy productive of abundant labors. Faith was more than an attitude. It was an energy creative of mighty endeavor. Hope was more than a posture. It was an energy generative of a most enduring patience. All these are dynamics, to be counted as active allies, cooperating in the ministry of the kingdom. And so the epistles abound in the recital of mystic ministries at work. The Holy Spirit worketh! Grace worketh! Faith worketh! Love worketh! Hope worketh! Prayer worketh! And there are other allies robed in less attractive garb. "Tribulation worketh!" "This light affliction worketh." "Godly sorrow worketh!" On every side of him the apostle conceives cooperative and friendly powers. "The mountain is full of horses and chariots of fire round about him." He exults in the consciousness of abounding resources. He discovers the friends of God in things which find no place among the scheduled powers of the world. He finds God's raw material in the world's discarded waste. "Weak things," "base things," "things that are despised," "things that are not," mere nothings; among these he discovers the operating agents of the mighty God. Is it any wonder that in this man, possessed of such a wealthy consciousness of multiplied resources, the spirit of a cheery optimism should be enthroned? With what stout confidence he goes into the fight! He never mentions the enemy timidly. He never seeks to underestimate his strength. Nay, again and again he catalogs all possible antagonisms in a spirit of buoyant and exuberant triumph. However numerous the enemy, however subtle and aggressive his devices, however towering and well-established the iniquity, however black the gathering clouds, so sensitive is the apostle to the wealthy resources of God that amid it all he remains a sunny optimist, "rejoicing in hope," laboring in the spirit of a conqueror even when the world was exulting in his supposed discomfiture and defeat.

And, finally, in searching for the springs of this man's optimism, I place alongside his sense of the reality of redemption and his wealthy consciousness of present resources his impressive sense of the reality of future glory. Paul gave himself time to think of heaven, of the home of God, of his own home when time should be no more. He loved to contemplate "the glory that shall be revealed." He mused in wistful expectancy of the day "when Christ who is our life shall be manifested," and when we also "shall be manifested with him in glory." He pondered the thought of death as "gain," as transferring him

to conditions in which he would be "at home with the Lord," "with Christ, which is far better." He looked for "the blest hope and appearing of the glory of our great God and Savior Jesus Christ," and he contemplated "that great day" as the "henceforth," which would reveal to him the crown of righteousness and glory. Is any one prepared to dissociate this contemplation from the apostle's cheery optimism? Is not rather the thought of coming glory one of its abiding springs? Can we safely exile it from our moral and spiritual culture? I know that this particular contemplation is largely absent from modern religious life, and I know the nature of the recoil in which our present impoverishment began. "Let us hear less about the mansions of the blest and more about the housing of the poor!" Men revolted against an effeminate contemplation, which had run to seed, in favor of an active philanthropy which sought the enrichment of the common life. But, my brethren, pulling a plant up is not the only way of saving it from running to seed. You can accomplish by a wise restriction what is wastefully done by severe destruction. I think we have lost immeasurably by the uprooting, in so many lives, of this plant of heavenly contemplation. We have built on the erroneous assumption that the contemplation of future glory inevitably unfits us for the service of man. It is an egregious and destructive mistake. I do not think that Richard Baxter's labors were thinned or impoverished by his contemplation of "The Saint's Everlasting Rest." When I consider his mental output, his abundant labors as father-confessor to a countless host, his pains and persecutions and imprisonments, I can not but think he received some of the powers of his optimistic endurance from contemplations such as he counsels in his incomparable book. "Run familiarly through the streets of the heavenly Jerusalem; visit the patriarchs and prophets, salute the apostles, and admire the armies of martyrs; lead on the heart from street to street, bring it into the palace of the great king; lead it, as it were, from chamber to chamber. Say to it, 'Here must I lodge, here must I die, here must I praise, here must I love and be loved. My tears will then be wiped away, my groans be turned to another tune, my cottage of clay be changed to this palace, my prison rags to these splendid robes'; 'for the former things are passed away.'" I can not think that Samuel Rutherford impoverished his spirit or deadened his affections, or diminished his labors by mental pilgrimages such as he counsels to Lady Cardoness: "Go up beforehand and see your lodging. Look through all your Father's rooms in heaven. Men take a sight of the lands ere they buy them. I know that Christ hath made the bargain already; but be kind

to the house ye are going to, and see it often.''
I can not think that this would imperil the
fruitful optimisms of the Christian life. I
often examine, with peculiar interest, the
hymn-book we use at Carr's Lane. It was
compiled by Dr. Dale. Nowhere else can I
find the broad perspective of his theology and
his primary helpmeets in the devotional life
as I find them there. And is it altogether
unsuggestive that under the heading of
"Heaven" is to be found one of the largest
sections of the book. A greater space is
given to "Heaven" than is given to "Christian duty.'' Is it not significant of what a
great man of affairs found needful for the
enkindling and sustenance of a courageous
hope? And among the hymns are many which
have helped to nourish the sunny endeavors of
a countless host.

> There is a land of pure delight
>   Where saints immortal reign;
> Infinite day excludes the night,
>   And pleasures banish pain.

> What are these, arrayéd in white,
>   Brighter than the noonday sun?
> Foremost of the suns of light,
>   Nearest the eternal throne.

> Hark! hark, my soul! Angelic songs are swelling
>   O'er earth's green fields and ocean's wave-beat shore
> Angelic songs to sinful men are telling
>   Of that new life when sin shall be no more.

My brethren, depend upon it, we are not
impoverished by contemplations such as these.
They take no strength out of the hand, and
they put much strength and buoyancy into
the heart. I proclaim the contemplation of
coming glory as one of the secrets of the
apostle's optimism which enabled him to labor
and endure in the confident spirit of rejoicing hope. These, then, are some of the springs
of Christian optimism; some of the sources in
which we may nourish our hope in the newer
labors of a larger day: a sense of the glory of
the past in a perfected redemption, a sense of
the glory of the present in our multiplied resources, a sense of the glory of to-morrow in
the fruitful rest of our eternal home.

> O blest hope! with this elate
> Let not our hearts be desolate;
> But, strong in faith and patience, wait
>   Until He come!

JOHN KNOX

1505-1572

THE FIRST TEMPTATION OF CHRIST

BIOGRAPHICAL NOTE

JOHN KNOX, the great Scottish reformer, was born at Giffordgate, four miles from Haddington, Scotland, in 1505. He first made his appearance as a preacher in Edinburgh, where he thundered against popery, but was imprisoned and sent to the galleys in 1546. In 1547 Edward VI secured his release and made him a royal chaplain, when he acquired the friendship of Cranmer and other reformers. On the accession of Mary (1553) he took refuge on the Continent. In 1556 he accepted the charge of a church in Geneva, but, after three years of tranquillity, returned to Scotland and became a popular leader of the Reformation in that country. His eloquence lashed the multitude to enthusiasm and acts of turbulent violence. As a preacher his style was direct and fearless, often fiery, and he had a habit of pounding the pulpit to emphasize particular truths. He died in 1572.

Then was Jesus led up of the Spirit into the wilderness, to be tempted of the devil.—Matt. iv., 1.

THE cause moving me to treat of this place of Scripture is, that such as by the inscrutable providence of God fall into divers temptations, judge not themselves by reason thereof to be less acceptable in God's presence. But, on the contrary, having the way prepared to victory by Jesus Christ, they shall not fear above measure the crafty assaults of that subtle serpent Satan; but with joy and bold courage, having such a guide as here is pointed forth, such a champion, and such weapons as here are to be found (if with obedience we will hear, and unfeigned faith believe), we may assure ourselves of God's present favor, and of final victory, by the means of Him, who, for our safeguard and deliverance, entered in the battle, and triumphed over His adversary, and all his raging fury. And that this being heard and understood, may the better be kept in memory; this order, by God's grace, we propose to observe, in treating the matter: First, What this word temptation meaneth, and how it is used within the Scriptures. Secondly, Who is here tempted and at what time this temptation happened. Thirdly, How and by what means He was tempted. Fourthly, Why He should suffer these temptations, and what fruits ensue to us from the same.

First, Temptation, or to tempt, in the Scriptures of God, is called to try, to prove, or to assault the valor, the power, the will, the pleasure, or the wisdom—whether it be of God, or of creatures. And it is taken sometimes in good part, as when it is said that God tempted Abraham; God tempted the people of Israel; that is, God did try and examine them, not for His own knowledge, to whom nothing is hid, but to certify others how obedient Abraham was to God's commandment, and how weak and inferior Israelites were in their journey toward the promised land. And this temptation is always good, because it proceeds immediately from God, to open and make manifest the secret motions of men's hearts, the puissance and power of God's word, and the great lenity and gentleness of God toward the iniquities (yea, horrible sins and rebellions) of those whom He hath received into His regimen and care. For who could have believed that the bare word of God could so have moved the heart and affections of Abraham, that to obey God's commandment he determined to kill, with his own hand, his best-beloved son Isaac? Who could have trusted that, so many torments as Job suffered, he should not speak in all his great temptation one foolish word against God? Or who could have thought that God so mercifully should have pardoned so many and so manifest transgressions committed by His people in the desert, and yet that His mercy never utterly left them, but still continued with them, till at length he performed His promise made to Abraham? Who, I say, would have been persuaded of these things, unless by trials and temptations taken of His creatures by God, they had come by revelation made in His holy Scriptures to our knowledge? And so this kind of temptation is profitable, good, and necessary, as a thing proceeding from God, who is the fountain of all goodness, to the manifestation of His own glory, and to the profit of the suffered, however the flesh may judge in the hour of temptation. Otherwise temptation, or to tempt, is taken in evil part; that is, he that assaults or assails intends destruction and confusion to him that is assaulted. As when Satan tempted the women in the garden, Job by divers tribulations, and David by adultery. The scribes and Pharisees tempted Christ by divers means, questions, and subtleties. And of this matter, saith St. James, "God tempteth no man"; that is, by temptation proceeding immediately from Him He intends no man's destruction. And here you shall note, that altho Satan appears sometimes to prevail against God's elect, yet he is ever frustrated of his final purpose. By temptation He led Eve and David from the obedience of God, but He could not retain them forever under His thraldom. Power was granted to Him to spoil Job of his substance and children, and to strike his body with a plague and sickness most vile and fearful, but He could not compel his mouth to blaspheme God's majesty; and, therefore, altho we are laid open sometimes, as it were, to tribulation for a time, it is that when He has poured forth the venom of His malice against God's elect it may return to His own confusion, and that the deliverance of God's children may be more to His glory, and the comfort of the afflicted: knowing that His hand is so powerful, His mercy and good-will so prompt, that He delivers His little ones from their cruel enemy, even as David did his sheep and lambs from the mouth of the lion. For a little benefit received in extreme danger more moves us than the preservation from ten thousand perils, so that we fall not into them. And yet to preserve from dangers and perils so that we fall not into them, whether they are of body or spirit, is no less the work of God than to deliver from them; but the weakness of our faith does not perceive it: this I leave at the present.

Also, to tempt means simply to prove or try without any determinate purpose or profit or damage to ensue; as when the mind doubteth of anything, and therein desires to be satisfied, without great love or extreme hatred of the thing that is tempted or tried. David tempted; that is, tried himself if he could go in harness. (I Sam. xvii.) And Gideon said, "Let not thine anger kindle against me, if I tempt thee once again." So the Queen of Sheba came to tempt Solomon in subtle questions. This famous queen, not fully trusting the report and fame that was spread of Solomon, by subtle questions desired to prove his wisdom; at the first, neither extremely hating nor fervently loving the person of the king. And David, as a man not accustomed to harness, would try how he was able to go, and behave and fashion himself therein, before he would hazard battle with Goliath so armed. And Gideon, not satisfied in his conscience by the first that he received, desired, without contempt or hatred of God, a second time to be certified of his vocation. In this sense must the apostle be expounded when he commands us to tempt; that is, to try and examine ourselves, if we stand in the faith. Thus much for the term.

Now to the person tempted, and to the time and place of his temptation. The person tempted is the only well-beloved Son of God; the time was immediately after His baptism; and the place was the desert or wilderness. But that we derive advantage from what is related, we must consider the same more profoundly. That the Son of God was thus tempted gives instructions to us, that temptations, altho they be ever so grievous and fearful, do not separate us from God's favor and mercy, but rather declare the great graces of God to appertain to us, which makes Satan to rage as a roaring lion; for against none does He so fiercely fight as against those of whose hearts Christ has taken possession.

The time of Christ's temptation is here most diligently to be noted. And that was, as Mark and Luke witness, immediately after the voice of God the Father had commended His Son to the world, and had visibly pointed to Him by the sign of the Holy Ghost; He was led or moved by the Spirit to go to a wilderness, where forty days he remained fasting among the wild beasts. This Spirit which led Christ into the wilderness was not the devil, but the holy Spirit of God the Father, by whom Christ, as touching His human and manly nature, was conducted and led; likewise by the same Spirit He was strengthened and made strong, and, finally, raised up from the dead. The Spirit of God, I say, led Christ to the place of His battle, where He endured the combat for the whole forty days and nights. As Luke saith, "He was tempted," but in the end most vehemently, after His continual fasting, and that He began to be hungry. Upon this forty days and this fasting of Christ do our Papists found and build their Lent; for, say they, all the actions of Christ are our instructions; what He did we ought to follow. But He fasted forty days, therefore we ought to do the like. I answer, that if we ought to follow all Christ's actions, then ought we neither to eat nor drink for the space of forty days, for so fasted Christ; we ought to go upon the waters with our feet; to cast out devils by our word; to heal and cure all sorts of maladies; to call again the dead to life; for so did Christ. This I write only that men may see the vanity of those who, boasting themselves of wisdom, have become fools.

Did Christ fast those forty days to teach us superstitious fasting? Can the Papists assure me, or any other man, which were the forty days that Christ fasted? plain it is he fasted the forty days and nights that immediately followed His baptism, but which they were, or in what month was the day of His baptism, Scripture does not express; and altho the day were express, am I or any Christian bound to counterfeit Christ's actions as the ape counterfeits the act or work of man? He Himself requires no such obedience of His true followers, but saith to the apostles, "Go and preach the gospel to all nations, baptizing them in the name of the Father, the Son, and the Holy Ghost; commanding them to observe and keep all that I have commanded you." Here Christ Jesus requires the observance of His precepts and commandments, not of His actions, except in so far as He had also commanded them; and so must the apostle be understood when he saith, "Be followers of Christ, for Christ hath suffered for us, that we should follow His footsteps," which can not be understood of every action of Christ, either in the mystery of our redemption, or in His actions and marvelous works, but only of those which He hath commanded us to observe. But where the Papists are so diligent in establishing their dreams and fantasies, they lose the profit that here is to be gathered; that is, why Christ fasted those forty days; which were a doctrine more necessary for Christians than to corrupt the simple hearts with superstition, as tho the wisdom of God, Christ Jesus, had taught us no other mystery by His fasting than the abstinence from flesh, or once on the day to eat flesh, for the space of forty days. God hath taken a just vengeance upon the pride of such men, while He thus confounds the wisdom of those that do most glory in wisdom, and strikes with blindness such as will be guides and lanterns to the feet of others, and yet refuse themselves to hear or follow the light of God's word. From such deliver thy poor flock, O Lord!

The uses of Christ's fasting these forty days I find chiefly to be two: The first, to witness to the world the dignity and excellence of His vocation, which Christ, after His baptism, was to take upon Him openly; the other, to declare that he entered into battle willingly for our cause, and does, as it were, provoke his adversary to assault Him: altho Christ Jesus, in the eternal counsel of His Father, was appointed to be the Prince of Peace, the angel (that is, the messenger) of His testament, and He alone that could fight our battles for us, yet He did not enter in execution of it, in the sight of men, till He was commended to mankind by the voice of His heavenly Father; and as He was placed and anointed by the Holy Ghost by a visible sign given to the eyes of men. After which time He was led to the desert, and fasted, as before is said; and this He did to teach us with what fear, carefulness, and reverence the messengers of the Word ought to enter on their vocation, which is not only most excellent (for who is worthy to be God's ambassador?) but also subject to most extreme troubles and dangers. For he that is appointed pastor, watchman, or preacher, if he feed not with his whole power, if he warn and admonish not when he sees the snare come, and if, in doctrine, he divide not the Word righteously, the blood and souls of those that perish for lack of food, admonition, and doctrine shall be required of his hand.

But to our purpose; that Christ exceeded not the space of forty days in His fasting, He did it to the imitation of Moses and Elias; of whom, the one before the receiving of the law, and the other before the communication and reasoning which he had with God in Mount Horeb, in which He was commanded to anoint Hazael king over Syria, and Jehu king over Israel, and Elisha to be prophet, fasted the same number of days. The events that ensued and followed this supernatural fasting of these two servants of God, Moses and Elias, impaired and diminished the tyranny of the kingdom of Satan. For by the law came the knowledge of sin, the damnation of such impieties, specially of idolatry, and such as the devil had invented; and, finally, by the law came such a revelation of God's will that no man could justly afterward excuse his sin by ignorance, by which the devil before had blinded many. So that the law, altho it might not renew and purge the heart, for that the Spirit of Christ Jesus worketh by faith only, yet it was a bridle that did hinder and stay the rage of external wickedness in many, and was a schoolmaster that led unto Christ. For when man can find no power in himself to do that which is commanded, and perfectly understands, and when he believes that the curse of God is pronounced against those that abide not in everything that is commanded in God's law to do them—the man, I say, that understands and knows his own corrupt nature and God's severe judgment, most gladly will receive the free redemption offered by Christ Jesus, which is the only victory that overthrows Satan and his power. And so by the giving of the law God greatly weakened, impaired, and made frail the tyranny and kingdom of the devil. In the days of Elias, the devil had so prevailed that kings and rulers made open war against God, killing His prophets, destroying His ordinances, and building up idolatry, which did so prevail that the prophet complained that of all the true fearers and worshipers of God he was left alone, and wicked Jezebel sought His life also. After this, his fasting and complaint, he was sent by God to anoint the persons aforenamed, who took such vengeance upon the wicked and obstinate idolaters that he who escaped the sword of Hazael fell into the hands of Jehu, and those whom Jehu left escaped not God's vengeance under Elisha.

The remembrance of this was fearful to Satan, for, at the coming of Christ Jesus, impiety was in the highest degree among those that pretended most knowledge of God's will; and Satan was at such rest in his kingdom that the priests, scribes and Pharisees had taken away the key of knowledge; that is, they had so obscured and darkened God's Holy Scriptures, by false glosses and vain traditions, that neither would they themselves enter into the kingdom of God, nor suffer and permit others to enter; but with violence restrained, and with tyranny struck back from the right way, that is, from Christ Jesus Himself, such as would have entered into the possession of life everlasting by Him. Satan, I say, having such dominion over the chief rulers of the visible Church, and espying in Christ, such graces as before he had not seen in man, and considering Him to follow in fasting the footsteps of Moses and Elias, no doubt greatly feared that the quietness and rest of his most obedient servants, the priests, and their adherents, would be troubled by Christ. And, therefore, by all engines and craft, he assaults Him to see what advantage he could have of Him. And Christ did not repel him, as by the power of His Godhead He might have done, that he should not tempt Him, but permitted him to spend all his artillery, and received the strokes and assaults of Satan's temptations in His own body, to the end He might weaken and enfeeble the strength and tyrannous power of our adversary by His long suffering. For thus, methinks, our Master and Champion, Jesus Christ, provoked our enemy to battle: "Satan, thou gloriest of thy power and victories over mankind, that there is none able to withstand thy assaults, nor escape thy darts, but at one time

or other thou givest him a wound: lo! I am a man like to my brethren, having flesh and blood, and all properties of man's nature (sin, which is thy venom, excepted); tempt, try, and assault me; I offer you here a place most convenient—the wilderness. There shall be no mortal to comfort me against thy assaults; thou shalt have time sufficient; do what thou canst, I shall not fly the place of battle. If thou become victor, thou shalt still continue in possession of thy kingdom in this wretched world; but if thou canst not prevail against me, then must thy prey and unjust spoil be taken from thee; thou must grant thyself vanquished and confounded, and must be compelled to leave off from all accusation of the members of my body; for to them appertains the fruit of my battle, my victory is theirs, as I am appointed to take the punishment of their sins in my body."

What comfort ought the remembrance of these signs to be to our hearts! Christ Jesus hath fought our battle; He Himself hath taken us into His care and protection; however the devil may rage by temptations, be they spiritual or corporeal, he is not able to bereave us out of the hand of the almighty Son of God. To Him be all glory for His mercies most abundantly poured upon us!

There remains yet to be spoken of the time when our Lord was tempted, which began immediately after His baptism. Whereupon we have to note the mark, that altho the malice of Satan never ceases, but always seeks for means to trouble the godly, yet sometimes he rages more fiercely than others, and that is commonly when God begins to manifest His love and favor to any of His children, and at the end of their battle, when they are nearest to obtain final victory. The devil, no doubt, did at all times envy the humble spirit that was in Abel, but he did not stir up the cruel heart of Cain against him till God declared His favor toward him by accepting his sacrifice. The same we find in Jacob, Joseph, David, and most evidently in Christ Jesus. How Satan raged at the tidings of Christ's nativity! what blood he caused to be shed on purpose to have murdered Christ in His infancy! The evangelist St. Matthew witnesses that in all the coasts and borders of Bethlehem the children of two years old and less age were murdered without mercy. A fearful spectacle and horrid example of insolent and unaccustomed tyranny! And what is the cause moving Satan thus to rage against innocents, considering that by reason of their imperfections they could not hurt his kingdom at that instant? Oh, the crafty eye of Satan looked farther than to the present time; he heard reports by the three wise men, that they had learned by the appearance of a star that the King of the Jews was born;

and he was not ignorant that the time prophesied of Christ's coming was then instant; for a stranger was clad with the crown and scepter of Judah. The angel had declared the glad tidings to the shepherds, that a Savior, which was Christ the Lord, was born in the city of David. All these tidings inflamed the wrath and malice of Satan, for he perfectly understood that the coming of the promised Seed was appointed to his confusion, and to the breaking down of his head and tyranny; and therefore he raged most cruelly, even at the first hearing of Christ's birth, thinking that altho he could not hinder nor withstand His coming, yet he could shorten his days upon earth, lest by long life and peaceable quietness in it, the number of good men, by Christ's doctrine and virtuous life, should be multiplied; and so he strove to cut Him away among the other children before He could open His mouth on His Father's message. Oh, cruel serpent! in vain dost thou spend thy venom, for the days of God's elect thou canst not shorten! And when the wheat is fallen on the ground, then doth it most multiply.

But from these things mark, what hath been the practise of the devil from the beginning—most cruelly to rage against God's children when God begins to show them His mercy. And, therefore, marvel not, dearly beloved, altho the like come unto you. If Satan fume or roar against you, whether it be against your bodies by persecution, or inwardly in your conscience by a spiritual battle, be not discouraged, as tho you were less acceptable in God's presence, or as if Satan might at any time prevail against you. No; your temptations and storms, that arise so suddenly, argue and witness that the seed which is sown is fallen on good ground, begins to take root and shall, by God's grace, bring forth fruit abundantly in due season and convenient time. That is it which Satan fears, and therefore thus he rages, and shall rage against you, thinking that if he can repulse you now suddenly in the beginning, that then you shall be at all times an easy prey, never able to resist his assaults. But as my hope is good, so shall my prayer be, that so you may be strengthened, that the world and Satan himself may perceive or understand that God fights your battle. For you remember that being present with you and treating of the same place, I admonished you that Satan could not long sleep when his kingdom was threatened. And therefore I willed you, if you were in mind to continue with Christ, to prepare yourselves for the day of temptation. The person of the speaker is wretched, miserable, and nothing to be regarded, but the things that were spoken are the infallible and eternal truth of God; without observation of which, life neither can or

shall come to mankind. God grant you continuance to the end.

This much have I briefly spoken of the temptation of Christ Jesus, who was tempted; and of the time and place of His temptation. Now remains to be spoken how He was tempted, and by what means. The most part of expositors think that all this temptation was in spirit and in imagination only, the corporeal senses being nothing moved. I will contend with no man in such cases, but patiently will I suffer every man to abound in his own knowledge; and without prejudice of any man's estimation, I offer my judgment to be weighed and considered by Christian charity. It appears to me by the plain text that Christ suffered this temptation in body and spirit. Likewise, as the hunger which Christ suffered, and the desert in which He remained, were not things offered to the imagination, but that the body did verily remain in the wilderness among beasts, and after forty days did hunger and faint for lack of food; so the external ear did hear the tempting words of Satan, which entered into the knowledge of the soul, and which, repelling the venom of such temptations, caused the tongue to speak and confute Satan, to our unspeakable comfort and consolation. It appears also that the body of Christ Jesus was carried by Satan from the wilderness unto the temple of Jerusalem, and that it was placed upon the pinnacle of the same temple, from whence it was carried to a high mountain and there tempted. If any man can show to the contrary hereof by the plain Scriptures of God, with all submission and thanksgiving I will prefer his judgment to my own; but if the matter stand only in probability and opinion of men, then it is lawful for me to believe as the Scripture here speaks; that is, that Satan spake and Christ answered, and Satan took Him and carried Him from one place to another. Besides the evidence of the text affirming that Satan was permitted to carry the body of Christ from place to place, and yet was not permitted to execute any further tyranny against it, is most singular comfort to such as are afflicted or troubled in body or spirit. The weak and feeble conscience of man under such temptations, commonly gathers and collects a false consequence. For man reasons thus: The body or the spirit is vexed by assaults and temptations of Satan, and he troubles or molests it, therefore God is angry with it, and takes no care of it. I answer, tribulations or grievous vexations of body or of mind are never signs of God's displeasure against the sufferer; neither yet does it follow that God has cast away the care of His creatures because He permits them to be molested and vexed for a time. For if any sort of tribulation were the infallible sign of God's displeasure, then should we condemn the best beloved children of God. But of this we may, speak hereafter. Now to the temptation.

Verse 2. "And when he fasteth forty days and forty nights, He was afterwards an hungered." Verse 3. 'Then came to Him the tempter,' and said, 'If you be the Son of God, command that these stones be made bread," etc. Why Christ fasted forty days and would not exceed the same, without sense and feeling of hunger, is before touched upon, that is, He would provoke the devil to battle by the wilderness and long abstinence, but He would not usurp or arrogate any more to Himself in that case than God had wrought with others, His servants and messengers before. But Christ Jesus (as St. Augustine more amply declares), without feeling of hunger, might have endured the whole year, or to time without end, as well as He did endure the space of forty days. For the nature of mankind was sustained those forty days by the invisible power of God, which is at all times of equal power. But Christ, willing to offer further occasion to Satan to proceed in tempting of Him, permitted the human nature to crave earnestly that which it lacked, that is to say, refreshing of meat; which Satan perceiving took occasion, as before, to tempt and assault. Some judge that Satan tempted Christ to gluttony, but this appears little to agree with the purpose of the Holy Ghost; who shows us this history to let us understand that Satan never ceases to oppugn the children of God, but continually, by one mean or other, drives or provokes them to some wicked opinions of their God; and to have them desire stones to be converted into bread, or to desire hunger to be satisfied, has never been sin, nor yet a wicked opinion of God. And therefore I doubt not but the temptation was more spiritual, more subtle, and more dangerous. Satan had respect to the voice of God, which had pronounced Christ to be His well-beloved Son, etc. Against this voice he fights, as his nature is ever to do against the assured and immutable Word of God; for such is his malice against God, and against His chosen children, that where and to whom God pronounces love and mercy, to these he threatens displeasures and damnation; and where God threatens death, there is he bold to pronounce life; and for this course is Satan called a liar from the beginning. And so the purpose of Satan was to drive Christ into desperation, that he should not believe the former voice of God His Father; which appears to be the meaning of this temptation: "Thou hast heard," would Satan say, "a voice proclaimed in the air, that Thou wast the beloved Son of God, in whom His soul was pleased; but mayst Thou not be judged more than mad, and weaker than the brainless fool if Thou believest any

such promise? Where are the signs of His love? Art Thou not cast out from comfort of all creatures? Thou art in worse case than the brute beasts, for every day they hunt for their prey, and the earth produces grass and herbs for their sustenance, so that none of them are pined and consumed away by hunger; but Thou hast fasted forty days and nights, ever waiting for some relief and comfort from above, but Thy best provision is hard stones! If Thou dost glory in thy God, and dost verily believe the promise that is made, command that these stones be bread. But evident it is that so Thou canst not do; for if Thou couldst, or if Thy God would have showed Thee any such pleasure, Thou mightest long ago have removed Thy hunger, and needest not have endured this languishing for lack of food. But seeing Thou hast long continued thus, and no provision is made for Thee, it is vanity longer to believe any such promise, and therefore despair of any help from God's hand, and provide for Thyself by some other means!"

Many words have I used here, dearly beloved, but I can not express the thousandth part of the malicious despite which lurked in this one temptation of Satan. It was a mocking of Christ and of His obedience. It was a plain denial of God's promise. It was the triumphing voice of him that appeared to have gotten victory. Oh, how bitter this temptation was no creature can understand but such as feel the grief of such darts as Satan casts at the tender conscience of those that gladly would rest and repose in God, and in the promises of His mercy. But here is to be noted the ground and foundation. The conclusion of Satan is this: Thou art none of God's elect, much less His well-beloved Son. His reason is this: Thou art in trouble and findest no relief. There the foundation of the temptation was Christ's poverty, and the lack of food without hope of remedy to be sent from God. And it is the same temptation which the devil objected to Him by the princes of the priests in His grievous torments upon the cross; for thus they cried, "If he be the Son of God, let him come down from the cross and we will believe in him; he trusted in God, let him deliver him, if he have the pleasure in him." As tho they would say, God is the deliverer of His servants from troubles; God never permits those that fear Him to come to confusion; this man we see in extreme trouble; if He be the Son of God, or even a true worshiper of His name, He will deliver Him from this calamity. If He deliver Him not, but suffer Him to perish in these anguishes, then it is an assured sign that God has rejected Him as a hypocrite, that shall have no portion of His glory. Thus, I say, Satan takes occasion to tempt, and moves also others to judge and condemn God's elect and chosen children, by reason that troubles are multiplied upon them.

But with what weapons we ought to fight against such enemies and assaults we shall learn in the answer of Christ Jesus, which follows: But He, answering, said ".It is written, man shall not live by bread alone, but by every word which proceedeth out of the mouth of God." This answer of Christ proves the sentence which we have brought of the aforesaid temptation to be the very meaning of the Holy Ghost; for unless the purpose of Satan has been to have removed Christ from all hope of God's merciful providence toward Him in that His necessity, Christ had not answered directly to his words, saying, "Command that these stones be made bread." But Christ Jesus, perceiving his art and malicious subtility, answered directly to his meaning, His words nothing regarded; by which Satan was so confounded that he was ashamed to reply any further.

But that you may the better understand the meaning of Christ's answer, we will express and repeat it over in more words. "Thou laborest, Satan," would Christ say, "to bring into my heart a doubt and suspicion of My Father's promise, which was openly proclaimed in My baptism, by reason of My hunger, and that I lack all carnal provision. Thou art bold to affirm that God takes no care for Me, but thou art a deceitful and false corrupt sophister, and thy argument, too, is vain, and full of blasphemies; for thou bindest God's love, mercy, and providence to the having or wanting of bodily provision, which no part of God's Scriptures teach us, but rather the express contrary. As it is written, 'Man doth not live by bread alone, but by every word that proceedeth out of the mouth of God,' that is, the very life and felicity of man consists not in the abundance of bodily things, or the possession and having of them makes no man blest or happy; neither shall the lack of them be the cause of his final misery; but the very life of man consists in God, and in His promises pronounced by His own mouth, unto which whoso cleaves unfeignedly shall live the life everlasting. And altho all creatures in earth forsake him, yet shall not his bodily life perish till the time appointed by God approach. For God has means to feed, preserve, and maintain, unknown to man's reason, and contrary to the common course of nature. He fed His people Israel in the desert forty years without the provision of man. He preserved Jonah in the whale's belly; and maintained and kept the bodies of the three children in the furnace of fire. Reason and the natural man could have seen nothing in these cases but destruction and death, and could have judged nothing but that God had cast away the care of these, His creatures, and yet His providence was most vigilant toward them in the extremity of their dangers, from which He did so deliver them, and in the midst of them did so assist them, that His glory, which is His mercy and goodness, did more appear and shine after their troubles than it could have done if they had fallen in them. And therefore I measure not the truth and favor of God by having or by lacking of bodily necessities, but by the promise which He has made to me. As He Himself is immutable, so is His word and promise constant, which I believe, and to which I will adhere, and so cleave, whatever can come to the body outwardly."

In this answer of Christ we may perceive what weapons are to be used against our adversary the devil, and how we may confute his arguments, which craftily, and of malice, he makes against God's elect. Christ might have repulsed Satan with a word, or by commanding him to silence, as He to whom all power was given in heaven and earth; but it pleased His mercy to teach us how to use the sword of the Holy Ghost, which is the word of God, in battle against our spiritual enemy. The Scripture which Christ brings is written in the eighth chapter of Deuteronomy. It was spoken by Moses a little before His death, to establish the people in God's merciful providence. For in the same chapter, and in certain others that go before, He reckons the great travail and divers dangers with the extreme necessities that they had sustained in the desert the space of forty years, and yet, notwithstanding how constant God had been in keeping and performing His promise, for throughout all perils He had conducted them to the sight and borders of the promised land. And so this Scripture more directly answers to the temptation of Satan; for thus does Satan reason, as before is said, "Thou art in poverty and hast no provision to sustain thy life. Therefore God takes no regard nor care of Thee, as He doth over His chosen children." Christ Jesus answered: "Thy argument is false and vain; for poverty or necessity precludes not the providence or care of God; which is easy to be proved by the people of God, Israel, who, in the desert, oftentimes lacked things necessary to the sustenance of life, and for lack of the same they grudged and murmured; yet the Lord never cast away the providence and care of them, but according to the word that He had once pronounced, to wit, that they were His peculiar people; and according to the promise made to Abraham, and to them before their departure from Egypt, He still remained their conductor and guide, till He placed them in peaceable possession of the land of Canaan, their great infirmities and manifold transgressions notwithstanding."

Thus are we taught, I say, by Christ Jesus, to repulse Satan and his assaults by the Word of God, and to apply the examples of His mercies, which He has shown to others before us, to our own souls in the hour of temptation, and in the time of our trouble. For what God doth to one at any time, the same appertains to all that depend upon God and His promises. And, therefore, however we are assaulted by Satan, our adversary, within the Word of God is armor and weapons sufficient. The chief craft of Satan is to trouble those that begin to decline from his obedience, and to declare themselves enemies to iniquity, with divers assaults, the design whereof is always the same; that is, to put variance betwixt them and God into their conscience, that they should not repose and rest themselves in His assured promises. And to persuade this, he uses and invents divers arguments. Sometimes he calls the sins of their youth, and which they have committed in the time of blindness, to their remembrance; very often he objects their unthankfulness toward God and present imperfections. By sickness, poverty, tribulations in their household, or by persecution, he can allege that God is angry, and regard them not. Or by the spiritual cross which few feel and fewer understand the utility and profit of, he would drive God's children to desperation, and by infinite means more. he goeth about seeking, like a roaring lion, to undermine and destroy our faith. But it is imposible for him to prevail against us unless we obstinately refuse to use the defense and weapons that God has offered. Yea, I say, that God's elect can not refuse it, but seek for their Defender when the battle is most strong; for the sobs, groans, and lamentations of such as fight, yea, the fear they have lest they be vanquished, the calling and prayer for continuance, are the undoubted and right seeking of Christ our champion. We refuse not the weapon, altho sometimes, by infirmity, we can not use it as we would. It suffices that your hearts unfeignedly sob for greater strength, for continuance, and for final deliverance by Christ Jesus; that which is wanting in us, His sufficiency doth supply; for it is He that fighteth and overcometh for us. But for bringing of the examples of the Scriptures, if God permit, in the end we shall speak more largely when it shall be treated why Christ permitted Himself thus to be tempted. Sundry impediments now call me from writing in this matter, but, by God's grace, at convenient leisure I purpose to finish, and to send it to you. I grant the matter that proceeds from me is not worthy of your pain and labor to read it; yet, seeing it is a testimony of my good mind toward you, I doubt not but you will accept it in good part. God, the Father of our Lord Jesus Christ, grant unto you to find favor and mercy of the Judge, whose eyes and knowledge pierce through the secret cogitations of the heart, in the day of temptation, which shall come upon all flesh, according to that mercy which you (illuminated and directed by His Holy Spirit) have showed to the afflicted. Now the God of all comfort and consolation confirm and strengthen you in His power unto the end. Amen.

HUGH LATIMER

1485-1555

ON CHRISTIAN LOVE

BIOGRAPHICAL NOTE

HUGH LATIMER, reformer and martyr, was born in Leicestershire, England, in 1485, or two years later than Luther. On completing an education at Cambridge, he took holy orders and preached strenuously in favor of the Lutheran views. As a profound canonist, he was placed on the commission appointed to decide on the legality of Henry VIII's marriage with Katharine of Aragon. His decision in favor of Henry gained him a royal chaplaincy and a living.

Appointed Bishop of Worcester in 1535, he preached boldly the reformed doctrines, but lost favor at court, and when Gardiner and Bonner pushed a reactionary movement to the front, he retired from his see (1539). Latimer lived in peaceful retirement under Edward VI, but under Mary he, with other reformers, was arrested and thrown into the Tower. Brought to Oxford for examination, he refused to recant, and was confined for a year in the common prison, and on October 16, 1555, put to death by fire, along with Ridley, at a place opposite Balliol College, where the Martyr's Memorial was subsequently erected.

This is my commandment, that ye love one another, as I have loved you.—John xv., 12.

SEEING the time is so far spent, we will take no more in hand at this time than this one sentence; for it will be enough for us to consider this well, and to bear it away with us. "This I command unto you, that ye love one another." Our Savior himself spake these words at His last supper: it was the last sermon that He made unto His disciples before His departure; it is a very long sermon. For our Savior, like as one that knows he shall die shortly, is desirous to spend that little time that He has with His friends, in exhorting and instructing them how they should lead their lives. Now among other things that He commanded this was one: "This I command unto you, that ye love one another." The English expresses as tho it were but one, "This is my commandment." I examined the Greek, where it is in the plural number, and very well; for there are many things that pertain to a Christian man, and yet all those things are contained in this one thing, that is, love. He lappeth up all things in love.

Our whole duty is contained in these words, "Love together." Therefore St. Paul saith, "He that loveth another fulfilleth the whole law"; so it appeareth that all things are contained in this word love. This love is a precious thing; our Savior saith, "By this shall all men know that ye are my disciples, if ye shall love one another."

So Christ makes love His cognizance, His badge, His livery. Like as every lord commonly gives a certain livery to his servants, whereby they may be known that they pertain unto him; and so we say, yonder is this lord's servants, because they wear his livery: so our Savior, who is the Lord above all lords, would have His servants known by their liveries and badge, which badge is love alone. Whosoever now is endued with love and charity is His servant; him we may call Christ's servant; for love is the token whereby you may know that such a servant pertaineth to Christ; so that charity may be called the very livery of Christ. He that hath charity is Christ's servant; he that hath not charity is the servant of the devil. For as Christ's livery is love and charity, so the devil's livery is hatred, malice and discord.

But I think the devil has a great many more servants than Christ has; for there are a great many more in his livery than in

331

Christ's livery; there are but very few who are endued with Christ's livery; with love and charity, gentleness and meekness of spirit; but there are a great number that bear hatred and malice in their hearts, that are proud, stout, and lofty; therefore the number of the devil's servants is greater than the number of Christ's servants.

Now St. Paul shows how needful this love is. I speak not of carnal love, which is only animal affection; but of this charitable love, which is so necessary that when a man hath it, without all other things it will suffice him. Again, if a man have all other things and lacketh that love it will not help him, it is all vain and lost. St. Paul used it so: "Tho I speak with tongues of men and angels, and yet had no love, I were even as sounding brass, or as a tinkling cymbal. And tho I could prophesy and understand all secrets and all knowledge; yet if I had faith, so that I could move mountains out of their places, and yet had no love, I were nothing. And tho I bestowed all my goods to feed the poor, and tho I gave my body even that I were burned, and yet had no love, it profiteth me nothing" (I Cor. xiii). These are godly gifts, yet St. Paul calls them nothing when a man hath them without charity; which is a great commendation, and shows the great need of love, insomuch that all other virtues are in vain when this love is absent. And there have been some who taught that St. Paul spake against the dignity of faith; but you must understand that St. Paul speaks here not of the justifying faith, wherewith we receive everlasting life, but he understands by this word faith the gift to do miracles, to remove hills; of such a faith he speaks. This I say to confirm this proposition. Faith only justifieth; this proposition is most true and certain. And St. Paul speaks not here of this lively justifying faith; for this right faith is not without love, for love cometh and floweth out of faith; love is a child of faith; for no man can love except he believe, so that they have two several offices, they themselves being inseparable.

St. Paul has an expression in the 13th chapter of the first of the Corinthians, which, according to the outward letter, seems much to the dispraise of this faith, and to the praise of love; these are his words, "Now abideth faith, hope and love, even these three; but the chiefest of these is love." There are some learned men who expound the greatness of which St. Paul speaketh here as if meant for eternity. For when we come to God, then we believe no more, but rather see with our eyes face to face how He is; yet for all that love remains still; so that love may be called the chiefest, because she endureth forever. And tho she is the chiefest, yet we must not attribute unto her the office which pertains

unto faith only. Like as I can not say, the Mayor of Stamford must make me a pair of shoes because he is a greater man than the shoemaker is; for the mayor, tho he is a greater man, yet it is not his office to make shoes; so tho love be greater, yet it is not her office to save. Thus much I thought good to say against those who fight against the truth.

Now, when we would know who are in Christ's livery or not, we must learn it of St. Paul, who most evidently described charity, which is the only livery, saying, "Love is patient, she suffereth long." Now whosoever fumeth and is angry, he is out of this livery: therefore let us remember that we do not cast away the livery of Christ our Master. When we are in sickness, or any manner of adversities, our duty is to be patient, to suffer willingly, and to call upon Him for aid, help and comfort; for without Him we are not able to abide any tribulation. Therefore we must call upon God, He has promised to help: therefore let me not think Him to be false or untrue to His promises, for we can not dishonor God more than by not believing or trusting in Him. Therefore let us beware above all things of dishonoring God; and so we must be patient, trusting and most certainly believing that He will deliver us when it seems good to Him, who knows the time better than we ourselves.

"Charity is gentle, friendly, and loving; she envieth not." They that envy their neighbor's profit when it goes well with him, such fellows are out of their liveries, and so out of the service of God; for to be envious is to be the servant of the devil.

"Love doth not frowardly, she is not a provoker"; as there are some men who will provoke their neighbor so far that it is very hard for them to be in charity with them; but we must wrestle with our affections; we must strive and see that we keep this livery of Christ our master; for "the devil goeth about as a roaring lion seeking to take us at a vantage," to bring us out of our liveries, and to take from us the knot of love and charity.

"Love swelleth not, is not puffed up"; but there are many swellers nowadays, they are so high, so lofty, insomuch that they despise and contemn all others; all such persons are under the governance of the devil. God rules not them with His good spirit; the evil spirit has occupied their hearts and possest them.

"She doth not dishonestly; she seeketh not her own; she doth all things to the commodity of her neighbors." A charitable man will not promote himself with the damage of his neighbor. They that seek only their own advantage, forgetting their neighbors, they are not of God, they have not His livery. Further, "Charity is not provoked to anger; she thinketh not evil." We ought not to think evil of our neighbor, as long as we see not open wickedness; for it is written, "You shall not judge"; we should not take upon us to condemn our neighbor. And surely the condemners of other men's works are not in the livery of Christ. Christ hateth them.

"She rejoiceth not in iniquity"; she loveth equity and godliness. And again, she is sorry to hear of falsehood, of stealing, or such like, which wickedness is now at this time commonly used. There never was such falsehood among Christian men as there is now, at this time; truly I think, and they that have experience report it so, that among the very infidels and Turks there is more fidelity and uprightness than among Christian men. For no man setteth anything by his promise, yea, and writings will not serve with some, they are so shameless that they dare deny their own handwriting; but, I pray you, are those false fellows in the livery of Christ? Have they His cognizance? No, no; they have the badge of the devil, with whom they shall be damned world without end, except they amend and leave their wickedness.

"She suffereth all things; she believeth all things." It is a great matter that should make us to be grieved with our neighbor; we should be patient when our neighbor doth wrong, we should admonish him of his folly, earnestly desiring him to leave his wickedness, showing the danger that follows, everlasting damnation. In such wise we should study to amend our neighbor, and not to hate him or do him a foul turn again, but rather charitably study to amend him: whosoever now does so, he has the livery and cognizance of Christ, he shall be known at the last day for his servant.

"Love believeth all things"; it appears daily that they who are charitable and friendly are most deceived; because they think well of every man, they believe every man, they trust their words, and therefore are most deceived in this world, among the children of the devil. These and such like things are the tokens of the right and godly love; therefore they that have this love are soon known, for this love can not be hid in corners, she has her operation: therefore all that have her are well enough, tho they have no other gifts besides her. Again, they that lack her, tho they have many other gifts besides, yet is it to no other purpose, it does then no good: for when we shall come at the great day before him, not having this livery (that is love) with us, then we are lost; he will not take us for His servants, because we have not His cognizance. But if we have this livery, if we wear His cognizance here in this world; that is, if we love our neighbor, help him in his distress, are charitable, loving, and friendly unto him, then we shall be known at the last

day: but if we be uncharitable toward our neighbor, hate him, seek our own advantage with His damage, then we shall be rejected of Christ and so damned world without end.

Our Savior saith here in this gospel, "I command you these things"; He speaketh in the plural number, and lappeth it up in one thing, which is that we should love one another, much like St. Paul's saying in the 13th to the Romans, "Owe nothing to any man, but to love one another. Here St. Paul lappeth up all things together, signifying unto us that love is the consummation of the law; for this commandment, "Thou shalt not commit adultery," is contained in this law of love: for he that loveth God will not break wedlock, because wedlock-breaking is a dishonoring of God and a serving of the devil. "Thou shalt not kill"; he that loveth will not kill, he will do no harm. "Thou shalt not steal"; he that loveth his neighbor as himself will not take away his goods. I had of late occasion to speak of picking and stealing, where I showed unto you the danger wherein they are that steal their neighbor's goods from them, but I hear nothing yet of restitution. Sirs, I tell you, except restitution is made, look for no salvation. And it is a miserable and heinous thing to consider that we are so blinded with this world that, rather than we would make restitution, we will sell unto the devil our souls which are bought with the blood of our Savior Christ. What can be done more to the dishonoring of Christ than to cast our souls away to the devil for the value of a little money?—the soul which He has bought with His painful passion and death. But I tell you those that will do so, and that will not make restitution when they have done wrong, or taken away their neighbor's goods, they are not in the livery of Christ, they are not his servants; let them go as they will in this world, yet for all that they are foul and filthy enough before God; they stink before His face; and therefore they shall be cast from His presence into everlasting fire; this shall be all their good cheer that they shall have, because they have not the livery of Christ, nor His cognizance, which is love. They remember not that Christ commanded us, saying, "This I command you, that ye love one another." This is Christ's commandment. Moses, the great prophet of God, gave many laws, but he gave not the spirit to fulfil the same laws: but Christ gave this law, and promised unto us, that when we call upon Him He will give us His Holy Ghost, who shall make us able to fulfil His laws, tho not so perfectly as the law requires; but yet to the contention of God, and to the protection of our faith: for as long as we are in this world, we can do nothing as we ought to do, because our flesh leadeth us, which is ever bent against the law of God;

yet our works which we do are well taken for Christ's sake, and God will reward them in heaven.

Therefore our Savior saith, "my yoke is easy, and my burden is light," because He helpeth to bear them; else indeed we should not be able to bear them. And in another place He saith, "His commandments are not heavy"; they are heavy to our flesh, but being qualified with the Spirit of God, to the faithful which believe in Christ, to them, I say, they are not heavy; for tho their doings are not perfect, yet they are well taken for Christ's sake.

You must not be offended because the Scripture commends love so highly, for he that commends the daughter commends the mother; for love is the daughter, and faith is the mother: love floweth out of faith; where faith is, there is love; but yet we must consider their offices, faith is the hand wherewith we take hold on everlasting life.

Now let us enter into ourselves, and examine our own hearts, whether we are in the livery of God, or not: and when we find ourselves to be out of this livery, let us repent and amend our lives, so that we may come again to the favor of God, and spend our time in this world to His honor and glory, forgiving our neighbors all such things as they have done against us.

And now to make an end: mark here who gave this precept of love—Christ our Savior Himself. When and at what time? At His departing, when He should suffer death. Therefore these words ought the more to be regarded, seeing He Himself spake them at His last departing from us. May God of His mercy give us grace so to walk here in this world, charitably and friendly one with another, that we may attain the joy which God hath prepared for all those that love Him. Amen.

HENRY P. LIDDON

1829-1890

INFLUENCES OF THE HOLY SPIRIT

BIOGRAPHICAL NOTE

HENRY PARRY LIDDON was born at North Stoneham, Hampshire, in 1829. His intellectual power and fearless and earnest preaching attracted immense congregations to St. Paul's Cathedral, London. He sought to meet the speculative fallacies of his day by truth clearly and boldly proclaimed. Probably his greatest fault in delivery was that he tied himself slavishly to a manuscript in all his preaching. There was a force and intensity to his delivery, however, that often projected his words towards his hearers like great projectiles across a battlefield. Dr. Arthur S. Hoyt recommends him for study in these words: "Canon Liddon brings the riches of exegesis and theology and philosophy to the pulpit, and gives to the sermon the distinction of his refined and spiritual personality." He died in 1890.

The wind bloweth where it listeth, and thou hearest the sound thereof, but canst not tell whence it cometh, and whither it goeth.—St. John iii., 8.

WHO has not felt the contrast, the almost tragic contrast, between the high station of the Jewish doctor, member of the Sanhedrin, master in Israel, and the ignorance of elementary religious truth, as we Christians must deem it, which he displayed in this interview with our blest Lord? At first sight it seems difficult to understand how our Lord could have used the simile in the text when conversing with an educated and thoughtful man, well conversed in the history and literature of God's ancient people; and, indeed, a negative criticism has availed itself of this and of some other features in the narrative, in the interest of the theory that Nicodemus was only a fictitious type of the higher classes in Jewish society, as they were pictured to itself by the imagination of the fourth Evangelist. Such a supposition, opposed to external facts and to all internal probabilities, would hardly have been entertained, if the critical ingenuity of its author had been seconded by any spiritual experience. Nicodemus is very far from being a caricature; and our Lord's method here, as elsewhere, is to lead on from familiar phrases and the well-remembered letter to the spirit and realities of religion. The Jewish schools were acquainted with the expression "a new creature"; but it had long since become a mere shred of official rhetoric. As applied to a Jewish proselyte, it scarcely meant more than a change in the outward relations of religious life. Our Lord told Nicodemus that every man who would see the kingdom of God which He was founding must undergo a second birth; and Nicodemus, who had been accustomed to the phrase all his life, could not understand it if it was to be supposed to mean anything real. "How," he asks, "can a man be born when he is old? Can he enter a second time into his mother's womb, and be born?" Our Lord does not extricate him from this blundering literalism; He repeats His own original assertion, but in terms which more fully express His meaning: "Verily, verily, I say unto thee, Except a man be born of water and of the Spirit, he can not enter into the kingdom of God. That which is born of the flesh is flesh; and that which is born of the Spirit is spirit. Marvel not that I said unto thee, Ye must be born again." Our Lord's reference to water would not have been unintelligible to Nicodemus; every one in

Judæa knew that the Baptist had insisted on immersion in water as a symbol of the purification of the soul of man. Certainly, in connecting "water" with the Spirit and the new birth, our Lord's language, glancing at that of the prophet, went very far beyond this. He could only be fully understood at a later time, when the sacrament of baptism had been instituted, just as the true sense of His early allusions to His death could not have been apprehended until after the crucifixion. But Nicodemus, it is plain, had not yet advanced beyond his original difficulty; he could not conceive how any second birth was possible, without altogether violating the course of nature. And our Lord penetrates His thoughts and answers them. He answers them by pointing to that invisible agent who could achieve, in the sphere of spiritual and mental life, what the Jewish doctor deemed so impossible a feat as a second birth. Nature, indeed, contained no force that could compass such a result; but nature in this, as in other matters, was a shadow of something beyond itself.

It was late at night when our Lord had this interview with the Jewish teacher. At the pauses in conversation, we may conjecture, they heard the wind without as it moaned along the narrow streets of Jerusalem; and our Lord, as was His wont, took His creature into His service—the service of spiritual truth. The wind was a figure of the Spirit. Our Lord would not have used the same word for both. The wind might teach Nicodemus something of the action of Him who is the real Author of the new birth of man. And it would do this in two ways more especially.

On a first survey of nature, the wind arrests man's attention, as an unseen agent which seems to be moving with entire freedom. "The wind bloweth where it listeth." It is fettered by none of those conditions which confine the swiftest bodies that traverse the surface of the earth; it sweeps on as if independent of law, rushing hither and thither, as tho obeying its own wayward and momentary impulse. Thus it is an apt figure of a self-determining invisible force; and of a force which is at times of overmastering power. Sometimes, indeed, its breath is so gentle, that only a single leaf or blade of grass will at distant intervals seem to give the faintest token of its action; yet, even thus, it "bloweth where it listeth." Sometimes it bursts upon the earth with destructive violence; nothing can resist its onslaught; the most solid buildings give way; the stoutest trees bend before it; whatever is frail and delicate can only escape by the completeness of its submission. Thus, too, it "bloweth where it listeth." Beyond anything else that strikes upon the senses of man, it is suggestive of free supersensuous power; it is an appropriate symbol of an irruption of the invisible into the world of sense, of the action, so tender or so imperious, of the divine and eternal Spirit upon the human soul.

But the wind is also an agent about whose proceedings we really know almost nothing. "Thou hearest the sound thereof"; such is our Lord's concession to man's claim to knowledge. "Thou canst not tell whence it cometh, and whither it goeth"; such is the reserve which He makes in respect of human ignorance. Certainly we do more than hear the sound of the wind; its presence is obvious to three of the senses. We feel the chill or the fury of the blast; and, as it sweeps across the ocean, or the forest, or the field of corn, we see how the blades rise and fall in graceful curves, and the trees bend, and the waters sink and swell into waves which are the measure of its strength. But our Lord says, "Thou hearest the sound thereof." He would have us test it by the most spiritual of the senses. It whispers, or it moans, or it roars as it passes us; it has a pathos all its own. Yet what do we really know about it? "Thou canst not tell whence it cometh, and whither it goeth." Does the wind then obey no rule; is it a mere symbol of unfettered caprice? Surely not. If, as the psalmist sings, "God bringeth the winds out of his treasuries," He acts, we may be sure, here as always, whether in nature or in grace, by some law, which his own perfections impose upon His action. He may have given to us of these later times to see a very little deeper beneath the surface of the natural world than was the case with our fathers. Perchance we explain the immediate antecedents of the phenomenon; but can we explain our own explanation? The frontier of our ignorance is removed one stage farther back; but "the way of the wind" is as fitting an expression for the mysteries now as it was in the days of Solomon. We know that there is no cave of Æolus. We know that the wind is the creature of that great Master who works everywhere and incessantly by rule. But, as the wind still sweeps by us who call ourselves the children of an age of knowledge, and we endeavor to give our fullest answer to the question, "Whence it cometh, and whither it goeth?" we discover that, as the symbol of a spiritual force, of whose presence we are conscious, while we are unable to determine, with moderate confidence, either the secret principle or the range of its action, the wind is as full of meaning still as in the days of Nicodemus.

When our Lord has thus pointed to the freedom and the mysteriousness of the wind, He adds, "So is every one that is born of the Spirit." The simile itself would have led us to expect—"So is the Spirit of God." The man born of the Spirit would answer not to the wind itself, but to the sensible effect of the wind. There is a break of correspondence between the simile and its application. The simile directs attention to the divine Author of the new birth in man. The words which follow direct attention to the human subject upon whom the divine agent works. Something similar is observable when our Lord compares the kingdom of heaven to a merchantman seeking goodly pearls; the kingdom really corresponds not to the merchantman, but to the pearl of great price which the merchantman buys. In such cases, we may be sure, the natural correspondence between a simile and its application is not disturbed without a motive. And the reason for this disturbance is presumably that the simile is not adequate to the full purpose of the speaker, who is anxious to teach some larger truth than its obvious application would suggest. In the case before us, we may be allowed to suppose, that by His reference to the wind our Lord desired to convey something more than the real but mysterious agency of the Holy Spirit in the new birth of man. His language seems designed, not merely to correct the materialistic narrowness of the Jewish doctor, not merely to answer by anticipation the doubts of later days as to the spiritual efficacy of His own sacrament of regeneration, but to picture, in words which should be read to the end of time, the general work of that divine person whose mission of mercy to our race was at once the consequence and the completion of His own.

It may be useful to trace the import of our Lord's simile in three fields of the action of the holy and eternal Spirit; His creation of a sacred literature, His guidance of a divine society, and His work upon individual souls.

I. As, then, we turn over the pages of the Bible, must we not say, "The wind of heaven bloweth where it listeth"? If we might reverently imagine ourselves scheming beforehand what kind of a book the Book of God ought to be, how different would it be from the actual Bible. There would be as many bibles as there are souls, and they would differ as widely. But in one thing, amid all their differences, they would probably agree; they would lack the variety, both in form and substance, of the holy Book which the Church of God places in the hands of her children. The self-assertion, the scepticism, and the fastidiousness of our day would meet like the men of the second Roman triumvirate on that island in the Reno, and would draw up their lists of proscription. One would condemn the poetry of Scripture as too inexact; another its history as too largely secular; another its metaphysics as too transcendental, or as hostile to some fanciful ideal of "simplicity," or as likely to quench a purely moral enthusiasm. The archaic history of the Pentateuch, or the sterner side of the ethics of the psalter, or the supernaturalism of the histories of Elijah or of Daniel, or the so-called pessimism of Ecclesiastes, or the alleged secularism of Esther, or the literal import of the Song of Solomon, would be in turn condemned. Nor could the apostles hope to escape: St. John would be too mystical in this estimate; St. James too legal in that; St. Paul too dialectical, or too metaphysical, or too easily capable of an antinomian interpretation; St. Peter too undecided, as if balancing between St. Paul and St. James. Our new Bible would probably be uniform, narrow, symmetrical; it would be entirely made up of poetry, or of history, or of formal propositions, or of philosophical speculation, or of lists of moral maxims; it would be modeled after the type of some current writer on English history, or some popular poet or metaphysician, or some sentimentalist who abjures history and philosophy alike on principle, or some composer of well-intentioned religious tracts for general circulation. The inspirations of heaven would be taken in hand, and instead of a wind blowing where it listeth, we should have a wind, no doubt, of some kind, rustling earnestly enough along some very narrow crevices or channels, in obedience to the directions of some one form of human prejudice, or passion, or fear, or hope.

The Bible is like nature in its immense, its exhaustless variety; like nature, it reflects all the higher moods of the human soul, because it does much more; because it brings us face to face with the infinity of the divine life. In the Bible the wind of heaven pays scant heed to our anticipations or our prejudices; it "bloweth where it listeth." It breathes not only in the divine charities of the gospels, not only in the lyrical sallies of the epistles, not only in the great announcements scattered here and there in Holy Scripture of the magnificence, or the compassion, or the benevolence of God; but also in the stern language of the prophets, in the warnings and lessons of the historical books, in the revelations of divine justice and of human responsibility which abound in either Testament. "Where it listeth." Not only where our sense of literary beauty is stimulated, as in St. Paul's picture of charity, by lines which have taken captive the imagination of the world, not only where feeling and conscience echo the verdict of authority and the promptings of reverence, but also where this is not the case; where neither precept nor example stimulates us, and we are left face to face with historical or ethical material, which appears to us to inspire no spiritual enthusiasm, or which is highly suggestive of critical difficulty. Let us be patient; we shall understand, if we will only wait, how these features of the Bible too are integral parts of a living whole; here, as elsewhere, the Spirit breathes; in the genealogies of the

Chronicles as in the last discourse in St. John, though with an admitted difference of manner and degree. He "bloweth where He listeth." The apostle's words respecting the Old Testament are true of the New: "All Scripture is given by inspiration of God, and is profitable for doctrine, for reproof, for correction, for instruction in righteousness." And, " Whatsoever things were written aforetime were written for our learning, that we through patience and comfort of the Scriptures might have hope."

" But thou hearest the sound thereof, and canst not tell whence it cometh, and whither it goeth." The majesty of Scripture is recognized by man, wherever there is, I will not say a spiritual faculty, but a natural sense of beauty. The "sound" of the wind is perceived by the trained ear, by the literary taste, by the refinement, by the humanity of every generation of educated men. But what beyond? What of its spiritual source, its spiritual drift and purpose, its half-concealed but profound unities, its subtle but imperious relations to conscience? Of these things, so precious to Christians, a purely literary appreciation of Scripture is generally ignorant; the sacred Book, like the prophet of the Chebar, is only "as a very lovely song of one that hath a pleasant voice, and can play well on an instrument." Or again, the "sound" thereof" is heard in the admitted empire of the Bible over millions of hearts and consciences; an empire the evidences of which strike upon the ear in countless ways, and which is far too wide and too secure to be affected by the criticisms that might occasionally seem to threaten it. What is the secret of this influence of Scripture? Not simply that it is the Book of Revelation; since it contains a great deal of matter which lay fairly within the reach of man's natural faculties. The Word or eternal Reason of God is the Revealer; but Scripture, whether it is a record of divine revelations or of naturally observed facts, is, in the belief of the Christian Church, throughout "inspired" by the Spirit. Inspiration is the word which describes the presence and action of the Holy Spirit everywhere in Scripture. We know not how our own spirits, hour by hour, are acted upon by the eternal Spirit, though we do not question the fact; we content ourselves with recognizing what we can not explain. If we believe that Scripture is inspired, we know that it is instinct with the presence of Him whose voice we might hear in every utterance, but of whom we cannot tell whence He cometh or whither He goeth.

II. The history of the Church of Christ from the days of the apostles has been a history of spiritual movements. Doubtless it has been a history of much else; the Church has been the scene of human passions, human speculations, human errors. But traversing these, He by whom the whole body of the Church is governed and sanctified, has made His presence felt, not only in the perpetual proclamation and elucidation of truth, not only in the silent, never-ceasing sanctification of souls, but also in great upheavals of spiritual life, by which the conscience of Christians has been quickened, or their hold upon the truths of redemption and grace made more intelligent and serious, or their lives and practise restored to something like the ideal of the Gospels. Even in the apostolic age it was necessary to warn Christians that it was high time to awake out of sleep; that the night of life was far spent, and the day of eternity was at hand. And ever since, from generation to generation, there has been a succession of efforts within the Church to realize more worthily the truth of the Christian creed, or the ideal of the Christian life. These revivals have been inspired or led by devoted men who have represented the highest conscience of Christendom in their day. They may be traced along the line of Christian history; the Spirit living in the Church has by them attested His presence and His will; and has recalled lukewarm generations, paralyzed by indifference or degraded by indulgence, to the true spirit and level of Christian faith and life.

In such movements there is often what seems, at first sight, an element of caprice. They appear to contemporaries to be onesided, exaggerated, narrow, fanatical. They are often denounced with a passionate fervor which is so out of proportion to the reality as to border on the grotesque. They are said to exact too much of us, or to concede too much. They are too contemplative in their tendency to be sufficiently practical, or too energetically practical to do justice to religious thought. They are too exclusively literary and academical, as being the work of men of books; or they are too popular and insensible to philosophical considerations, as being the work of men of the people. Or, again, they are so occupied with controversy as to forget the claims of devotion, or so engaged in leading souls to a devout life as to forget the unwelcome but real necessities of controversy. They are intent on particular moral improvements so exclusively as to forget what is due to reverence and order; or they are so bent upon rescuing the Church from chronic slovenliness and indecency in public worship as to do less than justice to the paramount interests of moral truth. Sometimes these movements are all feeling; sometimes they are all thought; sometimes they are, as it seems, all outward energy. In one age they produce a literature like that of the fourth and fifth centuries; in another they found orders of men devoted to preaching or to works of mercy, as in the twelfth; in another they enter the lists, as in the thirteenth century, with a hostile philosophy; in another they attempt a much-needed reformation of the Church; in another they pour upon the heathen world a flood of light and warmth from the heart of Christendom. It is easy, as we survey them, to say that something else was needed; or that what was done could have been done better or more completely; or that, had we been there, we should not have been guilty of this onesidedness, or of that exaggeration. We forget, perhaps, who really was there, and whose work it is, though often overlaid and thwarted by human weakness and human passion, that we are really criticizing. If it was seemingly onesided, excessive or defective, impulsive or sluggish, speculative or practical, esthetic or experimental, may not this have been so because in His judgment, who breatheth where He listeth, this particular characteristic was needed for the Church of that day? All that contemporaries know of such movements is "the sound thereof"; the names with which they are associated, the controversies which they precipitate, the hostilities which they rouse or allay, as the case may be. Such knowledge is superficial enough; of the profound spiritual causes which really engender them, of the direction in which they are really moving, of the influence which they are destined permanently to exert upon souls, men know little or nothing. The accidental symptom is mistaken for the essential characteristic; the momentary expression of feeling for the inalienable conviction of certain truth. The day may come, perhaps, when more will be known; when practise and motive, accident and substance, the lasting and the transient, will be seen in their true relative proportions; but for the time this can hardly be. He is passing by, whose way is in the sea, and His paths in the deep waters, and His footsteps unknown. The Eternal Spirit is passing; and men can only say, "He bloweth where He listeth."

III. Our Lord's words apply especially to Christian character. There are some effects of the living power of the Holy Spirit which are invariable. When He dwells with a Christian soul, He continually speaks in the voice of conscience; He speaks in the voice of prayer. He produces with the ease of a natural process, without effort, without the taint of self-consciousness, "love, joy, peace, long-suffering, gentleness, goodness, faith, meekness, temperance." Some of these graces must be found where He makes His home. There is no mistaking the atmosphere of His presence: in its main features it is the same now as in the days of the apostles. Just as in natural morality the main elements of "goodness" do not change; so in religious life, spirituality is, amid great varieties of detail, yet, in its leading constituent features, the same thing from one generation to another. But in the life of the individual Christian, or in that of the Church, there is legitimate room for irregular and exceptional forms of activity or excellence. Natural society is not strengthened by the stern repression of all that is peculiar in individual thought or practise; and this is not less true of spiritual or religious society. From the first, high forms of Christian excellence have often been associated with unconscious eccentricity. The eccentricity must be unconscious, because consciousness of eccentricity at once reduces it to a form of vanity which is entirely inconsistent with Christian excellence. How many excellent Christians have been eccentric, deviating more or less from the conventional type of goodness which has been recognized by contemporary religious opinion. They pass away, and when they are gone men do justice to their characters; but while they are still with us how hard do many of us find it to remember that there may be a higher reason for their peculiarities than we think. We know not the full purpose of each saintly life in the designs of Providence; we know not much of the depths and heights whence it draws its inspirations; we can not tell whence it cometh or whither it goeth. Only we know that He whose workmanship it is bloweth where He listeth; and this naturally leads us to remark the practical interpretation which the Holy Spirit often puts upon our Lord's words by selecting as His chosen workmen those who seem to be least fitted by nature for such high service. The apostle has told us how in the first age He set Himself to defeat human anticipations. "Not many wise men after the flesh, not many mighty, not many noble, are called"; learned academies, powerful connections, gentle blood did little enough for the gospel in the days when it won its first and greatest victories. The Holy Spirit, as Nicodemus knew, passed by the varied learning and high station of the Sanhedrin, and breathed where He listed on the peasants of Galilee; He breathed on them a power which would shake the world. And thus has it been again and again in the generations which have followed. When the great Aquinas was a student of philosophy under Albertus Magnus at Cologne, he was known among his contemporaries as "the dumb Ox"; so little did they divine what was to be his place in the theology of Western Christendom. And to those of us who can look back upon the memories of this University for a quarter of a century or more, few things appear more remarkable than the surprizes which the later lives of men constantly afford; sometimes it is a failure of early natural promise, but more often a rich development of intellectual and practical capacity where there had seemed to be no promise at all. We can remember, perhaps, some dull quiet man who seemed to be without a ray of genius, or, stranger still, without anything interesting or marked in character, but who now exerts, and most legitimately, the widest influence for good, and whose name is repeated by thousands with grateful respect. Or we can call to mind another whose whole mind was given to what was frivolous, or even degrading, and who now is a leader in everything that elevates and improves his fellows. The secret of these transfigurations is ever the same. In those days these men did not yet see their way; they were like travelers through the woods at night, when the sky is hidden and all things seem to be other than they are.

Since then the sun has risen and all has changed. The creed of the Church of Christ, in its beauty and its power, has been flashed by the Divine Spirit upon their hearts and understandings; and they are other men. They have seen that there is something worth living for in earnest; that God, the soul, the future, are immense realities, compared with which all else is tame and insignificant. They have learned something of that personal love of our crucified Lord, which is itself a moral and religious force of the highest order, and which has carried them forwards without their knowing it. And what has been will assuredly repeat itself.

GEORGE C. LORIMER

1838-1904

THE FALL OF SATAN

BIOGRAPHICAL NOTE

GEORGE C. LORIMER was born at Edinburgh, Scotland, in 1838. He was brought up by his stepfather who was associated with the theater, and in this relation he received a dramatic education and had some experience on the stage. In 1855 he came to the United States, where he joined the Baptist Church and abandoned the theatrical profession. Later he studied for the Baptist ministry, being ordained in 1859. He died in 1904. His direct and dramatic pulpit style brought him into great popularity in Boston, Chicago, and New York. At Tremont Temple, Boston, he frequently spoke to overflowing congregations. He is the author of several well-known books, from one of which the sermon here given is taken as indicating his familiarity with and liking for dramatic literature. His pulpit manner always retained a flavor of dramatic style that contributed to his popularity.

I beheld Satan, as lightning, fall from heaven.—Luke x., 18.

WHETHER the "glorious darkness" denoted by the name Satan is an actual personage or a maleficent influence, is of secondary moment as far as the aim and moral of this discourse are concerned. If the ominous title applies to an abstraction, and if the event so vividly introduced is but a dramatical representation of some phase in the mystery of iniquity, the spiritual inferences are just what they would be were the words respectively descriptive of an angel of sin, and of his utter and terrible overthrow. I shall not, therefore, tax your patience with discussions on these points, but shall assume as true that literal reading of the text which has commended itself to the ripest among our evangelical scholars.

The Scriptures obscurely hint at a catastrophe in heaven among immortal intelligences, by which many of them were smitten down from their radiant emerald thrones. Their communications on the subject are not specific and unambiguous, and neither can they escape the suspicion of being designedly figurative; intended, probably, as much to veil as to reveal. One of the clearest statements is made by Jude, where he says: "And the angels which kept not their first estate, but left their own habitation, he hath reserved in everlasting chains, under darkness, unto the judgment of the great day"; and Peter, in like manner, speaks of God sparing not the angels that sinned, "but cast them down to hell"; and yet these comparatively lucid passages suggest a world of mist and shadow, which becomes filled with strange images when we confront the picture, presented by John, of war in heaven, with Michael and his angels fighting against the dragon, "that old serpent called the devil." Back of them there doubtless lies a history whose tragic significance is not easily measured. The sad, imperishable annals of our race prove that sin is a contingency of freedom. Wherever creatures are endowed with moral liberty, transgression is impliedly possible. It is, consequently, inherently probable that celestial beings, as well as man, may have revolted from the law of their Maker; and a fall accomplished among the inhabitants of heaven should no more surprise us than the fall of mortals on earth. Perhaps, after all, there is as much truth as poetry in Milton's conception of the rebellion, and of the fearful defeat that overtook its leader:

341

"Him the almighty Power
Hurled headlong flaming from the ethereal sky,
With hideous ruin and combustion, down
To bottomless perdition: there to dwell
In adamantine chains and penal fire,
Who durst defy the Omnipotent to arms."

An apostle, admonishing a novice, bids him beware of pride, "lest he fall into the condemnation of the devil." Here presumptuous arrogance and haughtiness of spirit are specified as the root and source of the great transgression. Shakespeare takes up this thought:

"Cromwell, I charge thee, fling away ambition.
By that sin fell the angels: how can man, then,
The image of his Maker, hope to win by't?"

And Milton repeats it in the magnificent lines:

"What time his pride
Had cast him out of heaven, with all his host
Of rebel angels; by whose aid, aspiring
To set himself in glory above his peers,
He trusted to have equalled the Most High,
If He opposed; and, with ambitious aim,
Against the throne and monarchy of God
Raised impious war in heaven and battle proud,
With vain attempt."

Our Savior, also, sanctions this idea in the text. Joining His disciples again, after their brief separation, He finds them elated and exultant. They rejoiced, and, apparently, not with modesty, that devils were subject unto them, and that they could exorcize them at their pleasure. While they acknowledged that their power was due to the influence of His name, they evidently thought more of themselves than of Him. They were given to unseemly glorifying and self-satisfaction, and were met by the Master's words—half warning, half rebuke—"I beheld Satan, as lightning, fall from heaven." He thus identifies their pride with that evil spirit which led to angelic ruin, and seeks to banish it from their hearts: "Rejoice not that the demons are subject unto you, but, rather, rejoice because your names are written in heaven." Rejoice not on account of privilege and power, but on account of grace; for the memory of grace must promote humility, as it will recall the guilt of which it is the remedy.

We have, here, a lesson for all ages and for all classes of society—a lesson continually enforced by Scripture, and illustrated by history. It deals with the insanity of pride and the senselessness of egotism. It reminds us, by repeated examples, of the temptations to self-inflation, and of the perils which assail its indulgence. "Ye shall be as gods," was the smiling, sarcastic allurement which beguiled our first parents to their ruin. They thought that before them rose an eminence which the foot of creaturehood had never trodden; that from its height the adventurous climber would rival Deity in the sweep of his knowledge and the depth of his joy. Elated and dazzled by the prospect, they dared tread through sin to its attainment, vainly dreaming that wrong-doing would lead to a purer paradise and to a loftier throne. One step, and only one, in the gratification of their desires, converted their enchanting mountain into a yawning gulf, and in its horrid wastes of darkness and of sorrow their high-blown pride was shamed and smothered. The haughty king walked on the terrace heights of Babylon, and, beneath the calm splendor of an Assyrian sky, voiced the complacent feeling which dulled his sense of dependence upon God—as the perfumes of the East lull into waking-slumber the faculties of the soul. Thus ran his self-glorifying soliloquy: "Is not this great Babylon that I have built for the house of the kingdom by the might of my power, and for the honor of my majesty?" Alas for the weakness of the royal egotist! In an hour his boasting was at an end, and, reduced by the chastening judgment of the Almighty to the level of the brute creation, he was compelled to learn that "those who walk in pride the King of heaven is able to abase." Similar the lesson taught us by the overthrow of Belshazzar when, congratulating himself on the stability of his throne, and in his excess of arrogance, he insulted the sacred vessels which his father had plundered from the temple at Jerusalem. I say taught us, for the foolhardy braggart was past learning anything himself. Like the yet more silly Herod, who drank in the adulation of the mob as he sat shimmering in his silver robe and slimed his speech from his serpent-tongue, he was too inflated and bloated with vanity to be corrected by wholesome discipline. Both of these rulers were too self-satisfied to be reproved, and God's exterminating indignation overtook them. Like empty bubbles, nothing could be done with them, and hence the breath of the Almighty burst and dispersed their glittering worthlessness. Pope John XXI., according to Dean Milman, is another conspicuous monument of this folly. "Contemplating," writes the historian, "with too much pride the work of his own hands"— the splendid palace of Viterbo—"at that instant the avenging roof came down on his head." And Shakespeare has immortalized the pathetic doom which awaits the proud man, who, confident in his own importance and in the magnitude of his destiny, is swallowed up in schemes and plans for his personal aggrandizement and power. Wolsey goes too far in his self-seeking, is betrayed by his excess of statecraft, and, being publicly disgraced, laments, when too late, his selfish folly:

"I have ventured,
Like little wanton boys that swim on bladders,
These many summers on a sea of glory,
But far beyond my depth: my high-blown pride
At length broke under me; and now has left me,
Weary, and old with service, to the mercy
Of a rude stream, that must forever hide me."

It is not difficult to discern the fatal effects of this spirit in the lives of the great and mighty; but we are frequently blind to its pernicious influence on the lowly and weak. We do not realize, as we ought, that the differences between men lie mainly in their position, not in their experiences and dangers. The leaders of society are merely actors, exhibiting on the public stage of history what is common to mankind at large. However insignificant we may be, and however obscure our station, our inner life is not far removed from that of the exalted personages who draw to themselves the attention of the world. The poorest man has his ambitions, his struggles and his reverses; and the first may take as deep a hold upon his heart, and the second call forth as much cunning or wisdom to confront, and the last as much bitterness to endure, as are found in the vicissitudes of a Richelieu or a Napoleon. The peasant's daughter, in her narrow circle, feels as keenly the disappointment of her hopes, and mourns as intensely the betrayal of her confidence, or the rude ending of her day-dreams, as either queen or princess, as either Katharine of England or Josephine of France. We do wrong to separate, as widely as we do in our thoughts, ranks and conditions of society. The palace and the hovel are nearer to each other than we usually think; and what passes beneath the fretted ceiling of the one, and the thatched roof of the other, is divided by the shadowy line of mere externalities. And so it happens that the fall of an angel may be pertinent to the state of a fisherman-disciple, and the fall of a prime minister or ruler have its message of warning for the tradesman and mechanic.

Indeed, it will generally be found that the failures of life, and the worse than failures, are mainly due to the same cause which emptied heavenly thrones of their angelic occupants. What is it, let me ask, that comes into clearer prominence as the Washington tragedy [1] is being investigated and scrutinized? Is it not that a diseased egotism, or perhaps it would be more correct to say, a stalwart egotism, robbed this country of its ruler, committed "most sacrilegious murder," and "broke ope"

"The Lord's anointed temple, and stole thence
    The life o' the building."

Like bloody Macbeth, who greedily drank in the prognostications of the weird sisters, tho he feared that the "supernatural soliciting" could not be good, because they pandered to his monstrous self-infatuation, Guiteau, having wrought himself up through many years of self-complacency, claims to have believed that the divine Being had chosen him to do a deed which has filled the earth

[1] The assassination of President Garfield.

with horror. Thus the growth of self-conceit into mammoth proportions tends to obscure the rights of others, and to darken with its gigantic shadow the light of conscience. If we are to admit the prisoner's story, as the expression of his real condition prior to the assassination, we look on one so intoxicated with the sense of his own importance that he would "spurn the sea, if it could roar at him," and hesitate not to perform any deed of darkness that would render him more conspicuous. Others, less heinous offenders than this garrulous murderer, have, from similar weakness, wrought indescribable mischief to themselves. The man, for instance, who frets against providence because his standing is not higher and his influence greater, has evidently a better opinion of his deservings than is wholesome for him. He imagines he is being wronged by the Creator—that his merits are not recognized as they should be—never, for a moment, remembering that, as a sinner, he has no claims on the extraordinary bounty of his heavenly Father. From murmuring he easily glides into open rebellion, and from whispered reproaches to loud denunciations. There are people in every community whose pride leads them into shameful transactions. They would not condescend to mingle with their social inferiors, but they will subsist on the earnings of their friends, and consider it no disgrace to borrow money which they have no intention of returning. Their vanity, at times, commits them to extravagances which they have no means of supporting. They ought to have carriages and horses, mansions and pictures, with all the luxuries of affluence —at least so they think—and, being destitute of the resources requisite to maintain such state, they become adepts in those arts which qualify for the penitentiary. Others have such confidence in the strength of their virtue, such commanding arrogance of integrity, that, like a captain who underestimates the force of an enemy and overrates his own, they neglect to place a picket-guard on the outskirts of their moral camp, and in such an hour as they think not they are surprised and lost. Even possessors of religion are not always clear of this folly, or safe from its perils. They "think more highly of themselves than they ought to think"; they come to regard themselves as specially favored of heaven; they talk of the Almighty in a free and easy manner, and of Jesus Christ as tho He were not the Judge at all. When they pray, it is with a familiarity bordering on irreverence, and when they deal with sacred themes it is with a lightness that breeds contempt. When they recount the marvels which they have wrought in the name of Christ, it is hardly possible for them to hide their self-complacency; for, while they profess to give Him the glory, the manner of their speech shows that they are taking it to themselves. They are like the disciples, who were as proud of their prowess in casting out devils as children are with their beautiful toys, and they are as much in need of the Savior's warning: "I beheld Satan, as lightning, fall from heaven." And because they have failed to give heed unto it, they have oftentimes followed the Evil One in his downward course, and in a moment have made shipwreck of their faith.

"As sails, full spread, and bellying with the wind,
    Drop, suddenly collapsed, if the mast split;
    So to the ground down dropp'd the cruel fiend";

and earthward have the unsaintly saints of God as swiftly sped, when they have fostered the pride which changed angels into demons.

"How art thou fallen from heaven, O Lucifer, son of the morning!" What more pitiable spectacle than the ruin of an angel! We have seen the forsaken halls of time-worn and dilapidated castles, have stood in the unroofed palaces of ancient princes, and have gazed on the moss-covered and ivy-decked towers of perishing churches, and the sight of them has filled our hearts with melancholy, as we thought of what had been, and of the changes that had swept over the fair, valiant and pious throngs whose laughter, bravery and prayers once made these scenes so gay and vocal. All is hushed now, and the silence is broken only by the hoot and screech of the owl, or by the rustle of the nightbat's leathern wing. But how much sadder is the form of the mighty spirit, who once sat regnant among the sons of light, emptied of his innocence, filled with foul, creeping, venomous thoughts and feelings, uncrowned, dethroned only with malignity and throned in evil! The Bible calls him the prince and the god of this world; and everywhere we are surrounded with evidences of his despotic sway. Unlike earthly rulers, whose exhausted natures exact repose, he is ever sleepless, and his plotting never ends. Enter his somber presence-chamber, and commotion, bustle, activity will confront and amaze you. He is continually sending his emissaries forth in every direction. The perpetual wranglings, ceaseless distractions, irreconcilable contradictions, disquieting doubts, discouraging outlooks, inharmonious and jangling opinions, unaccountable delusions, clashing and crashing dissonances, cruel hatreds, bitter enmities and stormful convulsions, which so largely enter and deface the course of human history, proceed mainly from his influence. We know that "the heart of a lost angel is in the earth," and as we know its throbbings carry misery and despair to millions of our fellow-beings, we can surmise the intensity of wo wherewith it afflicts himself. Mrs. Browning's Adam thus addresses Lucifer:

"The prodigy
Of thy vast brows and melancholy eyes,
Which comprehend the heights of some great fall.
I think that thou hast one day worn a crown
Under the eyes of God."

But now the vast brow must wear a heavier gloom, and the eyes betray a deeper sorrow, as in his ruin he has sought to bury the hopes and joys of a weaker race. How different his dealings with the race from those which mark the ministry of Christ! Immortal hate on the one side of humanity; immortal love on the other; both struggling for supremacy. One sweeping across the soul with pinions of dark doubts and fears; the other, with the strong wing of hope and fair anticipations. One seeking to plunge the earth-spirit into the abysmal depths of eternal darkness; the other seeking to bear it to the apex of light, where reigns eternal day. And of the two, Christ alone is called "the blest." In the agony and anguish of His sufferings He yet can exclaim, "My joy I leave with thee"; and in the lowest vale of His shame can calmly discourse on peace. The reason? Do you ask the question? It is found in His goodness. He is good, and seeks the good of all; and goodness crowns His lacerated brow with joy. This Satan sacrificed in his fall; this he antagonizes with, in his dreary career, and so remains in the eyes of all ages the monument of melancholy gloom. Thus, also, is it with man, whose haughtiness thrusts him into evil. He is morose and wretched, crusht beneath a burden of wo, which weighs the eyelids down with weariness and the heart with care, and which constrains him to curse the hour of his birth. Next to the grief-crowned angel, there is no more pitiable object in all God's fair creation than a human soul tumbled by its own besotted pride into sin and shame. "How is the gold become dim! how is the most fine gold changed!" aye, changed to dross, which the foot spurns, and which the whirlwind scatters to the midnight region of eternity.

In view of these reflections, we can understand the stress laid by the inspired writers on the grace of humility. We are exhorted to be like Jesus, who was meek and lowly in heart; and we are commanded to esteem others better than ourselves. These admonitions are not designed to cultivate a servile or an abject spirit, but to promote a wholesome sense of our own limitations, weaknesses and dependence. They would foster such a state of mind as will receive instruction, as will lean on the Almighty, and recognize the worthiness and rights of all. Just as the flower has to pass its season entombed in the darkness of its calyx before it spreads forth its radiant colors and breathes its perfume, so the soul must veil itself in the consciousness of its own ignorance and sinfulness before it will be able to expand in true greatness, or shed around it the aroma of pure goodness. Crossing the prairies recently between this city and St. Louis, I noticed that the trees were nearly all bowed in the direction of the northeast. As our strongest winds blow from that quarter, it was natural to inquire why they were not bent to the southwest. The explanation given was, that the south winds prevail in the time of sap, when the trees are supple with life and heavy with foliage, and consequently, that they yield before them. But when the winter comes they are hard and firm, rigid and stiff, and even the fury of the tempest affects them not. Thus is it with human souls. When humility fills the heart, when its gentleness renders susceptible its thoughts and feelings, the softest breath of God's Spirit can bend it earthward to help the needy, and downward to supplicate and welcome heaven's grace. But when it is frozen through and through with pride, it coldly resists the overtures of mercy, and in its deadness is apathetic even to the storm of wrath. Nothing remains but for the wild hurricane to uproot it and level it to the ground. Such is the moral of my brief discourse. God grant we may have the wisdom of humility to receive it!

MARTIN LUTHER

1483-1546

THE METHOD AND FRUITS OF JUSTIFICATION

BIOGRAPHICAL NOTE

MARTIN LUTHER, leader of the Reformation, was born at Eisleben in 1483, and died there 1546. His rugged character and powerful intellect, combined with a strong physique, made him a natural orator, so that it was said "his words were half battles."

Of his own method of preaching he once remarked:

"When I ascend the pulpit I see no heads, but imagine those that are before me to be all blocks. When I preach I sink myself deeply down; I regard neither doctors nor masters, of which there are in the church above forty. But I have an eye to the multitude of young people, children, and servants, of which there are more than two thousand. I preach to them. When he preaches on any article a man must first distinguish it, then define, describe, and show what it is; thirdly, he must produce sentences from the Scripture to prove and to strengthen it; fourthly, he must explain it by examples; fifthly, he must adorn it with similitudes; and lastly, he must admonish and arouse the indolent, correct the disobedient, and reprove the authors of false doctrine."

Now I say, that the heir, as long as he is a child, differeth nothing from a servant, though he be Lord of all; but is under tutors and governors until the time appointed of the father. Even so we, when we were children, were in bondage under the elements of the world: but when the fullness of the time was come, God sent forth His Son, made of a woman, made under the law, to redeem them that were under the law, that we might receive the adoption of sons. And because ye are sons, God hath sent forth the Spirit of His Son into your hearts, crying, Abba, Father. Wherefore thou art no more a servant, but a son, and if a son, then an heir of God through Christ.—Gal. iv., 1-7.

THIS text touches the very pith of Paul's chief doctrine. The cause why it is well understood but by few is, not that it is so obscure and difficult, but because there is so little knowledge of faith left in the world; without which it is not possible to understand Paul, who everywhere treats of faith with such earnestness and force. I must, therefore, speak in such a manner that this text will appear plain; and that I may more conveniently illustrate it, I will speak a few words by way of preface.

First, therefore, we must understand the doctrine in which good works are set forth, far different from that which treats of justification; as there is a great difference between the substance and its working; between man and his work. Justification pertains to man, and not to works; for man is either justified and saved, or judged and condemned, and not works. Neither is it a controversy among the godly, that man is not justified by works, but righteousness must come from some other source than from his own works: for Moses, writing of Abel, says, "The Lord had respect unto Abel, and to his offering." First, He had respect to Abel himself, then to his offering; because Abel was first counted righteous and acceptable to God, and then for his sake his offering was accepted also, and not he because of his offering. Again, God had no respect to Cain, and therefore neither to his offering: therefore thou seest that regard is had first to the worker, then to the work.

From this it is plainly gathered that no work can be acceptable to God, unless he which worketh it was first accepted by Him: and again, that no work is disallowed of Him unless the author thereof be disallowed before. I think these remarks will be sufficient concerning this matter at present, by which it is easy to understand that there are two sorts of works, those before justification and those after it; and that these last are good works indeed, but the former only appear to be good. Hereof cometh such disagreement between God and those counterfeit holy ones; for this cause nature and reason rise and rage against the Holy Ghost; this is that of which almost the whole Scripture treats. The Lord in His Word defines all works that go before justification to be evil, and of no importance, and requires that man before all things be justified. Again, He pronounces all men which are unregenerate, and have that nature, which they received of their parents unchanged, to be righteous and wicked, according to that saying "all men are liars," that is, unable to perform their duty, and to do those things which they ought to do; and "Every imagination of the thoughts of his heart are only evil continually"; whereby he is able to do nothing that is good, for the fountain of his actions, which is his heart, is corrupted. If he do works which outwardly seem good, they are no better than the offering of Cain.

Here again comes forth reason, our reverend mistress, seeming to be marvelously wise, but who indeed is unwise and blind, gainsaying her God, and reproving Him of lying; being furnished with her follies and feeble honor, to wit, the light of nature, free will, the strength of nature; also with the books of the heathen and the doctrines of men, contending that the works of a man not justified are good works, and not like those of Cain, yea, and so good that he that worketh them is justified by them; that God will have respect, first to the works, then to the worker. Such doctrine now bears the sway everywhere in schools, colleges, monasteries wherein no other saints than Cain was, have rule and authority. Now from this error comes another: they which attribute so much to works, and do not accordingly esteem the worker, and sound justification, go so far that they ascribe all merit and righteousness to works done before justification, making no account of faith, alleging that which James saith, that without works faith is dead. This sentence of the apostle they do not rightly understand; making but little account of faith, they always stick to works, whereby they think to merit exceedingly, and are persuaded that for their work's sake they shall obtain the favor of God: by this means they continually disagree with God, showing themselves to be the posterity of Cain. God hath respect unto man, then unto the works of man; God alloweth the work for the sake of him that worketh, these require that for the work's sake the worker may be crowned.

But here, perhaps, thou wilt say, what is needful to be done? By what means shall I become righteous and acceptable to God? How shall I attain to this perfect justification? Those the gospel answers, teaching that it is necessary that thou hear Christ, and repose thyself wholly on Him, denying thyself and distrusting thine own strength; by this means thou shalt be changed from Cain to Abel, and being thyself acceptable, shalt offer acceptable gifts to the Lord. It is faith that justifies thee, thou being endued therewith; the Lord remitteth all thy sins by the mediation of Christ His Son, in whom this faith believeth and trusteth. Moreover, He giveth unto such a faith His Spirit, which changes the man and makes him anew, giving him another reason and another will. Such a one worketh nothing but good works. Wherefore nothing is required unto justification but to hear Jesus Christ our Savior, and to believe in Him. Howbeit these are not the works of nature, but of grace.

He, therefore, that endeavors to attain to these things by works shutteth the way to the gospel, to faith, grace, Christ, God, and all things that help unto salvation. Again, nothing is necessary in order to accomplish good works but justification; and he that hath attained it performs good works, and not any other. Hereof it sufficiently appears that the beginning, the things following, and the order of man's salvation are after this sort; first of all it is required that thou hear the Word of God; next that thou believe; then that thou work; and so at last become saved and happy. He that changes this order, without doubt is not of God. Paul also describes this, saying, "Whosoever shall call upon the name of the Lord shall be saved. How then shall they call on Him in whom they have not believed? and, how shall they believe in Him of whom they have not heard? and, how shall they hear without a preacher? and, how shall they preach except they be sent?"

Christ teaches us to pray the Lord of the harvest to send forth laborers into His harvest; that is, sincere preachers. When we hear these preach the true Word of God, we may believe; which faith justifies a man, and makes him godly indeed, so that he now calls upon God in the spirit of holiness, and works nothing but that which is good, and thus becomes a saved man. Thus he that believeth shall be saved; but he that worketh without faith is condemned; as Christ saith, he that doth not believe shall be condemned, from which no works shall deliver him. Some say, I will now endeavor to become honest. It is meet surely that we study to lead an honest life, and to do good works. But if one ask them how we may apply ourselves unto honesty, and by what means we may attain it, they answer, that we must fast, pray, frequent temples, avoid sins, etc. Whereby one becomes a Carthusian monk, another chooses some other order of monks, and another is consecrated a priest; some torment their flesh by wearing hair-cloth, others scourge their bodies with whips, others afflict themselves in a different manner; but these are of Cain's progeny, and their works are no better than his; for they continue the same that they were before, ungodly, and without justification: there is a change made of outward works only, of apparel, of place, etc.

They scarce think of faith, they presume only on such works as seem good to themselves, thinking by them to get to heaven. But Christ said, "Enter in at the strait gate, for I say unto you, many seek to enter in, and can not." Why is this? because they know not what this narrow gate is; for it is faith, which altogether annihilates or makes a man appear as nothing in his own eyes, and requires him not to trust in his own works, but to depend upon the grace of God, and be prepared to leave and suffer all things. Those holy ones of Cain's progeny think their good works are the narrow gate; and are not, therefore, extenuated or made less, whereby they might enter.

When we begin to preach of faith to those that believe altogether in works, they laugh and hiss at us, and say, "Dost thou count us as Turks and heathens, whom it behooves now first to learn faith? is there such a company of priests, monks, and nuns, and is not faith known? who knoweth not what he ought to believe? even sinners know that." Being after this sort animated and stirred up, they think themselves abundantly endued with faith, and that the rest is now to be finished and made perfect by works. They make so small and slender account of faith, because they are ignorant what faith is, and that it alone doth justify. They call it faith, believing those things which they have heard of Christ; this kind of faith the devils also have, and yet they are not justified. But this ought rather to be called an opinion of men. To believe those things to be true which are preached of Christ is not sufficient to constitute thee a Christian, but thou must not doubt that thou art of the number of them unto whom all the benefits of Christ are given and exhibited; which he that believes must plainly confess, that he is holy, godly, righteous, the son of God, and certain of salvation; and that by no merit of his own, but by the mere mercy of God poured forth upon him for Christ's sake: which he believes to be so rich and plentiful, as indeed it is, that altho he be as it were drowned in sin, he is notwithstanding made holy, and become the son of God.

Wherefore, take heed that thou nothing doubt that thou art the son of God, and therefore made righteous by His grace; let all fear and care be done away. However, thou must fear and tremble that thou mayest persevere in this way unto the end; but thou must not do this as tho it consisted in thy own strength, for righteousness and salvation are of grace, whereunto only thou must trust. But when thou knowest that it is of grace alone, and that thy faith also is the gift of God, thou shalt have cause to fear, lest some temptation violently move thee from this faith.

Every one by faith is certain of this salvation; but we ought to have care and fear that we stand and persevere, trusting in the Lord, and not in our own strength. When those of the race of Cain hear faith treated of in this manner, they marvel at our madness, as it seems to them. God turn us from this way, say they, that we should affirm ourselves holy and godly; far be this arrogance and rashness from us: we are miserable sinners; we should be mad, if we should arrogate holiness to ourselves. Thus they mock at true faith, and count such doctrine as this execrable error; and thus try to extinguish the Gospel. These are they that deny the faith of Christ, and persecute it throughout the whole world; of whom Paul speaks: "In the latter times many shall depart from the faith," etc., for we see by these means that true faith lies everywhere opprest; it is not preached, but commonly disallowed and condemned.

The pope, bishops, colleges, monasteries, and universities have more than five hundred years persecuted it with one mind and consent most obstinately, which has been the means of driving many to hell. If any object against the admiration, or rather the mad senselessness of these men, if we count ourselves even holy, trusting the goodness of God to justify us, or as David prayed, "Preserve Thou me, O Lord, for I am holy," or as Paul saith, "The Spirit of God beareth witness with our spirit that we are the children of God"; they answer that the prophet and apostle would not teach us in these words, or give us an example which we should follow, but that they, being particularly and specially enlightened, received such revelation of themselves. In this way they misrepresent the Scripture, which affirms that they are holy, saying that such doctrine is not written for us, but that it is rather peculiar miracles, which do not belong to all. This forged imagination we account of as having come from their sickly brain. Again, they believe that they shall be made righteous and holy by their own works, and that because of them God will give them salvation and eternal blessedness.

In the opinion of these men it is a Christian duty to think that we shall be righteous and sacred because of our works; but to believe that these things are given by the grace of God, they condemn as heretical; attributing that to their own works which they do not attribute to the grace of God. They that are endued with true faith, and rest upon the grace of the Lord, rejoice with holy joy, and apply themselves with pleasure to good works, not such as those of Cain's progeny do, as feigned prayers, fasting, base and filthy apparel, and such like trifles, but to true and good works whereby their neighbors are profited.

Perhaps some godly man may think, if the matter be so, and our work do not save us, to what end are so many precepts given us, and why doth God require that they be obeyed? The present text of the apostle will give a solution of this question, and upon this occasion we will give an exposition thereof. The Galatians being taught of Paul the faith of Christ, but afterward seduced by false apostles, thought that our salvation must be finished and made perfect by the works of the law; and that faith alone doth not suffice. These Paul calls back again from works unto faith with great diligence; plainly proving that the works of the law, which go before faith, make us only servants, and are of no importance toward godliness and salvation; but that faith makes us the sons of God, and from thence good works without constraint forthwith plentifully flow.

But here we must observe the words of the apostle; he calls him a servant that is occupied in works without faith, of which we have already treated at large; but he calls him a son which is righteous by faith alone. The reason is this, altho the servant apply himself to good works, yet he does it not with the same mind as doth the son; that is, with a mind free, willing, and certain that the inheritance and all the good things of the Father are his; but does it as he that is hired in another man's house, who hopes not that the inheritance shall come to him. The works indeed of the son and the servant are alike; and almost the same in outward appearance; but their minds differ exceedingly: as Christ saith, "The servant abideth not in the house forever, but the son abideth ever."

Those of Cain's progeny want the faith of sons, which they confess themselves; for they think it most absurd, and wicked arrogancy, to affirm themselves to be the sons of God, and holy; therefore as they believe, even so are they counted before God; they neither become holy nor the sons of God, nevertheless are they exercised with the works of the law; wherefore they are and remain servants forever. They receive no reward except temporal things; such as quietness of life, abundance of goods, dignity, honor, etc., which we see to be common among the followers of popish religion. But this is their reward, for they are servants, and not sons; wherefore in death they shall be separated from all good things, neither shall any portion of the eternal inheritance be theirs, who in this life would believe nothing thereof. We perceive, therefore, that servants and sons are not unlike in works, but in mind and faith they have no resemblance.

The apostle endeavors here to prove that the law with all the works thereof makes us but mere servants, if we have not faith in Christ; for this alone make us sons of God. It is the word of grace followed by the Holy Ghost, as is shown in many places, where we read of the Holy Ghost falling on Cornelius and his family while hearing the preaching of Peter. Paul teaches that no man is justified before God by the works of the law; for sin only cometh by the law. He that trusts in works condemns faith as the most pernicious arrogancy and error of all others. Here thou seest plainly that such a man is not righteous, being destitute of that faith and belief which is necessary to make him acceptable before God and His Son; yea, he is an enemy to this faith, and therefore to righteousness also. Thus it is easy to understand that which Paul saith, that no man is justified before God by the works of the law.

The worker must be justified before God before he can work any good thing. Men judge the worker by the works; God judges the works by the worker. The first precept requires us to acknowledge and worship one God, that is, to trust Him alone, which is the true faith whereby we become the sons of God. Thou canst not be delivered from the evil of unbelief by thine own power, nor by the power of the law; wherefore all thy works which thou doest to satisfy the law can be nothing but works of the law; of far less importance than to be able to justify thee before God, who counteth them righteous only who truly believe in Him; for they that acknowledge Him the true God are His sons, and do truly fulfil the law. If thou shouldst even kill thyself by working, thy heart can not obtain this faith thereby, for thy works are even a hindrance to it, and cause thee to persecute it.

He that studieth to fulfil the law without faith is afflicted for the devil's sake; and continues a persecutor both of faith and the law, until he come to himself, and cease to trust in his own works; he then gives glory to God, who justifies the ungodly, and acknowledges himself to be nothing, and sighs for the grace of God, of which he knows that he has need. Faith and grace now fill his empty mind, and satisfy his hunger; then follow works which are truly good; neither are they works of the law, but of the spirit, of faith and grace; they are called in the Scripture the works of God, which He worketh in us.

Whatsoever we do of our own power and strength, that which is not wrought in us by His grace, without doubt is a work of the law, and avails nothing toward justification; but is displeasing to God, because of the unbelief wherein it is done. He that trusts in works does nothing freely and with a willing mind; he would do no good work at all if he were not compelled by the fear of hell, or allured by the hope of present good. Whereby it is plainly seen that they strive only for gain, or are moved with fear, showing that they rather hate the law from their hearts, and had rather there were no law at all. An evil heart can do nothing that is good. This evil propensity of the heart, and unwillingness to do good, the law betrays when it teaches that God does not esteem the works of the hand, but those of the heart.

Thus sin is known by the law, as Paul teaches; for we learn thereby that our affections are not placed on that which is good. This ought to teach us not to trust in ourselves, but to long after the grace of God, whereby the evil of the heart may be taken away, and we become ready to do good works, and love the law voluntarily; not for fear of any punishment, but for the love of righteousness. By this means one is made of a servant, a son; of a slave an heir.

We shall now come to treat more particularly of the text. Verse 1. "The heir, as long as he is a child, differeth nothing from a servant, tho he be lord of all." We see that the children unto whom their parents have left some substance are brought up no otherwise than if they were servants. They are fed and clothed with their goods, but they are not permitted to do with them, nor use them according to their own minds, but are ruled with fear and discipline of manners, so that even in their own inheritance they live no otherwise than as servants. After the same sort it is in spiritual things. God made with His people a covenant, when He promised that in the seed of Abraham, that is in Christ, all nations of the earth should be blest. That covenant was afterward confirmed by the death of Christ, and revealed and published abroad by the preaching gospel. For the gospel is an open and general preaching of this grace, that in Christ is laid up a blessing for all men that believe.

Before this covenant is truly opened and made manifest to men, the sons of God live after the manner of servants under the law; and are exercised with the works of the law, altho they can not be justified by them; they are true heirs of heavenly things, of this blessing and grace of the covenant; altho they

do not as yet know or enjoy it. Those that are justified by grace cease from the works of the law, and come unto the inheritance of justification; they then freely work those things that are good, to the glory of God and benefit of their neighbors. For they have possest it by the covenant of the Father, confirmed by Christ, revealed, published, and as it were delivered into their hands by the gospel, through the grace and mercy of God.

This covenant Abraham, and all the fathers which were endued with true faith, had no otherwise than we have: altho before Christ was glorified this grace was not openly preached and published: they lived in like faith, and therefore obtained the like good things. They had the same grace, blessing, and covenant that we have; for there is one Father and God over all. Thou seest that Paul here, as in almost all other places, treats much of faith; that we are not justified by works, but by faith alone. There is no good thing which is not contained in this covenant of God; it gives righteousness, salvation, and peace. By faith the whole inheritance of God is at once received. From thence good works come; not meritorious, whereby thou mayest seek salvation, but which with a mind already possessing righteousness thou must do with great pleasure to the profit of thy neighbors.

Verse 2. "But is under tutors and governors until the time appointed of the Father." Tutors and governors are they which bring up the heir, and so rule him and order his goods that he neither waste his inheritance by riotous living, nor his goods perish or be otherwise consumed. They permit him not to use his goods at his own will or pleasure, but suffer him to enjoy them as they shall be needful and profitable to him. They keep him at home, and instruct him whereby he may long and comfortably enjoy his inheritance: but as soon as he arrives to the years of discretion and judgment, it can not but be grievous to him to live in subjection to the commands and will of another.

In the same manner stands the case of the children of God, which are brought up and instructed under the law, as under a master in the liberty of sons. The law profits them in this, that by the fear of it and the punishment which it threatens, they are driven from sin, at least from the outward work: by it they are brought to a knowledge of themselves, and that they do no good at all with a willing and ready mind as becomes sons; whereby they may easily see what is the root of this evil, and what is especially needful unto salvation; to wit, a new and living spirit to that which is good: which neither the law nor the works of the law is able to give; yea, the more they apply themselves to it, the more unwilling they find themselves to work those things which are good.

Here they learn that they do not satisfy the law, altho outwardly they live according to its precepts. They pretend to obey it in works, altho in mind they hate it; they pretend themselves righteous, but they remain sinners. These are like unto those of Cain's progeny, and hypocrites; whose hands are compelled to do good, but their hearts consent unto sin and are subject thereto. To know this concerning one's self is not the lowest degree toward salvation. Paul calls such constrained works the works of the law; for they flow not from a ready and willing heart; howbeit the law does not require works alone, but the heart itself; wherefore it is said in the first psalm of the blest man, "But his delight is in the law of the Lord: and in His law doth he meditate day and night." Such a mind the law requires, but it gives it not; neither can it of its own nature: whereby it comes to pass that while the law continues to exact it of a man, and condemns him as long as he hath such a mind, as being disobedient to God, he is in anguish on every side; his conscience being grievously terrified.

Then, indeed, is he most ready to receive the grace of God; this being the time appointed by the Father when his servitude shall end, and he enter into the liberty of the sons of God. For being thus in distress, and terrified, seeing that by no other means he can avoid the condemnation of the law, he prays to the Father for grace; he acknowledges his frailty, he confesses his sin, he ceases to trust in works, and humbles himself, perceiving that between him and a manifest sinner there is no difference at all except of works, that he hath a wicked heart, even as every other sinner hath. The condition of man's nature is such that it is able to give to the law works only, and not the heart; an unequal division, truly, to dedicate the heart, which, incomparably excels all other things, to sin, and the hand to the law: which is offering chaff to the law, and the wheat to sin; the shell to God, and the kernel to Satan; whose ungodliness if one reprove, they become enraged, and would even take the life of innocent Abel, and persecute all those that follow the truth.

Those that trust in works seem to defend them to obtain righteousness; they promise to themselves a great reward for this, by persecuting heretics and blasphemers, as they say, who seduce with error, and entice many from good works. But those that God hath chosen, learn by the law how unwilling the heart is to conform to the works of the law; they fall from their arrogancy, and are by this knowledge of themselves brought to see their own unworthiness. Hereby they receive that covenant of the eternal blessing and the Holy Ghost which renews the heart: whereby they are delighted with the law, and hate sin; and are willing and ready to do those things which are good. This is the time appointed by the Father, when the heir must no longer remain a servant, but a son; being led by a free spirit, he is no more kept in subjection under tutors and governors after the manner of a servant; which is even that which Paul teaches in the following:

Verse 3. "Even so we, when we were children, were in bondage under the elements of the word." By the word elements thou mayest here understand the first principles or law written; which is as it were the first exercises and instructions of holy learning; as it is said: "As concerning the time ye ought to be teachers, ye have need that one teach you again which be the first principles of the oracles of God." "Beware lest any man spoil you through philosophy and vain deceit, after the tradition of men, after the rudiments of the world." "How turn ye again to the weak and beggarly elements, whereunto ye desire again to be in bondage."

Here Paul calls the law rudiments; because it is not able to perform that righteousness which it requires. For whereas it earnestly requires a heart and mind given to godliness, nature is not able to satisfy it: herein it makes a man feel his poverty, and acknowledge his infirmity: it requires that of him by right which he has not, neither is able to have. "The letter killeth, but the Spirit giveth life." Paul calls them the rudiments of the world, which, not being renewed by the Spirit, only perform worldly things; to wit, in places, times, apparel, persons, vessels, and such like. But faith rests not in worldly things, but in the grace, word, and mercy of God: counting alike, days, meats, persons, apparel, and all things of this world.

None of these by themselves either help or hinder godliness or salvation. With those of Cain's progeny, faith neither agrees in name or anything else; one of them eats flesh, another abstains from it; one wears black apparel, another white; one keeps this day holy, and another that; every one has his rudiments, under which he is in bondage: all of them are addicted to the things of the world, which are frail and perishable. Against these Paul speaks, "Wherefore, if ye be dead with Christ from the rudiments of the world, why, as tho living in the world, are ye subject to ordinances: touch not, taste not, handle not, which all are to perish with the using, after the commandments and doctrines of men? Which things have indeed a show of wisdom in will-worship and humility, and neglecting of the body; not in any honor to the satisfying of the flesh."

By this and other places above mentioned,

it is evident that monasteries and colleges, whereby we measure the state of spiritual men as we call them, plainly disagree with the Gospel and Christian liberty: and therefore it is much more dangerous to live in this kind of life than among the most profane men. All their works are nothing but rudiments and ordinances of the world; neither are they Christians but in name, wherefore all their life and holiness are sinful and most detestable hypocrisy. The fair show of feigned holiness which is in those ordinances does, in a marvelous and secret manner, withdraw from faith more than those manifest and gross sins of which open sinners are guilty. Now this false and servile opinion faith alone takes away, and teaches us to trust in, and rest upon, the grace of God, whereby is given freely that which is needful to work all things.

Verse 4. "But when the fulness of the time was come, God sent forth His Son, made of a woman, made under the law, to redeem them that were under the law, that we might receive the adoption of sons." After Paul had taught us that righteousness and faith can not come to us by the law, neither can we deserve it by nature, he shows us by whom we obtain it; and who is the author of our justification. The apostle saith, "When the fulness of the time was come"; here Paul speaks of the time which was appointed by the Father to the Son, wherein He should live under tutors, etc. This time being come to the Jews, and ended, Christ came in the flesh; so it is daily fulfilled to others, when they come to the knowledge of Christ, and change the servitude of the law for the faith of sons. Christ for this cause came unto us, that believing in Him we may be restored to true liberty; by which faith they of ancient times also obtained the liberty of the Spirit.

As soon as thou believest in Christ, He comes to thee, a deliverer and Savior; and now the time of bondage is ended; as the apostle saith, the fulness thereof is come.

Verse 6. "And because ye are sons, God hath sent forth the Spirit of His Son into your hearts, crying, Abba, Father." Here we see plainly that the Holy Ghost cometh to the saints, not by works, but by faith alone. Sons believe, while servants only work; sons are free from the law, servants are held under the law, as appears by those things that have been before spoken. But how comes it to pass that he saith "because ye are sons, God hath sent forth the Spirit," etc., seeing it is before said that by the coming of the Spirit we are changed from servants to sons: but here, as tho we could be sons before the coming of the Spirit, he saith "because ye are sons," etc. To this question we must answer, that Paul speaks here in the same manner that he did before, that is, before the fulness of

the time came, we were in bondage under the rudiments of the world: all that shall become sons are counted in the place of sons with God: therefore he saith rightly, "because ye are sons," that is, because the state of sons is appointed to you from everlasting, "God hath sent forth the Spirit of His Son," to wit, that He might finish it in you, and make you such as He hath long since of His goodness determined that He would make you.

Now if the Father give unto us His Spirit, He will make us His true sons and heirs, that we may with confidence cry with Christ, Abba, Father; being His brethren and fellow heirs. The apostle has well set forth the goodness of God which makes us partakers with Christ, and causes us to have all things common with Him, so that we live and are led by the same Spirit. These words of the apostle show that the Holy Ghost proceeds from Christ, as he calls Him his Spirit. So God hath sent forth the Spirit of His Son, that is, of Christ, for He is the Spirit of God, and comes from God to us, and not ours, unless one will say after this manner, "my Holy Spirit," as we say, "my God," "my Lord," etc. As He is said to be the Holy Spirit of Christ, it proves Him to be God of whom that Spirit is sent, therefore it is counted His Spirit.

Christians may perceive by this whether they have in themselves the Holy Ghost, to wit, the Spirit of sons; whether they hear His voice in their hearts: for Paul saith, He crieth in the hearts which He possesseth, Abba, Father; he saith also, "We have received the Spirit of adoption, whereby we cry Abba, Father." Thou hearest this voice when thou findest so much faith in thyself that thou dost assuredly, without doubting, presume that not only thy sins are forgiven thee, but also that thou art the beloved Son of God, who, being certain of eternal salvation, durst both call Him Father, and be delighted in Him with a joyful and confident heart. To doubt these things brings a reproach upon the death of Christ, as tho He had not obtained all things for us.

It may be that thou shalt be so tempted as to fear and doubt, and think plainly that God is not a favorable Father, but a wrathful revenger of sins, as it happened with Job, and many other saints: but in such a conflict this trust and confidence that thou art a son ought to prevail and overcome. It is said "The Spirit itself maketh intercession for us with groanings which can not be uttered; and that He beareth witness with our spirit that we are the children of God." How can it therefore be that our hearts should not hear this cry and testimony of the Spirit? But if thou dost not feel this cry, take heed that thou be not slothful and secure; pray constantly, for thou art in an evil state.

Cain saith, "My punishment is greater than I can bear. Behold, Thou hast driven me out this day from the face of the earth, and from Thy face shall I be hid; 'and it shall come to pass that every one that findeth me shall slay me." This is a dreadful and terrible cry, which is heard from all Cain's progeny, all such as trust to themselves and their own works, who put not their trust in the Son of God, neither consider that He was sent from the Father, made of a woman under the law, much less that all these things were done for their salvation. And while their ungodliness is not herewith content, they begin to persecute even the sons of God, and grow so cruel that, after the example of their father Cain, they can not rest until they slay their righteous brother Abel, wherefore the blood of Christ continually cries out against them nothing but punishment and vengeance; but for the heirs of salvation it cries by the Spirit of Christ for nothing but grace and reconciliation.

The apostle here uses a Syrian and Greek word, saying, Abba, Pater. This word Abba, in the Syrian tongue, signifies a father, by which name the heads of monasteries are still called; and by the same name, hermits in times past, being holy men, called their presidents: at last, by use, it was also made a Latin word. Therefore that which Paul saith is as much as Father, Father; or if thou hadst rather, "my Father."

Verse 7. "Wherefore thou art no more a servant, but a son, and if a son, then an heir of God through Christ." He saith, that after the coming of the Spirit, after the knowledge of Christ, "thou art not a servant." A son is free and willing, a servant is compelled and unwilling; a son liveth and resteth in faith, a servant in works. Therefore it appears that we can not obtain salvation of God by works, but before thou workest that which is acceptable to Him, it is necessary that thou receive salvation; then good works will freely flow, to the honor of thy heavenly Father, and to the profit of thy neighbors; without any fear of punishment, or looking for reward.

If this inheritance of the Father be thine by faith, surely thou art rich in all things, before thou hast wrought any thing. It is said "Your salvation is prepared and reserved in heaven, to be showed in the last time," wherefore the works of a Christian ought to have no regard to merit, which is the manner of servants, but only for the use and benefit of our neighbors, whereby we may truly live to the glory of God. Lest that any think that so great an inheritance cometh to us without cost (altho it be given to us without our cost or merit), yet it cost Christ a dear price, who, that He might purchase it for us, was made under the law, and satisfied it for us, both by life and also by death.

Those benefits which from love we bestow upon our neighbor, come to him freely, without any charges or labor of his, notwithstanding they cost us something, even as Christ hath bestowed those things which are His upon us. Thus hath Paul called back the Galatians from the teachers of works, which preached nothing but the law, perverting the Gospel of Christ. Which things are very necessary to be marked of us also: for the Pope, with his prelates and monks hath for a long time intruded, urging his laws, which are foolish and pernicious, disagreeing in every respect with the Word of God, seducing almost the whole world from the gospel of Christ, and plainly extinguishing the faith of sons, as the Scripture hath in diverse places manifestly prophesied of His kingdom. Wherefore let every one that desires salvation, diligently take heed of him and his followers, no otherwise than Satan himself.

HUGH ROSS MACKINTOSH

1870-1936

THE HIDDEN LIFE

BIOGRAPHICAL NOTE

PROFESSOR of systematic theology, New College, Edinburgh, 1904-1931; born October 31, 1870; educated Neilson Institution, Paisley; Tain Royal Academy; George Watson's College, Edinburgh; Edinburgh University; New College, Edinburgh; Universities of Freiburg, Halle and Marburg; entered the ministry of the Free Church of Scotland, 1896; assistant to the Rev. Charles Watson, D.D., of Largs, 1896,7; minister of Tayport, 1897-1901; Beechgrove church, Aberdeen, 1901-04; author of translation (joint) of Ritschl's "Justification and Reconciliation," of Loof's "Anti-Haeckel," edited with Prof. Caldecott "Selections from the Literature of Theism."

" Ye are dead, and your life is hid with Christ in God."—Col. 3 : 3.

No one can suppose a saying like this to be addrest indiscriminately to the world at large. The class of persons whom it indicates, the audience who will grasp and appreciate its meaning, is limited in kind. It is not that the text is obscure. It is not that it belongs to an age so far away from ours. It is not that it raises needless barriers. Only it takes for granted that we have passed through a great experience, and that this experience has brought us into a new world. In short, it touches as very few verses even of the Bible do the vital source and center of the Christian life. It tells the open secret of discipleship, and lays its finger on the pulse of personal religion.

Now there is something remarkable in the calmness with which Paul utters this great truth. Is it not one of the plain marks of its higher origin upon the Bible that it speaks of the most stupendous themes with this quiet, assured power, with the composure of eternity? When men get hold of a great idea, or an idea that seems to them great, how they fret and fume over it, raising such a dust and commotion as if the like of the new theory had never been heard. But few things are more wonderful than the calm, strong tranquillity of the apostles. The message they brought was not a message of their own. The gospel was not their happy discovery. Hence they did not need to claim a place for it with loud protest and urgency, as tho jealous that their voices should be drowned amid the countless voices of the world. It was the truth of God; so that their simple duty was to make it known, and it would do its own work and bear its own witness. With the same quiet, sure restraint of tone Paul says to his readers now: " Your life is hid with Christ in God." He is so certain of it that he needs no appeal or argument. For him the Christian's hidden life is a thing so real and substantial that proof may be dispensed with. Like the beauty of the sunlight, like the sweet freshness of morning, it is not an inference at all; it is the clear presupposition on which everything rests. It is the great immovable fact on which we take our stand, and look out from it with settled faith over the moving scene of the world and up to the glory that shall follow.

We have a wonderful proof of the power of Christianity to touch hearts and change lives in the fact that Paul should have felt it possible to write thus to people whose home was

Colossæ. Colossæ was no worse, perhaps, than the average Asian city of the time, but it can hardly have been much better. And a few years before the idea of sending a message like this to any of the inhabitants of the place would have been a sad irony. So it was a year or two back, but mark the difference now. In the meantime, the gospel of Christ had come, and the tide of its power and joy was flowing thro their lives. All things had become new. They were risen with Christ now, and the very springs of their being were hid with Him in God. Once their life had no hidden depths about it at all; it had all been shallow, specious, concerned with the surface only, busy about things that mattered little, infinitely occupied with trifles, running to waste pathetically over poor and passing aims. But the grace of God had called them, as it calls us, into a new life. In that old barren experience wells had been sunk, and now fountains of living water were springing up clear and fresh. Mines of infinite wealth had been opened in what before had seemed an unprofitable land, and the gold and precious stones of faith and hope and love were being yielded now. Once they had been content with a poor, starveling, hand-to-mouth morality, always precarious, always unequal to any sharp and sudden strain; but to-day their best stores of power, and their deepest springs of joy, were away far and beyond the reach of sorrow or temptation, because held and guarded by Christ in the unseen.

Believers leave the old life behind them. " Ye are dead," Paul says to these Colossians; or even, as it is in stricter accuracy, " ye died." Sometimes the passage of a soul into the kingdom of God is like the flight of a bird in its swiftness. It arrives as the revolution of a moment. " Within ten paces, as I walked, life was transformed to me," says one to whom the change had happened thus. We lie down some night our old selves, and ere we sleep again the great disclosure has broken on the soul. Yet in itself the text says nothing of this suddenness. It speaks of an event in the past; it does not describe it as either swift or slow. Men may die swiftly, and men may die slowly; it matters nothing, when they have wakened on " the immortal side of death." When the ship comes to the equator, no visible line is there which all see as they cross over; yet in point of fact the crossing is made; they pass from the one hemisphere into the other. So when God's eye reads our past many things stand clear before Him which it was not given to us to perceive. He has watched the rise and progress of our life in Christ from the beginning. And where to our eyes there showed nothing but a gentle imperceptible advance, He, it well might be, may discern a cleavage, sharp as though made by a scimitar, between the old life and the new.

The best metaphor to illustrate this change that Paul can think of, is the passage from one world to another which we name death.

You see the thought which is moving in his mind. Union to Christ Jesus produces a moral and spiritual transfiguration analogous to death and resurrection. At death the soul does not cease to be; rather by the great transition it enters a new environment, like the buds rising through the sod in spring. Just so in regeneration the soul does not lose its identity, but its attachment to Christ lifts it into a new and higher realm. He died for sin —to break its power, to undo the awful ruin, to rectify the wrong: we, through Him, die to sin, in response to His holiness, caught up and borne on by His power, compelled by His love. It is not that we become sinless. We are under no such delusion. But whatever sin remains, we still may have the glad and honest certainty that our fixed desire and choice are now one in will with the will of Jesus Christ. He has made us new creatures, in whom the tyranny of sin is broken. He has given us a new self, the only self worth having or worth keeping. And formidable as the world, the flesh, and the devil are, we know that from this time on there is a Brother beside us in the battle, and a Presence within us that will be ours for ever and ever. So through Him, lives that were so hopeless will become blest; the barren will become fruitful, and the weak strong. The old life dies on the birthday of faith.

Brethren, surely it is a great thing to have this settled once for all. The old life is dead; its day is over. The channels in which its waters used of old to flow may still at times seem to run as freely as ever; but the parent spring is failing, and one day it will have ceased, to flow no more again. You who have the new heart, but are sadly opprest by the old, remember that. Do not say that the conflict avails nothing. If holiness and faith in you have never ceased to wrestle with sin and doubt, it is the greatest triumph you could win. And besides, the battle is not to be unending. Your hour of victory, final and complete, and drawing ever nearer, is marked for you on God's plan. Some day—as surely as once you crossed the line that severs Christ from sin, and chose your side with Him for ever—some day you will overcome, and the crown of perfect righteousness will be set upon your head.

Note, secondly, the Christian's hidden life. " Your life is hid with Christ." There is something in every true disciple, even the meekest and plainest, which it would tax the wisest onlooker to account for. You cannot explain the Christian character by anything that shows upon the surface. To unveil the secret of it you must go down into the buried depths, beneath a man's common words and thoughts. Frequently, as you cross a highland moor, you come upon a bright streak of green, winding in and out among the heather, its pure and shining verdure in strange relief against the dull brown of its surroundings. What can it be, you ask? How came it there? Whence rises the sap to feed this soft ribband of elastic turf? There is a tiny stream below; a rill of sweet water flowing down there out of sight, only hinting its presence by the greenness and beauty above. So the springs of Christian life are hidden—hidden with Christ in God.

For one thing, they are hidden from the unchristian world; but I will not speak much of this. Something mysterious and inscrutable must always appear to a man of the world in those who live by faith in the Son of God. He may merely wonder at the mystery, or he may resent it, but he is always conscious of its presence. And when he asks himself how personal religion is to be accounted for, any explanation but the right one often will suffice. Fear, self-interest, hoary tradition, weak delusion—we know the theories by which outsiders have sought to explain Christian faith, and by the explanation to rob it of its power. It has always been their plan. Even of the Master they whispered, " He is beside himself "; and of the apostles, with the fire and life of Pentecost throbbing in their veins, they deemed it enough to say, " These men are full of new wine." All that the believer can plead—and how much it is!—of aid sent him in temptation, or light that visits him in darkness, or consolations that draw the poison out of bitter grief, is counted a tale of little meaning. The existence of all that deep life is not perceived. The Christian secret is a secret from the world.

But more than this may be said. There is some profounder meaning here. For my text declares, or, at least, it implies, does it not, that a believer's deepest life is somehow a secret from himself? Is this not so at the origin and birth of religion in the soul, when the Spirit quickens the dead to life? " The wind bloweth where it listeth; thou hearest the sound thereof, but canst not tell whence it cometh or whither it goeth "—thou canst not tell; no, not tho it be in thy heart that it is blowing! Regeneration makes us God's in a deeper fashion than we dream. And if it be so at the first, it is so ever after. To-day men of science are obviously moving about in worlds not realized, among half-comprehended forces which only now and then flash an isolated token of their nature into the realm of knowledge. Do we not see that the same holds good of the experience of every true believer in Christ? He sees and loves the fruits that spring from fellowship with God, and in his own heart he knows the joy of it; but the roots go far down out of sight. He

is conscious that God is offering him grace and love each day, and bringing him to respond with trust and longing; but how the two, the grace and trust, meet and mingle in his soul, he cannot tell. He knows that communion with God sets his mind perfectly at rest, and that this strange inward power is never so effectual as just in the midst of distress; but the rationale of it all is beyond him. He can feel the power of Christ resting upon him, raising him above himself, turning his very weakness into strength; but how it comes to pass he knows not, or as little as he does the relations of soul and body. He can say what the causes are, he cannot say how the causes work. His life in Christ, at its deepest, is hidden in a measure from himself.

What is this but to say that the sources of our very life are in Christ's keeping, not in ours? He guards for us the springs of faith and love. The reservoir in which our supplies are stored is yonder, not here; and enough for each day's necessity is given. All that Christ has, He has for those who love Him; and one sometimes imagines that His greatest sorrow, if perchance He sorrows still, must be that we draw upon Him so sparingly, with the fear lest we are asking too much. Cases of hallucination have been known in which men who had a fortune in the bank dreamed they were paupers, and could hardly be got to draw a check for the essentials of life; and one is reminded of them now and then by our own neglect of the treasures laid up in Jesus Christ. Never judge of your Redeemer's grace and power by what you have yet received from Him. Had you suffered Him, He would have done far more. And if He has not done it, the reason always is not that Christ is less bountiful than we believed, but that our heart is much shallower and our faith far less open and simple than it might be.

But if a Christian is thus in direct correspondence with the infinite nature of Christ, it follows that he is a man with great reserves of power. Like some great commercial houses, which have the more in the warehouse the less there is of open display, a believing life is a far richer thing than it seems. You have noticed how the secret of the charm and power of certain pictures lies in the suggestion they give of a wide, illimitable background, in which eye and fancy lose themselves as we gaze; and the same subtle impression clings about everyone whose character is rooted in the love of God. God in Christ is the great background of the life of faith. Yet how often worldly men have taken a simple, quiet Christian at an utterly false valuation, and deemed him weak because he is unpretending. They gathered round him with their promises and threats, looking for his fall as a thing of course; yet within that soul there were hidden stores of fearless power they never dreamed of, and the foiled assault drew back as harmless as the waves that fall from the rock shattered into spray. What is the reason? It is that his life is hid with Christ in God. He has access, and we all have access, to the comforts of a love so deep and broad and high that it passeth knowledge. And the task of the Christian is so to walk before men that they shall say: "There must be springs in such a life. That steady, sustained gladness and peace could not be without roots somewhere." Thus the experience that came from Christ must be employed to point men back to Christ again, and the circle of believing witness return to glorify Him who made it what it is.

Then, besides that, the sources of our life, thus being hid in Christ, are protected against dispeace and trouble. Here, it is true, we must distinguish between what goes on upon the surface and that which is passing in the depths. Take the experience of any Christian man, and even after a close study you might be tempted to think it very like that of anyone else. The believer is not spared the common vicissitudes of life. Like his neighbor, he must enter the struggle of business and bear its disappointments. He, too, may know what it is to labor long in hope, and wait in vain for the harvest that never comes. He, too, must bear the pain of suspense and daily care, and perplexity of conscience, and fear for those he loves. He, too, may feel the weight of the dread law of God which rends loving hearts asunder and makes havoc of our plans. All this is true, and more; it is the common lot of man. But yet, let us remember with thankfulness and proclaim it with joy—this, tho it were multiplied and intensified a hundredfold, need not touch the true life seated in the depths of the heart. The storm may rage upon the coast, yet not a breath of its fury reach the sequestered valley that sleeps in the bosom of the hills. The ocean surface may be torn and buffeted by billows that race from shore to shore, and all the while the untroubled depths be still. And just so, amid his cares and occupations, and even his adversity, the believer may have a mind at perfect peace; for his life, his true life, the life that really makes the man, is hid with Christ in God. And this is our unspeakable privilege, this is the perpetual miracle we may put in force, that it is open to us to fall back upon this indestructible peace. In a moment, without a sound, wherever we are, we can pass from the street into the sanctuary, from the world into the presence of our Lord; and there find our true life, calm and safe with Him.

The life that is hid with Christ is not to be hidden for ever. It is hidden thus, because Christ is yonder and we are here. But like the bud that sleeps in its sheath and waits for the call of the spring, the life of the man of faith is big with promise. One day the secret will be out. The vestments that wrapt it round will be taken off, for the present is but a stage that passes. When Christ who is our life shall appear, then shall we also appear with Him in glory.

Take an instance. Take the life of one of our countrymen in India. Soldier perhaps, or missionary, or merchant, he labors on with brain and hand, doing his work as only a true man can. But his home—his home is in Scotland. Those he loves best of all are there; and where a man's treasure is, there will his heart be also. He would scorn to neglect his duty; yet all the time his true life is circling not round the routine of his station, but round his home far away. And often, as he rides from post to post his thoughts go a-wandering over the sea to some cottage on the hill where his children are, and he hears them shout in their play amid the heather and the bracken, or sees the mother stooping over them as they sleep. It is an inner life unperceived by those around him, but from it rise all but the very highest incentives of brave and honest manhood. And as he toils and labors on, it is with a great hope that the day will come when, foreign service over, he will go back to his home. And then, and ever after, what used to be only the private luxury of quiet thought will, please God, be the open and endless interest of every hour and every day.

Is there one of us who does not feel this to be only a parable of the Christian life? We give thanks to God for the supplies of love and grace that are ours now; we bless the good hand that gives them, and we strive to use them for His glory. But all the while the thought is uppermost with us that something better—far better—is yet to be revealed. Not that we should long for death, not that, in our haste, we should call the world a barren, weary desert. The earth is the Lord's, and the fulness thereof; and the time and the coming of death we gladly leave to the secret love of God. But more and more, if we are Christians at all, we are coming to be sure, and ever surer, that God has kept the best to the last. Here we draw from the stream, but one day we shall stand by the very fountainhead. We shall leave the foreign land, and travel to God, who is our home.

Our life is hidden now, because Christ is hidden; hidden, not in darkness, but in the light where He dwells with the Father. It is better that it should be so, is it not? It is better that our stores and treasures should be outside of ourselves. Yes, and every new gift that comes from Christ, every new grasp of His hand, every reminder of His love, only stirs us to think how much He has laid up in store for the trusting heart, awaiting the disclosure of the great day. How deep and broad must be the ocean of that hidden life and love, when out of it flows this clear, deep river, so full of water, making glad the city of God!

ALEXANDER MACLAREN

1826-1910

THE PATTERN OF SERVICE

BIOGRAPHICAL NOTE

ALEXANDER MACLAREN was born in 1826, educated at Glasgow University, for twelve years preached at Southampton, and afterwards for many years in Manchester. Besides an impressive face and figure he brought to the pulpit a ripe scholarship, an almost perfect English style, and an uncommonly vigorous personality. The keynote of his life and character is disclosed in his own words, uttered in Manchester:

"I have been so convinced that I was best serving all the varied social, economical, and political interests that are dear to me by preaching what I conceived to be the gospel of Jesus Christ, that I have limited myself to that work. I am sure, with a growing conviction day by day, that so we Christian ministers best serve our generation. My work, whatever yours may be, is, and has been for thirty-eight years, and I hope will be for a little while longer yet, to preach Jesus Christ as the King of England and the Lord of all our communities, and the Savior and friend of the individual soul."

He touched his tongue; and looking up to heaven, He sighed, and saith, Ephphatha, that is, Be opened.—Mark vii., 33, 34.

FOR what reason was there this unwonted slowness in Christ's healing works? For what reason was there this unusual emotion ere He spoke the word which cleansed?

As to the former question, a partial answer may perhaps be that our Lord is here on half-heathen ground, where aids to faith were much needed, and His power had to be veiled that it might be beheld. Hence the miracle is a process rather than an act; and, advancing as it does by distinct stages, is conformed in appearance to men's works of mercy, which have to adapt means to ends, and creep to their goal by persevering toil. As to the latter, we know not why the sight of this one poor sufferer should have struck so strongly on the ever-tremulous chords of Christ's pitying heart; but we do know that it was the vision brought before His spirit by this single instance of the world's griefs and sicknesses, in which mass, however, the special case before Him was by no means lost, that raised His eyes to heaven in mute appeal, and forced the groan from His breast.

The missionary spirit is but one aspect of the Christian spirit. We shall only strengthen the former as we invigorate the latter. Harm has been done, both to ourselves and to this great cause, by seeking to stimulate compassion and efforts for heathen lands by the use of other excitements, which have tended to vitiate even the emotions they have aroused, and are apt to fail us when we need them most. It may therefore be profitable if we turn to Christ's own manner of working, and His own emotions in His merciful deeds, set forth in this remarkable narrative, as containing lessons for us in our missionary and evangelistic work. I must necessarily omit more than a passing reference to the slow process of healing which this miracle exhibits. But that, too, has its teaching for us, who are so often tempted to think ourselves badly used, unless the fruit of our toil grows up, like Jonah's gourd, before our eyes. If our Lord was content to reach His end of blessing step by step, we may well accept patient continuance in well-doing as the condition indispensable to reaping in due season.

But there are other thoughts still more

needful which suggest themselves. Those minute details which this evangelist ever delights to give of our Lord's gestures, words, looks, and emotions, not only add graphic force to the narrative, but are precious glimpses of the very heart of Christ. That fixed gaze into heaven, that groan which neither the glories seen above nor the conscious power to heal could stifle, that most gentle touch, as if removing material obstacles from the deaf ears, and moistening the stiff tongue that it might move more freely in the parched mouth, that word of authority which could not be wanting even when His working seemed likest a servant's, do surely carry large lessons for us. The condition of all service, the cost of feeling at which our work must be done, the need that the helpers should identify themselves with the sufferers, and the victorious power of Christ's word over all deaf ears—these are the thoughts which I desire to connect with our text, and to commend to your meditation to-day.

We have here set forth the foundation and condition of all true work for God in the Lord's heavenward look.

The profound questions which are involved in the fact that, as man, Christ held communion with God in the exercise of faith and aspiration, the same in kind as ours, do not concern us here. I speak to those who believe that Jesus is for us the perfect example of complete manhood, and who therefore believe that He is "the leader of faith," the head of the long procession of those who in every age have trusted in God and been lightened. But, perhaps, tho that conviction holds its place in our creeds, it has not been as completely incorporated with our thoughts as it should have been. There has, no doubt, been a tendency, operating in much of our evangelical teaching, and in the common stream of orthodox opinion, to except, half unconsciously, the exercises of the religious life from the sphere of Christ's example, and we need to be reminded that Scripture presents His vow, "I will put my trust in Him," as the crowning proof of His brotherhood, and that the prints of His kneeling limbs have left their impressions where we kneel before the throne. True, the relation of the Son to the Father involves more than communion—namely, unity. But if we follow the teaching of the Bible, we shall not presume that the latter excludes the former, but understand that the unity is the foundation of perfect communion, and the communion the manifestation, so far as it can be manifested, of the unspeakable unity. The solemn words which shine like stars—starlike in that their height above us shrinks their magnitude and dims their brightness, and in that they are points of radiance partially disclosing, and separated by, abysses of unlighted infinitude—tell us that in the order of eternity, before creatures were, there was communion, for "the Word was with God," and there was unity, for "the Word was God." And in the records of the life manifested on earth the consciousness of unity loftily utters itself in the unfathomable declaration, "I and my Father are one"; whilst the consciousness of communion, dependent like ours on harmony of will and true obedience, breathes peacefully in the witness which He leaves to Himself: "The Father has not left me alone for I do always the things that please him."

We are fully warranted in supposing that that wistful gaze to heaven means, and may be taken to symbolize, our Lord's conscious direction of thought and spirit to God as He wrought His work of mercy. There are two distinctions to be noted between His communion with God and ours before we can apply the lesson to ourselves. His heavenward look was not the renewal of interrupted fellowship, but rather, as a man standing firmly on firm rock may yet lift his foot to plant it again where it was before, and settle himself in his attitude before he strikes with all his might; so we may say Christ fixes Himself where He always stood, and grasps anew the hand that He always held, before He does the deed of power. The communion that had never been broken was renewed; how much more the need that in our work for God the renewal of the —alas! too sadly sundered—fellowship should ever precede and always accompany our efforts! And again, Christ's fellowship was with the Father. Ours must be with the Father through the Son. The communion to which we are called is with Jesus Christ, in whom we find God.

The manner of that intercourse, and the various discipline of ourselves with a view to its perfecting, which Christian prudence prescribes, need not concern us here. As for the latter, let us not forget that a wholesome and wide-reaching self-denial cannot be dispensed with. Hands that are full of gilded toys and glass beads cannot grasp durable riches, and eyes that have been accustomed to glaring lights see only darkness when they look up to the violet heaven with all its stars. As to the former, every part of our nature above the simply animal is capable of God, and the communion ought to include our whole being.

Christ is truth for the understanding, authority for the will, love for the heart, certainty for the hope, fruition for all the desires, and for the conscience at once cleansing and law. Fellowship with Him is no indolent passiveness, nor the luxurious exercise of certain emotions, but the contact of the whole nature with its sole adequate object and rightful Lord.

Such intercourse, brethren, lies at the foundation of all work for God. It is the condition of all our power. It is the measure of all our success. Without it we may seem to realize the externals of prosperity, but it will be all illusion. With it we may perchance seem to spend our strength for naught; but heaven has its surprizes; and those who toiled, nor left their hold of their Lord in all their work, will have to say at last with wonder, as they see the results of their poor efforts, "Who hath begotten me these? behold, I was left alone; these, where had they been?"

Consider in few words the manifold ways in which the indispensable prerequisite of all right effort for Christ may be shown to be communion with Christ.

The heavenward look is the renewal of our own vision of the calm verities in which we trust, the recourse for ourselves to the realities which we desire that others should see. And what is equal in persuasive power to the simple utterance of your own intense conviction? He only will infuse his own religion into other minds, whose religion is not a set of hard dogmas, but is fused by the heat of personal experience into a river of living fire. It will flow then, not otherwise. The only claim which the hearts of men will listen to, in those who would win them to spiritual beliefs, is that ancient one: "That which we have seen with our eyes, which we have looked upon, declare we unto you." Mightier than all arguments, than all "proofs of the truth of the Christian religion," and penetrating into a sphere deeper than that of the understanding, is the simple proclamation, "We have found the Messias." If we would give sight to the blind, we must ourselves be gazing into heaven. Only when we testify of that which we see, as one might who, standing in a beleaguered city, discerned on the horizon the filmy dust-cloud through which the spearheads of the deliverers flashed at intervals, shall we win any to gaze with us till they too behold and know themselves set free.

Christ has set us the example. Let our prayers ascend as His did, and in our measure the answers which came to Him will not fail us. For us, too, "praying, the heavens" shall be "opened," and the peace-bringing spirit fall dove-like on our meek hearts. For us, too, when the shadow of our cross lies black and gaunt upon our paths, and our souls are troubled, communion with heaven will bring the assurance, audible to our ears at least, that God will glorify Himself even in us. If, after many a weary day, we seek to hold fellowship with God as He sought it on the Mount of Olives, or among the solitudes of the midnight hills, or out in the morning freshness of the silent wilderness, like Him we shall have men gathering around us to hear us speak when we come forth from the secret place of the Most High. If our prayer, like His, goes before our mighty deeds, the voice that first pierced the skies will penetrate the tomb, and make the dead stir in their grave-clothes. If our longing, trustful look is turned to the heavens, we shall not speak in vain on earth when we say, "Be opened."

Brethren, we cannot do without the communion which our Master needed. Do we delight in what strengthened Him? Does our work rest upon the basis of inward fellowship with God which underlay His? Alas! that our pattern should be our rebuke, and the readiest way to force home our faults on our consciences should be the contemplation of the life which we say that we try to copy!

We have here pity for the evils we would remove set forth by the Lord's sigh.

What was it that drew that sigh from the heart of Jesus? One poor man stood before Him, by no means the most sorely afflicted of the many wretched ones whom He healed. But He saw in him more than a solitary instance of physical infirmities. Did there not roll darkly before His thoughts that whole weltering sea of sorrow that moans round the world, of which here is but one drop that He could dry up? Did there not rise black and solid against the clear blue, to which He had been looking, the mass of man's sin, of which these bodily infirmities were but a poor symbol as well as a consequence? He saw as none but He could bear to see, the miserable realities of human life. His knowledge of all that man might be, of all that the most of men were becoming, His power of contemplating in one awful aggregate the entire sum of sorrows and sins, laid upon His heart a burden which none but He has ever endured. His communion with Heaven deepened the dark shadow on earth, and the eyes that looked up to God and saw Him could not but see foulness where others suspected none, and murderous messengers of hell walking in darkness unpenetrated by mortal sight. And all that pain of clearer knowledge of the sorrowfulness of sorrow, and the sinfulness of sin, was laid upon a heart in which was no selfishness to blunt the sharp edge of the pain nor any sin to stagnate the pity that flowed from the wound. To Jesus Christ, life was a daily martyrdom before death had "made the sacrifice complete," and He bore our griefs, and carried our sorrows through many a weary hour before He "bare them in his own body on the tree." Therefore, "Bear ye one another's burden, and so fulfil the law" which Christ obeyed, becomes a command for all who would draw men to Him. And true sorrow, a sharp and real sense of pain, becomes indispensable as preparation for, and accompaniment to, our work.

Mark how in us, as in our Lord, the sigh of compassion is connected with the look to heaven. It follows upon that gaze. The evils are more real, more terrible, by their startling contrast with the unshadowed light which lives above cloudracks and mists. It is a sharp shock to turn from the free sweep of the heavens, starry and radiant, to the sights that meet us in "this dim spot which men call earth." Thus habitual communion with God is the root of the truest and purest compassion. It does not withdraw us from our fellow feeling with our brethren, it cultivates no isolation for undisturbed beholding of God. It at once supplies a standard by which to measure the greatness of man's godlessness, and therefore of his gloom, and a motive for laying the pain of these upon our hearts, as if they were our own. He has looked into the heavens to little purpose who has not learned how bad and how sad the world now is, and how God bends over it in pitying love.

And that same fellowship, which will clear our eyes and soften our hearts, is also the one consolation which we have when our sense of all the ills that flesh is heir to becomes deep, near to despair. When one thinks of the real facts of human life, and tries to conceive of the frightful meanness and passion and hate and wretchedness, that has been howling and shrieking and gibbering and groaning through dreary millenniums, one's brain reels, and hope seems to be absurdity, and joy a sin against our fellows, as a feast would be in a house next door to where was a funeral. I do not wonder at settled sorrow falling upon men of vivid imagination, keen moral sense, and ordinary sensitiveness, when they brood long on the world as it is. But I do wonder at the superficial optimism which goes on with its little prophecies about human progress, and its rose-colored pictures of human life, and sees nothing to strike it dumb for ever in men's writhing miseries, blank failures, and hopeless end. Ah! brethren, if it were not for the heavenward look, how could we bear the sight of earth! "We see not yet all things put under him." No, God knows, far enough off from that. Man's folly, man's submission to the creatures he should rule, man's agonies, and man's transgression, are a grim contrast to the psalmist's vision. If we had only earth to look to, despair of the race, exprest in settled melancholy apathy, or in fierce cynicism, were the wisest attitude. But there is more within our view than earth; "we see Jesus"; we look to the heaven, and as we behold the true man, we see more than ever, indeed, how far from that pattern we all are; but we can bear the thought of what men as yet have been, when we see that perfect example of what men shall be. The root and the consolation of our sorrow for man's evils is communion with God.

We have here loving contact with those whom we would help, set forth in the Lord's touch.

The reasons for the variety observable in Christ's method of communicating superna-

tural blessing were, probably, too closely connected with unrecorded differences in the spiritual conditions of the recipients to be distinctly traceable by us. But tho we cannot tell why a particular method was employed in a given case, why now a word, and now a symbolic action, now the touch of His hand, and now the hem of His garment, appeared to be the vehicles of His power, we can discern the significance of these divers ways, and learn great lessons from them all.

His touch was sometimes obviously the result of what one may venture to call instinctive tenderness, as when He lifted the little children in His arms and laid His hands upon their heads. It was, I suppose, always the spontaneous expression of love and compassion, even when it was something more. The touch of His hand on the ghastly glossiness of the leper's skin was, no doubt, His assertion of priestly functions, and of elevation above all laws of defilement; but what was it to the poor outcast, who for years had never felt the warm contact of flesh and blood? It always indicated that He Himself was the source of healing and life. It always exprest His identification of Himself with sorrow and sickness. So that it is in principle analogous to, and may be taken as illustrative of, that transcendent act whereby He became flesh, and dwelt among us. Indeed, the very word by which our Lord's taking the blind man by the hand is described in the chapter following our text is that employed in the Epistle to the Hebrews when, dealing with the true brotherhood of Jesus, the writer says, "He took not hold of angels, but of the seed of Abraham he taketh hold." Christ's touch is His willing contact with man's infirmities and sins, that He may strengthen and hallow.

And the lesson is one of universal application. Wherever men would help their fellows, this is a prime requisite, that the would-be helper should come down to the level of those whom he desires to aid. If we wish to teach, we must stoop to think the scholar's thoughts. The master who has forgotten his boyhood will have poor success. If we would lead to purer emotions, we must try to enter into the lower feelings which we labor to elevate. It is of no use to stand at the mouth of the alleys we wish to cleanse, with our skirts daintily gathered about us, and smelling-bottle in hand, to preach homilies on the virtue of cleanliness. We must go in among the filth, and handle it, if we want to have it cleared away. The degraded must feel that we do not shrink from them, or we shall do them no good. The leper, shunned by all, and ashamed of himself because everybody loathes him, hungers in his hovel for the grasp of a hand that does not care for defilement, if it can bring cleansing. Even in regard to common material helps the principle holds good. We are too apt to cast our doles to the poor like the bones to a dog, and then to wonder at what we are pleased to think men's ingratitude. A benefit may be so conferred as to hurt more than a blow; and we cannot be surprized if so-called charity which is given with contempt and a sense of superiority, should be received with a scowl, and chafe a man's spirit like a fetter. Such gifts bless neither him who gives nor him who takes. We must put our hearts into them, if we would win hearts by them. We must be ready, like our Master, to take blind beggars by the hand, if we would bless or help them. The despair and opprobrium of our modern civilization, the gulf growing wider and deeper between Dives and Lazarus, between Belgravia and Whitechapel, the mournful failure of legalized help, and of delegated efforts to bridge it over, the darkening ignorance, the animal sensuousness, the utter heathenism that lives in every town of England, within a stone's throw of Christian houses, and near enough to hear the sound of public worship, will yield to nothing but that sadly forgotten law which enjoins personal contact with the sinful and the suffering, as one chief condition of raising them from the black mire in which they welter.

The effect of much well-meant Christian effort is simply to irritate. People are very quick to catch delicate intonations which reveal a secret sense, "how much better, wiser, more devout I am than these people!" and wherever a trace of that appears in our work, the good of it is apt to be marred. We all know how hackneyed the charge of spiritual pride and Pharisaic self-complacency is, and, thank God, how unjust it often is. But averse as men may be to the truths which humble, and willing as they may be to assume that the very effort to present these to others on our parts implies a claim which mortifies, we may at least learn from the threadbare calumny, what strikes men about our position, and what rouses their antaganism to us. It is allowable to be taught by our enemies, especially when it is such a lesson as this, that we must carefully divest our evangelistic work of apparent pretensions to superiority, and take our stand by the side of those to whom we speak. We cannot lecture men into the love of Christ. We can but win them to it by showing Christ's love to them; and not the least important element in that process is the exhibition of our own love. We have a gospel to speak of which the very heart is, that the Son of God stooped to become one with the lowliest and most sinful; and how can that gospel be spoken with power unless we, too, stoop like Him?

We have to echo the invitation, "Learn of me, for I am lowly in heart"; and how can such divine words flow from lips into which like grace has not been poured? Our theme is a Savior who shrunk from no sinner, who gladly consorted with publicans and harlots, who laid His hand on pollution, and His heart, full of God and of love, on hearts reeking with sin; and how can our message correspond with our theme if, even in delivering it, we are saying to ourselves, "The temple of the Lord are we: this people which knoweth not the law is curst"? Let us beware of the very real danger which besets us in this matter, and earnestly seek to make ourselves one with those whom we would gather into Christ, by actual familiarity with their condition, and by identification of ourselves in feeling with them, after the example of that greatest of Christian teachers who became "all things to all men, that by all means he might gain some"; after the higher example, which Paul followed, of that dear Lord who, being highest, descended to the lowest, and in the days of His humiliation was not content with speaking words of power from afar, nor abhorred the contact of mortality and disease and loathsome corruption; but laid His hands upon death, and it lived; upon sickness, and it was whole; on rotting leprosy, and it was sweet as the flesh of a little child.

The same principle might be further applied to our Christian work, as affecting the form in which we should present the truth. The sympathetic identification of ourselves with those to whom we try to carry the gospel will certainly make us wise to know how to shape our message. Seeing with their eyes, we shall be able to graduate the light. Thinking their thoughts, and having in some measure succeeded, by force of sheer community of feeling, in having as it were got inside their minds, we shall unconsciously, and without effort, be led to such aspects of Christ's all-comprehensive truth as they most need. There will be no shooting over people's heads, if we love them well enough to understand them. There will be no toothless generalities, when our interest in men keeps their actual condition and temptations clear before us. There will be no flinging fossil doctrines at them from a height, as if Christ's blest gospel were, in another than the literal sense, "a stone of offense," if we have taken our place on their level. And without such sympathy, these and a thousand other weaknesses and faults will certainly vitiate much of our Christian effort.

We have here the true healing power and the consciousness of wielding it set forth in the Lord's authoritative word.

All the rest of His action was either the spontaneous expression of His true participation in human sorrow, or a merciful veiling of His glory that sense-bound eyes might see it the better. But the word was the utterance of His will, and that was omnipotent. The hand laid on the sick, the blind or the deaf was not even the channel of His power. The bare putting forth of His energy was all-sufficient. In these we see the loving, pitying man. In this blazes forth, yet more loving, yet more compassionate, the effulgence of manifest God. Therefore so often do we read the very syllables with which His "voice then shook the earth," vibrating through all the framework of the material universe. Therefore do the gospels bid us listen when He rebukes the fever, and it departs; when He says to the demons, "Go," and they go; when one word louder in its human articulation than the howling wind hushes the surges; when "Talitha cumi" brings back the fair young spirit from dreary wanderings among the shades of death. Therefore was it a height of faith not found in Israel when the Gentile soldier, whose training had taught him the power of absolute authority, as heathenism had driven him to long for a man who would speak with the imperial sway of a god, recognized in His voice an all-commanding power. From of old, the very signature of divinity has been declared to be "He spake, and it was done"; and He, the breath of whose lips could set in motion material changes, is that eternal Word, by whom all things were made.

What unlimited consciousness of sovereign dominion sounds in that imperative from His autocratic lips! It is spoken in deaf ears, but He knows that it will be heard. He speaks as the fontal source, not as the recipient channel of healing. He anticipates no delay, no resistance. There is neither effort nor uncertainty in the curt command. He is sure that He has power, and He is sure that the power is His own.

There is no analogy here between us and Him. Alone, fronting the whole race of man, He stands—utterer of a word which none can say after Him, possessor of unshared might, and of His fulness do we all receive. But even from that divine authority and solitary sovereign consciousness we may gather lessons not altogether aside from the purpose of our meeting here to-day. Of His fulness we have received, and the power of the word on His lips may teach us that of His word, even on ours, as the victorious certainty with which He spake His will of healing may remind us of the confidence with which it becomes us to proclaim His name.

His will was almighty then. Is it less mighty or less loving now? Does it not gather all the world in the sweep of its mighty purpose of mercy? His voice pierced then into the dull cold ear of death, and has it become weaker since? His word spoken by Him was enough to banish the foul spirits that run riot, swine-like, in the garden of God in man's soul, trampling down and eating up its flowers and fruitage; is the word spoken of Him less potent to cast them out? Were not all the mighty deeds which He wrought by the breath of His lips on men's bodies prophecies of the yet mightier which His Will of love, and the utterance of that Will by stammering lips, may work on men's souls. Let us not in our faint-heartedness number up our failures, the deaf that will not hear, the dumb that will not speak, His praise; nor unbelievingly say Christ's own word was mighty, but the word concerning Christ is weak on our lips. Not so; our lips are unclean, and our words are weak, but His word—the utterance of His loving will that men should be saved—is what it always was and always will be. We have it, brethren, to proclaim. Did our Master countenance the faithless contrast between the living force of His word when He dwelt on earth, and the feebleness of it as He speaks through His servant? If He did, what did He mean when He said, "He that believeth on me, the works that I do shall he do also, and greater works than these shall he do, because I go unto the Father"?

NORMAN MACLEOD

1812-1872

THE TRUE CHRISTIAN MINISTRY

BIOGRAPHICAL NOTE

NORMAN MACLEOD, the eminent Scotch preacher, was born at Campbeltown, in Argyleshire, in 1812. In his preaching he departed from the rigid conventionality of the Scottish Church. His large vision and broad culture gave unusual distinction both to his writings and to his pulpit oratory. He was conspicuous for philanthropic efforts, and frequently held evening services for workingmen. He distinguished himself by his popular Christian writing and by his pulpit oratory. He was practical and manly, of godly nature, with extreme adaptability, and greatly esteemed by Queen Victoria, who made him her chaplain in 1857. He died in 1872.

Neither pray I for these alone, but for them also which shall believe on me through their word;

That they all may be one; as thou, Father, art in me, and I in thee, that they also may be one in us; that the world may believe that thou hast sent me.
—John xvii., 20, 21.

"THESE words spake Jesus, and lifted up his eyes to heaven, and said, Father, the hour is come!" The hour was indeed come for which the whole world had been in travail since creation, and which was for ever to mark a new era in the history of the universe. The hour was come when, having finished the work given Him to do, He was to return to His Father, but only after ending His earthly journey along the awful path on which He was now entering, and which led through Gethsemane, the cross, and the grave. At such a moment in His life He lifted up His eyes in perfect peace, from the sinful and sorrowful world, to the heavens glorious in their harmony and soothing in their silence, and said, "Father!" One feels a solemn awe, as if entering the holy of holies, in seeking to enter into the mind of Christ as exprest in this prayer. Never were such words spoken on earth, never were such words heard in heaven. I ask no other evidence to satisfy my spirit that they are the truth of God than the evidence of their own light, revealing as it does the speaker as being Himself light and life, who verily came from God and went to God.

But let me in all reverence endeavor to express a few thoughts, as to the general meaning of this prayer, with reference more especially to that portion of it which I have selected as the subject of my discourse.

The one all-absorbing desire of our Lord, as here exprest—the ultimate end sought to be realized by Him—is that God might be glorified as a Father, and that by the world seeing His love revealed in sending His Son into the world to save sinners. "God is love," but "In this was manifested the love of God toward us, because that God sent his only-begotten Son into the world that we might live through him"—a love which, when spiritually seen and possest by us, is itself life eternal; for "This is life eternal that they might know thee, the only true God, and Jesus Christ, whom thou hast sent;" but "He that loveth not, knoweth not God; for God is love."

All "religion" accordingly, all good, all righteousness, peace, joy, glory, to man and to the universe, are bound up in this one thing, knowing God as a Father. Out of this right condition of love to God, must necessarily come our right condition towards man, that of love to man as a brother with special love, the love of character, to Christian brethren. Such a religion as this was never possest as an idea even by the greatest thinkers among the civilized heathen nations; far less was it realized by any. Whatever knowledge many had about God, they knew Him not as a Father to be loved and trusted, and therefore obeyed. When St. Paul addrest the Athenians, he could find such a thought exprest by a poet only, who had said, "We are also His offspring." It is only in the line of supernatural revelation of God to man, as given to and received by Abraham, "the friend," and perfected by Christ the Son, that this knowledge of God has been possest by man. But even among those to whom this true revelation was given about God, how few truly knew Him!

The want of this religion, whatever else might exist that was called by that name, was the complaint made by God against His people of old, "They do not know me!" "They proceed from evil to evil," He cries, for "they know not me, saith the Lord." "Through deceit they refuse to know me, saith the Lord;" and again: "Thus saith the Lord, Let not the wise man glory in his wisdom, neither let the mighty man glory in his might, let not the rich man glory in his riches; but let him that glorieth glory in this, that he understandeth and knoweth me, that I am the Lord which exercise loving-kindness, judgment, and righteousness, in the earth: for in these things I delight, saith the Lord." (Jer. ix., 23, 24.)

This was the sorrowing cry of Christ, "O righteous Father, the world hath not known thee!" This was His joy, "I have known thee, and these have known that thou hast sent me!"

But if Christ desired that His Father's name should be glorified, how was this to be accomplished? By what medium, or means? Now I would here observe that God's method of revealing Himself to man has ever been to do so by living men; and the Bible is a true record of such revelations in the past. Christianity is not the philosophy of life, but life itself; and is a revelation, not of abstract truth, but of the living personal God to living persons as His children, whom He hath created to glorify and enjoy Him for ever. The first grand medium of this revelation is the eternal Son of God. The very essence of God's character being love, He did not exist from all eternity with a mere capacity of loving, but without an object to love; like an eye capable of seeing light, but with no light to see. The object of His love was His Son,

who from all eternity responded to that love and rejoiced in His Father. This eternal Son, when manifested in the flesh, revealed His Father directly, so that He could say, in all He was, and in all He did, and, in a true sense, in all He suffered, "He that hath seen me, hath seen the Father;" and men could say of Him, "We beheld His glory, the glory as of the only-begotten of the Father, full of grace and truth;" "The glory of God" was "in the face of Jesus Christ." Again, He had also, as the Son of Man, glorified His Father; and, by His reverence for, confidence in, and obedience to, Him, and by His joy in Him, had indirectly revealed what he knew God to be to Him and to all as a Father. "I have glorified Thee on the earth: I have finished the work which Thou gavest me to do." Such was His finished work. But something more was yet to be accomplished. Ere He descends to Gethsemane, He desires anew to have the joy of revealing a Father's heart by revealing to the world His own heart of love as a Son to that Father. Hence His prayer, "Glorify thy Son, that thy Son also may glorify thee." He does not prescribe the new circumstances in which His long-tried and perfect filial confidence and love as a Son were to be manifested. With the absolute consecration of true sonship He leaves these circumstances to be determined by His Father. Now, as on the cross, He commits His spirit, as a little child, into His Father's hands. He desires only that in any way, by any means, He may have the joy of showing forth the reality, the endurance, and the triumph of His Sonship. His Father may fill His cup according to His own will, the Son will drink it. The Father may permit a crown of thorns to be placed on His brow, and every conceivable horror of great darkness from the hate of men and devils to be cast over Him like a funeral-pall; He may be rejected by all His brethren and by the Church and by the State —"Amen!" He cries. Let His body be broken and His blood shed, He will give thanks! One thing only He prays for, "Glorify thy Son, that thy Son also may glorify thee!" As a further end to be accomplished, He prays that He may have the joy of making others share the same divine love and joy, and therefore adds, "As thou hast given him power over all flesh, that he should give eternal life to as many as thou hast given him. And this is life eternal, that they might know thee, the only true God, and Jesus Christ, whom thou hast sent."

But while He as the Son was to be the first revealer of God the Father, He was not, therefore, to be the only revealer. He was the first-born of many brethren in whom the same love was to be reproduced, and by whom the same high duty was to be performed. If the light of the glory of God shone directly in the face of Jesus Christ, that light was to be transmitted to those who were to shine as lights in the world, that others seeing them might glorify the same God. For now, as ever, God in a real sense manifests Himself in the flesh. Hence our Lord's desire that His brethren should, as sons, reveal the Father, like Himself the Son. He says accordingly, "As thou hast sent me into the world, even so have I also sent them into the world." Sent whom? Not apostles only, but those also who should believe through their word; not ministers of the Church only, but members also; all, in short, who were qualified to convince the world that God was a Father, by convincing it of this truth, that God had sent His Son to save sinners—the "faithful saying, worthy of all acceptation."

But the question is further suggested, What is this qualification? What is this which men must possess in order to accomplish Christ's purpose of inducing the world to believe? What is this evidence of Christianity which they are to present to the eyes of unbelieving men, by seeing which these are to know and glorify God as their Father in Christ? We reply, it is the oneness of those who are to be ambassadors from God and fellow-workers with Christ. "I pray for them," He says, and not for them only, but "for them also who shall believe on me through their word; that they all may be one; as thou, Father, art in me, and I in thee, that they may be one in us; that the world may believe that thou hast sent me."

Now this leads me to consider more particularly the nature of this oneness which is essential for such a successful mission as will convince the world of the truth of Christ's mission from the Father. What is meant by this oneness, or this union?

We are guided in our inquiry by three features which characterize it. First, It is a oneness such as subsists between Christ and God; secondly, It is a oneness which can be seen or appreciated; thirdly, It is a oneness which is calculated from its nature to convince the world of the truth of Christ's mission.

Now there are many kinds of union among men, which, however wonderful or excellent, may be set aside as obviously not fulfilling these conditions, and not such, therefore, as Christ prayed for. There is, e. g., the unity of an army which marches as one man, implicitly obeying its commander even unto death and without a question. Yet, however grand this is, and however illustrative of the character of good soldiers of Jesus Christ, it does not fulfil the conditions specified. Nor does the wonderful unity of a State, which makes and imposes laws, proclaims war or peace, administers justice, and executes its judgments. In neither case is there any union

such as subsists betwixt God and Christ; nor such as is in any sense adapted to convince the world that God has sent His Son to save sinners. The same may be alleged of any outward and visible unity of a body of men which might be called a Church. Its organization might be as wonderful, and its members as disciplined, and its power as remarkable, as those of an army; it might be held together like a state by its laws and its enactments, its rewards and punishments, and might energetically advance until it possess the dominion of the world, and attracted such attention as that all men might marvel at it; its members might assent to all the details of a creed however large; the same rights and ceremonies and modes of worship might be repeated throughout all its parts; and it might be able to continue its organized existence from age to age,—yet it would by no means follow that any such system, however remarkable, possest that inward spiritual unity desired in Christ's prayer, no more than the compact unity of Brahminism does, nor the still more extraordinary unity of Buddhism, with its temples, its priesthood, its creed, its rites and ceremonies, continuing unchanged during teeming centuries, and dominating over hundreds of millions of the human race. May not all these and many similar unities be fully and satisfactorily accounted for by principles in human nature, altogether irrespective of the fact of a supernatural power having come into the world to which their origin or continuance is owing? For there is a oneness in the churchyard as well as in the church. There might be a oneness of assent amongst a deaf multitude with regard to the beauty of music, because determined by the fiat of authority, but not as the result of hearing and of taste; and the same kind of oneness of judgment as to the beauty of pictures, on the part of those who were blind. Unity alone proves nothing, apart from its nature and its origin.

There is but one kind of unity or oneness which fulfils the specified conditions, and that is, oneness of character or of spiritual life—in one word, the oneness of love;—for this is the highest condition of a personal spirit. It is such love as God had and has to Christ; "That the love wherewith thou has loved me may be in them;" such love as the Son has to the Father, and such as He manifested to His disciples that very evening when, conscious of His divine glory, and "knowing that he was come from God, and went to God," He girded Himself with a towel and washed His disciples' feet. Hence the declaration, "The glory," that is, of character, "which thou gavest me I have given them, that they," through its possession, "may be one, even as we are one: I in them, and thou in me." Hence again His saying, "They are not of the world, even as I am not of the world;'' and His prayer, ''I pray not that thou shouldst take them out of the world, but that thou shouldst keep them from the evil.'' Such love as this, when in the soul of ordinary men, does not originate in their own hearts, however naturally benevolent or affectionate these may be. Our Lord in this prayer recognizes it as inseparable from faith in His own teaching, and from personal conviction of the truth which they themselves were to preach; for they had received His words, and had ''known surely that I came out from thee, and they have believed that thou didst send me''; and so He prays, ''Sanctify them through thy truth; thy word is truth.''

Now, if we would divide, as with a prism, this pure light of love, we might discern it as being composed, as it were, of at least two colors, or features—first, love to God, exprest in the desire that He should be known; secondly, love to man, exprest in self-sacrifice that all should share this true love. But these very features we discern as first existing in God the Father and in Christ the Son; for God desires, from the necessity of His own nature, that He should be known, and that all His rational creatures should see the glory of His character, and, in seeing it, should live. God has also manifested His love, according to the law of love, by giving and by self-sacrifice, inasmuch as He ''spared not his own Son, but delivered him up for us all.'' In like manner, the Son desired that His Father might be known, and to accomplish this He became incarnate. He has manifested His love also in the form of self-sacrifice, in that His whole life and death were an offering up of Himself as a sacrifice unto God, and as an atonement for the sins of the world, in order that all men might be made partakers of His own eternal life in God. This, too, is the ''mind'' of the Holy Spirit, for He glorifies the Son, that the Son may glorify the Father, and glorifies Him in and by His true Church. Hence, wherever true love exists in man, it will manifest itself in these two forms; it will ever desire that God may be known, and will never ''seek its own,'' but sacrifice itself that this end may be attained. In such oneness as this of mind, spirit, character—in one word, love—there is realized the first condition of that oneness for which our Lord prayed.

Secondly, This unity of character fulfils the second condition in its being such as the world can in some degree see and appreciate. Blind as the world is, it can see love in the form of self-sacrifice at least, seeking its good, even tho it may not at once see in this a revelation of such love as has its origin in the love of God to man. The world's heart can perceive more things and greater things than can its intellect. The child of the statesman or man of science may not be able to comprehend the world-politics of the one or the scientific discoveries of the other; but it can see and feel the love revealed in the glance of the eye, in the smile on the lips, or in the arms that clasp it to the bosom; and in seeing this, it sees an infinitely greater thing than the politics of the one or the scientific discoveries of the other. It sees, too, in this, tho unconsciously, the love of the Father's heart which fills the universe with glory, even as its eye, when opened to a little light, sees the same light which illumines a thousand worlds. And thus can the world see the light of love. Those who are in prison, in nakedness, or in thirst, are quite able to see and to appreciate the love that, for Christ's sake, visits them, clothes them, and gives them drink. The wretched lepers in the lazar-house, into which no one could enter and ever return to the world, could see and appreciate the love of the Moravian missionary who visited them, and who shut the door for ever between him and all he knew and loved, that he might share and alleviate the horrors of his wretched brethren whom he loved more than all. Blind as the world is, it can see this or nothing; bad as it is, it can appreciate this goodness or none.

Thirdly, Such a character is calculated also to convince the world that God has sent Christ to save sinners. Observe again what is our Lord's idea of the mission which was to convert the world; it is this, that those whom He sends, even as God had sent Himself, whether as apostles or as disciples, should give to their fellow men what they have first received from their living Head, Jesus Christ. They were to give ''the words'' which they received from Him, and which He had received from God— they were to give ''the truth'' which they received from Him, and which He Himself had glorified in His life and death, that God had sent Him to be the Savior of the world. They were also to manifest that life which they had received from Him, and which He had received from God, and which in them was the necessary result of their faith. Now, it is in the seeing of this life in those who proclaim the truth that the truth itself appears worthy of all acceptation, and that God verily, who has sent His Son to save sinners, is love. It is thus, you perceive, that the mission of the Church, whether of its ministers or its members, is not only to preach glad tidings, but to show their reality in their actual results; not only to preach salvation, but to preach it by saved men; not only to preach eternal life, but to preach it by those who possess it; not only to preach about a Father, but to reveal also that Father through His regenerated sons, who themselves know and love Him. Further, the idea of a Church is that of a society whose members are united through faith in the same truth, and are in possession of the same life. Such a society necessarily springs out of faith and love, and its members cannot choose but unite outwardly because united inwardly. Our Lord assumes its future existence and provides for its continuance. A Church realizing Christ's ideal would, therefore, possess, as its creed this, at least, of believing Christ's words, and the truth that "God had sent his Son to be the Savior of the world." For "every spirit that confesseth not that Christ hath come in the flesh is not of God." "And whosoever shall confess that Jesus is the Son of God, God dwelleth in him, and he in God." Its initiatory sacrament, that of baptism, does but express the nature of this society—viz., that its members are the children of God the Father through Christ the Son, and by the indwelling of the Holy Spirit—their character being a spiritual baptism into the possession of "God's name," which is "love."

Another characteristic of it is their possession of that eternal life which is exprest as well as maintained by the "communion" in which its members meet together as brethren, their bond of union being a common union with God in Christ and one another, through the constant partaking of Him, the living bread; eating His flesh and drinking His blood —that is, His whole life of self-sacrifice and love becoming a part of their very being. Worship in spirit and in truth is also necessarily involved in the idea of such a society; and I might add, worship, not from a command merely, but as a necessary result of spiritual character, becoming in a true sense "infallible" as to religion; but religion in this sense,—that of knowing God because of its members being able to say, "We know that he dwelleth in us, and we in him, because he hath given us his Spirit, and we know and testify that he sent his Son to be the Savior of the world." Such a Church would likewise, in a true sense, have an apostolical succession— that is, a succession of teachers and members who had the apostolic spirit, or the oneness as described by our Lord; for it would be able, from its possessing the Spirit of God, to discern those who were like-minded, and to select such as were specially fitted for the work of the ministry. This is the ideal of the Church.

But has such a Church been realized? Has there ever been a visible organized body of men who carried out this sublime purpose? Once, indeed, there was. For we perceive, more or less clearly, all these features in the early Church when it had received the Spirit on the day of Pentecost, and when its members met together and "had all things in common," and manifested such sonship towards God, and brotherhood towards each other; and sent forth everywhere its public minister and its members also to bring men into the same blessed unity. But supposing the ideal had no

more been realized since that time than God's ideal as described by Moses had been fully realized in the Jewish Church;—yet must the ideal, nevertheless, be ever kept before the spiritual eye. For we do not produce high art by keeping a low rather than a high standard before the artist; neither can we reach to great things in the Church unless we keep a high standard before its members. It is unnecessary here to inquire how it came to pass that the Church, to such a great extent, lost this ideal as one visible society, and became so corrupt as to substitute innumerable vain appearances of spiritual realities for that which alone could satisfy a true and righteous God. But as things now are, the "Church" is broken up into various "churches" or societies, striving more or less to realize the ideal. Each society does so just in proportion as it is able to carry out our Lord's purpose as to its ministry being one in faith, believing Christ's words, in its knowing truly that He came from God to save sinners, and in its seeking, from love to God and man, to make all men know their Father, in the knowledge of whom is salvation.

But to confine myself to our own particular duties, let me remind you, fathers and brethren, of our high calling as profest ministers of Christ's Church. The cry of earnest souls, weary of their many burthens, unsatisfied with their husks, conscious of being in a distant land, and finding nothing which men can give to allay their hungering and thirsting, is this: "Show us the Father, and it sufficeth us!" Now supposing an earnest spirit, seeking after the Father, comes to us as His profest ministers in order to discover the truth of what we preach, he might very naturally say, "You preach to me a Savior who came a long time ago into the world professing to save sinners, and you tell me that He is coming again at some future period to judge the world and to bestow salvation upon many; but I want to know whether there is a Savior now; or is it all empty space between that past and that future? You tell me about salvation from the suffering of sin; I ask, 'Is there salvation from sin itself, without which I feel there can be no deliverance from suffering'? You tell me about a medicine that is an infallible cure for 'this ineradicable taint of sin,' and describe the terrible consequences of the disease to me if I be not cured, and the blessed results of joyous spiritual health and peace; but 'Can you show me any person who has actually been restored from disease to health by this divine medicine'? Is all this preaching a mere idle theory of life? Or if not, where is the life itself? Art thou thyself saved? If not— 'physician, heal thyself'; for until then thou canst not cure me." But suppose, further, that this same person comes into close contact with the mind of the preacher, and that the more he sees and knows it the more he discerns in the man such thoughts regarding God, such a knowledge of Him, such a love to Him, as convince him that here at least is a reality and not a pretense; suppose that the more he discerns his whole inner life, the things which give him pain and joy, the things which he desires and loves, with his whole feelings towards his fellow-men—feelings expressed in a life of action, which, in spite of infirmities and shortcomings belonging to all human beings, the questioner cannot but recognize as a kind of life he never saw before—a life, too, which commends itself, from what it is, as being the most real and the most satisfactory to reason, conscience, and heart: can anything, I ask, be more calculated to convince him of the account which its possessor gives him as to its origin, when he says, "The life I now live in the flesh, I live by faith in the Son of God, who loved me, and gave himself for me." "It is a faithful saying, and worthy of all acceptation, that Christ came into the world to save sinners, of whom I am the chief." What then? What else must be the result of such a vision of true life than the conviction that God is our Father and that God is love, because it is evident from observation as well as from testimony that He hath sent His Son to save men, not in the past only, but to save them now—not to save only those who are called "good," but to save those who are the chief of sinners? If a man truly believes all this, then does he know God, and in so doing possesses eternal life. But more than this, how will his convictions be deepened if, in searching for others who may have the same life, and if, tho failing to discover any one visible body of Christians that show it forth in the unity of the Spirit and in the bond of peace, he is yet able to satisfy himself that there have been, during the last eighteen centuries, and that there are now, in every church, in every land, among all races of men, among those of different temperaments, different culture, and amidst a variety of all possible outward circumstances, men with like passions as himself, who have faith in the same Lord, and are thereby possest of a true love of God and of one another—how will this, I say, deepen in him the conviction that God is a Father, because a Savior, who "gave his Son, not that any should perish, but that all should possess everlasting life?" Will he not be thus led to "believe the record that God has given us eternal life, and that this life is in his Son?" I am persuaded that a man of the highest intellectual culture and the greatest learning, earnestly searching after God and Christ, and the truth of Christianity, would be more convinced of the love of the one as manifested in the truth of the other, by coming into contact with one true soul which, without perhaps intellectual culture or

learning, yet truly loved God and man, than he would be by all the volumes on the evidence of Christianity ever written, without such a spiritual vision of a holy life.

On the other hand, supposing that no such evidence of the truth of Christianity could be discovered in the preacher of Christianity; nay, if his character contradicted his preaching; if, while he preached love to God and man, he manifested neither, but indifference, to say the least of it, to both; if, while he preached the necessity and the excellence of the Christian life, he himself revealed its very opposite—what effect would this have upon an earnest spirit, but that Christianity was a mere ideal system unsuited to the world, a philosophy of life that might be believed in, but not a life itself that might be possest?

This want of personal character, however imperfect, yet real, may account for the want of success in the mission of the Church to convince the world, whether at home or abroad. We may give religion but not godliness; the means of grace, as they are called, but not the grace seen and exprest in the living man. We would thus hear of Christianity without seeing it; hear about the love of God, and the love of Christ as a Savior, without being convinced even by those who send missionaries to India, who, altho they may individually reveal this life, yet how often are looked upon as mere official teachers; while the "Christians" from "Christendom" may, in coming into contact with the heathen, show by their denial of Christianity that it is a matter for the priesthood, not for all men; a book theology, but not an actual power working in humanity: and of such persons it may be said that they have profaned God's great name among the heathen.

And this, too, may also account for the secret of success by many a minister of whom the world knows nothing: "For greatest minds are those of whom the noisy world hears least." They may not be great in the ordinary sense of the word—great as thinkers, great as orators, or great in the possession of any remarkable gifts; but they are nevertheless great in the kingdom of heaven; great because little children—great in meekness, in patience, in humility, in love of God and man, and who carry this music in their heart, "through dusky land and wrangling mart." What is the secret of their power? What but an eternal reality! the reality of a godly, godlike life obtained from God, and sustained by God, and seen in the eye, felt in the hand, heard in the words—a light of life which shines beside many a dying bed in many a home of sorrow, as well as in the pulpit. This is a kind of life whose biography will be written with the tears of the grateful orphan and widow, and of many a saved soul which remembers its possessor as its spiritual father. Such a ministry as this can no more fail than the love of God which gives it birth. Let us thank God, therefore, that such a secret power as this is within the reach of us all. We may not be men of talent, and for that we are not responsible; but we may be good men because little children towards God, and for that we are responsible: "I thank thee, heavenly Father, that thou hast hid these things from the wise and prudent, and revealed them unto babes."

And now, fathers and brethren, such is our high calling, to proclaim the glad tidings that God has sent Christ into the world to save sinners. Our chief authority for doing this is that we know it to be true; and if so, no one can deprive us of the high privilege and joy of proclaiming it. A glorious work is thus given us to do; we are ambassadors for God, beseeching men to be reconciled to Him, and we are fellow-workers with our Lord Himself. But this involves a great responsibility, corresponding to the greatness of our calling. For it is at once a glorious and a tremendous thought that Christ perils the chief evidence of the truth of Christianity, not upon what we say, but more upon what we are; and what we are is neither more nor less than what God knows us to be. Our preaching may, nevertheless, fail in some cases to convince the world, as it has done before; for the glory of Christ Himself was not seen by Judas. Indeed the light of life, when it shines, requires the single eye to see it. But in so far as the ministry of men, as an instrumentality, can convince the world, let our ministry be such as is calculated according to Christ's purpose to produce this result. Let it consist of those who can say, "We know whom we have believed." "We know and believe the love that God hath to us." "We testify that he sent his Son to be the Savior of the world."

But I must bring my sermon to a close.

Pardon me, my brethren, if I have appeared to address you in any other spirit than that of one who would with you confess his sins and shortcomings, and lament with shame and sorrow how much time and power have been lost never to be regained; how many gifts and noble opportunities have been neglected and perverted through unbelief and sloth, which might have been used for our own good and that of our fellow-men. Verily the day is far spent with many of us, and the night is near in which no man can work. Whatever our hands find to do must be done now or never. Let us pray that the living Spirit of God, given to all who seek Him, and whose work it is to glorify the Son, may take of His things and show them to our souls, and open our spiritual eye to see the glory of God in the face of Christ, so that we may be changed into the same glory. May we strive to keep the unity of the Spirit in the bond of peace, and be enabled so to preach and so to live that the world may be convinced, by what it sees and hears, of the reality of the love of God the Father in giving us and all men eternal life through Jesus Christ His Son! May He who makes us sons of God enable us, as sons, to be glorified in the perfection and revelation of our characters, so that with our elder Brother we may glorify His Father and our Father!

And now, to Father, Son and Holy Ghost, one God, be glory, dominion, and praise for evermore. Amen!

WILLIAM C. MAGEE

1821-1891

THE MIRACULOUS STILLING OF THE STORM

Lord save us: we perish. . . . Then he arose, and rebuked the winds and the sea; and there was a great calm.—Matt. viii., 25, 26.

THE story of this miracle reveals to us Christ entering into peril together with His Church. It records for us her faith and her prayer. It reveals to us His presence and His power. That faith has been her faith, that prayer has been her prayer, from that hour until now. In all the long perilous voyage of the Church from that hour, never has she unlearned yet her first prayer; never has she become entirely unconscious of her Lord. Sometimes with a great and a fearless faith that defied the most terrible tempests, sometimes with a little and a timid faith, that shrank from the first ripple upon the deep, but ever with her real faith have Christ's Church and Christ's disciples turned in the hour of their tribulation to seek their Lord. And never has that prayer been said in vain. Never from the Church at large, or from the solitary disciple in his terror, has that prayer gone up without an answer. Never has the eye of faith sought, and sought in vain, the Savior. Ever has the praying Church or the praying disciple found the still present Christ; and we believe that it is so now. We believe that Christ our Lord is here in the midst of us now, and that our eye of faith may see Him, and our prayer of faith may reach Him. And if this be so now—if Christ's presence be a real fact amongst us now, and our prayer have really a might to reveal that presence—then, above all things, it concerns us, that we understand the nature of that prayer, and the manner of that presence, that we understand what it is we mean, and what will come of it when we say: "Lord, save us, or we perish."

We ask you, then, to-night, brethren, to consider these two things: the meaning of the Church's prayer; the manner of her Lord's presence. Now, when we use these words: "Lord, save: we perish," we are really rehearsing two articles of our belief. We are declaring, first of all, that we believe there is a Lord —that in the visible world there is an invisible God with His overruling, and controlling, and appointing will; and, in the next place, we believe that this God is our Lord Jesus Christ. In the first of these, we Christians agree with every religion that ever has been. In the second, we differ from all other religions. When we say that above nature there is a will and a personality, we say what every religion says. Religion is nothing else than the belief in the supernatural, in something above nature, in a person, in a will; and prayer is nothing but the speech of our spirit to that will, and the submission of our will to it. Prayer is the effort of the spirit of man to rise above the visible up to the region of the invisible and the personal, there to speak out his care or his need. There can, therefore, be no prayer without this element of religion; and there can be no religion without this fact of prayer. Without it, you have philosophy, you may have sentiment; but you cannot have a real, practical, every-day religion. And, therefore, all religions have believed in a God or gods, a Lord or lords. Turk, Jew, heathen, in like case, would have said to some lord or other: "Save, or we perish." But the Christian believes something more. He believes that his Lord has come down amongst men; that He has taken to Him human flesh, and lived a human life, and died, and risen again, for his salvation. He worships not only a lord, but the incarnate Lord; and so the Church speaks her twofold faith in her great hymn from the first to Christ as God: "We praise Thee, O God; we acknowledge Thee to be the Lord"—Thee, and none other, to be the God, and Thee to be the Lord, and Ruler, and Master of all things. You see, then, that there is something different in Christian prayer from all other prayer and worship, and that the difference consists in this: that it is distinctively and avowedly the prayer to an incarnate Christ.

Now, if there be this difference between this prayer and all other prayer, then there must be a corresponding difference in the feelings and in the practical results of such a religion; and I am about to ask you now to follow me while I endeavor to trace for you this difference between Christian prayer and all other prayer. It seems as if the story in the gospel of this miracle exactly sets out this difference—exactly shows us the distinctive nature of Christian prayer. The story, you observe, divides itself, naturally, into three parts. There is, first of all, the voyage before the storm; there is, then, the storm; and there is, then, the miraculous stilling of the storm. Now, you observe that in each of these three parts, we have one thing in common. We have man, in some way or other, encountering, or encountered by, the outward and visible world. The third of these—the stilling of the storm—differs from the other two in this, that it is miraculous and supernatural. Now, let us, for a moment, leave out this third part. There are some, you know, who say, that we should always leave it out, and be better without it. Let us leave out, then, this third or miraculous part of the story; and let us contrast the first and the second parts. And what have we got? We have got a most re-markable contrast between the two scenes. What is it we see in the first scene? We see a man subduing nature. It was by the knowledge of the elements and the laws of nature, that man learned thus to sail upon the deep; and in that one fact you have represented for you the whole of the material progress of humanity—all the triumphs of science, all the glory and the beauty of art, all that marvelous mastery that man obtains by his inventive and creative will over the secret powers of nature, as he unlocks them one by one, and compels her to tell him her deepest mysteries—all that man has done as he has advanced from horizon to horizon of discovery, finding still new worlds to conquer, until we stand amazed at our own progress and the infinity of it, and we say of man: "What manner of being is this, that even the winds and the sea obey him?" Yes, there is the man the lord of nature. There is nothing supernatural there. All is natural, all is orderly. Man is lord and master. Nature is man's servant; and, therefore, there seems no room, there seems no need for prayer. There is nothing, seemingly, there to be had for the asking; there is everything, seemingly, there to be had for working. Man is to be seen walking in the garden of his own planting and his own fencing; and he reaches out hands to unforbidden fruits of knowledge; and he believes that at last he shall gather even of the tree of life. He is a god unto himself, and he sees no need for prayer.

And now we turn to the second scene, and what have we there? We have the direct contrast with this scene. We have there, not man subduing nature, but nature subduing man. We have the storm in which the elements are man's masters and not his servants; and he that one minute before was the boasting lord of nature is its toy and its sport. The very foam upon the crest of those billows is not more helpless in the grasp of the elements than the lord and the king of them; and they toss him to and fro, as the wind drives the stubble in the autumn. This is the terrible aspect of nature. This is nature in her might, and in her majesty, and in her pitilessness, and in her capriciousness—when nature seems everything, and man, in her awful presence, dwindles and dwarfs into very nothingness —when man, in the presence of the vastness of her solitude, and the might of her storms, and the terror of her earthquakes, seems no more before her, with his little cares and his sorrows, than the wee bubbles upon the head of the cataract. This is nature as she masters man. Is it, then, any wonder that, in the early struggles of mankind with this terrible visible power of the creature, men came to worship the creature—that they ascribed to every one of these powers a divinity, that in the voice of the wind, and in the roar of the sea, and in the raging of the fire, they saw the signs of a divine presence, and they said to these elements: "Spare us," or "Save us, or else we perish"? And so all creation became peopled with gods—cruel gods, capricious gods, vengeful gods, gods whom men bribed with blood, gods whom, even while they bribed them, they could not love, and did not believe that they loved them. This is the first and most terrible form of creature worship; this was the idolatry of the heathen. But mark this, that such a worship as this could not continue forever, could not continue long, because it is the worship of ignorance; it is the belief in the supernatural, only because it confuses the unknown with the supernatural. Ever as science advances must this faith melt away. Ever must the domain of the known push itself forward into the domain of the unknown. Ever does the man of science take one by one the gods of the man of superstition and break them upon their pedestals, and tell him this: "What you worship is no god. What you worship is no lord. It is not your lord. It is a servant of yours; and I class it in this or that rank of your servants." So, one by one, like ghosts and fantoms in the dawning of the day—one by one, the fantoms of gods that haunted the night of the old world vanish before the dawn of knowledge. But then it is a terrible daylight that breaks on men—a blank, dreary world in which men have no sight of the invisible, no sense of the supernatural. It is that last and most terrible aspect of nature, when she appears, not as many gods, or many wills, but as the great soulless piece of mechanism, of which we are only part—a terrible machinery in which we are, somehow or other, involved, and in the presence of which the sense of our free-will leaves us. The pith, and the manhood, and the vigor of men, and the beauty and the freedom of their life die out of them as they stand appalled before this passionless, this terrible, this awful face of a soulless world. This is the last and the most terrible form of creature worship. And mark this, that between these two aspects of nature, if you have no assured faith, there is no logical resting-place. Without the act of faith, you must take your choice between the superstition of ignorance or the atheism of knowledge.

And now we have seen these, we turn to the third portion of our story; and what is that we see there? We see, again, in this world of men, the miraculous and the supernatural. We hear a prayer, and we see a miracle. In the face of the might of nature and the terrors of her elements there arises up a Man in answer to man's cry—there is heard a Man's voice, which is yet the voice of God; and it rebukes the winds and the sea, and the elements of nature own their real Lord; and

immediately there is a great calm. What is it, then, that we see? We see a miracle, and a miracle that answers to prayer; we see the living spirits of living men, in the hour of their agony and their distress, appealing from nature to the God of nature; and we have recorded the answer of God to man's prayer. The answer is, that God is Lord both of man and of nature; and we say, therefore, that the miracle, and the miracle alone, sufficiently justifies the prayer. We say that the reason why men may pray is, and can only be, that they know and believe, that there is a will which rules the visible. If you have not this belief, then believe us that all prayer, whatever men may say about it, is an unreality and a miserable mockery. To what am I to pray if I see no living God to pray to? Am I to pray to a law? Am I to pray to a system? Am I to pray to the winds, or to the waves, as men prayed of old? Am I to pray for physical blessings and deliverances? Men tell us we are not to pray, or to give thanks, concerning the rain or fruitful seasons, for that science has told us that the supernatural has no place there. Am I to pray then (for men do tell me that I may pray) only for spiritual and for moral gifts? Am I to pray only to be made wise, and good, and pure, and true, and holy? Ah! science is beginning to meet us there, too; for she is telling us, and telling us loudly, and telling us shamelessly, that here, too, there is no room, so far as she can tell, for prayer, as our mind is but a part of our body, and that our spiritual condition is a necessary result of our past history and of our present temperament—that we are what we are by virtue of birth and education, and country, and clime, and other things over which we have no control. And so the very spirit of man, all that is left of the invisible, vanishes before the approach of science. The knife of the anatomist lays bare, as he tells you, the secrets of man's being; and he finds no soul—he finds only the gray matter of the brain and the white threads of the nerves; and this is all that is left. Then, if we are not to pray, may we at least praise? Men say that if it is a folly to pray, at least it is a wisdom to praise; and they tell us this is the sentimental theory of the modern gospel. They tell you: "You may not pray,—prayer has no place in our system,—but you may praise; you may lift up your heart in hymns of joy and gratitude to the great Father of your being; you may have festival and flower-crowned processions in honor of the Supreme Being; yes, you may in fine weather, when you are sailing over summer seas, and the pleasant summer wind is filling the sails of your bark, and is wafting sweet odors from the flower-crowned shores along which youth, and hope, and joy are passing—then you may lift up your hearts in thanks to the Father that gave all these, if you do not forget it. But how is it in foul weather? How is it when the sky above us darkens, and the white crests of the waves beneath us are swelling sharp and fierce, and the jagged edges of the rocks are projecting for our shipwreck, and the wild waste of the waters is yawning below us, and we tremble and shudder at their depths, and the wild wind blows our prayer back into our bosoms—is that the time to sing sentimental hymns to our great supreme Father and Giver of all good? It is a time (thank God, thank Christ, for this) when the Christian, when the disciple of Christ, may hold fast his faith and say, "Tho he slay me, yet will I trust in him"; but it is not a time when the deist has breath to sing his hymns to the supreme Author of his being. No, we believe that there is a miracle that justifies, and alone justifies prayer. We know that there are those (and they are good and wise men, many of them) who contrive nice adjustments and philosophical explanations how prayer may be reconciled with universal law. We do not greatly care for these. They may be right; they may be wrong. In some future state and higher condition of our being we may know how far they are true, how far they are false; but, meanwhile, we need not be too nervously anxious to make room for almighty God to work His own will in His own world. We believe in the miracle of creation; we believe that there was once a voice that said, "Let there be light, and there was light"; we believe that at the sound of that voice the universe leapt into life; and we believe in the miracle of the Incarnation, when God took human flesh and dwelt amongst men; we believe in the miracle of the descent of the Spirit of God, when, with the miraculous sound of the rushing wind and the miraculous gleam of the fire, God once more came down to dwell amongst men; we believe in the miracles that are written for us in this Book, were they ten times as many as they are; we believe that the sea has stood on one side like a wall, and that the waters have gushed forth from the rock; we believe that bread has been rained from heaven; we believe that a touch has awakened the dead—we believe all this; and, because we believe it, we believe the voice when it says to us, "Pray"; and because we hear that voice still amongst us, and because we know it to be the same voice, we say, as we hear it, "Lord, save, or we perish."

But still, in the last place, it may be said to us: If you do believe that there is this power of miracle amongst you still, and that it will answer to your prayer, why is it that we do not see more miracles than we do? Why is not the world filled with strange miracles every day, considering the infinite number of men's needs, and the infinite number of human prayers? My brethren, it does seem to me that if we were merely deists, and did not believe in Christ, it would be difficult for us to answer this objection. The spirit of man has, however (thanks be to God for it), in all ages been deeper and truer in its instincts than his mere logical power. Even the deist (and we thankfully acknowledge it), tho inconsistently and illogically, yet really and truly prays. For us Christians there is not any difficulty. There is that difference in our prayer of which I spoke. To whom is it that we pray? Not merely to the invisible Lord or Creator of the past, but to the incarnate Lord of the present. We believe that Christ our Lord, to whom we pray, took flesh and dwelt amongst us, and we believe that He did so that He might work the greatest of all miracles—the salvation of the souls of men; and we believe that He wrought it by dying and by living again. We believe that He established in the world this great and miraculous law, that it is possible out of death to bring life—nay, that death is the way to life. If this be so, that by His death life was purchased for us, then He teaches us that there is another life than this, and that there is another death and a deeper death than that we fear; and He tells us, it may be, that even by dying we shall be saved, that He will not always save us from death—nay, that He may save us by death. And so it comes to pass that we understand how, by losing life, we may miraculously save it; and yet, on the other hand, by trying to save life, we may naturally lose it. So we come to understand this fact, how the beginning of His kingdom was full of miracles, and how, in the history of His kingdom, miracles have since ceased. The kingdom began with miracles that He might teach us that He was able to save; the miracles ceased in order that He might work a greater miracle. The lesser miracle of ruling nature ceased in order that the greatest of all miracles might perpetually be wrought—the regeneration, the redemption, and the glorification of the nature of man. And so we understand that Christ our Lord, because He is our Lord, may save us, even while we seem to perish, and to perish in His presence. He saved us of old by His agony and bloody sweat, by His cross and passion; and He will save us now, and He does save every child of His. Through agony and sweating, through cross and passion—through the agony of our long nights of spiritual darkness, through the sweat of long days of sore trouble and labor, beneath the weight of sharp and heavy crosses and sorrow, and through the bitterness of spiritual or bodily passion, does Christ our Lord still save those who cry to Him, even while He seems to sleep and not to hear them, as, in the bitterness of their souls, thinking themselves Christ-forsaken, they cry,

"Our Christ, our Christ, why hast Thou forsaken us? Dost Thou sleep, Lord? Save us, or we perish." And so you understand the peculiarity, the blest and the glorious peculiarity, of our Christian prayer. You understand the meaning of those deep words of Scripture—patience and the faith of the saints. You understand how the Christian man may pray and wait, and wait and pray still. If prayer were always followed by a miraculous answer, then prayer would be easy enough; or, on the other hand, if there were no thought of an answer, then it might be possible, tho not easy, to submit ourselves to the inevitable. But to pray and not to receive an answer, and yet to believe that the very not receiving is an answer; to cry, "Save, or we perish," and to seem about to perish; to believe that in what seems perishing is really salvation; to look for the living and watchful Christ, and to see what seems only the living and regardless Christ, and yet to believe that the time will come when, at His word, there shall be a great calm—this is the patience, this is the faith of those who worship an incarnate Lord. And so we trace the history of Christ's Church, and so we strive to trace the history of our own lives. Comparatively easy it is to trace the Church's history along her voyage. The Church gives time for comparing events and testing faith; and so, believing still in the presence of her living Lord, the litanies of His Church ring out, as they have ever rung, clearly and loudly, and high above the roar of the tempest and the rushing of the waters, still the prayer is heard, "Good Lord, deliver us"; and still, again and again, as the storm sweeps by, and the Church passes out into calmer waters, still comes the voice of thanksgiving: "He hath delivered us." Even in our shorter voyage, are there none of us who can remember times when we have knelt in agony and wrestled in prayer with the Savior, who seemed to have forgotten us, when the mighty storm of temptation and the billows of calamity seemed about to destroy us, and when we have cried (oh, how men do cry in those storms of the soul, in those tempests and terrors of the heart, "Lord, save us, or we perish!" to Him to save us, and He has seemed to sleep and to refuse to save? But at the last we can remember how He did reveal Himself, not stilling the raging storm when we would have had Him still the terrible tempest, not sparing, it may be, the precious bark that we had rigged, and manned, and launched ourselves with trembling hopes and loving prayers, and watched with eyes tearless with agony, as we saw it about to sink before us; and we have been led to see and believe that the living and the loving Lord was answering even then our prayer, for the bark has, at length, entered that haven where we would be, and where the vexed waters of our voyage never awake a ripple on the calm depths of its eternal peace. This has been the experience of more than one of this great multitude that I see. And there is another experience that each one of you may have: it is when, in the troubles of your own spirit, when in the agonies of your own grief-stricken heart, when in the depths of your own repentance, when in the storms of your own fear and your own doubt, you cry to Christ the Savior—when you bring your sins as some men bring their sorrows, as anxious to have them removed as the others—when you cry to Christ your Savior: "Lord, save me, a sinner! Save me, an unprayerful man hitherto! Save me, an unbelieving man hitherto! Save me, not merely from the hell hereafter, but the present storm and depth of my own sins that threaten to destroy me! Save me, or I perish!" For, brethren, be sure of this, sooner or later this will be the experience of every such vexed and terrified soul—that, after he shall have endured, so long as his Lord sees good, the terrifying storm and the threatening deep that drive him in closer and closer search and seeking after his Lord, then, at last, there will appear the form of the Son of man, the form of Him who hung upon the cross, that He might for ever in the world's history work this great and, to Him, dearest of all miracles; and, at last, He will rebuke the winds and the waves in that troubled soul, and there will be a great calm—a calm that may not last for ever, a calm that will not last for ever, for we have not yet reached the haven of perfect rest, but a calm that is a foretaste of the eternal rest. And so, praying with all our hearts to Christ our Lord, setting our will in submission to His will, pouring out our spirit in prayer to His Spirit, laying bare our hearts before His pure and loving eyes, through calm and through storm, praying still that we suffer not death in either, that we neither rot in the calm nor founder in the storm, praying still for His presence, praying still for grace to realize that presence, crying still for that deeper and yet deeper faith which is the result of more and more constant experience, crying still, "Lord, save, or we perish," wait in patience and in faith until He shall send His last messenger in this world, His angel of death, and bid him for us and in His name rebuke for the last time the winds that have vexed us, and the waves that have terrified us, and then with Him for ever there shall be a great calm.

GEORGE CURRIE MARTIN

1865-1937

THE LIFE THAT KNOWS NO DEFEAT

BIOGRAPHICAL NOTE

PROFESSOR of New Testament language, etc., and patristics in the United College, Bradford, Yorks, and Lancashire Independent College, 1903-1909; born Portobello, Scotland, July 9, 1865; educated George Watson's College, Edinburgh; Knox Institute, Haddington; Edinburgh and Marburg universities; New College, London; minister of Congregational churches, Nairn, N. B., 1890-95; Reigate, Surrey, 1895-1903; author of " Foreign Missions in Eras of Non-conformity," " A Catechism on the Teaching of Jesus," editor of " Ephesians, Proverbs," etc., in " The Century Bible," " New Guinea," " How Best to Read the New Testament," etc.

" I can do all things in him that strengtheneth me."
—Phil. 4 : 13.

THESE words constitute a great boast. Boasting is common enough, but justifiable boasting is not so common. It is true that humility is not the very highest quality in character, and that the greatest men have frequently astounded their contemporaries by the confidence of their utterances about their ability. Our Lord Himself found that one cause of the people's enmity lay in the statements He made about His own personality, and the claims He assumed as His own right. But here we find His great apostle Paul speaking in a note of absolute assurance that staggers us. The only justification of such a claim is that it should be verified in experience.

First, then, we want to look at the verification of this boast. At first sight, it is true, there does not seem very much justification for it. Paul writes this letter from prison. Now it would appear that the most obvious thing for him to do at the moment, if he were possest of the power to which he lays claim, would be to escape from prison and go to the assistance of his various converts and churches. This very letter shows us that he had a longing so to do. To break prison only requires a certain amount of ingenuity. It is said that there are no bolts so strong, no fetters so heavy, no arrangement of a prison-house so ingenious that men cannot escape if they set themselves to accomplish the task. Paul never attempted it. If the most obvious and simple thing was not done, how are we to find a justification of the statement?

It will be remembered that a century or two ago one of our English poets was in prison, and in his cell he wrote a song that has floated down the years to our own day:

" Stone walls do not a prison make,
Nor iron bars a cage;
Hearts innocent and quiet take
That for a hermitage."

This was a wonderful accomplishment of the poet's imagination. To him the constraint of the prison became the refuge of the solitary, and he found reasons for thankfulness in the very circumstances of compulsory solitude.

When, in the days of the Scottish Covenant, they exiled Samuel Rutherford from his lovely parish of Anworth to the cold, gray desolation of Aberdeen, he was wont to write letters of comfort and consolation to his parishioners. and sometimes he dated them, not, as we might expect, from the dreary prison-house at Aberdeen, but from "My Lord's Palace at Aberdeen." This was what his faith taught Rutherford, and transformed the place of confinement to a room in which he held high converse with his Lord. But Paul's accomplishment is more wonderful than either of these. For him the prison becomes a pulpit. They had confined him in Rome, that they might silence what the Roman historian called "the mischievous superstition" of Christianity, and, behold, he finds the prison a better place for extending his evangel than the free travel that had formerly been his lot. In this letter he tells us how the whole company of the imperial guard had heard the word of Christ, and those letters of his reached the utmost limits of the empire. Not only so, but they come down through all the centuries, until to-day we read in this word the same message of indomitable courage, and unconquerable confidence.

But, says someone, at any rate the apostle could not escape suffering and trial. No, he could not, but let us read that great autobiographical self-revelation—the Second Epistle to the Corinthians—and we find the way in which Paul dealt with such circumstances. Once on his missionary journeys the multitude stoned him. His attitude to every form of suffering is just as if he had been able to take the stones his persecutors threw at him, raise them in his hands, and as he did so the stones had turned to bright and flashing gems, which he set upon his forehead as a triumphal diadem. This was the manner in which he treated all the trials that befell him. He made them subjects of boasting. "If I must boast I will boast of my suffering, my weakness, and my trial," he said. Here again, much more truly than had he escaped all, he overcomes in the power of his Lord.

Nor is death any terror to him. Again, in the pages of this letter we find him saying, "To me to live is Christ, and to die is gain." It is simply impossible to do anything with a man like this. There is no form of barrier known to human skill which will stop him, no form of terror the most demoniacal ingenuity can invent that will in the least degree dissuade him. Truly we find in Paul's experience this great boast completely verified —"I can do all things in him that strengtheneth me."

Secondly, there lies in the words a note of victory. Paul is a victorious man, and I beg you to think for a moment or two of the forces that were arrayed against him. I speak of the special forms of enmity with which the apostle in his peculiar work was conversant. In the main there were three: First, the power of the Jew was a mighty force. It was the force of his own countrymen, and we all know how intense a patriot Paul was, and how difficult

it is for the patriot to resist the persuasion or the pressure of those he loves with such intense devotion. But not only were they his own countrymen—they were the people who possess the finest and most spiritual religion of that day—in fact, the most spiritual religion of any day, except that which grew out of it—Christianity itself. It was a religion not only hoary with antiquity, but able to point to vast achievements, and to a large element of spiritual power. Secondly, there were the Greeks. Now the Greeks stood for two things—the religion of beauty, and the religion of pleasure. They taught the world such lessons of loveliness, as it has not been able to surpass in all the centuries since. Even to-day we have to go to the school of Greek sculpture and the Greek architects in order to know some of the secrets of purest beauty. And they were the pleasure-loving folk. They preached the doctrine of enjoyment of life to the full. All the world had listened to the message and thereby it increased its stock of joy. And, thirdly, there was the might of Rome. Rome stood for many things, but in this particular connection let us confine our attention to two—her sense of justice, and her might of civilization. Rome had evolved such a system of law that upon it is based the great legal systems of modern Europe. And the effectiveness of her civilization was such that probably never from that day to this has the world been so safe a place in which to travel.

Now, these three mighty powers were arrayed against the apostle, and he had to contend with them, and, if the words of the text are true, he not only contended with them but felt he had the secret of their subjugation. This might only be an interesting historical fact, if it were not that these same forces are arrayed against the Church of Christ to-day, and the individual Christian has now a battle upon which to enter similar to that the apostle had to fight. We do not indeed call the forces by the same names, but the realities are there. Do we not all know of churches which pride themselves upon their past achievement, upon the correctness of their creed, or the antiquity of their ritual, or the splendor of their worldly power? Has Christendom ever been free from such conflict, and is it not one of the hardest tasks of the spiritual church to-day to resist and vanquish such enemies within her own ranks? Was it only the Greeks that preached the popular gospel of pleasure? Are there no echoes of it amongst ourselves? Have not young men and women ever in their ears the voices which bid them fill life with beauty, with gaiety, and with gladness? Take the cup of life, and fill up to the brim, and drain it, care for nothing but pleasure! say these voices. If ever an age listened to that message it is our own. And, finally, the gospel of the might of empire, and the greatness of civilization has never been so loudly proclaimed as to-day. Are there not many who suppose that the great glory of England lies in the extension of her imperial might? Are the English people not told to acquire by any means, but certainly to acquire; and to hold what they have acquired, with an iron hand, if it must be, but certainly to hold? And, further, those who are most keenly interested in the spread of the gospel of Christ in foreign lands are often met with the argument that might well have come from an old Roman. " Go to China, or to India," we are told, " and take there all that Western science has taught you, all that modern discovery has been able to find, share with these people all knowledge except the knowledge of the cross." Often, when we are brought into relation with primitive peoples, men will tell us, " Yes, make them good citizens of the empire, teach them how to increase our commerce, how to be of advantage to our money-making endeavor, and once you have civilized them, perhaps one day, far off, you may speak the message of Christ." To a very large number the order of events is, civilization first, Christianity afterwards. There are many even within the ranks of the Church who seem to hold that view. It is said that the religion of the Sikhs in northern India is sometimes phrased by its followers in one brief utterance —" Victory! Victory! " That is the " good morning " and " good evening " of Sikhdom. Such is their phrase of confident assurance. I have sometimes wondered whether the modern Church of Christ dare say the same thing. Could we, in the face of the world, declare " Victory! Victory! That is the ' good morning ' and ' good evening ' of Christendom? " But if we cannot do so, ought we not to feel ashamed for Paul to do so? For have not we the intervening centuries to add their witness to the faith which he preached, and in the power of which he lived?

Thirdly, in these words we find the note of vision. " In him that strengtheneth me." All Paul's religion centered in the person of his Lord. Whenever you come into the secret places of Paul's inner life you are made aware of one unforgetable event—the event which altered the whole current of his experience— the vision of his Lord on the way to Damascus. Not only before King Agrippa, but in face of all inquiries, Paul would have said " I was not disobedient unto the heavenly vision." There is no great religion in the world that has not acquired its power, and so long as it had any vitality, preserved it through the strength of its vision. Buddha was able to reach his great achievements, because of the vision he had seen of the world's need, and the means whereby he felt that it might be met. Mohammed found in his religion the light of the vision of the one God he had beheld in the solitudes of the trackless desert, and whatever might has attached to that great faith has been found where such a vision has been renewed. It is not the power of the sword, but the power of its vision that has made Islam what it is, and Christianity is a religion of vision. The older faith of Judaism said that " To see God was to die," the new religion says " To see God is to live." " He that hath seen me hath seen the Father," said its Founder. " No one knoweth the Father save the Son, and he to whomsoever the Son willeth to reveal him," and he who knoweth God and Him whom God hath sent has the secret of eternal life.

From vision, then, comes power. Power, in the first instance, of pardon, in the second instance, of peace, and, in the third instance, of achievement. But the vision must not be only for one occasion—it must be a vision that is perpetually renewed. For Paul there was nothing so certain as the presence of Christ, and the lives that are lived in that consciousness are the lives that know conquest. It is said that there was once a great musician visiting this country, and that his host took him to church with him on one occasion. A week later he extended the invitation again, but the musician replied, " No, I will not go with you unless you can take me to hear someone who will tempt me to do the impossible." " Tempt us to do the impossible "—that is what Christ is ever doing. Nothing can have seemed more hopeless than the quest upon which He sent Paul. Standing on the threshold of the Roman world, He beckoned to the apostle to follow Him in order that He might bring all that proud Roman empire to His feet. Nothing could have seemed more quixotic and unpractical than that, yet the apostle not only accepted the challenge, but here, after long years of experience, not any more a young man with untried enthusiasm and untested zeal, he says, " I can do all things," and, as we have seen, the boast was no vain one, but a reality that can be tested by his life.

These, then, are the tests of a true Christian experience. Are they to be found in our lives—these notes of verification, of victory and vision? If not, it must be ours to catch them, or to recall them, and the only secret of their acquirement or renewal is to come into close and intimate fellowship with Jesus Christ through His Spirit, whereby our hearts also will be assured in the day of conflict, strengthened in the hour of temptation, and made more than conqueror through Him that loveth us.

ROBERT MURRAY McCHEYNE

1813-1843

ORDINATION SERMON

BIOGRAPHICAL NOTE

ROBERT MURRAY McCHEYNE, who often said, "Live so as to be missed," was born May 21, 1813 in Edinburgh, Scotland. Twenty-nine years later he succumbed to typhoid fever, but how God used him!

With a mind quick in attainment, he could name and write the Greek alphabet at the age of 4 and later memorized long passages of Scripture. He graduated from the University of Edinburgh in 1830 with training in music, geography and modern languages and entered Divinity Hall at the age of eighteen to prepare for the Christian ministry.

Licensed to preach at the age of twenty-two and ordained at twenty-three, he was Minister of St. Peter's Church, Dundee and served as the Secretary of Association of Church Extension.

Although busy day and night with his growing flock, the needs of the world at large lay heavy on his soul. He grasped every opportunity to preach and travelled much. His philosophy was "there is a great difference between preaching doctrine and preaching Christ"; which apparently God honored as shortly before his passing, God's Spirit broke forth in his church in Dundee with a mighty revival and in many other places he had visited.

"I charge thee therefore before God, and the Lord Jesus Christ, who shall judge the quick and the dead at His appearing and His kingdom, preach the word; be instant in season, out of season; reprove, rebuke, exhort with all long-suffering and doctrine." 2 Tim. iv. 1, 2.

1. WHERE *faithful ministers stand:* "Be*fore God and the Lord Jesus Christ."* There is no more responsible situation in the whole world than that in which a faithful minister stands.

(1) *Before God.* This is true in two ways.

First, *As a sinner saved by grace.* He was once far off, but is now brought nigh by the blood of Jesus. Having "boldness to enter into the holiest by the blood of Jesus, by a new and living way which He hath consecrated for us through the veil, that is to say, His flesh," he draws near. He stands within the veil, in the holiest of all, in the love of God. He is justified before God. A faithful minister is *an example to his flock of a sinner saved.* God says to him as He did to Abraham, "Walk before Me, and be thou perfect." He can say with Paul, "I was a blasphemer, and a persecutor, and injurious, but I obtained mercy." A faithful minister is like Aaron's rod, that was laid up beside the ark of God and budded there.

Second, *As a servant.* In the East, servants always stand in the presence of their master, watching his hand. The Queen of Sheba said to Solomon: "Happy are these Thy servants, which stand continually before Thee, and hear Thy wisdom." So it is said of the angels, that "they do always behold the face of My Father which is in heaven." Even when most engaged in the service of the saints, they feel under His all-seeing, holy, living eye. So *ought* faithful ministers to feel. They should feel constantly in His presence: under His soul-piercing, gentle-guiding, holy, living eye. "I will guide thee with Mine eye." "The eyes of the Lord are over the righteous." Ah! how often we feel we are before *man!* Then all power withers, and we become weak as other men; but oh, how sweet to feel in the presence of God, as if there were no eye on us but God's! *In prayer,* how sweet to feel before Him; to kneel at His footstool, and to put our hand upon the mercy-seat — no curtain, no veil, no cloud between the soul and God! *In preaching,* how sweet to say, like Elijah, when he stood before Ahab, "I stand before the Lord God of Israel!" To stand at His feet, in His family, in His pavilion, oh, believers, it is then we get above the billows! The applause of men, the rage and contempt of men, then pass by us like the idle wind which we regard not. Thus is a minister like a rock in the ocean; the mountain-billows dash upon its brow, and yet it stands unshaken.

(2) *Before Jesus Christ.* This also is true in two ways:

First, The faithful minister has a present sight of Christ as his Righteousness. He is like John the Baptist. "Seeing Jesus coming unto him, he saith, Behold the Lamb of God!" Or like Isaiah, he saw "His glory and spake of Him." His own soul is ever watching at Gethsemane and at Golgotha. Oh, brethren, it is thus only we can ever speak with feeling, or with power, or with truth, of the unsearchable riches of Christ! We must have the taste of the manna in our mouth, "milk and honey under our tongue," else we cannot tell of its sweetness. We must be drinking the living water from the smitten rock, or we cannot speak of its refreshing power. We must be hiding our guilty souls in the wounds of Jesus, or we cannot with joy speak of the peace and rest to be found there. This is the reason why unfaithful ministers are cold and barren in their labours. They speak, like Balaam, of a Saviour whose grace they do not feel. They speak, like Caiaphas, of the blood of Christ, without having felt its power to speak peace to the troubled heart. This is the reason why many good men have a barren ministry. They speak from clear head-knowledge, or from past experience, but not from a present grasp of the truth nor from a present sight of the Lamb of God. Hence their words fall like a shower of snow: fair and beautiful but cold and freezing. The Lord give us to stand in the presence of the Lord Jesus.

Second, The faithful minister should feel the presence of a living Saviour. A minister should be like the bride in the Song: "Leaning upon her beloved." This was Jeremiah's strength (i. 8): "Be not afraid of their faces, for I am with thee to deliver thee, saith the Lord." So it was with Paul (Acts xviii. 9, 10): "Be not afraid, but speak, and hold not thy peace: for I am with thee, and no man shall set on thee to hurt thee: for I have much people in this city." So Jesus told all the disciples: "Yet a little while, and the world seeth Me not; but ye see Me: because I live, ye shall live also." And again He says expressly "Lo, I am with you alway, even to the end of the world." Yes, brethren, Christ is as truly walking in the midst of the seven golden candlesticks, as truly in this place to-day, as if you saw Him with your bodily eyes. His humanity is at the right hand of God, appearing in the presence of God for us. His Godhead fills all in all. Thus He is with us, standing at our right hand, so that we cannot be moved. It is sweet to know and feel this. Thus only can we be sustained amid all the trials of the ministry. Are we weary? we can lean, like John, upon His bosom. Are we burdened with a sense of sin? we can hide in

the clefts of that Rock of Ages. Are we empty? we can look up to Him for immediate supply. Are we hated of all men? we can hide under His wings. Stand before the Lord Jesus Christ, and then you may smile at Satan's rage, and face a frowning world. Learn here also the guilt of refusing a gospel ministry: "He that refuseth you, refuseth Me; and he that refuseth Me, refuseth Him that sent Me."

(3) *Within sight of judgment — "Who shall judge the quick and dead."* Ministers and their flocks shall meet together before the throne of the Lord Jesus. That will be a solemn day. They have many solemn meetings on earth. An ordination day is a solemn day. Their meetings from Sabbath to Sabbath are solemn meetings; and sacrament days are very solemn days. But their meeting at the judgment-seat will be by far the most solemn of all. Then:

First, The minister will give his account, either with joy or with grief. He will no more meet to plead with the people, or to pray with them, but to bear witness how they received the word. Of some he will give account with a joyful countenance: that they received the word with all readiness of mind, that they were converted and became like little children; these will be his joy and crown. Of most with grief: that he carried the message to them, but they would not come — they make light of it; or perhaps they listened for a while, but drew back into perdition. He will be a swift witness against them in that day. "Depart, ye cursed."

Second, Then the people will give their account of the minister. If he was faithful, if he made it his meat and drink to do the will of God, if he preached the whole truth with seriousness, urgency, love, if he was holy in his life, if he preached publicly, and from house to house: then that minister shall shine like the stars. If he was unfaithful, if he fed himself, but not the flock, if he did not seek the conversion of souls, did not travail in birth, if he sought his own ease, his own wealth, his own praise, and not their souls: then shall the loud curses of ruined souls fall on that wretched man; and God shall say, Take the unfaithful servant, and bind him hand and foot, and cast him into outer darkness. Oh, believers, it is the duty of ministers to preach with this solemn day in mind! We should stand, like Abraham, looking down on the smoke of Sodom; like John, listening to the new song and golden harps of the New Jerusalem. Would not this take away the fear of man? Would not this make us urgent in our preaching? You must either get these souls into Christ, or you will yet see them lying down in everlasting burnings. Oh, brethren, did I not say truly that the place where a minister stands is the most solemn spot in all this world!

2. THE *grand business of the faithful minister.* Described in two ways: *First,* Generally: Preach the Word; *Second,* More in detail: Reprove, rebuke, exhort.

(1) *Preach the Word.* The grand work of the minister, in which he is to lay out his strength of body and mind, is preaching. Weak and foolish as it may appear, this is the grand instrument which God has put into our hands, by which sinners are to be saved, and saints fitted for glory. It pleased God, by the foolishness of preaching, to save them that believe. It was to this *our blessed Lord* devoted the years of His own ministry. Oh, what an honour has He put upon this work, by preaching in the synagogues, in the temple, and by the blue waves of Galilee, under the canopy of heaven! Has He not consecrated this world as preaching ground? This was the grand work of Paul and all the apostles, for this was our Lord's command: "Go ye into all the world, and preach the gospel." Oh, brethren, this is our great work! It is well to visit the sick, and well to educate children and clothe the naked. It is well to attend presbyteries. It is well to write books or read them. But here is the main thing: preach the Word. The pulpit is, as George Herbert says, "our joy and throne." This is our watchtower. Here we must warn the people. The silver trumpet is put into our hand. Woe be unto us if we preach not the gospel!

The Matter — The Word. It is in vain we preach, if we preach not the Word, the truth as it is in Jesus.

First, Not *other* matters. "Ye are My witnesses." "The same came to *bear witness* of that light." We are to speak of nothing but what we have seen and heard from God. It is not the work of the minister to open up schemes of human wisdom or learning, not to bring his own fancies, but to tell the facts and glories of the gospel. We must speak of what is within the word of God.

Second, Preach the *Word,* the most essential parts especially. If you were with a dying man, and knew he had but half an hour to live, what would you tell him? Would you open up some of the curiosities of the Word, or enforce some of the moral commands of the Word? Would you not tell him his undone condition by nature and by wicked works? Would you not tell him of the love and dying of the Lord Jesus? Would you not tell him of the power of the Holy Spirit? These are the essential things which a man must receive or perish. These are the great subject-matters of preaching. Should we not preach as Jesus did when He went to Emmaus, when He began at Moses and all the prophets, and expounded to them the things concerning Himself? Let there be much of Christ in your ministry, says the excellent Eliot. Rowland Hill used to say, "See there be no sermon without *three R's* in

it: Ruin by the fall, Righteousness by Christ, and Regeneration by the Spirit." Preach Christ for awakening, Christ for comforting, Christ for sanctifying. "God forbid that I should glory, save in the cross of our Lord Jesus Christ."

Third, Preach *as* the Word. I would humbly suggest for the consideration of all ministers, whether we should not preach more in the manner of God's word. Is not the Word the sword of the Spirit? Should not our great work be to take it from its scabbard, to cleanse it from all rust, and then to apply its sharp edge to the consciences of man? It is certain the fathers used to preach in this manner. Brown of Haddington used to preach as if he had read no other book than the Bible. It is the truth of God in its naked simplicity that the Spirit will most honour and bless. "Sanctify them through Thy truth: Thy Word is truth."

(2) *Reprove, rebuke, exhort.* — The first work of the Spirit on the natural heart is to *reprove the world of sin.* Although He is the Spirit of love, although a dove is His emblem, although He be compared to the soft wind and gentle dew; still His first work is to convince of sin. If ministers are filled with the same Spirit, they will begin in the same way. It is God's usual method to awaken them, and bring them to despair of salvation by their own righteousness, before He reveals Christ to them. So it was with the jailor. So it was with Paul: he was blind three days. A faithful minister must lay himself out for this. Plough up the fallow ground, and sow not among thorns. Men must be brought down by law work to see their guilt and misery, or all our preaching is beating the air. Oh, brethren, is this our ministry? Let us do this plainly. The most, I fear, in all our congregations are sailing easily down the stream into an undone eternity, unconverted and unawakened. Brethren, they will not thank us in eternity for speaking smooth things: for sewing pillows to their arm-holes, and crying, Peace, peace, when there is no peace. No, they may praise us now, but they will curse our flattery in eternity. Oh, for the bowels of Jesus Christ in every minister, that we might long after them all! *Exhort.* — The original word means to comfort: to speak as the Comforter does. This is the second part of the Spirit's work, to lead to Christ, to speak good news to the soul. This is the most difficult part of the Christian ministry. Thus did John: "Behold the Lamb of God." Thus did Isaiah: "Comfort ye, comfort ye." Thus did our Lord command: "Go, preach the gospel to every creature." It is true this makes the feet of the gospel messenger beautiful on the mountains. He has to tell of a full, free, Divine Saviour.

And here I would observe what appears to me *a fault in the preaching of our beloved*

Scotland. Most ministers are accustomed to set Christ before the people. They lay down the gospel clearly and beautifully, but they do not urge men to enter in. Now God says, Exhort, beseech men, persuade men; not only point to the open door, but compel them to come in. Oh to be more merciful to souls, that we would lay hands on men and draw them in to the Lord Jesus!

3. *The manner.*
(1) *With long-suffering.* There is no grace more needed in the Christian ministry than this. This is the heart of God the Father towards sinners: "He is long-suffering to usward, not willing that any should perish." This is the heart of the Lord Jesus. How tenderly does He cry, "O Jerusalem, Jerusalem, how often would I," etc. This is the mind of the Holy Spirit in striving with men. He will not always strive, but oh, how long He does strive with men! Dear believers, had He not striven long with us, we would this day have been like Lot's wife, monuments of grace resisted. Now, such ought ministers to be. Above all men, we need "love that suffers long and is kind." Sometimes, when sinners are obstinate and hard-hearted, we are tempted to give up in despair, or to lose temper and scold them, like the disciples calling down fire from heaven. But, brethren, we must be of another spirit. The wrath of man worketh not the righteousness of God. Only be filled with the Spirit of Christ, and it will make us patient toward all. It will make us cry, "How often would I," etc.

(2) *With doctrine.* Some good men cry, Flee, flee, without showing the sinner what he is to flee from; and again, they cry, Come, come, without showing plainly the way of pardon and peace. These men act as one would do who should run through the streets crying, Fire, fire, without telling where. In the preaching of the apostles you will observe the clear and simple statement of the truth preceding the warm and pathetic exhortation. This has always been followed by the most judicious and successful divines.

It behoves ministers to unite the cherub and the seraph in their ministry: the angel of knowledge and the angel of burning zeal. If we would win souls, we must point clearly the way to heaven, while we cry, Flee from the wrath to come. I believe we cannot lay down the guilt of man, his total depravity, and the glorious gospel of Christ too clearly; that we cannot urge men to embrace and flee too warmly. Oh for a pastor who unites the deep knowledge of Edwards, the vast statements of Owen, and the vehement appeals of Richard Baxter!

(3) *With urgency.* If a neighbour's house were on fire, would we not cry aloud and use every exertion? If a friend were drowning, would we be ashamed to strain every nerve to save him? But alas! the souls of our neighbors are even now on their way to everlasting burnings, — they are ready to be drowned in the depths of perdition. Oh, shall we be less earnest to save their never-dying souls, than we would be to save their bodies? How anxious was the Lord Jesus in this! When He came near and beheld the city, He wept over it. How earnest was Paul! "Remember that by the space of three years I ceased not to warn every one night and day with tears." Such was George Whitfield; that great man scarcely ever preached without being melted into tears. Brethren, there is need of the same urgency now. Hell is as deep and as burning as ever. Unconverted souls are as surely rushing to it. Christ is as free and pardon is as sweet as ever! Ah! how we shall be amazed at our coldness when we do get to heaven!

(4) *At all times.* Our Lord went about continually doing good; He made it His meat and drink. "Daily in the temple." So should we. *Satan is busy* at all times; he does not stand upon ceremony; he does not keep himself to Sabbath-days or canonical hours. *Death is busy.* Men are dying while we are sleeping. About fifty die every minute; nearly one every second entering into an unchangeable world! *The Spirit of God is busy.* Blessed be God, He hath cast our lot in times when there is the moving of the great Spirit among the dry bones. Shall ministers then be idle, or stand upon ceremony? Oh that God would baptize us this day with the Holy Ghost and with fire, that we might be all changed as into a flame of fire, preaching and building up Christ's Church till our latest, our dying hour!

CHARGE TO THE MINISTER.

MY DEAR BROTHER, It is not many years ago since you and I played together as children, and now, by the wonderful providence of God, I have been appointed to preside at your ordination to the office of the holy ministry. Truly His way is in the sea, and His path in the deep waters. Do not think, then, that I mean to assume an authority which I have not. I cannot speak to you as a father, but as a brother beloved in the Lord let me address a few words of counsel to you.

(1) *Thank God for putting you into the ministry* — "I thank Christ Jesus my Lord for that He counted me faithful, putting me into the ministry." "To me, who am less than the least of all saints," etc. Oh, brother, thank God for saving your soul; for sending His Spirit into your heart, and drawing you to Christ! But this day you have a new cause of thankfulness in being put into the ministry. It is the greatest honour in this world. "Had I a thousand lives, I would willingly spend

them in it; and had I a thousand sons, I would gladly devote them to it." True, it is an awfully responsible office: the eternity of thousands depends on your faithfulness; but ah! the grace is so full, and the reward so glorious. "If," said the dying Payson, "If ministers only saw the preciousness of Christ, they would not be able to refrain from clapping their hands with joy, and exclaiming, I am a minister of Christ! I am a minister of Christ!" Do not forget, then, dear brother, amid the broken accents of confession from a broken heart, to pour out a song of thankfulness. Thanks be to God, for my own part, during the few years I have been a minister; I can truly say that I desire no other honour upon earth ' than to be allowed to preach the everlasting gospel. Thanks be to God for His unspeakable gift.

(2) *Seek the anointing of the Holy Spirit.* The more anointing of the Holy Spirit you have, the more you will be a happy, holy, and successful minister. You remember *the two olive-trees* that stood close by the golden candlestick, and emptied the golden oil out of themselves. These represent successful ministers, anointed ones that stand by the Lord of the whole earth. The Lord make you like one of them. Remember *John the Baptist:* "He shall be filled with the Holy Ghost, and many of the children of Israel shall he turn to the Lord their God." The Lord fill you in like manner, and then you will be a converting minister. Remember *the apostles.* Before the day of Pentecost they were dry, sapless trees, — they had little fruit; but when the Spirit came on them like a mighty rushing wind, then three thousand people were pricked to the heart.

Oh, brother, plead with God to fill you with the Spirit, that you may stand in His counsel, and cause the people to hear His words, and turn many from the evil of their ways. You know that a heated iron, though blunt, can pierce its way ever where a much sharper instrument, if cold, could not enter. Pray that you may be filled with the fire of the Spirit, that you may pierce into the hard hearts of unconverted sinners.

(3) *Do not rest without success in your ministry.* Success is the rule under a living ministry; want of success is the exception. *"The want of ministerial success,"* says Robinson, *"is a tremendous circumstance never to be contemplated without horror."* Your people will be of two kinds:

First, The Lord's people, those who are already in Christ, seek for success among them. He gave some pastors and teachers for the perfecting of the saints. Never forget Christ's words: "Feed My sheep, feed My lambs." Be like Barnabas, a son of consolation. Exhort them to cleave to the Lord. Do not say, "They are safe, and I will let them alone." This is a great mistake. See how Paul laid out his strength in confirming the disciples. Be a helper of their joy. Do not rest till you get them to live under the pure, holy rules of the gospel.

Second, The great mass you will find to be unconverted. Go, brother, leaving the ninety-nine, go after the one sheep that was lost. Leave your home, your comforts, your bed, your ease, your all, to feed lost souls. The Lord of glory left heaven for this; it is enough for the disciple to be as his Master. It is said of Alleine, that "He was infinitely and insatiably greedy for the conversion of souls." Rutherford wrote to his dear people, "My Witness is above, that your heaven would be two heavens to me, and the salvation of you all as two salvations to me." The Lord give you this heavenly compassion for this people. Do not be satisfied without conversion. You will often find that there is a shaking among the dry bones, a coming together bone to his bone, skin and flesh come upon them, but no breath in them. Oh, brother, cry for the breath of heaven! Remember a moral sinner will lie down in the same hell with the vilest.

(4) *Lead a holy life.* I believe, brother, that you are born from above, and therefore I have confidence in God touching you, that you will be kept from the evil. But oh, study universal holiness of life! Your whole usefulness depends on this. Your sermon on Sabbath lasts but an hour or two; your life preaches all the week. Remember, ministers are standard-bearers. Satan aims his fiery darts at them. If he can only make you a covetous minister, or a lover of pleasure, or a lover of praise, or a lover of good eating, then he has ruined your ministry for ever. Ah! let him preach on fifty years, he will never do me any harm. Dear brother, cast yourself at the feet of Christ, implore His Spirit to make you a holy man. Take heed to thyself, and thy doctrine.

(5) *Last of all, be a man of prayer.* Give yourself to prayer, and to the ministry of the Word. If you do not pray, God will probably lay you aside from your ministry, as He did me, to teach you to pray. Remember Luther's maxim, *"Bene orâsse est bene studuisse."* Get your texts from God, your thoughts, your words, from God. Carry the names of the little flock upon your breast, like the High Priest; wrestle for the unconverted. Luther spent his three best hours of the day in prayer. John Welch prayed seven or eight hours a day. He used to keep a plaid on his bed, that he might wrap himself in it when he rose during night. Sometimes his wife found him on the ground lying weeping. When she complained, he would say, "Oh, woman, I have the souls of three thousand to answer for, and I know not how it is with many of them!" Oh that God would pour down this spirit of prayer on you and me, and all the ministers of our beloved Church, and then we shall see better days in Scotland. I commend you to God, etc.

CHARGE TO THE PEOPLE.

DEAR BRETHREN: I trust that this is to be the beginning of many happy days to you in this place. Gifts in answer to prayer are always the sweetest. I believe your dear pastor has been given you in answer to prayer, for I do not think your wonderful unanimity can be accounted for in any other way.

(1) *Love your pastor.* So far as I know him, he is worthy of your love. I believe he is one to whom the Lord has been very merciful, that God has already owned his labours, and I trust will a thousand times more. Esteem him very highly in love for his work's sake. You little know the anxieties, temptation, pains and wrestlings, he will be called on to bear for you. Few people know the deep wells of anxiety in the bosom of a faithful pastor. Love and reverence him much. *Do not make an idol of him;* that will destroy his usefulness. It was said of the Erskines, the men could not see Christ over their heads. Remember, look beyond him and above him. Those that would have worshipped Paul were the people who stoned him. Do not stumble at his infirmities. There are spots upon the sun and infirmities in the best of men. Cover them, do not stumble at them. Would you refuse gold because it was brought you in a ragged purse? Would you refuse pure water because it came in a chipped bowl. The treasure is in an earthen vessel.

(2) *Make use of your pastor.* He has come with good news from a far country. Come and hear.

First, Wait patiently on his minstry. He does not come in his own name. The Lord is with him. If you refuse him, you will refuse Christ; for he is the messenger of the Lord of Hosts.

Second, Welcome him into your houses. He is coming, like his Master, to seek that which was lost, and to bind up that which is broken; to strengthen that which was sick, and to bring again that which was driven away. You all have need of him, whether converted or not. Remember there is an awful curse against those who receive not gospel messages. He will shake the dust off his feet against you, and that dust will rise against you in judgment.

Third, Do not trouble him about worldly matters. His grand concern is to get your soul saved. He is not a man of business but a man of prayer. He has given himself to prayer and to the ministry of the Word.

Fourth, Go freely to him about your souls. "The minister's house was more thronged than ever the tavern had wont to be." These were happy days. There is no trade I would like to see broken in this place but that of the taverners. It is a soul-destroying trade. I would like to see the taverns emptied, and the minister's house thronged. Do not hesitate to go to him. It is your duty and your privilege. It is your duty. It will encourage him, and show him how to preach to your souls. It is your privilege. I have known many who got more light from a short conversation than from many sermons.

Fifth, Be brief. Tell your case. Hear his word and be gone. Remember his body is weak, and his time precious. You are stealing his time from others or from God. I cannot tell you what a blessing it will be if you will be very short in your calls. The talk of the lips tendeth to penury.

(3) *God's children, pray for him.* Pray for his body, that he may be kept strong, and spared for many years. Pray for his soul, that he may be kept humble and holy, a burning and a shining light, that he may grow. Pray for his ministry, that it may be abundantly blessed, and that he may be anointed to preach good tidings. Let there be no secret prayer without naming him before your God and no family prayer without carrying your pastor in your hearts to God. Hold up his hands so that Israel will prevail against Amalek.

(4) *Unconverted souls, prize this opportunity.* I look on this ordination as a smile of Heaven upon you. God might have taken away ministers from this town instead of giving us more. I believe the Lord Jesus is saying, "I have much people in this city." The door is begun to be opened this day. The Spirit is beginning to shine. Oh that you would know the day of your visitation! This is the market-day of grace beginning in this end of the town, and you should all come to buy. Oh that you knew the day of your visitation! Some, I fear, will be the worse for this ministry and not the better. The election will be saved and the rest be blinded. Some will yet wish they had died before this church was opened. Be sure, dear souls, that you will either be saved, or more lost, by this ministry. Your pastor comes with the silver trumpet of mercy. Why will ye turn it into the trumpet of judgment? He comes with glad tidings of great joy. Why should you turn them into sad tidings of endless woe? He comes to preach the acceptable day of the Lord. Why will ye turn it into the day of vengeance of our God?

16th December 1840.

JOHN WILLIAM McGARVEY

1829-1911

THE PRAYERS OF JESUS

BIOGRAPHICAL NOTE

PRESIDENT of the College of the Bible, Lexington, Ky. 1895-1911; born Hopkinsville, Ky., March 1, 1829; graduated from Bethany College, W. Va., 1850; resided and preached for twelve years at Fayette and Dover, Mo.; at Lexington, Ky., 1863; since 1865 professor of sacred history; author of commentaries on "Acts of Apostles," and "Matthew and Mark," "Lands of the Bible," "Text and Canon of the New Testament," "Credibility and Inspiration of the New Testament," etc.

"Who in the days of his flesh, when he had offered up prayers and supplications with strong crying and tears unto him that was able to save him from death, and was heard in that he feared; though he were a Son yet learned he obedience by the things which he suffered."—Hebrews 5 : 7, 8.

WHY did Jesus pray? Scoffers have said that if He was divine He prayed to himself, and His prayers were not real. They forget that while He was here He was less than Himself—that tho, before His advent He was " in the form of God, and counted it not a prize to be on an equality with God," He " emptied himself, taking the form of a servant, being made in the likeness of men; and being found in fashion as a man, He humbled himself, becoming obedient unto death, yea, even the death of the cross " (Phil. 2 : 6-8). This is the representation from which to regard Him. Having thus made Himself in a measure dependent on His Father, it was proper for Him to pray.

Others have said that He prayed, not because He needed, as we do, the benefits of prayer, but simply to set us an example. This answer is little better than the other; for if He prayed only to set an example, it was a bad example, for it would teach us also to offer prayers for which we would feel no need. That His prayers were real and heartfelt, is manifest from the passage cited as my text in which it is said that " in the days of his flesh he offered up prayers and supplications with strong crying and tears." When prayers are accompanied by " strong crying and tears " on the part of a sane man, there can be no possible doubt of their sincerity and reality.

The question still confronts us, Why did Jesus pray? We are told that He was tempted in all points like as we are, yet without sin (Heb. 4 : 15). If this is true, He must have employed with unfailing success the means of resisting temptation which we employ so ineffectually. One of these is prayer; for He said to His disciples, " Watch, and pray that ye enter not into temptation." To " enter into temptation," is to come under its controlling power. To watch and to pray guards us against this. We watch, in order to see the temptation ere it assails us. We pray for strength to resist it when it comes. If we study the prayers of Jesus with reference to the occasions on which they were offered, I think we shall see very plainly that He faithfully practised the precept which He gave to His disciples.

He began His public career by solemnly submitting to John's baptism. Whatever may have been His trials and temptations before this, He knew that this act would introduce Him into a career in which they would be more severe and would end in a struggle testing the utmost strength of His soul. He perhaps knew also that immediately after His baptism He would be subjected to the strongest temptations which Satan's ingenuity could invent for that moment in His career. Most wisely then was His baptism followed immediately by prayer. And it was while He was praying that the heavens were opened above Him, and the Holy Spirit came down upon Him in the form of a dove, and entered into Him (Luke 3:21, 22; Mark 1:10, 11). He was now prepared for the worst that Satan could do, and when, after forty days He triumphed and drove Satan from Him, angels came and ministered to Him.

We know not to what extent Jesus was dependent on His Father for wisdom and guidance respecting the affairs of His coming kingdom; but we know that He made His most important administrative act the subject of protracted prayer. That act was the selection of the twelve men to whom He would entrust the establishment and ordering of His kingdom on earth after He should have returned to the world whence He came. No selection of subordinate officers in any kingdom since the world began has been of so momentous importance. Suppose, if we can, that all had proven as false to their trust as did Judas Iscariot, who can begin to imagine the consequences? We may not be able to see any temptation that beset Him in making this choice, unless it was in regard to placing among the twelve the thief who was to betray Him; but we learn that before making the selection He spent the whole of the preceding night in prayer (Luke 6:12-16). Who can tell to what extent the unequaled fidelity and amazing triumph of those men in the inauguration and administration of the kingdom of God resulted from the efficacy of that prayer? The answer is wrapt up in the secrets of eternity.

On the morning of the day in which the five thousand were fed the twelve apostles returned to Jesus from their first tour of preaching and healing (Luke 9:1-17). They had not yet eaten their morning meal. An agitated throng gathered about them and prest them so that they could not do so. As Mark expresses it, " Many were coming and going, and they had no leisure so much as to eat " (6:30, 31). At the same early hour an excited group of John's disciples came to Jesus with the crushing announcement that John the Baptist had been beheaded by Herod, and that they had taken his headless body and laid it in a tomb (Matt. 14:12-14; Mark 6:29). Either of these reports was enough to excite the people; and when they heard both, they were wild. The people were already thrilled by what the twelve had been doing, and when they heard of the bloody deed of Herod they went wild; for all counted John as a prophet. The more they heard the details of the bloody deed the more exasperated they became.

But if this fateful announcement was exasperating to the multitude of the Galileans, what must it have been to Jesus? John had been the best friend He had on earth next to his mother. He had baptized Him, had given Him honor in the presence of the multitude, and had secured for Him His first disciples. He was also a kinsman in the flesh, and even his murderer had acknowledged him to be " a holy man and just." No one who has not been suddenly informed of the cruel murder of a dear friend and kinsman, can realize the conflict of emotions which agitated the soul of Jesus when this announcement was made. The pang was all the keener in that it foreshadowed what was soon to come upon Himself. He said nothing. Not a word of comment is quoted from Him by any of the narrators. What He was tempted to say we can conjecture only by our knowledge of human nature, and the apostle's statement that He was " tempted in all points like as we are, yet without sin." He only said to His apostles, " Come ye yourselves apart into a desert place, and rest awhile " (Matt. 14:34). What other purpose He had in going to the desert place we learn farther on. They quietly entered their boat and struck out for the pasture lands belonging to Bethsaida Julias, at the northeastern curve of the lake (Luke 9:10). The people soon saw to what point the boat was headed, and with a common impulse they started on a rush around the northwestern curve and northern end of the lake for the same spot. The news spread like wild-fire through the villages, and almost the whole population ran out to join the race. Soon the largest multitude that ever gathered about Jesus was before Him, and the rest for which He had started was prevented. His compassion for them and for the sick whom they brought with them overpowered His desire for rest and quiet, so He spent the day in teaching and healing until it was too late for the people to return to their homes without suffering from hunger. Then came the feeding. So wildly excited had the people been, that they had come to this uninhabited plain without food; and, reckless of consequences, had remained all day.

At this point an incident mentioned only by John added immensely to the temptation which had been oppressing Jesus since the early morning. He perceived that the people " were about to come and take him by force and make him king" (6:15). This was a renewal of Satan's third temptation in the wilderness. The people believed that He intended to set up a political kingdom; and such was the exasperation now felt toward Herod that the moment for an uprising seemed to have come. The five thousand men present were ready to strike the first blow. Herod's capital city, Tiberias, was in full view across the lake, and it could be taken in a few hours. With five thousand men ready to move at His command and the whole of Galilee in a popular ferment, it would have been easy and quick work to dethrone the murderer of His friend, and then march with accumulating forces upon Pontius Pilate and Judea. If His soul had been fired with such passions as are universal with men, how strong the temptation would have been! But no; the disciples are hastily ordered into their boat with orders to cross the lake, the multitude are formally dismissed, and Jesus retires into the mountain at the base of which He had spent the day. Not till now did He find that for which He had started in the morning. Alone in the solitude of the mountain He spends the night in prayer. Once more He applies the safeguard against temptation; once more the tempest within His soul, like that on the lake a few days previous, hears the rebuke, " Peace, be still "; and there is a " great calm." It was now about the fourth watch of the night; the full moon of the passover week was shining (John 6 : 4); and a very strong wind was blowing from the west; but Jesus, knowing that His disciples were struggling in the middle of the lake against that wind, walks out to them on the boiling waves, a distance of nearly three miles (John 6 : 1). The boat soon glided over the remaining three miles, but when it landed another day had dawned, and the whole company had passed twenty-four hours without rest, without food, unless they partook with the multitude of the cold barley bread and fish, and without sleep. This is a specimen of the laborious life which Jesus was leading, and into the hardships of which His disciples were initiating the twelve.

Not long after this occurred that ever memorable occasion on which Jesus was first formally acknowledged by His disciples as the " Christ, the Son of the living God." He was " praying alone " when the disciples came to Him and heard from Him the searching question, " Who do you say that I am? " (Luke 9 : 18-20). What the especial occasion of that prayer was, we are not informed; but it illustrates at least His prayerful habit.

About eight days after these sayings Jesus went up into another mountain to pray, and now He takes with Him Peter, James and John (Luke 9 : 28). Matthew calls it " a high mountain " (17 : 1), and as one of the sayings from which the eight days are counted was spoken near Caesarea Philippi, which stands at the base of Mount Hermon, the highest mountain in Palestine, it was proba-

bly this or some of its outlying spurs that He now ascended. It was a laborious climb to reach the spot, and here was another night of prayer. The three disciples soon completed their short prayers, and fell asleep. They were awakened by the sound of voices; and on looking up they beheld Jesus transfigured in glory and two other men in glory deeply absorbed in conversation with Him. They soon learn by hearing their names called, that the other two were Moses and Elijah. They learn, too, that the subject of conversation was " the decease which he was about to accomplish at Jerusalem." They had first heard of this about eight days before from the lips of Jesus Himself (Luke 9 : 22, 28). Now, to their amazement they hear it spoken of again by these mighty men whose abode had been for many centuries in the land of departed spirits. What they said of it we may never know; but may we not safely conclude that the purpose of Jesus in that night of prayer was to plead for an increase of fortitude as the shadow of His final agony was now growing deeper as He approached it? His prayer was answered by the words of sympathy which came to Him from men almost divine. How I would love to know what they said. If my courage shall fail not when I meet with Moses or Elijah, I shall inquire what they said to Jesus; and I shall also ask how they knew that He would be on that mountain that night, and how they knew that He was going to die in Jerusalem.

Although Jesus was so prayerful Himself, He was not persistent like the apostle Paul in urging this duty on the disciples. Even in His well-known remarks on the subject in the Sermon on the Mount, He did not exhort them to pray; but, assuming that they would pray, He was content with telling them how. And so, in the subsequent course of His ministry He depended on the force of His example, rather than on repeated precept for their training in this respect. His method had the desired effect; for after what I have thus far narrated, " it came to pass, as he was praying in a certain place that when he ceased, one of his disciples said to him, ' Lord, teach us to pray, as John also taught his disciples ' " (Luke 11 : 1-4). Having been a disciple of John, this man knew what John had taught on the subject, and he also knew what Jesus Himself had taught in the Sermon on the Mount. Why then was he not satisfied? Evidently he thought from the protracted prayers of Jesus, and perhaps from what he saw, or thought he saw, of their effects on the life of Jesus, that there was yet a secret in prayer which he had not discovered. None of the disciples could as yet pray all night; and none since then have learned to do so. Who ever tried it without falling asleep? And who has prayed so effectually as to guard himself against all sin? It is a high credit to this disciple—and probably he spoke for the others as well as for himself—that he aspired to his Master's devotion in this respect. He was disappointed. Jesus answered only by repeating the major part of the simple prayer which He had taught them before, and by adding a parable to show the value of importunity in pleading for what we need (Luke 11 : 5-13).

While seated at the last supper, Peter met with a surprise greater, perhaps, than any he had ever known. Jesus said to him: " Simon, Simon, behold, Satan asked to have you that he might sift you like wheat: but I made supplication for thee, that thy faith fail not: and do thou, when once thou art turned again, establish thy brethren '' (Luke 22 : 32). What a revelation to Simon! How startling to know that Satan had thus reached for him, that he might toss him up and down like a farmer winnowing his wheat! What could be meant by his future turning again that he might strengthen his brethren; and how watchful the Master had been to intercede for his safety when he was unmindful of danger. Who knows to what extent the final salvation of Peter depended on that supplication? How sweet it is to know that we too may be objects of similar solicitude in our days of peril. While praying for Himself, Jesus did not forget to pray for others. Did He pray for Judas? He gave the traitor blood-curdling warnings on that same fateful night, but not a word about praying for him. Was it true of Him, as the old preachers were once accustomed to say, that He was no longer on " praying ground or pleading terms with God? "

The longest prayer ever quoted from the lips of Jesus followed after Judas had left the upper room and the solemn feast. It contains few words for Himself, and the rest for the faithful to whom the destinies of His kingdom were now to be entrusted till the final day without His visible presence. Then followed the silent moonlit walk through the deserted streets and down the steep declivity to the Kidron and Gethsemane. On reaching the garden it was observed that " He began to be sorrowful and sore troubled." The composure that He had maintained thus far broke down as He directed Peter and the sons of Zebedee to go farther with Him, and said to the rest, " Sit ye here, while I go yonder and pray." His supreme hour had come, and what could He do but pray? To the three He said, " My soul is exceeding sorrowful, even unto death ''—death, unless He could find relief. " Abide ye here and watch " (stay awake) " with me." Three times He went from them a short distance to pray, and three times came back to find them asleep. He could not endure to be thus left alone in His anguish. But wakeful angels were watching over the scene and at the moment of His keenest anguish one of them was permitted to appear to Him and strengthen Him. The reported words of this prayer are few. It was doubtless now that His words were attended with strong crying and tears, and by these He was choked almost into silence. I can almost hear the sob with which he prayed, " Father, if it be possible, let this cup pass from me." Who can fathom the depth of meaning in that utterance, or weigh the temptation which it implied? It was offered to " him who was able to save him from death," and He was heard (Heb. 5 : 8)—heard not by saving Him from death, but by sending the angel to strengthen Him. How I long to know what that angel said! Some day I hope to ask him. It did strengthen Him; for when He next returned to the sleeping disciples, instead of waking them, as before, He said, " Sleep on now, and take your rest." Without another cry, or another groan, He passed through the arrest, the trial, the mocking, the scourging, the crucifixion, till the moment when He cried out, " My God, my God, why hast thou forsaken me? " In another moment we hear the last prayer He ever uttered: " Father, into thy hands I commend my spirit." His Father had not forsaken Him. His temptations, His prayers and His tears were now ended forevermore.

ARTHUR CUSHMAN McGIFFERT

1861-1933

THE KINGDOM OF GOD IN THE MODERN WORLD

BIOGRAPHICAL NOTE

PROFESSOR of Church history, Union Theological Seminary, New York, 1893-1927; born Sauquoit, N. Y., March 4, 1861; graduated Western Reserve College; D.D., 1892; D.D., Harvard, 1906; graduated from Union Theological Seminary, 1885; University of Marburg, Germany, Ph.D., 1888; studied in Germany, France and Italy; instructor of Church history, Lane Theological Seminary, Cincinnati, 1888-90; professor from 1890-93; author of "A Dialogue Between a Christian and a Jew," a translation of Eusebius "Church History," "A History of Christianity in the Apostolic Age," "The Apostles' Creed," etc.

" Go thou and publish abroad the kingdom of God."
—Luke 9 : 60.

THE age in which we live is notably religious. I will not say that there is more religion within the Christian Church than in other days, or that we Christians are distinguished above our fathers by the sincerity and vigor of our religious life, but certainly the multiform religious sects that are springing up all about us, the growing discontent with existing forms of faith, and the eagerness of many both within and without the established religious communities to listen to those who have anything new to offer in religious lines are evidence of a deep and wide stirring of religious impulse and interest. Humanity at large is so constituted that religion of some sort may fairly be regarded as permanently necessary to it, but as the needs of men change the religions in which they have been trained may easily cease to meet their new demands, and a new faith may come to be substituted for the old. This has occurred repeatedly in history. The displacement of the Greek and Roman paganism by Christianity is one of the most notable and familiar instances. Christianity won its victory in the Roman Empire and became finally the religion of the state simply because it met the needs of the age as the older cults were unable to do. The faiths of Greece and Rome were the fruit of ancient conditions and even before Christianity appeared new needs had developed which made new religious conceptions and practises a necessity. The result was that foreign cults of all sorts became popular and the old ones underwent large changes in the effort, conscious or unconscious, to meet the new situation. Had Christianity not come upon the scene the traditional paganism, radically modified to meet the demands of the day, might have retained a permanent hold upon the Roman Empire. But the new faith, born in the new age, and responsive from the beginning to its new needs, was fitted as the older could not be to become the religion of the new world and its victory was inevitable.

It has often been remarked that our age bears a striking resemblance to the period in which Christianity first saw the light. The eager curiosity, the social unrest, the lively intercourse between different parts of the world, the developing spirit of cosmopolitanism and sense of human brotherhood, the disappearance of old and familiar landmarks, the common questioning of traditional standards, the multiplying of religious sects, the prevalence both of rationalism and of superstition, the loss of faith and the search for certainty—in all these and many other respects there is a close kinship between the earliest and the latest of the Christian centuries. It was a period of change on a vast scale and so is this. Are we to suppose then that as the ancient paganism gave way before the young and lusty Christianity so Christianity in its turn is to be crowded off the field by some new faith or by no faith? There are many who think so and who talk about Christianity as an outworn system fitted only for an age that is gone. In reply to them it is not enough to show that Christianity still meets many needs of many hearts, needs which remain ever much the same—that it comforts the sorrowing, strengthens the weak, raises the fallen as it has always done. It must be shown rather that Christianity not only does this but also meets the new needs of the new age. What then is this new age? What are its characteristic features and its peculiar needs?

The modern age is marked by a vast confidence in the powers of man. For many centuries it was the custom to think of man as a weak and puny thing. Humility and self-distrust were the cardinal virtues, pride and self-reliance and independence the root of all vice. The change is not the fruit of speculation, a mere philosophical theory as to man's relation to the universe, but the result of the actual and growing conquest of the world in which we live. We are not completely its masters to be sure, but we understand it far better and control it far more effectively than our fathers did. The past century has given the most brilliant demonstration the world has ever seen of what human power can actually accomplish in the material realm, the realm of the tangible and the visible and the audible. Science and mechanics have combined to give the modern man a sense of mastery undreamed of in other ages. What such a man most needs from Christianity (and he is the representative man of the modern age, whose presence in overwhelming numbers chiefly distinguishes this age from those that have preceded it) is not condemnation for the pride of accomplishment, exhortations to humility, and the offer of healing from above, but the chance to use his strength in ways that are most worth while—higher ideals, larger opportunities, vaster realms of service.

Another marked characteristic of the modern age is its widespread and controlling interest in the present world. With all its sorrow and suffering and distress, the world seems to the representative modern man a better and a more satisfying place than it did to the representative man of an older day. It is not simply that this earth has become more interesting as we have learned more

about it, and the present life more comfortable as material conditions have improved, but that the future possibilities of human life upon this planet seem so tremendous. Characteristic of a former time was its conviction that all had been learned and accomplished that man was capable of, that the golden age lay in the past and that nothing better was to be looked for. Characteristic of the present time is its unbounded faith in the future, based upon its solid experience of the past. Pessimism there is in plenty, as in every age of the world, but optimism not pessimism is the dominant temper of this young and confident century. And again, what the age needs from Christianity is not a demonstration that this earth is a poor and unsatisfying place, but the vision of a work worth doing now and here, a work worth doing for this world, in which the thought and interest of the modern age so largely center.

Another characteristic of our age is its growing social concern, which is the fruit in part of the modern interest in the present life just referred to, in part of the general emphasis on solidarity and unity which succeeded the eighteenth century emphasis on individuality. The social conscience of Europe and America is now more wide awake and more generally active than ever before. Opportunities for social service are steadily multiplying, character is more and more interpreted in social terms, and their obligation to labor for the promotion of the welfare of society is increasingly felt both by individuals and by institutions. Our generation is burning with zeal for social, economic and civic reform, and is controlled by the idea of human brotherhood and marked by its practise as no generation ever was before. And again, what such an age needs from Christianity is not to be told the supreme importance of personal salvation, but to be given a social ideal grand enough to fire its imagination, to arouse its enthusiasm and to enlist its devotion.

Has Christianity then a message for the modern world, or does it belong wholly to the past and minister only to the same needs it always has? If so, it may expect to find itself more and more disregarded by modern men. All too many indeed disregard it now. It is not that they are hostile to Christianity but that they care nothing about it. It seems to address itself only to interests which they do not share. The old needs as experience shows, may be revivified, or even recreated on a larger or a smaller scale where they do not already exist, but to create artificial needs in order to meet them when the modern world is full of real needs of another kind is a sorry business. If Christianity cannot do more than this it is an outworn faith and the past only not the future belongs to it. But Christianity is not an outworn faith and the future does belong to it, for it has a message for the representative men of this modern age. It ministers not only to permanent human needs which are common to all times and places, but also to the new and peculiar needs of this twentieth century.

The greatest fact in modern Christian history is the rediscovery of Jesus. He is better known and understood to-day than He has ever been before. The recent development of historical study and criticism which has revolutionized traditional opinion upon all sorts of matters has given us a new insight into the origin and growth of Christianity. The Jesus of the synoptic gospels has been finally set free from the integuments in which the devotion and the misunderstanding of the Christian Church early enswathed Him, and has been allowed for the first time to speak for Himself. And the striking feature of the situation is that He speaks a language which the modern age, with its genial confidence in men, its vivid interest in the present world and its profound concern for social betterment, is peculiarly fitted to understand. His message is just the message that the modern world is looking for.

The kingdom of God was the burden of His preaching, not a kingdom lying simply in another world beyond the skies, but established here and now—" Thy kingdom come, thy will be done in earth "; not a kingdom made up of isolated human lives moving along their several and separate paths toward heaven, but of the society of all human kind banded together in common labor under the control of a common purpose; and not by some supernatural and miraculous means was the kingdom to come, while men sat by and gazed in awe upon the power of the Almighty, but by the work of Jesus Himself and of those that came after Him, by the devotion and energy of human lives working at one with the divine will. When Jesus said, " Follow me," He meant nothing else than laboring with Him at the same task in the same spirit.

The kingdom of God on earth—what does it mean? We answer perhaps glibly enough: the control of the lives of all men and of all their relationships one with another and of all the institutions in which those relationships find expression by the spirit of Jesus Christ who has shown us what God is and what He would have this world be. The answer is profoundly true, but it needs to be given a more definite content. What is actually involved in the kingdom of God on earth? Is it only a vague form of words, a beautiful but intangible mirage; or is it really something concrete and practical? Does it affect only ethics and religion, or social, economic and civic matters as well? Does it mean merely the improvement of individual character or also the transformation of society and the State; the mod-

ification of details in our existing systems or their radical reconstruction; the grafting of new principles on the old or the repudiation of all we have and the birth of a new world? Can our present civilization really be Christianized or must it give way to an altogether different order? Is it a dangerous thing, this kingdom of God? Does it cut too deep to be welcome or is it simply the fulfilment of our faith and hope? And how is the kingdom to be established? What methods are to be adopted, what principles followed and along what lines must the work proceed? It is not to answer them that I have propounded such momentous questions as these. Who indeed can answer them to-day? It is only to emphasize the importance of the problem. All other problems pale beside it. In it the Church of the twentieth century, to which has been committed the responsibility of leadership has the most difficult, the most complicated, the most pressing problem that it has to face. We Protestants have hardly more than played with it hitherto. In the Middle Ages the Catholics grappled with it and actually evolved an international state which they called the kingdom of God and which dominated western Europe for centuries. It was a grand conception, magnificently carried out, but it was not the kind of kingdom Jesus was thinking of nor the kind of a kingdom the world needs to-day. We live in the modern age and the modern age has turned its back forever on medievalism whether in State or Church. We do not want the spirit of otherworldliness to distract men from their duty to this world, but to inspire them to it. We do not want the future to overshadow the present, but to transfigure it. We do not want the supernatural to crowd out the natural, but to fill it with divine meaning. We do not want a recrudescence of priestly or ecclesiastical authority, but the birth of the spirit of Christian service. Freedom, spontaneity, individuality, opportunity, confidence and self-reliance, all these precious gains of the modern age we must preserve. But we must have also love, sympathy, fellowship, cooperation and an ideal worthy of our common devotion, our common effort and our common sacrifice.

The kingdom for which medieval Christians toiled was for still another reason quite a different thing from the kingdom of God which Jesus had in mind. He did not mean another institution, set up in the midst of the existing institutions of the world into which a man could enter from without. The kingdom of God which Jesus revealed is not identical with the Christian Church. It is the reign of God, of His purposes, of His ideals, of His Spirit, in the lives of men and in the relationships and institutions of the world. It is the world itself brought into harmony with God's will; not a dualism of two kingdoms, but one kingdom only—God's world and ours—controlled by the spirit of Christ. For this the Christian Church is called to labor; not to enlarge and glorify itself and to seek to dominate, but to make itself the most efficient instrument for the transformation of the world into the kingdom of God.

It is a vast and splendid thing, this kingdom of God of which Jesus dreamed. It is not for one type of mind, one form of character, one sort of temperament alone, but for all the sons of God the wide world over. It is rich enough to supply the most varied needs. It offers opportunity to the strong, activity to the strenuous, visions to the seer, comfort to the sorrowing, peace to the troubled, to all service by doing or enduring, by giving or receiving, by the spirit of Christ in active conflict or in quiet meditation.

It is a divine thing, this kingdom of God. In it God's supreme purpose finds expression, His purpose to promote the reign of the spirit of love among men. It is for this that God is, and this is what God's love for the world means. In human brotherhood the divine Fatherhood finds fulfilment. Through human brotherhood alone the Father's purpose for His children comes to accomplishment, and through human brotherhood alone His children discover Him. God Himself is back of the kingdom. We did not invent it. Its ideals are not of our making. They have been given us. They are higher than we could have dreamed of. They lift us above ourselves. We rise to meet them and find exprest in them the best that we can know. In this kingdom the divine and the human are inextricably interwoven. In it there is communion with God as His desires fill our souls and His purposes are made our own, and in it there is the power of God as the inspirations of His presence lay hold upon us. And yet it realizes itself only in the experience of man. We do not find it by turning our backs upon the world and ceasing to be human, we find it only here in human life itself. It is rooted in the inner man, in his affections, his will, his character, but it comes to visible expression in all sorts of ways as the external relationships of life are brought one after another under the control of the inner disposition.

It is both material and spiritual, this kingdom of God. It ministers to the body and to the soul. Not as in earlier days when the Church thought only of the spirit and looked upon the body with contempt; not as to-day so many social reformers, even Christians, seem to think only of the body and disregard altogether the higher things of the spirit. Unlike both, Jesus ministered at once to the outer and the inner man, and the kingdom of God which He proclaimed means the weal of the one as of the other, means a social order in which there shall be food and drink and cloth-

ing and shelter, a just share of the physical goods of life for all God's children, and in which there shall be also for all of them the consolations of divine communion, the inspirations of human fellowship, the glow of sympathy, the joy of service, the trinity of faith and hope and love.

It is a Christian thing, this kingdom of God. The greatest gift of God to the world is Jesus Christ. It is just this which differentiates the kingdom we proclaim from all man-made Utopias. His life, His character, His teaching, His work, His spirit of service dominating the world—this is what the kingdom means. In it is not merely our self-taught love and devotion, but the love and devotion of the Christ, kindled in our hearts as we have looked upon Him and caught the inspiration of His vision of God. The prophets too preached the kingdom of God, and exalted their conception was; but they had not seen the Christ, and it is not the kingdom of the prophets we proclaim to the world but the kingdom of the Christ. In Him God has given the full revelation of His purpose for the world, and His aims, His motives, His estimate of values, His hopes are those that we would have the world share.

It is a uniting, not a dividing force, this kingdom of God. Not setting the present over against the past, the Church over against the world, the conservative over against the radical, one community, one nation, one sect over against another. It gathers them all up into one; for it is broad enough to include all the best of the past and of the present and of the future yet to come; grand enough to enlist the devotion of men of every people, clime and faith; and large enough to unite the whole world in a vast confederation of labor, not for the greatest good of the greatest number but for the greatest good of all; not the good of competition, which blesses one at the expense of another, but the good of cooperation which blesses both alike. Not by jealousy and envy, not by sectarian zeal and religious fanaticism, not by national bigotry and class prejudice, not by the forcing of opinions and customs upon others, but by the union of all men of good will of every race and condition, by the sharing of their visions and by the linking of their faiths and hopes and efforts shall the kingdom of God come.

The great task of the Christian Church of the twentieth century is ready to its hand. Upon the Church devolves the chief responsibility for the bringing of the kingdom, for to it has been vouchsafed the supreme vision, in Jesus' revelation of His Father's will. The Church has had many large tasks in the past which it has met in a spirit of consecrated heroism—the conversion of the Roman Empire, the planting of a Christian civilization among the barbarian people of western Europe, the establishment of the world Church of the Middle Ages, the recovery of the gospel of Christ and its incarnation in new institutions in the sixteenth century. It is in the face of great tasks that the Church has always shown itself at its best and it may well be grateful when they come. If ever there was such a task it is before us now.

We are on the eve of great happenings. No one familiar with history and able to read the signs of the times can for a moment doubt it. Unfortunately the Church, as too often in the past, has temporarily lost its leadership. It continues to minister beautifully and efficiently to its own members and to bless the lives of multitudes of them, but it is not in the van of progress and much of the best life of the world has turned its back upon it and is pushing on alone. There have been periods when the world lagged behind the Church and the Church's one task was to urge it forward. To-day no small part of the world is ahead of the Church.

We Christians are apt to be much too easily satisfied. We are complacent if our churches hold their own, if our better families can still be counted on, if respectability still dictates, even tho hardly so imperatively as in other days, connection with the church and attendance upon its services. But this is not to be in command of the situation and it gives no large promise for the future. We are content with too little and the great modern world with its teeming masses, its eager enthusiasms, its burning problems and its untold possibilities, is in danger of slipping away from us. And yet what a message we have for it! The kingdom of God on earth, the control of all the relationships of life and of all the institutions of society by the spirit of Jesus Christ.

Is it a mere idle dream, the coming of God's kingdom on this our earth? It is the dream of Jesus Himself, and shall not His disciples share His faith? Is it vain after all the efforts of these nineteen centuries to hope that the thing can ever be done? But the thing has never been tried with that singleness of purpose to which Jesus summoned His followers. That is a momentous fact to be taken account of in every estimate of the future. The Christian Church has tried to do all sorts of things and in many of them has been remarkably successful. But it has never made the kingdom of God on earth, the reign of the spirit of Christ in all the relationships of life and in all the institutions of society its supreme aim. And so we need not be discouraged because the work is still unaccomplished. It is a new task to which the new insight of the Church summons it. Made wise by all the experiences of the past, endowed with a new charity and breadth of vision, taught the evils of disunion and the necessity of cooperation with all the forces of goodness everywhere, the Church is justified in entering upon its new mission with courage and with confidence.

Let us no longer stand upon the defensive; let us no longer regret a past forever gone; let us no longer be content to minister to the needs only of a small and select portion of the community; let us no longer indeed think so much about needs and think more about opportunities and obligations; let us keep our eyes fixed upon Jesus' glorious vision of the kingdom of God, of a new earth in which dwelleth righteousness, of a regenerated society controlled by His spirit. So will Christianity again as in the days of its youth rise exultant to a world-wide task. And this strong, manly, eager, busy age will respond with enthusiasm to an ideal worthy of its wisest planning and its best effort, the transformation not merely of individual lives into the image of Jesus Christ, but of this great earth into the kingdom of God, His Father and ours.

PHILIP MELANCHTHON

1497-1560

THE SAFETY
OF THE VIRTUOUS

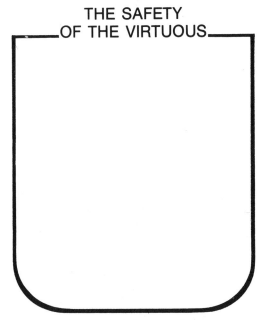

BIOGRAPHICAL NOTE

PHILIP MELANCHTHON (Schwarzerd) was born at Bretten, in Baden, in 1497. His name is noteworthy as first a fellow laborer and eventually a controversial antagonist of Luther. At the Diet of Augsburg, in 1530, he was the leading representative of the Reformation. He formulated the twenty-eight articles of the evangelical faith known as the "Augsburg Confession." The Lutherans of extreme Calvinistic views were alienated by Melanchthon's subsequent modifications of this confession, and by his treatises in ethics. He and his followers were bitterly assailed, but his irenic spirit did not forsake him. He was a true child of the Renaissance, and is styled by some writers "the founder of general learning throughout Europe." While he was never called or ordained to the ministry of the Church, he was in the habit of addressing the local religious assemblies or collegia from time to time, and, being a man of profound piety, his sympathetic and natural style of delivery made him an impressive speaker. He died in 1560, and his body was laid beside that of Martin Luther.

Neither shall any man pluck them out of my hand.
—John x., 28.

To THEE, almighty and true God, eternal Father of our Lord Jesus Christ, maker of heaven and earth, and of all creatures, together with Thy Son our Lord Jesus Christ, and the Holy Ghost—to Thee, the wise, good, true, righteous, compassionate, pure, gracious God, we render thanks that Thou hast hitherto upheld the Church in these lands, and graciously afforded it protection and care, and we earnestly beseech Thee evermore to gather among us an inheritance for Thy Son, which may praise Thee to all eternity.

I have in these, our assemblies, often uttered partly admonitions and partly reproofs, which I hope the most of you will bear in mind. But since I must presume that now the hearts of all are wrung with a new grief and a new pang by reason of the war in our neighborhood, this season seems to call for a word of consolation. And, as we commonly say, "Where the pain is there one claps his hand," I could not, in this so great affliction, make up my mind to turn my discourse upon any other subject. I do not, indeed, doubt that you yourselves seek comfort in the divine declarations, yet will I also bring before you some things collected therefrom, because always that on which we had ourselves thought becomes more precious to us when we hear that it proves itself salutary also to others. And because long discourses are burdensome in time of sorrow and mourning, I will, without delay, bring forward that comfort which is the most effectual.

Our pains are best assuaged when something good and beneficial, especially some help toward a happy issue, presents itself. All other topics of consolation, such as men borrow from the unavoidableness of suffering, and the examples of others, bring us no great alleviation. But the Son of God, our Lord Jesus Christ, who was crucified for us and raised again, and now sits at the right hand of the Father, offers us help and deliverance, and has manifested this disposition in many declarations. I will now speak of the words: "No man shall pluck my sheep out of my hand." This expression has often raised me up out of the deepest sorrow, and drawn me, as it were, out of hell.

The wisest men in all times have bewailed the great amount of human misery which we see with our eyes before we pass into eternity —diseases, death, want, our own errors, by which we bring harm and punishment on ourselves, hostile men, unfaithfulness on the part of those with whom we are closely connected, banishment, abuse, desertion, miserable children, public and domestic strife, wars, murder, and devastation. And since such things appear to befall good and bad without distinction, many wise men have inquired whether there were any Providence, or whether accident brings everything to pass independent of a divine purpose? But we in the Church know that the first and principal cause of human wo is this, that on account of sin man is made subject to death and other calamity, which is so much more vehement in the Church, because the devil, from the hatred toward God, makes fearful assaults on the Church and strives to destroy it utterly.

Therefore it is written: "I will put enmity between the serpent and the seed of the woman." And Peter says: "Your adversary, the devil, as a roaring lion, walketh about and seeketh whom he may devour."

Not in vain, however, has God made known to us the causes of our misery. We should not only consider the greatness of our necessity, but also discern the causes of it, and recognize His righteous anger against sin, to the end that we may, on the other hand, perceive the Redeemer and the greatness of His compassion; and as witnesses to these, His declarations, He adds the raising of dead men to life, and other miracles.

Let us banish from our hearts, therefore, the unbelieving opinions which imagine that evils befall us by mere chance, or from physical causes.

But when thou considerest the wounds in thy own circle of relations, or dost cast a glance at the public disorders in the State, which again afflict the individual also (as Solon says: "The general corruption penetrates even to thy quiet habitation"), then think, first, of thy own and others' sins, and of the righteous wrath of God; and, secondly, weigh the rage of the devil, who lets loose his hate chiefly in the Church.

In all men, even the better class, great darkness reigns. We see not how great an evil sin is, and regard not ourselves as so shamefully defiled. We flatter ourselves, in particular, because we profess a better doctrine concerning God. Nevertheless, we resign ourselves to a careless slumber, or pamper each one his own desires; our impurity, the disorders of the Church, the necessity of brethren, fills us not with pain; devotion is without fire and fervor; zeal for doctrine and discipline languishes, and not a few are my sins, and thine, and those of many others, by reason of which such punishments are heaped upon us.

Let us, therefore, apply our hearts to repentance, and direct our eyes to the Son of God, in respect to whom we have the assurance that, after the wonderful counsel of God, He is placed over the family of man, to be the protector and preserver of his Church.

We perceive not fully either of our wretchedness or our dangers, or the fury of enemies, until after events of extraordinary sorrowfulness. Still we ought to reflect thus: there must exist great need and a fearful might and rage of enemies, since so powerful a protector has been given to us, even God's Son. When He says: "No man shall pluck my sheep out of my hand," He indicates that He is no idle spectator of wo, but that mighty and incessant strife is going on. The devil incites his tools to disturb the Church or the political commonwealth, that boundless confusion may enter, followed by heathenish desolation. But the Son of God, who holds in His hands, the congregation of those who call upon His name, hurls back the devils by His infinite power, conquers and chases them thence, and will one day shut them up in the prison of hell, and punish them to all eternity with fearful pains. This comfort we must hold fast in regard to the entire Church, as well as each in regard to himself.

If, in these distracted and warring times, we see States blaze up and fall to ruin, then look away to the Son of God, who stands in the secret counsel of the Godhead and guards His little flock and carries the weak lambs, as it were, in His own hands. Be persuaded that by Him thou also shalt be protected and upheld.

Here some, not rightly instructed, will exclaim: "Truly I could wish to commend myself to such a keeper, but only His sheep does He preserve. Whether I also am counted in that flock, I know not." Against this doubt we must most strenuously contend, for the Lord Himself assures us in this very passage, that all who "hear and with faith receive the voice of the gospel are His sheep"; and He says expressly: "If a man love me, he will keep my words, and my Father will love him, and we will come to him and make our abode with him." These promises of the Son of God, which can not be shaken, we must confidently appropriate to ourselves. Nor shouldst thou, by thy doubts, exclude thyself from this blest flock, which originates in the righteousness of the gospel. They do not rightly distinguish between the law and the gospel, who, because they are unworthy, reckon not themselves among the sheep. Rather is this consolation afforded us, that we are accepted "for the Son of God's sake," truly, without merit, not on account of our own righteousness, but through faith, because we are unworthy, and impure, and far from having fulfilled the law of God. That is, moreover, a universal promise, in which the Son of God saith: "Come unto me, all ye that labor and are heavy laden, and I will give you rest.''

The eternal Father earnestly commands that we should hear the Son, and it is the greatest of all transgressions if we despise Him and do not approve His voice. This is what every one should often and diligently consider, and in this disposition of the Father, revealed through the Son, find grace.

Altho, amid so great disturbances, many a sorrowful spectacle meets thine eye, and the Church is rent by discord and hate, and manifold and domestic public necessity is added thereto, still let not despair overcome thee, but know thou that thou hast the Son of God for a keeper and protector, who will not suffer either the Church, or thee, or thy family, to be plucked out of His hand by the fury of the devil.

With all my heart, therefore, do I supplicate the Son of God, our Lord Jesus Christ, who, having been crucified for us, and raised again, sits at the right hand of the Father, to bless men with His gifts, and to Him I pray that He would protect and govern this little church and me therein. Other sure trust, in this great flame when the whole world is on fire, I discern nowhere. Each one has his separate hopes, and each one with his understanding seeks to repose in something else; but however good that may all be, it is still a far better, and unquestionably a more effectual, consolation to flee to the Son of God and expect help and deliverances from Him.

Such wishes will not be in vain. For to this end are we laden with such a crowd of dangers, that in events and occurrences which to human prudence are an inexplicable enigma, we may recognize the infinite goodness and presentness of God, in that He, for His Son's sake, and through His Son, affords us aid. God will be owned in such deliverance just as in the deliverance of your first parents, who, after the fall, when they were forsaken by all the creatures, were upheld by the help of God alone. So was the family of Noah in the flood, so were the Israelites preserved when in the Red Sea they stood between the towering walls of waters. These glorious examples are held up before us, that we might know, in like manner, the Church, without the help of any created beings, is often preserved. Many in all times have experienced such divine deliverance and support in their personal dangers, as David saith: ''My father and my mother have forsaken me, but the Lord taketh me up''; and in another place David saith: ''He hath delivered the wretched, who hath no helper.'' But in order that we may become partakers of these so great blessings, faith and devotion must be

kindled within us, as it stands written, ''Verily, I say unto you!'' So likewise must our faith be exercised, that before deliverance we should pray for help and wait for it, resting in God with a certain cheerfulness of soul; and that we should not cherish continual doubt and melancholy murmuring in our hearts, but constantly set before our eyes the admonition of God: ''The peace of God which passeth all understanding keep your heart and mind''; which is to say, be so comforted in God, in time of danger, that your hearts, having been strengthened by confidence in the pity and presentness of God, may patiently wait for help and deliverance, and quietly maintain that peaceful serenity which is the beginning of eternal life, and without which there can be no true devotion.

For distrust and doubt produce a gloomy and terrible hate toward God, and that is the beginning of the eternal torments, and a rage like that of the devil.

Now you must guard against these billows in the soul, and these stormy agitations, and, by meditation on the precious promises of God, keep and establish your hearts.

Truly these times allow not the wonted security and the wonted intoxication of the world, but they demand that with honest groans we should cry for help, as the Lord saith, ''Watch and pray that ye fall not into temptation,'' that ye may not, being overcome by despair, plunge into everlasting destruction. There is need of wisdom to discern the dangers of the soul, as well as the safeguard against them. Souls go to ruin as well when, in epicurean security, they make light of the wrath of God as when they are overcome by doubt and cast down by anxious sorrow, and these transgressions aggravate the punishment. The godly, on the other hand, who by faith and devotion keep their hearts erect and near to God, enjoy the beginning of eternal life and obtain mitigation of the general distress.

We, therefore, implore Thee, Son of God, Lord Jesus Christ, who, having been crucified and raised for us, standest in the secret counsel of the Godhead, and makest intercession for us, and hast said: ''Come unto me, all ye that labor and are heavy laden, and I will give you rest.'' I call upon Thee, and with my whole heart beseech Thee, according to Thine infinite compassion, forgive us our sins. Thou knowest that in our great weakness we are not able to bear the burden of our wo. Do Thou, therefore, afford us aid in our private and public necessities; be Thou our shelter and protector, uphold the churches in these lands, and all which serves for their defense and safeguard.

JAMES MOFFATT

1870-1944

THE COURAGE OF RELIGION

BIOGRAPHICAL NOTE

On the editorial staff of the *Hibbert Journal;* minister of the United Free Church of Scotland; born Glasgow, July 4, 1870; educated at the academy, university and Free Church College, Glasgow; ordained in 1896; Jowett lecturer, London, 1907; author of "The Historical New Testament," "English Edition and Translation of Harnack's '*Ausbreitung des Christentums,*'" "The Golden Book of Owen," "Literary Illustrations of the Bible."

" And David said in his heart, I shall now perish one day by the hand of Saul."—1 Sam. 27 : 1.

BUT he did not perish by the hand of Saul. He lived to pronounce a eulogy, and a generous eulogy, upon his dead foe. Saul perished first; his attack seemed irresistible, but it came to nothing, and David's fear proved vain.

Thus do even strong, religious natures often make trouble for themselves out of a future about which they know next to nothing. David was terribly discouraged at this moment. The fond hope which he had cherished of succeeding to a high position in the kingdom had ebbed away. Wherever he turned, he saw nothing but the prospect of further peril and privation, whose end, sooner or later, meant defeat. Saul's resources were so numerous, and his power was so versatile, that the result of the struggle seemed to David to be merely a question of time.

Now, forethought is one thing. We have to be on the alert against the risks of life and open-eyed in face of any horrible combination which may threaten our position or affect our interests injuriously. But it is another thing altogether to collapse weakly in despair of heart before apprehensions and anxieties which may turn out to be quite unfounded. In the early part of last century a young scientist once wrote: " It has been a bitter mortification to me to digest the conclusion that the race is for the strong, and that I shall practically do little more but be content to admire the strides others make in science." It was Charles Darwin. He was in bad health, and bad health is apt to bring low spirits. Yet Darwin lived to do work which made others only too glad to follow his strides in science. That is one instance of the misjudgments which we are prone to make about our future, and David's bitter cry is just another.

We can all see how wrong it is for a religious man to yield thus to depression, and how foolish this perverse habit is, but surely we can also feel how natural it is to lose heart and courage for the moment. Only those who have had to make the effort know how difficult it is to be brave at certain times in life. I am speaking not of the courage required for some enterprise or heroic action, but of the quieter courage which holds depression at bay, which braces the soul against anxiety and which enables people to be composed and firm under circumstances of hardship, when doubts as to our own usefulness and prospects occur, or when the pressure of things seems to thwart and even to deny any providence of God within our sphere of life. At such moments, the strain almost overpowers us. David was living the anxious life of a hunted creature, like Hereward the Wake, or Bruce in the Athole country, or Wallace in Ayrshire and the North, obliged to be on his guard against repeated surprises, his nerves aquiver with the tension of pursuit. As he bitterly complained, Saul was chasing him like a partridge among the hills. True, he had first succeeded in outwitting his foe, but at night reaction came over him like a wave. How long could this guerrilla warfare go on? One day the fugitive pretender would be sure to fall into an ambush! He could not expect always to foil the attack of his enemies! And so thinking he lost his heart. "I shall now perish one day by the hand of Saul."

We must be on our guard against such moments of reaction, especially toward evening, when after the tiring day the body is too exhausted to help the mind against the inroad of oracle fears. Then doubts about our faith and health and work and income rise and shape themselves into dark possibilities of evil, and feelings are apt to get the better of our self-possession, and faith is shaken for the moment. It is a great part of life's management to be on our guard against such apprehensions. Towards night, or when you are run down, whenever reaction sets in, the judgment and the content of faith are apt to be disturbed by fears which either vanish or at any rate shrink to their true proportions in the light of the morning. You are bound to remember that, and to lay your account with it.

The mood is almost constitutional with some. Owing to inherited disposition or to imperfect training, some are tempted to dwell repeatedly upon the darker side of things. They are highly strung, by nature. Their sensitive hearts get easily deprest. The sense of danger, which acts upon certain people like a pacific stimulus, only serves to damp their courage. They belong to the class for which Bunyan, with all the generosity of a strong nature, felt such evident sympathy—Mrs. Despondency, Miss Much-Afraid, Mr. Fearing, Mr. Feeble-Mind, the ready inaction of Giant Despair and of Castle Doubting.

At the same time, neither circumstances nor character can altogether explain the occasional failure of moral courage in life. David, for example, lived in the open air; his body was strong; there was nothing morbid about his habits of life; he loved music and fighting. But nevertheless he was subject to fits of depression and dismay, which discolored life and made God seem actually indifferent or hostile to him. Now, what is to be done, when the spirit is thus overwhelmed within us?

In the first place, there is usually something that can be done. Action is one of the best means of banishing idle shadows from the path. There is this to be said for David, that he never allowed self-pity to benumb his faculties. Despair made him energetic; it drove him at this crisis to seek shelter outside the boundaries of the country for himself and his household. Instead of folding his hands and letting things drift, he did his best to secure a haven for his family and to provide as well as he could for himself. Such is the first note of practical courage in our religious life. Often, to lose heart means, with us, to lose vigor. People brood on their difficulties and perplexities until hardship is allowed to paralyze their faculties of resistance. Now David's example summons us to face our troubles and to make the best of them, instead of sitting down to bemoan ourselves as the victims of fate. We all have our moments of cowardice. Thank God if they are only moments. Thank God if we have enough faith and nerve left to rise, as David did, even with a heavy heart, and put our hand to some business of the day. The mere feeling of movement will help to raise our courage. It will inspire us with the conviction that we are not meant to be mere driftwood, at the mercy of the wild risks and chances of the current. Our very proverb about "rising to the occasion" is based upon this truth. And to rise to the occasion means that we shake off the selfish torpor of self-pity and depression, standing up to grapple somehow with the difficulties of our lot.

The second mark of returning courage is to get away from the circle of our own feelings, and this is the escape of faith. Remember what David forgot for the moment—God's purpose and God's faithfulness. Long ago he had been chosen from the sheepfold for a career which neither he nor anyone else anticipated. God had lifted him from the country to the court. His vocation had opened up, and now, altho everything appeared to contradict this purpose, could it have failed? Could the will of God be shattered or recalled? Was the past experience of His favor accidental or delusive? Such is the heart's logic of the religious man. It is in fact the underlying faith in providence which rallies and restores our nature in its broken hours. Newman once called it the true religion of Great Britain. "What Scripture illustrates from its first page to its last," he declared, "is God's providence; and that is nearly the only doctrine held with a real assent by the mass of religious Englishmen. Hence the Bible is so great a solace and refuge to them in trouble." The reason why people draw hope and encouragement in this way is that religion means not simply an ordered view of the universe, which excludes caprice and tyranny alike, but a sense of the divine control and care for the individual. A vague impression of providence would not rally anybody. What is needed to reinforce our moral strength is the conviction of God's personal interest in the single life, and of a wise, loving Will which never fails anyone who loyally follows it at all hazards. No outsider can form any idea of the change produced in a human soul by this resolute trust in the higher responsibility of God. The center is changed from nervous worry about oneself to a pious reliance on the care of the Lord, and a real but unaccountable sense of security passes into the very secrets of the soul. According to our temperament it takes many forms, from quiet calm to an exulting confidence, but in every form this faith does its perfect work by putting the entire concern of life into God's sure keeping.

Here, then, lies another remedy for nervousness and agitation about our prospects. Even in your hours of panic, when life seems brought to nothing, you can reflect: " After all, I am the object of my Father's care and purpose. I can trust Him absolutely. He has put me here and been with me hitherto. I am not left to myself. I cannot, I will not, believe that He has grown weary of the responsibility for what He made." To say that in your heart is not vanity; it is the sheer trust of faith, won from long experience and still to be verified during the days to come. Unknown as your future may be, you are at the disposal of One whom you have learned to trust, whose management of life you are prepared to accept, not coldly but with a steady and even a cheerful consent. The deepest thing you know about your life is that you are His choice and charge and handiwork.

That naturally opens out into a third source of courage, namely, gratitude. Faith, in order to do its perfect work, needs to pass from dull submission and acquiescence into a habit of thankfulness to God. The spirit of praise ministers to our sense of God's reality by calling up before our mind and heart those acts in which we see His character and from which we are intended to gain a firmer impression of His continuous and personal interest in ourselves. When we thank God, we realize Him more profoundly and intimately than ever. Too often, I am afraid, most of us are thankful to get past some difficulty, and if we remember it at all it is to congratulate ourselves secretly upon the skill and good fortune which carried us over the jolt in the road. But these steps and stages should be precious to the soul. They ought to be accumulating for us, as the years go by, a steady faith in God's sure faithfulness. Now that is impossible unless we are in the habit of saying to ourselves, as each favor comes: " This is the doing of God. I thank thee for this my Father. Thou art very good to me." Dejection is frequently the result of nothing more

than a failure to practise this habit of thankfulness. We forget to praise God for His daily mercies, and so they pass away from us without leaving any rich deposit of assurance, as they would have done if we had owned His hand in every one. Now the full good of any deliverance and help is not merely the outward benefit which it confers upon our life. The relief is something. But surely we are also intended to win from it a new confirmation of our faith in God's character and a deeper apprehension of His purpose in relation to ourselves. The repeated acts of God within our personal experience are so many glimpses into the constancy and truth of His will, and it is our privilege to use those, from time to time, in order to learn how surely He can be depended upon. David seems to have forgotten this, for the time being. He had rejoiced over his recent exploit, but he had not allowed it to bear home to him the sense of God's unfailing care, and that was one reason why he lay open to misgivings and fear. It is always so, in human experience, when we face the future without having won from the past a more settled faith in the continuity of God's living will.

Such are some of the methods by means of which religion ministers to strength and constancy of life. Courage indeed varies with our disposition and our training. " The French courage," Byron wrote once to Murray, " proceeds from vanity, the German from phlegm, the Turkish from fanaticism and opium, the Spanish from pride, the English from custom, the Dutch from obstinacy, the Russian from insensibility, but the Italian from anger." A generalization like this is always loose, but it serves to remind us how many forces in life will call out courage; an inspiriting example, sympathy, indignation, pity, the sense of self-respect—any of these will often keep us from breaking down and giving way. Faith can pour strength along these and other channels, but most directly of all it helps us, if it is real, to be self-possessed and brave by calling up before us the entire compass of the situation. Where we fail is in forgetting to include the greatest element of all, or in undervaluing it. We leave God out of our estimate. David said, " I shall now perish one day by the hand of Saul." Was there no more in his life than that? I and Saul? What about God? Had life resolved itself into a mere trial of strength between David and his foe? Was there no longer any providence in it? What of the splendid confession before Goliath, " The Lord who delivered me from the power of the lion and the bear will deliver me out of the hand of this Philistine? " Ah, there spoke the true David, the man after God's own heart, who recognized God's hand in the action and passion of his days, and who was no more sure of his own existence than of God's answer to the faith and effort of the soul.

The sterling courage of religion is to be satisfied with this assurance, to win it from experience and to hold it by due care of the mind and body and by a habit of sincere thankfulness to God. It may be that for a time your life is very different from what you expected. You may have to face difficult passages and dark turns when it is not easy to feel much more than the annoyance and uncertainty and strain that sometimes crowd upon you with disturbing force. There are days when you scarcely venture to look ahead, in case you are unnerved by the prospect. It seems as if almost everything conspired to strip life of its just hope and vitality. When such clouds of physical reaction and brain-weariness come down, will you believe that God has not abandoned you? Do not reckon up nervously this chance and that, pitting the one against the other, but fall back on what you know of God's character and goodness in the past, till His word and witness put some fresh hope into your soul.

> Say not, The struggle naught availeth,
> The labor and the wounds are vain;
> The enemy faints not, nor faileth
> And as things have been, they remain;

say it not, even in your heart. Believe it not. What does remain is the undying interest of God in you. What faints not, nor faileth, is this redeeming purpose. Don't give way. Whatever you do, do not lose heart and hope, under the gray sky. Tell yourself to wait, to wait for the living God, and see. And you will see what thousands of men and women have rejoiced to see, that, whoever fails you, whatever may be thrust on you or taken from you, nothing, neither life nor death, nor things present, nor things to come, will be able to separate you from the love of God which is in Christ Jesus, our Lord.

DWIGHT L. MOODY

1837-1899

WHAT THINK YE OF CHRIST?

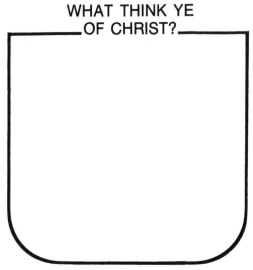

BIOGRAPHICAL NOTE

DWIGHT LYMAN MOODY, the evangelist, was born at Northfield, Massachusetts, in 1837, and died in 1899. As a business man he brought to his evangelistic work exceptional tact, initiative, and executive ability, but the main source of his power lay in his knowledge of the Bible, his constant companion. In preaching he largely disregarded form, and thought little of the sermon as such. His one overwhelming and undeviating purpose was to lead men to Christ. His speaking was in a kind of monotone, but his straightforward plainness never failed to be effective. He usually held the Bible in his hand while speaking, so that there was little of gesture. His great sympathetic nature is spoken of by Henry Drummond in these words:

"If eloquence is measured by its effect upon an audience, and not by its balanced sentences and cumulative periods, then this is eloquence of the highest sort. In sheer persuasiveness Mr. Moody has few equals, and rugged as his preaching may seem to some, there is in it a pathos of a quality which few orators have ever reached, and an appealing tenderness which not only wholly redeems it, but raises it, not unseldom, almost to sublimity."

What think ye of Christ?—Matt. xxii., 42.

I SUPPOSE there is no one here who has not thought more or less about Christ. You have heard about Him, and read about Him, and heard men preach about Him. For eighteen hundred years men have been talking about Him and thinking about Him; and some have their minds made up about who He is, and doubtless some have not. And altho all these years have rolled away, this question comes up, addresst to each of us, to-day, "What think ye of Christ?"

I do not know why it should not be thought a proper question for one man to put to another. If I were to ask you what you think of any of your prominent men, you would already have your mind made up about him. If I were to ask you what you thought of your noble queen, you would speak right out and tell me your opinion in a minute.

If I were to ask about your prime minister, you would tell me freely what you had for or against him. And why should not people make up their minds about the Lord Jesus Christ, and take their stand for or against Him? If you think well of Him, why not speak well of Him and range yourselves on His side? And if you think ill of Him, and believe Him to be an impostor, and that He did not die to save the world, why not lift up your voice and say you are against Him? It would be a happy day for Christianity if men would just take sides—if we could know positively who is really for Him and who is against Him.

It is of very little importance what the world thinks of any one else. The queen and the statesman, the peers and the princes, must soon be gone. Yes; it matters little, comparatively, what we think of them. Their lives can only interest a few; but every living soul on the face of the earth is concerned with this Man. The question for the world is, "What think ye of Christ?"

I do not ask you what you think of the Established Church, or of the Presbyterians, or the Baptists, or the Roman Catholics; I do not ask you what you think of this minister or that, of this doctrine or that; but I want to ask you what you think of the living person of Christ?

I should like to ask, Was He really the Son of God—the great God-Man? Did He leave heaven and come down to this world for a purpose? Was it really to seek and to save? I should like to begin with the manger, and to follow Him up through the thirty-three years He was here upon earth. I should ask you what you think of His coming into this world and being born in a manger when it might have been a palace; why He left the grandeur and the glory of heaven, and the royal retinue of angels; why He passed by palaces and crowns and dominion and came down here alone.

I should like to ask you what you think of Him as a teacher. He spake as never man spake. I should like to take Him up as a preacher. I should like to bring you to that mountain-side, that we might listen to the words as they fall from His gentle lips. Talk about the preachers of the present day! I would rather a thousand times be five minutes at the feet of Christ than listen a lifetime to all the wise men in the world. He used just to hang truth upon anything. Yonder is a sower, a fox, a bird, and He just gathers the truth around them, so that you cannot see a fox, a sower, or a bird, without thinking what Jesus said. Yonder is a lily of the valley; you cannot see it without thinking of His words, "They toil not, neither do they spin."

He makes the little sparrow chirping in the air preach to us. How fresh those wonderful sermons are, how they live to-day! How we love to tell them to our children, how the children love to hear! "Tell me a story about Jesus," how often we hear it; how the little ones love His sermons! No story-book in the world will ever interest them like the stories that He told. And yet how profound He was; how He puzzled the wise men; how the scribes and the Pharisees would never fathom Him! Oh, do you not think He was a wonderful preacher?

I should like to ask you what you think of Him as a physician. A man would soon have a reputation as a doctor if he could cure as Christ did. No case was ever brought to Him but what He was a match for. He had but to speak the word, and disease fled before Him. Here comes a man covered with leprosy.

"Lord, if thou wilt thou canst make me clean," he cried.

"I will," says the Great Physician, and in an instant the leprosy is gone. The world has hospitals for incurable diseases; but there were no incurable diseases with Him.

Now, see Him in the little home at Bethany, binding up the wounded hearts of Martha and Mary, and tell me what you think of Him as a comforter. He is a husband to the widow and a father to the fatherless. The weary may find a resting-place upon that breast, and the friendless may reckon Him their friend. He never varies, He never fails, He never dies. His sympathy is ever fresh, His love is ever free. Oh, widow and orphans, oh, sorrowing and mourning, will you not thank God for Christ the comforter?

But these are not the points I wish to take up. Let us go to those who knew Christ, and ask what they thought of Him. If you want to find out what a man is nowadays, you inquire about him from those who know him best. I do not wish to be partial; we will go to His enemies, and to His friends. We will ask them, What think ye of Christ? We will ask His friends and His enemies. If we only went to those who liked Him, you would say: "Oh, he is so blind; he thinks so much of the man that he can't see His faults. You can't get anything out of him unless it be in His favor; it is a one-sided affair altogether."

So we shall go in the first place to His enemies, to those who hated Him, persecuted Him, curst and slew Him. I shall put you in the jury-box, and call upon them to tell us what they think of Him.

First, among the witnesses, let us call upon the Pharisees. We know how they hated Him. Let us put a few questions to them. "Come, Pharisees, tell us what you have against the Son of God, What do you think of Christ?" Hear what they say! "This man receiveth sinners." What an argument to bring against Him! Why, it is the very thing that makes us love Him. It is the glory of the gospel. He receives sinners. If He had not, what would have become of us? Have you nothing more to bring against Him than this? Why, it is one of the greatest compliments that was ever paid Him. Once more: when He was hanging on the tree, you had this to say to Him, "He saved others, but He could not save Himself and save us too." So He laid down His own life for yours and mine. Yes, Pharisees, you have told the truth for once in your lives! He saved others. He died for others. He was a ransom for many; so it is quite true what you think of Him—He saved others, Himself He cannot save.

Now, let us call upon Caiaphas. Let him stand up here in his flowing robes; let us ask him for his evidence. "Caiaphas, you were chief priest when Christ was tried; you were president of the Sanhedrin; you were in the council-chamber when they found Him guilty; you yourself condemned Him. Tell us; what did the witnesses say? On what grounds did you judge Him? What testimony was brought against Him?" "He hath spoken blasphemy," says Caiaphas. "He said, 'Hereafter you shall see the Son of Man sitting on the right hand of power, and coming in the clouds of heaven.' When I heard that, I found Him guilty of blasphemy; I rent my mantle and condemned Him to death." Yes, all that they had against Him was that He was the Son of God; and they slew Him for the promise of His coming for His bride!

Now let us summon Pilate. Let him enter the witness-box.

"Pilate, this man was brought before you; you examined Him; you talked with Him face to face; what think you of Christ?"

"I find no fault in him," says Pilate. "He said he was the King of the Jews [just as He wrote it over the cross]; but I find no fault in him." Such is the testimony of the man who examined Him! And, as He stands there, the center of a Jewish mob, there comes along a man elbowing his way in haste. He rushes up to Pilate, and, thrusting out his hand, gives him a message. He tears it open; his face turns pale as he reads—"Have thou nothing to do with this just man, for I have suffered many things this day in a dream because of him." It is from Pilate's wife—her testimony to Christ. You want to know what His enemies thought of Him? You want to know what a heathen thought? Well, here it is, "no fault in him"; and the wife of a heathen, "this just man."

And now, look—in comes Judas. He ought to make a good witness. Let us address him. "Come, tell us, Judas, what think ye of Christ? You knew the Master well; you sold Him for thirty pieces of silver; you betrayed Him with a kiss; you saw Him perform those miracles; you were with Him in Jerusalem. In Bethany, when He summoned up Lazarus, you were there. What think you of Him? I can see him as he comes into the presence of the chief priests; I can hear the money ring as he dashes it upon the table, "I have betrayed innocent blood!" Here is the man who betrayed Him, and this is what he thinks of Him! Yes, those who were guilty of His death put their testimony on record that He was an innocent man.

Let us take the centurion who was present at the execution. He had charge of the Roman soldiers. He told them to make Him carry His cross; he had given orders for the nails to be driven into His feet and hands, for the spear to be thrust in His side. Let the centurion come forward. "Centurion, you had charge of the executioners; you saw that the order for His death was carried out; you saw Him die; you heard Him speak upon the cross. Tell us, what think you of Christ?" Hark! Look at him; he is smiting his breast as he cries, "Truly, this was the son of God!"

I might go to the thief upon the cross, and ask what he thought of Him. At first he railed upon Him and reviled Him. But then he thought better of it: "This man hath done nothing amiss," he says.

I might go further. I might summon the very devils themselves and ask them for their testimony. Have they anything to say of Him? Why, the very devils called Him the Son of God! In Mark we have the unclean spirit crying, "Jesus, thou Son of the most high God." Men say, "Oh, I believe Christ to be the Son of God, and because I believe it intellectually I shall be saved." I tell you the devils did that. And they did more than that, they trembled.

Let us bring in His friends. We want you to hear their evidence. Let us call that prince of preachers. Let us hear the forerunner; none ever preached like this man—this man who drew all Jerusalem and all Judea into the wilderness to hear him; this man who burst upon the nations like the flash of a meteor. Let John the Baptist come with his leathern girdle and his hairy coat, and let him tell us what he thinks of Christ. His words, tho they were echoed in the wilderness of Palestine, are written in the Book forever, "Behold the Lamb of God which taketh away the sin of the world!" This is what John the Baptist thought of him. "I bear record that He is the Son of God." No wonder he drew all Jerusalem and Judea to him, because he preached Christ. And whenever men preach Christ, they are sure to have plenty of followers.

Let us bring in Peter, who was with Him on the mount of transfiguration, who was with Him the night He was betrayed. Come, Peter, tell us what you think of Christ. Stand in this witness-box and testify of Him. You denied Him once. You said, with a curse, you did not know Him. Was it true, Peter? Don't you know Him? "Know Him!" I can imagine Peter saying: "It was a lie I told then. I did know Him." Afterward I can hear him charging home their guilt upon these Jerusalem sinners. He calls Him "both Lord and Christ." Such was the testimony on the day of Pentecost. "God had made that same Jesus both Lord and Christ." And tradition tells us that when they came to execute Peter he felt he was not worthy to die in the way his Master died, and he requested to be crucified with the head downward. So much did Peter think of Him!

Now let us hear from the beloved disciple John. He knew more about Christ than any other man. He had laid his head on his Savior's bosom. He had heard the throbbing of that loving heart. Look into his Gospel if you wish to know what he thought of Him.

Matthew writes of Him as the royal king come from His throne. Mark writes of Him as the servant, and Luke of the Son of Man. John takes up his pen, and, with one stroke, forever settles the question of Unitarianism. He goes right back before the time of Adam. "In the beginning was the Word, and the Word was with God, and the Word was God." Look into Revelation. He calls him "the bright and the morning star." So John thought well of Him—because he knew Him well.

We might bring in Thomas, the doubting

disciple. You doubted Him, Thomas? You would not believe He had risen, and you put your fingers into the wound in His side. What do you think of Him?

"My Lord and my God!" says Thomas.

Then go over to Decapolis and you will find Christ has been there casting out devils. Let us call the men of that country and ask what they think of Him. "He hath done all things well," they say.

But we have other witnesses to bring in. Take the persecuting Saul, once one of the worst of his enemies. Breathing out threatenings he meets Him. "Saul, Saul, why persecutest thou me?" says Christ. He might have added, "What have I done to you? Have I injured you in any way? Did I not come to bless you? Why do you treat Me thus, Saul?" And then Saul asks, "Who art thou, Lord?"

"I am Jesus of Nazareth, whom thou persecutest." You see, He was not ashamed of His name, altho He had been in heaven; "I am Jesus of Nazareth." What a change did that one interview make to Saul! A few years afterward we hear him say, "I have suffered the loss of all things, and do count them but dross that I may win Christ." Such a testimony to the Savior!

But I shall go still further. I shall go away from earth into the other world. I shall summon the angels and ask what they think of Christ. They saw Him in the bosom of the Father before the world was. Before the dawn of creation, before the morning stars sang together, He was there. They saw Him leave the throne and come down to the manger. What a scene for them to witness! Ask these heavenly beings what they thought of Him then. For once they are permitted to speak; for once the silence of heaven is broken. Listen to their song on the plains of Bethlehem, "Behold, I bring you good tidings of great joy, which shall be to all people. For unto you is born this day, in the city of David, a Savior, which is Christ the Lord." He leaves the throne to save the world. Is it a wonder the angels thought well of Him?

Then there are the redeemed saints—they that see Him face to face. Here on earth He was never known, no one seemed really to be acquainted with Him; but He was known in that world where He had been from the foundation. What do they think of Him there? If we could hear from heaven we should hear a shout which would glorify and magnify His name. We are told that when John was in the Spirit on the Lord's Day, and being caught up, he heard a shout around

him, ten thousand times ten thousand, and thousands and thousands of voices, "Worthy is the Lamb that was slain, to receive power, and riches, and wisdom, and strength, and honor, and glory, and blessing!" Yes, He is worthy of all this. Heaven cannot speak too well of Him. Oh, that earth would take up the echo and join with heaven in singing, "Worthy to receive power, and riches, and wisdom, and strength, and honor, and glory, and blessing!"

But there is still another witness, a higher still. Some think that the God of the Old Testament is the Christ of the New. But when Jesus came out to Jordan, baptized by John, there came a voice from heaven. God the Father spoke. It was His testimony to Christ: "This is my beloved Son, in whom I am well pleased." Ah, yes! God the Father thinks well of the Son. And if God is well pleased with Him, so ought we to be. If the sinner and God are well pleased with Christ, then the sinner and God can meet. The moment you say, as the Father said, "I am well pleased with Him," and accept Him, you are wedded to God. Will you not believe the testimony? Will you not believe this witness, this last of all, the Lord of hosts, the King of kings himself? Once more he repeats it, so that all may know it. With Peter and James and John, on the mount of transfiguration, He cries again, "This is my beloved Son; hear him." And that voice went echoing and reechoing through Palestine, through all the earth from sea to sea; yes, that voice is echoing still, Hear Him! Hear Him!

My friend will you hear Him to-day? Hark! what is He saying to you? "Come unto me, all ye that labor and are heavy laden, and I will give you rest. Take my yoke upon you and learn of me; for I am meek and lowly in heart; and ye shall find rest unto your souls. For my yoke is easy, and my burden is light." Will you not think well of such a Savior? Will you not believe in Him? Will you not trust in Him with all your heart and mind? Will you not live for Him? If He laid down His life for us, is it not the least we can do to lay down ours for Him? If He bore the cross and died on it for me, ought I not to be willing to take it up for Him? Oh, have we not reason to think well of Him? Do you think it is right and noble to lift up your voice against such a Savior? Do you think it is just to cry, "Crucify Him! crucify Him!" Oh, may God help all of us to glorify the Father, by thinking well of His only-begotten Son.

EDWARD CALDWELL MOORE

1857-1943

THE CONSCRIPT CROSS-BEARER

BIOGRAPHICAL NOTE

PARKMAN professor of theology, Harvard, 1902-1929; born September 1, 1857, in Westchester, Pa.; educated at Marietta College, Ohio, 1877; A.M., in same, 1880; B.D., Union Theological Seminary, 1884; fellow of Union Seminary, 1884-86, studying in Giessen, Gottingen and Berlin; Ph.D., Brown University, 1891; D.D., Yale University, 1909; minister of the Westminster Presbyterian church, Yonkers, N. Y., 1886-89; Central Congregational church, Providence, R. I., 1889-1902; preacher to Harvard University and chairman of the board of preachers to the university, 1905; lecturer in Mansfield College, Oxford, England, 1894; in Yale Divinity School, 1906-7; Lowell lecturer in Boston, 1903; author of " The New Testament in the Christian Church."

" And they compel one Simon, a Cyrenian, who passed by, coming out of the country, the father of Alexander and Rufus, to bear his cross."—Mark 15:21.

THIS is one of the little touches in the story of the crucifixion which it would be easy for us quite to overlook. The climax overshadows everything. Our minds, like the feet of the crowd which followed Jesus, hurry to the issue. The tide which is rushing toward that great event drags us also with it, just as it seized the people of that quarter of Jerusalem and swept them up the slope of Calvary, with no thought but of one person and one awful spectacle. Later, we discover that, as often under great excitement, we had noted many things we did not know we noticed. So is it here. In truth, it seems to me that there are in the whole gospel few more touching and instructive episodes than this one of the Cyrenian who, at that moment of Christ's need, by chance came by.

He is mentioned in three gospels. Some things that are said of him suggest that he was, later on, a follower of Jesus. The manner of his mention here makes plain he was no follower as yet. He was just passing by, when they laid hold on him. He was going into the city as the rabble with the Sufferer came out. He may have had knowledge of Jesus and no interest in Him. He may have had very little knowledge. He was a foreigner, a Jew by name but African by residence. There were hosts of Jews engaged in business in Egypt and thence westward now three hundred years, since Alexander gave the race commercial privileges which the Ptolemies and the Romans never took away. This man's family may have been for generations thus merchants in self-chosen exile, and not pining much in exile. There were strangers from Cyrene present at the Pentecost a few weeks after the crucifixion. There was a synagog of the Cyrenians in Jerusalem. This man may have been attending one of the few feasts of his lifetime in the sacred city of his nation. Or he may have been a man who did not trouble much the feasts and synagogs.

He was coming out of the country in most natural fashion, intent upon his own affairs. He was perhaps no more than curious about this mob which was going out to see an execution. He must have been astonished and indignant thus to be laid hold of. The word is a rough one. It is the word for impressing a man into the service. It is to be taken in all its harsh literalness, no doubt.

The man to be executed often added this to

his torment and humiliation, that he had to carry on his own back the rough beam on which he was to suffer. John says Jesus went forth thus bearing His cross. After a time perhaps, overwrought, His strength had yielded. He had faltered, may be fallen, underneath the load. There was no time to look about for one of Jesus' followers, to force him to do the service. I fear none was nigh. Any back would do. But the mere man of the rabble never gets this sort of thing on his back. And so it was, I fancy, that this clean-washed, neutral stranger, on his little morning journey, found himself one moment well at the roadside, a mere spectator, and the next dragged by some mailed hand into the midst, faced sharp about and forced to follow Jesus with that accursed beam upon his neck. After all, Jesus was hardly to blame. The crowd jeered if Simon showed discomfiture. One might as well remonstrate with wild beasts as with the soldiers. What was to be done? What but to go on, to get done, and, soon as possible, to slip away?

Imagine for this man any relation to Jesus that you choose, it was a trying experience. It was most trying if he had had no relation. So far as we know, nothing could have been farther from Simon's purpose for himself. Few things could have been less characteristic, so far as he yet understood his own character. And here, right out of the even tenor of his chosen way, there has seized him bodily this absolutely unexpected force. Here he is, Simon of Cyrene, toiling up Calvary after Jesus, with that strange thing, the latter's cross, upon his neck.

Now the lot of this all but unknown man would not be worth to us the time that we have spent in trying to imagine it, were it not for the fact that it seems to me to picture, in most interesting and suggestive fashion, the lot and life of many a man and woman whom we have known, to illuminate some fragment of experience which we may ourselves have had.

It suggests, namely—this story of the Cyrenian—a holy and spiritual interpretation of some events in our lives, of certain whole aspects of those lives. They were unexpected events, they were forced, unwelcome aspects, when they came. They have continued unmeaning, tho they have been long time with us. They bid fair to remain unfruitful, tho we should carry them to the end of our days. Perhaps they have continued unmeaning and unfruitful to us because we have persisted in regarding them as merely the net result of the misfortunes, the stupidities and iniquities of our fellow-men, instead of seeing, as we might, that in these very things we are being suffered to bear after Him a part of the true cross of Jesus Christ. For what was the cross of Jesus Christ, in one way of looking at

it, but just the net result of the misfortunes, the stupidities, the iniquities of his fellow-men? And who are we that we should feel ourselves thus injured at being asked to bear a part? We might come to healing of our own torn souls and reconciliation with a mysterious hard lot, we might come to joy in it and be glorified through it, did we but realize that what has happened to us is precisely what befel this Simon, when he was so unceremoniously compelled to put his flinching shoulders and his bewildered and rebellious spirit under the Lord's load.

A good part of the load in life which serious men and women find themselves carrying was not created by themselves, it was not due to themselves, it was not chosen for themselves. Do I not accurately describe the case when I say they find themselves carrying it? This load was not created by Simon, it was not due to Simon, it was not chosen of Simon. He found himself carrying it. For that matter it was not created by Jesus, it was not due to Jesus. But you will say to me that it was, at least, freely chosen for Himself of Jesus. He was not simply caught under the load of the misfortunes and iniquities of His fellow-men, He had the insight and the courage freely to accept His cross before He came to it. And that makes a difference. Yes, and His followers have learned to do even that after Him. But sometimes, apparently, God asks no harder thing of you and me than this, that we shall have the insight and the courage to accept our cross after we get it. Get a good deal of it we shall, anyway, if we are true men and women, this cross hewn by the mistakes, the miseries and sins of men. Get a good deal of it, I say, we shall anyway, if there is any manhood in us. So that what we choose, after all, is merely this, whether we ourselves shall be curst or else blest and glorified in the bearing of it.

Or let us look at the matter in another way. This story of what happened to the Cyrenian affords us some rational and natural and everyday explanation of what we mean by the phrase, "the cross of Christ." The phrase through much use has often become hackneyed and conventional. Jesus laid great stress upon the thought. We are sure it is a thing we ought to do, to take up some cross. But we have most vague and mythological notions as to how it is to be done. Superficial people talk most arrant platitudes. They manufacture some absurdity. They put this holy name upon some trivial and artificial thing. They rack imagination and bring forth some small asceticism. Zealots do unreal and unnecessary things, bigots even wrong ones, and call that the bearing after Him of the cross of Jesus Christ. And all the while the grand course of life has been trying to force on us something which perhaps we never thought of save as an imposition upon us, our ill-luck, blunder or badness of somebody in which we have got tangled, violence, wrong, even if unintentional, which someone has done us. We are still animated by the paltry hope that some day we shall give the soldiers the slip, or even get redress. We have spent a good part of our life in trying to be rid of this burden. Or, we have gone on bearing it grimly, embittered against men, and all the space dark between us and God.

I have seen men and women do this thing grandly, bear loads for men in general and men in particular, for parents unfortunate, brothers foolish, friends treacherous, or even wicked—loads which they neither had part in making nor could escape part in bearing. I bow in reverence before them. But all the time my heart goes out to them. They do not seem to know what they are doing. They do not realize that this was just what Jesus did, and that in thus doing, they most closely follow Him. They probably have manhood and womanhood enough not to say anything. But in their hearts, at least in tired moments and by wakeful nights, they dwell on the gross injustice which was done them. They cannot forget that they have been rudely laid hold of. They were passing innocent along the road. They have been by unseen and unloved hands compelled. It rankles. It rankles enough to make men and women who bear grandly all their lives just miss the transfiguration of their own characters, the glorification of their own spirits, which ought to go therewith.

Do not you know men and women who have carried just as much lumber up a lifelong Calvary, have set their shoe soles in the still warm footprints of the Christ of God, and hardly got more good out of it, just now, you might say, than one of the thieves? It cannot fail but that they will get that good by and by, in that day when all eyes are opened. But one could mourn for them, whoever they may be, that they do not get that blessedness now. So near is the glory of life to some who do not seem to know it. So far is it from some who prate most about it but shun these galling loads.

The Christian life is, at bottom, no new life which we lead after we are converted. It is rather, a new and noble and blessed way of looking at the same old life which, if we are half way true men and women, we have to lead in any case. And the cross of Christ is no pious decoration of our existence which we carpenter together or cast of gold and set with sharp points of steel and put next our skin. Nay, but it is the same old bloody, wooden thing which the weakness, folly, wickedness of mankind has been forever creating, and the true part of mankind has been forever carrying, and the one perfect Man bore perfectly, happily, triumphantly, and longs only to teach us how to do the same.

The same heavy wood is with us still. I think that one day we shall give thanks, that, as Paul put it, there are things behind of the sacrifice of Christ which we are to fill up. I think that some day we shall give thanks that we took life as it was, or rather that life took us as we were. The soldiers dragged us whither we were not wise enough or had not sufficient grace to wish to go. So much of the meaning of life opens to us only as life opens. And all is good that opens life to us. Ah, they were our ministers, those soldiers who took us by the throat, the mob who jeered at us, the clean people who got behind us. They did not exactly mean us the good. But now that we are calm we see also that they did not mean us all the harm. They were our ministers, I say, and we could pour out our thanks to them, only, I fear, they might not understand. Surely the day came when the Cyrenian gave thanks to God for nothing so much, as that the brave Christ's flesh proved, for a moment, insufficient, and that, at that moment, he, Simon, chanced to be passing by.

And now I think that you will have seen coming all the rest that I have to say. Almost I am of divided mind, whether it is better to draw examples or to let you draw them for yourselves. Your own are best. You are a man whose bit of wood, dropt from the shoulders of the Christ, and forced on you in the rough soldiering of life, goes back to your very youth. It weighed on your sensitive spirit when you were a child. You wanted an education, you had a right to a start in business, an opening in a loved profession. And the money which should have gone into that, may be God did not let your father earn, or let him earn and lose. And may be that was part of his cross, that he could not do for you as he hoped. And you and he might clasp hands over that bit of wood instead of misunderstanding one another as perhaps you have done.

Or somebody was a fool or wicked and squandered that money, or frittered away a commercial or personal influence, forfeited a reputation. Some family shame overshadows us, some sin or crime is committed by one to whom we ought always to have been able to refer with pride. Somebody's over sanguine temperament in business and loose sense of responsibility involves a whole wide circle in lawsuit or indebtedness. Somebody's towering and unscrupulous ambition, or again somebody's sheer inefficiency, improvidence, laziness or plain vice, piles up loads of obligations which almost break the faithful souls to earth. Sickness, misery, fall within our circle so closely that even the world says, there is something for you manfully to bear. Sickness, misery, misfortune, fall outside what we have called our circle, but which somebody has to bear. You see, it is only a matter of the size of the circle and the strength of the carrying sense. And Christ was only He to whom the whole race was but the circle of His brethren, and every mortal wo lay on His willing heart.

You will feel that I have described not some lives, but some aspect of every life which rises into seriousness or worthiness of any sort. And that is true. That is only to say what I have said before, that the opportunity of Christliness almost forces itself upon us so soon as our eyes are open to see. Every true man or woman knows the sensation, knows the shame which for affection's sake we tenderly cover, knows the patience called for by the faults of those we should revere, knows the burden which is borne for those who cannot, and sometimes even for those who will not, bear it for themselves, knows the complication and annoyance, lifelong pain and embarrassment into which somebody's thoughtlessness, vanity, obstinacy, may have plunged a whole connection, knows the debts that must be paid, the weakness that must be shielded, the wrongs that, so far as may be, must be atoned for, the wretched consequences that must be kept from others, must be taken quietly upon ourselves. That is life to those who deeply live.

Jest has been made of the fact alleged that there is enough wood of the true cross in Europe alone to build several ships. The jest is a sorry underestimate. Of the real stuff of the true cross, of the kind of material we have just been speaking of, there has been enough to give to every man and woman, every child, in every generation since the Christ, a good large piece. And so far as one can judge, there will be enough to last till Christ shall come again.

You stand by the wayside some bright morning of your life. We all do it in our turn. Fresh from your rest in the country, you are going into the city of your choice, perchance to worship in some synagog or offer in the high temple, as befits your state. So stood the Cyrenian. And he wist not of what sort the offering and worship of that day should be.

You are intent on business, your own profitable, pleasant business. Has not every man a right to his own successful business? And what a monstrous wrong it is that all the wretched business of others should be made into a load for you to bear. You have your own clear right and privileges, your own bright plans. So had the Cyrenian. He had no idea what his real business and privilege of that day should be.

And suddenly someone starts out of the crowd. You have hardly time to know what it is all about, no questions asked, no remonstrance heeded. Resistless hands are on you. The tide of the world is bearing you along with it. It would all seem a bad dream were it not for the plain duty, too prosaic and urgent to admit of being dreamed about. You never proposed to do it. But you are going to do it. You are too much of a man, too true a woman not to do it. There is that responsibility. It was not you who incurred it. But it is you who are going to have to carry it. There are the consequences which you even warned your friend against. There is that unending patience to be shown, that unfaltering faithfulness to be manifested, there is that wisdom to be exercised, loved, cherished, even against greatest odds. There is the wood. And there is the Christ going before us, bearing what He can of all the burden of the world, and leaving behind Him just enough to make all men great and Christlike if they will but follow in His steps. Perhaps you never said that you were going to follow Him. But you will. You are too much of a man not to. You may not have called your following by that name. That makes but little difference. It is the Christ that goes before us in all noblest human life. And we follow Him when we do nobly bear.

And now, are we going to accept this interpretation of the things that have been wearing upon us? Shall we not let all the rebellion in our hearts be healed, and then go out to take up those tasks again, rejoicing in Christ as we had never done before?

We noted at the start that trait in our text which makes us feel reasonably sure that this Simon stood near to the Christian circle, later on. Mark, writing for that circle, brings his man forward out of all uncertainty with one swift stroke—"the father of Alexander and Rufus"—he it was whom they compelled to bear the cross. He assumes that these names are well known to his readers. One cannot help letting his imagination play with this fact. Simon's sons would seem to have been Christians, and his family one of standing among the supporters of Christ's cause. Does it seem unlikely that the father was a Christian from that April day?

I think that at the first he meant, when, with the cross, he should have reached the top of Calvary, to slip away. I think that as he watched the holy Sufferer the world was changed. I think that the clean rebellious man whom we saw at the foot of the hill, Simon of Cyrene, was all changed. I think that the soiled and stricken man, believing and transfigured, that crucifixion evening, would not have changed his lot with that of any man on earth. It was a strange way to become a follower of Jesus, was it not? And yet I am sure the like has happened since. I think that through the mist of years and dust of other services, he looked back to that morning and to the violence then done him, as the pinnacle of mortal privilege and only wondered why the heavenly privilege should have fallen just to him. I think he was reconciled.

But you will say to me it is easier to be reconciled to my own cross than to that part of it which projects into my children's lives. It is easy to see the spiritual profit for me. But what of them? That is the last straw upon the weight of many a man's cross. You think on some fair morning as you go into the city, that the blessing for your children will lie in the fortune that you make for them, in the position, public or social, that you win. You are often thinking of them far more than of yourself when you say you cannot bear this cross. " My father, there is the wood for the burnt offering, but where is the lamb? " said little Isaac. " My son, God will provide himself a lamb," said Abraham. But who shall say what was in his heart as he looked at his only boy?

Oh, my friend, those things we named are good—sometimes. But I do also know that there is no heritage on earth like that which those children do enjoy who have seen their father or mother go bravely up life's Calvary with the cross of Christ upon their backs. I think they would not change the lot. I think they are reconciled. It is rather a strange way of ensuring that one's children will be followers of Jesus. But it is rather a common way, and rather sure. Never fear. Your Alexander and Rufus will bless you. And the world will have cause to bless your Alexander and Rufus. The world will never know— there are many things which the world need never know—that it all goes back, this grace and benediction which those lives have been, that it all goes back to a morning when you were dragged from your vantage by the highway, as Christ passed to be crucified so long ago. But in the stillness of your heart you may know, and in that will be happiness enough for earth and almost enough for heaven.

My friends, these things are a parable. We think our crosses wooden. It is we who are wooden and do not see. We curse men when we ought to be blessing God. We are cast down when we should be lifted up. Let us have done. Let us appreciate that what then in the wood could happen to but one man, may happen, in the spirit of it, to every soul of us, to be allowed to bear after Him a little of the burden of the true cross of Jesus Christ.

WILLIAM GALLOGLY MOOREHEAD

1836-1914

MEN SENT FROM GOD

BIOGRAPHICAL NOTE

PROFESSOR of New Testament literature and exegesis, from 1899-1914 president of the faculty in Xenia Theological Seminary, Ohio; born Rix Mills, Muskingum Co., Ohio, 1836; educated Allegheny Theological Seminary, 1858,9; Xenia Theological Seminary, 1859-62; ordained to the ministry, 1862; missionary of the American and Foreign Christian Union, Italy, 1862-69; pastor of First United Presbyterian church, Xenia, 1870; author of "Outline Studies in Old Testament," "Studies in the Mosaic Institutions," "Studies in the Four Gospels," "Outline Studies in Acts—Ephesians," "Outline Studies in Philippians—Hebrews."

" There was a man sent from God whose name was John."—John 1 : 6.

THIS is a short but significant description of the mission of John the Baptist. Few men whose names appear in the Bible receive such honorable mention as he. His place in the divine record is most conspicuous and the commendation of him unqualified. He whose judgment is always exact, founded as it is on His unerring knowledge of men, declared him to be a prophet and more than a prophet: of women-born none was greater (Luke 7 : 25-28). His coming and his ministry were the subject of prediction centuries before he appeared in the world. His birth was supernatural, as truly so as that of Isaac, for he came to gladden the hearts of his parents when they were old and well-stricken in years. His name of John was given him by the angel who announced his birth to his astonished father in the Temple.

That which arrests attention in this verse and which is its prominent feature is the fact that John the Baptist was sent from God and by God into the world. His ministry was of heavenly origin, and himself likewise was heaven-sent. Both himself and his mission were of divine appointment and ordainment. John seems to have regarded this as the chief part of his commission, and he refers to it again and again as the essential feature of his life and work (comp. John 1 : 33; 3 : 28; Mark 1 : 2). The same thing is made prominent in the prophecy which announced his advent (Mal. 3 : 1). This, then, is the main idea in the text, viz.: a man sent from God. But this element, so marked in his case, is not peculiar or exceptional. It is also true of all who are commissioned to do God's work in the world. The mark by which they are distinguished, whether in Old or New Testament times, whether ancient or modern, is precisely this, they are men sent from God. Be it Moses or Samuel, Paul or Peter, Martin Luther or John Knox; be it any and every genuine servant of Christ in our own day; they are alike distinguished by this sign; they have divine authority for their mission.

Of those whom the Lord in His great mercy sends forth upon His errands there are two classes; the ordinary laborers whose ministry is occupied with the common duties, the everyday toil which the gospel imposes, without which all testimony for God would ultimately cease. We cannot rate too highly those faithful men whose lives are spent largely in quietness and obscurity and who are contented, even happy in their lot, and to whom the

Church and the world owe more than can ever
be paid. Besides these who make up the vast
mass of God's workers there are the extraordinary laborers who are raised up for special
service, for supreme emergencies, and who are
correspondingly equipped therefor. To this
class, the extraordinary messengers of God,
John the Baptist belonged, and it is of these
we are to speak more especially.

One of the most precious gifts heaven bestows on the earth is a man with a message for
his fellows. A man sent to deliver tidings of
great joy, to acquaint us with God's thoughts
and purposes about us, to pour light into our
darkness, and to fill the heart with a song of
gladness—what greater boon could be ours,
or should be more acceptable? Such a gift
ranks above every earthly good, ranks next to
God's " unspeakable gift " with which indeed
it is closely associated. And such men do now
and then appear; genuine messengers from
God, envoys extraordinary from the court of
heaven. Their advents are occasional, their
visits rare. Long stretches of time often lie
between the presence of one and that of his
fellow. Their coming is like that of the
highest poets and heroes, infrequent and exceptional. There is no regular succession of
them. Sometimes they appear in groups, and
they deliver their messages contempora-
neously, as in the deportation of the Israelites
to Babylon when great prophets like Jeremiah,
Ezekiel, and Daniel were on the world's stage
together; as in the beginning of Christianity
when a whole cluster of them united in giving
their testimony to men; as in the Reformation
of the sixteenth century. Sometimes one appears alone, as in the instance of Moses, Samuel, and Elijah. But whether in groups or
singly, God in His gracious pity and love does
ever and anon enrich our race with the gift
of a man from Himself. To spend a little
while in the company of such men is profitable. We cannot look, however inadequately,
on a man sent from God without gaining somewhat from him. He is a living light-fountain
which it is good and pleasant to be near, in
whose radiance all souls must feel that it is
well with them. On any terms whatsoever we
should not grudge to stay for awhile in his
neighborhood.

These men receive their commission directly
from the Lord Himself. He furnishes them
with their message and He equips them for
their ministry. They are sent by Him, hence
their mission is authoritative; they are sent
from Him, therefore they have the needed
gifts. Our Lord reserves to Himself the sovereign right to select and to commission His
laborers. It is His prerogative as the Master
in His own house, a prerogative that He has
not delegated to any mere man or body of
men. Thus He speaks, " Ye have not chosen
me, but I have chosen you, and ordained you,

that ye should go and bring forth fruit, and
that your fruit should remain " (John
15 : 16). Thus likewise we are told that having ascended up on high " he led captivity
captive, and gave gifts unto men. . . .
And he gave some, apostles; and some, prophets; and some, evangelists; and some, pastors
and teachers; for the perfecting of the saints,
for the work of the ministry, for the edifying
of the body of Christ " (Eph. 4 : 13). All
gifts and graces, offices and office-bearers flow
from Him. Christ is the ruler in His own
house under whose hand the order of the
house proceeds and the servants, great and
small, come and go. Primarily they are not
man-made nor man-appointed. They receive
not their commission from mitered priest, nor
at the hands of Presbytery. The ministerial
call and function are not imparted by any
holy chrism or imposition of human hands,
nor by education or theological lore. Properly speaking man has nothing to do with the
great office save gladly to recognize what God
in His sovereign good pleasure has given,
chosen, and sent forth.

Two important results flow from this truth.
One is this: they whom the Lord sends forth
into His work are clothed with divine authority. The Lord Jesus invests His servants with
the like authority He Himself has, for in His
intercessory prayer He says, " As thou hast
sent me into the world, even so have I also
sent them into the world " (John 17 : 18).
He had His commission from God, the fountain and source of all power and lordship.
His apostles share with Him in their appointment and mission. Wherever they go they
carry with them heavenly credentials, and
their message is authenticated by a power that
is extra-human. It is not they who speak but
the Spirit of their Lord. Men therefore listen
to their voice, hang upon their words, follow
them with joy that they may hear and learn,
and have peace.

The other is this: their whole-hearted devotion to their great task. Each of these sent
men is swayed by an impulse, a force that
ever impels him to fulfil his mission, to finish
his work. It is the burden laid upon him by
his Master, a burden he cannot lift from his
shoulders and would not if he could. It is
the will, the voice of God heard in the central
deeps of his being, ever insistent, urgent, irresistible. Paul refers to it in language that
may well be that of every one sent of God:
" Necessity is laid upon me; yea, wo is me if
I preach not the gospel." That strange, compelling necessity drove him a glad and willing
servant over much of Asia, over large sections
of Europe, amid privation, suffering, victories
and defeats, that he might make men know
the love of God which surpasses knowledge.
These men cannot do otherwise; they must
accomplish their mission, fulfil their task, or

die. One of them, the prophet Jeremiah, actually sought to stifle the voice within his soul, and said to himself, I will speak no more, I will sit in silence and witness no more, but the mighty word within him became as a burning flame in his bones, he was weary of forbearing, he could not contain (Jer. 20:9). Ease, comfort, home often, wealth, social position, friends are all secondary, and are sacrificed without a pang of grief when they would thrust themselves between the man and his mission, when they would arrest his feet. He is God's messenger, and he cannot be stayed nor linger.

Men sent from God are endowed with the noblest talents and gifts. The magnitude of the errand upon which they come necessitates this. All workers for God may justly be said to be sent by Him, and by Him they are fitted for their task. But there come occasionally into our race those who create epochs in history, who set loose new forces that change the course of things, who become light-centers that fling their radiance far out into the surrounding darkness, whose life and teaching mold the thoughts and beliefs of generations. He who sends them takes care that they are supplied with the gifts and filled with the talents, the greatness and the difficulties of their mission demand. From their birth they are girded by Him with power. John the Baptist was filled with the Holy Spirit from his mother's womb (Luke 1:15). The angel that announced his advent said, " He shall go before him in the spirit and power of Elijah." He was born great; enriched with supreme gifts from the beginning. Thus, likewise, when Moses was born, we are told his parents hid him for they saw he was " a goodly child." In Heb. 11 : 23 we learn that they saw he was " a proper child." Stephen explains what the attractiveness in the face of the little Moses was that arrested the attention and aroused the hope of his parents—he " was exceeding fair " (Acts 7 : 20)—" beautiful unto God " is Stephen's fine term. There was that in his face which faith read, for God had set His stamp upon him and so parted him from other children. From his birth Moses had the marks of one chosen of God and equipped with the most extraordinary talents. Amram and Jochebed interpreted the divine purpose which providence traced in the face of their gifted child, and they feared not the king's commandment.

The like supernatural endowment appears in the case of the prophets, notably in Jeremiah and Isaiah. We learn that Jeremiah was set apart to his high office before he began to exist. His choice as the messenger of God antedated his birth. As his mission was to be a most unwelcome and perilous one, a ministry of admonition and of antagonism, God fitted him for it by the richest bestow-

ments. He was to be the solitary fortress, the column of iron, the wall of brass, the one immovable figure standing athwart the path of the apostatizing nation, struggling to arrest and turn them back; and he was girded with the strength his hard mission imposed. In the remarkable vision of Isaiah (Chap. 6) the prophet saw the Lord high and lifted up and heard the ceaseless chant of the seraphim, and he fell on his face overwhelmed with the sense of his own and his people's sinfulness. His cry was, " Wo is me! for I am undone." The swift seraph laid the flaming coal from the altar on his defiled lips. Thereby his pollution was purged away, and the marvelous style and sublime diction which have entranced the world were created. The like equipment is seen in the primitive Christian disciples. The Spirit in the form of disparted tongues of fire sat upon each of them. It was the fulfilment of the promise that they should be endued with power from on high. It symbolized the supernatural gift of speech, of burning, invincible speech that none could gainsay or resist.

We find evidences of an impartation of extraordinary gifts for extraordinary service, in other men whose names are not recorded in the Scriptures. One or two examples must suffice. The first is Martin Luther. A child of the people, of obscure and humble origin, the son of a miner, all his ancestors back to his great-grandfather peasants, without fame or fortune, Luther was set to grapple in a death-struggle with the most gigantic power, the most consummate organization in existence. What were his gifts that he single-handed should smite the Colossus to the ground, free the race from its cruel domination, unchain the Bible and give it unfettered to the world? God was in the mighty struggle, we cannot doubt; it was His battle, not Luther's alone, and His was the victory. But He took care that the man sent to accomplish the mighty task should be girded with His strength. If the trenchant words of John smote on the ears of Israel as a voice from the other world and stirred the heart of the nation, we may well say with Richter that Luther's words were " half battles." He flashed out illumination from him; his striking idiomatic phrases and sentences pierced to the very heart of the controversy. There was in him insight, profound insight that betokens genius and more than genius, even the presence and the power of the Spirit of God. Frenchmen do not appreciate perhaps how much they owe to John Calvin and his fellow reformers, as Beza and Farrel, for the copious, firm, precise and accurate speech they wield with such elegance and power, just as the English-speaking people but feebly recognize the debt they owe to John Wyclif, John Knox, and William Tindale for our splendid English tongue.

The same truth is seen in the equipment of William Carey, the pioneer in modern missions. Sydney Smith sneeringly named him the "consecrated cobbler." A maker and mender of shoes he was, and he honestly and heroically maintained his family thereby when the little flock of Christians to whom he ministered could but scantily support him. Notwithstanding the pressure of poverty, he managed to acquire Latin, Greek, Hebrew, and a goodly amount of other useful knowledge, especially in natural history and botany. But it was in India that his true mission opened to him, and his marvelous capacity for the mastering of difficult languages was displayed. His translation of the Bible, in whole or in part, either alone or with others, into some twenty-six Indian languages; his Serampur press rendering the Scripture accessible to more than a hundred million human beings; his composition of grammars and dictionaries of several tongues; his professorship of thirty years at Fort William College in Calcutta—all this and much more exhibit something of the marvelous talents with which God had enriched His servant, William Carey.

Two lessons we may learn from the facts thus set forth. One is, that no emergency or crisis in human affairs finds God unprepared. He has His chosen instruments ready for every circumstance and every exigency that may arise. Even the fall of Adam was not a surprise, nor was redemption an afterthought. When Messiah is about to appear among men His forerunner is sent to prepare His way for Him. When Egyptian bondage has reached its climax, then Moses arrives. Grateful Jewish hearts have coined the magnificent proverb that has cheered many an opprest one since: "When the tale of bricks is doubled and there is no straw, then Moses comes." When the papal cup of abomination was brim-full and running over, heaven-sent men struck the filthy thing to the ground. When the gospel was to be carried to the regions beyond, when the age of missions had arrived, William Carey and Adoniram Judson were sent forth, and the churches of Britain and of America sprang to their feet to help in the blessed work. "God never is before His time, He never is too late."

The other lesson is, that the Lord alone can impart the gifts needed for extraordinary service. No man nor body of men can bestow them. Money can not buy them. Station furnishes them not. Education cannot secure them. They cannot be bought nor wrought by the hand of man. Education may whet the scythe, it cannot make it.

Another characteristic of such men is that they receive special training from the Lord Himself.

It is not enough that they be endowed with great natural talents and capacities; they must enter God's school that their powers may be developed, their acquaintance with Him and His truth be made sure and absolute. They are always sent to that school and set down to those lessons which will fit them for their tasks. John the Baptist was in the desert until his showing unto Israel. His wilderness sojourn was one of thirty years. God led him there and there schooled and disciplined him for his dangerous and difficult mission. There in the profound solitude afar from the enervating influences of hollow formalism and artificial life, with none near but God, his spirit was chastened and tempered for the solemn duties that awaited him. This is characteristic of all sent of God. When He would fit His servants for some vast work requiring spiritual might and heroic self-sacrifice, He takes them afar from the distracting cares of the world to commune with Himself in the grandeur of solitude. Forty years Moses spent in the desert of Midian, a keeper of sheep, the best years of his life wasted utterly, worldly wisdom would say—but rashly. That sojourn qualified Moses to become the deliverer of Israel, the leader of the Exodus, the conqueror of Egypt and the lawgiver of his nation. His education in Pharaoh's court might be valuable; this of the wilderness was indispensable. "All the wisdom of Egypt" could not have prepared him for his future path. No man is fit to do God's work who has not had some training with the Lord Himself. Nothing can take its place, nothing make up for its loss.

All God's servants have been taught in this stern school. Elijah at Cherith, Ezekiel at Chebar, David in exile, Paul in Arabia, Savonarola in St. Mark's Convent, Luther in Erfurth, are eminent examples of the immense value of being taught of God. The divine Servant, the Lord Jesus, spent by far the largest part of His earthly sojourn in the privacy and obscurity of Nazareth. Even in His public ministry He often retreated from the gaze of men to enjoy the sweet and sacred retirement of the Father's presence. None can teach like the Lord. The man whom He educates is educated, and none other. It lies not within the range of man's ability to prepare an instrument for the service of God. Man's hand can never mold "a vessel meet for the Master's use." Ordinarily great truths are not revealed to men in an instant of time; these are not thrust into the mind as if fired from a catapult. The truths a man can live and die on are wrought in the fires of the heart, in bitterest soul-agonies often, in plash of tears and sobs of secret longing. In silence and loneliness generally the true world workers are trained for their mission. Men who have learned to nurse their souls on truth in solitary meditation and communion with the

Invisible speak at length words that men must hear and heed.

A firm persuasion of the absolute truth of their message is another characteristic of those who are sent from God. It is conviction of its truth and more than conviction; it is assurance of faith profound, immovable, unalterable. God has spoken to them, and in the central deeps of their being His word is enshrined. More certain than life or death, more stable than the everlasting hills, firm as the throne itself, they know the message to be. We see this feature prominent in John. The period of the desert discipline was over; his difficulties and his struggles were ended. He had reached convictions, had learned truths on which to live and die, and he came forth from his retirement with his message, every word and syllable of which was to him a living verity, the eternal word of God. For in the solitude of the wilderness his spirit had been hardened into the temper a reformer needs. His locust food, his garment of camel's hair cloth, his indifference to worldly comforts, his contempt of luxurious ease, his separation and his loneliness, his bronzed face and unfaltering tongue, all told how real his ministry was. If ever men saw a sincere and genuine man it was John the Baptist. Now this is true of all men who are sent from God. Standing in the midst of a world full of uncertainty, of doubt and skepticism, they know whom they have believed and what they affirm. Each of them uses the little but significant word "know"—"we know"; "I know." There is not the slightest taint of agnosticism in their creed; agnostics they are not nor can be. They have all caught a gleam of the infinite glory; to some of them, to almost all of them, the King in His beauty has been revealed; to them heaven itself has been opened, and the ineffable light has streamed down upon their faces. That light, that blessed vision is never forgotten; it stays with them to the end, through all their vicissitudes and their discouragements, their victories and defeats. They have received the message of God, have felt the powers of the world to come, the Spirit of God has borne witness with their spirits: therefore they cannot be flattered nor argued nor sneered nor persecuted out of their faith and their testimony.

This assured confidence of the infallible certainty of the message is what the world wants. Multitudes are weary and sick of speculations, of barren idealities, and hollow formalism. They want realities, not hypotheses, food, not husks nor stones. God's chosen messengers bear precisely such messages, and their faith in them is unwavering. They know that they know. It is easy to denounce the evil and evil tendencies of our age, and to extol the virtues and excellencies of former days. While there are not wanting the evidence of much good, of genuinely heroic self-sacrifice on the part of multitudes of Christian men and women, it must sorrowfully be acknowledged that sinister assailants of no common sort threaten the cause and people of God on every side. There are principles and tendencies at work in modern society which if left unchecked will ere long result in disaster and ruin. A lawless drift is already on us, precurser of worse to come. Who does not perceive that the ax is already aimed at the chief hoops that bind together the staves of the civil polity? The restlessness under restraint, the revolt against authority and even law, the growth of agnosticism, the assaults on the Bible the anchor of all true religion, the prevalence of materialism, fostered as this is by the philosophy and the commercialism of the time, the enormous greed of those who have and who want still more, the deep ominous growl of those who have not, who want and will have—all this betokens the breaking down of the barriers and the near approach of the "falling away," the apostasy, of which prophecy speaks with most solemn warning (2 Thess. 2:3, 4). Men sent from God, with their living personal apprehension of God never perhaps were more needed than now; men who believe, with their whole mind and heart, soul and strength; believe, and endure as seeing Him who is invisible.

Some other features of these men may be grouped together and briefly treated. These are men of ardent love, of deep and abiding affection for their fellows. Paul had a continual heaviness and sorrow in his heart for his unbelieving countrymen. One may well doubt whether he had unalloyed happiness for a single day during the whole period of his Christian career. Wherever he went he carried this burden of grief, a heart full of tears. Nor was his solicitude confined to the descendants of Abraham. How pathetic are the terms in which he addresses certain Gentile converts who were slipping away from the truth and the liberty of Christ in which he had set them: "My little children, of whom I am again in travail until Christ be formed in you. . . . I am perplexed about you." "Now we live if ye stand fast in the Lord." Knox's midnight cry, "Give me Scotland or I die," discloses the like passionate, tearful love and yearning. It reminds us of His tears who wept over guilty, impenitent Jerusalem, "O Jerusalem, Jerusalem, that killeth the prophets, and stoneth them that are sent unto her! How often would I have gathered thy children together, even as a hen gathereth her chickens under her wings, and ye would not!"

Strength and courage are always found allied with the tenderest feelings and emotions. Luther could be as strong and fearless as a

lion in the presence of the great and mighty
of earth, and yet be as a little child with children. He loved music, loved to sing his even-
song, to play soft melodies on his flute. He
delighted in birds, in the still starry nights,
and in the flowers and shrubs and trees.
Many a tree he planted with his own hands.
Strong, courageous, but tender withal, and
gentle as a little child. He used what seems
in our day violent and awful words against
the pope, against Henry VIII and against
others, yet words that the circumstances demanded and the tyrannies and despotisms of
these exalted potentates made necessary. He
called them the swine of hell, and told them
he, Martin, would grind their brazen foreheads into powder! He writes: " I have seen
and defied innumerable devils. Duke George
of Leipzic "—a great enemy of his—" is not
equal to one devil. If I had business at Leipzig, I would ride into Leipzig, tho it rained
Duke Georges for nine days running." " He
lies there," said the Earl of Morton at Knox's
grave, " who never feared the face of man."
They may appear harsh, intolerant, these
heaven-sent men, but it must never be forgotten that the mission imposed on them, the
solemn, awful message they have to deliver,
and their fidelity to Him who commissions
them, forbid absolutely all softness, compromise, and pliability. The message as often contains lamentations and mourning and woe
as good tidings of great joy. It is the Lord's
word they speak, and it is one of truth always,
often of stern reproof and dreadful denunciation. Whatever the message, let it be ours to
welcome the messenger, and be glad for the
heaven-sent man.

G. CAMPBELL MORGAN

1863-1945

THE PERFECT IDEAL OF LIFE

BIOGRAPHICAL NOTE

GEORGE CAMPBELL MORGAN, Congregational divine and preacher, was born in Tetbury, Gloucestershire, England, in 1863, and was educated at the Douglas School, Cheltenham. He worked as a lay-mission preacher for the two years ending 1888, and was ordained to the ministry in the following year, when he took charge of the Congregational Church at Stone, Staffordshire. After occupying the pulpit in several pastorates (including four years in America), in 1904 he became pastor of the Westminster Congregational Chapel, Buckingham Gate, London, a position which he held until 1917. Besides being highly successful as a pulpit orator, Dr. Morgan has published many works of a religious character, among which may be enumerated: "God's Methods with Man," "The Spirit of God," "The Crises of the Christ," "The Practice of Prayer," and "The Analysed Bible."

Jesus therefore said, When ye have lifted up the son of man, then shall ye know that I am he, and that I do nothing of myself, but as the Father taught me, I speak these things. And he that sent me is with me; he hath not left me alone; for I do always the things that are pleasing to him. As he spake these things, many believed on him.—John viii., 28-30.

THE Master, you will see, in this verse lays before us three things. First of all, He gives us the perfect ideal of human life in a short phrase, and that comes at the end, "the things that please him." Those are the things that create perfect human life, living in the realm of which man realizes perfectly all the possibilities of his wondrous being—"the things that please him." So I say, in this phrase, the Master reveals to us the perfect ideal of our lives. Then, in the second place, the Master lays claim—one of the most stupendous claims that He ever made—that He utterly, absolutely, realizes that ideal. He says, "I do always the things that please him." And then, thirdly, we have the revelation of the secret by which He has been able to realize the ideal, to make the abstract concrete, to bring down the fair vision of divine purpose to the level of actual human life and experience, and the secret is declared in the opening words: "He that sent me is with me; my Father hath not left me alone."

The perfect ideal for my life, then, is that I live always in the realm of the things that please God; and the secret by which I may do so is here unfolded—by living in perpetual, unbroken communion with God: communion with which I do not permit anything to interfere. Then it shall be possible for me to pass into this high realm· of actual realization.

It is important that we should remind ourselves in a few sentences that the Lord has indeed stated the highest possible ideal for human life in these words: "The things that please him." Oh, the godlessness of men! The godlessness that is to be found on every hand! The godlessness of the men and women that are called by the name of God! How tragic, how sad, how awful it is! because godlessness is always not merely an act of rebellion against God, but a falling short in our own lives of their highest and most glorious possibilities.

Here is my life. Now, the highest realm for me is the realm where all my thoughts, and all my deeds, and all my methods, and everything in my life please God. That is the highest realm, because God only knows what

I am; only perfectly understands the possibilities of my nature, and all the great reaches of my being. You remember those lines that Tennyson sang—very beautifully, I always think:

> Flower in the crannied wall,
> I pluck you out of the crannies;—
> Hold you here, root and all, in my hand,
> Little Flower—but if I could understand
> What you art, root and all, and all in all,
> I should know what God and man is.

Beautiful confession! Absolutely true. I hold that flower in my hand, and I look at it, flower and leaves and stem and root. I can botanize it, and then I tear it to pieces—that is what the botanist mostly does—and you put some part of it there, and some part of it there, and some part of it there. There is the root, there the stem, and there are the leaves, and there is everything; but where is the flower? Gone. How did it go? When did it go? Why, when you ruthlessly tore it to bits. But how did you destroy it? You interfered with the principle that made it what it was—you interfered with the principle of life. What is life? No man can tell you. "If I could but know what you are, little flower, root and all, and all in all," I would know what life is, what God is, what man is. I can not.

Now, if you lift that little parable of the flower into the highest realm of animal life, and speak of yourself—we don't know ourselves; down in my nature there are reaches that I have not fathomed yet. They are coming up every day. What a blest thing it is to have the Master at hand, to hand them over to Him as they come up, and say, "Lord, here is another piece of Thy territory; govern it; I don't know anything about it." But there is the business. I don't know myself, but God knows me, understands all the complex relationships of my life, knows how matter affects mind, and physical and mental and spiritual are blended in one in the high ideal of humanity. Oh, remember, man is the crowning and most glorious work of God of which we know anything as yet. And God only knows man.

But here is a Man that stands amid His enemies, and He looks out upon His enemies, and He says, "I do the things that please him"—not "I teach them," not "I dream them," not "I have seen them in a fair vision," but "I do them." There never was a bigger claim from the lips of the Master than that: "I do always the things that please him."

You would not thank me to insult your Christian experience, upon whatever level you live it, by attempting to define that statement of Christ. History has vindicated it. We believe it with all our hearts—that He always did the things that pleased God. But I have got on to a level that I can touch now. The great ideal has come from the air to the earth. The fair vision has become concrete in a Man. Now, I want to see that Man; and if I see that Man I shall see in Him a revelation of what God's purpose is for men, and I shall see, therefore, a revelation of what the highest possibility of life is. Now this is a tempting theme. It is a temptation to begin to contrast Him with popular ideals of life. I want to see Him; I want, if I can, to catch the notes of the music that make up the perfect harmony which was the dropping of a song out of God's heaven upon man's earth, that man might catch the key-note of it and make music in his own life. What are the things in this Man's life? He says: "I have realized the ideal—I do." There are four things that I want to say about Him, four notes in the music of His life.

First, spirituality. That is one of the words that needs redeeming from abuse. He was the embodiment of the spiritual ideal in life. He was spiritual in the high, true, full, broad, blest sense of that word.

It may be well for a moment to note what spirituality did not mean in the life of Jesus Christ. It did not mean asceticism. During all the years of His ministry, during all the years of His teaching, you never find a single instance in which Jesus Christ made a whip of cords to scourge Himself. And all that business of scourging oneself—an attempt to elevate the spirit by the ruin of the actual flesh—is absolutely opposed to His view of life. Jesus Christ did not deny Himself. The fact of His life was this—that He touched everything familiarly. He went into all the relationship of life. He went to the widow. He took up the children and held them in His arms, and looked into their eyes till heaven was poured in as He looked. He didn't go and get behind walls somewhere. He didn't get away and say: "Now, if I am going to get pure I shall do it by shutting men out." You remember what the Pharisees said of Him once. They said: "This man receiveth sinners." You know how they said it. They meant to say: "We did hope that we should make something out of this new man, but we are quite disappointed. He receives sinners."

And what did they mean? They meant what you have so often said: "You can't touch pitch without being defiled." But this Man sat down with the publican and He didn't take on any defilement from the publican. On the other hand, He gave the publican His purity in the life of Jesus Christ. Things worked the other way. He was the great negative of God to the very law of evil that you have—evil contaminates good. If you will put on a plate one apple that is getting bad among twelve others that are pure, the bad one will influence the others. Christ came to drive back every force of disease and every force of evil by this strong purity of His own person, and He said: "I will go among the bad and make them good." That is what He was doing the whole way through. So His spirituality was not asceticism. And if you are going to be so spiritual that you see no beauty in the flowers and hear no music in the song of the birds; if the life which you pass into when you consent to the crucifixion of self does not open to you the very gates of God, and make the singing of the birds and the blossoming of the flowers infinitely more beautiful, you have never seen Jesus yet.

What was His spirituality? The spirituality of Jesus Christ was a concrete realization of a great truth which He laid down in His own beatitudes. What was that? "Blest are the pure in heart, for they shall see God." Now, the trouble is we have been lifting all the good things of God and putting them in heaven. And I don't wonder that you sing:

> My willing soul would stay
> In such a frame as this,
> And sit and sing itself away
> To everlasting bliss.

No wonder you want to sing yourself away to everlasting bliss, because everything that is worth having you have put up there. But Jesus said: "Blest are the pure in heart, for they shall see God." If you are pure you will see Him everywhere—in the flower that blooms, in the march of history, in the sorrows of men, above the darkness of the darkest cloud; and you will know that God is in the field when He is most invisible.

Second, subjection. The next note in the music of His life is His absolute subjection to God. You can very often tell the great philosophies which are governing human lives by the little catchwords that slip off men's tongues: "Well, I thank God I am my own master." That is your trouble, man. It is because you are your own master that you are in danger of hell. A man says: "Can't I do as I like with my own?" You have got no "own" to do what you like with. It is because men have forgotten the covenant of God, the kingship of God, that we have all the wreckage and ruin that blights this poor earth of ours. Here is the Man who never forgot it.

Did you notice those wonderful words: "I do nothing of myself, but as my Father taught me, I speak." He neither did nor spoke anything of Himself. It was a wonderful life. He stood forevermore between the next moment and heaven. And the Father's voice said, "Do this," and He said "Amen, I came to do thy will," and did it. And the Father's voice said, "Speak these words to men," and He, "Amen," and He spoke.

You say: "That is just what I do not want to do." I know that. We want to be independent; have our own way. "The things that please God—this Man was subject to the divine will." You know the two words—if you can learn to say them, not like a parrot, not glibly, but out of your heart—the two words that will help you "Halleluiah" and "Amen." You can say them in Welsh or any language you like; they are always the same. When the next dispensation of God's dealings faces you look at it and say: "Halleluiah! Praise God! Amen!" That means, "I agree."

Third, sympathy. Now, you have this Man turned toward other men. We have seen something of Him as He faced God: Spirituality, a sense of God; subjection, a perpetual amen to the divine volition. Now, He faces the crowd. Sympathy! Why? Because He is right with God, He is right with men; because He feels God near, and knows Him, and responds to the divine will; therefore, when He faces men He is right toward men. The settlement of every social problem you have in this country and in my own land, the settlement of the whole business, will be found in the return of man to God. When man gets back to God he gets back to men. What is behind it? Sympathy is the power of putting my spirit outside my personality, into the circumstances of another man, and feeling as that man feels.

I take one picture as an illustration of this. I see the Master approaching the city of Nain, and around Him His disciples. He is coming up. And I see outside the city of Nain, coming toward the gate a man carried by others, dead, and walking by that bier a mother. Now, all I want you to look at is that woman's face, and, looking into her face, see all the anguish of those circumstances. She is a widow, and that is her boy, her only boy, and he is dead. Man can not talk about this. You have got to be in the house to know what that means. But look at her face—there it is. All the sorrow is on her face. You can see it.

Now, turn from her quickly and look into the face of Christ. Why, I look into His face —there is her face. He is feeling all she is feeling; He is down in her sorrow with her; He has got underneath the burden, and He is feeling all the agony that that woman feels because her boy is dead. He is moved with compassion whenever human sorrow crosses His vision and human need approaches Him. And now I see Him moving toward the bier. I see Him as He touches it. And He takes the boy back and gives him to his mother. Do you see in yon mountain a cloud, so somber and sad, and suddenly the sun comes from behind the cloud, and all the mountain-side laughs with gladness? That is that woman's face. The agony is gone. The tear that remains there is gilded with a smile, and joy is on her face. Look at Him. There it is. He is in her joy now. He is having as good a time as the woman. He has carried her grief and her sorrow. He has given her joy. And it is His joy that He has given to her. He is with her in her joy.

Wonderful sympathy! He went about gathering human sorrow into His own heart, scattering His joy, and having fellowship in agony and in deliverance, in tears and in their wiping away. Great, sympathetic soul! Why? Because He always lived with God, and, living with God, the divine love moved Him with compassion. Ah, believe me, our sorrows are more felt in heaven than on earth. And we had that glimpse of that eternal love in this Man, who did the things that pleased God, and manifested such wondrous sympathy.

Fourth, strength. The last note is that of strength. You talk about the weakness of Jesus, the frailty of Jesus. I tell you, there never was any one so strong as He. And if you will take the pains of reading His life with that in mind you will find it was one tremendous march of triumph against all opposing forces. About His dying—how did He die? "At last, at last," says the man in his study that does not know anything about Jesus; "at last His enemies became too much for Him, and they killed Him." Nothing of the sort. That is a very superficial reading. What is the truth? Hear it from His own lips: "No man taketh my life from me. I lay, it down of myself. And if I lay it down I have authority to take it again." What do you think of that? How does that touch you as a revelation of magnificence in strength?

And then, look at Him, when He comes back from the tomb, having fulfilled that which was either an empty boast or a great fact—thank God, we believe it was a great fact! Now He stands upon the mountain, with this handful of men around Him, His disciples, and He is going away from them. "All authority," He says, "is given unto me. I am king not merely by an office conferred, but by a triumph won. I am king, for I have faced the enemies of the race—sin and sorrow and ignorance and death—and my foot is upon the neck of every one. All authority is given to me."

Oh, the strength of this Man! Where did He get it? "My Father hath not left me alone. I have lived with God. I have walked with God. I always knew him near. I always responded to his will. And my heart went out in sympathy to others, and I mastered the enemies of those with whom I sympathized. And I come to the end and I say, All authority is given to me." Oh, my brother, that is the pattern for you and for me! Ah, that is life! That is the ideal! Oh, how can I fulfil it? I am not going to talk about that. Let me only give you this sentence to finish with. "Christ in you, the hope of glory." If Christ be in me by the power of the Spirit, He will keep me conscious of God's nearness to me. If Christ be in me by the consciousness of the spirit reigning and governing, He will take my will from day to day, blend it with His, and take away all that makes it hard to say, "God's will be done."

JAMES B. MOZLEY

1813-1878

THE REVERSAL OF HUMAN JUDGMENT

Many that are first shall be last; and the last shall be first.—Matthew xix., 30.

PERHAPS there is hardly any person of reflection to whom the thought has not occurred at times, of the final judgment turning out to be a great subversion of human estimates of men. Society forms its opinions of men, and places some on a high pinnacle; they are favorites with it, religious and moral favorites. Such judgments are a necessary and proper part of the present state of things; they are so, quite independently of the question whether they are true or not; it is proper that there should be this sort of expression of the voice of the day; the world is not nothing, because it is transient; it must judge and speak upon such evidence as it has, and is capable of seeing. Therefore those characters of men are by all means to be respected by us, as members of this world; they have their place, they are a part of the system. But does the idea strike us of some enormous subversion of human judgments in the next world, some vast rectification, to realize which now, even if we could, would not be good for us? Such an idea would not be without support from some of those characteristic prophetic sayings of our Lord, which, like the slanting strokes of the sun's rays across the clouds, throw forward a tract of mysterious light athwart the darkness of the future. Such is that saying in which a shadow of the Eternal Judgment seems to come over us— "Many that are first shall be last; and the last shall be first." It is impossible to read this saying without an understanding that it was intended to throw an element of wholesome scepticism into the present estimate of human character, and to check the idolatry of the human heart which lifts up its favorites with as much of self-complacency as of enthusiasm, and in its worship of others flatters itself.

Indeed, this language of Scripture, which speaks of the subversion of human judgments in another world, comes in connection with another language with which it most remarkably fits in, language which speaks very decidedly of a great deception of human judgments in this world. It is observable that the gospel prophecy of the earthly future of Christianity is hardly what we should have expected it beforehand to be; there is a great absence of brightness in it; the sky is overcast with clouds, and birds of evil omen fly to and fro; there is an agitation of the air, as if dark elements were at work in it; or it is as if a fog rose up before our eyes, and treacherous lights were moving to and fro in it, which we could not trust. Prophecy would fain presage auspiciously, but as soon as she casts her eye forward, her note saddens, and the chords issue in melancholy and sinister cadences which depress the hearer's mind. And what is the burden of her strain? It is this. As soon as ever Christianity is cast into the world to begin its history, that moment there begins a great deception. It is a pervading thought in gospel prophecy—the extraordinary capacity for deceiving and being deceived that would arise under the gospel; it is spoken of as something peculiar in the world. There are to be false Christs and false prophets, false signs and wonders; many that will come in Christ's name, saying, I am Christ, and deceive many; so that it is the parting admonition of Christ to His disciples—"Take heed, lest any man deceive you"—as if that would be the greater danger. And this great quantity of deception was to culminate in that one in whom all power of signs and lying wonders should reside, even that Antichrist, who as God should sit in the temple of God, showing himself that he is God. Thus before the true Christ was known to the world, the prophecy of the false one was implanted deep in the heart of Christianity.

When we come to the explanation of this mass of deception as it applies to the Christian society, and the conduct of Christians, we find that it consists of a great growth of specious and showy effects, which will in fact issue out of Christianity, not implying sterling goodness. Christianity will act as a great excitement to human nature, it will communicate a great impulse, it will move and stir man's feelings and intellect; this impulse will issue in a great variety of high gifts and activities, much zeal and ardor. But this brilliant manifestation will be to a large extent lacking in the substance of the Christian character. It will be a great show. That is to say, there will be underneath it the deceitful human heart—the *natura callida*, as Thomas à Kempis calls it, *quæ se semper pro fine habet*. We have even in the early Christian Church that specious display of gifts which put aside as secondary the more solid part of religion, and which St. Paul had so strongly to check. Gospel prophecy goes remarkably in this direction, as to what Christianity would do in the world; that it would not only bring out the truth of human nature, but would, like some powerful alchemy, elicit and extract the falsehood of it; that it would not only develop what was sincere and sterling in man, but what was counterfeit in him too. Not that Christianity favors falsehood, any more than the law favored sin because it brought out sin. The law, as St. Paul says, brought out sin because it was spiritual, and forced sin to

be sin against light. So in the case of Christianity. If a very high, pure, and heart-searching religion is brought into contact with a corrupt nature, the nature grasps at the greatness of the religion, but will not give up itself; yet to unite the two requires a self-deception the more subtle and potent in proportion to the purity of the religion. And certainly, comparing the hypocrisy of the Christian with that of the old world, we see that the one was a weak production in comparison with the other, which is indeed a very powerful creation; throwing itself into feeling and language with an astonishing freedom and elasticity, and possessing wonderful spring and largeness.

There is, however, one very remarkable utterance of our Lord Himself upon this subject, which deserves special attention. "Many will say to me in that day, Lord, Lord, have we not prophesied in thy name, and in thy name cast out devils, and in thy name done many wonderful works? And then I will profess unto them, I never knew you." Now this is a very remarkable prophecy, for one reason, that in the very first start of Christianity, upon the very threshold of its entrance into the world, it looks through its success and universal reception, into an ulterior result of that victory—a counterfeit profession of it. It sees, before the first nakedness of its birth is over, a prosperous and flourishing religion, which it is worth while for others to pay homage to, because it reflects credit on its champions. Our Lord anticipates the time when active zeal for Himself will be no guaranty. And we may observe the difference between Christ and human founders. The latter are too glad of any zeal in their favor, to examine very strictly the tone and quality of it. They grasp at it at once; not so our Lord. He does not want it even for Himself, unless it is pure in the individual. But this statement of our Lord's is principally important, as being a prophecy relating to the earthly future of Christianity. It places before us public religious leaders, men of influence in the religious world, who spread and push forward by gifts of eloquence and powers of mind, the truths of His religion, whom yet He will not accept, because of a secret corruptness in the aim and spirit with which they did their work. The prophecy puts forth before us the fact of a great deal of work being done in the Church, and outwardly good zealous work, upon the same motive in substance, upon which worldly men do their work in the world, and stamps it as the activity of corrupt nature. The rejection of this class of religious workers is complete, altho they have been, as the language itself declares, forward and active for spiritual objects, and not only had them on their lips. Here then we have a remarkable subversion of human judgments in the next world foretold by our Lord Himself; for those men certainly come forward with established religious characters to which they appeal; they have no doubt of their position in God's kingdom, and they speak with the air of men whose claims have been acquiesced in by others, and by numbers. And thus a false Christian growth is looked to in gospel prophecy, which will be able to meet even the religious tests of the current day, and sustain its pretensions, but which will not satisfy the tests of the last day.

We are then perhaps at first surprized at the sternness of their sentence, and are ready to say with the trembling disciple, "Who then shall be saved?" But when we reflect upon it, we shall see that it is not more than what meets the case; i. e., that we know of sources of error in the estimate of human character which will account for great mistakes being made; which mistakes will have to be rectified.

One source of mistakes then is, that while the gospel keeps to one point of its classification of men,—viz., the motive, by which alone it decides their character, the mass of men in fact find it difficult to do so. They have not that firm hold of the moral idea which prevents them from wandering from it, and being diverted by irrelevant considerations, they think of the spirituality of a man as belonging to the department to which he is attached, the profession he makes, the subject matter he works upon, the habitual language he has to use. The sphere of these men, of whom the estimate was to be finally reversed, was a religious one,—viz., the Church, and this was a remarkable prop to them. Now, with respect to this, it must be observed that the Church is undoubtedly in its design a spiritual society, but it is also a society of this world as well; and it depends upon the inward motive of a man whether it is to him a spiritual society or a worldly one. The Church, as soon as ever it is embodied in a visible collection or society of men, who bring into it human nature, with human influences, regards, points of view, estimates, aims, and objects—I say the Church, from the moment it thus embodies itself in a human society, is the world. Individual souls in it convert into reality the high profest principles of the body, but the active stock of motives in it are the motives of human nature. Can the visible Church indeed afford to do without these motives? Of course it cannot. It must do its work by means of these to a great extent, just as the world does its work. Religion itself is beautiful and heavenly, but the machinery for it is very like the machinery for anything else. I speak of the apparatus for conducting and administering the visible system of it. Is not the machinery for all causes and objects

much the same, communication with others, management, contrivance, combination, adaptation of means to end? Religion then is itself a painful struggle, but religious machinery provides as pleasant a form of activity as any other machinery possesses; and it counts for and exercises much the same kind of talents and gifts that the machinery of any other department does, that of a government office, or a public institution, or a large business. The Church, as a part of the work, must have active-minded persons to conduct its policy and affairs; which persons must, by their very situation, connect themselves with spiritual subjects, as being the subjects of the society; they must express spiritual joys, hopes, and fears, apprehensions, troubles, trials, aims, and wishes. These are topics which belong to the Church as a department. A religious society, then, or religious sphere of action, or religious sphere of subjects, is irrelevant as regards the spirituality of the individual person, which is a matter of inward motive.

One would not of course exclude from the sphere of religion the motive of *esprit de corps*: it is undoubtedly a great stimulus, and in its measure is consistent with all simplicity and singleness of heart; but in an intense form, when the individual is absorbed in a blind obedience to a body, it corrupts the quality of religion; it ensnares the man in a kind of self-interest; and he sees in the success of the body the reflection of himself. It becomes an egotistic motive. There has been certainly an immense produce from it; but the type of religion it has produced is a deflection from simplicity; it may possess striking and powerful qualities, but it is not like the free religion of the heart; and there is that difference between the two, which there is between what comes from a second-hand source and from the fountain head. It has not that naturalness (in the highest sense) which alone gives beauty to religion.

Again, those who feel that they have a mission may convert it into a snare to themselves. Doubtless, if, according to St. Paul, "he who desireth the office of a bishop desireth a good work," so one who has a mission to do some particular work has a good office given him. Still, where life is too prominently regarded in this light, the view of life as a mission tends to supersede the view of it as trial and probation. The mission becomes the final cause of life. The generality may be born to do their duty in that station of life in which it has pleased God to call them; but in their own case the mission overtops and puts into the shade the general purpose of life as probation; the generality are sent into the world for their own moral benefit, but they are rather sent into the world for the benefit of that world itself. The outward object with its display and machinery is apt to reduce to a kind of insignificance the inward individual end of life. It appears small and commonplace. The success of their own individual probation is assumed in embarking upon the larger work, as the less is included in the greater; it figures as a preliminary in their eyes, which may be taken for granted; it appears an easy thing to them to save their own souls, a thing, so to speak, for anybody to do.

What has been dwelt upon hitherto as a source of false magnifying and exaltation of human character, has been the invisibility of men's motives. But let us take another source of mistake in human judgment.

Nothing is easier, when we take gifts of the intellect and imagination in the abstract, than to see that these do not constitute moral goodness. This is indeed a mere truism; and yet, in the concrete, it is impossible not to see how nearly they border upon counting as such; to what advantage they set off any moral good there may be in a man; sometimes even supplying the absence of real good with what looks extremely like it. On paper these mental gifts are a mere string of terms; we see exactly what these terms denote, and we cannot mistake it for something else. It is plain that eloquence, imagination, poetical talent, are no more moral goodness than riches are, or than health and strength are, or than noble birth is. We know that bad men have possest them just as much as good men. Nevertheless, take them in actual life, in the actual effect and impression they make, as they express a man's best moods and highest perceptions and feelings, and what a wonderful likeness and image of what is moral do they produce. Think of the effect of refined power of expression, of a keen and vivid imagination as applied to the illustration and enrichment of moral subjects,—to bringing out, e. g., with the whole force of intellectual sympathy, the delicate and high regions of character,—does not one who can do this seem to have all the goodness which he expresses? And it is quite possible he may have; but this does not prove it. There is nothing more in this than the faculty of imagination and intelligent appreciation of moral things. There enters thus unavoidably often into a great religious reputation a good deal which is not religion, but power.

Let us take the character which St. Paul draws. It is difficult to believe that one who had the tongue of men and of angels would not be able to persuade the world that he himself was extraordinarily good. Rather it is part of the fascination of the gift, that the grace of it is reflected in the possessor. But St. Paul gives him, besides thrilling speech which masters men's spirits and carries them away, those profound depths of imagination which

still and solemnize them; which lead them to the edge of the unseen world, and excite the sense of the awful and supernatural; he has the understanding of all mysteries. And again, knowledge unfolds all its stores to him with which to illustrate and enrich spiritual truths. Let one then, so wonderful in mental gifts, combine them with the utmost fervor, with boundless faith, before which everything gives way; boundless zeal, ready to make even splendid sacrifices; has there been any age in which such a man would have been set down as sounding and empty? St. Paul could see that such a man might yet be without the true substance—goodness; and that all his gifts could not guarantee it to him; but to the mass his own eloquence would interpret him, the gifts would carry the day, and the brilliant partial virtues would disguise the absence of the general grace of love.

Gifts of intellect and imagination, poetical power, and the like, are indeed in themselves a department of worldly prosperity. It is a very narrow view of prosperity that it consists only in having property; a certain kind of gifts are just as much worldly prosperity as riches; nor are they less so if they belong to a religious man, any more than riches are less prosperity because a religious man is rich. We call these gifts worldly prosperity, because they are in themselves a great advantage, and create success, influence, credit, and all which man so much values; and at the same time they are not moral goodness, because the most corrupt men may have them.

But even the gifts of outward fortune themselves have much of the effect of gifts of mind in having the semblance of something moral. They set off what goodness a man has to such immense advantage, and heighten the effect of it. Take some well-disposed person, and suppose him suddenly to be left an enormous fortune, he would feel himself immediately so much better a man. He would seem to himself to become suddenly endowed with a new large-heartedness and benevolence. He would picture himself the generous patron, the large dispenser of charity, the promoter of all good in the world. The power to become such would look like a new disposition. And in the eyes of the others, too, his goodness would appear to have taken a fresh start. Even serious piety is recognized more as such; it is brought out and placed in high relief, when connected with outward advantages; and so the gifts of fortune become a kind of moral addition to a man.

Action, then, on a large scale, and the overpowering effect of great gifts, are what produce, in a great degree, what we call the canonization of men—the popular judgment which sets them up morally and spiritually upon the pinnacle of the temple, and which professes to be a forestalment, through the mouth of the Church or of religious society, of the final judgment. How decisive is the world's, and, not less confident, the visible Church's note of praise. It is just that trumpet note which does not bear a doubt. How it is trusted! With what certainty it speaks! How large a part of the world's and Church's voice is praise! It is an immense and ceaseless volume of utterance. And by all means let man praise man, and not do it grudgingly either; let there be an echo of that vast action which goes on in the world, provided we only speak of what we know. But if we begin to speak of what we do not know, and which only a higher judgment can decide, we are going beyond our province. On this question we are like men who are deciding irreversibly on some matter in which everything depends upon one element in the case, which element they cannot get at. We appear to know a great deal of one another, and yet, if we reflect, what a vast system of secrecy the moral world is. How low down in a man sometimes (not always) lies the fundamental motive which sways his life? But this is what everything depends on. Is it an unspiritual motive? Is there some keen passion connected with this world at the bottom? Then it corrupts the whole body of action. There is a good deal of prominent religion then, which keeps up its character, even when this motive betrays itself; great gifts fortify it, and people do not see because they will not. But at any rate there is a vast quantity of religious position which has this one great point undecided beneath it; and we know of tremendous dangers to which it is exposed. Action upon a theater may doubtless be as simple-minded action as any other; it has often been; it has been often even childlike action; the apostles acted on a theater; they were a spectacle to men and to angels. Still, what dangers in a spiritual point of view does it ordinarily include—dangers to simplicity, inward probity, sincerity! How does action on this scale and of this kind seem, notwithstanding its religious object, to pass over people, not touching one of their faults, leaving—more than their infirmities—the dark veins of evil in their character as fixed as ever. How will persons sacrifice themselves to their objects? They would benefit the world, it would appear, at their own moral expense; but this is a kind of generosity which is perilous policy for the soul, and is indeed the very mint in which the great mass of false spiritual coinage is made.

On the other hand, while the open theater of spiritual power and energy is so accessible to corrupt motives, which, tho undermining its truthfulness, leave standing all the brilliance of the outer manifestation; let it be considered what a strength and power of

goodness may be accumulating in unseen quarters. The way in which man bears temptation is what decides his character; yet how secret is the system of temptation? Who knows what is going on? What the real ordeal has been? What its issue was? So with respect to the trial of griefs and sorrows, the world is again a system of secrecy. There is something particularly penetrating, and which strikes home, in those disappointments which are especially not extraordinary, and make no show. What comes naturally and as a part of our situation has a probing force grander strokes have not; there is a solemnity and stateliness in these, but the blow which is nearest to common life gets the stronger hold. Is there any particular event which seems to have, if we may say so, a kind of malice in it which provokes the Manichean feeling in our nature, it is something which we should have a difficulty in making appear to any one else any special trial. Compared with this inner grasp of some stroke of providence, voluntary sacrifice stands outside of us. After all, the self-made trial is a poor disciplinarian weapon; there is a subtle masterly irritant and provoking point in the genuine natural trial, and in the natural crossness of events, which the artificial thing cannot manage; we can no more make our trials than we can make our feelings. In this way moderate deprivations are in some cases more difficult to bear than extreme ones. "I can bear total obscurity," says Pascal, "well enough; what disgusts me is semi-obscurity; I can make an idol of the whole, but no great merit of the half." And so it is often the case that what we must do as simply right, and which would not strike even ourselves, and still less anybody else, is just the hardest thing to do. A work of supererogation would be much easier. All this points in the direction of great work going on under common outsides where it is not noticed; it hints at a secret sphere of growth and progress; and as such it is an augury and presage of a harvest which may come some day suddenly to light, which human judgments had not counted on.

It is upon such a train of thought as this which has been passing through our minds that we raise ourselves to the reception of that solemn sentence which Scripture has inscribed on the curtain which hangs down before the judgment-seat—"The first shall be last, and the last shall be first." The secrets of the tribunal are guarded, and yet a finger points which seems to say—"Beyond, in this direction, behind this veil, things are different from what you will have looked for."

Suppose, e. g., any supernatural judge should appear in the world now, and it is evident that the scene he would create would be one to startle us; we should not soon be used to it; it would look strange; it would shock and appal; and that from no other cause than simply its reductions; that it presented characters stripped bare, denuded of what was irrelevant to goodness, and only with their moral substance left. The judge would take no cognizance of a rich imagination, power of language, poetical gifts and the like, in themselves, as parts of goodness, any more than he would of riches and prosperity; and the moral residuum would appear perhaps a bare result. The first look of divine justice would strike us as injustice; it would be too pure a justice for us; we should be long in reconciling ourselves to it. Justice would appear, like the painter's gaunt skeleton of emblematic meaning, to be stalking through the world, smiting with attenuation luxuriating forms of virtue. Forms, changed from what we knew, would meet us, strange unaccustomed forms, and we should have to ask them who they are—"You were flourishing but a short while ago, what has happened to you now?" And the answer, if it spoke the truth, would be—"Nothing, except that now, much which lately counted as goodness, counts as such no longer; we are tried by a new moral measure, out of which we issue different men; gifts which have figured as goodness remain as gifts, but cease to be goodness." Thus would the large sweep made of human canonizations act like blight or volcanic fire upon some rich landscape, converting the luxury of nature into a dried-up scene of bare stems and scorched vegetation.

So may the scrutiny of the last day, by discovering the irrelevant material in men's goodness, reduce to a shadow much exalted earthly character. Men are made up of professions, gifts, and talents, and also of themselves, but all so mixed together that we cannot separate one element from another; but another day must show what the moral substance is, and what is only the brightness and setting off of gifts. On the other hand, the same day may show where, tho the setting off of gifts is less, the substance is more. If there will be reversal of human judgment for evil, there will be reversal of it for good too. The solid work which has gone on in secret, under common exteriors, will then spring into light, and come out in a glorious aspect. Do we not meet with surprizes of this kind here, which look like auguries of a greater surprize in the next world, a surprize on a vast scale. Those who have lived under an exterior of rule, when they come to a trying moment sometimes disappoint us; they are not equal to the act required from them; because their forms of duty, whatever they are, have not touched in reality their deeper fault of character, meanness, or jealousy, or the like, but have left them where they were; they have gone on thinking themselves good because they did particular things, and used certain

language, and adopted certain ways of thought, and have been utterly unconscious all the time of a corroding sin within them. On the other hand, some one who did not promise much, comes out at a moment of trial strikingly and favorably. This is a surprize, then, which sometimes happens, nay, and sometimes a greater surprize still, when out of the eater comes forth meat, and out of a state of sin there springs the soul of virtue. The act of the thief on the cross is a surprize. Up to the time when he was judged he was a thief, and from a thief he became a saint. For even in the dark labyrinth of evil there are unexpected outlets; sin is established by the habit in the man, but the good principle which is in him also, but kept down and supprest, may be secretly growing too; it may be undermining it, and extracting the life and force from it. In this man, then, sin becomes more and more, tho holding its place by custom, an outside and a coating, just as virtue does in the deteriorating man, till at last, by a sudden effort and the inspiration of an opportunity, the strong good casts off the weak crust of evil and comes out free. We witness a conversion.

But this is a large and mysterious subject— the foundation for high virtue to become apparent in a future world, which hardly rises up above the ground here. We cannot think of the enormous trial which is undergone in this world by vast masses without the thought also of some sublime fruit to come of it some day. True, it may not emerge from the struggle of bare endurance here, but has not the seed been sown? Think of the burden of toil and sorrow borne by the crowds of poor: we know that pain does not of itself make people good; but what we observe is, that even in those in whom the trial seems to do something, it yet seems such a failure. What inconstancy, violence, untruths! The pathos in it all moves you. What a tempest of character it is! And yet when such trial has been passed we involuntarily say—has not a foundation been laid? And so in the life of a soldier, what agonies must nature pass through in it! While the present result of such a trial is so disappointing, so little seems to come of it! Yet we cannot think of what has been gone through by countless multitudes in war, of the dreadful altar of sacrifice, and the lingering victims, without the involuntary idea arising that in some, even of the irregular and undisciplined, the foundation of some great purification has been laid. We hear sometimes of single remarkable acts of virtue, which spring from minds in which there is not the habit of virtue. Such acts point to a foundation, a root of virtue in man, deeper than habit; they are sudden leaps which show an unseen spring, which are able to compress in a moment the growth of years.

To conclude. The gospel language throws doubt upon the final stability of much that passes current here with respect to character, upon established judgments, and the elevations of the outward sanctuary. It lays down a wholesome scepticism. We do not do justice to the spirit of the gospel by making it enthusiastic simply, or even benevolent simply. It is sagacious, too. It is a book of judgment. Man is judged in it. Our Lord is Judge. We cannot separate our Lord's divinity from His humanity; and yet we must be blind if we do not see a great judicial side of our Lord's human character;—that severe type of understanding, in relation to the worldly man, which has had its imperfect representation in great human minds. He was unspeakably benevolent, kind, compassionate; true, but He was a Judge. It was indeed of His very completeness as man that He should know man; and to know is to judge. He must be blind who, in the significant acts and sayings of our Lord as they unroll themselves in the pregnant page of the gospel, does not thus read His character; he sees it in that insight into pretensions, exposure of motives, laying bare of disguises; in the sayings—"Believe it not"; Take heed that no man deceive you"; "Behold, I have told you"; in all that profoundness of reflection in regard to man, which great observing minds among mankind have shown, tho accompanied by much of frailty, anger, impatience, or melancholy. His human character is not benevolence only; there is in it wise distrust—that moral sagacity which belongs to the perfection of man.

Now then, as has been said, this scepticism with regard to human character has had, as a line of thought, certain well-known representatives in great minds, who have discovered a root of selfishness in men's actions, have probed motives, extracted aims, and placed man before himself denuded and exposed; they judged him, and in the frigid sententiousness or the wild force of their utterances, we hear that of which we cannot but say, how true! But knowledge is a goad to those who have it; a disturbing power; a keenness which distorts; and in the sight it gives it partly blinds also. The fault of these minds was that in exposing evil they did not really believe in goodness; goodness was to them but an airy ideal, the dispirited echo of perplexed hearts,—returned to them from the rocks of the desert, without bearing hope with it. They had no genuine belief in any world which was different from theirs; they availed themselves of an ideal indeed to judge this world, and they could not have judged it without; for anything, whatever it is, is good, if we have no idea of anything better; and therefore the conception of a good world was necessary to judge the bad one. But the ideal held loose to their minds—not anything to be substantiated, not as a type in which a real world was to be cast, not as anything of structural power, able to gather into it, form round it, and build up upon itself; not, in short, as anything of power at all, able to make anything, or do anything, but only like some fragrant scent in the air, which comes and goes, loses itself, returns again in faint breaths, and rises and falls in imperceptive waves. Such was goodness to these minds; it was a dream. But the gospel distrust is not disbelief in goodness. It raises a great suspense, indeed, it shows a curtain not yet drawn up, it checks weak enthusiasm, it appends a warning note to the pomp and flattery of human judgments, to the erection of idols; and points to a day of great reversal; a day of the Lord of Hosts; the day of pulling down and plucking up, of planting and building. But, together with the law of sin, the root of evil in the world, and the false goodness in it, it announces a fount of true natures; it tells us of a breath of Heaven of which we know not whence it cometh and whither it goeth; which inspires single individual hearts, that spring up here and there, and everywhere, like broken gleams of the supreme goodness. And it recognizes in the renewed heart of man an instinct which can discern true goodness and distinguish it from false; a secret discrimination in the good by which they know the good. It does not therefore stand in the way of that natural and quiet reliance which we are designed by God to have in one another, and that trust in those whose hearts we know. "Wisdom is justified of her children"; "My sheep hear my voice, but a stranger will they not follow, for they know not the voice of strangers."

EDGAR YOUNG MULLINS

1860-1928

THE GLORY OF CHRIST

BIOGRAPHICAL NOTE

PRESIDENT of the Southern Baptist Theological Seminary, Louisville, Ky., 1899-1928; born Franklin County, Miss., January 5, 1860; educated at Corsicana, Tex., 1870-76; Agricultural and Mechanical College of Texas, 1876-79; ordained to Baptist ministry, 1885; graduated Southern Baptist Theological Seminary, 1885, D.D. and LL.D.; pastor at Harrodsburg, Ky., 1885-88; Lee Street church, Baltimore, 1888-95; editor of *The Evangel*, Baltimore, 1890-95; pastor of First church, Newton, Mass., 1896-99; author of " Why is Christianity True," " The Axioms of Religion."

" We beheld his glory."—John 1 : 14.

SOME years ago a painter who admired the moral beauty of Christ's character, but who refused to acknowledge that He was God, resolved to paint Christ's portrait from the evangelical records. For weeks he read these simple gospels and opened his soul to every suggestion of beauty and moral impulse, permitting himself to be moved and swayed by all the grandeur and radiance of that matchless life, knowing that only thus could he catch and reproduce on canvas the face he would portray. But in his process of sympathetic study of Jesus his unbelief slowly passed away. First one doubt and then another was consumed, burned up, so to speak, in the flaming splendor of that marvelous life, and ere long the painter bowed before Christ in adoration and worship. Like a man who has gazed into a holy mystery, he came forth among his friends, a look of wonder and of praise upon his face, and exclaimed, " I beheld His glory."

Men are denying to-day that Christ is divine. They are seeking to undermine that faith which has healed broken hearts, and has destroyed the power of sin, and comforted the dying for two thousand years. It is well that we ask and answer the question, Was He what He claimed to be, the divine son of God and Savior of the world?

As evidence that Christ cannot be classed with other men, I invite your attention to the threefold glory of Jesus which we have beheld. First of all, we will glance at that glory as seen in the gospel records where the painter saw it.

If a meteoric stone should fall upon the calm bosom of the sea, the energy of its impact might be measured by the diameter of the circling waves which it would set in motion when those waves had reached their limit. So the claims of Jesus may be tested by the rôle He enacted while on earth and by the effects which He produced. Let us study, then, the circling waves of His power in a series of relationships sustained by Him.

Note, first, His relation to sin. He was Himself sinless. His inner life was a flawless mirror of stainless purity reflecting the image of God. He has challenged criticism for two thousand years to discover a flaw in His character. " Which of you convicteth me of sin ? " remains as He spoke it, the unanswered challenge of divine holiness. As has been said, He is the sun on which all the telescopes of time have failed to find a spot.

He was not only sinless—He forgave sin in

others. Well did His enemies accuse Him of blasphemy when He pronounced the words to the paralytic, " Son, thy sins are forgiven thee," unless indeed and in truth He was God, for God alone can forgive sins.

He transformed sinners. As a sunbeam falls on a mud puddle and draws up a drop of water into the clouds, distils it and purifies it of all foulness and sends it back as a snowflake, even so could He lay His finger on the stained life of a Magdalen and make it white as snow.

He shed His blood on the cross for the remission of sins, and He declared that remission of sins should be preached in His name to the end of time.

But sin is a violation of law, and this relation of sin raises another question, that of His relation to law. And so we find Him claiming to be lawgiver and king. " He that heareth these sayings of mine and doeth them," " Ye have heard it said, but I say unto you," are forms of speech familiar on His lips.

But law suggests a kingdom and a scepter and a throne. So we find that He is King of a new kingdom among men. He claims that His kingdom shall endure forever and He shall reign in righteousness.

But a kingdom set up on earth implies control of providential events. For how shall such a kingdom survive through the ages unless the ruler can control the course of history? Read the twenty-fourth and twenty-fifth chapters of Matthew, and see how calmly He anticipates the course of history, of earthquakes and wars, of famines and pestilences. Yet He says he that endureth to the end shall be saved, and that He himself shall come again at the consummation.

Providence, again, is but part of a vaster system of nature. And we find that He is Lord of nature. He spoke to the water, and it blushed into wine; He spoke to the barren figtree, and it withered from the roots upward; He spoke to the loaves and fishes, and they were multiplied and fed the thousands; He spoke to the tempest, and it was hushed into silence. Nature was His servant. He was its Master.

Towards man He asserts the sublimest claims. He is the object of human faith; for Him all human ties must be severed if need be; for Him death is to be welcomed. He extends His arms and invites the race to come to Him for peace. " Come unto me, all ye that labor and are heavy laden, and I will give you rest."

How sublime is this role enacted by the Nazarene! And to crown it all, He claims equality with God. Before " Abraham was I am." " I and my Father are one." Well has it been said: Jesus was either God or a bad man; for He claimed to be God.

And how simple the picture in the gospels; how consistent; how transparent and clear the story. His words about God are like the spontaneous warblings of some strange and wonderful bird. His deeds of power, His miracles of grace are as sparks emitted by some great fire. Yet how unaffected He is in it all! There is never any attempt at dramatic effect. In the moments of His greatest majesty He is as quiet and as unassuming as the shining of a softly beaming star. Homer's gods are represented as shaking the heavens by their least act. The poet produces his effects by physical disturbances when his gods stir. Jove gives an affirmative answer to a petitioner, and this is Homer's description of it:

" He spoke and awful bends his sable brows,
Shakes his ambrosial curls and gives the nod,
The stamp of fate and sanction of a god.
High heaven with trembling the dread signal took,
And all Olympus to the center shook."

Contrast this with the quiet majesty and moral grandeur of Jesus stilling the tempest as He rises from His slumber and says to the rolling billows and raging winds, " Peace, be still." Sometimes He unites in a single act the perfectly human and the perfectly divine in His nature. Humility nestles up by the side of majesty. Grandeur is adorned by lowliness, and extremes meet in perfect harmony. He is worn out with toil and asleep on the boat like any other, and in an instant stills a tempest. He stands weeping at the grave of Lazarus, like any other broken-hearted friend, and at once hurls the voice of command into the tomb and raises the dead to life. He allows Himself to be led away captive by his foes, but restores the severed ear of the high-priest's servant, and says to the impetuous disciple, " Knowest thou not that I could call to my side twelve legions of angels? " He allows Himself to be nailed to the cross, and to be laid away in the tomb, and then in undaunted might quietly opens his eyes and lays aside the grave-clothes, rises from the dead and ascends to the Father.

Surely we have beheld His glory in these pages, and any man will repeat the painter's experience who allows Christ's image, as there portrayed, to have room in his mind and heart. I have read the tragedies of Shakespeare, and awe and horror have fallen upon my spirit at their close; I have gazed upon the Sistine Madonna, that masterpiece of the artistic genius of Raphael, and a sense of beauty has mastered me. I have been swung on shipboard by the mighty rhythmic force of the ocean, and a sense of its power has filled me. I have gazed on a clear night at the dazzling splendor of the milky way, and adoration and humility have combined to sway my soul with emotion. I have stood on the Gorner Grat, surrounded by cloud-piercing sentinels of snow-clad Alpine peaks keeping guard like tall archangels over diminutive man below, and wonder and awe have opprest me. But the image of Jesus Christ, as it towers in solitary grandeur before me in the New Testament surpasses them all. He inspires me with greater awe than Shakespeare, and greater majesty than ocean or Alps. He is more splendid than the milky way, and not afar from me, as it is, but near me. And if a human writer invented His picture as recorded in Matthew, then a Galilean peasant wears the literary crown of the ages and the genius of Raphael and Michelangelo pale into insignificance by the side of his. Nay, as Rousseau said, it would take a Jesus to forge a Jesus.

Again, " we beheld his glory " in history. The marvel of the ages is the Rock of Ages. The supremacy of Christ as compared with other teachers in all our civilization of the West is as the supremacy of the giant oak in the midst of a forest of saplings, or as the supremacy of the sun as compared with the planets in our solar system.

Dr. Fairbairn says, men have attempted in recent years to get rid of Christ in two ways. One is by critical analysis. They have taken the knife of criticism, and with it have cut and slashed at the gospel records, until one of them has said that there are but six or seven authentic sayings of Jesus in the entire New Testament. The other way is by logical analysis. They have tried to show that the decisions of the early Christian councils declaring Jesus to be God are unreasonable and absurd. But when they have completed their destructive work and done their worst, there stands Christ towering above the troubled sea of human speculation and doubt like a great and lofty rock at whose solid base the angry waves foam out their rage and dash themselves in vain. There stands Jesus in the firmament of human hope like a star of the first magnitude, above the multitudes of hungering and sorrowing and sinning humanity, growing larger and brighter and more splendid with each generation, until to-day all over the earth the nations are in commotion as they gaze upward and point with the trembling finger of yearning and hope to Him as the lodestar of their lives.

Look for a moment at His achievements in history. See Him as He moves westward in the person of the apostle to the Gentiles. He kindles a flame of faith in the islands of the Mediterranean. He plants His banner at Antioch. He sweeps through Lystra and Derbe, and Asia Minor begins to prostrate herself before Him. He plants His foot in Ephesus, and Diana begins to totter from her throne. Restless, He crosses the Hellespont, and at Philippi, amid the quakings of the earth, He wins trophies. In Athens, amid

classic surroundings of the Acropolis and Parthenon and the chiseled beauties of Phidias and the glories of Praxiteles, His voice is heard calling men to repentance. At length in Rome itself He grapples with the world power. His crown flashes in moral beauty by the side of the crown of the Cæsars; His throne rises, mystic, silent and invisible, but mighty in its movement as the silent stars in the bending heavens. When the empire is broken up and barbarians come in hosts, sweeping like a conflagration over that ancient empire, He lays His hand on their untamed spirits. Clovis is converted. The Goths are evangelized. The Franks and Gauls and Scandinavians come bending to Him. England owns His sway. America, through cavalier and Puritan and Pilgrim, is founded, and when the feet of those men touch our shores, the " sounding aisles of the dim woods rang with the anthems of the free " and in praise of the Nazarene.

A humble prophet of Nazareth has done all this. He has done it by the use of a single principle—indeed, by means of one despised virtue, self-denial. The cross is the keystone in the arch of His power. It is a true saying that, as chemistry is organized around the principle of affinity, as political economy is based on the single idea of value, as astronomy owes its origin and progress to the one law of gravitation, so Christ founded His religion on the one idea embodied in the cross, dying to live.

See, then, how He dominates the world; not, indeed, perfectly yet, but with increasing power. Look at the great creeds of Christendom, the Lutheran, the Calvinistic, the Westminster, the Philadelphia and New Hampshire confessions of faith. He is the center of them all. If you should go through the forest with an ax and cut a ring around the great trees, all of them would die. To take Christ's name from these great creeds would be to do the same for them. They would wither, their leaves lose their life and color, their sap cease to flow. They would perish.

The Church is His monument. She has had a long and checkered career, sometimes persecuted and driven into the wilderness, sometimes unworthy of her high calling, but even to-day she is the fairest among ten thousand institutions and the chief glory of this earth.

The Lord's Supper, beautiful impressive memorial of His death, so simple that any child can understand it, yet so profound in its suggestions of divine love that no philosopher has ever fathomed its mystery to its depths, monument of quenchless love and gentle solicitude on His part and expressive of tender love on the part of His disciples, it stretches back through eighteen centuries to Calvary, filled with the aroma of His presence at every step of the way, and shining to the eye of faith through the ages like a chain of roses bedewed with tears of saints and woven by the hands of angels.

He dominates the greatest art of the world. This fact has often been pointed out, and has become commonplace. Go yonder to the art galleries of Europe. Gaze upon those yards upon yards, and furlongs upon furlongs, and miles upon miles of flaming canvas, the very crown and blossom of human genius, and what do you see? His figure, His mother's figure, His brethren's figures, His disciples, His enemies. They portray Him as babe in Bethlehem with the light bursting from His infant form, as boy in the temple, as teacher, as cleanser of the temple, as healer, being raised on the cross, being crucified, descending, ascending to glory, judging the world. As I stand there gazing I interrogate those great masters, and from their graves I seem to hear the answer from Murillo and Rubens and Raphael and the rest. "It was He," they say, "who touched my brush with celestial fire; His hands mingled the colors, and His spirit inspired mine to its great achievements."

So, too, as I listen to the great masters of music, to Handel and Hayden and Beethoven, as the billows of harmony roll in upon me and catch me up and sweep me on, as the sublime strains of the "Messiah" take my spirit captive and chain me to the flaming chariot of triumphant melody, I seem to hear the master of composition say: "It was His breath through my soul which first fanned the flame of harmony; His hands first smote the chords of my being until they thrilled with the very echoes of heaven."

What shall I say more? He is in our modern life everywhere: in our political economy seeking justice in all industrial conditions, in our politics seeking to purge it of greed and graft, in our social life, in our literature shedding a moral radiance over it; in modern missions He is not yet conqueror, but He presides over the struggle.

> " Careless seems the great avenger.
>   History's pages but record
> One death grapple in the darkness
>   'Twixt false systems and the Word.
>
> Truth forever on the scaffold,
>   Wrong forever on the throne;
> But that scaffold sways the future,
>   And behind the dim unknown
> Standeth Christ within the shadow
>   Keeping watch above His own."

In the third place, we have beheld His glory in the realm of Christian experience. His glory shines on the pages of the New Testament. It rises to a new brilliancy as He marches triumphantly through history. But for the individual believer, that glory attains to its noonday splendor in the experience of his own heart.

Christianity adopts the scientific method of demonstration, viz., the method of experiment. Christian experience means Christian experiment. Make a trial of Christ and He will prove to you that He is real, a living Christ doing a divine work in the soul.

We have all seen the triumph of Christ in debased lives, men and women plucked as brands from the burning. A diamond and a piece of charcoal are essentially the same thing, or at least diamonds were made of charcoals; in her own mysterious workshop nature accomplishes this wonder. That is interesting, but it would be far more interesting if my scientific friend could tell me how I can transform charcoal into diamonds. Now this is the glory of Christ, that He does just that. Jerry McAuley was a charcoal, and Christ changed him into a diamond. S. H. Hadley, the bum, the drunkard and reprobate, was a black piece of charcoal, and so was George Muller, of England, who began life as a burglar. Christ touched their lives and made them spiritual jewels, fit to adorn His own crown of glory.

Christ predicted that He would do just that. He said that men would believe on Him, that prayer in His name would open the gates of Paradise, that a cup of water given in His name would have eternal reward. What a magic name it is to-day in its power to renew human lives! According to the old story, George Washington while a boy went into his father's garden one morning in spring and found to his wonder and delight that his name was growing on a garden bed, spelled out by the plants. His father, of course, had planned the surprise for George. But suppose the father had foretold that hundreds of years later his name, Washington, would be found spelled out by growing plants in other garden beds, and suppose the prophecy had come true, then we would conclude that he was in league with the cosmos, that he had supernatural power. Now Jesus has done a more wondrous thing. He predicted that His name would be written in human hearts to the end of time, and that that name in the garden of the soul would keep it clean from weeds and briars, and to-day tens of thousands of men and women are witnesses to His power.

Experiment, I say, not in the vainly curious fashion, but in the high aim of moral purpose. Try Christ thus and He will give the proof of His power. The school children will recall the way the books prove that we have a blind spot. Hold a white piece of cardboard with black marks on it before the eyes, and move it up and down and back and forth until when it reaches a given point the black marks will vanish. Try this and prove it. Now Christianity says turn the soul towards Christ in all sincerity, and suddenly it will appear that you have not a blind but a seeing spot. You will behold His glory. A young woman scientist who was a skeptic denied Christ's resurrection. The pastor in the neighborhood told her to give up speculation and try experiment, offer herself to Christ. She returned soon with radiant face, exclaiming, " I cannot yet prove by argument that Christ arose from the dead, but I know He is alive, for He has come to me and manifested Himself to me." She beheld His glory in the holy place of experience.

Here, then, is the ground of our confidence. First, we believe because, as Professor James says, we will to believe, or because the Bible tells us to believe, or because some friend witnesses to us of Christ's power. But at length we believe because of what He does in us and for us. That is the reason why destructive criticism cannot fundamentally shake our confidence in the Bible. In it we find reflected our own experience. If I look into a mirror which changes or distorts my face, I know it is an untrue mirror, but if it gives me back my own image, I know the mirror is true. Such a mirror is the Bible. It reflects truly my spiritual image.

Blind Bartimaeus, of Jericho, was healed by Jesus, and Dr. Dale has suggested that conceivably his faith at first was based on the healing of the man born blind in Jerusalem, of which he had heard. Imagine a doubter seeking to destroy his faith by calling in question the story of the man in Jerusalem who was healed. " The story looks suspicious," says the skeptic. " Why did Jesus put clay on the man's eyes, and send him off to wash in a pool? There must have been fraud somewhere." What answer would Bartimaeus have given to such a doubter? He would have pointed to his own eyes. He would have declared, as the other declared, " Whereas I was blind, now I see." I see the fair forms of nature and they all tell me I am no longer blind. The daisies that blossom at my feet, they tell as I gaze at their beauty that I am no longer blind; the white blossoms on the trees, the bloom on the grapes, and the hues of the pomegranate; the blue haze on yonder mountain, the fiery splendor of yonder evening cloud, and those burning stars above— these all are my witnesses; the faces of my friends which I now see, of my brothers and sisters, and the dear face of my mother—these all are my witnesses, all this beautiful wondrous earth of God's, fashioned by His fingers, all proclaim my testimony. Yes, yes, I believe not because of what Jesus did to someone else, but because of what He has done to me that He is the divine son of God. I have beheld His glory with the eyes to which He unlocked the gates of light and bade me enter.

This, then, is the witness of experience, and every believer knows what it is in some measure. I went to Him in my bondage and sin, and He broke off the shackles and set me free. I went to Him in doubt and perplexity, and the light of day fell on my darkened path; in the lonely night of sorrow when friends and helpers failed me, He came into my life and bound up my broken heart. In doubt and despair and dread of the future, He gives me life and hope. We have seen His glory, then, on the pages of the New Testament record. It has flashed before us through eighteen centuries of history, as the rider on the white horse went forth conquering and to conquer. That glory has also shone forth within us, and we see it in the lives of others. We have seen it as it breaks forth in the faces of the dying who in His name greet death with a triumphant shout, and we seem to catch it in the notes of the redeemed host above who sing His praises and who proclaim that they owe their victory to Him, and shall spend eternity in telling it.

JOHN H. NEWMAN

1801-1890

GOD'S WILL
THE END OF LIFE

BIOGRAPHICAL NOTE

JOHN HENRY NEWMAN was born in London in 1801. He won high honors at Oxford, and in 1828 was appointed vicar of the University Church, St. Mary's, and with Keble and Pusey headed the Oxford Movement. In the pulpit of St. Mary's he soon showed himself to be a power. His sermons, exquisite, tho simple in style, chiefly deal with various phases of personal religion which he illustrated with a keen spiritual insight, a sympathetic glow, an exalted earnestness and a breadth of range, unparalleled in English pulpit utterances before his time. His extreme views on questions of catholicity, sacerdotalism and the sacraments, as well as his craving for an infallible authority in matters of faith, shook his confidence in the Church of England and he went over to Rome in 1845. He was made Cardinal in 1879 and died in 1890.

I came down from heaven not to do mine own will but the will of him that sent me.—John vi., 38.

I AM going to ask you a question, my dear brethren, so trite, and therefore so uninteresting at first sight, that you may wonder why I put it, and may object that it will be difficult to fix the mind on it, and may anticipate that nothing profitable can be made of it. It is this: "Why were you sent into the world?" Yet, after all, it is perhaps a thought more obvious than it is common, more easy than it is familiar; I mean it ought to come into your minds, but it does not, and you never had more than a distant acquaintance with it, tho that sort of acquaintance with it you have had for many years. Nay, once or twice, perhaps you have been thrown across the thought somewhat intimately, for a short season, but this was an accident which did not last. There are those who recollect the first time, as it would seem, when it came home to them. They were but little children, and they were by themselves, and they spontaneously asked themselves, or rather God spake in them, "Why am I here? how came I here? who brought me here? What am I to do here?" Perhaps it was the first act of reason, the beginning of their real responsibility, the commencement of their trial; perhaps from that day they may date their capacity, their awful power, of choosing between good and evil, and of committing mortal sin. And so, as life goes on, the thought comes vividly, from time to time, for a short season across their conscience; whether in illness, or in some anxiety, or at some season of solitude, or on hearing some preacher, or reading some religious work. A vivid feeling comes over them of the vanity and unprofitableness of the world, and then the question recurs, "Why then am I sent into it?"

And a great contrast indeed does this vain, unprofitable, yet overbearing world present with such a question as that. It seems out of place to ask such a question in so magnificent, so imposing a presence, as that of the great Babylon. The world professes to supply all that we need, as if we were sent into it for the sake of being sent here, and for nothing beyond the sending. It is a great favor to have an introduction to this august world. This is to be our exposition, forsooth, of the mystery of life. Every man is doing his own will here, seeking his own pleasure, pursuing his own ends; that is why he was brought into existence. Go abroad into the streets of the populous city, contemplate the continuous outpouring there of human energy, and the countless varieties of human character, and be satisfied! The ways are thronged, carriage-way and pavement; multitudes are hurrying to and fro, each on his own errand, or are loitering about from listlessness, or from want of work, or have come forth into the public concourse, to see and to be seen, for amusement or for display, or on the excuse of business. The carriages of the wealthy mingle with the slow wains laden with provisions or merchandise, the productions of art or the demands of luxury. The streets are lined with shops, open and gay, inviting customers, and widen now and then into some spacious square or place, with lofty masses of brickwork or of stone, gleaming in the fitful sunbeam, and surrounded or fronted with what simulates a garden's foliage. Follow them in another direction, and you find the whole groundstead covered with large buildings, planted thickly up and down, the homes of the mechanical arts. The air is filled, below, with a ceaseless, importunate, monotonous din, which penetrates even to your innermost chamber, and rings in your ears even when you are not conscious of it; and overhead, with a canopy of smoke, shrouding God's day from the realms of obstinate, sullen toil. This is the end of man!

Or stay at home, and take up one of those daily prints, which are so true a picture of the world; look down the columns of advertisements, and you will see the catalog of pursuits, projects, aims, anxieties, amusements, indulgences which occupy the mind of man. He plays many parts: here he has goods to sell, there he wants employment; there again he seeks to borrow money, here he offers you houses, great seats or small tenements; he has food for the million, and luxuries for the wealthy, and sovereign medicines for the credulous, and books, new and cheap, for the inquisitive. Pass on to the news of the day, and you will learn what great men are doing at home and abroad: you will read of wars and rumors of wars; of debates in the legislature; of rising men, and old statesmen going off the scene; of political contests in this city or that country; of the collision of rival interests. You will read of the money market, and the provision market, and the market for metals; of the state of trade, the call for manufactures, news of ships arrived in port, of accidents at sea, of exports and imports, of gains and losses, of frauds and their detection. Go forward, and you arrive at discoveries in art and science, discoveries (so-called) in religion, the court and royalty, the entertainments of the great, places of amusement, strange trials, offenses, accidents, escapes, exploits, experiments, contests, ventures. Oh, this curious, restless, clamorous, panting being,

which we call life!—and is there to be no end to all this? Is there no object in it? It never has an end, it is forsooth its own object!

And now, once more, my brethren, put aside what you see and what you read of the world, and try to penetrate into the hearts, and to reach the ideas and the feelings of those who constitute it; look into them as closely as you can; enter into their houses and private rooms; strike at random through the streets and lanes: take as they come, palace and hovel, office or factory, and what will you find? Listen to their words, witness, alas! their works; you will find in the main the same lawless thoughts, the same unrestrained desires, the same ungoverned passions, the same earthly opinions, the same wilful deeds, in high and low, learned and unlearned; you will find them all to be living for the sake of living; they one and all seem to tell you, "We are our own center, our own end." Why are they toiling? why are they scheming? for what are they living? "We live to please ourselves; life is worthless except we have our own way; we are not sent here at all, but we find ourselves here, and we are but slaves unless we can think what we will, believe what we will, love what we will, hate what we will, do what we will. We detest interference on the part of God or man. We do not bargain to be rich or to be great; but we do bargain, whether rich or poor, high or low, to live for ourselves, to live for the lust of the moment, or, according to the doctrine of the hour, thinking of the future and the unseen just as much or as little as we please."

Oh, my brethren, is it not a shocking thought, but who can deny its truth? The multitude of men are living without any aim beyond this visible scene; they may from time to time use religious words, or they may profess a communion or a worship, as a matter of course, or of expedience, or of duty, but, if there was sincerity in such profession, the course of the world could not run as it does. What a contrast is all this to the end of life, as it is set before us in our most holy faith! If there was one among the sons of men, who might allowably have taken his pleasure, and have done his own will here below, surely it was He who came down on earth from the bosom of the Father, and who was so pure and spotless in that human nature which He put on Him, that He could have no human purpose or aim inconsistent with the will of His Father. Yet He, the Son of God, the Eternal Word, came, not to do His own will, but His who sent Him, as you know very well is told us again and again in Scripture. Thus the Prophet in the Psalter, speaking in His person, says, "Lo, I come to do thy will, O God." And He says in the Prophet Isaiah, "The Lord God hath opened mine ear, and I do not resist; I have not gone back." And in the gospel, when He hath come on earth, "My food is to do the will of him that sent me, and to finish his work." Hence, too, in His agony, He cried out, "Not my will, but thine, be done;" and St. Paul, in like manner, says, that "Christ pleased not himself;" and elsewhere, that, "tho he was God's Son, yet learned he obedieice by the things which he suffered." Surely so it was; as being indeed the eternal coequal Son, His will was one and the same with the Father's will, and He had no submission of will to make; but He chose to take on Him man's nature and the will of that nature; he chose to take on Him affections, feelings, and inclinations proper to man, a will innocent indeed and good, but still a man's will, distinct from God's will; a will, which, had it acted simply according to what was pleasing to its nature, would, when pain and toil were to be endured, have held back from an active cooperation with the will of God. But, tho He took on Himself the nature of man, He took not on Him that selfishness, with which fallen man wraps himself round, but in all things He devoted Himself as a ready sacrifice to His Father. He came on earth, not to take His pleasure, not to follow His taste, not for the mere exercise of human affection, but simply to glorify His Father and to do His will. He came charged with a mission, deputed for a work; He looked not to the right nor to the left, He thought not of Himself, He offered Himself up to God.

Hence it is that He was carried in the womb of a poor woman, who, before His birth, had two journeys to make, of love and of obedience, to the mountains and to Bethlehem. He was born in a stable, and laid in a manger. He was hurried off to Egypt to sojourn there; then He lived till He was thirty years of age in a poor way, by a rough trade, in a small house, in a despised town. Then, when He went out to preach, He had not where to lay His head; He wandered up and down the country, as a stranger upon earth. He was driven out into the wilderness, and dwelt among the wild beasts. He endured heat and cold, hunger and weariness, reproach and calumny. His food was coarse bread, and fish from the lake, or depended on the hospitality of strangers. And as He had already left His Father's greatness on high, and had chosen an earthly home; so again, at that Father's bidding, He gave up the sole solace given Him in this world, and denied Himself His mother's presence. He parted with her who bore Him; He endured to be strange to her; He endured to call her coldly "woman," who was His own undefiled one, all beautiful, all gracious, the best creature of His hands, and the sweet nurse of His infancy. He put her aside, as Levi, His type, merited the sacred ministry, by saying to His parents and kins-

men, "I know you not." He exemplified in His own person the severe maxim, which He gave to His disciples, "He that loveth more than me is not worthy of me." In all these many ways He sacrificed every wish of His own; that we might understand, that, if He, the Creator, came into His world, not for His own pleasure, but to do His Father's will, we too have most surely some work to do, and have seriously to bethink ourselves what that work is.

Yes, so it is; realize it, my brethren;—every one who breathes, high and low, educated and ignorant, young and old, man and woman, has a mission, has a work. We are not sent into this world for nothing; we are not born at random; we are not here, that we may go to bed at night, and get up in the morning, toil for our bread, eat and drink, laugh and joke, sin when we have a mind, and reform when we are tired of sinning, rear a family and die. God sees every one of us; He creates every soul, He lodges it in the body, one by one, for a purpose. He needs, He deigns to need, every one of us. He has an end for each of us; we are all equal in His sight, and we are placed in our different ranks and stations, not to get what we can out of them for ourselves, but to labor in them for Him. As Christ had His work, we too have ours; as He rejoiced to do His work, we must rejoice in ours also.

St. Paul on one occasion speaks of the world as a scene in a theater. Consider what is meant by this. You know, actors on a stage are on an equality with each other really, but for the occasion they assume a difference of character; some are high, some are low, some are merry, and some sad. Well, would it not be simple absurdity in any actor to pride himself on his mock diadem, or his edgeless sword, instead of attending to his part? what, if he did but gaze at himself and his dress? what, if he secreted, or turned to his own use, what was valuable in it? Is it not his business, and nothing else, to act his part well? Common sense tells us so. Now we are all but actors in this world; we are one and all equal, we shall be judged as equals as soon as life is over; yet, equal and similar in ourselves, each has his special part at present, each has his work, each has his mission,—not to indulge his passions, not to make money, not to get a name in the world, not to save himself trouble, not to follow his bent, not to be selfish and self-willed, but to do what God puts on him to do.

Look at the poor profligate in the gospel, look at Dives; do you think he understood that his wealth was to be spent, not on himself, but for the glory of God?—yet forgetting this, he was lost for ever and ever. I will tell you what he thought, and how he viewed things: he was a young man, and had succeeded to a good estate, and he determined to enjoy himself. It did not strike him that his wealth had any other use than that of enabling him to take his pleasure. Lazarus lay at his gate; he might have relieved Lazarus; that was God's will; but he managed to put conscience aside, and he persuaded himself he should be a fool, if he did not make the most of this world, while he had the means. So he resolved to have his fill of pleasure; and feasting was to his mind a principal part of it. "He fared sumptuously every day"; everything belonging to him was in the best style, as men speak; his house, his furniture, his plate of silver and gold, his attendants, his establishments. Everything was for enjoyment, and for show, too; to attract the eyes of the world, and to gain the applause and admiration of his equals, who were the companions of his sins. These companions were doubtless such as became a person of such pretensions; they were fashionable men; a collection of refined, high-bred, haughty men, eating, not gluttonously, but what was rare and costly; delicate, exact, fastidious in their taste, from their very habits of indulgence; not eating for the mere sake of eating, or drinking for the mere sake of drinking, but making a sort of science of their sensuality; sensual, carnal, as flesh and blood can be, with eyes, ears, tongue steeped in impurity, every thought, look, and sense, witnessing or ministering to the evil one who ruled them; yet, with exquisite correctness of idea and judgment, laying down rules for sinning;—heartless and selfish, high, punctilious, and disdainful in their outward deportment, and shrinking from Lazarus, who lay at the gate, as an eye-sore, who ought for the sake of decency to be put out of the way. Dives was one of such, and so he lived his short span, thinking of nothing but himself, till one day he got into a fatal quarrel with one of his godless associates, or he caught some bad illness; and then he lay helpless on his bed of pain, cursing fortune and his physician that he was no better, and impatient that he was thus kept from enjoying his youth, trying to fancy himself mending when he was getting worse, and disgusted at those who would not throw him some word of comfort in his suspense, and turning more resolutely from his Creator in proportion to his suffering;—and then at last his day came, and he died, and (oh! miserable!) "was buried in hell." And so ended he and his mission.

This was the fate of your pattern and idol, oh, ye, if any of you be present, young men, who, tho not possess of wealth and rank, yet affect the fashions of those who have them. You, my brethren, have not been born splendidly, or nobly; you have not been brought up in the seats of liberal education; you have no high connections; you have not learned the manners nor caught the tone of good society; you have no share of the largeness of mind, the candor, the romantic sense of honor, the correctness of taste, the consideration for others, and the gentleness which the world puts forth as its highest type of excellence; you have not come near the courts of the mansions of the great; yet you ape the sin of Dives, while you are strangers to his refinement. You think it the sign of a gentleman to set yourselves above religion; to criticize the religious and professors of religion; to look at Catholic and Methodist with impartial contempt; to gain a smattering of knowledge on a number of subjects; to dip into a number of frivolous publications, if they are popular; to have read the latest novel; to have heard the singer and seen the actor of the day; to be well up with the news; to know the names and, if so be, the persons of public men, to be able to bow to them; to walk up and down the street with your heads on high, and to stare at whatever meets you; and to say and do worse things, of which these outward extravagances are but the symbol. And this is what you conceive you have come upon the earth for! The Creator made you, it seems, oh, my children, for this work and office, to be a bad imitation of polished ungodliness, to be a piece of tawdry and faded finery, or a scent which has lost its freshness, and does not but offend the sense! O! that you could see how absurd and base are such pretenses in the eyes of any but yourselves! No calling of life but is honorable; no one is ridiculous who acts suitably to his calling and estate; no one, who has good sense and humility, but may, in any state of life, be truly well-bred and refined; but ostentation, affectation, and ambitious efforts are, in every station of life, high or low, nothing but vulgarities. Put them aside, despise them yourselves. Oh, my very dear sons, whom I love, and whom I would fain serve; —oh, that you could feel that you have souls! oh, that you would have mercy on your souls! oh, that, before it is too late, you would betake yourselves to Him who is the source of all that is truly high and magnificent and beautiful, all that is bright and pleasant and secure what you ignorantly seek, in Him whom you so wilfully, so awfully despise!

He, alone, the Son of God, " the brightness of the Eternal Light, and the spotless mirror of His Majesty," is the source of all good and all happiness to rich and poor, high and low. If you were ever so high, you would need Him; if you were ever so low, you could offend Him. The poor can offend Him; the poor man can neglect his divinely appointed mission as well as the rich. Do not suppose, my brethren, that what I have said against the upper or the middle class will not, if you happen to be poor, also lie against you. Though a man were as poor as Lazarus, he could be as guilty as Dives. If you were resolved to degrade yourselves to the brutes of the field, who have no reason and no conscience, you need not wealth or rank to enable you to do so. Brutes have no wealth; they have no pride of life; they have no purple and fine linen, no splendid table, no retinue of servants, and yet they are brutes. They are brutes by the law of their nature: they are the poorest among the poor; there is not a vagrant and outcast who is so poor as they; they differ from him, not in their possessions, but in their want of a soul, in that he has a mission and they have not, he can sin and they can not. Oh, my brethren, it stands to reason, a man may intoxicate himself with a cheap draft, as well as with a costly one; he may steal another's money for his appetites, though he does not waste his own upon them; he may break through the natural and social laws which encircle him, and profane the sanctity of family duties, tho he be not a child of nobles, but a peasant or artisan, —nay, and perhaps he does so more frequently than they. This is not the poor's blessedness, that he has less temptations to self-indulgence, for he has as many, but that from his circumstances he receives the penances and corrections of self-indulgence. Poverty is the mother of many pains and sorrows in their season, and these are God's messengers to lead the soul to repentance; but, alas! if the poor man indulges his passions, thinks little of religion, puts off repentance, refuses to make an effort, and dies without conversion, it matters nothing that he was poor in this world, it matters nothing that he was less daring than the rich, it matters not that he promised himself God's favor, that he sent for the priest when death came, and received the last sacraments; Lazarus too, in that case, shall be buried with Dives in hell, and shall have had his consolation neither in this world nor in the world to come.

My brethren, the simple question is, whatever a man's rank in life may be, does he in that rank perform the work which God has given him to do? Now then, let me turn to others, of a very different description, and let me hear what they will say, when the question is asked them. Why, they will parry it thus: "You give us no alternative," they will say to me, "except that of being sinners or saints. You put before us our Lord's pattern, and you spread before us the guilt and ruin of the deliberate transgressor; whereas we have no intention of going so far one way or the other; we do not aim at being saints, but we have no desire at all to be sinners. We neither intend to disobey God's will, nor to give up our own. Surely there is a middle way, and a safe one, in which God's will and our will may both be satisfied. We mean to enjoy both this world and the next. We will

guard against mortal sin; we are not obliged to guard against venial; indeed it would be endless to attempt it. None but saints do so; it is the work of a life; we need have nothing else to do. We are not monks, we are in the world, we are in business, we are parents, we have families; we must live for the day. It is a consolation to keep from mortal sin; that we do, and it is enough for salvation. It is a great thing to keep in God's favor; what indeed can we desire more? We come at due time to the sacraments; this is our comfort and our stay; did we die, we should die in grace, and escape the doom of the wicked. But if we once attempted to go further, where should we stop? how will you draw the line for us? The line between mortal and venial sin is very distinct; we understand that; but do you not see that, if we attended to our venial sins, there would be just as much reason to attend to one as to another? If we began to repress our anger, why not also repress vainglory? Why not also guard against niggardliness? Why not also keep from falsehood, from gossiping, from idling, from excess in eating? And, after all, without venial sin we never can be, unless indeed we have the prerogative of the Mother of God, which it would be almost heresy to ascribe to any one but her. You are not asking us to be converted; that we understand; we are converted, we were converted a long time ago. You bid us aim at an indefinite vague something, which is less than perfection, yet more than obedience, and which, without resulting in any tangible advantage, debars us from the pleasures and embarrasses us in the duties of this world."

This is what you will say; but your premises, my brethren, are better than your reasoning, and your conclusions will not stand. You have a right view why God has sent you into the world; viz., in order that you may get to heaven; it is quite true also that you would fare well indeed if you found yourselves there, you could desire nothing better; nor, it is true, can you live any time without venial sin. It is true also that you are not obliged to aim at being saints; it is no sin not to aim at perfection. So much is true and to the purpose; but it does not follow from it that you, with such views and feelings as you have exprest, are using sufficient exertions even for attaining purgatory. Has your religion any difficulty in it, or is it in all respects easy to you? Are you simply taking your own pleasure in your mode of living, or do you find your pleasure in submitting yourself to God's pleasure? In a word, is your religion a work? For if it be not, it is not religion at all. Here at once, before going into your argument, is a proof that it is an unsound one, because it brings you to the conclusion that, whereas Christ came to do a work, and all saints, nay, nay, and sinners to do a work too, you, on the contrary, have no work to do, because, forsooth, you are neither sinners nor saints; or, if you once had a work, at least that you have despatched it already, and you have nothing upon your hands. You have attained your salvation, it seems, before your time, and have nothing to occupy you, and are detained on earth too long. The work days are over, and your perpetual holiday is begun. Did then God send you, above all other men, into the world to be idle in spiritual matters? Is it your mission only to find pleasure in this world, in which you are but as pilgrims and sojourners? Are you more than sons of Adam, who, by the sweat of their brow, are to eat bread till they return to the earth out of which they are taken? Unless you have some work in hand, unless you are struggling, unless you are fighting with yourselves, you are no followers of those who "through many tribulations entered into the kingdom of God." A fight is the very token of a Christian. He is a soldier of Christ; high or low, he is this and nothing else. If you have triumphed over all mortal sin, as you seem to think, then you must attack your venial sins; there is no help for it; there is nothing else to do, if you would be soldiers of Jesus Christ. But, oh, simple souls! to think you have gained any triumph at all! No; you cannot safely be at peace with any, even the

least malignant, of the foes of God; if you are at peace with venial sins, be certain that in their company and under their shadow mortal sins are lurking. Mortal sins are the children of venial, which, tho they be not deadly themselves, yet are prolific of death. You may think that you have killed the giants who had possession of your hearts, and that you have nothing to fear, but may sit at rest under your vine and under your fig-tree; but the giants will live again, they will rise from the dust, and, before you know where you are, you will be taken captive and slaughtered by the fierce, powerful, and eternal enemies of God.

The end of a thing is the test. It was our Lord's rejoicing in His last solemn hour, that He had done the work for which He was sent. "I have glorified thee on earth." He says in His prayer, " I have finished the work which thou gavest me to do; I have manifested thy name to the men whom thou hast given me out of the world." It was St. Paul's consolation also, "I have fought the good fight, I have finished the course, I have kept the faith; henceforth there is laid up for me a crown of justice, which the Lord shall render to me in that day, the just judge." Alas! alas! how different will be our view of things when we come to die, or when we have passed into eternity, from the dreams and pretenses with which we beguile ourselves now! What

will Babel do for us then? Will it rescue our souls from the purgatory or the hell to which it sends them? If we were created, it was that we might serve God; if we have His gifts, it is that we may glorify Him; if we have a conscience, it is that we may obey it; if we have the prospect of heaven, it is that we may keep it before us; if we have light, that we may follow it, if we have grace, that we may save ourselves by means of it. Alas! alas! for those who die without fulfilling their mission; who were called to be holy, and lived in sin; who were called to worship Christ, and who plunged into this giddy and unbelieving world; who were called to fight, and who remained idle; who were called to be Catholics, and who did but remain in the religion of their birth! Alas for those who have had gifts and talent, and have not used, or have misused, or abused them; who have had wealth, and have spent it on themselves; who have had abilities, and have advocated what was sinful, or ridiculed what was true, or scattered doubts against what was sacred; who have had leisure, and have wasted it on wicked companions, or evil books, or foolish amusements! Alas! for those of whom the best can be said is, that they are harmless and naturally blameless, while they never have attempted to cleanse their hearts or to live in God's sight!

The world goes on from age to age, but the Holy Angels and Blessed Saints are always crying Alas, alas! and Wo, wo! over the loss of vocations, and the disappointment of hopes, and the scorn of God's love, and the ruin of souls. One generation succeeds another, and whenever they look down upon earth from their golden thrones, they see scarcely anything but a multitude of guardian spirits, downcast and sad, each following his own charge, in anxiety, or in terror, or in despair, vainly endeavoring to shield him from the enemy, and failing because he will not be shielded. Times come and go, and man will not believe, that that is to be which is not yet, or that what now is only continues for a season, and is not eternity. The end is the trial; the world passes; it is but a pageant and a scene; the lofty palace crumbles, the busy city is mute, the ships of Tarshish have sped away. On heart and flesh death is coming; the veil is breaking. Departing soul, how hast thou used thy talents, thy opportunities, the light poured around thee, the warnings given thee, the grace inspired into thee? Oh, my Lord and Savior, support me in that hour in the strong arms of Thy sacraments, and by the fresh fragrance of Thy consolations. Let the absolving words be said over me, and the holy oil sign and seal me, and Thy own body be my food, and Thy blood my sprinkling; and let my sweet mother Mary breathe on me, and my angel whisper peace to me, and my glorious saints, and my own dear father, Philip, smile on me; that in them all, and through them all, I may receive the gift of perseverance, and die, as I desire to live, in Thy faith, in Thy Church, in Thy service, and in Thy love.

WILLIAM R. NICOLL

1851-1923

GETHSEMANE
THE ROSE GARDEN
OF GOD

BIOGRAPHICAL NOTE

WILLIAM ROBERTSON NICOLL, Presbyterian minister and author, was born at Lumsden, Aberdeenshire, 1851. He was educated at the University of Aberdeen, where he took his degree in 1870. He was Free Minister of Dufftown, 1874-1877; of Kelso, 1877-1885. In 1886 he became editor of *British Weekly*, *Bookman*, *Expositor* and *Woman at Home*, and was a prolific book writer, mostly theological.

Without shedding of blood is no—Heb. ix., 22.

I HAD a strange feeling, dear brethren, this morning, in busy London, on a week-day, in the sunshine, reading these words from the Epistle to the Hebrews; and it struck me that some few would think they were strangely antique, that they contrasted violently with your morning newspapers. And then it passed through my mind again that there could not be anything so vitally modern, so close and quick to the moment in London as just my text—"Without shedding of blood there is no" —no anything; nothing; no mighty result, no achievement, no triumph, no high thing accomplished without shedding of blood. That is just on the lowest plane what we are getting to know as a nation, and if we are taught it as Christians, then we shall come to know at last what Christianity means.

Dear brethren, life is just our chance of making this great and strange discovery, that without shedding of blood there is nothing, nothing at all. How do young people begin, most of them? They begin by doing little or nothing; they begin by trifling. And then they begin to find that they are not making progress. And if so, they are wise, gradually they put more strength into it; and then more, till at last they have put all their strength into it. And then they say they have not succeeded, have not gained their point. And they say, What have we got to do now? You take off your coat to your work. A man may disrobe; what more can be done? What more have I got left? Left? You have got your blood left, and until you begin to part with that you will never do any great work at all. I mean by that, if you leave a mark in life; to fulfil a mission in life there is wanted something more than the concentration of life. I appeal to you, there is wanted, besides, the pruning of life, aye, and even the maiming of life. There must be for success, even in the business world, I say, in the world of commercial achievement, there must be more and more an actual parting with the life before it is reached. And we are being sternly taught this lesson as a nation. But I want to teach it this morning to the Church as Christians.

Well, let me go back to the very beginning. I find that there is in the primitive elemental religion a profound and solemn witness to this truth; "Without shedding of blood there is no remission," no peace with God, no life in Christ. And I look upon these early and crude and distorted ideas as God's deep preparation of the mind and heart of man by the grand gospel of the substitution under the law of Jesus Christ for guilty sinners. And we can not get those thoughts out, they are embodied in our very language. Do you know what the word "bless" means, what it was derived from? The word "bless" comes from the Anglo-Saxon word for "blood." And the idea dimly aimed at is this: that before you can really bless a fellow creature you must part with your life, or part of your life, for him; shed blood. We can do a great deal by little things; our Lord said so—by smiles, by gifts, by kind words, by cups of cold water. Christ will never forget these things. But at the same time, if you are to bless a soul in the superlative sense, you can not do it in that easy way; you have to sprinkle the soul with blood, and with your own blood. You know what I mean. Oh, some of you know it who have labored for another soul for weary years; you know it too well. But part with your life and you will win a soul at last. It will cover a multitude of sins.

I wish I had time to quote from the primitive religions; but I would remind you of the old legend of the building of Copenhagen. The builders could not make progress with their work; the sea came in and took it away, until at last they took a human life, and by the sacrifice of that human life they gave to the city stability. And you know the old idea of primitive religion, that the corn will not grow in the seed ground unless the body of a dead man is buried there—life coming out of death. Now, I say all these things point on to the supreme Author of the universe; Jesus died, the Just for the unjust, that He might bring us to God. Now do you not think you can see how it is that the eternal Son shed His blood in Gethsemane, and offered Himself immaculate to God on Calvary?

But we shall never know quite—none of the ransomed ever know—how deep were the waters crost, or how dark was the night that the Lord passed through ere He found the sheep that was lost. But we read with hearts bowed the prayer offered up with strong crying and tears—the prayer, "If it be possible let this cup pass." There is no prayer like that, when you feel that a life is hanging in the balance, that the issues are not quite decided, that your prayer might turn it. Then you understand what prayer can be. And we hear those dim, overcome witnesses who heard afar the broken moaning, the long-drawn sighs, who saw the hard-won victory which seemed defeat, and we read—I love to read—about that all-pitying but undimmed angel who appeared to strengthen at last. God made His minister a flame of fire in the dark and cold, else could Christ have conquered? His prayer was answered; the cup was not taken away, but His lips were made brave to drink it, and He drank it and opened the kingdom of heaven to all believers. Some of my friends think that the real crowning-point in the suffering of Christ was Gethsemane, that it was over there that the cross was more the public and open manifestation which the world, passing by the wayside, could see. I do not know. Christ quivered a lament upon the cross too.

And now I come to the two thoughts of my sermon.

In the first place, partly from etymology, we learn that the shedding of our own blood is the condition of our blessing others. And then my second point is, that since bloom and blossom, the perfection of life, are also associated with the root, with the word blood, then I say that the bloom and perfection of our own lives depend upon our parting with the natural life and having it replaced by the resurrection life. I hope it is simple enough. Without shedding of blood there is no blessing to others; without shedding of blood there is no blessing to ourselves. Take these two great ruling missionary ideas.

I. Bloodshed for blessing others.

I spoke about Gethsemane because I wanted you to understand that I was referring not merely to absolute physical death, but to the death which leads a man to go on, and perhaps to live more abundantly than before. But still, dear friends, we have been most solemnly and impressively reminded in these times, that, whatever has failed in the Church of Christ, the race of martyrs has not failed. Great names have been written there, the names of those who have been received in heaven. And, for my part, I love the way in which the Church of Rome reverences the martyrs. You know that that Church never prays for the martyrs, but makes requests for their prayers; you know that that Church pictures in the assembly of the redeemed before the throne the martyrs in their robes of crimson and the saints in white. The blood of the martyrs is the seed of the Church. We can not atone for others, but we can bless others. We can not, dear friends, have any part in the one perfect oblation and substitution in the sacrifice of the world, but we fill up that which is behind of the afflictions of Christ. We know Him and the fellowship of His sufferings as well as the power of His resurrection. And when Christ first laid His hand on His well-beloved He said: "I will show him how great things he must suffer for my name's sake." This is the chief work of the martyr, to suffer; and it is the chief work of every Christian to suffer for Christ's name's sake. And I sometimes think the whole of Christianity, for the present generation, is summed up in this: fill up that which is behind of the afflictions of Christ, for until that is filled up He can not have His triumph.

But, dear brethren, of course I do not confuse labor and suffering in the Christian servant's life. The labor is effective in proportion as there is suffering, and the suffering by itself is nothing without the labor. But, oh, how Christ's great servants have suffered! Have you ever thought how St. Paul was actually driven to use the awful language of the passion when he described his own life? He did not like to do it; he always drew the line sharp and clear between himself and the Master. He said, "Was Paul crucified for you?" Yes; but he was driven to say, "I am crucified with Christ"—always bearing about the body and its death—"I die daily." Oh, they have suffered by way of bloodshed. Yes; but, dear brethren, I think that in the lives of the great servants of Christ, the elect servants, there is always one Gethsemane above the rest, far above the rest; one shedding of blood, one parting with life which makes all the rest comparatively easy. We can not tell, I think, about other people's Gethsemane; and we can not tell, will not tell, nothing would make us tell, about our own.

How does the Gethsemane come? Often it is passed with very little sign or show. You have read in "The Bonny Brier Bush" that when George Howe came home to die, his mother hid herself beneath the laburnum, and as the cat stood beneath the stile, it told the plain fact, as she had feared. And Margaret passed through her Gethsemane with the gold blossoms falling on her face. I believe there are some of you who are passing through your Gethsemane in this chapel while I am speaking to you now. There is little to show—some absence of manner, some twitching of the lips, some unwonted pallor, some strange abstraction, but no more. And you will never tell anybody about it, and nobody will discover it when you are dead. You sometimes suspect— do you not?—about another man what his Gethsemane has been. You are almost sure to be wrong. That surrender which you see was accomplished almost without murmur or reluctance. Sometimes in biographies I think I can see where the Gethsemane is. It may be, and often is, the rooting out of some cherished ambition that has filled the heart and occupied every thought, every dream for years and years. It may be the shattering of some song, the breaking of some dream. It may be, and often is, a great rending of the affections, the cutting the soul free from some detaining human tenderness. Well, we do not know— the real Gethsemane never lasts long. I think an hour is the longest that anybody could bear it—"Could ye not watch with me one hour?" True, the heartache may go on to the end, but the Gethsemane, that can not last a long time.

We have in biographies some instances of Gethsemanes, and sometimes in very unexpected places. You would not imagine that a prosperous suburban minister, with a rich congregation, and every earthly ambition realized, would have his Gethsemane as a missionary far among the heathen has. But in the "Life of Dr. Raleigh," of Kensington, whom many of you remember, there is a significant passage. When he was at the zenith of his fame he said that ministers came and looked around at his crowded church and envied his position. "They do not know," he said, "what it has cost me to come to this." In the "Life" of the beloved James Hamilton, of Regent Square, there is a passage which always touches me. It shows how he parted, for Christ's sake, with the great ambition of his life. He longed to write a life of Erasmus, but other things came and he was balked of his desire. He says:

"So this day, with a certain touch of tenderness, I restored the eleven tone folios to the shelf and tied up my memoranda, and took leave of a project which has often cheered the hours of exhaustion, the mere thought of which has always been enough to overcome my natural indulgence. It is well. It is the only chance I ever had of attaining a small measure of literary distinction, and where there is so much pride and naughtiness of heart it is better to remain unknown."

I think we may all easily see where the Gethsemane came in in Henry Martyn's life, and—I say it with great diffidence—I think we may see where the Gethsemane came in in John Wesley's life, tho I should not care to indicate it. But the heart knoweth its own bitterness. What we know is that the Gethsemanes in the Christian life are in the course of duty, and in obedience to God's will, as it is revealed from day to day.

Go back to John Wesley's Journal. On one occasion he had the claim of a reputed saint, and he rejected it, and said—mark these words: "No blood of the martyrs is here, no scandal of the cross, no persecution of them that love God." No blood is here, no saint. When Adam Clarke was speaking in the City-Road Chapel in 1816, at the establishment of a missionary society in London, he told the people about the Moravians. And I need not tell you how great the Moravian influence was on early Methodism. He told his hearers at that time that the Moravians, when all told, only numbered six hundred members, but they had missionaries in every part of the globe to which it was then possible to send them. Dr. Clarke told them of the beginning, which was in the far-away place of St. Thomas. A negro slave escaped from St. Thomas somehow, and he came into contact with Zinzendorf, and found the way of salvation, and rejoiced in Christ. Well, this negro came to the Moravians, and he told them that among his fellow slaves in St. Thomas there were several—his own sister was one, I think—who were feeling after God. "But," he said, "nobody can go out to tell them the gospel unless they sell themselves as slaves and go out as slaves." Whereupon two brethren immediately offered themselves, and exprest their willingness to be sold as slaves, that they might preach Christ. Yes, we may be sure that no life will bring forth fruit to God if it is without its Gethsemane, with the great drops of blood in it; and I believe that just as the Savior's blood dropt in Gethsemane and the ground blest it, so the blood of the surrendered soul makes its Gethsemane a garden, if not now, then hereafter; but the time must be, whenever a martyr's blood has been shed, upon that ground the fruits of righteousness must spring.

II. Bloodshed for self-perfection.

I have just my other point. The second point is that there must be bloodshedding for the bloom and perfection of our own lives before they can come to their flower, to God's ideal beauty; there must be the expenditure of the natural life.

Now, what is it that should follow when we have parted with our life and lived our Gethsemane; what should be the effect upon our lives? Well, what ought to follow is, that the resurrection life, which the shedding of blood has made room for, should take the place of the other. But what does follow? I think three things, often:

First, it often happens that a real Gethsemane of the soul means a brief tarrying in this world. It seems as if too much life had gone, as if the spirit could not recover its energies. There are a few books which the heart of the Church has always loved. I call them Gethsemane books. They are books about Gethsemane, about the bloodshedding in the early days and what was gone through. They are chiefly the lives of David Brainerd, Henry Martyn, and McCheyne. But there are many others that I have no time to name. All of these died young, not without signs of the divine blessing, but their rich, fervent natures were prematurely exhausted and burned out. Have you read the memoir of Brainerd? John Wesley published it, slightly abridged, for his people, and I have a copy. Read it, mark its reserved passion, its austere tenderness; read the story of young Miss Edwards, who followed her betrothed so soon. You will then feel that you have done business in great waters. The pages of this book are all spotted with blood. Read Brainerd's aspirations:

"Oh, that I might be a flaming fire in the service of my God! Here I am, Lord, send me; send me to the ends of the earth; send me to the rough and savage pagan, to the wilderness; send me from all that is called earthly, comfort; send me even to death itself if it be but in Thy service and to promote Thy Kingdom."

But sometimes the earthly life is parted with and not fully replaced by the resurrection life, and the long-drawn melancholy ensues. You really must not believe that I am speaking as an enemy of Methodism when I say I venture to think there is something of that in the life of that great saint and supreme Christian poet, Charles Wesley. I think it will be granted by his most ardent admirers that the last thirty years of his life will not compare with those of his mighty brother. They were sad years in the main, spent in comparative inaction, with many, many wearisome discontented days. Dear friends, there is no such thing as melancholy in the New Testament—nothing. And Charles Wesley's melancholy is the most attractive in the world—

Oh, when shall we sweetly move?
Oh, when shall our souls be at rest?

And there is this view of life: "Suffer out my threescore years till the Deliverer come; and then this soul appeals to God to explain my life of misery with all Thy love's designs in Thee." Those are awful matters—"explain my life of misery with all Thy love's designs in Thee." But, dear friends, am I right in saying that this frame is a Christian frame? When Charles Wesley was in his last years his favorite text was—and it is a text which will always go with his name—"I will bring the third part through the fire." That is, he thought that God would bring to glory one-third part of Methodists, that one-third of them would endure to the end. Compare that with "God is with us who seeth the end." Who is right? And he never sought an abundant entrance into the kingdom. What he used to say over and over again was: "Oh, that I might escape safe to land on a broken piece of the ship. This is my daily, hourly prayer, that I may escape safe to land." In his latter days he was always warning those about him that a flood was coming out over the country which would sweep much of this religion away. You know it was said on another death-bed, "Clouds drop fatness."

It is always necessary that the bloom of life should come out of death. What Christ means is that as the natural life goes, as the veins are depleted, there is the resurrection life which should fill them and pour into them to strengthen. There is no book in the world, I think, like John Wesley's "Journal," because it is the book of the resurrection life, and I do not know another in all literature; the resurrection life lived in this world almost as Christ might have gone on living it if the forty years had been prolonged into fifty years. As a book it stands out solitary in all literature, clear, detached, columnar. It is a tree that is ever green before the Lord. It tells us of a heart that kept to the last its innocent pleasures, but held them so lightly, while its Christian renunciation and its passionate peace grew and grew to the end, the old wistfulness, the old calm fiery and revealed eloquence.

John Wesley was indeed one of those who had attained the inward stillness, who had entered the second rest, who, to use his own fine words, was "of those who are at rest before they go hence, possessors of that rest which remaineth even here"—even here—"for the people of God." With what emotion one comes to his closing days, and follows him to that last sermon at Leatherhead, on the word: "Seek ye the Lord while he may be found, call ye upon him while he is near!" And watch by his triumphant deathbed and hear him say, "The clouds drop fatness." The only one I can compare him with in all the history of the Church is the apostle Elliot, the missionary to the Indians, whose life was written by Cotton Mather. You know that in that day they had a tradition that the country was safe as long as the apostle was there. Some of you will remember that Nathaniel Hawthorne, in his great book, "The Scarlet Letter," tells us of how the poor children of Arthur Dimsdale pleaded to see the apostle Elliot, for the testimony is that there was an unearthly light upon his face to the last of his long life. We read about that great apostle, fit to be named with Wesley, that he had his bitter sorrows. Two sons died before him, and Cotton Mather says they were desirable preachers of the gospel. But the old man sacrificed them. Now, note Cotton Mather's phrase, "sacrificed with such a sacred indifference." And he was so nailed to the cross and the Lord Jesus Christ that the grandeur of this world would seem to him just what it would be to a dying man, when at a great age and nearing the end he grew, with John Wesley, still more heavenly, more Saviorly, more divine and scented more and more of that spicy country at which he was ready to put ashore. His last words were, "Welcome, joy," and he died. Such a life of sacrifice is the gateway of the eternal city.

2. It is likewise necessary that the conversion of the world should come out of death. I for one believe in the ancient promise, "The knowledge of the Lord shall cover the earth as the waters cover the sea." Yes, but before the knowledge of the Lord shall cover the earth, the earth must be covered with the blood falling upon it from faithful souls. "Without shedding of blood there is no—." Some young men whom I love have started societies for the evangelization of the world in the present generation. I love that; let us try.

But what is evangelization? To send Bibles, to deliver the message to everybody? No, not that, but the shedding of the servants' blood on every field, with the world as one great Gethsemane. We shall see over it the flowers that grew only in the garden where Christ's brow dropt blood. At this meeting, in this chapel, there will be some sweet mother who is going through her Gethsemane. She is resolving to give up a son who has heard the call: "Depart, for I will send them far hence to the heathen." One in widow's weeds was asked if she had subscribed to the missionary society. She said: "Yes, I gave my only son, and he died in the field." That is my text: "Without shedding of blood there is no—."

Yes, and there is some young heart here that has a great deal to give up, a great deal at home. And he is hearing me, and he has made up his mind that he will make the sacrifice, too; that he will go forth to Christ. And what are the rest of us doing? Well, dear brethren, there is to be a collection, and we will put our hands in our pockets in the old way, half thinking what we will spend, and how we are to spend it before we go home; and select a coin and put it in. And then we shall go home and see a missionary magazine on the table, and express our regret that missionary magazines are not better edited and not more interesting. Of course, there will be something for the collector when the collector goes round. It will not be much; and perhaps, owing to the war, you know, we can not give quite so much as last year.

And do you really think that the world will ever be converted in that way? Do you believe it? Have you any right to expect that it should be converted in that way? No right at all. The world will never be converted until the Church is in agony, and prays more earnestly, and sweats, as it were, great drops of blood; never, never! "Without shedding of blood there is no remission of sins."

JAMES ORR

1844-1913

THE ABIDING WORD

BIOGRAPHICAL NOTE

PROFESSOR of apologetics and theology at Theological College of United Free church, Glasgow, 1891-1901; born in Glasgow, April 11, 1844; educated at Glasgow University, Theological Hall of United Presbyterian church; minister of East Bank United Presbyterian Church, Hawick, 1874-91; professor of Church history at Theological College, Glasgow, of the United Presbyterian Church, 1891-1901; author of "The Christian View of God and the World," "The Supernatural in Christianity," "The Ritschlian Theology and the Evangelical Faith," "Neglected Factors in the Study of the Early Progress of Christianity," "Early Church History and Literature," "Elliot Lectures on the Progress of Dogma," "Essays on Ritschlianism," "The Image of God in Man and Its Defacement," "The Problem of the Old Testament," "The Bible Under Trial," "The Virgin Birth of Christ," one of the editors of the "Pulpit Commentary," etc.

" Heaven and earth shall pass away, but my words shall not pass away."—Matt. 24 : 35.

A WORD seems a light and fragile thing put in comparison with this mighty and glorious fabric of heaven and earth. " Heaven and earth," Jesus says, " shall pass away," yet nothing in itself might seem more unlikely. The first impression which the great objects of nature make upon us is that of strength, solidity, enduringness. The earth we tread on, the hills girding us, the rocks frowning down upon us, the stars in their nightly watch above us, all give the idea of objects which are the opposite of transient—which may be depended on to outlast all human generations.

And this at first sight seems the verdict of history. " One generation cometh and another goeth; but the earth abideth forever." The constellations which the Chaldean astronomer dim ages past noted in his book; the planets to which he gave their names; the Pleiades and Orion spoken of by Job; all meet the gaze of the student of the skies just as they used to do. The traveler, as he visits the spots famous in ancient history, marks the mounds where lie buried the ruins of once great cities, and views the wasteness and desolation around, has the same reflection forced on him—the shortness of human life, the transiency of human affairs, and, as contrasted with this the enduringness of nature.

Over against this lasting reality of heaven and earth how frail, how perishable a thing seems a word! Of the numberless myriads of words spoken every day, how few have the faintest chance of living in memory even for an hour. Words, speaking generally, are the lightest, most trivial, most evanescent, least substantial of all entities. Words written are hardly more enduring than words spoken. Look at the mass of old books which cumber the shelves of any of our libraries, and ask the question, Who ever reads them? Our own day has its thick crop of authors and of books, but how many of them will be remembered or heard of twenty or fifty or one hundred years hence?

Yet Jesus says in this passage of the text that heaven and earth shall pass away, but His words shall not pass away. He deliberately puts His words in contrast with this mighty material fabric of the physical universe, and declares that while it is not eternal, His words are; that His words shall last while it perishes; that they are more enduring than it. It was a calm, great utterance, and the wonder of it is only increased when we think of what Jesus was as He appeared to His contemporaries. In any ordinary man in Christ's worldly position such words would have been the height of madness; and so probably they would have been regarded by the Herods and Pilates and Caiaphases of his time. Yet history has verified this saying of Christ; His words have taken deeper and deeper hold upon the minds of men as the centuries have advanced; and thereby we have been taught to see the difference between Christ's outward seeming and His real greatness.

We are to try now to see for ourselves that what Christ says in this wonderful saying of His is true. And we may begin by reminding ourselves of the falsity of the conception into which we so easily glide in thinking the material world to be more enduring than the spiritual. Christ's saying teaches us to recast our first impressions. That is a thing we are constantly under the necessity of doing. We are constantly being deceived by the outward appearances and shows of things, and have to learn the art—a great part of the wisdom of life just consists in learning the art—of getting behind appearances, and judging reality by other than material standards. When we do this we learn that mind is greater than matter, truth more enduring than the material order, thoughts and the words that embody them more permanent than even heaven and earth.

"Heaven and earth," Jesus says, "shall pass away." Now this, notwithstanding the apparent enduringness, is, as we know to-day, a simple and literal scientific fact. Stable as this great material universe seems to be, it is really in constant process of change. Only slowly and by prolonged and gradual steps has the universe been built up to what it is now. It had its beginning and it will have its end. Science makes perfectly clear to us that the existing conditions of things is not a permanent one; that the world, to use an illustration of its own, is in the position of a clock running down, and that it is as impossible for the present system of things to go on forever, without renewed supply of energy, as it would be for a clock to go on forever without renewed winding up. And there is nearly as little hesitation in science as there is in Scripture in saying in general terms what the end shall be. The end, in the view of men of science, may be postponed to an indefinitely distant period, but they no less than the believer in revelation most surely look forward and hasten unto the coming of a day—he may not call it a day of the Lord—when the heavens being on fire shall be dissolved and the elements shall melt with fervent heat, and the earth also and the works that are therein shall be burned up. No truth is therefore more certain than this, testified long ago by the prophet Isaiah—"Lift up your eyes to the heavens and look upon the earth beneath; for the heavens shall vanish away like smoke, and the earth shall wax old like a garment, and they that dwell therein shall die in like manner"—tho the prophet is able gloriously to add—and it is but the Old Testament anticipation of this New Testament saying—"But my salvation shall be forever and my righteousness shall not be abolished."

Look now at words. It may be true that many words are mere breath and nothing else; true also that most books often are destined to a very brief term of existence. But this is not true of all words. There are words which the world reckons among its choicest treasures and which it will not willingly let die—words of wisdom so imperishable, of truth so rare, of thought so deep, of counsel so wise, that they can never pass away. The Bible is a book of very old words, and what freshness and vitality still belong to them. But even outside the Bible there are words in other literature, words great and wise and noble and beautiful, to which this same quality of permanence in their degree belongs. They are the words into which the race has distilled its choicest wisdom, and they are bound to live. And let us not undervalue the might of words. The thoughts they embody may be invisible; you may not be able to see or weigh or measure them, but the force which resides in them is, for all that, incalculable. Words have power to kill and make alive. The ideas embodied in words are the forces which make and unmake societies. Masses of men are moved by the ideas which gain possession of their minds and these ideas are implanted in them and propagated through winged words. Mere physical force avails little in the end against the growth of ideas. It is ideas which govern the world. We come to see then, that it is not the material but the immaterial in which resides the greatest vitality and permanence. Heaven and earth shall pass away but it may very well be that there are some words which shall not pass away.

This quality of permanence we speak of belongs preeminently to the words of Christ. Jesus says it does and we are to try to see that what He says is true.

To show this, glance for a moment at what kind of words they are which do endure and what kind of words they are which do not endure. There are three kinds of words regarding which we may say with all confidence that they cannot endure. The first is false words. Falsehoods, indeed, have often a surprising vitality. They live long, are hard to kill, and in the interval do an infinite amount of mischief. Nay, so greedily do the minds of men sometimes receive error, so easily are they led away by sophistry and by appeals to their passions and prejudices, that we might be tempted to think that it is error, not truth, which rules the world, and that the still, small voice of truth is scarcely heard in the noise and confusion of unwisdom and falsehood. But only a little thought is necessary to dispel this illusion. We cannot doubt that under the government of a God of truth the ultimate fate of everything false in this world is to be found out, exposed, condemned. An error, a superstition, may have a reign of centuries, but by and by, as thought widens and discovery advances, it is sure to be exploded. Every year sees the interment of some old-world fallacy, and if it also sees the springing up of some new fallacy of its own, future generations in like manner will see that buried.

A second class of words which cannot endure is trivial words. How few of the words spoken every day have even the remotest right to continued existence. They relate to the mere trifles or accidents of life: what so and so thought; how he felt; what he did; our passing impression about this and about that; the news of the day; where we were; what we saw; whom we met—so a stream of irresponsible talk flows on. Words of this kind are not meant to live—you can compare them to nothing more appropriately than to those swarms of gnats which circle round your heads in the sunlight on a warm summer evening, to which nature allots but a brief hour or day of existence.

The third class of words which cannot endure are those which relate to subjects of but temporary importance. They need not be trivial words; the subjects to which they relate may be of the very highest interest and importance for the immediate present, but their interest is not a permanent one. There comes a day when they are things of the past and live only in history. Of what interest to us, e. g., except for historical purposes, are the questions of life and law and government affecting the Middle Ages? We have our own questions of political and social reform which are to us of great moment, but even these will become things of the past and will cease to interest our successors. Prophecies will fail, for they shall be fulfilled; tongues shall cease, for they shall no longer be spoken; knowledge shall pass away, for that to which our knowledge and ordered sciences relate shall have vanished from existence!

From these considerations we can gradually infer by contrast the character of the words which must and shall endure. They must be true words; they must be weighty words; and they must be words which refer to subjects of perpetual and eternal interest. Now what we say is that this is preeminently the character of the words of the Lord Jesus Christ. It is upon the fact that His words are true, that they are weighty, and that they relate to subjects of infinite and everlasting moment, that He bases His assertion that heaven and earth shall pass away, but His words shall not pass away. Can we refuse the claim?

Christ's words are true. He came forth from the bosom of the Father to proclaim the truth to a world which had in large measure lost the knowledge of the true God and of the way of life. He can say of His words what no other could say, "I am the truth." Approach Christ even from the human side and this quality in Him is apparent. The light of true knowledge of the Father shone in His soul and as it shone in no other. He had the clearest insight into the facts and laws of the spiritual world. Every chord of His nature vibrated in harmony with holiness and responded in delicate sympathy to impulses from above. What says even a skeptic of Christ (Greg): "In reading His words we feel that we are holding converse with the wisest, purest, noblest being that ever clothed thought in the poor language of humanity; in studying His life we are following in the footsteps of the highest ideal yet presented to us on earth." Christ spake as never man spake; and in this way, by his words, as well as by all else about Him, He vindicated His claim to be not son of man alone, but Son of God Most High.

If Christ's words are true do they not also possess the other qualities of permanence? They are certainly weighty words. No light, trivial, shallow utterances are they. They embody deep enduring principles; set forth more than master truths; move in a region as high above the ordinary teachings of man as heaven is high above earth. When a man asked Jesus to bid his brother divide his inheritance with him, He said, "Man, who made me a judge and divider over you?" It was not Christ's mission to occupy Himself with these petty controversies. It is this which give His words weight. Each age, as it comes round, finds them fruitful in applications to itself. Christ commits Himself to no side in party politics; to no one denomination or party in the Church; to no one form of Church government or action; to no one mode of social organization; to no one solution of the questions of capital and labor, of rulers and subjects, of rich and poor. And the reason is that the solution of these questions proper to one age and stage of society, would not be the solution proper to another age and stage of society, and Christ is not the Teacher of one age only, else His words would, like those of other teachers, have long since become obsolete, but the Teacher of all times and of all ages. Hence He contents Himself with enunciating great truths, unfolding great principles which underlie and are to guide us in all our studies of these subjects and ought to regulate us in our thought and legislation upon them.

I was much struck in reading the

" Thoughts on Religion " by the late Mr. Romanes, that eminent scientific man who, during the greater part of his life, was under an absolute eclipse of his faith, who lost his faith even in God and wrote against belief in God, but who the last year or two of his life came back to the full Christian confession, and he tells us in these " Thoughts on Religion " that one thing that most profoundly influenced him was the discovery that Christ's words did not become obsolete as the words of other great teachers did; that while the words of Plato and others had passed away so far as actual living influence was concerned, the words of Jesus endured, and it was just this truth, that His words did not and do not pass away, that produced so remarkable an effect upon his mind.

But even this is not the most essential part of Christ's teaching. It is not the kingdom of earth but the kingdom of God concerning which He specially came to enlighten men, and it is to this higher and eternal region that most of His teachings belong. Here most of all we see the truth of the statement " Heaven and earth shall pass away, but my words shall not pass away."

What are the special themes to which Christ's words relate? He speaks to man above all of God His Father, and truth about God—if only it be truth—can in the nature of the case never pass away. Truth about other things may pass away; but truth about eternal God, His being, character, love, grace—this can never pass so long as God Himself endures.

Christ speaks to us again about man, but about man under what aspect and in what relations? Not from the point of view of man in any of his natural characteristics, as rank, age, sex, race, culture; but solely of man as a spiritual and immortal being, in his capacity of enduring existence, in his relation to God and eternity. Christ speaks of that which is universal in man, therefore His teaching endures and applies to all grades of civilization and all stages of culture. In Christ Jesus there is neither Greek, or Jew, or Barbarian, or Scythian, or bond, or free, or male or female, or any of those things; but Christ regards man as a spiritual and immortal being; in his enduring aspect; in his relations to God and to eternity. Christ looked at man always and altogether in that one light, set man before Him in that light as He went through the world, taught about man in that light, legislated for man in that light, never looked at man in any other light than that. It might be the poorest beggar on the street; it might be the greatest sinner in the city; Christ always looked on that man or that woman in the light of their relation to God and to eternity, and therefore Christ's teaching about man endures. It cannot become obsolete;

it goes down deeper than all these distinctions that divide us. Oceans divide nations, interest divides nations, but Christ's teaching about man, about the soul, goes deeper than all these things. His teachings are fitted for every race—experience proves that—for every age, for every civilization. The little child begins to lisp " Our Father " and takes in these teachings of Jesus, and the sage in the heights of his loftiest speculations feels that he can never get beyond them, and so Christ's words about man endure.

Christ speaks again of spiritual truth and duty, of the righteousness of the kingdom of God, and this is truth which in its nature is eternal. There is no inherent necessity, so far as we can see, for the laws of the material universe, of the heaven and the earth, being precisely what they are. The planets, had the Creator willed it, might have revolved in other orbits, might have moved in different directions, the properties, laws and relations of substances might have been different from what they are. The fabric of the world is thus contingent on the Creator's decree, and so is alterable and can be thought of as passing away. But it is not so with spiritual and moral truth. That is eternal as the nature of God Himself. No decree of heaven could ever make that which is essentially right wrong or that which is essentially wrong right; could ever make falsehood, deceit or treachery into virtues, or make love, affection, fidelity into vices. But it is in this region of eternal truth that throughout His gospel Christ specially legislates.

Finally, Christ speaks to man of salvation, and one of His favorite names for salvation is eternal life. It needs no proof that words of truth about eternal life are words that must and shall endure; that after all sums up the whole nature of Christ's mission to the world. He came to seek and to save the lost. He came that He might redeem and save us and bring us back to God, and what is Christ's own great name, or one of His great names for this salvation He came to bring? Is it not just this eternal life: " I give unto my sheep eternal life," he says. He came that we might have life, that we might have it more abundantly. In the very nature of the case truth about eternal life is truth that cannot pass away. Truth about earthly, temporal things may pass away; truth about eternal life cannot pass away. All that Christ came into this world to do had for its end the bestowing upon us of that life which is everlasting. His coming, His living, His dying, His rising again, the gift of His Spirit, everything else, all has this for its end, that we poor, perishing sinners may be lifted up into participation with that pure, holy, incorruptible, blessed life of God Himself, which is just the other name for eternal life; and truth about this eternal life, as I say, is truth that can never pass away.

Thus we have turned these words of Jesus round and round. The more closely we look at them the more clearly we see that from their very nature they cannot pass away. They remain to us the touchstone of eternal truth, in all spiritual things, the rock foundation on which alone if men build they shall stand secure in that dread day, which shall try every man's work of what sort it is. May God grant that at long and last, when our persons and characters and life work are brought unto judgment, they may be found enduring because resting on this rock of the eternal words of Christ!

JOSEPH PARKER

1830-1902

A WORD TO THE WEARY

BIOGRAPHICAL NOTE

JOSEPH PARKER was born at Hexham-on-Tyne, England, in 1830. He was a prodigious worker, writer, and preacher. His "The People's Bible," in twenty-eight large volumes, a popular commentary on the Scriptures, is his greatest work. To a naturally energetic personality he added great originality and resourcefulness. He gave much time to the preparation of sermons, reading them aloud as he wrote in order to test their effect upon the ear. A strong personal quality pervaded all his preaching. "If I have not seen Him myself," he said, "I cannot preach Him." In lectures to students he gave much valuable advice gathered from the storehouse of his own varied experience. He gave particular attention to the use of the voice. "It is not enough," he said, "that you be heard; you must be effective as well as audible; you must lighten and thunder with the voice; it must rise and fall like a storm at times; now a whisper, now a trumpet, now the sound of many waters. There is an orator's voice, and there is a bellman's. The auctioneer talks; the orator speaks." Dr. Parker's sermons are published in numerous volumes. He died in 1902.

The Lord God hath given me the tongue of the learned, that I should know how to speak a word in season to him that is weary.—Isaiah 50 : 4.

THE power of speaking to the weary is nothing less than a divine gift. As we see the divinity in our gifts shall we be careful of them, thankful for them: every gift seems to enshrine the giver, God. But how extraordinary that this power of speaking to the weary should not be taught in the schools. It is not within the ability of man to teach other men how to speak to the weary-hearted, the wounded in spirit, the sore in the innermost feelings of the being. But can we lay down directions about this and offer suggestions? Probably so, but we do not touch the core of the matter. There is an infinite difference between the scholar and the genius. The scholar is made, the genius is inspired. Information can be imparted, but the true sense, the sense that feels and sees God, is a gift direct from heaven.

It is a common notion that anybody can sing. Why can you sing? Why, because I have been taught. That is your mistake. You can sing mechanically, exactly, properly, with right time, right tune, but really and truly you can not sing. Here is a man with his music and with the words; he sings every note, pronounces every word, goes through his lesson, finishes his task, and nobody wants to hear him any more. Another man takes up the same music, the same words, and the same hearers exclaim, "Oh, that he would go on for ever!" How is that?—the words exactly the same, the notes identical—how? Soul, fire, ever-burning, never consuming, making a bush like a planet. The great difficulty in all such cases is the difficulty of transferring to paper a proper or adequate conception of the power of the men who thus sway the human heart. There are some men whose biographies simply belie them, and yet every sentence in the biography is true in the letter; but the biography is little else than a travesty and a caricature, because the power was personal, it was in the face, in the voice, in the presence, in the gait, in the touch—an incommunicable power; the hem of the garment trembled under it, but no biographer could catch it in his scholarly ink.

Very few ministers can enter a sick chamber with any probability of doing real and lasting good. They can read the Bible, and they can pray, and yet, when they have gone, the room seems as if they had never been there. There is no sense of emptiness or desolation. Other men, probably not so much gifted in some other directions, will enter the sick room, and there will be a light upon the wall, summer will gleam upon the window-pane, and angels will rustle in the air, and it will be a scene of gladness and a vision of triumph. How is that? The Lord God hath given me the tongue of the learned that I might know how—*how* to speak a word in season to him that is weary. The Lord God hath not only given me a word to say, but hath given me learning to teach me how to speak it. Place the emphasis upon the how, and then you develop all the mystery, all the tender music, all the infinite capacity of manner.

We may say the right word in the wrong tone; we may preach the gospel as if it were a curse. The common notion is that anybody can go into the Sunday-school and teach the young. We sometimes think that it would be well if a great many persons left the Sunday-school all over the world. Teach the young—would God I had that great gift, to break the bread for the children, and to be able to lure and captivate opening minds, and to enter into the spirit of the words—

"Delightful task! to rear the tender thought,
To teach the young idea how to shoot."

It requires to be father and mother and sister and nurse and genius to speak to the young. They may hear you and not care for you: they may understand your words, and be repelled by your spirit. You require the tongue of the learned to know how to speak, and that tongue of the learned is not to be had at school, college, university—it is not included in any curriculum of learning—it is a gift divine, breathing an afflatus, an inspiration—the direct and distinct creation of God, as is the star, the sun. The speaker, then, is Jesus Christ, the Son of God, the representative of the Father, the incarnate Deity—He it is who is charged with the subtle learning; He it is whose lips tremble with the pathos of this ineffable music.

Tho the gift itself is divine, we must remember that it is to be exercised seasonably. The text is, "that I should know how to speak a word in season." There is a time for everything. It is not enough to speak the right word, it must be spoken at the right moment. Who can know when that is! We can not be taught. We must feel it, see it hours beyond: nay, must know when to be silent for the whole twenty-four hours and to say, "To-morrow, at such and such a time, we will drop that sentence upon the listening ear." "The day after to-morrow, he will probably be in circumstances to admit of this communication being delivered with sympathy and effect."

How few persons know the right time—the right time in conversation. Some people are never heard in conversation tho they are talking all the time. They talk so unseasonably, they talk when other people are talking; they can not wait; they do not know how to come in along the fine line of silence: they do not understand the German expression "Now an angel has passed," and they do not quickly enough follow in his wake. Consequently, tho chattering much they are saying nothing—tho their words be multitudinous, the impression they make is a blank.

I have a ripe seed in my hand. As an agriculturist I am going to sow it. Any laborer in the field can tell me that I should be acting foolishly in sowing it just now. Why? "It is out of season," the man says. "There is a time for the doing of that action: I will tell you when the time returns—do it then, and you may expect a profitable result of your labor."

Then I will change the character and be a nurse, and I will attend to my patient (perhaps I will over attend to him—some patients are killed by over nursing), and I will give the patient this medicine—it is the right medicine. So it is, but you are going to give it at the wrong time, and if you give the medicine at the wrong time, tho itself be right, the hour being wrong you will bring suffering upon the patient, and you yourself will be involved in pains and penalties. Thus we touch that very subtle and sensitive line in human life, the line of refined discrimination. You may say "I am sure I told him." You are right—you did tell him and he did not hear you. You may reply, "I am perfectly confident I delivered the message,—I preached the exact words of the gospel." So you did, but you never got the hearing heart, your manner was so unsympathetic, so ungentle, so cruel (not meant to be—unconsciously so), that the man never understood it to be a gospel. You spoilt the music in the delivery, in the giving of the message. The Lord God giveth the tongue of the learned, that he to whom it is given may know how to speak—how to speak the right word—how to speak the right word at the right point of time. You want divine teaching in all things, in speech not least.

This is a curious word to find in the Bible. Does the Bible care about weary people? We have next to no sympathy with them. If a man be weary, we give him notice to quit: if he ask us to what place he can retire, we tell him that it is his business not ours. Now the tenderness of this Book is one of the most telling, convincing arguments on behalf of its inspiration, and its divine authority. This Book means to help us, wants to help us, it says, "I will try to help you, never hinder you: I will wait for you, I will soften the wind into a whisper, I will order the thunder to be silent, I will quiet the raging sea; I will wait upon you at home, in solitude, at midnight, anywhere—fix the place, the time, yourself, and when your heart most needs me I will be most to your heart." Any book found in den, in gutter, that wants to do this, should be received with respect. The purpose is good: if it fail, it fails in a noble object.

Everywhere in this Book of God we find a supreme wish to help man. When we most need help the words are sweeter than the honeycomb. When other books are dumb, this Book speaks most sweetly. It is like a star, it shines in the darkness, it waits the going down of the superficial sun of our transient prosperity, and then it breaks upon us as the shadows thicken. This is the real greatness of God: he will not break the bruised reed. Because the reed is bruised, therefore the rude man says he may break it. His argument in brief is this: "If the reed were strong, I should not touch it, but seeing that it is bruised what harm can there be in completing the wound under which it is already suffering? I will even snap it and throw the sundered parts away." That is the reasoning of the rude man—that is the vulgar view of the case. The idea of the healing is the idea of a creator. He who creates also heals. Herein we see God's estimate of human nature: if He cared only for the great, the splendid, the magnificent, the robust, and the everlasting, then He would indeed be too like ourselves. The greatness of God and the estimate which He places upon human nature are most seen in all these ministrations in reference to the weak and the weary and the young and the feeble and the sad. Made originally in the image of God, man is dear to his Maker, tho ever so broken. Oh, poor prodigal soul with the divinity nearly broken out of thee, smashed, bleeding, crushed, all but in hell—while there is a shadow of thee outside perdition, He would heal thee and save thee. Thou art a ruin, but a grand one,—the majestic ruin of a majestic edifice, for knowest thou not that thou wast the temple of God?

When we are weary, even in weariness, God sees the possibility of greatness that may yet take place and be developed and supervene in immortality. How do we talk? Thus: "The survival of the fittest." It is amazing with what patience and magnanimity and majestic disregard of circumstances we allow people to die off. When we hear that thousands have perished, we write this epitaph on their white slate tombstones: "The survival of the fittest required the decay of the weakest and the poorest." We pick off the fruit which we think will not come to perfection. The gardener lays his finger and thumb upon the tree, and he says, "This will not come to much"—he wrenches the poor unpromising piece of fruit off the twig and throws it down as useless. In our march we leave the sick and wounded behind. That is the great little, the majestic insignificant, the human contradiction. We go in for things that are fittest, strongest, most promising, healthy, self-complete, and therein we think we are wise. God says, "Not a lamb must be left out—bring it up: not a sick man must be omitted: not a poor publican sobbing his 'God be merciful to me a sinner' must be omitted from the great host. Bring them all in, sick, weary, wounded, feeble, young, illiterate, poor, insignificant, without name, fame, station, force—all in: gather up the fragments that nothing be lost." Let us go to that Shepherd—He will spare us and love us. When our poor strength gives out, He will not set His cruel heel upon us and kill us, He will gather us in His arms and make the whole flock stand still till He has saved the weakest one.

Did we but know the name for our pain we should call it Sin. What do we need, then, but Christ the Son of God, the Heart of God, the Love of God? He will in very deed give us rest. He will not add to the great weight which bows down our poor strength. He will give us grace, and in His power all our faintness shall be thought of no more. Some of us know how dark it is when the full shadow of our sin falls upon our life, and how all the help of earth and time and man does but mock the pain it can not reach. Let no man say that Christ will not go so low down as to find one so base and vile as he. Christ is calling for thee; I heard His sweet voice lift itself up in the wild wind and ask whither thou hadst fled, that He might save thee from death and bring thee home. There is no wrath in His face or voice, no sword is swung by His hand as if in cruel joy, saying, "Now at last I have My chance with you." His eyes gleam with love: His voice melts in pity: His words are gospels, every one. Let Him but see thee sad for sin, full of grief because of the wrong thou hast done, and He will raise thee out of the deep pit and set thy feet upon the rock.

THEODORE PARKER

1810-1860

THE
TRANSIENT AND PERMANENT
IN CHRISTIANITY

BIOGRAPHICAL NOTE

THEODORE PARKER, American divine and reformer, was born at Lexington, Mass., in 1810. He was educated at Harvard and graduated from the Divinity School of that University in 1836. The following year he was ordained pastor of Roxbury Christian Church, and first attracted attention by his sermon on the "Transient and Permanent in Christianity," preached in 1841. This sermon was ultimately the cause of his practical exclusion from the Unitarian body, and in 1846 he became minister to the Twenty-eighth Congregational Society in Boston.

In this pastorate he became well known to all denominations from the remarkable sermons he preached for seven years in Music Hall. He died of consumption at Florence, Italy, in 1860. His powerful intellect and vigorous eloquence were exhibited in the many controversial sermons he preached, both as a believer in the non-supernaturalism of present Christianity and as a practical humanitarian. He figured as one of the leading abolitionists of New England.

Heaven and earth shall pass away; but My words shall not pass away.—Luke xxi., 33.

IN this sentence we have a very clear indication that Jesus of Nazareth believed the religion He taught would be eternal, that the substance of it would last forever. Yet there are some who are affrighted by the faintest rustle which a heretic makes among the dry leaves of theology; they tremble lest Christianity itself should perish without hope. Ever and anon the cry is raised, "The Philistines be upon us, and Christianity is in danger." The least doubt respecting the popular theology, or the existing machinery of the Church; the least sign of distrust in the religion of the pulpit, or the religion of the street, is by some good men supposed to be at enmity with faith in Christ, and capable of shaking Christianity itself. On the other hand, a few bad men, and a few pious men, it is said, on both sides of the water, tell us the day of Christianity is past. The latter, it is alleged, would persuade us that hereafter piety must take a new form; the teachings of Jesus are to be passed by; that religion is to wing her way sublime, above the flight of Christianity, far away, toward heaven, as the fledged eaglet leaves forever the nest which sheltered his callow youth. Let us therefore devote a few moments to this subject, and consider what is transient in Christianity, and what is permanent therein.

In actual Christianity,—that is, in that portion of Christianity which is preached and believed,—there seems to have been, ever since the time of its earthly Founder, two elements, the one transient, the other permanent. The one is the thought, the folly, the uncertain wisdom, the theological notions, the impiety of man; the other, the eternal truth of God. These two bear, perhaps, the same relation to each other that the phenomena of outward nature, such as sunshine and cloud, growth, decay and reproduction, bear to the great law of nature, which underlies and supports them all. As in that case more attention is commonly paid to the particular phenomena than to the general law, so in this case more is generally given to the transient in Christianity than to the permanent therein.

It must be confest, tho with sorrow, that transient things form a great part of what is commonly taught as religion. An undue place has often been assigned to forms and doctrines, while too little stress has been laid on the divine life of the soul, love to God, and love to man. Religious forms may be useful and beautiful. They are so, whenever they speak to the soul, and answer a want thereof. In our present state some forms are perhaps necessary. But they are only the accident of Christianity, not its substance. They are the robe, not the angel, who may take another robe quite as becoming and useful. One sect has many forms; another, none. Yet both may be equally Christian, in spite of the redundance or the deficiency. They are a part of the language in which religion speaks, and exist, with few exceptions, wherever man is found. In our calculating nation, in our rationalizing sect, we have retained but two of the rites so numerous in the early Christian Church, and even these we have attenuated to the last degree, leaving them little more than a specter of the ancient form. Another age may continue or forsake both; may revive old forms, or invent new ones to suit the altered circumstances of the times, and yet be Christians quite as good as we, or our fathers of the dark ages. Whether the apostles designed these rites to be perpetual seems a question which belongs to scholars and antiquarians,—not to us, as Christian men and women. So long as they satisfy or help the pious heart, so long they are good. Looking behind or around us, we see that the forms and rites of the Christians are quite as fluctuating as those of the heathens, from whom some of them have been, not unwisely, adopted by the earlier Church.

Any one, who traces the history of what is called Christianity, will see that nothing changes more from age to age than the doctrines taught as Christian, and insisted on as essential to Christianity and personal salvation. What is falsehood in one province passes for truth in another. The heresy of one age is the orthodox belief and "only infallible rule" of the next. Now Arius, and now Athanasius, is lord of the ascendant. Both were excommunicated in their turn, each for affirming what the other denied. Men are burned for professing what men are burned for denying. For centuries the doctrines of the Christians were no better, to say the least, than those of their contemporary pagans. The theological doctrines derived from our fathers seem to have come from Judaism, heathenism, and the caprice of philosophers, far more than they have come from the principle and sentiment of Christianity. The doctrine of the Trinity, the very Achilles of theological dogmas, belongs to philosophy and not religion; its subtleties cannot even be expressed in our tongue. As old religions became superannuated, and died out, they left to the rising faith, as to a residuary legatee, their forms and their doctrines; or rather, as the giant in the fable left his poisoned garment to work the overthrow of his conqueror. Many tenets that pass current in our theology seem to be the refuse of idol temples, the off-scourings of Jewish and heathen cities rather than the sands of virgin gold which the stream of Christianity has worn off from the rock of ages, and brought in its bosom for us. It is wood, hay, and stubble, wherewith men have built on the corner-stone Christ laid. What wonder the fabric is in peril when tried by fire? The stream of Christianity, as men receive it, has caught a stain from every soil it has filtered through, so that now it is not the pure water from the well of life which is offered to our lips, but streams troubled and polluted by man with mire and dirt. If Paul and Jesus could read our books of theological doctrines, would they accept as their teaching what men have vented in their name? Never, till the letters of Paul had faded out of his memory, never, till the words of Jesus had been torn out from the book of life. It is their notions about Christianity men have taught as the only living word of God. They have piled their own rubbish against the temple of truth where piety comes up to worship; what wonder the pile seems unshapely and like to fall? But these theological doctrines are fleeting as the leaves on the trees. They—

> "Are found
> Now green in youth, now withered on the ground;
> Another race the following spring supplies;
> They fall successive, and successive rise."

Like the clouds of the sky, they are here to-day; to-morrow, all swept off and vanished; while Christianity itself, like the heaven above, with its sun, and moon, and uncounted stars, is always over our head, tho the cloud sometimes debars us of the needed light. It must of necessity be the case that our reasonings, and therefore our theological doctrines, are imperfect, and so perishing. It is only gradually that we approach to the true system of nature by observation and reasoning, and work out our philosophy and theology by the toil of the brain. But meantime, if we are faithful, the great truths of mortality and religion, the deep sentiment of love to man and love to God, are perceived intuitively, and by instinct, as it were, tho our theology be imperfect and miserable. The theological notions of Abraham, to take the story as it stands, were exceedingly gross, yet a greater than Abraham has told us, "Abraham desired to see my day, saw it, and was glad." Since these notions are so fleeting, why need we accept the commandment of men as the doctrine of God?

This transitoriness of doctrines appears in many instances, of which two may be selected for a more attentive consideration. First, the doctrine respecting the origin and authority of the Old and New Testaments. There has been a time when men were burned for asserting doctrines of natural philosophy which rested on evidence the most incontestable, because those doctrines conflicted with sentences in the Old Testament. Every word of that Jewish record was regarded as miraculously inspired, and therefore as infallibly true. It was believed that the Christian religion itself rested thereon, and must stand or fall with the immaculate Hebrew text. He was deemed no small sinner who found mistakes in the manuscripts. On the authority of the written word man was taught to believe impossible legends, conflicting assertions; to take fiction for fact, a dream for a miraculous revelation of God, an Oriental poem for a grave history of miraculous events, a collection of amatory idyls for a serious discourse "touching the mutual love of Christ and the Church"; they have been taught to accept a picture sketched by some glowing Eastern imagination, never intended to be taken for a reality, as a proof that the infinite God spoke in human words, appeared in the shape of a cloud, a flaming bush, or a man who ate, and drank, and vanished into smoke; that He gave counsels to-day, and the opposite to-morrow; that He violated His own laws, was angry, and was only dissuaded by a mortal man from destroying at once a whole nation,—millions of men who rebelled against their leader in a moment of anguish. Questions in philosophy, questions in the Christian religion, have been settled by an appeal to that book. The inspiration of its authors has been assumed as infallible. Every fact in the early Jewish history has been taken as a type of some analogous fact in Christian history. The most distant events, even such as are still in the arms of time, were supposed to be clearly foreseen and foretold by pious Hebrews several centuries before Christ. It has been assumed at the outset, with no shadow of evidence, that those writers held a miraculous communication with God, such as He has granted to no other man. What was originally a presumption of bigoted Jews became an article of faith, which Christians were burned for not believing. This has been for centuries the general opinion of the Christian Church, both Catholic and Protestant, tho the former never accepted the Bible as the only source of religious truth. It has been so. Still worse, it is now the general opinion of religious sects at this day. Hence the attempt, which always fails, to reconcile the philosophy of our times with the poems in Genesis writ a thousand years before Christ. Hence the attempt to conceal the contradictions in the record itself. Matters have come to such a pass that even now he is deemed an infidel, if not by implication an atheist, whose reverence for the Most High forbids him to believe that God commanded Abraham to sacrifice his son,—a thought at which the flesh creeps with horror; to believe it solely on the authority of an Oriental story, written down no-

body knows when or by whom, or for what purpose; which may be a poem, but can not be the record of a fact, unless God is the author of confusion and a lie.

Now, this idolatry of the Old Testament has not always existed. Jesus says that none born of a woman is greater than John the Baptist, yet the least in the kingdom of heaven is greater than John. Paul tells us the law —the very crown of the old Hebrew revelation—is a shadow of good things which have now come; only a schoolmaster to bring us to Christ; and when faith has come, that we are no longer under the schoolmaster; that it was a law of sin and death, from which we are made free by the law of the spirit of life. Christian teachers themselves have differed so widely in their notion of the doctrines and meaning of those books that it makes one weep to think of the follies deduced therefrom. But modern criticism is fast breaking to pieces this idol which men have made out of the Scriptures. It has shown that here are the most different works thrown together; that their authors, wise as they sometimes were, pious as we feel often their spirit to have been, had only that inspiration which is common to other men equally pious and wise; that they were by no means infallible, but were mistaken in facts or in reasoning,—uttered predictions which time has not fulfilled; men who in some measure partook of the darkness and limited notions of their age, and were not always above its mistakes or its corruptions.

The history of opinions on the New Testament is quite similar. It has been assumed at the outset, it would seem with no sufficient reason, without the smallest pretense on its writers' part, that all of its authors were infallibly and miraculously inspired, so that they could commit no error of doctrine or fact. Men have been bid to close their eyes at the obvious difference between Luke and John, the serious disagreement between Paul and Peter; to believe, on the smallest evidence, accounts which shock the moral sense and revolt the reason, and tend to place Jesus in the same series with the Hercules and Appollonius of Tyana; accounts which Paul in the Epistles never mentions, tho he also had a vein of the miraculous running quite through him. Men have been told that all these things must be taken as part of Christianity, and if they accepted the religion, they must take all these accessories along with it; that the living spirit could not be had without the killing letter. All the books which caprice or accident had brought together between the lids of the Bible were declared to be the infallible Word of God, the only certain rule of religious faith and practise. Thus the Bible was made not a single channel, but the only certain rule of religious faith and practise. To disbelieve any of its statements, or even the common interpretation put upon those statements by the particular age or church in which the man belonged, was held to be infidelity, if not atheism. In the name of Him who forbids us to judge our brother, good men and pious men have applied these terms to others, good and pious as themselves. That state of things has by no means passed away. Men who cry down the absurdities of paganism in the worst spirit of the French "free thinkers" call others infidels and atheists, who point out, tho reverently, other absurdities which men have piled upon Christianity. So the world goes. An idolatrous regard for the imperfect scripture of God's word is the apple of Atalanta, which defeats theologians running for the hand of divine truth.

But the current notions respecting the infallible inspiration of the Bible have no foundation in the Bible itself. Which evangelist, which apostle of the New Testament, what prophet or psalmist of the Old Testament, ever claims infallible authority for himself or for others? Which of them does not in his own writings show that he was finite, and, with all his zeal and piety, possess but a limited inspiration, the bound whereof we can sometimes discover? Did Christ ever demand that men should assent to the doctrines of the Old Testament, credit its stories, and take its poems for histories, and believe equally two accounts that contradict one another? Has He ever told you that all the truths of His religion, all the beauty of a Christian life should be contained in the writings of those men who, even after His resurrection, expected Him to be a Jewish king; of men who were sometimes at variance with one another, and misunderstood His divine teachings? Would not those modest writers themselves be confounded at the idolatry we pay them? Opinions may change on these points, as they have often changed—changed greatly and for the worse since the days of Paul. They are changing now, and we may hope for the better; for God makes man's folly as well his wrath to praise Him, and continually brings good out of evil.

Another instance of the transitoriness of doctrines taught as Christian is found in those which relate to the nature and authority of Christ. One ancient party has told us that He is the infinite God; another, that He is both God and man; a third, that He was a man, the son of Joseph and Mary, born as we are; tempted like ourselves; inspired as we may be, if we will pay the price. Each of the former parties believed its doctrine on this head was infallibly true, and formed the very substance of Christianity, and was one of the essential conditions of salvation, tho scarce any two distinguished teachers, of ancient or modern times, agree in their expression of this truth.

Almost every sect that has ever been, makes Christianity rest on the personal authority of Jesus, and not the immutable truth of the doctrines themselves, or the authority of God, who sent Him into the world. Yet it seems difficult to conceive any reason why moral and religious truths should rest for their support on the personal authority of their revealer, any more than the truths of science on that of him who makes them known first or most clearly. It is hard to see why the great truths of Christianity rest on the personal authority of Jesus, more than the axioms of geometry rest on the personal authority of Euclid or Archimedes. The authority of Jesus as of all teachers, one would naturally think, must rest on the truth of His words, and not their truth on His authority.

Opinions respecting the nature of Christ seem to be constantly changing. In the three first centuries after Christ, it appears, great latitude of speculation prevailed. Some said He was God, with nothing of human nature, His body only an illusion; others that He was man, with nothing of the divine nature, His miraculous birth having no foundation in fact. In a few centuries it was decreed by councils that He was God, thus honoring the divine element; next, that He was man also, thus admitting the human side. For some ages the Catholic Church seems to have dwelt chiefly on the divine nature that was in Him, leaving the human element to mystics and other heretical persons, whose bodies served to flesh the swords of orthodox believers. The stream of Christianity has come to us in two channels,— one within the Church, the other without the Church,—and it is not hazarding too much to say that since the fourth century the true Christian life has been out of the established Church, and not in it, but rather in the ranks of dissenters. From the Reformation till the latter part of the last century, we are told, the Protestant Church dwelt chiefly on the human side of Christ, and since that time many works have been written to show how the two—perfect Deity and perfect manhood —were united in His character. But, all this time, scarce any two eminent teachers agree on these points, however orthodox they may be called. What a difference between the Christ of John Gerson and John Calvin,— yet were both accepted teachers and pious men. What a difference between the Christ of the Unitarians and the Methodists,—yet may men of both sects be true Christians and acceptable with God. What a difference between the Christ of Matthew and John,— yet both were disciples, and their influence is wide as Christendom and deep as the heart of man. But on this there is not time to enlarge.

Now, it seems clear that the notions men form about the origin and nature of the Scriptures, respecting the nature and authority of Christ, have nothing to do with Christianity except as its aids or its adversaries; they are not the foundation of its truths. These are theological questions, not religious questions. Their connection with Christianity appears accidental; for if Jesus had taught at Athens, and not at Jerusalem; if He had wrought no miracle, and none but the human nature had ever been ascribed to them; if the Old Testament had forever perished at His birth,—Christianity would still have been the word of God; it would have lost none of its truths. It would be just as true, just as beautiful, just as lasting, as now it is; tho we should have lost so many a blessed word, and the work of Christianity itself would have been, perhaps, a long time retarded.

To judge the future by the past, the former authority of the Old Testament can never return. Its present authority can not stand. It must be taken for what it is worth. The occasional folly and impiety of its authors must pass for no more than their value; while the religion, the wisdom, the love, which make fragrant its leaves, will still speak to the best hearts as hitherto, and in accents even more divine when reason is allowed her rights. The ancient belief in the infallible inspiration of each sentence of the New Testament is fast changing, very fast. One writer, not a skeptic, but a Christian of unquestioned piety, sweeps off the beginning of Matthew; another, of a different church and equally religious, the end of John. Numerous critics strike off several epistles. The Apocalypse itself is not spared, notwithstanding its concluding curse. Who shall tell us the work of retrenchment is to stop here; that others will not demonstrate what some pious hearts have long felt, that errors of doctrine and errors of fact may be found in many parts of the record, here and there, from the beginning of Matthew to the end of Acts? We see how opinions have changed ever since the apostles' time; and who shall assure us that they were not sometimes mistaken in historical as well as doctrinal matters; did not sometimes confound the actual with the imaginary; and that the fancy of these pious writers never stood in the place of their recollection?

But what if this should take place? Is Christianity then to perish out of the heart of the nations, and vanish from the memory of the world, like the religions that were before Abraham? It must be so, if it rest on a foundation which a scoffer may shake, and a score of pious critics shake down. But this is the foundation of a theology, not of Christianity. That does not rest on the decision of councils. It is not to stand or fall with the infallible inspiration of a few Jewish fishermen, who have writ their names in characters of light all over the world. It does not

continue to stand through the forbearance of some critic, who can cut when he will the thread on which its life depends. Christianity does not rest on the infallible authority of the New Testament. It depends on this collection of books for the historical statement of its facts. In this we do not require infallible inspiration on the part of the writers, more than in the record of other historical facts. To me it seems as presumptuous, on the one hand, for the believer to claim this evidence for the truth of Christianity, as it is absurd, on the other hand, for the skeptic to demand such evidence to support these historical statements. I can not see that it depends on the personal authority of Jesus. He was the organ through which the Infinite spoke. It is God that was manifested in the flesh by Him, on whom rests the truth which Jesus brought to light, and made clear and beautiful in His life; and if Christianity be true, it seems useless to look for any other authority to uphold it, as for some one to support Almighty God. So if it could be proved—as it can not—in opposition to the greatest amount of historical evidence ever collected on any similar point, that the Gospels were the fabrication of designing and artful men, that Jesus of Nazareth had never lived, still Christianity would stand firm, and fear no evil. None of the doctrines of that religion would fall to the ground; for, if true, they stand by themselves. But we should lose—oh, irreparable loss!—the example of that character, so beautiful, so divine, that no human genius could have conceived it, as none, after all the progress and refinement of eighteen centuries, seems fully to have comprehended its lustrous life. If Christianity were true, we should still think it was so, not because its record was written by infallible pens, nor because it was lived out by an infallible teacher; but that it is true, like the axioms of geometry, because it is true and is to be tried by the oracle God places in the breast. If it rest on the personal authority of Jesus alone, then there is no certainty of its truth if He were ever mistaken in the smallest matter,—as some Christians have thought He was in predicting His second coming.

These doctrines respecting the Scriptures have often changed, and are but fleeting. Yet men lay much stress on them. Some cling to these notions as if they were Christianity itself. It is about these and similar points that theological battles are fought from age to age. Men sometimes use worst the choicest treasure which God bestows. This is especially true of the use men make of the Bible. Some men have regarded it as the heathen their idol, or the savage his fetish. They have subordinated reason, conscience, and religion to this. Thus have they lost half the treasure it bears in its bosom. No doubt the time will come when its true character shall be felt. Then it will be seen that, amid all the contradictions of the Old Testament,—its legends, so beautiful as fictions, so appalling as facts; amid its predictions that have never been fulfilled; amid the puerile conceptions of God which sometimes occur, and the cruel denunciations that disfigure both psalm and prophecy,—there is a reverence for man's nature, a sublime trust in God, and a depth of piety, rarely felt in these cold northern hearts of ours. Then the devotion of its authors, the loftiness of their aim, and the majesty of their life, will appear doubly fair, and prophet and psalmist will warm our hearts as never before. Their voice will cheer the young, and sanctify the grayheaded; will charm us in the toil of life, and sweeten the cup death gives us when he comes to shake off this mantle of flesh. Then will it be seen that the words of Jesus are the music of heaven sung in an earthly voice, and that the echo of these words in John and Paul owe their efficacy to their truth and their depth, and to no accidental matter connected therewith. Then can the Word, which was in the beginning and now is, find access to the innermost heart of man, and speak there as now it seldom speaks. Then shall the Bible—which is a whole library of the deepest and most earnest thoughts and feelings, and piety, and love, ever recorded in human speech—be read oftener than ever before,—not with superstition, but with reason, conscience, and faith, fully active. Then shall it sustain men bowed down with many sorrows; rebuke sin, encourage virtue, sow the world broadcast and quick with the seed of love, that man may reap a harvest for life everlasting.

With all the obstacles men have thrown in its path, how much has the Bible done for mankind! No abuse has deprived us of all its blessings. You trace its path across the world from the day of Pentecost to this day. As a river springs up in the heart of a sandy continent, having its father in the skies, and its birthplace in distant unknown mountains; as the stream rolls on, enlarging itself, making in that arid waste a belt of verdure wherever it turns its way; creating palm groves and fertile plains, where the smoke of the cottager curls up at eventide, and marble cities send the gleam of their splendor far into the sky, —such has been the course of the Bible on the earth. Despite of idolaters bowing to the dust before it, it has made a deeper mark on the world than the rich and beautiful literature of all the heathen. The first book of the Old Testament tells man he is made in the image of God; the first of the New Testament gives us the motto, Be perfect as your Father in heaven. Higher words were never spoken. How the truths of the Bible have blest us! There is not a boy on all the hills of New England; not a girl born in the filthiest cellar

which disgraces a capital in Europe, and cries to God against the barbarism of modern civilization; not a boy nor a girl all Christendom through, but their lot is made better by that great book.

Doubtless the time will come when men shall see Christ also as He is. Well might He still say, "Have I been so long with you, and yet hast thou not known me?" No! we have made Him an idol, have bowed the knee before Him, saying, "Hail, king of the Jews!" called Him "Lord, Lord!" but done not the things which He said. The history of the Christian world might well be summed up in one word of the evangelist—"and there they crucified him"; for there has never been an age when the men did not crucify the Son of God afresh. But if error prevail for a time and grow old in the world, truth will triumph at the last, and then we shall see the Son of God as He is. Lifted up, He shall draw all nations unto Him. Then will men understand the word of Jesus, which shall not pass away. Then shall we see and love the divine life that He lived. How vast has His influence been! How His spirit wrought in the hearts of His disciples, rude, selfish, bigoted, as at first they were! How it has wrought in the world! His words judge the nations. The wisest son of man has not measured their height. They speak to what is deepest in profound men, what is holiest in good men, what is divinest in religious men. They kindle anew the flame of devotion in hearts long cold. They are spirit and life. His truth was not derived from Moses and Solomon; but the light of God shone through Him, not colored, not bent aside. His life is the perpetual rebuke of all time since. It condemns ancient civilization; it condemns modern civilization. Wise men we have since had, and good men; but this Galilean youth strode before the whole world thousands of years, so much of divinity was in Him. His words solve the question of this present age. In Him the Godlike and the human met and embraced, and a divine life was born. Measure Him by the world's greatest sons—how poor they are! Try Him by the best of men— how little and low they appear! Exalt Him as much as we may, we shall yet perhaps come short of the mark. But still was He not our brother; the son of man, as we are; the son of God, like ourselves? His excellence—was it not human excellence? His wisdom, love, piety,—sweet and celestial as they were,—are they not what we also may attain? In Him, as in a mirror, we may see the image of God, and go on from glory to glory, till we are changed into the same image, led by the spirit which enlightens the humble. Viewed in this way, how beautiful is the life of Jesus! Heaven has come down to earth, or rather, earth has become heaven. The Son of God, come of age, has taken possession of His birthright. The brightest revelation is this of what is possible for all men,—if not now, at least hereafter. How pure is His spirit, and how encouraging its words! "Lowly sufferer," he seems to say, "see how I bore the cross. Patient laborer, be strong; see how I toiled for the unthankful and the merciless. Mistaken sinner, see of what thou art capable. Rise up, and be blest."

But if, as some early Christians began to do, you take a heathen view, and make Him a God, the Son of God in a peculiar and exclusive sense, much of the significance of His character is gone. His virtue has no merit, His love no feeling, His cross no burthen, His agony no pain. His death is an illusion, His resurrection but a show. For if He were not a man, but a god, what are all these things? What His words, His life, His excellence of achievement? It is all nothing, weighed against the illimitable greatness of Him who created the worlds and fills up all time and space! Then His resignation is no lesson, His life no model, His death no triumph to you or me, who are not gods, but mortal men, that know not what a day shall bring forth, and walk by faith "dim sounding on our perilous way." Alas! we have despaired of man, and so cut off his brightest hope.

In respect of doctrines as well as forms, we see all is transitory. "Everywhere is instability and insecurity." Opinions have changed most on points deemed most vital. Could we bring up a Christian teacher of any age, from the sixth to the fourteenth century, for example, tho a teacher of undoubted soundness of faith, whose word filled the churches of Christendom, clergymen would scarce allow him to kneel at their altar, or sit down with them at the Lord's table. His notions of Christianity could not be exprest in our forms, nor could our notions be made intelligible to his ears. The questions of his age, those on which Christianity was thought to depend,—questions which perplexed and divided the subtle doctors,—are no questions to us. The quarrels which then drove wise men mad now only excite a smile or a tear, as we are disposed to laugh or weep at the frailty of man. We have other straws of our own to quarrel for. Their ancient books of devotion do not speak to us; their theology is a vain word. To look back but a short period,—the theological speculations of our fathers during the last two centuries, their "practical divinity," even the sermons written by genius and piety are, with rare exceptions, found unreadable; such a change is there in the doctrines.

Now who shall tell us that the change is to stop here; that this sect or that, or even all sects united, have exhausted the river of life, and received it all in their canonized urns, so that we need draw no more out of the eternal well, but get refreshment nearer at hand?

Who shall tell us that another age will not smile at our doctrines, disputes, and unchristian quarrels about Christianity, and make wide the mouth at men who walked brave in orthodox raiment, delighting to blacken the names of heretics, and repeat again the old charge, "He hath blasphemed"? Who shall tell us they will not weep at the folly of all such as fancied truth shone only into the contracted nook of their school, or sect, or coterie? Men of other times may look down equally on the heresy-hunters, and men hunted for heresy, and wonder at both. The men of all ages before us were quite as confident as we, that their opinion was truth, that their notion was Christianity and the whole thereof. The men who lit the fires of persecution, from the first martyr to Christian bigotry down to the last murder of the innocents, had no doubt their opinion was divine. The contest about transubstantiation and the immaculate purity of the Hebrew and Greek texts of the Scriptures was waged with bitterness unequaled in these days. The Protestant smiles at one, the Catholic at the other, and men of sense wonder at both. It might teach us all a lesson, at least of forbearance. No doubt an age will come in which ours shall be reckoned a period of darkness, like the sixth century,—when men groped for the wall, but stumbled and fell, because they trusted a transient notion, not an eternal truth; an age when temples were full of idols, set up by human folly; an age in which Christian light had scarce begun to shine into men's hearts. But while this change goes on, while one generation of opinions passes away, and another rises up, Christianity itself, that pure religion, which exists eternal in the constitution of the soul and the mind of God, is always the same. The Word that was before Abraham, in the very beginning, will not change, for that Word is truth. From this Jesus subtracted nothing; to this He added nothing. But He came to reveal it as the secret of God, that cunning men could not understand, but which filled the souls of men meek and lowly of heart. This truth we owe to God; the revelation thereof to Jesus, our elder brother, God's chosen son.

To turn away from the disputes of the Catholics and the Protestants, of the Unitarian and the Trinitarian, of old school and new school, and come to the plain words of Jesus of Nazareth,—Christianity is a simple thing, very simple. It is absolute, pure morality; absolute, pure religion,—the love of man; the love of God acting without let or hindrance. The only creed it lays down is the great truth which springs up spontaneous in the holy heart,—there is a God. Its watchword is, Be perfect as your Father in heaven. The only form it demands is a divine life,—doing the best thing in the best way, from the highest motives; perfect obedience to the great law of God. Its sanction is the voice of God in your heart; the perpetual presence of Him who made us and the stars over our head; Christ and the Father abiding within us. All this is very simple—a little child can understand it; very beautiful—the loftiest mind can find nothing so lovely. Try it by reason, conscience, and faith,—things highest in man's nature,—we see no redundance, we feel no deficiency. Examine the particular duties it enjoins,—humility, reverence, sobriety, gentleness, charity, forgiveness, fortitude, resignation, faith, and active love; try the whole extent of Christianity, so well summed up in the command, "Thou shalt love the Lord thy God with all thy heart, and with all thy soul, and with all thy mind; thou shalt love thy neighbor as thyself"; and is there anything therein that can perish? No, the very opponents of Christianity have rarely found fault with the teachings of Jesus. The end of Christianity seems to be to make all men one with God as Christ was one with Him; to bring them to such a state of obedience and goodness that we shall think divine thoughts and feel divine sentiments, and so keep the law of God by living a life of truth and love. Its means are purity and prayer; getting strength from God, and using it for our fellow-men as well as ourselves. It allows perfect freedom. It does not demand all men to think alike, but to think uprightly, and get as near as possible at truth; not all men to live alike, but to live holy, and get as near as possible to a life perfectly divine. Christ set up no Pillars of Hercules, beyond which men must not sail the sea in quest of truth. He says, "I have many things to say unto you, but ye cannot bear them now. . . . . Greater works than these shall ye do." Christianity lays no rude hand on the sacred peculiarity of individual genius and character. But there is no Christian sect which does not fetter a man. It would make all men think alike, or smother their conviction in silence. Were all men Quakers or Catholics, Unitarians or Baptists, there would be much less diversity of thought, character, and life, less of truth active in the world, than now. But Christianity gives us the largest liberty of the sons of God; and were all men Christians after the fashion of Jesus, this variety would be a thousand times greater than now; for Christianity is not a system of doctrines, but rather a method of attaining oneness with God. It demands, therefore, a good life of piety within, of purity without, and gives the promise that whoso does God's will shall know of God's doctrine.

LEWIS BAYLES PATON

1864-1932

THE GREATEST QUESTION

BIOGRAPHICAL NOTE

PROFESSOR of Old Testament exegesis and criticism, and instructor in the Assyrian language in Hartford Theological Seminary; born in New York City, June 27, 1864; educated in the high schools of Des Moines and Keokuk, Iowa, and in Parson's College, Fairfield, Iowa; graduated from the University of New York in 1884 with the degree of B.A.; spent three years in study and travel in Europe; student in Princeton Theological Seminary, 1887-90; Old Testament fellow of the same for two years which were spent in Berlin, Germany; Ph.D., University of Marburg, Germany, 1897; D.D., University of New York, 1906; director of the American school of Oriental Study and Research in Jerusalem, 1903,4; author of "The Early History of Syria and Palestine," "Jerusalem in Bible Times," "Esther" in "International Critical Commentary," editor of "Recent Christian Progress."

" Who say ye that I am? "—Matt. 16 : 15.

CHRIST'S question, " Who say ye that I am? " is so familiar that we do not always realize its extraordinary character. Why should He ask His disciples who He was? Was not that perfectly apparent to everybody? So thought the Jews in His day, when they said, " We know this man whence he is " (John 7 : 27). " Is not this the carpenter's son? Is not his mother called Mary? and his brethren, James, and Joseph, and Simon, and Judas? And his sisters, are they not all with us? (Matt. 13 : 55 f.). Other religious teachers and leaders have not felt constrained to ask this question of their disciples. In spite of their genius and the dignity that their message conferred upon them, they have understood that they differed so little from the rest of mankind that it would be absurd for them to ask, Who say ye that I am? But Jesus was conscious of a mysterious something about Himself that differentiated Him from all other men, and that made it imperative for Him to put this question; and so, from beginning to end of His ministry, we find Him directing the attention of His disciples not so much to His doctrine as to His person. He does not say, " Come to my way of thinking," but, " Come unto me "; not, " Follow my rule of life," but, " Follow thou me "; not, " What say ye of my doctrine? " but, " Who say ye that I am? "

No less extraordinary than the question of Jesus is the way in which men everywhere have felt compelled to answer this question. If other men should put this question to us, we should pay no attention to it. We are under no compulsion to define the other great teachers and leaders of humanity, and to come to a decision in regard to their claims; but there has always been a strange power about this question of Jesus. Men cannot escape it, they cannot ignore it. Those to whom it first came were obliged to give it an answer of some sort, and throughout the succeeding centuries, wherever the story of the gospel has been told, men have been constrained to say to themselves, Who is this Jesus of Nazareth, what is He, and what is His claim upon me?

The gospel narrative shows us four answers to Jesus' question that were given by the men of His own day. They are representative of the answers that men have been giving ever since.

First, there was the answer of the scribes and the Pharisees. They were the religious leaders of the nation, the makers of public opinion. They had long been considering this question of Jesus, and their minds were fully made up as to the answer that they should give to it. They said, He is an impostor, "He deceiveth the people." They were sure that they were correct in their ideas about religion, and when they learned that He differed from them, they at once pronounced Him a heretic. They laid emphasis upon the ritual commandments of the law, but Jesus emphasized the message of the prophets, "I desire mercy and not sacrifice, and the love of God rather than burnt offerings"; and He denounced the scribes and the Pharisees as hypocrites, who bound heavy burdens around the necks of other men, but who would not touch them with one of their fingers. This was enough to convince them that He was a dangerous character, who ought to be put out of the way lest He should pervert the minds of the people. When their attention was called to His healings of those diseased in mind or in body, they said, "He casteth out devils through Beelzebub, the prince of the devils" (Matt. 12:24).

This answer of the religious authorities of Jesus' day to His question concerning Himself has been the answer of official Judaism ever since. The Talmud, that huge repository of Jewish thought during the first six centuries of our era, has only scorn for Jesus as an arch-heretic who caused a great apostasy from the religion of Moses. Down to our own day the common Jewish name for Him has been the contemptuous title "he who was hung," which expresses the thought that He suffered justly as a deceiver of mankind. In modern times, however, Judaism has come for the most part to take a higher view of Him and, outside of Judaism, the view that He was an impostor has been exceedingly rare. Two centuries ago, at the time of the French "illumination," there were some who regarded all religious teachers as impostors, Jesus along with the rest; and who were ready to say of Him with Voltaire, "Crush the wretch." There may be some to-day who hold this view; but if there are such, they exert little influence in the world of thought.

Second, there was the answer of a few of the Jewish leaders. Men like Nicodemus and Joseph of Arimathea were not willing to pronounce Jesus an impostor, but regarded Him rather as a great religious teacher. When Nicodemus came to Jesus by night, he said to him, "Rabbi, we know that thou art a teacher come from God." That is to say, he regarded Him as an expounder of the law like himself, and was willing to admit that He possest both genius and truth in His views concerning religion and ethics.

This has been the attitude of the heathen world in general. The Greeks and the Romans would have been quite willing to admit Jesus to a place among their own wise men, philosophers, and poets, and to have adopted many of His teachings, if the early Church had made no higher claim for Him than that He was a teacher, like the world's other great teachers. The people of India, China, and Japan are willing to-day to accept Jesus on the same basis. They will put Him alongside of Buddha and Confucius, but they will not accord Him a higher place. This is the attitude also of modern liberal Judaism. It regards Jesus as a great and a good man, one of the rabbis, like Hillel or Gamaliel, who taught men how to keep the law of Moses, and who did not differ essentially from other teachers of Judaism. This is also the common opinion of most men who to-day stand outside of the Christian Church. They have no doubt of Jesus' purity or of His sincerity. They think that He uttered many noble ethical maxims which are worthy of obedience, but they can see no essential difference between Him and Socrates, or Plato, or Mohammed, or Dante, or Shakespeare.

Third, there was the answer of the mass of the common people in the time of Christ. When Jesus said to Peter, "Who do men say that the Son of man is?" Peter replied, "Some say John the Baptist; some, Elijah; and others, Jeremiah, or one of the prophets." The Book of Malachi had predicted that Elijah should return, to turn the hearts of the fathers to the children, and the hearts of the children to the fathers; and many of the people thought that this prediction was fulfilled in Jesus. Others noticed that He came with the same message as John the Baptist, "Repent ye, for the kingdom of heaven is at hand," and they concluded that John had come to life again. Others thought that He most resembled Jeremiah, and still others did not try to identify Him with a particular character of the Old Testament, but said simply, He is one of the prophets; that is, they recognized in Him a divine inspiration that lifted Him above all ordinary teachers, but they could not see that He differed in any essential way from Moses, or Elijah, or Isaiah, or any of the other prophets of the Old Covenant.

This view concerning Jesus has been widely prevalent at different times in the Christian Church. It is the view of our Unitarian brethren, and of large numbers in other denominations. They see that Jesus is more than an ordinary sage, that a special divine illumination must be recognized in Him, but they can see no fundamental distinction between Him and other prophets whom from time to time God has raised up to bring a message to men.

Fourth, there was the answer of Peter and the other apostles. When, after asking, "Who say men that I am?" Jesus continued, "But who say ye that I am?" Peter as the spokesman of the Twelve replied,

" Thou art the Messiah, the Son of the living God." That is to say, he recognized in Jesus the fulfilment of all the Old Testament predictions concerning the coming of a glorious personage, endued with the sevenfold spirit of God, who should appear in the name and in the majesty of God to overcome the enemies of Israel, to destroy sin, and to establish the kingdom of righteousness, peace, and truth for evermore upon earth; and more than this, he recognized in Him such a unique relation to God, that it was possible to speak of Him as " the Son of the living God " in a sense in which it was possible to speak of no other man.

This was the view of the early Church when it went forth to conquer the world for Jesus. It was the view of Paul, the apostle of the Gentiles, and it has been the view of the great multitude of Christians in all ages since.

These, then, were the answers that men gave to Jesus' question, " Who say ye that I am? " at the time when that question was first put; and they are the answers that men have been giving ever since. The fact that there are so many different replies cannot fail to perplex the thoughtful mind. If even the men of Christ's own day could not agree in regard to Him, and if ever since men have not been able to agree, how can we hope in these latter days to answer this question with certainty for ourselves? The problem is formidable, but much light is shed upon it when we consider who the people were that gave these different answers to Christ's question, and observe that those who gave the lowest definition were those who knew least about Him, and that those who gave the highest definition were those who knew most about Him. Let us look at each of the answers from this point of view.

Those who pronounced Jesus an impostor were the scribes and the Pharisees who knew little or nothing about Him except that He did not agree with their views. They would have scorned to have stood with the common crowd in the market-place, or on the sea-shore, and to have listened to His words. That would have been as strange as for an archbishop to sit at the feet of a street preacher of the Salvation Army. They would not follow Jesus about from town to town to hear all that He had to say and to see all His wonderful works. It was enough for them to know that He did not agree with them for them to condemn Him; they did not find it necessary to look more closely into His doctrine. They had their paid spies out watching Him, and they sent some of their number from time to time to propound questions through which they hoped He would be entrapped into saying something that could be construed as blasphemy or treason; but, beyond the garbled stories that these emissaries brought back,

they had no knowledge of Him. These blind, prejudiced men, who had no first-hand knowledge of Jesus, and whose sole effort was to destroy Him, were the only ones who pronounced Him an impostor. Their opinion is of little importance in the matter.

Those who pronounced Jesus a great teacher were the men who knew a little more about Him. They felt that it was unfair to condemn anyone without a hearing, and they resolved to investigate the young teacher of Galilee on their own behalf. Men like Nicodemus came to Him by night to learn more about His doctrine; and as they listened to Him, and saw the nobility of His thought and the sincerity of His purpose, they became convinced that, whatever else He was, He was not an impostor. No man could teach as He taught unless He were good and true. Accordingly, with their more perfect knowledge, they felt compelled to give up the theory of their associates that Jesus was a deceiver, and to advance the theory that He was a pious rabbi sent by God to help men understand and keep the law.

Those who pronounced Jesus a prophet were the multitude that accompanied Him from town to town. They had heard all of His sermons, they had seen all of His mighty deeds, they knew Him far more completely than the timid rabbis who came to Him only occasionally by night. They knew Him better than any others, except the inner circle of the Twelve; and, in the light of that fuller knowledge, they saw that they could not stop short with the theory that He was only a great teacher. No man could speak as He spoke, no man could do the miracles of healing that He did, unless God were with Him in a peculiar way. They saw that He spoke with authority, and not as the scribes; that they could not classify Him among the rabbis whose business it was to expound an already given law, but that they must at least recognize Him as standing on an equality with the prophets of the Old Covenant as one enlightened in peculiar measure by the Spirit of God.

Those who pronounced Jesus the Messiah, the Son of the living God, were the Twelve, who knew Jesus with an intimacy that is without a parallel in the history of human relationships. They were His constant companions throughout the whole of His ministry. Together they trudged with Him over the dusty roads of Syria, beneath the blazing light of an unclouded sun. Together they watched with Him on the lonely mountainside in the cold Syrian nights. They saw Him in the hour of triumph and in the hour of apparent defeat. They saw Him at the wedding-feast and by the bedside of the dying, in joy and in sorrow, in strength and in weakness, in health and in sickness, by day and by night. Every phase of His thought and character was familiar to them, and through all, the wonderful impression was made upon them that He was a sinless man. One of them speaking of Him said, " He was holy, harmless, undefiled, separate from sinners "; and another said, " He was tempted in all points like as we are, yet without sin." Other men may have been saints to the world at large, but never to their intimate associates. The members of their families, their close companions, their servants, have been only too well aware of their shortcomings. But these associates of Jesus, who had the opportunity to watch Him so closely, could find no flaw in Him.

We cannot say that they esteemed Him thus highly because their standards of judgment were low. They were Jews, who had been trained in the righteousness of the law and of the prophets, and that was no low sort of righteousness. Besides, they had been under the tuition of Jesus Himself, and no one ever set the standard of conduct so high as He. He taught that righteousness consisted in the inner state of the heart, rather than in the outer act, and He said to His disciples, " Except your righteousness shall exceed the righteousness of the scribes and the Pharisees, ye shall in no wise see the kingdom of God." Judged by His own lofty standard they found Him faultless.

Nor can we say that the standard of the age in which the first disciples lived was a low one, and that, judged by the higher standards of our own day, Jesus does not stand the test. This is true of many other teachers of the Church. Luther, in spite of all his glorious service, was a rough, violent man, for many of whose acts his followers need to apologize. Calvin, in spite of all the good that he did, burnt Servetus at the stake; and many a loyal Calvinist of to-day would give his right hand if he could blot that deed from the page of history. But in the life of Jesus there is nothing for which His followers need to apologize. The ages have come and have gone, mankind has progressed wonderfully in the arts and the sciences, but no higher moral ideal has been attained than that exprest in His life. Far from being left behind by the advance of civilization, He still remains the unattained ethical ideal toward which the world is struggling. The verdict of the first disciples has been the verdict of each succeeding age. As we study closely the story of His life recorded in the gospels, we are constrained to acknowledge with those who knew Him so intimately that He was a sinless man.

Recognizing the sinlessness of Jesus, the Twelve were forced to give some explanation of this fact, and they saw clearly that all the other theories that were held in their day were inadequate to explain the personality of their Master. A sinless man could not be an impostor. A sinless man was more than a great teacher, more even than a prophet of the Old Testament, for the prophets were men of like passions with ourselves. The unblemished purity of Jesus they could explain only by recognizing that He stood in a relation to God different from that held by any other man, that God was manifest in Him in a unique way, that He was one with the Father in a unique sense; and, therefore, when Jesus solemnly put the question to them, " Who say ye that I am? " the only answer that they could give was, " Thou art the Messiah, the Son of the living God."

Intimate as was the relation of the Twelve to Jesus, there was one who knew Him even better than they, and that one was Jesus Himself. Long before the mystery of His sinlessness had dawned upon them it had dawned upon Him, and had prest for an interpretation. From earliest childhood He had been conscious of an unbroken fellowship with God, which enabled Him to look up and say, " My Father," in a way that none of us can say, who bear in our consciences the burden of sin. At His baptism in Jordan He had heard a voice saying, " Thou art my beloved Son in whom I am well pleased." In the wilderness He was subjected to the three chief temptations to which men fall a prey, and was victorious. Throughout His life He never once knew an interruption of perfect communion with His Father, and He was able to pray, " Father I know that thou hearest me always." Many of Jesus' prayers are recorded for us in the gospels, but in no one of them do we find the note of contrition that is so fundamental in the prayers of all other holy men. Judged by His own lofty standard of character, He could find no sin to confess. Other religious leaders have prayed often with their disciples, and have taught them by example how they ought to pray, but there is no record that Jesus ever prayed with His disciples. He could not do so, because He could not join in the cry of penitence that must be the first word of the petition of other men. To His disciples He said, " After this manner pray ye, Forgive us our debts, as we forgive our debtors," but He never joined in that prayer, for He knew that He had no sin to confess. Even at the end of His life, when the shadows were closing in about Him, and He knew that the cross stood immediately before—even then we see no sign of contrition. In the presence of death, if never before, other men are constrained to cry out, " God be merciful to me a sinner "; but, instead of that, we find Jesus praying, " I have glorified thee on the earth, I have finished the work which thou gavest me to do. And now, O Father, glorify thou me with the glory which I had with thee before the world was " (John 17 : 4).

It was this consciousness of sinlessness that forced home upon Jesus the same question that He put to His disciples, "Who say ye that I am?" and, long before they had been able to give an answer to that question, He had answered it for Himself. He knew that His sinlessness and unbroken fellowship with God could have no explanation except that, in a unique way, true of no other man, He was one with the Father. Long before the confession of Peter He had said to Himself, "Thou art the Messiah, the Son of the living God." But He did not force this conviction upon His disciples. Faith that rested merely upon His authority would have little value. He wished rather to have His followers reach this conclusion for themselves on the basis of their own observation; then their faith would be a possession that could not be taken from them. Accordingly, He waited until the very end of His ministry before He called upon them to decide who He was. After they had heard all His gracious words, after they had seen all His miracles, after they had come to know Him under every circumstance of life,

then, when all the evidence that He had to offer was in, He turned solemnly to them and said, "Who say ye that I am?" and when Peter as the spokesman of the Twelve replied, "Thou art the Messiah, the Son of the living God," that answer came as no surprise to Jesus. We do not find Him putting it away from Him as a temptation, and saying to Peter, "No Peter, you must not speak of me in that way." Nor do we find Him dallying with the thought, as something in regard to which He Himself was in perplexity, and saying to Peter, "Do you really think that I am so great a personage as that?" Instead of this, we find only the prompt and glad acceptance of the confession, as of something that He had long hoped to hear, "Blessed art thou Simon Bar-Jonah, for flesh and blood hath not revealed it unto thee, but my Father which is in heaven. . . . Upon this rock I will build my Church and the gates of Hades shall not prevail against it."

FRANCIS L. PATTON

1843-1932

GLORIFICATION THROUGH DEATH

BIOGRAPHICAL NOTE

FRANCIS LANDEY PATTON, Presbyterian minister and educator, was born in Bermuda in 1843. He studied at Knox College, Toronto, and Princeton Seminary, New Jersey. From 1865 to 1871 he held many pastorates, but in the latter year his work as a controversialist and educator began. He took a prominent part in the ecclesiastical trials of Prof. David Swing and Dr. C. A. Briggs, and was elected to succeed Dr. McCosh in the presidency of Princeton in 1888, but resigned in 1902, after which he was elected president of the Princeton Seminary. He was a deep thinker and dialectician, and a vigorous speaker on the theological subjects in which he was interested.

Verily, verily, I say unto you, except a corn of wheat fall into the ground and die, it abideth alone; but if it die, it bringeth forth much fruit.—John xii., 24.

WE all know that it was necessary for Christ to die, and that his path lay through the valley of the shadow of death. I do not take this text to illustrate this idea, but to concern myself with a line of illustration which has no reference to His death, and so will avoid the suggestion. We have here, in the first place, the enunciation of a principle which goes far toward unifying the moral and spiritual history of our world. Glorification through death is a principle that may be seen in various spheres of observation, and in the relation of the individual to the race. For instance, a man of ordinary education has a family of boys and girls. He has reached that time of life, the sure sign of middle age, perhaps a little beyond, when he ceased to raise the question that he has been raising about himself, How shall I make the best of myself? and he begins to raise the question—the only question he thinks of after that—What shall I do for them? "Well," he says, "I had but a limited education; they shall have the best the country can give or they are willing to take. I had but few opportunities; there is no lack of opportunity for them. I had many a rough encounter when I first set out in the world; they shall have the advantage of my accumulated earnings to set them up in life."

Sure enough, the boys grow up and fill positions that the father and mother did not fill, and could not fill; and by and by they all come home again, and as they look on the dead man's face they say, or rather they seem to say, "Father did well by us," and they may very well say it. His hand had wrought for them; his head had thought for them; his heart had beat for them; this is the long result—the father lies in his coffin, and the children go their several ways in life, and repeat in their own experience the story; and so "the individual withers, and the world is more and more."

And this principle of glorification through death is illustrated further in the fact that, when the lower forms of life or civilization disappear to make room for the higher, the one dominating phase of the doctrine of evolution is the seeming unity with which it invests everything; because, imagine it true, and there at once you see how moving are the poet's words:

I held it truth, with him who sings
  To one clear harp in divers tones,
  That men may rise on stepping-stones
Of their dead selves to higher things.

This is the story not of the potential, but of the actual. And what is true of the material world is true of the spiritual world. The history of the spiritual world is a history of displacement. You may account for it by the love of glory or by the sentiment of revenge, but we know that God's glory is the final cause, and it is all explicable upon the great scale of divine providence. We all understand that there is a definite relationship between our present and the past, and that we to-day are the heirs of all that civilization that has gone. Our acts are the result of all that has gone before. They were the seed and we are the harvest: "Except a corn of wheat fall into the earth and die, it abideth alone; but if it die, it bringeth forth much fruit." The mass of this early civilization survives in the civilization of to-day. Where do you go to find the origin of the great principle of civil liberty? Where do you go, but to that crowd of sturdy peoples who lived along the banks of the Rhine, and whom Tacitus describes, or to those sturdy barons at Runnymede who extorted the Magna Charta from King John? It is just as true in the sphere of science or philosophy. It is a far cry back to Thales of Miletus, and yet our own boasted century, the nineteenth, and this which may have boasts of its own, has a close relation to the civilization of the very far past. Our astronomy is different from their astrology, and our chemistry is different from their alchemy, but they are closely associated. We see further than they did sometimes, just because we are as pigmies borne on the shoulders of a giant.

This principle of glorification through death is illustrated once more in that a new and expanded form of life is the fruit of death. Take the railroad at the proper season of the year, and see the corn standing as a dazzling glory in the fertile fields of the golden West. Mark how towers herald the approach to the towns and cities, and ask what they stand there for? These are the nation's treasure-houses. These are the storehouses of the world. This is the annual coronation of nature, and simply so many illustrations of the text: "Except a corn of wheat fall into the earth and die, it abideth alone; but if it die it bringeth forth much fruit."

Change the illustration and borrow one from the humbler phases of the animal world, like the caterpillar, which eats up the floor of the leaf on which it creeps, until, by and by, as it begins to realize that its life is nearly done, it sets its house in order, turns undertaker, weaves itself a silken shroud, and awaits the dawning of its resurrection day, and soars away a bright-winged butterfly—a beautiful illustration of the text: "Except a corn of wheat fall into the earth and die, it abideth alone; but if it die, it bringeth forth much fruit." That is the story of our life. We are born, and we grow; we go on our way, renew our infancy with impaired faculties, and then we pass away. Life is a battle, and we win our greatest victory when we lie down on that battle-field and die. Life is a race, and the goal is at the grave. Life is a journey, and the path that we take lies straight for the valley of the shadow of death. The valley is dark, but beyond the darkness and across the river I see the lights of the celestial city; I get an echo of the angels' song, and the glimpse that I get tells me that it is worth all it costs to die.

The principle of glorification through death is illustrated in the death of Judaism. Judaism was a divinely founded institution—a theological seminary. The purpose of it was to disseminate the knowledge of the one living and true God. With the approach of the pagan world and Christianity it gathered up its energies to give birth to Jesus of Nazareth. That is what it existed for; and in the throes of the birth-struggle Judaism died. Let us not speak reproachfully of Judaism, for the glory of Christianity is the glory of Judaism with an added glory: "Except a corn of wheat fall into the earth and die, it abideth alone; but if it die, it bringeth forth fruit."

Once more (for this is our Lord's own illustration concerning Himself), the principle of glorification through death is illustrated in the death and resurrection of our Lord Jesus Christ Himself. We see Jesus made a little lower than the angels and crowned with glory and honor. He suffered that we might conquer. He drank the bitter cup in order that we might taste something of the sweetness of the joys of His Father's house. He has settled the question of His own place, and of our place too, in the scale of being. The question whether the finite and the infinite can ever come together has been solved in the doctrine of the incarnation. We do not want any more to sing the old song, which never amounted to very much in the way of music or poetry:

I want to be an angel,
  And with the angels stand,
A crown upon my forehead,
  A harp within my hand.

We do not want anything of the sort. Angels never rise so high nor stand so low as man. They know nothing about sin or repentance or salvation through Jesus Christ, and are not worthy to sit with Him who judges the ten tribes of Israel.

This text not only fastens on us this principle of glorification through death, but, in the second place, it gives us a twofold vindication of death: the first being the perils of survivorship, and the second being the promise of grace. Death is one of the most philosophical things in the world; and if you put yourselves in the right attitude toward it, it is one of the kindest agencies in nature. There is such a thing as a time to die; for two reasons at least.

One is the solitude of old age—the peril of survivorship—"Except, a corn of wheat fall into the ground and die, it abideth alone"; it abideth alone. You can imagine a person very old. His eyes have grown dim. Generations have grown old and died, but he still lives on. He is too old to take kindly to the new ideas, or to see much reason for the changes taking place. He is too old to have an interest in the present, too old to have any friends, and at last he lives, and lives, and lives, until he seems like a monumental intrusion into the present, an object that people stop to look at when they are in a reflective mood and wish to mark the flight of years. Who would not court a new-made grave rather than risk the perils of survivorship?

Then there is the promise of grace. Our blest Lord hallowed the grave by His presence, and left it upon the morning of the third day. The promise of Christ gives us a connection with His own glorious resurrection; and planted with Him in His death, we shall be with Him in His glory. And so the message comes to you and to me: Be not afraid. Do not hesitate to go down, even into the grave. Our Lord has not made it unnecessary for us to die, but He has robbed death of its terrors. He has made easy the approach; He has festooned the entrance with flowers; and we ride through its portals, singing as we go, "O grave, where is thy victory? O death, where is thy sting?" and we turn to discover that the door of death is the gate of heaven.

Again, this text teaches one other truth. As we read it, we can not very well help being imprest with the idea that there is embodied in it the thought that there are two contrasted modes of being: a fruitless conservation and a prolific decay. The seed corn is very tenacious of life, and there is a story that grains taken from an Egyptian mummy have been planted and have germinated in English gardens. I believe that this is not so, but the tenacity of wheat in respect to life is true. It abideth; but it abideth alone. Let it reproduce itself, and by and by there will be enough of harvest to feed a nation. We must make a choice between a fruitless conservation and prolific decay. And this choice comes to us in so many ways. We see it in the sphere of prejudice. Prejudice is often, but it is not always, right. It is very often misplaced or perpetuated beyond a time when it does any good. (You never find a man cherishing a prejudice, because he says he is "standing up for a principle.") It was good enough when

he started; it served its purpose at first; but it has outlived its usefulness, and is now just a prejudice. A good many years ago, at the foundation of the London Missionary Society, a speaker said, "We stand to-day at the funeral of bigotry." There is not a word of objection to that, except that these obsequies have been so unduly protracted. God send the day when men shall recognize the lineament of Jesus Christ in one another's face, whether they be Presbyterians, Episcopalians, or what! And this principle, this choice, whether there shall be a conservation that is fruitless, or an expenditure that is generous, meets us everywhere. It meets us in our relationship to the past. There is a sort of medievalism cherished and fostered by some people with an odor of sanctity—they love things which are old. And there is a vandalism that destroys the old, and worships the new, because it is new. My friends, they are both wrong. Let us look at our inheritance of the past in proof of this. Hold fast to that which is true, and do not hold anything that is not. Read the great formularies of worship with the critical light of modern thought, and hold on to that which is true. The Jerusalem Chamber is not holy ground, the Westminster divines were not inspired. If they said what was true, it is because of the truth of what they say that we hold on to it, not because they said it. And what is true in regard to these formulas holds true in reference to our own individual life. But there are times, I suppose, when people who live in a city as busy as this is, and where the engagements of the week run over into two weeks, and where every hour has its own employment, there are times, I suppose, even here that people have leisure to sit still while the fire burns; and in these choice stolen hours, I suppose, figures of long ago come out upon the canvas, and stand there in bold relief; and we say that they were happy days. Imagine that dear old room, and those pictures of long ago coming before us, when our imagination was all aglow. I can imagine that the door-bell might ring, and that one of those that we have not seen for fifty years was announced. I can imagine the conversation that would ensue. We would talk excitedly for twenty minutes, and then the conversation would flag, and before the hour was up we would be completely disillusioned, and would see that our paths had diverged. All that sort of thing was good in its way and time, but it is not the time for it now. Of course, we must have a foundation for the house. Still we do not live in the cellar. We live upstairs in the sunlight, and experience says we do well. These past incidents of life are just the foundation, and it is the superstructure after all that you build upon; and unless a man is willing to part with the past, he is going to make a mistake. Unless we learn to do better to-day the things that we did yesterday, and paint a better picture to-day, and write a better poem than the last, and are more proficient in our arts, we are just as good as dead. We are eternally improving and moving on. There is a conservation, stedfast and still; and there is a forgetfulness and a generous prodigality of past attainments that is prolific of vast results. There is your health. What are you going to do with it? You had better wear out than rust out any day. You can see people who make themselves obnoxious to you by their everlasting attitude of complaint. There is something better for a man to do than to take care of his health, and he will probably live longer if he does not. Is a man who has an intellect expected to have nothing better to do than to play nurse to his body that he has to summer in the North, and winter in the South, and to clothe with purple and fine linen, and fare sumptuously every day, and give it now and then a trip to Europe—a body that is bound to die? There is your life. What are you going to do with it? There is your money. What are you going to do with it? Why, invest it, and be careful about your security, and don't be careful about the interest, and keep on investing and reinvesting, until it will take the figures of astronomy to count it. As fortunes go now, astronomy is not in it. Invest it, and then what do you do? There are so many things that some people might do and do do, that so many more people might do. They might perpetuate their names by doing some-

thing for the Church, for education, and for the world, and its moral, spiritual, and intellectual advance. God be praised for this! You, who have cast your bread of benevolence upon the waters of Christian philanthropy hope that you will receive it after many days. This world's history shows that our forests have not been cleared by the brawn of men who lived in comfortable homes. How have our liberties been secured? By the blood of men who counted no service too great. Can we do that? William of Orange might have lived a long life, but he stript himself of land and fortune, and planted himself in deadly opposition to Alva, and died a monument to the fall of Spanish tyranny. Yes, my friends, in humbler spheres it is your privilege, and mine, in the house of this tabernacle, to choose between the alternative of a conservation which is fruitless and an expenditure that is substantial, generous, and prodigal. It is a choice for us to make. Wrap yourselves in your mummy folds, and live for yourself or, in generous forgetfulness, live for God and country, and for fellow men while you live, and when the hour comes, without fear, if need be, drop into the ground and die.

Help us, O Lord, to endure as good soldiers of Jesus Christ. Help us to do our duty so completely that every day we do better and become better and be with Christ. Help us that we may be ready for death, and in that last encounter may be as brave as in all the other encounters of our lives. Give us this faith to the end. For Christ's sake. Amen.

ARTHUR T. PIERSON

1837-1911

OUR LORD'S PRIMARY LESSON IN THE SCHOOL OF PRAYER

BIOGRAPHICAL NOTE

EDITOR-IN-CHIEF of *The Missionary Review of the World;* born in New York City, March 6, 1837; graduated Hamilton College, 1857; and Union Theological Seminary, 1860; ordained to the gospel ministry as an evangelist in May the same year; pastor of the First Congregational church, Binghamton, N. Y., 1860-63; Presbyterian church, Waterford, N. Y., 1863-69; Fort Street Presbyterian church, Detroit, Mich., 1869-82; Second Presbyterian church, Indianapolis, Ind., 1882,3; Bethany Presbyterian church, Philadelphia, 1883-89; Metropolitan Tabernacle, London, England, 1891-93; Duff lecturer on missions in Scotland, 1891-94; Graves lecturer at New Brunswick, etc.; author of "Miracles of Missions," "Crisis of Missions," "George Müller of Bristol," "Forward Movements of the Last Half Century," etc.

" Thou, when thou prayest, enter into thy closet."—Matt. 6 : 6.

THREE things stand out prominently in this brief injunction; first, the individual approach to God; second, the secret place of communion; third, the specific object, prayer.

The word, " closet," is unusual. The original word is found but four times in the New Testament, in one instance being rendered, " secret chambers," and in another, " storehouse." The words here used by our Lord closely resemble those of Isaiah 26 : 20: " Come, my people, enter thou into thy chambers, and shut thy doors about thee."

There is in both cases marked emphasis on the singular number of the second personal pronoun. In Isaiah, the opening call is plural, or collective, " Come, my people," but immediately changes to the singular, " Enter thou into thy chambers," and so, in our Lord's adaptation of these words, conspicuous stress is laid on the singular, " thou." The injunction is intensely individual. " But *thou,* when *thou* prayest, enter into *thy* closet; and when *thou* hast shut *thy* door pray to *thy* Father, who is in secret, and *thy* Father shall reward *thee* openly." Eight times, in so brief a space, is the singular pronoun used, surely not without purpose.

What do these four words suggest: " Enter into thy closet "? Closet means simply a close, a closed place, shut in for privacy, shut out from intrusion and interruption. To Jewish hearers such language would naturally suggest the one place that was preeminently a secret chamber—the inmost court of tabernacle and temple, where God specially dwelt, known as the holy of holies.

That was preeminently a secret chamber, a closed place, having neither door nor window; unlike many an Oriental court which is open to the sky, it was roofed in and without skylight. It was always shut. A door which we open, as we enter a room, we must also close behind us; but the veil in front of the holiest of all, raised as the high priest went in, fell back as soon as it was released, and so kept the secrecies of God's chamber shut out from mortal eyes.

Here then was one place, peculiarly marked by silence, secrecy, solitude and separation. Only one person ever entered here, at a time, " the high priest, once every year, alone." Two parties never met there save himself and God. It was, in a unique sense, the place of which God could say, " Thou and I "—the one closet, shut-in place, secret chamber for the meeting of one man with his Maker.

Moreover, its one conspicuous solitary article of furniture was the mercy-seat, the appointed meeting place, the basis of fellowship between the suppliant and the Hearer of prayer. And thus the three conditions, suggested by the injunction, " Enter into thy closet," were met here as nowhere else; here was the secret chamber, the individual approach and the prayerful communion.

Here we have the key to this first lesson on prayer: the " closet " is the holy of holies where the praying soul meets God alone, and communes with Him at the blood-sprinkled mercy-seat.

The highest prayer is impossible, save as the human suppliant deliberately seeks to meet God absolutely alone. To secure such aloneness we are bidden to " enter into the closet," to find some place and time where we may shut ourselves in with Him. This is made emphatic by repetition in another form: " And when thou hast shut thy door, pray to thy Father, who is in secret," a second word here used meaning essentially the same as closet—a secret place.

In praying, we need some place and time, free from needless interruption and intrusion. The eyelid drops over the organ of vision, shutting out all external objects; and, if the ear were similarly supplied with an earlid, to shut out all sounds, as the eyelid does all sights, a closet could be instantly found and entered even in the throng, and the spirit might secretly commune with God in the crowded streets or assemblies.

But, in the absence of any such natural provision for such complete seclusion and exclusion, our Lord counsels us, when we pray, to get somehow, somewhere, a silent, secret communing place with God, as not only the very basis of prayer, but of all holy living built upon prayer. The more completely we can separate ourselves from all others, worldly pursuits and pleasures, distracting cares and diverting thoughts, shutting out all else but God, the more perfect is the fitness of the hour and place to the purpose. Those who know how needful and helpful such a secret time and place for prayer are, will secure, at any cost, the silent season even tho, like the psalmist, they rise before others wake, and " prevent the dawning of the morning."

Every praying soul needs to meet God absolutely alone. There are inner secrets which no other human being however intimate ought to know, or indeed can know.

" The heart knoweth his own bitterness;
 And a stranger doth not intermeddle with his joy."

We turn ourselves inside out not even to a bosom friend: we would not if we could, and could not if we would. To the inmost secret chambers there is no open door; they are locked and sealed; words supply no key to them, and the seal of silence and secrecy is inviolable. But " all things are naked and opened unto the eyes of Him with whom we have to do "; and so the closet, where we meet God alone and only, is the one place for all such secrets. Nothing else will supply its place. Public worship, the " family altar," or the more private prayer in which only husband and wife join before God—none of these can take the place of the solitary closet. In one respect they who are " one flesh," are still " twain "; for neither can ever fully know the other. But while, to our most intimate friend we cannot reveal everything, from God we can conceal nothing. His omniscient eye pierces to the secret chambers, despite the lock which no man can pick, the seal which no man dares break. He reads the thoughts yet " afar off," like forms faintly seen in the dim distance, and hears the word yet unspoken " in the tongue," And it is as to these secrets which must be brought to the light in His presence, exposed, confessed, renounced, corrected before Him, that the closet is meant to give facility and freedom for converse with God. Hence this initial command to cultivate habitual aloneness with Him. Like Jacob at Peniel, each suppliant must be " left alone " at times: the " thou " must be absolute and not the " ye," when the closet is entered.

Why now is such stress laid, in our Lord's primary lesson on prayer, upon this shutting out of all else, and closing in of the suppliant with God?

It is, first of all, in order to what, as his third instrument of " Holy Living," Jeremy Taylor calls " the practise of the presence of God."

Nothing else has such an effect upon character and conduct, as this sense of God's presence; and nothing is so difficult, nay impossible of attainment, so long as we neglect God's appointed means.

God is a Spirit, and must be worshiped in the spirit. Invisible, inaudible, intangible, He cannot be tested by the senses: they utterly fail as channels of impression or communication. His subtle essence evades all carnal approach or analysis. He must therefore be otherwise known, if at all: the spirit alone has the higher senses which, being exercised to discern good and evil, can enable us to perceive God and hold communication with Him. Hence, to those who live a sinful or even worldly life, and are carnally minded, even the reality and verity of His existence become matters of practical, if not theoretical, doubt. There is much virtual atheism in mere unbelief. It is possible to recite the creed, " I believe in God, the Father Almighty," without ever for one moment having had a real, true sense of the presence of God. Many who do not deny that God is, do not know that He is.

Such sense of the divine existence, and realization of the divine presence may be cultivated. God has appointed two means, which, when used jointly, never fail: first a meditative reading of Holy Scripture, and secondly a habitual communion with Him in the closet. These two are so closely related, that they are not only mutually helpful, but operate upon us in ways almost precisely alike Both introduce us into God's secret chambers.

When a devout disciple takes up God's Word for studious thought, he naturally lifts his heart to Him who alone can unveil the eyes of his understanding to behold wondrous things out of His law. As he reads and searches, meditating therein, the same Spirit who first inspired the Word, illumines his mind. New light is thrown upon the sacred page, so that what was obscure or hidden, becomes visible and legible; and new clearness of sight and insight is given so that spiritual vision becomes more capable of seeing, more keen-sighted and far-sighted.

Those who have felt this double effect of the Spirit's teaching bear witness that the Bible becomes a transformed book. Best of all books before, it is now the Book of God—a house of many mansions, in which new doors constantly open into new apartments, massive and magnificent, God's art galleries, museums of curious things, chambers of disclosed mysteries, treasuries of celestial gems. The devout student is transported with wonder and delight. Words open with new meanings, affording glimpses into depths and heights, breadths and lengths, that are infinite. Looking at a firmament which was before clouded, the clouds are parting and heavenly constellations are visible. Meanwhile the eye has become telescopic; and where before were seen a few scattered stars or an indistinct nebulous cloud, everything is ablaze with the glories of countless and many colored lights. When the Author of the Word becomes Instructor and Interpreter of His own text-book, heaven's great classic is read with the notes and comments of the divine Author himself; and so he who devoutly searches the Scriptures, finds in them both eternal life and the testimony of Jesus; the reverent, prayerful study of the Word of God is the cure of all honest doubt as to its divine origin, and the all-convincing proof of its plenary inspiration.

But, as the First Psalm reminds us, to find such delight in the law of the Lord, one must meditate therein day and night; be a sort of sacramental tree of life, planted by the rivers of water. Mark the instructive, emphatic

metaphor. A tree is permanently planted in the soil. Its roots are fixed organs of nutrition, constantly subordinate to the double purpose of growth and fruitfulness. Through the spongelets at the extremities of the roots, the tree takes up the water of the river into itself, transmuting it into sap which deposits woody fiber in the branches and becomes juice in the fruit. The disciple, planted by the river of God—the Word which goeth forth out of His mouth, takes up into himself the very water of life, translating truth into character, and precepts and promises into practise. He reads God's Word and, like the cattle that chew the cud, ruminates upon it; and so comes to know God through His Word, as we know men through candid and self-revealing utterances. To meditate on God's words introduces us to the secret chambers of God's thoughts, and imparts insight into God's character. One becomes sure there is a God, who sees Him unveiled in the Scriptures, hears His still small voice in their audience chambers, traces His footprints on their golden pavements; and, in times of temptation, trial, sorrow, or doubt, God's words, brought to remembrance, and applied by the Spirit to his needs, become, individually, God's words to him. He consults the oracles of God, and they give answer. This is to the unbelieving one of the closed mysteries, a stumbling-block of mysticism, or the foolishness of fanaticism; but, to him whose experience has been enriched by it, an open mystery, a fact as indisputable as any in the realm of matter.

The other method of the practise of the presence of God is communion with Him in the closet. And how like to Scripture study is the process whereby prayer introduces to His fellowship! It implies meditation; opens the secret chambers and reveals God; discloses marvels and unlocks mysteries; makes one sure that God " is and is a rewarder of them that diligently seek him," which is the divinely declared condition of all acceptable, prevailing approach!

Upon this method of cultivating acquaintance with God, the great Teacher would specially fix attention in this, His primary lesson on prayer.

All other presence hinders the practise of the presence of God. The thought of human auditors or observers prevents the closest approach and the highest power in prayer. At the very moment when the supreme need is that all the faculties and activities of the being shall be converged and concentrated, centralized and facilized, as are scattered rays of light by a concave speculum or a convex lens, the mind is diverted and distracted, and the attention divided, by the thought that another human being hears or sees. Such divided attention must hinder the realization of the presence of the unseen God. Nor is it hard to see the reason why.

That profound lesson, taught the Samaritan woman on the subject of worship, includes prayer as one of its highest forms or acts. God, being a spirit, must be worshiped as such, and can be approached only by what is spiritual in man. There is among men bodily contact and communion, as when hand joins hand, eye looks into eye, or words pass from one mouth to another ear. But, as God can neither be seen, heard, nor touched, there can be no such sensible contact between man and God; being a spirit, He can be approached only spiritually, that is by contact between our spirits and His.

In order to such contact, and that it may be real, recognized and conscious, all the spiritual faculties need to be active, on the alert; and all diversions or distractions of mind must be avoided which make impossible exclusive attention to the divine object of thought. But we are so constituted as to be unable really to fix attention on more than one subject or object at a time. Hence, in God's economy of nature, many necessary acts are so provided for as to be automatic, like walking, only half conscious and semi-voluntary; for, were it needful to concentrate all attention upon every step, we could, while walking, give heed to nothing else.

Moreover, we cannot fully exercise any one sense while any of the others is fully exercised and occupied, there being room for but one thorough sense-impression at a time. We cannot fix the eye upon a picture so as to study its effects in drawing and coloring, and yet at the same time give our ears to the hearing of a masterpiece of music, so as to observe critically its melody and harmony.

Especially do we find that, to occupy the physical senses is so far to divert the mind from purely intellectual processes however simple. For instance, in some late experiments in psychology, the test was made, how far an observer, watching rapid changes of color, could detect the delicate transitions from one shade to another; and it was found that if, while so engaged, the simplest exercise in mental arithmetic were attempted, tho only the addition or multiplication table, the power to discern these gradual changes of color was arrested. Man is constituted to do properly and thoroughly, but one thing at once.

Acquaintance with the unseen God is the first of all acquisitions. To attain the closest approach, to get the most vivid sense of His presence, and so, the greatest power and blessing at the mercy-seat, all thought of men and of this world must be shut out, and all interruptions avoided that come through the senses or the imagination. So far only as we learn the art of thinking only of God, will this great lesson of closet prayer be learned, for, on the

measure of our realization of the unseen Presence, all else must depend.

Our Lord's first lesson on prayer gives another hint of great value, tho rather implied than openly exprest. He tells us that the Father who is in secret, or in the secret place, and who sees in the darkness of the soul's holy of holies, rewards the suppliant openly—"in the open." When the high priest approached to God it is neither recorded nor intimated that he was wont to offer up supplication; the element of petition is nowhere prominent. He seems to have gone in to the holiest, to "appear before God"—to present himself, with the blood, before the mercy-seat—his presence constituting his plea; and the blood of atonement, both the sign of his obedience and the pledge of his acceptance. There he seems to have waited not so much to offer up to God prayers and supplications, as to receive from God impressions and revelations.

The "Urim and Thummim" may have some connection with this revealing of God's mind and will. Some think that the light of the Shekinah fire, shining on the breast-plate of the high priest, made successive letters of the names with which its stones were graven, stand out conspicuous, so that he could, in characters of light, spell out the divine message; and it is a curious fact that the twelve names, taken together, contain nearly every letter of the Hebrew alphabet.

However this be, the mercy-seat was mainly a place, not of petition but of communication, of impartation from God, of divine revelation. The high priest waited there for a message which he bore back to the people in benediction.

The closet is not only an oratory—a place for prayer—but an observatory, where we may get new views and revelations of God. There is a quest higher than mere request—a search after knowledge of God and communication from Him. Here devout souls learn what is meant by communion—which is always mutual—implying not only prayer offered, but answer received. The praying soul speaks to God, and hears God speak—gets as well as gives—and finds the most precious part of this communion, not in requests imparted Godward, but in returns imparted manward, the reception of divine impressions and communications. The reward, promised, comes while yet he speaks and waits before the Lord: believing he receives, and receiving enjoys. Such a reward cannot be kept secret. It makes the heart to overflow and even the face to shine.

True prayer, in its highest form and reach, is not only impartive but receptive: the whole nature going out in adoration, thanksgiving, confession, supplication, intercession; but also opening all its channels for the incoming of blessing. Communion becomes intercommunication—Jacob's ladder resting in the closet and reaching to the throne—and angels descend to bring blessing, as well as ascend to bear petition; or, as a simple Japanese convert puts it, prayer is like the well where one bucket comes down while the other goes up, only that it is always the empty bucket that goes up and the full one that comes back.

Of this aspect of prayer, as a revelation of God to the suppliant, the current definitions take little notice. The Westminster standards define prayer as "the offering up of our desires unto God, in the name of Christ, by the help of His Spirit, with confession of our sins and thankful acknowledgment of His mercies." Here is no recognition of meditative communion with the divine Presence for the sake of a present communication from God to the soul.

With most praying people, the fundamental if not exhaustive conception of prayer is asking somewhat of God. This is surely not the whole of prayer; little more than a beginning is made without some disclosure of God to the soul. Our Lord himself at times withdrew from all human companionships, for secret communion with the Father, as when He went out "into a mountain to pray and continued all night in prayer to God." Such all-night interviews mark all great crises of His life on earth; but it cannot be supposed that He spent all these hours in continuous supplication, but rather, like Gideon, on the plains of Jezreel, spread out His whole being like fleece, to drink in the heavenly dew of the Father's presence, and in the strength of this celestial nectar confront new duties, trials and temptations.

Thus meditative prayer, like reflective reading of the Word of God, becomes a perpetual means and medium of communion with God, and so, also, of revelation of God, communion both leading to, and itself becoming, revelation. He who converses with a friend, habitually, cannot doubt his existence and presence; and God meant this simple converse with Himself to be a demonstration that He is, and is a rewarder of them that diligently seek Him—so convincing as to dispel all doubts, itself the sufficient proof of His reality and verity as the ever present, living, helping God.

The humblest believer, however unlettered or unlearned, may thus, in this school of prayer attain to practical certainty in divine things; he needs no volumes of apologetics or evidences of Christianity: in practising the presence of God, the proofs, tho he cannot always formulate them for others, become convincing to himself. Indeed we oftenest find such assurance in the humbler, simpler disciples, the ignorant and unlearned, rather than the princes or great scholars of the Church, and so there is a proneness to associate such faith with credulity, if not with superstition. Witness that abominable lying maxim, "Ignorance is the mother of devotion." But the inference is wrong; for, while the more intelligent and intellectual often lean to their own understanding, and depend on human logic and philosophy for confirmation of their faith, he who, being untaught of men and books, has no other means of strengthening his assurance save converse with God, is compelled to learn in His school, where logic and philosophy are never perverted to the purposes of fallacy and sophistry. "He that dwelleth in the secret place of the most High, abides under the shadow of the Almighty"; and no darts of Satanic doubt can pierce him, save as they first pass through the divine "wings" which are his covering and shelter.

Here, then, is our Lord's initial lesson upon prayer; and as, in any first lesson, a master teacher naturally lays down fundamental laws or first principles, here He lays the cornerstone of all true prayer, namely: Prayer is at bottom the meeting of a human suppliant alone with God, for supplication and communion at the mercy-seat, and revelation of the existence, presence and character of God.

It is plain why His preliminary caution is directed against hypocritical ostentation. The hypocrites "love to pray, standing in the synagogs and in the corners of the streets that they may be seen of men. Verily I say unto you, they have their reward." In praying, as in almsgiving and fasting, hypocrisy courts publicity—it is all "to be seen of men." The hypocrite's prayer is addrest to a human audience rather than to the divine ear; it has reference mainly to outward appearance and transient impression. Hence publicity is an object; and in the synagogs where the crowds throng, at the street corners or crossways commanding all points of the compass at once, he takes his stand that he may be seen of men. The formalist may not be a hypocrite, but his mind is taken up with the externals, and here again "the letter killeth," and only "the spirit giveth life."

Christ would have praying souls learn, first of all, that being seen of men is to be avoided rather than courted. To concentrate all thought and desire upon God, forget all else in order not to forget Him, and so be lost in the absorbing sense of His presence—this is the first secret of power in prayer, as also of all power in holy living and serving.

This first lesson is also the last, for there is no higher fruit of habitual closet communion with God than this new sense of divine realities. Paul gently rebukes those who have not, by reason of use, exercised their senses—trained them to keenness—to discern good and evil. The spirit as well as the body, has its senses and they are trained to acuteness and exactness by holy exercise. Imagination is the sense of the unseen; reason, the sense of truth and falsehood; conscience, the sense of right and wrong; sensibility, the sense of the attractive and repulsive; memory, the sense of the past. The understanding and heart have eyes with which to see God's beck and glance, ears with which to hear His still small voice, organs of touch wherewith to " handle " Him and see that it is He Himself. The closet is the school for the exercise and education of these senses. There we go to learn to look at things unseen, eternal; to hear the divine whisper; to catch the scent of heavenly gardens; to taste and see that the Lord is good. And to reach such results, we need aloneness with God, senses fixed upon Himself.

The closet supplies a key to many mysteries of Scripture biography, like Jacob's experience at Bethel—" Surely God was in this place and I knew it not; this "—a desert place with a stone pillow—" is none other but the house of God, and this is the gate of Heaven ": and particularly, at Peniel, where later on, he saw " the face of God " and got a lifelong blessing, the supplanter of men becoming the prince of God. It is when we are " left alone " that revelations come. Elijah was bidden first to hide himself, and then show himself unto Ahab; it was the hiding that made the showing such a power. When Elisha " went in and shut the door upon them twain and prayed unto the Lord," there came out from that secret chamber a dead child, brought back to life. Nathanael under the fig tree was holding secret converse with God; and, when Christ said to him, " Before that Philip called thee, when thou wast under the fig tree I saw thee," the guileless Israelite recognized in Him One whom he had met in the secret place, and who now as then read his thoughts.

To get such impressions of God, in closet communion, there is needful the time-element. Rapid glances always leave comparatively transient impressions, but a gaze, which takes time to fix itself on an object, takes in its whole impress so as to leave its image permanently in the mind.

True, our Lord warns us that we are not heard for our much speaking: it is not by many words or long prayers that we prevail. It is nevertheless also true that haste or hurry in prayer defeats the main end, preventing that calmness, concentration, peace and quiet of soul which helps to revelation. The word, " reflection," suggests a power to mirror divine verities and realities. To all such reflection hurry and worry are fatal. He who rushes into the presence of God, hastens through a few formal petitions, and then hastens back to outside cares and pursuits, does not tarry long enough in the secret chamber, to lose the impression of what is without, and get the impress of what is within. He does not take time to fix his gaze on the unseen and eternal, and many a so-called praying man has never once really met and seen God in the closet. His spirit, disturbed and perturbed, tossed up and down and driven to and fro by worldly thoughts and cares, can no more reflect God than a ruffled lake can mirror the heavens above it. To see God reflected in the heart-depths, one must stay long enough for the storm to be calmed, and the soul to become placid enough to mirror heaven.

When such communion does become real, prayer ceases to be mere duty and becomes delight, all sense of obligation lost in privilege. Love seeks the company of its object. If we cultivate human companionship for its own sake, mutely sitting in the presence of one whom we devotedly love, shall not our love to God make it an object to shut ourselves in with Him at times just to enjoy Him? Is there no taint of selfishness in prayer which knows no higher motive than to ask some favor? Jude bids us " pray in the Holy Ghost " as one means to keep ourselves in the love of God; as Archbishop Usher, in his last days, when his animal heat failed, kept himself in the warm sunshine. In the closet one learns to keep himself in the love of God, finding there the Sunbeam whose light illumines, whose love warms, whose life quickens. God's presence becomes the atmosphere without which spiritual life has no breath. Such habitual abiding in the presence of God, and dwelling upon His perfections develops an enamoring love, which led Zinzendorf and Tholuck to say, " I have but one passion: and it is He and He alone! "

Such God-revealing habits of prayer lay the very corner-stone of all holy living. Everything vital to godliness is nourished on closet air. Prayer is spiritual respiration and the secret place supplies its oxygen and ozone.

For example, what a power both to reveal and to prevent sin is this sense of the presence of God which is learned in secret prayer.

We must not be surprised when the communion with God that reveals Him unveils ourselves: " Whatsoever doth make manifest is light." That same Shekinah fire, which makes the golden wings and faces of the cherubim shine, pierces every disguise and shows the very thoughts and intents of the heart, like a sword piercing to the dividing asunder of soul and spirit. Secret prayer is a revelation of self as well as of God. We must endure and even invoke its searching ray:

" Search me, O God, and know my heart;
Try me and know my thoughts;
And see if there be in me any wicked way,
And lead me in the everlasting way."

Daniel was so faultless that even enemies could find nothing in him to accuse save his faith in God and his prayer to God; yet, in the presence of that Glory, even his " comeliness was turned into corruption," and Isaiah in that Presence, cried, " Wo is me; for I am a man of unclean lips and dwell in the midst of a people of unclean lips; for mine eyes have seen the King, the Lord of hosts." But all such self-revelation and self-condemnation are only blessings, for they are the result of a divine vision, and the divine answer to such self-abasement is a new communication and exaltation. When Daniel abhorred himself, he heard a voice, saying, " O Daniel, a man greatly beloved, fear not; for from the first day that thou didst set thine heart to understand and to chasten thyself before thy God, thy words were heard and I am come for thy words." When Isaiah bewailed his unclean lips, the seraph touched those same lips with a live coal from off God's altar, and said, " Lo, this hath touched thy lips, and thine iniquity is taken away, and thy sin is purged." When Peter felt so unfit for the Lord's companionship that he involuntarily besought Him to depart from him, he heard only the assuring answer, " Fear not, from henceforth thou shalt capture men alive."

This sense of the divine Presence, which reveals sin, also prevents it. In the crisis of temptation Joseph's answer to the syren voice of the tempter evinced his habit of thinking of God, and it was natural to say with himself, " How can I do this great thing and sin against God? " Paul reminds Corinthian disciples that they are the very temple—the holy of holies—of God, because His Spirit dwelleth in them; and, on the basis of this awe-inspiring fact, he builds that exhortation, " Having therefore these promises, let us cleanse ourselves from all filthiness of the flesh and spirit, perfecting holiness in the fear of God." In the hour of temptation, sudden, overwhelming, overpowering, what a safeguard is the thought, the conviction, the consciousness, " Thou, God, seest me." I can go nowhere from Thy presence. The wings of the morning are not swift enough, nor the uttermost parts of the earth far enough, to remove me from Thine eye and Thine hand. Such are the profound, devout meditations suggested by that psalm of the presence of God unsurpassed for poetry or piety. When one feels God near, searching the inmost depths of being with omniscient glance; by omnipresent companionship with us because in us, always and everywhere; and with omnipotent energy creating, upholding, strengthening—how easy and natural to do what pleases God, and say to all seductive allurements, " My heart is fixed." Only when the sense of God's presence is lost, can voluntary sin be possible.

Again, what intrepid courage in witness for God and heroic duty, this sense of His presence imparts!

Elijah, the great reformer of abuses, and rebuker of idolatry and iniquity in high places, cultivated this consciousness of God. His characteristic phrase was, " Jehovah, God of Israel, before whom I stand "—as tho he felt himself to be constantly standing in the presence of his divine Master—a servant whose eyes were to the eye and hand of that Master, watching and waiting to be guided by a beck or even a glance. Because he thus stood before God, he could stand unabashed before Ahab and Jezebel.

In the old days it was customary to open the Connecticut legislature with an " election sermon." On one occasion the chosen preacher was one of the Strong brothers, and his modesty shrank from the grave responsibility. On the way to the place of assembly, he disclosed to his brother his oppressive burden of reluctance to face such an audience, a body among whom would be found lawyers and judges, generals and statesmen, doctors of divinity and doctors of law, governors and ex-governors—the flower of the commonwealth. " How can I venture before such an audience? " " You have only to remember," answered his brother, " that other Presence, so august, that in comparison all human presence becomes utterly insignificant, and preach as in that Presence. alone." With this thought, he went fearlessly to the discharge of his duty. Rev. Dr. Samuel H. Cox recalled this incident when in a momentous crisis of his life he addrest the Evangelical Alliance with its representatives of all nations, and the thought of that same Presence nerved his fainting spirit.

So went John Baptist before Herod, Paul before Agrippa, Felix, Nero; Luther before the Diet of Worms, Knox before Queen Mary. This same sense of the Father, who never left Him alone, enabled Him whom the prophet called " The Servant of Jehovah," to go with infinite calmness before Herod, Caiaphas and Pilate, utterly careless of human opinion, indifferent alike to censure or applause, because He could say, " I do always those things which please Him! " After a severe rebuke to those who made void the commandments of God through their tradition, His disciples said, " Knowest thou that the Pharisees were offended after they heard this saying? " but He calmly answered, " Every plant which my heavenly Father hath not planted shall be rooted up." He could not modify His message on account of the opposition of the hearer, but the hearer must accommodate himself to the message; and so will every true messenger of God answer human opposers, if he is wont to cultivate and cherish the sense of the presence of God.

This practise of the presence of God is the secret of both fidelity and cheerfulness in the discharge of common duty.

Whatever helps us to holy living must be found in those secret chambers of devout study of the Word and habitual communion with a prayer-hearing God. Any burden can be borne, any trial endured, any responsibility assumed, when this sense of God is active and constant. To be about His " Father's business " was our Lord's secret of untiring service and unalloyed satisfaction; and we, His followers, work out the mission of a complete life while we feel that God works in us to will and to do!

Hence Paul wrote to Corinth: " Let every man, in that calling wherein he is found, therein abide with God." When renewing grace finds one engaged in an honest calling, however humble, he has no need to change his vocation, but only to take a new and divine partner, henceforth abiding with God in his daily sphere of work. Jesus of Nazareth wrought at the bench of a carpenter until, at thirty, He entered on His public ministry, teaching us that no workman need be ashamed of his craft when he follows it as God's servant; whether it be the bench of the carpenter, the shoemaker, or the judge; the loom of the weaver or the wheel of the potter; the desk of the author, the studio of the artist, or the throne of the emperor—wherever service is rendered to God there is a pulpit of witness, a shrine of worship.

From the letters of a humble monk, known as Brother Lawrence, it appears that, in a menial office, as cook in a convent, he was led, by this suggestion of Jeremy Taylor about the practise of God's presence, so to cultivate the habit of thinking of God as ever with him, a partner in his lowly calling, that it became easier to think of Him as present than as absent; and that convent kitchen became as another garden of Eden, and every day as one of the days of heaven upon earth.

This sense of the divine presence is in every way so helpful to prayer that in exact proportion to its vividness and constancy is prayer effective and powerful.

Every element and exercise of prayer is dependent upon it. It prompts the highest thanksgiving, for it proves that God is and reveals Him as He is: we get glimpses of His character and glory which are the inspiration of gratitude. To know what God is, is of far more consequence than to know what He does. He is love, and therefore all His outgoings are lovely and loving: the stream is as the spring.

We have seen that to realize the divine presence leads to most heart-searching contrition and confession, because in the light of His purity and holiness sin's enormity and deformity are most clearly seen; and in the contrast of the glory of His goodness our unworthiness and ungratefulness become awfully apparent. In like manner, when the mind is filled with new views of God, of His

truth and grace, and the reality and verity of His promise, supplications and intercessions become the confident appeals of those who " have boldness and access with confidence by the faith of Him."

There is thus no side or aspect of true prayer which this vision of God in the closet does not touch. Contemplation of God compels contemplation of self; a new sense of destitution, degradation, depravity; a deeper contrition, a sincerer confession; a more importunate entreaty; a new repentance toward God, a new faith in God, a new separation unto God, a new power with God.

Prayer in its highest reach, is worship—worth-ship—ascribing worth to God, describing His worth in adoring praise, inscribing His worth on the forefront of the miter, the palms of the hands, the door-posts of the house, the gates whereby we go out and in; keeping before us and others His infinite excellence. Worship is more than thanksgiving and praise, including both, but above both in adoration, the whole being going out to Him in devout words, or in groanings and raptures which cannot be 'uttered, the mute language of emotions and affections which find no adequate articulate utterance.

Worship is the form of prayer which echoes in the Apocalypse when the door is opened into heaven: " Thou art worthy, O Lord! " Redeemed throngs and angelic hosts, lost in the vision of infinite excellence and worthiness, rest not day or night from such adoration. To get new apprehension and appreciation of these adorable perfections is the ideal of prayerful communion.

In the Twenty-ninth Psalm, the Psalm of Nature, all creation is figuratively viewed as God's temple, the vast cathedral where He is throned, and all the forces of the material universe are vocal with His praise. The boom of the great waters sounds the deep diapason, the gentle breezes breathe melodies, and the peal of the thunders rolls its pedal bass, while cyclones and whirlwinds add majesty to the chorus. Lightnings flash like electric lamps, and giant oaks and immortal cedars bow like worshipers. In this Psalm of Nature it is declared that " In his temple, everything doth shout, glory! "

To devout souls who abide in the secret chambers with God, the closet itself becomes another grand cathedral, where every power and faculty of body and mind, soul and spirit, shout " Glory! " Memory brings her grateful stores to lay them at God's feet; imagination, the poet and painter, weaves choicest tributes and paints glorious pictures, as aids to faith; reason, the logician, constructs its most eloquent arguments to set forth God's claim on universal homage and love; the understanding, overawed before the infinite Mind, can only mutely confess its own insignificance; conscience, the judge, pronounces Him perfect in all moral beauty; the will, the sovereign of man, lays down its imperial scepter at His feet who is alone worthy to rule; and affection, despairing of ever responding fully to such perfect love, breaks her alabaster flask and fills the whole house with the odor of her anointing. It is the closet's revelings that prompt us to cry, " Who is like, O Lord, unto thee! "

Our Lord's first lesson on prayer, is, therefore, Enter into thy closet. The first rung in the ladder of ascent is faith in the actuality, reality, verity of the divine existence. As the primary condition of prayer, " he that cometh to God must believe that he is, and is a rewarder of them that diligently seek him." Of what use indeed to pray—nay, what but an affront, rather than an approach, to God— if we do not believe that He exists; and what is the closet for, if not to cultivate those spiritual senses which alone can perceive and receive Him?

Let us not dismiss this primary lesson without once more recalling and impressing its central truth, that communion with God is the essential secret of all holiness of character, conduct and service; and that meditation on the divine character and perfections prepares us not only for prevailing supplication but for reception of divine blessing. Let us think of the secret chamber as a place of vision—of contemplation of God, making possible new impressions, discoveries into His nature, revelations of His goodness, impartations of His power. Thus it comes to pass that before we call He answers, and while we are yet speaking He hears. Communion proves mutual— both an outgo, and an income—a voice that answers as well as a voice that cries.

What a new factor in our spiritual life would such prayer prove!

The most devout find it not only profitable but natural to make the first exercise in closet devotion mute meditation. The prayer of Habakkuk hints that this is becoming to all true worship:

" The Lord is in his holy temple!
    Let all the earth keep silence before him."

So, when, in the Apocalypse, that vision of the prayers of saints in the golden censer is about to be disclosed, the mysterious announcement which precedes it is:

" There was silence in Heaven about the space of
    half an hour,"

as though such silence were the only fit prelude and preparation for a revelation of such magnificence and significance.

God is here; but what if I know it not? Let me tarry till I do know it. Then how much added power will come into my communing, and with what new anointing shall I go forth to life's work and witness and warfare!

ALFRED PLUMMER

1841-1926

CHRISTIAN UNITY

BIOGRAPHICAL NOTE

EX-PRINCIPAL of Durham University (retired, 1902); born Heworth, near Gateshead, England, Feb. 17, 1841; educated at Lancing College, Exeter College, Oxford; Fellow Trinity College, Oxford, 1865-75; tutor and dean 1867-74; Master of University College, Durham, 1874-1902; sub-warden University of Durham, 1896-1902; author of translations of several of Dr. Dollinger's works; commentaries on 2 Peter, and Jude, John's Gospel and Epistles, The Pastoral Epistles, Epistles of James and Jude, Luke's Gospel, 2 Corinthians, "Introduction to Joshua and Nehemiah," "Handbook on the Church of the Early Fathers," "Lectures on English Church History."

" Other sheep I have which are not of this fold: them also I must bring, and they shall hear my voice; and they shall become one flock, one shepherd."—John 10 : 16.
" A new commandment I give unto you, that ye love one another; even as I have loved you, that ye also love one another. By this shall all men know that ye are my disciples, if ye have love one to another."—John 13 : 34-35.

THE second of these passages tells us the necessary result of the fulfilment of the prediction and promise made in the first. When all the sheep have been gathered in and they have become one flock under one Shepherd, then the component members of the flock will find that their relation to the Shepherd involves a similar relation to one another. Love, especially on the Shepherd's part, is the bond which connects each one of them with the Shepherd—a love so strong, that He is ready to die for them: love, therefore, is the bond which must unite each member of the flock with his fellows, and in this each ought to aim at imitating the love of the Shepherd.

But perhaps, with almost equal truth, we might reverse this, and make the mutual love not the result of the oneness of the flock, but the means of producing the oneness. Christ predicts that a time will come when the sheep who are not in the fold will be united with those who are in the fold, and that they will become one body, with Him at its head. And we may say that, when He gives to His followers the new commandment to love one another, even as He has loved them, He is telling them how to become one flock under Himself.

Perhaps it does not matter much which we regard as cause, and which as effect. The important point is, that the two facts are indissolubly connected by some law of divine causation. If there is love such as His there will be unity, and if there is unity under Him there will be love. Consequently, the presence of either fact may, in proportion to the fulness of its presence, be taken as evidence of the presence of the other; and, what is an equally important influence for our guidance, the absence of either fact may, in proportion to the completeness of its absence, be regarded as evidence of the absence of the other. If there is no love there will be no vital unity, and unless there is vital unity there will be no real love.

Unity, not uniformity. The two things are widely different, and either may exist without the other. Indeed, it may be doubted whether uniformity is not more of a hindrance than a help to unity. Uniformity is certainly a serious limitation of liberty; and liberty is the soil in which living unity is likely to flourish. Liberty is a sign of the presence of God's Spirit; " Where the spirit of the Lord is, there is liberty; " and where the spirit of the Lord is not, neither the unity which Christ promised, nor the love which He commanded, is likely to spring up.

And it is very unfortunate that, in one of the two texts which we are considering, our Bibles have made us familiar with a mis-translation, which seems to imply that Christ promised, and therefore enjoined, uniformity, when He does nothing of the kind. The Authorized Version makes Him say that, when the sheep which are not of this fold are brought, " there shall be one fold, one shepherd." What He does say is, that, when the others are brought, " they shall become one flock, one shepherd." Few corrections made in the Revised Version are more important than this. The mistake originated in Jerome's translation, where we have the same Latin word to represent two different Greek words. Wyclif followed him; and, although Tyndale and Coverdale corrected the error, the Authorized Version unfortunately followed Wyclif. Christ says nothing about there being one fold, which would imply uniformity: what He promises, and encourages us to work for and to pray for, is " one flock," in which there may be large measures of diversity along with the essential unity of belonging to one and the same Shepherd.

It is impossible to estimate the mischief that has been done by this unhappy substitution of " fold " for " flock " in this important text. Throughout the Middle Ages, few people in Western Europe knew Greek, and Jerome's Vulgate led them to believe that Christ had used the word " fold " in both places, and that He had inculcated a doctrine, which the change of word was perhaps intended to exclude. The doctrine, that the sheep not in the fold must be brought in, until there is one fold, with all the sheep penned within it, gave immense support to the claims of the Roman Catholic Church to be the one church, outside which there is no salvation. What Christ says is that those outside the then existing fold, equally with those who were in the fold, shall become one flock, of which He is the Shepherd. Christ had come to break down " the wall of partition " between the Jewish Church and the Gentiles. In the gospel, the distinction between Jew and Gentile was to cease, and the salvation, which had been offered first to the Jew, became the common inheritance of all.

In what sense than was the command which Christ gave to His followers, to love one another, " a new commandment? "

It may be said to be as old as the human race, a fundamental instinct, known even to the heathen. Wherever human beings lived together, the obligation to mutual affection existed, and was attested by inward promptings, of which each was conscious, and by inward reproaches, whenever the law of mutual affection was grossly violated, as by grievous injury or murder. Even to the Gentile, whose life was often one long transgression of it, the commandment to love his fellows was not, in the strictest sense, new.

Still less was it new to the Israelite. Every well-instructed Jew knew that it stood written in the book of Leviticus: " Thou shalt not take vengeance, nor bear any grudge against the children of thy people, but thou shalt love thy neighbor as thyself." If the obligation to love one's fellow-man was as old as the human race, the obligation to love him as oneself was as old as Judaism. It lies at the basis of many of the minute ordinances of the Jewish code.

What then does our Lord mean by calling it new?

First, it had been promulgated afresh, and in much clearer language. The original instinct of mutual affection, born in heaven and renewed in Paradise, had long since been almost forgotten. Even by those who dimly remembered it, and at times feebly recognized it, it was constantly ignored. In most men, other instincts far more congenial to man's fallen will, had stifled it or driven it out of court. Its faint whisperings were scarcely heard among the strident voices of selfishness and passion. A Plato or a Seneca might here and there suggest precepts of self-restraint and benevolence. But " what were they among so many? " And what chance had they against the self-indulgence which generations of practise had stereotyped into a habit, and which philosophers had formulated into a system?

Nor did the Jew need a new proclamation of the law of love much less than the heathen did. The Jew had so narrowed the scope of the command to love his neighbor, and had so overlaid it with qualifications and exceptions, that the word of God was made of none effect. He was quick to raise the previous question: " And who is my neighbor? " And when it was evident that, at any rate, a man's own parents must be considered as among his neighbors, there was the monstrous device of Corban to free him from obligation. And, as regards all mankind outside Judaism, the divine command had been not merely evaded, but reversed, by the unholy addition, " hate thine enemy."

But Christ's law of love was new for other reasons than because it had been published anew with greater clearness and emphasis. It was not merely the old instinct of our unfallen nature, dragged from oblivion, and quickened into new life. It was not merely the old Jewish precept, freed from glosses and perversions, and set forth once more in its original simplicity and comprehensiveness. It was all this; but it was a great deal more. It was the old instinct, the old precept, so transfigured, enlarged, and glorified, as to be indeed "a new commandment"; new in its extent; new in its sanction. It was no longer the old standard of loving one's neighbor as oneself. It was no longer the old sanction of loving him, because God would punish us if we did not. "Even as I have loved you, that ye also love one another": that is the new standard; that is the new sanction. Not the measure of our love for ourselves is to be our standard, but the measure of Christ's love for us. Not fear of God's judgments, not even obedience to His commands, is to be the mainspring of our love, but love itself. His love is to kindle our love; and the newborn fire is to know no limit but that of the fire that kindled it. "Even as I have loved you." In determining our duty to others, it is not enough to ask, "What, if our positions were reversed, should I wish them to do to me?" That is a very practical and useful question: it will help to clear the ground. But it is not the final question; and it may lead to serious mistakes; for we sometimes wish others to do to us what would be anything but beneficial. The final and the safe question is this: "What would Jesus Christ have me to do?" And, when we have answered it, and find our selfish wills shrinking back from the answer, let us confront them with another question: "What has Jesus Christ done for me? What is He still doing for me?" "Even as I have loved you, that ye also love one another."

Let us ask ourselves what we are doing towards the fulfilment of the divine promise, "one flock, one shepherd," and the fulfilment of the divine command, "that ye love one another, even as I have loved you." It is a test question. Nay, by the declaration of Christ Himself, it is the test question. "By this shall all men know that ye are my disciples, if ye have love one to another." This is the true note of the Church; not miracles; miracles are no absolute test of truth; "there shall arise false Christs and false prophets, and shall show great signs and wonders, so as to lead astray, if possible, even the elect;" not formularies nor discipline, for both of these may change, and a past discipline may be a present heresy; not numbers, numbers are no test of truth; truth may be on the side of an Athanasius or a Galileo against the large majority of Christians. The ultimate absolute test is love. Where is the man who loves his neighbors, loves his opponents, and loves them because Christ has loved him, and as Christ has loved him? There, in the noblest form, is the true Christian.

What have we done, what are we doing day by day, to produce this character in ourselves? What are we doing to produce that peace and unity among Christians, which depends, not upon uniformity of worship, or identity of dogma, but upon fervency of love? What are we doing to make mankind, and especially those with whom we come most closely in contact, healthier, happier, and holier? Those of us who keep any kind of watch over our thoughts, and words, and actions will hardly be able to reply to questions such as these in a way that would produce solid self-satisfaction.

Those unworthy suspicions of the motives of others; those pitiful jealousies of our neighbor's advancement; that diabolical gloating over what brings shame or loss to others—are thoughts of this kind quite unknown to us? And then, those impatient rejoinders, which seem to imply that the whole world is bound to satisfy us; those outbursts of anger, when our wills have been crossed; those harsh criticisms of the conduct of other people; that readiness to repeat what is discreditable to our neighbor, without any certainty that it is true, or that any good can come of repeating it—can we honestly plead "not guilty" to such things as these? And if we made even a rough calculation of the amount of time and energy we day by day expend upon unselfish attention to the wants of others, and the amount which we devote to the promotion of our own personal interests and pleasures, what kind of a balance sheet could we present to our consciences and to God? How many of our prayers are directed towards alleviating the sufferings and strengthening the characters of others rather than towards getting our own personal wants supplied? We often read newspapers as a mere amusement; and among the things that we find interesting are the records of the calamities, and it may be the disgrace, of other people. How callously we read it all, with scarcely a moment's sympathy, and altogether without even a momentary prayer for those whose sufferings have been a pastime to us!

In short, the love of Christ does not constrain us, does not fence us in, so as to keep us from squandering upon self those affections and energies which ought to be devoted to the service of others; and thus the divine law of love is only fitfully and feebly fulfilled by us, if at all. We look perhaps with indignation upon the animosities which separate class from class, and with contempt upon the controversial bitterness which divides Christian from Christian. But we forget how largely our own lack of the spirit of love and unity has contributed towards perpetuating the obstacles, which still hinder the realization of the divine ideal of "one flock, one Shepherd."

WILLIAM M. PUNSHON

1824-1881

ZEAL IN THE CAUSE OF CHRIST

BIOGRAPHICAL NOTE

WILLIAM MORLEY PUNSHON, English Methodist divine, was born at Doncaster, in Yorkshire, in 1824. His style was brilliant and elaborate, and while his sermons were written out in the minutest detail and carefully committed to memory, they were delivered with a freshness and vigor that rivaled the charm of extemporaneous eloquence. Every word he uttered was charged with the force and vitality of his great personality. At the Metropolitan Church, Toronto, Canada, he preached for many years, drawing thousands of people to Christ by the zeal, magnetism and power of his pulpit oratory. He died in 1881.

For whether we be beside ourselves, it is to God: or whether we be sober, it is for your cause. For the love of Christ constraineth us; because we thus judge, that if one died for all, then were all dead; and that he died for all, that they who live should not henceforth live unto themselves, but unto him who died for them, and rose again.—2 Cor. v., 13-15.

IT is always an advantage for the advocate of any particular cause to know the tactics of his adversary. He will be the better prepared for the onset, and repel the attack the more easily. Forewarned of danger, he will intrench himself in a position from which it will be impossible to dislodge him. The apostle Paul possest this advantage in a very eminent degree. In the earlier years of his apostleship, the Jew and the Greek were the antagonists with whom he had to contend. Having been himself a member of the straitest sect of the Jews, he knew full well the antipathy with which they regarded anything which set itself by its simplicity in contrast with their magnificent ritual; and he knew also the haughty scorn with which they turned away from what they deemed the unworthy accessories of the Nazarene. And, well read as he was in classic literature, and acquainted with all the habits and tendencies of the Grecian mind, he could readily understand how the restraints of the gospel would be deemed impertinent by the voluptuous Corinthian, and how the philosophic Athenian would brand its teachers mad. And yet, rejoicing in the experimental acquaintance with the gospel, he says, for his standing-point of advantage: "We preach Christ crucified, to the Jews a stumbling-block and to the Greeks foolishness, but to them that are called, the power of God and the wisdom of God." And in the words of the text, addressing some of those very Corinthians upon whom the gospel had exerted its power, he seems to accept the stigma and vindicate the glorious madness: "For whether we be beside ourselves, it is to God: or whether we be sober it is for your cause. For the love of Christ constraineth us; because we thus judge, that if one died for all, then were all dead; and that he died for all, that they who live should not henceforth live unto themselves, but unto him who died for them, and rose again." The great purpose of the apostle in these words is to impress upon us the fact that the cause of Christ in the world, sanctioned by the weight of so many obligations, fraught with the destinies of so many

482

millions, should be furthered by every legitimate means; that for it, if necessary, should be employed the soberest wisdom; and for it, if necessary, the most impassioned zeal. He vindicates the use of zeal in the cause of Christ by the three following considerations: First, from the condition of the world; secondly, from the obligations of the Church; and, thirdly, from the master-motive of the Savior's constraining love. To illustrate and enforce this apostolic argument, as not inappropriate to the object which has called us together, will be our business for a few brief moments to-night.

I. The apostle argues and enforces the use of zeal in the cause of Christ, in the first place, from the condition of the world. The apostle speaks of the world as in a state of spiritual death. He argues the universality of this spiritual death from the universality of the atonement of Christ. "For the love of Christ constraineth us, because we thus judge, that if one died for all, then were all dead"—dead in sin, with every vice luxuriant and every virtue languishing; dead in law, judicially in the grasp of the avenger; nay, "condemned already," and hastening to the second death. We need not remind you that this is by no means the world's estimate of its own condition. It is short-sighted, and, therefore, self-complacent. There is a veil over its eye; there is a delusion at its heart. In that delusion it fancies itself enthroned and stately, like some poor lunatic, an imaginary monarch under the inflictions of its keeper. The discovery of its true position comes only when the mind is enlightened from on high. "We thus judge," not because there is in us any intuitional sagacity, or any prophetical foresight, by which our judgment is made more accurate than the judgment of others; but the Holy Spirit has come down, has wrought upon us—has shown us the plague of our own hearts—and from the death within us we can the better argue the death which exists around. And that this is the actual condition of the world, Scripture and experience combine to testify. The Bible, with comprehensive impartiality, concludes all "under sin"; represents mankind as a seed of evil-doers—"children that are corrupters"—sheep that have wandered away from the Shepherd and Bishop of their souls. In the adjudication of Scripture there is no exemption from this common character of evil, and from this common exposure to danger. The men of merciful charities, and the woman of abandoned life—the proudest peer, and the vilest serf in his barony—the moralist observer of the decalogue, and the man-slayer, red with blood, all are comprehended in the broad and large denunciation: "Ye were by nature children of wrath, even as others." And out in the broad world, wherever the observant eye travels, you have abundant confirmation of the testimony of Scripture. You have it in your own history. The transgressions and sins which constitute this moral death abound in our age no less than in any former age of mankind. There are thousands around you who revel in undisguised corruption. There are thousands more externally reputable who have only a name to live. You have this confirmation in the nations of the Continent—some safely bound by the superstition of ages; others subsiding into a reactionary skepticism. You have this confirmation further away in the countries which own Mohammedan rule, and cherish the Mohammedan's dream—where you have unbridled lust, and a tiger's thirst for blood. You have this confirmation in the far-off regions of heathenism proper, where the nature, bad in itself, is made a thousand fold worse by its religion—where the man is the prey of every error, and the heart the slave of every cruelty—where men live in destruction, and where men die in despair. Travel where you will, visit the most distant regions, and search under the shadow of the highest civilization—penetrate into the depths of those primeval forests, into whose original darkness you might have imagined the curse would hardly penetrate, and the result is uniformly the same. Death is everywhere. You see it, indeed, in all its varieties now in the rare and fading beauty which it wears just after the spirit has fled from the clay, when its repose seems the worn-out casket, which the soul has broken, and thrown away; now, when there is shed over it a hue of the sublime, and it is carried amid the tears to burial, and now, when corruption has begun its work, and its ill odor affects the neighborhood, and spreads the pestilence—you see it in all its varieties, but uniformly death is there. We gather from our melancholy pilgrimage no vestige of spiritual life. Mourners go about the streets, and there are mourners over many tombs.

Altho, as we have observed just now, a thorough and realizing estimate of the world's condition comes only when the judgment is enlightened from on high, the wise men of the world, the minds that have in all ages towered above their fellows, have felt an unsatisfactoriness for which they could hardly account; they have had a vague and morbid consciousness that all was not right somehow, either with themselves or with their race; they have met with disturbing forces, signs of irregularity, tokens of misery and of sin that have ruffled, somewhat, the philosophic evenness of their minds. Each in his own way, and from his own standpoint, has guessed at the solution of the problem, and has been ready with a suggested remedy. The peoples are imbruted; educate them. The nations are barbarous; civilize them. Men grovel in sensual pleasure; cultivate the esthetic faculty; open to them galleries of pictures; bring them under the humanizing influences of art. Men groan in bondage; emancipate them, and bid them be free! Such are some of the tumultuous cries that have arisen from earnest but blind philanthropists, who have ignored the spiritual part of man's nature, and forgotten altogether the Godward relations of his soul. All these, as might have been expected, valuable enough as auxiliaries, worth something to promote the growth and comfort of a man when life has been once imparted, fail, absolutely fail to quicken the unconscious dead. In all cases the bed has been shorter than that a man could lie on it, and the covering narrower than that he could wrap himself in it. The inbred death lay too deep for such superficial alchemy; corpses can not by any possibility animate corpses; and the compassionate bystander from other worlds, sickened with the many inventions, might be constrained to cry, "Amid all this tumult of the human, O for something divine!" And the divine is given—Christ has died for all men. There is hope for the world's life. This is a death whereby we live; this is a remedy commensurate with existing need, and intended entirely to terminate and extinguish that need.

That squalid savage, whose creed is a perpetual terror, and whose life is a perpetual war—Christ hath died for him. That fettered and despairing slave, into whose soul the iron has entered, valued by his base oppressor about on a par with the cattle he tends, or with the soil he digs—Christ hath died for him. That dark blasphemer, who lives in familiar crime, whose tongue is set on fire of hell, whose expatriation would be hailed by the neighborhood around him as a boon of chiefest value—Christ has died for him. That dark recluse, whom an awakened conscience harasses, and who, in the vain hope of achieving merit by suffering, wastes himself with vigilant penance well-nigh to the grave—Christ has died for him. Oh, tell these tidings to the world, and it will live. Prophesy of this name in the motionless valley, and the divine Spirit who always waits to do honor to Jesus will send the afflatus from the four winds of heaven, and they shall leap into life to His praise.

Now take these two points. Think in the first place, of the condition of the world—a condition so disastrous, that nothing but death can illustrate it—a condition which prostrates every faculty, which smites the body with unnumbered cruelties, which dwarfs the mind with prejudices or distorts it into unholy passion, which banishes the soul and mind within a man in hopeless estrangement from happiness and God; and then think of the death of Christ, providing for the furthest need,

overtaking the utmost exile, pouring its abundant life upon the sepulchered nations, diffusing light, liberty, hope, comfort, heaven: and I appeal to your enlightened judgment whether you are not bound, those of you who believe in Jesus, to labor for the world's conversion with intensest energy and zeal. Oh, if temporal miseries elicit sympathy, and prompt to help; if the anxieties of a neighborhood gather around a drowning child, or are fastened upon the rafters of a burning house, where, solitary and imploring, stands a single man, already charred by the flame, how much of sympathy, of effort, of liberality, of zeal, of prayer, are due to a world lying in the wicked one, and panting after the second death! You will agree with me, that there is more than license for the poet's words:

"On such a theme,
'Tis impious to be calm!"

And you will rejoice—will you not? to take your stand to-night by the apostle's side, and to cry, when men deem your zeal impertinence and your efforts fanaticism, "If we be beside ourselves, it is to God: and if we be sober, it is for your cause."

II. The apostle argues the necessity for zeal in the cause of Christ, secondly, from the obligations of the Church, in that He died for all, that they should live—should not henceforth live unto themselves, but for Him who died for them and rose again. The apostle's argument is this—none of us has life in himself; if we live at all, we live by imparted life; we live because life has been drafted into our spirits from on high. Then it is not our own; it belongs to Him who has purchased it for us with His own blood, and we are bound to employ it in His service, and for His glory. This also is the conclusion of an enlightened judgment. We judge this as well as the other, and this is in accordance with the whole tenor of Scripture. Time would fail us to mention a tithe of the passages in which devotion—the devotion of the heart and of the service of God are made matter of constant and of prominent demand. I will just mention one passage that may serve as an illustration of all: "I beseech you therefore, brethren, by the mercies of God, that ye give your bodies as a living sacrifice." Have you ever gaged the depth of consecration that slumbers in the heart of those words —"a living sacrifice"; to be absolutely and increasingly devoted to God, as if the knife were at the throat, and the life-blood streamed forth in votive offering? Nay, better than that; because the life-blood could stream out but once, but the living sacrifice may be a perpetual holocaust, repeated daily for a lifetime—a living sacrifice, holy and acceptable unto God, which is your reasonable service. From the doctrine of this passage, and of numberless others kindred to it, it would appear that the regenerate heart is not at liberty to live for itself, nor to aim supremely at its own gratification; it must live for Him who has died for it, and who has risen again. You can not fail, I think, to perceive that compliance with this exhortation is utterly antagonistic to the ordinary procedure of mankind.

In the age of organization against idolatry, there is one proud, rampant idolatry which retains its ascendency amongst us. Selfishness is the most patronized idolatry in the world. It is the great image whose brightness is exceeding terrible, and before which all men bow; it is a throne, and an empire, and the likeness of a kingly crown; it equips armies and mans armaments to gratify its lust of power. Fastnesses have been explored and caverns ransacked to appease its thirst for gold. It presides over the councils of kings and over the diplomacy of cabinets; for it the merchantman grindeth down his manhood, for it the treader-under-foot of nations marcheth in his might and in his shame; its votaries are of all handicrafts—of the learned professions, and of every walk in life. It hath sometimes climbed on to the judgment-seat, and perverted justice there. The cowled monk hath hidden it beneath his robe, and it hath become for him an engine of oppression, and it hath occasionally robed itself in holy vestments, and entered the priest's office for a morsel of bread. No grace or virtue of humanity is free from its contamination. It has breathed, and patriotism has degenerated into partisanship; it has breathed, and friendship has been simulated for policy; it has breathed, and charity has been blemished by ostentation; it has breathed, and religion has been counterfeited for gold; its sway is a despotism—its territory wherever man hath trodden, and it is the undisputed anarch of the world. Now it is against this principle in human nature, throned within us all, doggedly contesting every inch of ground, that Christianity goes forth to combat. The gospel absolutely refuses to allow self to be the governing power, and assaults it in all its strongholds with precepts of sublime morality. To the selfishness of avarice it goes up boldly, even while the miser clutches his gold, and says: "Give to him that asketh of thee, and from him that would borrow of thee turn not thou away." To the selfishness of anger it addresses itself, even when the red spot is yet on the brow of the angry: "Let not the sun go down upon thy wrath"; "Bless them that curse you, pray for them that despitefully use you and persecute you." To the selfishness of pride, even in its haughtiness and arrogance, it says: "In honor preferring one another, be clothed with humility, let each esteem another better than himself." To the selfishness of indifference to the concerns of others, "Look not on thine own things, but likewise upon the things of others"; and to the selfishness of souls and criminal neglect of the great salvation, it speaks in tones of pathos which that must be a callous heart that can withstand, "Ye know the graces of our Lord Jesus Christ, who, tho he was rich, yet for our sins he became poor, that we, through his poverty, might be made rich." Oh, how small, alongside of august and heavenly precepts like these, are the sublimest maxims of any merely ethical morality!

It is said that, once, during the performance of a comedy in the Roman theater, one of the actors gave utterance to the sentiment, "I am a man; nothing, therefore, that is human can be foreign to me," and the audience were so struck by the disinterestedness, or so charmed by the novelty, that they greeted it with thunders of applause. How much greater wealth of kindly wisdom and prompting to unselfish action lies hidden in the gospel of Christ, shrined there as every-day utterances passed by the most of us very slightingly by! Oh! let there be anything like the genial practise of this divine morality, and the world would soon lose its aspect of desolation and of blood; oppression and over-reaching, and fraud and cruelty, would be frowned out of the societies of men, and this earth would be once more an ample and a peopled paradise. By selfishness, as we have thus endeavored to describe it, we mean that grasping, monopolizing spirit which gets all and gives nothing; heedful enough of its own fortunes, careless of the concerns and interests of others. This is the principle in our nature which Christianity opposes, and with which it ceaselessly wages war. But there is a sort of selfishness which, for the sake of distinction, we may call self-love, which is instinctive, and therefore innocent—that merciful provision by which we are prompted to the care of our own lives and to the avoidance of everything that would disquiet or abridge them. This principle in our nature Christianity encourages; to this principle Christianity addresses itself; and hence it has connected, married in indissoluble union, man's chiefest duty and man's highest pleasure. Godliness is profitable unto all things, having the promise of the life that now is. What has the dark, morbid, unhappy sensualist to do with it? Godliness hath the promise of the life "that now is," as well as "that which is to come." In keeping Thy commandments there is a present reward. "Take my yoke upon you and learn of me, for I am meek and lowly in heart, and ye shall find rest unto your souls; for my yoke is easy and my burden is light." "In thy presence there is fulness of joy; at thy right hand there are pleasures for evermore.'' Just as it is in man's physical organization, and its adaptation to the material world around him, when body and mind are alike in health, we can neither eat, nor drink, nor walk, nor sleep, nor sing, nor perform any of the commonest actions of life without a sensation of pleasure; so it is in the spiritual life: there is pleasure in its every motion. There is pleasure even in the sting of penitence; it is

"A godly grief and pleasing smart,
That melting of a broken heart."

There is pleasure in the performance of duty; there is pleasure in the enjoyment of privilege; there is pleasure in the overcoming of temptations, a grand thrill of happiness to see trampled under foot a vanquished lust or slain desire; there is pleasure in the exercise of benevolence; there is pleasure in the importunity of prayer. Hence it is that the apostle seeks to rivet the sense of personal obligation by the remembrance of personal benefit. "We thus judge, that he died for all, that they which live should not henceforth live unto themselves, but unto him who"—owns them? No. Claims them? No. Will judge them? No; but—"to him who died for them and rose again." Gratitude is to be the best prompter to our devotion. Those who live to Christ, those who live by Christ, will not tamely see His altars forsaken, His Sabbaths desecrated, His name blasphemed, the blood of the covenant wherewith He was sanctified accounted an unholy thing. Brethren, are you of that happy family? Have you obtained life from the dead through His name? Then you are bound to spend it for His honor, and, watching with godly jealousy for every possible opportunity of doing good, to spend and be spent for them who have not yet your Master known. I call on you to answer this invocation; it belongs to you. There is no neutrality, believe me, in this war —and if there be some of you that would like to be dastardly and half-hearted trimmers, you will find by and by that you have got the hottest place in the battle, exposed to the cross-fire from the artillery of both parties. I call on you decisively to-night to answer this invocation. Call up before your minds the benefits you have individually received; think of the blessings which the death of Christ has procured for you—the removal of the blighting curse which shadowed all your life, the present sense of pardon, mastery over self and over sin, light in the day of your activity, and songs in the night of your travail; the teaching Spirit to lead you into still loftier knowledge, and the sanctifying Spirit to impress upon you the image of the heavenly; that divine fellowship which lightens the present, and that majestic hope which makes the future brighter far. Think of the

benefits which the resurrection of Christ has conferred upon you; light in the shadowed valley, the last enemy destroyed, support amid the swellings of Jordan, a guide upon the hither side of the flood, angelic welcomes, the King in his beauty, and "a house not made with hands, eternal in the heavens." And then, as the sum of favor is presented, and gratitude arises and the fire burns, and the heart is full, and the frame quivers with the intensity of its emotions, just remember that there is a world lying in the wicked one, that there are multitudes, thousands upon thousands, in your own city, at your own doors, for whom the Savior died, who never heard His name; that there are multitudes for whom He has abolished death who have never felt His resurrection's power. Let your tears flow; better, far better a tear for God's sake and the world's sake than the hard-heartedness and darkness of sin. Lift up your voice in the midst of them; lift it up, be not afraid. Say unto the cities of Judah, "Behold your God." Men will call you mad, but you can give them the apostle's answer, "If we be beside ourselves, it is to God; if we be sober, it is for your cause."

III. The apostle argues the necessity of zeal in the cause of Christ, in the third place, from the master motive of the Savior's constraining love. "The love of Christ constraineth us" —forces us along, carries us away as with the impetuosity of a torrent, or rather as when cool heavens and favoring air speed the vessel steadily to the haven. Love is at once man's most powerful motive and his highest inspiration, both in the life that now is and that which is to come. From love to Christ spring the most devoted obedience, the most untiring efforts in His service. There are other springs of action, I know, by which men are influenced to a profession of religion. Interest can occasionally affect godliness from sordid aims, and behave itself decorously amid the respectabilities of the temple-going and almsgiving religion; but it will give its arm to any man that goes down to the house of Rimmon; and if there is a decree that at the sound of all kinds of music they are to fall down before another image which has been erected in the plains of Dura, they will be the most obsequious benders of the knee. Men sometimes practise obedience under the influence of fear. A sudden visitation, a prevailing epidemic, an alarming appeal, will strike into momentary concern; but when the indignation is overpast, and the craven soul has recovered from its paroxysms of terror, there will often be a relapse into more than the former atrocities of evil. Convictions of duty may and sometimes will induce a man, like an honest Pharisee of the olden time, to observe rigidly the enactments of the law; but there will be no heart in his obedience, and no holy passion in his soul; but let the love of God be shed abroad in his heart by the Holy Ghost given unto him, let there be a perception of love in God, let there be sight of the Crucified as well as of the cross, and there will be disinterested, and cheerful, and hearty obedience. Zeal for God will become at once a passion and a principle, intensifying every purpose into ardor, and filling the whole soul with vehemence of absorbing desire. This is the emotion from whose natural and inevitable outflow the apostle vindicates impassioned zeal.

Opinions are divided as to whether the constraining love spoken of in the text refers to Christ's love to us or to our love to Him, which the sense of His love has enkindled in the soul. I do not think we can go far wrong if we take both meanings, inasmuch as no principle of exposition is violated, and as we need the pressure of a combination of motive, that we may be zealously affected always in this good thing. Ye, then, if there are any of you here who need rousing to energy in the service of Christ, think of His love to you; how rich its manifestations, and how unfeigned; how all other love of which it is possible for you to conceive shrinks in the comparison! There have been developments in the histories of years of self-sacrificing affection, which has clung to the loved object amid hazard and suffering, and which has been ready even to offer up life in its behalf. Orestes and Pylades, Damon and Pythias, David and Jonathan, what lovely episodes their histories give us amid a history of selfishness and sin! Men have canonized them, partly because such instances are rare, and partly because they are like a dim hope of redemption looming from the ruins of the fall. We have it on inspired authority, indeed, ''Greater love hath no man than this'' —this is the highest point which man can compass, this is the culminating point of that affection which man can by possibility attain, the apex of his loftiest pyramid goes no higher than this—''greater love hath no man than this, that a man lay down his life for his friend; but God commendeth his love toward us, in that while we were yet sinners Christ died for us.'' A brother has sometimes made notable efforts to retrieve a brother's fortunes, or to blanch his sullied honor; but there is a Friend that sticketh closer than a brother. A father has bared his breast to shield his offspring from danger, and a mother would gladly die for the offspring of her womb; but a father's affection may fail in its strength, and yet more rarely a mother's in its tenderness.

And ''can a woman forget her sucking child, that she should not have compassion on the son of her womb? Yea, they may forget, yet will I not forget thee.'' O Jesus of Nazareth, who can declare Thee? ''Herein is love, not that we loved God, but that he loved us, and sent his Son to be a propitiation for our sins.'' Think of that love—love which desertion could not abate—love which ingratitude could not abate—which treachery could not abate—love which death could not destroy—love which, for creatures hateful and hating one another, stooped to incarnation, and suffered want, and embraced death, and shrank not even from the loathesomeness and from the humiliation of burial; and then, with brimming eye, and heart that is full of wonder: ''Why such love to me?'' you will indeed be ungrateful if you are not stirred by it to an energy of consecration and endeavor, which may well seem intemperate zeal to cool reckoners with worldly wisdom.

Then take the other side of the argument; take it as referring to your love to Christ, which the sense of His love has enkindled in the soul. The deepest affection in the believing heart will always be the love of Jesus. The love of home, the love of friends, the love of letters, the love of rest, the love of travel, and all else, are contracted by the side of this master passion. ''A little deeper,'' said one of the veterans of the first Napoleon's old guard, when they were probing in his bosom for a bullet that had mortally wounded him, and he thought they were getting somewhere in the region of the heart— ''a little deeper and you will find the Emperor.'' Engraven on the Christian's heart deeper than all other love of home or friends, with an ineffaceable impression that nothing can erase, you find the loved name of Jesus. Oh! let this affection impel us, and who shall measure our diligence or repress our zeal? Love is not bound by rule; there is no law that can bind it; it is never below the precept, it is always up to the precept, but it always has a margin of its own. It does not calculate, with mathematical exactitude, with how little of obedience it can escape penalty and secure recompense; like its Master it gives in princely style; it is exuberant in its manifestations; there is always enough and to spare. And if meaner motive can prompt to heroic action—if from pure love of science astronomers can cross the ocean familiarly, and dare encounter dangers, just that they may watch in distant climes the transit of a planet across the disc of the sun—and if botanists can travel into inhospitable climes and sojourn among inhospitable men, only to gather specimens of their gorgeous flora—and if, with no motive but love of country, and no recompense save bootless tears and an undying name, a Willoughby could sacrifice himself to blow up a magazine, and a Sarkeld could fire the Cashmere Gate at Delhi, surely we, with obligations incomparably higher, with the vows of profession on our lips, with death busy in the midst of us, and souls going down from our doors into a joyless and blasted immortality, ought to present our life-blood, if need be, for the cause of Christ, and for the good of souls. Let the scoffers spurn at us as they will; we are far superior to such poor contumely. Heaven applauds our enthusiasm, and we vindicate it in the apostle's words: "If we be beside ourselves, it is to God; and if we be sober, it is for your cause."

WALTER RAUSCHENBUSCH

1861-1918

THE UNSPOKEN THOUGHTS OF JESUS

BIOGRAPHICAL NOTE

PROFESSOR of Church history Rochester Theological Seminary 1902-1918; born Rochester, N. Y., October 4, 1861; graduated with first honors in classical gymnasium, Gutersloh, Germany, 1883; University of Rochester, 1884; graduated from Rochester Theological Seminary, 1886, D.D.; studied abroad 1891,2, 1907,8; ordained to the Baptist ministry, 1886; author of " Christianity and the Social Crisis."

" I have yet many things to say unto you, but ye can not bear them now. Howbeit when he, the Spirit of truth, is come, he shall guide you into all the truth." —John 16 : 12-13.

WE all have our unspoken thoughts. Some are thoughts so envious, mean, or despairing that we are ashamed to utter them. Some are thoughts so righteous, brave, and far-reaching that we are afraid to express them for fear of social consequences. Jesus had no Bluebeard's chamber to lock up, nor was He afraid of the prophet's martyrdom. His silences, like His words, were prompted by love and pedagogic wisdom. " I have many things to say, but ye can not bear them now." His pupils were not yet out of fractions, and He was not going to burden them with quadratic equations. In regard to the truth, too, His yoke was easy and His burden light.

Some of His thoughts were so sad that they would have bruised His friends with grief. All great minds have a subsoil of profound melancholy. Jesus saw the cross from afar, gaunt and threatening, first as a possibility, finally as a certainty, but it was a long time before He told His friends that His career was not to end in a triumphal march and royal enthronement, but in apparent failure and an outlaw's death. One of His most pathetic words, through which we catch a glimpse of His continued spiritual sufferings, is this: " When the Son of man comes, shall he find faith on earth? " But if He foresaw this, He did not tell His friends that after nineteen hundred years only a fraction of humanity would own Him king, and that only a fraction of that fraction would be serious about it.

There were other thoughts so radical and far-reaching that they would have unsettled the foundations of faith for His followers. He did not tell them that the Jewish nation would be superseded and the kingdom given to the Gentiles. He did not tell them outright that the temple and its worship and all the ceremonial ritual of their ancestral religion were to be laid away like the kindergarten material of childhood. There are plain indications that He knew and that His mind was working more and more consciously in that direction, but He did not force these ideas upon His followers.

But while Jesus had His silences, like every reserved mind and like every wise teacher, He looked forward to the time when the truths withheld would be revealed. " When the Spirit of truth is come, he shall guide you into all the truth.'' One of the finest facts about Judaism and about Christianity is that both are unfinished religions. The Old Testament does not claim that the revelation of God is completed; on the contrary, the air of expectancy is through it all: a new prophet like Moses, a greater king than David, a new covenant of the Spirit written in the hearts of men, a fuller outpouring of the Spirit, a perfect reign of God were to come. In the same way in the New Testament every face is turned to the better future. Christianity at the outset was quite as much a religion of hope as a religion of love. But if you consider how prone the great leaders, and especially the great system-makers, are to think they know it all, the more does this spiritual modesty, this unquenchable hopefulness, this sense of the inexhaustible resources of God, seem proof that the Christian religion really was illuminated by the light of God.

We know that the expectation of Jesus came to pass. Nothing is more remarkable about the beginnings of the Church than the capacity for growth inherent in its leaders. This crude human material from Galilee was transformed by an inward power that lifted them beyond themselves and turned fishermen into apostles and initiators of a new spiritual era. They had three propulsive forces upon them: a great aim, a real human brotherhood, and the mysterious Spirit of God within. I believe in the Spirit of God. When He brooded over the waters, He turned chaos into form and beauty, and when He broods over a human soul, the creative force is present which works miracles on human nature. Other men merely rearrange what is already present in human life. The rare men who listen to the inner voice, whose vision is clarified by conscious contact with God, and whose will is hardened to the steel-edge by leaning back on the Eternal—they introduce new forces into the stale world. The individuals and the religious bodies who have trusted to the mystic enlightenment have usually been distrusted and derided by their contemporaries, but somehow the subsequent progress of religion and of morality swings over into the track marked out by these pioneers who followed God and not tradition. They have often anticipated the social evolution of mankind by centuries. There is no teacher like the Spirit.

Jesus said the Spirit '' shall take of mine and shall declare it unto you.'' Truths which Jesus had foreshadowed, suggestions which He had thrown out, corollaries which He had left unformulated, would stand out and loom up as great compelling truths. The spring only quickens the seeds dropped by autumn. The Spirit came like a shower of rain on the seeds that lay dormant in the tropical dust and they woke to life. Every truth contains new truth for a mind stimulated by outward occasion and inward impulse, just as every leaf of the calla lily is a sheath from which the next leaf grows. Our new psychology has shown that the human memory is a vast storehouse of unassimilated information and impressions. The observations made in our childhood, the chance utterances made by our teachers, which seemed so irrelevant or even foolish when we heard them—there they lie. By and by comes some great change in our life, some great impulse of human love or divine aspiration, and the sleeping seeds of truth awaken and take root. Great masses of truth in the New Testament were practically useless to the Church for centuries, and then the Spirit and the occasion met, and they sprang to life. Paul's thought about the uselessness of the law and the power of faith to justify was unintelligible for the Middle Ages, but it became vivid and vital when the aroused Church of the Reformation was stripping off the inherited legalism of medieval religion. The social contents of the Bible have been lying unrecognized and the social purpose of Jesus was slighted or denied, till the modern world began to agonize over the social problems and the Spirit summoned our generation imperiously to carry into effect the holy will of Christ. Thus the Spirit unfolds and quickens the historical heritage left by Christ in the individual, in the Church, and in humanity, and the unbearable truths become bearable and dear.

Would it be possible to divine what the unspoken thoughts of Jesus were? Could we work back now into the inner recesses of His mind? If the subsequent teachings of the Spirit have really thus unfolded the germinal truths that lay locked in His mind, it might be possible to trace them back to Him; especially if some passing utterance of His showed that He harbored the thought. The undertaking is venturesome, but even if our exploration ends in '' Perhaps,'' it will carry some reward.

Almost the first great advance step which the Church took, was the recognition of the universal mission of Christianity. The Jewish disciples set out by assuming as a matter of course that salvation was for the Jews, and that heathen could share in it only by becoming Jews. The book of Acts is a bright account of the triumphal transition from Jerusalem to Rome. But from the letters of Paul we learn the dark background of obstinate orthodoxy and pious intrigue which resisted this process at every step. It took the best fighting strength of one of the world's great fighters to beat down the national barriers and let Christianity out on its world-wide career. Now, I take it that this was one of the truths germinating in the mind of Jesus and unfolded by the Spirit. So far as I remember He nowhere expressly announced it except in one saying ascribed to the time after His resurrection. But His mind was working in that direction. When He met the Roman centurion and saw his spiritual susceptibility, He at once had a vision of heathen coming from East and West to share in the Messianic table round. He emphasized the fact that the one leper who had moral refinement enough to come back and thank Him was a Samaritan, and when He wanted to hold up a model of brotherly kindness, He picked out an heretical alien and set him in lurid contrast to the religious pillars of His own nation. With a mind so little bound by national prejudices and so swift to recognize human worth in outsiders, there were surely daring and hopeful glances across the wall of partition into the vast fields of humanity outside of His nation.

A second truth into which the Spirit had to lead the Church was the great law of development. The common Jewish expectation was that the kingdom of the Messiah would come in suddenly. It was all fixed up and ready in heaven, and some day they would open their eyes and say: '' Lo, there it is.'' The early Christians shared this catastrophic hope and all their doctrinal thought, their preaching, their moral endeavor and church discipline centered about the great consummation when the Lord should return. It would have shattered their faith if they had known that nineteen centuries would run on without a break. Jesus on the other hand had comprehended the law of spiritual evolution. His parables discouraged the theory of catastrophe and insisted that growth takes time and will not be hurried. But He had to wrap that disappointing truth into parabolic form or they would have resented and repudiated it. The Spirit has had to lead the Church into this truth, and it has not yet comprehended it fully. In its conception of conversion for the individual, and in its outlook for social regeneration the rank and file of the Church have not yet outgrown the youthful hopes of brilliant suddenness.

A third truth which was familiar to Jesus and veiled to His disciples was the pure spirituality of the new religion. All primitive religions were so embedded in traditional forms that form and essence were indistinguishable for most of the worshipers. To the rabbis and Pharisees Jesus seemed to be undermining religion itself when He neglected the ritual fastings and washings. Jesus nowhere called

His disciples out of Judaism. He did not tell them to cease the observance of the old rites. Yet He was emancipated from the old forms Himself. He scarcely mentions the temple, the center of religion. He foretold the time when all questions of holy places would be antiquated. He treated the Sabbath from a totally new point of view. The whole business of clean and unclean food He regarded as irrelevant and without religious basis. Forms of prayer were of great moment to His countrymen; Jesus taught only one prayer and the distinguishing characteristic of that is its utter simplicity and directness. To strip religion of all forms and make it purely a matter of love to God and man was so immense an innovation that we have hardly come in sight of it yet. But wherever the tuition of the Spirit can be discerned in the past, we see humanity veering in that direction so far as the professional exponents of religion will permit, and to those who are following the leading of the Spirit, it is indisputably clear that Jesus is with them in it.

Thus we have tried in three instances to divine the unspoken thoughts of Jesus by working back from the later development of the Church to the inner mind of Jesus. Whether we have been successful or not, it is impossible to escape a sense of the affectionate patience of Jesus in giving them only what they could bear. He was a superb teacher, because He loved superbly. Nor can we escape a feeling of our own dulness and slowness. Singly and collectively we have bickered about trivialities and heroically resisted everything that might by chance make Christians of us. We have all been guilty of keeping back the progress of truth. The progress has been so slow that it takes only a fit of melancholy to make a man doubt if there has been any real progress at all. But against our moral stupidity Christ sets his unwavering determination to have us learn. If not to-day, then to-morrow. Without haste and without rest the great Teacher is urging us on. Learn we must, for some day we are to see God. But for anyone to whom spiritual education is no longer the unwilling task of a slave, but to whom truth is the glad sunlight of the soul, this saying of Jesus opens an endless vista of truth, an ever-expanding horizon, mystery after mystery coming out of the grayness of the dawn and breaking into glory.

ARCHIBALD THOMAS ROBERTSON

1863-1934

THE TRANSFORMING POWER OF THE VISION OF CHRIST

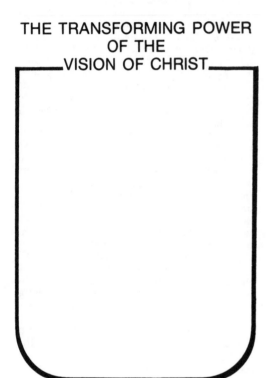

BIOGRAPHICAL NOTE

PROFESSOR of interpretation of the New Testament in the Southern Baptist Theological Seminary 1895-1934; born near Chatham, Va., November 6, 1863; graduated from Wake Forest College, N. C., 1885; Southern Baptist Theological Seminary, Louisville, 1888; assistant instructor of New Testament interpretation, 1888; professor Biblical introduction, 1892; author of "Life and Letters of John A. Broadus," "Syllabus for New Testament Greek Syntax," "Syllabus for New Testament Study," "Teaching of Jesus Concerning God the Father," "The Students' Chronological New Testament," "Keywords to the Teaching of Jesus," "Epochs in the Life of Jesus," "A Short Grammar in Greek New Testament," "Epochs in the Life of Paul."

" But we all, with unveiled face beholding as in a mirror the glory of the Lord, are transformed into the same image from glory to glory, even as from the Lord the Spirit."—2 Cor. 3 : 18.

THE verse chosen for discussion is the culmination of the argument in 2 Cor. 3 : 4-18. Paul is engaged in setting forth the glories of the Christian ministry. He had been in the depths of despondency while at Troas over not seeing Titus (2 Cor. 2 : 12). In Macedonia, however, he had met Titus who greatly refreshed his spirit by the news from Corinth. As a result Paul's spirit rebounds to its normal buoyancy, if it does not go higher than normal (2 Cor. 2 : 14). Under the spell of this new enthusiasm Paul discourses at length concerning the dignity and glory of the Christian ministry. He casts no reflection upon the ministry of the Old Testament dispensation. That was glorious indeed. But the moon gets its light from the sun and fades before it. In the verse here under discussion he broadens the treatment to include all Christians (" we all ") and touches the fundamental thing—Christian experience, the believer's relation to Jesus.

The verb " transformed " is the heart of the verse and it is in the present tense. It is therefore a process that is here described. The metamorphosis, to use the exact Greek word, is not yet complete. The work has been begun, the end is still ahead. It is noticeable that Paul here, as often, appeals to the common experience of believers in Christ. His own theology was grounded securely—his own great experience of grace. The subject that naturally presents itself, therefore, is the transforming power of the vision of Christ. The text will respond to several questions:

Into what are we transformed? The answer is, " into the same image." Whose image? It is clearly the Lord's image whose glory the disciple beholds. By " the Lord " here, as is usual with Paul, is meant the Lord Jesus. The Christian then is represented as transformed into the likeness of the Lord Jesus. One cannot doubt that the apostle has in mind the creation of man's spirit in the likeness of God. That likeness has been greatly marred by sin, but not wholly destroyed. Jesus has come to restore the image of God in men.

The implication is that the image needs restoration. A new artist must work upon the old picture, now so badly injured. If it be replied that evolution has overthrown this doctrine of man's likeness to God and fall from that likeness, one may reply that this is not so certain. I am perfectly willing to assume evolution as a working hypothesis or as a fact. I am sure that God made the universe in His own way. It is too late now for our theories to alter the facts. If God brought the bodies of men up by way of monkeys there is nothing in that process to cause protest on the part of a believer in God. Besides it is entirely possible to have a lapse into sin after a rise from a lower state. The spirit of man is all that is claimed to have been made in the likeness of God. It is not shown to be impossible for that likeness to come at a high stage in the process of evolution. Indeed evolution is in perfect harmony with that conception. Sin comes with moral consciousness. Sin is a fact. When did it enter the life of man? Certainly not before moral consciousness. There is plenty of room for the " fall."

It is a fact to-day that many men and women do undergo the transformation claimed by Paul as a reality. Christianity makes the appeal to life. It is life. The change took place in Paul's day and takes place now. Men are down. They can be lifted up. Christ lays hold of the spirit of man, which was made in the image of God, and restores the likeness to the Father. Christianity to-day stands the scientific test of experience. The great doctrine of grace is in perfect accord with modern knowledge. Life is always open to this appeal. Paul was certain that he and others were being transformed into the image of the Lord Jesus and so of God.

How is the transformation wrought? Here the answer is twofold: " Beholding as in a mirror the glory of the Lord," and " from the Lord the Spirit." There are two factors in the great change, the divine and the human. There is some doubt as to the exact meaning in both of these phrases, but the central fact remains true in each instance. It is not clear whether we should translate " Spirit of the Lord," or " the Lord the Spirit." The order of words in the Greek favors the American Revision. In this sense the deity of the Holy Spirit is asserted and, in a sense, almost identity with Jesus. But the point of importance is that the great change is wrought by the Holy Spirit. This is the basal doctrine of regeneration. The new birth is the truth here firmly set forth. Evidently Paul held the same opinion as the Lord Jesus on this matter. He had no sympathy with the common " fads " of the time which denied the reality of sin and the need of such a radical course. The modern " Christian Science " has some of its roots in the Oriental cults of Paul's time. The term " mind-cure " has one element of truth at least. Some minds certainly need a " cure." But it is very difficult for a diseased mind to cure itself. The other point

here is found in the word " beholding." This word is ambiguous and may mean " reflecting." But even so, it reflects what falls upon it. This 'is the human side of the matter. The heart of the believer must turn to the Lord. The sinner looks upon Christ. As he beholds the glory of the Lord the change is wrought. The Lord draws him away from himself. He gazes upon the majesty of Christ. Thus no mere human expedients will satisfy the conditions. Reformation will come, of course, but mere reformation will not cause this inward change. Ascetic practises will not necessarily lead to the life of piety. Self-torture may lead away from Christ. Hence no church, no ordinance, no priest, no creed must come between the soul and his Lord. It is the vision of Christ Himself in His glory that brings the wondrous transformation. This is the Pauline principle. All Christians are priests in this holy place. The soul of man finds God in Christ, is won back to God by the sight of Christ, is made like God by communion with Christ, who is God. This is the fellowship with the eternal God that saves the soul from sin.

Is the change instantaneous or gradual? It is both. It is an act and a process. Regeneration is an act, sanctification is a process. Both are in view here. " Beholding as in a mirror the glory of the Lord " we " are transformed." The new life springs up in the heart that looks upon Jesus as Lord and Savior. The new life grows as the soul continues to look upon Jesus. He is the bread of life, the true manna from heaven. There must be constant fellowship with Jesus if the growth is to be normal and wholesome. Sporadic looking means imperfect development. James in his Epistle (1 : 24) pictures the mere hearer who " beholdeth himself, and goeth his way, and straightway forgetteth what manner of man he was." " But he that looketh into the perfect law, the law of liberty, and so continueth, being not a hearer that forgetteth but a doer that worketh, this man shall be blest in his doing " (James 1 : 25).

The law of environment applies to the spiritual world. Birds, butterflies, snakes, rabbits, often become like their surroundings. Nature protects from harm or equips for conflict as the case may be. The Christian is inevitably influenced by his surroundings. It is the law of life. It was the main concern of Jesus in His prayer for the disciples (John 17) that they might be in the world, but not of it. Two great laws are in conflict. The spiritual plant is brought as an exotic into an unspiritual environment. If it is left alone, disaster will come. Jesus promises to be with the disciples. He will create a new environment " in the world, but not of it." Never alone can the work of transformation be carried on in the Christian. Never alone can the world itself be transformed. The only hope that the Christian has is to be in constant fellowship with Jesus. He must not wander from "base" as the children understand in their games. In a word, if one aims to be like God he must live with God. If he is not at all like God, he cannot help the world back to God. The Christian then is constantly drawn away from God by the very world that he is endeavoring to lead to God. The drowning man seeks to destroy his rescuer.

Will the change last? Will it be permanent? The answer of Paul is in the words "with unveiled face." The Christian has no need of a veil upon his face. Moses indeed (2 Cor. 3 : 7) put a veil over his face as he came down the mount that the people might not see the glory fade from his countenance. He had been upon the mount with God. He was afraid that the glory upon his face would not last. The Christian is free from that fear. "Where the spirit of the Lord is, there is liberty" or freedom from apprehension on that score. The glory remains on the face of the Christian for he is in constant fellowship with God in Christ. He continually beholds the glory. He continually reflects the glory. Thus both ideas of the word come round. He needs no veil. The change is a permanent one. It will last.

What is the destiny of the Christian? It is "from glory to glory." The best is yet ahead. We go from grace to grace, from strength to strength, from glory to glory. That is our destiny. Here is an answer to the professional "perfectionist." He is the only one who has discovered his "perfection!" The culmination is still ahead. The goal is indeed the fulness of God. Will there not be progress in heaven? Sometimes indeed a saint may be granted here a foretaste of the glory that is to be. Jesus on the Mount of Transfiguration is a case in point. Stephen also "saw the glory of God, and Jesus standing on the right hand of God" (Acts 7 : 55).

No wonder that the bystanders had already noticed that his face shone as the face of an angel (Acts 6 : 15). Sometimes an aged saint, a mother in Israel, has the glory of God on her face, she has looked so long upon the face of the Lord. Mont Blanc will catch the light of the sun after his light has paled from the hills, and cast it upon the country round —the glorious Alpine after-glow. I once saw this beautiful sight on Lake Geneva. It was like a glimpse of the other world.

The mirror is something to be grateful for. But for the mirror we might not see God at all. But the mirror is not like the person himself. "For now we see in a mirror darkly; but then face to face" (1 Cor. 13 : 12). "That will be glory for me" indeed to look upon His face, to see Jesus as He is. The Christian life thus begins with a look. The life is developed by looking at Jesus, living with Him. The consummation will come with a look. "Beloved, now are we the sons of God, and it doth not yet appear what we shall be: but we know that, when he shall appear, we shall be like him, for we shall see him as he is" (1 John 3 : 2). That is it, "We shall be like him." We are somewhat like Christ now. Then we shall have the full family likeness of the household of God. The final reason for John's faith is that "we shall see him even as he is." That is enough.

John Jasper, the famous negro preacher of Richmond, Virginia, used to tell a dream. He dreamed that he went to heaven, and sat down just inside the gate. After a while he was asked by an angel if he did not want to come up closer and see the glories of heaven. "Do you not want your golden crown, John Jasper? Do you not want your harp and your white robe?" "Oh, yes," he answered, "but not yet. Time enough for all that. But now just let me stay where I am ten thousand years and gaze and gaze and gaze at the face of Jesus."

FREDERICK W. ROBERTSON

1816-1853

THE LONELINESS OF CHRIST

BIOGRAPHICAL NOTE

FREDERICK WILLIAM ROBERTSON, was born in London in 1816, educated at Edinburgh University and took his degree at Oxford in 1841. From a law office he passed into the ministry, where his career, tho brief, was exceptionally brilliant. His English style commends itself to the preacher's study for its naturalness, poetic beauty, lucidity, and strength. It is the style of a man of unique genius. He died of consumption at Brighton in 1853, little more than thirty-six years of age.

Perhaps the most remarkable feature in the career of Robertson was the influence he exercised over the workingmen. This class had in his day become estranged from the Church of England, few of whose clergy had any power to attract their attention and adherence. He was denounced as a socialist because of his foundation of a workingmen's institute, and the opposition and vilification which he thus met with no doubt helped to shorten his life.

Jesus answered them, Do ye now believe? Behold, the hour cometh, yea, is now come, that ye shall be scattered every man to his own, and shall leave me alone; and yet I am not alone, because the Father is with me.
—John xvi., 31, 32.

THERE are two kinds of solitude: the first consisting of isolation in space; the other, of isolation of the spirit. The first is simply separation by distance. When we are seen, touched, heard by none, we are said to be alone. And all hearts respond to the truth of that saying, This is not solitude; for sympathy can people our solitude with a crowd. The fisherman on the ocean alone at night is not alone, when he remembers the earnest longings which are rising up to heaven at home for his safety. The traveler is not alone, when the faces which will greet him on his arrival seem to beam upon him as he trudges on. The solitary student is not alone, when he feels that human hearts will respond to the truths which he is preparing to address to them.

The other is loneliness of soul. There are times when hands touch ours, but only send an icy chill of unsympathizing indifference to the heart; when eyes gaze into ours, but with a glazed look which can not read into the bottom of our souls; when words pass from our lips, but only come back as an echo reverberated without reply through a dreary solitude; when the multitude throng and press us, and we can not say, as Christ said, "Somebody hath touched me"; for the contact has been not between soul and soul, but only between form and form.

And there are two kinds of men, who feel this last solitude in different ways. The first are the men of self-reliance—self-dependent—who ask no counsel, and crave no sympathy; who act and resolve alone, who can go sternly through duty, and scarcely shrink, let what will be crushed in them. Such men command respect: for whoever respects himself constrains the respect of others. They are invaluable in all those professions of life in which sensitive feeling would be a superfluity; they make iron commanders, surgeons who do not shrink, and statesmen who do not flinch from their purpose for the dread of unpopularity. But mere self-dependence is weakness; and the conflict is terrible when a human sense of weakness is felt by such men. Jacob was alone when he slept on his way to Padan Aram, the first night that he was away from his father's roof, with the world before him, and all the old broken up; and Elijah was alone in the wilderness when the court had deserted him, and he said, "They have digged down thine altars, and slain thy prophets with the sword: and I, even I, only am left, and they seek my life to take it away." But the loneliness of the tender Jacob was very different from that of the stern Elijah. To Jacob the sympathy he yearned for was realized in the form of a gentle dream. A ladder raised from earth to heaven figured the possibility of communion between the spirit of man and the Spirit of God. In Elijah's case, the storm, and the earthquake, and the fire did their convulsing work in the soul, before a still, small voice told him that he was not alone. In such a spirit the sense of weakness comes with a burst of agony, and the dreadful conviction of being alone manifests itself with a rending of the heart of rock. It is only so that such souls can be taught that the Father is with them, and that they are not alone.

There is another class of men, who live in sympathy. These are affectionate minds, which tremble at the thought of being alone; not from want of courage nor from weakness of intellect comes their dependence upon others, but from the intensity of their affections. It is the trembling spirit of humanity in them. They want not aid, not even countenance, but only sympathy. And then trial comes to them not in the shape of fierce struggle, but of chill and utter loneliness, when they are called upon to perform a duty on which the world looks coldly, or to embrace a truth which has not found lodgment yet in the breasts of others.

It is to this latter and not to the former class that we must look, if we could understand the spirit in which the words of the text were pronounced. The deep humanity of the soul of Christ was gifted with those finer sensibilities of affectionate nature which stand in need of sympathy. He not only gave sympathy, but wanted it, too, from others. He who selected the gentle John to be His friend, who found solace in female sympathy, attended by the women who ministered to Him out of their substance—who in the trial hour could not bear even to pray without the human presence, which is the pledge and reminder of God's presence, had nothing in Him of the hard, merely self-dependent character. Even this verse testifies to the same fact. A stern spirit never could have said, "I am not alone: the Father is with me"; never would have felt the loneliness which needed the balancing truth. These words tell of a struggle, an inward reasoning, a difficulty and a reply, a sense of solitude—"I shall be alone"; and an immediate correction of that: "Not alone: the Father is with me."

There is no thought connected with the life of Christ more touching, none that seems so peculiarly to characterize His spirit, as the solitariness in which He lived. Those who understood Him best only understood Him half. Those who knew Him best scarcely could be said to know Him. On this occasion the disciples thought, Now we do understand, now we do believe. The lonely spirit answered, "Do ye now believe? Behold the hour cometh that ye shall be scattered, every man to his own, and shall leave me alone."

Very impressive is that trait in His history. He was in this world alone.

I. First, then, we meditate on the loneliness of Christ.

The loneliness of Christ was caused by the divine elevation of His character. His infinite superiority severed Him from sympathy; His exquisite affectionateness made that want of sympathy a keen trial.

There is a second-rate greatness which the world can comprehend. If we take two who are brought into direct contrast by Christ Himself, the one the type of human, the other that of divine excellence, the Son of Man and John the Baptist, this becomes clearly manifest. John's life had a certain rude, rugged goodness, on which was written, in characters which required no magnifying-glass to read, spiritual excellence. The world, on the whole, accepted him. Pharisees and Sadducees went to his baptism. The people idolized him as a prophet; and, if he had not chanced to cross the path of a weak prince and a revengeful woman, we can see no reason why John might not have finished his course with joy, recognized as irreproachable. If we inquire why it was that the world accepted John and rejected Christ, one reply appears to be, that the life of the one was infinitely simple and one-sided, that of the other divinely complex. In physical nature, the naturalist finds no difficulty in comprehending the simple structure of the lowest organizations of animal life, where one uniform texture, and one organ performing the office of brain and heart and lungs, at once, leave little to perplex. But when he comes to study the complex anatomy of men, he has the labor of a lifetime before him. It is not difficult to master the constitution of a single country; but when you try to understand the universe, you find infinite appearances of contradiction: law opposed by law; motion balanced by motion; happiness blended with misery; and the power to elicit a divine order and unity out of this complex variety is given to only a few of the gifted of the race. That which the structure of man is to the structure of the limpet, that which the universe is to a single country, the complex and boundless soul of Christ was to the souls of other men. Therefore, to the superficial observer, His life was a mass of inconsistencies and contradictions. All thought themselves qualified to point out the discrepancies. The Pharisees could not comprehend how a holy Teacher could eat with publicans and sinners. His own brethren could not reconcile His assumption of a public office with the privacy which He aimed at keeping. "If thou doest these things, show thyself to the world." Some thought He was "a good man"; others said, "Nay, but he deceiveth the people." And hence it was that He lived to see all that acceptance which had marked the earlier stage of His career—as, for instance, at Capernaum—melt away. First, the Pharisees took the alarm; then the Sadducees; then the political party of the Herodians; then the people. That was the most terrible of all: for the enmity of the upper classes is impotent; but when that cry of brute force is stirred from the deeps of society, as deaf to the voice of reason as the ocean in its strength churned into raving foam by the winds, the heart of mere earthly oak quails before that. The apostles, at all events, did quail. One denied; another betrayed; all deserted. They "were scattered, each to his own": and the Truth Himself was left alone in Pilate's judgment hall.

Now learn from this a very important distinction. To feel solitary is no uncommon thing. To complain of being alone, without sympathy, and misunderstood, is general enough. In every place, in many a family, these victims of diseased sensibility are to be found, and they might find a weakening satisfaction in observing a parallel between their own feelings and those of Jesus. But before that parallel is assumed, be very sure that it is, as in His case, the elevation of your character which severs you from your species. The world has small sympathy for divine goodness; but it also has little for a great many other qualities which are disagreeable to it. You meet with no response; you are passed by; find yourself unpopular; meet with little communion. Well! Is that because you are above in the world—nobler, devising and executing grand plans, which they can not comprehend; vindicating the wronged; proclaiming and living on great principles; offending it by the saintliness of your purity, and the unworldliness of your aspirations? Then yours is the loneliness of Christ. Or is it that you are wrapped up in self, cold, disobliging, sentimental, indifferent about the welfare of others, and very much astonished that they are not deeply interested in you? You must not use these words of Christ. They have nothing to do with you.

Let us look at one or two of the occasions on which this loneliness was felt.

The first time was when He was but twelve years old, when His parents found Him in the temple, hearing the doctors and asking them questions. High thoughts were in the Child's soul: expanding views of life; larger views of duty, and His own destiny.

There is a moment in every true life—to some it comes very early—when the old routine of duty is not large enough; when the parental roof seems too low, because the Infinite above is arching over the soul; when the old formulas, in creeds, catechisms, and articles, seem to be narrow, and they must either be thrown aside, or else transformed into living and breathing realities; when the earthly father's authority is being superseded by the claims of a Father in Heaven.

That is a lonely, lonely moment, when the young soul first feels God—when this earth is recognized as an "awful place, yea, the very gate of heaven"; when the dream-ladder is seen planted against the skies, and we wake, and the dream haunts us as a sublime reality.

You may detect the approach of that moment in the young man or the young woman by the awakened spirit of inquiry; by a certain restlessness of look, and an eager earnestness of tone; by the devouring study of all kinds of books; by the waning of your own influence, while the inquirer is asking the truth of the doctors and teachers in the vast temple of the world; by a certain opinionativeness, which is austere and disagreeable enough; but the austerest moment of the fruit's taste is that in which it is passing from greenness into ripeness. If you wait in patience, the sour will become sweet. Rightly looked at, that opinionativeness is more truly anguish; the fearful solitude of feeling the insecurity of all that is human; the discovery that life is real, and forms of social and religious existence hollow. The old moorings are torn away, and the soul is drifting, drifting, drifting, very often without compass, except the guidance of an unseen hand, into the vast infinite of God. Then come the lonely words, and no wonder. "How is it that ye sought me? Wist ye not that I must be about my Father's business?"

That solitude was felt by Christ in trial. In the desert, in Pilate's judgment hall, in the garden, He was alone; and alone must every son of man meet his trial-hour. The individuality of the soul necessitates that. Each man is a new soul in this world: untried, with a boundless "Possible" before him. No one can predict what he may become, prescribe his duties, or mark out his obligations. Each man's own nature has its own peculiar rules; and he must take up his life-plan alone, and persevere in it in a perfect privacy with which no stranger intermeddleth. Each man's temptations are made up of a host of peculiarities, internal and external, which no other mind can measure. You are tried alone; alone you pass into the desert; alone you must bear and conquer in the agony; alone you must be sifted by the world. There are moments known only to a man's own self, when he sits by the poisoned springs of existence, "yearning for a morrow which shall free him from strife." And there are trials more terrible than that. Not when vicious inclinations are opposed to holy, but when virtue conflicts with virtue, is the real rending of the soul in twain. A temptation, in which the lower nature struggles for mastery, can be met by the whole united force of the spirit. But it is when obedience to a heavenly Father can be only paid by disobedience to an earthly one; or fidelity to duty can be only kept by infidelity to some entangling engagement; or the straight path must be taken over the misery of others; or the counsel of the affectionate friend must be met with a "Get thee behind me, Satan":—Oh! it is then, when human advice is unavailable, that the soul feels what it is to be alone.

Once more: the Redeemer's soul was alone in dying. The hour had come—they were all gone, and He was, as He predicted, left alone. All that is human drops from us in that hour. Human faces flit and fade, and the sounds of the world become confused. "I shall die alone"—yes, and alone you live. The philosopher tells us that no atom in creation touches another atom; they all approach within a certain distance; then the attraction ceases, and an invisible something repels—they only seem to touch. No soul touches another soul except at one or two points, and those chiefly external—a fearful and lonely thought, but one of the truest of life. Death only realizes that which has been fact all along. In the central deeps of our being we are alone.

II. The spirit or temper of that solitude.

Observe its grandeur. I am alone, yet not alone. This is a feeble and sentimental way in which we speak of the Man of sorrows. We turn to the cross, and the agony, and the loneliness, to touch the softer feelings, to arouse compassion. You degrade that loneliness by your compassion. Compassion! compassion for Him! Adore if you will—respect and reverence that sublime solitariness with which none but the Father was—but no pity; let it draw out the firmer and manlier graces of the soul. Even tender sympathy seems out of place.

For even in human beings, the strength that is in a man can only be learnt when he is thrown upon his own resources and left alone. What a man can do in conjunction with others does not test the man. Tell us what he can do alone. It is one thing to defend the truth when you know that your audience are already prepossest, and that every argument will meet a willing response; and it is another thing to hold the truth when truth must be supported, if at all, alone—met by cold looks and unsympathizing suspicion. It is one thing to rush on to danger with the shouts and the sympathy of numbers; it is another thing when the lonely chieftain of the sinking ship sees the last boat-full disengage itself, and folds his arms to go down into the majesty of darkness, crushed, but not subdued.

Such and greater far was the strength and majesty of the Savior's solitariness. It was not the trial of the lonely hermit. There is a certain gentle and pleasing melancholy in the life which is lived alone. But there are the forms of nature to speak to him; and he has not the positive opposition of mankind, if he has the absence of actual sympathy. It is a solemn thing, doubtless, to be apart from men, and to feel eternity rushing by like an arrowy river. But the solitude of Christ was the solitude of a crowd. In that single human bosom dwelt the thought which was to be the germ of the world's life, a thought unshared, misunderstood, or rejected. Can you not feel the grandeur of those words, when the Man, reposing on His solitary strength, felt the last shadow of perfect isolation pass across His soul:—"My God, my God, why hast thou forsaken me?"

Next, learn from these words self-reliance. "Ye shall leave me alone." Alone, then, the Son of Man was content to be. He threw Himself on His own solitary thought: did not go down to meet the world; but waited, tho it might be for ages, till the world should come round to Him. He appealed to the future, did not aim at seeming consistent, left His contradictions unexplained: I came from the Father: I leave the world, and go to the Father. "Now," said they, "Thou speakest no proverb"; that is enigma. But many a hard and enigmatical saying before He had spoken, and He left them all. A thread runs through all true acts, stringing them together into one harmonious chain: but it is not for the Son of God to be anxious to prove their consistency with each other.

This is self-reliance, to repose calmly on the thought which is deepest in our bosoms, and be unmoved if the world will not accept it yet. To live on your own convictions against the world, is to overcome the world—to believe that what is truest in you is true for all: to abide by that, and not be over-anxious to be heard or understood, or sympathized with, certain that at last all must acknowledge the same, and that, while you stand firm, the world will come round to you, that is independence. It is not difficult to get away into retirement, and there live upon your own convictions; nor is it difficult to mix with men, and follow their convictions; but to enter into the world, and there live out firmly and fearlessly according to your own conscience—that is Christian greatness.

There is a cowardice in this age which is not Christian. We shrink from the consequences of truth. We look round and cling dependently. We ask what men will think; what others will say; whether they will stare in astonishment. Perhaps they will; but he who is calculating that will accomplish nothing in this life. The Father—the Father which is with us and in us—what does He think? God's work can not be done without a spirit of independence. A man has got some way in the Christian life when he has learned to say humbly, and yet majestically, "I dare to be alone."

Lastly, remark the humility of this loneliness. Had the Son of Man simply said, I can be alone, He would have said no more than any proud, self-relying man can say; but when He added, "because the Father is with me," that independence assumed another character, and self-reliance became only another form of reliance upon God. Distinguish between genuine and spurious humility. There is a false humility which says, "It is my own poor thought, and I must not trust it. I must distrust my own reason and judgment, because they are my own. I must not accept the dictates of my own conscience; for is it not my own, and is not trust in self the great fault of our fallen nature?"

Very well. Now, remember something else. There is a Spirit which beareth witness in our spirits; there is a God who "is not far from any one of us"; there is a "Light which lighteth every man which cometh into the world." Do not be unnaturally humble. The thought of your own mind perchance is the thought of God. To refuse to follow that may be to disown God. To take the judgment and conscience of other men to live by, where is the humility of that? From whence did their conscience and judgment come? Was the fountain from which they drew exhausted for you? If they refused like you to rely on their own conscience, and you rely upon it, how are you sure that it is more the mind of God than your own which you have refused to hear?

Look at it in another way. The charm of the words of great men—those grand sayings which are recognized as true as soon as heard —is this, that you recognize them as wisdom which passed across your own mind. You feel that they are your own thoughts come back to you, else you would not at once admit them: "All that floated across me before, only I could not say it, and did not feel confident enough to assert it, or had not conviction

enough to put into words." Yes, God spoke to you what He did to them: only they believed it, said it, trusted the Word within them, and you did not. Be sure that often when you say, "It is only my own poor thought, and I am alone," the real correcting thought is this, "Alone, but the Father is with me,"—therefore I can live by that lonely conviction.

There is no danger in this, whatever timid minds may think—no danger of mistake, if the character be a true one. For we are not in uncertainty in this matter. It has been given us to know our base from our noble hours: to distinguish between the voice which is from above, and that which speaks from below, out of the abyss of our animal and selfish nature. Samuel could distinguish between the impulse—quite a human one— which would have made him select Eliab out of Jesse's sons, and the deeper judgment by which "the Lord said, Look not on his countenance, nor on the height of his stature, for I have refused him." Doubtless deep truth of character is required for this: for the whispering voices get mixed together, and we dare not abide by our own thoughts, because we think them our own, and not God's: and this because we only now and then endeavor to know in earnest. It is only given to the habitually true to know the difference. He knew it, because all His blessed life long He could say, "My judgment is just, because I seek not my own will, but the will of him who sent me."

The practical result and inference of all this is a very simple, but a very deep one: the deepest of existence. Let life be a life of faith. Do not go timorously about, inquiring what others think, and what others believe, and what others say. It seems the easiest, it is the most difficult thing in life to do this. Believe in God. God is near you. Throw yourself fearlessly upon Him. Trembling mortal, there is an unknown light within your soul, which will wake when you command it. The day may come when all that is human, man and woman, will fall off from you; as they did from Him. Let His strength be yours. Be independent of them all now. The Father is with you. Look to Him, and He will save you.

GEORGE LIVINGSTONE ROBINSON

1864-1958

THE KINGSHIP OF CHRIST

BIOGRAPHICAL NOTE

PROFESSOR of Old Testament literature and exegesis in McCormick Theological Seminary, Chicago, 1898 - 1938; born August 19, 1864, at West Hebron, Washington County, N. Y.; educated at Salem Washington Academy and Fort Edward Collegiate Institute; graduated B.A., from Princeton University in 1887; instructor in the Syrian Protestant College, Beirut, Syria, 1887-90; won, upon graduation from Princeton Theological Seminary in 1893, the Old Testament fellowship in Hebrew which afforded him two years' study in Germany; Ph.D., University of Leipsic, 1895; D.D., Grone City College, 1904; pastor of the Roxbury Presbyterian church, Boston, Mass.; professor of Old Testament literature and exegesis in Knox College, Toronto, Canada, 1896-98.

" Jesus of Nazareth, the King of the Jews."—John 19 : 19.

THESE words upon the cross were an accusation against Christ. " Pilate wrote a title and put it on the cross and the writing was, Jesus of Nazareth, the King of the Jews." It seems striking, when we think of it, that our Lord should have been crucified as king, when by the very act of His sacrifice He was performing His priestly office and, at the same time, fulfilling His own prophecy. Yet in three languages over His cross were written the words, " Jesus of Nazareth, the king of the Jews."

The word " king " signifies sovereignty, authority, power; and traced to its origin seems to denote one to whom superior knowledge has given superior power. In the civil world various other words are employed to designate the sovereigns of particular states. Thus there is the " shah " of Persia, the " sultan " of Turkey, the " emperor " of China, and formerly there were the " dey " of Algiers, and the " doge " of Venice. Jesus was called " king." We are accustomed to think of Him as Savior and too little to contemplate Him as king, yet the Bible clearly sets forth His kingship. The Gospel of Matthew especially emphasizes His regal power. The writer of this gospel evidently sought to prove to the unbelieving Jews that Jesus was their expected king. The Old Testament had long before declared the coming of a monarch. In Genesis He is denominated " lawgiver ": " The scepter shall not depart from Judah nor a lawgiver from between his feet until Shiloh come: and unto him shall the gathering of the people be."

The prophet Isaiah invests Him with judicial and executive functions: " For unto us a child is born, unto us a son is given: and the government shall be upon his shoulders. Of the increase of his government and peace there shall be no end, upon the throne of David and upon his kingdom to order it and to establish it with judgment and with justice from henceforth even forever." Daniel ascribes to Him eternal and unlimited dominion over all: " And there was given him dominion and glory and a kingdom, that all peoples, nations and languages should serve him. His dominion is an everlasting dominion which shall not pass away and his kingdom that which shall not be destroyed." David enthrones Him at the right hand of God: " The Lord said unto my Lord, Sit thou on my right hand until I make thine enemies thy footstool."

Christ Himself claimed kingly authority. The Sermon on the Mount resounds with those commanding words: " But I say unto you." " Ye have heard that it was said by them of old time, Thou shalt love thy neighbor and hate thine enemy. But I say unto you, Love your enemies, bless them that curse you, do good to them that hate you and pray for them which despitefully use you and persecute you." As Jesus went up and down through Galilee, He said to one and another, " Follow me," and His disciples followed Him. To the sick He said, " Arise "; to the dead Lazarus, " Come forth." His great commission, " Go ye into all the world and preach the gospel to every creature," was based upon His kingly authority. In all His teaching and in all His words there was an air of command. The gospel picture we have of Him is quite the contrast of king or prince, yet, as has been said, " All his words were kingly, all his acts a succession of the kingliest deeds, decisions, commands." When He preached, He spoke with authority; when He taught He showed divine wisdom, and when He healed, He evinced divine power. Christ needed no excuse and made no apology. He was a ruler and He came to rule; He was a monarch and He performed the functions of a monarch; He was a king and He spoke like a king.

Christ was recognized as king. On the first day of what we call " Passion week," He made His triumphal entry into Jerusalem. That day saw His formal inauguration as king of the Jews. His humanity was then exalted. Starting from Bethany, He was borne on an ass' colt—not upon a war-horse, but an animal the symbol of peace—over the Mount of Olives, down across the valley of the Kedron on the way to the Holy City. It was Passover week. Thousands of Jews had come up from all parts of the Roman Empire to attend the feast. The city was crowded to its utmost. Our Lord was escorted by His disciples. As He approached the city, throngs came out to meet Him. Multitudes gazed with eager eyes from lofty eminences. The city began to resound with the cries and shouts of the people. Branches of palm trees were broken down and strewed before the new monarch. Adoring followers spread their garments in the way that the new-hailed king might tread upon them. The shout of hosannas to the Son of David rent the air. Jesus was entering the capital. We read much of the pomp and splendor with which earthly kings are escorted through their realms. History relates that the way before the conquering Xerxes, as he led his troops across the bridge over the Hellespont, was strewed with green branches of myrtle while the incense of burning spices and aromatic perfumes filled the air. Travelers, even in these modern days, tell of Per-

sian rulers passing in wonderful pageants along a road of roses miles in extent, and of glass vessels with symbols of mysterious fashion—tokens of supreme prosperity—broken at every step beneath the horses' feet. But look at Christ's retinue! What a resplendent pageant! Look at the crowded capital! Hear the people cry hosannas to their triumphal monarch! Watch the jealous rabbis as they endeavor to hush the exultant throng. Jesus is making His triumphal entry and the world is for the first time beginning to grasp the meaning of His person and work.

And yet the admiring hosts only saw in Him His temporal power. Even His disciples understood not the spiritual import of His kingship. They had but a vague conception of the kingdom of heaven. By the " kingdom of God" a Jew understood human society perfected, where God was visible and ruled. They failed to comprehend His spiritual rule; they failed to acknowledge His divine lordship; they failed to recognize Him as the great king and head of the Church. Christ was more than temporal king. His loyalty commenced in heaven's eternal purpose. He was to be monarch of men's hearts as well as minds. He was to be the governor and controller of human destiny. Not only this, but He was to reign in love. He was to be a king of love. He was to win His followers through love. He was to found His kingdom on love. Napoleon, conversing in exile one day at St. Helena, as his custom was, about the great men of antiquity and comparing himself with them, said: " Alexander, Cæsar, Charlemagne, and myself founded great empires, but upon what did the creations of our genius depend? Upon force. Jesus alone founded His kingdom upon love, and to this day millions would die for Him." True indeed! Upon love Jesus established His monarchy. His empire is a monarchy of love, not a democracy, not a republic, but an absolute monarchy based upon supreme loyalty to Him, and governed throughout by love. Broad and extended, yet never exceeding the limits of love. This is Christ's kingdom, and this is the manner of His government; a kingdom worthy of a human, and worthy, also, in every way of a divine Christ.

Let us consider briefly His kingly offices: Earthly kings exercise various functions. In a word, they make subjects, found kingdoms, govern their people, protect and defend their empires, and conquer their enemies. Our Lord has similar functions. Our catechism tells us that " Christ executeth the office of a king in subduing us to himself, in ruling and defending us and in restraining and conquering all his and our enemies."

As a king, therefore, Christ's first office is the subjection of His people. Such is the natural condition of the human heart, that without the almighty power of a divine ruler men would not be brought into subjection. "The carnal mind is enmity against God: for it is not subject to the law of God, neither indeed can be." Men are obstinate and refused to be governed, and it requires kingly power and kingly love to conquer such rebellious hearts. Yet Christ effects His purpose and men become His loyal subjects. Paul is a good example of such subjection. He was on his way to Damascus. His heart was set against Christianity. His mission was to visit the synagogs and bring any disciples of Christ that he might find bound unto Jerusalem. He was, therefore, in absolute rebellion against the Savior. But, "suddenly there shone from heaven a great light round about him, and he fell unto the ground and heard a voice saying unto him, Saul, Saul, why persecutest thou me?" Not until he heard the voice from heaven was his heart changed. Not until the divine effulgence was manifested to Paul in miraculous power did he inquire, "Who art thou, Lord?" Not until Paul was smitten to the earth was he led to ask, "Lord, what wilt thou have me do?" Then it was the King of men softened Paul's heart; then it was that Christ conquered his rebellious will; then it was that Paul became the *doulos,* purchased servant, of Jesus Christ. Even so Christ subdues us. He speaks with authority to the conscience. He questions our lives; He interrogates our motives; He visits us in secret; He speaks to us when alone; He follows us into the darkness; He haunts our slumbers; He makes us dissatisfied with self; and He reveals Himself to us in such a way that He conquers our stubborn wills, wins our rebellious hearts, and makes us His obedient and willing subjects. This is the first work of the Christ-king.

As a king, Christ rules his people. After the Macedonian had conquered the East, after the renowned Roman had subjected the world, after the hero of France had overrun Europe, their common difficulty was to know how to govern. To have left those foreign nations to govern themselves would have meant disloyalty and revolt. So in the kingdom of grace. The great King does not leave us to govern ourselves. Having become citizens of His realm, we are placed under new laws, bound by new obligations and subject to new restrictions. We are citizens of a new commonwealth. "Old things have passed away." New thoughts, better feelings, higher aspirations are our possession. Duties that once we deemed a burden now become a joy. Things we once hated, now we love. Whenever He calls, we are ready to obey. We are no longer our own masters. We belong to His moral empire. He gives laws and He expects obedience. He holds the right and He demands the service of every human life. "His will be-

comes the common rule of all; His life our common motive; His glory our common end." He governs in righteousness. He fills our hearts with love. He infuses into us a feeling of sympathy. He makes us philanthropic. He rids us of social selfishness. He inspires us with Christian fellowship. He delivers us from caste. He allays strife. He promotes peace. He opens up before us the great avenues of Christian love; strengthens us in weakness, comforts us in sorrow; corrects us when sinful; and helps us and encourages us in times of perplexity and discouragement— all for the praise of His glorious name. Christ governs, and His government is a government of love; Christ reigns, and His reign is a reign of love.

Again, Christ protects His people from their enemies. His citizens are surrounded by adversaries on every side. Foes from within and without beset the child of God. Sin, Satan, the world and the grave are all enemies of Christ's subjects. His people are continually being tempted; but, "The Lord knoweth how to deliver the godly out of temptations." He has promised to do so. To the Church of Philadelphia he declared: "I will keep thee from the hour of temptation." And again, Paul says: "God is faithful who will not suffer you to be tempted above that ye are able, but will with the temptation also make a way of escape that ye may be able to bear." Christ unhesitatingly told those entering His kingdom that, "they should be hated of all men for his name's sake." But He added, "There shall not a hair of your head perish." He it is who "is able to keep us from falling and to present us faultless before the presence of his glory with exceeding joy; the only wise God our Savior," and King. He it was who "delivered the apostle out of the mouth of the lion." He it was who enabled martyrs to die with feelings of triumphant victory in their hearts, and made them ready and willing to be burnt at the stake or be tortured in body on the rack because of their confidence in His protection. Just so He will protect us. If we are loyal subjects of King Jesus, nothing can overcome us. "Even the gates of hell shall not prevail against us." Sin shall not have dominion over us. Through Him will come salvation. Through Him we shall have the victory. What blessed assurance have His people! What secure protection! What perfect safety in the empire of such a sovereign! What unspeakable joy under the governorship of Jesus!

But He does more than subdue, control and defend His subjects: Christ restrains His own and His peoples'-enemies. The birth of this monarch made the great Herod tremble upon his throne. Christ's reply to Satan: "Get thee hence" thwarted further temptation. His rejoinders in the temple silenced the priests and elders of the people. His "woes" recorded in Matthew caused the Pharisees and hypocrites to falter and retreat. And to-day His voice, speaking through the conscience, checks the enemies of the cross in their wicked plots to overthrow the Church. He strikes terror into wicked hearts. Rebels become cowards in carrying out their schemes against the children of God. Their hearts fail them in prosecuting their plots against the citizens of the kingdom of Christ. Wicked men falter when they come to the threshold of righteousness. The wretch trembles when he reaches the crisis of his contemplated crime. Sin totters as it undertakes to ruin the child of God. The Psalmist says: "When the wicked even my enemies and my foes came upon me to eat up my flesh, they stumbled and fell." Christ restrains and intimidates His enemies. He frustrates the assaults of sin. How? By the barracks and castles and fortresses, I mean the churches, chapels and cathedrals, reared in all parts of the world for the drill and discipline of His soldiers; by the immense fortifications of holiness—the schools of the prophets—erected against the onsets of Satan; by the lighthouses planted along the coast, by which are meant the sailors' rests and hospitals and other charitable institutions to be found in almost every quarter of the globe; by the war-ships sent out into the enemy's territory, by which I mean the missionaries of the gospel who have gone forth to battle for truth; by the standing army of the Church of Christ, with its ministers and officers, its Sabbath-school teachers and Christian workers; who stand armed with the whole armor of God, their loins girt about with truth, having on the breastplate of righteousness, their feet shod with the preparation of the gospel of peace, on their arms the shield of faith, on their heads the helmet of salvation, and in their hands the sword of the Spirit which is the word of God; confronted by these, the adversaries of Christ's kingdom hesitate and grow faint at heart; before these the world becomes weak, vice is restrained, the evil one is thwarted, Satan stand dumb, every adversary trembles, and Christ's people are made to prosper. I verily believe that there is enough wickedness in the world to overthrow the Church were it not for the restraining power of King Jesus.

As a king Christ conquers His own and His peoples' enemies. Restraining is not sufficient. The enemy must be completely overthrown. This is the final achievement of our King. Christ is a conqueror. His kingdom is an eternal kingdom. "The kings of the earth set themselves, and the rulers take counsel together against the Lord and against his anointed, saying, Let us break their bands asunder, and cast away their cords from us," but Christ is a conqueror of kings. No weapon formed against His kingdom shall prosper. The contest which once seemed doubtful will then betoken His victory, and it will be a complete victory. At His name, "every knee shall bow of things in heaven and things in earth and things under the earth: and every tongue shall confess that Jesus Christ is Lord." All the agents of Satan, all devils, "Beelzebub the sovereign of devils, Lucifer the brilliant devil, Mammon the money devil, Pluto the fiery devil, Baal the military devil," all will fall prostrate before His conquering power. Before Him the nations will bow, for He will come as judge. At His feet angels and archangels will kneel. "A crown will be given to him as he goes forth conquering and to conquer"; "and great voices" will be heard "in heaven, saying, the kingdoms of this world are become the kingdom of our Lord and of his Christ and he shall reign forever and ever." We read of the triumphs of the Cæsars; of the triumphal arches erected in ancient Rome in honor of returning conquerors. But compare with these the triumph of Jesus. Behold the heavenly Cæsar, as saints and angels celebrate His universal victory! For Him the arch of triumph is nothing less than the arc of heaven itself; His city, the heavenly Jerusalem; His triumph a universal celebration. "The kings of Tarshish and of the isles shall bring presents, the kings of Sheba and Seba shall offer gifts. Yea, all kings shall fall down before him, all nations shall serve him. He shall have dominion from sea to sea and from the river unto the ends of the earth. They that dwell in the wilderness shall bow before him; and his enemies shall lick the dust." "All things shall be put in subjection under his feet." "For he must reign till he hath put all enemies under his feet." The last enemy shall be conquered. As victor, He shall reign, and to Him will be ascribed glory, and majesty, and power for ever and ever.

Let us pause and contemplate such a victory. Let us picture to ourselves that celestial coronation scene. Jesus our King seated on the throne of heaven, surrounded with glory, His kingdom universal, His enemies under His feet, Satan vanquished, earthly magistrates and potentates, sages and kings, armies and emperors, bowing submissively before Him as King of Kings and Lord of Lords; hymns of praise chanted by the heavenly choir; tributes of adoration by the saints clothed in white; His elect singing hallelujahs to Him that sitteth upon the throne of God most high, and worshiping multitudes raising their voices in songs of triumph, as God the Father places upon His brow the crown of victory. What a glorious coronation! What a supreme triumph! What an unparalleled victory! Oh, Jesus, thou art the monarch of the skies, thou art king of heaven and of earth!

JACQUES SAURIN

1677-1730

PAUL BEFORE FELIX AND DRUSILLA

BIOGRAPHICAL NOTE

JACQUES SAURIN, the famous French Protestant preacher of the seventeenth century, was born at Nismes in 1677. He studied at Geneva and was appointed to the Walloon Church in London in 1701. The scene of his great life work was, however, the Hague, where he settled in 1705. He has been compared with Bossuet, tho he never attained the graceful style and subtilty which characterize the "Eagle of Meaux." The story is told of the famous scholar Le Clerc that he long refused to hear Saurin preach, on the ground that he gave too much attention to mere art. One day he consented to hear him on the condition that he should be permitted to sit behind the pulpit where he could not see his oratorical action. At the close of the sermon he found himself in front of the pulpit, with tears in his eyes. Saurin died in 1730.

And before certain days, when Felix came with his wife Drusilla, which was a Jewess, he sent for Paul, and heard him concerning the faith of Christ. And as he reasoned of righteousness, temperance, and judgment to come, Felix trembled, and answered, Go thy way for this time; when I have a convenient season, I will call for thee.—Acts xxiv., 24, 25.

My brethren, tho the kingdoms of the righteous be not of this world, they present, however, amidst their meanness, marks of dignity and power. They resemble Jesus Christ. He humbled Himself so far as to take the form of a servant, but frequently exercised the rights of a sovereign. From the abyss of humiliation to which He condescended, emanations of the Godhead were seen to proceed. Lord of nature, He commanded the winds and seas. He bade the storm and tempest subside. He restored health to the sick, and life to the dead. He imposed silence on the rabbis; He embarrassed Pilate on the throne; and disposed of Paradise at the moment He Himself was pierced with the nails, and fixt on the cross. Behold the portrait of believers! "They are dead. Their life is hid with Christ in God." (Col. iii., 3.) "If they had hope only in this life, they were of all men most miserable." (I Cor. xv., 19.) Nevertheless, they show I know not what superiority of birth. Their glory is not so concealed but we sometimes perceive its luster! just as the children of a king, when unknown and in a distant province, betray in their conversation and carriage indications of illustrious descent.

We might illustrate this truth by numerous instances. Let us attend to that in our text. There we shall discover that association of humility and grandeur, of reproach and glory, which constitutes the condition of the faithful while on earth. Behold St. Paul, a Christian, an apostle, a saint. See him hurried from tribunal to tribunal, from province to province; sometimes before the Romans, sometimes before the Jews, sometimes before the high-priest of the synagog, and sometimes before the procurator of Cæsar. See him conducted from Jerusalem to Cæsarea, and summoned to appear before Felix. In all these traits, do you not recognize the Christian walking in the narrow way, the way of tribulation, marked by his Master's feet? But consider him nearer still. Examine his discourse, look at his countenance; there you will see a fortitude, a courage, and a dignity which constrain you to acknowledge that there was something really grand in the person of St. Paul. He preached Jesus Christ at the very moment he was persecuted for having preached Him. He preached even when in chains. He did more; he attacked his judge on the throne. He reasoned, he enforced, he thundered. He seemed already to exercise the function of judging the world, which God has reserved for His saints. He made Felix tremble. Felix felt himself borne away by a superior force. Unable to hear St. Paul any longer without appalling fears, he sent him away. "After certain days, when Felix came with his wife Drusilla, he sent for Paul, and heard him concerning the faith in Christ," etc.

We find here three considerations which claim our attention: An enlightened preacher, who discovers a very peculiar discernment in the selection of his subject; a conscience appalled and confounded on the recollection of its crimes and of that awful judgment where they must be weighed, a sinner alarmed, but not converted; a sinner who desires to be saved, but delays his conversion: a case, alas! of but too common occurrence.

You perceive already, my brethren, the subject of this discourse: first, that St. Paul reasoned before Felix and Drusilla of righteousness, temperance, and judgment to come; second, that Felix trembled; third, that he sent the apostle away; three considerations which shall divide this discourse. May it produce on your hearts, on the hearts of Christians, the same effects St. Paul produced on the soul of this heathen; but may it have a happier influence on your lives. Amen.

Paul preached before Felix and Drusilla "on righteousness, temperance, and judgment to come." This is the first subject of discussion. Before, however, we proceed further with our remarks, we must first sketch the character of this Felix and this Drusilla, which will serve as a basis to the first proposition.

After the scepter was departed from Judah, and the Jewish nation subjugated by Pompey, the Roman emperors governed the country by procurators. Claudius filled the imperial throne while St. Paul was at Cæsarea. This emperor had received a servile education from his grandmother Lucia, and from his mother Antonia; and having been brought up in obsequious meanness, evinced, on his elevation to the empire, marks of the inadequate care which had been bestowed on his infancy. He had neither courage nor dignity of mind. He who was raised to sway the Roman scepter, and consequently to govern the civilized world, abandoned his judgment to his freedmen, and gave them a complete ascendency over his mind. Felix was one of those freedmen. "He exercised in Judea the imperial functions with a mercenary soul." Voluptuous-

ness and avarice were the predominant vices of his heart. We have a proof of his avarice immediately after our text, where it is said he sent for Paul,—not to hear him concerning the truth of the gospel which this apostle had preached with so much power; not to inquire whether this religion, against which the Jews raised the standard, was contrary to the interest of the State; but because he hoped to have received money for his liberation. Here is the effect of avarice.

Josephus recited an instance of his voluptuousness. It is his marriage with Drusilla. She was a Jewess, as is remarked in our text. King Azizus, her former husband, was a heathen; and in order to gain her affections, he had conformed to the most rigorous ceremonies of Judaism. Felix saw her, and became enamored of her beauty. He conceived for her a violent passion; and in defiance of the sacred ties which had united her to her husband, he resolved to become master of her person. His addresses were received. Drusilla violated her former engagements, and chose rather to contract with Felix an illegitimate marriage than to adhere to the chaste ties which united her to Azizus. Felix the Roman, Felix the procurator of Judea and the favorite of Cæsar appeared to her a noble acquisition. It is indeed a truth, we may here observe, that grandeur and fortune are charms which mortals find the greatest difficulty to resist, and against which the purest virtue has need to be armed with all its constancy. Recollect these two characters of Felix and Drusilla. St. Paul, before those two personages, treated concerning "The faith in Christ"; that is, concerning the Christian religion, of which Jesus Christ is the sum and substance, the author and the end: and from the numerous doctrines of Christianity, he selected "righteousness, temperance, and judgment to come."

Here is, my brethren, an admirable text; but a text selected with discretion. Fully to comprehend it, recollect the character we have given of Felix. He was covetous, luxurious, and governor of Judea. St. Paul selected three subjects, correspondent to the characteristics. Addressing an avaricious man, he treated of righteousness. Addressing the governor of Judea, one of those persons who think themselves independent and responsible to none but themselves for their conduct, he treated of "judgment to come."

But who can here supply the brevity of the historian, and report the whole of what the apostle said to Felix on these important points? It seems to me that I hear him enforcing those important truths he has left us in his works, and placing in the fullest luster those divine maxims interspersed in our Scriptures. "He reasoned of righteousness." There he maintained the right of the widow and the orphan. There he demonstrated that kings and magistrates are established to maintain the rights of the people, and not to indulge their own caprice; that the design of the supreme authority is to make the whole happy by the vigilance of one, and not to gratify one at the expense of all; that it is meanness of mind to oppress the wretched, who have no defense but cries and tears; and that nothing is so unworthy of an enlightened man as that ferocity with which some are inspired by dignity, and which obstructs their respect for human nature, when undisguised by worldly pomp; that nothing is so noble as goodness and grandeur, associated in the same character; that this is the highest felicity; that in some sort it transforms the soul into the image of God; who, from the high abodes of majesty in which He dwells, surrounded with angels and cherubim, deigns to look down on this mean world which we inhabit, and "Leaves not Himself without witness, doing good to all."

"He reasoned of temperance." There he would paint the licentious effects of voluptuousness. There he would demonstrate how opposite is this propensity to the spirit of the gospel; which everywhere enjoins retirement, mortification, and self-denial. He would show how it degrades the finest characters who have suffered it to predominate. Intemperance renders the mind incapable of reflection. It debases the courage. It debilitates the mind. It softens the soul. He would demonstrate the meanness of a man called to preside over a great people, who exposes his foibles to public view; not having resolution to conceal, much less to vanquish them. With Drusilla, he would make human motives supply the defects of divine; with Felix, he would make divine motives supply the defects of human. He would make this shameless woman feel that nothing on earth is more odious than a woman destitute of honor, that modesty is an attribute of the sex; that an attachment, uncemented by virtue, can not long subsist; that those who receive illicit favors are the first, according to the fine remark of a sacred historian, to detest the indulgence: "The hatred wherewith 'Ammon, the son of David,' hated his sister, after the gratification of his brutal passion, was greater than the love wherewith he had loved her" (II Sam. xiii., 15). He would make Felix perceive that, however the depravity of the age might seem to tolerate a criminal intercourse with persons of the other sex, with God, who has called us all to equal purity, the crime was not less heinous.

"He reasoned," in short, "of judgment to come." And here he would magnify his ministry. When our discourses are regarded as connected only with the present period, their force, I grant, is of no avail. We speak for a Master who has left us clothed with infirmities, which discover no illustrious marks of Him by whom we are sent. We have only our voice, only our exhortations, only our entreaties. Nature is not averted at our pleasure. The visitations of Heaven do not descend at our command to punish your indolence and revolts: that power was very limited, even to the apostle. The idea of a future state, the solemnities of a general judgment, supply our weakness, and St. Paul enforced this motive; he proved its reality, he delineated its luster, he displayed its pomp. He resounded in the ears of Felix the noise, the voices, the trumpets. He showed him the small and the great, the rich man and Lazarus, Felix the favorite of Cæsar, and Paul the captive of Felix, awakened by that awful voice: "Arise, ye dead, and come to judgment."

But not to be precipitate in commending the apostle's preaching. Its encomiums will best appear by attending to its effects on the mind of Felix. St. Jerome wished, concerning a preacher of his time, that the tears of his audience might compose the eulogy of his sermons. We shall find in the tears of Felix occasion to applaud the eloquence of our apostle. We shall find that his discourses were thunder and lightning in the congregation, as the Greeks used to say concerning one of their orators. While St. Paul preached, Felix felt I know not what agitations in his mind. The recollection of his past life; the sight of his present sins; Drusilla, the object of his passion and subject of his crime; the courage of St. Paul—all terrified him. His heart burned while that disciple of Jesus Christ expounded the Scriptures. The word of God was quick and powerful. The apostle, armed with the two-edged sword, divided the soul, the joints, and the marrow, carried conviction to the heart. Felix trembled, adds our historian, Felix trembled! The fears of Felix are our second reflection.

What a surprising scene, my brethren, is here presented to your view. The governor trembled, and the captive spoke without dismay. The captive made the governor tremble. The governor shuddered in the presence of the captive. It would not be surprising, brethren, if we should make an impression on your hearts (and we shall do so, indeed, if our ministry is not, as usual, a sound of empty words); it would not be surprising if we should make some impression on the hearts of our hearers. This sanctuary, these solemnities, these groans, this silence, these arguments, these efforts,—all aid our ministry, and unite to convince and persuade you. But here is an orator destitute of these extraneous aids: behold him without any ornament but the truth he preached. What do I say? that he was destitute of extraneous aids? See him in a situation quite the reverse,—a captive, loaded with irons, standing before his judge. Yet he made Felix tremble. Felix trembled! Whence proceeded this fear, and this confusion? Nothing is more worthy of your inquiry. Here we must stop for a moment: follow us while we trace this fear to its source. We shall consider the character of Felix under different views; as a heathen, imperfectly acquainted with a future judgment, and the life to come; as a prince, or governor, accustomed to see every one humble at his feet; as an avaricious magistrate, loaded with extortions and crimes; in short, as a voluptuous man, who has never restricted the gratification of his senses. These are so many reasons of Felix's fears.

First, we shall consider Felix as a heathen, imperfectly acquainted with a future judgment and the life to come: I say, imperfectly acquainted, and not as wholly ignorant, the heathens having the "work of the law written in their hearts" (Rom. ii., 15). The force of habit had corrupted nature, but had not effaced its laws. They acknowledged a judgment to come, but their notions were confused concerning its nature.

Such were the principles of Felix, or rather such were the imperfections of his principles, when he heard this discourse of St. Paul. You may infer his fears from his character. Figure to yourselves a man hearing for the first time the maxims of equity and righteousness inculcated in the gospel. Figure to yourselves a man who heard corrected the immorality of pagan theology; what was doubtful, illustrated; and what was right, enforced. See a man who knew of no other God but the incestuous Jupiter, the lascivious Venus, taught that he must appear before Him, in whose presence the seraphim veil their faces, and the heavens are not clean. Behold a man, whose notions were confused concerning the state of souls after death, apprized that God shall judge the world in righteousness. See a man who saw described the smoke, the fire, the chains of darkness, the outer darkness, the lake of fire and brimstone; and who saw them delineated by one animated by the Spirit of God. What consternation must have been excited by these terrific truths!

This we are incapable adequately of comprehending. We must surmount the insensibility acquired by custom. It is but too true that our hearts—instead of being imprest by these truths, in proportion to their discussion—become more obdurate. We hear them without alarm, having so frequently heard them before. But if, like Felix, we had been brought up in the darkness of paganism, and if another Paul had come and opened our eyes, and unveiled those sacred terrors, how exceedingly should we have feared! This was the case with Felix. He perceived the bandage which conceals the sight of futurity drop in a moment. He heard St. Paul, that herald of grace and ambassador to the Gentiles, he heard him reason on temperance and a judgment to come. His soul was amazed; his heart trembled; his knees smote one against another.

Amazing effects, my brethren, of conscience! Evident argument of the vanity of those gods whom idolatry adorns after it has given them form! Jupiter and Mercury, it is true, had their altars in the temples of the heathens; but the God of heaven and earth has His tribunal in the heart: and, while idolatry presents its incense to sacrilegious and incestuous deities, the God of heaven and earth reveals His terrors to the conscience, and there loudly condemns both incest and sacrilege.

Secondly, consider Felix as a prince; and you will find in this second office a second cause of his fear. When we perceive the great men of the earth devoid of every principle of religion, and even ridiculing those very truths which are the objects of our faith, we feel that faith to waver. They excite a certain suspicion in the mind that our sentiments are only prejudices, which have become rooted in man, brought up in the obscurity of humble life. Here is the apology of religion. The Caligulas, the Neros, those potentates of the universe, have trembled in their turn as well as the meanest of their subjects. This independence of mind, so conspicuous among libertines, is consequently an art,—not of disengaging themselves from prejudices, but of shutting their eyes against the light, and of extinguishing the purest sentiments of the heart. Felix, educated in a court fraught with the maxims of the great instantly ridicules the apostle's preaching. St. Paul, undismayed, attacks him, and finds a conscience concealed in his bosom: the very dignity of Felix is constrained to aid our apostle by adding weight to his ministry. He demolishes the edifice of Felix's pride. He shows that if a great nation was dependent on his pleasure, he himself was dependent on a Sovereign in whose presence the kings of the earth are as nothing. He proves that dignities are so very far from exempting men from the judgment of God that, for this very reason, their account becomes the more weighty, riches being a trust which Heaven has committed to the great: and "where much is given, much is required." He makes him feel this awful truth, that princes are responsible, not only for their own souls, but also for those of their subjects; their good or bad example influencing, for the most part, the people committed to their care.

See then Felix in one moment deprived of his tribunal. The judge became a party. He saw himself rich and in need of nothing; and

yet he was "blind, and naked, and poor."
He heard a voice from the God of the whole
earth, saying unto him, "Thou profane and
wicked prince, remove the diadem and take
off the crown. I will overturn, overturn,
overturn it, and it shall be no more" (Ezekiel
xxi., 25-27). "Tho thou exalt thyself as the
eagle, and tho thou set thy nest among the
stars, thence will I bring thee down, saith the
Lord" (Obadiah, 4). Neither the dignity
of governor, nor the favor of Cæsar, nor all
the glory of empire shall deliver thee out of
My hand.

Thirdly, I restrict myself, my brethren, as
much as possible in order to execute without
exceeding my limits the plan I have conceived; and proceed to consider Felix as an
avaricious man: to find in this disposition a
further cause of his fear. Felix was avaricious, and St. Paul instantly transported him
into a world in which avarice shall receive
its appropriate and most severe punishment.
For you know that the grand test by which we
shall be judged is charity. "I was hungry,
and ye gave me meat"; and of all the construc-
tions of charity covetousness is the most obstinate and insurmountable.

This unhappy propensity renders us insensible of our neighbor's necessities. It magnifies the estimate of our wants; it diminishes
the wants of others. It persuades us that we
have need of all, that others have need of
nothing. Felix began to perceive the iniquity
of this passion, and to feel that he was guilty
of double idolatry: idolatry in morality, idolatry in religion; idolatry in having offered incense to gods, who were not the makers of
heaven and earth; idolatry in having offered
incense to Mammon. For the Scriptures
teach, and experience confirms, that "covetousness is idolatry." The covetous man is not
a worshiper of the true God. Gold and
silver are the divinities he adores. His heart
is with his treasure. Here then is the portrait of Felix: a portrait drawn by St. Paul
in the presence of Felix, and which reminded
this prince of innumerable prohibitions, innumerable frauds, innumerable extortions; of
the widow and the orphan he opprest. Here
is the cause of Felix's fears. According to
an expression of St. James, the "rust of his
gold and silver began to witness against him,
and to eat his flesh as with fire" (James v., 3).

Fourthly, consider Felix as a voluptuous
man. Here is the final cause of his fear.
Without repeating all we have said on the
depravity of this passion, let one remark suffice, that, if the torments of hell are terrible
at all, they must especially be so to the voluptuous. The voluptuous man never restricts
his sensual gratification; his soul dies on the
slightest approach of pain. What a terrific
impression must not the thought of judgment
make on such a character. Shall I, accus-

tomed to indulgence and pleasure, become a
prey to the worm that dieth not and fuel to
the fire which is not quenched? Shall I, who
avoid pain with so much caution, be condemned to eternal torments? Shall I have
neither delicious meats nor voluptuous delights? This body, my idol, which I habitu-
ate to so much delicacy, shall it be "cast into
the lake of fire and brimstone, whose smoke
ascendeth up forever and ever?" And this
effeminate habit I have of refining on pleasure, will it render me only the more sensible
of my destruction and anguish?

Such are the traits of Felix's character;
such are the causes of Felix's fear. Happy,
if his fear had produced that "godly sorrow,
and that repentance unto salvation not to be
repented of." Happy if the fear of hell had
induced him to avoid its torments. But, ah
no! he feared, and yet persisted in the causes
of his fear. He trembled, yet said to St.
Paul, "Go thy way for this time." This is
our last reflection.

How preposterous, my brethren, is the sinner! What absurdities does he cherish in his
heart! For, in short, had the doctrines St.
Paul preached to Felix been the productions
of his brain:—had the thought of a future
judgment been a chimera, whence proceeded
the fears of Felix? Why was he so weak as
to admit this panic of terror? If, on the contrary, Paul had truth and argument on his
side, why did Felix send him away? Such
are the contradictions of the sinner. He
wishes; he revolts; he denies; he grants; he
trembles; and says, "Go thy way for this
time." Speak to him concerning the truths
of religion, open hell to his view, and you
will see him affected, devout, and appalled:
follow him in life, and you will find that these
truths have no influence whatever on his conduct.

But are we not mistaken concerning Felix?
Did not the speech of St. Paul make a deeper
impression upon him than we seem to allow?
He sent the apostle away, it is true, but it
was "for this time" only. And who can censure this delay? The infirmities of human
nature require relaxation and repose. Felix
could afterward recall him. "Go thy way
for this time; when I have a convenient season, I will send for thee."

It pains me, I confess, my brethren, in entering on this head of my discourse, that I
should exhibit to you in the person of Felix
the portrait of whom? Of wicked men?
Alas! of nearly the whole of this assembly;
most of whom seem to us living in negligence
and vice, running with the children of this
world "to the same excess of riot." One
would suppose that they had already made
their choice, having embraced one or the other
of these notions: either that religion is a fantom, or that, all things considered, it is better

to endure the torments of hell than to be restricted to the practise of virtue. Oh no! that is not their notion. Ask the worse among them. Ask whether they have renounced their salvation. You will not find an individual who will say that he has renounced it. Ask them again whether they think it attainable by following this way of life. They will answer, No. Ask them afterward how they reconcile things so opposite as their life and their hopes. They will answer that they are resolved to reform, and by and by they will enter on the work. They will say, as Felix said to St. Paul, "Go thy way for this time; when I have a convenient season, I will call for thee." Nothing is less wise than this delay. At a future period I will reform. But who has assured me that at a future period I shall have opportunities of conversion? Who has assured me that God will continue to call me, and that another Paul shall thunder in my ears?

I will reform at a future period. But who has told me that God at a future period will accompany His word with the powerful aids of grace? While Paul may plant and Apollos may water, is it not God who gives the increase? How then can I flatter myself that the Holy Spirit will continue to knock at the door of my heart after I shall have so frequently obstructed His admission?

I will reform in future. But who has told me that I shall ever desire to be converted? Do not habits become confirmed in proportion as they are indulged? And is not an inveterate evil very difficult to cure? If I can not bear the excision of a slight gangrene, how shall I sustain the operation when the wound is deep?

I will reform in future! But who has told me that I shall live to a future period? Does not death advance every moment with gigantic strides? Does he not assail the prince in his palace and the peasant in his cottage? Does he not send before him monitors and messengers: acute pains, which wholly absorb the soul; deliriums, which render reason of no avail; deadly stupors, which benumb the brightest and most piercing geniuses? And what is still more awful, does He not daily come without either warning or messenger? Does He not snatch away this man without allowing him time to be acquainted with the essentials of religion; and that man, without the restitution of riches ill acquired; and the other, before he is reconciled to his enemy?

Instead of saying "Go thy way for this time" we should say, Stay for this time. Stay, while the Holy Spirit is knocking at the door of my heart; stay, while my conscience is alarmed; stay, while I yet live; "while it is called to-day." The arguments confounded my conscience: no matter. "Thy hand is heavy upon me": no matter still.

Cut, strike, consume; provided it procure my salvation.

But, however criminal this delay may be, we seem desirous to excuse it. "Go thy way for this time; when I have a convenient season, I will call for thee." It was Felix's business then which induced him to put off the apostle. Unhappy business! Awful occupation! It seems an enviable situation, my brethren, to be placed at the head of a province; to speak in the language of majesty; to decide on the fortunes of a numerous people; and in all cases to be the ultimate judge. But those situations, so happy and so dazzling in appearance, are in the main dangerous to the conscience. Those innumerable concerns, this noise and bustle, entirely dissipate the soul. While so much engaged on earth, we can not be mindful of heaven. When we have no leisure we say to St. Paul, "Go thy way for this time; when I have a convenient season, I will call for thee."

Happy he who, amid the tumult of the most active life, has hours consecrated to reflection, to the examination of his conscience, and to insure the "one thing needful." Or, rather, happy he who, in the repose of the middle classes of society,—places between indigence and affluence, far from the courts of the great, having neither poverty nor riches according to Agur's wish,—can in retirement and quietness see life sweetly glide away, and make salvation, if not the sole, yet his principal, concern.

Felix not only preferred his business to his salvation, but he mentions it with evasive disdain. "When I have a convenient season, I will call for thee." "When I have a convenient season!" Might we not thence infer that the truths discust by St. Paul were not of serious importance? Might we not infer that the soul of Felix was created for the government of Judea; and that the grand doctrines of righteousness, temperance, and a judgment to come ought to serve at most but to pass away the time, or merely to engross one's leisure—"when I have a convenient season?" . . .

Yes, Christians, this is the only moment on which we can reckon. It is, perhaps, the only acceptable time. It is, perhaps, the last day of our visitation. Let us improve a period so precious. Let us no longer say by and by— at another time; but let us say to-day—this moment—even now. Let the pastor say: I have been insipid in my sermons, and remiss in my conduct; having been more solicitous, during the exercise of my ministry, to advance my family than to build up the Lord's house, I will preach hereafter with fervor and zeal. I will be vigilant, sober, rigorous, and disinterested. Let the miser say: I have riches ill acquired. I will purge my house of illicit wealth. I will overturn the altar of Mammon and erect another to the supreme Jehovah. Let the prodigal say: I will extinguish the unhappy fires by which I am consumed and kindle in my bosom the flame of divine love. Ah, unhappy passions, which war against my soul; sordid attachments; irregular propensities; emotions of concupiscence; law in the members,—I will know you no more. I will make with you an eternal divorce, I will from this moment open my heart to the eternal Wisdom, who condescends to ask it.

If we are in this happy disposition, if we thus become regenerate, we shall enjoy from this moment foretastes of the glory which God has prepared. From this moment the truths of religion, so far from casting discouragement and terror on the soul, shall heighten its consolation and joy; from this moment heaven shall open to this audience, paradise shall descend into your hearts, and the Holy Spirit shall come and dwell there. He will bring that peace, and those joys, which pass all understanding.

GIROLAMO SAVONAROLA

1452-1498

THE ASCENSION OF CHRIST

BIOGRAPHICAL NOTE

GIROLAMO SAVONAROLA was born at Ferrara in 1452, and was admitted in 1475 into the novitiate of the Dominican Order, where he soon made himself conspicuous for eloquence, and in Florence attracted many hearers by his diatribes against corruption. Florence, having lost its independence as a republic, was completely under the sway of the Medici, who became arrayed against Savonarola, who aimed at establishing an ideal Christian commonwealth. When he attacked the Pope Alexander VI. his doom was practically sealed. In 1495 he was forbidden to appear in the pulpit, and four years later was excommunicated. He rebelled against papal authority, but the people of Florence grew tired of the strict rule of conduct imposed by his teaching, and he was imprisoned and tried for heresy and sedition. On May 23, 1498, he was hanged and his body burned. His puritanism, his bold rebuking of vice, his defiance of every authority excepting that of his own conscience, seem to anticipate the efforts made by Calvin to regenerate Geneva. Both men failed in their splendid attempts at social reformation, but both left an example of heroic altho somewhat short-sighted unselfishness, which has borne fruit in history.

While He blessed them, He was parted from them, and carried up into heaven.—St. Luke xxiv., 51.

BELOVED in Christ Jesus, the wise men of this world divide all created things into two classes; one class they name substances, the other accidents. The substances are those things that exist through themselves without requiring anything else on which to rest, as the earth, water, air, the heavens, animals, stones, plants, and similar things. The accidents can not exist by themselves, but only by resting on something else, as color, odor, taste, and other such things. But because our knowledge is entirely through the senses, and we are able to know anything only when its accidents fall upon our senses, we have, therefore, knowledge of the accidents rather than of the substances. The eyes are for colors, the ears for sounds, the nose for scents, the tongue for flavors, the touch for heat and cold, for hard and soft. Each sense has its own sphere of knowledge and brings what it has perceived before the imagination, and this hands it over to the reason within, which reads and illuminates the productions of the imagination, judges them, and in this way comes to a knowledge of the substances. But the reason has little light if it is separated from the body, for God has joined soul and body together; and so by means of the senses knowledge becomes definite and complete. For if the soul out of the body were richer in knowledge, it would be in vain that it should be in the body. God and nature have done nothing in vain, and therefore the soul's union with the body ministers to its perfection.

The soul's knowledge, however, will not be complete so long as it lives in this mortal body. It does not while here come to the fundamental distinctions and causes of the substances, because it is obliged to know the inner side of things through their externals. Therefore man is able only imperfectly to know an incorporeal substance; how much less can he know the uncreated infinite being of God? But if he can not know the being of God, he will not be able to know many other infinite things which are in Him. We ought therefore not to be surprised that there is much in God which we can not understand, and that very many truths of the faith we can not yet prove since we do not yet know everything. The great God in His rich mercy saw our poor knowledge and came into our flesh and assumed it that He might work for us, die, and rise again from the dead; until after a life full of love He raised Himself above the world of sense into His eternity. But so long as our Redeemer lived with His apostles they loved too much that which they saw of Him, because they were bound down to their senses, and were therefore unable to rise to the knowledge of His Spirit. It was necessary that He should disappear in the heavens that He might lift their souls far above the world of sense up to Himself. Their natural powers could not do this; therefore He gave to His elect a light from above. Ascending on high He led captivity captive, for ascending into the heavens He took with Him the prey which the devil had made of the soul of men ever since the fall of our parents. The Lord has given gifts unto men (Eph. iv. 8), inasmuch as He has imparted to them the seven gifts of the Holy Ghost. Now they leave everything of this world, and rise above by following Christ, who gives to them for a light the light of faith. Let us speak this morning of this faith which leads to the Savior.

"Awake thou that sleepest and Christ shall give thee light." Be not held captive by flesh and sense, which hold thee fast in sleep; rise to Christ, He will give thee light. See, His flesh is above. What do ye say to that, ye wise men of this world? Everything that has weight tends downward, but His flesh is on high above all heavens. This time your laws have been set at nought. But see what hope Almighty God rouses in us: if our head has gone above, we, His members, will follow Him. In that we hope; of that we preach; on that we live. Know, O man, that if thou wilt thou canst go to Paradise, for thither has thy Savior Christ gone; but know this also, that not by thine own nature, not by means of silver and gold, not by thy virtue, wilt thou reach that place. He has given gifts unto men, and through these thou mayest reach Paradise, if thou only wilt. He has given thee the gifts of His Holy Ghost, and before all the gift of knowledge by which He enlightens thee and shows thee by that light thy goal. Thereupon He gives thee the gift of wisdom, by which thou learnest to love thy goal, and perceivest how much thou needest love. Christ then says to man: Remain in My love, leave the things of this world, follow Me to heaven. And because it is needful for thee to know that this world amounts to nothing, He gives thee experience that it may say to thee that thou must soon leave this world in which nothing lasts. Through many difficulties and doubts, man must get so far and know what to do; therefore thou hast the gift of counsel. Hold fast to this counsel, and follow Christ, who will always give thee good counsel. He will give thee not the treasures of this world, but eternal glory and undying happiness. What wilt thou do, O child of man? Leave this world, enter the service of Christ. He is waiting for thee, and will reward thy service, for He is a bountiful rewarder. Let every one then hasten to serve Him. But because each one is bound to care for the salvation of his brother, and to lead him to Christ, therefore the Lord gives thee the gift of love, by which thou shouldst warn thy brother, thy neighbor, thy friend, thy wife, every one, and with all thy strength and zeal shouldst lead them to Christ. But in this world man must go through joy and sorrow. To oppose the joys of earth, Christ gives thee fear, that thou mightest always be careful lest thou shouldst fall, and not let thy joyous days separate thee from the grace of Christ: to oppose unhappiness, He gives thee strength to resist.

What do ye want, O children of men; will ye not follow Christ who has gone up on high and has departed to prepare a place for you in glory? Thou comest not into the service of the Lord, because thou art not able to believe these words. If thou didst but believe thou wouldst stand no longer indifferent. Thou art unbelieving, thou art unthankful, and the Lord will punish thy unbelief even as on the morning of His ascension He punished the unbelief of His apostles. Because I have explained to thee this morning this Gospel, I must punish the hardness and unthankfulness of thy heart. Thou hast refused the service of the Lord, who has ascended to prepare for thee the highest glory.

I call upon all men and women, all whose lives are ruined in sorrows and troubles. What do ye fear? He who believes that Christ is above no longer fears anything. Come then all ye into His service. Jesus reproved the unbelief and the hard-heartedness of His disciples, because they did not believe those who had seen Him after He had risen. Without faith it is impossible to please God. No doubt the apostles said: How can we believe these women? But these women were of pure heart before God, and therefore the Savior reproved His disciples. Ye deserve still sharper reprimands. To the disciples a few women announced the news that He had risen. Ye hear all this, and in addition all the glorious revelations in which the Lord after this manifested Himself on earth. Why do ye not come to serve Christ? Ye do not truly believe, because ye are so full of sin, and despise God's commandments. Ye do not deserve the gift of faith. He who has faith should show it in his deeds, that he may have what he says he has, and may know what he has; namely, the certainty of the divine word, which can not err, the goodness of God, and His guidance into all goodness. On account of thy sins, thou hast not the true light which would have enabled thee to see all goodness. Thou art sunk in vice, drunken with greed and luxury, and all the works of this world. Thou seekest only power and glory. And wherefore? If thou hadst faith, thou wouldst not seek such things, for thou wouldst know that faith would give thee a much higher crown. From these sins have come thy unbelief and thy hardness of heart. Therefore the words of faith do not touch thy heart: it is a heart of stone and iron. Throw off thy load of sin and give thy will to righteousness; then will thy hard-heartedness end, and God will bestow on thee the gift of faith. What wilt thou? Why standest thou so uncertain and irresolute? Why dost thou not hasten to Him, and see how He leaves thy life, how He goes into the heavens, to which He bids thee come up. Leave at length thy sensual life and enter the pathway of Christ. Hesitate no longer, begin to-day, put it not off until to-morrow. If thou hast faith, thou canst not delay longer, and if thy heart is right before God, He will give thee the light of faith which will enable thee to distinguish the false from the true faith, and so when on the right road not to fall into error. Then wilt thou know for thyself that the Gospel makes good men out of those who truly believe, and thine experience will tell thee that thou hast no occasion to doubt.

A story from the Old Testament might perhaps serve as a parable and make clearer what I mean. When Balak heard of Israel's march, he was afraid and sent to call Balaam to curse Israel for him. Balaam set out on his way with his ass, accompanied by an angel of the Lord, because Balaam was going to Balak with an evil intention. The beast sought in vain to turn into the field, and finally fell down between two walls, and suffered under blows and curses, until the prophet saw the angel and perceived his sin. Balak is the devil who would ruin the people of God; by Balaam we can understand the nobles, the prelates, the preachers, the learned, who are held captive by their arrogance. The two servants are those who follow the proud, serve them, and flatter them, especially the lazy clergy and monks, who so far as outward show goes live a virtuous life, but who live for ceremonies and take care not to speak the truth. To these belong many citizens who live apparently virtuously and hide their pride. Because they commit no sins of the flesh which can be noticed, they are full of piety in their outward ceremonies, but within full of arrogance. These are the members of the devil, for the devil neither eats, drinks, nor sleeps, he is neither a miser nor a wanton, but is within full of pride as are these. By the ass we are to understand the simple people. They are led in the way of sin by the ceremonies of the lazy, since they are not thought fit for the worship of the heart, and

must be led by masses, penance, and indulgences, and they throw away what might be of profit for money and for candles. The lazy give them council in their sermons: Give some vestment, build a chapel, and thou wilt be freed from any danger of going to hell. Do not believe these mountebanks; no outward act can bring you to Paradise, not even miracles and prophecy, but only the grace of God, if you have humility and love . . . . Before the ass stood an angel with a sword. This is Christ, who speaks to the ass: Walk no longer in the path of sin, for I have ready for you a great scourge. The ass alone saw the angel; for the simple first hear the word of the Lord, but Balaam and such as are with him will hear nothing of it. The ass left the path of captivity and went out into the field, into the way of the Lord. "For the kingdom of heaven is like treasure hid in a field; which when a man found he sold all that he had and bought that field." So the simple go into the holy field of the Scriptures and say: "Let me look around a little, for the flowers of this field bear fruit." Yea, our fathers, the prophets, apostles, and martyrs bore fruit, they who died with joy for the truth. These are they who go into the field and speak the truth in the face of death. Come into the city, where the nobles and the masters taken captive by sin crowd together, cry the lazy troop of monks: O fathers, it would be well if when you spoke of these things, you touched not this string, by which you allow yourselves to fall into disgrace and disfavor. They have said that already to me. Our persecution begins if we begin to preach. But Jesus was willing to die for the truth of what He said; should we forsake the truth in order not to displease men? No, we will say it in every way, and with Balaam's ass go into the field.

Think not that I am such a fool as to undertake these things without good reason. I call heaven and earth to witness against me if I do not speak the truth. For against all the world is my sermon; every one contradicts it. If I go about with lies, then I have Christ against me; therefore I have heaven and earth against me, and how then could I stand? As such a trifler with holy things how should I dare rise up? Believe me, I speak the truth, I have seen it with my eyes, and touched it with my hands. Believe it! If I speak not the truth, I consign myself body and soul to destruction; but I tell you I am certain of the truth, and I would that all were as I am. I say that of the truth on which I stand, not as tho I wished that others had my failings as well. So come then into the service of Jesus; come to the truth, come here, I bid you. Do ye not know how I explained the revelation of St. John? There were many who said that I spoke too much in detail, and went too deep into it. There stood the angel before the ass, and wanted it to go out into the field, but Balaam smote it; and ye know not how much opposition I must yet undergo. The lazy monks were the first who called me a fool and revolutionist, and on the other side stood the weak and the simple, who said in their innocent faith: "Oh, if we could only do what He teaches!" Then I had war with the citizens and the great judges of this time, whom my manner of preaching did not please. I was between two walls; the angel warned me, threatening eternal death from this road, and I received Balaam's blows. Ye know my persecution and my danger; but I knew that I was on the way to victory and said always: No human being can drive my cause from the world. Balaam, thou leanest thy foot against the walls, but do as thou wilt, I will crush thy foot; I leaned on the wall, on Christ, I leaned on His grace, I hoped; leave off thine anger and threatening, thou canst not get me away from the wall. I say to all of you: Come to the truth, forsake your vice and your malice, that I may not have to tell you of your grief. I say it to you, O Italy, I say it to you, O Rome, I say it to all of you; return and do penance. There stands before you the holy truth; she can not fall; she can not bend or give way; wait not until the blows fall.

In everything am I opprest; even the spiritual power is against me with Peter's mighty key. Narrow is my path and full of trouble; like Balaam's ass, I must throw myself on the ground and cry: "See, here I am; I am ready to die for the truth." But when Balaam beat his fallen beast, it said to him: "What have I done to thee?" So I say to you: "Come here and tell me: what have I done to you? Why do you beat me? I have spoken the truth to you; I have warned you to choose a virtuous life; I have led many souls to Christ." But you answer: "Thou hast spoken evil of us, therefore, thou shouldst suffer the stripes thou deservest." But I named no one, I only blamed your vices in general. If you have sinned, be angry with yourselves, not with me. I name none of you, but if the sins I have mentioned are without question yours, then they and not I make you known. As the smitten beast asked Balaam, so I ask you: "Tell me, am I not your ass? and do you not know that I have been obedient to you up to this very moment, that I have even done what my superiors have commanded, and have always behaved myself peaceably?" You know this, and because I am now so entirely different, you may well believe that a great cause drives me to it. Many knew me as I was at first; if I remained so I could have had as much honor as I wanted. I lived six years among you, and

now I speak otherwise, nevertheless I announce to you the truth that is well known. You see in what sorrows and what opposition I must now live, and I can say with Jeremiah: "O, my mother, that thou hast borne me a man of strife and contention to the whole earth!" But where is a father or a mother that can say I have led their son into sin; one that can say I have ruined her husband or his wife? Everybody knows my manner of life, therefore it is right for you to believe that I speak the truth which everybody knows. You think that it is impossible for a man to do what the faith I have preached tells him to do: with God it would be easy for you.

The ass alone saw the angel, the others did not; so open your eyes. Thank God, many have them open. You have seen many learned men whom you thought wise, and they have withstood our cause: now they believe; many noted masters who were hard and proud against us: now humility casts them down. You have also seen many women turn from their vanity to simplicity; vicious youths who are now improved and conduct themselves in a new way. Many, indeed, have received this doctrine with humility. That doctrine has stood firm, no matter how attacked with the intention of showing that it was a doctrine opposed to Christ. God does that to manifest His wisdom, to show how it finally overcomes all other wisdom. And He is willing that His servants be spoken against that they may show their patience and humility, and for the sake of His love not be afraid of martyrdom.

O ye men and women, I bid you to this truth; let those who are in captivity contradict you as much as they will, God will come and oppose their pride. Ye proud, however, if you do not turn about and become better, then will the sword and the pestilence fall upon you; with famine and war will Italy be turned upside down. I foretell you this because I am sure of it: if I were not, I would not mention it. Open your eyes as Balaam opened his eyes when the angel said to him: "Had it not been for thine ass, I would have slain thee." So I say to you, ye captives: Had it not been for the good and their preaching, it would have been wo unto you. Balaam said: "If this way is not good, I will return." You say likewise, you would turn back to God, if your way is not good. And to the angel you say as Balaam said: "What wilt thou that we should do?" The angel answers thee as he answered Balaam: "Thou shalt not curse this people, but shalt say what I put in thy mouth." But in thy mouth he puts the warning that thou shouldst do good, convince one another of the divine truth, and bear evil manfully. For it is the life of a Christian to do good and to bear wrong and to continue stedfast unto death, and this is the Gospel, which we, according to the text of the Gospel for to-day, shall preach in all the world.

What wilt thou have of us, brother? you ask. I desire that you serve Christ with zeal and not with sloth and indifference. I desire that you do not mourn, but in thankfulness raise your hands to heaven, whenever your brother or your son enters the service of Christ. The time is come when Christ will work not only in you but through you and in others; whoever hears, let him say: "Come brother. Let one draw the other. Turn about, thou who thinkest that thou art of a superior mind and therefore canst not accept the faith." If I could only explain this whole Gospel to thee word for word, I would then scourge thy forehead and prove to thee that the faith could not be false and that Christ is thy God who is enthroned in heaven, and waits for thee. Or dost thou believe? Where are thy works? Why dost thou delay about them? Hear this: There was once a monk who spoke to a distinguished man about the faith, and got him to answer why he did not believe. He answered thus: "You yourself do not believe, for if you believed you would show other works." Therefore, to you also I say: If you believe, where are your works? Your faith is something every one knows, for every one knows that Christ was put to death by the Jews, and that everywhere men pray to Him. The whole world knows that His glory has not been spread by force and weapons, but by poor fishermen. O wise man, do you think the poor fishermen were not clever enough for this? Where they worked, there they made hearts better; where they could not work, there men remained bad; and therefore was the faith true and from God. The signs which the Lord had promised followed their teaching: in His name they drove out the devil; they spoke in new tongues; if they drank any deadly drink, they received therefrom no harm. Even if these wonders had not occurred, there would have been the wonder of wonders, that poor fishermen without any miracle could accomplish so great a work as the faith. It came from God, and so is Christ true and Christ is thy God, who is in heaven and awaits thee.

You say you believe the Gospel, but you do not believe me. But the purer anything is, so much the nearer it stands to its end and purpose. The Christian life purifies the heart, and places it very near to the truth. To the Christian life will I lead you, if you would have the knowledge of the truth. If I had wished to deceive you, why should I have given you as the chief of my gifts the means of discovering my fraud? I would be verily a fool to try to impose upon you with a falsehood which you would soon de-

tect; only because I offered you the truth, did I call you. Come here, I fear you not; the closer you examine, the clearer the truth will become to you.

There are some, however, who are ashamed of the cross of Jesus Christ, and say: If we should believe that, we should be despised everywhere, especially by the wisest. But if you would know the truth, look only on the lives of those who would have to cry wo on their unbelief if they should be measured by deeds. If you are ashamed of the cross, the Lord was not ashamed to bear that cross for you, and to die on that cross for you. Be not ashamed of His service and of the defense of the truth. Look at the servants of the devil, who are not ashamed in the open places, in the palaces, and everywhere to speak evil and to revile us. Bear then a little shame only for your Lord; for whoever follows Him will, according to our gospel, in His name drive out the devil; that is, he will drive out his sins, and lead a virtuous life; he will drive out serpents; he will throw out the lazy who come into the houses, and say evil things under the pretense of right-eousness, and so are like poisonous serpents. You will see how children can withstand them with the truth of God, and drive them away. If a believer drinks anything deadly it will not hurt him: this deadly drink is the false doctrines of the lazy, from whom, as you con-tend with them, a little comes also to you. But he who stands unharmed in the faith, cries to you: See that you do good; seek God's glory, not your own. He that does that is of the truth, and remains unharmed. The Lord says further of the faithful: They shall lay their hands on the sick and shall heal them. The hands are the works, and the good lay such hands on the weak that they may support them when they totter. Do I not teach you according to the Gospel? Why do you hesitate and go not into the service of the Lord? Do you ask me still what you ought to do? I will, in conclusion, tell you.

Look to Christ and you will find that all He says concerns faith. Ask the apostle; he speaks of nothing else than of faith. If you have the ground of all, if you have faith, you will always do what is good. Without faith man always falls into sin. You must seek faith in order to be good, or else your faith will become false. Christ commanded His disciples to preach the Gospel to all the world, and your wise men call a man a little world, a microcosm. So then preach to yourself, O man, woman, and child. Three parts the world has in you also. Preach first of all to your knowledge, and say to it: If you draw near this truth, you will have much faith; wherefore do you hesitate to use it? To your will, say: Thou seest that everything passes away; therefore love not the world, love Christ. Thereupon turn to the second part of your world, and say to it: Be thankful, O my memory, for the mercies God has shown thee, that thou thinkest not of the things of this world but of the mercy of thy creation, and thy redemption through the blood of the Son of God. Then go to the third part, to thy imagination, and proclaim to it: Set nothing before my eyes but my death, bring nothing before me but the Crucified, embrace Him, fly to Him. Then go through all the cities of thy world and preach to them. First say to thine eyes: Look not on vanity. To thy ears say: Listen not to the words of the lazy, but only to the words of Jesus. To thy tongue say: Speak no more evil. For thy tongue is as a great rock that rolls from the summit of a mountain, and at first falls slowly, then ever faster and more furiously. It begins with gentle murmuring, then it utters small sins, and then greater, until it finally breaks forth in open blasphemy. To thy palate say: It is necessary that we do a little penance. In all thy senses be clean, and turn to the Lord, for He it is who will give you correction and purity. To thy hands say: Do good and give alms; and let thy feet go in the good way. Our reformation has begun in the Spirit of God, if you take it to heart that each one has to preach to himself. Then will we in the name of Jesus drive out the devils of temptation. Yes, call upon Jesus as often as temptation approaches: call upon Him a hundred times and believe firmly, and the temptation will depart. Then will we speak with new tongues; we will speak with God. We shall drive away serpents; the enticement of the senses are these serpents. If we drink anything deadly it will not hurt us; if anger and lust arise in us, at the name of Jesus they will have to give way. We shall lay our hands upon the sick and heal them; with good deeds shall we strengthen the weak soul. If thou feelest thy weakness, flee to God, and He will strengthen; therefore He is thy only refuge. He is thy Savior and thy Lord, who went into the heavens to prepare a place for thee, and to wait thee there. What do you intend to do? Go and follow Jesus, who is praised from everlasting to everlasting. Amen.

FRIEDRICH E.D. SCHLEIERMACHER

1768-1834

CHRIST'S RESURRECTION AN IMAGE OF OUR NEW LIFE

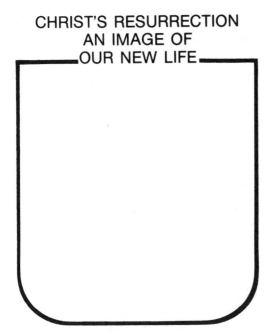

BIOGRAPHICAL NOTE

FRIEDRICH ERNST DANIEL SCHLEIER-
MACHER, German theologian and philosopher, was born at Breslau in 1768. He
was brought up in a religious home and
in 1787 went to the University of Halle,
and in 1789 became a Privat-Docent.
In 1794 he was ordained and preached
successively at Landsberg and Berlin.
The literary and philosophical side of
his intellect developed itself in sympathy
with the Romanticists, but he never lost
his passion for religion, a subject on
which he published five discourses in 1799.
We find in them a trace of the pantheism
of Spinoza. His translation of Plato,
accomplished between 1804 and 1806, gave
him high rank as a classical scholar. In
1817 he joined the movement toward the
union of the Lutheran and Reformed
churches. As a preacher he was unpre-
possessing in appearance, being sickly
and hunchbacked, but his simplicity of
manner, and his clear, earnest style endeared him to many thousands. He died
in Berlin in 1834.

As Christ was raised up from the dead by the glory of the Father, even so we should walk in newness of life.—Romans vi., 4.

IT is natural, my friends, that the glorious festival of our Savior's resurrection should attract the thoughts of believers to a far remote time, and that it should make them rejoice to think of the time when they shall be with Him who, after He had risen from the dead, returned to His and our Father. But the apostle, in the words of our text, recalls us from what is far off to what is close to us—to the immediate present of our life here. He takes hold of what is the most immediate concern, of what we are at once to share in and which is to form us, even here, into the likeness of Christ's resurrection. We are buried with Him, He says, unto death, that as He was raised from the dead through the glory of the Father, we also might walk in newness of life. And this new life is that which, as the Lord Himself says, all who believe in Him possess even now as having passed through death to life. The apostle compares this with those glorious days of our Lord's resurrection; and how could we more appropriately keep this feast—a feast in which, above all others, many Christians draw renewed strength for this new life from the most intimate union with our heavenly Head—how could we better celebrate it than by endeavoring to receive this directly for ourselves from the words of the apostle? Let us then, according to the teaching of these words, consider the resurrection life of our Lord, as the apostle presents it to us, as a glorious, tho it may be unattainable, model of the new life in which we are all to walk through Him.

1. This new life is like that of our risen Savior, first, in the manner of His resurrection. In order to appear to His disciples in that glorified form, which already bore in it the indications of the eternal and immortal glory, it was necessary that the Savior should pass through the pains of death. It was not an easy transformation; it was necessary for Him, tho not to see corruption, yet to have the shadow of death pass over Him; and friends and enemies vied with each other in trying to retain Him in the power of the grave; the friends rolling a stone before it, to keep the beloved corpse in safety, the enemies setting a watch lest it should be taken away. But when the hour came which the

Father had reserved in His own power, the angel of the Lord appeared and rolled away the stone from the tomb, and the watch fled, and at the summons of omnipotence life came back into the dead form.

Thus, my friends, we know what is the new life that is to be like the resurrection life of the Lord. A previous life must die; the apostle calls it the body of sin, the law of sin in our members, and this needs no lengthened discussion. We all know and feel that this life, which Scripture calls a being dead in sins, pleasant and splendid as may be the form it often assumes, is yet nothing but what the mortal body of the Savior also was, an expression and evidence of the power of death, because even the fairest and strongest presentation of this kind lacks the element of being imperishable. Thus with the mortal body of the Savior, and thus also with the natural life of man, which is as yet not a life from God.

And this our old man must die a violent death in the name of the law, such as the Savior died, not without severe suffering and painful wounds. For if the body of sin dies out in a man of itself, through satiety of earthly things, and because no excitement can any longer affect his exhausted powers, that is a death from which we see no new life proceed. The power of sin must be slain in a man by violence; a man must go through the torture of self-knowledge, showing him the contrast between his wretched condition and the higher life to which he is called; he must hear the cry, and accept it as an irrevocable sentence; that an end is to be put to this life; he must groan and almost sink under the preparations for the execution of that sentence; all his accustomed habits of life must cease; he must be conscious of the wish that he were safely through it all, and it were at an end.

And when he has yielded up the old life to a welcome death, and the old man is crucified with Christ, then the world, which knows nothing better than that previous life, if it only goes on well and easily, uses all kinds of efforts to hinder the rising up of the new life, some of them well-meaning, others self-interested and therefore hostile. Some, with good intentions, like those friends of the Savior, consult together, and try all in their power, keeping away all extraneous influences, to preserve at least the appearance of their friend from being defaced, and tho no joyful movement can ever again be awakened, to preserve the form of the old life. Others, seeking their own interest and pleasure in a way by which they almost certainly accuse themselves, try to prevent an abuse being practised in this state of things, and also to guard against the gay, merry life which they lead, and into which they like so much to lead

others, being brought into contempt by a question of a new life arising after this dying off of the old man, when, as they think, there is really nothing else and nothing better here on earth and when it is a vain pretense for some to assert that they know this new life, and a mischievous delusion for others to attempt attaining it. Therefore wherever they perceive such a state of things, they have their spies to watch against every deception that might be practised about such a new life, or at least at once to discover and publish what kind of delusions prevail in connection with it.

But when the hour has come which the Father has kept in His own power, then in one form or another His life-bringing angel appears to such a soul. Yet how little do we know about what part the angel had in the Savior's resurrection! We do not know if the Savior saw him or not; we can not determine the moment at which he rolled away the stone from the tomb and the reanimated Savior came forth; no one witnessed it, and the only persons of whom we are told that they might have been able to see it with their bodily eyes were smitten with blindness. And in like manner, neither do we know how the soul, lying, so to speak, in the tomb of self-destruction, is wrought upon by the angel of the Lord in order to call forth the life of God in it. It arises unseen in that grave-like silence, and can not be perceived until it is actually present; what is properly the beginning of it is hidden, as every beginning usually is, even from him to whom the life is imparted. But this is certain, as the apostle says, that the Lord was raised from the dead by the glory of the Father, and thus also, according to the words of the Savior, no man comes to the Son except the Father draw him; that same glory of the ·Father, which then called forth the Savior from the tomb, still awakens in the soul that has died to sin the new life, like the resurrection life of the Lord. Indeed, among all the proofs of the Father's glory in heaven and earth, there is none greater than this, that he has no pleasure in the death-like condition of the sinner, but that at some time or another the almighty, mysterious, life-giving call sounds in his ears —Arise and live.

2. And, secondly, this new life resembles its type and ideal, the resurrection life of Christ, not only in being risen from death, but also in its whole nature, way and manner. First, in this respect, that tho a new life, it is, nevertheless, the life of the same man, and in the closest connection with his former life. Thus, with our Savior; He was the same, and was recognized by His disciples as the same, to their great joy; His whole appearance was the very same; even in the glory of His resurrection He bore the marks of His wounds as a remembrance of His sufferings and as the

tokens of His death; and the remembrance of His former state was most closely and constantly present with Him. And just so it is with the new life of the Spirit. If the old man has died in sin, and we now live in Christ, and with Him in God, yet we are the same persons that we were before. As the resurrection of the Lord was no new creation, but the same man, Jesus, who had gone down into the grave, come forth again from it; so in the soul before it died the death which leads to life in God, there must have lain the capability of receiving that life when the body of sin should die and perish; and that life is developed in the same human soul amid the same outward circumstances as before, and with its other powers and faculties remaining unchanged. We are entirely the same persons, only that the fire of the higher life is kindled in us, and also that we all bear the signs of death, and that the remembrance of our former state is present with us. Yes, in manifold ways we are often reminded of what we were and what we did before the call to new life sounded in our hearts; and it is not so easy to efface the scars of the wounds, and the numberless traces of the pains under which the old man had to die that the new man might live. And as the glad faith of the disciples rested on the very fact that they recognized the Lord as being, in the glory of His resurrection, the same person that He was before; so also in us, the confidence in this new life, as a permanent and now natural state with us, rests only on this—that we recognize ourselves in it as the same persons that we were before; that there are the same faculties, lower and higher, of the human soul, which formerly served sin, but are now created anew as instruments of righteousness. Indeed, all the traces of that death, as well as of the former life, make us more vividly conscious of the great change that the life-giving call of God has produced in us, and call for the most heartfelt gratitude.

And as the Savior was the same person in the days of His resurrection, so His life was also again of course a vigorous and active life; indeed, we might almost say it bore the traces of humanity, without which it could be no image of our new life, even in this, that it gradually grew stronger and acquired new powers. When the Savior first appeared to Mary, He said, as if His new life had been, as it were, timid and sensitive, "Touch me not, for I am not yet ascended to my God and your God." But after a few days He showed Himself to Thomas, and bade him boldly touch Him, put his hand in the Master's side, and his fingers into the marks left by the nails of the cross, so that He did not shrink from being touched even on the most sensitive spots. And also even in the earliest days, and as if the new life were to be fully strengthened by

doing so, we find Him walking from Jerusalem to Emmaus, and from Emmaus back to Jerusalem, as well as going before His disciples into Galilee, and leading them back to Jerusalem, where He then ascended to heaven in their sight. And as He thus walked among them, living a life with them, human in every part, and exercising a human influence on them; so also His most important business was to talk with them of the kingdom of God, to reprove and rouse them up from their slowness of heart, and to open the eyes of their minds. Now so it is, my friends, with our new life— that is like the resurrection life of the Lord. Oh, how very gradually it gains its faculties in us, grows and becomes strong, only bearing still more than the new life of the Lord the traces of earthly imperfection. I can appeal on this point to the feeling of us all, for assuredly it is the same in all. How intermittent at first are the manifestations of this new life, and how limited the sphere of its action! How long does it retain its sensitive spots, which can not be touched without pain, or even without injurious consequences, and those are always the places in which the old man has been most deeply wounded in his dying hours! But in proportion as it becomes stronger, this new life ought the less to give the impression of being a mere fantom life, —the impression the Lord's disciples had when in the first moments they thought in their fear that they saw a spirit, so that He was obliged to appeal to the testimony of all their senses, that they might perceive He was no spirit, but had flesh and bones. And thus if our new life in God consisted in mere states of feeling and emotions, which were not in the least capable of passing into action, or perhaps did not even aim at doing so; which were too peculiar and special to ourselves to be actually communicated to others or to move them with good effect, but rather might touch them with a chill sense of awe; what would such a life be but a ghost-like apparition that would no doubt excite attention, but would find no credence, and would make men uneasy in their accustomed course, but without producing any improvement in it? No, it is a life of action, and ought to be ever becoming more so; not only being nourished and growing stronger and stronger through the word of the Lord and through heart-communion with Him, to which He calls us, giving Himself to us as the meat and drink of eternal life, but every one striving to make his new life intelligible to others about him, and to influence them by it. Oh, that we had our eyes more and more steadily fixt on the risen Savior! Oh, that we could ever be learning more and more from Him to breathe out blessing, as He did when He imparted His Spirit to the disciples! Oh, that we were more and more learning like Him to encourage the foolish and slow of heart to joyful faith in the divine promises, to active obedience to the divine will of their Lord and Master, to the glad enjoyment and use of all the heavenly treasures that He has thrown open to us! Oh, that we were ever speaking more effectively to all connected with us, of the kingdom of God and of our inheritance in it, so that they might see why it was necessary for Christ to suffer, but also into what glory He has gone! These are our desires, and they are not vain desires. The life-giving Spirit, whom He has obtained for us, effects all this in each in the measure that pleases Him; and if once the life of God is kindled in the human soul if we have once, as the apostle says, become like Him in His resurrection, then His powers are also more and more abundantly and gloriously manifested in us through the efficacy of His Spirit for the common good.

But along with all this activity and strength, the life of the risen Savior was yet, in another sense, a secluded and hidden life. It is probable that when, in order to show Himself to His disciples, He went here and there from one part of the land to another, He was seen by many besides them, who had known Him in His previous life. How could it be otherwise? But the eyes of men were holden, that they did not recognize Him; and He made Himself known only to those who belonged to Him in faithful love. At the same time, however, He said to them, Blest are they who do not see, yet believe! And what was the little number of those who were counted worthy of seeing Him, even if we add to them the five hundred whom Paul mentions, compared with the number of those who afterward believed in their testimony to the Lord's resurrection? And thus it is also, my friends, with the new life in which we walk, even if it is, as it ought to be, strong and vigorous, and ever at work for the kingdom of God; yet it is at the same time an unknown and hidden life, unrecognized by and hidden from the world, whose eyes are holden; and he who should set himself to force the knowledge of it upon them, who should hit upon extraordinary proceedings in order to attract their attention to the difference between the life of sin and the resurrection life, would not be walking in the likeness of the Lord's resurrection. As the people in the time of Christ had opportunity enough to inquire about His resurrection, in seeing how His disciples continued to hold together, so our neighbors also see our close alliance, which has nothing to do with the affairs of this world; and if they, because of this, inquire about what unites us, the answer will not be lacking to them. But our inner history we will as little thrust upon them as the risen Christ thrust His presence

on those who had slain Him, and who had therefore no desire to see Him. Instead of this, as He showed Himself only to His own, we also will make known our inner life only to those who are just in the same way our own; who, glowing with the same love, and cheered by the same faith, can tell us in return how the Lord has revealed Himself to them. Not by any means as if we followed some mysterious course, and that those only whose experiences had been entirely alike should separate themselves into little exclusive groups; for even the days of the Lord's resurrection present examples of various kinds of experience, and of one common inner fellowship connected with them all. And not only so, but even those who as yet have experienced nothing at all are not sent empty away. Only they must first become aware, by what they see without our thrusting it upon them, that here a spirit is breathing to which they are strangers, that here is manifested a life as yet unknown to them. Then will we, as was done then, lead them by the word of our testimony to the foundation of this new life; and as, when the word of preaching pierced men's hearts, when to some of them the old man began to appear as he really is, and they felt the first pangs that precede the death of the sinful man, there also sprang up faith in the resurrection of Him whom they had themselves crucified; so will it always be with the knowledge of the new life proceeding from Him who has risen. Therefore let us have no anxiety; the circle of those who recognize this life will always be widening, just because they are beginning to share in it. And as soon as the slightest premonition of it arises in a man's soul, as soon as he has come only so far as to be no longer pleased and satisfied with the perishing and evil things of the world, as soon as his soul absorbs even the first ray of heavenly light, then his eyes are opened, so that he recognizes this life, and becomes aware what a different life it is to serve righteousness, from living in the service of sin.

3. And lastly, my friends, we can not feel all these comforting and glorious things in which our new life resembles the resurrection life of our Lord, without being at the same time, on another side, moved to sorrow by this resemblance. For if we put together all that the evangelists and apostles of the Lord have preserved for us about His resurrection life, we still can not out of it all form an entirely consecutive history. There are separate moments and hours, separate conversations and actions, and then the Risen One vanishes again from the eyes that look for Him; in vain we ask where He can have tarried, we must wait till He appears again. Not that in Himself there was anything of this broken or uncertain life, but as to our

view of it, it is and can not be but so; and we try in vain to penetrate into the intervals between those detached moments and hours. Well, and is it not, to our sorrow, with the new life that is like Christ's resurrection life? I do not mean that this life is limited to the few hours of social worship and prayer, glorious and profitable as they are; for in that case there would be cause to fear that it was a mere pretense; nor to the services, always but small and desultory, that each of us, actively working through the gifts of the Spirit, accomplishes, as it were, visibly and tangibly according to his measure, for the kingdom of God. In manifold ways besides these we become conscious of this new life; there are many quieter and secret moments in which it is strongly felt, tho only deep in our inmost heart. But notwithstanding this, I think all, without exception, must confess that we are by no means conscious of this new life as an entirely continuous state; on the contrary, each of us loses sight of it only too often, not only among friends, among disturbances and cares, but amid the commendable occupations of this world. But this experience, my dear friends, humbling as it is, ought not to make us unbelieving, as if perhaps our consciousness of being a new creature in Christ were a delusion, and what we had regarded as indications of this life were only morbid and overstrained emotions. As the Lord convinced His disciples that He had flesh and bones, so we may all convince ourselves and each other that this is an actual life; but in that case we must believe that, tho in a hidden way and not always present to our consciousness, yet it is always in existence, just as the Lord was still in existence even at the times when He did not appear to His disciples; and had neither returned to the grave, nor as yet ascended to heaven. Only let us not overlook this difference. In the case of Christ we do not apprehend it as a natural and necessary thing that during those forty days He led a life apparently so interrupted; but each of us must easily understand how, as the influence of this new life on our outward ways can only gradually become perceptible, it should often and for a long time be quite hidden from us, especially when we are very busy with outward work, and our attention is taken up with it. But this is an imperfection from which as time goes on we should be always becoming more free. Therefore always go back, my friends, to Him who is the only fountain of this spiritual life! If, ever and anon, we can not find it in ourselves, we always find it in Him, and it is always pouring forth afresh from Him the Head to us His members. If every moment in which we do not perceive it is a moment of longing, as soon as we become conscious of the void, then it is also a moment in which the Risen One appears to our spirit, and breathes on us anew with His life-giving power. And thus drawing only from Him, we shall attain to having His heavenly gifts becoming in us more and more an inexhaustible, continually flowing fountain of spiritual and eternal life. For this He rose from the dead by the glory of the Father, that we should be made into the likeness of His resurrection. That was finished in His return to the Father; our new life is to become more and more His and the Fathers return into the depths of our souls; there they desire to make their abode; and the life of God is to be ever assuming a more continuous, active and powerful form in us, that our life in the service of righteousness may become, and continue even here, according to the Lord's promise, an eternal life.

JOSEPH A. SEISS

1823-1904

THE WONDERFUL TESTIMONIES

BIOGRAPHICAL NOTE

JOSEPH A. SEISS, Lutheran divine, was born in 1823, at Graceham, Md. He received his theological education as a private pupil of several clergymen and was first settled over churches at Martinsburg and Shepherdstown, Va. In 1843 he was transferred to Cumberland, then to Baltimore, Md., and finally became pastor of St. John's Church, Philadelphia, and for twelve years was editor of "The Lutheran." He died in 1904.

Thy testimonies are wonderful.—Psalms, cxix., 129.

THE Psalmist here addresses himself to God. The testimonies of which he speaks are God's testimonies. As collected and arranged in one book, they are known to us as the Bible. For the contents of these holy oracles the royal singer expresses his admiration. He pronounces them "wonderful."

It was not an unworthy theme with which he was occupied at the time, neither was it an extravagant opinion which he uttered. It is impossible that there should be for man a more important subject than the communications made to him from his God. And if ever there was a marvelous thing submitted to human inspection, it is this book, the holy Bible. It lies before us like an ocean, boundless and unfathomable,—like a Himalayan mountain, whose summit no foot of man has trod, and whose foundation is in the undiscovered heart of the world. To make a full survey of it is not possible in the present condition of the human faculties. Even the inspired Paul, when he came to look into it, found himself gazing into profundities at which he could do no more than exclaim, "Oh, the depth of the riches both of the wisdom and the knowledge of God!" And yet there are many beautiful shells and pebbles lying on the shore of this sea, and as many precious flowers blooming on this mountain side, which any one may gather, and which, whosoever attentively contemplates, must feel himself impelled to join the admiring exclamation, "The testimonies of the Lord are wonderful."

Let us look briefly at a few particulars by which to verify this declaration, praying that God may open our eyes to behold wondrous things out of His law.

I. The testimonies of the Lord are wonderful in age and preservation.

The Bible is the oldest of books. Some portions of it are much more recent than others, but a large part of it has come down from the remotest antiquity and antedates all other writings in the world. It contains a journal of events which transpired centuries before the building of the Pyramids. The book of Job existed before Cadmus carried letters into Greece. The five books of Moses were read in holy assemblies two hundred years before Sanchoniathon wrote. David and Solomon had uttered their sacred songs and prophecies half a century before Homer enraptured the Greeks with his verses or Lycurgus had given laws to Lacedæmon. Dozens of the books of Scripture were complete a hundred years before the first public library was founded at Athens; and the last of the prophets had ended his message before Socrates, Plato, and Aristotle had propounded their philosophies. When the elements of society were but forming in the womb of the far-distant past, the Bible was there. When the foundations of earth's present greatness were laid, it was there. And when we go back to the very beginnings of history, even there does its hand lead us and its right hand uphold us.

Nor is it as a mere lifeless fossil that this book has come down to us from such remote antiquity. Tho hoary with age, its youthful vigor remains, and its natural force is not abated. It has only grown fresher with age, and strengthened with every new trial. It has been at the births and deaths of a hundred mighty nations, and seen empires rise, flourish, and fall, and coexisted with the longest lines of earthly kings, and beheld some of the sublimest monuments of human effort come forth and disappear, and passed a hundred generations in reaching us; but, withal, it still lives, in all nations, in all languages, the most precious legacy of departed ages, and the only thing that remains to us from some of them. Tho it has encountered many a fierce conflict with the hate of men and the spite of devils,—tho the object of many a concerted scheme to blot it from the earth,—tho often held up to ridicule, with "gigantic apes like Voltaire chattering at it, men of genius turned by some Circean spell into swine, like Mirabeau and Paine, casting filth at it, demoniacs whom it had half rescued and half inspired, like Rousseau, making mouths in its face,"and all the varied passions of unsanctified men continually arrayed against it,—it still holds its place as the most uncorrupt and authentic of histories, the most august and controlling of records, the most universal, venerable, and potent of books, imagining in its very history the stupendous majesty of the God whom it reveals.

II. The testimonies of the Lord are wonderful in their authorship.

They are not of man, but of God. We can not now refer to the varied and multitudinous considerations which enter into the proofs of this. It is capable, however, of being established by the very highest moral evidences. The wisest and best men of every age have concurred in receiving the Scriptures as from God. And it is not possible to give a rational account of their origin, and the source of their contents, without ascribing them to the divine authorship which they claim.

It may seem strange that the infinite God should condescend to put His great thoughts into the poor language of mortals, to communicate with creatures so dull and stupid as the sons of men; but this He has done. Portions of the Scriptures are made up of the very words of God, articulated by Himself in the hearing of men commissioned to declare them. One chapter, which embodies the moral essence of all the rest, was engraven by His own finger upon tables of rock, and delivered to Moses all ready formed and set in the alphabetic signs employed by men. Other parts consist of communications of celestial messengers sent directly from heaven's throne to declare God's will and purposes to the dwellers upon earth. A still larger portion was taken down as it fell from the lips of One in whom God had incarnated Himself, and whose every word and act in this world was a revelation from the unknown Deity. Even those parts which were written by men were produced by mysterious motion and illumination of the Holy Ghost,—by inspiration of God. Indeed, the whole book is a literary aerolite, all the characteristics of which are unearthly, and whose own superior attributes are so many demonstrations of its superhuman source. Its very address is so far above that of man, that no mortal, unprompted, could ever have risen to it. Its subjects are all treated after an unearthly manner. Every leaf of it bears the sunlight of some higher sphere. Every page has on it the imprimatur of God. And all its words are instinct with divine fires, flashing the admonition upon every reader, "Put off thy shoes from off thy feet, for the place whereon thou standest is holy ground." They that look upon it look upon expressions of the eternal Spirit. They that rightly take its lessons drink in living emanations from unsearchable Godhead. It is the abiding miracle of *rapport* with the Mind which projected, upholds, and governs the universe. It is the Word of God.

III. The testimonies of the Lord are wonderful in their originality and instructiveness.

The Bible depends upon no discoveries of man, and leans upon no other books. If it says some things which may be learned elsewhere, its utterances are always independent and peculiarly its own. The world through which it ranges is much wider than that of man's thoughts. It goes back to a remoter antiquity; it takes in a broader space; it extends to a vaster future; it introduces to sublimer spheres and forms of being; and it exhibits a much profounder wisdom. It opens arcana of which no earthly powers ever dreamed, and is at home in regions where the sublimest imaginings of man had hardly extended a guess. On all the great questions of theology, life, death, and futurity, it speaks with a familiarity, comprehensiveness, and propriety which at once command our confidence and satisfy our hearts. What it touches, it touches with a master's hand. It never speaks without pregnant meaning in all its words. And there is nothing in human science, poetry, or tradition which it does not exceed in knowledge, wisdom, and real value.

In its account of the creation, and the origin of things, there is nothing to compare with it. In all the historians, philosophers, and secular authors,—the books of Zoroaster, the records of Phœnicia and Egypt, the Dialogues of Plato and Lucian, the annals of China, the treatises of Plutarch, the Shastras of India, the Edda of Scandinavia, and all the schemes that have ever been given in explanation of the earth's primal history,—there is nothing so natural, so magnificent, so simple, so appropriate, so reliable, so satisfactory, as the first chapter of Genesis. Nor have all the discoveries of modern geology brought forward anything to convict Moses of a false cosmogony. If it is a truth that the history of the earth's formation runs back through uncounted ages, he leaves an interval for it, between "the beginning" and the period when God caused light to appear upon its dark and misty surface. If it is true that vast eras have been traversed by each separate order of living things, one after the other, we find precisely the same succession in the Mosaic account which is found preserved in the different layers of the earth's crust. And if it be true that there was life upon our world ages and cycles of ages before the period noted in Genesis as that in which man was created, it is also true that no traces of human existence are found except in the most recent deposits. A certain stonemason of the village of Cromartie, with sledge and chisel, himself delved through every formation, from the surface-mold down through the old red sandstone to the Silurian, gneiss, and granite, and, having mastered all that is known concerning each, has written it down as the result of his marvelous explorations, that the truthfulness of the Mosaic record is engraven upon the rocks forever.

And so in every department of science the Bible is always true to nature, and has invariably been in advance of all human investigations and discoveries. How many thousands of years have metaphysicians and psychologists been at work to map out, classify, and gauge the various capacities and powers of the human mind and soul! But they have found no way of approach to the heart so masterly and effective as that taken by the Scriptures; and the more that is known of the nature of the man, the more clearly is it seen that the Bible comprehended it from the commencement. It has been but a few years since Newton laid open the laws of gravitation; and yet the Scriptures spoke of the earth being hung "upon nothing," as if familiar with the whole subject, before human science had begun to form even its feeblest guesses in the case. It has only been since the invention of the telescope enabled men to search through the starry spaces that Sir John Herschel has discovered in the northern sky a peculiar barrenness; but more than three thousand years ago Job told Bildad the Shuhite that "God stretched out the north over the empty place." It has been but a few years since science discovered "that the sun is not the dead center of motion, around which comets sweep and planets whirl," but that "the earth and sun, with their splendid retinue of comets, satellites, and planets, are all in motion around some point or center of attraction inconceivably remote, and that that point is in the direction of the star Alcyone, one of the Pleiades"; which would hence seem to be "the midnight throne" in which the whole system of gravitation has its central seat and from which all material orbs are governed. But the Bible asked the question, more than thirty centuries ago, "Canst thou bind the sweet influences of Pleiades?" as if the speaker knew all about the facts in the case. How long has it been since the doctrine of the rotundity of the earth has been settled by scientific men? yet the Psalmist spoke of "the round world"; and Solomon described in brief the true theory of wind-currents, and strongly hinted the circulation of the blood, at least twenty-five hundred years ago. And, with all the advances of knowledge which have so wonderfully marked the last three hundred years, in which the spirit of philosophic inquiry has ranged the universe, searched heaven, earth, and sea, knocked at every door, peered into every recess, consulted every oracle of nature, and gathered trophies of power and treasures of wisdom and sublimities of knowledge at which the world has been amazed,—in all the motions which the experimentist has traced, in all the principles of power which the master of physics has discovered, in all the combinations which the chemist has detected, in all the forms which the naturalist has recorded, in all the spiritual phenomena which the metaphysician has described, and in all the conditions and relations of mind or matter, past or present, which human research has found out,—there has not come to light one truth to contradict these holy records, or to require the relinquishment or change of one word in all the great volume of Scripture.

IV. The testimonies of the Lord are wonderful in beauty and literary excellence.

The Bible is a casket of jewelry of the richest hues and the most exquisite workmanship. Sir William Jones, that great Orientalist and scholar, has said, "I have regularly and attentively perused these Holy Scriptures, and am of the opinion that this volume, independently of its divine origin, contains more true sublimity, more exquisite beauty, more pure morality, more important history, and finer strains of poetry and eloquence, than can be collected from all other books, in whatever age or language they may have been written.'' Even Rousseau wrote, "The majesty of the Scriptures strikes me with admiration. The works of our philosophers, with all their pomp of diction, how mean, how contemptible, in comparison with them! ''

Nor does it matter much what part of the Scriptures we take, or in what department of rhetoric we test them. Whether it be history or prophecy, the Old Testament or the New, narrative or description, poetry or prose, the same characteristics are to be seen. Moses is as pure and simple as Adam and Eve in Paradise, and yet as majestic and grand as that great creation which he describes. Job contains a drama which is without a parallel,—a drama of facts in which heaven and earth, visible and invisible, with all their wonderful interpenetrations, are set out in their connection with a suffering saint upon his couch, and in which the spirit of earnest inquiry urges itself forward until everything comes forth to declare the majesty of God, and all the might and goodness of man lies prostrate before Him who "bringeth forth Mazzaroth in his season" and speaketh comfortably to them that trust in Him. Under the leadership of David's muse, we pass through varied scenes of beauty and grandeur, —pastures and glens, still waters and roaring floods, dismal swamps and silent wildernesses, forests crashing with the lightnings of God and tempests that convulse the seas, the smoke and fury of battle and the shoutings of glad multitudes, by dells of lonely sorrow and along the starry archways of the sky,—until at length we take our places in a temple high as heaven and wide as space, with all objects of creation as living worshipers around us, each with its separate hymn of grateful joy, blending in one almighty adoration. Isaiah rises upon us like some "mighty orb of song," whose rays are streaming minstrelsies, that have thrilled upon the hearts of men for seventy generations, and which must needs thrill on, unrivaled in their kind, while earth and time endure. Ezekiel is a very comet of fire, flaming his impetuous way across the heavens, and, like the living spirits in his own first vision, going and returning as a flash of lightning. And throughout,—the Evangelists with their simple story of Jesus, and Paul in his epistles and orations, and John in his loving letters and apocalyptic visions,—from the first words, "In the beginning," onward to the last "amen," we find variety, beauty, pathos, dignity, sweetness, magnificence, and glory, such as are contained in no other composition. Here are the sublimest heights and the profoundest depths, and all the gradations from the one to the other. From the worm that grovels in the dust, to the leviathan in the foaming deep, and the supreme archangel, and the eternal God; from the hyssop on 'the wall, to the cedars of Lebanon, and the healing trees which shade life's eternal river; from the pearl-drops which trickle from the mountain rock, to the noise of dashing torrents, and the wide waters of the deluge; from the glowworm under the thorn, to the sun in the heavens, and the great Father of Lights; from the lone pilgrim to the triumphing host, and the gathering multitude which no man can number; from the deepest sorrows of the lost, to the probation scenes of earth and the seraphic visions of the blest,—there is nothing known to mortals which God hath not brought into requisition to intensify and adorn the precious book which He has given to men. As an eloquent preacher beyond the sea remarks, "He has filled it with marvelous incident and engaging history, with sunny pictures from Old-World scenery and affecting anecdotes from patriarchal times. He has replenished it with stately argument and thrilling verse, and sprinkled it over with sententious wisdom and proverbial pungency. It has the gracefulness of high utility; it has the majesty of intrinsic power; it has the charm of its own sanctity: it never labors, never strives, but, instinct with great realities and bent on blessed ends, has all the translucent beauty and unstudied power which you might expect from its lofty object and all-wise Author.''

Some call these Scriptures dull and uninviting; but there is no book in being with so many real attractions. There is no classic equal to it,—no historian like Moses, no poet like Job or Isaiah, no singer like David, no orator like Paul, no character like Jesus, and no revelation of God or nature like that which these venerable pages give. Not without reason has Sir Thomas Browne said, "Were it of man, I could not choose but say it was the singularest and superlative piece that hath been extant since the creation. Were I a pagan, I should not refrain the lecture of it, and can not but commend the judgment of Ptolemy, that thought not his library complete without it.''

V. The testimonies of the Lord are wonderful in their influences and effects.

The Bible has been, for three thousand years, one of the greatest potencies on earth. It has been, and is to this moment, a greater power than Rome, or Greece, or Babylon ever was. Though it has not conquered the world, it has advanced further towards it than Alexander ever did. It has done more to govern and renew the human heart than all the laws enacted by legislators, and all the maxims devised by uninspired sages, and all the lessons, apart from itself, that were ever given to the race. It is the chief stay of a society which for a thousand years has been the most widespread, the most important, and the most powerful association on the earth. It has controlled the religious opinions of a large part of mankind for nearly forty centuries. It has molded characters and directed the efforts of men whose lives and labors introduced new eras and shaped the destinies of nations and turned the course of the world's entire history. It has begotten and fostered the purest virtue, the sublimest manhood, the noblest beneficence, the sincerest charity, the tenderest kindness, and all the blessed saintship, that have ever been upon earth.

Its vast influence upon the welfare of nations may be estimated in part from the bloody codes, and infamous administrations, and social degradations, and far-reaching wretchedness, of those countries where it is rejected or unknown, contrasted with the blessedness and peace of those who have received it. It was the great Milton who said, "There are no politics like those which the Scriptures teach"; and in proof we need only look at Judea when it knew no laws but those which this book contains. How smooth and steady were the wheels of public justice, and how beautiful was the flow of national peace, in those golden days of the old Hebrew commonwealth! How did the joyous vines, and fields of waving ears, and gold of Ophir, and flocks and cattle abiding on a thousand hills, and cities full of peace and plenty, proclaim abroad the wealth and blessedness of that goodly land! How did the voice of singing and the fragrance of virtue linger round each habitation, and the sacrifices of praise crowd all the temple's courts from tribes rejoicing in the smiles of God!

In the sphere of learning and thought-creations, also, the influence of the Bible is equally marked and wonderful. It is to the world of letters what the sun is to the solar system, the fountain of the purest light and brightest wisdom. It has produced more books than any other one thing in existence. It has fostered learning when there was no other stimulation to its cultivation felt. Even the heathen classics owe their preservation to it. As a book written in other times, places, and languages, it has called forth the most laboriously compiled lexicons, grammars, and works on archeology by which the world of the present communes with the world of the past. As a book claiming the faith and obedience of men, it has created a world of learned apology, comment, and exposition, and some of the noblest specimens of argument, eloquence, and appeal which are known to man. And, simply as a book among books, it has wrought wondrously upon the thoughts and productions of authors of all classes. The Visions of Dante are largely drawn from it.

Every canto of the Faerie Queene bears the impress of its influence. Milton's matchless songs of Paradise are from an inspiration which the Bible alone could give. From the same source came the immortal dream of Bunyan, the Pauline reasonings of Barrow, the flaming zeal of Richard Baxter, the "molten wealth" and "lava of gold and gems" which poured down "the russet steep of Puritan theology," the songs of Cowper, and "Thoughts" of Young, and visions of Pollok, and mighty eloquence of the Luthers, the Knoxes, the Massillons, the Whitefields, and the Halls. Addison, and Thomson, and Burke, and Dryden, and Wordsworth, and Coleridge, and Southey, and Campbell, and Goethe, all are vastly indebted to the Scriptures for whatever excellences are found in their works. Shakespeare drew largely from this same precious mine, and also even Hobbes, and Shelley, and Byron. That prince of modern orators, Daniel Webster, once said, "If there be anything in my style or thoughts to be commended, the credit is due to my kind parents in instilling into my mind an early love of the Scriptures." Indeed, if we were to destroy the Bible, and take from the world of literature and thought all that it has contributed directly or indirectly, half the history of the race would be swept out of mind, the noblest ideas that have swelled man's heart would be gone, some of the proudest monuments of human genius would be buried in oblivion, and thick darkness would settle down upon the world forever.

VI. The testimonies of the Lord are wonderful as a fountain of consolation, hope and salvation.

The Bible to all its other excellences adds this, that it is the Book of Life. It is not only a basket of silver network, but it contains apples of gold. It is the record of glad tidings to a perishing world, a message of joy to all people. In it, Wisdom hath mingled her wine, and slain her fatlings, and furnished her table, and calls all the hungry and needy to come and partake. The entrance of its words giveth light and imparteth understanding to the simple, and maketh wise unto salvation. It is a balm from Gilead for the sick, oil for the bruises of the wounded, reprieve for the prison-bound, and bread for them that are ready to perish. Its different books are but so many angels of mercy, carrying contentment into the abodes of poverty, enabling even the children of want to lift up their eyes to God who ordereth all things well, and to eat their scanty meals in peace; staying the hearts of the persecuted and opprest, causing them to rejoice and sing under the yoke, at the stake, and in the hottest of the fires, as on their passage-way to crowns immortal in the world to come; calming the minds of the fevered, mollifying where all earthly medicines fail, and kindling glad hopes of recompense yet to be revealed; lighting up comforts in the breasts of those that mourn for their dead, and assuring them of blessed reunions in a better life; and kindling even the dying eye and inspiring the dying heart with thoughts of speedy triumph, causing lips already closed for death to open once more in utterances of victory.

We may talk of the venerable age of the Bible, and its scientific accuracy, and its literary beauty and sublimity, and its wonderful influences upon the ideas, laws, governments, and general order of society and mankind; but it is all nothing in comparison with the spiritual good and immortal hopes and consolations which it begets in those who receive it as a message from their God. Are we voyagers upon a troubled and a dangerous sea? Here is a chart by which to steer in safety to the happy shores. Are we soldiers, beset with foes and required to endure the shocks of battle? This is an armory from which all needed weapons may be drawn at will, and by the right use of which we may hew our way to immortal triumph. Are we pilgrims and strangers, worn and weary in our search for the home from which we are exiles? In this book gush out the pure, fresh waters of life, the cooling shades from the Rock of salvation appear, and the guiding word is heard from pilgrims in advance, to cheer and encourage us till we reach the mansion of our Father. Indeed, it is beyond the power of language to express the excellency and richness of spiritual treasure which we have in this holy Book. It is the miraculous cruse of the Shunamitess which never exhausts. It is the wand of Moses which swallows the serpents of life, and parts the sea of trouble, and brings forth waters in the thirsty wilderness. It is the ladder of Jacob on which our spirits ascend to commune with God and angels. It is the telescope of faith by which we look on things invisible, survey even the third heavens, and have present to our view what is to be in afterages. It is the chariot of Elijah in which to ride up the starry way to immortality unhurt of death. It is the channel of the almighty Spirit as it goes forth for the sanctification of the race,—the very gulf-stream of eternal life

as it pours out for the resuscitation of our wilted and decaying world.

Allusion has been made to the dreadful eclipse it would be to the world of letters and thought, for the Bible, and what it has done for man, to be blotted out. But that were nothing to the moral and spiritual night that would go along with such a calamity. Besides carrying away with it a vast proportion of the intellectual and moral life of the last eighteen centuries, it would silence every preacher of salvation, and abolish at once his office and his text. It would stop every work of mercy and plan of philanthropy in the world.

It would transmute into a lie all our fond anticipations of the return of Jesus to renew the world, restore our dead, complete our salvation, and bring us to an eternal heaven. It would hush forever the glad tidings with which men have comforted themselves for these many weary ages. It would put out the mother's hopes of her dead babes, quench the wife's fond desires for her husband's everlasting peace, destroy the widow's consolation as she lingers by the grave of her buried love, and extinguish the matron's last comfort as she trembles on the verge of eternity.

It would take with it all the reliefs and blessedness which prayer in the name of Jesus gives, and leave the sinner without pardon in the extremities of life. It would take away the last appeal of the slave against his oppressor, remove the last check of tyranny, and lift from the wicked hearts of men the last restraints, giving carnival to every lust and play to every passion, without correction, without limit, and without end!

We stagger, and are horrified, at the mere idea of the loss that would be inflicted. Chills run down our pulses at the contemplation of the despair and wretchedness which would ensue.

Let us, then, learn to value the possession of such a precious book. Let us bind it to our hearts as our chief treasure in this sin-darkened world. And, whilst we admire its beauty and revere its mysteries, let us abide by its precepts, and, as far as in us lies, practise its sacred mandates.

WILLIAM SELBIE

1862-1944

THE NEW COVENANT

BIOGRAPHICAL NOTE

PRINCIPAL of Mansfield College, Oxford, England; born, Chesterfield, December 24, 1862; educated, Manchester grammar school, Brasenose and Mansfield Colleges, Oxford; lecturer in Hebrew and Old Testament, Mansfield, Oxford, 1889,90; minister of Highgate Congregational church, London, 1890-1902; Emmanuel Congregational church, Cambridge, after 1902; editor of *The British Congregationalist;* lecturer on pastoral theology at Cheshunt College, Cambridge.

" Behold, the days come, saith the Lord, that I will make a new covenant with the house of Israel, and with the house of Judah: Not according to the covenant that I made with their fathers, in the day that I took them by the hand to bring them out of the land of Egypt; which my covenant they brake, although I was a husband unto them, saith the Lord: But this shall be the covenant that I will make with the house of Israel; After those days, saith the Lord, I will put my law in their inward parts, and write it in their hearts; and will be their God, and they shall be my people. And they shall teach no more every man his neighbor, and every man his brother, saying, Know the Lord: for they shall all know me, from the least of them unto the greatest of them, saith the Lord: for I will forgive their iniquity, and I will remember their sin no more."—Jer. 31: 31-34.

HERE is the message of a new time, the message of brightest hope and of fullest regeneration in the whole of the Old Testament. This promise of hope our Lord laid hold of as He approached His hour of darkest trial. He held it before the eyes of His disciples when the dread hour of parting from him weighed like a nightmare upon their souls. He planted it at the heart of the sacrament of life and of death which he sent down the Christian ages to bear His remembrance before the eyes of men; " This cup is the new covenant in my blood."

It is the message of a new time for every age and for every soul. It awakens in man's soul the consciousness that he is the master and not the slave of years and centuries. To the old and weary it holds out the promise of newness. He ceases to move mechanically from day to day, allowing the custom and circumstance of the times and period to decide his action and determine his fate, it reveals to him that he is a son of eternity as well as a child of time. He stands above the flow of time, guides its course, determines its character, and gives it an ever new content of worth and meaning out of his own eternal spirit. He looks before and after, and learns that his mastery of the future has not been forfeited to the debts and bonds of the past. He finds that in repentance and forgiveness he may even recover the lordship of the past, and the future opens up before him as a broad heritage upon which he may enter and where he may reign as monarch of the morning and springtide.

How natural to every man is the longing for newness and freshness! It often appears as mere trivial curiosity or superficial love of novelty, but even these are strong intimations of the hope revealed in the new covenant. More solemn and serious are the ever-recurring new vows, new resolves, new

promises, which men make in critical and
crucial hours and events of their lives, and
tho the vows and promises be often broken,
and great resolves come to naught, so long
as a spark of humanity glows in the soul, man,
feeling his mastery over time, renews his
hopes, his vows and his covenants. But the
justification and power of every new hope, of
every regeneration, lie only in the broad principles of the message of the new covenant.

The first and most important fact about the
new covenant is that it is God that makes it;
" Behold, the days come, saith the Lord, that
I will make a new covenant." This is the
fundamental religious idea in the Old Testament, and indeed in all religion. Behind
every law and ordinance and promise of the
Old Testament lies the covenant relation between Jehovah and His people. It is proclaimed with fresh emphasis and with a new
wealth of gracious meaning by Jeremiah, but
it was implied and often exprest in God's
dealing with Adam, with Noah, with Abraham, with Moses, with Saul and with David.
It means that Jehovah of His own free will
and loving kindness began a friendship with
these men, that He graciously condescended
to enter into a bond of mutual fellowship and
faithfulness with His people. We are not to
think of this covenant as a bargain or agreement between equals, but as the offering of
gracious terms by the absolute Sovereign, by
which, however, He bound Himself in mutual
compact with the true Israelites, who received
the covenant. The present colloquial usage of
the term " covenant " is apt to lead the mind
into the market-place, when two parties meet,
each having something which the other needs.
One man has corn and the other has money,
and the man who has corn needs money and
the man who has money needs corn. They
each make an offer, and improve their offers
until they have found common terms upon
which they agree, strike the bargain and make
the covenant. But God's covenant with man
is not of this kind; there is no market-place
wherein we can stand to make terms with God,
nor have we any price that He needs us to
offer Him. The Hebrew figure of speech
which expresses God's covenant relation with
man is derived from a different and an older
custom of life—from the battlefield. The picture at the back of the figure is that of the
victorious leader, after the battle. He passes
over the field of conquest and finds his enemy
lying at his feet, beaten, wounded, helpless,
and he does not now draw the hostile sword to
kill, but bends down to the stricken man, takes
him by the hand, sets him on his feet, restores
to him life, friendship and hope, and of his
free power bestows upon him again the territory, the throne, the crown he had lost. It
is so that God finds men, poor, helpless, lying
in sin and ruin, and out of his free grace He
sets him upon his feet, and bestows upon him
the friendship of God and all the hope, joy
and riches involved in that. Such is God's
new covenant; it is the truth exprest in more
technical terms by Paul in his doctrine of
justification by faith; it is the truth exprest
in language at once more intimate and universal in our Lord's doctrine of the divine fatherhood. God begins the new relation, and all
it involves. In Him is the fountain of all new
beginnings and out of Him proceeds the binding force of all new covenants. The making of
new covenants, the formation of new characters, the acquisition of new powers and riches
of life is therefore not so much a matter for
us to make new resolves, new vows, new promises, as it is for us to allow God to make the
terms of his covenant with our souls. And
here is man's hope, the hope for every man,
even the man who has often promised, often
determined to reform, to rise higher, and who
has failed as often. Broken resolutions, the
bondage of old habit, and the despair of failure may weigh heavily on his soul; he may
have said, " I have tried so often to overcome
the same temptation, I have so many times
vowed to renounce my besetting sin, but all
the vows are broken, and I dare not try
again." But there is still one way, an infallible way, the only way—to open wide the
gates of the soul, to let God come in to make
His own covenant with man.

The next feature of the new covenant is
that it becomes for man a covenant of inward
principle as distinguished from one of outward rules; " Not according to the covenant
that I made with their fathers in the day that
I took them by the hand, to bring them out of
the land of Egypt,"—not like the mosaic
covenant of laws and ordinances, " but this is
the covenant. . . . I will put my law in
their inward parts and in their hearts will I
write it." For the child it is good that he
should live by rules which he has neither assimilated nor understood, under commands
which derive their authority from the knowledge and experience of others who have lived
them, but that is not good for the man, because character, moral worth and spiritual
strength are only acquired to the extent that
virtue and holiness have become spontaneous
forces within the soul. There may be a kind
of prudence and safety in keeping within the
boundaries laid down by law and custom,
without knowing or feeling anything of their
inner authority, but that is a weak and poor
life to live, with no freshness, no growth, no
springtide to it, and one easily disturbed by
the fascinations of temptation and the storms
of passion. But such is not the life of the
people of the covenant. God works from
within outward; He establishes the fortress
of the soul on the foundations of His ever
present love, He binds man to Himself in

bonds of never-ceasing friendship and faithfulness that become for man principles of life and conduct, convictions of mind and heart that form the very fiber of the soul's being. The life of the covenant is not a constant effort, an uncertain endeavor to observe more minutely the rules of good conduct, or to keep more faithfully the laws of acknowledged morality, but it is the free outflow in life and conduct of the work of God in the heart within; it is not the painful and regular practise of the bondage of an established law, but the practise of submission to the working of God upon the springs of conduct. Moral progress and growth of the soul are to make inward and subjective those objective ideals and realities of truth, beauty and goodness revealed in God while He impresses His covenant ever deeper upon the human spirit. The morality of the covenant is not something to be adopted and assumed each time we act, and to be neglected when we dwell in repose, but it is in us, as the breath of life in the body, even the power and spirit urging and determining our every act.

From this follows a third feature of the new covenant, that it establishes between God and man a relation of mutual possession as distinguished from mutual obligation; "and I will be their God, and they shall be my people." Law enforces obligations—of man to obey God, and of God to reward or punish man according to his deserts. Such was the relation between God and man conceived under the old legal covenant, now to be superseded. But the new covenant creates a deeper relation. First, God is ours; He not merely undertakes to do this and that for us, but He binds Himself to be ours in all that He is; all His resources and powers are pledged to the service of our salvation. This is the invincible, irresistible might of the new covenant. The power and enthusiasm of Puritanism was derived from its Calvinistic doctrine of predestination and election, for whatever defects in form may have pertained to that doctrine, it meant to them at least that God had given Himself to His people so that He was irrevocably pledged to save them and make them victorious.

And then, we are God's—His own, His property. We are bound, if we accept the covenant bond, not merely to fulfil this or that duty, to keep a number of covenants, perform a number of services, but to give Him ourselves, all that we are, nay more, all that we can be. We make not merely a passive surrender, but give Him our best selves. And this is the place for man's activity to give to God the largest possession possible of himself. By vows and covenants of his own he will not save his soul, but there are fitting responses to the covenant which God makes with us, so that when He has given Himself to us, we shall not be sparing, and shall never cease giving ourselves to Him.

And this mutual possession of one another by living spirits, as God and man are, involves one deeper and greater relation yet, the final feature of the new covenant; it is a covenant of intimate personal communion as distinguished from one of mediation. "And they shall teach no more every man his neighbor, and every man his brother, saying, Know the Lord: for they shall all know me." This is the climax of the new covenant; it contains and creates all that has gone before.

The old covenant of the law had been given by the mediator of men and of angels; and it was itself rather a medium of separation than a bond of union between God and man. Its institutions likewise, the priesthood and the sacrifices rather stood between man and God than brought man to God. But all this belongs to an elementary stage of revelation, fitted for the shy childhood of the race. It obscures the true attitude of God to man, conceals His grace and mercy, and represents Him as a remote avenging Deity, only to be propitiated by the acts of a priestly order which therefore will stand to man as more gracious and powerful than God Himself. But the revelation of the new covenant rends the veil, scatters the clouds, and removes out of the way all mediating agencies, for in it, God Himself comes to man in such a way that they may have personal knowledge of one another. The only mediator of the new covenant is God Himself in Jesus Christ who comes to all in form and manner so near and so intimate that man can receive Him, know Him and hold converse of spirit with Him. In this intimate friendship with God, iniquity is forgiven and sin is forgotten, so that man may know all the freshness, sweetness and joy of the new life which God makes for him and forms within him, by giving Himself unto him in the loving bonds of unfailing friendship and communion.

MATTHEW SIMPSON

1810-1884

THE RESURRECTION OF OUR LORD

BIOGRAPHICAL NOTE

MATTHEW SIMPSON, Methodist Episcopal minister, was born at Cadiz, Ohio, in 1810. He early distinguished himself as an orator, his style being that of spontaneous unpremeditated eloquence, in which he carried his congregation to heights of spiritual fervor and enthusiasm. He visited Europe in 1878 as delegate to the World's Evangelical Alliance in Berlin, which served to widen his reputation as a public speaker. He officiated at the funeral of Abraham Lincoln at Springfield, Illinois. His "Lectures on Preaching" delivered before the divinity students at Yale have been widely read. He died in 1884.

But now is Christ risen from the dead, and become the first fruits of them that slept.—1 Cor. xv., 20.

A LITTLE more than eighteen hundred years ago, as the light of the morning was breaking around the walls of Jerusalem, there was a guard placed about a sepulcher in a small garden near the walls of the city. They were guarding a grave. Some strange scenes had occurred on the Friday before. While a man whom they had taken from the hills of Galilee and around the little lake of Capernaum had been hanging on the cross crucified as a malefactor, strange signs appeared in the heavens, and on the earth and in the temple.

It was rumored that he had said he would rise the third morning. The third morning was coming, and as the light began to break in the East, there came two women silently and sadly wending their way among the tents that were pitched all around the city of Jerusalem; they had sojourned all night in the tents, for as yet the gates of the city had not been opened. They came to see the sepulcher and were bringing spices in their hands. They loved the man who had been crucified as a malefactor, because of his goodness, his purity, and his compassion. They seemed to be almost the only hearts on earth that did love him deeply, save the small circle of friends who had gathered around him. There had been curses upon his head as he hung on the cross—curses from the bystanders, curses from the soldiers, curses from the people. They cried: "Away with him; his blood be on us and on our children!" and on that morning there were none but a few feeble, obscure, heart-broken friends that dared to come near his grave.

A little more than eighteen hundred years have passed and on the anniversary of that day, the morning of the first day of the week, the first Sabbath after the full moon and the vernal equinox, at the same season, the whole world comes to visit that grave. The eyes of princes and of statesmen, the eyes of the poor and the humble in all parts of the earth are turned toward that sepulcher.

All through Europe men and women are thinking of that grave and of Him who lay in it. All over western lands, from ocean to ocean, on mountain top and in valley, over broad prairies and deep ravines, the eyes and hearts of the people are gathered round that grave. In the darkness of Africa, here and there, we see them stretching out their hands

531

toward it. Along the coasts of India and the heights of the Himalayas they have heard of that grave and are bending toward it. The Chinese, laying aside their prejudices, have turned their eyes westward and are looking toward that sepulcher. Along the shores of the seas, over the mountain tops and in the valleys, the hearts of the people have not only been gathering around that grave, but they have caught a glimpse of the rising inmate who ascended in His glory toward heaven.

The song of jubilee has gone forth, and the old men are saying, "The Lord is risen from the dead." The young men and matrons catch up the glowing theme, and the little children around our festive boards, scarcely comprehending the source of their joy, with glad hearts are now joyful, because Jesus has risen from the dead. All over the earth tidings of joy have gone forth, and as the valleys have been ringing out their praises on this bright Sabbath morning how many hearts have been singing—

"Our Jesus is going up on high!"

Why this change? What hath produced such a wonderful difference in public feeling? The malefactor once curst, now honored; the obscure and despised, now sought for; the rising Redeemer, not then regarded by men, now universally worshiped. What is the cause of this great change?—how brought about? The subject of this morning, taken from the associations of this day, call us to consider as briefly as we may the fact of the resurrection of Christ from the dead and some of the consequences which flow to us from that resurrection.

It is important for us to fix clearly in our minds the fact that this is one reason why such days are remembered in the annals of the Church as well as in the annals of nations; for our faith rests on facts, and the mind should clearly embrace the facts that we may feel that we are standing on firm ground. This fact of the resurrection of Christ is the foundation of the Christian system; for the apostle says: "And if Christ be not raised, your faith is vain, ye are yet in your sins; then they also which are fallen asleep in Christ will perish." If Christ be not risen, we shall never see the fathers and the mothers who have fallen asleep in Jesus; we shall never see the little ones who have gone up to be, as we believe, angels before the throne of God. If Christ be not raised, we are of all men the most miserable, because we are fancying future enjoyment, which never can be realized; but if Christ be raised, then shall we also rise, and them that sleep in Jesus will God bring with Him. And that our minds may rest as to the fact of Christ's resurrection, let us notice how God hath arranged the evidences to secure the knowledge of this fact clearly to man.

The first point to which our attention is invited is the fact of Christ's death. Were not this fact clearly established it would be in vain to try to prove His resurrection from the dead. Christ might have suffered for man in some obscure place; He might have laid down His life as a ransom, and yet there would have been no legal evidence of it. God allowed the wrath of man to become the instrument of praising Him, in that He suffered Christ to be taken under what was then the legal process—arrested first by the great council of the Jews, and then by the authority of the Roman governor, so that the matter became of public record—a legal transaction. The highest power, both of the Jewish and Roman governments, united in this fact of His arrest, His trial, and His condemnation to death.

Not only was this permitted, but the time of the occurrence was wisely arranged. It was at the feast of the Jews, the Passover, when all the Jews came up to keep the Passover. They came not only from Egypt but from all the country through which they were scattered. Jerusalem could not hold the people that came together; they pitched their tents all around the city, on the hills and in the valleys. It was the time of full moon, when there was brightness all night, and they came together with safety and security. The multitude, then, was there to witness the scene, so that it might be attested by people from all parts of Judea and from all countries round about Judea.

Then, again, the form of the death was such as to be not a sudden one, but one of torture, passing through many hours. Had the execution been a very sudden one, as it might have been, the death would have been equally efficacious, yet it would not have been witnessed by so many; but as He hung those dreadful hours, from nine until three, the sun being darkened, what an opportunity was given to the people passing by to be imprest with the scene! The crucifixion was near the city; the crowd was there; the temple worship was in process; the strangers were there; and as one great stream passes on some festive day through the great thoroughfare of your city, so passed the stream of men, women, and children by that cross on which the Savior hung. They wagged their heads and reviled as they passed by. The very ones whom Jesus had healed, whose fathers had been cured of leprosy or fever, whose mothers' eyes had been opened; the ones who had been raised up from beds of sickness by the touch of that Savior, passed by and reviled, and said: "He saved others, Himself He cannot save." The multitude saw Him as He hung suffering on the cross.

Then, again, the circumstances attending

His death were such as to invite universal attention. It was not designed that the death should be a private one; not merely a legal transaction, a matter soon over, but a protracted and agonizing spectacle—one to be seen and known by the multitude; but, in addition, that man's attention should be drawn to something to be connected with that wonderful scene; hence God called upon the heavens and the earth, the air and the graves, and the temple itself for testimony. It is said that before the coronation of a prince in olden time in Europe—and in some kingdoms the custom is still observed—there is sent forth a herald, sometimes three days in advance, at different periods according to the custom, to issue a challenge to anyone that dares to claim the kingdom to come and prove his right, and to announce that the coronation of this prince is to take place.

Methinks it was such a challenge God gave to all the powers of humanity and to all the powers of darkness. There hung suffering on the cross He who died for human wo, and as He hung God was about to crown Him King of Kings and Lord of Lords on the morning of the third day. He sends forth His voice of challenge, and as He speaks the earth rocks to its center; that ground, shaking and convulsing, was a call to man to witness what was about to occur.

Not only is there a voice of earth. Yonder the sun clothed himself in sackcloth for three hours, as much as to say: "There may be gloom for three days; the great Source of light hath veiled Himself, as in a mantle of night, for three days. As for three hours this darkness hangs, but as out of the darkness the light shines forth, so at the end of the three days shall the Sun of Righteousness shine out again, the great center of glory, with that glory which He had with the Father from the foundation of the world." It was the herald's voice that passed through the heavens, and that spoke through all the orbs of light, "Give attention, ye created beings, to what is to happen!" But it was not alone in the earth, which is the great center, nor in the heavens, which is the great source of light, that the tidings were proclaimed.

Look in yonder valley. The tombs are there; the prophets have been buried there. Yon hillside is full of the resting-places of the dead; generations on generations have been buried there; friends are walking in it, and they are saying, "Yonder is a mighty judge in Israel; there is the tomb of a prophet." They were passing to and fro through that valley of death when the earthquake's tread was heard, and behold! the tombs were opened, the graves displayed the dead within, and there was a voice that seemed to call from the very depths of the graves, "Hear, O sons of men!"

What feelings must have thrilled through the hearts of those who stood by those monuments and bended over those graves, when, thrown wide open, the doors bursting, and the rocks giving way, they saw the forms of death come forth and recognized friends that once they had known. What was to occur? What could all this mean? Then the great sacrifice was offered. It was three o'clock in the afternoon when Christ was to give up the ghost. Yonder the multitude of pious people were gathered toward the temple. The outer court was full; the doors and gates which lead into the sanctuary were crowded; the lamb was before the altar; the priest in his vestments had taken the sacrificial knife; the blood was to be shed at the hour of three; the multitude were looking.

Yonder hangs a veil; it hides that inner sanctuary; there are cherubim in yonder with their wings spread over the mercy-seat; the shekinah once dwelt there; God Himself in His glory was there and the people are bending to look in. No one enters into that veil save the high priest, and he, with blood and in the midst of incense, but once a year; but it was the mercy-seat and the eye of every pious Jew was directed toward that veil, thinking of the greater glory which lay beyond it.

As the hour of three came and as the priest was taking the sacrificial knife from the altar and was about to slay the lamb, behold! an unseen hand takes hold of that veil and tears it apart from top to bottom, and has thrown open the mercy-seat, not before seen by men. The cherubim are there; the altar with its covering of blood is there; the resting-place of the ark is there; it is the holiest of holies. Methinks the priest drops the knife, the lamb goes free, for the Lamb that was slain from the foundation of the world is suffering for man. The way to the holy of holies is open, —a new and living way, which men may not close, which priest alone can not enter; but a way is open whereby humanity, opprest and downtrodden, from all parts of the earth, may find its way to the mercy-seat of God. There was a call to the pious worshiper by voices which seemed to say: "An end to all the sacrifices, an end to all the suffering victims, an end to all the sprinkled hyssop that is used in purification, for One has come to do the will of God on whom the burden of man had been laid."

Now here were all these calls to humanity from all parts, as if to announce the great transaction. While all this was occurring Christ was on the cross, suffering the agony of crucifixion. How deep that agony we need not attempt to tell you; it was fearful; and yet no complaint escaped His lips, no murmuring was there. He bore the sins of many in His own flesh on the tree. He heard the multitudes revile Him; He saw them wag their heads; He remembered that the disciples had fled from Him—one followed afar off, but the rest had gone; and yet He complained not. Friends and kindred had all left Him and He trod the wine-press alone. He drank the cup in all its bitterness and no complaint escaped from Him. One left Him that .had never forsaken Him before. ''The world is gone, the disciples I have fed and taught have all fled and passed away,—all have forsaken Me.''

But there was no time until that moment of fearful darkness came, when all the load of guilt was upon Him and for our sins He was smitten, that His spirit was crusht, and He called out, ''My God, my God, why hast thou forsaken me?'' All else might go—it were little; ''Why hast thou forsaken me?'' But it is over; the darkness is past; the load is borne; and I hear Him say, ''It is finished''; He bows His head and dies.

Now there is publicity for the transaction. It demanded public investigation, it received it. There was not only the mental agony united with the agony of crucifixion, but there was the voluntary giving up of His life; yet, lest there might be some suspicion, to all this was added the proof of the fact of His death. When the limbs of the others were broken and He was perceived to be dead, the soldier thrust the spear into His side and there came out of that side both water and blood.

There is a peculiarity in the sacred writings. A little incident that seems to be mentioned without care becomes the strongest possible proof, not only of the fact of Christ's death, but of the nature of His death. When that sentence was written the human frame was not understood, the circulation of the blood was not understood. Anatomists had not then, as they have now, unveiled the human system; the great science of pathology had not yet been clearly taught to man; and yet in that sentence we have almost a world of meaning. For it is well attested now that where persons die from violent mental emotion, by what is termed a broken heart, a crusht spirit, there is always formed a watery secretion around the heart. It was not known then to the soldier who lifted up the spear and pierced the body; but so much of that water had secreted around the heart that he saw it issuing forth from the pierced side, unstained by blood, which showed that the great heart had been crusht by agony within.

When taken from the cross He was put in the sepulcher. His friends had given Him up, His disciples had forsaken Him; some of them saw Him die; they knew that He was crucified and they abandoned Him. They were returning to their former employments; but His enemies remembered He had said He would rise the third day, and they put a guard around Him. The Roman soldiers were there; the king's seal was on the stone rolled over the mouth of the sepulcher; they made everything secure. Here again God ordered that we should have abundant proof of Christ's crucifixion.

He was crucified on Friday, which was to them the last day of the week, resting in the grave on our Saturday, which is their Sabbath, and then comes the first day of the week, our Sabbath morning, made our Sabbath because of Christ's resurrection from the dead. There came an humble visitant to the tomb, Mary Magdalene; she had been healed of much, forgiven much and she loved Him. Mary, the mother of James, came also and beheld the scenes that occurred; but there had been strange commotions elsewhere.

Heaven had been gathering around that grave. Angels had been watching there; they had seen the Roman guard; they had seen the shining spear and polished shield; they had seen that Christ was held as a prisoner by the greatest powers on earth. Methinks I see the angelic host as they gathered round the throne of God and looked up into the face of Omnipotence, and if ever there was a time when there was silence in heaven for half an hour, it was before the morning light of the third day dawned. I hear them say ''How long shall man triumph? How long shall human power exalt itself? How long shall the powers of darkness hold jubilee? Let us away and roll away the stone; let us away and frighten yonder Roman guard and drive them from the sepulcher.''

They waited until permission was given. I see the angel coming down from the opening doors of glory; he hastens outside the walls of Jerusalem and down to the sepulcher; when they saw him coming the keepers shook, they became like dead men; he rolls away the stone and sets himself by the mouth of the sepulcher. Christ, girding Himself with all the power of His divinity, rises from the grave. He leads captivity captive, tears the crown from the head of death, and makes light the darkness of the grave. Behold Him as He rises just preparatory to His rising up to glory. Oh, what a moment was that! Hell was preparing for its jubilee; the powers of earth were preparing for a triumph; but as the grave yields its prey, Christ, charged with being an impostor, is proved to be the Son of God with power; it is the power of His resurrection from the dead.

There was Christ's resurrection from the dead. He became the first fruits of them that slept. But to give the amplest proofs of His resurrection He lingered on earth to be seen of men, and to be seen in such a manner as to show that He was still the Savior Christ. In my younger days I used to often wonder why was it that Mary Magdalene came first to the sepulcher, and the mother of James that stood there—why He should appear to them; but in later days I have said it was to show that He was the Savior still; that the same nature was there which had made Him stoop to the lowliest of the low—the power that enabled Him to heal the guiltiest of the guilty; that that power, that compassion, were with Him still.

Tho now raised beyond death and triumphing over hell, He still had within Him the Savior's heart. Methinks I see, when Peter had run in anxiety to tell the news, Mary remained there; she could not fully comprehend it; the grave was open, the napkins were there; it was said He was not there, but He was risen. And yet, there was a darkness upon her; she could not fully conceive, it seems to me, the resurrection of the dead. She stood wondering, when she heard a voice behind her which said, "Woman, why weepest thou?" Bathed in tears as she was, she turned round and saw the man standing, and taking him to be the gardener, and supposing that he had taken the body and carried it away as not fit to lie in that tomb or be in that garden, she said: "If thou hast taken him away, tell me where thou hast laid him, and I will take him away." If He must not lie in this tomb, if He can not lie in the garden, if as a malefactor He must be cast out from man, tell me where the body is and I will take it away. It was a proof of her affection.

A voice said, "Mary, Mary." Oh, she recognized it, and her heart cried out: "Rabboni, my Lord and my God!" and then she would have thrown herself at His feet and bathed those feet again with her tears, but He said, "Touch me not, I am not ascended to my Father; go and tell the disciples and Peter that I am risen from the dead." See the compassion of the Savior! and then that message! "Tell the disciples and Peter." Why send a message to him? Because he curst and swore and denied the Master. The other disciples might have said, "If Christ is risen, He may receive and bless us all; but Peter is gone, hopelessly and irretrievably gone; he that forsook his Master and denied Him, there is no hope for him." And yet said Jesus, "Go and tell the disciples and Peter"—poor backslidden Peter.

Jesus knew his sorrow and anguish and almost felt the throbbings of his broken heart, and He sent a message to Peter. He may be a disciple still—may come back and be saved through the boundless love of Christ. Oh, the compassion of the Son of God! Thank God that Peter's Savior is on the throne this morning!

Not only was He seen by these, but He met with the disciples journeying by the way and explained the Scriptures to them; and as they met in the upper room He was there. When the doors were unopened He came in their midst and said, "Peace!" breathed on them and said, "Receive ye the Holy Ghost." Thus He met with them and said to Thomas, "Reach hither thy fingers, and be not faithless but believing."

Then afterward He was seen by five hundred, and from the Mount of Olives, while the disciples were gathered around Him, He was received up into glory. They saw Him and as He went He blest them. The last vision that ever humanity had of the Son of God ere he ascended to heaven was that of spreading out His hands in blessing. Oh, my Savior hath thus gone up, and He dropt from those outstretched hands a blessing which falls to-day like the gentle dew all over the earth; it reaches heart after heart. It hath reached patriarchs, apostles, martyrs, fathers, and mothers and little children, and, thank God, the heavenly dew, as from those outstretched hands, is coming down on our assembly this very morning. On this glad day blessings are dropping from the throne of God upon us from this risen Savior. He hath ascended up on high, the gates have opened for Him, and He hath gone to His throne in glory.

Let us look at a few of the results that flow to us from these facts thus sustained of His death and resurrection from the dead!

In the first place it established all Bible declarations. It had been predicted that He should not stay in the grave, and when He arose it put the seal to the Old Testament as the Word of God. The prophecy in Him fulfilled gave glorious proof that the other parts of it should be also fulfilled as the word of an unchanging God.

Again, in His resurrection we see a proof of His divine power. No man hath been raised from the dead by his own power. All died, from Adam to Moses, with the exception of Enoch and Elijah, who, because of their devotion and acknowledgment of the divine head, themselves became prophets of a coming Savior. He rose by His own power. He conquered death itself, the grave, and the whole powers of humanity.

Jupiter is represented by an old classic writer as saying to the lesser gods that if all of them combined together and should endeavor to throw down his throne—if all power was arrayed against him—he, by his own might, would be able to overcome them all. What was fiction with the ancients becomes gloriously realized in Christ. Take all the powers of humanity—the Jewish power, the Roman power; the power of learning, of art, of public opinion; take all the powers of earth and hell, death and the grave, and combine them all against the Savior and, without one effort, without one single apparent movement —the Sleeper lies in death, His eyes are sealed, and, as if all unconscious, for the warning had not been given before—in an instant those eyes were opened, that frame rises, the grave yields up its prey, death retires conquered, and Christ demonstrates Himself to be the ruler of the whole universe. He made the earth to tremble, the sun to put on sackcloth, the very air to grow dark, the graves to open, the dead to come forth, and proclaimed Himself to be the conqueror of death and hell. So we have proof of His being the Son of God with power.

In that resurrection from the dead we have a pledge of our own resurrection. Christ has become the first-fruits of them that slept. You know the figure of the first-fruits as understood by the Jews. Their religion was connected with the seasons of the year—with the harvest crops; one of their feasts was called the feast of the first-fruits, and was on this wise: When the first heads of grain began to ripen in the field, and there was thus a pledge of harvest, they cut off those first ripened heads and went up to Jerusalem.

Before that the grain was not crusht, no bread was baked out of it, and nothing was done to appropriate that crop to man's use until those ripened heads of grain were brought up to Jerusalem and presented to the Lord as a thank-offering. He was acknowledged as Lord of the harvest and they were laid up as a kind of thank-offering before God. They were the first-fruits. Then they went away to the fields and all through Judea the sickle was thrust in, the grain was reaped and gathered into sheaves, and when the harvest was secured they baked the bread for their children out of this first grain. They came up to the temple, where the first-fruits had been laid, and they held a feast of thanksgiving and shouted harvest home. The old harvest feast seems to be descended from this ancient custom.

Christ rose as the first-fruits, and there is to be a glorious resurrection. Christ came, the first man to rise in this respect, by His own power, from the grave, having snatched the crown from death, having thrown light into the grave, having Himself ascended up toward glory. He goes up in the midst of the shouts of angels; the heavens open before Him; yonder is the altar; there is the throne, and around it stand the seraphim and the cherubim; and Christ enters, the victor, and sits down upon the throne, from henceforth expecting until His enemies be made His footstool. He is the first-fruits of the harvest, but the angels are to be sent out like the reapers, and by and by humanity is coming.

As Christ, the first-fruits, passed through the grave and went up to glory, so there shall come forth from their sleeping dust in Asia, in Africa, in Europe, and in America, from every mountain top, from the depths of the sea, from deep ravines, and from plains outspread—oh, there shall come in the time of the glorious harvest—the uprising of humanity, when all the nations, waking from their long sleep, shall rise and shall shout the harvest home! Thank God! At that time none shall be wanting.

Oh, they come, they come, from the nations of the past and from the generations yet unborn! I see the crowd gathering there. Behold the angels are waiting, and as the hosts rise from the dead they gather round the throne. Christ invites His followers to overcome and sit down with Him on His throne, as He overcame and sat down with the Father on His throne. In that is the pledge of our resurrection from the dead. Can I not suffer, since Christ suffered? Can I not die, since Christ died? Let the grave be my resting-place, for Christ rested there. Is it cold? The warmth of His animation is in it. He shall be beside me in all His spirit's power. Does the load of earth above me and beneath which I am placed press upon me? Christ hath power to burst the tomb, tho deep it be, and I shall rise through His almighty power.

Yet, let the malice of men be directed against me; let me be taken, if it must be, as a martyr and be bound to the stake; let the fagots be kindled, let the flame ascend, let my body be burned; gather my ashes, grind my bones to powder, scatter them on the ocean's surface; or carry those ashes to the top of yonder volcano and throw them within its consuming fire—let them be given to the dust —and yet I can sing:

"God my Redeemer lives,
  And ever from the skies
Looks down and watches all my dust,
  Till He shall bid it rise."

Thank God! it may be scattered on the wings of the wind—Christ is everywhere present; He has marked every particle and it shall rise again by His own almighty power. And what is it to sleep awhile if I am Christ's? To die, if I am like Christ in dying? and be buried, if I am like Christ in being buried? I trust I shall be like Him when He comes forth in His glory. I shall be like Him, for the apostle says, "We shall be like him, for we shall see him as he is"; "We shall be changed from glory into glory, into the same image as by the Spirit of God."

It would be a great change to be changed from glory to glory, from saints to angels, from angels to cherubim, from cherubim to seraphim, from glory to glory; but, thank God! we shall not stop being changed; for the change shall go on from glory to glory until we shall be transformed into the likeness of the Son of God, brighter than angels ever shone, more glorious than were ever cherubim.

We shall be near the throne; we shall sit beside Him, for He hath made room for us on the other side, thank God! death is passed forever; we shall then put our feet on the neck of the monster and shall be able to say:

"Oh death, where is thy sting?
Oh grave, where is thy victory?"

Looking at the resurrection of Christ we exclaim, Thanks be unto God who hath given us the victory! Such is the eternity and blessedness that awaits us. Thank God for a spiritual body! Here some of us long to triumph over nature. We would grasp, if we could, angelic wisdom; but our brows will ache with pain, our frames decay, our eyes grow dim, our hearing fail. This flesh of ours will not stand hours of painful study and seasons of protracted labor; but, thank God! when the body that now oppresses us is laid in the grave a spiritual body will be given to us, pure, ethereal, and holy. Oh, what an extent of knowledge shall flash upon us; what light and glory; what spirituality and power! Then we shall not need to ask an angel anything. We shall know as we are known. Jesus will be our teacher; the Everlasting God, the Man whose name is Wonderful, the Counselor, the Prince of Peace. He Himself shall be our Leader. We shall know then as also we are known.

Then rejoice in God. Dry up those tears. Cast away that downcast look. Child of the dust, you are an heir of glory. There is a crown all burnished for you; there is a mansion all ready for you; there is a white robe prepared for you; there is eternal glory for you; angels are to be your servants and you are to reign with the King of Kings forever. But while you wait on earth, be witnesses for God; attest the glory of your Master; rise in the greatness of His strength; bind sin captive to your chariot wheels; go onward in your heavenly career, and be as pure as your ascended Head is pure. Be active in works of mercy; be angels of light; be flames of fire; go on your mission of mercy and convert the world unto God before you go up higher. When you go, not only go forward to present yourself, but may every one of you be able to say: "Here am I and those which Thou hast given me."

GEORGE ADAM SMITH

1856-1942

ASSURANCE IN GOD

BIOGRAPHICAL NOTE

GEORGE ADAM SMITH, divine, educator and author, was born at Calcutta in 1856, and educated at New College, Edinburgh, Scotland. For years he was professor of Old Testament Language, Literature and Theology in the United Free Church College, Glasgow. He is author of "The Historical Geography of the Holy Land," "Jerusalem, the Topography, Economics and History from the Earliest Time to A.D. 70"(1908). He was generally regarded as one of the most gifted preachers of Scotland.

Preserve me, O God.—Psalm xvi., 16.

THE psalmist lived in a period when belief in the reality of many gods was still strong, and when a man who would follow the one true God had to prefer to do so against the attractions of other deities and against the convictions of a great number of his fellow countrymen that these deities were living and powerful. That stage of religion is so distant from ourselves that we may imagine the psalmist's example to be of no practical value for our faith, yet in such an imagination we should be very much mistaken indeed, for, to begin with, consider how much you and I to-day owe to those believers who so many centuries ago rejected all the gods that offered themselves to the hearts of men except the true God, and who chose to cleave to Him alone with all that passionate loyalty which breathes through these verses. But for them you and I could not be standing where we are in religion to-day. As the eleventh of Hebrews reminds us, we are the spiritual heir of such believers. It is to their struggles and their faith and their victories that we greatly owe it that we have been born into an atmosphere in which no religious belief is possible to us save in one God who is Spirit and Righteousness and all Truth.

That, then, was the great choice that the psalmist's faith was turning to—a choice that was no mere assent to a creed that had been fought for and established by previous generations of believers. It was the man's own proving of things unseen and his own preference of those against the crowd and a system of things seen, palpable, and very powerful in their attraction for the senses of humanity. But we are not to suppose that the rival deities, from which this man turned to the unseen God, were to his mind or to the mind of his day the heap of dead and ugly idols which we know them to be. They were not dead things that he could kick away with his feet that these believers had to reject when they sought the living God, but things which he and his contemporaries felt to be alive and powerful; powerful alike in their seduction and in their vengeance. They were believed to be identical, as you know, with the forces of nature; they were supposed to be indispensable to the welfare of the individual and of society, and they were fanatically supported at the time by the mass of this man's own countrymen; so that to break from them in those days meant to abandon ancient opinions and habits, to resist many pleasant

538

and natural temptations and to incur the hostility, as was believed, of the powers of nature, to break with customs and with rites that had fortified and consoled the individual heart for generations and been the support and sanction of society and of the state as well. Yet this man did it. From all that living crowd and system, from all those visible temptations and terrors he turned to the unseen, fully conscious of his danger, for he opens his Psalm with a great cry, "Preserve me, preserve me, O God!" but yet deliberately, and with all his heart: "I have said unto the Lord, Thou art my Lord." I have no goodness, no happiness, that is outside Thee or outside the saints that are in the land, "the excellent in whom is all my delight." Here we touch another great characteristic of all true faith which is full of example to ourselves. It is remarkable how, when a man really turns to God, he turns to God's people as well, and how he includes them in the loyalty and in the devotion which he feels toward his Redeemer. His confidence and the sensitiveness of his faith in and toward God become almost an equal confidence and an equal sensitiveness toward his fellow believers. So it is throughout Scripture; you remember that other psalmist who tells us how he had been tempted to doubt God's providence and God's power to help the good man—"does God know and is there knowledge in the Most High? Verily I have cleansed my heart in vain and washed my hands in innocency." The psalmist immediately adds: "If I had spoken thus, behold I had dealt treacherously with the generation of God's children." If I had spoken thus, denying God, I had dealt treacherously with the generation of God's children. Unbelief toward God meant to him treason toward God's people; and the author of the Epistle to the Hebrews affirms the same double character of true faith when he emphasizes just these two points in the faith of Moses: "choosing to suffer affliction with the people of God," and "enduring as seeing Him who is invisible," and God Himself through Jesus Christ has accepted this partnership of His people in our loyalty—"Inasmuch as ye have done it unto one of the least of these my brethren ye have done it unto me." I do not believe in the full faith of any man who does not extend the loyalty he professes to God to God's people as well, who does not feel as sensitive to his brethren on earth as he does to his Father in heaven, who does not practise piety toward the Church as he does toward her Head, or find in her fellowship and her service a joy and a gladness which is one with his deep joy in God, his Redeemer. Nay, is it not just in loving people who are still imperfect, often disappointing, and far from their ideal it may be, that in our relations to them we are to find the

greater proof and test of our religious faith? In these days such a duty is unfortunately more complicated than with the psalmist. The lines between God's Church and the world is not so clear as it was to him, and the Church is divided into many and often hostile factions. All the more it becomes the test of our religion if our hearts feel and rejoice in the fellowship of God's simpler and more needy and more devoted believers, however unattractive they may otherwise be.

Consider the way in which the psalmist reached this pure faith in God and in His people. A factor in the process was distaste for the ugly rites of idolatry—"Their drink-offerings of blood will I not offer." Idolatry always develops a loathsome ritual. Sometimes it is cruel and sometimes it is horribly unclean, but it always debases the worshiper's mind, confuses his conscience, and hampers his freedom and energy by the burdensome ceremonies it imposes upon them. Standing afar off from them as we do, and knowing that there is no heathen religion but has something good in it, we are apt to think that it does not in the least matter how crude or how material a nation's faith be if only it be faith in something more powerful than themselves, if it satisfy their consciences and have some influence in disciplining society and helping the individual to control himself. But you have only to see idolatry at work, and at work with the habits of ages upon it, to recognize how terrible it can be in its identification of sheer filth and cruelty with the interests of religion, and how it at once demoralizes and paralyzes its adherents. To see it thus is to understand the passionate horror of these words: "Their drink-offering of blood will I not offer."

It is, however, no mere recoil from the immoral which started the spring of this psalmist's faith in God. That faith was formed on personal experience of God Himself. In simple but pregnant phrases the psalmist tells us how sure he has become, first, of God's providence in his life; secondly, of God's intimate communion with his soul. God, he says, had been everything in his life. One does not know whether the psalmist was a prosperous man or a poor one; the inference that he was prosperous and rich has sometimes been drawn, but wrongly drawn, from one of the verses of the Psalm. His indifference to that is clear, but what he did have he knew he had from God. God, he says, is all his happiness and all his strength—"The Lord is the portion of mine inheritance and of my cup; thou maintainest my lot." Whether poor or prosperous he could say: "The lines are fallen unto me in pleasant places; yea, I have a goodly heritage." Now that assurance of divine leading is not analyzable, but we know that it does grow up solid and sure in the experience of simple men who have put their trust in God, who have felt life to be a commission from Him and who have done their duty obeying His call. With such men "all things work together for good." Tho life about them shake and darken, they feel their own solidity and have light enough to read the future. Tho stript and stark, they feel the Lord Himself to be the portion of their inheritance and of their cup. The portion of my inheritance the Lord is, *i.e.*, the little bit of land that fell to each Israelite as his share in the promised inheritance of the nation. "The Lord is the portion of mine inheritance," as we might say in our Scotch language, "The Lord is my croft and my cup," so they find in Him all the ground and the freedom they need to do their work, fulfil their relationships, and develop their manhood.

It is, however, with the psalmist's second reason for his faith we have most to do. "I will bless the Lord, who hath given me counsel: my reins also instruct me in the night seasons." This man held close communion with God. Is it not great to find the testimony of a brother man coming down all through those ages, from that dim and distant past, clear and sure as to this, that he had God's counsel and that God kept communion with him? God had spoken to this man and shown him His will. Yes, he had received what we call inspiration and revelation, and had proved the truth of these in his life. They had led and they had lifted him. Nor had they come to him as many men falsely suppose revelation and inspiration exclusively have come to mankind, by means, namely, that were extraordinary and miraculous. The psalmist tells us of no vision of angels, of no voice from heaven. The Lord had not appeared to him in dreams nor by any marvelous signs; on the other hand, he tells us simply that the divine counsel of which he was so sure, and which he passes on to us, came to him through the workings of his inner spiritual life. That is what he means by the emphatic statement "yea, my reins instruct me in the night seasons," which he adds parallel with the thought, "I will bless the Lord, who hath given me counsel." According to the primitive physiology of this man's nation and times, the reins of a man fulfil the same intellectual function which we, with our larger knowledge, know are discharged by the brain. This was how God's revelation came to this brother of ours, through the working of his mind and conscience, but it was in the night seasons that they worked, not in the day and in the sunshine, but in the night when a man is left to himself with only this advantage to his thought: that like the blind he is yet undistracted by the influences which are seen. When he lies down he thinks soberly and quietly about himself and about life and about God, and about the great hidden future that is waiting for him. He was communing with God, who had made his brain and used it as an instrument of revelation. In these thoughts God was communing with man through his reason and through his conscience. You and I are always contrasting God's providence and His grace. We are always attempting to oppose reason and revelation; to this man they were one. God's great grace had come to him through God's own providence, and God's revelation was ministered to him through the reason with which he had endowed the creature He had made in His own image. This psalmist's chief and practical help to us men and women to-day is that he became sure of God not because of any miracle or supernatural sign, on his report of which we might be content indolently to rest our faith, but in God's own providence in his life and in God's quiet communion with him through the organs God Himself has created in every one of us. For all time, whether before or after Christ, these are the chief grounds and foundations of faith in God. So it was in the Old Testament—"stand in awe and sin not," "commune with your own heart upon your bed and be still," "be still and know that I am God." So with Christ, "for the kingdom of heaven cometh not with observation, but the kingdom of heaven is within you," and so with Paul, "the Spirit itself beareth witness with our spirit, that we are the children of God, and if children then heirs, heirs of God and joint heirs with Christ." "For this cause I bow my knees unto the Father of our Lord Jesus Christ, . . . that he would grant you according to the riches of his glory.to be strengthened with might by his spirit in the inner man; that Christ may dwell in your hearts by faith, to the end that ye being rooted and grounded in love may come to apprehend with all saints what is the breadth and length and depth and height and to know the love of Christ."

God's guidance of his life, first of all, produces in a man a great sense of stability. "I have set the Lord always before me: because he is at my right hand I shall not be moved." He who has found God so careful of him, he whom God hath regarded as worth speaking to and counseling and disciplining, will be certain that he shall endure, provided he is sure of his own loyalty. The life so loved of God, so provided for, and in such close communion with the Eternal is not, can not be the creature of the day, and this assurance stands firm in face of even death and the horrible corruption of the body. The psalmist refuses to believe that he is to dwell in the horrible under-world forever—either himself or any of God's believers. "Thou must not, thou wilt not leave my soul in sheol, thou must not, thou wilt not suffer thy loved ones to see the pit.'' To this man it is incredible, and our hearts bear witness to the truth if we have had any experience of God's blessing and guidance.   To this man it is incredible that the life God has cared for and guided and spoken to and brought into such intimate communion with himself can find its end in death.   Those whom God has loyally loved and who have loyally loved God—for this word badly translated ''holy'' in the psalms really has that actual significance—those whom God has loyally loved and who have loyally loved God shall never die.   As He lives so shall they; they shall never be absent from His presence.   Be the future unknown and unknowable, be we ourselves incapable of conceiving the processes by which this mortal shall put on immortality, or where heaven is, or what eternity can possibly be to those who have never lived outside time, yet that future is secure and its immortal character is indubitable—where God is there shall His servants be, and because He is there their life shall be peace and joy, and because He is eternal it shall last forevermore.   That thought is the whole of the hope and argument.   We are assured of the future life because we have known God, and as we have found Him to be true to us and proved ourselves true to Him.

ROBERT SOUTH

1638-1716

THE IMAGE OF GOD IN MAN

BIOGRAPHICAL NOTE

ROBERT SOUTH, who was born in the borough of Hackney, London, England, in 1638, attracted wide attention by his vigorous mind and his clear, argumentative style in preaching. Some of his sermons are notable specimens of pulpit eloquence. A keen analytical mind, great depth of feeling, and wide range of fancy combined to make him a powerful and impressive speaker. By some critics his style has been considered unsurpassed in force and beauty. What he lacked in tenderness was made up in masculine strength. He was a born satirist. Henry Rogers said of him: "Of all the English preachers, South seems to furnish, in point of style, the truest specimens of pulpit eloquence. His robust intellect, his shrewd common sense, his vehement feelings, and a fancy always more distinguished by force than by elegance, admirably qualified him for a powerful public speaker." South became prebendary of Westminster in 1663, canon at Oxford in 1670, and rector of Islip in 1678. An edition of his writings was published in 1823. He died in 1716.

So God created man in his own image, in the image of God created he him.—Genesis i., 27.

HOW HARD it is for natural reason to discover a creation before revealed, or, being revealed, to believe it, the strange opinions of the old philosophers, and the infidelity of modern atheists, is too sad a demonstration. To run the world back to its first original and infancy, and, as it were, to view nature in its cradle, and trace the outgoings of the Ancient of Days in the first instance and specimen of His creative power, is a research too great for any mortal inquiry; and we might continue our scrutiny to the end of the world, before natural reason would be able to find out when it began.

Epicurus's discourse concerning the original of the world is so fabulous and ridiculously merry that we may well judge the design of his philosophy to have been pleasure, and not instruction. Aristotle held that it streamed by connatural result and emanation from God, the infinite and eternal Mind, as the light issues from the sun; so that there was no instant of duration assignable of God's eternal existence in which the world did not also coexist. Others held a fortuitous concourse of atoms—but all seem jointly to explode a creation, still beating upon this ground, that the producing something out of nothing is impossible and incomprehensible; incomprehensible, indeed, I grant, but not therefore impossible. There is not the least transaction of sense and motion in the whole man, but philosophers are at a loss to comprehend, I am sure they are to explain it. Wherefore it is not always rational to measure the truth of an assertion by the standard of our apprehension.

But, to bring things even to the bare preception of reason, I appeal to any one who shall impartially reflect upon the ideas and conceptions of his own mind, whether he doth not find it as easy and suitable to his natural notions to conceive that an infinite Almighty power might produce a thing out of nothing, and make that to exist *de novo*, which did not exist before, as to conceive the world to have had no beginning, but to have existed from eternity, which, were it so proper for this place and exercise, I could easily demonstrate to be attended with no small train of absurdities. But then, besides that the acknowledging of a creation is safe, and the denial of it dangerous and irreligious, and yet not more, perhaps much less, demonstrable

542

than the affirmative; so, over and above, it gives me this advantage, that, let it seem never so strange, uncouth, and incomprehensible, the nonplus of my reason will yield a fairer opportunity to my faith.

The work that I shall undertake from these words shall be to show what this image of God in man is, and wherein it doth consist. Which I shall do these two ways: 1. Negatively, by showing wherein it does not consist. 2. Positively, by showing wherein it does.

For the first of these we are to remove the erroneous opinion of the Socinians. They deny that the image of God consisted in any habitual perfections that adorned the soul of Adam, but, as to his understanding, bring him in void of all notion, a rude, unwritten blank; making him to be created as much an infant as others are born; sent into the world only to read and to spell out a God in the works of creation, to learn by degrees, till at length his understanding grew up to the stature of his body; also without any inherent habits of virtue in his will; thus divesting him of all, and stripping him of his bare essence; so that all the perfection they allowed his understanding was aptness and docility, and all that they attributed to his will was a possibility to be virtuous.

But wherein, then, according to their opinion, did this image of God consist? Why, in that power and dominion that God gave Adam over the creatures; in that he was vouched His immediate deputy upon earth, the viceroy of the creation, and lord-lieutenant of the world. But that this power and dominion is not adequately and formally the image of God, but only a part of it, is clear from hence, because then he that had most of this would have most of God's image; and consequently Nimrod had more of it than Noah, Saul than Samuel, the persecutors than the martyrs, and Cæsar than Christ Himself, which, to assert, is a blasphemous paradox. And if the image of God is only grandeur, power, and sovereignty, certainly we have been hitherto much mistaken in our duty, and hereafter are by all means to beware of making ourselves unlike God by too much self-denial and humility. I am not ignorant that some may distinguish between a lawful authority and actual power, and affirm that God's image consists only in the former, which wicked princes, such as Saul and Nimrod, have not, tho they possess the latter. But to this I answer,

1. That the Scripture neither makes nor owns such a distinction, nor anywhere asserts that when princes begin to be wicked they cease of right to be governors. Add to this, that when God renewed this charter of man's sovereignty over the creatures to Noah and his family we find no exception at all, but that Shem stood as fully invested with this right as any of his brethren.

2. But, secondly, this savors of something ranker than Socinianism, even the tenants of the fifth monarchy, and of sovereignty founded only upon saintship, and therefore fitter to be answered by the judge than the divine, and to receive its confutation at the bar of justice than from the pulpit.

Having now made our way through this false opinion, we are in the next place to lay down positively what this image of God in man is. It is, in short, that universal rectitude of all the faculties of the soul, by which they stand apt and disposed to their respective offices and operations, which will be more fully set forth by taking a distinct survey of it in the several faculties belonging to the soul.

1. In the understanding. 2. In the will. 3. In the passions or affections.

I. And, first, for its noblest faculty, the understanding: it was then sublime, clear, and aspiring—and, as it were, the soul's upper region, lofty and serene, free from vapors and disturbances of the inferior affections. It was the leading, controlling faculty; all the passions wore the colors of reason; it was not consul, but dictator. Discourse was then almost as quick as intuition; it was nimble in proposing, firm in concluding; it could sooner determine than now it can dispute. Like the sun, it had both light and agility; it knew no rest but in motion, no quiet but in activity. It did not so properly apprehend, as irradiate the object; not so much find, as make things intelligible. It did not arbitrate upon the several reports of sense, and all the varieties of imagination, like a drowsy judge, not only hearing, but also directing their verdict. In sum, it was vegete, quick, and lively, open as the day, untainted as the morning, full of the innocence and sprightliness of youth, it gave the soul a bright and a full view into all things, and was not only a window, but itself the prospect. Briefly, there is as much difference between the clear representations of the understanding then and the obscure discoveries that it makes now as there is between the prospect of a casement and of a keyhole.

Now, as there are two great functions of the soul, contemplation and practise, according to that general division of objects, some of which only entertain our speculation, others also employ our actions, so the understanding, with relation to these, not because of any distinction in the faculty itself, is accordingly divided into speculative and practical; in both of which the image of God was then apparent.

1. For the understanding speculative. There are some general maxims and notions in the mind of man which are the rules of discourse and the basis of all philosophy: as, that the same thing can not at the same time be and not be; that the whole is bigger

than a part; that two dimensions, severally equal to a third, must also be equal to one another. Aristotle, indeed, affirms the mind to be at first a mere *tabula rasa*, and that these notions are not ingenit, and imprinted by the finger of nature, but by the later and more languid impressions of sense, being only the reports of observation, and the result of so many repeated experiments.

(1.) That these notions are universal, and what is universal must needs proceed from some universal, constant principle, the same in all particulars, which here can be nothing else but human nature.

(2.) These can not be infused by observation, because they are the rules by which men take their first apprehensions and observations of things, and therefore, in order of nature, must needs precede them; as the being of the rule must be before its application to the thing directed by it. From whence it follows that these were notions not descending from us, but born with us, not our offspring, but our brethren; and, as I may so say, such as we were taught without the help of a teacher.

Now it was Adam's happiness in the state of innocence to have these clear and unsullied. He came into the world a philosopher, which sufficiently appeared by his writing the nature of things upon their names; he could view essences in themselves, and read forms without the comment of their respective properties; he could see consequents yet dormant in their principles, and effects yet unborn and in the womb of their causes; his understanding could almost pierce into future contingents; his conjectures improving even to prophecy, or the certainties of prediction; till his fall, it was ignorant of nothing but sin, or at least it rested in the notion, without the smart of the experiment. Could any difficulty have been proposed, the resolution would have been as early as the proposal; it could not have had time to settle into doubt. Like a better Archimedes, the issue of all his inquiries was a *eureka*, a *eureka*, the offspring of his brain without the sweat of his brow. Study was not then a duty, night-watchings were needless, the light of reason wanted not the assistance of a candle. This is the doom of fallen man, to labor in the fire, to seek truth *in profundo,* to exhaust his time and impair his health, and perhaps to spin out his days and himself into one pitiful, controverted conclusion. There was then no poring, no struggling with memory, no straining for invention; his faculties were quick and expedite, they answered without knocking, they were ready upon the first summons.

2. The image of God was no less resplendent in that which we call man's practical understanding; namely, that storehouse of the soul in which are treasured up the rules of action and the seeds of morality; where,

we must observe, that many who deny all connate notions in the speculative intellect, do yet admit them in this. Now of this sort are these maxims, "That God is to be worshiped, that parents are to be honored, that a man's word is to be kept," and the like; which, being of universal influence, as to the regulation of the behavior and converse of mankind, are the ground of all virtue and civility, and the foundation of religion.

It was the privilege of Adam innocent, to have these notions also firm and untainted, to carry his monitor in his bosom, his law in his heart, and to have such a conscience as might be its own casuist; and certainly those actions must needs be regular where there is an identity between the rule and the faculty. His own mind taught him a due dependence upon God, and chalked out to him the just proportions and measures of behavior to his fellow creatures. He had no catechism but the creation, needed no study but reflection, read no book but the volume of the world, and that too, not for the rules to work by, but for the objects to work upon. Reason was his tutor, and first principles his *magna moralia*. The decalogue of Moses was but a transcript, not an original. All the laws of nations, and wise decrees of states, the statutes of Solon, and the twelve tables, were but a paraphrase upon this standing rectitude of nature, this fruitful principle of justice, that was ready to run out and enlarge itself into suitable demonstrations upon all emergent objects and occasions.

And this much for the image of God, as it shone in man's understanding.

II. Let us in the next place take a view of it as it was stamped upon the will. It is much disputed by divines concerning the power of man's will to good and evil in the state of innocence: and upon very nice and dangerous precipices stand their determinations on either side. Some hold that God invested him with a power to stand so that in the strength of that power received, he might, without the auxiliaries of any further influence, have determined his will to a full choice of good. Others hold that notwithstanding this power, yet it was impossible for him to exert it in any good action without a superadded assistance of grace actually determining that power to the certain production of such an act; so that whereas some distinguish between sufficient and effectual grace, they order the matter so as to acknowledge some sufficient but what is indeed effected, and actually productive of good action. I shall not presume to interpose dogmatically in a controversy which I look never to see decided. But concerning the latter of these opinions, I shall only give these two remarks:

1. That it seems contrary to the common and natural conceptions of all mankind, who acknowledge themselves able and sufficient

to do many things which actually they never do.

2. That to assert that God looked upon Adam's fall as a sin, and punished it as such when, without any antecedent sin of his, he withdrew that actual grace from him upon the withdrawing of which it was impossible for him not to fall, seems a thing that highly reproaches the essential equity and goodness of the divine nature.

Wherefore, doubtless the will of man in the state of innocence had an entire freedom, a perfect equipendency and indifference to either part of the contradiction, to stand, or not to stand; to accept, or not to accept the temptation. I will grant the will of man now to be as much a slave as any one who will have it, and be only free to sin; that is, instead of a liberty, to have only a licentiousness; yet certainly this is not nature, but chance. We were not born crooked; we learned these windings and turnings of the serpent: and therefore it can not but be a blasphemous piece of ingratitude to ascribe them to God, and to make the plague of our nature the condition of our creation.

The will was then ductile and pliant to all the motions of right reason; it met the dictates of a clarified understanding half way. And the active informations of the intellect, filling the passive reception of the will, like form closing with matter, grew actuate into a third and distinct perfection of practise; the understanding and will never disagreed; for the proposals of the one never thwarted the inclinations of the other. Yet neither did the will servilely attend upon the understanding, but as a favorite does upon his prince, where the service is privilege and preferment; or as Solomon's servants waited upon him: it admired its wisdom, and heard its prudent dictates and counsels—both the direction and the reward of its obedience. It is indeed the nature of this faculty to follow a superior guide—to be drawn by the intellect; but then it was drawn as a triumphant chariot, which at the same time both follows and triumphs: while it obeyed this, it commanded the other faculties. It was subordinate, not enslaved to the understanding: not as a servant to a master, but as a queen to her king, who both acknowledges a subjection and yet retains a majesty.

III. Pass we now downward from man's intellect and will to the passions, which have their residence and situation chiefly in the sensitive appetite. For we must know that inasmuch as man is a compound, and mixture of flesh as well as spirit, the soul, during its abode in the body, does all things by the mediation of these passions and inferior affections. And here the opinion of the Stoics was famous and singular, who looked upon all these as sinful defects and irregularities, as so many devia-

tions from right reason, making passion to be only another word for perturbation. Sorrow in their esteem was a sin scarce to be expiated by another; to pity, was a fault; to rejoice, an extravagance; and the apostle's advice, "to be angry and sin not," was a contradiction in their philosophy. But in this they were constantly outvoted by other sects of philosophers, neither for fame nor number less than themselves: so that all arguments brought against them from divinity would come in by way of overplus to their confutation. To us let this be sufficient, that our Savior Christ, who took upon Him all our natural infirmities, but none of our sinful, has been seen to weep, to be sorrowful, to pity, and to be angry: which shows that there might be gall in a dove, passion without sin, fire without smoke, and motion without disturbance. For it is not bare agitation, but the sediment at the bottom, that troubles and defiles the water; and when we see it windy and dusty, the wind does not (as we used to say) make, but only raise a dust.

Now, tho the schools reduce all the passions to these two heads, the concupiscible and the irascible appetite, yet I shall not tie myself to an exact prosecution of them under this division; but at this time, leaving both their terms and their method to themselves, consider only the principal and noted passions, from whence we may take an estimate of the rest.

And first for the grand leading affection of all, which is love. This is the great instrument and engine of nature, the bond and cement of society, the spring and spirit of the universe. Love is such an affection as can not so properly be said to be in the soul as the soul to be in that. It is the whole man wrapt up into one desire; all the powers, vigor, and faculties of the soul abridged into one inclination. And it is of that active, restless nature that it must of necessity exert itself; and, like the fire to which it is so often compared, it is not a free agent, to choose whether it will heat or no, but it streams forth by natural results and unavoidable emanations. So that it will fasten upon any inferior, unsuitable object, rather than none at all. The soul may sooner leave off to subsist than to love; and, like the vine, it withers and dies if it has nothing to embrace. Now this affection, in the state of innocence, was happily pitched upon its right object; it flamed up in direct fervors of devotion to God, and in collateral emissions of charity to its neighbor. It was not then only another and more cleanly name for lust. It had none of those impure heats that both represent and deserve hell. It was a vestal and a virgin fire, and differed as much from that which usually passes by this name nowadays as the vital heat from the burning of a fever.

Then for the contrary passion of hatred.

This we know is the passion of defiance, and there is a kind of aversation and hostility included in its very essence and being. But then (if there could have been hatred in the world when there was scarce anything odious) it would have acted within the compass of its proper object; like aloes, bitter indeed, but wholesome. There would have been no rancor, no hatred of our brother: an innocent nature could hate nothing that was innocent. In a word, so great is the commutation that the soul then hated only that which now only it loves, that is, sin.

And if we may bring anger under this head, as being, according to some, a transient hatred, or at least very like it, this also, as unruly as now it is, yet then it vented itself by the measures of reason. There was no such thing as the transports of malice or the violences of revenge, no rendering evil for evil, when evil was truly a nonentity and nowhere to be found. Anger, then, was like the sword of justice, keen, but innocent and righteous: it did not act like fury, then call itself zeal. It always espoused God's honor, and never kindled upon anything but in order to a sacrifice. It sparkled like the coal upon the altar with the fervors of piety, the heats of devotion, the sallies and vibrations of a harmless activity.

In the next place, for the lightsome passion of joy. It was not that which now often usurps this name; that trivial, vanishing, superficial thing, that only gilds the apprehension and plays upon the surface of the soul. It was not the mere crackling of thorns or sudden blaze of the spirits, the exultation of a tickled fancy or a pleased appetite. Joy was then a masculine and a severe thing; the recreation of the judgment, the jubilee of reason. It was the result of a real good, suitably applied. It commenced upon the solidity of truth and the substance of fruition. It did not run out in voice or indecent eruptions, but filled the soul, as God does the universe, silently and without noise. It was refreshing, but composed, like the pleasantness of youth tempered with the gravity of age; or the mirth of a festival managed with the silence of contemplation.

And, on the other side, for sorrow: Had any loss or disaster made but room for grief, it would have moved according to the severe allowances of prudence, and the proportions of the provocation. It would not have sallied out into complaint of loudness, nor spread itself upon the face, and writ sad stories upon the forehead. No wringing of hands, knocking the breast, or wishing oneself unborn; all which are but the ceremonies of sorrow, the pomp and ostentation of an effeminate grief, which speak not so much the greatness of the misery as the smallness of the mind! Tears may spoil the eyes, but not wash away the affliction. Sighs may exhaust the man, but not eject the burden. Sorrow, then, would have been as silent as thought, as severe as philosophy. It would have been rested in inward senses, tacit dislikes; and the whole scene of it been transacted in sad and silent reflections. . . .

And, lastly, for the affection of fear: It was then the instrument of caution, not of anxiety; a guard, and not a torment to the breast that had it. It is now indeed an unhappiness, the disease of the soul: it flies from a shadow, and makes more dangers than it avoids; it weakens the judgment and betrays the succors of reason: so hard is it to tremble and not to err, and to hit the mark with a shaking hand. Then it fixt upon Him who is only to be feared, God; and yet with a filial fear, which at the same time both fears and loves. It was awe without amazement, dread without distraction. There was then a beauty even in this very paleness. It was the color of devotion, giving a luster to reverence and a gloss to humility.

Thus did the passions then act without any of their present jars, combats, or repugnances; all moving with the beauty of uniformity and the stillness of composure; like a well-governed army, not for fighting, but for rank and order. I confess the Scripture does not expressly attribute these several endowments to Adam in his first estate. But all that I have said, and much more, may be drawn out of that short aphorism, "God made man upright." And since the opposite weaknesses infest the nature of man fallen, if we will be true to the rules of contraries we must conclude that these perfections were the lot of man innocent. . . .

Having thus surveyed the image of God in the soul of man, we are not to omit now those characters of majesty that God imprinted upon the body. He drew some traces of His image upon this also, as much as a spiritual substance could be pictured upon a corporeal. As for the sect of the Anthropomorphites, who from hence ascribe to God the figure of a man, eyes, hands, feet, and the like, they are too ridiculous to deserve a confutation. They would seem to draw this impiety from the letter of the Scripture sometimes speaking of God in this manner. Absurdity! as if the mercy of Scripture expressions ought to warrant the blasphemy of our opinions; and not rather to show us that God condescends to us only to draw us to Himself; and clothes Himself in our likeness only to win us to His own. The practise of the papists is much of the same nature, in their absurd and impious picturing of God Almighty; but the wonder in them is the less since the image of a deity may be a proper object for that which is but the image of a religion. But to the purpose: Adam was then no less glorious in his externals; he had a beautiful body, as well as an immortal soul. The whole compound was like a well-built temple, stately without, and sacred within. The elements were at perfect union and agreement in His body; and their contrary qualities served not for the dissolution of the compound, but the variety of the composure. Galen, who had no more divinity than what his physic taught him, barely upon the consideration of this so exact frame of the body, challenges any one, upon a hundred years' study, to find out how any the least fiber, or most minute particle, might be more commodiously placed, either for the advantage of use or comeliness. His stature erect, and tending upward to his center; his countenance majestic and comely, with the luster of a native beauty that scorned the poor assistance of art or the attempts of imitation; His body of so much quickness and agility that it did not only contain but also represent the soul; for we might well suppose that where God did deposit so rich a jewel He would suitably adorn the case. It was a fit workhouse for sprightly, vivid faculties to exercise and exert themselves in; a fit tabernacle for an immortal soul, not only to dwell in, but to contemplate upon; where it might see the world without travel, it being a lesser scheme of the creation, nature contracted a little cosmography or map of the universe. Neither was the body then subject to distempers, to die by piecemeal, and languish under coughs, catarrhs, or consumptions. Adam knew no disease so long as temperance from the forbidden fruit secured him. Nature was his physician, and innocence and abstinence would have kept him healthful to immortality.

The two great perfections that both adorn and exercise man's understanding, are philosophy and religion: for the first of these, take it even among the professors of it where it most flourished, and we shall find the very first notions of common-sense debauched by them. For there have been such as have asserted, "that there is no such thing in the world as motion: that contradictions may be true." There has not been wanting one that has denied snow to be white. Such a stupidity or wantonness had seized upon the most

raised wits that it might be doubted whether the philosophers or the owls of Athens were the quicker sighted. But then for religion; what prodigious, monstrous, misshapen births has the reason of fallen man produced! It is now almost six thousand years that far the greater part of the world has had no other religion but idolatry: and idolatry certainly is the first-born of folly, the great and leading paradox, nay, the very abridgment and sum total of all absurdities. For is it not strange that a rational man should worship an ox, nay, the image of an ox? That he should fawn upon his dog? Bow himself before a cat? Adore leeks and garlic, and shed penitential tears at the smell of a deified onion? Yet so did the Egyptians, once the famed masters of all arts and learning. And to go a little further, we have yet a stronger instance in Isaiah, "A man hews him down a tree in the wood, and a part of it he burns, with the residue thereof he maketh a god." With one part he furnishes his chimney, with the other his chapel. A strange thing that the fire must first consume this part and then burn incense to that. As if there was more divinity in one end of the stick than in the other; or, as if he could be graved and painted omnipotent, or the nails and the hammer could give it an apotheosis! Briefly, so great is the change, so deplorable the degradation of our nature, that whereas we bore the image of God, we now retain only the image of man.

In the last place, we learn hence the excellency of Christian religion, in that it is the great and only means that God has sanctified and designed to repair the breaches of humanity, to set fallen man upon his legs again, to clarify his reason, to rectify his will, and to compose and regulate his affections. The whole business of our redemption is, in short, only to rub over the defaced copy of the creation, to reprint God's image upon the soul, and, as it were, to set forth nature in a second and fairer edition; the recovery of which lost image, as it is God's pleasure to command, and our duty to endeavor, so it is in His power only to effect; to whom be rendered and ascribed, as is most due, all praise, might, majesty, and dominion, both now and forever more. Amen.

CHARLES H. SPURGEON

1834-1892

SONGS IN THE NIGHT

BIOGRAPHICAL NOTE

CHARLES HADDON SPURGEON was born at Kelvedon, Essex, England, in 1834. He was one of the most powerful and popular preachers of his time, and his extraordinary force of character and wonderful enthusiasm attracted vast audiences. His voice was unusually powerful, clear and melodious, and he used it with consummate skill. In the preparation of sermons he meditated much but wrote scarcely a word, so that he was in the truest sense a purely extemporaneous speaker. Sincerity, intensity, imagination and humour, he had in pre-eminent degree, and an English style that has been described as "a long bright river of silver speech which unwound, evenly and endlessly, like a ribbon from a revolving spool that could fill itself as fast as it emptied itself." Thirty-eight volumes of his sermons were issued in his lifetime and are still in increasing demand. Dr. Robertson Nicoll says: "Our children will think more of these sermons than we do ; and as I get older I read them more and more." He died in 1892.

But none saith, Where is God my maker, who giveth songs in the night?—Job xxxv., 10.

ELIHU was a wise man, exceeding wise, tho not as wise as the all-wise Jehovah, who sees light in the clouds, and finds order in confusion; hence Elihu, being much puzzled at beholding Job thus afflicted, cast about him to find the cause of it, and he very wisely hit upon one of the most likely reasons, altho it did not happen to be the right one in Job's case. He said within himself— "Surely, if men be tried and troubled exceedingly, it is because, while they think about their troubles and distress themselves about their fears, they do not say, 'Where is God my maker, who giveth songs in the night?' " Elihu's reason was right in the majority of cases. The great cause of the Christian's distress, the reason of the depths of sorrow into which many believers are plunged, is this —that while they are looking about, on the right hand and on the left, to see how they may escape their troubles, they forget to look to the hills whence all real help cometh; they do not say, "Where is God my maker, who giveth songs in the night?" We shall, however, leave that inquiry, and dwell upon those sweet words, "God my maker, who giveth songs in the night."

The world hath its night. It seemeth necessary that it should have one. The sun shineth by day, and men go forth to their labors; but they grow weary, and nightfall cometh on, like a sweet boon from heaven. The darkness draweth the curtains, and shutteth out the light, which might prevent our eyes from slumber; while the sweet, calm stillness of the night permits us to rest upon the lap of ease, and there forget awhile our cares, until the morning sun appeareth, and an angel puts his hand upon the curtain, and undraws it once again, touches our eyelids, and bids us rise, and proceed to the labors of the day. Night is one of the greatest blessings men enjoy; we have many reasons to thank God for it. Yet night is to many a gloomy season. There is "the pestilence that walketh in darkness"; there is "the terror by night"; there is the dread of robbers and of fell disease, with all those fears that the timorous know, when they have no light wherewith they can discern objects. It is then they fancy that spiritual creatures walk the earth; tho, if they knew rightly, they would find it to be true, that

"Millions of spiritual creatures walk this earth,
Unseen, both when we sleep and when we wake,"

and that at all times they are round about us —not more by night than by day. Night is the season of terror and alarm to most men. Yet even night hath its songs. Have you never stood by the seaside at night, and heard the pebbles sing, and the waves chant God's glories? Or have you never risen from your couch, and thrown up the window of your chamber, and listened there? Listened to what? Silence—save now and then a murmuring sound, which seems sweet music then. And have you not fancied that you heard the harp of God playing in heaven? Did you not conceive, that yon stars, that those eyes of God, looking down on you, were also mouths of song—that every star was singing God's glory, singing, as it shone, its mighty Maker, and His lawful, well-deserved praise? Night hath its songs. We need not much poetry in our spirit, to catch the song of night, and hear the spheres as they chant praises which are loud to the heart, tho they be silent to the ear—the praises of the mighty God, who bears up the unpillared arch of heaven, and moves the stars in their courses. . . .

If we are going to sing of the things of yesterday, let us begin with what God did for us in past times. My beloved brethren, you will find it a sweet subject for song at times, to begin to sing of electing love and covenanted mercies. When thou thyself art low, it is well to sing of the fountain-head of mercy; of that blest decree wherein thou wast ordained to eternal life, and of that glorious Man who undertook thy redemption; of that solemn covenant signed, and sealed, and ratified, in all things ordered well; of that everlasting love which, ere the hoary mountains were begotten, or ere the aged hills were children, chose thee, loved thee firmly, loved thee fast, loved thee well, loved thee eternally. I tell thee, believer, if thou canst go back to the years of eternity; if thou canst in thy mind run back to that period, or ere the everlasting hills were fashioned, or the fountains of the great deep scooped out, and if thou canst see thy God inscribing thy name in His eternal book; if thou canst see in His loving heart eternal thoughts of love to thee, thou wilt find this a charming means of giving thee songs in the night. No songs like those which come from electing love; no sonnets like those that are dictated by meditations on discriminating mercy. Some, indeed, cannot sing of election: the Lord open their mouths a little wider! Some there are that are afraid of the very term; but we only despise men who are afraid of what they believe, afraid of what God has taught them in His Bible. No, in our darker hours it is our joy to sing:

"Sons we are through God's election,
  Who in Jesus Christ believe;
By eternal destination,
  Sovereign grace we now receive.
Lord, thy favor,
  Shall both grace and glory give.''

Think, Christian, of the yesterday, I say, and thou wilt get a song in the night. But if thou hast not a voice tuned to so high a key as that, let me suggest some other mercies thou mayest sing of; and they are the mercies thou hast experienced. What! man, canst thou not sing a little of that blest hour when Jesus met thee; when, a blind slave, thou wast sporting with death, and He saw thee, and said: "Come, poor slave, come with me"? Canst thou not sing of that rapturous moment when He snapt thy fetters, dashed thy chains to the earth, and said: "I am the Breaker; I came to break thy chains, and set thee free"? What tho thou art ever so gloomy now, canst thou forget that happy morning, when in the house of God thy voice was loud, almost as a seraph's voice, in praise? for thou couldst sing: "I am forgiven; I am forgiven":

"A monument of grace,
  A sinner saved by blood.''

Go back, man; sing of that moment, and then thou wilt have a song in the night? Or if thou hast almost forgotten that, then sure thou hast some precious milestone along the road of life that is not quite grown over with moss, on which thou canst read some happy inspiration of His mercy toward thee! What! didst thou never have a sickness like that which thou art suffering now, and did He not raise thee up from that? Wast thou never poor before, and did He not supply thy wants? Wast thou never in straits before, and did He not deliver thee? Come, man! I beseech thee, go to the river of thine experience, and pull up a few bulrushes, and weave them into an ark, wherein thy infant faith may float safely on the stream. I bid thee not forget what God hath done. What! hast thou buried thine own diary? I beseech thee, man, turn over the book of thy remembrance. Canst thou not see some sweet hill Mizar? Canst thou not think of some blest hour when the Lord met with thee at Hermon? Hast thou never been on the Delectable Mountains? Hast thou never been fetched from the den of lions? Hast thou never escaped the jaw of the lion and the paw of the bear? Nay, O man, I know thou hast; go back, then, a little way, and take the mercies of yesterday; and tho it is dark now, light up the lamps of yesterday, and they shall glitter through the darkness, and thou shalt find that God hath given thee a song in the night.

But I think, beloved, there is never so dark a night, but there is something to sing about, even concerning that night; for there is one thing I am sure we can sing about, let the night be ever so dark, and that is, "It is of the Lord's mercies that we are not consumed, and because His compassions fail not." If we cannot sing very loud, yet we can sing a little low tune, something like this—"He hath not dealt with us after our sins, nor rewarded us according to our iniquities.''

"Oh!" says one, "I do not know where to get my dinner from to-morrow. I am a poor wretch." So you may be, my dear friend; but you are not so poor as you deserve to be. Do not be mightily offended about that; if you are, you are no child of God; for the child of God acknowledges that he has no right to the least of God's mercies, but that they come through the channel of grace alone. As long as I am out of hell, I have no right to grumble; and if I were in hell I should have no right to complain, for I feel, when convinced of sin, that never creature deserved to go there more than I do. We have no cause to murmur; we can lift up our hands, and say, "Night! thou art dark, but thou mightst have been darker. I am poor, but, if I could not have been poorer, I might have been sick. I am poor and sick—well, I have some friend left, my lot cannot be so bad, but it might have been worse." And therefore, Christian, you will always have one thing to sing about —"Lord, I thank Thee, it is not all darkness!" Besides, Christian, however dark the night is, there is always a star or moon. There is scarce ever a night that we have, but there are just one or two little lamps burning up there. However dark it may be, I think you may find some little comfort, some little joy, some little mercy left, and some little promise to cheer thy spirit. The stars are not put out, are they? Nay, if thou canst not see them, they are there; but methinks one or two must be shining on thee; therefore give God a song in the night. If thou hast only one star, bless God for that one, perhaps He will make it two; and if thou hast only two stars, bless God for the two stars, and perhaps He will make them four. Try, then, if thou canst not find a song in the night.

But, beloved, there is another thing of which we can sing yet more sweetly; and that is, we can sing of the day that is to come. I am preaching to-night for the poor weavers of Spitalfields. Perhaps there are not to be found a class of men in London who are suffering a darker night than they are; for while many classes have been befriended and defended, there are few who speak up for them, and (if I am rightly informed) they are generally ground down within an inch of their lives. I suppose that their masters intend that their bread shall be very sweet, on the principle, that the nearer the ground, the sweeter the grass; for I should think that no people have their grass so near the ground as the weavers of Spitalfields. In an inquiry by the House of Commons last week, it was given in evidence that their average wages amount to seven or eight shillings a week; and that they have to furnish themselves with a room, and work at expensive articles, which my friends and ladies are wearing now, and which they buy as cheaply as possible; but

perhaps they do not know that they are made with the blood and bones and marrow of the Spitalfields weavers, who, many of them, work for less than man ought to have to subsist upon. Some of them waited upon me the other day; I was exceedingly pleased with one of them. He said, "Well, sir, it is very hard, but I hope there is better times coming for us." "Well, my friend," I said, "I am afraid you cannot hope for much better times, unless the Lord Jesus Christ comes a second time." "That is just what we hope for," said he. "We do not see there is any chance of deliverance, unless the Lord Jesus Christ comes to establish His kingdom upon the earth; and then He will judge the opprest, and break the oppressors in pieces with an iron rod, and dash them in pieces like a potter's vessel." I was glad my friend had got a song in the night, and was singing about the morning that was coming. Often do I cheer myself with the thought of the coming of the Lord. We preach now, perhaps, with little success; "the kingdoms of this world" are not "become the kingdoms of our Lord and of his Christ"; we send out missionaries; they are for the most part unsuccessful. We are laboring, but we do not see the fruits of our labors. Well, what then? Try a little while; we shall not always labor in vain, or spend our strength for naught. A day is coming, and now is, when every minister of Christ shall speak with unction, when all the servants of God shall preach with power, and when colossal systems of heathenism shall be scattered to the winds. The shout shall be heard, "Alleluia! Alleluia! the Lord God Omnipotent reigneth." For that day do I look; it is to the bright horizon of that second coming that I turn my eyes. My anxious expectation is, that the sweet Sun of righteousness will arise with healing beneath His wings, that the opprest shall be righted, that despotisms shall be cut down, that liberty shall be established, that peace shall be made lasting, and that the glorious liberty of the gospel shall be extended throughout the known world. Christian! if thou art in a night, think of the morrow; cheer up thy heart with the thought of the coming of thy Lord.

There is another sweet to-morrow of which we hope to sing in the night. Soon, beloved, you and I shall lie on our dying bed, and we shall want a song in the night then; and I do not know where we shall get it, if we do not get it from the to-morrow. Kneeling by the bed of an apparently dying saint, last night, I said, "Well, sister, He has been precious to you; you can rejoice in His covenant mercies, and His past loving-kindnesses." She put out her hand, and said, "Ah! sir, do not talk about them now; I want the sinner's Savior as much now as ever; it is not a saint's I want; it is still a sinner's

Savior that I am in need of, for I am a sinner still." I found that I could not comfort her with the past; so I reminded her of the golden streets, of the gates of pearl, of the walls of jasper, of the harps of gold, of the songs of bliss; and then her eyes glistened; she said, "Yes, I shall be there soon; I shall meet them by-and-by;" and then she seemed so glad! Ah! believer, you may always cheer yourself with that thought. Thy head may be crowned with thorny troubles now, but it shall wear a starry crown directly; thy hand may be filled with cares—it shall grasp a harp soon, a harp full of music. Thy garments may be soiled with dust now; they shall be white by-and-by. Wait a little longer. Ah! beloved, how despicable our troubles and trials will seem when we look back upon them! Looking at them here in the prospect, they seem immense; but when we get to heaven, we shall then,

> "With transporting joys recount
> The labors of our feet."

Our trials will seem to us nothing at all. We shall talk to one another about them in heaven, and find all the more to converse about, according as we have suffered more here below. Let us go on, therefore; and if the night be ever so dark, remember there is not a night that shall not have a morning; and that morning is to come by and by.

And now I want to tell you, very briefly, what are the excellences of songs in the night above all other songs.

In the first place, when you hear a man singing a song in the night—I mean in the night of trouble—you may be quite sure it is a hearty one. Many of you sang very prettily just now, didn't you? I wonder whether you would sing very prettily, if there was a stake or two in Smithfield for all of you who dared to do it? If you sang under pain and penalty, that would show your heart to be in your song. We can all sing very nicely indeed when everybody else sings. It is the easiest thing in the world to open your mouth, and let the words come out; but when the devil puts his hand over your mouth, can you sing then? Can you say, "Tho he slay me, yet will I trust in him"? That is hearty singing; that is real song that springs up in the night. The nightingale singeth most sweetly because she singeth in the night. We know a poet has said that, if she sang by day, she might be thought to sing no more sweetly than the wren. It is the stillness of the night that makes her song sweet. And so doth a Christian's song become sweet and hearty, because it is in the night.

Again: the songs we sing in the night will be lasting. Many songs we hear our fellow-creatures singing in the streets will not do to sing by-and-by; I guess they will sing a different kind of tune soon. They can sing nowadays any rollicking, drinking songs; but they will not sing them when they come to die; they are not exactly the songs with which to cross Jordan's billows. It will not do to sing one of those light songs when death and you are having the last tug. It will not do to enter heaven singing one of those unchaste, unholy sonnets. No; but the Christian who can sing in the night will not have to leave off his song; he may keep on singing it forever. He may put his foot in Jordan's stream, and continue his melody; he may wade through it, and keep on singing still, and land himself safe in heaven; and when he is there, there need not be a gap in his strain, but in a nobler, sweeter strain he may still continue singing His power to save. There are a great many of you that think Christian people are a very miserable set, don't you? You say, "Let me sing my song." Ay, but, my dear friends, we like to sing a song that will last; we don't like your songs; they are all froth, like bubbles on the beaker, and they will soon die away and be lost. Give me a song that will last; give me one that will not melt. Oh, give me not the dreamster's gold! he hoards it up, and says, "I'm rich"; and when he waketh, his gold is gone. But give me songs in the night, for they are songs I sing forever.

Again: the songs we warble in the night are those that show we have real faith in God. Many men have just enough faith to trust God as far as they can see Him, and they always sing as far as they can see providence go right; but true faith can sing when its possessors cannot see. It can take hold of God when they cannot discern Him.

Songs in the night, too, prove that we have true courage. Many sing by day who are silent by night; they are afraid of thieves and robbers; but the Christian who sings in the night proves himself to be a courageous character. It is the bold Christian who can sing God's sonnets in the darkness.

He who can sing songs in the night, too, proves that he has true love to Christ. It is not love to Christ to praise Him while everybody else praises Him; to walk arm in arm with Him when He has the crown on His head is no great deed, I wot; to walk with Christ in rags is something. To believe in Christ when He is shrouded in darkness, to stick hard and fast by the Savior when all men speak ill of Him and forsake Him—that is true faith. He who singeth a song to Christ in the night, singeth the best song in all the world; for He singeth from the heart.

I am afraid of wearying you; therefore I shall not dwell on the excellences of night songs, but just, in the last place, show you their use.

It is very useful to sing in the night of our

troubles, first, because it will cheer ourselves. When you were boys living in the country, and had some distance to go alone at night, don't you remember how you whistled and sang to keep your courage up? Well, what we do in the natural world we ought to do in the spiritual. There is nothing like singing to keep your spirits alive. When we have been in trouble, we have often thought ourselves to be well-nigh overwhelmed with difficulty; and we have said, "Let us have a song." We have begun to sing; and Martin Luther says, "The devil cannot bear singing." That is about the truth; he does not like music. It was so in Saul's days: an evil spirit rested on Saul; but when David played on his harp, the evil spirit went away from him. This is usually the case: if we can begin to sing we shall remove our fears. I like to hear servants sometimes humming a tune at their work; I love to hear a plowman in the country singing as he goes along with his horses. Why not? You say he has no time to praise God; but he can sing a song —surely he can sing a Psalm, it will take no more time. Singing is the best thing to purge ourselves of evil thoughts. Keep your mouth full of songs, and you will often keep your heart full of praises; keep on singing as long as you can; you will find it a good method of driving away your fears.

Sing, again, for another reason: because it will cheer your companions. If any of them are in the valley and in the darkness with you, it will be a great help to comfort them. John Bunyan tells us, that as Christian was going through the valley he found it a dreadful dark place, and terrible demons and goblins were all about him, and poor Christian thought he must perish for certain; but just when his doubts were the strongest, he heard a sweet voice; he listened to it, and he heard a man in front of him saying, "Yea, when I pass through the valley of the shadow of death, I will fear no evil." Now, that man did not know who was near him, but he was unwittingly singing to cheer a man behind. Christian, when you are in trouble, sing; you do not know who is near you. Sing, perhaps you will get a companion by it. Sing! perhaps there will be many a heart cheered by your song. There is some broken spirit, it may be, that will be bound up by your sonnets. Sing! there is some poor distrest brother, perhaps, shut up in the Castle of Despair, who, like King Richard, will hear your song inside the walls, and sing to you again, and you may be the means of getting him a ransom. Sing, Christian, wherever you go; try, if you can, to wash your face every morning in a bath of praise. When you go down from your chamber, never go to look on man till you have first looked on your God; and when you have looked on Him, seek to come down with a face beaming with joy; carry a smile, for you will cheer up many a poor way-worn pilgrim by it.

One more reason; and I know it will be a good one for you. Try and sing in the night, Christian, for that is one of the best arguments in all the world in favor of your religion. Our divines nowadays spend a great deal of time in trying to prove Christianity against those who disbelieve it. I should like to have seen Paul trying that! Elymas the sorcerer withstood him: how did our friend Paul treat him? He said, "Oh, full of all subtlety and all mischief, thou child of the devil, thou enemy of the righteousness, wilt thou not cease to pervert the right ways of the Lord?" That is about the politeness such men ought to have who deny God's truth. We start with this assumption: we will prove that the Bible is God's word, but we are not going to prove God's word. If you do not like to believe it, we will shake hands, and bid you good-by; we will not argue with you. The gospel has gained little by discussion. The greatest piece of folly on earth has been to send a man round the country, to follow another up who has been lecturing on infidelity just to make himself notorious.

Why, let them lecture on; this is a free country; why should we follow them about? The truth will win the day. Christianity need not wish for controversy; it is strong enough for it, if it wishes it; but that is not God's way.

God's direction is, "Preach, teach, dogmatize." Do not stand disputing; claim a divine mission; tell men that God says it, and there leave it. Say to them, "He that believeth shall be saved, and he that believeth not shall be damned"; and when you have done that, you have done enough. For what reason should our missionaries stand disputing with Brahmins? Why should they be wasting their time by attempting to refute first this dogma, and then another, of heathenism? Why not just go and say, "The God whom ye ignorantly worship, I declare unto you; believe me, and you will be saved; believe me not, and the Bible says you are lost." And then, having thus asserted God's word, say, "I leave it, I declare it unto you; it is a thing for you to believe, not a thing for you to reason about."

Religion is not a thing merely for your intellect; a thing to prove your own talent upon, by making a syllogism on it; it is a thing that demands your faith. As a messenger of heaven, I demand that faith; if you do not choose to give it, on your own head be the doom, if there be such, if there be not, you are prepared to risk it. But I have done my duty; I have told you the truth; that is enough, and there I leave it. Oh, Christian, instead of disputing, let me tell thee how to prove your religion. Live it out!

Live it out! Give the external as well as the internal evidence; give the external evidence of your own life. You are sick; there is your neighbor who laughs at religion; let him come into your house. When he was sick, he said, "Oh, send for the doctor"; and there he was fretting, and fuming, and whining, and making all manner of noises. When you are sick, send for him, tell him that you are resigned to the Lord's will; that you will kiss the chastening rod; that you will take the cup, and drink it, because your Father gives it.

You do not need to make a boast of this, or it will lose all its power; but do it because you cannot help doing it. Your neighbor will say, "There is something in that." And when you come to the borders of the grave—he was there once, and you heard how he shrieked, and how frightened he was—give him your hand, and say to him, "Ah! I have a Christ that will do to die by; I have a religion that will make me sing in the night." Let me hear how you can sing, "Victory, victory, victory!" through Him that loved you. I tell you, we may preach fifty thousand sermons to prove the gospel, but we shall not prove it half so well as you will through singing in the night. Keep a cheerful frame; keep a happy heart; keep a contented spirit; keep your eye up, and your heart aloft, and you prove Christianity better than all the Butlers, and all the wise men that ever lived. Give them the analogy of a holy life, and then you will prove religion to them; give them the evidence of internal piety, developed externally, and you will give the best possible proof of Christianity.

JAMES STALKER

1848-1927

SIX ATTITUDES OF TEMPTATION

BIOGRAPHICAL NOTE

JAMES STALKER, professor of Church
History in the United Free Church College, Aberdeen, was born at Crieff in
1848, and was educated at the universities
of Edinburgh, Halle, and Berlin. He has
been an incumbent of many pastorates in
Scotland, and has published "Life of Jesus
Christ"; "Life of St. Paul"; "The
Preacher and His Models," etc. In 1891
he delivered the Lyman Beecher Lectures
on Preaching, at Yale, and was examiner
for the degree of B.D. in Aberdeen
University.

*There hath no temptation taken you but such as is
common to men; but God is faithful, who will not
suffer you to be tempted above that ye are able; but
will with temptation also make a way to escape, that
ye may be able to bear it.—I Cor. x., 13.*

ONCE, when I was going to address a
gathering of young men, I asked a
friend what I should speak to them
about. His answer was: There is only one
subject worth speaking to young men about,
and that is temptation.

Of course, he did not mean this literally: he
only meant to emphasize the importance of
this subject. Was he not right? You remember, in the story of the Garden of Eden, where
the tree which represented temptation stood?
It stood in the midst of the garden—just at
the point where all the walks converged, where
Adam and Eve had to pass it every day. This
is a parable of human life. We are out of
paradise now; but the tree of temptation still
stands in our life where it stood then—in the
midst; where all the roads meet; where we
must pass it every day—and every man's weal
of wo depends on the attitude to it which
he takes up.

There are six attitudes in any of which we
may stand to temptation—first, we may be
tempted; second, we may have fallen before
temptation; third, we may be tempting others;
or, fourth, we may be successfully resisting
temptation; fifth, we may have outlived temptation; sixth, we may be assisting others to
overcome their temptations.

As I should like these six attitudes to be
remembered, let me give them names; and
these I will borrow from the politics of the
continent of Europe. Any of you who may
glance at times into the politics of France
or Germany will be aware that in their legis-
lative assemblies there prevails a more minute
division into parties, or groups as they are
called, than we are accustomed to. In your
politics you are content with two great historical parties—Republicans and Democrats.
But, as I have said, in Continental parliaments
the members are divided into groups. You
read of the group of the left center,
the group of the left, and the group
of the extreme left; the group of the
right center, the group of the right, and the
group of the extreme right. I do not pretend that even these are all; but I will take
these as the six names I need for character-
izing the six attitudes in which men may
stand to temptation.

On the left there are three—first, the group of the left center, by which I mean those who are being tempted; second, the group of the left, by which are meant those who have fallen before temptation; third, the group of the extreme left, or those who are tempters of others. And on the right there are three groups—the fourth group, that of the right center, containing those who are successfully resisting temptation; the fifth, the group of the right, or those who have outlived their temptations; and the sixth and last, the group of the extreme right, that is to say, those who are helping others to resist their temptations.

Let me run rapidly over these six groups.

I. The group of the left center or those who are being tempted.

With this one I begin; because we have all been in it. Whether we have been in the other groups or not, we have all been in this one: we have all been tempted. One of the first things we were told when we were quite young was that we should be tempted—that we should have to beware of evil companions; and there is not one of us in whose case this prediction has not come true.

There is, indeed, no greater mystery of providence than to understand the unequal proportions in which temptation is distributed. Some are comparatively little tempted; others are thrown into a fiery furnace of it seven times heated. There are in the world sheltered situations in which a man may be compared to a ship in the harbor, where the waves may sometimes heave a little, but a real storm never comes; there are other men like the vessel which has to sail the high seas and face the full force of the tempest. Many here must know well what this means. Perhaps you know it so well that you feel inclined to say to me, Preacher, you know nothing about it; if you had to live where we live—if you had to associate with the companions whom we have to work with, and hear the kind of language which we have to listen to every hour of the day—you would know better the truth of what you are saying. Do not be too sure of that. Perhaps I know as well about it as you do. Perhaps my library is as dangerous a place for me as your workshop is for you. Solitude has its temptations as well as society. St. Anthony, before his conversion, was a gay and fast young man of Alexandria; and, when he was converted, he found the temptations of the city so intolerable that he fled into the Egyptian desert and became a hermit; but he afterward confest that the temptations of a cell in the wilderness were worse than those of the city. It would not be safe to exchange our temptations for those of another man; every one has his own.

I believe, further, that every man has his own tempter or temptress. Every man on his journey through life meets with some one who deliberately tries to ruin him. Have you met your tempter yet? Perhaps he is sitting by your side at this moment. Perhaps it is some one in whose society you delight to be, and of whose acquaintance you are proud; but the day may come when you will curse the hour in which you ever saw that face. Some of us, looking back, can remember well who our tempter was; and we tremble yet, sometimes, as we remember how nearly we were over the precipice.

One of the chief powers of temptation is the power of surprise. It comes when you are not looking for it; it comes from the person and from the quarter you least suspect. The day dawns which is to be the decisive one in our life; but it looks like any other day. No bell rings in the sky to give warning that the hour of destiny has come. But the good angel that watches over us is waiting and trembling. The fiery moment arrives; do we stand; do we fall? Oh, if we fall, that good angel goes flying away to heaven, crying, fallen, fallen!

II. The group of the left or those who have fallen before temptation.

Tho I do not know this audience, I know human nature well enough to be certain that there are some hearing me who are whispering sadly in their hearts, This is the group I belong to: I have fallen before temptation; it may not be known; it may not even be suspected; but it is true.

To such I bear a message of hope to-day.

The great tempter of men has two lies with which he plies us at two different stages. Before we have fallen, he tells us that one fall does not matter; it is a trifle; we can easily recover ourselves again. And, after we have fallen, he tells us that it is hopeless: we are given over to sin, and need not attempt to rise.

Both are false.

It is a terrible falsehood to say that to fall once does not matter. Even by one fall there is something lost that can never be recovered again. It is like the breaking of an infinitely precious vessel, which may be mended, but will never again be as if it had not been broken. And, besides, one fall leads to others; it is like going upon very slippery ice on the face of a hill; even in the attempt to rise you are carried away again farther than ever. Moreover, we give others a hold over us. If we have not sinned alone, to have sinned once involves a tacit pledge that we will sin again; and it is often almost impossible to get out of such a false position. God keep us from believing the devil's lie, that to fall once does not matter.

But then, if we have fallen, he plies us with the other lie: It is of no use to attempt to rise; you can not overcome your besetting sin. But this is falser still. To those who feel themselves fallen I come, in Christ's name, to say,

Yes, you may rise. If we could ascend to heaven to-day and scan the ranks of the blest, should we not find multitudes among them who were once sunk low as man can fall? But they are washed, they are justified, they are sanctified, in the name of our Lord Jesus and by the Spirit of our God. And so may you be.

It is, I know, a doctrine which may be abused; but I will not scruple to preach it to those who are fallen and sighing for deliverance. St. Augustine says that we may out of our dead sins make stepping-stones to rise to the heights of perfection. What did he mean by that? He meant that the memory of our falls may breed in us such a humility, such a distrust of self, such a constant clinging to Christ as we never could have had if we had not fallen.

Does not the Scripture itself go even further? David fell—deep as man can fall; but what does he say in that great fifty-first Psalm, in which he confesses his sin? Anticipating forgiveness, he says:

> Then will I teach Thy ways unto
> Those that transgressors be,
> And those that sinners are, shall then
> Be turned unto Thee.

And what did our Lord Himself say to St. Peter about his fall? "When thou art converted, strengthen thy brethren." A man may derive strength to give to others from having fallen. He may have a sympathy with the erring; he may be able to describe the steps by which to rise, as no other can. Thus, by God's marvelous grace, out of the eater may come forth meat, and out of the strong may come forth sweetness.

III. The group of the extreme left or those who are tempters of others.

These three groups on the left form three stages of a natural descent. First, tempted; secondly, fallen; then, if we have fallen, we tempt others to fall.

This is quite natural. If we are down ourselves, we try to get others down beside us. There is a satisfaction in it. To a soul that has become black a soul that is still white is an offense. It is said of some, "They rest not except they have done mischief, and their sleep is taken away, except they cause some to fall." There is nothing else, I think, in human nature so diabolical as the delight which the wicked feel in making others like themselves. Have you never seen it? Have you never seen a group of evil-doers deliberately set themselves to ruin a newcomer, scoffing at his innocence and enticing him to their orgies? And, when they succeeded, they rejoiced over his fall as if they had won a great triumph. So low can human nature sink.

Sometimes it may be self-interest that makes man a tempter. The sin of another may be

necessary to secure some end of his own. The dishonest merchant, for his own gain, undermines the honesty of his apprentice; the employer, making haste to be rich, tempts his employees to break the Sabbath; the tyranical landlord forces his tenants to vote against their conscience. Why, there are trades which flourish on other people's sins.

But perhaps the commonest way to become a tempter is through thoughtlessness. I protest, we have no pity for each other's souls. We trample about among these most brittle and infinitely precious things, as if they were common ware, and we tempt one another and ruin one another without even being aware of it. Perhaps, indeed, no one who goes to the place of wo goes there alone; perhaps every one takes at least one with him. I hear it said nowadays that the fear of hell no longer moves men's minds; and that preachers ought no longer to make use of it as a motive in religion. Well, I confess, I fear it myself; it is a motive still to me. But I will tell you what I fear ten times more. What! is there anything which a man can fear ten times more than the fire that never shall be quenched? Yes! it is to meet there any one who will say, You have brought me here; you were my tempter; and but for you I might never have come to this place of torment. God forbid that this should ever be said to me by any one. Will it be said to any of you?

But now let us turn away from this side of our subject and look at the bright side—at the three groups on the right.

IV. The group of the right center, or those who are successfully resisting temptation.

Not very long ago a letter chanced to come under my eye. It was by a young man attending one of the great English universities. One day two or three fellow students had come into his rooms and asked him to join them in some amusement of a questionable kind, which they were contemplating. On the spur of the moment he promised; but, when they had gone, he thought what his parents would say if they knew. It was a godly home he belonged to and a very happy one, in which the children were bound to the parents in such a way that they kept no secrets from them. He thought of his home, and he had doubts whether what he had promised to do might not cause pain there. He was afraid it would; and he promptly and frankly went and told his companions that his engagement was off till he should inquire. The letter I saw was the inquiry. It affected me deeply to read it; for it was easy to understand how much manliness was required to do that which might be interpreted as unmanly.

The memory of that man's home came to him in the hour of temptation and made him strong to resist. I wonder this influence does not prove a rescuing power oftener than it does. Young men, when you are tempted, think of home. I have been a minister away in a provincial town; and, I think, if you could realize the mother's terror, and the father's stricken frame, and the silent tearful circle, as I have seen them—it would make you fling the cup of temptation from your lips, however persuasive was the hand that proffered it.

Yet this will not always be a strong enough motive in the struggle with temptation. There will come times when you are tempted to great sin which will appear to you absolutely safe from discovery and not likely to inflict the slightest injury on your fortunes. In such circumstances nothing will sustain you if you do not respect your own nature and stand in awe of your own conscience. Nay, even this is not enough; the only effective defense is that of one who was surely tempted in this very way, "How can I do this great wickedness and sin against God?"

There are secret battles fought and victories won on this ground, never heard of on earth, but essentially more glorious than many victories which are trumpeted far and wide by the breath of fame. There is more of courage and manhood needed for them than for walking up to the cannon's mouth? Many a soldier could do that who could not say "No" to two or three companions pressing him to enter the canteen. Not long ago I was speaking to a soldier who told me that many a time in the barracks he was the only man to go down on his knees out of twenty or thirty; and he did it among showers of oaths and derision. Do you think walking up to the cannon's mouth would have been difficult to that man? Such victories have no record on earth; but be sure of this, they are widely heard of in heaven, and there is One there who will not forget them.

V. The group of the right or those who have outlived their temptations.

On this point I do not mean to dwell; but I should like at least to mention it, as there is contained in it a great encouragement to some who may be enduring the very hottest fires of temptation. Perhaps your situation is so intolerable that you often say, I can not stand this much longer; if it lasts as it is, I must fall—"One day I shall fall into the hands of Saul."

No, you will not. I bid you take courage; and as one encouragement I say, you will yet outlive your temptation.

That which is a temptation at one period of life may be no temptation at all at another. To a child there may be an irresistible temptation in a sweetmeat which a man would take a good deal to touch; and some of the temptations which are now the most painful to you will in time be as completely outlived. God may lift you, by some turn of providence,

out of the position where your temptation lies; or the person from whom you chiefly suffer may be removed from your neighborhood. The unholy fire of passion, which now you must struggle to keep out of your heart, may, through the mercy of God who setteth men in families, be burnt away and replaced by the holy fire of love burning on the altar of a virtuous home. The laughter and scorn which you may now be bearing for your Christian profession will, if you only have patience, be changed into respect and veneration; for even the ungodly are forced at last to do honor to a consistent Christian life.

In these and other ways, if you only have patience, you will outlive temptation; tho I do not suppose we shall ever in this world be entirely out of its reach, or be beyond the need of these two admonitions: "Watch and pray that ye enter not into temptation," and, "Let him that thinketh he standeth take heed lest he fall."

VI. The group of the extreme right, or those who are helping others to overcome temptation.

You see, on the right there is an upward progress, as on the left there was a downward one. The first step is to be successfully resisting temptation; a higher one is to have outlived temptation; the highest of all is to be helping others to resist it; tho I do not say that this must be the chronological order. It is the order of honor.

This group of the extreme right is the exact opposite of the group of the extreme left. Those in the latter group are tempting others to fall; those in this one are encouraging and aiding others to stand fast. No man ought to be satisfied till he is in this noble group.

There are many ways in which we may assist others with their temptations. A big-hearted man will often be doing so without being aware of it. His very presence, his attractive manhood, his massive character act as an encouragement to younger men and hold them up. I do not know anything so much to be coveted as in old age to have men coming to say, Your example, your presence, your sympathy were like a protecting arm put round my stumbling youth and helped me over the perilous years. My brothers, if a few men can honestly say this to us in the future, will it not be better than Greek and Roman fame?

Many are helping the young against their temptations by providing them with means of spending their leisure innocently and profitably. Our leisure time is the problem. While we are at work, there is not so much fear of us; but it is in the hours of leisure—the hours between work and sleep—that temptation finds men, and they are lost; and therefore I say, there is no more Christian work than providing men with opportunities of spending leisure profitably.

But by far the best way to help men with their temptations is to bring them to Christ. It may be of some service to a man if, in the time of trial, I put round him the sympathetic arm of a brother; but it is infinitely better if I can get him to allow Christ to put round him His strong arm. This is the effectual defense; and no other can be really depended on. . . .

AUGUSTUS HOPKINS STRONG

1836-1921

THE HOLY SPIRIT THE ONE AND ONLY POWER IN MISSIONS

BIOGRAPHICAL NOTE

PRESIDENT and professor of systematic theology, Rochester Theological Seminary, 1872-1912; born in Rochester, N. Y., August 3, 1836; graduated from Yale, 1857; pastor of the First Baptist church, Haverhill, Mass., 1861-65; First Baptist church, Cleveland, Ohio, 1865-72; D.D., Brown University, Yale and Princeton; LL.D., Bucknell and Alfred universities; author of "Systematic Theology," "Philosophy and Religion," "The Great Poets and their Theology," "Christ in Creation and Ethical Monism," etc.

" The power of the Holy Ghost."—Rom. 15 : 13.

WHO is the Holy Spirit? He is the third person of the blessed Trinity. In opposition to much of the false and pernicious teaching of our day, I emphasize the truth that the Holy Spirit is a person, not an influence—some One, and not some thing. I do not need to tell you that the tripersonality of the divine nature is essential to the life, communion, and blessedness of God. Because God is Father, Son, and Holy Spirit, He is independent of creation; He does not need the universe. The world has had a beginning; it is the work of His sovereignty and grace, but the Holy Spirit is eternal, and before the world was He existed, coequal with the Father and the Son. He is not only a person, but He is that person of the Godhead who comes nearest to us in our needs, who brings the Creator not only to, but into, the creature. He is personal love in its tenderest form, and only when we appreciate the depths of our own ingratitude and His holy shrinking from our sin, can we understand " the love of the Spirit " that bears with our manifold provocations and still persists in His healing and purifying work. As Christ in Gethsemane " began to be sorrowful and very troubled," so the Holy Spirit is sorrowful and very troubled, at the ignoring, despising, resisting of His work, on the part of those whom He is trying to rescue from sin and to lead out into the activities of the Christian life. Multiply this experience by millions, and conceive how great must be the suffering and sorrow of the third person of the Trinity, as He struggles with the apathy and unbelief of the Church, endeavors to replace the spirit of selfishness by the spirit of missions, and strives to turn the weakness of His people into power!

But tho the Holy Spirit is the third person of the Trinity, He is more than this; He is also the Spirit of the incarnate Christ. We cannot understand this without reflecting upon the nature of the change in Christ Himself when He took upon Him human flesh. Before His incarnation He was the eternal Word of God, the Revealer of God in nature and in history. But when He was born of a virgin, He condensed His glory, so to speak, and manifested Himself within the limits of humanity. What was before abstract and far away now became concrete and near. In Christ we see the Godhead in our own likeness, speaking to us with a brother's voice

559

and feeling for us with a brother's heart. Christ is now Son of man as well as Son of God. And what I wish to say with regard to the Holy Spirit, is, that He is the Spirit, not of the preincarnate but of the incarnate Christ, with just as much more power than He had before as Christ had more power after His incarnation.

The Holy Spirit had wrought in some measure before the incarnation, just as Christ had wrought. But as Christ the Word of God, was abstract and hard to recognize so the Spirit of Christ partook of the same disabilities. The Holy Spirit, who always manifested Christ, could in Old Testament times manifest only the divine side of Christ, because there was as yet no human side to manifest. But when Christ's person had become complete by taking humanity into its divinity and when Christ's work had become complete by taking all our sins and penalties and bearing them for us, then the Holy Spirit, the Spirit of Christ, had more to manifest than He ever had before. From being the Spirit of God alone, He became the Spirit of the God-man, the Spirit of the incarnate Jesus, the revealer through all space and time of the humanity that had been taken up into the divinity.

We can understand now how it can be said in John's Gospel that before the crucifixion and resurrection " the Spirit was not yet given "—or was not yet—" because Jesus was not yet glorified." The proper work of the Holy Spirit is to take of the things of Christ and show them to men. Until Christ's work was accomplished the Holy Spirit had comparatively little to show. Not only was His influence limited in its degree, but it was also limited in its kind: the Holy Spirit as the revealer of the incarnate Jesus did not as yet exist. We might illustrate this by the pride and joy of the mother in showing off her son: she can exhibit him after he has reached his majority and has education and character, as she never could when he was a babe in arms. One might even say that while she was caring for him in his infancy her time for showing him off had not yet come. The mother was not yet exhibitor. So the Holy Spirit could not exhibit Christ until there was a full-grown Christ to exhibit. While our Lord retained the form of a servant and was subject to the Holy Spirit here on earth, the Holy Spirit could not make Him known, any more than the mother could publish abroad the greatness of her son, before the time of his greatness had come. But when Christ's humiliation was ended and His exaltation had begun, then the Holy Spirit's work could begin also. Only when the Savior was glorified in heaven, could the Spirit glorify Him on earth.

But we must not separate the Spirit from Christ as if the two were independent of each other like Peter and Paul. The persons are one in essence. As the Father dwells in and reveals Himself through the Son, so the Son dwells in and reveals through the Spirit. As Christ could say: " He that hath seen me hath seen the Father," so the Holy Spirit might say: " He that hath seen me hath seen Christ. In the Holy Spirit we have Christ Himself, no longer far away and unintelligible, but possest of a human soul and touched with the feeling of our infirmities as He could never be if He had not passed through the temptation and the sorrow of an actual human life. The Holy Spirit is the same incarnate Christ now made omnipresent and omnipotent. You can appreciate how great a truth this is, when you remember the sorrow of the disciples at the taking from them of their Lord. To part with Him, their Teacher and Helper, seemed to them to be the loss of all. How hard it was for them to realize that it was expedient for them that He should go away! Yet it was best for them to lose His visible, bodily presence, because only thus could they have His invisible, spiritual omnipresence. Unless He went away in body, He could not send His Spirit. But if He departed from their eyes, He could come into their hearts. Hence He can say indifferently, " I will send the Comforter," and " I will come unto you," for the Comforter is only Christ in another, more spiritual, more universal form.

It was to educate the disciples to this faith in His invisible presence through the Holy Spirit that Jesus appeared to them so mysteriously in the upper chamber, on the way to Emmaus and by the seaside of Galilee. A moment ago He seemed absent, but now He is here, stretching out His hands in blessing. Has He come through the solid walls, or through the circumambient air? Ah, not so! The lesson to be learned is rather that He has been here all the while, and now He only manifests His presence. And the disciples do learn the lesson that, while seemingly absent, the Savior is ever present with them—while invisible, by the eye of faith He can be seen. The Holy Spirit is the incarnate Christ not only, but the incarnate Christ spiritualized, freed from all the limitations of space and time, no longer subject to the conditions of His humiliation, but omnipresent and glorified. While here on earth in human flesh He could heal the lepers and feed the hungry and raise the dead and walk the sea; but He could not be in two places at the same time, nor teach Peter in Galilee at the same time that He taught John at Jerusalem. Now, by His Holy Spirit, He can be present with the little knot of believers that worships in Swatow, at the same time that He meets with us here in America. And as the Holy Spirit is the omnipresent

Christ, so He is the omnipotent Christ also, with every restraint upon His working removed, except the restraints of infinite wisdom and infinite love.

We begin to see the greatness of the Holy Spirit. And yet we shall not understand how great He is, unless we remember how great this Christ is who works through Him. Jesus said that all power was committed to Him in heaven and in earth. This means nothing less than that nature, with all her elements and laws, is under His control and manifests His will; that history, with all her vicissitudes, including the rise and fall of empires and civilizations is the working out of His plan; and that the Church, with her witnessing for the truth, her martyrdoms, her love and anguish for men's souls, her struggling after righteousness, is the engine by which He is setting up His kingdom. The incarnate Christ is now on the throne of the universe, and the hand that was nailed to the cross now holds the scepter over all.

Who, then, is the Holy Spirit? He is the incarnate and divine Redeemer wielding all this infinite power, in the realm of spirit, and for spiritual ends. He is the organ of internal revelation, as Christ is the organ of external revelation. Just so far as Christ does anything for intelligent and moral beings He does it through the Holy Spirit. We can make no exceptions. As the Spirit of God in the beginning brooded over chaos and brought forth forms of life and beauty, so still He works in nature to complete and restore the creation which sin has marred; as He strove with men before the flood, so He strives with them all along the course of time, in every nation and in every conscience giving witness of Christ's law and grace; as with Noah and Abraham and Moses and David and Isaiah He renewed the heart by presenting the truth made known by the preincarnate Logos, so now He takes the clearer truth of Christ's incarnation and sacrifice and resurrection and makes it the means of establishing the kingdom of God in human hearts. Pentecost could come only after the Passover. The feast of jubilation and first fruits dated back to the other feast when the lamb was slain in every household. So Christ had first to die, before the Holy Spirit could show to John on Patmos the Lamb that had been slain, sitting upon the very throne of God and with all the crowns of the universe upon His brow. In other words, the Holy Spirit is the divine but incarnate Savior omnipresent and omnipotent to subdue to Himself the hearts of earth's revolted millions and to go forth conquering and to conquer until every spiritual enemy has been put beneath His feet.

If what I have said is true, then I think we shall be obliged greatly to enlarge our ordinary conceptions of the power of the Holy Ghost. I think we cannot confine it, as we sometimes do, to the power exerted in the conversion of the individual, tho that is its most common and impressive exhibition. There is a larger agency of the Spirit in the leavening of society, the shaping of public opinion, the raising of ethical standards, the quickening of the moral sense throughout whole communities and decades, throughout whole nations and ages. Just as there is a preliminary work in the individual which prepares the way for his regeneration so there is a preliminary work in the masses of mankind that prepares the way for the coming of the kingdom; and this preliminary work is the work of the Holy Spirit, just as much as the work of consummation is.

There are times when financial depression is succeeded by a strange awe and expectation of the coming of God. There are times when the sudden solution of vexed problems of State, when great public deliverances and great public judgments, are recognized even by ungodly men as due to the finger of God. Then it is the Holy Spirit that draws the curtain aside and lets men see the living God behind the wheels. In the movements and enterprises of the Church there is a work of the Holy Spirit quite aside from His enlightening and sanctifying of individuals. At times a multitude of believers, widely separated from each other, seemed moved to pray for the removal of some mountain-like obstacle that prevents the progress of God's cause. Then slavery is abolished, walls of heathen exclusion are broken down, civil reforms are instituted, great revivals of religion and great missionary efforts are inaugurated. And yet it is true that even these broad and general influences upon the heart of humanity and of the Church are connected with renewals of single individuals, like the conversion of Paul and the conversion of Luther; and these turnings of individuals become the means of turning whole communities.

Regeneration is a spiritual work, in the sense that it takes place in man's spiritual nature, is wrought by a spiritual Being, and makes use of spiritual means and agencies. The Holy Spirit changes men's natures by bringing truth to bear upon them—the truth with regard to their sin, with regard to Christ's salvation, with regard to God's judgment. He convinces of sin, and of righteousness, and of judgment. As a flash of lightning shows the nightly wanderer that he is on the edge of a precipice when before he thought himself safe, so the Holy Spirit lights up all the heart's ungodliness and reveals its danger. As the rising sun discloses the glories of an Alpine landscape which the darkness has hidden and shows snowy mountain and deep blue lake in all their beauty, so the Holy Spirit draws aside the veil of unbelief and enables the lost and helpless to perceive the divine compassion and the infinite sufficiency of Jesus Christ, the Savior of sinners. And then He convinces of judgment also—the certainty and awfulness of God's judgment against sin; the Holy Spirit teaches this, and enables the sinner to renounce sin utterly and thus to make the judgment of God his own.

So, while Christ is the life, the Holy Spirit is the life-giver. The Holy Spirit presents Christ to the soul, or, if you prefer the phrase, in and through the Holy Spirit, Christ comes to the soul and takes up His abode in it, makes it holy, gives it new views of truth and new power of will. Before the Holy Spirit began His work Christ was outside, and we looked upon Him as a foreign, perhaps even as a distant, Redeemer. After the Holy Spirit has done His work, we have Christ within, the soul of our soul and the life of our life. A union is established between Christ and us, so that none can separate us from Him or from His love. In fact, there is nothing more marked in the New Testament than the way in which He is identified with His body, the Church, unless it is the way in which the Holy Spirit is identified with our spirit. The Holy Spirit so passes into our spirits that we are said to have the spirit of Christ, and it is sometimes difficult to tell whether our spirit or the divine Spirit is meant, the two are so merged the one in the other. All this renewing and transforming shows what power the Holy Spirit exercises. It is power compared with which the mightiest physical changes sink into insignificance. You can more easily create a world than recreate a soul. Only God can regenerate. It is only God, who causes the light to shine out of darkness at the beginning, who can shed abroad in a sinful soul the light of the knowledge of the glory of God in the face of Jesus Christ.

And yet physical images are employed to illustrate the Holy Spirit's power. His agency is compared to that of air, of water, and of fire, at their highest pitch of efficiency. Take the air, that is often so still and apparently impotent about us that we absolutely forget its existence. Would you believe that this air, when stirred, is capable of taking up cattle and carrying them half a mile over fences and trees? Would you believe that this air could absolutely prostrate the strongest houses, and even lay low the largest trees, cutting a clear swath for miles and miles through the forest? Yet the eastern tornado or the western cyclone is nothing but "wild air," as Helen Keller beautifully said. So in the ordinary quiet workings of the Holy Spirit, we get no idea of the mighty effects He is able to produce. The same divine Agent who comforts the sorrowing and speaks in whispers of peace to the heart of a child is able to come like a mighty rushing wind at Pentecost and in a single day convert three thousand unto God.

The agency of the Holy Spirit is compared to that of water. The rain is a symbol of His influence. Sometimes it is the gentle showers that water the mown grass and cause the thirsty field to revive. So the Holy Spirit encourages the believer whose earthly hopes have been cut down. But there are larger manifestations of His power. In this country and latitude we know little of what rain can accomplish. Years ago I was traveling in Palestine and happened to be caught in the last rain of the springtime, just before the long dry season from April to November set in. I had heard of rain coming down in the tropics in sheets and bucketsful, but I had never expected to see anything like it But there, on the way from Carmel to Cæsarea, I had the experience. The water seemed to descend in masses. Those exposed to it were drenched as if they had been plunged into the sea. Then I understood what the psalmist meant by "the river of God which is full of water": he meant the rain, that came down like floods from heaven. And then I understood the promise of Malachi: "Bring ye all the tithes into the storehouse, and prove me now herewith, saith the Lord, if I will not open the windows of heaven and pour you out a blessing, so that there shall not be room to receive it." The opening of the windows of heaven is an allusion to the deluge of old; and the prophet assures us that, when God's people are faithful and put His promise to the test, the Holy Spirit whose ordinary influences are so gentle will descend like the floods of Noah, so that the fountains of the great deep are broken up, and rivers of blessing flow forth from God's sanctuary, to water the earth.

The agency of the Holy Spirit is compared to fire. The flame kindled in the heart by the blessèd Spirit may be so slight and low that a single breath of coldness and opposition may suffice to quench it. But it may also become a consuming blaze that carries everything before it. It is only a match that sets the dry wood burning in the hunter's campfire, but that fire may spread till the whole forest for miles and miles is swept by the roaring flames. A kerosene lamp overturned is a little thing, but Chicago devoured by conflagration is the result—the greatest structures of wood and iron melt and crumble in that heat. So in the common operations of the Holy Spirit we get no conception of what the Spirit can do in melting hard hearts and in bringing to nothing the pride and opposition of men. How often has He swept whole communities with religious anxiety and zeal that could only be compared with fire from heaven! The college revivals, and the great awakenings on a larger scale which this country has witnessed in days gone by, are evidence that the Holy Spirit has a power beyond all our ordinary estimates. Why should we be so slow to believe in His power?

Was Pentecost the limit of His working? What was Pentecost but the feast of first-fruits, the bringing in of the first few ripened ears of the mighty harvest? Shall we limit the harvest by the first fruits, or think that the first ingathering is the greatest possible? Ah, no! Pentecost was but the beginning and the power of the Spirit of God will be fully seen only when a nation is born in a day.

There is no measure of the Holy Spirit's power except the greatness of the Holy Spirit Himself. The Holy Spirit is as great as Christ—in fact, He is Christ, not now absent but present, with us and with His Church alway even unto the end of the world, and all things in heaven and earth are given into His hand. And since Christ is God revealed, deity manifested, divinity brought down to our comprehension and engaged in the work of our salvation, the Holy Spirit is this same God in the hearts of believers and pushing the conquests of Christ's kingdom in the world. Wherever God is by His omnipresence, there the Holy Spirit is, to make men will and do according to His will, and whatever God can do by His omnipotence in the spirits of men, that the Holy Spirit can do, to convert the world to Christ. Is the Holy Spirit equal to the work of missions? Ah, the Holy Spirit is God Himself, engaged in this very work. More pervasive than electricity or magnetism, His power encircles the globe, and hence the touch of prayer in America can produce results in Africa or in Japan.

He is one, and He is almighty. He can weave together all the prayers and all the labors of the Christian Church into the complex structure of His kingdom, and He can make the least breath of desire, and the widow's mite of contribution, most potent agencies for the salvation of the world. All the wealth of Christendom is His, and He can prompt His people to use it. The storms of war and the oppositions of the nations are only surface movements of the great sea of humanity, beneath which the vast ocean of God's Spirit is ever resting and waiting with power to bring the waves to calm or to drive them with one consent to engulf and overwhelm the shore. And the day shall come when, in answer to His people's prayers and through their very efforts, this ocean-like Spirit shall show His power and the work of a thousand years shall be done in one day. Men may fail and be discouraged, but the mighty Spirit of God shall not fail nor be discouraged, till He has set judgment in the earth, and the kingdoms of this world have become the kingdoms of our God and of His Christ.

"It is the mistake and disaster of the Christian world that effects are sought instead of causes." These weighty words of a recent writer have deeply imprest me. I wish to apply them to the subject of missions. The Holy Spirit is the one and only power in missions, and to expect success in missions while we ignore the Holy Spirit, is to look for an effect without a cause. How evident it is that this great agent, this renewer of hearts, this regenerator of the world, has been largely neglected and ignored! We have been trying to carry on missions without the Spirit of missions. We have trusted our own wisdom, instead of trusting Him. We have invoked earthly helps, instead of invoking the Helper, the Advocate, who has been called to this work by God. And so our zeal has slackened, and our faith has grown weak, and our love has become cold. Neither faith nor love will survive, if hope does not go with them. We cannot do this work ourselves, and when we lose sight of the Holy Spirit, Christian activity dwindles and dies.

The success of missions is dependent upon our recognition of the Spirit of missions. The conversion of the world must be preceded by new faith in Him who effects conversion. The Holy Spirit will show His greatest power only when the Church seeks His power. The Spirit of missions is also the Spirit of prayer. How may we secure the power of the Holy Spirit in missions and in prayer? Ah, we cannot pray that He will take to Himself His great power and reign supreme in the world, until we ourselves admit Him to complete dominion in our hearts and lives. So long as we are full of other things that He abhors —our own selfish plans, our impure desires, our worldly ambitions—He will not work in us that mighty praying, that mighty effort, that mighty sacrifice, that alone will save the world. You might put a corked bottle under Niagara, but you could never fill it. The flood of spiritual influence may be descending like Niagara, but the love of sin may completely prevent it from entering our souls. Let us open our hearts then that we may receive. Let us put away the evil that offends God and prevents Him from doing His work in us. Let us ask for His coming and indwelling. Let us take Him, by the act of our wills, once more to be our Lord.

On his last birthday but one, Livingstone wrote: "My Jesus, my King, my Life, my All, I again dedicate my whole self to Thee!" No wonder that he died on his knees, with his face buried in his hands, praying for the regeneration of Africa. The Spirit of missions is also the Spirit of consecration. He prompts to various kinds of service. He puts it into the heart of one to say: "Here am I, send me!" He moves another to say: "The half of my goods I give, to send the gospel across the sea!'' He impels still another to spend days and nights in prayer for the conversion of Madras, or for the spiritual revolutionizing of New York.

We are responsible for the bringing of the world to God, because we have this connection and partnership with the Spirit of God. It is not so much a question of giving as it is a question of receiving.

The Savior even now utters His command as He did in the company of those disciples on the evening of His resurrection. ''Receive ye—take ye—the Holy Ghost!'' He says to each one of us. But we make two mistakes with regard to His words. First, they are a command, and not a mere permission; and secondly, it is not a passive receiving, but an active taking that is required of us. Shall we thus take the Holy Spirit—the Spirit of missions, the Spirit of power? May God the Father grant it! May Christ the Son bestow it! May the Holy Spirit Himself vouchsafe it! Then from us, tho of ourselves we are hard and dry as rocks in the desert, shall flow rivers of living water like that which sprang forth at the touch of Moses' rod! Then shall be set in motion divine influences which shall flow like ocean tides around the world, until every land shall be bathed in their flood and the knowledge of the Lord shall fill the earth as the waters cover the sea!

JOHN SUMMERFIELD

1798-1825

THE HEAVENLY INHERITANCE

BIOGRAPHICAL NOTE

JOHN SUMMERFIELD was born in England in 1798, and came to New York in 1821, where he soon became one of the most popular and eloquent preachers of that day. He belonged to the Methodist Communion and his name is still perpetuated in the names of many Methodist churches. He was unusually simple and modest in his tastes and habits, but when he spoke from the pulpit he produced a great impression by the force and daring of his style. He gave promise of equaling Whitefield as a pulpit orator, but he was subject to delicate health and prematurely died in 1825, twenty-seven years of age.

For so an entrance shall be ministered unto you abundantly into the everlasting kingdom of our Lord and Saviour Jesus Christ.—2 Peter i., 11.

OF all the causes which may be adduced to account for the indifference which is so generally manifested toward those great concerns of eternity, in which men are so awfully interested, none appears to me so likely to resolve the mystery, as that unbelief which lies at the core of every heart, hindering repentance, and so making faith impossible. Men hear that there is a hell to shun, a heaven to win; and, though they give their assent to both these truths, they never impress them on their mind. It is plain that, whatever their lips may confess, they never believed with the heart, otherwise some effect would have been produced in the life. The germ of unbelief lies within, and discovers itself in all that indifference which is displayed, in the majority of that class of beings whose existence is to be perpetuated throughout eternity. If these thoughts do sometimes obtrude themselves on their serious attention, they are immediately banished from their minds; and the dying exclamation of Moses may be taken up with tears by every lover of perishing sinners: "O! that they were wise, that they understood this, that they would consider their latter end!" When God, by His prophet Isaiah, called the Israelites to a sense of their awful departure from Him, His language was, "My people do not know: My people do not consider." How few are there like Mary, who "ponder those things in their heart," who are willing to look at themselves, to pry into eternity, to put the question home,

"Shall I be with the damn'd cast out,
Or numbered with the bless'd?"

This question must sooner or later have a place in your minds, or awful will be your state indeed; let it reach your hearts to-day; and if you pray to the Father of light, you will soon be enabled in His light to discern so much of yourselves as will cause you to cry, "What shall I do to be saved?" While we shall this morning attempt to point out some of the privileges of the sons of God, oh! may your hearts catch the strong desire to be conformed to the living Head, that so an abundant entrance may be administered unto you also, into the everlasting kingdom of our Lord and Savior, Jesus Christ.

The privilege to which our text leads us, is

exclusively applicable to those to whom that question has been solved by the Spirit of God; those who have believed to the saving of their souls; who have experienced redemption through His blood, and the forgiveness of sins; and who are walking in the fear of the Lord and in the comfort of the Holy Ghost.

I. The state to which we look forward: the "everlasting kingdom of our Lord and Savior."

1. It is a kingdom. By this figurative expression our Lord has described the state of grace here and of glory hereafter; our happiness in time and our happiness in eternity. They were wisely so called: Jesus has said, as well as done, all things well; for these two states differ not in kind, but in degree; the one is merely a preparative for the other, and he who has been a subject of the former kingdom will be a subject of the latter. Grace is but the seed of glory, glory is the maturity of grace; grace is but the bud of glory, glory is grace full blown; grace is but the blossom of glory, glory is the ripe fruit of grace; grace is but the infant of glory, glory is the perfection of grace. Hence our hymn beautifully says, "The men of grace have found glory begun below," agreeing with our Lord's own words, "He that believeth hath everlasting life"; he feels even here its glories beginning —a foretaste of its bliss.

Now the propriety with which these two states are called kingdoms is manifest from the analogy which might be traced between them and the model of a human sovereignty. Two or three of the outlines of this model will be sufficient.

In the idea of a kingdom it is implied that in some part of its extent there is the residence of a sovereign; for this is essential to constitute it. Now in the kingdom of grace the heart of the believer is made the residence of the King invisible! "Know ye not that your body is the temple of the Holy Ghost which is in you?" Such know what that promise means, "I will dwell in them, and they shall be my people." St. Paul exultingly cries, "Christ liveth in me."

Again, it is essential that the inhabitants of a kingdom be under the government of its laws. An empire without laws is no sovereignty at all; it ceases to be such, for every inhabitant has an equal right to do that which seems good in his own eyes. Now the subjects of Christ's kingdom of grace are "not without law, but are under a law to Christ"; they do His righteous will!

Lastly, it is essential that the subjects of a kingdom be under the protection of the presiding monarch, and that they repose their confidence in him. To the subjects of the kingdom of grace, Christ imparts His kingly protection; this is their heritage: "No weapon formed against them shall prosper"; nay, He imparts to them of His royal bounty, and they enjoy all the blessings of an inward heaven.

But how great the perfection of the kingdom of glory mentioned in our text! Does He make these vile bodies His residence here? How much more glorious is His temple above! how splendid the court of heaven! There, indeed, he fixes His throne, and they see Him as He is. Does He exercise His authority here and rule His happy subjects by the law, the perfect law of love? How much more in heaven! He reigns there forever over them; His government is there wholly by Himself; He knows nothing of a rival there; His rule is sole and perfect: there they serve Him day and night. Are His subjects here partakers of His kingly bounty? Much more in heaven! He calls them to a participation of all the joys, the spiritual joys which are at His right hand, and the pleasures which are there forevermore. Yet, after all our descriptions of that glory, it is not yet revealed, and, therefore, inconceivable. But who would not hail such a Son of David? who would not desire to be swayed by such a Prince of Peace? Whose heart would not ascend with the affections of our poet, "O! that with yonder sacred throng, we at His feet may fall"?

2. But it is an everlasting kingdom! Here it rises in the scale of comparison. Weigh the kingdoms of this world in this balance, and they are found wanting; for on many we read their fatal history, and ere long we shall see them all branded with the writing of the invisible Agent, "The kingdom is taken from thee, and given to a nation bringing forth the fruits thereof"; "For the kingdoms of this world have become the kingdoms of our Lord and of his Christ"; they will be absorbed and swallowed up in the fulness of eternity, and leave not a wrack behind! Every thing here is perishable! The towering diadem of Caesar has fallen from his head and crumbled into dust; and that kingdom whose scepter once swayed the world, betwixt whose colossal stride all nations were glad to creep to find themselves dishonored graves, is now forgotten, or, if its recollection be preserved, its history is emphatically called "The Decline and Fall."

But bring the matter nearer home; apply it not to multitudes of subjects, but to your individual experience, and has not that good teacher instructed you in this sad lesson? We tremble to look at our earthly possessions and employments, lest we should see them in motion, spreading their wings to fly away! How many are there already who, in talking of their comforts, are obliged to go back in their reckoning! Would not this be the language of some of you: "I had—I had a husband, the sharer of my joys, the soother of my sorrows; but he is not! I had a wife, a helpmeet for me; but where is she? I had children to whom I looked up as my support and staff in the decline of life, while passing down the hill; but I am bereaved of my children! I had health, and I highly prized its wealth; but now my emaciated frame, my shriveled system, and the pains of nature bespeak that comfort fled! I had, or fondly thought I had, happiness in possession! Then I said with Job, 'I shall die in my nest!' but ah! an unexpected blast passed over me, and now my joys are blighted! 'They have fled as a shadow, and continued not.'" Yes! time promised you much! perhaps it performed a little; but it can not do any thing for you on which it can grave "eternal." Its name is mortal, its nature is decay; it was born with man, and when the generations of men shall cease to exist, it will cease also: "Time shall be no longer!" We know concerning these that, "All flesh is as grass, and all the glory of man as the flower of grass. The grass withereth, and the flower fadeth, but the word of the Lord endureth forever." Yes! His kingdom is an everlasting kingdom; glory can not corrupt! the crown of glory can not fade! Why? Death will be destroyed; Christ will put this last enemy under His feet, and all will then be eternal life! Oh, happy, happy kingdom; nay, thrice happy he who shall be privileged to be its subject!

3. It is the everlasting kingdom of our own Lord and Savior Jesus Christ. It is His by claim: "Him hath God the Father highly exalted"; yea, Him hath He appointed to be "the judge of quick and dead"; for tho by the sufferings of death He was made a little lower than the angels, yet immediately after His resurrection He declares that now "All power is given unto him in heaven and in earth"! The Father hath committed all judgment unto the Son, and He has now the disposal of the offices and privileges of the empire among His faithful followers. This is the idea that the penitent dying thief had on the subject: "Lord, remember me when thou comest into thy kingdom"; and St. Paul expresses the same when he says to Timothy in the confidence of faith, "The Lord shall deliver me and preserve me unto his heavenly kingdom." Oh! how pleasing the thought to the child of God, that his ruler to all eternity will be his elder Brother; for He who sanctifieth and they who are sanctified are all of one; and though He is heir of all things, yet we, as younger branches of the same heavenly family, shall be joint heirs, fellow-heirs of the same glorious inheritance How great will be our joy to behold Him who humbled Himself for us to death, even the death of the cross, now exalted God over all, blest for evermore; and while contemplating Him under the character of our Lord and Savior Jesus Christ, how great the relish which will be given to that feeling of the re-

deemed which will constrain them to cry, "Thou alone art worthy to receive glory, and honor, and power."

II. But the apostle reminds us of the entrance into this kingdom!

1. The entrance into this kingdom is death: "By one man sin entered into the world, and death by sin:"

> "Death, like a narrow sea, divides
> That heavenly land from ours!"

"A messenger is sent to bring us to God, but it is the King of Terrors. We enter the land flowing with milk and honey, but it is through the valley of the shadow of death." Yet fear not, O thou child of God! there is no need that thou, through the fear of death, shouldst be all thy lifetime subject to bondage.

2. No; hear the apostle: the entrance is ministered unto thee! Death is but His minister; he can not lock his ice-cold hand in thine till He permit. Our Jesus has the keys of hell and death; and till He liberates the vassal to bring thee home, not a hair of thy head can fall to the ground! Fear not, thou worm! He who minds the sparrows appoints the time for thy removal: fear not; only be thou always ready, that, whenever the messenger comes to take down the tabernacle in which thy spirit has long made her abode, thou mayest be able to exclaim, "Amen! even so, Lord Jesus, come quickly." Death need have no terrors for thee; he is the vassal of thy Lord, and, however unwilling to do Him reverence, yet to Him that sits at God's right hand shall even death pay, if not a joyful, yet a trembling homage; nay, more:

> "To Him shall earth and hell submit,
> And every foe shall fall,
> Till death expires beneath His feet,
> And God is all in all."

Christ has already had one triumph over death; His iron pangs could not detain the Prince who has "life in himself"; and in His strength thou shalt triumph, for the power of Christ is promised to rest upon thee! He has had the same entrance; His footsteps marked the way, and His cry to thee is, "Follow thou me." "My sheep," says He, "hear my voice, and they do follow me"; they follow Me gladly, even into this gloomy vale; and what is the consequence? "They shall never perish, neither shall any man pluck them out of my hand."

3. It is ministered unto you abundantly. Perhaps the apostle means that the death of some is distinguished by indulgences and honors not vouchsafed to all. In the experience of some, the passage appears difficult; in others it is comparatively easy; they gently fall asleep in Jesus. But we not only see diversities in the mortal agony—this would be a

small thing. . . . Some get in with sails full spread and carrying a rich cargo indeed, while others arrive barely on a single plank. Some, who have long had their conversation in heaven, are anxious to be wafted into the celestial haven; while others, who never sought God till alarmed at the speedy approach of death, have little confidence,

> " And linger shivering on the brink,
> And fear to launch away.''

This doctrine must have been peculiarly encouraging to the early converts to whom St. Peter wrote. From the tenor of both of his epistles it is clear that they were in a state of severe suffering, and in great danger of apostatizing through fear of persecution. He reminds them that if they hold fast their professions, an abundant entrance will be administered unto them. The death of the martyr is far more glorious than that of the Christian who concealed his profession through fear of man. Witness the case of Stephen: he was not ashamed of being a witness for Jesus in the face of the violent death which awaited him, and which crushed the tabernacle of his devoted spirit; his Lord reserved the highest display of His love and of His glory for that awful hour! "Behold!" says he to his enemies, while gnashing on him with their teeth, "Behold! I see heaven opened, and the Son of man standing on the right hand of God''; then, in the full triumph of faith, he cries out, "Lord Jesus! receive my spirit!"

But did these things apply merely to the believers to whom St. Peter originally wrote? No; you are the men to whom they equally apply; according to your walk and profession of that gospel will be the entrance which will be ministered unto you. Some of you have heard, in another of our houses, during the past week, the dangerous tendency of the spirit of fear, the fear of man. I would you had all heard that discourse: alas! many who have a name and a place among us are becoming mere Sabbath-day worshipers in the courts of the Lord, and lightly esteem the daily means of grace. I believe this is one cause at least why many are weak and sickly among us in divine things. The inner man does not make due increase; the world is stealing a march unawares upon us. May God revive among us the spirit of our fathers!

These things, then, I say, equally apply to you. Behold the strait, the royal, the king's highway! Are you afraid of the reproach of Christ?

> " Ashamed of Jesus, that dear Friend,
> On whom our hopes of heaven depend? ''

How soon would the world be overcome if all who profess that faith were faithful to it!

Wo to the rebellious children who compromise truth with the world, and in effect deny their Lord and Master! Who hath required this at their hands? Do they not follow with the crowd who cry, "Lord, Lord! and yet do not the things which He says"? Will they have the adoption and the glory? Will they aim at the honor implied in these words, "Ye are my witnesses?" Will ye indeed be sons? Then see the path wherein His footsteps shine! The way is open! see that ye walk therein! The false apostles, the deceitful workers shall have their reward; the same that those of old had, the praise and esteem of men; while the faith of those who truly call Him Father and Lord, and who walk in the light as He is in the light, who submit, like Him and His true followers, to be counted as "the filth of the world, and the offscouring of all things, shall be found unto praise, and honor, and glory!

The true Christian does not seek to hide himself in a corner; he lets his light shine before men, whether they will receive it or not; and thereby is his Father glorified. Having thus served, by the will of God, the hour of his departure at length arrives. The angels beckon him away; Jesus bids him come; and as he departs this life he looks back with a heavenly smile on surviving friends, and is enabled to say, "Whither I go, ye know, and the way ye know." An entrance is ministered unto him abundantly into the everlasting kingdom of his Lord and Savior.

III. Having considered the state to which we look, and the mode of our admission, let us consider the condition of it. This is implied in the word "so." "For so an entrance shall be ministered unto you." In the preceding part of this chapter, the apostle has pointed out the meaning of this expression, and in the text merely sums it all up in that short mode of expression.

The first condition he shows to be, the obtaining like precious faith with him, through the righteousness of God and our Savior Jesus Christ. Not a faith which merely assents to the truths of the gospel record, but a faith which applies the merits of the death of Christ to expiate my individual guilt; which lays hold on Him as my sacrifice, and produces, in its exercises, peace with God, a knowledge of the divine favor, a sense of sin forgiven, and a full certainty, arising from a divine impression on the heart, made by the Spirit of God, that I am accepted in the Beloved and made a child of God.

If those who profess the Gospel of Christ were but half as zealous in seeking after this enjoyment as they are in discovering creaturely objections to its attainment, it would be enjoyed by thousands who at present know nothing of its happy reality. Such persons, unfortunately for themselves, employ much more assiduity in searching a vocabulary to find out epithets of reproach to attach to those who maintain the doctrine than in searching that volume which declares that "if you are sons, God has sent forth the Spirit of his Son into your hearts, crying Abba, Father"; and that "he that believeth hath the witness in himself." In whatever light a scorner may view this doctrine now, the time will come when, being found without the wedding garment, he will be cast into outer darkness.

O sinner! cry to God this day to convince thee of thy need of this salvation, and then thou wilt be in a condition to receive it:

"Shalt know, shalt feel thy sins forgiven,
Bless'd with this antepast of heaven."

But, besides this, the apostle requires that we then henceforth preserve consciences void of offense toward God and toward man. This faith which obtains the forgiveness of sin unites to Christ, and by this union we are made, as St. Peter declares, "partakers of the divine nature": and as He who has called you is holy, so you are to be holy in all manner of conversation. For yours is a faith which not only casts out sin, but purifies the heart—the conscience having been once purged by the sprinkling of the blood of Christ, you are not to suffer guilt to be again contracted; for the salvation of Christ is not only from the penalty, but from the very stain of sin; not only from its guilt, but from its pollution; not only from its condemnation, but from its very in-being"; "The blood of Jesus Christ cleanseth from all sin"; and "For this purpose was the Son of God manifested, that he might destroy the works of the devil." You are therefore required by St. Peter, "to escape the corruption that is in the world through lust," and thus to perfect holiness in the fear of the Lord!

Finally, live in progressive and practical godliness. Not only possess, but practise, the virtues of religion; not only practise, but increase therein, abounding in the work of the Lord! Lead up, hand in hand, in the same delightful chorus, all the graces which adorn the Christian character. Having the divine nature, possessing a new and living principle, let diligent exercise reduce it to practical holiness; and you will be easily discerned from those formal hypocrites, whose faith and religion are but a barren and unfruitful speculation.

To conclude: live to God—live for God—live in God; and let your moderation be known unto all men—the Lord is at hand: "Therefore giving all diligence, add to your faith virtue; and to virtue, knowledge; and to knowledge, temperance; and to temperance, patience; and to patience, godliness; and to godliness, brotherly kindness; and to brotherly kindness, charity."

HENRY BARCLAY SWETE

1835-1917

THE TEACHING OF JESUS ABOUT THE FATHER

BIOGRAPHICAL NOTE

REGIUS professor of divinity, Cambridge, England; born Redlands, Bristol, March 14, 1835; D.D., Cambridge and Glasgow; Litt.D., Dublin; educated, King's College, London; Caius College, Cambridge; deacon, 1858; priest, 1859; dean, tutor and theological lecturer, Caius College, 1869-77; rector, Ashdon, Essex, 1877-90; professor of pastoral theology, King's College, London, 1882-90; fellow of Caius College, 1858-77; honorary fellow, 1886-90; fellow of King's College, 1891, of British Academy, 1902; honorary canon of Ely, 1906; author of "The Old Testament in Greek," "The Akhmim Fragment of the Gospel of Peter," "The Apostles' Creed in Relation to Primitive Christianity," "Faith in Relation to Creed, Thought and Life," "Church Services and Service Books before the Reformation," "The Gospel According to St. Mark: the Greek Text with Introduction, Notes and Indices," "An Introduction to the Old Testament in Greek," "Patristic Study," "Studies in the Teaching of our Lord," "The Apocalypse of St. John," etc.

" These things have I spoken unto you in proverbs. The hour cometh when I shall no more speak unto you in proverbs, but shall tell you plainly of the Father."—John 16 : 25.

IN what sense is it true that our Lord spoke to His disciples in proverbs? His teaching, as it is represented in the gospels, falls almost entirely under the two heads of discourse and parable, and neither of these answers to the usual conception of the proverb. But the proverb in its Biblical acceptation has a wider reference; it comprehends not merely the brief aphorisms and trite sayings current on the lips of man, but all sayings which contain more than they express; which, simple in form and phrase, are packed with thought that eludes the hearer because it lies beyond the range of his personal experience. Such sayings normally turn upon the analogy which exists between the outer form of things and the inner truth; they lead the mind on from what it knows or can imagine to that which lies as yet beyond its grasp. The parallelism may be locked up in a few pregnant words, or worked out at length. In the latter case the proverb grows into the parable, the parable being merely an extended proverb, as the proverb is a contracted parable. Even the words are interchanged; the parable of the Good Shepherd is called by John παροιμία, while Luke gives the name of παραβολή to the proverb, " Physician, heal thyself." If we examine our Lord's Galilean teaching in the light of these facts, the truth of His saying in the text becomes apparent. Parables were the chief vehicle of instruction during the greater part of the ministry; " without a parable spake He not unto " the crowds that flocked to hear Him; " all things " were " done in parables," *i. e.*, the whole business of the ministry was transacted in this form.

But the parables, it may be urged, were not enigmatic; their purpose was to teach truth in the only shape in which a mixed multitude could receive it. This is widely different from our Lord's own account of them. The primary end of the parable, as He explained it, was not to assist the mental vision but to darken it: "·that seeing they may see and not perceive, and hearing they may hear and not understand." Doubtless the parable served to keep the word alive in men's hearts till the time came for growth, even as the seed preserves the germ which it conceals; but its immediate effect was not to reveal the truth but to hide it. How well it served this purpose may be gathered from the fact that even the Twelve, to whom was given the mystery of the kingdom, were compelled to ask for an interpretation of the Parable of the Sower. It was our Lord's habit to explain to them in private the meaning of His public teaching; without this help even the inner circle of His disciples would have failed to understand it. The parable, notwithstanding its apparent simplicity, is of the nature of a veil; the obscurity which belongs to it is not accidental, but of its essence. Christ's design was to postpone full knowledge where definite teaching would be premature, and thereby to stimulate thought and provoke inquiry. As the son of Sirach says: "He that hath applied his soul . . . will seek out the hidden meaning of proverbs, and be conversant in the dark sayings of parables." Such inquirers there doubtless were among our Lord's hearers, men who had ears to hear and truly heard; but even in their case the proverb or parable was but preparatory to the fuller teaching which was to follow.

The Fourth Gospel creates at first a different impression of Christ's method. In the Johannine discourses He seems to drop parable and proverb, and to use a directness of teaching which is in strong contrast with His manner in the Synoptic Gospels. The difference is perhaps especially noticeable in the great discourse of the fourteenth and two following chapters. Here our Lord is represented as speaking only to the apostles, neither uninstructed peasants nor captious scribes being present; even Judas, it is expressly said, has left the upper room and gone out into the night. If ever there was an occasion upon which Jesus could pour out His mind freely, it was this. Yet it is of the discourse delivered at this gathering that He says, towards the end, "These things have I spoken unto you in proverbs." It seems, then, that while the literary form in which the Johannine sayings are cast differs widely from that to which we are accustomed in the Synoptists, they claim to possess a true affinity, an essential oneness with the curt sentences and enigmatic parables of the Galilean ministry. There is a note which is common to the Johannine and the Synoptic reports, a note which is deeper than manner or form and can be heard in all Christ's teaching down to the eve of the passion. Whether He instructed a crowd of fishermen, taxgatherers, traders, and peasants by the shore of the lake, or the chosen eleven in the sanctuary of the supper-chamber at Jerusalem, His method was substantially the same. From the day when He began to teach until the night before He suffered He followed a uniform plan. His plan was always to go beyond the immediate comprehension of His hearers—not indeed by the use of unintelligible words, for His

words are ever of the plainest—but by making simple words hold more than they seem to hold; by so speaking that, either in form or substance or in both, He spoke in proverbs which concealed more than they disclosed. No one who has occupied himself with the attempt to expound the gospels will fail to recognize the truth of this remark. The simplest of our Lord's sayings is found to be inexhaustible; when the student has done his best, he is constrained to leave it with the conviction that there are depths in it which he cannot fathom, and suggestions of half-revealed truths which for the present baffle inquiry.

It was, then, characteristic of our Lord to speak in proverbs; and the Christ of the Fourth Gospel does not differ herein materially from the Christ of the Synoptists. But when we have said this, we must be careful to add that the words hold true only of His teaching before the passion. Christ Himself has told us that His use of this method was only for a time; "the hour cometh when I shall no more speak unto you in proverbs." The great Master will not limit Himself to a single method; He will adapt Himself to circumstances. If He used proverbs and parables throughout His earthly ministry, even when speaking to the innermost circle of His disciples, this was because the time had not come for employing any other vehicle of teaching. But He distinctly foresees the arrival of the moment when proverbs may be flung to the winds, and He will be free to speak to these same apostles plainly and directly—οὐκέτι ἐν παροιμίαις · · · ἀλλὰ παρρησίᾳ [no longer in parables, but plainly]. The alliteration, which is repeated a few verses below, seems to show that the writer of the gospel wished forcibly to contrast the two methods. The proverb excludes plain speaking, and plain speaking, when it comes, will abandon the use of the proverb. In the future, Christ foretells, obscurity, whether of words or of thought, will give place to a luminous clearness, extending both to the form and the substance of the message. This is to be the main distinction between Christ's earlier teaching and His later, between the ministry which preceded the passion and that which will follow, between the teaching of Christ in the flesh and His teaching in the Spirit.

It follows that our Lord saw, beyond the rapidly approaching end of His earthly mission, the dawn of a fresh period of teaching under other conditions, and therefore after another method. His passion marked only the end of the first stage of His work as the Teacher of mankind. We call these chapters in John the "Last Discourse," but they are the last only of one series of the great Master's lessons. The days were past when excited crowds exclaimed, "What is this? a new teaching!" and hung upon His lips as if afraid to lose a word; when hostile officials declared " Never man spake like this man," and could lay no hands upon Him, such was the fascination of His voice. The days were past when, alone with His disciples, He taught them, as they could bear it, the mystery of the kingdom of God. But all this has been but the prelude; the richest harmonies of Christ's teaching are yet to be heard. When? and how? He answers only, " The hour cometh," and the Church is left to interpret those words by the event. The phrase is one which occurs not seldom in the Gospel of John. " The hour cometh in which all that are in the tombs shall hear His voice "; " the hour cometh that whosoever killeth you shall think that he offereth service to God "; " the hour cometh, yea is come, that ye shall be scattered, every man to his own." It is clear from these examples that " the hour " which is intended may be remote or close at hand. Jesus does not say plainly which He means; He is still speaking in proverbs. But looking back at His words over the centuries we may venture to interpret them by the light of experience.

" The hour cometh when I shall tell you plainly of the Father." The words reveal both the subject and the manner of the Lord's future teaching. The subject will be the revelation of the Father; the manner, that of one who brings a clear and full report from firsthand observation of the facts. In the earlier part of this discourse the Lord had announced that He was going to the Father, but would come again. He now adds that when He returns, He will bring back word of the Father.

To reveal the Father had been the purpose of His personal teaching from the first. Even in the days of His flesh He could tell men of that which He knew, and bear witness of that which He had seen in His preexistent life with God. He was Himself a living revelation of God; so that John, looking back from the end of the first century to the days of the Son of man, could say: " We beheld his glory, glory as of an only begotten from a Father." When on the night before the passion Philip thoughtlessly exclaimed, " Lord, shew us the Father," the Lord with a touch of infinite sadness answered, " Have I been so long time with you, and dost thou not know me, Philip? He that hath seen me hath seen the Father." All His teaching, all His life, had been directed to this one end, to show men the Father. Never before had man been taught so plainly the fatherhood of God. He had taught them to call daily upon " Our Father which is in Heaven," to look to the Father for daily bread, to imitate Him " as dear children," to prepare for their place in His presence. Yet this teaching, sufficient as it was to awaken a consciousness of the divine love and of human responsibility, left the mystery of divine paternity unrevealed. In what sense God was the Father of Jesus Christ, in what sense He was the Father of Christ's disciples, were questions which still awaited an answer. There are those who bid us be content with the theology of the Sermon on the Mount. Christ Himself, be it said with reverence, was not content with it; He recognized that there was a plainer, fuller, more explicit report to be given when He returned from the Father, and to that future teaching He referred those who had heard all His earlier words.

Did our Lord then resume the office of Teacher after His return from the dead? Luke enables us to answer the question, as far as regards the immediate sequel to the passion. During the forty days that followed the resurrection, the Lord appeared from time to time and spoke to His apostles " the things concerning the kingdom of God." The old teaching began again; the subject was the same as before the passion. But was it handled in the same way? Only a few fragments of this post-resurrection teaching remain; but in them I think we can discern greater plainness of speech than in the sayings of the ministry. Take for example the words spoken on the first Easter night: " As the Father hath sent me, even so send I you. . . . Receive ye the Holy Ghost; whosoever sins ye forgive they are forgiven." Or those spoken after the return to Galilee: " All authority hath been given unto me in heaven and on earth. Go ye, therefore, and make disciples of all the nations, baptizing them into the name of the Father and of the Son and of the Holy Ghost." This is assuredly plain speaking, and if there is nothing in either saying which is wholly new, the manner is new; it is παρρησία, not παροιμία any more. Indeed, the critics have so generally recognized the change of manner that in the second saying they have thought they discovered an idealized report, into which the next generation had infused its own beliefs and hopes. The hypothesis would have been unnecessary, if they had but remembered Christ's promise to convert proverb into plainness of speech, or if they had believed the words of the text to be truly Christ's.

But the forty days were only the beginning of the new order. The ascension which terminated the visible presence of Christ on earth, inaugurated His presence in the Spirit. The Bridegroom was taken away only to return at once in the power of the Holy Ghost. The " other Paraclete " who was promised was yet not another, for He was the very Spirit of the Son, of the Christ, of the sacred humanity of Jesus. When He spoke to the Church, He spoke not from Himself, but as the Vicar of Jesus Christ, teaching in Christ's stead, carrying on and completing Christ's ministry. Hence the Lord speaks of the

Spirit's teaching as His own. " I have yet many things to say unto you, but ye cannot bear them now; howbeit when he, the Spirit of truth, is come, he shall guide you into all the truth . . . he shall take of mine and shall declare it unto you. All things whatsoever the Father hath are mine; therefore said I, that he taketh of mine, and shall declare it unto you. . . . These things have I spoken unto you in proverbs; the hour cometh when I shall tell you plainly of the Father."

The hour came, then, when the Spirit came; and the first results of the new παῤῥησία are to be seen in the teaching of the apostles, and especially in the epistles of Paul.

It is a fashion of our time to attach an excessive importance to the personality of Paul as a factor in the evolution of the Christian religion. Undoubtedly that personality is the most striking in the apostolic age—perhaps it may be added, in the whole history of the Church. Undoubtedly also, the teaching of Paul was colored by his mental habits, and these owed much to the influences of his Pharisaic upbringing. The relation of Paul to contemporary thought is a legitimate subject for inquiry, and we have recently been reminded how much may be gleaned by a diligent worker in this field.* But it is impossible to ascribe Paul's presentation of Christianity as a whole to any such source; the only question that can arise with regard to it, is whether we are to consider it as a product of the apostle's own mind, or as due, in the last analysis, to the Spirit of Jesus Christ. The former of these alternatives is often taken for granted; men speak of the gospel which Paul preached as " Paulinism," as if it were a type of Christianity which owes more to Paul than to Christ; and of Paul himself as a second founder of the Christian faith. But to speak thus is to claim that our own age understands Paul better than he understood himself. In all his epistles he styles himself " the servant," nay " the bond-slave," of Jesus Christ; he assures us that the gospel which he preached was " not after man," but had come to him " through revelation of Jesus Christ "; that Christ lived in him, worked in him, spoke in him, through the Spirit. On this point I gladly quote the judgment of Professor Harnack:

" Paul understood the Master, and continued His work. . . . Those who blame him for corrupting the Christian religion have never felt a breath of his spirit . . . those who extol or criticize him as the founder of a religion are forced to make him bear witness against himself on the main point."

I would add to this that those who thus misjudge Paul's position, either forget or ignore the Lord's promise that His Spirit should

* See H. St. J. Thackeray, " The Relation of St. Paul to Contemporary Jewish Thought," Macmillan, 1900.

guide His Church into all the truth, telling her plainly of the Father. In the light of that magnificent promise Paulinism is seen to be, in its essence, nothing else than a continuation of the teaching of Christ. It is the voice of Christ, speaking at length παῤῥησία, with a new directness and comprehensiveness. If utterance was given to Paul to make known the mystery of the gospel more fully than it was taught by the other apostles, more plainly than it had been taught by the Master Himself, he was in this simply a witness of things wherein Christ revealed Himself to him through the Spirit. Thus, when Paul proclaims his great doctrine of justification by faith, while the arguments by which he defends it rest here and there on methods which belong to his age and mental training, we are assured that the doctrine itself, in its inner verity, is but the teaching of Christ brought out into the clearer light of the Spirit. Or again, when he unfolds his doctrine of the person of Christ, and teaches the divine preexistence of the Son and the meaning of the incarnation, we know ourselves to be listening to the very Spirit of Christ, who through the apostle's words is glorifying Christ as Christ foretold. The same is true of the other great apostolic teachers. We hear the voice of the Spirit of Jesus Christ in John's doctrine of the Word made flesh, and not less clearly in the doctrine of the Lord's high-priestly office as it is set forth in the Epistle to the Hebrews. The apostolic letters speak plainly where Christ spoke in proverbs; but the Teacher is the same, tho the method is changed.

A Paul or a John comes but once in the life of the Church. But it is a shallow unbelief which would limit the teaching of the Spirit of Christ to the first century; and such unbelief is refuted, if refutation be necessary, by the promises " I am with you always, even unto the end of the world "; " the Father . . . shall give you another Comforter that he may be with you forever." The Spirit was not granted only to the first generation. Nor was He granted only to the ante-Nicene Church, or to the age of the great councils, or to the medieval saints, or to the reformers. The grant is for all time. Christ teaches His Church to-day as truly as He taught the apostles and the fathers and the schoolmen and the reformers; the Spirit speaks now as certainly as He spoke in the days when dogma was being made in the yet undivided Church. His instruments, His manner of teaching, vary from age to age. To-day, He does not teach, as some hold, by creating fresh articles of faith; still less by proclaiming new gospels, messages of peace and healing for· the world which were unknown to the ancient Church. The Spirit of Christ will never proclaim any other gospel than that which Christ proclaimed on the first day of His preaching in

Galilee; will never teach any other faith than that which was once for all delivered to the saints. But as the world grows older, the Spirit of Christ may be expected to tell men more and more plainly of the Father. There have been and there will be fresh interpretations of the original message, new lights thrown on the teaching of Scripture and on the doctrine of the Church. The Light of the world is ever bringing on the dawn of the perfect day; the unchangeable truth grows clearer in the growing light of knowledge and experience.

There has been in the best theological teaching of the last fifty years, within our memory, a marvelous extension of Christian thought, an opening up of new or forgotten avenues of truth, a lifting of clouds which had long obscured the field of vision, a casting away of unsound opinions and mere presuppositions, which marks a real advance in spiritual knowledge. We have had our prophets, even if we have not ventured, while they were with us, to call them by that name; we have had teachers to whom it has been given to look into the mysteries of life and of grace with an insight not wholly due to strength of intellect or length of experience. If for the moment they have been taken from us, and we seem to-day to have no prophet amongst us any more, they have at least taught us that the Spirit of Christ in His illuminating power has not been withdrawn from the modern Church.

Nor is it only in the province of theology that our Lord's great promise is fulfilling itself to our own age. Indeed it is perhaps chiefly by the discoveries of physical science that He is to-day telling us plainly of the Father. It is true, alas! that to many of the discoverers themselves these new marvels bring as yet no message from the Father of their spirits, or seem rather to exclude the possibility of His personal existence. They cannot see the sun for the glory of the light; their vision is darkened by the brightness of this new revelation of God. But we have reason to hope that this first effect of physical research will pass with fuller knowledge and reflection. Meanwhile it is for the Church to welcome these great accessions to knowledge as a true fulfilment of the Lord's word. To us at least He is speaking in them more plainly than before, telling us of the Father in His relation to the visible world. We know and believe that it is the Only Begotten who declares the Father, whatever the revelation may be, through whatever channel it may come.

It is impossible to foresee the surprises which even the near future may have in store for not a few of us. Within the lifetime of the younger men new lights may break upon the Church, bringing new fulfilments of

Christ's words. Such a hope may well inspire life with a buoyancy which will stimulate the next generation to new endeavors. In view of the promise of progressive teaching which the Church has received from Christ, no problem need be abandoned as hopeless, and all lines of legitimate study may be pursued with confidence. " I will tell you plainly," is a word which will fulfil itself ever more and more to those who are patient workers in every part of the great field of knowledge.

Yet its complete fulfilment must lie beyond the present order. Come what may, there are limits imposed by human infirmity which cannot be removed in the present life; limits partly of the spirit, partly of the intellect, partly due to the inability of human words to express the highest truths. No one has recognized this more clearly than Paul, notwithstanding the abundance of the revelations vouchsafed to him. " When I was a child, I spake as a child, I felt as a child, I thought as a child . . . now we see in a mirror darkly . . . now I know in part." The proverb, the enigma, must enter largely even into the teaching of the Spirit, so long as we are here. The plainest words that can be used to express our faith are not free from obscurity; the most carefully balanced statements of Christian doctrine are, in the last analysis, found to be in some respects confessions of our ignorance. There is in every great article of our faith an ultimate enigma which baffles our efforts to construct a perfect theory. Sometimes we seem to be on the verge of a solution, but further reflection throws us back; the mystery eludes us still. It has been so in every age of the Church; it will be so, we may be very sure, to the end. The " proverb " is with us still, notwithstanding Christ's greater and growing " plainness of speech."

But the fact is suggestive of hope and not of despair. There must be a more magnificent fulfilment of Christ's promise reserved for the future state. There must be a teaching in store for us which will exceed our present knowledge, as the teaching of the Spirit exceeded the parables of our Lord's ministry.

How our Lord will teach His Church in the great future is altogether beyond present comprehension. The apocalyptic imagery of the New Testament, largely based on Old Testament conceptions of the world to come, speaks of Him as coming in the clouds of heaven with the glory of God; of a throne set and books opened; of a new Jerusalem descending from God out of heaven; of God tabernacling with men, and men seeing God day and night in His temple, or made pillars therein, and bearing upon them an inscription which reveals the name of God and His Christ; of a Shepherd who is Himself a Lamb, leading His flock to fountains of waters of life, and of God wiping away every tear from their eyes. We recognize at once the symbolical character of these descriptions. But what are the facts which lie behind the symbolism? One thing can be clearly made out. The future holds for us a presence of Christ not altogether such as we now have through the indwelling of His Spirit, but such as will be a new manifestation of the risen Christ to the risen Church. It is not another coming of the Spirit which is the hope of the future, but another coming of the Christ in person; not a *vicaria vis Spiritus sancti,* but the very power of the incarnate Lord revealing in Himself the fulness of the divine glory. How this can be we can no more understand than the apostles could understand the coming of the other Paraclete before He actually came. Nor again can we see the relation which the second coming of the Son will bear to the mission of the Spirit. Will the teaching of the Spirit be merged in the personal teaching of the Lord, visibly present with His Church? We know not. But we are sure that in the perfect life Christ will at length tell us plainly of the Father. The last riddle will be solved, the full measure of the divine παρρησία attained. If I may venture to carry John's alliteration one step further, the παρρησία of the Spirit which succeeded to the παροιμία of the ministry, will culminate in the παρουσία. The silence of God will be broken at last; the final mystery will become, as Ignatius has it, a μυστήριον κραυγῆς, a truth proclaimed aloud that all may hear.

Yet it is not to be thought that all truth will be flashed in a moment upon the soul that has reached the presence of Christ. The analogies of God's dealings with mankind in the past point to a progressive illumination in the world to come. Teaching will not cease because mystery has vanished away. "The Lamb shall guide them." The metaphor speaks of an endless advance in the knowledge of the Infinite.

The prospect is one which ought to appeal with especial force to us whose daily life here is spent in the endeavor to learn and read the lower lessons of truth. All truth is one, and every truth is in its measure a revelation of God. Thus we may, if we will, connect our pursuit of exact knowledge in letters or history or philosophy or physics with our eternal work of learning to know God in Christ. Habits of mind, of character, of life, can be formed here which we may carry with us into the eternal order. With such an end in view, nothing is trivial, nothing is to be despised. "He that is faithful in a very little"—how little it is that we can learn or teach here!— "is faithful also in much."

One thing is needful in order that our studies may be linked on to the eternal. The conscience must be kept bright and clear; the ear of the soul must lie open to the voice of

Christ. His plainest words fall like muffled sounds on hearts that are preoccupied by sin or self. "Blessed are the pure in heart, for they shall see God"; they shall hear all that the divine Word will tell them of the Father.

THOMAS DE WITT TALMAGE

1832-1901

A BLOODY MONSTER

BIOGRAPHICAL NOTE

THOMAS DE WITT TALMAGE was born at Bound Brook, N. J., in 1832. For many years he preached to large and enthusiastic congregations at the Brooklyn Tabernacle. At one time six hundred newspapers regularly printed his sermons. He was a man of great vitality, optimistic by nature, and particularly popular with young people. His voice was rather high and unmusical, but his distinct enunciation and earnestness of manner gave a peculiar attraction to his pulpit oratory. His rhetoric has been criticized for floridness and sensationalism, but his word pictures held multitudes of people spellbound as in the presence of a master. He died in 1901.

It is my son's coat; an evil beast hath devoured him.—Gen. xxxvii., 33.

JOSEPH'S brethren dipt their brother's coat in goat's blood, and then brought the dabbled garment to their father, cheating him with the idea that a ferocious animal had slain him, and thus hiding their infamous behavior. But there is no deception about that which we hold up to your observation to-day. A monster such as never ranged African thicket or Hindustan jungle hath tracked this land, and with bloody maw hath strewn the continent with the mangled carcasses of whole generations; and there are tens of thousands of fathers and mothers who could hold up the garment of their slain boy, truthfully exclaiming, "It is my son's coat; an evil beast hath devoured him." There has, in all ages and climes, been a tendency to the improper use of stimulants. Noah took to strong drink. By this vice, Alexander the Conqueror was conquered. The Romans at their feasts fell off their seats with intoxication. Four hundred millions of our race are opium-eaters. India, Turkey, and China have groaned with the desolation; and by it have been quenched such lights as Halley and De Quincey. One hundred millions are the victims of the betelnut, which has specially blasted the East Indies. Three hundred millions chew hashish, and Persia, Brazil, and Africa suffer the delirium. The Tartars employ murowa; the Mexicans, the agave; the people at Guarapo, an intoxicating product taken from sugarcane; while a great multitude, that no man can number, are the votaries of alcohol. To it they bow. Under it they are trampled. In its trenches they fall. On its ghastly holocaust they burn. Could the muster-roll of this great army be called, and could they come up from the dead, what eye could endure the reeking, festering putrefaction? What heart could endure the groan of agony? Drunkenness! Does it not jingle the burglar's key? Does it not whet the assassin's knife? Does it not cock the highwayman's pistol? Does it not wave the incendiary's torch? Has it not sent the physician reeling into the sick-room; and the minister with his tongue thick into the pulpit? Did not an exquisite poet, from the very top of his fame, fall a gibbering sot, into the gutter, on his way to be married to one of the fairest daughters of New England, and at the very hour the bride was decking herself for the altar; and did he not die of delirium tremens, almost unattended, in a hospital? Tamerlane asked for one hundred and sixty thousand skulls with which to build a pyramid to his own honor. He got the skulls, and built the pyramid. But if the bones of all those who have fallen as a prey to dissipation could be piled up, it would make a vaster pyramid. Who will gird himself for the journey and try with me to scale this mountain of the dead—going up miles high on human carcasses to find still other peaks far above, mountain above mountain white with the bleached bones of drunkards?

The Sabbath has been sacrificed to the rum traffic. To many of our people, the best day of the week is the worst. Bakers must keep their shops closed on the Sabbath. It is dangerous to have loaves of bread going out on Sunday. The shoe store is closed: severe penalty will attack the man who sells boots on the Sabbath. But down with the window-shutters of the grog-shops. Our laws shall confer particular honor upon the rum-traffickers. All other trades must stand aside for these. Let our citizens who have disgraced themselves by trading in clothing and hosiery and hardware and lumber and coal take off their hats to the rum-seller, elected to particular honor. It is unsafe for any other class of men to be allowed license for Sunday work. But swing out your signs, and open your doors, O ye traffickers in the peace of families and in the souls of immortal men. Let the corks fly and the beer foam and the rum go tearing down the half-consumed throat of the inebriate. God does not see! Does He? Judgment will never come! Will it?

It may be that God is determined to let drunkenness triumph, and the husbands and sons of thousands of our best families be destroyed by this vice, in order that our people, amazed and indignant, may rise up and demand the extermination of this municipal crime. There is a way of driving down the hoops of a barrel so tight that they break. We have, in this country, at various times, tried to regulate this evil by a tax on whisky. You might as well try to regulate the Asiatic cholera or the smallpox by taxation. The men who distil liquors are, for the most part, unscrupulous; and the higher the tax, the more inducement to illicit distillation. Oh! the folly of trying to restrain an evil by government tariff! If every gallon of whisky made —if every flask of wine produced, should be taxed a thousand dollars, it would not be enough to pay for the tears it has wrung from the eyes of widows and orphans, nor for the blood it has dashed on the Christian Church, nor for the catastrophe of the millions it has destroyed for ever.

I sketch two houses in one street. The first is bright as home can be. The father comes at nightfall, and the children run out to meet him. Bountiful evening meal! Gratulation and sympathy and laughter! Music in the parlor! Fine pictures on the wall! Costly books on the table! Well-clad household! Plenty of everything to make home happy!

House the second! Piano sold yesterday by the sheriff! Wife's furs at pawnbroker's shop! Clock gone! Daughter's jewelry sold to get flour! Carpets gone off the floor! Daughters in faded and patched dresses! Wife sewing for the stores! Little child with an ugly wound on her face, struck by an angry blow! Deep shadow of wretchedness falling in every room! Doorbell rings! Little children hide! Daughters turn pale! Wife holds her breath! Blundering step in the hall! Door opens! Fiend, brandishing his fist, cries, "Out! out! What are you doing here?" Did I call this house second? No; it is the same house. Rum transformed it. Rum embruted the man. Rum sold the shawl. Rum tore up the carpets. Rum shook his fist. Rum desolated the hearth. Rum changed that paradise into a hell.

I sketch two men that you know very well. The first graduated from one of our literary institutions. His father, mother, brothers and sisters were present to see him graduate. They heard the applauding thunders that greeted his speech. They saw the bouquets tossed to his feet. They saw the degree conferred and the diploma given. He never looked so well. Everybody said, "What a noble brow! What a fine eye! What graceful manners! What brilliant prospects!"

Man the second: Lies in the station-house. The doctor has just been sent for to bind up the gashes received in a fight. His hair is matted and makes him look like a wild beast. His lip is bloody and cut. Who is this battered and bruised wretch that was picked up by the police and carried in drunk and foul and bleeding? Did I call him man the second? He is man the first! Rum transformed him. Rum destroyed his prospects. Rum disappointed parental expectation. Rum withered those garlands of commencement day. Rum cut his lip. Rum dashed out his manhood. Rum, accurst rum!

This foul thing gives one swing to its scythe, and our best merchants fall; their stores are sold, and they sink into dishonored graves. Again it swings its scythe, and some of our physicians fall into suffering that their wisest prescriptions cannot cure. Again it swings its scythe, and ministers of the gospel fall from the heights of Zion, with long resounding crash of ruin and shame. Some of your own households have already been shaken. Perhaps you can hardly admit it; but where was your son last night? Where was he Friday night? Where was he Thursday night? Wednesday night? Tuesday night? Monday night? Nay, have not some of you in your own bodies felt the power of this habit? You think that you could stop? Are you sure you could? Go on a little further, and I am sure you cannot. I think, if some of you should try to break away, you would find a chain on the right wrist, and one on the left; one on the right foot, and another on the left. This serpent does not begin to hurt until it has wound 'round and 'round. Then it begins to tighten and strangle and crush until the bones crack and the blood trickles and the eyes start from their sockets, and the mangled wretch cries. "O God! O God! help! help!" But it is too late; and not even the fires of wo can melt the chain when once it is fully fastened.

I have shown you the evil beast. The question is, who will hunt him down, and how shall we shoot him? I answer, first, by getting our children right on this subject. Let them grow up with an utter aversion to strong drink. Take care how you administer it even as medicine. If you must give it to them and you find that they have a natural love for it, as some have, put in a glass of it some horrid stuff, and make it utterly nauseous. Teach them, as faithfully as you do the truths of the Bible, that rum is a fiend. Take them to the almshouse, and show them the wreck and ruin it works. Walk with them into the homes that have been scourged by it. If a drunkard hath fallen into a ditch, take them right up where they can see his face, bruised, savage, and swollen, and say, "Look, my son. Rum did that!" Looking out of your window at some one who, intoxicated to madness, goes through the street, brandishing his fist, blaspheming God, a howling, defying, shouting, reeling, raving, and foaming maniac, say to your son, "Look; that man was once a child like you." As you go by the grog-shop let them know that that is the place where men are slain and their wives made paupers and their children slaves. Hold out to your children warnings, all rewards, all counsels, lest in afterdays they break your heart and curse your gray hairs. A man laughed at my father for his scrupulous temperance principles, and said: "I am more liberal than you. I always give my children the sugar in the glass after we have been taking a drink." Three of his sons have died drunkards, and the fourth is imbecile through intemperate habits.

Again, we will grapple this evil by voting only for sober men. How many men are there who can rise above the feelings of partizanship, and demand that our officials shall be sober men? I maintain that the question of sobriety is higher than the question of availability; and that, however eminent a man's services may be, if he have habits of intoxication, he is unfit for any office in the gift of a Christian people. Our laws will be no better than the men who make them. Spend a few days at Harrisburg or Albany or Washington and you will find out why, upon these subjects, it is impossible to get righteous enactments.

Again, we will war upon this evil by organized societies. The friends of the rum traffic have banded together; annually issue their circulars; raise fabulous sums of money to advance their interests; and by grips, passwords, signs, and strategems, set at defiance public morals. Let us confront them with organizations just as secret, and, if need be, with grips and pass-words and signs, maintain our position. There is no need that our beneficent societies tell all their plans. I am in favor of all lawful strategy in the carrying on of this conflict. I wish to God we could lay under the wine-casks a train which, once ignited, would shake the earth with the explosion of this monstrous iniquity!

Again, we will try the power of the pledge. There are thousands of men who have been saved by putting their names to such a document. I know it is laughed at; but there are some men who, having once promised a thing, do it. "Some have broken the pledge." Yes; they were liars. But all men are not liars. I do not say that it is the duty of all persons to make such signature; but I do say that it would be the salvation of many of you. The glorious work of Theobald Mathew can never be estimated. At this hand four millions of people took the pledge, and multitudes in Ireland, England, Scotland, and America, have kept it till this day. The pledge signed has been to thousands the proclamation of emancipation.

Again, we expect great things from asylums for inebriates. They have already done a glorious work. I think that we are coming at last to treat inebriation as it ought to be treated, namely, as an awful disease, self-inflicted, to be sure, but nevertheless a disease. Once fastened upon a man, sermons will not cure him, temperance lectures will not eradicate it; religious tracts will not remove it; the Gospel of Christ will not arrest it. Once under the power of this awful thirst, the man is bound to go on; and, if the foaming glass were on the other side of perdition, he would wade through the fires of hell to get it. A young man in prison had such a strong thirst for intoxicating liquors that he had cut off his hand at the wrist, called for a bowl of brandy in order to stop the bleeding, thrust his wrist into the bowl, and then drank the contents. Stand not, when the thirst is on him, between a man and his cups. Clear the track for him. Away with the children! he would tread their life out. Away with the wife! he would dash her to death. Away with the cross! he would run it down. Away with the Bible! he would tear it up for the winds.

Away with heaven! he considers it worthless as a straw. "Give me the drink! Give it to me! Tho the hands of blood pass up the bowl, and the soul trembles over the pit—the drink! Give it to me! Tho it be pale with tears; tho the froth of everlasting anguish float on the foam—give it to me! I drink to my wife's wo to my children's rags; to my eternal banishment from God and hope and heaven! Give it to me! the drink!"

Again, we will contend against these evils by trying to persuade the respectable classes of society to the banishment of alcoholic beverages. You who move in elegant and refined associations; you who drink the best liquors; you who never drink until you lose your balance, let us look at each other in the face on this subject. You have, under God, in your power the redemption of this land from drunkenness. Empty your cellars and wine-closets of the beverage, and then come out and give us your hand, your vote, your prayers, your sympathies. Do that, and I will promise three things: first, that you will find unspeakable happiness in having done your duty; secondly, you will probably save somebody—perhaps your own child; thirdly, you will not, in your last hour, have a regret that you made the sacrifice, if sacrifice it be. As long as you make drinking respectable, drinking customs will prevail, and the plowshare of death, drawn by terrible disasters, will go on turning up this whole continent, from end to end, with the long, deep, awful furrow of drunkards' graves.

This rum fiend would like to go and hang up a skeleton in your beautiful house, so that, when you opened the front door to go in, you would see it in the hall; and when you sat at your table you would see it hanging from the wall; and, when you opened your bedroom you would find it stretched upon your pillow; and, waking at night, you would feel its cold hand passing over your face and pinching at your heart. There is no home so beautiful but it may be devastated by the awful curse. It throws its jargon into the sweetest harmony. What was it that silenced Sheridan, the English orator, and shattered the golden scepter with which he swayed parliaments and courts? What foul sprite turned the sweet rhythm of Robert Burns into a tuneless babble? What was it that swamped the noble spirit of one of the heroes of the last war, until, in a drunken fit, he reeled from the deck of a Western steamer, and was drowned. There was one whose voice we all loved to hear. He was one of the most classic orators of the century. People wondered why a man of so pure a heart and so excellent a life should have such a sad countenance always. They knew not that his wife was a sot.

I call upon those who are guilty of these indulgences to quit the path of death! Oh! what a change it would make in your home! Do you see how everything there is being desolated? Would you not like to bring back joy to your wife's heart, and have your children come out to meet you with as much confidence as once they showed? Would you not like to rekindle the home-lights that long ago were extinguished? It is not too late to change. It may not entirely obliterate from your soul the memory of wasted years and a ruined reputation, nor smooth out from your anxious brow the wrinkles which trouble has plowed. It may not call back unkind words uttered or rough deeds done; for perhaps in those awful moments you struck her! It may not take from your memory the bitter thoughts connected with some little grave. But it is not too late to save yourself, and secure for God and your family the remainder of your fast-going life.

But perhaps you have not utterly gone astray. I may address one who may not have quite made up his mind. Let your better nature speak out. You take one side or other in war against drunkenness. Have you the courage to put your foot down right, and say to your companions and friends, "I will never drink intoxicating liquor in all my life; nor will I countenance the habit in others"? Have nothing to do with strong drink. It has turned the earth into a place of skulls, and has stood opening the gate to a lost world to let in its victims; until now the door swings no more upon its hinges, but, day and night, stands wide open to let in the agonized procession of doomed men.

Do I address one whose regular work in life is to administer to this appetite? For God's sake get out of that business! If a wo be pronounced upon the man who gives his neighbor drink, how many woes must be hanging over the man who does this every day and every hour of the day!

Do not think that because human government may license you that therefore God licenses you. I am surprized to hear men say that they respect the "original package" decision by which the Supreme Court of the United States allows rum to be taken into States like Kansas, which decided against the sale of intoxicants. I have no respect for a wrong decision, I care not who makes it; the three judges of the Supreme Court who gave minority report against that decision were right, and the chief justice was wrong. The right of a State to defend itself against the rum traffic will yet be demonstrated, the Supreme Court notwithstanding. Higher than the judicial bench at Washington is the throne of the Lord God Almighty. No enactment, national, State, or municipal, can give you the right to carry on a business whose effect is destruction.

God knows better than you do yourself the number of drinks you have poured down. You keep a list; but a more accurate list has been kept than yours. You may call it Burgundy, Bourbon, cognac, Heidsieck, sour mash, or beer. God calls it "strong drink." Whether you sell it in low oyster-cellar or behind the polished counter of a first-class hotel, the divine curse is upon you. I tell you plainly that you will meet your customers one day when there will be no counter between you. When your work is done on earth, and you enter the reward of your business, all the souls of the men whom you have destroyed will crowd around you, and pour their bitterness into your cup. They will show you their wounds and say, "You made them"; and point to their unquenchable thirst and say, "You kindled it"; and rattle their chain and say, "You forged it." Then their united groans will smite your ear; and with the hands out of which you once picked the sixpences and the dimes they will push you off the verge of great precipices; while rolling up from beneath, and breaking away among the crags of death, will thunder, "Wo to him that giveth his neighbor drink!"

JEREMY TAYLOR

1613-1667

CHRIST'S ADVENT TO JUDGMENT

BIOGRAPHICAL NOTE

JEREMY TAYLOR, born in Cambridge, England, in 1613, was the son of a barber. By his talents he obtained an entrance into Caius College, where his exceptional progress obtained for him admission to the ministry in his twenty-first year, two years before the canonical age. He was appointed in succession fellow of All Souls, Oxford, through the influence of Laud, chaplain to the King, and rector of Uppingham. During the Commonwealth he was expelled from his living and opened a school in Wales, employing his seclusion in writing his memorable work "The Liberty of Prophesying."

At the Restoration, Charles II raised him to the bishopric of Down and Connor (1660), in which post he remained until his death in 1667. His *"Ductor Dubitantium,"* dedicated to Charles II, is a work of subtilty and ingenuity; his "Holy Living" and "Holy Dying" (1652), are unique monuments of learning and devotion. His sermons form, however, his most brilliant and most voluminous productions, and fully establish his claims to the first place among the learned, witty, fanciful, ornate and devotional prose writers of his time.

For we must all appear before the judgment seat of Christ, that every one may receive the things done in his body, according to that he hath done, whether it be good or bad.—II Cor., v., 10.

IF we consider the person of the Judge, we first perceive that He is interested in the injury of the crimes He is to sentence: "They shall look on Him whom they have pierced." It was for thy sins that the Judge did suffer such unspeakable pains as were enough to reconcile all the world to God; the sum and spirit of which pains could not be better understood than by the consequence of His own words, "My God, my God, why hast thou forsaken me?" meaning, that He felt such horrible, pure, unmingled sorrows, that, altho His human nature was personally united to the Godhead, yet at that instant he felt no comfortable emanations by sensible perception from the Divinity, but He was so drenched in sorrow that the Godhead seemed to have forsaken Him. Beyond this, nothing can be added: but then, that thou hast for thy own particular made all this sin in vain and ineffective, that Christ thy Lord and Judge should be tormented for nothing, that thou wouldst not accept felicity and pardon when he purchased them at so dear a price, must needs be an infinite condemnation to such persons. How shalt thou look upon Him that fainted and died for love of thee, and thou didst scorn His miraculous mercies? How shall we dare to behold that holy face that brought salvation to us, and we turned away and fell in love with death, and kissed deformity and sins? And yet in the beholding that face consists much of the glories of eternity. All the pains and passions, the sorrows and the groans, the humility and poverty, the labors and watchings, the prayers and the sermons, the miracles and the prophecies, the whip and the nails, the death and the burial, the shame and the smart, the cross and the grave of Jesus, shall be laid upon thy score, if thou hast refused the mercies and design of all their holy ends and purposes. And if we remember what a calamity that was which broke the Jewish nation in pieces, when Christ came to judge them for their murdering Him who was their King and the Prince of Life, and consider that this was but 'a dark image of the terrors of the day of judgment, we may then apprehend that there is some strange unspeakable evil that attends them that are guilty of this death, and of so much evil to their

Lord. Now it is certain if thou wilt not be saved by His death, you are guilty of His death; if thou wilt not suffer Him to have thee, thou art guilty of destroying Him; and then let it be considered what is to be expected from that Judge before whom you stand as His murderer and betrayer. But this is but half of this consideration.

Christ may be crucified again, and upon a new account, put to an open shame. For after that Christ has done all this by the direct actions of His priestly office, of sacrificing himself for us, He hath also done very many things for us which are also the fruits of His first love and prosecutions of our redemption. I will not instance the strange arts of mercy that our Lord uses to bring us to live holy lives; but I consider, that things are so ordered, and so great a value set upon our souls since they are the images of God, and redeemed by the blood of the Holy Lamb, that the salvation of our souls is reckoned as a part of Christ's reward, a part of the glorification of His humanity. Every sinner that repents causes joy to Christ, and the joy is so great that it runs over and wets the fair brows and beauteous looks of cherubim and seraphim, and all the angels have a part of that banquet; then it is that our blest Lord feels the fruits of His holy death; the acceptation of His holy sacrifice, the graciousness of His person, the return of His prayers. For all that Christ did or suffered, and all that He now does as a priest in heaven, is to glorify His Father by bringing souls to God. For this it was that He was born and died, that He descended from heaven to earth, from life to death, from the cross to the grave; this was the purpose of His resurrection and ascension, of the end and design of all the miracles and graces of God manifested to all the world by Him; and now what man is so vile, such a malicious fool, that will refuse to bring joy to his Lord by doing himself the greatest good in the world? They who refuse to do this, are said to crucify the Lord of Life again, and put him to an open shame—that is, they, as much as in them lies, bring Christ from His glorious joys to the labors of His life and the shame of His death; they advance His enemies, and refuse to advance the kingdom of their Lord; they put themselves in that state in which they were when Christ came to die for them; and now that He is in a state that He may rejoice over them (for He hath done all His share towards it), every wicked man takes his head from the blessing, and rather chooses that the devils should rejoice in his destruction, than that his Lord should triumph in his felicity. And now upon the supposition of these premises, we may imagine that it will be an infinite amazement to meet that Lord to be our Judge whose person we have murdered, whose honor we have disparaged, whose purposes we have destroyed, whose joys we have lessened, whose passion we have made ineffectual, and whose love we have trampled under our profane and impious feet.

But there is yet a third part of this consideration. As it will be inquired at the day of judgment concerning the dishonors to the person of Christ, so also concerning the profession and institution of Christ, and concerning His poor members; for by these also we make sad reflections upon our Lord. Every man that lives wickedly disgraces the religion and institution of Jesus, he discourages strangers from entering into it, he weakens the hands of them that are in already, and makes that the adversaries speak reproachfully of the name of Christ; but altho it is certain our Lord and Judge will deeply resent all these things, yet there is one thing which He takes more tenderly, and that is, the uncharitableness of men towards His poor. It shall then be upbraided to them by the Judge, that Himself was hungry and they refused to give meat to Him that gave them His body and heart-blood to feed them and quench their thirst; that they denied a robe to cover His nakedness, and yet He would have clothed their souls with the robe of His righteousness, lest their souls should be found naked on the day of the Lord's visitation; and all this unkindness is nothing but that evil men were uncharitable to their brethren, they would not feed the hungry, nor give drink to the thirsty nor clothe the naked, nor relieve their brothers' needs, nor forgive their follies, nor cover their shame, nor turn their eyes from delighting in their affronts and evil accidents; this is it which our Lord will take so tenderly, that His brethren for whom He died, who sucked the paps of His mother, that fed on His body and are nourished with His blood, whom He hath lodged in His heart and entertains in His bosom, the partners of His spirit and co-heirs of His inheritance, that these should be denied relief and suffered to go away ashamed, and unpitied; this our blest Lord will take so ill, that all those who are guilty of this unkindness, have no reason to expect the favor of the Court.

To this if we add the almightiness of the Judge, His infinite wisdom and knowledge of all causes, and all persons, and all circumstances, that He is infinitely just, inflexibly angry, and impartial in His sentence, there can be nothing added either to the greatness or the requisites of a terrible and an almighty Judge. For who can resist Him who is almighty? Who can evade His scrutiny that knows all things? Who can hope for pity of Him that is inflexible? Who can think to be exempted when the Judge is righteous and impartial? But in all these annexes of the Great Judge, that which I shall now remark, is that indeed which hath terror in it, and that is, the severity of our Lord. For then is the day of vengeance and recompenses, and no mercy at all shall be showed, but to them that are the sons of mercy; for the other, their portion is such as can be expected from these premises.

If we remember the instances of God's severity in this life, in the days of mercy and repentance, in those days when judgment waits upon mercy, and receives laws by the rules and measures of pardon, and that for all the rare streams of loving kindness issuing out of paradise and refreshing all our fields with a moisture more fruitful than the floods of Nilus, still there are mingled some storms and violences, some fearful instances of the divine justice, we may more readily expect it will be worse, infinitely worse, at that day, when judgment shall ride in triumph, and mercy shall be the accuser of the wicked. But so we read, and are commanded to remember, because they are written for our example, that God destroyed at once five cities of the plain, and all the country, and Sodom and her sisters are set forth for an example, suffering the vengeance of eternal fire. Fearful it was when God destroyed at once twenty-three thousand for fornication, and an exterminating angel in one night killed one hundred and eighty-five thousand of the Assyrians, and the first-born of all the families of Egypt, and for the sin of David in numbering the people, three score and ten thousand of the people died, and God sent ten tribes into captivity and eternal oblivion and indistinction from a common people for their idolatry. Did not God strike Korah and his company with fire from heaven? and the earth opened and swallowed up the congregation of Abiram? And is not evil come upon all the world for one sin of Adam? Did not the anger of God break the nation of the Jews all in pieces with judgments so great, that no nation ever suffered the like, because none ever sinned so? And at once it was done, that God in anger destroyed all the world, and eight persons only escaped the angry baptism of water, and yet this world is the time of mercy; God hath opened here His magazines, and sent His Holy Son as the great channel and fountain of it, too: here He delights in mercy, and in judgment loves to remember it, and it triumphs over all His works, and God contrives instruments and accidents, chances and designs, occasions and opportunities for mercy. If, therefore, now the anger of God makes such terrible eruptions upon the wicked people that delight in sin, how great may we suppose that anger to be, how severe that judgment, how terrible that vengeance, how intolerable those inflictions which God reserves for the full effusion of indignation on the great day of vengeance!

We may also guess at it by this: if God upon all single instances, and in the midst of our sins, before they are come to the full, and sometimes in the beginning of an evil habit, be so fierce in His anger, what can we imagine it to be in that day when the wicked are to drink the dregs of that horrid potion, and count over all the particulars of their whole treasure of wrath? "This is the day of wrath, and God shall reveal, or bring forth, His righteous judgments." The expression is taken from Deut. xxxii., 34: "Is not this laid up in store with me, and sealed up among my treasures? I will restore it in the day of vengeance, for the Lord shall judge His people, and repent Himself for His servants." For so did the Lybian lion that was brought up under discipline, and taught to endure blows, and eat the meat of order and regular provision, and to suffer gentle usages and the familiarities of societies; but once He brake out into His own wildness, and killed two Roman boys; but those that forage in the Lybian mountains tread down and devour all that they meet or master; and when they have fasted two days, lay up an anger great as is their appetite, and bring certain death to all that can be overcome. God is pleased to compare himself to a lion; and though in this life He hath confined Himself with promises and gracious emanations of an infinite goodness, and limits himself by conditions and covenants, and suffers Himself to be overcome by prayers, and Himself hath invented ways of atonement and expiation; yet when He is provoked by our unhandsome and unworthy actions, He makes sudden breaches, and tears some of us in pieces, and of others He breaks their bones or affrights their hopes and secular gaieties, and fills their house with mourning and cypress, and groans and death. But when this Lion of the tribe of Judah shall appear upon His own mountain, the mountain of the Lord, in His natural dress of majesty, and that justice shall have her chain and golden fetters taken off, then justice shall strike, and mercy shall hold her hands; she shall strike sore strokes, and pity shall not break the blow; and God shall account with us by minutes, and for words, and for thoughts, and then He shall be severe to mark what is done amiss; and that justice may reign entirely, God shall open the wicked man's treasure, and tell the sums, and weigh grains and scruples. Said Philo upon the place of Deuteronomy before quoted: As there are treasures of good things, and God has crowns and scepters in store for His saints and servants, and coronets for martyrs, and rosaries for virgins, and vials full of prayers, and bottles full of tears, and a register of sighs and penitential groans, so God hath a treasure of wrath and fury, of scourges and scorpions, and then shall be produced the shame of lust, and the malice of envy, and the groans of the opprest, and the persecutions of the saints, and the cares of covetousness, and the troubles of ambition, and the insolencies of traitors, and the violence of rebels, and the rage of anger, and the uneasiness of impatience, and the restlessness of unlawful desires; and by this time the monsters and diseases will be numerous and intolerable, when God's heavy hand shall press the *sanies* and the intolerableness, the obliquity and the unreasonableness, the amazement and the disorder, the smart and the sorrow, the guilt and the punishment, out from all our sins, and pour them into one chalice, and mingle them with an infinite wrath, and make the wicked drink of all the vengeance, and force it down their unwilling throats with the violence of devils and accurst spirits.

We may guess at the severity of the Judge by the lesser strokes of that judgment which He is pleased to send upon sinners in this world, to make them afraid of the horrible pains of doomsday—I mean the torments of an unquiet conscience, the amazement and confusions of some sins and some persons. For I have sometimes seen persons surprised in a base action, and taken in the circumstances of crafty theft and secret injustices, before their excuse was ready. They have changed their color, their speech hath faltered, their tongue stammered, their eyes did wander and fix nowhere, till shame made them sink into their hollow eye-pits to retreat from the images and circumstances of discovery; their wits are lost, their reason useless, the whole order of their soul is decomposed, and they neither see, nor feel, nor think, as they used to do, but they are broken into disorder by a stroke of damnation and a lesser stripe of hell; but then if you come to observe a guilty and a base murderer, a condemned traitor, and see him harassed first by an evil conscience, and then pulled in pieces by the hangman's hooks, or broken upon sorrows and the wheel, we may then guess (as well as we can in this life) what the pains of that day shall be to accurst souls. But those we shall consider afterward in their proper scene; now only we are to estimate the severity of our Judge by the intolerableness of an evil conscience; if guilt will make a man despair—and despair will make a man mad, confounded, and dissolved in all the regions of his senses and more noble faculties, that he shall neither feel, nor hear, nor see anything but specters and illusions, devils and frightful dreams, and hear noises, and shriek fearfully, and look pale and distracted, like a hopeless man from the horrors and confusions of a lost battle, upon which all his hopes did stand—then the wicked must at the day of judgment expect strange things and fearful, and such which now no language can express, and then no patience can endure. Then only it can truly be said that he is inflexible and inexorable. No

prayers then can move Him, no groans can cause Him to pity thee; therefore pity thyself in time, that when the Judge comes thou mayest be one of the sons of everlasting mercy, to whom pity belongs as part of thine inheritance, for all else shall without any remorse (except His own) be condemned by the horrible sentence.

That all may think themselves concerned in this consideration, let us remember that even the righteous and most innocent shall pass through a severe trial. Many of the ancients explicated this severity by the fire of conflagration, which say they shall purify those souls at the day of judgment, which in this life have built upon the foundation (hay and stubble) works of folly and false opinions, states of imperfection. So St. Augustine's doctrine was: "The great fire at doomsday shall throw some into the portion of the left hand, and others shall be purified and represented on the right." And the same is affirmed by Origen and Lactantius; and St. Hilary thus expostulates: "Since we are to give account for every idle word, shall we long for the day of judgment, wherein we must, every one of us, pass that unwearied fire in which those grievous punishments for expiating the soul from sins must be endured; for to such as have been baptized with the Holy Ghost it remaineth that they be consummated with the fire of judgment." And St. Ambrose adds: "That if any be as Peter or as John, they are baptized with this fire, and he that is purged here had need to be purged there again. Let him also purify us, that every one of us being burned with that flaming sword, not burned up or consumed, we may enter into Paradise, and give thanks unto the Lord who hath brought us into a place of refreshment." This opinion of theirs is, in the main of it, very uncertain; relying upon the sense of some obscure place of Scripture is only apt to represent the great severity of the Judge at that day, and it hath in it this only certainty, that even the most innocent person hath great need of mercy, and he that hath the greatest cause of confidence, altho he runs to no rocks to hide him, yet he runs to the protection of the cross, and hides himself under the shadow of the divine mercies: and he that shall receive the absolution of the blest sentence shall also suffer the terrors of the day, and the fearful circumstances of Christ's coming. The effect of this consideration is this: That if the righteous scarcely be saved, where shall the wicked and the sinner appear? And if St. Paul, whose conscience accused him not, yet durst not be too confident, because he was not hereby justified, but might be found faulty by the severer judgment of his Lord, how shall we appear, with all our crimes and evil habits round about us? If there be need of much mercy to the servants and friends of the Judge, then His enemies shall not be able to stand upright in judgment.

Let us next consider the circumstances of our appearing and his sentence; and first I consider that men at the day of judgment that belong not to the portion of life, shall have three sorts of accusers: 1. Christ Himself, who is their judge; 2. Their own conscience, whom they have injured and blotted with characters of death and foul dishonor; 3. The devil, their enemy, whom they served.

Christ shall be their accuser, not only upon the stock of those direct injuries (which I before reckoned) of crucifying the Lord of Life, once and again, etc., but upon the titles of contempt and unworthiness, of unkindness and ingratitude; and the accusation will be nothing else but a plain representation of those artifices and assistances, those bonds and invitations, those constrainings and importunities, which our dear Lord used to us to make it almost impossible to lie in sin, and necessary to be saved. For it will, it must needs be, a fearful exprobration of our unworthiness, when the Judge Himself shall bear witness against us that the wisdom of God Himself was strangely employed in bringing us safely to felicity. I shall draw a short scheme which, altho it must needs be infinitely short, of what God hath done for us, yet it will be enough to shame us. God did not only give His Son for an example, and the Son gave Himself for a price for us, but both gave the Holy Spirit to assist us in mighty graces, for the verifications of faith, and the entertainments of hope, and the increase and perseverance of charity. God gave to us a new nature, He put another principle into us, a third part of a perfective constitution; we have the spirit put into us, to be a part of us, as properly to produce actions of a holy life, as the soul of man in the body does produce the natural. God hath exalted human nature, and made it in the person of Jesus Christ, to sit above the highest seat of angels, and the angels are made ministering spirits, ever since their Lord became our brother. Christ hath by a miraculous sacrament given us His body to eat and His blood to drink; He made ways that we may become all one with Him. He hath given us an easy religion, and hath established our future felicity upon natural and pleasant conditions, and we are to be happy hereafter if we suffer God to make us happy here; and things are so ordered that a man must take more pains to perish than to be happy. God hath found out rare ways to make our prayers acceptable, our weak petitions, the desires of our imperfect souls, to prevail mightily with God, and to lay a holy violence and an undeniable necessity upon Himself; and God will deny us nothing but when we ask of Him to do us ill offices, to give us poisons and dangers, and evil nourish-

ment, and temptations; and He that hath given such mighty power to the prayers of His servants, yet will not be moved by those potent and mighty prayers to do any good man an evil turn, or to grant him one mischief—in that only God can deny us. But in all things else God hath made all the excellent things in heaven and earth to join toward the holy and fortunate effects; for He that appointed an angel to present the prayers of saints, and Christ makes intercession for us, and the Holy Spirit makes intercession for us with groans unutterable, and all the holy men in the world pray for all and for every one, and God hath instructed us with scriptures, and precedents, and collateral and direct assistances to pray, and He encouraged us with divers excellent promises, and parables, and examples, and teaches us what to pray, and how, and gives one promise to public prayer, and another to private prayer, and to both the blessing of being heard.

Add to this account that God did heap blessings upon us without order, infinitely, perpetually, and in all instances, when we needed and when we needed not. He heard us when we prayed, giving us all, and giving us more, than we desired. He desired that we should ask, and yet He hath also prevented our desires. He watched for us, and at His own charge sent a whole order of men whose employment is to minister to our souls; and if all this had not been enough, He had given us more also. He promised heaven to our obedience, a province for a dish of water, a kingdom for a prayer, satisfaction for desiring it, grace for receiving, and more grace for accepting and using the first. He invited us with gracious words and perfect entertainments; He threatened horrible things to us if we would not be happy; He hath made strange necessities for us, making our very repentance to be a conjugation of holy actions, and holy times, and a long succession; He hath taken away all excuses from us; He hath called us from temptation; He bears our charges; He is always beforehand with us in every act of favor, and perpetually slow in striking, and His arrows are unfeathered; and He is so long, first, in drawing His sword, and another long while in whetting it, and yet longer in lifting His hand to strike, that before the blow comes the man hath repented long, unless he be a fool and impudent; and then God is so glad of an excuse to lay His anger aside, that certainly, if after all this, we refuse life and glory, there is no more to be said; this plain story will condemn us; but the story is very much longer; and, as our conscience will represent all our sins to us, so the Judge will represent all His Father's kindnesses, as Nathan did to David, when he was to make the justice of the divine sentence appear against him. Then it shall be remembered that the joys of every day's piety would have been a greater pleasure every night than the remembrance of every night's sin could have been in the morning; that every night the trouble and labor of the day's virtue would have been as much passed and turned to as the pleasure of that day's sin, but that they would be infinitely distinguished by the effects. The offering ourselves to God every morning, and the thanksgiving to God every night, hope and fear, shame and desire, the honor of leaving a fair name behind us, and the shame of dying like a fool,—everything indeed in the world is made to be an argument and an inducement to us to invite us to come to God and be saved; and therefore when this, and infinitely more shall by the Judge be exhibited in sad remembrances, there needs no other sentence; we shall condemn ourselves with a hasty shame and a fearful confusion, to see how good God hath been to us, and how base we have been to ourselves. Thus Moses is said to accuse the Jews; and thus also He that does accuse, is said to condemn, as Verres was by Cicero, and Claudia by Domitius her accuser, and the world of impenitent persons by the men of Nineveh, and all by Christ, their Judge. I represent the horror of this circumstance to consist in this, besides the reasonableness of the judgment, and the certainty of the condemnation, it can not but be an argument of an intolerable despair to perishing souls, when He that was our advocate all our life, shall, in the day of that appearing, be our Accuser and our Judge, a party against us, an injured person in the day of His power and of His wrath, doing execution upon all His own foolish and malicious enemies.

Our conscience shall be our accuser. But this signifies but these two things: First, That we shall be condemned for the evils that we have done and shall then remember, God by His power wiping away the dust from the tables of our memory, and taking off the consideration and the voluntary neglect and rude shufflings of our cases of conscience. For then we shall see things as they are, the evil circumstances and the crooked intentions, the adherent unhandsomeness and the direct crimes; for all things are laid up safely, and tho we draw a curtain of cobweb over them, and a few fig-leaves before our shame, yet God shall draw away the curtain, and forgetfulness shall be no more, because, with a taper in the hand of God, all the corners of our nastiness shall be discovered. And, secondly, it signifies this also, that not only the justice of God shall be confest by us in our own shame and condemnation, but the evil of the sentence shall be received into us, to melt our bowels and to break our heart in pieces within us, because we are the authors of our own death, and our own

inhuman hands have torn our souls in pieces. Thus far the horrors are great, and when evil men consider it, it is certain they must be afraid to die. Even they that have lived well, have some sad considerations, and the tremblings of humility, and suspicion of themselves. I remember St. Cyprian tells of a good man who in his agony of death saw a fantasm of a noble and angelical shape, who, frowning and angry, said to him: "Ye can not endure sickness, ye are troubled at the evils of the world, and yet you are loath to die and to be quit of them; what shall I do to you?" Altho this is apt to represent every man's condition more or less, yet, concerning persons of wicked lives, it hath in it too many sad degrees of truth; they are impatient of sorrow, and justly fearful of death, because they know not how to comfort themselves in the evil accidents of their lives; and their conscience is too polluted to take death for sanctuary, and to hope to have amends made to their condition by the sentence of the day of judgment. Evil and sad is their condition who can not be contented here nor blest hereafter, whose life is their misery and their conscience is their enemy, whose grave is their prison and death their undoing, and the sentence of doomsday the beginning of an intolerable condition.

The third sort of accusers are the devils, and they will do it with malicious and evil purposes. The prince of the devils hath Diabolus for one of his chiefest appellatives. The accuser of the brethren he is by his profest malice and employment; and therefore God, who delights that His mercy should triumph and His goodness prevail over all the malice of men and devils, hath appointed one whose office is to reprove the accuser and to resist the enemy, and to be a defender of their cause who belong to God. The Holy Spirit is a defender; the evil spirit is the accuser; and they that in this life belong to one or the other, shall in the same proportion be treated at the day of judgment. The devil shall accuse the brethren, that is, the saints and servants of God, and shall tell concerning their follies and infirmities, the sins of their youth and weakness of their age, the imperfect grace and the long schedule of omissions of duty, their scruples and their fears, their diffidences and pusillanimity, and all those things which themselves by strict examination find themselves guilty of and have confest all their shame and the matter of their sorrows, their evil intentions and their little plots, their carnal confidences and too fond adherences of the things of this world, their indulgence and easiness of government, their wilder joys and freer meals, their loss of time and their too forward and apt compliances, their trifling arrests and little peevishnesses, the mixtures of the world with the thing of the Spirit, and all the incidences of humanity he will bring forth and aggravate them by circumstances of ingratitude, and the breach of promise, and the evacuating all their holy purposes, and breaking their resolutions, and rifling their vows, and all these things, being drawn into an entire representment, and the bills clogged by numbers, will make the best man in the world seem foul and unhandsome, and stained with the characters of death and evil dishonor. But for these there is appointed a defender. The Holy Spirit that maketh intercession for us shall then also interpose, and against all these things shall oppose the passion of our blest Lord, and upon all their defects shall cast the robe of righteousness; and the sins of their youth shall not prevail so much as the repentance of their age, and their omissions be excused by probable intervening causes, and their little escapes shall appear single and in disunion, because they were always kept asunder by penitential prayers and sighings, and their seldom returns of sin by their daily watchfulness, and their often infirmities by the sincerity of their souls, and their scruples by their zeal, and their passions by their love, and all by the mercies of God and the sacrifice which their Judge offered and the Holy Spirit made effective by daily graces and assistances. These, therefore, infallibly go to the portion of the right hand, because the Lord our God shall answer for them. But as for the wicked, it is not so with them; for altho the plain story of their life be to them a sad condemnation, yet what will be answered when it shall be told concerning them, that they despised God's mercies, and feared not His angry judgments; that they regarded not His Word, and loved not His excellences; that they were not persuaded by the promises nor affrighted by His threatenings; that they neither would accept His government nor His blessings; that all the sad stories that ever happened in both the worlds (in all which Himself did escape till the day of His death, and was not concerned in them save only that He was called upon by every one of them, which He ever heard or saw or was told of, to repentance), that all these were sent to Him in vain? But can not the accuser truly say to the Judge concerning such persons, "They were Thine by creation, but mine by their own choice; Thou didst redeem them indeed, but they sold themselves to me for a trifle, or for an unsatisfying interest; Thou diedst for them, but

they obeyed my commandments; I gave them nothing, I promised them nothing but the filthy pleasures of a night, or the joys of madness, or the delights of a disease; I never hanged upon the cross three long hours for them, nor endured the labors of a poor life thirty-three years together for their interest; only when they were Thine by the merit of Thy death, they quickly became mine by the demerit of their ingratitude; and when Thou hadst clothed their soul with Thy robe, and adorned them by Thy graces, we stript them naked as their shame, and only put on a robe of darkness, and they thought themselves secure and went dancing to their grave like a drunkard to a fight, or a fly unto a candle; and therefore they that did partake with us in our faults must divide with us in our portion and fearful interest." This is a sad story because it ends in death, and there is nothing to abate or lessen the calamity. It concerns us therefore to consider in time that he that tempts us will accuse us, and what he calls pleasant now he shall then say was nothing, and all the gains that now invite earthly souls and mean persons to vanity, was nothing but the seeds of folly, and the harvest in pain and sorrow and shame eternal. But then, since this horror proceeds upon the account of so many accusers, God hath put it in our power by a timely accusation of ourselves in the tribunal of the court Christian, to prevent all the arts of aggravation which at doomsday shall load foolish and undiscerning souls. He that accuses himself of his crimes here, means to forsake them, and looks upon them on all sides, and spies out his deformity, and is taught to hate them, he is instructed and prayed for, he prevents the anger of God and defeats the devil's malice, and, by making shame the instrument of repentance, he takes away the sting, and makes that to be his medicine which otherwise would be his death: and, concerning this exercise, I shall only add what the patriarch of Alexandria told an old religious person in his hermitage. Having asked him what he found in that desert, he was answered, "Only this, to judge and condemn myself perpetually; that is the employment of my solitude." The patriarch answered, "There is no other way." By accusing ourselves we shall make the devil's malice useless, and our own consciences clear, and be reconciled to the Judge by the severities of an early repentance, and then we need to fear no accusers.

WILLIAM M. TAYLOR

1829-1895

CHRIST BEFORE PILATE
PILATE BEFORE CHRIST

BIOGRAPHICAL NOTE

WILLIAM MACKERGO TAYLOR, Congregational divine, was born at Kilmarnock, Scotland, in 1829. He was for many years pastor of the Broadway Tabernacle, New York. He had an impressive presence and his delivery was marked by a magnetic earnestness. During the first ten years of his ministry he spoke memoriter, but subsequently wrote out his sermons with detailed care and preached them from manuscript, but their delivery was without the freedom and freshness of extemporaneous address. He came to regret this, for he said: "If I might speak from my own experience I would say, that memoriter preaching is the method which has the greatest advantages, with the fewest disadvantages." He died in 1895.

Pilate saith unto them, What shall I do, then, with Jesus, which is called Christ?—Matthew xxvii., 22.

DURING my late visit to my native land I had the great enjoyment of seeing, and somewhat carefully studying, Munkacsy's famous picture of "Christ Before Pilate." Rarely, if ever, had I been so much moved by a work of art; and I propose to give, as nearly as I can recall it, the sermon which it reached to me as I sat silently contemplating the figures, which, even as I looked at them, seemed to grow before me into life.

But, first, I must try to describe to you the picture itself. The canvas is large, and the figures, all of which are on the line of sight, are of life size. The scene is in the pavement or open court before the governor's palace, which was called in the Hebrew tongue Gabbatha, and in which, after all his efforts to wriggle out of the responsibility of dealing with the case, Pilate ultimately gave up Jesus to be crucified. At one end of the court, on a raised bench, and drest in a white toga, Pilate sits. On either side of him are Jews, each of whom has a marked and special individuality. The two on his left are gazing with intense eagerness at Christ. They are evidently puzzled, and know not well what to make of the mysterious prisoner. On his right, standing on one of the seats, and with his back against the wall, is a Scribe, whose countenance is expressive of uttermost contempt, and just in front of this haughty fellow are some Pharisees, one of whom is on his feet, and passionately urging that Jesus should be put to death, presumably on the ground that, if Pilate should let Him go, he would make it evident that he was not Cæsar's friend. Before them again is a usurer, sleek, fat and self-satisfied, clearly taking great comfort to himself in the assurance that, however the matter may be settled, his well-filled money-bags will be undisturbed. Beyond him stands the Christ in a robe of seamless white, and with His wrists firmly bound; while behind, kept in place by a Roman soldier, standing with his back to the spectator, and making a barricade with his spear, which he holds horizontally, is a motley group of onlookers, not unlike that which we may still see any day in one of our criminal courts. Of these, one more furious than the rest is wildly gesticulating, and crying, as we may judge from his whole attitude, "Crucify Him! crucify Him!" and another, a little to the Savior's left, but in the second row behind Him, is leaning forward with mockery in his leering look, and making almost as if he would spit upon the saintly one. There is but one really compassionate face in the crowd, and that is a face of a woman who, with an infant in her arms, most fitly represents those gentle daughters of Jerusalem who followed Jesus to Calvary with tears. Then, over the heads of the on-lookers, and out of the upper part of the doorway into the court, we get a glimpse of the quiet light of the morning as it sleeps upon the walls and turrets of the adjacent buildings. All these figures are so distinctly seen that you feel you could recognize them again if you met them anywhere; and a strange sense of reality comes upon you as you look at them, so that you forget that they are only painted, and imagine that you are gazing on living and breathing men.

But, as you sit awhile and look on, you gradually lose all consciousness of the presence of the mere on-lookers and find your interest concentrated on these two white-robed ones, as if they were the only figures before you. The pose of Christ is admirable. It is repose blended with dignity; self-possession rising into majesty. There is no agitation or confusion; no fear or misgiving; but, instead, the calm nobleness of Him who has just been saying, "Thou couldst have no power at all against me, except it were given thee from above; therefore he that delivered me unto thee hath the greater sin." The face alone disappoints. Perhaps that may be owing to the lofty ideal we have of the divine Man, so that no picture of our Lord would entirely please. But tho the painter has wisely abandoned the halo, and all similar conventionalisms of art, and has delineated a real man, for all which he is to be highly commended, yet the eyes which look so steadily at Pilate, as if they were looking him through, seem to me to be cold, keen, and condemnatory, rather than compassionate and sad. It is a conception of the Lord of the same sort as that of Doré, in his well-known picture of the leaving of the Prætorium, and the eyes have not in them that deep well of tenderness out of which came the tears which He shed over Jerusalem, and which we expect to see in them when He is looking at the hopeless struggle of a soul which will not accept His aid. It is said that the artist, dissatisfied with his first attempt, has painted the Christ face twice; but this, also, is a partial failure, and here, so at least it seemed to me as I looked at it, is the one defect in his noble work. But if there is this defect, it is one which it shares with every other effort that human art has made

to delineate the Lord. The Pilate, however, is well-nigh faultless. Here is a great, strong man, the representative of the mightiest empire the world has ever seen, with a head indicating intellectual force, and a face, especially in its lower part, suggestive of sensual indulgence. There is ordinarily no want of firmness in him, as we may see from the general set of his features; but now there is in his countenance a marvelous mixture of humiliation and irresolution. He cannot lift his eyes to meet the gaze of Christ; and while one of his hands is nervously clutching at his robe he is looking sadly into the other, whose fingers, even as we look at them, almost seem to twitch with perplexed irresolution. He is clearly pondering for himself the question which a few moments before he had addrest to the multitude, "What shall I do with Jesus which is called Christ?" He is annoyed that the case has been brought to him at all, and as he feels himself drifting on, against his own better judgment, toward yielding to the clamor of the multitude, he falls mightily in his own conceit, and begins to despise himself. He would, at that moment, give, oh, how much! to be rid of the responsibility of dealing with the Christ, but he cannot evade it; and so he sits there, drifting on to what he knows is a wrong decision, the very incarnation of the feeling which his own national poet described when he said, "I see and approve the better course; I follow the worse." Thus, as we look at these two, we begin to discover that it was not Christ that was before Pilate so much as Pilate was before Christ. His was the testing experience. His was the trial; his too, alas! was the degradation; and at that coming day when the places shall be reversed, when Christ shall be on the judgment seat, and Pilate at the bar, there will still be that deep self-condemnation which the painter here has fixt upon his countenance. It is a marvelous picture, in many respects the most remarkable I ever looked upon, and, even from this imperfect description of it, you will easily understand how, as I sat intent before it, it stirred my soul to the very depths.

But now, with this portrayal of the scene before us let us see if we can account, first, for the hesitation of Pilate to give up the Lord, and then for his final yielding to the clamor of the people. Why all this reluctance on his part to send Jesus to the cross? He was not usually so scrupulous. A human life more or less gave him generally very little concern. He had all a Roman's indifference for the comfort of those who stood in any respect in his way; and had no compunction, as we know, in mingling the blood of certain turbulent Jews with the very sacrifices which at the moment they were offering. Had Christ been a Roman citizen, indeed, he would most likely have been very watchful over His safety, for in regard to all such the imperial law was peculiarly strict, but the life of a mere Jew was a very small thing in his estimation. Wherefore, then, this unwonted squeamishness of conscience? It was the result of a combination of particulars, each of which had a special force of its own, and the aggregate of which so wrought upon his mind that he was brought thereby to a stand.

There was, in the first place, the peculiar character of the prisoner. A very slight examination had been sufficient to convince him that Christ was innocent of the charge which had been brought against Him. But in the course of that examination much more than the innocence of Christ had come to view. He had manifested a dignified patience altogether unlike anything that Pilate had ever seen; and His answers to certain questions had been so strangely suggestive of something higher and nobler than even the most exalted earthly philosophy that he could not look upon Him as a common prisoner. He was no mere fanatic; neither was He after the pattern of any existing school, whether Jewish, Greek, or Roman. There was about Him an "other-worldliness" which brought those near Him into close proximity, for the time, with the unseen; and an elevation which lifted Him above the tumult that was howling for His destruction. Probably Pilate could not have described it to himself, but there was something which he felt unusual and exceptional in this man, marking Him out from every other he ever had before him, and constraining him to take a special interest in His case. Add to this that his wife had sent to him that singular message—"Have thou nothing to do with that just man, for I have suffered many things this day in a dream because of him,"—a message which, in those days of mingled scepticism and superstition —for the two always go hand in hand—must have produced a deep impression on his mind. Moreover, there seemed some fatality about the case. He had tried to roll it over upon Herod, but that wily monarch sent the prisoner back upon his hands. He had attempted to release Him, as the Passover prisoner for the year, but neither was there any outlet for him in that, for the people had preferred Barabbas. And so the responsibility had come again to his own door, and could not be passed on to another. Still again, he saw that the Jews were acting most hypocritically in the matter. It was a new thing for them to be zealous for the honor of Cæsar, and he could easily see through the mask they wore into the envy and malice which were the motives for their conduct. The deeper he went into the case he discovered only the more reason for resisting their importunity, and, however, he looked at it, his plain duty was to set the prisoner free.

Why then, again we ask, was his perplexity? The answer is suggested by the taunt of the Jews, "If thou let this man go thou art not Cæsar's friend; whosoever maketh himself a king speaketh against Cæsar." He foresaw that if he resisted the will of the rulers he would make them his enemies, and so provoke them to complain of him to the emperor, who would then institute an inquiry into the administration of his office—and that he was not prepared to face. He had done things as a governor which would not bear the light, and so at the crisis of his life he was fettered by deeds of the past from doing that which he felt to be the duty of the present. You may, perhaps, remember that expression of the prophet, which thus reads in the margin: "Their doings will not suffer them to turn unto their God": and that other, which affirms, concerning Israel: "Their own doings have beset them about." Now these descriptions most accurately define the cause of Pilate's perplexity here. His conduct in the past had been such that he had not the courage to take any course which might lead to an investigation of that. If he could deliver Christ without provoking that, then he would most cheerfully do so; but if by delivering Christ he would provoke that, then Christ must be given up to the cross. Hence his perplexity at the first, and hence, also, his yielding in the end. His past misdeeds had put him virtually into the power of those who were now so eager for the condemnation of the Christ. On three several occasions his arbitrariness had been such as all but to instigate a rebellion among the people, and his cruelty and contempt for justice, when he had a personal end to gain, were sure, upon appeal to the emperor, to be severely punished; so to save himself from banishment and disgrace, if not even death, he delivered over Jesus to the will of the Jews. He wished to do right in this case more than ever he had wished before; there was something about it which in his view made it more important that he should do right now than ever before; but through all his past official life he had, by his enormities and oppressions, been unconsciously weaving round himself a net, in the meshes of which he was now inextricably caught. His guilty conscience made him a coward at the very time when most of all he wanted to be brave. He had come to his "narrow place," where he could turn neither to the right hand nor to the left, but must face the naked alternative "yes" or "no"; and he fell because in his former life, when he was thinking of no such ordeal, he had sold himself by his evil deeds into the power of the enemy.

Now, what a lesson there is in all this for us! Men think that they may live for the time being as they please, and that at a convenient season they can repent and turn to God. But the present is conditioning the future, and making it either possible or the reverse for us to do right in the future. He who neglects the laws of health every day, and lives in intemperance and excess of all kinds, is only making it absolutely certain that when fever lays him low he will die, for he has eaten out the strength of his constitution by his follies. And, in the same way, he who sets all morality at defiance in his ordinary conduct only makes it inevitable that when his convenient season does come, when his time of privilege and testing does arrive, he will fail to rise to the occasion, and be swept away into perdition. The tenor of our ordinary life determines how we shall pass through exceptional and crucial occasions, therefore let us bring that up to the highest level by doing everything as unto God, and then we shall be ready for any emergency.

Nor let me forget to add here, that in spite of all his efforts to keep back investigation, Pilate's day of reckoning with the emperor did come. The Jews complained of him after all, in spite of his yielding to them now; and as the result he was banished, and afterwards, so tradition says, he committed suicide. Thus the ordeal and the disgrace came, notwithstanding all he did to avert them, and he had not under them the solace which he might have enjoyed if only he had stood firm on this great and memorable occasion. Therefore let us all, and especially the young, take to ourselves, as the first lesson from this deeply interesting history, that we should be careful not to hamper ourselves for the discharge of duty in the future by guilt of the present. By our conduct now we are either coiling cords around us which shall hold us fast at the very time when we most desire to be free, or we are forming and fostering a strength of character which, through God, will triumph over every temptation. If "to be weak is to be miserable," it is no less true that to be guilty is to be weak. Preserve yourselves, therefore, from this danger, and seek above all other things to keep your consciences clean; then when you will need all your strength for a crisis, you will not sit, like Pilate here, in nervous perplexity bemoaning your helplessness even while you yield to the adversary; but you will shake the temptation from you with as much ease as the eagle shakes the dewdrop from his wing. Keep yourselves pure: so shall your youth be full of happiness, and you shall go forth out of it with no encumbering past to clog the wheels of your endeavor. How happy he whose youth thus leaves him with a smile and sends him forth upon the duties of manhood with a benediction! But he, how miserable! whose early years heap bitter maledictions on his head, and push him forward into active life with a conscience already laden with guilt, and a soul as weak before temptation as a reed is before the wind.

But while there is thus in this history a lesson for all time, I think Munkacsy, by the appearance of his wondrous picture now, has made it evident that there is also something in it specially adapted to these modern days. It is with artists in the choice of their subjects as it is with ministers in the selection of their themes. Both alike, consciously and unconsciously, and most frequently perhaps unconsciously, are affected by the spirit of their age. The atmosphere—literary, moral, political, and religious—which is round about them, and which they are daily breathing, does, insensibly to themselves, so influence them that their thoughts are turned by it into a channel different from that in which those of a former generation flowed. Hence, whether the painter would admit it or not, I see in this picture, at this juncture, at once a mirror of the times and a lesson for them. The question of Pilate, "What shall I do, then, with Jesus which is called the Christ?" is preeminently the question of the present age. No doubt we may say with truth that it has been the question of all the Christian centuries, and each one of them has faced it and solved it after its own fashion. It has tested the centuries even as it tested Pilate, and those in which Christ was rejected have been the darkest in the world's history; while those in which He has been hailed as the incarnate God have been the brightest which the earth has ever seen, because irradiated with truth, and justice, and benevolence and purity. But tho we are always prone to exaggerate that in the midst of which we are ourselves, it seems to me that in no one age since that of the primitive Church has this jesting question been so prominent as in our own. All the controversies of our times, social, philosophical, and theological, lead up to and find their ultimate hinge in the answer to this inquiry, "Who is this Jesus Christ?" If He be a mere man, then there is for us nothing but uncertainty on any subject, outside of the domain of the exact sciences; and we must all become agnostics, holding this one negative article of belief, that nothing can be known about anything save that of which we can take cognizance with the bodily sense. But if He be incarnate God, then He brings with Him from heaven the final word on all subjects concerning which He has spoken; and tho in His person He is the mystery of mysteries, yet, at once received, He becomes forthwith the solution of all mysteries, and faith in Him is at once the satisfaction of the intellect and the repose of the heart. It is perfectly natural, therefore, that all the controversies of the day should turn on Him. The lives of Christ which have been written during the last thirty or forty years would make in themselves a very respectable library; and the cry even of the sceptic is, "I could get on very well with unbelief, if I only knew what to make of Christ." Yes, that is just the difficulty. Christ is here in the Scriptures a character portrayed in literature; He was in the world for thirty-three years, and lived a life exceptional in every respect, but most of all in the moral and spiritual departments, so that of Him alone perfection can be predicated; He has been ever since a most potent factor in history, for through His influence all that is pure, and noble, and exalted, and lovely and of good report, has come into our civilization. Now, these things have to be accounted for. If He was only a man, how shall we explain them? And if He was more than a man shall we not take His own testimony as to His dignity and mission? If we are to be unbelievers, we must account for Christ on natural principles; but if we cannot do that, then we must conceive Him as He claims to be conceived. There is no alternative. Those in the age who have the spirit and dispositon of Pilate will anew reject Him! but those who are sincere and earnest in their inquiries will come ultimately out into the light, for "if any man be willing to do his will, he shall know of the doctrine whether it be of God."

And what is true of the age, as a whole, is true also of every individual to whom the gospel is proclaimed. For each of us, my hearers, this is the question of questions, "What shall I do with Jesus which is called Christ?" Shall I reject Him and live precisely as if I had never heard His name? or shall I accept Him as the Lord from heaven in human nature, trust in Him as my Savior, and obey Him as my King? I must do the one or the other; and yet how many are seeking, like Pilate, to evade the question? They try to escape the responsibility of dealing with it as a direct alternative of yes or no. But as one has well said, "necessity is laid upon us. The adversaries of Christ press upon us to give our verdict against Him. We are troubled and perplexed, for we have long heard about Him, and have had each of us his own convictions. We would still remain neutral. We try—and try in vain—to escape from the

mission? If we are to be unbelievers, we must account for Christ on natural principles; but if we cannot do that, then we must conceive Him as He claims to be conceived. There is no alternative. Those in the age who have the spirit and dispositon of Pilate will anew reject Him! but those who are sincere and earnest in their inquiries will come ultimately out into the light, for "if any man be willing to do his will, he shall know of the doctrine whether it be of God."

And what is true of the age, as a whole, is true also of every individual to whom the gos- It is this: You can not evade the decision, but be sure that you look at the Christ before you give Him up. Nothing is so remarkable in the picture to which I have so often this day referred as the evident persistency with which Pilate keeps his eyes from Christ; and few things are so saddening as to meet with men who profess to have, and really have, difficulties about Christ, but who have never read the gospels or the New Testament with any attention.

Let me urge you earnestly, therefore, to study these gospels and epistles before you give your voice against the Lord, and I am very sure that if you ponder them thoroughly you will soon accept Him. Give over trying to solve all the difficulties and so-called discrepancies in the Scriptures which form the stock-in-trade of the infidel lecturer—all these are but as dust which he raises that he may blind your eyes to the really important question, "Who is Christ?" Settle that, and if you do, all other difficulties will vanish. Turn your face to the light, and the shadow will fall behind you. Look at the Christ before you give Him up. And remember, if you do reject Christ, you have still to account for Him. It is unreasonable for you, if you believe only in the natural and material, to leave such a phenomenon as Christ unexplained.

Yes, and I must add here that if you reject Him you must yet account to Him. Go, then, and ponder this text; yea, may it continue sounding in your inmost heart until you have determined to receive and rest upon Him as your only Savior, and say to Him, like Thomas, "My Lord and my God."

MILTON SPENSER TERRY

1840-1914

THE APOSTOLIC INTERPRETATION OF CHRIST

BIOGRAPHICAL NOTE

PROFESSOR of Christian doctrine, Garrett Biblical Institute, Northwestern University, Evanston, Ill., 1885-1914; born near Albany, N. Y., February 22, 1840; studied at Charlottesville Seminary, Troy University, Yale Divinity School, and the University of Berlin, Germany; pastor of Methodist Episcopal churches in New York, from 1863-84; author of popular commentaries on several books of the Old Testament, "Moses and the Prophets," "The New Apologetic," "Biblical Hermeneutics," "Biblical Apocalyptics," "Biblical Dogmatics," translation of the Greek "Sibylline Oracles" into English blank verse, etc.

"I am the light of the world."—John 9 : 5.
"Ye are the light of the world."—Matt. 5 : 14.
"Forasmuch as many have taken in hand to draw up a narrative concerning those matters which have been fully established among us, even as they delivered them unto us, who from the beginning were eyewitnesses and ministers of the word, it seemed good to me also, having traced the course of all things accurately from the first, to write unto thee in orderly sequence, most excellent Theophilus; that thou mightest know the certainty concerning the things wherein thou wast instructed."—Luke 1 : 1-4.
"How shall we escape, if we neglect sc great salvation? which having at the first been spoken through the Lord, was confirmed unto us by them that heard; God also bearing witness with them, both by signs and wonders, and by manifold powers, and by distributions of the Holy Spirit, according to his own will."—Hebrews 2 : 3, 4. [Private translation.]

THESE various scriptures of the New Testament have obvious bearing on the question which I propose to discuss, namely: How far the apostolic interpretation of Christ is trustworthy and authoritative? It is conceded at the start that whatever Christ Himself clearly taught is authoritative. He is the light of the world. He is the great divine Teacher; the supreme Personality among the many master minds that have spoken with authority. But He lived and taught well nigh two thousand years ago. What do we certainly know now of the words, the exact teachings of Jesus Christ? It is reported that he once wrote with His finger on the ground, but what He wrote is unknown, and even the passage which records the story is set aside by the majority of recent critics as no part of the Fourth Gospel. Aside from the statements of that disputed and rejected text, there is no evidence that Jesus ever wrote a word.

But it is commonly supposed that the four gospels, aside from all disputed texts, contain to a great extent the very words of Jesus. There are the Sermon on the Mount, the parables, the long discourses recorded in Matthew and John, and numerous other teachings which are reported as having been spoken by the Lord. But these reported words of Jesus are so conspicuously at variance in the different gospels that the most devout reader may often search in vain to find the exact language of the great Teacher. Even the title put upon the cross, and the words of Jesus at the last supper, are reported differently by each of the evangelists. The whole cast of thought, tone and style of the Fourth Gospel are so notably different from the Synoptic gospels that numerous writers of the present time do not hesitate to say that it is a product of

Alexandrian thought rather than a trustworthy record of the sayings of Jesus.

Paul's writings, moreover, possess a marked originality in their presentation of the doctrines of grace, human depravity, justification by faith, atonement in Christ, and the eternal purposes of God, so that some modern teachers do not hesitate to say that the bulk of systematic theology, as enunciated in the later creeds of Christendom, is Paulinism rather than the doctrine of Christ. It is maintained that the Epistle of James teaches a doctrine of justification by works, directly opposite to Paul's doctrine of faith, and that the Epistle to the Hebrews defines faith as the substance of things hoped for, in a manner differing from both James and Paul. To all this add the statement of the ancient church-historian Eusebius that some in his day doubted the apostolic origin and authority of the epistles of James, Jude, 2 Peter, 2 and 3 John, and the book of Revelation.

I think this is a fair, and for our present purpose a sufficient, statement of the difficulties which are supposed to detract from the value and authority of the apostolic writings. Unquestionably these statements, maintained as positive propositions by not a few influential writers of the present time, have disturbed the faith of many. The devout Christian, upon hearing such apparent disparagement of books which he has ever regarded as sacred, and has been accustomed to call the word of God, is apt to feel that the foundations of his faith have been assailed, and that if such statements can be shown to be true, we can no longer appeal to evangelists and apostles as final authority.

How, now, shall we meet the difficulties of this problem, and what measure of authority are we to recognize in the apostolic interpretation of Christ? There are several methods of dealing with a question of this kind. One is to make uncompromising war upon the methods and results of scientific criticism. Another is to ignore the points at issue, and as far as possible withhold from the common people all knowledge of critical controversy. There are a few who appear to view the battle afar off, and if they find occasion to say anything, act the part of artful fencers by a dodging of real issues, avoiding the thrusts of the adversary, and " playing fast and loose." The only true method is that which proceeds on the principle of " proving all things, and holding fast that which is good." We must first of all insist upon a clear statement of the points at issue, and a clear definition of the terms we employ in argument. Half of our difficulties may arise from a misunderstanding of the real nature of the question before us, and a failure to define the terms we use.

Our first care in the discussion of the subject before us is to repudiate certain extravagant and untenable claims touching the nature of the writings of the apostles. What do we mean by authoritative apostolic interpretation of Jesus Christ? We certainly ought not to claim for the New Testament writers an authority or an infallibility which they do not claim for themselves. Are there not many pious people who treat the entire Bible as if it were God Himself? They have somehow acquired the notion that every line and word of it is the direct gift of the almighty Father. Nor is this notion confined to the ignorant and credulous alone. It has grown out of a sort of a priori reasoning about the Scriptures: " These holy oracles are a gift of God; therefore they must needs be perfect." In the seventeenth century the absolute perfection of the Bible in all its parts was insisted on as an article of the true faith, and it is affirmed in one of the Swiss confessions that the inspiration of the Hebrew Scriptures extends to " the consonants, the vowels and the vowel points." The purists of that period and as late as the eighteenth century insisted that the Greek of the New Testament was deficient in no element of perfection as compared with the classical Greek. All these extravagant claims for the literal perfection and infallibility of the Bible sprang from a priori assumptions of what those theologians imagined the written word of God ought to be.

Those controversies are obsolete and half forgotten now. But other issues of a similar character are kept alive by reason of similar assumptions as to the infallibility and inerrancy of the Scriptures. Other current ideas of a traditional character have so far possessed men's minds that when one affirms that the Psalms are not all from David, nor the book of Proverbs by Solomon; that Ecclesiastes is a pseudograph written in the name of Solomon long after the Babylonian exile, and the Pentateuch is not the composition of Moses—many hold up their hands in holy horror, and seem to think that such opinions are essentially at war with the teachings and the religion of Jesus Christ.

Would it not be better to inquire, What are the facts upon which these assertions are based? Some of them are so positive and simple that one marvels how sundry current notions about the authorship of the Psalms and Proverbs ever became so general. The Psalter contains psalms ascribed to Asaph, and Heman, and Solomon, and Moses; and the book of Proverbs contains at least seven different collections, one of which consists of " the words of Agur," and another of " the words of Lemuel, which his mother taught him." As for the authorship of the Pentateuch, one may naturally hesitate to affirm that Moses wrote the account of his own death and burial, or to believe that a meek and modest man would write what we read in Numbers 12 : 3:

" Now the man Moses was very meek above all the men which were upon the face of the earth.'' So extravagant are the notions of some people about the perfection of the Biblical writers that it is affirmed that Solomon knew all about the modern telephone, Daniel was acquainted with the rise and power of the American republic, and Paul was fully aware, when he wrote his epistles, that they were destined to become a part of the Bible, and a divine authority for the world. An earnest Christian and well-educated man assured me that his faith in God and the Bible was disturbed by the statement of a Biblical scholar in whom he had had much confidence that the Epistle to the Hebrews was not the work of Paul the apostle. Others are perplexed and confounded on being told that the doxology of the Lord's prayer, and the story of the angel that troubled the waters of Bethesda are rejected by the latest criticism, and are even omitted from the Revised Version of our English Bible. " I do not see,'' said a venerable man to me some time ago, " but that this modern criticism is going on to wipe out the old Bible altogether.''

Is it not evident, in view of these things, that our first duty in attempting to show the nature of apostolic authority is to disabuse the popular mind of sundry current vague and erroneous notions of what the Bible is? How can we faithfully and securely build the people up in the true knowledge of the Scriptures without laying again the foundation of elementary facts and principles?

We inquire in the second place what the New Testament writers claim for themselves as interpreters of Christ. What have the written gospels and the apostolic epistles to say or imply as to their nature and authority? Are the letters of James and John and Peter and Paul natural or supernatural, human or superhuman? If they embody a divine or supernatural element, wherein is that element to be discerned?

Let us begin with a brief study of the preface to the Gospel of Luke. " It seemed good to me,'' he writes Theophilus, " having traced the course of all things from the first, to write unto thee in orderly sequence.'' Here we find no claim of supernatural assistance. Like any other historian who aims to put on record a trustworthy narrative of facts, he also made diligent search to obtain the best accredited testimony of eyewitnesses. Why should we or any one make a claim of infallibility or of supernatural help for a writer who seems not only to make no pretension to such assistance, but rather implies that he has prepared his narrative in an ordinary human way?

If now we turn to Matthew and Mark, we find much of the same matter as that recorded by Luke, but no assertion whatever of careful inquiry after the certainty of the matters recorded, or of divine assistance in the work. John's Gospel, however, differs notably from the other three, and has produced the conviction that its language and style are those of its author rather than of Jesus, so that when it makes record of the sayings of our Lord, those sayings are not the very words of Christ, but His teachings as apprehended and translated by the evangelist. He claims to have written these things " that ye may believe that Jesus is the Christ, the Son of God; and that believing ye may have life in his name.'' In another place he says, " He that hath seen hath borne witness, and his witness is true: and he knoweth that he saith true, that ye also may believe '' (19:35). At the close of the gospel we find a postscript which seems to have been appended by the first readers of the gospel rather than the author himself: " This is the disciple who bears witness of these things, and wrote these things; and we know that his witness is true.'' But whether these words were written by the apostle John himself or some other hand, their utmost claim is that the record is altogether true and trustworthy.

The First Epistle of John begins with a statement so important and impressive that I quote it in full: " That which was from the beginning, that which we have heard, that which we have seen with our eyes, that which we beheld, and our hands handled, concerning the word of life (and the life was manifested, and we have seen, and bear witness, and declare unto you the life, the eternal life, which was with the Father, and was manifested unto us) that which we have seen and heard declare we unto you also, that ye also may have fellowship with us: yea, and our fellowship is with the Father, and with his Son Jesus Christ: and these things we write, that our joy may be fulfilled.'' This passage is the most positive kind of testimony of personal contact with Jesus Christ. The writer testifies that he has seen and heard and touched and carefully examined the one adorable Personage in whom the word of life was incarnate. The entire epistle is in keeping with this lofty claim, but at the same time the author admonishes his readers " not to believe every spirit, but prove the spirits, whether they are of God: because many false prophets are gone out into the world.'' We must accordingly in every case, reserve the right of conscientious judgment, and determine on rational grounds what is true and what is false.

The epistles of James and Peter make no claim of other or greater authority than that of " servants and apostles of Jesus Christ.'' They are of the nature of pastoral letters addrest to communities of Christians, and filled with godly counsel and instruction.

Turning now to the epistles of Paul, we

find him everywhere confessing himself an apostle and bond-servant of Jesus Christ. He has no message but that which he claims to have received by divine revelation, and he speaks and writes as one who is gifted with a notable measure of divine authority. Hear him as he writes to the Galatians: "Tho we, or an angel from heaven, should preach unto you any gospel other than that which we preached unto you, let him be anathema. For I make known to you, brethren, as touching the gospel which was preached by me, that it is not after man. For neither did I receive it from man, nor was I taught it, but through revelation of Jesus Christ. For I persecuted the church of God, and made havoc of it. But when it was the good pleasure of God to reveal his Son in me, that I might preach him among the Gentiles; immediately I conferred not with flesh and blood; neither went I up to Jerusalem to them who were apostles before me; but I went away into Arabia; and again I returned unto Damascus. Then after three years I went up to Jerusalem to become personally acquainted with Cephas, and tarried with him fifteen days. But other of the apostles saw I none, save James the Lord's brother. Now touching the things I write you, behold, before God, I do not lie." Here is a profession of divine illumination and authority which is too explicit to be misunderstood. His fifteen days of personal interview with Peter afforded a great opportunity to verify and supplement the current tradition of Jesus Christ, but he insists that his divine call and apostleship were not dependent upon any mortal man. And this fact is not to be set aside or weakened by his saying elsewhere that he was least of all the apostles, and unfit to be called an apostle, because of his persecuting the Church of God (1 Cor. 15 :9), and that Christ appeared unto him last of all as to the child untimely born. In the matter of illumination and teaching, his claim was to be "not a whit behind the very chiefest apostles." This positive claim of revelation and authority directly from God is, therefore, a conspicuous feature in the writings of Paul.

It has been repeatedly asserted in modern times that the theology of Paul has been a controlling element in Christian thought, and so far dominated the life and teaching of the churches that the real doctrines of Jesus have been overshadowed. The saying of the famous Frenchman has been repeated many times, and with apparent approval, that when Phebe the deaconess carried Paul's Epistle to the Romans from Cenchrea to Rome, she held, wrapt in the folds of her mantle, the theology of nineteen centuries. Well, it need not be disputed that the apostle of the Gentiles, as he himself affirms in that great epistle (11 : 13), "magnified his office." He glorified his ministry by an unquenchable zeal to preach the gospel of which he was not ashamed. But so far from misrepresenting or changing the gospel of the Lord, he determined to know nothing among the people he instructed save Jesus Christ and him crucified (1 Cor. 2 : 2). He is no independent and superior dogmatist, but the bond-slave of Jesus, and he utters his anathema against any and all who preach another gospel.

But while we thus make due note of the apostle's claims of divine authority, we ought also to observe that the larger portions of Paul's epistles are not of a doctrinal character. In fact he always writes more as a pastor than a theologian. His letters abound in personal greetings, in statements of personal experience, in words of rebuke and admonition. He speaks of baptizing several persons in Corinth, but he is uncertain whether he baptized any others than those named. He requests Timothy to bring him the cloak which he left at Troas, and also the books and parchments. He writes to Philemon in most affecting tenderness about his son Onesimus, whom he had begotten in his bonds. He tells the saints at Rome how often he had purposed coming unto them, and how much he longed to see them. On certain questions of Christian expediency he frankly said that he had no commandment of the Lord to offer, but he gave his judgment as one who had obtained mercy of the Lord to be faithful. In short, he is a man among men. The human element in his writings, as in his person and nature, is as conspicuous as we have seen it in the other apostles. He is a man compassed with infirmities, asking the churches to pray for him. He subjects his body to painful discipline, lest by any means, after having been a herald to others, he himself should be rejected.

Paul the apostle, therefore, like all the other apostles, was a man called and anointed of God for a most important ministry. He did not contravene, nor misinterpret and pervert the doctrines of his Lord. He accepted as certain all the great facts and truths which came as a blesséd inheritance to the churches from those "who from the beginning were eyewitnesses and ministers of the word." He had received his own special revelations from Jesus Christ, but in common with all the apostles he declared, "We preach not ourselves, but Christ Jesus as Lord, and ourselves as your servants for Jesus' sake. Seeing it is God who said, Light shall shine out of darkness, who shined in our hearts to give the light of the knowledge of the glory of God in the face of Jesus Christ" (2 Cor. 4 : 5, 6).

We are now prepared to deal directly with our main question: How far the apostolic interpretation of Christ is authoritative? And our answer is, in a word, just so far as it goes. That is, just so far as apostolic tradition and teaching, fairly interpreted, assume to be a faithful setting forth of the person, character, sayings and revelations of Jesus, they are to be accepted as altogether true and trustworthy. None of the apostles give us reason to believe that they followed cunningly devised fables, or had the slightest desire to misrepresent that which they declare to be the doctrine of their Lord. There is now no higher external authority to which we can appeal. If any one say, "Away from the apostles and back to Jesus," he has still to face the fact that we are dependent on the apostolic tradition for all we know of Jesus' words and works. The four gospels and the apostolic writings are so many reports, traditions and interpretations of Jesus Christ, and they are authoritative so far as they convey convictions of truth to our conscience and our heart.

The authority and value of the apostolic testimony may be seen in the light of the three following propositions: (1) The apostles of Jesus were evidently captivated and carried along in their work by the supreme conviction that their Lord was the true Messiah, the very Christ of God and the Savior of the world. (2) The Christ they preached is a character so perfect that it is impossible for us to believe that their interpretation of Him is a product of their own imagination or invention. (3) The variety in types of doctrine among the New Testament writers, so far from presenting incongruities and contradictions, discloses rather the manifold fulness and riches of the gospel of Jesus.

One of the most impressive facts in the apostolic writings is the supreme devotion to Christ which His first heralds everywhere evince. The love of Christ has over them an all-constraining power. They are ready to go to prison or to death for the sake of His name. He is the source of their authority; He is their wisdom, their strength, their hope, their joy. James calls himself "a servant of God and of the Lord Jesus Christ," and counts it all joy to fall into divers tests and proofs of faith that lead to the divine approval and the crown of life. Peter declares it blesséd to be reproached for the name of Christ, and so to be partakers of Christ's sufferings. John glories in the loving witness that "God gave unto us eternal life, and this life is in his Son. He that hath the Son hath the life; and he that hath not the Son of God hath not the life." Paul cries in an exultant tone, "I have been crucified with Christ: yet I live; and yet no longer I, but Christ liveth in me; and the life which I now live in the flesh I live in faith which is in the Son of God, who loved me, and gave himself up for me." The Acts of the Apostles records that "with great power gave the apostles their witness of the resurrection of the Lord Jesus,

and great grace was upon them all." One obvious purpose of the Gospel of Matthew is to show that Jesus of Nazareth is the Messiantic king, the son of David and son of Abraham, the hope of Israel and of the world. And apostolic heralds of this Son of God and Son of man went everywhere preaching the word. and turning the world upside down. Stephen was stoned to death; James the brother of John was killed with the sword; others were imprisoned and threatened. But they counted not their lives dear unto themselves, but took joyfully the spoiling of their goods, and were ready to undergo any sacrifice and peril for the name of Christ. Now I deem it important, first of all to emphasize these facts. For while it is very possible for religious enthusiasts to become fanatical, and even to go bravely to a martyr's death for a delusion which they believe to be the truth of God, the testimony and doctrine and work of the apostles are without a real parallel in history. The fall of Judaism and the beginning of the going forth of the gospel of Christ form a most conspicuous turning-point in the ages. That was the opening of a new era in the history and civilization of mankind. We insist that the first apostles, even if they were enthusiasts, were the most sane of men, the most removed from anything like fanatical delusion, and the most deliberate, rational and intelligent interpreters of God in history, that can be found in the religious annals of the world.

In the next place we aver that the Christ of the apostles is a character so perfect that it is impossible to believe their interpretation of Him is a product of their own imagination. The various theories which have been devised in modern times to explain away the miraculous element in the gospel narratives have not succeeded in satisfying the common sense of Christendom. I venture to say that the ingenious naturalistic explanations of Jesus' miracles by Paulus, the mythical hypothesis of Strauss, and the several modifications of these theories by other writers have never really satisfied the honest critical judgment of any large number of thoughtful minds. Whatever theory of the miracles one may adopt, there stands the peerless Christ of the apostles forever greater than His miracles. His commanding personality, as mirrored in the gospels, is inexplicable on any naturalistic principles. Let us look a moment at a few of the most striking facts which the apostles affirm of Jesus Christ:

(1) The authority of His teaching. He boldly assumed to supplement and even to set aside that which was said by them of old time. He made himself greater than Abraham, Moses, Solomon and the prophets. The officers of the chief priests and Pharisees testified that man never spoke like this man. He

scandalized the Jewish teachers of His time by His authoritative attitude towards the national institutions and customs. He spoke in parables which remain to this day jewels in the literature of the world. Surely no rabbi, sage, lawgiver or philosopher ever taught with such commanding authority as Jesus.

(2) His marvelous self-assumption and self-expression. He assumed power on earth to forgive sins, and declared that the Father had committed all judgment into His hands. What other teacher or prophet ever presumed to say, " I am the light of the world." " I am the bread of life." " If I be lifted up from the earth, I will draw all men unto me." " I am the resurrection and the life, and whosoever liveth and believeth in me shall never die." " Come unto me all ye that labor and are heavy laden, and I will give you rest "? Such assumptions as these sayings involve would be treated as the extravagance of insanity in any other person, but they seem perfectly natural in Jesus.

(3) His sinlessness. One of His most memorable sayings is: " Which of you convinceth me of sin?" The uniform apostolic testimony is that He was holy, harmless, undefiled, tempted in all points as we are, and yet without sin. He is called the righteous and holy one, a lamb without blemish and without spot. The entire portraiture of His spotless character as presented in the four gospels accords with these ideals. Although He assumed the power to forgive the sins of others, He nowhere acknowledges any need of repentance on His own part. He is the one unchallengeable sinless man of history.

(4) These facts become the more impressive and wonderful in view of the conditions of His obscure birth, His short period of public life, and His shameful crucifixion. A great genius may, indeed, rise to notoriety and honor in spite of poverty and reproach. He may triumph over strong and malicious opposition. But we have looked in vain for the record of another man, who, with all these conditions against him, in a career of three years, cut off by ignominious crucifixion, has commanded the thousandth part of the power which the name of Jesus holds in the world to-day. The late Philip Schaff is credited with the following words: " Jesus of Nazareth, without money and arms, conquered more millions than Alexander, Cæsar, Mohammed and Napoleon; without science and learning, He shed more light on things human and divine than all the philosophers and scholars combined; without the eloquence of schools, he spoke words of life such as were never spoken before or since, and produced effects which lie beyond the reach of orator or poet; without writing a single line, he has set more pens in motion, and furnished themes for more sermons, orations, discussions, learned volumes, works of art and sweet songs of praise than the whole army of great men of ancient and modern times. Born in a manger, and crucified as a malefactor, He now controls the destines of the civilized world, and rules a spiritual empire which embraces one third of the inhabitants of the globe."

Our third proposition is that the apostolic interpretation of Christ, so far from being disparaged or weakened in authority by reason of variety of types of doctrine found in the New Testament, is rather by that very fact exhibited in greater fulness and beauty than if it had come down to us in a stereotyped uniformity of statement.

I think our older theologians too generally failed to make the important distinction between unity of doctrine and uniformity of doctrine. They of course observed the varieties of thought and expression among the different Biblical writers, but their ideas of inspiration were generally so mechanical and unbending that any real progress of doctrine in the New Testament was rarely supposed to be possible. The human element in Scripture, with its conflicting tendencies, its various points of view and methods of statement, was often quite ignored. Luther's hasty rejection of the Epistle of James is a striking illustration of the assumption that uniformity of doctrine must needs be found in all authoritative Scripture. Many of the attempts to harmonize all the statements of the four gospels have proceeded on the supposition that real discrepancies in matters of detail would seriously weaken the authority and credibility of the evangelists. But the fact is that there is a remarkable lack of uniformity in the four gospels in their representation of the Christ. Take for example their several reports of our Lord's temptation. John makes no mention of it. Mark says that after the baptism " straightway the Spirit driveth him forth into the wilderness. And he was in the wilderness forty days tempted of Satan; and he was with the wild beasts; and the angels ministered unto him." Matthew adds to this simple record a kind of dramatic picture of three distinct temptations, and writes down particular conversations between Jesus and the devil. Luke repeats the story of the three temptations, but records them in a different order, and with noticeable verbal variations. For another example, take Matthew's report of the parable of the talents and Luke's report of the parable of the ten pounds. These parables obviously inculcate the same great lesson, but differ in the occasion of their utterance, and in their language and imagery. They may be regarded as varying reports of one and the same parable of Jesus, or as two independent parables uttered on different occasions. Add to these examples all we have previously referred to, as the remarkable diversities of statement and teaching among the evangelists and apostles, and we are compelled to acknowledge that there is a striking lack of uniformity in the apostolic interpretation of Christ.

But while we are careful to note the variety of types of teaching in the New Testament, we maintain that they nowhere involve essential contradictions, or misinterpret the real teaching of Christ. A fundamental unity of doctrine is apparent back of all this variety of types. We have not only gospels according to Matthew, Mark, Luke and John, but a Gospel according to Peter, and a Gospel according to James, and another according to the unknown author of the Epistle to the Hebrews. These are not opposing and irreconcilable gospels. Their differences are but the natural and normal idiosyncrasies of so many individuals, each captivated and controlled by the spirit of their one common Lord. Paul and Barnabas differed in judgment and separated from each other in their missionary work; Paul also resisted Peter to his face at Antioch, charged him with dissimulation and inconsistency so that he stood condemned. The Second Epistle of Peter declares that Paul's epistles contain some things hard to be understood. All the apostles were men of like passions with us, and incidental confusion of thought and errors may be found in their writings. But on all the great matters of fact and doctrine they are at one. There is substantial unity in their concept of Christ, but notable variety in the manner in which they preach the one living gospel of the common salvation. We should expect the same differences in result if Shakespeare, Milton, Tennyson and Browning had written on one great theme.

We shall obtain the true idea of this variety of interpretation when we come to look upon it as God's own method of revealing His eternal truth. Not rigid uniformity, but conspicuous variety of method is a leading feature of the entire Biblical revelation. God spoke in old time to the fathers in the prophets " by divers portions and in divers manners." And when in the fulness of time He spoke in His Son, He caused that the new word of life should go forth into all the world in just such variety of thought and form as appear in the word of the ancient prophets. The gospel of Peter is not the gospel of John, nor that of Paul. But these apostles all present the gospel of Christ as truly as Amos, and Isaiah, and Jeremiah spoke the word of God. Their differences of conception and expression show that the human is to be recognized in their writings as well as the divine. We possess the heavenly treasure in earthen vessels, and the treasure is none the less heavenly because it is thus enshrined. It is, I think, a mis-

chievous error, and can only lead to trouble and confusion in the Church of Christ, for over-zealous defenders of the faith to go about declaring that the vessel is not earthen. It will not add one whit to the honor and value of the vessel to insist on its being something which it is not. We possess the heavenly illumination, so to speak, in a great variety of human forms. Peter had his natural limitations, and his more exclusive ministry to the circumcision imposed a corresponding limitation upon his interpretation of the gospel of Jesus. Paul's wider mission to the Gentiles enlarged his range of vision. John's esoteric mode of thought, intensified by long contact with Alexandrian theosophy, produced the most profound and spiritual version of the teaching of Jesus. But old-fashioned James, " a servant of God and of the Lord Jesus Christ," keeps well within his Jewish environment, and insists that " the twelve tribes which are of the Dispersion " exhibit the practical godliness of visiting the fatherless and widows in their affliction, and fulfilling the royal law of love to one's neighbor. We gain nothing for the gospel of Christ by ignoring the human limitations of all these blesséd apostles. Even Paul, generally supposed to be the most catholic of them all, betrays in his epistles at times a measure of unconscious bondage to his Pharisaic training and to rabbinical habits of thought. Our contention is that the gospel of Jesus is none the less authoritative, but vastly the fuller and richer by reason of its transmission through many apostles and ministers of God.

We shall perhaps obtain our best ideal of apostolic authority from the words which Jesus Himself addrest to Simon Peter: " Thou art Peter, and upon this rock (petra) I will build my church; and the gates of Hell shall not prevail against it. I will give unto thee the keys of the kingdom of heaven; and whatsoever thou shalt bind on earth shall be bound in heaven; and whatsoever thou shalt loose on earth shall be loosed in heaven." I understand that what is here directly addrest to Peter because of his representative leadership among the twelve and the significance of his name (which is by interpretation a stone), is also by implication true of the other apostles. The same thing in substance was said to them on other occasions (see Matt. 18 : 18; 19 : 28; John 20 : 23). They were the anointed leaders, chosen by the Lord to lay the foundations of Christianity. Whatsoever they did in fulfilment of this holy office and ministry was ratified in heaven. And Peter, afterward writing to the Christians scattered abroad in Asia Minor, tells them that, coming unto Christ as to a living stone, they also as living stones are built up a spiritual house. Paul also teaches that the Christian Church is the " household of God, being built upon the foundation of the apostles and prophets, Christ Jesus Himself being the chief cornerstone.'' In beautiful harmony with this imagery we have the vision of the city of God, the new Jerusalem, coming down out of heaven and made ready as a bride adorned for her husband, '' and the wall of the city had twelve foundations, and on them twelve names of the twelve apostles of the Lamb.'' The visional symbolism is enhanced by the further statement that these foundations were adorned with all manner of precious stones, like the jasper, the sapphire and the amethyst. For the apostles of our Lord were privileged above all other men to look with unveiled face upon the Christ Himself. It was their unspeakable glory to have seen and heard and handled the very word of life as manifested in the personality of Jesus. They became transfigured by His adorable presence, and exalted by the power of His Spirit. Their personal contact with the Son of God, and their special commission from Him place them apart from and above all other men as interpreters of the Christ. And we thank God to-day that there were twelve apostles of Christ rather than one or two. They are like a crown of twelve stars upon the head of the Church during all her period of travail and persecution. They are the light of the world, for tho their luster is but a reflection of that greater light which lighteth every man coming into the world, it is a true and reliable reflection.

Years ago I made a journey to the capital of Denmark mainly for the purpose of looking on Thorwaldsen's great masterpiece of sculpture—the Christ and His apostles. There they stand, in '' the Church of our Lady,'' wonderful in their impressive silence. The figure of Christ is placed under a massive canopy back of the high altar, and the apostles, in two rows, stand facing each other down the long nave of the church. Each apostle bears some distinctive symbol. There is Peter with the keys, and John with book and pen in hand and an eagle at his feet. James holds a staff, and Andrew a cross and a roll. Judas Iscariot is not represented, but Paul is substituted for him, and stands at the right hand of Jesus, pointing upward with his right finger and resting his left hand on a sword. But even more impressive than the attitudes and symbols are the distinct expressions wrought upon those marble faces. In their presence I learned some new and deeper lessons of the Saviour. To me those twelve apostles symbolized twelve gospels of the Son of God, each one a separate ideal of His heavenly kingdom in the human soul. And since that day, time and again, I have found myself saying, If those mute forms of marble can speak so much to a passing traveler, how much more shall the living thoughts of apostolic teaching interpret Christ to men? Nay, how much more shall the eternal Spirit of the Christ Himself speak through His own apostles to the Church, and guide her into all the truth?

JOHN TILLOTSON

1630-1694

THE REASONABLENESS OF A RESURRECTION

BIOGRAPHICAL NOTE

JOHN TILLOTSON, archbishop of Canterbury, renowned as a preacher, was born at Sowerby, in Yorkshire, in 1630, the son of an ardent Independent. After graduating from Clare College, Cambridge, he began to preach in 1661, in connection with the Presbyterian wing of the Church of England. He, however, submitted to the Act of Uniformity the following year, and in 1663 was inducted into the rectory of Veddington, Suffolk. He was also appointed preacher to Lincoln's Inn, was made prebendary of Canterbury in 1670 and dean in 1672. William III regarded him with high favor, and he succeeded the nonjuring Sancroft in the arch-see of Canterbury. His sermons are characterized by stateliness, copiousness and lucidity, and were long looked upon as models of correct pulpit style. He died in 1694.

Why should it be thought a thing incredible with you that God should raise the dead?—Acts xxvi., 8.

THE resurrection of the dead is one of the great articles of the Christian faith; and yet so it hath happened that this great article of our religion hath been made one of the chief objections against it. There is nothing that Christianity hath been more upbraided for withal, both by the heathens of old and by the infidels of later times, than the impossibility of this article; so that it is a matter of great consideration and consequence to vindicate our religion in this particular. But if the thing be evidently impossible, then it is highly unreasonable to propose it to the belief of mankind.

I know that some, more devout than wise, and who, it is to be hoped, mean better than they understand, make nothing of impossibilities in matters of faith, and would fain persuade us that the more impossible anything is, for that very reason it is the fitter to be believed; and that it is an argument of a poor and low faith to believe only things that are possible; but a generous and heroical faith will swallow contradictions with as much ease as reason assents to the plainest and most evident propositions. Tertullian, in the heat of his zeal and eloquence, upon this point of the death and resurrection of Christ, lets fall a very odd passage, and which must have many grains of allowance to make it tolerable: "*prosus credible est* (saith he), *quia ineptum est; certum est, quia impossible*—it is therefore very credible, because it is foolish, and certain, because it is impossible"; "and this (says he) is *necessarium dedecus fidei,*" that is, "it is necessary the Christian faith should be thus disgraced by the belief of impossibilities and contradictions." I suppose he means that this article of the resurrection was not in itself the less credible because the heathen philosophers caviled at it as a thing impossible and contradictious, and endeavored to disgrace the Christian religion upon that account. For if he meant otherwise, that the thing was therefore credible because it was really and in itself foolish and impossible; this had been to recommend the Christian religion from the absurdity of the things to be believed; which would be a strange recommendation of any religion to the sober and reasonable part of mankind.

I know not what some men may find in themselves; but I must freely acknowledge that I could never yet attain to that bold and hardy degree of faith as to believe anything for this reason, because it was impossible: for this would be to believe a thing to be because I am sure it can not be. So that I am very far from being of his mind, that wanted not only more difficulties, but even impossibilities in the Christian religion, to exercise his faith upon.

Leaving to the Church of Rome that fool-hardiness of faith, to believe things to be true which at the same time their reason plainly tells them are impossible, I shall at this time endeavor to assert and vindicate this article of the resurrection from the pretended impossibility of it. And I hope, by God's assistance, to make the possibility of the thing so plain as to leave no considerable scruple about it in any free and unprejudiced mind. And this I shall do from these words of St. Paul, which are part of the defense which he made for himself before Festus and Agrippa, the substance whereof is this, that he had lived a blameless and inoffensive life among the Jews, in whose religion he had been bred up; that he was of the strictest sect of that religion, a Pharisee, which, in opposition to the Sadducees, maintained the resurrection of the dead and a future state of rewards and punishments in another life; and that for the hope of this he was called in question, and accused by the Jews. "And now I stand here, and am judged, for the hope of the promise made unto the fathers; unto which promise our twelve scribes, instantly serving God day and night, hope to come; for which hope's sake, King Agrippa, I am accused of the Jews." That is, he was accused for preaching that Jesus was risen from the dead, which is a particular instance of the general doctrine of the resurrection which was entertained by the greatest part of the Jews, and which to the natural reason of mankind (however the heathen in opposition to the Christian religion were prejudiced against it), hath nothing in it that is incredible. And for this he appeals to his judges, Festus and Agrippa: "why should it be thought a thing incredible with you that God should raise the dead?"

Which words being a question without an answer, imply in them these two propositions:

First, That it was thought by some a thing incredible that the dead should be raised. This is supposed in the question, as the foundation of it: for he who asks why a thing is so, supposeth it to be so.

Secondly, That this apprehension, that it is a thing incredible that God should raise the dead, is very unreasonable. For the question being left unanswered, implies its own answer, and is to be resolved into this affirmative, that there is no reason why they or any man else should think it a thing incredible that God should raise the dead.

I shall speak to these two propositions as briefly as I can; and then show what influence this doctrine of the resurrection ought to have upon our lives.

First, that it was thought by some a thing incredible that God should raise the dead. This St. Paul has reason to suppose, having from his own experience found men so averse from the entertaining of this doctrine. When he preached to the philosophers at Athens, and declared to them the resurrection of one Jesus from the dead, they were amazed at this new doctrine, and knew not what he meant by it. They said, "he seemeth to be a setter forth of strange gods, because he preached unto them Jesus and the resurrection." He had discoursed to them of the resurrection of one Jesus from the dead; but this business of the resurrection of one Jesus from the dead was a thing so remote from their apprehensions that they had no manner of conception of it; but understood him quite in another sense, as if he had declared to them two new deities, Jesus and Anastasis; as if he had brought a new god and a new goddess among them, Jesus and the Resurrection. And when he discoursed to them again more fully of this matter, it is said that, "when they heard of the resurrection of the dead, they mocked." And at the twenty-fourth verse of this twenty-sixth chapter, when he spake of the resurrection, Festus told him he would hear him no further, and that he looked upon him as a man beside himself, whom much learning had made mad. Festus looked upon this business of the resurrection as the wild speculation of a crazy head. And indeed the heathens generally, even those who believed the immortality of the soul, and another state after this life, looked upon the resurrection of the body as a thing impossible. Pliny, I remember, reckons it among those things which are impossible, and which God himself can not do; "*revocare defunctos*, to call back the dead to life"; and in the primitive times the heathen philosophers very much derided the Christians, upon account of this strange doctrine of the resurrection, looking always upon this article of their faith as a ridiculous and impossible assertion.

So easy it is for prejudice to blind the minds of men, and to represent everything to them which hath a great appearance of difficulty in it as impossible. But I shall endeavor to show that if the matter be thoroughly examined, there is no ground for any such apprehension.

I proceed therefore to the second proposition, namely, that this apprehension, that it is an incredible thing that God should raise the dead, is very unreasonable: "why should it be thought a thing incredible with you, that God should raise the dead?" That is, there is no sufficient reason why any man should look upon the resurrection of the dead as a thing impossible to the power of God; the only reason why they thought it incredible being because they judged it impossible; so that nothing can be vainer than for men to pretend to believe the resurrection; and yet at the same time to grant it to be a thing in reason impossible, because no man can believe that which he thinks to be incredible; and the impossibility of a thing is the best reason any man can have to think a thing incredible. So that the meaning of St. Paul's question is, "why should it be thought a thing impossible that God should raise the dead?"

To come then to the business: I shall endeavor to show that there is no sufficient reason why men should look upon the resurrection of the dead as a thing impossible to God. "Why should it be thought a thing incredible (that is, impossible) with you, that God should raise the dead?" which question implies in it these three things:

1. That it is above the power of nature to raise the. dead.

2. But it is not above the power of God to raise the dead.

3. That God should be able to do this is by no means incredible to natural reason.

First. This question implies that it is above the power of nature to raise the dead; and therefore the apostle puts the question very cautiously, "why should it be thought incredible that God should raise the dead?" by which he seems to grant that it is impossible to any natural power to raise the dead; which is granted on all hands.

Secondly. But this question does plainly imply that it is not above the power of God to do this. Tho the raising of the dead to life be a thing above the power of nature, yet why should it be thought incredible that God, who is the author of nature, should be able to do this? and indeed the apostle's putting the question in this manner takes away the main ground of the objection against the resurrection from the impossibility of the thing. For the main reason why it was looked upon as impossible was, because it was contrary to the course of nature that there should be any return from a perfect privation to a habit, and that a body perfectly dead should be restored to life again: but for all this no man that believes in a God who made the world, and this natural frame of things, but must think it very reasonable to believe that He can do things far above the power of anything that He hath made.

Thirdly. This question implies that it is not a thing incredible to natural reason that God should be able to raise the dead. I do not say that by natural light we can discover that God will raise the dead; for that, depending merely upon the will of God, can not other-

wise be certainly known than by divine revelation: but that God can do this is not at all incredible to natural reason. And this is sufficiently implied in the question which St. Paul asks, in which he appeals to Festus and Agrippa, neither of them Christians, "why should it be thought a thing incredible with you that God should raise the dead?" And why should he appeal to them concerning the credibility of this matter if it be a thing incredible to natural reason?

That it is not, I shall first endeavor to prove, and then to answer the chief objections against the possibility of it.

And I prove it thus: it is not incredible to natural reason that God made the world, and all the creatures in it; that mankind is His offspring; and that He gives us life and breath, and all things. This was acknowledged and firmly believed by many of the heathens. And indeed, whoever believes that the being of God may be known by natural light, must grant that it may be known by the natural light of reason that God made the world; because one of the chief arguments of the being of God is taken from those visible effects of wisdom, and power, and goodness, which we see in the frame of the world. Now He that can do the greater can undoubtedly do the less; He that made all things of nothing, can much more raise a body out of dust; He who at first gave life to so many inanimate beings, can easily restore that which is dead to life again. It is an excellent saying of one of the Jewish rabbis: He who made that which was not, to be, can certainly make that which was once, to be again. This hath the force of a demonstration; for no man that believes that God hath done the one, can make any doubt but that He can, if He please, do the other.

This seems to be so very clear, that they must be strong objections indeed, that can render it incredible.

There are but two that I know of, that are of any consideration, and I shall not be afraid to represent them .to you with their utmost advantage; and they are these:

First, against the resurrection in general: it is pretended impossible, after the bodies of men are resolved into dust, to re-collect all the dispersed parts and bring them together, to be united into one body.

The second is leveled against a resurrection in some particular instances, and pretends it to be impossible in some cases only—viz., when that which was the matter of one man's body does afterward become the matter of another man's body; in which case, say they, it is impossible that both these should, at the resurrection, each have his own body.

The difficulty of both these objections is perfectly avoided by those who hold that it is not necessary that our bodies at the resurrection should consist of the very same parts of matter that they did before. There being no such great difference between one parcel of dust and another; neither in respect of the power of God, which can easily command this parcel of dust as that to become a living body, and being united to a living soul to rise up and walk; so that the miracle of the resurrection will be all one in the main, whether our bodies be made of the very same matter they were before, or not; nor will there be any difference as to us; for whatever matter our bodies be made of, when they are once reunited to our souls, they will be then as much our own as if they had been made of the very same matter of which they consisted before. Besides that, the change which the resurrection will make in our bodies will be so great that we could not know them to be the same, tho they were so.

Now upon this supposition, which seems philosophical enough, the force of both these objections is wholly declined. But there is no need to fly to this refuge; and therefore I will take this article of the resurrection in the strictest sense for the raising of a body to life, consisting of the same individual matter that it did before; and in this sense, I think, it has generally been received by Christians, not without ground, from Scripture. I will only mention one text, which seems very strongly to imply it: "and the sea gave up the dead which were in it; and death and the grave delivered up the dead which were in them; and they were judged every man according to his works." Now why should the sea and the grave be said to deliver up their dead, if there were not a resurrection of the same body; for any dust formed into a living body and united to the soul, would serve the turn? We will therefore take it for granted that the very same body will be raised, and I doubt not, even in this sense, to vindicate the possibility of the resurrection from both these objections.

First, against the resurrection in general of the same body; it is pretended impossible, after the bodies of men are moldered into dust, and by infinite accidents have been scattered up and down the world, and have undergone a thousand changes, to re-collect and rally together the very same parts of which they consisted before. This the heathens used to object to the primitive Christians; for which reason they also used to burn the bodies of the martyrs, and to scatter their ashes in the air, to be blown about by the wind, in derision of their hopes of a resurrection.

I know not how strong malice might make this objection to appear; but surely in reason it is very weak; for it wholly depends upon a gross mistake of the nature of God and his providence, as if it did not extend to the smallest things; as if God did not know all things that He hath made, and had them not always in His view, and perfectly under His command; and as if it were a trouble and burden to infinite knowledge and power to understand and order the least things; whereas infinite knowledge and power can know and manage all things with as much ease as we can understand and order any one thing; so that this objection is grounded upon a low and false apprehension of the Divine nature, and is only fit for Epicurus and his herd, who fancied to themselves a sort of slothful and unthinking deities, whose happiness consisted in their laziness, and a privilege to do nothing.

I proceed therefore to the second objection, which is more close and pressing; and this is leveled against the resurrection in some particular instances. I will mention but two, by which all the rest may be measured and answered.

One is, of those who are drowned in the sea, and their bodies eaten up by fishes, and turned into their nourishment: and those fishes perhaps eaten afterward by men, and converted into the substance of their bodies.

The other is of the cannibals; some of whom, as credible relations tell us, have lived wholly or chiefly on the flesh of men; and consequently the whole, or the greater part of the substance of their bodies is made of the bodies of other men. In these and the like cases, wherein one man's body is supposed to be turned into the substance of another man's body, how should both these at the resurrection each recover his own body? So that this objection is like that of the Sadducees to our Savior, concerning a woman that had seven husbands: they ask, "whose wife of the seven shall she be at the resurrection?" So here, when several have had the same body, whose shall it be at the resurrection? and how shall they be supplied that have it not?

This is the objection; and in order to the answering of it, I shall premise these two things:

1. That the body of man is not a constant and permanent thing, always continuing in the same state, and consisting of the same matter; but a successive thing, which is continually spending and continually renewing itself, every day losing something of the matter which it had before, and gaining new; so that most men have new bodies oftener than they have new clothes; only with this difference, that we change our clothes commonly at once, but our bodies by degrees.

And this is undeniably certain from experience. For so much as our bodies grow, so much new matter is added to them, over and beside the repairing of what is continually spent; and after a man come to his full growth, so much of his food as every day turns into nourishment, so much of his yesterday's body is usually wasted, and carried off by insensible perspiration—that is, breathed out at the pores of his body; which, according to the static experiment of Sanctorius, a learned physician, who, for several years together, weighed himself exactly every day, is (as I remember) according to the proportion of five to eight of all that a man eats and drinks. Now, according to this proportion, every man must change his body several times in a year.

It is true indeed the more solid parts of the body, as the bones, do not change so often as the fluid and fleshy; but that they also do change is certain, because they grow, and whatever grows is nourished and spends, because otherwise it would not need to be repaired.

2. The body which a man hath at any time of his life is as much his own body as that which he hath at his death; so that if the very matter of his body which a man had at any time of his life be raised, it is as much his own and the same body as that which he had at his death, and commonly much more perfect; because they who die of lingering sickness or old age are usually mere skeletons when they die; so that there is no reason to suppose that the very matter of which our bodies consists at the time of our death shall be that which shall be raised, that being commonly the worst and most imperfect body of all the rest.

These two things being premised, the answer to this objection can not be difficult. For as to the more solid and firm parts of the body, as the skull and bones, it is not, I think, pretended that the cannibals eat them; and if they did, so much of the matter even of these solid parts wastes away in a few years, as being collected together would supply them many times over. And as for the fleshy and fluid parts, these are so very often changed and renewed that we can allow the cannibals to eat them all up, and to turn them all into nourishment, and yet no man need contend for want of a body of his own at the resurrection—viz., any of those bodies which he had ten or twenty years before; which are every whit as good and as much his own as that which was eaten.

Having thus shown that the resurrection is not a thing incredible to natural reason, I should now proceed to show the certainty of it from divine revelation. For as reason tells us it is not impossible, so the word of God hath assured us that it is certain. The texts of Scripture are so many and clear to this purpose, and so well known to all Christians, that I will produce none. I shall only tell you that as it is expressly revealed in the gospel, so our blest Savior, for the confirmation of our faith and the comfort and

encouragement of our hope, hath given us the experiment of it in his own resurrection, which is "the earnest and first-fruits of ours." So St. Paul tells us that "Christ is risen from the dead, and become the first-fruits of them that slept." And that Christ did really rise from the dead, we have as good evidence as for any ancient matter of fact which we do most firmly believe; and more and greater evidence than this the thing is not capable of; and because it is not, no reasonable man ought to require it.

Now what remains but to conclude this discourse with those practical inferences which our apostle makes from this doctrine of the resurrection; and I shall mention these two:

The first for our support and comfort under the infirmities and miseries of this mortal life.

The second for the encouragement of obedience and a good life.

1. For our comfort and support under the infirmities and miseries of this mortal state. The consideration of the glorious change of our bodies at the resurrection of the just can not but be a great comfort to us, under all bodily pain and sufferings.

One of the greatest burdens of human nature is the frailty and infirmity of our bodies, the necessities they are frequently prest withal, the manifold diseases they are liable to, and the dangers and terrors of death, to which they are continually subject and enslaved. But the time is coming, if we be careful to prepare ourselves for it, when we shall be clothed with other kind of bodies, free from all the miseries and inconveniences which flesh and blood is subject to. For "these vile bodies shall be changed, and fashioned like to the glorious body of the Son of God." When our bodies shall be raised to a new life, they shall become incorruptible; "for this corruptible shall put on incorruption, and this mortal must put on immortality; and then shall be brought to pass the saying that is written, death is swallowed up in victory." When this last enemy is conquered, there shall be no "fleshly lusts" nor brutish passions "to fight against the soul; no law in our members to war against the laws of our minds"; no disease to torment us; no danger of death to amaze and terrify us. Then all the passions and appetites of our outward man shall be subject to the reason of our minds, and our bodies shall partake of the immortality of our souls. It is but a very little while that our spirits shall be crusht and clogged with these heavy and sluggish bodies; at the resurrection they shall be refined from all dregs of corruption, and become spiritual, and incorruptible, and glorious, and every way suited to the activity and perfection of a glorified soul and the "spirits of just men made perfect."

2. For the encouragement of obedience and

a good life. Let the belief of this great article of our faith have the same influence upon us which St. Paul tells it had upon him. "I have hope toward God that there shall be a resurrection of the dead, both of the just and unjust; and herein do I exercise myself always to have a conscience void of offense toward God and toward man." The firm belief of a resurrection to another life should make every one of us very careful how we demean ourselves in this life, and afraid to do anything or to neglect anything that may defeat our hopes of a blest immortality, and expose us to the extreme and endless misery of body and soul in another life.

Particularly, it should be an argument to us, "to glorify God in our bodies and in our spirits"; and to use the members of the one and the faculties of the other as "instruments of righteousness unto holiness." We should reverence ourselves, and take heed not only how we defile our souls by sinful passions, but how we dishonor our bodies by sensual and brutish lusts; since God hath designed so great an honor and happiness for both at the resurrection.

So often as we think of a blest resurrection to eternal life, and the happy consequences of it, the thought of so glorious a reward should make us diligent and unwearied in the service of so good a Master and so great a Prince, who can and will prefer us to infinitely greater honors than any that are to be had in this world. This inference the apostle makes from the doctrine of the resurrection. "Therefore, my beloved brethren, be ye steadfast, unmovable, always abounding in the work of the Lord; for as much as ye know that your labor is not in vain in the Lord."

Nay, we may begin this blest state while we are upon earth, by "setting our hearts and affections upon the things that are above, and having our conversation in heaven, from whence also we look for a Savior, the Lord Jesus Christ, who shall change our vile bodies, that they may be fashioned like unto his glorious body, according to the working whereby he is able to subdue all things to himself."

"Now the God of peace, who brought again from the dead our Lord Jesus Christ, the great Shepherd of the sheep, through the blood of the everlasting covenant, make us perfect in every good work to do his will, working in us always that which is pleasing in his sight, through Jesus Christ, to whom be glory forever. Amen."

HENRY VAN DYKE

1852-1933

THE MEANING OF MANHOOD

BIOGRAPHICAL NOTE

HENRY VAN DYKE was born in Germantown, Pa., in 1852. He is a graduate of Princeton Theological Seminary and of Berlin University. From 1882 to 1900 he was pastor of the Brick Presbyterian Church, New York, since which time he has been Professor of English Literature in Princeton University. As a preacher he is generally regarded as a model, and as the author of many books he enjoys the highest literary reputation. Doctor Brastow calls him "the pulpit artist of his school," and adds: "In skilful handling of the manuscript, in clearness, force, chasteness, and felicity of diction, and in a directness and cogency of moral appeal which seemingly his later literary interests have not enhanced, he stands in the front line of American preachers."

How much, then, is a man better than a sheep!
—Matt. xii., 12.

ON the lips of Christ these noble words were an exclamation. He knew, as no one else has ever known, "what was in man." But to us who repeat them they often seem like a question. We are so ignorant of the deepest meaning of manhood, that we find ourselves at the point to ask in perplexity, how much, after all, is a man better than a sheep?

It is evident that the answer to this question must depend upon our general view of life. There are two very common ways of looking at existence that settle our judgment of the comparative value of a man and a sheep at once and inevitably.

Suppose, in the first place, that we take a materialistic view of life. Looking at the world from this standpoint, we shall see in it a great mass of matter, curiously regulated by laws which have results, but no purposes, and agitated into various modes of motion by a secret force whose origin is, and forever must be, unknown. Life, in man as in other animals, is but one form of this force. Rising through many subtle gradations, from the first tremor that passes through the gastric nerve of a jellyfish to the most delicate vibration of gray matter in the brain of a Plato or a Shakespeare, it is really the same from the beginning to the end—physical in its birth among the kindred forces of heat and electricity, physical in its death in cold ashes and dust. The only difference between man and other animals is a difference of degree. The ape takes his place in our ancestral tree, and the sheep becomes our distant cousin.

It is true that we have somewhat the advantage of these poor relations. We belong to the more fortunate branch of the family, and have entered upon an inheritance considerably enlarged by the extinction of collateral branches. But, after all, it is the same inheritance, and there is nothing in humanity which is not derived from and destined to our mother earth.

If, then, we accept this view of life, what answer can we give to the question, how much is a man better than a sheep? We must say: He is a little better, but not much. In some things he has the advantage. He lives longer, and has more powers of action and capacities of pleasure. He is more clever, and has succeeded in making the sheep subject to his domination. But the balance is not all on one side. The sheep has fewer pains as well as fewer pleasures, less care as well as less power. If it does not know how to make a coat, at least it succeeds in growing its own natural wool clothing, and that without taxation, Above all, the sheep is not troubled with any of those vain dreams of moral responsibility and future life which are the cause of such great and needless trouble to humanity. The flocks that fed in the pastures of Bethlehem got just as much physical happiness out of existence as the shepherd, David, who watched them, and, being natural agnostics, they were free from David's delusions in regard to religion. They could give all their attention to eating, drinking, and sleeping, which is the chief end of life. From the materialistic standpoint, a man may be a little better than a sheep, but not much.

Or suppose, in the second place, that we take the commercial view of life. We shall then say that all things must be measured by their money value, and that it is neither profitable nor necessary to inquire into their real nature or their essential worth. Men and sheep are worth what they will bring in the open market, and this depends upon the supply and demand. Sheep of a very rare breed have been sold for as much as five or six thousand dollars. But men of common stock, in places where men are plenty and cheap (as, for example, in Central Africa), may be purchased for the price of a rusty musket or a piece of cotton cloth. According to this principle, we must admit that the comparative value of a man and a sheep fluctuates with the market, and that there are times when the dumb animal is much the more valuable of the two.

This view, carried out to its logical conclusion, led to slavery, and put up men and sheep at auction on the same block, to be disposed of to the highest bidder. We have gotten rid of the logical conclusion. But have we gotten rid entirely of the premise on which it rested? Does not the commercial view of life still prevail in civilized society?

There is a certain friend of mine who often entertains me with an account of the banquets which he has attended. On one occasion he told me that two great railroads and the major part of all the sugar and oil in the United States sat down at the same table with three gold-mines and a line of steamships. "How much is that man worth?" asks the curious inquirer. "That man," answers some walking business directory, "is worth a million dollars; and the man sitting next to him is not worth a penny." What other answer can be given by one who judges everything

by a money standard? If wealth is really the measure of value, if the end of life is the production or the acquisition of riches, then humanity must take its place in the sliding scale of commodities. Its value is not fixt and certain. It depends upon accidents of trade. We must learn to look upon ourselves and our fellow men purely from a business point of view and to ask only: What can this man make? how much has that man made? how much can I get out of this man's labor? how much will that man pay for my services? Those little children that play in the squalid city streets—they are nothing to me or to the world; there are too many of them; they are worthless. Those long-fleeced, high-bred sheep that feed upon my pastures—they are among my most costly possessions; they will bring an enormous price; they are immensely valuable. How much is a man better than a sheep? What a foolish question! Sometimes the man is better; sometimes the sheep is better. It all depends upon the supply and demand.

Now these two views of life, the materialistic and the commercial, always have prevailed in the world. Men have held them consciously and unconsciously. At this very day there are some who profess them, and there are many who act upon them, altho they may not be willing to acknowledge them. They have been the parents of countless errors in philosophy and sociology; they have bred innumerable and loathsome vices and shames and cruelties and oppressions in the human race. It was to shatter and destroy these falsehoods, to sweep them away from the mind and heart of humanity, that Jesus came into the world. We can not receive His gospel in any sense, we can not begin to understand its scope and purpose, unless we fully, freely, and sincerely accept His great revelation of the true meaning and value of man as man.

We say this was His revelation. Undoubtedly it is true that Christ came to reveal God to man. But undoubtedly it is just as true that He came to reveal man to himself. He called Himself the Son of God, but He called Himself also the Son of man. His nature was truly divine, but His nature was no less truly human. He became man. And what is the meaning of that lowly birth, in the most helpless form of infancy, if it be not to teach us that humanity is so related to Deity that it is capable of receiving and embodying God Himself? He died for man. And what is the meaning of that sacrifice, if it be not to teach us that God counts no price too great to pay for the redemption of the human soul? This gospel of our Lord and Savior Jesus Christ contains the highest, grandest, most ennobling doctrine of humanity that ever has been proclaimed on earth. It is the only certain cure for low and debasing views of life. It is the only doctrine from which we can learn to think of ourselves and our fellow men as we ought to think. I ask you to consider for a little while the teachings of Jesus Christ in regard to what it means to be a man.

Suppose, then, that we come to Him with this question: How much is a man better than a sheep? He will tell us that a man is infinitely better, because he is the child of God, because he is capable of fellowship with God, and because he is made for an immortal life. And this threefold answer will shine out for us not only in the words, but also in the deeds, and above all in the death, of the Son of God and the Son of man.

1. Think, first of all, of the meaning of manhood in the light of the truth that man is the offspring and likeness of God. This was not a new doctrine first proclaimed by Christ. It was clearly taught in the magnificent imagery of the book of Genesis. The chief design of that great picture of the beginnings is to show that a personal Creator is the source and author of all things that are made. But next to that, and of equal importance, is the design to show that man is incalculably superior to all the other works of God—that the distance between him and the lower animals is not a difference in degree, but a difference in kind. Yes, the difference is so great that we must use a new word to describe the origin of humanity, and if we speak of the stars and the earth, the trees and the flowers, the fishes, the birds, and the beasts, as "the works" of God, when man appears we must find a nobler name and say, "This is more than God's work; he is God's child."

Our human consciousness confirms this testimony and answers to it. We know that there is something in us which raises us infinitely above the things that we see and hear and touch, and the creatures that appear to spend their brief life in the automatic workings of sense and instinct. These powers of reason and affection and conscience, and above all this wonderful power of free will, the faculty of swift, sovereign, voluntary choice, belong to a higher being. We say not to corruption, "Thou art my father," nor to the worm, "Thou art my mother"; but to God, "Thou art my father," and to the great Spirit, "In thee was my life born."

> Not only cunning casts in clay:
> Let science prove we are, and then
> What matters science unto men,
> At least to me? I would not stay.
>
> Let him, the wiser man who springs
> Hereafter, up from childhood shape
> His action like the greater ape;
> But I was born to other things.

Frail as our physical existence may be, in some respects the most frail, the most defenseless among animals, we are yet conscious of something that lifts us up and makes us supreme. "Man," says Pascal, "is but a reed, the feeblest thing in nature; but he is a reed that thinks. It needs not that the universe arm itself to crush him. An exhalation, a drop of water, suffice to destroy him. But were the universe to crush him, man is yet nobler than the universe; for he knows that he dies, and the universe, even in prevailing against him, knows not its power."

Now the beauty and strength of Christ's doctrine of man lie, not in the fact that He was at pains to explain and defend and justify this view of human nature, but in the fact that He assumed it with an unshaken conviction of its truth, and acted upon it always and everywhere. He spoke to man, not as the product of nature, but as the child of God. He took it for granted that we are different from plants and animals, and that we are conscious of the difference. "Consider the lilies," He says to us; "the lilies can not consider themselves: they know not what they are, nor what their life means; but you know, and you can draw the lesson of their lower beauty into your higher life. Regard the birds of the air; they are dumb and unconscious dependents upon the divine bounty, but you are conscious objects of the divine care. Are you not of more value than many sparrows?" Through all His words we feel the thrilling power of this high doctrine of humanity. He is always appealing to reason, to conscience, to the power of choice between good and evil, to the noble and godlike faculties in man.

And now think for a moment of the fact that His life was voluntarily, and of set purpose, spent among the poorest and humblest of mankind. Remember that He spoke, not to philosophers and scholars, but to peasants and fishermen and the little children of the world. What did He mean by that? Surely it was to teach us that this doctrine of the meaning of manhood applies to man as man. It is not based upon considerations of wealth or learning or culture or eloquence. Those are the things of which the world takes account, and without which it refuses to pay any attention to us. A mere man, in the eyes of the world, is a nobody. But Christ comes to humanity in its poverty, in its ignorance, stript of all outward signs of power, destitute of all save that which belongs in common to mankind; to this lowly child, this very beggar-maid of human nature, comes the king, and speaks to her as a princess in disguise, and lifts her up and sets a crown upon her head. I ask you if this simple fact ought not to teach us how much a man is better than a sheep.

2. But Christ reveals to us another and a still higher element of the meaning of manhood by speaking to us as beings who are

capable of holding communion with God and reflecting the divine holiness in our hearts and lives. And here also His doctrine gains clearness and force when we bring it into close connection with His conduct. I suppose that there are few of us who would not be ready to admit at once that there are some men and women who have high spiritual capacities. For them, we say, religion is a possible thing. They can attain to the knowledge of God and fellowship with Him. They can pray, and sing praises, and do holy work. It is easy for them to be good. They are born good. They are saints by nature. But for the great mass of the human race this is out of the question, absurd, impossible. They must dwell in ignorance, in wickedness, in impiety.

But to all this Christ says, "No!" No, to our theory of perfection for the few. No, to our theory of hopeless degradation for the many. He takes His way straight to the outcasts of the world, the publicans and the harlots and sinners, and to them He speaks of the mercy and the love of God and the beauty of the heavenly life; not to cast them into black despair, not because it was impossible for them to be good and to find God, but because it was divinely possible. God was waiting for them, and something in them was waiting for God. They were lost. But surely they never could have been lost unless they had first of all belonged to God, and this made it possible for them to be found again. They were prodigals. But surely the prodigal is also a child, and there is a place for him in the Father's house. He may dwell among the swine, but he is not one of them. He is capable of remembering his Father's love. He is capable of answering his Father's embrace. He is capable of dwelling in his Father's house in filial love and obedience.

This is the doctrine of Christ in regard to fallen and disordered and guilty human nature. It is fallen, it is disordered, it is guilty; but the capacity of reconciliation, of holiness, of love to God, still dwells in it, and may be quickened into a new life. That is God's work, but God Himself could not do it if man were not capable of it.

Do you remember the story of the portrait of Dante which is painted upon the walls of Bargello, at Florence? For many years it was supposed that the picture had utterly perished. Men had heard of it, but no one living had seen it. But presently came an artist who was determined to find it again. He went into the place where tradition said that it had been painted. The room was used as a storehouse for lumber and straw. The walls were covered with dirty whitewash. He had the heaps of rubbish carried away. Patiently and carefully he removed the whitewash from the wall. Lines and colors long hidden began to appear; and at last the grave,

lofty, noble face of the poet looked out again upon the world of light.

"That was wonderful," you say, "that was beautiful!" Not half so wonderful as the work which Christ came to do in the heart of man—to restore the forgotten likeness of God and bring the divine image to the light. He comes to us with the knowledge that God's image is there, tho concealed; He touches us with the faith that the likeness can be restored. To have upon our hearts the impress of the divine nature, to know that there is no human being in whom that treasure is not hidden and from whose stained and dusty soul Christ can not bring out that reflection of God's face—that, indeed, is to know the meaning of manhood, and to be sure that a man is better than a sheep!

3. There is yet one more element in Christ's teaching in regard to the meaning of manhood, and that is His doctrine of immortality. This truth springs inevitably out of His teaching in regard to the origin and capacity of human nature. A being formed in the divine image, a being capable of reflecting the divine holiness, is a being so lofty that he must have also the capacity of entering into a life which is spiritual and eternal, and which leads onward to perfection. All that Christ teaches about man, all that Christ offers to do for man, opens before him a vast and boundless future.

The idea of immortality runs through everything that Jesus says and does. Never for a moment does He speak to man as a creature who is bound to this present world. Never for a moment does He forget, or suffer us to forget, that our largest and most precious treasures may be laid up in the world to come. He would arouse our souls to perceive and contemplate the immense issues of life.

The perils that beset us here through sin are not brief and momentary dangers, possibilities of disgrace in the eyes of men, of suffering such limited pain as our bodies can endure in the disintegrating process of disease, of dying a temporal death, which at the worst can only cause us a few hours of anguish. A man might bear these things, and take the risk of this world's shame and sickness and death, for the sake of some darling sin. But the truth that flashes on us like lightning from the word of Christ is that the consequence of sin is the peril of losing our immortality. "Fear not them which kill the body," said he, "but are not able to kill the soul; but rather fear him which is able to destroy both soul and body in hell."

On the other hand, the opportunities that come to us here through the grace of God are not merely opportunities of temporal peace and happiness. They are chances of securing endless and immeasurable felicity, wealth that can never be counted or lost, peace that the world can neither give nor take away. We must understand that now the kingdom of God has come near unto us. It is a time when the doors of heaven are open. We may gain an inheritance incorruptible, and undefiled, and that fadeth not away. We may lay hold not only on a present joy of holiness, but on an everlasting life with God.

It is thus that Christ looks upon the children of men: not as herds of dumb, driven cattle, but as living souls moving onward to eternity. It is thus that He dies for men: not to deliver them from brief sorrows, but to save them from final loss and to bring them into bliss that knows no end. It is thus that He speaks to us, in solemn words before which our dreams of earthly pleasure and power and fame and wealth are dissipated like unsubstantial vapors: "What shall it profit a man if he gain the whole world and lose his own soul? Or what shall a man give in exchange for his soul?"

There never was a time in which Christ's doctrine of the meaning of manhood was more needed than it is to-day. There is no truth more important and necessary for us to take into our hearts, and hold fast, and carry out in our lives. For here we stand in an age when the very throng and pressure and superfluity of human life lead us to set a low estimate upon its value. The air we breathe is heavy with materialism and commercialism. The lowest and most debasing views of human nature are freely proclaimed and unconsciously accepted. There is no escape, no safety for us, save in coming back to Christ and learning from Him that man is the child of God, made in the divine image, capable of the divine fellowship, and destined to an immortal life. I want to tell you just three of the practical reasons why we must learn this.

(1) We need to learn it in order to understand the real meaning, and guilt, and danger, and hatefulness of sin.

Men are telling us nowadays that there is no such thing as sin. It is a dream, a delusion. It must be left out of account. All the evils in the world are natural and inevitable. They are simply the secretions of human nature. There is no more shame or guilt connected with them than with the malaria of the swamp or the poison of the nightshade.

But Christ tells us that sin is real, and that it is the enemy, the curse, the destroyer of mankind. It is not a part of man as God made him; it is a part of man as he has unmade and degraded himself. It is the marring of the divine image, the ruin of the glorious temple, the self-mutilation and suicide of the immortal soul. It is sin that casts man down into the mire. It is sin that drags him from the fellowship of God into the company of beasts. It is sin that leads him into the far country of famine, and leaves him among the swine, and makes him fain to fill his belly with the husks that the swine do eat. Therefore we must hate sin, and fear it, and abhor it, always and everywhere. When we look into our own heart and find sin there, we must humble ourselves before God and repent in sackcloth and ashes. Every sin that whispers in our heart is an echo of the world's despair and misery. Every selfish desire that lies in our soul is a seed of that which has brought forth strife, and cruelty, and murder, and horrible torture, and bloody war among the children of men. Every lustful thought that defiles our imagination is an image of that which has begotten loathsome vices and crawling shames throughout the world. My brother-men, God hates sin because it ruins man. And when we know what that means, when we feel that same poison of evil within us, we must hate sin as He does, and bow in penitence before Him, crying, "God, be merciful to me a sinner."

(2) We need to learn Christ's doctrine of the meaning of manhood in order to help us to love our fellow men.

This is a thing that is easy to profess, but hard, bitterly hard, to do. The faults and follies of human nature are apparent. The unlovely and contemptible and offensive qualities of many people thrust themselves sharply upon our notice and repel us. We are tempted to shrink back, wounded and disappointed, and to relapse into a life that is governed by disgusts. If we dwell in the atmosphere of a Christless world, if we read only those newspapers which chronicle the crimes and meannesses of men, or those realistic novels which deal with the secret vices and corruptions of humanity, and fill our souls with the unspoken conviction that virtue is an old-fashioned dream, and that there is no man good, no woman pure, I do not see how we can help despising and hating mankind. Who shall deliver us from this spirit of bitterness? Who shall lead us out of this heavy, fetid air of the lazar-house and the morgue?

None but Christ. If we will go with Him, He will teach us not to hate our fellow men for what they are, but to love them for what they may become. He will teach us to look, not for the evil which is manifest, but for the good which is hidden. He will teach us not to despair, but to hope, even for the most degraded of mankind. And so, perchance, as we keep company with Him, we shall learn the secret of that divine charity which fills the heart with peace and joy and quiet strength. We shall learn to do good unto all men as we have opportunity, not for the sake of gratitude or reward, but because they are the children of our Father and the brethren of our Savior. We shall learn the meaning of that blest death on Calvary, and be willing to give ourselves as a sacrifice for others, knowing that he that turneth a sinner from the error of his ways shall save a soul from death and cover a multitude of sins.

(3) Finally, we need to accept and believe Christ's doctrine of the meaning of manhood in order that it may lead us personally to God and a higher life.

You are infinitely better and more precious than the dumb beasts. You know it, you feel it; you are conscious that you belong to another world. And yet it may be that there are times when you forget it and live as if there was no God, no soul, no future life. Your ambitions are fixt upon the wealth that corrodes, the fame that fades. Your desires are toward the pleasures that pall upon the senses.

You are bartering immortal treasure for the things which perish in the using. You are ignoring and despising the high meaning of your manhood. Who shall remind you of it, who shall bring you back to yourself, who shall lift you up to the level of your true being, unless it be the Teacher who spake as never man spake, the Master who brought life and immortality to light.

Come, then, to Christ, who can alone save you from the sin that defiles and destroys your manhood. Come, then, to Christ, who alone can make you good men and true, living in the power of an endless life. Come, then, to Christ, that you may have fellowship with Him and realize all it means to be a man.

CHARLES J. VAUGHAN

1816-1897

GOD CALLING TO MAN

And the Lord God called unto Adam, and said unto him, Where art thou?—Genesis iii., 9.

"I WISH," said a great man of our day, "that some one would preach under the dome of St. Paul's, on the text, 'Where art thou, Adam?'" A noble subject, my brethren, when we think of it! But who is equal to the task of handling it? The work of God is quick and powerful—may it be so now, He Himself using it, and prospering it in the thing whereto He sent it.

I shall ask you to look very closely into the text itself. I need not tell anyone whence it comes; from the midst of that awful story which tells us of the first sin, and of its immediate consequences. That same story is in substance acted over and over again in every marked sin that is ever done by any man: the same mode of temptation; first inward question, "Yea, hath God said? is this thing which I wish to do really forbidden?" and then the thought of the hardship; "God doth know that this which He has forbidden is something desirable, something delightful; it is hard that it should be denied me;" and then the growing confidence, "I shall not surely die for it;" and then the last review of all the advantages, "good for food—pleasant to the eyes—to be desired to make me wise, or to make me happy, or to make me independent;" and then the act itself—the taking and eating; and then the sense of leanness entering into the very soul. But that is not all which sin brings after it. The next tells us of a summons, and after the context of an arraigning, and an examination, and at first a self-excusing, and then of a conviction, and a silencing, and a judgment: only one little word of comfort, one little streak of light, amidst all the sorrow, and all the curse, and all the gloom.

But I intend to sever the text now somewhat from its context, and to look into it, with you, by itself alone. "The Lord God called unto Adam, and said unto him, Where art thou?" There is the speaker—God, the Lord God. There is the person spoken to—Adam, the first man; Adam, from whom we all sprang; the father, and the likeness, and the representative of us all. There is the nature of the address—a call, a summons, decisive, authoritative, majestic. There are, at last, the words uttered—few and plain, yet, when looked into, big with meaning—"Where art thou?" And we shall not end without appealing to all of you, to each of you separately, to answer that question; to answer it truly, as we shall all have to answer it one day.

Now I shall not occupy your time, or use many words, about the speaker. There are those who profess to doubt the being of God; and there are those, on the other hand, who profess to prove it. I shall not suspect you of the one, and I shall not endeavor to do the other. I am quite sure that in your inmost hearts you do not doubt His being; and I am quite certain that, if you do, I cannot prove it to you. The being of God is not a matter of argument, it is a matter of instinct. The doubt or denial of it may pass muster with scoffing men in robust health and prosperous circumstances; but nine out of ten of those same men, finding themselves in sudden danger, by land or sea, from accident or disease, will be heard praying: they may conceal it, they may disown it, they may be ashamed of it afterwards—but they did it: and that prayer was a witness, an unimpeachable witness, that down in the depths of their heart there was a belief in God all the time; in their works alike and in their words they deny Him, but in their inmost souls, like the very spirits of evil, they believe and tremble. God, then, speaks here. I tell you not who He is: you know it; you know that there is such a person, your creator, your ruler, your judge: happy if you know also that He is the God and Father of our Lord Jesus Christ!

Now, to whom does He here speak? I will say two things of His call as here described: First, that it is an individual call; and, secondly, that it is a universal call. We try to make God's call a vague one. It is for some one, no doubt; but every natural man tries to put it away from himself. In hearing a sermon, everyone thinks how suitable this reproof or that warning is to his neighbor; he goes away to wish that such a person had heard it, to hope that such a person listened to it; but the person who thus hopes, and probably, too, the person thus hoped about, never thought of taking it home—never said to himself, tho he was but too ready to say to another, "Thou art the man." Nevertheless, God's call is an individual one. The only use of it is to be so. O that we could hear it in that spirit! O that we could practise ourselves in so hearing it! Where art thou? not, where is he? still less, generally, where are they? Read the Bible thus, my brethren, as written for you, for your learning, for your reproof, for your comfort—yours individually and personally—and you will never need it in vain.

But this individual call is also universal. Let us not flatter ourselves that we are more to God than others are: it is a very common, tho a well-disguised notion. We think that our souls are more important than any others; and that is the least form of the error:

but we go on to think our faults are more excusable, our sins more venial, than those of others; we go on to think that God will spare us when He does not spare others; we go on to think that our virtues are greater, our self-denials more meritorious, than those of others; and by this time we have got farther away from the truth and the gospel, than the poor self-condemning sinner who feels, and denies it not, that he is yet in the gall of bitterness, in the very bond of iniquity.

The call of God, like the care of God, is universal. It is to the race. It is to His creatures. Hear the word—"The Lord God called unto Adam, and said unto him." If it had been, God called to Abraham, or to Moses, or to David, there would have been some particularity, perhaps some limitation, in the summons; but none of us can say he is not included when Adam is spoken to; he is, indeed, the father of us all: of him we all come. What God says to him, He certainly says to us—to us all, as to each of us.

But we ask, perhaps, thirdly: How does God call to us? I will say, in three ways. He calls within—in conscience. Can you tell me what that thing is in each of us which seems at once so intimate with us, yet so independent of us, that it knows everything we do, or say, or even think, and yet sits in judgment upon us for everything? Is it not a strange thing? We should expect that the whole man would move together; that, if we did a thing, if we said a thing, if we thought a thing, we should go along with it, we should approve that thing: but is it so? No; we carry about within us a whole machinery of judicature; a witness, a jury, a judge, yes, an executioner, too; and, strange to say, it is in early life that the process is most perceptible, just while we are most ignorant, least reflecting, least logical in our judgments. It is the work of many men through life to stifle the voice within, and at last they almost succeed: but do not tell me that you have no such voice within—certainly you will not say that you never had it; and I will tell you what that voice is, or was. It was the voice of the Lord God within, calling to Adam, and saying, "Where art thou?"

He calls also without—in providence. I really know not whether this be not the most persuasive of all His modes of calling to us; certainly it is the most authoritative of all. Conscience may be stifled, but providence grasps us very tightly—we cannot escape from it. Tell me, who caused you to be born where and what you were? Who settled that you should be born in this country and not in that? Who decided that you were to have poor parents or rich, Christian parents or unChristian? Who has managed your circumstances for you since you had a being? Who gave you, who has continued to give you, your vigor of mind and body, your power of enjoyment, or your experience of kindness, or your principles of judgment, or your instincts of affection? Who took away from you that friend for whom you are now mourning—that parent, that brother, that sister, that wife, that child? Yes, we may forget it, or we may fret under it, but in the hands of a providence we all are; we are utterly powerless in that grasp: and whether we will believe it or no, that power is a voice too—a call from God without, even as conscience is His voice and His call within.

Once more, God calls from above also—in revelation. My friend, believest thou the Scriptures? I know that thou believest. Your presence here seems to say that you do. And yet in this multitude how many must there be who do not in their hearts believe! Let me rather say, who do not in their lives believe; for in your hearts I think you do: sure I am that there are some parts of the Bible which you cannot read and disbelieve; of course you may leave them unread, that is always possible—easier than to read them—but I do not think you can read the fifty-third chapter of Isaiah, for example, in the Old Testament, and I do not think you can read one chapter of St. John's Gospel in the New Testament, and shut the book, saying, "There is nothing in it." I suspect that is why we so often leave the Bible unread—just because we believe it; we feel, when we do read it, that it is God's voice, and we do not want to hear that voice. The Bible is more its own witness than we like oftentimes to admit.

> "Who that has felt its glance of dread
>   Thrill through his heart's remotest cells,
> About his path, about his bed,
>   Can doubt what spirit in it dwells?"

God speaks; and speaks to us—to each of us and to all of us; and speaks, chiefly in three ways—in conscience, in providence, in revelation: and now, fourthly, what is His call? How is it here briefly exprest? It might have been put, it is put in the Bible, in different forms—but how is it here exprest? "The Lord called unto Adam, and said unto him, Where art thou?" This is a call, first, to attention. As tho God had said, Listen to Me. That is the first step in all religion. What we want first is a spirit of attention. It is the great art of our enemy to keep our thoughts off religion. That is the meaning of the overwhelming cares of life. The devil would occupy our whole time and thoughts with something which is not, and has nothing (as he persuades us) to do with God. That is the meaning of the excessive amusements of life. The cares of life are not enough to engross the attention of all men always; and therefore the enemy provides something which shall al-

ternate with them for some men, and take the place of them for others. It is this art which God, in His mercy, in His long-suffering, in His desire that we should not perish, has to counteract by His divine skill. He takes a man aside now and then, from time to time—blest be His name for it!—and makes him listen. He interposes by some chastisement, some sickness, some bereavement, and constrains him to hearken to what He, the Lord God, has to say concerning him and to him. This is the first point gained. Behold, he listens! better still, Behold, he prayeth! It is a call, next, to the recognition of God's being, and of our responsibility to Him. "Where art thou?" It is as if He had said, I am, and thou art Mine. As if He has said, I have a right to know about thee, and thou canst not evade Me. As if He had said, I am about, now, to enter into judgment with thee: give an account of thy stewardship. Yes, my brethren, it is an awful moment, when a man first becomes distinctly conscious that God is, and is something to him. He may have talked of God before: he may have fancied that he knew all about Him: he may even have prayed before, and confest himself before, and asked grace and help before: but now, for the first time, he sees how much more there is in all this than he has yet dreamed of; and the only words which he can find at all to express his new feeling, are those of the patriarch of old —"I have heard of thee by the hearing of the ear, but now mine eye seeth thee: wherefore I abhor myself, and repent in dust and ashes."

It is a call, once more, and yet more particularly, to reflect upon our place or our position. I know not how else to express the force of the inquiry, "Where art thou?" It may be read literally—of place. May not some one of those here assembled have been, ere now, perhaps often, perhaps quite recently, in some place in which the question, "Where art thou?" would have had a startling and condemning sound?—some place where he was sinning? some place where he had gone to sin? some place where he would not for the world have been seen by any human eye, and where he gladly forgot that there was yet one eye which did see him? Oh, if God stood this night upon earth, and called aloud to the "Adam" of this generation—to the men and women who form now the sum of the living human creation; if He should call them suddenly from the east and from the west to avow exactly where they were, and to come forth from that place as they were, without an instant allowed them to cover up and disguise themselves; oh, what a revelation would it be of action and of character! Oh, who might abide the scrutiny of that question? Oh, who could stand when that inquirer appeared! But, even if the literal local question could be well answered, there would remain yet another behind applicable to all men. "Where art thou?" is an inquiry as to position no less than place. It says, "What is thy present place as a man with a soul, as an immortal being? What is thy present standing, thy present state? Art thou safe? Art thou happy? Art thou useful? Art thou doing the work I gave thee to do? Is it well with thee in the present? Is it well with thee in the future? Say not, I can not answer, I know not. I have taught thee how to judge of thyself; now therefore advise, and see what answer thou wilt return to Him that made thee."

My brethren, I propose, in the last place, that we all answer this question. It is a very serious thing to do; and it is what no man can do for his brother. Each one of us has one secret place, one sanctuary within the veil, into which, not even once a year, not even in the character of a high priest, can earthly foot ever enter. Yet in that secret place shines forth the light of God's presence; a light never put out altogether in any man, so far at least as its disclosing and revealing character is concerned, until sin and perverseness have done their perfect work, and the awful words are at length fulfilled, "If the light that is in thee be darkness, how great is that darkness!" At present, we will humbly hope, that this last ruin has not been wrought in any one who hears me. And if not, I repeat it, we can all, if we will, answer God's question, when He calls to each of us, as He does this night, and says, "Where art thou?"

One of us, perhaps, answers, if he speaks truly, I am wandering. I have left my Father's home; I took my portion of His goods, and carried them away into a far country. Yes, He was very generous to me; He grudged me nothing; life and health, food and clothing, even success in the world, even human friendship and human love, He gave me all these, and upbraided not: He warned me that I should be sorry one day if I left Him; He cautioned me against the perils of my way; He told me that I should not find happiness; He bade me, if I wished for that, to stay; He bade me, if I should ever be sorry that I had gone, to arise instantly and return. My heart was young then, and I thought I knew best; I left Him, with little feeling, with much expectation; His last look was one of regretful love that I left Him and I am a wanderer still. Sometimes I have arisen to go to my Father, but I went not: I was ashamed, I was afraid, I thought I was too sinful, I felt myself unstable, I feared that I might relapse, I dreaded reproach, I dreaded ridicule, I dreaded, above all, the sight of that face:—and thus stayed where I was, in the far country— I am a wanderer, an outcast still. And another answers, like him to whom the question

in the text was first put, I am hiding. I have sinned and I have not repented. I have eaten of the tree of which God said to me, "Thou shalt not eat of it, neither shalt thou touch it, lest thou die." I believed the creature more than the Creator—the tempter more than the Savior. I went to the edge of temptation; I desired forbidden knowledge first, and then I could not rest until I knew by experience also; and now my heart is defiled, my conscience is defiled, my life is defiled; I have lost all right to the beatific vision, for I am no longer pure in heart; now, when I hear the voice of the Lord God, I hide myself, because I know myself sinful, and because I know that He is of purer eyes than to look upon or tolerate iniquity. And another answers, I am resting. Earth is very pleasant to me; I have toiled and I have reaped, I have gathered myself a competence; I have found the happiness of lawful love; I have built myself a nest here, I have fenced it against the blasts of fortune, I am warm and tranquil within: let me alone a little while; it is not long that I can enjoy it; soon calamity may come, loss, sickness, death, into my peaceful home; then I will turn and seek Thee—not yet, O not just yet! And another says, I am working. Am I not doing Thy work? Am I not discharging the duties of my station? Am I not setting an example of diligence and sobriety? Am I not availing myself of the faculties which Thou has given to make myself respectable, and useful, and exemplary in my generation? How can I do all this, and yet be religious? How can I find time for both worlds at once? But yet, indeed, am I not providing for that other world in making a proper use of this? Let me alone a little while; when I have a convenient season, I will call for Thee. And another says, honestly, I am trifling. The world is so gay, so amusing, so exciting: hast Thou not made it so for our enjoyment? Oh, grudge me not my brief time of mirth and forgetfulness; I shall be serious enough one day. And another says, I am coming. Yes, I am on my way. This is no world, I see it, of rest for me. There is no peace but in God: I sought it once elsewhere, and found it not: now I know my error; yes, I am coming, I am coming, I am on my way: but give me time: so great a change cannot be wrought all at once: heaven cannot be won in a day: give me time, and I will reach Thee. I am now using the means: I pray, I read the Bible, I go to Thy House, I partake in Christ's supper: surely this is the way to Thee!

Yes, my brother, but why this delay? Why this postponement of the desired result? Wilt thou be any fitter to-morrow than to-day for that step across the barrier which now seems so premature, so presumptuous? The word is very nigh thee: it is in thy mouth, it is in thy heart—thou knowest it well, even the word of faith—"Believe on the Lord Jesus Christ," at once, "and thou shalt be saved. Come unto me"—not to-morrow, but to-day—"all ye that labor and are heavy laden, and I will give you rest." Are there any here present—God grant that they be many!—who have yet one other answer to return to the question on which we have dwelt? Thou sayest to me, O Lord, "Where art thou?" Lord, I am a sinner in a world of danger; and I have learned that danger in myself; for I have fallen, and I have sinned against Thee, times without number; yet by Thy grace I have risen, and I have returned to Thee, and Thou hast accepted me in Thy Son, and hast endued me, according to my need, with Thy Holy Spirit. And now, Lord, my life is hid with Christ in Thee: He is my trust, He is my life, He is my hope, and the life that I now live upon earth, I live by faith in Him. Under Thy care, doing Thy work, thankful for Thy mercies, trusting in Thy strength, even now I am Thine, and hereafter I shall see Thee. Guide Thou my steps, make Thy way plain before me, in the days that remain to me, and at last receive me to Thyself, disciplined, humbled, sanctified, that I may rest in Thee forever, and forever see Thy glory!

My brethren, the work of God in each of us would be almost accomplished if this one call were heard within. Once let us know that God is speaking to us, and that He waits an answer; once let us feel that He is, and that He will have us to be saved, and all the rest will follow. May it be so now! May some wanderer this night return to his Father; some hiding soul this night come forth from its lurking place; some builder upon the sand lay this night his foundations upon the rock; some trifler be made serious; some worldly man turned heavenward—so that all may have cause to bless God for His word here spoken, and ascribe to Him, through eternal ages, thanksgiving, and blessing, and praise!

ALEXANDER R. VINET

1797-1847

THE MYSTERIES OF CHRISTIANITY

Things which have not entered into the heart of man. —1 Cor. ii., 9.

"I DO not comprehend, therefore I do not believe." "The gospel is full of mysteries, therefore I do not receive the gospel:"—such is one of the favorite arguments of infidelity. To see how much is made of this, and what confidence it inspires, we might believe it solid, or, at least, specious; but it is neither the one nor the other; it will not bear the slightest attention, the most superficial examination of reason; and if it still enjoys some favor in the world, this is but a proof of the lightness of our judgments upon things worthy of our most serious attention.

Upon what, in fact, does this argument rest? Upon the claim of comprehending every thing in the religion which God has offered or could offer us—a claim equally unjust, unreasonable, useless. This we proceed to develop.

1. In the first place, it is an unjust claim. It is to demand of God what He does not owe us. To prove this, let us suppose that God has given a religion to man, and let us further suppose that religion to be the gospel: for this absolutely changes nothing to the argument. We may believe that God was free, at least, with reference to us, to give us or not to give us a religion; but it must be admitted that in granting it He contracts engagements to us, and that the first favor lays Him under a necessity of conferring other favors. For this is merely to say that God must be consistent, and that He finishes what He has begun. Since it is by a written revelation He manifests His designs respecting us, it is necessary He should fortify that revelation by all the authority which would at least determine us to receive it; it is necessary He should give us the means of judging whether the men who speak to us in His name are really sent by Him; in a word, it is necessary we should be assured that the Bible is truly the Word of God.

It would not indeed be necessary that the conviction of each of us should be gained by the same kind of evidence. Some shall be led to Christianity by the historical or external arguments; they shall prove to themselves the truth of the Bible as the truth of all history is proved; they shall satisfy themselves that the books of which it is composed are certainly those of the times and of the authors to which they are ascribed. This settled, they shall compare the prophecies contained in these ancient documents with the events that have happened in subsequent ages; they shall assure themselves of the reality of the miraculous facts related in these books, and shall thence infer the necessary intervention of divine power, which alone disposes the forces of nature, and can alone interrupt or modify their action. Others, less fitted for such investigations, shall be struck with the internal evidence of the Holy Scriptures. Finding there the state of their souls perfectly described, their wants fully exprest, and the true remedies for their maladies completely indicated; struck with a character of truth and candor which nothing can imitate; in fine, feeling themselves in their inner nature moved, changed, renovated, by the mysterious influence of these holy writings, they shall acquire, by such means, a conviction of which they can not always give an account to others, but which is not the less legitimate, irresistible, and immovable. Such is the double road by which an entrance is gained into the asylum of faith. But it was due from the wisdom of God, from His justice, and, we venture to say it, from the honor of His government, that He should open to man this double road; for, if He desired man to be saved by knowledge, on the same principle He engaged Himself to furnish him the means of knowledge.

Behold, whence come the obligations of the Deity with reference to us, which obligations He has fulfilled. Enter on this double method of proof. Interrogate history, time and places, respecting the authenticity of the Scriptures; grasp all the difficulties, sound all the objections; do not permit yourselves to be too easily convinced; be the more severe upon that book, as it professes to contain the sovereign rule of your life, and the disposal of your destiny; you are permitted to do this, nay, you are encouraged to do it, provided you proceed to the investigation with the requisite capacities and with pure intentions. Or, if you prefer another method, examine, with an honest heart, the contents of the Scriptures; inquire, while you run over the words of Jesus, if ever man spake like this Man; inquire if the wants of your soul, long deceived, and the anxieties of your spirit, long cherished in vain, do not, in the teaching and work of Christ, find that satisfaction and repose which no wisdom was ever able to procure you; breathe, if I may thus express myself, that perfume of truth, of candor and purity, which exhales from every page of the gospel; see, if, in all these respects, it does not bear the undeniable seal of inspiration and divinity. Finally, test it, and if the gospel produces upon you a contrary effect, return to the books and the wisdom of men, and ask of them what Christ has not been able to give you.

But if, neglecting these two ways, made accessible to you, and trodden by the feet of ages, you desire, before all, that the Christian religion should, in every point, render itself comprehensible to your mind, and complacently strip itself of all mysteries; if you wish to penetrate beyond the veil, to find there, not the aliment which gives life to the soul, but that which would gratify your restless curiosity, I maintain that you raise against God a claim the most indiscreet, the most rash and unjust; for He has never engaged, either tacitly or expressly, to discover to you the secret which your eye craves; and such audacious importunity is fit to excite His indignation. He has given you what He owed you, more indeed than He owed you; the rest is with Himself.

If a claim so unjust could be admitted, where, I ask you, would be the limit of your demands? Already you require more from God than He has accorded to angels; for these eternal mysteries which trouble you, the harmony of the divine prescience with human freedom, the origin of evil and its ineffable remedy, the incarnation of the eternal Word— the relations of the God-man with His Father —the atoning virtue of His sacrifice, the regenerating efficacy of the Spirit-comforter, all these things are secrets, the knowledge of which is hidden from angels themselves, who, according to the word of the Apostle, stoop to explore their depths, and can not.

If you reproach the Eternal for having kept the knowledge of these divine mysteries to Himself, why do you not reproach Him for the thousand other limits He has prescribed for you? Why not reproach Him for not having given you wings like a bird, to visit the regions, which, till now, have been scanned only by your eyes? Why not reproach Him for not giving you, besides the five senses with which you are provided, ten other senses which He has perhaps granted to other creatures, and which procure for them perceptions of which you have no idea? Why not, in fine, reproach Him for having caused the darkness of night to succeed the brightness of day invariably on the earth? Ah! you do not reproach Him for that. You love that night which brings rest to so many fatigued bodies and weary spirits; which suspends in so many wretches, the feeling of grief; that night, during which orphans, slaves, and criminals cease to be, because over all their misfortunes and sufferings it spreads, with the opiate of sleep, the thick veil of oblivion; you love that night which, peopling the deserts of the heavens with ten thousand stars, not known to the day, reveals the infinite to our ravished imagination.

Well, then, why do you not, for a similar reason, love the night of divine mysteries; night, gracious and salutary, in which reason humbles itself, and finds refreshment and repose; where the darkness even is a revelation; where one of the principal attributes of God, immensity, discovers itself much more fully to our mind; where, in fine, the tender relations He has permitted us to form with Himself, are guarded from all admixture of familiarity by the thought that the Being who has humbled Himself to us, is, at the same time, the inconceivable God who reigns before all time, who includes in Himself all existences and all conditions of existence, the center of all thought, the law of all law, the supreme and final reason of every thing! So that, if you are just, instead of reproaching Him for the secrets of religion, you will bless Him that He has enveloped you in mysteries.

2. But this claim is not only unjust toward God; it is also in itself exceedingly unreasonable.

What is religion? It is God putting Himself in communication with man; the Creator with the creature, the infinite with the finite. There already, without going further, is a mystery; a mystery common to all religions, impenetrable in all religions. If, then, every thing which is a mystery offends you, you are arrested on the threshold, I will not say of Christianity, but of every religion; I say, even of that religion which is called natural, because it rejects revelation and miracles; for it necessarily implies, at the very least, a connection, a communication of some sort between God and man—the contrary being equivalent to atheism. Your claim prevents you from having any belief; and because you have not been willing to be Christians, it will not allow you to be deists.

"It is of no consequence," you say, "we pass over that difficulty; we suppose between God and us connections we can not conceive; we admit them because they are necessary to us. But this is the only step we are willing to take: we have already yielded too much to yield more." Say more, say you have granted too much not to grant much more, not to grant all! You have consented to admit, without comprehending it, that there may be communications from God to you, and from you to God. But consider well what is implied in such a supposition. It implies that you are dependent, and yet free: this you do not comprehend; it implies that the Spirit of God can make itself understood by your spirit: this you do not comprehend; it implies that your prayers may exert an influence on the will of God: this you do not comprehend. It is necessary you should receive all these mysteries, in order to establish with God connections the most vague and superficial, and by the very side of which atheism is placed. And when, by a powerful effort with yourselves you have done so much as to admit these mysteries, you recoil from those of Christianity! You have accepted the foundation, and refuse the superstructure! You have accepted the principle

and refuse the details! You are right, no doubt, so soon as it is proved to you, that the religion which contains these mysteries does not come from God; or rather, that these mysteries contain contradictory ideas. But you are not justified in denying them, for the sole reason that you do not understand them; and the reception you have given to the first kind of mysteries compels you, by the same rule, to receive the others.

This is not all. Not only are mysteries an inseparable part, nay, the very substance of all religion, but it is absolutely impossible that a true religion should not present a great number of mysteries. If it is true, it ought to teach more truths respecting God and divine things than any other, than all others together; but each of these truths has a relation to the infinite, and by consequence borders on a mystery. How should it be otherwise in religion, when it is thus in nature itself? Behold God in nature! The more He gives us to contemplate, the more He gives to astonish us. To each creature is attached some mystery. A grain of sand is an abyss! Now, if the manifestations which God has made of Himself in nature suggest to the observer a thousand questions which can not be answered, how will it be, when to that first revelation, another is added; when God the Creator and Preserver reveals Himself under new aspects as God the Reconciler and Savior? Shall not mysteries multiply with discoveries? With each new day shall we not see associated a new night? And shall we not purchase each increase of knowledge with an increase of ignorance? Has not the doctrine of grace, so necessary, so consoling, alone opened a profound abyss, into which, for eighteen centuries, rash and restless spirits have been constantly plunging?

It is, then, clearly necessary that Christianity should, more than any other religion, be mysterious, simply because it is true. Like mountains, which, the higher they are, cast the larger shadows, the gospel is the more obscure and mysterious on account of its sublimity. After this, will you be indignant that you do not comprehend every thing in the gospel? It would, forsooth, be a truly surprising thing if the ocean could not be held in the hollow of your hand, or uncreated wisdom within the limits of your intelligence! It would be truly unfortunate if a finite being could not embrace the infinite, and that, in the vast assemblage of things there should be some idea beyond its grasp! In other words, it would be truly unfortunate if God Himself should know something which man does not know!

Let us acknowledge, then, how insensate is such a claim when it is made with reference to religion.

But let us also recollect how much, in making such a claim, we shall be in opposition to ourselves; for the submission we dislike in religion, we cherish in a thousand other things. It happens to us every day to admit things we do not understand, and to do so without the least repugnance. The things, the knowledge of which is refused us, are much more numerous than we perhaps think. Few diamonds are perfectly pure; still fewer truths are perfectly clear. The union of our soul with our body is a mystery—our most familiar emotions and affections are a mystery—the action of thought and of will is a mystery—our very existence is a mystery. Why do we admit these various facts? Is it because we understand them? No, certainly, but because they are self-evident, and because they are truths by which we live. In religion we have no other course to take. We ought to know whether it is true and necessary; and once convinced of these two points, we ought, like the angels, to submit to the necessity of being ignorant of some things. And why do we not submit cheerfully to a privation which, after all, is not one?

3. To desire the knowledge of mysteries is to desire what is utterly useless; it is to raise, as I have said before, a claim the most vain and idle. What in reference to us is the object of the gospel? Evidently to regenerate and save us. But it attains this end wholly by the things it reveals. Of what use would it be to know those it conceals from us? We possess the knowledge which can enlighten our consciences, rectify our inclinations, renew our hearts; what should we gain if we possest other knowledge? It infinitely concerns us to know that the Bible is the Word of God; does it equally concern us to know in what way the holy men that wrote it were moved by the Holy Ghost? It is of infinite moment to us to know that Jesus Christ is the Son of God; need we know precisely in what way the divine and human natures are united in His adorable person? It is of infinite importance for us to know that unless we are born again we can not enter the kingdom of God, and that the Holy Spirit is the author of the new birth; shall we be further advanced if we know the divine process by which that wonder is performed? Is it not enough for us to know the truths that save? Of what use, then, would it be to know those which have not the slightest bearing on our salvation? "Tho I know all mysteries," says St. Paul, "and have not charity, I am nothing." St. Paul was content not to know, provided he had charity; shall not we, following his example, be content also without knowledge, provided that, like him, we have charity, that is to say, life?

But some one will say "If the knowledge of mysteries is really without influence on our salvation, why have they been indicated to us at all?" What if it should be to teach us not to be too prodigal of our "wherefores!," if it should be to serve as an exercise of our faith, a test of our submission! But we will not stop with such a reply.

Observe, I pray you, in what manner the mysteries of which you complain have taken their part in religion. You readily perceive they are not by themselves, but associated with truths which have a direct bearing on your salvation. They contain them, they serve to develop them; but they are not themselves the truths that save. It is with these mysteries as it is with the vessel that contains a medicinal draft—it is not the vessel that cures, but the draft; yet the draft could not be presented without the vessel. Thus each truth that saves is contained in a mystery, which, in itself, has no power to save. So the great work of expiation is necessarily attached to the incarnation of the Son of God, which is a mystery; so the sanctifying graces of the new covenant are necessarily connected with the effluence of the Holy Spirit, which is a mystery; so, too, the divinity of religion finds a seal and an attestation in the miracles, which are mysteries. Everywhere the light is born from darkness, and darkness accompanies the light. These two orders of truths are so united, so interlinked, that you can not remove the one without the other, and each of the mysteries you attempt to tear from religion would carry with it one of the truths which bear directly on your regeneration and salvation. Accept the mysteries, then, not as truths that can save you, but as the necessary conditions of the merciful work of the Lord in your behalf.

The true point at issue in reference to religion is this:—Does the religion which is proposed to us change the heart, unite to God, prepare for heaven? If Christianity produces these effects, we will leave the enemies of the cross free to revolt against its mysteries, and tax them with absurdity. The gospel, we will say to them, is then an absurdity; you have discovered it. But behold what a new species of absurdity that certainly is which attaches man to all his duties, regulates human life better than all the doctrines of sages, plants in his bosom harmony, order, and peace, causes him joyfully to fulfil all the offices of civil life, renders him better fitted to live, better fitted to die, and which, were it generally received, would be the support and safeguard of society! Cite to us, among all human absurdities, a single one which produces such effects. If that "foolishness" we preach produces effects like these, is it not natural to conclude that it is truth itself? And if these things have not entered the heart of man, it is not because they are absurd, but because they are divine.

Make but a single reflection. You are

obliged to confess that none of the religions which man may invent can satisfy his wants, or save his soul. Thereupon you have a choice to make. You will either reject them all as insufficient and false, and seek for nothing better, since man can not invent better, and then you will abandon to chance, to caprice of temperament or of opinion, your moral life and future destiny; or you will adopt that other religion which some treat as folly, and it will render you holy and pure, blameless in the midst of a perverse generation, united to God by love, and to your brethren by charity, indefatigable in doing good, happy in life, happy in death. Suppose, after all this, you shall be told that this religion is false; but meanwhile, it has restored in you the image of God, reestablished your primitive connections with that great Being, and put you in a condition to enjoy life and the happiness of heaven. By means of it you have become such that at the last day, it is impossible that God should not receive you as His children and make you partakers of His glory. You are made fit for paradise, nay, paradise has commenced for you even here, because you love. This religion has done for you what all religions propose, and what no other has realized. Nevertheless, by the supposition, it is false! And what more could it do, were it true? Rather do you not see that this is a splendid proof of its truth? Do you not see that it is impossible that a religion which leads to God should not come from God, and that the absurdity is precisely that of supposing that you can be regenerated by a falsehood?

Suppose that afterward, as at the first, you do not comprehend. It seems necessary, then, you should be saved by the things you do not comprehend. Is that a misfortune? Are you the less saved? Does it become you to demand from God an explanation of an obscurity which does not injure you, when, with reference to every thing essential, He has been prodigal of light? The first disciples of Jesus, men without culture and learning, received truths which they did not comprehend, and spread them through the world. A crowd of sages and men of genius have received, from the hands of these poor people, truths which they comprehended no more than they. The ignorance of the one, and the science of the other, have been equally docile. Do, then, as the ignorant and the wise have done. Embrace with affection those truths which have never entered into your heart, and which will save you. Do not lose, in vain discussions, the time which is gliding away, and which is bearing you into the cheering or appalling light of eternity. Hasten to be saved. Love now; one day you will know. May the Lord Jesus prepare you for that period of light, of repose, and of happiness!

WILLIAM L. WATKINSON

1838-1925

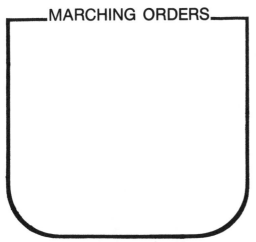

MARCHING ORDERS

BIOGRAPHICAL NOTE

WILLIAM L. WATKINSON, Wesleyan minister, was born at Hull, 1838, was educated privately and rose to eminence as a preacher and writer. The Rev. William Durban calls him "The classic preacher of British Methodism." "He ranks," says Dr. Durban, "with Dr. Dallinger and the Rev. Thomas Gunn Selby as the three most learned and refined of living preachers in the English Methodist pulpit. Dr. Watkinson is famous for the glittering illustrations which adorn his style. These are for the most part gathered from biography, the classics, and science, and of late years Dr. Watkinson has become more and more addicted to spiritualizing the aspects of modern scientific discovery. Dr. Watkinson never reads his utterances from a manuscript. Nor does he preach memoriter, as far as the language of his addresses is concerned. They are always carefully thought out and are never characterized by florid diction. His simple, strong Anglo-Saxon endears him to the people, for he is never guilty of an obscure sentence. He is in the habit of saying, 'I have always been aware that I have no power of voice for declamation, and therefore I can only hope for success in the pulpit by originality of thought.'" He was president of the Wesleyan Conference, 1897-1898, and editor of the *Wesleyan Church*, 1893-1890. He has published several volumes of sermons.

These shall first set forth.—Num. ii., 9.
And they shall set forth in the second rank.—Ver. 16.
And they shall go forward in the third rank.—Ver. 24.
They shall go hindmost with their standards.—Ver. 31.

SO God determined the order of the marching of the Israelites through the wilderness. The camp of Judah took the lead, followed by Reuben and Ephraim, whilst Dan brought up the rear. The tribes were not to travel as a rabble, but as a disciplined host under its several standards. A similar law prevails in society through all the generations, assigning to each individual his place and service, and resolving the multitude into great classes. These distinctive sections exist, they persist from age to age, and are not likely to be effaced. All attempts to abolish social gradations, to reduce society to a uniform mass, have hitherto proved abortive, whether those efforts were of a political, philosophical, or an ecclesiastical character. As by a great law society resolves itself into separate and graduated groups ; and no attempts to annul that law have succeeded, or are likely to succeed, for mainly the distinctions of society are first distinctions in nature.

I. These social distinctions must be accepted broadly as determinations of the government of God. Looking away from men, and contemplating the universe at large, we have no difficulty in recognizing and accepting the superiority and precedence, the inferiority and dependence, everywhere displayed. " There is one glory of the sun, and another glory of the moon, and another glory of the stars ; for one star differeth from another star in glory." In each department of creation the same law demonstrates itself in the diverse volume and virtue of whatever has been made ; all things and creatures vary in magnitude, energy, and splendor. God's shaping, sovereign hand is equally manifest in society.

Consider those who occupy the front by virtue of extraordinary genius, and we are compelled to recognize the divine election. Few who acknowledge God at all but will admit that He determined the power and place of these intellectual princes. How entirely was this the case with Shakespeare ! Like Melchizedec, he had neither father nor mother ; he owed nothing to society, universities, or parliaments. Heaven endowed him, placed him in the front rank, and there his stately figure shines until marching days are done. Handel is another conspicuous instance of the same sovereign ordination. As J. A. Symonds describes him : "Irritable and greedy, coarse and garrulous, fond of beer, destitute of affection, without a single intellectual taste. He never received any education. He had no experience. Yet he could interpret the deepest psychological secrets ; he could express the feelings of mighty nations, and speak with the voice of angels more effectually than even Milton ; he could give life to passion, and in a few changes of his melody lead love through all its variations from despair to triumph—there was nothing that he did not know. We shall never comprehend the mysteries of genius. It is a God-sent clairvoyance, inexplicable." The mighty musician with golden trumpet by right divine not to be gainsaid took his place with the foremost, and for ever animates the host by his glorious music. Turner is also an example of this marked election to greatness. Born of the poorest parents, reared in a squalid court, without scholastic or other advantage, he forthwith dipped his pencil into the radiances of nature, and left us those gorgeous gems of color which astonish and delight as do the splendors of the world. These marvellous masters received their gifts and glory directly and solely from God, as certainly as that He created the greater light to rule the day.

Acknowledging in the intellectual realm the sovereign Disposer, we cannot deny His authority in the political. President or king is a necessity of social organization, and the believer in the divine government must recognize its sway in dynasties and rulership. We cannot study revelation or history without discerning that God reigns in the political world equally with the intellectual, ordaining presidents as well as painters, princes as well as philosophers and poets. The wisest and noblest of mankind confess the mystic sanctity of the throne. If we are to affirm the absolute will of God in the solitary grandeur of Homer and Plato, of Shakespeare and Goethe, must we not concede the same supreme fiat in the royalty of Alexander and Caesar, of Napoleon and Washington ? He who assigns the magical pen or pencil to one, entrusts the sceptre or diadem to the other. We are free to admit that princes are not seldom in some sense sorry creatures ; but that does not disprove divine calling and office : the monarchs of the intellectual world have also been in certain respects unworthy, yet their royal gifts and vocation were indisputable for all that. How the anointed servants of God use their splendid prerogatives is another matter ; but that certain men are elected to majestic faculty and estate by Him who governs

all things is undeniable by those who recognize the divine government.

Allowing the sovereignty of God in intellect and rank, we cannot exclude it from the province of wealth. It is the fashion of our day to decry the very rich as necessarily enemies to the body politic ; and if this were true, it would be impossible to consider them as servants of God, for God has no servants who are not also servants of humanity ; but it is not true, and such an estimate of the status of the very rich is false. The millionaire in gold does not necessarily do us injustice any more than the millionaire in brains wrongs us. Aristotle, Plato, Shakespeare, Newton, and the rest of the mighty capitalists in genius, so far as they were faithful in the use of their extraordinary gifts, enriched us all ; so the world may yet come to see that the method of God for the happiness of the multitude follows the same lines in material things as it does in intellectual, and that the millionaire who is faithful in his stewardship is a blessing to society equally with the great thinker and the good king. It pleases God to endow the few with immense opulence, as it pleases Him to confer on others transcendent ability and the seats of the mighty ; and all attempts to discredit wealth and greatness, honestly attained, are prompted by ignorance or envy. " Thine is the kingdom, O Lord, and Thou art exalted as head above all. Both riches and honor come of Thee, and Thou reignest over all ; and in Thine hand is power and might ; and in Thine hand it is to make great, and to give strength unto all."

Having recognized the will of God in the great shapers of history, we cannot hesitate to confess it in the endowments and allocations of the second, third, and final ranks. He who gives to one ten talents, to another five, to another two, loans to the last one talent, to each according to his several ability ; for, as already said, the distinctions obtaining in society are owing first to the inequalities of personality. We greatly need in these days to remind ourselves of the divine sovereignty. The marching orders of the race are not enjoined by Acts of Parliament, the curriculum of universities, nor by the dogmas of science ; but, whatever some may think, we are dominated by a supernaturalism which fixes a great deal more in our lot beside the bounds of our habitation. If the ancient demarcations of society are to be annulled, it must be in those secret places where the primal Power gives to the embryo its character and bias ; education, sociologies, and politics come too late. God is likely to keep all things in His own hands, regulating the mighty host, maintaining a variegated world, assigning to each his place and standard. The rationalist is compelled to believe in something equivalent to this. According to his materialistic conception of things, nature is the potter and we are the clay; and if for unknown reasons, or without them, the supreme Force fashions one vessel modestly and another magnificently, the sceptic can not complain of these inequalities of mind and circumstance. "Nay, but, O man, who art thou that repliest against the partialities of cosmic law? Shall the thing formed say to him that formed it, Why hast thou made me thus?" The atheist can not remonstrate with the Power which, after evolving the infinite distinctions of heaven, earth and sea, has instituted the variety and contrasts of human power, status, and circumstance. The Christian finds no difficulty in acquiescing in the obvious order of the wise and gracious God. "He doeth according to His will in the army of heaven, and among the inhabitants of the earth; and none can stay His hand, or say unto Him, What doest Thou?"

Must we then conclude that every man is in his place? It is impossible to do so. No doubt, for various reasons, these Israelites from time to time missed their ranks; and it is very patent that men to-day are found in places where they ought not to be. By stratagem and the strange chances of life some figure in foremost places in which they are hopelessly outclassed; whilst others, through personal misconduct or social injustice, drop behind their true comrades. Many accidents, errors, usurpations, and vices afflict society and confuse its ranks. God's marching orders are imperfectly executed. Our contention is not that every person is in his place, but that for every one there is a place in which he will be specially happy and effective. That each may secure his billet it is necessary that the individual shall be true to himself, seeking personally to understand and prove the will of God. "Education is not the equalizer, but the discerner of men," writes Ruskin; and the more thoroughly we are educated, the more likely it will be that we find our fitting sphere. And, lastly, social and political justice must secure to every member of the community equality of opportunity. After this there is no more equality, for God has not predestinated the commonwealth to a dead uniformity, but provided for its perfection and happiness through a rich variety of gifts, offices, and orders. When each shall consult the divine will in his personal life; when education discriminates individual capacity, and indicates individual fitness; when a just government grants that equality of opportunity which allows and invites every citizen to strive unchecked for all that he is worth,—then shall be attained the grand ideal of society exprest

by St. Paul: "But now hath God set the members every one of them in the body, as it hath pleased Him."

II. The universal discontent which these social divisions appear to occasion next demands consideration. The dissatisfaction with the laws which govern society, and which group and grade us, is real, deep, and general. We wish to be something other than we are, to be appointed otherwise than we are. This friction with the environment is confined to no particular class; few, indeed, in any class, are fairly satisfied; all along the line the successive columns murmur at the Captain of the host, and resent His dispositions. In nature a delightful harmony exists between creatures and their environment—the fern enjoys the coolness of the dell, the rose glows in the sun, the water-lily drinks the pool, the violet hides in the grass, the orchid luxuriates in the summer glory; birds, flowers, and animals harmonize delicately with the landscapes and climes in which they sing, bloom, or roam. But the harmony of creation breaks off abruptly with man. Here everything is awry. The fern faints in the sun, the rose cankers in the shade, the water-lily thirsts in the desert, the violet frets in the glare, the orchid is bitten by the frost. We refuse to accept ourselves, we resent the conditions in which we must work out life; we believe ourselves to be misplaced, misinterpreted, misclassed, misused.

1. The first rank is the first to complain. The camp of Judah has burdens and difficulties, perils and sorrows, all its own. The greatest are not satisfied. In the very front rank they protest because they want to be in the rank before that—they are tormented by vague desires for an impossible greatness. The post of honor is also the place of special responsibility, temptation, and assault; whatever may be the coarse burdens of the porters in the rear, the princes in the front think them lighter than their own gilded sorrow. The cleverest are not satisfied. They who know the most resent most fiercely the limitations of the human understanding; they grow melancholy and cynical, plagued by the vision of the unattainable. The richest are not satisfied. Luxury and splendor pall on the senses. French purveyors, to tempt the eye and whet the appetite, paint the lovely fruits of summer, and heighten the flavor of the strawberry with ether. The epicure finds the cream of things insipid, and before long he will seek for the wherewithal to sprinkle the ether. The eye is not satisfied with seeing, nor the ear with hearing, nor the mouth with tasting. No; the nobles in place and genius have unique griefs. They who are farther in the rear, men of inferior station and

influence, have still the illusion left that riches and honor would satisfy had they more of them; but in the front rank no such illusion is possible—the bejewelled and laurel-crowned malcontents feel that life itself is a mockery. So the deepest wretchedness is the satiety of the rich; the bitterest cynicism is that of culture; and ages of extraordinary opulence and progress are ages of despair.

What is lacking in mortified greatness? Is it not that they ignore the great truth that "no man liveth to himself"? Judah was not nominated to the first place for its own glory and indulgence; the Keeper of Israel knew how the security and welfare of the whole host would be best served by its pre-eminence, and this was the sole basis of its election. The same reason and design explain all greatness to-day. The immortal few are not distinguished by genius, clothed in velvet, sceptred and crowned, that they may sate their personal pride and desire, but that they may greatly help and bless. Here the specially gifted too often make the mistake that turns life into wormwood—they make their personal indulgence and exaltation their exclusive object of solicitude. Out of this misconception springs the misery of the magnificent. How original and profound is the teaching of our Lord! "Ye know that they which are accounted to rule over the Gentiles exercise lordship over them. . . . But so it shall not be among you; but whosoever will be great among you shall be your minister." And just because the privileged too often can not receive this wonderful philosophy, they chafe and bleed.

No sooner, however, do the aristocracy enter into the view and spirit of our Lord than they realize the blessedness of illustrious birth and fortune. The very moment they begin to sympathize and serve, although in the first instance such magnanimity may not be called forth by high considerations, they experience a thrill which puts sensual, selfish pleasure to shame; and as their view and purpose of love attain clearness and largeness, they know the rich delight of high place and splendid power: they no longer require ether for their strawberries—the hips and haws of the hedgerows cloy with sweetness. The more they possess, the more they bless and are blessed. The millionaire in mind or treasure is a sympathetic sun, rejoicing in all the summer it creates; he is a self-conscious sea, exulting in the health and blessing it brings to many shores; he is a sentient Lebanon whose gladness is as diffusive as the ampler air it fills with fragrance. Greatness sanctified by love knows a blessedness akin to His who blesses all.

2. The middle ranks are not less unhappy. "The golden mean" of talent and station is certainly not golden in contentment. Mediocre ability is often resented with peculiar bitterness. Conscious of deficiency in intellectual independence, in originality, depth, or richness, thousands of educated men taste little pleasure in anything that they accomplish or attain. Dean Hole writes: "At a flower-show I have seen a competitor of the highest respectability tear a card in pieces on which he read 'Second Prize.'" This painful act was significant in an unusual degree of one of the diseases of our age: we are impatient with faculties and work which fall short of perfection. The second crown is scorned as a badge of disgrace; we would rather have none. Literary and artistic workers, together with handicraftsmen of all sorts, are fretted beyond expression because their work lacks the elements of popularity and fame. No one is willing to play the second fiddle. We have been made familiar with the most magnificent work of the human brain and hand, the prizes of eminent success are so immediate and splendid, the passion to excel is so intense, that mediocrity either in ourselves or others is intolerable; we despise fair, honest, medium, useful work. This essentially vain temper eats as doth a canker, disenchanting many a worthy worker, and making his indispensable work loveless and joyless.

The intermediate state socially is felt to be similarly vexatious. The artist paints the renowned at the top of the social scale, or the picturesque at the bottom, but never respectability. The poet and the dramatist find the fascination of life anywhere but in the middle. The social critic from a villa scorns villadom. So without poetry or pathos respectability misses distinction, and too often fails to respect itself. The severity of life is felt nowhere more than in these central bands. Their struggles hardly ever appear heroic; their successes are too petty to provoke applause; their sorrows excite no sympathy; they commonly acquire enough culture to be aware of their deficiencies; and by the time they reach competence they are too old to enjoy it. In the tribes of Reuben and Ephraim the strain, dullness, and chagrin of life are most acutely realized.

To reconcile themselves to their appointed rank the middle classes must recall the fact of their signal value to the community. When one of Darwin's correspondents remarked upon "the importance of our greatest men," the scientist responded finely, "I have been accustomed to think second, third, and fourth-rate men of very high importance, at least in the case of science." The masters of knowledge appreciate as brothers the second, third, and fourth-rate students, whose humbler work, wrought with poorer opportunity and inferior instruments, yet wrought in the spirit of love and patience, helps on the fuller interpretation of nature. What is true in science is yet more strikingly true in commerce. The ideal heroes of Greece and Rome were sought in the military sphere; but advancing civilization understands the immense import of the market-place and the traffic of the seas. Here the middle class are supreme. and their conduct is pregnant of national destiny. Were they struck out of the procession it would make a fatal gap. And how disastrous the consequences to the stability and evolution of society if the average is found wanting in character and faithfulness! That the middle classes are not less influential in patriotism is equally certain. They bring into public life an intelligence, a practical judgment, a sense of responsibility, and a sane enthusiasm which are of incalculable advantage in national life : in their sterling sense and virtue statesmen find the strength of the commonwealth. The importance of the middle classes as the religious factor of a nation is still more strongly marked. It required a Darwin justly to appreciate the importance of second, third, and fourth-rate men in science; but all can see how these classifications bear on the question of the religious faith and character of a nation. It is hardly too much to affirm that the scorned respectability of a nation is the backbone of Church and State.

This, then, is the great truth that the tribes of Reuben and Ephraim need to appreciate— their essential worth to God and humanity. Without the histrionic virtues and vices of the aristocracy, or the picturesque wretchedness of the ragged corps in the rear, they are not dramatically interesting; but on the loyalty of these drab troops depends the acquisition of Canaan. They lack the romance of the mighty and the pathos of the beggar; they tramp without either gay uniform or bizarre banner; the music is in the front, and the comedy and tragedy behind; yet if the patience, courage, and purity of this colorless rank and file are wanting, Armageddon will be lost. They constitute the nucleus in more senses than one; they are axial, for they maintain the integrity of the host first and last. This is the profound truth that must comfort and inspire the plebeian; and once conscious of what he is before God, and of the precious service he may render his generation, he will be more than content to belong to an order that has no distinction, to fulfil a mission that has no history. When the trumpet sounds the last réveillé, and the muster-roll is called out, no faithful soldier will be overlooked; and in the full assurance of this faith the undistinguished and unapplauded find the secret of peace.

3. The rear completes the chorus of discontent. The hindmost imagine that the disabilities of the premier ranks are chiefly imaginary, whilst their own sorrows are real

and overwhelming. Trumpets quicken the steps of the foremost, and they glitter like the Milky Way, whilst hardly a waft of music reaches the rearmost, painfully trudging through the mud with the impedimenta. The middle classes are comfortably posited in the center, the leading rank is far removed from the fear of evil; but the hindmost is closely menaced by terrible camp-followers and cruel foes— gaunt hunger, ghastly poverty, fell disease, winter's blast, desolate age, abject sickness, and death. So the fag-end is tormented by the sense of injustice, and loudly accuses kings, statesmen, capitalists, and priests.

It is no part of our purpose in this discourse to deny or condone the fact that the thoughtlessness, covetousness, and inhumanity of the stronger classes often inflict gratuitous suffering upon the sons and daughters of disadvantage. That fact is too obvious to be denied; it is one of the most tragic features of history, lamented by all noble souls. Nor are we to conclude that the miserable poor constitute any part of the program and procession of God; whereever the fault may lie, these ragged regiments and tattered banners do not belong to His kingly state. Yet even where no injustice is alleged, there is usually deep dissatisfaction with the common lot. The hindmost rebel at the simple fact of being the hindmost, apart from every other consideration. As the selfish rich disregard the poor, the discontented poor envy the rich. The foot has its perennial quarrel with the head, the hand aches and threatens because it is not the eye.

The hindmost need to lay to heart two great lessons, which are yet one. The camp of Dan was not dishonoured by coming last; the situation assigned it required the highest qualities, and the service it rendered to the host was of essential import. Two things the contemporary hindmost may remember to their deep consolation. They who fill the lowliest places, who do the rough work, who have the least silver and gold and the fewest changes of raiment, may nevertheless be men of the highest moral qualities. The intellectual limitations which involve social and civic subordination do not imply any inferiority in that moral character which is our chief glory; indeed, in the common people we find some of the noblest and saintliest of our fellows. A newspaper not long ago contained an article on "The Humbler Gems." It was directed to condemn the prevailing fashion of affecting rare and garish jewellery, whilst the more modest gems were neglected. The article proceeded to explain that numbers of jewels hitherto known only to the lapidary are yet of exceeding beauty. Just as there are heaps of modest jewels of special beauty entirely overlooked, so are there humbler gems of humanity whose strong, pure life is the poetry of city street and obscure hamlet. These lowly toilers reveal the rarest qualities of conscience and heart; and although they do not captivate the carnal eye as do fashionable brilliants and historic diamonds, yet are they His jewels who knows the exact value of us all, and they shall have their honored place in His diadem in the Great Day.

They who march in the rear, equally with the great, serve all the host by faithful service and sacrifice. The virtue of the humblest citizen adds to the splendor and stability of the commonwealth; and the influence, gifts, and prayers of nameless saints build up the kingdom of God. The happiness of the rich is found in cheerful unselfishness, and the happiness of the poor is in the same secret—the spirit of love and helpfulness. That the lowliest brother in the obscurest village may yet be a splendid servant of the race is one of the great lessons of the Carpenter of Nazareth.

It is impossible to predict the changes that may be brought about in the structure of society by the lapse of time. As the arrangements of to-day differ from the feudalism of the Middle Ages, so no doubt the manifold relations and interrelations of the community in ages to come will vary from the accepted social conditions of the present. As human nature itself is being ever more fully developed, and as advancing science is continually creating new conditions of human life and action, social readjustments are inevitable, and, in the course of generations, considerable. And we may justly hope and believe that successive readjustments will lessen friction, and finally bring about an ideal state, so far as the mechanism of the community is concerned. But we may just as confidently believe that the variations and gradations of power and position will continue. The scientist assures us that whilst nature is ever revealing itself in fresh forms and relations, yet many things remain the same thru all the ages, and in a high degree of probability these determinations and arrangements will remain for ever; there is permanence in mutation. So society may and will change in a thousand particulars, but its fundamental principles were settled early, and will continue as long as society itself.

Of this, we may be sure, that no period will ever arrive when room is not left for the virtues of humility, contentment, and obedience. No world is conceivable with which sloth, selfishness, and sensuality can be contented.

Nay, as the conditions of human life become more exquisitely perfect, and as human nature itself becomes more perfect, will not the obligations of humility, contentment, and obedience be more keenly felt, and be the more promptly responded to? The men of highest type to-day are precisely those who are readiest to render honor where honor is due, to do homage to genius, and unmurmuringly to accept their place and work in the service of humanity. The noblest of mankind least envy the gifts of others, and they find special delight in the vocation they can fill and adorn, whatever its conventional repute. The future we may expect to multiply these, and the world be the happiest, not when all varieties are lost in a vast monotony and all grades in a dead level, but when it is peopled throughout with Christian populations of variegated powers and situations, who in the love of God and humanity are alike utterly beyond the temptations of power and the sense of servility.

Do we not all need to think less, much less, of social distinctions, and more, much more, of moral qualities and faithfulness? Most of us are far more concerned about our conventional status than our standing before God; everything is supposed to depend upon the place we secure in the marshalled clusters. It is a serious error. Let every one by all means make the best of his personal powers; then let him seek out the niche in which he shall best disport himself: the faith of Jesus Christ has nothing to say contrary to this. This, however, being accomplished, let none yield to either pride or shame. We must concentrate our whole strength upon doing the will of God in the elected sphere. He is the Captain of the host; and, confiding in His wisdom and love, we must revere His sovereignty. Nothing but a sincere faith in God as our heavenly Father can reconcile us to our lot, and strengthen us for the long mysterious march through the wilderness. It is only as the heart is pure, simple, humble, patient, hopeful that we tranquilly accept our place, and adjust ourselves to the singularity and severity of circumstance. And lastly, if we are to march with songs, it can only be because we anticipate final victory and possession. If we are stepping to a funeral march and ending with a grave, there can be little joy in the wearied ranks. Marching orders! Marching whither? A great hope must charm our pained steps. Are we by faithfulness in things great and small becoming meet for the inheritance? It is only as we enter into these great and holy considerations that we have strength for the journey. The greater world, and nothing else, reconciles us to this. He has not brought us into the wilderness to kill us, but to school us for a kingdom. Let our whole concern be to play our part perfectly. We had little to do with fixing our style in this world; but we shall have a large share in deciding our place in the hierarchy of the next.

JOHN WATSON

1850-1907

OPTIMISM

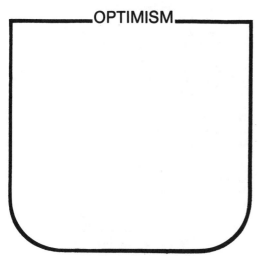

BIOGRAPHICAL NOTE

JOHN WATSON, widely known under his pen name of "Ian Maclaren," was born at Manningtree, Essex, England, in 1850. For many years he was pastor of Free St. Matthew's Church, Glasgow. He died in America in 1907. He enjoyed unusual popularity, both as a preacher and as a lecturer. In 1896 he gave a course of lectures to the students of Yale. "The Bonnie Brier Bush" is his best-known book. Another volume of his, "The Cure of Souls," is full of splendid practical suggestions for the minister and divinity student. Here is a sample of his satire directed toward certain speakers: "It is said that there are ingenious books which contain extracts—very familiar as a rule—on every religious subject, so that the minister, having finished his sermon on faith or hope, has only to take down this pepper-caster and flavor his somewhat bare sentences with literature. If this ignominious tale be founded on fact, and be not a scandal of the enemy, then the Protestant Church ought also to have an 'Index Expurgatorius,' and its central authorities insert therein books which it is inexpedient for ministers to possess. In this class should be included 'The Garland of Quotations' and 'The Reservoir of Illustrations.'"

Go ye therefore and teach all nations.—Matthew xxviii., 19.

AMONG the characteristics of Jesus' teaching which have passed into the higher consciousness of Christianity is an inextinguishable optimism. When He was only a village prophet, Jesus declared that the social Utopia of Isaiah was already being fulfilled; when He gave the Sermon on the Mount He spoke as a greater Moses, legislating not for a nation but for a race. If He called apostles, they were to disciple every creature, and if He died it was for a world. His generation might condemn Him, but they would see Him again on the clouds of heaven. His death would be celebrated in a sacrament unto every generation, and being lifted on a cross He would draw all men to Him. The apostles who failed in His lifetime would afterward do greater works than Himself, and He who departed from their sight would return in the Holy Ghost and be with them forever. He looks beyond His own land, and embraces a race in His plans. He ignores the defeats of His own ministry, and discounts the victory of His disciples. He teaches, commands, arranges, prophesies with a universal and eternal accent. This was not because he made light of His task or of His enemies; no one ever had such a sense of the hideous tyranny of sin or passed through such a Gehenna, but Jesus believed with all His heart and mind in the kingdom of God, that it was coming and must come. He held that the age of gold was not behind, but before humanity.

The high spirit has passed into the souls of Christ's chief servants. The directors and pioneers, the martyrs and exemplars of our faith have had no misgivings; the light of hope has ever been shining on their faces. St. Paul boasted that he was a free-born Roman, but he was prouder to be a member of Christ's commonwealth, whose capital was in heaven and in which all nations were one. He was loyal subject of Cæsar, but he owned a more magnificent emperor at God's right hand. Above the forces of this present world he saw the principalities and powers in the heavenly places fighting for his faith. Scourged and imprisoned he burst into psalms, and he looked beyond his martyrdom to the crown of righteousness. Shackled to a soldier he wrote letters brimming over with joy, and confined to a barrack room he caught through a narrow window the gleam of the eternal city. Never did he flinch before a hostile world, never was he browbeaten by numbers, never was he discouraged by failure or reverse. He knew that he was on the winning side, and that he was laying the foundation of an everlasting state. You catch the same grand note in St. Augustine with all his horror of prevailing iniquity; in the medieval hymn writers celebrating Jerusalem the Golden, when clouds of judgment hung over their heads; and in the missionaries of the faith who toiled their life through without a convert, and yet died in faith. They might be losing, but their commander was winning. The cross might be surrounded with the smoke of battle, it was being carried forward to victory.

They were right in this conviction, but do not let us make any mistake about the nature of this triumph, else we shall be caught by delusions, and in the end be discouraged. It will not be ecclesiastical, and by that one means that no single church, either the Church of Rome, or the Church of England, or the Church of Scotland will ever embrace the whole human race, or even its English-speaking province. One can not study church history since the Reformation, or examine the condition of the various religious denominations to-day without being convinced that there will always be diversity of organization, and any person who imagines the Church of the East making her humble submission to Rome, or the various Protestant bodies of the Anglo-Saxon race trooping in their multitude to surrender their orders to the Anglican Church has really lost touch with the possibilities of life. Nor will the triumph be theological in the sense that all men will come to hold the same dogma whether it be that of Rome or Geneva. There will always be many schools of thought within the kingdom of God just as there will be many nations. Neither one Church nor one creed will swallow up the others and dominate the world. He who cherishes that idea is the victim of an optimism which is unreasonable and undesirable. The kingdom of God will come not through organization but through inspiration. Its sign will not be the domination of a Church, but the regeneration of humanity. When man shall be brother to man the world over, and war shall no longer drench cornfields with blood: when women are everywhere honored, and children are protected: when cities are full of health and holiness, and when the burden of misery has been lifted from the poor, then the world shall know Christ has not died in vain, and His vision shall be fulfilled.

A fond imagination which only tantalizes and disheartens! It is natural to say so, but magnificent dreams have come true. Suppose you had been on the sorrowful way when Jesus was being led to His doom, and women were pitying this innocent prophet whose hopes had been so rudely dashed, and whose life had been so piteously wasted. "Ah!" they cry, "His illusions have been scattered, and His brief day is going down in darkness." It appeared so, but was it so?

Suppose while the kind-hearted people were talking, some one had prophesied the career of Jesus. They would have laughed and called him a visionary, yet which would have been right, the people who judged by Jesus' figure beneath the cross, or the man who judged Jesus' power through that cross? The people who looked at the mob of Jerusalem, or the man who saw the coming generations? There are two ideas of Christ's crucifixion in art, and each has its own place. There is the realistic scene with the cross raised only a few feet from the ground, a Jewish peasant hanging on it, a Roman guard keeping order, and a rabble of fanatical priests as spectators. That is a fact, if you please, down to the color of the people's garments and the shape of the Roman spears. Very likely that is how it looked and happened. There is also the idealistic scene with a cross high and majestic on which Christ is hanging with His face hidden. Behind there is an Italian landscape with a river running through a valley, trees against the sky, and the campanile of a village church. At the foot of the cross kneels St. Mary Magdalene, on the right at a little distance are the Blest Virgin and St. Francis, on the left St. John and St. Jerome. The Roman soldiers and the Jewish crowd and that poor cross of Roman making have disappeared as a shadow. The great cross of the divine Passion is planted in the heart of the Church and of the race forever. Facts? Certainly, but which is the fact, that or this? Which is nearer to the truth, the Christ of the sorrowful way or the Christ at God's right hand?

Have there been no grounds for optimism? Has the splendid hope of Christ been falsified? One may complain that the centuries have gone slowly, and that the chariot of righteousness has dragged upon the road. But Christ has been coming and conquering. There is some difference between the statistics of the Upper Room, and the Christian Church to-day; between slavery in the Roman Empire and to-day; between the experience of women in the pre-Christian period and to-day; between the reward of labor in Elizabeth's England and to-day; between the use of riches in the eighteenth century, and the beginning of the twentieth; between pity for animals in the Georgian period and to-day. If we are not uplifted by this beneficent progress, it is because we have grown accustomed to the reign of Christianity, and are impatient for greater things. We are apt to be pessimists, not because the kingdom of God is halting, but because it has not raced; not because the gospel has failed to build up native churches in the ends of the earth with their own forms, literature, martyrs, but because all men have not yet believed the joyful sound.

There are two grounds for the unbounded optimism of our faith, and the first is God. How did such ideas come into the human mind? Where did the imagination of the prophets and apostles catch fire? Where is the spring of the prayers and aspirations of the saints? Whence do all light and all love come? Surely from God. Can we imagine better than God can do? Can we demand a fairer world than God will make? Were not the Greek philosophers right in thinking that our ideals are eternal, and are kept with God? It is not a question of our imagining too much, but too little, of being too soon satisfied.

So soon made happy? Hadst thou learned
What God accounteth happiness
Thou wouldst not find it hard to guess
What hell may be his punishment
For those who doubt if God invent
Better than they.

The other ground for optimism is Jesus Christ. Does it seem that the perfect life for the individual, and for the race, is too sublime, that it is a distant and unattainable ideal? It is well enough to give the Sermon on the Mount, and true enough that if it were lived the world would be like heaven, but then has it ever been lived? Yes, once at least, and beyond all question. Christ lived as He taught. He bade men lose their lives and He lost His; He bade men trample the world underfoot and He trampled it; He commanded men to love, and He loved even unto death. This He did as the forerunner of the race. Why not again with Christ as Captain? Why not always, why not everywhere? Is not He the standard of humanity now, and is not He its Redeemer? Has He not been working in the saints who have reminded the world of God? Will He not continue to work till all men come to the stature of perfection?

Only one institution in human society carries the dew of its youth, and through the conflict of the centuries still chants its morning song. It is the religion of Jesus. I do not mean the Christianity which exhausts its energy in the criticism of documents or the discussion of ritual—the Christianity of scholasticism or ecclesiasticism, for there is no life in that pedantry. I do not mean the Christianity which busies itself with questions of labor and capital, meat and drink, votes and politics, for there is no lift in that machinery. I mean the Christianity which centers in the person of the Son of God, with His revelation of the Father, and His gospel of salvation, with His hope of immortality and His victory of soul. This Christianity endures while civilizations exhaust themselves and pass away, and the face of the world changes. Its hymns, its prayers, its heroism, its virtues, are ever fresh and radiant. If a man desires to be young in his soul let him receive the spirit of Jesus, and bathe his soul in the Christian hope. Ah, pessimism is a heartless, helpless spirit. If one despairs of the future for himself and for his fellows, then he had better die at once. It is despair which cuts the sinews of a man's strength and leaves him at the mercy of temptation. Do you say, What can I do, because the light round me is like unto darkness? Climb the mast till you are above the fog which lies on the surface of the water, and you will see the sun shining on the spiritual world, and near at hand the harbor of sweet content. True, we must descend again to the travail of life, but we return assured that the sun is above the mist. Do you say, What is the use of fighting, for where I stand we have barely held our own? Courage! It was all you were expected to do, and while you stood fast the center has been won, and the issue of the battle has been decided. It was a poet who had his own experience of adversity, and was cut down in the midst of his days, who bade his comrades be of good cheer.

Say not, the struggle naught availeth,
The labor and the wounds are vain,
The enemy faints not nor faileth,
And as things have been they remain.

If hopes were dupes, fears may be liars.
It may be in yon smoke concealed,
Your comrades chase e'en now the fliers,
And, but for you, possess the field.

For while the tired waves, vainly breaking,
Seem here no painful inch to gain,
Far back, through creeks and inlets making,
Comes silent, flooding in, the main.

And not by eastern windows only,
When daylight comes, comes in the light,
In front, the sun climbs slow, how slowly,
But westward look, the land is bright.

JOHN WESLEY

1703-1791

GOD'S LOVE TO FALLEN MAN

BIOGRAPHICAL NOTE

JOHN WESLEY was born at Epworth rectory in Lincolnshire, England, in 1703. He was educated at Charterhouse school and in 1720 entered Christ Church College, Oxford, where he graduated in 1724. He was noted for his classical taste as well as for his religious fervor, and on being ordained deacon by Bishop Potter, of Oxford, he became his father's curate in 1727. Being recalled to Oxford to fulfil his duties as fellow of Lincoln he became the head of the Oxford "Methodists," as they were called. He had the characteristics of a great general, being systematic in his work and a lover of discipline, and established Methodism in London by his sermons at the Foundery. His speaking style suggested power in repose. His voice was clear and resonant, his countenance kindly, and his tone extremely moderate. His sermons were carefully written, altho not read in the pulpit. They moved others because he was himself moved. At an advanced age he preached several times a day, and traveled many miles on horseback. At seventy years of age he had published thirty octavo volumes. He composed hymns on horseback, and studied French and mathematics in spare hours, and was never a moment idle until his death, in 1791.

Not as the transgression, so is the free gift.—
Romans v., 15.

HOW EXCEEDINGLY common, and how bitter is the outcry against our first parent, for the mischief which he not only brought upon himself, but entailed upon his latest posterity! It was by his wilful rebellion against God "that sin entered into the world." "By one man's disobedience," as the apostle observes, the many, as many as were then in the loins of their forefathers, were made, or constituted sinners: not only deprived of the favor of God, but also of His image; of all virtue, righteousness, and true holiness, and sunk partly into the image of the devil, in pride, malice, and all other diabolical tempers; partly into the image of the brute, being fallen under the dominion of brutal passions and groveling appetites. Hence also death entered into the world, with all his forerunners and attendants; pain, sickness, and a whole train of uneasy as well as unholy passions and tempers.

"For all this we may thank Adam," has been echoed down from generation to generation. The self-same charge has been repeated in every age and every nation where the oracles of God are known, in which alone this grand and important event has been discovered to the children of men. Has not your heart, and probably your lips too, joined in the general charge? How few are there of those who believe the Scriptural relation of the Fall of Man, and have not entertained the same thought concerning our first parent? severely condemning him, that, through wilful disobedience to the sole command of his Creator,

Brought death into the world and all our wo.

Nay, it were well if the charge rested here: but it is certain it does not. It can not be denied that it frequently glances from Adam to his Creator. Have not thousands, even of those that are called Christians, taken the liberty to call His mercy, if not His justice also, into question, on this very account? Some indeed have done this a little more modestly, in an oblique and indirect manner: but others have thrown aside the mask, and asked, "Did not God foresee that Adam would abuse his liberty? And did He not know the baneful consequences which this must naturally have on all his posterity? And why then did He permit that disobedience? Was it not easy for the Almighty to have prevented it?"

He certainly did foresee the whole. This can not be denied. "For known unto God are all His works from the beginning of the world." And it was undoubtedly in His Power to prevent it; for He hath all power both in heaven and earth. But it was known to Him at the same time, that it was best upon the whole not to prevent it. He knew that, "not as the transgression, so is the free gift"; that the evil resulting from the former was not as the good resulting from the latter, not worthy to be compared with it. He saw that to permit the fall of the first man was far best for mankind in general; that abundantly more good than evil would accrue to the posterity of Adam by his fall; that if "sin abounded" thereby over all the earth, yet grace "would much more abound"; yea, and that to every individual of the human race, unless it was his own choice.

It is exceedingly strange that hardly anything has been written, or at least published, on this subject: nay, that it has been so little weighed or understood by the generality of Christians: especially considering that it is not a matter of mere curiosity, but a truth of the deepest importance; it being impossible, on any other principle,

> To assert a gracious Providence,
> And justify the ways of God with men:

and considering withal, how plain this important truth is, to all sensible and candid inquirers. May the Lover of men open the eyes of our understanding, to perceive clearly that by the fall of Adam mankind in general have gained a capacity,

First, of being more holy and happy on earth, and,

Secondly, of being more happy in heaven than otherwise they could have been.

And, first, mankind in general have gained by the fall of Adam a capacity of attaining more holiness and happiness on earth than it would have been possible for them to attain if Adam had not fallen. For if Adam had not fallen, Christ had not died. Nothing can be more clear than this: nothing more undeniable: the more thoroughly we consider the point, the more deeply shall we be convinced of it. Unless all the partakers of human nature had received that deadly wound in Adam it would not have been needful for the Son of God to take our nature upon Him. Do you not see that this was the very ground of His coming into the world? "By one man sin entered into the world, and death by sin. And thus death passed upon all" through him, "in whom all men sinned." (Rom. v., 12.) Was it not to remedy this very thing that "the Word was made flesh"? that "as in Adam all died, so in Christ all might be made alive"? Unless, then, many had been made sinners by the disobedience of one, by the

obedience of one many would not have been made righteous (ver. 18); so there would have been no room for that amazing display of the Son of God's love to mankind. There would have been no occasion for His "being obedient unto death, even the death of the cross." It would not then have been said, to the astonishment of all the hosts of heaven, "God so loved the world," yea, the ungodly world, which had no thought or desire of returning to Him, "that he gave his Son" out of His bosom, His only begotten Son, to the end that "whosoever believeth on him should not perish, but have everlasting life." Neither could we then have said, "God was in Christ reconciling the world to himself"; or that He "made him to be sin," that is, a sin-offering "for us, who knew no sin, that we might be made the righteousness of God through him." There would have been no such occasion for such "an advocate with the Father" as "Jesus Christ the Righteous"; neither for His appearing "at the right hand of God, to make intercession for us."

What is the necessary consequence of this? It is this: there could then have been no such thing as faith in God, thus loving the world, giving His only Son for us men, and for our salvation. There could have been no such thing as faith in the Son of God, as loving us and giving Himself for us. There could have been no faith in the Spirit of God, as renewing the image of God in our hearts, as raising us from the death of sin unto the life of righteousness. Indeed, the whole privilege of justification by faith could have no existence; there could have been no redemption in the blood of Christ: neither could Christ have been "made of God unto us," "wisdom, righteousness, sanctification, or redemption."

And the same grand blank which was in our faith, must likewise have been in our love. We might have loved the Author of our being, the Father of angels and men, as our Creator and Preserver: we might have said, "O Lord our Governor, how excellent is Thy name in all the earth!" But we could not have loved Him under the nearest and dearest relation, as delivering up His Son for us all. We might have loved the Son of God, as being the "brightness of his Father's glory," the express image of His person (altho this ground seems to belong rather to the inhabitants of heaven than earth). But we could not have loved Him as "bearing our sins in his own body on the tree," and "by that one oblation of himself once offered, making a full oblation, sacrifice, and satisfaction for the sins of the whole world." We would not have been "made conformable to his death," nor have known "the power of his resurrection." We could not have loved the Holy Ghost as revealing to us the Father and the Son, as opening the eyes of our understanding, bringing us out of darkness into His marvelous light, renewing the image of God in our soul, and sealing us unto the day of redemption. So that, in truth, what is now "in the sight of God, even the Father," not of fallible men "pure religion and undefiled," would then have had no being: inasmuch as it wholly depends on those grand principles, "By grace ye are saved through faith"; and "Jesus Christ is of God made unto us wisdom, and righteousness, and sanctification, and redemption."

We see then what unspeakable advantage we derive from the fall of our first parent, with regard to faith: faith both in God the Father, who spared not His own Son, His only Son, but wounded Him for our transgressions and bruised Him for our iniquities; and in God the Son, who poured out His soul for us transgressors, and washed us in His own blood. We see what advantage we derive therefrom with regard to the love of God, both of God the Father and God the Son. The chief ground of this love, as long as we remain in the body, is plainly declared by the apostle, "We love him, because he first loved us." But the greatest instance of His love had never been given if Adam had not fallen.

And as our faith, both in God the Father and the Son, receives an unspeakable increase, if not its very being, from this grand event, as does also our love both of the Father and the Son: so does the love of our neighbor also, our benevolence to all mankind: which can not but increase in the same proportion with our faith and love of God. For who does not apprehend the force of that inference drawn by the loving apostle, "Beloved, if God so loved us, we ought also to love one another." If God so loved us—observe, the stress of the argument lies on this very point: so loved us! as to deliver up His only Son to die a curst death for our salvation. "Beloved, what manner of love is this," wherewith God hath loved us? So as to give His only Son! In glory equal with the Father: in majesty coeternal! What manner of love is this wherewith the only begotten Son of God hath loved us, as to empty Himself, as far as possible, of His eternal Godhead; as to divest Himself of that glory, which He had with the Father before the world began; as to take upon Him "the form of a servant, being found in fashion as a man"! And then to humble Himself still further, "being obedient unto death, even the death of the cross"! If God so loved us, how ought we to love one another? But this motive to brotherly love had been totally wanting if Adam had not fallen. Consequently we could not then have loved one another in so high a degree as we may now. Nor could there have been that height

and depth in the command of our blest Lord. "As I have loved you, so love one another."

Such gainers may we be by Adam's fall, with regard both to the love of God and of our neighbor. But there is another grand point, which, tho little adverted to, deserves our deepest consideration. By that one act of our first parent, not only "sin entered into the world," but pain also, and was alike entailed on his whole posterity. And herein appeared, not only the justice, but the unspeakable goodness of God. For how much good does He continually bring out of this evil! How much holiness and happiness out of pain!

How innumerable are the benefits which God conveys to the children of men through the channel of sufferings! so that it might well be said, "What are termed afflictions in the language of men, are in the language of God styled blessings." Indeed, had there been no suffering in the world, a considerable part of religion, yea, and in some respects, the most excellent part, could have no place therein: since the very existence of it depends on our suffering: so that had there been no pain it could have had no being. Upon this foundation, even our suffering, it is evident all our passive graces are built; yea, the noblest of all Christian graces, love enduring all things. Here is the ground for resignation to God, enabling us to say from the heart, and in every trying hour, "It is the Lord: let him do what seemeth him good." "Shall we receive good at the hand of the Lord, and shall we not receive evil?" And what a glorious spectacle is this? Did it not constrain even a heathen to cry out, "*Ecce spectaculum Deo dignum!* See a sight worthy of God: a good man struggling with adversity, and superior to it." Here is the ground for confidence in God, both with regard to what we feel, and with regard to what we should fear, were it not that our soul is calmly stayed on him. What room could there be for trust in God if there was no such thing as pain or danger? Who might not say then, "The cup which my Father hath given me, shall I not drink it?" It is by sufferings that our faith is tried, and, therefore, made more acceptable to God. It is in the day of trouble that we have occasion to say, "Tho he slay me, yet will I trust in him." And this is well pleasing to God, that we should own Him in the face of danger; in defiance of sorrow, sickness, pain, or death.

Again: Had there been neither natural nor moral evil in the world, what must have become of patience, meekness, gentleness, long-suffering? It is manifest they could have had no being: seeing all these have evil for their object. If, therefore, evil had never entered into the world, neither could these have had any place in it. For who could have returned good for evil, had there been no evil-doer in the universe? How had it been possible, on that supposition, to overcome evil with good? Will you say, "But all these graces might have been divinely infused into the hearts of men?" Undoubtedly they might: but if they had, there would have been no use or exercise for them. Whereas in the present state of things we can never long want occasion to exercise them. And the more they are exercised, the more all our graces are strengthened and increased. And in the same proportion as our resignation, our confidence in God, our patience and fortitude, our meekness, gentleness, and long-suffering, together with our faith and love of God and man increase, must our happiness increase, even in the present world.

Yet again: As God's permission of Adam's fall gave all his posterity a thousand opportunities of suffering, and thereby of exercising all those passive graces which increase both their holiness and happiness, so it gives them opportunities of doing good in numberless instances, of exercising themselves in various good works, which otherwise could have had no being. And what exertions of benevolence, of compassion, of godlike mercy, had then been totally prevented! Who could then have said to the lover of men,

> Thy mind throughout my life be shown,
> While listening to the wretches' cry,
> The widow's or the orphan's groan;
> On mercy's wings I swiftly fly
> The poor and needy to relieve;
> Myself, my all, for them to give?

It is the just observation of a benevolent man,

> ——All worldly joys are less,
> Than that one joy of doing kindnesses.

Surely in keeping this commandment, if no other, there is great reward. "As we have time, let us do good unto all men;" good of every kind and in every degree. Accordingly the more good we do (other circumstances being equal), the happier we shall be. The more we deal our bread to the hungry, and cover the naked with garments; the more we relieve the stranger, and visit them that are sick or in prison; the more kind offices we do to those that groan under the various evils of human life; the more comfort we receive even in the present world; the greater the recompense we have in our own bosom.

To sum up what has been said under this head: As the more holy we are upon earth, the more happy we must be (seeing there is an inseparable connection between holiness and happiness); as the more good we do to others, the more of present reward rebounds into our own bosom: even as our sufferings for God lead us to rejoice in Him "with joy unspeakable and full of glory"; therefore, the fall of Adam, first, by giving us an op-portunity of being far more holy; secondly, by giving us the occasions of doing innumerable good works, which otherwise could not have been done; and, thirdly, by putting it into our power to suffer for God, whereby "the spirit of glory and of God rests upon us": may be of such advantage to the children of men, even in the present life, as they will not thoroughly comprehend till they attain life everlasting.

It is then we shall be enabled fully to comprehend not only the advantages which accrue at the present time to the sons of men by the fall of their first parent, but the infinitely greater advantages which they may reap from it in eternity. In order to form some conception of this, we may remember the observation of the apostle, "As one star differeth from another star in glory, so also is the resurrection of the dead." The most glorious stars will undoubtedly be those who are the most holy; who bear most of that image of God wherein they were created. The next in glory to these will be those who have been most abundant in good works: and next to them, those that have suffered most, according to the will of God. But what advantages in every one of these respects will the children of God receive in heaven, by God's permitting the introduction of pain upon earth, in consequence of sin? By occasion of this they attained many holy tempers, which otherwise could have had no being: resignation to God, confidence in him in times of trouble and danger, patience, meekness, gentleness, long-suffering, and the whole train of passive virtues. And on account of this superior holiness they will then enjoy superior happiness. Again: every one will then "receive his own reward, according to his own labor." Every individual will be "rewarded according to his work." But the Fall gave rise to innumerable good works, which could otherwise never have existed, such as ministering to the necessities of the saints, yea, relieving the distress in every kind. And hereby innumerable stars will be added to their eternal crown. Yet again: there will be an abundant reward in heaven, for suffering as well as for doing, the will of God: "these light afflictions, which are but for a moment, work out for us a far more exceeding and eternal weight of glory." Therefore that event, which occasioned the entrance of suffering into the world, has thereby occasioned to all the children of God, an increase of glory to all eternity. For altho the sufferings themselves will be at an end: altho

> The pain of life shall then be o'er,
> The anguish and distracting care;
> The sighing grief shall weep no more;
> And sin shall never enter there:—

yet the joys occasioned thereby shall never

end, but flow at God's right hand for evermore.

There is one advantage more that we reap from Adam's fall, which is not unworthy our attention. Unless in Adam all had died, being in the loins of their first parent, every descendant of Adam, every child of man, must have personally answered for himself to God: it seems to be a necessary consequence of this, that if he had once fallen, once violated any command of God, there would have been no possibility of his rising again; there was no help, but he must have perished without remedy. For that covenant knew not to show mercy: the word was, "The soul that sinneth, it shall die." Now who would not rather be on the footing he is now; under a covenant of mercy? Who would wish to hazard a whole eternity upon one stake? Is it not infinitely more desirable, to be in a state wherein, tho encompassed with infirmities, yet we do not run such a desperate risk, but if we fall, we may rise again? Wherein we may say,

> My trespass is grown up to heaven!
> But, far above the skies,
> In Christ abundantly forgiven,
> I see Thy mercies rise!

In Christ! Let me entreat every serious person, once more to fix his attention here. All that has been said, all that can be said, on these subjects, centers in this point. The fall of Adam produced the death of Christ! Hear, O heavens, and give ear, O earth! Yea,

> Let earth and heaven agree,
> Angels and men be joined,
> To celebrate with me
> The Saviour of mankind;
> To adore the all-atoning Lamb,
> And bless the sound of Jesus' name!

If God had prevented the fall of man, the Word had never been made flesh: nor had we ever "seen his glory, the glory as of the only begotten of the Father." Those mysteries had never been displayed, "which the very angels desire to look into." Methinks this consideration swallows up all the rest, and should never be out of our thoughts. Unless "by one man, judgment had come upon all men to condemnation," neither angels nor men could ever have known "the unsearchable riches of Christ."

See then, upon the whole, how little reason we have to repine at the fall of our first parent, since herefrom we may derive such unspeakable advantages, both in time and eternity. See how small pretense there is for questioning the mercy of God in permitting that event to take place, since therein, mercy, by infinite degrees, rejoices over judgment! Where, then, is the man that presumes to blame God for not preventing Adam's sin? Should we not rather bless Him from the ground of the heart, for therein laying

the grand scheme of man's redemption, and making way for that glorious manifestation of His wisdom, holiness, justice, and mercy? If indeed God had decreed before the foundation of the world that millions of men should dwell in everlasting burnings, because Adam sinned, hundreds or thousands of years before they had a being, I know not who could thank him for this, unless the devil and his angels: seeing, on this supposition, all those millions of unhappy spirits would be plunged into hell by Adam's sin, without any possible advantage from it. But, blest be God, this is not the case. Such a decree never existed. On the contrary, every one born of a woman may be an unspeakable gainer thereby; and none ever was or can be a loser, but by his own choice.

We see here a full answer to that plausible account "of the origin of evil," published to the world some years since, and supposed to be unanswerable: that it "necessarily resulted from the nature of matter, which God was not able to alter." It is very kind in this sweet-tongued orator to make an excuse for God! But there is really no occasion for it: God hath answered for Himself. He made man in His own image, a spirit endued with understanding and liberty. Man abusing that liberty, produced evil, brought sin and pain into the world. This God permitted, in order to a fuller manifestation of His wisdom, justice, and mercy, by bestowing on all who would receive it an infinitely greater happiness than they could possibly have attained if Adam had not fallen.

"Oh, the depth of the riches both of the wisdom and knowledge of God!" Altho a thousand particulars of His judgments, and of His ways are unsearchable to us, and past our finding out, yet we may discern the general scheme running through time into eternity. "According to the council of his own will," the plan He had laid before the foundation of the world, He created the parent of all mankind in His own image. And He permitted all men to be made sinners by the disobedience of this one man, that, by the obedience of One, all who receive the free gift may be infinitely holier and happier to all eternity!

GEORGE WHITEFIELD

1714-1770

THE METHOD OF GRACE

BIOGRAPHICAL NOTE

GEORGE WHITEFIELD, evangelist and leader of Calvinistic Methodists, who has been called the Demosthenes of the pulpit, was born at Gloucester, England, in 1714. He was an impassioned pulpit orator of the popular type, and his power over immense congregations was largely due to his histrionic talent and his exquisitely modulated voice, which has been described as "an organ, a flute, a harp, all in one," and which at times became stentorian. He had a most expressive face, and altho he squinted, in grace and significance of gesture he knew perfectly how to "suit the action to the word." But he had not the style or scholarship of Wesley, and his printed sermons do not fully bear out his reputation. Whitefield died in 1770.

They have healed also the hurt of the daughter of my people slightly, saying, Peace, peace, when there is no peace.—Jeremiah vi., 14.

AS GOD can send a nation or people no greater blessing than to give them faithful, sincere, and upright ministers, so the greatest curse that God can possibly send upon a people in this world is to give them over to blind, unregenerate, carnal, lukewarm, and unskilful guides. And yet, in all ages, we find that there have been many wolves in sheep's clothing, many that daubed with untempered mortar, that prophesied smoother things than God did allow. As it was formerly, so it is now; there are many that corrupt the word of God and deal deceitfully with it. It was so in a special manner in the prophet Jeremiah's time; and he, faithful to his Lord, faithful to that God who employed him, did not fail from time to time to open his mouth against them, and to bear a noble testimony to the honor of that God in whose name he from time to time spake. If you will read his prophecy, you will find that none spake more against such ministers than Jeremiah, and here especially in the chapter out of which the text is taken he speaks very severely against them. He charges them with several crimes; particularly he charges them with covetousness: "For," says he, in the thirteenth verse, "from the least of them even to the greatest of them, every one is given to covetousness; and from the prophet even unto the priest, every one dealeth falsely."

And then, in the words of the text, in a more special manner he exemplifies how they had dealt falsely, how they had behaved treacherously to poor souls: says he, "They have healed also the hurt of the daughter of my people slightly, saying, Peace, peace, when there is no peace." The prophet, in the name of God, had been denouncing war against the people; he had been telling them that their house should be left desolate, and that the Lord would certainly visit the land with war. "Therefore," says he, in the eleventh verse, "I am full of the fury of the Lord; I am weary with holding in; I will pour it out upon the children abroad, and upon the assembly of young men together; for even the husband with the wife shall be taken, the aged with him that is full of days. And their houses shall be turned unto others, with their fields and wives together; for I will stretch out my hand upon the inhabitants of the land, saith the Lord."

The prophet gives a thundering message, that they might be terrified and have some convictions and inclinations to repent; but it seems that the false prophets, the false priests, went about stifling people's convictions, and when they were hurt or a little terrified, they were for daubing over the wound, telling them that Jeremiah was but an enthusiastic preacher, that there could be no such thing as war among them, and saying to people, Peace, peace, be still, when the prophet told them there was no peace.

The words, then, refer primarily unto outward things, but I verily believe have also a further reference to the soul, and are to be referred to those false teachers who, when people were under conviction of sin, when people were beginning to look toward heaven, were for stifling their convictions and telling them they were good enough before. And, indeed, people generally love to have it so; our hearts are exceedingly deceitful and desperately wicked; none but the eternal God knows how treacherous they are.

How many of us cry, Peace, peace, to our souls, when there is no peace! How many are there who are now settled upon their lees, that now think they are Christians, that now flatter themselves that they have an interest in Jesus Christ; whereas if we come to examine their experiences we shall find that their peace is but a peace of the devil's making— it is not a peace of God's giving—it is not a peace that passeth human understanding.

It is a matter, therefore, of great importance, my dear hearers, to know whether we may speak peace to our hearts. We are all desirous of peace; peace is an unspeakable blessing; how can we live without peace? And, therefore, people from time to time must be taught how far they must go and what must be wrought in them before they can speak peace to their hearts. This is what I design at present, that I may deliver my soul, that I may be free from the blood of all those to whom I preach—that I may not fail to declare the whole counsel of God. I shall, from the words of the text, endeavor to show you what you must undergo and what must be wrought in you before you can speak peace to your hearts.

But before I come directly to this give me leave to premise a caution or two.

And the first is, that I take it for granted you believe religion to be an inward thing; you believe it to be a work of the heart, a work wrought in the soul by the power of the Spirit of God. If you do not believe this, you do not believe your Bibles. If you do not believe this, tho you have got your Bibles in your hand, you hate the Lord Jesus Christ in your heart; for religion is everywhere represented in Scripture as the work of God in the heart. "The kingdom of God is within us," says our Lord; and, "he is not a Christian who is one outwardly; but he is a Christian who is one inwardly." If any of you place religion in outward things, I shall not perhaps please you this morning; you will understand me no more when I speak of the work of God upon a poor sinner's heart than if I were talking in an unknown tongue.

I would further premise a caution, that I would by no means confine God to one way of acting. I would by no means say that all persons, before they come to have a settled peace in their hearts, are obliged to undergo the same degrees of conviction. No; God has various ways of bringing His children home; His sacred Spirit bloweth when, and where, and how it listeth. But, however, I will venture to affirm this: that before ever you can speak peace to your heart, whether by shorter or longer continuance of your convictions, whether in a more pungent or in a more gentle way, you must undergo what I shall hereafter lay down in the following discourse.

First, then, before you can speak peace to your hearts, you must be made to see, made to feel, made to weep over, made to bewail, your actual transgressions against the law of God. According to the covenant of works, "the soul that sinneth it shall die"; curst is that man, be he what he may, be he who he may, that continueth not in all things that are written in the book of the law to do them.

We are not only to do some things, but we are to do all things, and we are to continue to do so, so that the least deviation from the moral law, according to the covenant of works, whether in thought, word, or deed, deserves eternal death at the hand of God. And if one evil thought, if one evil word, if one evil action deserves eternal damnation, how many hells, my friends, do every one of us deserve whose whole lives have been one continued rebellion against God! Before ever, therefore, you can speak peace to your hearts, you must be brought to see, brought to believe, what a dreadful thing it is to depart from the living God.

And now, my dear friends, examine your hearts, for I hope you came hither with a design to have your souls made better. Give me leave to ask you, in the presence of God, whether you know the time, and if you do not know exactly the time, do you know there was a time when God wrote bitter things against you, when the arrows of the Almighty were within you? Was ever the remembrance of your sins grievous to you? Was the burden of your sins intolerable to your thoughts? Did you ever see that God's wrath might justly fall upon you, on account of your actual transgressions against God? Were you ever in all your life sorry for your sins? Could you ever say, My sins are gone over my head as a burden too heavy for me to bear? Did you ever experience any such thing as this? Did ever any such thing as this pass between God and your soul? If not, for Jesus Christ's sake, do not call yourselves Christians; you may speak peace to your hearts, but there is no peace. May the Lord awaken you, may the Lord convert you, may the Lord give you peace, if it be His will, before you go home!

But, further, you may be convinced of your actual sins, so as to be made to tremble, and yet you may be strangers to Jesus Christ, you may have no true work of grace upon your hearts. Before ever, therefore, you can speak peace to your hearts, conviction must go deeper; you must not only be convinced of your actual transgressions against the law of God, but likewise of the foundation of all your transgressions. And what is that? I mean original sin, that original corruption each of us brings into the world with us, which renders us liable to God's wrath and damnation. There are many poor souls that think themselves fine reasoners, yet they pretend to say there is no such thing as original sin; they will charge God with injustice in imputing Adam's sin to us; altho we have got the mark of the beast and of the devil upon us, yet they tell us we are not born in sin. Let them look abroad and see the disorders in it, and think, if they can, if this is the paradise in which God did put man. No! everything in the world is out of order.

I have often thought, when I was abroad, that if there were no other arguments to prove original sin, the rising of wolves and tigers against man, nay, the barking of a dog against us, is a proof of original sin. Tigers and lions durst not rise against us unless it were as much as to say, "You have sinned against God, and we take up our master's quarrel." If we look inwardly, we shall see enough of lusts and man's temper contrary to the temper of God. There is pride, malice, and revenge in all our hearts; and this temper can not come from God; it comes from our first parent, Adam, who, after he fell from God, fell out of God into the devil.

However, therefore, some people may deny this, yet when conviction comes, all carnal reasonings are battered down immediately, and the poor soul begins to feel and see the fountain from which all the polluted streams do flow. When the sinner is first awakened, he begins to wonder, How came I to be so wicked? The Spirit of God then strikes in, and shows that he has no good thing in him by nature; then he sees that he is altogether gone out of the way, that he is altogether become abominable, and the poor creature is made to lie down at the foot of the throne of God and to acknowledge that God would be just to damn him, just to cut him off, tho he never had committed one actual sin in his life.

Did you ever feel and experience this, any of you—to justify God in your damnation—to own that you are by nature children of wrath, and that God may justly cut you off, tho you never actually had offended Him in all your life? If you were ever truly convicted, if your hearts were ever truly cut, if self were truly taken out of you, you would be made to see and feel this. And if you have never felt the weight of original sin, do not call yourselves Christians. I am verily persuaded original sin is the greatest burden of a true convert; this ever grieves the regenerate soul, the sanctified soul. The indwelling of sin in the heart is the burden of a converted person; it is the burden of a true Christian. He continually cries out: "Oh! who will deliver me from this body of death, this indwelling corruption in my heart?" This is that which disturbs a poor soul most. And, therefore, if you never felt this inward corruption, if you never saw that God might justly curse you for it, indeed, my dear friends, you may speak peace to your hearts, but I fear, nay, I know, there is no true peace.

Further, before you can speak peace to your hearts you must not only be troubled for the sins of your life, the sins of your nature, but likewise for the sins of your best duties and performances.

When a poor soul is somewhat awakened by the terrors of the Lord, then the poor creature, being born under the covenant of works, flies directly to a covenant of works again. And as Adam and Eve hid themselves among the trees of the garden and sewed fig-leaves together to cover their nakedness, so the poor sinner when awakened flies to his duties and to his performances, to hide himself from God, and goes to patch up a righteousness of his own. Says he, I will be mighty good now—I will reform—I will do all I can; and then certainly Jesus Christ will have mercy on me. But before you can speak peace to your heart you must be brought to see that God may damn you for the best prayer you ever put up; you must be brought to see that all your duties—all your righteousness—as the prophet elegantly expresses it—put them all together, are so far from recommending you to God, are so far from being any motive and inducement to God to have mercy on your poor soul, that He will see them to be filthy rags, a menstruous cloth—that God hates them, and can not away with them, if you bring them to Him in order to recommend you to His favor.

My dear friends, what is there in our performance to recommend us unto God? Our persons are in an unjustified state by nature; we deserve to be damned ten thousand times over; and what must our performance be? We can do no good thing by nature: "They that are in the flesh can not please God."

You may do things materially good, but you can not do a thing formally and rightly good; because nature can not act above itself. It is impossible that a man who is unconverted can act for the glory of God; he can not do anything in faith, and "whatsoever is not of faith is sin."

After we are renewed, yet we are renewed but in part, indwelling sin continues in us, there is a mixture of corruption in every one of our duties, so that after we are converted, were Jesus Christ only to accept us according to our works, our works would damn us, for we can not put up a prayer but it is far from that perfection which the moral law requireth. I do not know what you may think, but I can say that I can not pray but I sin—I can not preach to you or any others but I sin—I can do nothing without sin; and, as one expresseth it, my repentance wants to be repented of, and my tears to be washed in the precious blood of my dear Redeemer.

Our best duties are so many splendid sins. Before you can speak peace to your heart you must not only be sick of your original and actual sin, but you must be made sick of your righteousness, of all your duties and performances. There must be a deep conviction before you can be brought out of your self-righteousness; it is the last idol taken out of our heart. The pride of our heart will not let us submit to the righteousness of Jesus Christ. But if you never felt that you had no righteousness of your own, if you never felt the deficiency of your own righteousness, you can not come to Jesus Christ.

There are a great many now who may say, Well, we believe all this; but there is a great difference betwixt talking and feeling. Did you ever feel the want of a dear Redeemer? Did you ever feel the want of Jesus Christ, upon the account of the deficiency of your own righteousness? And can you now say from your heart Lord, thou mayest justly damn me for the best duties that ever I did perform? If you are not thus brought out of self, you may speak peace to yourselves, but yet there is no peace.

But then, before you can speak peace to your souls, there is one particular sin you must be greatly troubled for, and yet I fear there are few of you think what it is; it is the reigning, the damning sin of the Christian world, and yet the Christian world seldom or never think of it. And pray what is that?

It is what most of you think you are not guilty of—and that is, the sin of unbelief. Before you can speak peace to your heart, you must be troubled for the unbelief of your heart. But can it be supposed that any of you are unbelievers here in this churchyard, that are born in Scotland, in a reformed country, that go to church every Sabbath? Can any of you that receive the sacrament

once a year—oh, that it were administered oftener!—can it be supposed that you who had tokens for the sacrament, that you who keep up family prayer, that any of you do not believe in the Lord Jesus Christ?

I appeal to your own hearts, if you would not think me uncharitable, if I doubted whether any of you believed in Christ: and yet, I fear upon examination, we should find that most of you have not so much faith in the Lord Jesus Christ as the devil himself. I am persuaded that the devil believes more of the Bible than most of us do. He believes the divinity of Jesus Christ; that is more than many who call themselves Christians do; nay, he believes and trembles, and that is more than thousands amongst us do.

My friends, we mistake a historical faith for a true faith, wrought in the heart by the Spirit of God. You fancy you believe because you believe there is such a book as we call the Bible—because you go to church; all this you may do and have no true faith in Christ. Merely to believe there was such a person as Christ, merely to believe there is a book called the Bible, will do you no good, more than to believe there was such a man as Cæsar or Alexander the Great. The Bible is a sacred depository. What thanks have we to give to God for these lively oracles! But yet we may have these and not believe in the Lord Jesus Christ.

My dear friends, there must be a principle wrought in the heart by the Spirit of the living God. Did I ask you how long it is since you believed in Jesus Christ, I suppose most of you would tell me you believed in Jesus Christ as long as ever you remember—you never did misbelieve. Then, you could not give me a better proof that you never yet believed in Jesus Christ, unless you were sanctified early, as from the womb; for they that otherwise believe in Christ know there was a time when they did not believe in Jesus Christ.

You say you love God with all your heart, soul, and strength. If I were to ask you how long it is since you loved God, you would say, As long as you can remember; you never hated God, you know no time when there was enmity in your heart against God. Then, unless you were sanctified very early, you never loved God in your life.

My dear friends, I am more particular in this, because it is a most deceitful delusion, whereby so many people are carried away, that they believe already. Therefore it is remarked of Mr. Marshall, giving account of his experiences, that he had been working for life, and he had ranged all his sins under the ten commandments, and then, coming to a minister, asked him the reason why he could not get peace. The minister looked to his catalog. "Away," says he, "I do not find one word of the sin of unbelief in all your catalog.'' It is the peculiar work of the Spirit of God to convince us of our unbelief—that we have got no faith. Says Jesus Christ, ''I will send the comforter; and when he is come, he will reprove the world'' of the sin of unbelief; ''of sin,'' says Christ, ''because they believe not on me.''

Now, my dear friends, did God ever show you that you had no faith? Were you ever made to bewail a hard heart of unbelief? Was it ever the language of your heart, Lord, give me faith; Lord, enable me to lay hold on Thee; Lord, enable me to call Thee my Lord and my God? Did Jesus Christ ever convince you in this manner? Did he ever convince you of your inability to close with Christ, and make you to cry out to God to give you faith? If not, do not speak peace to your heart. May the Lord awaken you and give you true, solid peace before you go hence and be no more!

Once more, then: before you can speak peace to your heart, you must not only be convinced of your actual and original sin, the sins of your own righteousness, the sin of unbelief, but you must be enabled to lay hold upon the perfect righteousness, the all-sufficient righteousness, of the Lord Jesus Christ; you must lay hold by faith on the righteousness of Jesus Christ, and then you shall have peace. ''Come,'' says Jesus, ''unto me, all ye that are weary and heavy laden, and I will give you rest.''

This speaks encouragement to all that are weary and heavy laden; but the promise of rest is made to them only upon their coming and believing, and taking Him to be their God and their all. Before we can ever have peace with God we must be justified by faith through our Lord Jesus Christ, we must be enabled to apply Christ to our hearts, we must have Christ brought home to our souls, so as His righteousness may be made our righteousness, so as His merits may be imputed to our souls. My dear friends, were you ever married to Jesus Christ? Did Jesus Christ ever give Himself to you? Did you ever close with Christ by a lively faith, so as to feel Christ in your hearts, so as to hear Him speaking peace to your souls? Did peace ever flow in upon your hearts like a river? Did you ever feel that peace that Christ spoke to His disciples? I pray God he may come and speak peace to you. These things you must experience.

I am now talking of the invisible realities of another world, of inward religion, of the work of God upon a poor sinner's heart. I am now talking of a matter of great importance, my dear hearers; you are all concerned in it, your souls are concerned in it, your eternal salvation is concerned in it. You may be all at peace, but perhaps the devil has lulled you asleep into a carnal lethargy and security, and will endeavor to keep you there till he gets you to hell, and there you will be awakened; but it will be dreadful to be awakened and find yourselves so fearfully mistaken when the great gulf is fixt, when you will be calling to all eternity for a drop of water to cool your tongue and shall not obtain it.

ALEXANDER WHYTE

1837-1921

EXPERIENCE

BIOGRAPHICAL NOTE

ALEXANDER WHYTE, senior minister of St. George's Free Church, Edinburgh, was born at Kirriemuir (Thrums), Scotland, in 1837. He was educated at Aberdeen University (M. A., 1862), and at New College, Edinburgh (1862-66), and after being assistant minister of Free St. John's, Glasgow, from 1866 to 1870, became at first assistant minister, and later (1873) minister, of Free St. George's, Edinburgh, a position which he still retains, having had there an uninterrupted success. He is the author of a number of biographies, his most recent work being "An Appreciation of Newman."

And patience, experience; and experience, hope.— Romans v., 4.

THE deeper we search into the Holy Scriptures the more experimental matter do we discover in that divine Book. Both in the Old Testament and in the New Testament the spiritual experiences of godly men form a large part of the sacred record. And it gives a very fresh and a very impressive interest to many parts of the heavenly Book when we see how much of its contents are made up of God's ways with His people as well as of their ways with Him. In other words, when we see how much of purely experimental matter is gathered up into the Word of God. In a brilliant treatise published the other year, entitled, "The Gospel in the Gospels," the author applies this experimental test even to our Lord's teaching and preaching. Writing of the beatitudes in our Lord's Sermon on the Mount that fresh and penetrating writer says: "When our Savior speaks to us concerning what constitutes our true blessedness He is simply describing His own experience. The beatitudes are not the immediate revelation of His Godhead, they are much more the impressive testimony of His manhood. He knew the truth of what He was saying because He had verified it all in Himself for thirty experimental years." Now if that is so demonstrably true of so many of our Lord's contributions to Holy Scripture, in the nature of things, how much more must it be true of the experimental contributions that David and Paul have made to the same sacred record. And we ourselves are but imitating them in their great experimental methods when we give our very closest attention to personal and spiritual religion, both in ourselves and in all our predecessors and in all our own contemporaries in the life of grace in all lands and in all languages.

Now by far the deepest and by far the most personal experience of every spiritually minded man is his experience of his own inward sinfulness. The sinfulness of his sin; the malignity of his sin; the ungodliness and the inhumanity of his sin; the dominion that his sin still has over him; the simply indescribable evil of his sin in every way: all that is a matter, not of any man's doctrine and authority; all that is the personal experience and the scientific certainty, as we say, of every spiritually minded man; every man, that is, who takes any true observation of what goes on in his own heart. The simply unspeakable sinfulness of our own hearts is not the doctrine of David, and of Christ, and of Paul, and of Luther, and of Calvin, and of Bunyan, and of Edwards, and of Shepard only. It is their universal doctrine, indeed, it could not be otherwise; but it is also the every-day experience and the every-day agony of every man among ourselves whose eyes are open upon his own heart.

And then, if you are that spiritually enlightened man, from the day when you begin to have that heart-sore experience of yourself you will begin to search for and to discover those great passages of Holy Scripture that contain the recorded experiences of men like yourself. "I am but dust and ashes," said the first father of all penitent and believing and praying men. "I am vile," sobs Job. "Behold, I am vile, and I will lay my hand upon my mouth. I have heard of thee by the hearing of the ear, but now mine eye seeth thee. Wherefore I abhor myself and repent in dust and ashes." And David has scarcely heart or a pen for anything else. "There is no soundness in my flesh because of thine anger; neither is there any rest in my bones because of my sin. My loins are filled with a loathsome disease. For, behold, I was shapen in iniquity." And Daniel, the most blameless of men and a man greatly beloved in heaven and on earth: "I was left alone and there remained no strength in me: for my comeliness was turned to corruption, and I retained no strength." And every truly spiritually minded man has Paul's great experimental passage by heart; that great experimental and autobiographic passage which has kept so many of God's most experienced saints from absolute despair, as so many of them have testified. Yes! There were experimental minds long before Bacon and there was a great experimental literature long before the Essays and the "Advancement" and the *"Instauratio Magna."*

And then among many other alterations of intellectual insight and spiritual taste that will come to you with your open eyes, there will be your new taste, not only for your Bible, but also for spiritual and experimental preaching. The spiritual preachers of our day are constantly being blamed for not tuning their pulpits to the new themes of our so progressive day. Scientific themes are prest upon them and critical themes and social themes and such like. But your new experience of your own sinfulness and of God's salvation: your new need and your new taste for spiritual and experimental truth will not lead you to join in that stupid demand. As intelligent men you will know where to find all the new themes of your new day and you will be diligent students of them all, so far as your duty lies that way, and

so far as your ability and your opportunity go; but not on the Lord's Day and not in His house of prayer and praise. The more inward, and the more spiritual, and the more experimental, your own religion becomes, the more will you value inward, and spiritual, and experimental preaching. And the more will you resent the intrusion into the evangelical pulpit of those secular matters that so much absorb unspiritual men. There is another equally impertinent advice that our preachers are continually having thrust upon them from the same secular quarter. And that is that they ought entirely to drop the old language of the Scriptures, and the creeds, and the classical preachers, and ought to substitute for it the scientific and the journalistic jargon of the passing day. But with your ever-deepening knowledge of yourselves and with the disciplined and refined taste that will accompany such knowledge you will rather demand of your preachers more and more depth of spiritual preaching and more and more purity of spiritual style. And then more and more your estimates of preaching and your appreciations of preachers will have real insight and real value and real weight with us. "The natural man receiveth not the things of the Spirit of God: for they are foolishness to him: neither can he know them, because they are spiritually discerned." But he that is spiritual discerneth spiritual things and spiritual persons and he has the true authority to speak and to write about them.

And then, for all doubting and skeptically disposed persons among you, your own experience of your evil heart, if you will receive that experience and will seriously attend to it, that will prove to you the true apologetic for the theism of the Holy Scriptures and for the soul-saving faith of Jesus Christ. What is it about which you are in such debate and doubt? Is it about the most fundamental of all facts—the existence, and the nature, and the grace, and the government of Almighty God? Well, if you are really in earnest to know the truth, take this way of it: this way that has brought light and peace of mind to so many men. Turn away at once and forever from all your unbecoming debates about your Maker and Preserver and turn to what is beyond all debate, your own experience of yourselves. There is nothing else of which you can be so sure and certain as of the sin and the misery of your own evil hearts, your own evil hearts so full of self-seeking, and envy, and malice, and pride, and hatred, and revenge, and lust. And on the other hand, there is nothing of which you can be so convinced as that love, and humility, and meekness, and purity, and benevolence, and brotherly kindness, are your true happiness, or would be, if you could only attain to all these beatitudes. Well, Jesus Christ has attained to them all. And Jesus Christ came into this world at first, and He still comes into it by His Word and by His Spirit in order that you may attain to all His goodness and all His truth and may thus escape forever from all your own ignorance and evil. As William Law, the prince of apologists, has it: "Atheism is not the denial of a first omnipotent cause. Real atheism is not that at all. Real atheism is purely and solely nothing else but the disowning, and the forsaking, and the renouncing of the goodness, and the virtue, and the benevolence and the meekness, of the divine nature: that divine nature which has made itself so experimental and so self-evident in us all. And as this experimental and self-evident knowledge is the only sure knowledge you can have of God; even so, it is such a knowledge that cannot be doubted or debated away. For it is as sure and as self-evident as is your own experience." And so is it through all the succeeding doctrines of grace and truth: The incarnation of the divine Son: His life, His death, His resurrection, and His intercession: and then your own life of faith, and prayer, and holy obedience: and then your death, "dear in God's sight." Beginning with this continually experienced need of God, all these things will follow, with an intellectual, and a moral, and a spiritual demonstration, that will soon place them beyond all debate or doubt to you. Only know thyself and admit the knowledge: and all else will follow as sure as the morning sun follows the dark midnight.

And then in all these ways, you will attain to a religious experience of your own, that will be wholly and exclusively your own. It will not be David's experience, nor Paul's, nor Luther's, nor Bunyan's; much as you will study their experiences, comparing them all with your own. As you go deeper and ever deeper, into your own spiritual experience, you will gradually gather a select and an invaluable library of such experiences, and you will less and less read anything else with very much interest or delight. But your own unwritten experience will, all the time, be your own, and in your own spiritual experience you will have no exact fellow. For your tribulations, which work in you your experience,— as the text has it,—your tribulations are such that in all your experimental reading in the Bible, in spiritual biography, in spiritual autobiography, you have never met the like of them. Either the writers have been afraid to speak out the whole truth about their tribulations; or, what is far more likely, they had no tribulations for a moment to match with yours. There has not been another so weak and so evil heart as yours since weak and evil

hearts began to be; nor an evil life quite like yours; nor surrounding circumstances so cross-bearing as yours; nor a sinner, beset yours; nor surrounding circumstances so cross-bearing as your's; nor a sinner, beset with all manner of temptations and trials, behind and before, like you. So much are you alone that, if your fifty-first Psalm, or your seventh of the Romans, or your "Confessions," or your "Private Devotions," or your "Grace Abounding," could ever venture to be all honestly and wholly written and published, your name would, far and away, eclipse them all. You do not know what a singular and what an original and what an unheard-of experience your experience is destined to be; if only you do not break down under it; as you must not and will not do.

Begin, then, to make some new experiments upon a new life of faith, and of the obedience of faith. And begin to-day. If in anything you have been following a false and an unphilosophical and an unscriptural way of life, leave that wrong and evil way at once. Be true Baconians, at once, as all the true men of science will tell you to be. "If we were religious men like you," they will all say to you, "we would do, and at once, what you are now being told to do. We would not debate, or doubt, but we would make experiment, and would follow out the experience": so all the scientifically minded men will say to you. Come away then, and make some new experiments from this morning. For one thing, make a new experiment on secret prayer. And then come forth from your place of secret prayer and make immediate experiment on more love, and more patience, and more consideration for other men, and, especially, for the men of your own household. Be more generous-minded, and more open-handed, as God has been so generous-minded, and so open-handed toward you: if that has indeed been so. Make experiment upon the poor and the needy and help them according to your ability and opportunity and watch the result of the experiment upon yourself; and so on, as your awakened conscience, and as the regenerate part of your own heart, will prompt you and will encourage you to do.

Make such experiments as these and see if a new peace of conscience and a new happiness of heart does not begin to come to you, according to that great experimental psalm, —"Oh, that my people had hearkened unto me, and Israel had walked in my ways! I should soon have subdued their enemies, and turned my hand against their adversaries. He should have fed them also with the finest of the wheat: and with honey out of the rock should I have satisfied thee."

JOHN WYCLIF

1324-1384

CHRIST'S REAL BODY NOT IN THE EUCHARIST

BIOGRAPHICAL NOTE

JOHN WYCLIF, eminent as scholar, preacher, and translator, was born in 1324 in Spresswel, near Richmond, Yorkshire, England. Known as the "Morning Star of the Reformation" he was a vigorous and argumentative speaker, exemplifying his own definition of preaching as something which should be "apt, apparent, full of true feeling, fearless in rebuking sins, and so addrest to the heart as to enlighten the spirit and subdue the will." On these lines he organized a band of Bible preachers who worked largely among the common people.

Much of Wyclif's popularity was due to his clear and simple style. While not a great orator, he introduced a popular method of preaching that was widely copied. He died at Lutterworth in 1384. The Church considered him a heretic, for he taught the right of the individual to form his own opinions after personal study of the Scriptures. He was the first Englishman to translate the Bible systematically into his native Anglo-Saxon. In 1428, by order of Pope Martin V, his bones were exhumed and burned, and the ashes thrown into the river Swale.

This is my body.—Matt. xxvi., 26.

NOW UNDERSTAND ye the words of our Savior Christ, as He spake them one after another—as Christ spake them. For He took bread and blest, and yet what blest He? The Scripture saith not that Christ took the bread and blest it, or that He blest the bread which He had taken. Therefore it seemeth more that He blest His disciples and apostles, whom He had ordained witnesses of His passion; and in them He left His blest word, which is the bread of life, as it is written, "Not only in bread liveth man, but in every word that proceedeth out of the mouth of God." Also Christ saith, "I am the bread of life that came down from heaven." And Christ saith also in John, "The words that I have spoken to you are spirit and life." Therefore it seemeth more that He blest His disciples, and also His apostles, in whom the bread of life was left more than in material bread, for the material bread hath an end. As it is written in the Gospel of Matthew xv. that Christ said, "All things that a man eateth go down into the belly, and are sent down into the draught;" but the blessing of Christ kept His disciples and apostles, both bodily and [ghostly] spiritual. As it is written, that none of them perished but the son of perdition, that the Scriptures might be fulfilled, and often the Scripture saith that Jesus took bread and brake it, and gave it to his disciples, and said, "Take ye, eat ye, this is my body that shall be given for you." But He said not this bread is my body, or that bread should be given for the life of the world. For Christ saith, What and if ye shall see the Son of man ascend up where He was before? "It is the Spirit that quickeneth, the flesh profiteth nothing." Also Christ saith in the Gospel, "Verily, verily I say unto you except the wheat corn fall into the ground and die, it abideth alone, but if it die it bringeth forth much fruit."

Here men may see by the words of Christ that it behooved that He died in the flesh, and that in His death was made the fruit of everlasting life for all them that believe on Him, as it is written "For as by Adam they all die, even so by Christ shall all live, and every man in his own order; for as one clearness is in the sun, another in the moon, and a star in clearness is nothing in comparison to the sun; even so is the rising again of the dead for we are sown in corruption and shall rise again incorruptible, we are sown in infirmity, and shall rise again in strength; we are sown in natural bodies, and shall rise again spiritual bodies." Then if Christ shall change thus our deadly bodies by death, and God the Father spared not his own Son, as it is written, but that death should reign in him as in us, and that he should be translated into a spiritual body, as the first rising again of dead men; then how say the hypocrites that take on them to make our Lord's body? Make they the glorified body? Either make they again the spiritual body which is risen from death to life or make they the fleshy body as it was before he suffered death? And if they say also that they make the spiritual body of Christ, it may not be so, for what Christ said and did, He did as He was at supper before He suffered His passion; as it is written that the spiritual body of Christ rose again from death to life. Also that He ascended up to heaven, and that He will abide there till He come to judge the quick and the dead. And if they say that they make Christ's body as it was before He had suffered His passion, then must they needs grant that Christ is to die yet. For by all Holy Scriptures He was promised to die, and that He should give lordship of everlasting life.

Furthermore, if they say that Christ made His body of bread, I ask, With what words made He it? Not with these words, *Hoc est corpus meum;* that is to say in English, "This is my body," for they are the words of giving, and not of making, which He said after that He brake the bread; then parting it among His disciples and apostles. Therefore if Christ had made of that bread His body, [He] had made it in His blessing, or else in giving of thanks, and not in the words of giving; for if Christ had spoken of the material bread that He had in His hands when He said, *Hoc est corpus meum,* "This is my body," it was made before, or else the word had been a lie. For if I say, This is my hand, and if it be not a hand, then am I a liar; therefore seek carefully if ye can find two words of blessing, or of giving of thanks, wherewith Christ made his body and blood of the bread and wine. And that all the clerks of the earth know not, for if ye might find or know those words, then should ye wax great masters above Christ, and then ye might be givers of His substance, and as fathers and makers of Him, and that He should worship you, as it is written, Thou shalt worship thy father and mother. Of such as desire such worship against God's law, speaketh St. Paul of the man of sin, that enhanceth himself as if he were God. And he is worshiped over all things as God, and showeth himself as he were God. Where our clergy are guilty in this, judge ye or they that know most, for they say that when ye have said, *Hoc est corpus meum,* that is to say,

"This is my body;" which ye call the words of consecration, or else of making; and when they are said over the bread, ye say that there is left no bread, but it is the body of the Lord. So that in the bread there remaineth nothing but a heap of accidents, as witness ruggedness, roundness, savor, touching, and tasting, and such other accidents. Then, if thou sayest that the flesh and blood of Christ, that is to say, his manhood, is made more, or increased by so much as the ministration of bread and wine is, the which ye minister— if ye say it is so—then thou must needs consent that the thing which is not God to-day shall be God to-morrow; yea, and that the thing which is without spirit of life, but groweth in the field by kind, shall be God at another time. And we all ought to believe that He was without beginning, and without ending; and not made, for if the manhood of Christ were increased every day by so much as the bread and wine draweth to that ye minister, He should increase more in one day by cart-loads than He did in thirty-two years when He was here in earth.

And if thou makest the body of the Lord in those words, *Hoc est corpus meum;* that is to say, "This is my body"; and if thou mayest make the body of the Lord in those words, "This is my body," thou thyself must be the person of Christ, or else there is a false God; for if it be thy body as thou sayest, then it is the body of a false knave or of a drunken man, or of a thief, or of a lecherer, or full of other sins, and then there is an unclean body for any man to worship for God! For even if Christ had made there His body of material bread in the said words, as I know they are not the words of making, what earthly man had power to do as He did? For in all Holy Scripture, from the beginning of Genesis to the end of the Apocalypse, there are no words written of the making of Christ's body; but there are written that Christ was the Son of the Father, and that He was conceived of the Holy Ghost, and that He took flesh and blood of the Virgin Mary, and that He was dead, and that He rose again from death on the third day, and that He ascended to heaven very God and man, and that we should believe in all Scriptures that are written of Him, and that He is to come to judge the quick and the dead, and that the same Christ Jesus, King and Savior, was at the beginning with the Father and the Holy Ghost, making all things of naught, both heaven and earth, and all things that are therein; working by word of His virtue, for He said, Be it done, and it was done, whose works never earthly man might comprehend, either make. And yet the words of the making of these things are written in the beginning of Genesis, even as God spake them; and if ye can not make the work that He made, and have the word by which He made it, how shall ye make Him that made the works? You have no words of authority or power left you on earth by which ye should do this, but ye have feigned this craft of your false errors, which some of you understand not; for it is prophesied, "They shall have eyes and see not, and ears and hear not; and shall see prophesies, and shall not understand, less they be converted; for I hide them from the hearts of those people; their hearts are greatly fatted." And this thing is done to you for the wickedness of your errors in unbelief; therefore be ye converted from the worst sin, as it is written, "When Moses was in the hill with God," the people made a calf and worshiped it as God. And God spake to Moses, "Go, for the people have done the worst sin to make and worship alien gods."

But now I shall ask you a word; answer ye me, Whether is the body of the Lord made at once or at twice? Is it both the flesh and the blood in the host of the bread; or else is the flesh made at one time, and the blood made at another time; that is to say, the wine in the chalice? If thou wilt say it is full and wholly the manhood of Christ in the host of bread, both flesh and blood, skin, hair, and bones, then makest thou us to worship a false god in the chalice, which is unconjured when ye worship the bread; and if ye say the flesh is in the bread, and the blood in the wine, then thou must grant, if thy craft be true, as it is not indeed, that the manhood of Christ is parted, and that He is made at two times. For first thou takest the host of bread, or a piece of bread, and makest it as ye say, and the innocent people worship it. And then thou takest to thee the chalice, and likewise marrest, makest, I would have said, the blood in it, and then they worship it also, and if it be so as I am sure that the flesh and blood of Christ ascended, then are ye false harlots to God and to us; for when we shall be houselled ye bring to us the dry flesh, and let the blood be away; for ye give us after the bread, wine and water, and sometimes clean water unblest, or rather conjured, by the virtue of your craft; and yet ye say, under the host of bread is the full manhood of Christ. Then by your own confession must it needs be that we worship a false god in the chalice, which is unconjured when we worship the bread, and worship the one as the other; but where find ye that ever Christ or any of His disciples taught any man to worship this bread or wine?

Therefore, what shall we say of the apostles that were so much with Christ, and were called by the Holy Ghost; had they forgotten to set it in the creed when they made it, which is Christian men's belief? Or else we might say that they knew no such God, for they believe in no more gods but in Him that was at the beginning, and made of naught all things visible and invisible, which Lord took flesh and blood, being in the Virgin, the same God. But ye have many false ways, to beguile the innocent people with sleights of the fiend.

For ye say that in every host each piece is the whole manhood of Christ, or full substance of Him. For ye say as a man may take a glass, and break the glass into many pieces, and in every piece properly thou mayest see thy face, and yet thy face is not parted; so ye say the Lord's body is in each host or piece, and His body is not parted. And this is a full subtle question to beguile an innocent fool, but will ye take heed of this subtle question, how a man may take a glass and behold the very likeness of his own face, and yet it is not his face, but the likeness of his face; for if it were his very face, then he must needs have two faces, one on his body and another in the glass. And if the glass were broken in many places, so there should be many faces more by the glass than by the body, and each man shall make as many faces to them as they would; but as ye may see the mind or likeness of your face, which is not the very face; but the figure thereof, so the bread is the figure or mind of Christ's body in earth, and therefore Christ said, As oft as ye do this thing do it in mind of me.

Also ye say this, As a man may light many candles at one candle, and yet the light of that candle is never the more nor ever the less; so ye say that the manhood of Christ descendeth into each part of every host, and the manhood of Christ is never the more nor less. Where then becometh your ministrations? For if a man light many candles at one candle, as long as they burn there will be many candles lighted, and as well the last candle as the first; and so by this reason, if ye shall fetch your word at God, and make God, there must needs be many gods, and that is forbidden in the first commandment, Exod. xx. And as for making more, either making less, of Christ's manhood, it lieth not in your power to come there nigh, neither to touch it, for it is ascended into heaven in a spiritual body, which He suffered not Mary Magdalen to touch, when her sins were forgiven her.

Therefore all the sacraments that are left here in earth are but minds of the body of Christ, for a sacrament is no more to say but a sign or mind of a thing passed, or a thing to come; for when Jesus spake of the bread, and said to His disciples, As ye do this thing, do it in mind of me, it was set for a mind of good things passed of Christ's body; but when the angel showed to John the sacraments of the woman and of the beast that bare her, it was set for a mind of evil things to come on the face of the earth, and great destroying of the people of God. And in the old law there were many figures or minds of things to come. For before Christ, circumcision was commanded by a law; and he that kept not the law was slain. And yet St. Paul saith, "And neither is it circumcision that is openly in the flesh, but he that is circumcised of heart in spirit, not the letter whose praising is not of men, but of God." Peter saith in the third chapter of his epistle, "And so baptism of like form maketh not us safe, but the putting away of the filthiness of the flesh, and the having of good conscience in God by the rising again of our Lord Jesus Christ from death, that we should be made heirs of everlasting life, He went up into heaven, and angels, and powers, and virtues, are made subjects to Him.

And also the Scripture saith of John Baptist, that he preached in the wilderness and said, "A stronger than I shall come after me, and I am not worthy to kneel down and unlace His shoe;" and yet Christ said that he was more than a prophet. See also Isaiah xl., Matt. xi. How may ye then say that ye are worthy to make His body, and yet your works bear witness that ye are less than the prophets? for if ye were not, ye should not teach the people to worship the sacraments or minds of Christ for Christ himself; which sacraments or figures are lawful as God taught them and left them unto us, as the sacrifices or minds of the old law were full good. As it is written, "They that kept them should live in them." And so the bread that Christ brake was left to us for mind of things passed for the body of Christ, that we should believe He was a very man in kind as we are, but as God in power, and that His manhood was sustained by food as ours. For St. Paul saith He was very man, and in form he was found as man. And so we must believe that He was very God and very man together, and that He ascended up very God and very man to heaven, and that He shall be there till He come to doom the world. And we may not see him bodily, being in this life, as it is written, Peter i., for he saith, "Whom ye have not seen ye love, into whom ye now not seeing believe." And John saith in the first chapter of his Gospel, "No man saw God; none but the only begotten Son that is in the bosom of the Father, He hath told it out." And John saith in his first epistle, the third chapter, "Every man that sinneth seeth not him, neither knoweth him." By what reason then say ye that are sinners that ye make God? truly this must needs be the worst sin, to say that ye make God, and it is the abomination of discomfort that is said in Daniel the prophet to be standing in the holy place; he that readeth let him understand.

Also Luke saith that Christ took the cup after that He had supped, and gave thanks and said, "This cup is the new testament in my blood that shall be shed unto the remission of sins for man." Now, what say ye; the cup which He said was the new testament in His blood, was it a material cup in which the wine was that He gave his disciples wine of, or was it His most blest body in which the blest blood was kept till it was shed out for the sins of them that should be made safe by His passion? Needs must we say that He spake of His holy body, as He did when He called His passion or suffering in body a cup, when He prayed to His father, before He went to His passion, and said, "If it be possible that this cup pass from me, but if thou wilt that I drink it, thy will be done?" He spake not here of the material cup in which He had given His disciples drink; for it troubled not Him, but He prayed for His great sufferance and bitter death, the which He suffered for our sins and not for His own. And if He spake of His holy body and passion when He said, "This cup is the new testament in my blood," so He spake of His holy body when He said, "This is my body which shall be given for you," and not of the material bread which He had in His hand. Also in another place He called His passion a cup, where the mother of Zebedee's sons came to Him, and asked of Him that her two sons, when He came to His kingdom, might sit one on His right, and one at His left side. And He answered and said, "Woman, thou wottest not what thou asketh; then He said to them, May ye drink of the cup that I shall drink? and they said, Yea, Lord. And He said, Ye shall drink of my cup, but to sit on my right hand or left hand it is not mine to give, but to the Father it is proper." But in that He said, Ye shall drink of my cup, He promised them to suffer tribulation of this world as He did, by the which they should enter into life everlasting, and to be both on his right hand. And thus ye may see that Christ spake not of the material cup, neither of himself, nor of his apostles, neither of material bread, neither of material wine. Therefore let every man wisely, with meek prayers, and great study, and also charity, read the words of God and holy Scriptures; but many of you are like the mother of Zebedee's sons to whom Christ said, "Thou knowest not what thou askest." So, many of you know not what ye ask, nor what you do; for if ye did, ye would not blaspheme God as ye do, to set an alien God instead of the living God. Also Christ saith, "I am a very vine; wherefore then worship ye not the vine God, as ye do the bread? Wherein was Christ a very vine, or wherein was the bread Christ's body, in figurative speech, which is hidden to the understanding? Then if Christ became not a material or an earthly vine, neither did a material vine become His body. So neither the bread, material bread, was changed from its substance to the flesh and blood of Christ.

Have ye not read in John the second, when Christ came into the temple, they asked of Him what token He would show, that they might believe Him. And He answered them, "Cast down this temple, and in three days I shall raise it again;" which words were fulfilled in His rising again from death; but when He said, "Undo this temple," in that that He said this, they were in error, for they understood it fleshly, and had supposed that He had spoken of the temple of Jerusalem, because He stood in it. And therefore they accused Him at His passion full falsely. For He spake of the temple of His blest body, which rose again in the third day. And right so Christ spake of His holy body when He said, "This is my body which shall be given for you," which was given to death, and to rising again to bliss, for all that shall be saved by him. But like as they accused him falsely of the temple of Jerusalem, so now a days they accuse falsely against Christ, and say that Christ spake of the bread that He brake among His apostles; for in that Christ said this, they are deceived, take it fleshly, and turn it to the material bread, as the Jews did to the temple; and on this false understanding they make abomination of discomfort, as is said by Daniel the prophet, and in Matthew xxiv., to be standing in the holy place; he that readeth let him understand.

Now, therefore, pray we heartily to God, that this evil may be made short for the chosen men, as He hath promised in His blest Gospel; and the large and broad way that leadeth to perdition may be stopt, and the straight and narrow way that leadeth to bliss may be made open by Holy Scriptures, that we may know which is the will of God, to serve Him in truth and holiness in the dread of God, that we may find by Him a way of bliss everlasting. So be it.

ANDREW C. ZENOS

1855-1942

THE NEW HEAVENS AND THE NEW EARTH

BIOGRAPHICAL NOTE

PROFESSOR of Biblical theology, Presbyterian Theological Seminary, Chicago, 1894-1932; born, Constantinople, August 13, 1855; graduated from Robert College, Constantinople, 1872; Princeton, 1880; pastor of Presbyterian church, Brandt, Pa., 1881-83; professor of Greek, Lake Forest University, 1883-88; professor of New Testament exegesis, Hartford Theological Seminary, 1888-91; professor of Church history, McCormick Theological Seminary, 1891-94; author of " Elements of Higher Criticism," " Compendium of Church History," " The Teaching of Jesus Concerning Christian Conduct."

" We look for new heavens and a new earth, wherein dwelleth righteousness."—2 Pet. 3 : 13.

THESE words are a reminder rather than a piece of information. The belief in the destruction and reconstruction of the material universe was a general one among the early Christians. In the book of Revelation, this belief even seems to control the whole thought. A new heaven and a new earth stand before the seer as the goal of the whole movement of things. " For the first heaven and the first earth are passed away; and the sea is no more." " And he that sitteth on the throne said, Behold I make all things new." But the idea was not peculiarly Christian; it was a commonplace of prophetic preaching. As far back as the Exile period, the prophet heard Jehovah say, " Behold I create new heavens and a new earth, and the former things shall not be remembered nor come to mind." And in the two centuries, more or less, preceding the Christian era, the thought had been cherished and encouraged. There was much in the social and political world of the time to suggest corruption and decay and inevitable collapse. The world seemed to have reached its old age. Signs of decrepitude were visible. Wars and commotions were causing the destruction of cities hoary with antiquity, and an air of uncertainty prevailed. Old oracles were called to mind of " wonders in the heaven and on the earth: blood, and fire and pillar of smoke," " the sun turned into darkness and the moon into blood." Isaiah had said, " All the host of heaven shall be dissolved and the heavens shall be rolled together as a scroll, and all the host shall fade away." A class of prophetic writers, using the literary form of apocalypse, drew vivid pictures of the transformation which would bring about a new and fresh universe out of the ruins of the old.

At first glance the fact that the expectation of such a universal renovation of the world was not original with apostles and evangelists may appear to detract from its truth or value. But in view of the great amount borrowed by the earliest Christian teachers from their Jewish, and even from their heathen predecessors, we cannot think that it loses its value, when traced to a stage antecedent to the apostolic. Nevertheless there is a difference between the earlier expectation of " new heavens and a new earth " and the apostolic. For whereas to the former the predominant element is the outward and spectacular feature, to the latter the inner and moral reality rules. To the apocalyptists the method of transformation by a sudden, dazzling, overwhelming cataclysmic overthrow and magic creative reconstruction was in the foreground. To the Christian the main and essential fact was the regeneration of the moral content of the universe; and altho bold and picturesque ways of thinking of it were not discarded, these were means, not ends; they were vehicles to carry the thought of the moral restoration of the universe through Jesus Christ.

First of all, there was need for such renovation. And to feel this need was the first sign of a healthy moral nature. It was impossible to be satisfied with the world as it was. Does this mean that Peter and John regarded God's work a failure? Could they have been ignorant of the account in Genesis with its record that "God saw everything that he had made, and behold, it was good?" We can hardly think so. These men were too thorough Israelites to ignore God's part in the creation. It was rather because they knew too well what God had meant the world to be that they found in it a source of displeasure. God had created the heavens and the earth to be the home of a race which should know Him and honor Him. But instead of this, as the faithful saw it, the world was polluted by sin. Even the people of God's own choice had failed to redeem it from the power of evil. For generations the faithful had struggled and they had been worsted in the fight. Evil was not a mere influence diffused through society without a definite location. It was not hiding in the dark places and doing its work under cover. It was impersonated in the rulers of the world. Men like Tiberius, Caligula, Claudius, Nero, were openly defying God and disobeying His laws. Men like Herod and Caiaphas were controlling the destinies of the chosen people. And in their use of the forces of nature, they had seized upon all things and made them subject to their wicked wills. "The creation was subjected to vanity not of its own will." And it was groaning and travailing with pain in the hope of being delivered from the load of corruption.

Let us note that the spirit of discontent with the world for yielding to sin is a sign of health. All the prophets began by opening their eyes to the evil about them. There is a gospel abroad to the effect that men ought to be happy no matter what the circumstances about them. It is not a new gospel. Jeremiah and Ezekiel heard it and denounced it. Such a gospel promises no good. He who preaches it lacks the very first qualification for a true prophetic mission. It was because Moses saw evil in Egypt that he was used by God to lead the children of Israel from the land of bondage into that of promise. It was because the prophets saw the evil of the people that they

were sent with their burning messages to turn them to righteousness. It was because John the Baptist saw hypocrisy and wickedness that he was empowered to proclaim the coming Messiah. It was because Luther and Wesley saw spiritual deadness in the Church that they were given the vision of a new life in the body of Christ and helped to quicken it. Every great onward movement in the direction of bringing in "new heavens and a new earth" has sprung out of a feeling of discontent with the evil of the world. The eye which is blind to the evil is likely to be blind to the good also.

But while every prophet must begin with sensitiveness towards what ought not to be in the world; while he must realize the sting of sin, while he must appreciate its terrible power and destructive effect, he must not lapse into pessimism. No pessimist can become a true prophet. Far beyond the mere need of renovation, the prophet must see the possibility of it. The heavens and the earth as they are must pass away, because better heavens and a better earth are ready to take their place. If we shall fight sin and evil in the world as we ought, we must be dominated by the love of the better things awaiting us, which by their beauty and loveliness make the evil to appear all the more hateful. The prophet, like Hamlet, must hold before his own eye, and those of others, two pictures, ever calling "Look on this picture, and on this!" Thus only can he turn men from the old and decrepit, from the corrupt and decaying, to the fresh and powerful, to the beautiful and vital.

But the expectation of new heavens and a new earth is more than the offspring of discontent with present evil. It is rooted in an experience of change which one feels must culminate in a total transformation. The new heavens and the new earth are being even now created. There are scoffers as in Peter's day who say, "From the day that the fathers fell asleep all things continue as they were from the beginning of the creation." But they are exceedingly superficial observers and shallow thinkers. All things do not continue as they were. To be sure no change comes over nature such as seems to be pictured in the imaginative conception of these men of old. Looked at outwardly, the same heavens and the same earth are now about us which were about them. The same stars shine overhead; the same mountains bound the horizon at the same centers of observation; the same great rivers run their eternal courses into the same oceans. But we would be making a grievous mistake if we believed that the heavens and the earth to-day are after all the same as those of the days of Peter and John; for does not sameness depend on the inner view and the impression made on the seeing eye and the hearing ear rather than on identity of outward form or even substance? The youth leaves his home in the village, and after a score of years of wandering in the world, and perhaps of life in the great city, returns to the village. He looks on the same streets, the same houses, the same park, the same church; but are they the same for him? How they have shrunk and lost their glory! He may love them still, yea, and more than ever, but they no longer possess the same magnitude and significance in the world.

Something like this change has come over the world, and is ever coming. Were Peter and John to have seen as in a vision the world as it actually is to-day instead of dreaming their apocalyptic dreams, they could not have said more truly than they do, "I saw a new heaven and a new earth: for the first heavens and the first earth are passed away." The cities in which they lived, how different! The sounds that now would greet their ears, how unintelligible! The forms of life that would strike their eyes, how amazing! And even the stars in the firmament, tho apparently the same, and the landscape about so familiar, what a different story of power and glory they would tell.

The earth and the heavens are for us what we know them to be, and as revealed by telescope, microscope and spectroscope and modern science with its wonderful and intricate apparatus for observation, they are certainly other than they were in the days of the apostles. Instead of a vault in the shape of a huge inverted bowl resting on a flat surface, made irregular by mountains and lakes, the modern eye sees an infinite stretch of space, within which revolve countless myriads of burning spheres. Instead of a simple universe, consisting of four elements, earth, water, air and fire, the modern eye sees a vast multitude and variety of atoms and of still more primal electrons and ions. Surely to the eye of the present day student "old things have passed away, behold all things are new."

But more striking if possible is the change in the world of mankind. The same primal passions, the same inward hungerings and thirsts, the same quest for knowledge and power and happiness still burn and move in a restless turmoil, but the expressions of them, how different! The alignment of classes and masses, of races and tribes, of masters and slaves, of rich and poor, how utterly transformed!

But it may be said, Is this a legitimate interpretation of the apostolic thought? If we limit regard to mere external and imaginative garb of it, it may not be; but if we penetrate into the real motive and intent of it, it surely is. For the longing that led to such an ideal was much more than a hunger for change of material form. It looked forward to a more

harmonious universe, to one that would display God's glory more fully and serve as a suitable residence for God's immortal children. The world as it was, was too completely identified with the sin of man to serve any longer the purposes of its creation. Every portion of it, every element in it, was too full of evil associations, too heavily burdened with thoughts of lust and greed, selfishness and malice. It needed a complete purification; a perfect dissolution of its old associations, and when this was achieved it would in a true sense be destroyed and reconstructed.

Nevertheless the question of importance still remains, whether these new heavens and this new earth are better; whether the apostles would recognize in them the world of which they dreamed and for which they yearned. Men of Oriental civilizations coming into the midst of Western life may be made to give us the answer. Are they imprest with the superiority of the Western? Not always. Indeed the stronger the contrast with what they have been accustomed to the less their inclination to look upon the change with favor. Were Peter and John to pronounce upon our new world, it is certain they would not allow the facts of a more complex life, of larger knowledge and control of nature, keener pleasures and finer sensibilities, to influence their judgments. They would look beneath the surface into the strife of human passions, the degradation and misery caused by sin, the arrogance, the lust and greed, consuming, devouring and destroying all within their reach, and to the extent to which these ruled in the world, they would still long for and predict "new heavens and a new earth."

The earth which loomed into the vision of these ancient seers was one in which "dwelleth righteousness." The only world that will satisfy the child of God is that in which his Father's will is known and done. And what is righteousness? First of all it is a quality that pervades social relations, resulting in each person's giving to every other all that is right. Righteousness in the world means that men and women do not take advantage of one another, are honest in all transactions, pure and holy in character and in conduct. But all this is negative, and righteousness is something more than abstinence from evil.

The world has passed through two stages of moral life. In the first, the nearest to the brute, each one had regard to himself first of all, and tried to build himself at the expense of all others. How can I get the most and give the least? was his main question and concern. Alas, that so many still live in this stage. In the second stage, each regards every other and strives to be true and just to the interests of all. The question then is, How can I both give and take exact equivalents? How can I avoid being cheated, yet not cheat any other? How can I so adjust my relations as neither to get more than I give nor give more than I get? But there is a third stage to be reached. It is that in which the life and law of Jesus Christ will be the aim and achievement of all. According to this law each will strive to do for others as much as he can. The question will then be, How can I give the most in exchange for the least, for did not Jesus say, " It is more blessèd to give than to receive?" Men will not cease to strive to build themselves up either in riches or in wisdom or power, but it will be in order that they may spend themselves for the advantage of their brethren. Does this seem impracticable? John Wesley kept from his income just enough to meet the daily expenses of his household, and gave the remainder for the advancement of the kingdom of God.

But the righteousness which will fill and pervade the new heavens and the new earth is even more than a perfect conformity to standards and conceptions of right living for the sake of mere right living. It includes the recognition of God's holy character and holy will. It is the righteousness which the prophets preached to Israel of old, the righteousness, which Jesus Christ lived and exemplified. The writer of the text was an ardent Christian, and the golden age he anticipates is the golden age of the Christian mind and consciousness, the age of the reign of God through Jesus Christ. To the Christian, righteousness cannot be a mere abstraction alluring him by its own fascination, nor even a supreme law to be mechanically recognized and blindly obeyed. It can only be a living force drawn from an eternal personality and controlling all personal relations.

Hence to the Christian of the apostolic age the second coming of Christ in person to establish a reign of righteousness and peace upon earth was more than a glowing hope; it was a burning passion. And to the Christian of all ages the unconquerable faith that in some form or other the personal relation to Christ will lead in the molding of the character of His followers and result in the overwhelming predominance of the Christ-man, the man for whom the righteousness of God is at the same time an ideal, a goal and a law, must be ever indispensable.

But if so, the new heavens and the new earth for which the Christian looks cannot be expected in a merely passive way. We must do more than wait and prepare ourselves for them. We must in a large measure work out the transformation for which we are longing. It is at this point that the Christian's look forward into the golden age differs from the dreamer's Utopia. It is more than a creature of the imagination to be delighted in for its iridescent beauty. It is a land of promise, drawing through its charms; but it is also a building in process of erection, to which each day one may add what will bring it nearer completion.

Do we wish for the new heavens and the new earth? Are we looking and longing for them? If so, we may not be indifferent to the share we must have in their making. For while it is true that like the first heavens and the first earth they are to be the creation and gift of God to His own, it is also true that God is creating them even now through His own. God is not merely " the Power not ourselves making for righteousness "; He is also the Power in ourselves making for righteousness. And righteousness is not only to dwell in the renovated universe, but to be the force that shall reconstruct it.

SAMUEL MARINUS ZWEMER

1867-1952

BIBLE TEACHING ABOUT CONSCIENCE

BIOGRAPHICAL NOTE

FIELD secretary of the Board of Foreign Missions of the Reformed church in America. Born in Vriesland, Mich., 1867; graduated Hope College, Holland, Mich., 1887; New Brunswick (N. J.) Theological Seminary, 1890; ordained clergyman, Reformed church in America, 1890; missionary at Busrah, Bahrein, and other stations in Arabia, 1891-1905; D.D., Hope College, 1904; author of "Arabia, the Cradle of Islam," "Topsy-Turvy Land," "Raymond Lull," "Moslem Doctrine of God," "Islam, a Challenge to Faith."

" And herein do I exercise myself, to have always a conscience void of offence toward God, and toward men."—Acts 24 : 16.

THE Bible stands unique among all the other so-called sacred books of the East in that it reveals the fact of the conscience and addresses itself to the conscience. The Koran has not even a word to express the idea, and the idea itself is strangely absent from Moslem thought. Doctor Duff, if we are not mistaken, was the first to make the statement that the primary work of a missionary is to create a conscience; and this has been repeated often since by other thinkers and observers in India and the East. How rare is the blush of childhood, that first indication of a live conscience, seen in heathen lands; how weak is the moral sense among many in Christian lands!

A revival of conscience and of right views regarding its authority is one of the crying needs of the world to-day. A revival of conscience would be a revival of piety in the Church and would lead to deeper knowledge of sin and, consequently, higher ideas and ideals of holiness.

The apostle Paul in his defense before Felix gives us the keynote of Bible teaching regarding the Christian conscience and those words may well introduce our study of the subject. "Herein," he says, " do I exercise myself, to have always a conscience void of offense toward God, and toward men." Paul was always a conscientious man but Paul did not always have the same conscience. He was conscientious as a Pharisee and lived up to his moral light. He makes much of conscience in his preaching as an apostle; and, long after that his conversion, he says that he exerts himself, trains himself, exercises himself (the word is very strong in the Greek), " to have a conscience void of offense."

Man by creation was possest of threefold powers of soul, generally called the intellect, the affections, and the will. He was also created in holiness and righteousness. That is, his moral sense was enlightened so as to know God and know right perfectly. All his moral affections were inclined to the good and the pure. And his will was to obey God and His law. Adam's conscience in Paradise was void of offense, pure, good, and holy, as were all the other powers of his soul.

Even as from the ruins of Pompeii the historian can reconstruct an exact picture of the pomp and pride of Roman society, so from the universal testimony of fallen man in all ages it is possible to a degree to learn what a glorious gift conscience was before the fall—before the earthquake of sin overwhelmed its authority and integrity. The supreme place assigned to conscience by even heathen philosophers and sensual poets is remarkable. Byron calls it " the very oracle of God." Cicero described it as " God ruling in the human soul." And all the philosophers of modern times, tho they may reject the authority of a divine revelation, can not away with that which their great leader, Kant, calls " the categorical imperative " and " the eternal ought." The very terms used for conscience in Latin, Greek and other languages indicate something (*con science;* co-knowledge; the Greek, *suneidesis* has similar significance. The same idea occurs in the Teutonic languages, *e. g.,* the Dutch, *geweten*) of what unfallen man once knew with God. The ruined remnants of this knowledge of the right still bear witness to the grandeur of the human conscience before the fall. Paul refers to it when he writes: " For when the Gentiles which have not the law do by nature the things contained in the law, these having not the law are a law unto themselves; which show the work of the law written in their hearts, their conscience also bearing witness and their thoughts the meanwhile accusing or else excusing one another."

Not only was conscience intended to be a co-witness of God and an unerring guide to truth and right, but also to be a strong bulwark against temptations. The power of moral restraint which it still exercises must have been infinitely stronger and more authoritative at the first. The joy of an approving conscience must have been a powerful incentive to righteousness even in Paradise.

Man's conscience at creation was like a perfectly adjusted and compensated standard compass by which to direct his voyage of life. Or, to change the figure, his conscience resembled a delicate and costly barometer hanging in the chamber of his soul ready to warn him of the storms of the tempter. And yet that warning was unheeded; the voice of conscience was drowned in the tumult of appetite and desire; Adam fell. All his posterity shared in the awful heritage of moral ruin and moral corruption.

What effect had Adam's fall upon his conscience and that of his posterity? When a costly mercurial barometer falls from its support, be it ever so short a distance, no scientist longer trusts its indications of atmospheric pressure. It is still a barometer and still responds in a measure to the weight of an approaching storm; but for accurate and scientific use that barometer is ruined. It is a fallen barometer and cannot under all circumstances be relied upon. It is no longer stand-

ard. Even so with conscience. The fall of Adam was the fall of his whole soul with all its powers. Conscience of shame and guilt was awakened by the voice of God. " Who told thee that thou wast naked? " and " Where art thou? " These two questions of the Almighty showed Adam whence he had fallen. In the New Testament the fallen conscience or the conscience of the natural man is described by four adjectives which indicate at once the character and the degrees of ruin that came to conscience whether in individuals or in the mass of humanity.

In the eighth chapter of First Corinthians Paul speaks of a weak conscience. He tells of men among the Corinthians whose consciences were no longer strong and stedfast but weak and wavering; men whose consciences stumbled at things which in themselves were not wrong, and yet for whose sake those harmless things were to be avoided by stronger Christians. Now a weak conscience is not a healthy conscience. It is a troublesome guest and a more troublesome neighbor. Men and women with weak consciences should not attempt to set the standard for others. They are not only to be pitied but are blameworthy. Such a conscience may not perhaps call evil, good; but it comes under condemnation for calling good, evil. The Pharisees were so conscientious about the letter of the law that they trampled upon its spirit. They were afraid to break the ceremonial Sabbath laws but did not hesitate with perjured witnesses to condemn the Prince of Life before Pilate's judgment seat. What crimes have been committed in the name of religion by the power of " a weak conscience! " All the weight and the curse of ceremonialism and sacerdotalism may be traced back to weak consciences which did not distinguish between the shell and the core of religion and confounded the shadow with the substance. A weak conscience often " vaunteth itself, is easily provoked," and thinketh evil continually. It is scrupulous where it should be discriminating, and upright when it should be pliable. Paul did not have a weak conscience, and when Peter showed signs of one he withstood him to the face because he was to be blamed.

A stronger word for the fallen conscience is that used in the Epistle to the Hebrews. In the tenth chapter and twenty-second verse the conscience of the natural man is called evil. " Having our hearts sprinkled from an evil conscience." It is the same Greek word elsewhere used to describe fallen angels as evil spirits. In the case of conscience too the perversion of the best is the worst. When the compass has become evil there is little hope for the ship in a storm. The evil conscience no longer is guided by the infallible law of God but by the evil inclinations of its own imagination and desires. The scales of justice no longer hang even but moral judgment is perverted and the crooked is called straight.

The familiar picture of Gulliver, flat on his back and unable to rise, because of the hundreds of tiny cords with which the Lilliputians have bound him, contains an allegory. Gulliver is conscience and the tiny strands are evil habits, inherited or acquired, that prevent conscience from exerting its authority. The giant has been overcome by the dwarfs. An evil conscience, alas, is the inheritance of every son of Adam.

In Titus 1:15 we read of a third stage in the downward path of conscience. "Unto the pure all things are pure but unto them that are defiled and unbelieving is nothing pure but even their mind and conscience is defiled. They profess that they know God but in works they deny Him being abominable and disobedient and unto every good work reprobate." "Evil" refers to the general character and tendency of our conscience; "defiled" to some particular spot and blemish in our moral nature which, like an indellible stain on costly fabric, ruins the whole garment. How many there are whose consciences are defiled in some particular; men whose moral integrity is respected and their judgment upright in all points of the law, save one; and that one point proves how deep is the stain of a defiled conscience. Right here environment acts upon each one of us, while education or habit emphasizes its influence for good or ill. How hard it is for one to keep a pure and a sensitive conscience regarding the holy Sabbath day in an environment where everything relating to that day is lax and worldly. The insinuating power of the presence of moral leprosy on a pure conscience is described by Pope in these lines:

" Vice is a monster of such frightful mien,
  That to be hated needs but to be seen;
  But, seen too oft, familiar with her face,
  We first endure, then pity, then embrace."

Happy is the young man who has not experienced this awful truth in his own life. A morbid desire to know the taste of forbidden fruit is sure to lead on to a defiled conscience and a defiled life.

The last New Testament adjective used to describe the conscience of the unregenerate is the terrible word used by the apostle in 1 Tim. 4:1, 2. "Now the Spirit speaketh expressly, that in the latter times some shall depart from the faith, giving heed to seducing spirits and doctrines of devils; speaking lies in hypocrisy, having their conscience seared with a hot iron." A cauterized conscience; that is the word in the original. First weak, then evil, then defiled and finally dead, past feeling, seared with a hot iron, cauterized; such is the awful end of a conscience in a heart of unbelief and an environment of sin

and hypocrisy. The compass is not only inaccurate and unreliable in this case, but it has ceased to be a compass. The magnetic needle that once responded to the pole and oscillated at the slightest touch is now rusted fast to the pivot. The whole sense is gone. A man without a conscience is a man without a character. He can no longer be pricked in his conscience; it is cauterized. Such there are even in the bounds of the Christian Church and we call them gospel-hardened. Not hardened by the gospel but hardened against the gospel, because their consciences have ceased to respond to its appeals. Such there are among the Gentiles " having the understanding darkened, being alienated from the life of God through the ignorance that is in them, because of the blindness of their heart; who being past feeling have given themselves over unto lasciviousness to work all uncleanness with greediness." What missionary, what physician of souls, has not met with cases of cauterized consciences?

So far we have considered the effect of the fall on the individual conscience. Every natural conscience is imperfect and no two consciences are exactly alike. Each partakes of environment and heredity and education. A national conscience can only exist where the individual conscience is active and has authority; and its character depends on the conscience of individuals for its elements good or bad. By remembering this we understand how for example Spain and Scotland differ in their view of bull fights and how public morals are better in the twentieth than in the tenth century? The reason for this great contrast and change can only be the fact that conscience, however much fallen, can be regenerated and renewed by the Holy Spirit. There is no regeneration of the soul without a regeneration of the conscience.

This brings us to our third question. What should conscience be in a Christian? Paul's own life is the best illustration of the vast change regeneration makes in the conscience. The deeds of violence in persecuting the Church, which he once did conscientiously, he now abhors. His conscience is no longer weak, clinging to the beggarly elements of Judaism, but strong and manly.

A regenerate conscience is described in the New Testament by the words " good " (1 Tim. 1:5, 19), " pure " (1 Tim. 3:9), and " purged " (Heb. 9:14; 10:22). Although in the Old Testament the word " conscience " does not appear in the English version there is little doubt that the word translated " reins " would better be rendered " conscience." For example Ps. 73:21, " Thus my heart was grieved and I was pricked in my (reins) conscience." The same word translated " reins," in reference to the seat of the affections or the moral nature of man, is rendered " kidneys " in the account of the ceremonial offerings of the Pentateuch. A careful comparison of these passages leads me to conclude that because the kidneys were considered the seat of the moral sense in man, that part of the sacrificial victim was always put on the altar as pure (Exod. 29 : 13, 22; Lev. 3 : 4, 10, 15; 9 : 10, 19, etc.).

According to New Testament teaching the only power and instrument adequate to cleanse the conscience and renew it is the blood ˙of Christ. "Having your hearts sprinkled from an evil conscience " (Heb. 10 : 11). " How much more shall the blood of Christ purge your conscience from dead works to serve the living God " (Heb. 9 : 14).

The idea is often held that man's conscience both before and after conversion is identical; and that to be conscientious is to be possest of true piety. But both Scripture and experience teach the contrary. When the miracle of the new birth takes place conscience is aroused, enlightened, and once more given the throne of authority in the heart. How important is it then to have a good conscience, " a conscience void of offense toward God and man! "ʳ To this end Paul exercised himself daily. He put his conscience in training in the school of Christ. Notice the importance attached to conscience in Scripture.

In Heb. 13 : 18 a good conscience is made the subjective condition for intercessory prayer. " Pray for us; for we trust we have a good conscience; in all things willing to live honestly." You must be willing to live and act yourself, as you ask men to pray that you may live and act. Sincerity is the fruit of a good conscience.

Baptism, according to the apostle, is not only the sign and seal of regeneration in a general sense, but of a renewed conscience. " The like figure whereunto even baptism doth also now save us (not the putting away of the filth of the flesh but the answer of a good conscience toward God) by the resurrection of Jesus Christ " (1 Peter 3 : 21). A renewed life according to all the commandments of God is impossible unless we have a renewed conscience to respond gladly to all demands of holiness and an enlightened conscience to teach us the principles that underlie the moral law.

A good conscience is considered so important a gift and grace that it is repeatedly linked with love and faith. " Now the end of the commandment is charity out of a pure heart and of a good conscience and of faith unfeigned." Yet where we hear a hundred prayers for increase in love, and more strength of faith, we scarcely ever hear one offered for a better conscience; such a conscience as is the exact opposite of that weak, evil, defiled, and deadened thing which only the power of Christ can restore and purify.

The prayerful education of one's conscience by exercise and by the study of Christ's character, is the only road to piety.

Most striking of all, it is the teaching of Paul that without a good conscience, faith is vain and the Christian may suffer shipwreck when in sight of the harbor if he throws overboard this goodly compass. " War the good warfare; holding faith and a good conscience, which some having thrust from them made shipwreck concerning the faith " (1 Tim. 1 : 19 R. V.). A hypocrite sails not only under false colors but he sails on life's sea and into eternity without compass. " Why call ye me Lord, and do not the things which I say? " Why are ye so much religious and so little conscientious?

There is no power on earth equal to a sincere Christian character, a man who, like Paul, daily trains himself " to have a conscience void of offense toward God and toward men." Too often the world applies to the Church with truth the words of Emerson: " What you are is talking so loud that I cannot hear what you say." The Church needs a revival of conscience and that revival will come if we study the teaching of God's word on the subject.

From this teaching three things are very evident:

An unregenerate conscience is an unsafe guide. To live conscientiously is not to be saved. The words " Saul, Saul, why persecutest thou me " were addrest to a very conscientious man; but also to one whose conscience was blind and evil.

Even the regenerate conscience needs education. Like all the gifts and graces of the spirit it must grow more and more as we grow in knowledge. The standard of morals must become ever higher and purer as the years go by until we come " to the measure of the stature of the fulness of Christ " A firm grasp on this truth is the best antidote to an easy-going and unbiblical perfectionism. The command " Be ye perfect " means more and more according as our consciences become more tender, more holy, more like Christ. The growth in grace and in the knowledge of what God requires of us, are like the two sides of a parabolic curve, ever approaching but never meeting. Those who are living nearest to God see their own imperfections the more distinctly in the blinding light of His holy glory.

The kind of preaching that leads to conviction of sin, must be aimed at the conscience. Here it is, that even a bow drawn at a venture by a man in simplicity will send an arrow of conviction between the joints of the harness. Preaching to the intellect may be edifying but it never hits the bull's-eye nor makes sinners cry out, " What shall I do to be saved? " Preaching to the affections without reaching the conscience is like sowing on unplowed soil. But he who reaches a man's conscience has broken through to the very citadel and can demand an unconditional surrender. This was Paul's method. "Not handling the Word of God deceitfully but by manifestation of the truth commending ourselves to every man's conscience in the sight of God." "For we must all appear before the judgment seat of Christ . . . knowing therefore the terror of the Lord we persuade men. But we are made manifest unto God and I trust also are made manifest in your consciences." This kind of preaching made even Felix tremble when his conscience was put face to face with righteousness and judgment. It was the method of all the Old Testament prophets. David in royal purple and awful guilt was not proof against that one arrow of Nathan aimed at the conscience: "Thou art the man." The Fifty-first Psalm and the One Hundred and Thirty-ninth Psalm give us David's idea of an awakened conscience when the searchlight of God's eye lays bare every secret of his heart.

Christ's words to that sensual, self-righteous group of Pharisees, surrounding the woman who was a sinner, were so well aimed at the only vulnerable point of their proud panoply of hypocrisy, that we read: "They when they heard it, being convicted by conscience went out one by one beginning at the eldest, even unto the last."

INDEX OF TEXTS

INDEX OF SERMONS